MW01618148

招隠

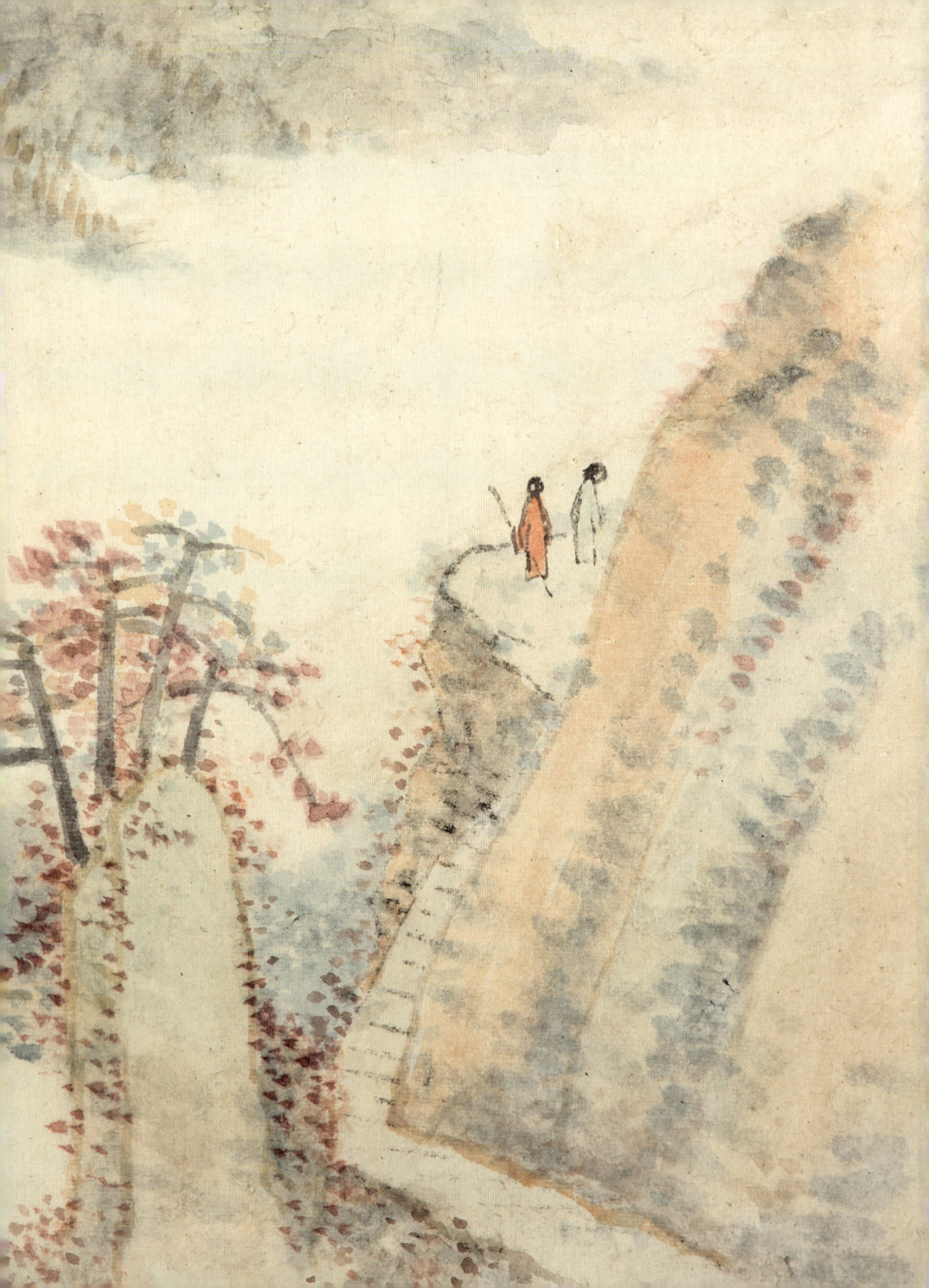

The Artful Recluse

Painting, Poetry, and Politics in Seventeenth-Century China

EDITED BY

Peter C. Sturman

Susan S. Tai

ESSAYS BY

Peter C. Sturman

Timothy Brook

Jonathan Chaves

Jonathan Hay

Hui-shu Lee

Santa Barbara Museum of Art

DelMonico Books • Prestel Munich London New York

Contents

This book is dedicated to the memory of F. Bailey Vanderhoef Jr.
1913–2008
Collector, Connoisseur, Benefactor, Trustee,
and Man of the World

This exhibition and catalogue are made possible by the China Guardian Auctions Co., Ltd., Beijing, China; Santa Barbara Museum of Art Women's Board; Robert and Mercedes Eichholz Foundation; Dr. Albert E. and Antoinette Gump Amorteguy Asian Publications Endowment; Cecille and Michael Pulitzer Foundation; Victor K. Atkins Jr.; Natalia and Michael Howe; Siri and Bob Marshall; The Charles Bloom Foundation; The Rong-Wu Foundation; Capital Group, Inc. Asian Lecture Fund Endowment; Robert and Christine Emmons; and Bruce G. Wilcox. Additional support is provided by Chen Chite; Amy Chu-hua O'Dowd; Pamela Melone; The Metropolitan Center for Far Eastern Art Studies, Kyoto; E. Rhodes and Leona B. Carpenter Foundation; and the Santa Barbara Museum of Art's Friends of Asian Art.

Foreword

The remarkable works assembled in this landmark exhibition are representative of one of the golden ages of Chinese painting. Produced by seventeenth-century painter-poet scholars of the late Ming and early Qing dynasties, these objects, in their complex explorations of the role of the individual during crisis and change, are unrivaled in drama, beauty, and sophistication. Like the compositions of seventeenth-century French artists Claude Lorrain and, to a greater degree, Nicholas Poussin, the Chinese paintings display an intimate knowledge of nature and a willful reworking of visual data toward an idealized, bucolic vision in accord with deeply held, philosophical tenets. The added textual components—inscriptions in masterful calligraphy—open intricate pathways into the artists' thoughts and sentiments.

Whether in residence at the imperial court or in self-imposed "reclusion"—as an escape from corrupt court politics or from foreign occupiers—these artist-poets fundamentally and ineluctably changed not only the course of painting in China but the entire culture through innovations that involved and encouraged personal expression and artistic freedom. They approached the art of the past with reverence, but also with a mind to improve upon and infuse new vitality into traditional genres. The present exhibition not only showcases the works of such major seventeenth-century talents as Dong Qichang, Xiang Shengmo, and the idiosyncratic monks Bada Shanren and Shitao, more fundamentally it helps refocus attention to the classical arts of China, which in recent years have been overshadowed by the contemporary Asian art scene.

A project of this scope and caliber requires the talents and hard work of many individuals. Particularly deserving commendation are the exhibition's co-curators Susan S. Tai, the Museum's Elizabeth Atkins Curator of Asian Art, and Peter C. Sturman, professor in the Department of the History of Art and Architecture, University of California, Santa Barbara (UCSB). Curator Tai and Professor Sturman not only brought to the show and catalogue the highest level of scholarship but also established a model of collaboration between a civic art museum and a distinguished university. Beyond the benefit to a national and international audience, this important and ambitious project served to educate and inspire many university graduate students—at UCSB; University of California, Los Angeles; and New York University—who were involved in the writing of catalogue entries.

We are grateful to the private individuals, who wish to remain anonymous, and the directors of the lending institutions for generously sharing masterpieces from their collections and for their implicit trust in the significance of our project: Michael Govan at the Los Angeles County Museum of Art, Stephan Jost at the Honolulu Museum of Art, Joseph Rosa of the University of Michigan Art Museum, Connie Wolf at the Iris & B. Gerald Cantor Center for Visual Arts at Stanford University, and Director and Senior Vice President of Global Arts and Cultural Programs Melissa Chiu at the Asia Society Museum. We are especially grateful to Dr. Chou Kung-shin (Julie), director of the National Palace Museum, Republic of China (Taiwan), for her institution's willingness to share the extraordinary set of twelve scrolls by Shitao—a true treasure shown for the first time in the United States.

It is fitting that *The Artful Recluse* was organized and will first open in Santa Barbara before it travels to the Asia Society in New York. In certain respects, the "ideal" living situation that the Chinese literati conjured up in their paintings and poetry resembles the tranquil and culturally sophisticated—for some, escapist—environment of Santa Barbara. Indeed, Santa Barbara has always attracted among its inhabitants cultured recluses (in the truest Chinese sense) who pursue lives at once close to nature and actively involved in the arts. Such was the case of the late SBMA trustee and benefactor and Asian art devotee F. Bailey (Billy) Vanderhoef Jr., to whom this volume is dedicated. Through this magnificent exhibition, the Museum hopes to continue to offer to its community inspiration and solace, particularly to those, like Billy, who seek a deeper, searching engagement with the more subtle, less accessible aspects of art, nature, and life.

Larry J. Feinberg
Robert and Mercedes Eichholz Director
Santa Barbara Museum of Art

Preface

The roots of this exhibition reach back less than three years to a seminar at the University of California, Santa Barbara. Students were provided the opportunity to learn about seventeenth-century Chinese art by working with the collections of the Santa Barbara Museum of Art (SBMA), the Los Angeles County Museum of Art, and a private collection in the region. Our modest plans for a small-scale exhibition became less so when additional public institutions and private collectors generously made available important works of art. As our plans developed, our ambitions grew. The small exhibition expanded beyond its designated space, and then, prompted by the suggestion that we produce a catalogue, our task became at once more serious and challenging.

A century is an arbitrary division of historical time; in premodern China, where time was measured in dynasties, reigns, and sixty-year cycles, it can be considered almost meaningless. Nonetheless, the period of time in China roughly corresponding to the West's seventeenth century is particularly rich in historical importance and drama. Halfway through the century the long-lived Ming dynasty (1368–1644) was destroyed by the Manchu people of the northeast, who would establish the equally long-lived Qing dynasty (1644–1911). The trauma of foreign conquest and dynastic change dominates the narrative of the seventeenth century, yet this is only a portion of the story. The last half century of Ming rule is equally engrossing. Though tainted by political crises centered on corruption at the imperial court, the late Ming witnessed a florescence of urban culture, with rich and diverse intellectual and artistic developments. This was especially true in the prosperous region known as Jiangnan (the Yangzi River Delta), where an atmosphere of exploration and experimentation reigned in cultural matters, including the introduction of Western learning by the Jesuits.

In Chinese painting, the seventeenth century is peerless. The quality, diversity, and intrinsic interest of paintings bridging the late Ming and early Qing—combined with the great number of extant works—provide an unparalleled opportunity for entering deeply into this profound and refined art. This was readily apparent to scholars of the previous generation and resulted in numerous important exhibitions and studies. Wai-kam Ho, Chu-tsing Li, Wen Fong, Richard Edwards, Richard Barnhart, and especially James Cahill (among a number of others) all produced important scholarship that laid the groundwork for today's understanding of Chinese painting. The seventeenth century was central, and not only for the art produced during that time; equally important was the lens it provided to the rich tradition that preceded it and the perspective it provided to what followed. It is not an exaggeration to say that what is known about Chinese painting today is largely owed to the seventeenth century's rich legacy.

In 1991 Wai-kam Ho spearheaded a blockbuster show and catalogue titled *The Century of Tung Ch'i-ch'ang, 1555–1636*, which in many respects was a grand statement about the importance of the seventeenth century. Erudite, broad, and impressively detailed, the monumental two-volume catalogue—together with the publication of the papers of its accompanying symposium—set a formidable standard for painting and calligraphy studies. *The Century of Tung Ch'i-ch'ang* also demonstrated how vast an undertaking it is to attempt an encapsulation of this vital period in Chinese art history, for outside of the central figure of Dong Qichang (the preferred romanization in this volume of Tung's name), the exhibition provided but an overview, pointing through the excellence of its selected pieces and their treatment in the catalogue how much more there was to discover. More than twenty years have passed since *The Century of Tung Ch'i-ch'ang*, and, despite a number of excellent monographic studies, the seventeenth century remains as daunting as ever.

In fact, in certain respects the challenge is greater, for with increased understanding and more accessible resources the standards of research in Chinese painting are higher today than ever before. While the overall terrain of seventeenth-century Chinese painting—styles, influences, regional schools, and general approaches of major figures—is understood, many of its details are not. Individual artists, not to mention works of art, remain understudied. What they and their paintings have to say remains unstated. This is ironic considering how verbal these artists were—their words and thoughts are recorded in the many inscriptions that accompany the paintings. Such relative silence deserves attention and remedy.

The present catalogue is our modest effort to explore the meanings of seventeenth-century Chinese painting by examining individual works of art closely and contextually. An overarching theme provides structural unity to allow these paintings and calligraphies to be understood in the broader matrix of late-Ming and early-Qing thought and society. The theme is reclusion or *yin* 隱, which can also be translated as "to hide or escape" or "to withdraw or disengage." The concept of reclusion may at first strike the average Western reader as strange. For the most part, hiding is not something we do in this country. Henry David Thoreau notwithstanding, disengagement is considered more an oddity than an attraction. In China, however, reclusion is a concept of such great antiquity and value that its ideals were retrospectively attached to the country's earliest legends. Disinterest in worldly gain was considered a mark of true sagacity, as was the recognition when "the times were not right" and a retreat to the hills was the proper course of action. Reclusion deeply informs the realms of philosophy, religion, even politics in China. It is of such age and influence that it literally can be counted as one of the founding blocks of traditional culture, pervasive in China's literature and art. So common is it that visitors familiar with the patterns of China's past may have precisely the opposite reaction of those who come uninformed—that reclusion is too ubiquitous a phenomenon to have any real significance.

In our opinion this is a mistake, for while it is true that the idea of disengaging from the world is a common topos throughout Chinese history, it is also a fact that the political ills and social trauma of the late Ming and early Qing greatly heightened interest in this time-honored ideal. The seventeenth century was a period of crisis, and in reaction the idea of escaping from the world provided comfort and attraction. The scholar-official painters who are at the center of this exhibition understood reclusion. From their readings of history and literature they knew the models of the past, they were familiar with its stories, and they understood the philosophical, moral, and social implications of worldly disengagement. Most importantly, they recognized that they lived in a period of crisis. Awareness prompted self-reflection, a heightened scrutiny of the historical past, and a desire to voice a response that asserted a sense of self. Poetry and painting were essential media for this purpose.

Reclusion is a common subject of the paintings included in the exhibition, described in idyllic landscapes of escape and through figures and flora that evoke such ideals through literary and historical allusion. More subtly, we find that engagement with art in the seventeenth century—the study of past traditions, the collecting and appreciation of famous paintings and calligraphies, and their emulation through one's own efforts—was also a notable form of reclusion. Art provided the means by which one could transcend the difficulties of one's times and connect to something permanent and meaningful. In many respects, the seventeenth century resembles other periods of dynastic decline and transition, but what makes it stand apart is an unparalleled urbanity marked by a deep familiarity with China's literary and art-historical past. The interweaving of the past with the present is a pervasive and enriching aspect of the art seen in this exhibition.

Reclusion signals escape to a private place, whether actual or imaginary. The paintings and calligraphies in this exhibition, many with accompanying poems, were in most cases forums for the expression of personal thoughts and desires intended to be shared with a highly select audience. The goal of this catalogue and its accompanying essays is to provide entrée to these thoughts, the private "reclusive" quarters of these artists' minds as expressed in images of great skill and subtlety. The path is not always easy. Figuratively speaking, some of these artists chose to reside in truly remote places. Nonetheless, immense reward accompanies the understanding of these paintings' intentions.

Any exhibition, large or small, that presents the art of seventeenth-century China almost by definition is not modest. The period—divided evenly by a change of dynasties—is one of great historical complexity and extraordinarily sophisticated literary, graphic, and material arts. For this reason we are especially blessed to have the scholarly contributions of professors Timothy Brook of University of British Columbia, Jonathan Chaves of George Washington University, Jonathan Hay of the Institute of Fine Arts at New York University (IFA), and Hui-shu Lee of the University of California at Los Angeles (UCLA). Their essays add immeasurably to the catalogue by exploring different aspects of the exhibition's thematic and historical structure in ways reflective of the authors' particular interests and approaches. Most gratifying is the manner in which the texts collectively bring seventeenth-century Chinese art into focus while maintaining their strong individual voices.

The Artful Recluse features what can unabashedly be called the elite art of China. Most of the paintings were produced by artists whose primary identification was as scholars, and the few whose orientation was more professional were still working in concert with literati ideals and taste. The results were scrolls, album leaves, and fans graced with copious amounts of writing that embed their images in the multi-faceted literary world of poetry, history, and philosophy. These are complex works of art whose full richness is apparent only with access to their textual elements. Toward that goal, we thank professors Xue Longchun of Nanjing Art Academy and Bai Qianshen of Boston University for their help in deciphering occasional passages of calligraphy and seals, and to Professor Jonathan Chaves for his translations of a number of poems. Graduate students from the University of California at Santa Barbara (UCSB), UCLA, and the IFA were responsible for writing the lion's share of catalogue entries. We are grateful to professors Hui-shu Lee and Jonathan Hay for the supervision they provided to their students and for their own catalogue entries. Philip Hu, associate curator of Asian art, Saint Louis Art Museum, graciously contributed the catalogue entries for Mi Wanzhong's landscapes. Whatever errors that may remain in the presentation of the objects in the catalogue are our responsibility.

Communication with institutions and private lenders for this exhibition and catalogue was greatly aided by Professor Shih Shou-chien of the Institute of History and Philology of Academica Sinica; Department Head Ho Chuan-hsing and Deputy Chief Curator Lee Yumin of the Department of Calligraphy and Painting, National Palace Museum (Taipei); curators Hyonjeong Kim-Han (now at the Asian Art Museum, San Francisco), Stephen Little, Christina Yu, and Curatorial Administrator Vanessa May Holterman at the Los Angeles County Museum of Art; Shawn Eichman of the Honolulu Museum of Art; Natsu Oyobe of the University of Michigan Art Museum; Xiaoneng Yang, Patrick J. J. Maveety Curator of Asian Art at the Iris & B. Gerald Cantor Center for the Visual Arts at Stanford University; Senior Curator of Traditional Art Adriana Proser and Director of Museum Operations Marion Kocot of the Asia Society, New York; Ms. Huang Wenling of Rock Publishing Company (Taipei); Professor Alfreda Murck, researcher of the Palace Museum (Beijing), and Ms. Zhang Ying of the museum's Digital Information Department; Research Specialist Stephen Allee of the Freer Gallery; Ms. Lü Weimin of the Shanghai Museum; and Arnold Chang of New Jersey. We are also grateful to the following for their generous support and enthusiasm throughout the project: Mr. Chen Chite of Rock Publishing, Mr. and Mrs. Shau-wai and Marie Lam, Mr. Tang Shi-fan, Dr. David Y. Wong, the Anna Fang Living Trust, Mr. and Mrs. Modo and Lily Chang, and Mr. and Mrs. Franklin and Lolita Tom.

Special gratitude is due to the graduate and undergraduate students of three seminars held by Professor Sturman at UCSB from 2010 through 2012. Without their feedback and contributions, this project would never have taken shape. Among these students, Seokwon Choi, Ph.D. candidate in the Department of the History of Art and Architecture at UCSB (who has also served as the Atkins Asian Art Research Intern at SBMA for the past two years), is deserving of special recognition. Both his scholarly contributions and invaluable administrative assistance in multiple aspects of this catalogue were truly indispensable.

For assistance in managing the countless organizational details of this project, we are most grateful to SBMA's staff. We especially thank Michelle Sullivan, senior curatorial assistant, who navigated the myriad details of this project with great skill and intelligence in addition to supporting the day-to-day affairs of the curatorial department. Many thanks also go to Sydney Hengst, curatorial assistant to Asian art, who joined the project in its last stages on the eve of Michelle's departure to attend graduate school. Their seamless transition was essential to the success of this project. Special thanks are also due to Cherie Summers and Ann Mersmann of Collections Management for their patience and the flawless arrangement of loans and logistics associated with traveling the exhibition; and Nancy Rogers, art preparator, for her attentiveness and consultation in handling these amazingly delicate works of art.

We are grateful to a number of people in the production of this catalogue. To Brian Forrest, for his superb photography of the majority of the works in the exhibition and his extraordinary skill in stitching together the numerous shots necessary to represent each of the long handscroll paintings. To Jane Hyun, our editor, who gave cohesion and clarity to our diverse styles and the multitude of details inherent to manuscripts that involve the study of literature in a foreign language. To Han-yun Chang, editor at the National Central Library in Taiwan, for her diligent review and editing of Chinese characters that appear in the catalogue and, in some cases, her further review of the Chinese readings in original sources. To Lorraine Wild of Green Dragon Office and her staff, Xiaoqing Wang and Amy Fortunato, for a book of truly elegant design that successfully integrates the images and texts so central to the expressions of the seventeenth-century literati artists. We are also indebted to Green Dragon Office for introducing to us Mary DelMonico of DelMonico Books, an imprint of Prestel Publishing, whose interest and participation in co-publishing gave us encouragement and the comfort that the catalogue would be made widely available.

Finally, our sincere thanks go to our families for their patience and support during the years this project occupied a large part of our daily lives.

Peter C. Sturman
Professor, Department of the History of Art and Architecture
University of California at Santa Barbara

Susan S. Tai
Elizabeth Atkins Curator of Asian Art
Santa Barbara Museum of Art

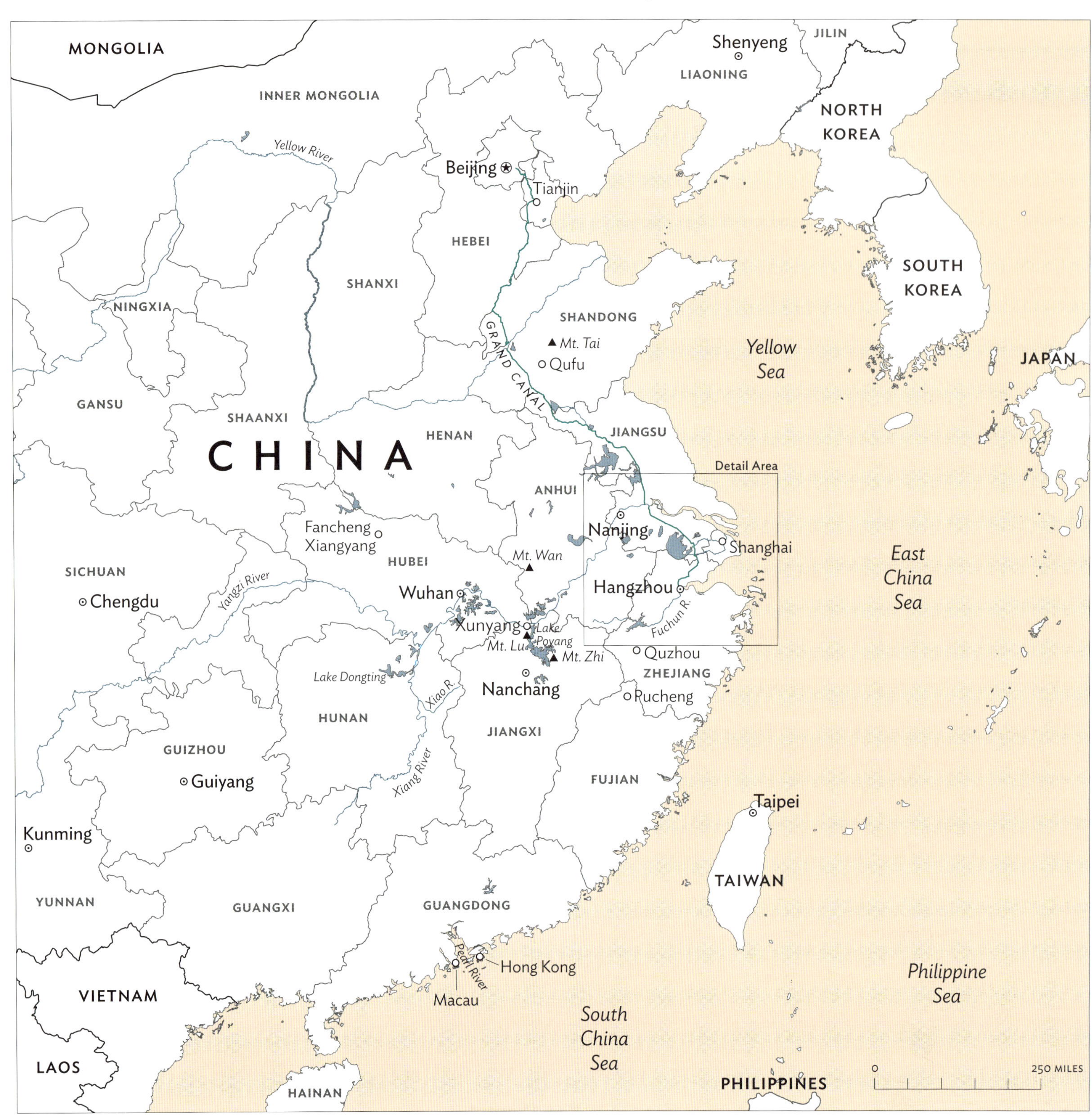

LEGEND

- ⊙ Province capitals
- ○ Cities
- ▲ Mountains

Maps and Chronology

Shang 商 c. 1600–c. 1100 BCE

Zhou 周 c. 1100–256 BCE

Qin 秦 221–207 BCE

Han 漢 206 BCE–220 CE
WESTERN HAN 西漢 206 BCE–8 CE
XIN 新 9–23
LIU XUAN 劉玄 23–25
EASTERN HAN 東漢 25–220

Three Kingdoms 三國 220–265
WEI 魏 220–265
SHU 蜀 221–263
WU 吳 222–280

Jin 晉 265–420
WESTERN JIN 西晉 265–316
EASTERN JIN 東晉 317–420

Northern and Southern Dynasties 南北朝 420–589

Northern Dynasties 北朝 386–581
NORTHERN WEI 北魏 386–534
EASTERN WEI 東魏 534–550
WESTERN WEI 西魏 535–557
NORTHERN QI 北齊 550–577
NORTHERN ZHOU 北周 557–581

Southern Dynasties 南朝 420–589
SONG 宋 420–479
QI 齊 479–502
LIANG 梁 502–557
CHEN 陳 557–589

Sui 隋 581–618

Tang 唐 618–907

Five Dynasties 五代 907–960

Song 宋 960–1279
NORTHERN SONG 北宋 960–1127
SOUTHERN SONG 南宋 1127–1279

Liao 遼 916–1125

Jin 金 1115–1234

Yuan 元 1279–1368

Ming 明 1368–1644
HONGWU 洪武 1368–1398
JIANWEN 建文 1398–1402
YONGLE 永樂 1402–1424
HONGXI 洪熙 1424–1425
XUANDE 宣德 1425–1435
ZHENGTONG 正統 1435–1449
JINGTAI 景泰 1449–1457
TIANSHUN 天順 1457–1464
CHENGHUA 成化 1464–1487
HONGZHI 弘治 1487–1505
ZHENGDE 正德 1505–1521
JIAJING 嘉靖 1521–1567
LONGQING 隆慶 1567–1572
WANLI 萬曆 1572–1620
TAICHANG 泰昌 1620
TIANQI 天啟 1620–1627
CHONGZHEN 崇禎 1627–1644

Southern Ming 南明
HONGGUANG 弘光 1644–1645
LONGWU 隆武 1645–1646
SHAOWU 紹武 1646
YONGLI 永曆 1646–1662

Qing 清 1644–1911
SHUNZHI 順治 1644–1661
KANGXI 康熙 1661–1722
YONGZHENG 雍正 1722–1735
QIANLONG 乾隆 1735–1796
JIAQING 嘉慶 1796–1820
DAOGUANG 道光 1820–1850
XIANFENG 咸豐 1850–1861
TONGZHI 同治 1861–1875
GUANGXU 光緒 1875–1908
XUANTONG 宣統 1908–1911

Central Coastal China, including the Yangzi River Delta (Jiangnan)

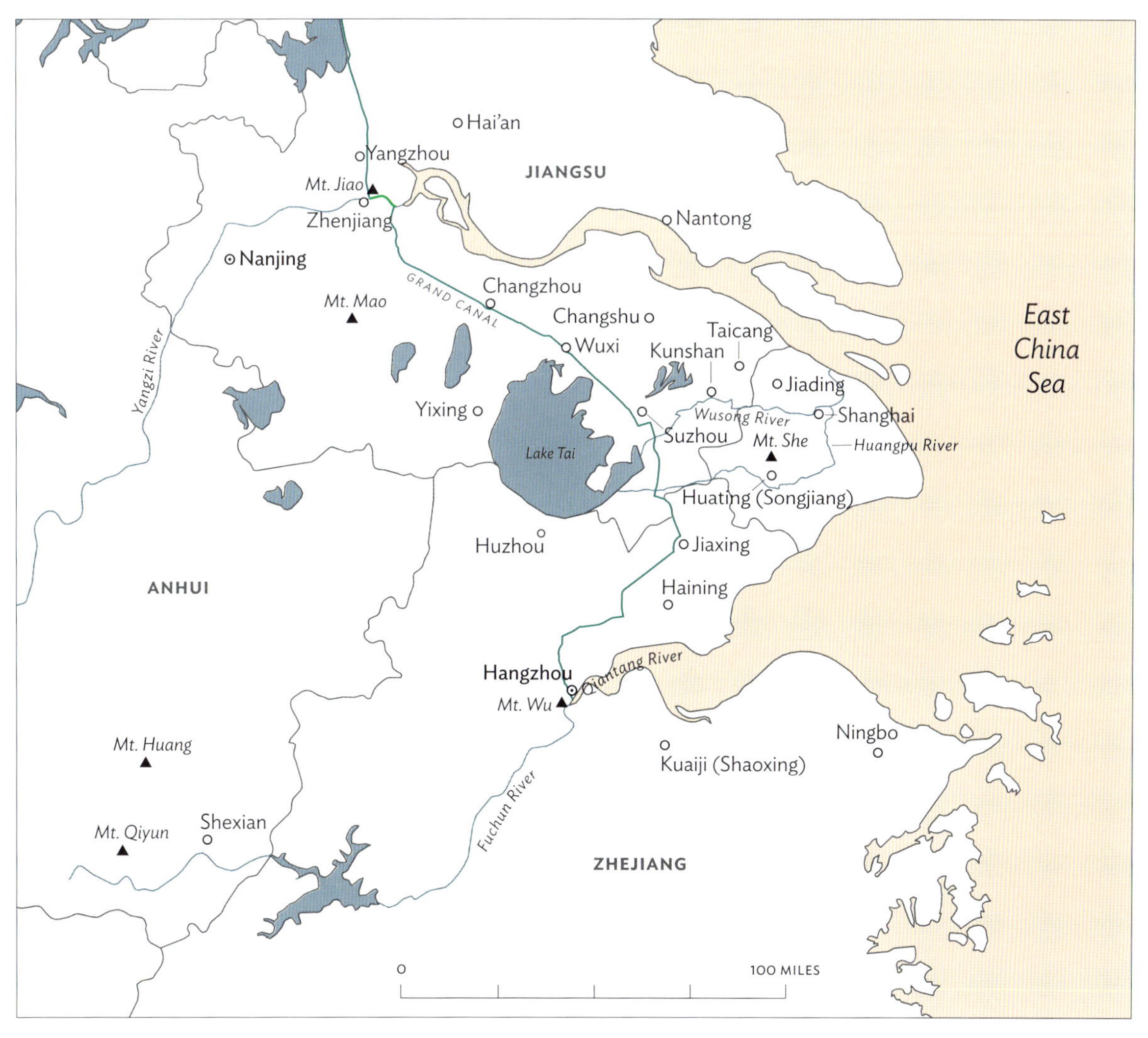

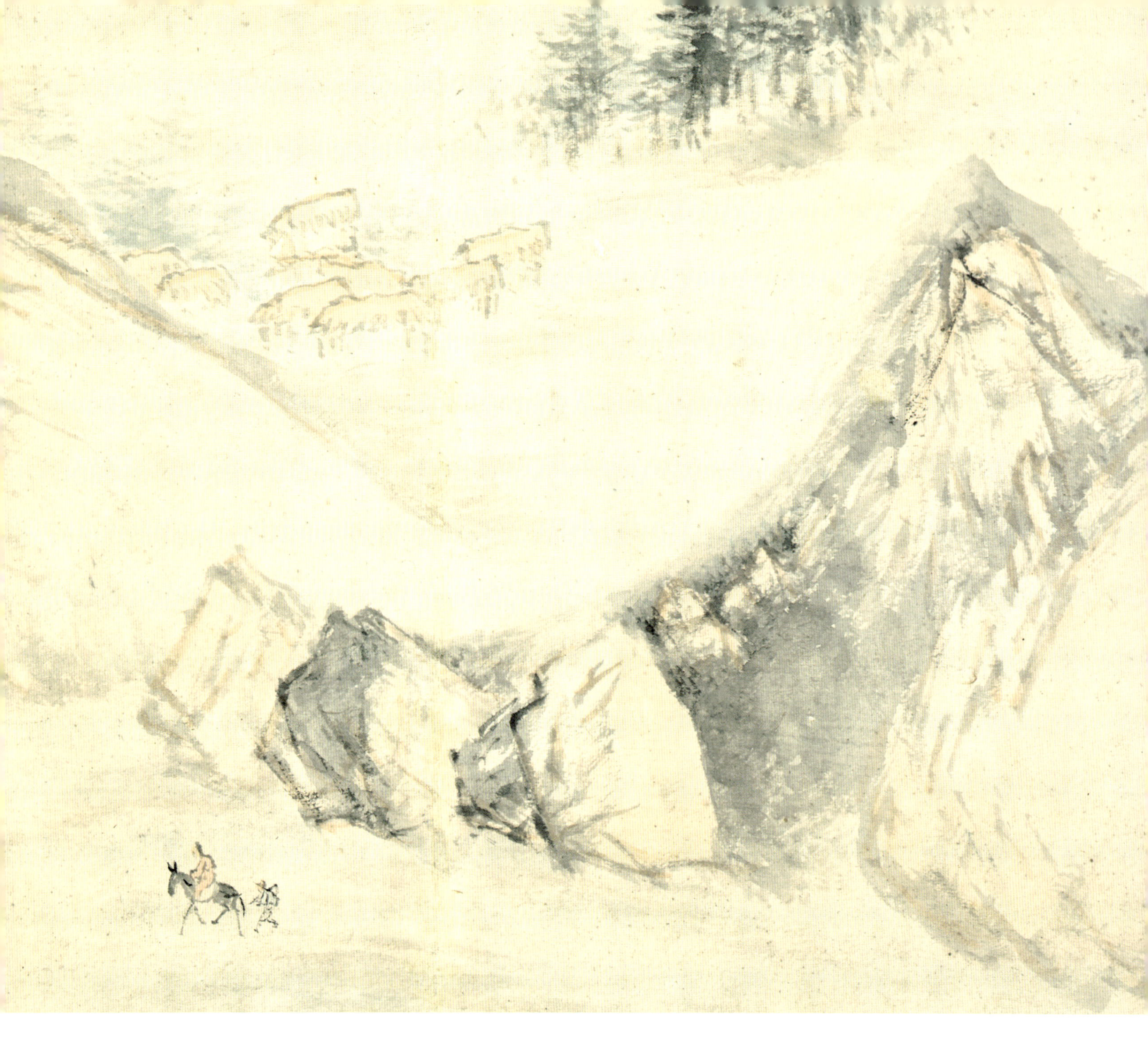

FIG. 1 Lu Wei, "Searching for Poetry" (detail), leaf from *Landscapes of Poetic Ideas*, before 1689 (cat. no. 52)

The Art of Reclusion

Peter C. Sturman

In February 1917, Chen Duxiu 陳獨秀 (1879–1942), the newly appointed dean of the School of Letters at Beijing University, published an article titled "Discourse on a Revolution in Literature" in *New Youth*, the magazine he helped found to serve as a platform for cultural reform. Writing only six years after the fall of the Qing dynasty (1644–1911), and for a nation still entombed by traditions that had developed over thousands of years of imperial rule, Chen was determined to establish guidelines for a new literature appropriate for a modern China. Consequently, he wielded his words not with the decorum one associates with high university administrators, but with the force of a sledgehammer:

I am willing to brave the enmity of all the pedantic scholars of the country, and hoist the great banner of the "Army of the Revolution in Literature" [promoting] these three great principles: Destroy the chiseled, obsequious writing of the aristocrat to establish the plain, expressive literature of the people. Destroy the putrid, formalistic prose of classicism and establish the refreshing, sincere literature of realism. Destroy the obscure and impenetrable writing of the hermit and recluse to establish the clear and popular literature of a living society! [1]

The last object of Chen Duxiu's angry attack provides the thematic center to the present exhibition, and his comment on the harmfulness of the hermit or recluse at the start of this introductory essay may thus strike the reader as misplaced. A closer look, however, reveals the usefulness of Chen's third principle as a way of introducing our subject. To begin with, it highlights the unusual status accorded the recluse in traditional Chinese culture—equal to, by Chen's reckoning, the aristocrat and the classicist as important foes in the task of modernizing China. How did the recluse, one whose solitary existence apart from society, come to be perceived as such a threat, and in the company of the most privileged and educated no less? And what is this obscure and impenetrable writing that the recluse creates?

The West has known its share of literary hermits, but such figures are more likely to be writers first, reclusive eccentrics second. Clearly, Chen Duxiu had something different in mind. This is not a phenomenon of occasional literary-minded individuals who chose to shun the world. Rather, he alludes to a greater subset of the social body that was perceived as collectively producing its own brand of literature. Religious hermits, perhaps? Disheveled monks lost in devotions and expressing the gleanings of their meditations in obtuse language? Hardly. While there certainly existed devout Buddhists and Daoists who sought solitary lives in order to pursue their spiritual beliefs, what Chen alludes to was far more widespread than these relatively few religious individuals, and decidedly secular as well.

The recluse that Chen Duxiu singles out as a hindrance to a new and modern culture in fact was hardly reclusive at all, which begs the question: how can a recluse not be reclusive? The answer is when he exists more in fiction than in fact. As Chen hoisted his revolutionary banner in the early years of the republic, he confronted in the recluse an ideal that was deeply embedded in the psyche of traditional Chinese culture. The pervasiveness of this ideal was such that for a reformist like himself, acting in a time of national crisis, what by definition should have been a non-entity was in fact a formidable opponent.

The recluse is such a familiar figure in Chinese culture that he is easily overlooked (fig. 1). He is the solitary fisherman plying his line by a river shore or the lone woodcutter ambling down a mountain path, a fagot of wood bundled to his back. The recluse is the donkey rider entering a forest grove; he is the figure seated in a rustic hut accompanied by books and scrolls. He is the mountain wanderer, the gentleman farmer, the flower-seeker. Not only does the recluse seem to populate every traditional-style landscape painting, he is a popular subject in figure painting and often alluded to through metaphor and association in a fair number of flower paintings as well. The ubiquity of the recluse suggests that he is truly a part of the fabric of Chinese painting and as such too broad a topic for particular inquiry.

For a modern audience, however, there is obvious value in learning about something so intrinsic to traditional Chinese culture. This is especially true in the West, where the concept of reclusion has attracted little attention, and the image of the recluse has most commonly been tied to famous eccentrics like Greta Garbo or Howard Hughes, whose reasons for disengagement rarely rose above the level of frivolous speculation. Our world today grows ever more crowded, ever more interconnected. As the world shrinks, outside affairs encroach, and our personal spaces become smaller, no doubt the notion of escape that reclusion embodies becomes attractive. There is, in other words, a universality to the images and ideas presented in these paintings that appears increasingly relevant to our own time and space.

Focusing solely on the universal, however, threatens to resurrect old misconceptions regarding the "timelessness" of Chinese art, and it certainly disserves the paintings and calligraphies gathered in this exhibition. For while reclusion is one of the oldest themes in China and the recluse a ubiquitous figure in the literary and visual arts, neither has much meaning unless considered within a specific historical matrix. Our concern is not with generalities but with the individual ways artists chose to explore and interpret the theme of reclusion in their own time. In this regard, the seventeenth century is both appropriate and special. Corresponding to the end of one dynasty (Ming, 1368–1644) and the beginning of another (Qing), the seventeenth century was dominated by the kind of social disorder that has long been considered one of the banes of Chinese history. All dynastic transitions were marked by periods of confusion and suffering, but the Ming-Qing cataclysm, as it has been called, was especially complex and prolonged.[2] The victors were the ethnically and culturally distinct Manchus from the north. The conquest of China by an outside people, and the survival of remnants of the Ming court for thirty years past the conquest date of 1644, heightened the issues of loyalty that accompany every dynastic transition. For the "remnants" or "leftover people" (*yimin* 遺民) who identified with the Ming, disengagement from the new polity was a time-honored option and one that was pursued earnestly by many.

For our purposes, however, what makes the seventeenth century particularly intriguing is the fact that reclusion did not suddenly emerge as a popular subject for artistic expression in the years following the Qing conquest. Well before there was any particularly pressing reason to take to the hills, a number of notable figures were already trumpeting the superiority of "mountain dwelling."

Reclusion thus proves to be a persistent and important theme throughout China's long and eventful seventeenth century. In fact, when Chen Duxiu railed against the obscure and impenetrable writing of the hermit and recluse as an obstacle to a new modern literature, for all intents and purposes he was pointing to what took place in the seventeenth century, as the cultural patterns established during that period of time were immensely influential over the remaining centuries of imperial rule. This exhibition focuses on paintings and calligraphy of seventeenth-century China, and in certain respects they fit the bill for Chen's criticism. However, lest the viewer worry that these objects are "obscure and impenetrable," we offer assurances to the contrary. Chen's comments belong to the very particular context of China's early modern years, when most of traditional culture seemed to exist in its own world, irrelevant to the urgent issues brought by foreign aggression. It is true that the objects displayed here represent the highest echelon of a culture built upon centuries of refinement: one, moreover, that was focused on a literary tradition of indubitable magnitude and density. And as such, particularly for an audience unschooled in the literary culture of China, there is much to learn in order to appreciate what is displayed. For the patient viewer, however, the rewards are great. Nothing rivals seventeenth-century Chinese painting for its combination of skill, inventiveness, complexity, and drama.

However, the best argument for the approachability of the paintings and calligraphies displayed here resides in an apparent conundrum of our topic: would a true recluse, one disengaged from the world, make the effort to express visually and verbally his disengagement? Is not the effort itself an act of engagement, a call for others to respond? Reclusion is an act of disengagement yet, ironically, pronouncing reclusion is the opposite: a calling out for individuals of sympathetic mind. However deeply certain individuals may have aspired to the ideal of the recluse and the solitary existence it implies, reclusion was primarily conceived as a broadly shared discourse that invited commentary within a like-minded community. In a manner of speaking, the paintings and calligraphies in this exhibition were intended to engage the viewer in a dialogue of disengagement, and their effectiveness is everywhere apparent in the many inscriptions added to the original works of art by contemporary and later admirers. Particularly with the handscrolls, these inscriptions can be extensive, and when written especially well or by a figure of renown they can draw almost as much attention as the original painting or calligraphy, thus providing all the more attraction for others to engage.

For the artist, reclusion represented a private space, a chamber within the mind, but it was a private space that was always intended to be shared. The goal of this exhibition is to enter those private spaces and explore the graphic and textual structures with which each artist conceived his or her place in a dynamically changing world.

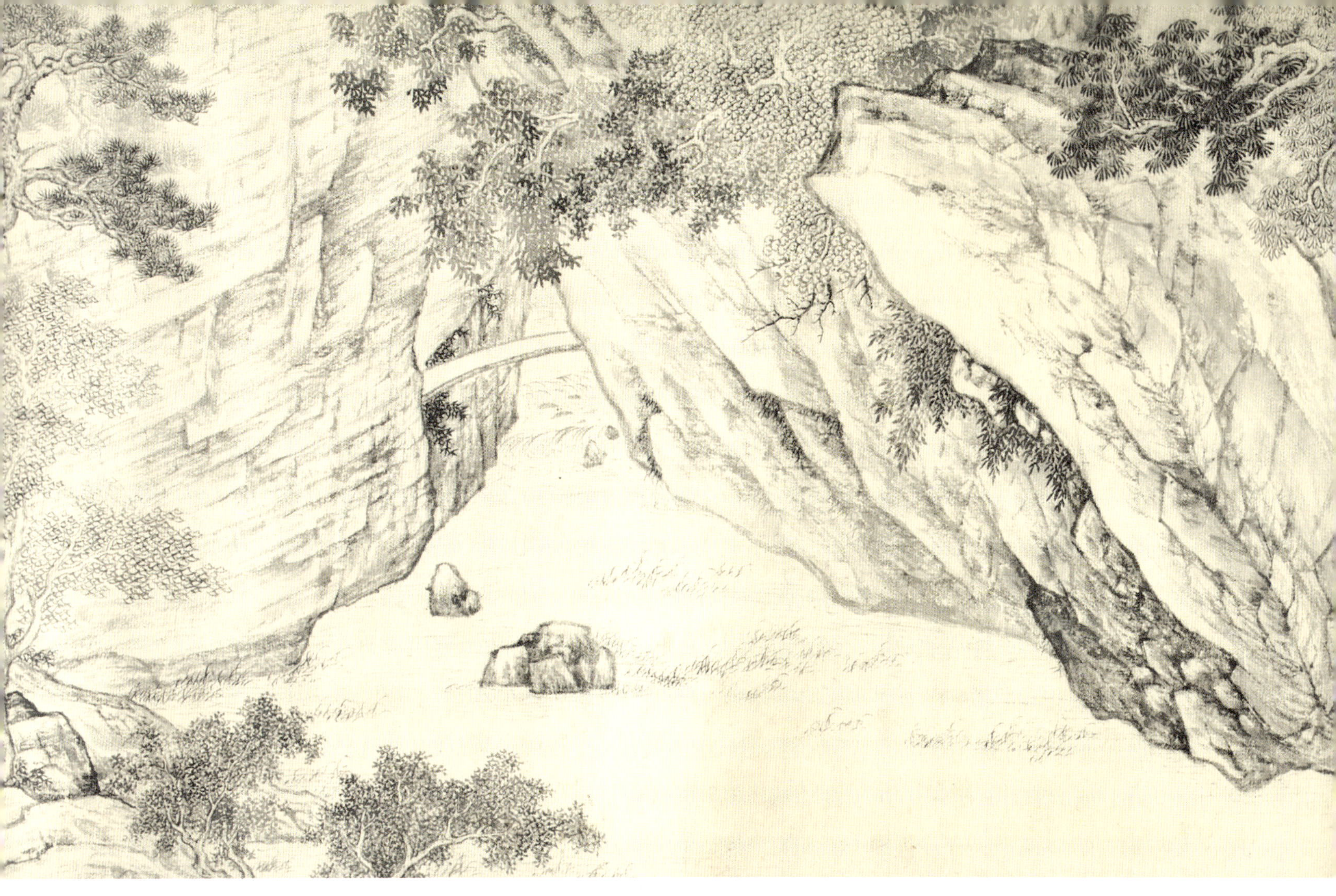

SUMMONING THE RECLUSE There is no better place to begin than with Xiang Shengmo's 項聖謨 (1597–1658) long and exquisitely painted landscape *Invitation to Reclusion* (1626; cat. no. 1, fig. 2). This is one of those rare works of art that immediately stands out as something different, what earlier Chinese connoisseurs would refer to as a "notable" or "famous" painting. The label is earned not only for the painting's quality but also its importance as a unique object. In this case, that uniqueness is largely owed to the youthfulness of the painter. According to his own lengthy inscription that follows the landscape, Xiang began the painting in the autumn of 1625 at the age of only twenty-eight while leisurely traveling by boat along waterways in the environs of Wu, between modern-day Suzhou and Shanghai. One of the enduring maxims of Chinese painting is that an artist does not mature until he reaches an advanced age. Maturity, however, does not necessarily correlate with excellence, and even less so with effort. Conversely, it is a lesser-known fact that the early work of well-trained artists often demonstrates the most ambition and skill, as the youthful artist works hard to impress senior colleagues and establish a reputation. That is certainly the case with *Invitation to Reclusion*, which boasts the literary adornments of three of the leading cultural figures of the late Ming dynasty. The painting's frontispiece title and a trailing inscription were done by Dong Qichang 董其昌 (1555–1636), the most celebrated calligrapher of the day; they are followed by the additions of another superb calligrapher, Chen Jiru 陳繼儒 (1558–1639), as well as one by Li Rihua 李日華 (1565–1635; see also cat. nos. 8–12). Dong, Chen, and Li, along with the younger Xiang, all hailed from the same area (Songjiang and Jiaxing) of Jiangsu Province, and there were longstanding and strong friendships between individuals and families that further added impetus to promote Xiang's painting.[3] Nonetheless, there were no shortcuts to fame here: Xiang's scroll is a tour de force, multifaceted demonstration of what it took to be an elite artist at the most demanding of levels in late-Ming China.

Following the painting to its left are twenty of Xiang Shengmo's own poems on the theme of reclusion; immediately after these is an inscription of almost equal length that details the circumstances of the painting. Poems and inscription are written neatly in a medium-sized standard script whose relative formality reinforces the impression that the scroll was intended to announce Xiang's matriculation into the ranks of serious scholar art. The poems provide the literary core for the painting's content and are essential for understanding his particular interpretation of reclusion.[4] Our attention, however, is drawn first to Xiang's inscription, as its narration of the process of the making of the scroll is one of the factors that make *Invitation to Reclusion* noteworthy. Xiang seems to have begun casually enough—some free time on the boat and some good paper leading to the start of a long handscroll composition—but his meticulous style of painting meant slow progress, and those six lengths of paper must have seemed to grow longer by the day after advance word got out to Dong Qichang, who insisted on monitoring its progress. Pressed to show something, Xiang hurriedly completed the first section of paper and shared it with Dong, who admired it and remarked:

FIG. 2 Xiang Shengmo, *Invitation to Reclusion* (detail), 1625–26 (cat. no. 1)

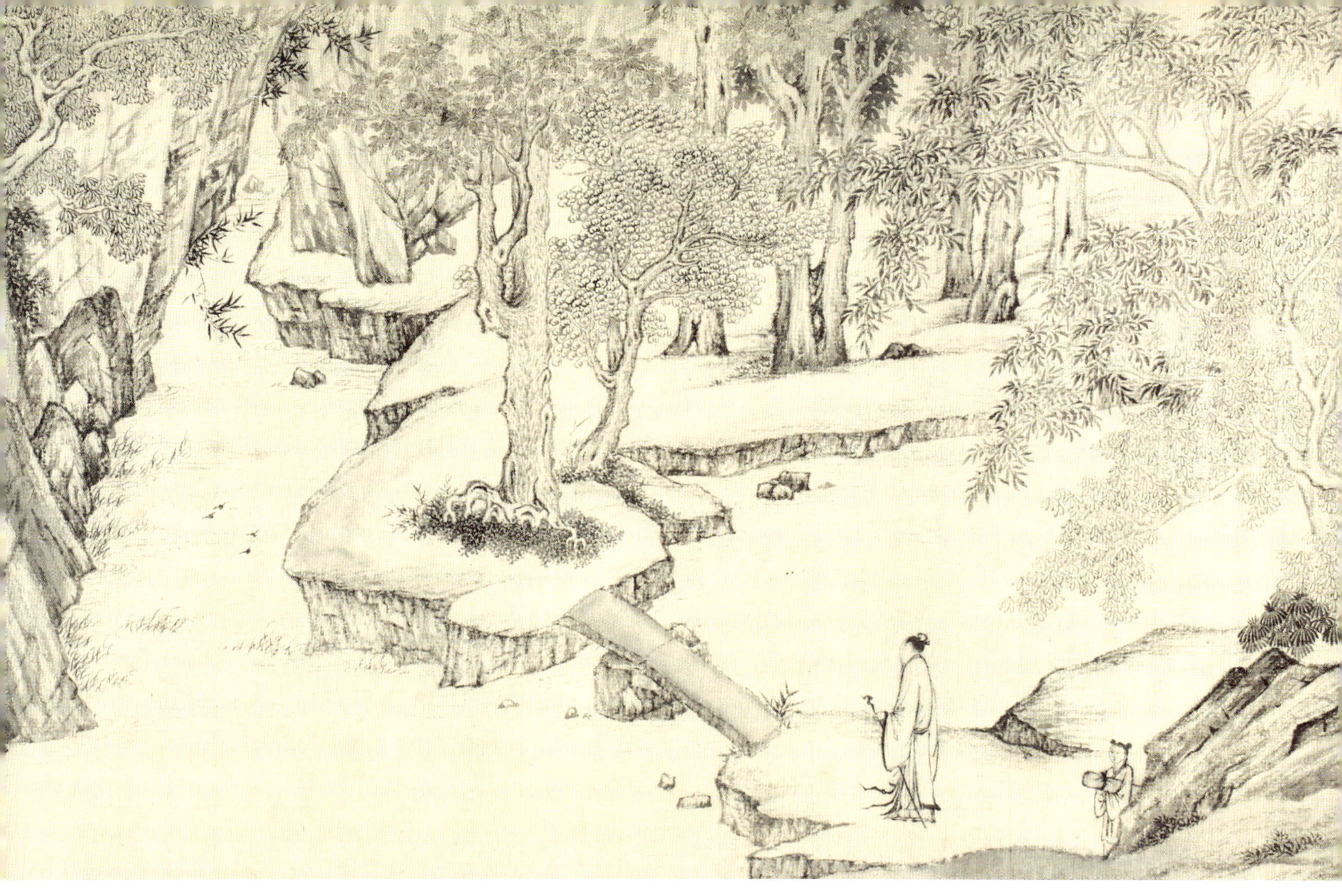

"The mountains are high, the valleys are beautiful. The forests are green and breezes caress the robes. The man does not look back and very much has an air of transcendence. What exactly is this painting?" I [Xiang] replied, "Because I read the poems on the invitation to reclusion by Lu Ji and Zuo Si I was very much inspired and painted this piece as an accompaniment."

「山高溪秀，林翠撲衣，人不回顧，甚有超逸之風．此何圖也?」曰：「因讀陸機，左思招隱詩，有興于懷，將補是圖.」

Following the scroll from its beginning (moving right to left), we can see where that first section of paper ends, just past the third water inlet right before a rustic dwelling with thatched huts and walls. We see the man that "does not look back" and thus, in a way that eerily compresses time, are able to revisit Dong's initial impression of Xiang's labors. And this truly was labor. According to the remainder of Xiang's inscription, it took at least nine more months to complete the painting. During this time he suffered from sickness, melancholy, and bothersome requests (presumably for paintings) along with other "worldly matters." He was reduced to working on the scroll in the evenings, oftentimes until midnight, and to meet the physical challenges he cut out wine and ate only "pine-flower cakes and tea-leaf soup." Contemporary readers of Xiang's inscription, with its description of the painting's long journey to completion and Dong's persistent inquiries, could well have been reminded of another long landscape handscroll with artist's inscription—Huang Gongwang's 黃公望 (1269–1354) *Dwelling in the Fuchun Mountains* (1347–50) of almost three centuries earlier, which Huang worked on for three to four years before finally being compelled to relinquish it to the promised recipient. Owned by Dong, *Dwelling in the Fuchun Mountains* was the most famous painting of the time and the ultimate benchmark by which any ambitious landscape scroll might be judged.[5]

Yet, it is really the differences between Huang Gongwang's famous landscape and Xiang Shengmo's *Invitation to Reclusion* that are striking. Few people embodied the reclusive ideal better than Huang, who wandered the landscape along the Fuchun River in the mid-fourteenth century and painted only when the mood was right. In contrast, Xiang's inscription describes physical, emotional, and possibly psychological struggles. There is a gap between Xiang's real life experiences and the image of reclusion he seeks to portray, a gap that was probably felt every time he contemplated earlier paragons of the eremitic ideal like Huang, for whom a seamless line between experience and art was generally assumed.

Awareness of the distance between the real and ideal is a recurring feature of seventeenth-century painting, though it is manifest in various and diverse ways. For Xiang Shengmo that awareness appears to have inspired an attempt at reconciliation or erasure of that breach, as he utilized a convincing visual vernacular to describe images of sublimity. This gentle balance is established at the painting's very beginning, with a gnarled and twisting tree that immediately pulls the viewer into its absorbing minutiae of forms and textures. The motifs multiply—shrubs, grasses, bamboo, a layered outcropping, all in the space of a few inches—yet are artfully composed to emphasize spatial depth. Rather than feel overwhelmed by details, we are seduced by the richness of this monochrome world, our eyes drawn to the plateaued shore of a riverbank and then left, in generous steps, to the scholar-recluse and his young zither-toting servant. Xiang's meticulous description makes a profound claim to an alternative reality, one that only deepens as we cross the stone bridge and his world slowly unfurls.

Throughout this initial section there is an astounding array of objects, textures, vistas, and movements. Receding inlets lure us deeply into the space of the paper. Birds on the wing, a recurring device throughout Xiang Shengmo's painting, help transform the paper's two dimensions into three. Our journey follows an unseen route behind an abrupt riverside cliff that pronounces the terrain's inaccessibility before a second bridge leads us directly into an even more precipitous rock face. Secluded in the foreground and backed by a telescoped torrent rushing through the mountainside is a stately grove of interlocking pines. Directly echoing the strolling scholar across the foreground water, these trees provide a metaphorical bookend—a statement of evergreen strength and virtue to symbolize the essential nature of this wanderer's reclusion.

This, more or less, is how much Dong Qichang first saw of the painting. There is so much care and detail described that this first section must already have seemed a complete painting. Yet, counting his poems, Xiang originally planned something five times again as long! Wisely, the plan also called for large expanses of open space. Moving through the scroll we encounter a country residence with riverside pavilion. We traverse sweeping terrains and deep grottoes, pass bucolic villages, remote temples, vegetable patches... the sights and tastes of a world apart. Punctuating our journey are the denizens of reclusion: immortal cranes, fishermen, scholars, and the young lads always ready to carry a zither or sweep a courtyard. The further we move through the landscape the more expansive it becomes, ending with a final elevated pavilion, from which we gaze into one last mysterious grotto where miniscule birds swoop and alight. A couplet in the fifth of Xiang's trailing verses nicely encapsulates the painting:

> Leave the world for a bounty of surpassing scenes;
> Return to the fields and escape from the crowd.
>
> 出世饒佳境，歸田有逸群.

In Xiang Shengmo's hands, reclusion was not to be equated with hiding but with transcendence—a crossing over into an alternative universe of exhilarating vistas and soaring horizons. So broad is the sweep of his landscape, and so convincing its descriptiveness, the viewer is easily lost in the immediacy of its sensory charms. Yet, other than a few brief comments from Chen Jiru on winding paths and tasty vegetables, Xiang's senior friends are remarkably silent about such things in their inscriptions. Dong Qichang, Chen Jiru, and Li Rihua focus instead on literary and artistic references. For those familiar with seventeenth-century Chinese painting this comes as little surprise, as Dong in particular was singularly absorbed by the polemics of painting theory and practice.[6] But while these scholars' comments clearly reflect issues of personal concern, they are also a reminder of how familiar and deeply layered the theme of reclusion was by the seventeenth century. Some things simply did not need to be mentioned, especially when there were subtle points to Xiang's art that could be emphasized to fit more immediate agendas. For our purposes, however, Xiang's painting provides an excellent vehicle by which we can introduce some of the different dimensions of reclusion in China.

According to Xiang, inspiration for his painting came from poems on the theme of "beckoning the recluse" (*zhao yin* 招隱) by Zuo Si 左思 (c. 253–c. 307) and Lu Ji 陸機 (261–303).[7] Zuo and Lu were both celebrated literary figures of the early Jin dynasty (Western Jin, 265–316).[8] Politically this was a tumultuous, unstable period of time, but if instability discouraged political engagement, conversely it prompted exploration of individuality through philosophical discourse as well as artistic expression. One development reflective of this important cultural movement was an interest in nature, landscape, and rural living as subjects for poetry. Zuo's and Lu's poems on the theme of beckoning the recluse are relatively early examples of this trend, which continued to grow and flourish in the fourth and fifth centuries.

How much Zuo Si's and Lu Ji's poems represent a new perspective on landscape in medieval China is clear when their verses are contrasted with an earlier poem of a very similar title that likely served as both model and point of departure. This "Beckoning the Recluse" (or "Summons for a Recluse"), included in the renowned *Chu ci* 楚辭 (Songs of the south) anthology and traditionally attributed to the tragic courtier Qu Yuan 屈原 (c. 340–278 BCE), describes a landscape of deep ravines and wild uneven mountains, where "tigers and leopards roar" 虎豹嗥 and "the heart stands still with awe aghast" 心淹留兮恫慌忽.[9] The poet seeks a prince who went wandering and mournfully calls out for him to return, insisting that in this god-forsaken place one cannot stay long. In utter contrast, Zuo's and Lu's poems of some centuries later beckon a hermit to emerge from a far more welcoming landscape, not to return to society but rather to serve as a companion in carefree wandering:

> Walking staff in hand, I beckon the man in reclusion,
> The wilderness path bridging past with present.
> A cliffside cave, free of intricate construction;
> Amid the hills, a resounding zither...[10]
>
> 杖策招隱士，荒塗橫古今.
> 巖穴無結構，丘中有鳴琴...

These are the opening lines of Zuo Si's first of two "Beckoning the Recluse" poems, and it is readily apparent that they served as the inspiration for the beginning of Xiang Shengmo's long handscroll. The figure walking forward with a staff, the same singled out by Dong Qichang, is Xiang's alter ego. Acting out Zuo's poetic voice, he leads us into the wilderness in search of a man in reclusion. This white-robed protagonist appears periodically throughout the scroll, but never more prominently than about midway in the painting, holding hands with a dark-shirted companion on a small bridge. The recluse has emerged! Arm outstretched, he gestures to the pleasures that a life of reclusion in the landscape promises.

Beyond the initial image of the figure with staff on a wilderness path and his zither-toting servant, it is hard to say if Xiang Shengmo singled out anything else in the poems by Zuo Si or Lu Ji for illustration. Indeed, the cozy signs of human habitation that follow in the painting are somewhat at odds with the naked cave that Zuo suggests as a place of dwelling. Their poems on reclusion may present a far more benign image of landscape than that presented in the *Chu ci* poem of centuries earlier, but Xiang's landscape is that much more domesticated, colored by additional layers of the reclusion tradition that became popularized not long after Zuo and Lu. Especially notable are the two rustic homesteads—models of country living with sturdy structures, tidy courtyards, and well-kept vegetable gardens.

The image of the agrarian idyll has deep, ancient roots in China, but in Xiang Shengmo's time it was indelibly associated with one reclusive figure in particular, the poet Tao Yuanming 陶淵明 (also known as Tao Qian 陶潛, 365?–427).

After serving in a number of relatively low-ranking civil posts, Tao retired in 405 and spent the rest of his life as a farmer-recluse at his home near Xunyang (modern Jiujiang, Jiangxi Province), where he enjoyed a life of self-sufficiency and wrote poetry that in time would become one of the most cherished bodies of writing in China. Irascible, independent, wine-loving, and plain-speaking, Tao was viewed by later scholar-officials, especially those encountering setbacks in their official careers, as an iconic hero.[11] More often than not, an association with Tao's legacy and his famous poem "Home Again!" celebrating his return was consciously intended when the kinds of rural dwellings we see in Xiang's painting were depicted.

Tao Yuanming's image loomed large in the seventeenth century, and he is evoked numerous times in this exhibition. Thoughts of his person and lifestyle were practically inevitable when viewers encountered the ubiquitous images of rustic domiciles in paintings like *Invitation to Reclusion*. He was a frequent subject in the eccentric figure painting of Chen Hongshou 陳洪綬 (1599–1652; cat. nos. 21–23). Portraits and self-portraits might allude to Tao through text and image. Even paintings of plants and flowers—chrysanthemums in particular but also willows and pines—could easily reference him through associations drawn from his biography and writings.

His most pervasive influence, however, is seen in the overall structure of many a landscape painting, especially those, like Xiang Shengmo's *Invitation to Reclusion*, in the long horizontal format of the handscroll. This is because of Tao Yuanming's authorship of the story of the Peach Blossom Spring, a beguilingly simple tale of a fisherman who, attracted to blossoming peach trees along a stream, inadvertently comes across a cavernous passageway that leads to a hidden valley of neat homes and orderly fields. The welcoming residents are a secreted community whose ancestors, six hundred years earlier, fled the tyrannical rule of the Qin dynasty (221–207 BCE) and established an idyllic society, totally ignorant of the passage of time and dynasties. The fisherman leaves, but the return path is never found again.[12]

The popularity of Tao's "Peach Blossom Spring" made it a common subject for painting.[13] More importantly, the story offered a spatial template for the fundamental theme of escape and transcendence that provides meaning to landscape in Chinese art. When Xiang planned the composition of *Invitation to Reclusion*, with its journey from dense wilderness to open vistas, there is little doubt that he had Tao's story in mind—not as a subject to illustrate but as inspiration to convey the idea of passage to another world. It is noteworthy that the last of Xiang's twenty verses following the painting specifically mentions the Peach Blossom Spring.

From the historical perspective of a seventeenth-century artist, the notion of reclusion was generally associated with figures like Tao Yuanming and, more broadly, with the complicated period of time that followed the fall of the Han dynasty (206 BCE–220 CE). Distance and the limitations of textual as well as material remains has blended much of the three centuries following the demise of the long-lived Han into a global image of political instability, reduced territory, and short-lived dynasties counterbalanced by brilliant achievements in the arts by untrammeled figures like Tao for poetry, Wang Xizhi 王羲之 (303–361) for calligraphy, and Gu Kaizhi 顧愷之 (c. 344–406) for painting. In addition to this generalized view of the distant past, reclusion had so insinuated itself into the mainstream of literati discourse that it was perfectly commonplace to evoke the image of a Tao Yuanming as a way to express the universal wish to just get away from it all and live a simple life. But Xiang Shengmo's *Invitation to Reclusion* is clearly something different. Far from polite posturing, the scroll is a dedicated reexamination of what reclusion means, and in this regard, Xiang's tracing back to Zuo Si's and Lu Ji's "Beckoning the Recluse" poems is significant. It suggests an effort, probably with the goal of imparting seriousness to his project, to get back to an earlier moment in the tradition of reclusion.

There is a slight irony in this, as recent scholarship has clarified that the third century of the Common Era, when Zuo and Lu were active, already represents a relatively late stage in the historical development of reclusion. Here, however, we distinguish between history and legend, for according to the latter, the patterns of reclusion are ascribed to some of the earliest moments of civilization. According to traditional accounts, hermits were already shaping political philosophy in the time of the sage kings Yao 堯 and Shun 舜 (traditional dates twenty-third–twenty-second centuries BCE).[14] The most famous are the recluses Xu You 許由 and "Nester" Chaofu 巢父 (who resided in trees). Recognizing Xu's innate virtue, Yao asked him to be his successor. Disgusted by this invitation to become embroiled in the grime of human affairs, Xu cleansed his ears in a nearby stream. Chaofu, one-upping his friend, thereupon led his cattle upstream to drink from its "unpolluted" waters.[15]

Stories like these highlight the superior quality of the recluse, who eschews wealth and fame in order to follow a solitary path. They also showcase the virtue of the ruler who, searching for a qualified successor, puts aside personal (clan) interests for those of the people. In a prominent variation of this model, the recluse bides his time until the proper opportunity presents itself and then accepts an invitation to serve at court, typically as an advisor. Well known of this type is Taigong Wang 太公望 (Lü Shang 呂尚, eleventh century BCE), a fisherman until he was discovered by Xibo Chang 西伯昌 (Chang, Earl of the West, posthumously known as King Wen of Zhou 周文王 [1099–1050 BCE]).[16] In such cases, the righteousness of the royal supplicant is a determining factor in enticing the superior man out of hiding. These two paragons—the uncompromising Chaofu, whose aversion to public involvement reached to the muzzle of his water buffalo, and the far more moderate Taigong Wang—together encapsulate the crux of the issue of reclusion in China and why it earned such prominence: it spoke to the personal choice of political and social engagement.

Scholars have pointed out that these early legends of exemplary recluses, and the various philosophical and political dimensions of eremitism, are not prominent in the textual record until the Warring States period (403–221 BCE). Aat Vervoorn more specifically points to a pivotal role played by Confucius 孔子 (traditional dates 551–479 BCE).[17] Emphasizing the concept of moral autonomy for an individual, Confucius turned the issue of service into a charged ethical matter. A subject would willingly serve under the right conditions and for the right ruler, as this would allow him to further the Way (*dao* 道). However, should service to a ruler result in moral compromise, then it would be better to retire. Confucius's "timely reclusion" reflects a belief in flexibility, a willingness to adjust one's actions according to circumstances. The lament of "not according with the times," commonly voiced in later periods by scholars who either lived during periods of chaos or simply were frustrated by circumstances that prevented advancement, reflects this fundamental Confucian precept that reclusion or retreat was an option when fate deemed service was not.

Interestingly, two of the earliest recluses who earned praise from Confucius were especially noted for their lack of flexibility. These are the brothers Boyi 伯夷 and Shuqi 叔齊 (both eleventh century BCE), who starved to death on Shouyang Mountain. The eldest and youngest sons, respectively, of the ruler of Guzhu (modern Hebei Province) during the rule of the last sovereign of the Shang dynasty (c. 1600–c. 1100 BCE), the two are said to have fled their native land upon their father's death. This was because of the father's desire, contrary to customary hereditary practice, to put the younger Shuqi on the throne.

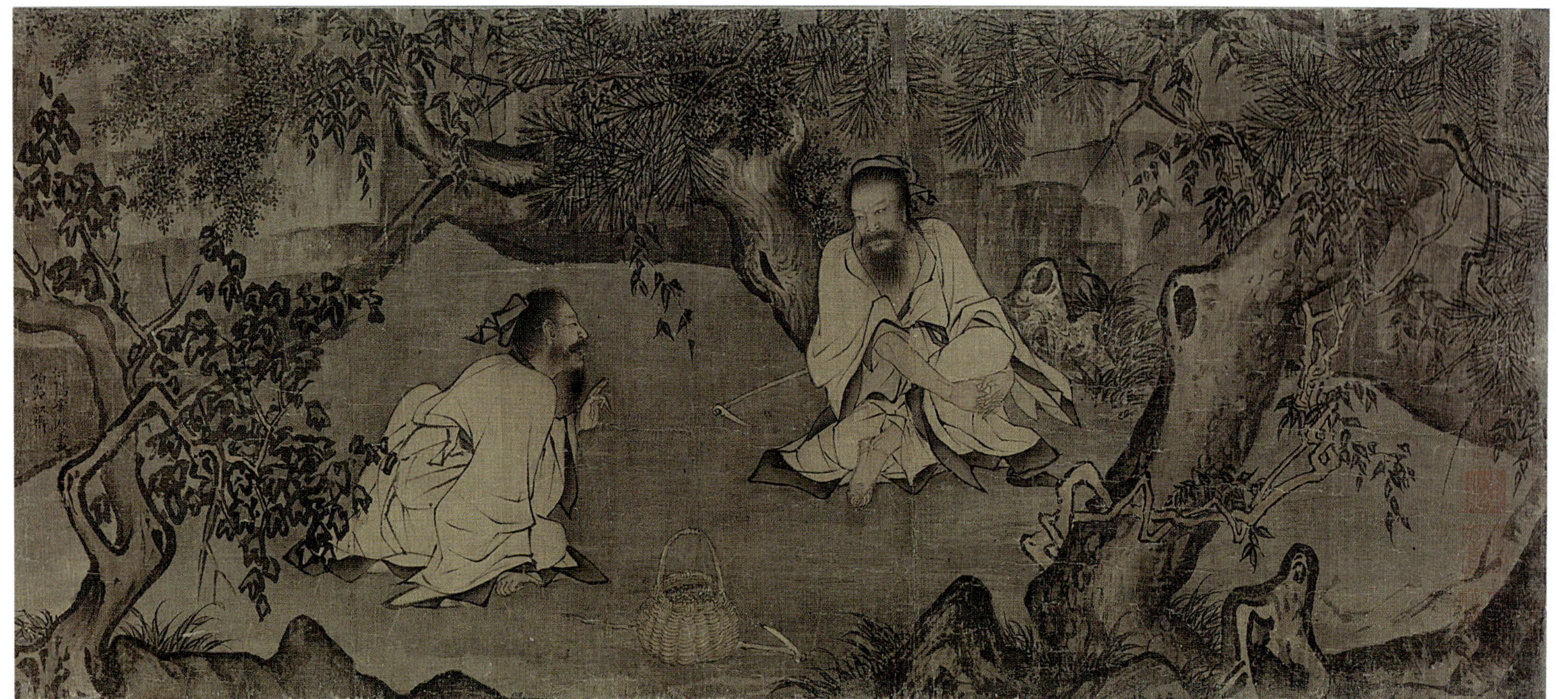

Boyi fled in order to remain filial to his father's wishes and avoid potential conflict. Shuqi joined him, unable to bear the thought of usurping Boyi's rightful position. The brothers traveled to Zhou, mindful of the sterling reputation of the aforementioned Xibo Chang, but by the time they arrived the king had died and his rule had passed to his son, King Wu (Zhou Wuwang 周武王, d. 1043 BCE). King Wu, from the perspective of the two brothers, failed critical litmus tests of moral propriety, and they thereupon fled to Shouyang Mountain, where they subsisted for some time on the *wei* 薇 plant before dying, refusing "to eat the grain of Zhou."[18] Confucius prominently called Boyi and Shuqi "famous men of old, who sought benevolence and attained it."[19]

These words may well have served as the inspiration for a portrayal of Boyi and Shuqi by Li Tang 李唐 (act. c. 1100–1150) in the middle of the twelfth century (fig. 3). The two brothers sit comfortably on a spotless ledge framed, metaphorically, by a twisting pine and cypress. Hand-hoes and a wicker basket of *wei* ferns for the moment are forgotten while the two engage in thoughtful conversation. Boyi clasps hands around knees and fixes his younger brother with an intense yet benign gaze. Shuqi's look is similarly concentrated. His left hand echoes his open mouth as he conveys vital words, right hand curling underneath to express passion and conviction. The portrayal is so skillful the viewer senses acuity to Shuqi's thoughts and personality and the rationale behind their father's desire to put him ahead of his brother. Equally well conveyed are Boyi's quiet wisdom and natural ease—a willingness to defer for the principle of filial piety. The one thing Li did not describe is any indication of the two brothers' misery, starving in the wilds of Shouyang Mountain. Painting for the court in the early years of the Southern Song (1127–1279), after the north had been lost to the invading armies of the non-Chinese Jurchen and the dynasty's survival remained precarious, Li Tang's sole interest was in portraying the unwavering strength of Boyi and Shuqi's convictions and the beauty of self-sacrifice for principle.

Not all saw Boyi and Shuqi in this way. Despite Confucius's praise, the brothers' uncompromising nature was a fulcrum for disagreement among later critics. The Daoist philosopher Zhuangzi 莊子 (fourth century BCE) was critical of Boyi for destroying his life and thus "blighting his inborn nature" 其於殘生傷性均也. From the Daoist's perspective, such strict adherence to a moral code was fundamentally unnatural.[20] Confucians too, however, could be critical of Boyi and Shuqi's inflexibility, or at least ambiguous. The great Han-dynasty historian Sima Qian 司馬遷 (c. 145–86 BCE) began his biographies of exemplary figures with Boyi and Shuqi, expressed admiration for their determination, and called them men of great virtue. Yet he also voiced disapproval—were it not for Confucius, he reasoned, who would know of their virtue? He ended their biography with some critical remarks:

> The hermit-scholars hiding away in their caves may be ever so correct in their givings and takings, and yet the names of them and their kind are lost and forgotten without receiving a word of praise. Is this not pitiful? Men of humble origin living in the narrow lanes strive to make perfect their actions and to establish a name for themselves, but if they do not somehow attach themselves to a great man, a "man of the blue clouds," how can they hope that their fame will be handed down to posterity?[21]
>
> 巖穴之士，趨舍有時，若此類名堙滅而不稱，悲夫．閭巷之人，欲砥行立名者，非附青雲之士，惡能施於後世哉?

Sima makes the point that a recluse by definition is someone hidden—out of sight, out of mind—and without traces of their exemplary conduct to follow, it is as if they never existed. The Daoist who proclaims the emptiness of fame and honor and champions withdrawal would not object, but most people did not subscribe to such purist ideals. Total disengagement from service, a full turning away from the world, held little attraction in a society where success was largely measured by how far one climbed and how much honor could be delivered to family and ancestors.

FIG. 3 Li Tang, *Picking Ferns* (detail); Handscroll: ink and color on silk; 27.2 × 90.5 cm; Palace Museum, Beijing

These early examples of reclusion already reveal various shades of behavior and motivation. Reclusion could be the result of an absolute conviction to have nothing to do with the world. More often, it seems to have been a reaction to circumstances, but the circumstances themselves could be varied and how precisely one reacted to them also diverse. The fundamental distinction is between the "true recluse," a Xu You or Chaofu, and those whose disengagement is conditional or qualified. The former, practitioners of what one scholar labels "substantive reclusion," have a very real and important presence in China. Their traces can still be seen (caves chiseled out of sheer cliffs) and their practices documented, despite the inherent difficulty of seeking those who choose to live apart.[22]

However, our interest is primarily with those of the latter category, for whom reclusion was less an absolutist's path than a role in a cultural discourse. It was a discourse that grew increasingly prominent as well as complex in the centuries that followed Confucius's affirmation of the idea of timely reclusion. For high-minded individuals, the idea of retreat as a moral imperative was fundamentally attractive. The complexity arises from the implications retreat might bring. The expression of disinterest in public service or outright refusal could reflect negatively on a ruler, who in turn possessed limited options. The recluse could always claim a true disinterest in worldly affairs, in which case the ruler would have to respect his wishes, but even in cases of open disapproval (as, for example, Boyi and Shuqi displayed toward King Wu) clearly a magnanimous response would serve a ruler better than a punitive one, as the latter would only confirm the wisdom of running as far away as possible. If, on the other hand, a qualified gentleman in reclusion answered a summons to serve, this return to engagement reflected positively on the ruler.

As the teachings of Confucius gained influence—especially during the Han dynasty, when Confucianism was embraced by the state—this most unlikely of relationships between those at the pinnacle of rule and those ostensibly furthest from it carried significant symbolic weight. During periods of turbulence or oppression reclusion was a natural option, but under a strong, unified dynasty with ostensibly enlightened emperors, prominent displays of disengagement demanded attention. Vervoorn points to the importance of the official recommendatory system during the Han for the emergence of what he labels "exemplary eremitism."[23] The system allowed individuals to be recommended to office on the basis of personal character and conduct within their communities. Various criteria of a largely subjective nature were used in determining individual merit, such as genuineness and sincerity. One thing was certain: the more one could present oneself as a high-minded, virtuous person, the more likely one would be recommended for office, and ironically one of the best ways to appear high-minded and virtuous was to profess no interest in worldly affairs: or, in other words, adopt the pose of a recluse.

From this arose two phenomena: the "styling" of reclusion, with its implications of insincere posturing, and the exemplary recluse—one who remains steadfast in the pursuit of eremitism but nonetheless appreciates the fact that he still wields influence as a *known* man of virtue. This is reclusion of a decidedly Confucian nature. Whereas Zhuangzi, the Daoist, repeatedly moralized against the pursuit of fame and wrote positively about those who pursued the Way in peaceful anonymity, the exemplary recluse sees the potential effect of his reputation and conduct for bettering the world. In other words, addressing Sima Qian's afore-cited concern, one can be a recluse *and* enjoy a lasting name.

From a skeptic's point of view, qualified reclusion is having it both ways: being a recluse while remaining embroiled in worldly affairs. And there is good reason to be skeptical. During the latter half of the Han dynasty (Eastern Han, 25–220) the prestige of eremitism was raised so high, and the *pas de deux* between emperor and recluse had reached such a level of decorum, that it was difficult to recognize high-minded gentlemen from those indulging in the fashion of appearing reclusive in order to attract attention. Arrogation of power by eunuchs in the latter half of this period increased the attraction of withdrawal from the world and helped to popularize further the rhetoric of reclusion.[24] Between those who aspired to be recluses in order to provide models for others, those who took on the pretensions of reclusion to attract commendation and official positions ("fake recluses"), and those who simply spoke the language of withdrawal as part of the intellectual discourse of the time, it appears that the whole idea of reclusion had ironically morphed into something exceedingly worldly.

By the late Han dynasty there were shades of reclusion as well as variations. Two that became popular were the "recluse of the marketplace" (*shiyin* 市隱) and the "recluse at the court" (*chaoyin* 朝隱). The former might work at any number of occupations while the latter, as the name implies, was involved at the highest levels of culture and politics. Both refer to a reclusion that is largely a state of mind, as there is no physical withdrawal to mountains or hills. As Vervoorn points out, the roots of this idea go back at least as far as Zhuangzi, who wrote of various lofty men of the Way engaged at menial trades in society.[25] Zhuangzi, however, was making the point that in the end perfect naturalness had to be a product of the self, regardless of place and activities. One suspects that a fair number of the espousers of marketplace and court reclusion, in contrast, were simply unwilling (or unable) to relinquish worldly ties.

Reclusion truly was an art in China. On the surface it was a simple act, a shedding of society's weight in order to pursue a solitary path of self-cultivation. In practice, however, it was malleable, manipulatable, nuanced, and expressive. Centered on the question of whether to serve the state, the act (or feint) of reclusion became a political tool employable by both ruler and subject. Moreover, with its deep philosophical roots and connection with the landscape of the wilderness—a landscape that was both imagined and experienced—reclusion offered an immensely attractive tableau for artistic expression. It was during the long era of political instability that followed the decline of the Han dynasty in the second century that poetry increasingly looked to landscape for inspiration. Painting followed, as artists grappled with the challenges of describing the natural world in two dimensions. It is difficult to separate these phenomena from the general discourse of reclusion—which, in concert with the perils of political involvement for which the Six Dynasties period is legend, continued to be voiced and practiced by a range of individuals.

Nor were developments in the arts limited only to subject matter: there were important aesthetic dimensions related to reclusion as well. One of the notable comments made of the great calligrapher Wang Xizhi is that his writing only became something truly marvelous in his late years after he retired from office in 355 due to a conflict with a superior. Happily wandering the beautiful landscape of the southeast in the company of fishermen and Daoists, his calligraphy shed its "constrained, dusty airs."[26] Reclusion—or in this case, retirement mimicking aspects of the recluse's life amidst mountains and forests (*shanlin* 山林)—presumes a purified body and mind capable of producing superior art.

Even assuming that most of the lore regarding Boyi, Shuqi, and other early paragons of reclusion was a product of the Warring States period, the chronological distance to the fully developed culture of eremitism of the post-Han world of Zuo Si, Lu Ji, Wang Xizhi, and Tao Yuanming was immense. Yet it is twice again as long before Xiang Shengmo painted his *Invitation to Reclusion* over twelve hundred years later in the seventeenth century. To those unfamiliar with the patterns of China's long history it may seem extraordinary that cultural influences could act out over such vast leaps of time, but this was only natural to scholar-officials. Comprehending antiquity through familiarity with the deep and vast literary traditions was the primary standard of knowledge. For the court, the past provided a constant and authoritative mirror for the present, to be used judiciously in establishing legitimacy and order. Especially during periods of transition, such as the early decades of a new dynasty, there was an impetus to utilize symbolic displays to affirm the ruling order's legitimacy.

In all likelihood, Li Tang's painting of Boyi and Shuqi fits into this category (fig. 3). The painting lacks confirming documentation, but given what is known of Li's role as a leading figure in reestablishing painting at the court of Emperor Gaozong (Song Gaozong 宋高宗, r. 1127–1162) following the near collapse of the Song dynasty, it is reasonable to assume some kind of public role for this moving portrayal of Confucian strength.[27] A more typical use of the recluse image by the court is the illustration of a "summoning," in which a noted hermit like Taigong Wang is lured from reclusion (in his case, as a fisherman) to serve an enlightened ruler. This and its converse, where the tolerant ruler permits a dedicated hermit to not answer the summons, provided the standard presentations of "good government." A number of such court-sponsored paintings from early in the Ming dynasty (1368–1644) are extant. The variety of the stories culled from the histories for illustration demonstrates thought and research on the part of the imperial advisors who were charged with this important task.[28]

More pertinent to the art of this exhibition is the relationship with the historical past as played out in the private sphere. The level of devoted study necessary to establish one's credentials as a scholar was so high that familiarity with the past bordered on intimacy. This was especially true for those who had the means and passion to chase after ancient works of calligraphy and painting—material traces of some of the same figures that were familiar from texts. The physical tangibility of old works of art could have the strange effect of compressing, or even erasing, time. This was the case with Mi Fu 米芾 (1052–1107/08), one of China's most famous connoisseurs as well as one of its greatest calligraphers. Single-mindedly focused on seeing and collecting calligraphy of the "golden age" of the fourth century, especially that of Wang Xizhi and son Wang Xianzhi 王獻之 (344–388), Mi celebrated his discoveries not only by emulating the writing styles of the two Wangs but also by composing poems that fictively engaged with members of Wang Xizhi's coterie. In a famous scroll of poems that Mi wrote in 1088, he conflated a gathering of friends of his own time with those of more than seven centuries earlier (see fig. 6)![29]

Calligraphy—which can be followed stroke by stroke, character by character, line by line—has an uncanny ability to bring a viewer into the immediacy of the original writing. This sense of authorial presence is one of the prized qualities of calligraphy and the single most important factor behind Mi Fu's fanciful flights to a much earlier time: when he encountered an epistle written by Wang Xizhi or Wang Xianzhi, he literally felt as if in their company. Nonetheless, the depth of Mi's immersion into fourth-century culture was also determined by his familiarity with the histories, anecdotes, and poetic writings of those earlier figures. Hence, he named his own collected writings *Shanlin ji* 山林集 (Writings of mountains and forests) after the expression used to characterize Wang Xizhi's period of retirement, when his calligraphy is said to have reached an unparalleled level of excellence.

When Xiang Shengmo painted *Invitation to Reclusion* he was following a pattern that was similarly retrospective in its orientation toward antiquity and earlier cultural and artistic traditions. His view of the distant past was that much further removed from when Mi Fu was active, but while the passing of centuries had taken its toll on the material remains of such treasures as Wang Xizhi's calligraphy and Gu Kaizhi's painting, their legacies remained vibrant. There were rare survivors, more often echoes (copies and attributions), but equally important were the chronicles of people like Mi who wrote extensively about their experiences collecting and the aesthetics of painting and calligraphy. Most importantly, artists like Mi left their own traces, which, by the seventeenth century, were also considered objects of immeasurable value.

The discussion has segued from reclusion back to art, but hopefully not in a way that appears unnatural. As the traditional critique of Wang Xizhi's late calligraphy suggests, there is a broad overlay between the ideas of reclusion and the making of art. Disentanglement from affairs was equated with clarity of mind and purity of intentions, which, according to conventional wisdom, were necessary conditions for superior art. Similarly, the collecting and appreciation of fine art were considered to belong to the domain of lofty living unencumbered by mundane concerns. These are idealized conceptions that do not stand up well to scrutiny, but that is beside the point. It was a broadly accepted idea that the fine arts were a refined activity that transcends the commonplace. In Xiang Shengmo's long account of his painting *Invitation to Reclusion* he describes a strict diet of pine-flower cakes and tea-leaf soup, of garden walks and moon-gazing—all to help him escape from the pressures of everyday life and put him in a frame of mind conducive to finishing his long scroll. He suggests very clearly that only a purified mind would allow, as he describes, a landscape of bright, smiling forests and hills, "far from vulgarity." He then ends his inscription with some strikingly honest words:

> I well realize that many people in the world are not recluses, and that they want to be recluses but are unable. Alas! There must have been others who became recluses before me. I say, "Please summon me for reclusion." I say: "I shall summon myself to reclusion." I can just say: "It is alright for me to summon myself for reclusion." I want to be a recluse of the city but cannot. I want to retreat into mountains and rivers but cannot. I want to retreat into poems and paintings, but they have been scattered around in the world, making it impossible for me to collect the names of those who own them. Thus, I must keep this in my arms and store it well in order to wait for one who shares my ideal.
>
> 我固知世人皆非隱者也，皆思隱而未肯者也．噫嘻哉！其必有先我而隱之者矣．曰招我隱可也；曰自我招隱可也；即曰自招亦無不可也．我將隱朝市，而不得；隱陵藪，而不得；將隱於詩畫，而詩畫已散落人間，又不得收拾姓字矣．亟懷此而善藏，以俟夫同志者．

This is a rather painful admission of failure to follow such a glorious painting. Xiang Shengmo desires to be a recluse, but that goal evades him. He remains enmeshed in worldly matters, and in the end the only reclusion he can manage is the one he creates for himself through his own painting. The three declarative statements beginning with "I say" are particularly striking. As if to suggest the distance he feels from his ideal of disengagement, his focus is not on reclusion but the intermediary step of calling him out to reclusion. "Who will do it?

Is there anyone qualified? Why, I'll do it myself! Yes! Why wait? I won't be breaking any rules, will I?" There seems to be an underlying hesitation as Xiang grants himself permission. He declares, yet conviction is still missing. The peacefulness that reclusion promises remains far away.

Invitation to Reclusion proved to be but the first of a series of long landscape paintings with poems on the theme of summoning the recluse that Xiang produced between 1626 and 1648. Their importance to the painter is established by the fact that they appear to have been personal possessions—to be shared with close friends but not given.[30] We thus recognize *Invitation to Reclusion* to be the first exploration into a subject that would prove to be an important touchstone for evaluating both the artist's place and ideals in the changing world of the late Ming and early Qing. The remainder of this essay will take a closer look at such paintings in that historical context.

But before proceeding, and as a way of concluding this short introduction to the rich topic of reclusion in China, let us briefly consider a curious phenomenon posed by the title of Xiang's painting and what it implies. Xiang gave his painting a simple two-character title: *zhaoyin* 招隱, rendered here as "invitation to reclusion." *Zhao* means to wave one's hand and call, invite, or beckon; *yin* can refer to both reclusion and the one who lives in reclusion. "Invitation to reclusion" is perfectly acceptable, but it is an interpretive translation determined by the context of Xiang's inscription. In fact, *zhaoyin* has the potential of having two precisely opposite meanings. Mirroring the historical ambiguity of the recluse in early China, *zhaoyin* can mean to call one *into* reclusion, yet the original meaning was to invite the virtuous hermit *out of* reclusion to serve at the court. Adding an element of complexity to the term is the semantic range of *zhao*—as informal as a hand-waving "beckoning" but also used more ritualistically, as in a "summons." This is how *zhao* is commonly translated for one of the most famous poems of the aforementioned *Chu ci* anthology: "Zhao hun," or "summons of the soul," in which the spirit of the deceased is repeatedly urged to end its dangerous wanderings and return to the comforts of its old abode.[31]

Following the precedents of Lu Ji's and Zuo Si's poems, it is clear that Xiang Shengmo intended his beckoning to be pointed towards the imagined recluse in the hills. At the same time, he blurs the distinction between this figure and himself. In the twenty poems that he composed for the painting, Xiang consistently adopts the voice of the person living in reclusion. Moreover, in two of them the summoning becomes the responsibility not of any human agent but of the landscape itself:

> Fine mountains begin to have a notion,
> And summon me...
>
> 好山始有意，招我欲如何...
>
> If the mountains do not summon me to reclusion,
> Then when would I become a Lord Recluse?
>
> 山不招人隱，何年得隱君.

The one constant is this act of summoning, *zhao*, and its imperative, ritual tone is clear. Whether it is to be summoned into or out of reclusion, the summoning is an existential call that cuts to the heart of how the scholar-official perceived and defined himself.

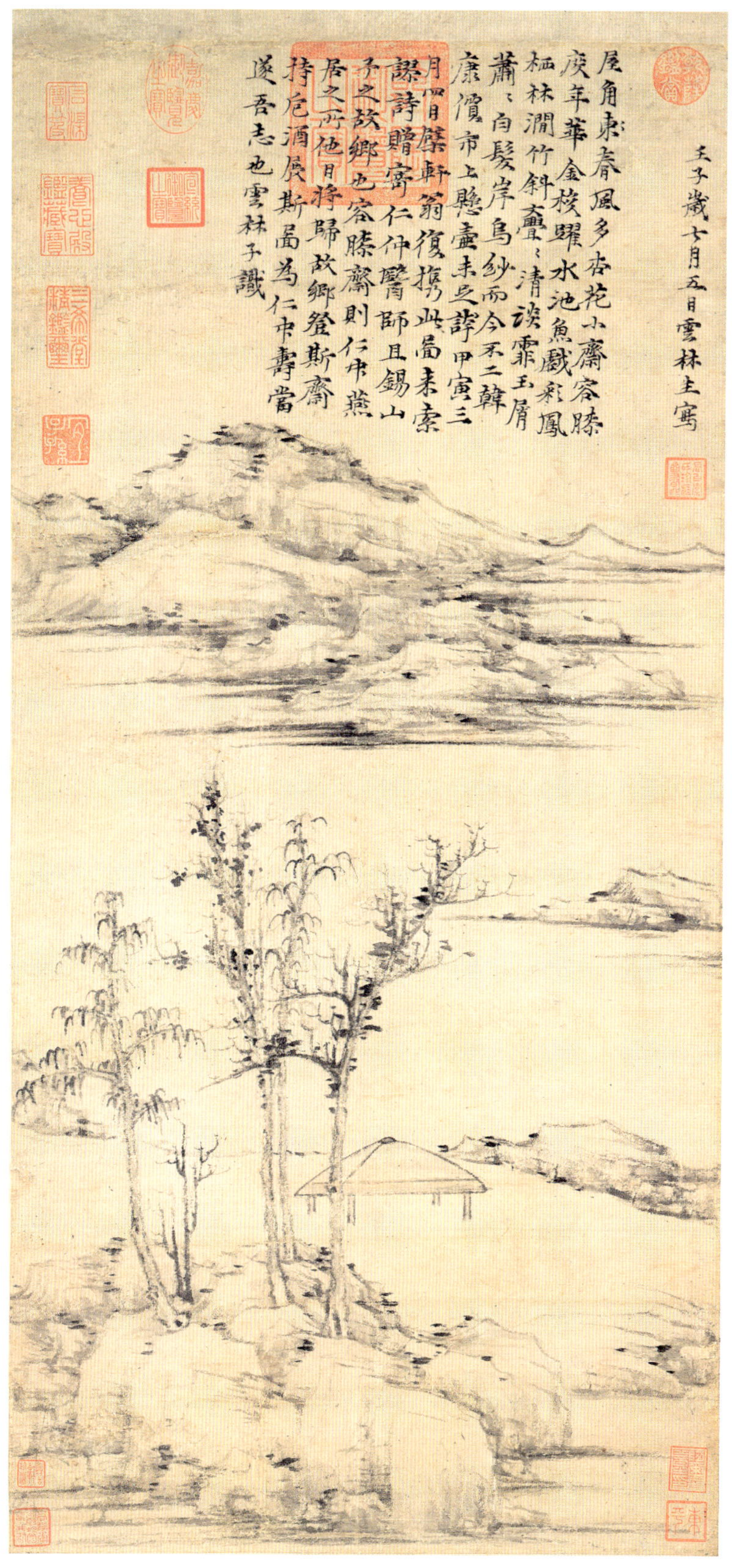

FIG. 4 Ni Zan, *The Rongxi Studio*, 1372; Hanging scroll: ink on paper; 74.7 × 35.5 cm; National Palace Museum, Republic of China (Taiwan)

RECLUSION IN ART Xiang Shengmo lived in a time when the prospect of being in reclusion became increasingly appealing. Through the first decades of the seventeenth century Emperor Shenzong (Ming Shenzong 明神宗, r. 1572–1620, often referred to as the Wanli emperor) became increasingly disengaged from his role at the court, frustrated and left bitter by the constraints imposed by a moralistic bureaucracy and in particular by his inability to procure agreement on his choice for a successor. Shenzong's alienation from his ministers led to a power vacuum that was partially filled by eunuchs and an increasingly poisonous atmosphere at the highest levels of government, where a career that took a lifetime to achieve could easily fall victim to factional politics and end in demotion or worse. Shenzong died in 1620, but the situation at the highest levels of government failed to improve—his successor, Guangzong 光宗, died under suspicious circumstances after only a month on the throne, followed by the young and manipulatable Emperor Xizong 熹宗 (r. 1620–1627). A power struggle ensued between a group of morally driven, reformist officials collectively known as the Donglin Party and an opposing faction of officials and eunuchs, the latter led by the notorious figure Wei Zhongxian 魏忠賢 (1568–1627). Wei and the eunuchs triumphantly ousted the leading Donglin figures at the court in late 1624, following this over the next couple of years with a thorough and brutal purging of those associated with the Donglin faction.[32] This was precisely the time Xiang painted his first *Invitation to Reclusion*.

Echoing Xiang Shengmo's long landscape in this exhibition is a monumentally sized landscape, painted only a month or so earlier, by Mi Wanzhong 米萬鍾 (1570–1628; cat. no. 4). Unlike the youthful Xiang, Mi was a well-established official in the center of the political maelstrom in Beijing. At odds with Wei, who attempted to wrest away desirable pieces of art from his collection, Mi fell victim to the eunuch's power grab. He painted this imposing landscape a few months before he would be impeached and nearly lose his life on trumped-up charges.[33] Sometime in the past the painting acquired the title *Landscape of Yangshuo*. However, nothing on the scroll substantiates an association with the famed karstic landscape of Yangshuo in distant Guilin Province. Rather, it appears that Mi Wanzhong intended this painting to be simply an emphatic statement of escape, away from the disintegrating situation at the capital to a hermitage deep in mountains that could be anywhere. His red-robed figure, abruptly entering from the right as if jumping from another, less pleasant landscape, nears the promised peace of a thatched compound shaded by bamboo. Tantalizingly close, its precise approach remains ambiguous.

The dysfunction of the late Ming court, excessive power of eunuchs, and precariousness of high office all echoed earlier patterns of dynastic decline. Consequently, a painting like Mi Wanzhong's tall landscape, which gives every appearance of being a reaction to immediate events, provides a predictable expression of the reclusion ideal. A closer look, however, reveals a more complex set of factors underlying a renewed interest in reclusion at this time, factors that predated the crisis at the court and are indicative of a far more developed society than existed earlier. Fundamental was the difficulty of climbing the ladder of officialdom. The grueling process of passing the series of examinations at the local, provincial, and national levels that led to a successful career as a ranked official was daunting and the competition increasingly stiff. Preparation involved years of studying the classics and histories at great family cost but towards an uncertain end. During the Wanli period in particular, not only did the bureaucracy fail to keep up with the pressures of a growing population and a large body of highly educated aspirants, vacated positions were left unfilled as well. To make matters worse, corruption polluted the waters of advancement, success at the examinations dependent as much on wealth as ability. Under such circumstances, widespread disenchantment must have been inevitable and the notion of separating oneself from the ills of contemporary society increasingly attractive.

For these well-educated, would-be officials, an additional factor must have been an intimate familiarity with the lore of reclusion through both literature and art. Compared to earlier epochs, the latter was of particular significance. A flourishing market economy boosted the value of collectibles, none more so than old paintings and calligraphies. This was especially true in Jiangnan (Yangzi River Delta), which boasted the greatest concentration of gentry wealth to go along with an extraordinary history of cultural achievements. The increased value of old paintings and calligraphy at this time, both culturally and materially, spurred demand as well as the less savory activities of altering and forging works of art. Much has been written about collecting activities of the first half of the seventeenth century, about the connoisseurship of old scrolls, of the surreptitious production of fakes, and especially about stylistic influence on late-Ming and early-Qing painting.

What is emphasized here is in some ways the most obvious by-product of the flourishing market in art: illustrations of reclusion. This is owed in particular to the relative abundance in the seventeenth century of paintings of the Yuan (1279–1368), the dynasty ruled by the Mongols that immediately preceded the Ming. The thirteenth-century subjugation of south China by the Mongols, the first such conquest by a foreign power in Chinese history, spurred widespread eremitic practice.[34] Images of reclusion dominate the subject matter of Yuan painting, especially that of the renowned masters who lived, traveled, and painted in the same Jiangnan region, such as the aforementioned Huang Gongwang, Wu Zhen 吳鎮 (1280–1354), Ni Zan 倪瓚 (1301–1374; fig. 4), and Wang Meng 王蒙 (c. 1308–1385). For seventeenth-century collectors, these were prime collectibles—little could rival painting by the Yuan masters in terms of desirability and status. Consequently, the urbane activity of appreciating paintings considered to be of the highest order amounted to a direct visual experience of an earlier era of reclusion. The prevalence and value of Yuan painting in circulation among scholars in the first decades of the seventeenth century surely played a significant role in the dissemination of the ideal of disengagement.

Few viewed this painting-inflected image of reclusion more clearly than Xiang Shengmo. Shengmo was the grandson of Xiang Yuanbian 項元汴 (1525–1590), a collector of such importance that a majority of the most important works of ancient painting and calligraphy extant in museums today carry his seals. The Xiang clan was wealthy, and it produced a number of prominent scholars and officials. However, there is no evidence that Xiang Shengmo passed any of the advanced examinations, and he certainly did not serve in any official positions of significance.[35] Rather, cushioned by family resources, and perhaps intimidated by the challenge of following the customary path to service, he devoted himself to the study and practice of painting. By conventional standards this was unusual: many among the scholar-official class took painting quite seriously but it was still perceived, idealistically, as an avocation, not as a singular devotion or means of support.

On the other hand, these were unconventional times. In an inscription he added to a painting of 1629, just a few years after his first *Invitation to Reclusion* scroll, Xiang Shengmo juxtaposes his failure as a student/official against his love of painting and describes a dream in which he climbs a celestial ladder in the form of a brush—a clear indication that this was Heaven's intended path.[36]

Having failed as a scholar-official, he relied upon his skill as a painter to establish a measure of personal accomplishment. It was a skill related to Xiang's access to earlier paintings through his family collection. As Chen Jiru remarks in his inscription to *Invitation to Reclusion*, Xiang was directly influenced by one of the more famous, and especially early, scrolls describing reclusion owned by his grandfather: *Ten Views of a Thatched Hut*, attributed to the Tang-dynasty painter Lu Hong 盧鴻 (act. first half eighth century; fig. 5).[37]

Chen was certainly in a position to know about the influence of Lu's *Ten Views of a Thatched Hut*. Thirty years senior to Xiang Shengmo, Chen was familiar with the Xiang family and its collection through his close friendship with Dong Qichang. Dong—who, we are reminded, added the title to Xiang's *Invitation to Reclusion* as well as his own inscription after the painting—was a frequent visitor to Xiang Yuanbian's residence and collection many years before Xiang Shengmo was born. This was precisely the time (late 1570s) that he and Chen first became acquainted. Over the course of their lifetimes Chen and Dong would forge a friendship intricately bonded to their close examination and appreciation of old paintings and calligraphy.

Dong in particular possessed a voracious appetite for acquiring knowledge from the study of art. So successful was he that a visit today to any major exhibition of early Chinese painting and calligraphy (especially works of art of the Song and Yuan dynasties) is almost like strolling through the galleries with Dong as a personal guide, so often does one find his inscriptions appended. Chen Jiru's inscriptions are often in tow, like a younger brother following his type-A sibling. Although not the kindest of analogies, this fits the perspective of most historians of Chinese art, who regard Dong as a titan—the kind of person of such ability and influence that he has a century named after him—and Chen as a satellite in Dong's circle.[38] However, this view of Chen is decidedly anachronistic. In the seventeenth century Chen carried plenty of weight, and his influence on Dong cannot be discounted. In fact, the argument will be made here that in order to achieve a fuller understanding of Dong's art, and his painting in particular, one needs to look at it through a particular prism provided by Chen that refracts its imagery into the world of the recluse.

Chen Jiru plays a central role in this exhibition, which includes one of his paintings, a superb example of his calligraphy, and inscriptions that he added to the work of others (cat. nos. 1, 2, 11, and 12). He also makes a surprise appearance in a landscape painting by his compatriot Zhao Zuo 趙左 (c. 1570s–1633 or later),

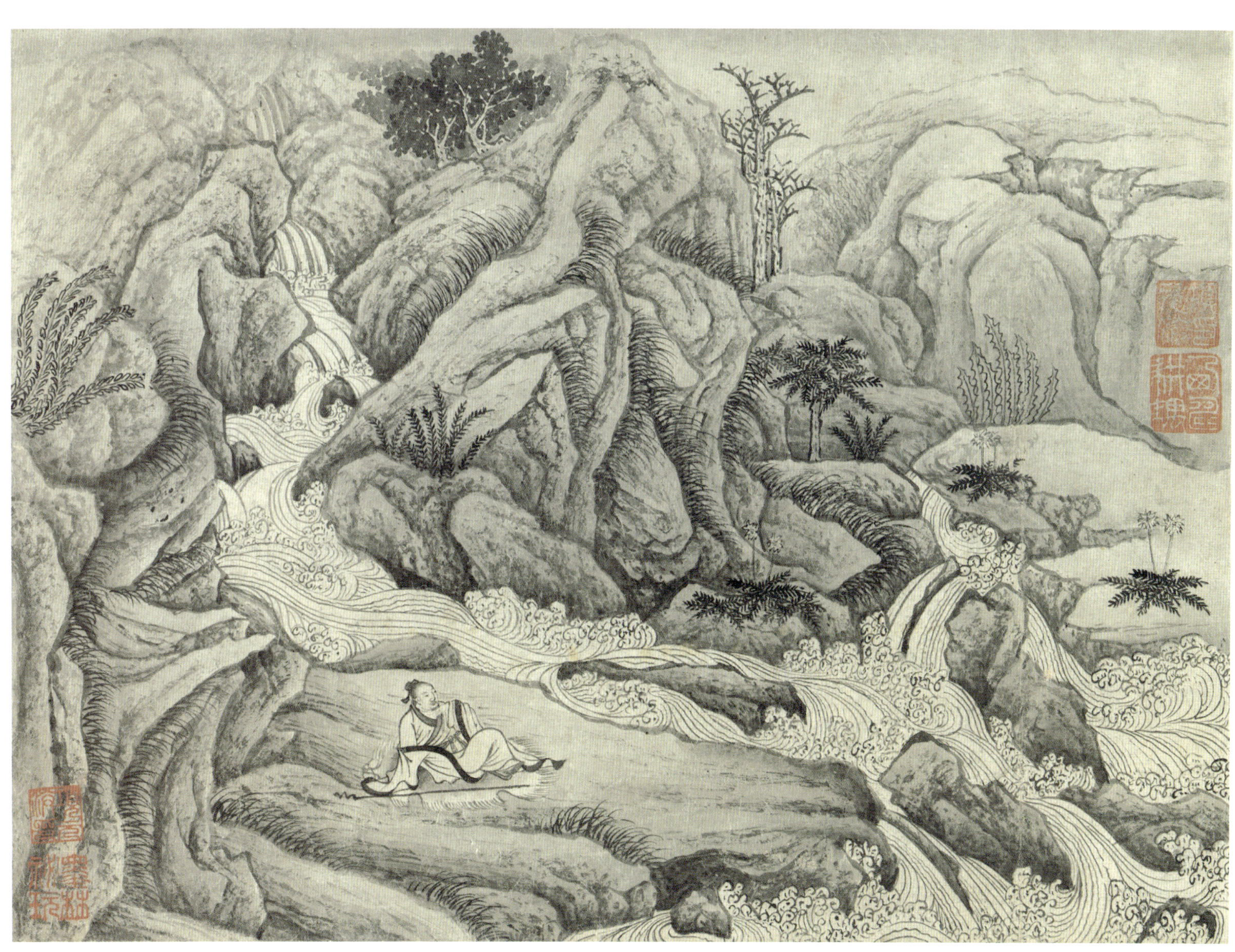

FIG. 5 Lu Hong (attributed), *Ten Views of a Thatched Hut* (detail); Handscroll: ink on paper; 29.4 × 600 cm; National Palace Museum, Republic of China (Taiwan)

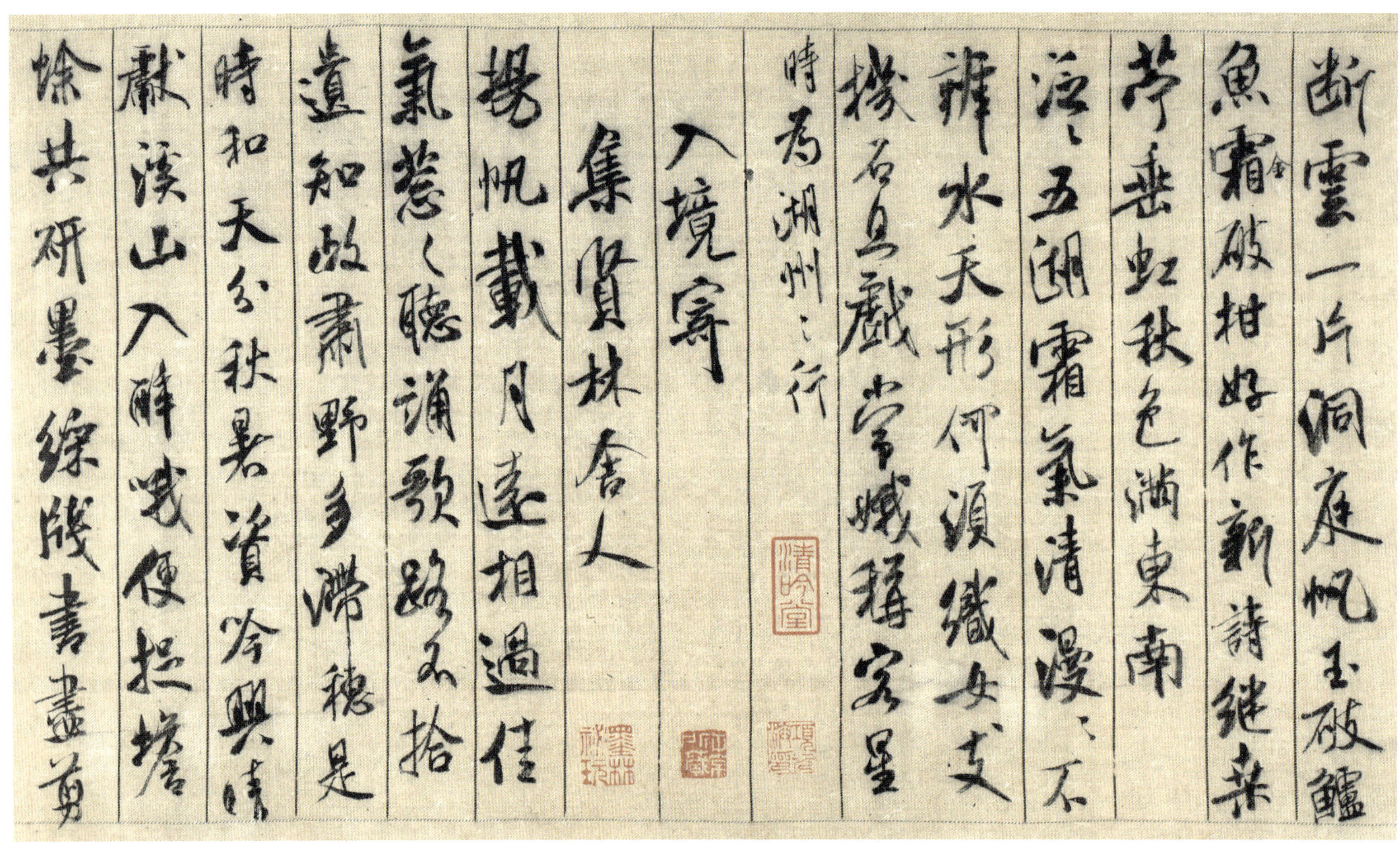

as described below. Graphic traces alone, however, hardly tell the story of Chen's influence. Already recognized as an important cultural figure in his own time, Chen was known in particular for his activities as a writer and bibliophile.[39] His success in this regard was tied to his celebrity status, one due in no small measure to his very public reputation as a recluse. Born in Songjiang (Jiangsu Province) to a family of relatively modest means, Chen proved to be an exceptional student and literary talent. He gained the notice of prominent scholars of the Jiangnan region and was introduced to many of the cultural elite. Unfortunately, success in scholarly and social circles did not translate to success in the official exams. Chen passed the low-level juvenile exam at the age of twenty in 1578, but that was it. He failed the provincial exams twice and, in dramatic fashion following his second disappointment, burned his scholar's robe and cap to renounce any possible future as an official.

In his own words explaining his rejection of the official's path, Chen Jiru wrote that he had already developed a dislike for the "vulgar world." Rejecting the calculation and compromise necessary to succeed in the constrained environment of the examination system, he proclaimed his intention to "take the rest of my life into my own hands and spend it happily, communing with nature."[40] In a manner of speaking, he hung up his shingle and became a professional tutor and writer. Prolific and versatile, he wrote, compiled, and edited a wide range of works on history, culture, and taste that purposely targeted a broad audience. His popularity was immense. One contemporary describes encountering Chen on a painting excursion—normally a private, intimate affair—in the company of a sizable entourage of admirers and celebrity-chasers.[41] So successful was Chen at marketing himself that his image was soon appropriated and used promotionally, hung in wine shops and teahouses to advertise wares. His name was attached to consumable goods as mundane as coverlets and sweet cakes.[42] We have already encountered the "recluse of the marketplace" of earlier Chinese history, descriptive of those who claimed a detached state of mind while remaining engaged in worldly affairs. Chen took the idea of engaged disengagement to a whole new level: he was the "marketable recluse."

As Jamie Greenbaum points out, the particular type of recluse that Chen Jiru represents was very much a product of the late Ming. Prosperity brought literacy to an expanded public, and there was a growing population hungry to digest matters of culture. Chen's talent and knowledge as a man of letters allowed him to seize this opportunity. People wanted to know his opinions about matters as diverse as tea-brewing, art objects, proper behavior, and withdrawal. They wanted to read about his experiences, his travels, his knowledge of others, past and present. In short, Chen lived in a time when culture was an expanding commodity and professionalized services for delivering it were in high demand. In this regard, he was an important precedent, if not model, for someone like Xiang Shengmo, who ultimately relied upon his skills as a painter for his livelihood. More significantly, in a very public manner Chen revived the ideal and image of the recluse. His reputation as a man of taste and erudition, intricately tied to the image he forged of himself as one disengaged from the travails of the world, must have had much to do with the resurgence in popularity of the recluse theme at the start of the seventeenth century.

Students of reclusion in China, especially those focused on its early history, tend to dismiss its significance for literati like Chen Jiru. By this late date the manners of disengagement had become too broadly and easily adopted, the ideals associated with reclusion too well known and their expression too well tread. Moreover, it seems inherently disingenuous when a figure as prominent in the public sphere as Chen cloaked himself in the guise of disengagement, especially when there is every reason to believe that doing so helped make his literary wares attractive. However, sitting in judgment of his reclusion misses the point. Clearly it mattered to him, and, whether it was dictated by his beliefs or calculation of a public persona, his efforts to present himself as a recluse were both considerable and considerably influential. In 1586, the same year

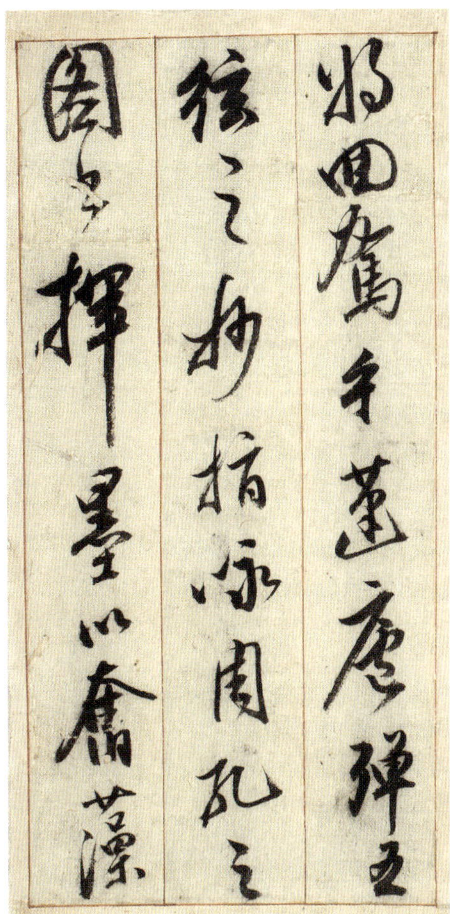
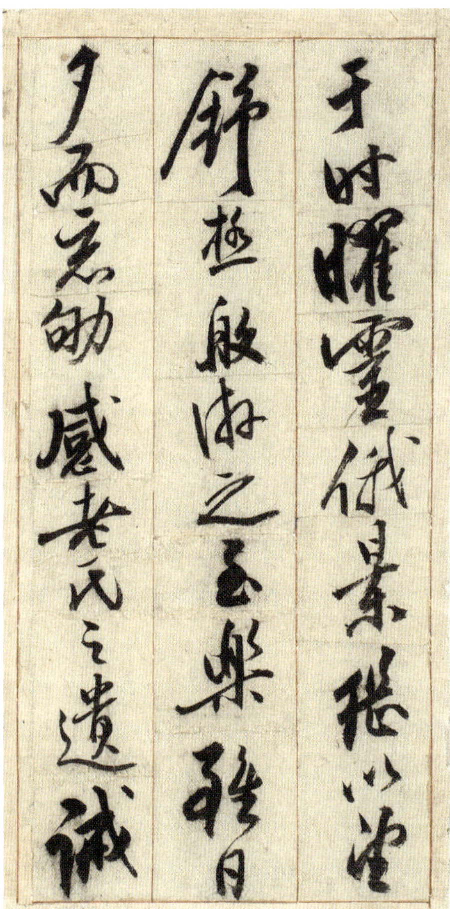

OPPOSITE: FIG. 6 Mi Fu, *Poems on Sichuan Silk* (detail), 1088; Handscroll: ink on silk; 27.8 × 270.8 cm; National Palace Museum, Republic of China (Taiwan)

LEFT: FIG. 7 Chen Jiru, leaves from *Zhang Heng's "Returning to the Field"* (cat. no. 12)

he burned his scholar's robe, an excursion with friends brought Chen to Little Mount Kun, outside of Huating (Songjiang). Here he discovered an attractive parcel of land that once belonged to the third-century literary figure Lu Ji, the same man whose beckoning-the-hermit poems served as inspiration for Xiang Shengmo's *Invitation to Reclusion*. Together with a friend, Chen purchased the property and immediately took steps to pronounce his allegiance with Lu and other paragons of reclusion of the Wei-Jin period (220–420), some thirteen centuries earlier, by dedicating a small shrine to Lu and his brother.[43] It was a definitive statement of trans-temporality. This was no mere borrowing of a suggestive allusion to give archaic piquancy to a poem or sobriquet; Chen was literally claiming the turf of ancient reclusion.

Chen Jiru's reclusion has been well described in the context of his life and activities, but the manner in which he gave it form through painting and calligraphy has largely been overlooked. It is easy to understand why. Cultural and literary historians rarely touch upon the graphic arts. Art historians, on the other hand, though aware of his appreciation and practice of painting and calligraphy, have not provided him his due because of the giant shadow cast by his lifelong friend, Dong Qichang.[44] This exhibition takes a step in correcting this oversight by highlighting a couple of Chen's works in the context of his adoption of the recluse persona. The first of these is his *Zhang Heng's "Returning to the Field"*, an excellent example of his calligraphy (cat. no. 12, fig. 7). Like Dong, Chen regarded himself heir to the classical tradition of calligraphy that could be traced back to Wang Xizhi and Wang Xianzhi of the fourth century. And, again like Dong, Chen's study of the classical tradition was largely filtered through the work of later calligraphers. Especially important to both were the Northern Song calligraphers of the late eleventh century. When it came to the two Wangs, Mi Fu's influence stood above all others because of his dedicated study of their calligraphy, the detailing of his experiences recorded in texts, and the survival of many pieces of his own calligraphy.

All of these elements played a role in Chen Jiru's writing of *Returning to the Field*, with the work briefly introduced earlier, Mi's *Poems on Sichuan Silk* (fig. 6), very possibly having direct bearing. *Poems on Sichuan Silk*, one of Mi's most celebrated works of calligraphy, was owned by both Xiang Yuanbian and Dong Qichang. Dong acquired it in 1604, but he had known of the scroll earlier and thought so highly of it as to include it in the compilation of model writings that he sponsored, *Xihongtang tie* 戲鴻堂帖 (1603).[45] Given these facts, it is certain that Chen too would have been familiar with this famous work by Mi. In general, Chen's writing style owed much to Mi, but the resemblance between *Returning to the Field* and *Poems on Sichuan Silk* is so close as to suggest an intentional echo. The content of the two writings reinforces this possibility. Mi's poems, written to commemorate an extended outing with friends, repeatedly evoke the image of Wang Xizhi and the fourth century. *Returning to the Field* is Chen's transcription of a classic poem on the theme of reclusion written by Zhang Heng 張衡 (78–139). Like Mi, Chen wrote it with comrades in mind: according to his trailing inscription, he was in the company of a number of "intimate recluses and monks." Evoking a famous work like this scroll by Mi to re-create, both in visual graphic form and content, a parallel journey back to the golden age of reclusion is precisely the kind of sophisticated engagement with art for which Chen and Dong were known.

Chen Jiru's transcription of Zhang's "Returning to the Field" was a gift presented to an accompanying friend who had made him a painting of a rustic thatched hut. That particular painting is no longer known, but the subject is certainly familiar from numerous other paintings, including one in this exhibition by Chen himself (cat. no. 11). Chen's painting is self-titled *Thatched Hut by Tall Pines*. Lacking any other documentation, we might presume that this painting too was meant as a gift, perhaps to someone whose studio name included the image of pine trees. It was a longstanding practice to see the personal space of the studio as an extension of its owner, and consequently a painting like this would have honored the personal qualities of the recipient. The thatched hut of Chen's painting, of course, is not a literal description but rather a metaphor for "rustic" values. Mature pines refer to longevity and youthful vigor, qualities in accord with the general conception of one who pursues the Dao or Way as a recluse. On the other hand, there is coincidental evidence that the studio belonged to Chen himself: the imagery of the painting is suggestively close to the description he provides of his residence in his inscription on *Returning to the Field*, especially the interlocking trees that seemingly form a gateway. In any case, even if *Thatched Hut by Tall Pines* was painted to honor someone else's studio, the best way to accomplish that would be to put as much of himself in the painting as possible. The value of the scroll would have been inextricably tied to Chen's celebrity status.

Thatched Hut by Tall Pines illustrates both the charm and limitations of the amateur tradition of literati painting. Chen Jiru was an exceptional calligrapher, but he probably had limited training as a painter. Paradoxically, that becomes one of the painting's strengths. Slight and unassuming, the painting deliberately maximizes, even celebrates, plainness. Plainness suggests evenness, a planing of emotions that coordinates well with the image of detachment. The brushwork may be unpolished, but that too benefits the particular aesthetic espoused by Chen—overt skill would suggest professionalism at odds with the "genuineness" associated with the touch of the amateur. *Thatched Hut by Tall Pines* may lack polish. Nonetheless, there is more to the painting than first apparent. The manner in which Chen built up the foreground rocks and composed his interlocking trees adds subtle layers of depth that countervail the painting's impression of flatness. The thought and effort indicated by these pictorial flourishes provide an all-important authorial presence.

Chen's presence also hovers throughout Zhao Zuo's long landscape of 1616, *Streams and Mountains without End* (cat. no. 13). The title, inscribed by Zhao at the end of the painting (and again, handsomely, in the frontispiece by the later calligrapher Wang Gong 汪恭 [late eighteenth–early nineteenth century]), has a long history in China, associated with landscapes in the handscroll format from as early as the twelfth century.[46] The idea was to create an extended pictorial journey that takes the viewer deeply into mountains, forests, and streams rendered with some degree of naturalism. This approach to landscape composition proved extremely popular among seventeenth-century artists, and it is well represented in this exhibition by paintings of similar intent though different titles (cat. nos. 1, 13, 17, and 24). In contrast to their predecessors, however, late-Ming and early-Qing painters created landscapes that were more deliberately and directly expressive of a particular viewpoint or vision.

This is precisely the case with Zhao Zuo's *Streams and Mountains without End*, which clearly reflects the artistic concepts of fellow townsmen Dong Qichang and Chen Jiru. The landscape, to begin with, is decidedly local. The grassy marshes, streams, and low-lying hills are clearly descriptive of the region south of the Yangzi River known as Jiangnan and specifically of the landscape around Huating, from which Zhao, Dong, and Chen all hailed.[47] Equally important is Zhao's implementation of specific brush modes and motifs that deliberately evoke earlier artists: Mi Fu, for one, associated with cloudy mountains, but also the Yuan-dynasty masters Zhao Mengfu 趙孟頫 (1254–1322), Ni Zan, Huang Gongwang, and Wu Zhen—all of whom painted the southern landscape of Jiangnan and figured prominently in Dong's and Chen's critical writings. However, what is noteworthy is Zhao's short inscription. After providing the title and date, Zhao details his location as the Hut of Vegetable Fragrance, where he was escaping the summer heat. This was one of Chen's studios, and, although not directly stated, we presume that Zhao painted this scroll in return for Chen's hospitality.[48] After traversing through the watery Jiangnan landscape past riverside villages, mountain hamlets, temples, and fishermen, nearing the end of the long landscape we encounter a single figure prominently seated in a rustic dwelling past a small bridge over a stream. This must be Chen Jiru (fig. 18).

Streams and Mountains without End is an extended, informed homage to Chen Jiru and his reclusion, coming from the hand of one who knew him well. Zhao Zuo's liberal use of Mi Fu's cloudy mountains motif is one indication of that intimacy—extant landscapes by Chen reveal Mi to have been one of his favored models for painting as well as calligraphy—but it is primarily the deft and varied brushwork of Zhao's painting that presents the strongest argument. Closely matching the tenor of Chen's *Thatched Hut by Tall Pines* but with far more professional skill, Zhao's brush-and-ink rendering is a virtuoso interpretation of the scholar's aesthetic as filtered through Yuan-dynasty styles. Among these, the one figure that stands out is Ni Zan, whose minimalist landscapes, in the minds of late-Ming aficionados, exemplified the ideal of the lofty and untrammeled scholar. The combination of Mi and Ni had particular resonance for Chen, who wrote a comment in one of his many miscellaneous jottings that almost seems tailored for this painting:

> Mi Xiangyang [Mi Fu] [lived] outside the commonly traversed streams and paths. All others come and go like so many cast vessels forged from this mold or that. In the Yuan there were many who were capable, but they still largely followed Song-dynasty methods, adding [only] a measure of loose, casual brushwork. Wu Zhonggui [Wu Zhen] possessed great spirit. Huang Zijiu [Huang Gongwang] had a particularly marvelous style, and Wang Shuming [Wang Meng] completely mastered the rules of his predecessors. Yet none of these three was able to wipe clean established habits. Only Yunlin [Ni Zan] was ancient, light, and natural. After Crazy Mi, there was only Ni.[49]

> 米襄陽在溪逕之外，餘皆從陶鑄而來，元之能者雖多，然承率宋法稍加蕭散耳. 吳仲圭大有神氣，黃子久特妙風格，王叔明奄有前規，而三家未洗縱橫習氣，獨雲林古淡天然，米癡後一人而已.

There is one last interesting point regarding Zhao Zuo's *Streams and Mountains without End*. Thirteen years later, with his death fast approaching, Chen Jiru chose the Hut of Vegetable Fragrance for sutra-chanting and a ritual of repentance to be conducted by famous Buddhist monks.[50] The fragrance of vegetables is a clear reference to the diet of a monk unsullied by impurities. Consequently, one can assume that the site was always invested with religious or spiritual value. Viewed retrospectively, the image of Chen in his hut gains otherworldly poignancy, as if shown reborn in his own personal Pure Land.

The most famous image honoring Chen's reclusion is also the most bizarre—a painting so unusual that its original eulogistic function has been almost entirely overlooked. This is *The Wanluan Thatched Hall*, painted by Dong Qichang a number of years earlier in 1597 to commemorate a second studio constructed by Chen on Little Mount Kun (fig. 8). Chen established the Wanluan Thatched Hall on the north side of Little Mount Kun about ten years after he first made a declarative statement of reclusion by following in the footsteps of Lu Ji and buying property in this area. Lu was still on Chen's mind—the name of his "thatched hall," Wanluan 婉孌 (literally, "to admire and envy"), appears to be a play on a poem presented to the third-century poet.[51] Chen chose this name in order to affirm his spiritual (as well as geographic) ties to an idealized reclusion of the distant past.

FIG. 8 Dong Qichang, *The Wanluan Thatched Hall*, 1597; Hanging scroll: ink on paper; 111.3 × 36.8 cm; Private collection, Taiwan

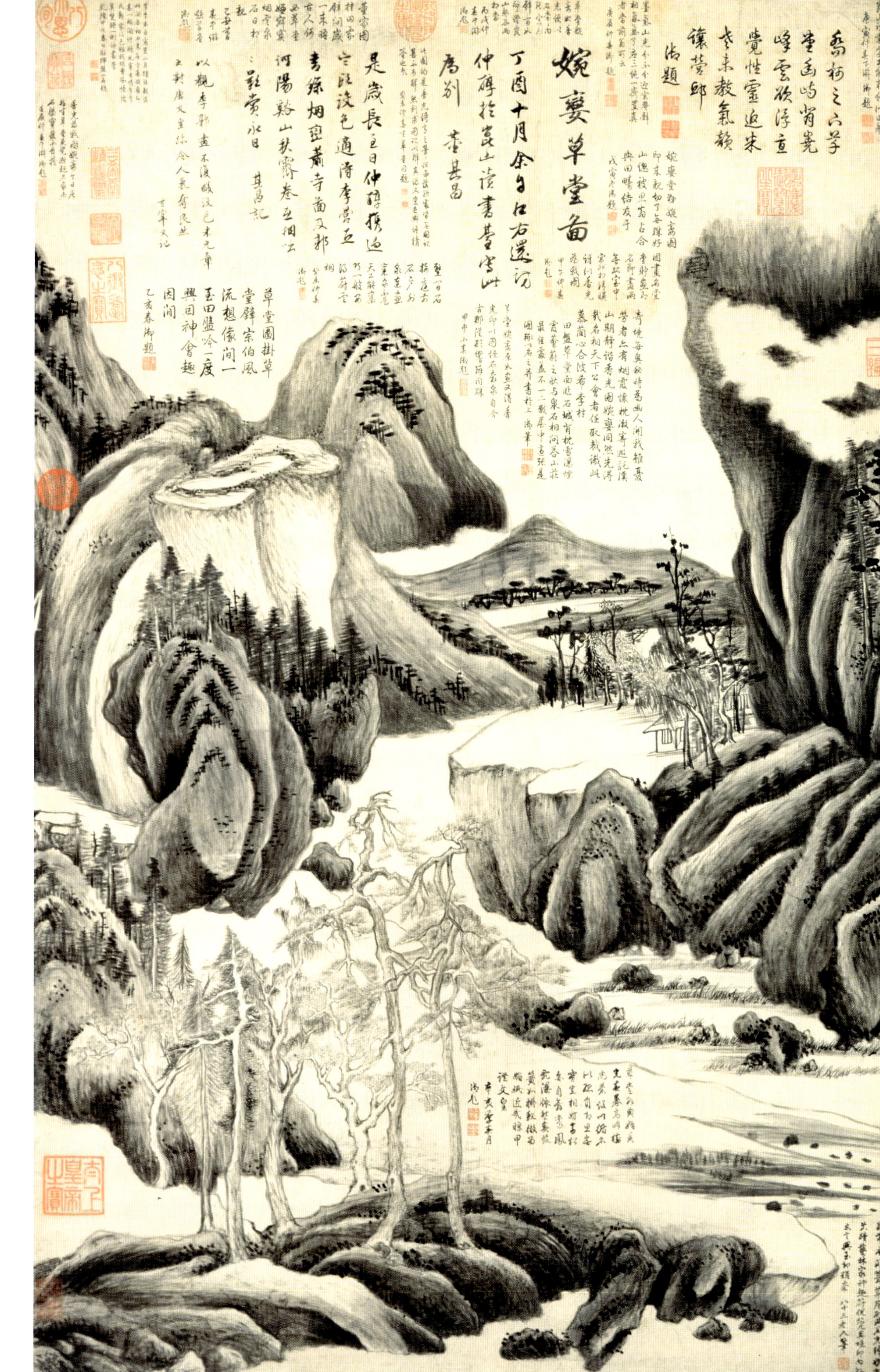
婉孌草堂圖

In a manner of speaking, Dong attempts the same with his painting. The small structure half hidden on the middle-ground ledge presumably is Chen's Wanluan Thatched Hall, but only symbolically—it is unlikely that this contorted jumble of twisted land formations has any ties to the actual landscape of Little Mount Kun outside of Songjiang. Rather, Dong created landscapes according to an approach that was uniquely his own. Drawing upon his extensive experiences viewing ancient paintings, he freely borrowed motifs, landscape passages, and brush modes from a number of scrolls that caught his interest and reassembled them into a new order. In this case, some of his inspiration apparently came from Song-dynasty landscape paintings by Li Cheng 李成 (919–967) and Guo Xi 郭熙 (c. 1000–c. 1090): in the second of his three inscriptions, he mentions recent purchases of brightly colored "blue-green" landscape paintings by these two famous masters that he and Chen admired all day long. The prominently displayed foreground trees allude to the Li-Guo tradition, thus suggesting some connection, and there are additional elements that seem to evoke other early painters.[52] However, the strangeness of this painting is so overwhelming that stylistic allusions alone simply do not suffice to explain its appearance.

Studies of Dong Qichang's paintings largely focus on stylistic influence, and with good reason. He saw so much and was so vocal with his opinions on attributions, quality, and importance that attention is naturally drawn to specific influences of earlier paintings. Yet by focusing on the minutiae we risk losing sight of the obvious. In the case of *The Wanluan Thatched Hall* the obvious is the painting's role in celebrating Chen Jiru's new study on Mount Kun or, in other words, its social function. Dong's inscriptions on the painting provide some interesting clues about how we might take this a step further. The first simply states the date and circumstances: returning from the north he visits Chen at his studio and paints this as a parting gift. The second, written shortly after, casually mentions that Chen brought the painting to Dong's studio and requested him to add some color. As Dong had recently acquired the aforementioned paintings by Li Cheng and Guo Xi, they spend the rest of the day enjoying them. In the third inscription, written in tiny characters, Dong explains that because of the distraction provided by Li's and Guo's paintings he never got around to adding color. He ends with an apparent non-sequitur: "Mi Yuanzhang [Fu], viewing Tang Wenhuang's [Tang Taizong 唐太宗 (r. 627–649)] calligraphy, commented that it takes one's breath away. Well said!" 米元章云，對唐文皇跡，令人氣奪，良然.

Dong's inscriptions appear casual to the point of almost being random, but they raise strange questions. For example, would Chen really come knocking with the temerity to ask Dong to add color to his painting? Color? A glance at Chen's *Thatched Hut by Tall Pines* and Zhao Zuo's *Streams and Mountains without End* reveals the incongruity.[53] In China, color was equated with luxuriousness and sensual pleasure—hardly qualities that a recluse would advertise, even one as socially active as Chen. Something going on here between the two friends is left unstated. I suspect it has to do with the rawness of Dong's painting, its unpalatability, and perhaps questions this raised for Chen regarding the manner in which it was representing his reclusion. Of course, there was never any intention of adding color. The last remark that Dong makes, borrowing from something Mi Fu wrote half a millennium earlier, must be directed towards his own painting: yes, it takes one's breath away.

Dong's *The Wanluan Thatched Hall* is not only an early image of Chen's reclusion; it is also a deeply personal one. Like Zhao's *Streams and Mountains without End* of some twenty years later, Dong's painting engages with earlier art to comment on Chen's eremitic image, but there is an important difference. Whereas Zhao's landscape defers to Chen's aesthetic preferences, *The Wanluan Thatched Hall* shows so little inclination to compromise that perhaps even Chen was a little unsure what to make of it.[54] The difference stems in part from the nature of Dong's relationship with Chen (they were virtual peers) but also from Dong's forceful personality. His paintings are deeply subjective, interpretive reactions to his experiences with ancient paintings and calligraphy. Those experiences were largely shared by Chen, and, as Dong's close friend and confidant, he was privy to Dong's creativity to a degree unmatched by anyone else. This painting should be understood as a record of their friendship, but according to terms dictated by Dong. Dong labored to make a challenging, ambitious image. Creating something inspired by shared experiences, and in such a manner that only someone truly knowledgeable would begin to grasp its aims, was his way of honoring his friend.

Dong presents us with a new interpretation of reclusion, though it is one based on an ancient concept—*zhiyin* 知音, "knowing the sounds." Drawn from the story of a talented *qin* (zither) player whose music was only understood by a single close friend—the *zhiyinzhe* 知音者, or "one who knows the sounds"—the painting refers to that one listener, or in this case viewer, who understands the utmost subtleties of one's art and consequently makes it meaningful.[55] The concept is elitist, presuming a shared knowledge or understanding limited to the artist and a select audience. Here Chen's superior understanding blends with his status as a lofty hermit who is disengaged from the world. But it is not a matter of Dong bringing his art into the world of the recluse. Rather, Dong and Chen created their own separate space—an idealized reclusion that was centered almost exclusively on art. As mentioned above, much of the art that was collected, both literally and figuratively, described the world of the recluse. For these two gentlemen, however, more than what the art presented, it was the pleasure of engaging with art of the highest order and at the highest level that determined this private space. Mi Fu again provides the most important historical model, not solely as a calligrapher or painter but as collector, connoisseur, and critic. In his own time, Mi's passion for art earned him a reputation for being eccentric, but by his own reckoning he considered his successful engagements with calligraphy and painting as an important counter to the relative failures he experienced as an official. This was an arena in which he was peerless, and it represented a world apart from the frustrations, constraints, and setbacks of court life.[56] Mi's precedent was well known in the seventeenth century and a source of great curiosity. Few, however, had the means to follow it like Dong.[57]

Reclusion in art is a concept borrowed from the term *huayin* 畫隱, "reclusion in painting," which was used to describe a person of superior virtue who eschews fame by choosing to limit the expression of his talents to this particular skill.[58] The model of the recluse in painting was itself derived from a well-established paradigm from *Zhuangzi*—the craftsman who attains oneness with the Dao (Way) despite the menial aspect of his craft.[59] As mentioned earlier, this curious archetype of the sage who resides among us, realizing perfection through some altogether ordinary profession, was the basis for the idea of the recluse in the marketplace or at the court, one whose reclusion is a state of mind rather than body. This was an important model for Dong Qichang. Unlike Chen Jiru, Dong successfully passed the examinations and climbed high up the ladder of officialdom. Earlier scholars questioned his commitment

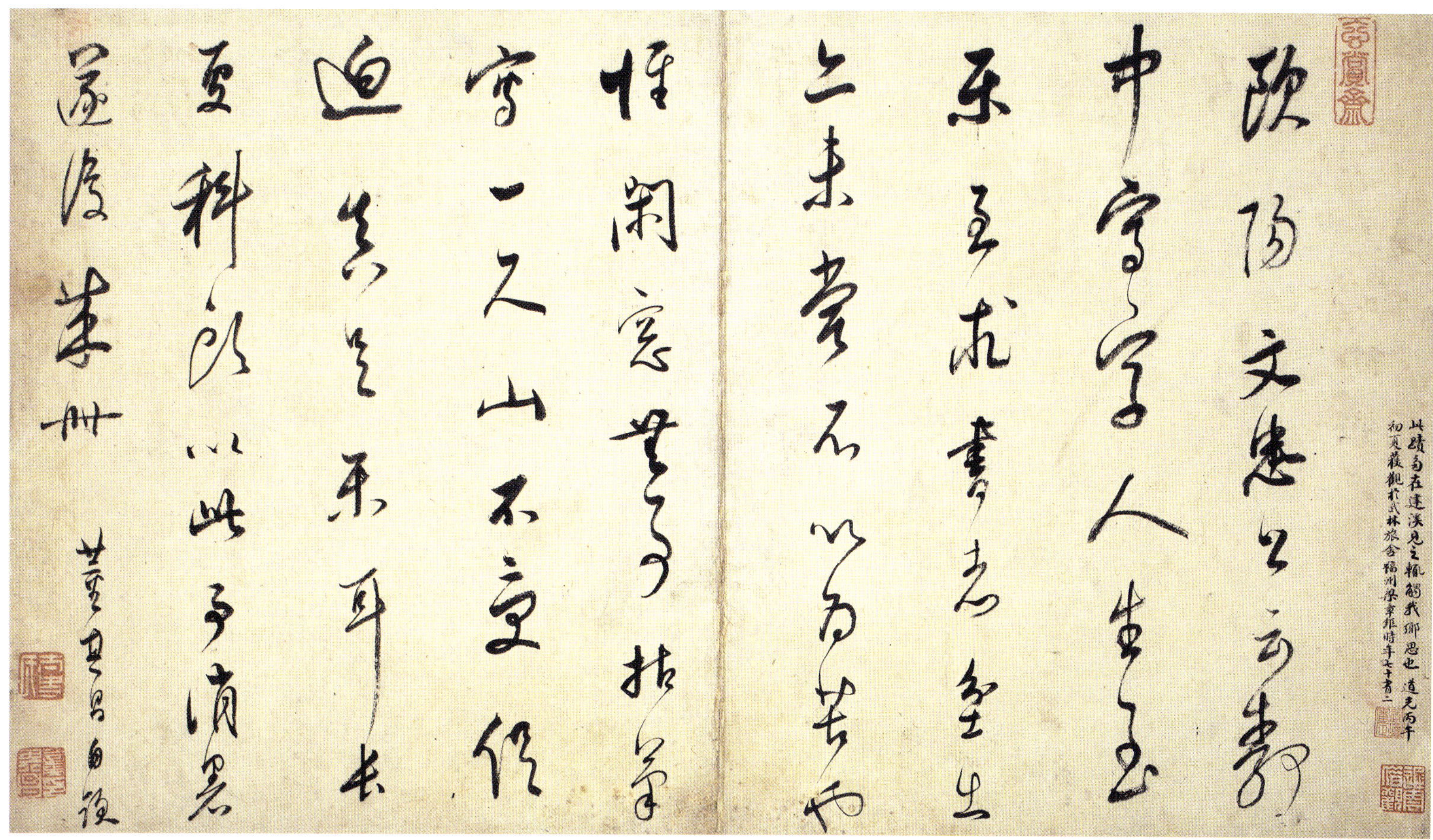

to official service, especially in consideration of his accomplishments as a painter, calligrapher, and theorist. The most thorough study of his life, however, has well established an unflagging ambition to succeed, even in the face of significant personal and professional setbacks.[60] For someone like Dong, who willfully navigated the treacherous waters of late-Ming politics, reclusion in art was doubly useful. On the one hand, deep immersion in matters of brush and ink must have provided a necessary escape—that notion of detachment while in the midst of worldly matters defining the recluse at the court. Much more important was the immense practical benefit provided by Dong's particular form of reclusion. His knowledge of ancient painting and calligraphy, not to mention his own abilities with the brush, placed him on a cultural pinnacle that few if any had a chance to reach. Like the skillful courtiers of the late Han period who could parlay their reputations as men of disengagement for political gain, Dong's mastery of painting and calligraphy established his credentials in the virtual world of high-culture reclusion.

Admittedly, it takes an extraordinarily forgiving definition of reclusion to fit someone with the ambition and social skills of Dong Qichang, who regarded disengagement less as an ideal than as a necessary statement of image when circumstances so dictated. An excellent example of this is a painting he did for a close friend, Wu Zhengzhi 吳正志 (d. c. 1619), titled *Invitation to Reclusion at Jingxi*. Originally painted in 1611 to commemorate Wu's decision to retire rather than take a remote provincial position, Dong changed his tune in an inscription he added two years later after Wu agreed to accept a more prestigious position that would set his career back on track. In a manner of speaking Dong proved as flexible as the term *zhaoyin*: after being invited into reclusion, the recluse is now being summoned out![61] Nonetheless, this is not to say that Dong was immune from the pleasures of retirement and their positive effect on painting and calligraphy. Like Wu, and in concert with him, Dong chose to retire rather than accept a provincial position unworthy of his talents in 1610. It was precisely at this important juncture of his life that he created the album of matching paintings and calligraphies that are included in this exhibition (cat. no. 8). The refreshing prospect of being free of the travails of office are clear in the inscription he added at the end (fig. 9):

> Ouyang Wenzhong [Ouyang Xiu 歐陽修, 1007–1072] said, "To be in a state of calm and write calligraphy is the utmost pleasure of life." As for pursuing the goals of calligraphy from the dust [of the world], has this not always been a kind of suffering? Idle by a window and without matters of concern, grasping a brush to sketch a foot-long mountain, free from any kind of outside pressure—that is true pleasure! On a long summer day and hatless, I engage in these matters to dispel the heat and compose this album.
>
> 歐陽文忠公云:「靜中寫字, 人生至樂」. 至求書志坌出, 亦未嘗不以爲苦也. 惟閑窓無事, 拈筆寫一尺山, 不受促迫, 眞是樂耳. 長夏科頭, 以此事消暑, 遂復成册.

This brilliant, heretofore unpublished album in circular format is titled by Dong in his own bold calligraphy "Contemplating the Dao with Emotions Cleansed" 澄懷觀道. Dispelling heat could be a euphemism for avoiding the problems of officialdom, and Dong's uncapped head reinforces the image of one far from social formalities. The result is a cleansing of the spirit and clarity of mind capable of penetrating the secrets of the Dao. The album's five jewel-like landscapes are composed on a decorative gold paper, the slick surface of which presents particular challenges. Yet Dong displayed such deft touch, sensitivity,

FIG. 9 Dong Qichang, inscription for *Contemplating the Dao with Emotions Cleansed*, c. 1610 (cat. no. 8)

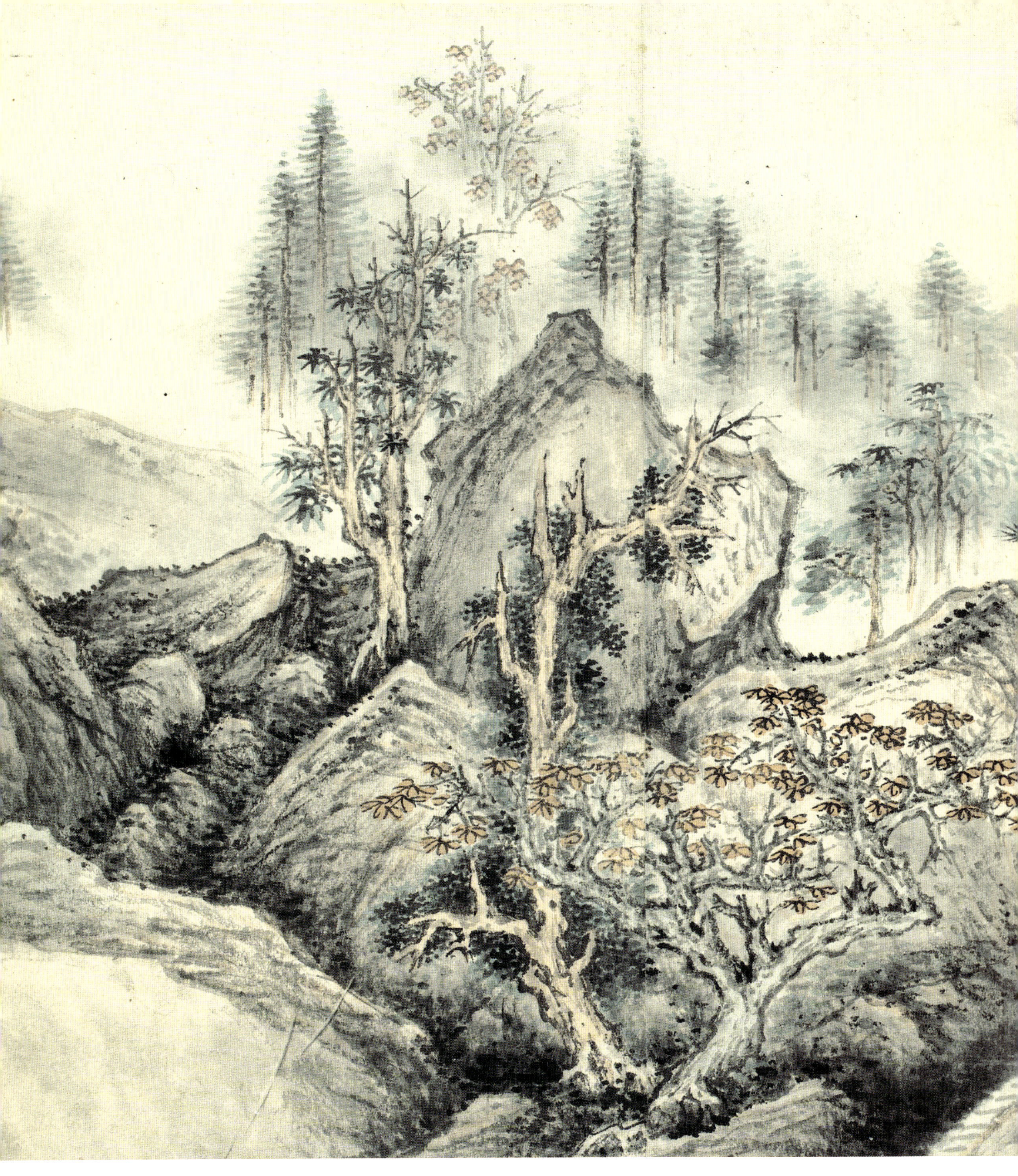

FIG. 10 Shen Shichong, *Landscape* (detail), 1631 (cat. no. 17)

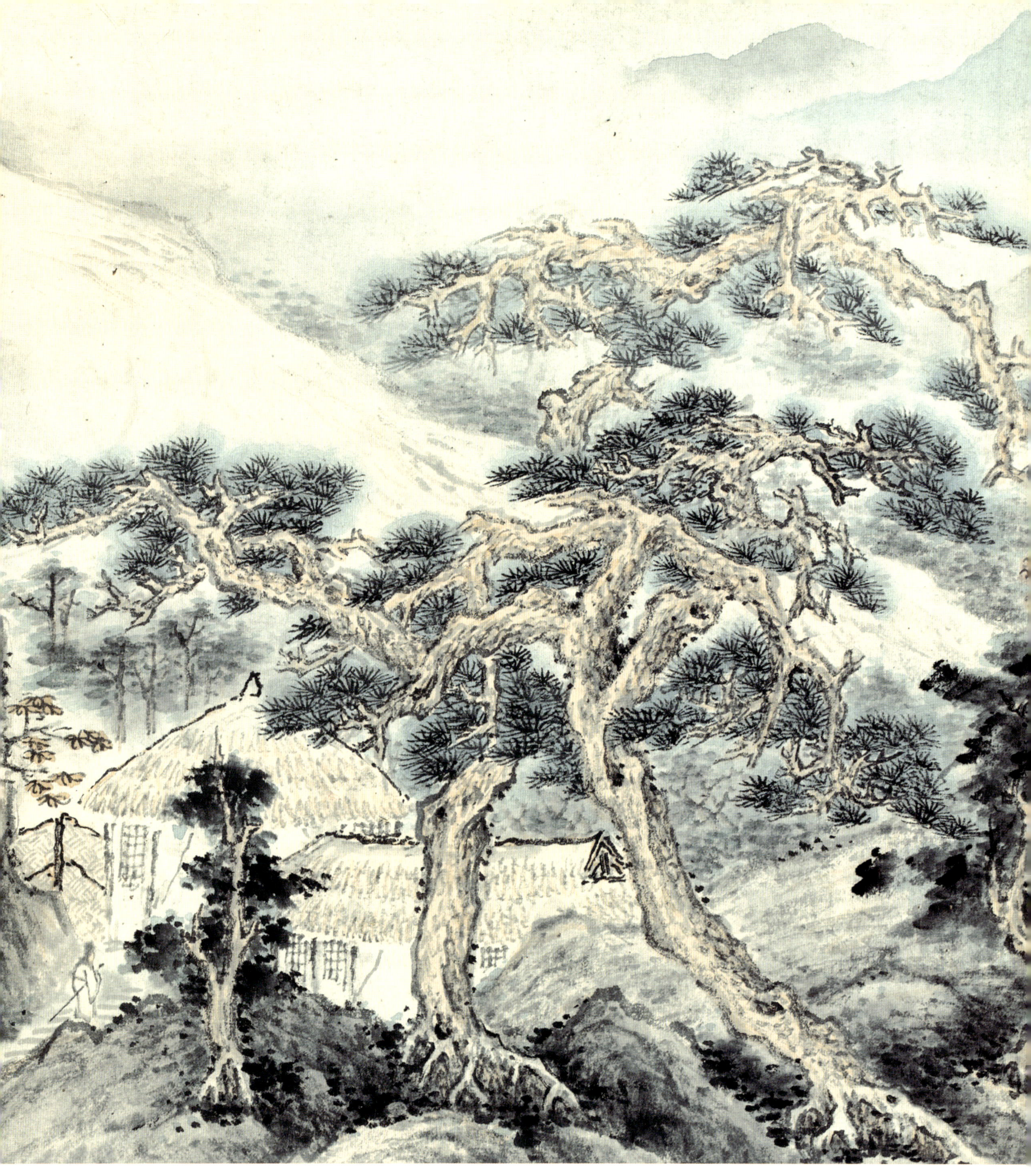

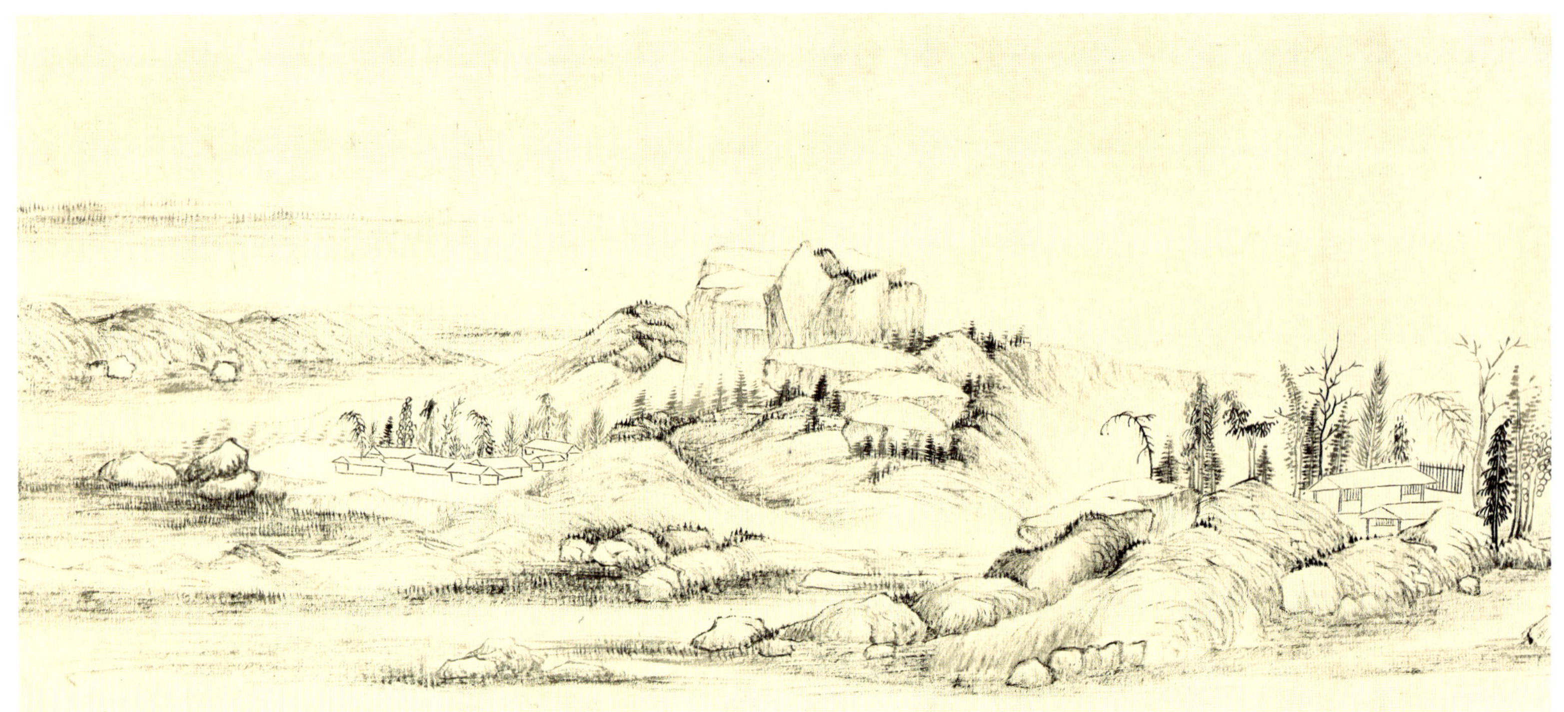

and thought that each small composition merits extended viewing. The matching inscriptions are written on a high-quality untreated paper chosen to maximize the presentation of his skill with the brush. Each painting carries a short inscription that sets a theme—a composition title, such as "Autumn Grove, Level Distance" 秋林平遠, or a simple phrase, such as "Brush ideas of the Yuan" 寫元人筆意. The text in the matching calligraphy roundel expands upon the theme. The connections between inscription and text are not always clear, but this is typical of Dong's work. This is his world, and we enter it with no expectation of being led gently by the hand. What *is* clear is his enjoyment and satisfaction, and the consequent value of this album. Few works by the artist reveal him creating so freely and yet with such obvious delight in the details of brushwork and composition. Headgear removed, the album presents Dong with a rare and impressive clarity.

The influence of Chen Jiru and Dong Qichang is pervasive throughout this exhibition. Chen was the model for modern disengagement in a period when reclusion subtly transformed from quaint and marketable topos to moral imperative. We sense his influence in Xiang Shengmo's *Invitation to Reclusion*. It must also have been a factor in Shen Shichong's 沈士充 (act. c. 1607–after 1640) long colorful *Landscape* of 1631 (cat. no. 17, fig. 10). A professional painter of about the same age as Xiang, Shen hailed from the same township as Dong and Chen and worked under their patronage. A year after he painted this landscape, he painted a very similar composition and explicitly titled it *Invitation to Reclusion*.[62] Whether or not *Landscape* was also intended to illustrate specifically the *zhaoyin* theme, the painting is filled with images of recluses and echoes Xiang's scroll of only five years earlier. Xiang and Shen both painted in a manner that is richly descriptive. Shen's painting, however, is more deeply sensual—a visual feast without complications of literary texts or narrations of personal journey.

If Chen's presence is felt through the image of the recluse, Dong's is known through the power of his opinions and the attraction of this notion of reclusion in art. A number of additional artists represented in the exhibition were in direct contact with Dong, including Lan Ying 藍瑛 (1585–1664 or later; cat. nos. 26–27), Shao Mi 邵彌 (c. 1595–1642; cat. no. 15), Yang Wencong 楊文驄 (1597–1646; cat. nos. 18–19), and Zhang Xuezeng 張學曾 (act. c. 1633–1657; cat. no. 25),[63] but his influence extended far beyond. His precept of learning from earlier painters and paintings became the foundation for an orthodoxy that dominated the later history of Chinese painting. We recognize his influence in the repeated evocation of the styles of such earlier artists as Huang Gongwang and Ni Zan, two of the key figures in Dong's heavily touted lineage of literati painters. Less obvious is the degree to which this process of engagement with earlier art must have been viewed as a form of escape in the troubled times of the late Ming. The Yuan artists in particular offered a window to an idealized existence. In this regard, Shao Mi's *Paintings in the Styles of Earlier Masters with Accompanying Poems of the Yuan Dynasty* (cat. no. 15) is particularly instructive. Despite the fact that three of the eight album leaves are ostensibly modeled after pre-Song painters, the entire album is profoundly "Yuan" in tone. This is partly due to the other five models—all famous Yuan painters—and partly to Shao's style of painting, but more significant is the fact that the accompanying texts all appear to be drawn from Yuan-dynasty poems.[64] Shao probably carefully chose them from some favorite collection of verses by Yuan poets and then painted the accompanying leaves—delicate scenes that represent his private journeys into the world of fourteenth-century letters.

History was particularly unkind to Shao's generation. Those born around the turn of the century in prosperous Jiangnan lived more than half of their lives amidst the sophistication of late-Ming society, only to see their world turned upside down with the events of the 1640s. Economic difficulties and resulting famines in the north led to rebel uprisings, one of which grew to such proportions that it threatened the capital at Beijing. Additional pressure came from the growing power and ambitions of the resurgent Jurchen (Manchu) people to the north. The capital fell to the rebel army of Li Zicheng 李自成 (Li Hongji 李鴻基, 1606–1645) in April 1644, which resulted in the suicide of the Ming emperor, Chongzhen (r. 1627–1644). The Chinese general Wu Sangui 吳三桂 (1612–1678) requested military assistance from the Jurchen to help restore the Ming dynasty, but the Jurchen took advantage of the situation and, after skillful political and military maneuvering, established sovereignty in the north under their dynasty called the Qing. Remnants of the Ming dynasty survived in the south for almost twenty more years, but after 1644 the world was fundamentally changed.

FIG. 11 Yang Wencong, *Water Village* (detail), 1644 (cat. no. 19)

One of the two paintings by Yang Wencong included in the exhibition, a delicate handscroll titled *Water Village* (1644), provides a particularly poignant face to this momentous change and suggests, perhaps, the limits of reclusion in art (cat. no. 19, fig. 11). A hint of the drama behind the painting can be read from its frontispiece, "Pure Winds of Lofty Character," written in reference to Yang by an early twentieth-century admirer. Like Xiang Shengmo, Shao Mi, and Zhang Xuezeng, Yang was a younger friend of Dong Qichang's and profoundly influenced by his approach to painting.[65] That is immediately apparent from this landscape, which, according to Yang's trailing inscription, combines the "brush ideas" of two famous fourteenth-century paintings that were well-known at the time: Zhao Mengfu's *Water Village* of 1302 (Beijing Palace Museum) and Huang Gongwang's *Sand Marsh* (fig. 12). Zhao's *Water Village*, owned by Dong, was especially well regarded because of its resemblance to the landscape around Huating; from what we can see of Huang's *Sand Marsh*, it too bore resemblance to the local topography.[66] Perhaps that sense of grounding in the familiar was important to Yang. What can be said with certainty is his *Water Village* was painted with immense care and thought. The allusions to its fourteenth-century models are erudite and cultured, and the painting's scholarly aesthetic as reflected through its Ni Zan–style lightness is duly noted. What really impresses, however, was his ability to marshal brush modes and motifs into a landscape of remarkable depth and atmosphere. This is a landscape of true reclusion, an escape to a world of profound stillness, where nothing is sullied.

Yang Wencong painted *Water Village* in the eleventh lunar month of 1644 in or near the city of Nanjing, the auxiliary capital and the seat of what remained of the Ming court. Talented and well connected, he was brought to the Southern Ming court and rose quickly up the ranks in the Ministry of War.[67] At precisely this time he was engaged in the important work of fortifying the defenses down the Yangzi River in nearby Zhenjiang in anticipation of an attack from the Manchus. The painting is dedicated to Gao Hongtu 高弘圖 (1583–1645), one of the Grand Secretaries to the Southern Ming court and a well-respected moderate whom the newly enthroned Hongguang emperor 弘光 (r. 1644–1645) relied heavily upon for counsel. Following the painting, Yang added a poem that contrasts markedly with the serenity of the landscape. He alludes directly to contemporary events and pointedly brings up Gao's petitions to retire from court. Gao was finally allowed to resign his position on November 4, 1644. It is apparent that Yang painted *Water Village* specifically to honor his respected friend's departure. Unfortunately for Gao, the only place of reclusion was the scene in Yang's painting. His biographies specify that he had "no home to which he could return," his native Shandong Province under the control of the Qing armies. Gao wandered about the Jiangnan region. When Nanjing fell to the Manchus half a year later he entered a temple in the wilderness and committed suicide by refusing food for nine days. Yang's fate was no better. Leading troops against the Qing armies, he was captured a few months later and put to death, along with his entire household, after refusing to capitulate.[68]

It is rare for paintings to mark important historical moments so clearly, but of course much of the poignancy of Yang's scroll is attached retrospectively: he had no idea of the sorry end that would befall Gao and himself. In fact, one gleans a sense of hope in Yang's dating of the scroll—the Hongguang reign date that he uses was set to start a month later, with the new lunar year.[69] A new reign symbolized a new beginning, and in November 1644 it could not begin soon enough. Whatever Yang's thoughts about the dynasty's survival, it is clear from the care he applied to *Water Village* that he intended it to provide Gao with a path to a better place. That path leads past Dong Qichang, Chen Jiru, and their rarefied world of privilege directly to a landscape envisioned and created by Zhao Mengfu and Huang Gongwang. The fourteenth century probably never seemed so tangible and relevant. From this point forward, reclusion in art would mean something different: more than a statement of detachment, it was a summoning to fashion a personal reality out of the imaginary.

A LANDSCAPE TRANSFORMED There could hardly be a better painting to illustrate how the trauma of dynastic change forced individuals to look inward than Xiang Shengmo's jarring *Self-Portrait in Red Landscape* (cat. no. 20; fig. 30). When he painted it, sometime after the fourth lunar month of 1644, Emperor Chongzhen had taken his life and the capital was occupied by Li Zicheng's army, but the Manchus had yet to assert their power. Xiang's painting and two poems thus were intended to express mourning but not necessarily despair. The red landscape, which may strike the modern viewer as bizarre, in fact is a statement of support for the Ming imperial family, whose surname, Zhu 朱, literally means crimson. Still, if Xiang's painting was intended to put a brave face forward, it does not exactly succeed. The strange scarlet landscape, however propitious its intent, is unlikely to have assuaged any contemporary viewer's fears for the present or future. Moreover, while there is certainly an element of defiance in Xiang's poems, self-doubts tend to dominate:

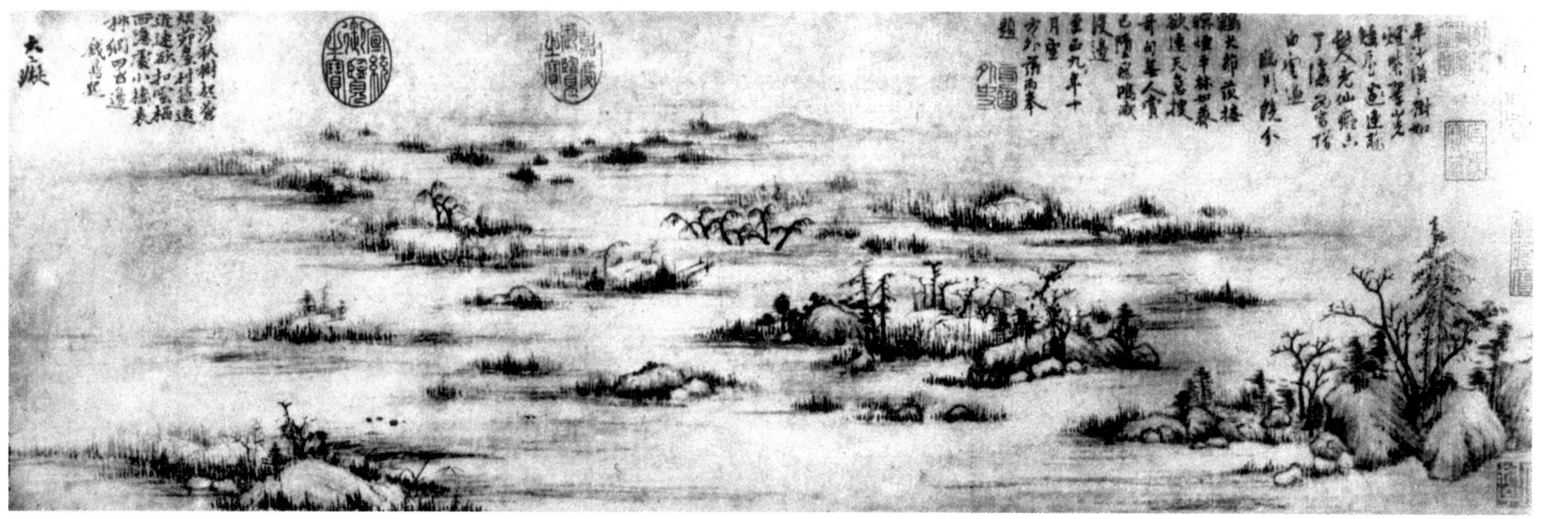

FIG. 12 Huang Gongwang (attributed), *Sand Marsh*; Whereabouts unknown. From Harada Kinjirō, ed., *Chūgoku meiga hōkan* (Tokyo: Ōtsuka Kogeisha, 1959), 337.

Remnant waters, leftover mountains—color still cinnabar red;
Murky heavens, darkened earth—shadow of a trifling body.
A flame ignites in my crimson heart, and I daub the ochre red;
But from this dry brush only careless words—I am ashamed
to paint pictures.
Men of mark are few and desolate; who is there to depict?
Valley clouds obscured in shadow—as if an ignorant fool.
In a change of heart, I laugh at my three "summons to the recluse";
Who would have believed that I was already one with the wild man?

剩水殘山色尚朱，天昏地黑影微軀.
赤心燄起塗丹雘，渴筆言輕愧畫圖.
人物寥寥誰可貌，谷雲杳杳亦如愚.
翻然自笑三招隱，孰信狂夫早與俱.

The last two lines from Xiang's first poem suggest that he has already achieved the sense of detachment that characterizes reclusion. His three "summons" must refer to the three "Summoning the Recluse" scrolls he had painted by this date, the last one only a few months before *Self-Portrait in Red Landscape*. The services of the "wild man" (*kuangfu* 狂夫), or in other words the recluse who is summoned to lead us into a better place, is no longer needed. In essence, Xiang is claiming that he is one and the same.[70] This little bit of bravado, however, does little to alleviate the concern evident in the first poem, nor the rather depressing series of observations, mostly about himself, that constitute his second poem. Frankly put, Xiang made a lousy recluse.

The events of 1644 and the long period of limbo that followed, as the Manchus dealt with the remnants of Ming resistance, altered the landscape in multiple ways. For many it was the end, as loyalists like Gao Hongtu, recipient of Yang Wencong's *Water Village*, chose suicide over life in the new dynasty. To state the obvious, suicide was the most radical form of withdrawal. It would seem to have little to do with the images of reclusion presented in the vast majority of Chinese paintings and poems, but as the two brothers Boyi and Shuqi of early times remind us, at the root of substantive reclusion is an adherence to principle that sometimes allowed only a single uncompromising pathway into the wilderness (see fig. 3).[71] Reclusion during the late Ming dynasty was more posture than reality. Surely there were many who chose the path of disengagement with the purest of aims, but how much can we expect to know of those who chose to disappear? Those from whom we do hear—the Chen Jirus and Xiang Shengmos—utilized the voice of reclusion to stake a philosophical and social claim. Regardless of motive or even depth of conviction, we recognize the calligraphy and painting of the late Ming as deeply engaged in what might be called the rhetoric of reclusion. In contrast, reclusion in the early decades of the Qing dynasty was a reality that many felt compelled to follow. How did the reality of reclusion translate into art?

It proves to be much easier to parse the rhetoric of reclusion than its reality. A painting like Zeng Jing's 曾鯨 (1564–1647) *Portrait of Pan Qintai* (1621; cat. no. 2), for example, unabashedly presents the subject—a scholar of Suzhou—as a man of the hills in a gentle masquerade that would have been immediately understood by all. For a portrait painting like this, fiction operates according to accepted formats and principles: plain white robe and hat indicate non-degree status, bamboo staff marks Pan as a wanderer in the landscape. But when we encounter an image like Xiang Shengmo's *Self-Portrait* and read the artist's poems we immediately sense the confusion that accompanied the events of 1644. Does one portray oneself as detached and aloof, stalwart and defiant, or simply mournful and ill? All of these qualities are suggested in Xiang's poems and perhaps in his image as well. For those like Xiang, who were well practiced in the rhetoric of reclusion, reality's intrusion must have compelled a reevaluation of self and its presentation. The trouble was the continued existence of Ming resistance to Manchu forces, even though increasingly weakened and geographically marginalized, made it that much more difficult to recognize the lay of the land.[72] For some, the landscape would always remain cinnabar red. For most it was only a matter of time before it returned to its natural state and there was reconciliation with the new dynasty.

In general, the events of 1644 did not precipitate immediate changes in the way paintings were composed. Rather, references to the new landscape tended to be subtle and often reliant more on literary allusion than pictorial content or style.[73] There are exceptions—one thinks especially of the dramatically moody landscape paintings of Gong Xian 龔賢 (1619–1689; cat. nos. 34–36) and the often puzzling images produced by Bada Shanren 八大山人 (1626–1705; cat. nos. 41–48)—but Gong in particular must also be seen in the context of experimentations in landscape painting that took place well before the fall of the Ming. Similarly, the misshapen figural depictions of Chen Hongshou were foremost a product of late Ming society (cat. nos. 21–23). Chen was a particularly sardonic chronicler of the posturing of reclusion. A precise contemporary of Xiang Shengmo, Chen too turned to painting for a livelihood after aborting an official career. Different personalities, however, led to radically different statements about self and society. There is an earnestness in Xiang's depiction of the recluse's existence, an apparent belief in the ideal even if the path to its attainment was unclear. Chen, on the other hand, seems to mock contemporary infatuations with this same ideal. His especially fine and late album of 1651, titled *Sixteen Views of Seclusion* (National Palace Museum, Taipei), depicts a series of figures echoing famous scholars of the past who, to one degree or another, were associated with reclusion. One typically awkward scholar is depicted playing with prized inkstones under a tree in the landscape, like a child with toy trucks in a sandbox (fig. 13). This might well be Su Shi 蘇軾 (1037–1101), who, despite professing detachment toward material objects, had a particular weakness for fine inkstones.[74] Given the extraordinary esteem with which Su, Mi Fu, and others of the late Northern Song were held by the likes of Chen Jiru and Dong Qichang in the late Ming, it is clear that the object of Chen Hongshou's playful ridicule was his own peers. The important thing to realize is Chen's ironic view toward contemporary habits and mores existed well before 1644. Dynastic change simply gave them a bitter edge. Chen's various adopted sobriquets, including Huichi 悔遲 (Regretting-to-Be-Late) and Wuchi 勿遲 (Don't Be Late), poignantly suggest the Ming loyalist's sense of inhabiting a dislocated space and time. The past continued into the present, but it was accompanied by a terrible sense of loss.

Dynastic collapse marks the disappearance of the center that psychologically and socially binds the country's subjects. In its absence the individual looks for alternative sources of strength and stability. It might be a cadre of like-minded peers—circles of friends for the sharing of thoughts and mutual support. Poetry, painting, and calligraphy all serve as important modes of communication to maintain a sense of identity and express communal sentiments. One interesting example is Zhang Xuezeng's undated *Fisherman Recluse* (cat. no. 25). Zhang is one of the forgotten painters of the seventeenth century. Counted among the so-called Nine Friends of Painting who knew and were deeply influenced by Dong Qichang, Zhang has not earned much scholarly attention. In part this is because his paintings are relatively rare, but it is also due to the nature of his work. Like the better-known Wang Shimin 王時敏 (1592–1680), with whom he was friends, Zhang adhered closely to Dong's theoretical tenets regarding models and simulation—too closely for those who prefer paintings less constrained by rules and principles.[75] Zhang's paintings, however, speak with conviction of the importance of the past and, at least in the case of his

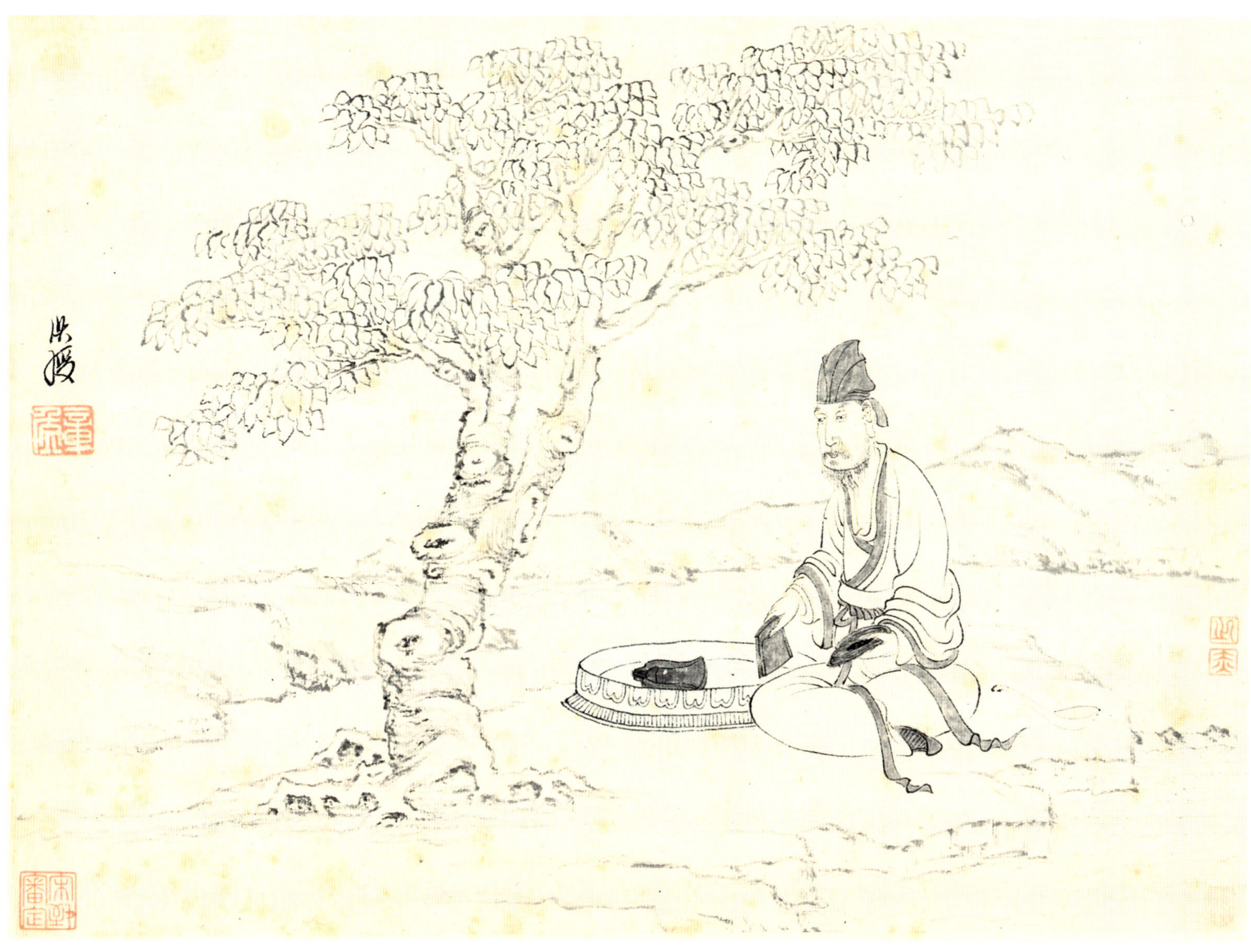

Fisherman Recluse, with more immediacy and relevance than is normally recognized. His inscription presents a short quatrain of "pure and new lines" that he credits to a Master Jian, who in all likelihood was the painter and noted Ming loyalist Jianjiang 漸江 (Jiang Tao 江韜, 1610–1664), better known by his Buddhist monk name Hongren 弘仁. The verse is a paean to reclusion, elevating the moral force of a solitary fisherman above the martial power of a general. Stimulated, Zhang used the stylistic idiom of Yuan-dynasty painter Wu Zhen to illustrate the "pure and new lines," and the iconic image of fourteenth-century reclusion thus spoke specifically to the loyalist community of Ming *yimin*. Zhang's painting is an important reminder that Dong's reclusion in art is not as far removed from the realities of the painter's everyday existence as may appear.

Another painting suggestive of networking within the Ming loyalist community is Zhang Feng's *Immortals' Secrets in a Stone Cave* of 1658 (cat. no. 30; fig. 14). Zhang Feng 張風 (d. 1662) was a native of Nanjing, and his paintings reflect the eclecticism and openness to experimentation that characterize painting from this urban center in the seventeenth century. Outside the circle of Dong's influence, he was less concerned with making statements of stylistic affiliation and more interested in visual effect, mood, and texture. His austere landscape is strangely configured, with bold outcroppings, stylized water, and sharp wintry trees. In his inscription, he describes a series of trips by boat between Nanjing, Zhenjiang, Suzhou, and Hangzhou, singling out in particular three scenic hills in Zhenjiang on the banks of the Yangzi River. His inscription ends with emphatic insistence that there is nothing more to the painting than its role commemorating a pleasant sightseeing trip with his friend, Da Chongguang 笪重光 (1623–1692; see cat. no. 31), but the landscape's solemnity and content suggest otherwise. Rather than portray any recognizable topographical scene (and out of keeping with the lush spring-summer season when the scroll was painted—it is signed the sixth lunar month), Zhang created a mysterious other-world and a hidden gathering in a cave where three figures and a servant ponder a game of *weiqi* 圍棋 (chess; fig. 14). The game of *weiqi* was commonly associated with the timeless world of immortals, with one of the stock figures of worldly disengagement—the woodcutter—playing the role of Rip Van Winkle–like witness (he enters the scene towards the end of Zhang's scroll).[76] During these early years of the Qing, however, when Manchu control remained uncertain, *weiqi* was used as a trope in loyalist circles for pondering strategy: one move might turn the tide of the match.[77]

FIG. 13 Chen Hongshou, "Figure with Inkstones," leaf from *Sixteen Views of Seclusion*, 1651; Album of sixteen leaves of painting and four leaves of calligraphy: ink and color on paper; 21.4 × 29.8 cm each; National Palace Museum, Republic of China (Taiwan)

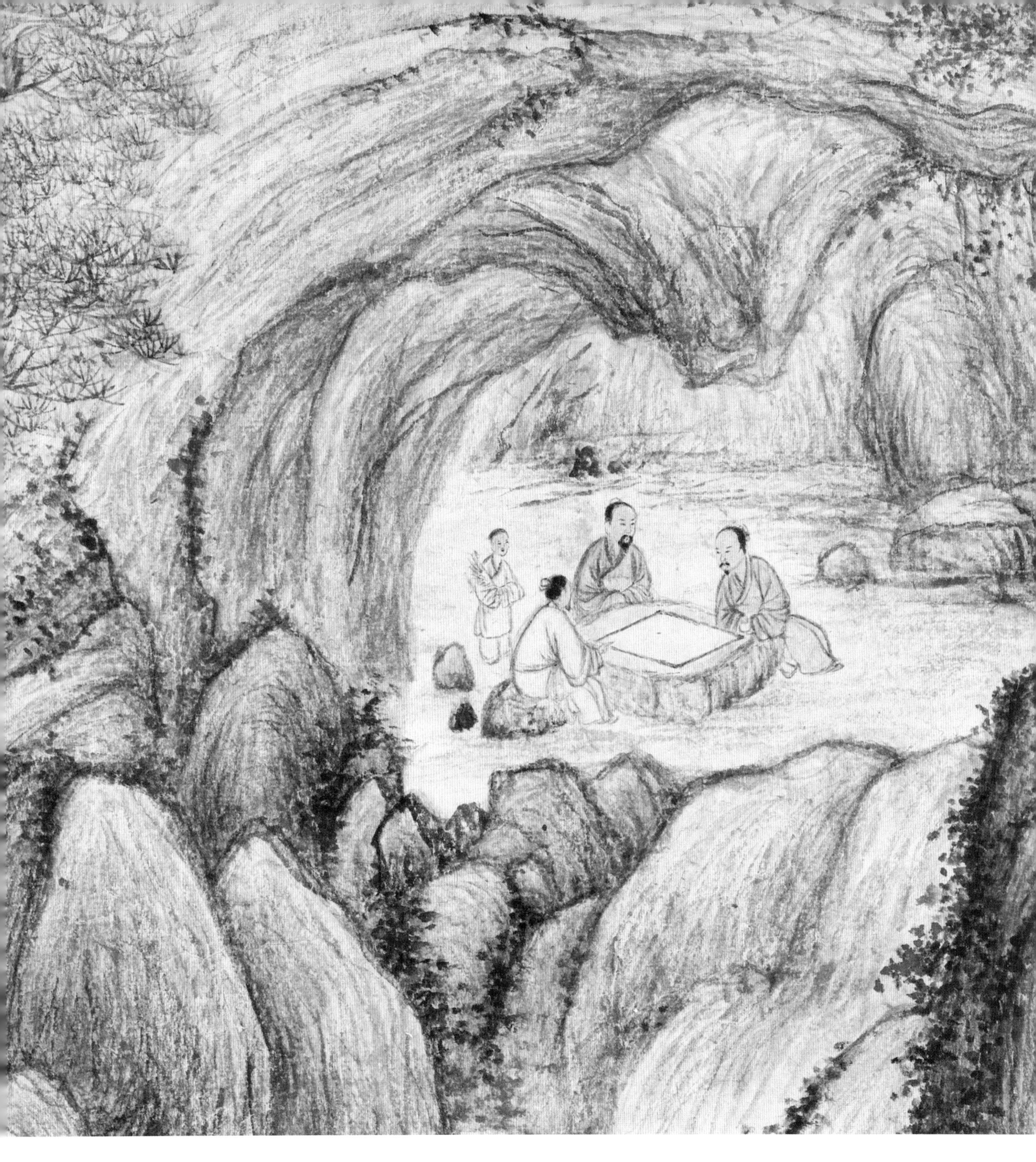

FIG. 14 Zhang Feng, *Immortals' Secrets in a Stone Cave* (detail), 1658 (cat. no. 30)

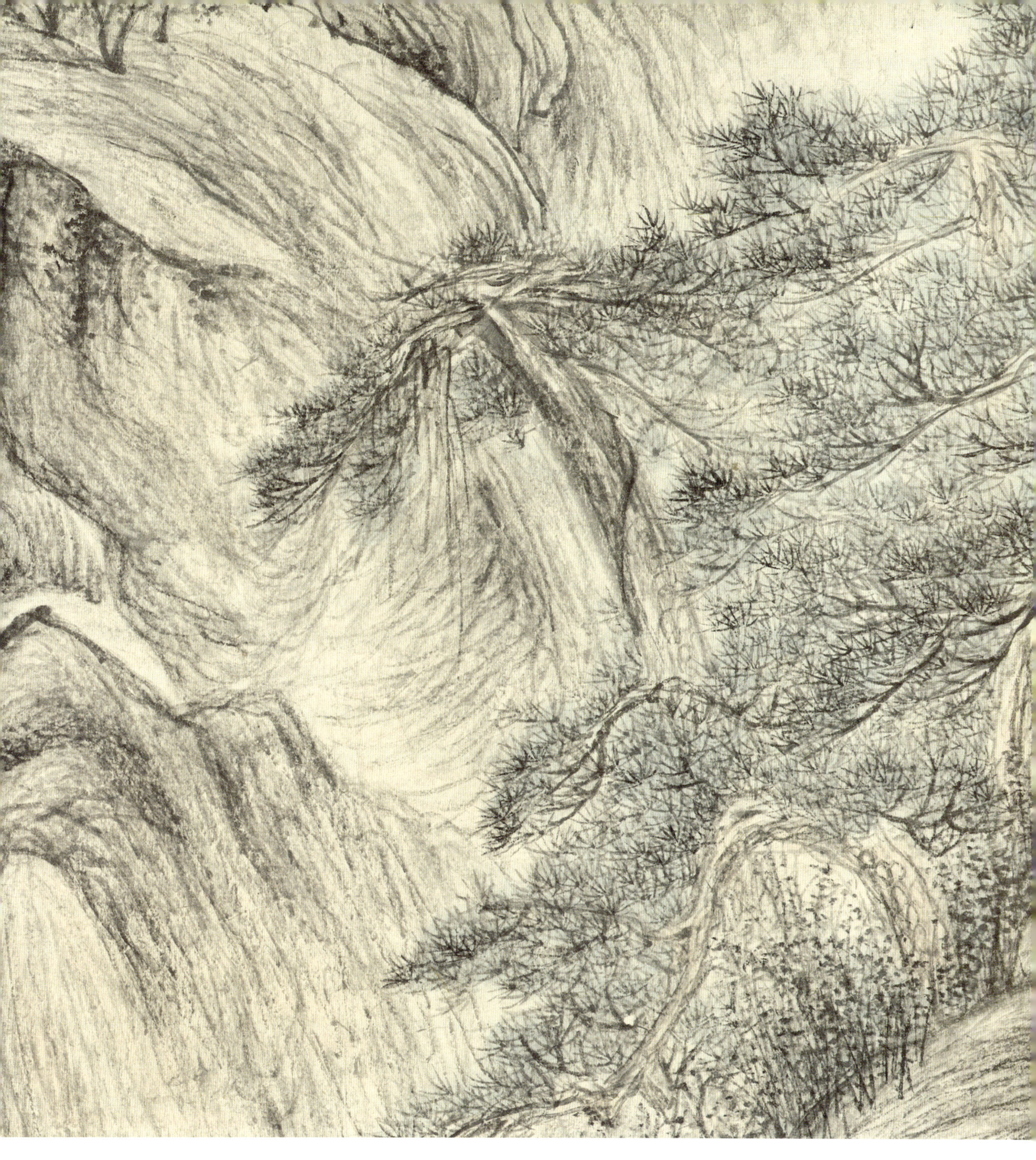

A separate scroll of calligraphy in the exhibition by the important literary figure Qian Qianyi 錢謙益 (1582–1664) transcribes a number of Qian's own poems, including two sets of quatrains on *weiqi* that have been interpreted as statements of hope for the anti-Qing movement (cat. no. 29). Qian's poems were first composed in 1648, at a critical moment in the Ming resistance. Precisely ten years later the loyalist commander Zheng Chenggong 鄭成功 (1624–1662), better known as Koxinga, moved his naval forces north from his base along the Fujian coast with the intention of attacking Qing garrisons in the Jiangnan region and specifically Nanjing. The timing of Zhang Feng's painting and its reference to precisely the same area where Zheng Chenggong would soon be engaged in battle with Qing forces is certainly not coincidental.[78] Despite the disclaimer in his inscription, Zhang's painting is all about contemporary affairs.

Immortals' Secrets in a Stone Cave takes a well-established motif from the lore of reclusion and uses it to mirror reality. The mirror, however, is purposely distorted, revealing a landscape that is a strange mix of local geography, myth, and emotion. As an ardent loyalist, Zhang appears to have been open about painting a scourged landscape, and in this regard he shared much with his fellow townsman, Gong Xian, whose paintings are typically bathed in a heavy, foreboding mood (cat. nos. 34–36). Others painted landscapes that offered solace and escape, though here too there is often an element of reality. During the years of conquest and resistance, Buddhist and Daoist temples were one of the few places of refuge from war. A painting like Zhang Zhengyue's 張正嶽 (b. c. 1590) *Mountain Landscape* (cat. no. 28)—pure escapist fare at a glance—may have been more grounded in the reality of the first decades of the Qing dynasty than one might otherwise expect from such a magical image. The blue-green landscape was a mode utilized by painters to create paradisiacal landscapes with strong archaistic value, but like Zhang Feng's *Immortals' Secrets in a Stone Cave*, the sense of timelessness in Zhang Zhengyue's *Landscape* should not mask the painting's relevance to the post-conquest world. Though the building complexes in the painting that the traveler approaches are not specifically recognizable, they suggest the kind of religious institutions that many turned to for refuge. This is to date the only known existing painting by Zhang Zhengyue, who is virtually unrecognized today, but was an artist of some repute in the seventeenth century. His colorful style well represents the taste and traditions of Hangzhou, shared by his better-known contemporaries Chen Hongshou and Lan Ying.

A very different and far more personal view of the landscape of Buddhist refuge is Xu Fang's 徐枋 (1622–1694) *Mount Qinyuhang* (cat. no. 38). This unusual landscape with figures by a small temple is one of a famous set of paintings (now scattered) titled *The Twelve Most Surpassing Mountains of Wu* that Xu painted in 1672 to illustrate the local landscape around Suzhou. Renowned among Ming loyalists for uncompromising behavior such as absolutely refusing to enter the city of Suzhou after the Qing conquest, Xu documented in quasi-topographical fashion the landscape of reclusion in which he lived. Mount Qinyuhang was one of his temporary dwellings in the early 1660s, and the place held such significance to him because of its historical associations with both reclusion and dynastic loss that he adopted its name for his sobriquet, the Mountain Man of Qinyu. His painting is unpolished, his brushwork simple, yet the methodical consistency of his style strangely suits what we know of this loyalist's sense of conviction. In his hands, the landscape of Wu is refashioned to reflect the blunt honesty of a true recluse.

Loyalism mixed with reclusion and Buddhism to form a distinctive mix in the art of the second half of the seventeenth century, though with results that are far from uniform. In the case of Kuncan 髡殘 (b. 1612), represented in the exhibition by *Temple on a Mountain Ledge* of 1661 (cat. no. 37; fig. 27), a serious commitment was made to the Buddhist church prior to the end of the Ming dynasty, and he remained a monk throughout his life. Thus, although deeply affected by the fall of the Ming, the primary effect of the dynastic transition may simply have been to deepen a fundamental Buddhist belief in the illusory nature of the world. According to his friend and chronicler Cheng Zhengkui 程正揆 (1604–1676), Kuncan spent three months deep in the southern wilderness of Hunan Province fleeing Qing forces in 1644:

> In the *jiashen* year [1644], he escaped the warfare by entering deeply into the wilds of Taoyuan. His travails brought him across mountains and rivers strange and remote, to trees and plants ancient and bizarre, amidst strange beasts and rare birds, uncanny sounds and ghostly shadows—all things that defy description. Finding places to rest in this homeless state he would sometimes pillow on rocks by clear-flowing streams or meander aimlessly on summit peaks where gibbons lay. Sometimes he would drink blood to quench his thirst, piss on his feet in search of warmth. Sometimes he would set a grass mat down where wild pigs root, avoid the rain in tigers' lairs. He suffered thus for some three months.[79]
>
> 甲申間避兵桃源深處，歷數山川奇僻，樹木古怪，與夫異獸珍禽，魑聲鬼影，不可名狀，寢處流離，或在溪澗枕石漱水，或在巒巘猿臥蛇委，或以血代飲，或以溺暖足，或藉草豕欄，或避雨虎穴，受諸苦惱凡三月.

Despite these miseries, or perhaps because of them, Kuncan sought spirituality in the landscape. In 1654 he moved back to the Nanjing region, where he had studied Buddhism years earlier, and settled in the Baoen Temple. Five years later he took an extended trip to the scenic region of Huangshan (Yellow Mountain) in nearby Anhui Province. Huangshan's landscape made a deep impression on the monk and played a central role in his paintings of the early 1660s.[80] Judging from the short poem that he added to *Temple on a Mountain Ledge*, this painting was no exception, as it uses precisely the kind of hyperbolic praise and immortal-tinged imagery that Huangshan typically inspired:

> Famous mountains! I, Monk Can, approach,
> First viewing them from beyond the clouds.
> That vast expanse encompasses Creation,
> That lofty majesty displays great dignity!
> Rows of peaks, like clustered bamboo,
> Flying mists, as if spit out by immortals...
>
> 名嶽殘僧近，先愷雲外瞻.
> 空濛亂造化，崒嵂闢尊巖.
> 列嶂紛如簇，飛霞噴若仙...

Nonetheless, while Huangshan may have been on Kuncan's mind, strictly speaking both painting and poem are less about Huangshan than Kuncan dreaming about Huangshan. Elaborate structures, boats, and an occasional person or two provide his paintings with a strong human presence reflective of the world that he inhabited as a prominent priest and cultural figure of Nanjing. As James Cahill has noted, occasionally, though not in this particular painting, he included himself in the scene as a meditating figure seated in a cave tucked away.[81] This subjective presence gives Kuncan's paintings a powerful autobiographical tone. He seems to equate landscape with spiritual enlightenment, but like that ultimate goal, it remains something on the horizon, not yet attained. His poem on *Temple on a Mountain Ledge* states as much in the first two lines. The subject of this painting is a journey. What he paints is one step along that journey's path, with a view that is as much introspective as it is inspired by what he saw and experienced.

Kuncan is something of an exception in this exhibition, as he represents a type of reclusion that seems almost detached from the realities of the seventeenth century. This may seem strange given the fact that he seems to have lived a fairly social life and was particularly active with members of the *yimin* community. His orientation, however, was shaped by serious religious convictions, and for the Buddhist monk this meant focusing on a spiritual quest that transcended the immediacy of worldly affairs. In other words, there is a certain purity and simplicity to his reclusion, a directness that we associate with those true hermits who lived among cliffs and caves. This is the image he attempted to convey in his paintings. His style is purposely unpolished and impressionistic—to speak of it in terms of the influence of earlier masters would simply miss the point. Kuncan's painting provides an unfiltered glimpse of landscape through his eyes, and in the warm luminosity of those peaks surrounding the mountain temple we sense the monk's spiritual glow.

In utter contrast to Kuncan's landscape is the striking set of four hanging scrolls depicting flowering plum blossoms by Fang Yizhi 方以智 (1611–1671; cat. no. 40). Buddhist imagery suffuses the poems Fang added to each scroll, but rather than narrate a path to serenity his verses bespeak troubled times, escape, and longing. "In Buddhist temples, over months and years, I've drawn the '106'; / In precincts of serenity, amid traces of snow, remain two or three" 梵宮歲月得百六，靜域香痕留二三. This couplet, from the poem on the scroll of twin branches opening to the left, is typical of his obtuse language. Both the ancient *Yi jing* 易經 (Book of changes) and Chinese calendric beliefs associate the number 106 with misfortune. "Two or three" presumably refers to blossoming plum trees (the *meihua* or *prunus mumae*), beloved in China for putting out delicate blossoms in the midst of winter and one of the most enduring of subjects in Chinese culture.[82] Fang's poems delve deeply into *meihua* lore, with allusions to ancient songs and persons, including one of the most famous of all recluses, Lin Bu 林逋 (967–1028), who was so enamored with the blossoming plum that he claimed her for his spouse. Plum as a feminized object of desire is one of the persistent themes of Fang's poems. The *meihua*, however, was also commonly used as a metaphor for lofty male virtue, able to endure the hardships of winter and blossom in solitude. Fang clearly intended this second meaning as well, specifically applying it to Ming loyalists like him ("two or three") who were scattered amongst mountain temples, blossoming in the wilderness.[83]

Fang's trees zig and zag on and off the scrolls, painted in a way unlike any other. One need only compare his manner of depicting plum blossoms with Gao Jian's 高簡 (1634–after 1708) lovely but far more conventional rendition of some decades later to recognize the fierce strangeness of Fang's vision (cat. no. 57). To augment the effect, he employed a strange, archaic style of calligraphy for his poems that is every bit as individual as the paintings. Sets of hanging scrolls like this commonly follow a prescribed arrangement that is visually apparent, but no matter how arranged, these four plum blossom compositions simply look uncomfortable together. Fang seems to emphasize separation and disjointedness, using these qualities as a metaphor for the loyalists' condition. This was the life he lived. One of the most prominent scholars of the seventeenth century and an active political figure, he remained steadfastly loyal to the fallen Ming regime throughout his life. He took the Buddhist tonsure in 1650, but his commitment to the religion was tempered by political activities and anti-Manchu sentiment. For much of the last twenty years of his life he moved restlessly from temple to temple throughout the south. Fang's poems on his plum blossom scrolls, with their striking imagery and allusions, vividly present this strange world of a Buddhist wilderness, at once filled with sadness, isolation, and displacement. Captured by Manchu forces, he died in 1671, likely by his own hand in a final display of loyalty.[84]

Fang Yizhi's fame as a profound thinker, as a scholar of far-reaching breadth, and as a patriot will always insure a certain curiosity in his artwork. To date, however, his paintings have received scant attention, relegated to the "scholar-amateur" category that barely qualifies as a backhanded compliment.[85] While his landscape paintings may deserve this characterization, these plum blossom scrolls suggest that a reevaluation of his art is in order. Maximizing his strong literary grounding, and perhaps liberated by the simplicity of his subject, Fang created images that are at once mysterious, disturbing, and dense with meaning. Perhaps most intriguing of all is how alike his approach and message are to what is seen in the art of Bada Shanren (cat. nos. 41–48). The two make an intriguing pair. Both were brilliant men from scholarly backgrounds, both were deeply loyal to the Ming house, and both spent years involved with the Buddhist church. Whether or not the two were personally acquainted, they shared so much in outlook and background that the similarities in their art should not be surprising. The more familiar Bada Shanren, however, is an artist whose skill is unquestioned. He is also an artist who took the artistic expression of reclusion to a level of profundity unmatched by any other.

One applies the word "familiar" to Bada Shanren with tongue in cheek. There is probably no painter in the history of China whose images are so immediately recognizable, yet his person is so cloaked in secrecy that his very identity remains a matter of speculation. Bada Shanren is the name by which he is most commonly known, but even this sobriquet—literally Eight-Great Mountain Man—is of obscure meaning and origins. What is known is that he was a member of a branch of the Ming imperial family located in Nanchang (Jiangxi Province), and that within a few years of the fall of the Ming dynasty in 1644 he disappeared into the Buddhist community. Determined scholarship in recent generations has done much to narrow down his identity and clarify his activities, but in some ways the more one knows about Bada Shanren the more one feels lost in a labyrinth of purposeful obscurity. He erased his birth identity and adopted names frequently—more than twenty over the course of his life.[86] Bada Shanren is the sobriquet that he used exclusively for his last twenty years, assuming it within a few years of leaving the monastic life in 1680. The decision to leave the temple and reenter the secular world was a difficult one. The Buddhist community had sustained him for over thirty years, and he had proven to be very much at home in the world of abstract intellectual discourse that characterizes Chan (Zen) philosophy. Most significantly, Buddhism shielded him from the very real dangers he had faced as a remnant member of the Ming imperial family. In the late 1670s, anticipating this momentous change, he solicited a number of inscriptions from friends to write on a portrait that he carried with him.[87] Over one such inscription he impressed a seal that boldly identifies his origins as a descendant of the Yiyang Prince of Jiangxi.

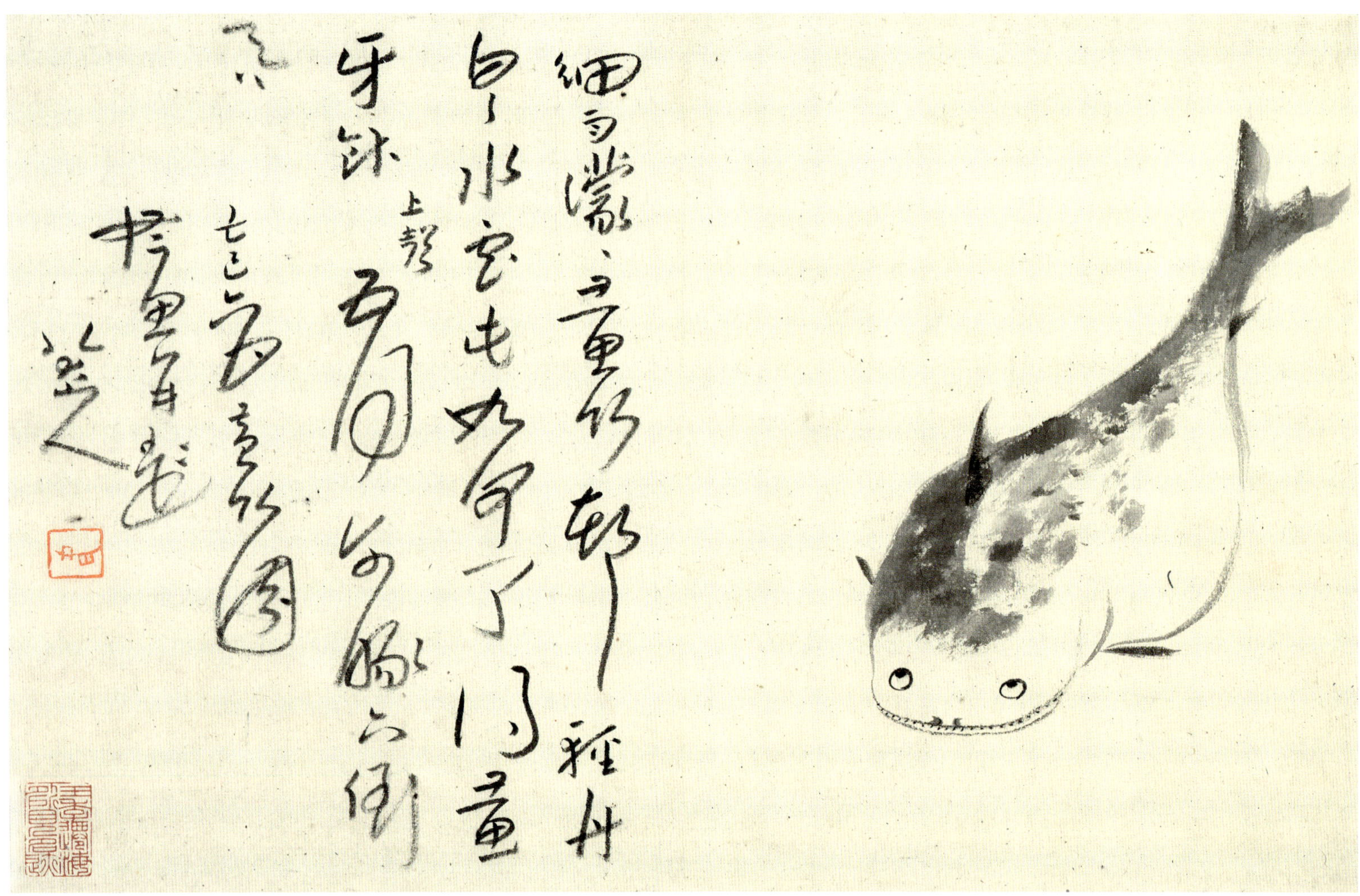

This is the one and only "public" proclamation of his imperial heritage (presumably, he showed the painting to a very select audience). At the same time, circa 1677–79, he began to exhibit bizarre behavior—alternately laughing and crying while aimlessly wandering about the marketplace disheveled. No one recognized him until he was discovered by a nephew, who brought him home and kept him for a long time, "releasing him only after the sickness got better."[88]

Bada Shanren's "madness" is one of the defining features of his art. His paintings are commonly of single subjects—such as birds, fish, or flowers—isolated and highlighted for concentrated effect. Settings, when added, are limited, and at times make little obvious sense. Bada composed his images with extraordinary attention to the picture frame, spacing his motifs for maximum tension, including inscriptions and seals that function like pictorial components. The result is a heightened awareness of the paintings' two dimensions, yet Bada's creativity and technical skills with the brush are so remarkable that with minimal strokes his images often appear to inhabit three-dimensional space. His whimsical *Globefish* (1689), for example, masterfully foreshortened, seems to emerge from the depths of the paper (cat. no. 42:1, fig. 15). In contrast, he purposely employed a largely unmodulated line in his writing so that his calligraphy has a distinctively flat appearance and seems to float right on the surface of the paper. Everything about his paintings is pictorially engaging—the lively and curious rendering of his subjects, the compositional and spatial tension, the distinctive style of his calligraphy—but when we try to read what he wrote our engagement dissolves in confusion. Here is his poem accompanying the grinning globefish, or "river pig" as he is known in China:

Fine rain drizzling in Yellow Bamboo Village,
Light boat bobbing in mounds of water and clouds.
How can one get a meal for yellow teeth?
In the fifth month the river pig is swallowed upside down!

細雨濛濛黄竹村，輕舟勺勺水雲屯.
如何了得黄牙飯，五月河豚下倒吞.

Typically, Bada Shanren's poems raise more questions than they answer, and this is presuming they can even be read. His contemporary biographer Shao Changheng 邵長蘅 (1637–1704) spoke of "difficult and mysterious words" in his writing, "not all of which can be understood" 間雜以幽澀語, 不盡可解.[89] Bada would use alternate versions of characters and employ homophonic puns; sometimes he twisted the syntactical structure of a poetic line so that even if all of the characters were readable one is left literally guessing at the meaning. Most commonly, as with the verse added to *Globefish*, the language of the poem can be read but its intent remains obscure. The isolation and reduction of his images gives them a sense of mystery and meaning—as if compacted to the status of icon or symbol. We are drawn to his texts for answers but left befuddled. With knowledge of his reputed breakdown, his paintings give the appearance of being products of an intensely creative but unstable mind.[90]

FIG. 15 Bada Shanren, "Globefish," leaf from *Golden Fish, Lotus Pods, Globefish, and Bamboo*, 1689 (cat. no. 42)

Research spearheaded by Wang Fangyu, who devoted many years to solving the riddles of Bada Shanren, has taken much of the air out of the issue of Bada's sanity. A number of the poems prove to be decipherable enough to demonstrate that his writings have very specific intentions. The problem is he does not seem to have wanted those intentions to be understood. He used language to shut doors, and the only way to open them is to have the kind of encyclopedic knowledge and flair for wordplay that he himself possessed (aided by years of training in Chan Buddhist discourse). Twenty years ago Wang made the argument that Bada feigned his madness, using "his eccentricity, consciously and selectively, as a device to conceal his inner feelings...and to avoid social interaction with those he chose to ignore."[91] In fact, feigning madness was a technique already employed in antiquity by principled individuals who sought to disengage themselves from social and political intercourse. Lu Tong 陸通 (sixth-fifth century BCE), better known as Jieyu 接輿, the Madman of Chu, is the classic example. He appears in the *Analects* as a vocal critic of Confucius and again in *Zhuangzi*, espousing the necessity of escape in times of misfortune.[92]

Bada Shanren's model, however, is more likely to come from texts of the medieval period. In one, a collection of biographies of recluses titled "Chushi zhuan," the compiler Yao Silian 姚思廉 (557–637) delineates in his introduction three different types of reclusion. The first consists of those paragons of great antiquity (like the aforementioned Xu You) who would never consider accepting positions at the court. Second are those who "hid in the marketplace and at the court," willing to "dwell in the worldly muck" as long as they could pursue the Dao. The third, and most relevant for Bada Shanren, "bared their bodies and feigned madness, and as though deaf and mute they cut off the world. . . These ones kept themselves intact, distancing themselves from harm, and attained the way of proper virtue" 或躶體佯狂，盲瘖絶世...此全身遠害，得大雅之道. After listing these three grades of reclusion, Yao praises the recluses in his account for knowing when to articulate and when to keep silent appropriate to the situation before asking, "How could we speak of them in the same breath along with those who pass their entire life in a disordered age contending for profit and striving for temporal success?" 與夫沒身亂世，爭利干時者，豈同年而語哉.[93]

There are specific things in Yao's introduction that presage Bada Shanren's behavior over a thousand years later. For example, Bada's biographer reports that he feigned dumbness to avoid unwanted social contacts, pasting the single character *ya* 啞 (dumb) on his door and refusing thereafter to speak.[94] But what really resonates with Bada's situation is Yao's rhetorical question. The issue of maintaining loyalty towards the Ming or collaborating with the new Qing dynasty was a matter of enormous concern for the *yimin* who lived well into the second half of the seventeenth century. With all periods of dynastic change, the question of remaining loyal to the past is simply a question of time: sooner or later sentiments change as the reality of a new world sets in, and what might have once been a stance of courage and principle loses relevance and becomes anachronistic. However, the Ming-Qing transition was prolonged. Hope for a return to the old dynasty was embodied by the continued existence of the Southern Ming court, at least until 1662, when it was finally extinguished with the capture of its last emperor in faraway Burma after lingering on in the deep southwest of China. There were other challenges to Manchu rule, but by 1683 the last of these was eliminated.[95] In some ways the most meaningful sign of the end of the Ming came a few years earlier, when the Qing emperor Kangxi (Shengzu 聖祖, r. 1661–1722) announced a special examination to be held in 1679. The intention of the *boxue hongci* exam was to facilitate reconciliation, and it was aimed precisely at Ming loyalists like Bada Shanren. Some of Bada's close acquaintances accepted invitations to participate. Bada's reaction appears to have been Yao Silian's third type of reclusion: cutting off the world by feigning madness.[96]

Not surprisingly, it is clear from those Bada Shanren poems whose meanings have been fully or partially unpacked that his art is fundamentally autobiographical; the focus is on himself, the *yimin* community, and the issue of displacement. His fish help demonstrate (cat. nos. 42–43). One of Bada's favorite subjects, in part because they lent themselves well to the kind of lively portrayal at which he excelled but also because of an intrinsic irony, fish were associated with happiness—or at least there was the presumption of their happiness according to a famous conversation recorded in *Zhuangzi*, in which the question was raised how one can know what fish are thinking or feeling.[97] Because the character for fish, *yu* 魚, has precisely the same pronunciation as the character *yu* 餘 ("surplus" or "extra"), Bada frequently used fish as a symbol of the *yimin*, the surplus or "left-over" subjects. One example of his use of homophones to embed intentions, this is only scratching the surface; he painted different kinds of fish, a number of which had their own distinct characteristics and a rich body of accompanying cultural lore that he was not averse to mining.[98]

Another character Bada used repetitively in his poems is *huang* 黃 (yellow), a homophone for *huang* 皇 (imperial). It appears twice in the *Globefish* poem, both times with puns likely intended. *Huangya* 黃牙, literally "yellow teeth," shows the artist poking fun at himself, but the two characters combined can also mean "wheat" as well as "gold," and more meanings are possible when the homophones for *ya* 牙 are considered. *Huangya* 黃芽 (yellow sprouts), for example, can refer to a medicinal potion for attaining immortality (refer to cat. no. 42). This would be a necessity if one indeed swallowed a globefish whole: also known as the blowfish or pufferfish (Japanese: *fugu*), the "river pig" is a delicacy that is deadly if not properly prepared! Interpreting this particular poem definitively remains a matter of conjecture. Nonetheless, it becomes clear how the artist played with language and utilized recondite allusions to provide his image with layers of meaning that point back to his own condition.

The preceding might suggest that Bada Shanren's paintings are puzzles, the solving of which depends largely on decoding his cryptic poems. Yet, while it is true that much can be learned from textual detective work in conjunction with an awareness of the issues that concerned the artist, treating his paintings only as solvable anagrams is shortsighted. These are complex works of art that bring us deeply into the mind of a complex person. As such, they are governed by unifying patterns of visual thought and expression. One of the overarching themes of Bada's art, as explored by Hui-shu Lee in an article some years ago and revisited in her essay for this catalogue, is transformation—the ability to change form, to morph from one creature to another and perhaps from one identity to another.[99] His paintings lure us in with their amusing creatures, with their superb displays of "brush and ink" and his intriguing calligraphy and puzzling texts, and we find ourselves entering a world where the laws of nature function differently. His paintings are undeniably attractive, but the more deeply one enters his world, the more disorienting and disturbing the effect.

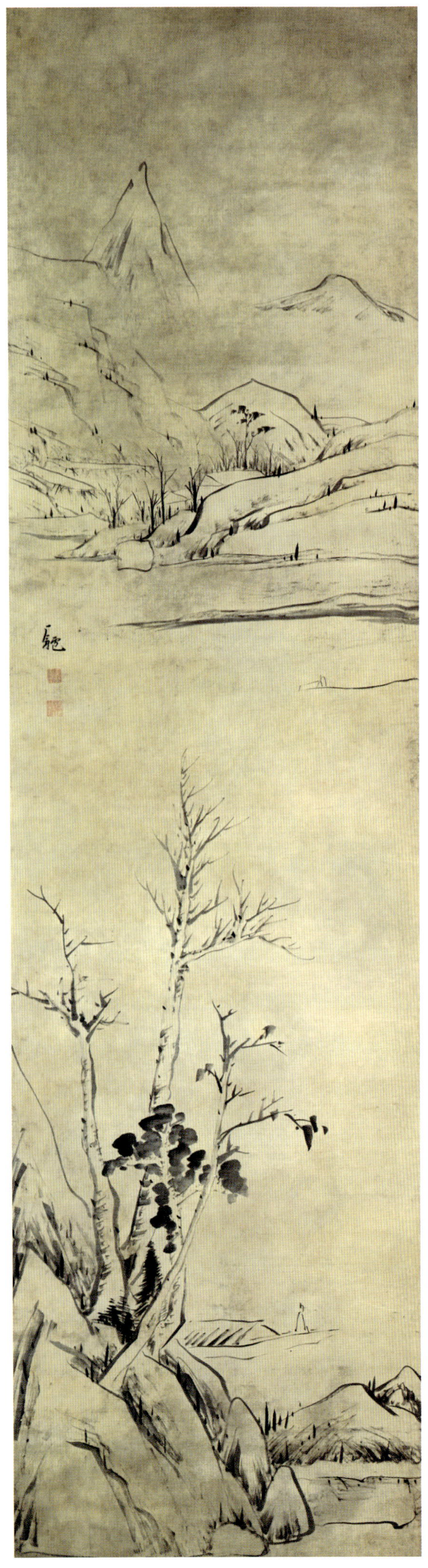

In my opinion, Bada Shanren provides the most compelling and purest pictorial expression of reclusion. All of the artists represented in this exhibition were intrigued by and attracted to the notion of reclusion. They idealized it, they depicted it, and they celebrated it. Some, like Xiang Shengmo, presented imagined paradises of forgotten, hidden-away idylls—reclusion as a place to be savored vicariously. Others overlaid their scenery with aesthetic values to make statements of exclusivity, thereby alluding to an abstracted reclusion of the mind. We see in the paintings of a number of those who lived on after 1644 intimations of how the world had changed and sense how reclusion was now refracted to reflect the realities of experience. All of these artists took some aspect of reclusion and made it the subject of their art. Only Bada Shanren took the subject of reclusion and made it the method of his art. He did not depict places of hiding; he depicted the process of hiding, and in so doing brings us into the mind of one who truly sought escape. Does this make Bada a true recluse? Presumably not—after all, true recluses are never heard from. For our purposes, however, he is something much more intriguing and valuable: an artist of startling ability and intelligence who provides a glimpse into what the pursuit of reclusion truly entailed.

No discussion of Bada Shanren and reclusion is complete without considering his landscape paintings, for these provide a curious coda to the story of his life and art. For the better part of his life he appears to have avoided painting landscapes. This is highly unusual, especially for someone of his ability with the brush, and one can only presume that his unwillingness to paint mountains and waters was a deliberate statement of alienation. The sense of isolation that he often created for his flora and fauna subjects supports the idea that he used space as a metaphor for personal displacement. Richard Barnhart makes note of the fact that it was not until 1690 that Bada painted a composition in which a fully defined and complete setting was suggested, and not until three years later, when the artist was approaching seventy, that he painted landscapes consistently.[100] In fact two extant hanging scrolls suggest that he experimented with landscape a decade earlier, circa 1681–83, but Barnhart's point is well taken: these two earlier paintings are nothing like what emerged in the mid-1690s and must be considered something fundamentally different (fig. 16).[101] In utter contrast, the veritable flood of landscapes that dominate Bada's artistic output until the end of his life represent an extraordinary transformation. How many artists are willing to remake who they are so late in the game?

For all intents and purposes, landscape *was* reclusion for the Chinese painter. It was the one subject that needed no explanation to suggest an alternate existence removed from worldly troubles. Consequently, as Barnhart notes, Bada's decision to explore this facet of artistic expression must have represented a significant shift in how he viewed himself and the world around him. Compared to his old compatriots, he must have been one of the very few to remain committed to the fallen dynasty so steadfastly and for so long, but there is evidence that around this time he must have become reconciled with his fate, if not with the new dynasty itself. Reconciliation allowed Bada a measure of peace that inspired him to create idealized places in which to dwell. Undoubtedly there were also friends, acquaintances, and admirers who were eager to share in his vision. The landscapes of his late years to some degree may have sustained him materially as well as spiritually.[102] Thus, when we approach Bada's landscapes we must take a number of factors

FIG. 16 Bada Shanren, *Fishing by a Wintry Grove*, c. 1681–83; Hanging scroll: ink on satin; 197.5 × 54.1 cm; Palace Museum, Beijing

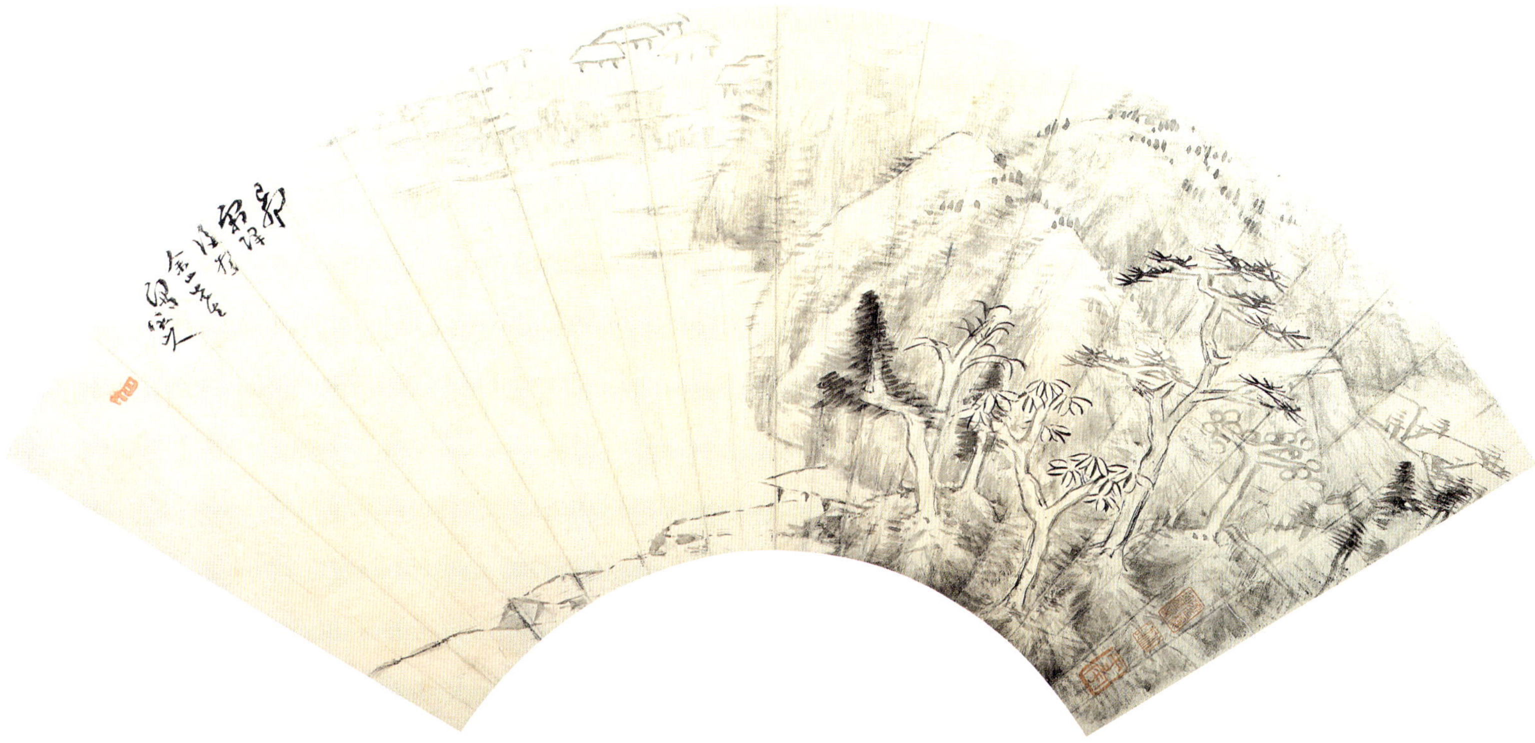

into consideration. Here was a mature artist whose life for so many years had been presented as puzzles and conundrums, electing to open doors and reveal a space, a landscape that represented his hopes for personal and communal serenity. What choices did he make?

One of the more obvious choices was to follow precedent. Many of his landscapes specifically designate models of earlier painting as sources of inspiration, such as the tenth-century landscape painter Dong Yuan 董源, Mi Fu, Huang Gongwang, and Ni Zan. These were the figures that loomed largest in the pantheon of preferred masters according to the theories of Dong Qichang. Bada would have had few if any chances to see genuine works by these Song and Yuan artists, and consequently there is little doubt that his orientation was reliant upon both Dong's dictums and practice of painting. This was a well-trodden and conservative path for many followers, but far from being constrained Bada used Dong's approach as a point of departure. Like so many others, he knew well the compositional structures, motifs, and brush-texturing systems that were associated with the distinctive styles of earlier painters. *Unlike* so many others, however, he was able to subordinate these features to his own well-developed methods of painting, and he seems to have genuinely enjoyed the challenge. The Honolulu album, a late work of around 1702, shows this clearly. Bada did not specify earlier models, but individual leaves distinctly echo Mi Fu and Huang Gongwang in particular. Huang's style is denoted by mountain sides built of boulders and flat-topped rock faces (cat. nos. 47B, F, and G), Mi's by wetter, mist-infused scenes (cat. nos. 47A, C, and H). In each leaf Bada picks up the recognizable schema of the earlier artists and plays with them, creating distinct abstract patterns and visual harmonies. He adds to these his own brand of curiously childlike trees and buildings, the latter often reduced to a few simple lines. Occasionally, he exaggerates the Ni Zan-style pavilion or isolates a small hut. These glyphlike renderings of human presence locate the artist in the landscape. In the case of the late fan from the very end of his life, Bada did this with a self-identifying tag: his signature, studio name, and seal are artfully placed directly above the hut (cat. no. 46). Most importantly, these buildings are thoroughly integrated into his landscapes—so much so that his buildings' roofs often mimic adjacent boulders and plateaus (cat. no. 45, fig. 17). If you look carefully in Bada's landscapes you will find other examples of how his brushwork creates ambiguities in the rendering of motifs—pine branches turning into a temple's roof, for example (cat. no. 47F), or foreground tree foliage transitioning into middle-ground grasses (cat. no. 47C). This is not simply a matter of the artist creating visual congruities to harmonize his compositions; Bada was deliberately exploring the theme of transformation, suggesting in his landscapes the presence of some overarching principle that ties one element to another, and all to the artist.

Painters such as Dong Yuan, Mi Fu, Huang Gongwang, and Ni Zan were symbols of the cultural bedrock, and recalling their presence was a means to tether one's own landscapes and provide them with meaning. Many artists did this, and while some were constrained by the rules of this emerging orthodoxy, a number succeeded in asserting individual voices. It was a relationship characterized by challenge—measuring oneself against the past. Yet, with Bada Shanren one senses that this relationship with the past was never so much of a struggle. His landscapes are so inviting, so engaging, that they feel very much like a homecoming. "Home, Again!," we are reminded, is the title of Tao Yuanming's famous paean to reclusion, written after retiring from office in the year 405. Tao's arrival home to his rural dwelling was more than simple retirement; it signaled a return to simple, honest values and a purer state of spiritual existence. I imagine that Tao was far from Bada's mind when he painted most of these landscapes. Yet perhaps in spirit these gentle, probing images documenting the recluse's journey to a personal sanctuary capture the true meaning of what Tao expressed so many years earlier.

FIG. 17 Bada Shanren, *Landscape for Yushan*, 1699 (cat. no. 45)

1 Chen Duxiu, "Wenxue geming lun" 文學革命論, from *Chen Duxiu zhuzuo xuan* 陳獨秀著作選 (Shanghai: Shanghai renmin chubanshe, 1993), 260–61. Chen's article was originally published in *Xin Qingnian* 新青年 (New youth) 2, no. 6 (February 1, 1917). My translation is adapted from that of the essayist and philosopher Hu Shi 胡適 (1891–1962), Chen's friend and one of the leading intellectuals of the early years of the Republic of China. See his *The Chinese Renaissance, The Haskell Lectures, 1933* (1934; reprint, New York: Paragon, 1963), 54.

2 Lynn Struve, ed., *Voices from the Ming-Qing Cataclysm: China in Tigers' Jaws* (New Haven, CT: Yale University Press, 1993).

3 This circle was the primary subject of the groundbreaking exhibition (and its accompanying catalogue) *The Chinese Scholar's Studio: Artistic Life in the Late Ming Period*, ed. Chu-tsing Li and James C. Y. Watt (New York: Thames and Hudson and the Asia Society, 1987).

4 To date, Xiang Shengmo's poems on reclusion have not drawn the full attention that they deserve, and few have been translated into English. For some thoughtful discussion on a select group of the many poems included on all of Xiang's reclusion paintings, see Eun-wha Park, "The World of Idealized Reclusion: Landscape Painting of Hsiang Sheng-mo (1597–1658)" (Ph.D. dissertation, University of Michigan, 1992), 92 and following.

5 Dong Qichang owned *Dwelling in the Fuchun Mountains* (collection of the National Palace Museum, Taipei) from 1596 until at least 1627. See Celia Carrington Riely, "Tung Ch'i-ch'ang's Ownership of Huang Kung-wang's 'Dwelling in the Fu-ch'un Mountains': With a Revised Dating for Chang Ch'ou's *Ch'ing-ho shu-hua fang*," *Archives of Asian Art* 28 (1974/75): 57–76. For a good introduction to this famous painting and its inscription, see Maxwell Hearn's discussion in Wen Fong and James Watt, eds., *Possessing the Past: Treasures from the National Palace Museum, Taipei* (New York: Metropolitan Museum of Art, 1996), 299–304. See also the catalogue that accompanied the recent blockbuster exhibition focused on Huang Gongwang and his Fuchun scroll at the National Palace Museum, *Shanshui hebi: Huang Gongwang yu Fuchun shanju tu tezhan* 山水合璧：黃公望與富春山居圖特展 (Taipei: Guoli Gugong bowuyuan, 2011).

6 Interested readers have many excellent choices for introductions to Dong Qichang's art and theory of painting, including James Cahill's chapter "Tung Ch'i-ch'ang and the Sanction of the Past" in his *The Compelling Image: Nature and Style in Seventeenth-Century Chinese Painting* (Cambridge, MA: Harvard University Press, 1982), 36–69; Cahill's *The Distant Mountains: Chinese Painting of the Late Ming Dynasty, 1570–1644* (New York: Weatherhill, 1982), 87–128; and the essays by Wai-kam Ho and Dawn Ho Delbanco and Wen C. Fong in Ho, ed., *The Century of Tung Ch'i-ch'ang, 1555–1636* (Kansas City: Nelson-Atkins Museum of Art, 1992), 3–42 and 43–54.

7 I am indebted to Alan Berkowitz's discussion of Lu Ji's and Zuo Si's poems on the *zhao yin* theme in his "Courting Disengagement: 'Beckoning the Recluse' Poems of the Western Jin," in Paul W. Kroll and David R. Knechtges, eds., *Studies in Early Medieval Chinese Literature and Cultural History, in Honor of Richard B. Mather and Donald Holzman* (Provo, UT: T'ang Studies Society, 2003), 81–116. As Berkowitz points out, Xiao Tong included three poems on the subgenre of *zhao yin* in his *Wen xuan* anthology, two by Zuo and one by Lu. These, no doubt, were the specific poems that Xiang Shengmo had in mind. For the original poems, see *Wen xuan* 文選 (reprint, Taipei: Wenjin chubanshe, 1987), 22:1027–29.

8 Lu Ji is particularly well known for his famous "Rhapsody on Literature," *Wen fu*.

9 See David Hawkes, *The Songs of the South: An Anthology of Ancient Chinese Poems by Qu Yuan and Other Poets* (Harmondsworth, England: Penguin, 1985), 243–45. As Hawkes and others point out, the *Chu ci* "Beckoning the Recluse" (*Zhao yinshi* 招隱士) is thought to have been written by a poet at the court of Liu An 劉安, Prince of Huainan (c. 179–122 BCE).

10 *Wen xuan*, 22:1027. Translation based on that of Berkowitz, "Courting Disengagement," 88–89.

11 Tao Yuanming's fame, both as a person and as a poet, escalated in the eleventh century and reached an apogee with Su Shi, who rhymed more than a hundred of Tao's poems when he experienced political exile late in his life. The literature on Tao is extensive. For a recent study of his image in later dynasties see Wendy Swartz, *Reading Tao Yuanming: Shifting Paradigms of Historical Reception (427–1900)* (Cambridge, MA: Harvard University Asia Center, 2008).

12 Tao Yuanming, "Taohua yuan ji" 桃花源記, in *Tao Yuanming ji* 陶淵明集, *Siku quanshu* ed., 5:1a–4b. See also Wolfgang Bauer, *China and the Pursuit of Happiness: Recurring Themes in Four Thousand Years of Chinese Cultural History*, trans. Michael Shaw (New York: Seabury Press, 1976), 190–92. For an interesting study regarding the pre-Tao origins of the story, see Stephen R. Bokenkamp, "The Peach Flower Font and the Grotto Passage," *Journal of the American Oriental Society* 106, no. 1 (January–March 1986): 65–77.

13 Susan Nelson, "On Through to the Beyond: The Peach Blossom Spring as Paradise," *Archives of Asian Art* 39 (1986): 23–47.

14 There is a rich body of scholarship on early reclusion in China that goes back a number of generations. Two studies of the current generation to which I am especially indebted are Aat Vervoorn's *Men of the Cliffs and Caves: The Development of the Chinese Eremitic Tradition to the End of the Han Dynasty* (Hong Kong: Chinese University Press, 1990), and Alan J. Berkowitz's *Patterns of Disengagement: The Practice and Portrayal of Reclusion in Early Medieval China* (Stanford, CA: Stanford University Press, 2000).

15 There are various versions of the Xu You and Chaofu story. This one is from Huangfu Mi's 皇甫謐 *Gaoshi zhuan* 高士傳 (*Siku quanshu* ed.), *shang*:4a–b. Berkowitz, *Patterns of Disengagement*, 44–45.

16 Taigong Wang possessed multiple identities, including butcher and boatman, but he is best known as the fisherman plying his line on the banks of the Wei River. See Sarah Allan, "The Identities of Taigong Wang in Zhou and Han Literature," *Monumenta Serica* 30 (1972–73): 57–99.

17 Vervoorn, *Men of the Cliffs and Caves*, 28–40.

18 The standard account of Boyi and Shuqi is found in Sima Qian's *Shi ji* 史記, where it occupies the first of the biographies of exemplary figures. Burton Watson, *Records of the Historian: Chapters from the Shih Chi of Ssu-ma Ch'ien* (reprint, New York: Columbia University Press, 1969), 11–15. Sima notes that the brothers objected to King Wu on two counts: he was proceeding with plans to attack King Zhou of Shang—who, despite his tyrannical rule, remained a rightful sovereign in their eyes—and was doing so before completion of the three-year mourning period following the death of his father. The story of Boyi and Shuqi, which has a number of variations, is critically examined by Aat Vervoorn in his "Boyi and Shuqi: Worthy Men of Old?" *Papers on Far Eastern History* 28 (September 1983): 1–22. See also Vervoorn, *Men of the Cliffs and Caves*, 35–37.

19 *Lunyu jijie yishu* 論語集解義疏 (*Siku quanshu* ed.), 4:9a.

20 *Zhuangzi jinzhu jinyi* 莊子今註今譯, ed. Chen Guying 陳鼓應 (reprint, Taipei: Taiwan Shangwu yinshuguan, 1984), 264. Burton Watson, trans., *The Complete Works of Chuang Tzu* (New York: Columbia University Press, 1968), 102. Later in *Zhuangzi* a very different picture of the two brothers is painted. Utilizing a variant of the story, in which Boyi and Shuqi are offended by King Wu's political dealings, their disdain for wealth and adherence to principle is fully applauded. *Zhuangzi jinzhu jinyi*, 840–41. Watson, *Chuang Tzu*, 321–22.

21 Sima Qian, *Shi ji* 史記 (*Siku quanshu* ed.), 61:7b–8a. Translation by Watson, *Records of the Historian*, 14–15.

22 Alan Berkowitz discusses substantive reclusion and its distinction from reclusion as a common mode of discourse adopted by scholar-officials ("abstract reclusion") in his "Topos and Entelechy in the Ethos of Reclusion in China," *Journal of the American Oriental Society* 114, no. 4 (October–December 1994): 632–38. It is also a major focus of his *Patterns of Disengagement*. For an engaging read tracing a contemporary's search for the "men of cliffs and caves," see Bill Porter, *Road to Heaven: Encounters with Chinese Hermits* (San Francisco: Mercury House, 1993).

23 Vervoorn, *Men of the Cliffs and Caves*, 116–25.

24 Ibid., 151–64.

25 Ibid., 108–9. See also Richard Mather's classic study "The Controversy over Conformity and Naturalness during the Six Dynasties," *History of Religions* 9, nos. 2/3 (November 1969–February 1970): 160–80. Two of the best recognized of Zhuangzi's blue-collar men of the Dao are Butcher Ding and Wheelwright Bian. See Watson, *Chuang Tzu*, 50–51, 152–53. On reclusion at the court see chapter four of Vervoorn's *Men of the Cliffs and Caves*, 203–27.

26 Fang Xuanling 方玄齡, *Jin shu* 晉書 (reprint, Beijing: Zhonghua shuju, 1974), 80:2100. See also my *Mi Fu: Style and the Art of Calligraphy in Northern Song China* (New Haven, CT: Yale University Press, 1997), 95–96.

27 Julia Murray discusses this painting in her *Mirror of Morality: Chinese Narrative Illustration and Confucian Ideology* (Honolulu: University of Hawaii Press, 2007), 80–81. Li Tang's role in the reaffirmation of the Song dynasty under Gaozong is established by his association with the painting *Duke Wen of Jin Recovering his State* (early 1140s, Metropolitan Museum of Art, New York). See Wen Fong, *Beyond Representation: Chinese Painting and Calligraphy 8th–14th Century* (New York: Metropolitan Museum of Art, 1992), 194–207.

28 Scarlett Ju-yu Jang, "Issues of Public Service in the Themes of Chinese Court Painting," (Ph.D. dissertation, University of California, Berkeley, 1989), 292 and following. See also Richard Barnhart, *Painters of the Great Ming: The Imperial Court and the Zhe School* (Dallas: Dallas Museum of Art, 1993), 113–15.

29 Mi Fu's inclination to engage with the past in such an exhibitionistic manner was especially pronounced in the late 1080s and is well represented by two extant scrolls of 1088: *Poems Playfully Written and Presented to My Friends, About to Embark for Tiao Stream* (Palace Museum, Beijing) and *Poems on Sichuan Silk* (National Palace Museum, Taipei). I discuss these scrolls and some of their poems in my *Mi Fu*, 68–86.

30 Three of these scrolls bear the same title, *Invitation to Reclusion*. The third of these, dated to the first lunar month of 1644, is no longer extant, though it is well recorded. Eun-wha Park documents and discusses these paintings in her dissertation, "The World of Idealized Reclusion."

31 Hawkes, *The Songs of the South*, 219–33. "Summons of the Soul," which in part was based on early burial rituals, served as the model for the thematically related "Summons for a Recluse" that is also anthologized in the *Chu ci*. "Summons of the Soul" is considered to be an older composition, possibly of the middle of the third century BCE.

32 John W. Dardess, *Blood and History in China: The Donglin Faction and its Repression, 1620–1627* (Honolulu: University of Hawaii Press, 2002). See also Harry Miller, *State versus Gentry in Late Ming Dynasty China, 1572–1644* (New York: Palgrave Macmillan, 2009), especially pages 125–38. Miller rightfully points out that the uncompromisingly black image of Wei Zhongxian that has been left to posterity by later scholars is harshly one sided.

33 Philip K. Hu, "The Paradise Landscape of Yangshuo: A Monumental Painting by Mi Wanzhong," *Cantor Arts Center Journal* 2 (2000–01): 6–21. Hu points out that Mi Wanzhong was sympathetic to the Donglin cause.

34 Frederick Mote, "Confucian Eremitism in the Yüan Period," in *The Confucian Persuasion*, ed. Arthur F. Wright (Stanford, CA: Stanford University Press, 1960), 202–40.

35 Xiang Shengmo accompanied Li Rihua to Beijing in 1628 and, through Li's services, appears to have secured a position as a designer in the imperial wardrobe. Unhappy, he returned to Jiaxing in 1629. Xiang was married to Li's niece. The trip to Beijing was probably related to Li's promotion to Vice Minister of the Court of the Imperial Stud. See Eun-wha Park, "The World of Idealized Reclusion," 28–29.

36 "When young, I enjoyed using the brush, but my late father charged me with the task of studying to pass the official examinations. So during the day I had no leisure, but at night I would shade my lamp and with all my attention, copy insects, plants, birds, animals, flowers and bamboo—I drew everything. Only when I had attained a likeness would I stop. One night, suddenly I dreamed of a brush standing like a column—a straight staff reaching up to the Milky Way. There were serried steps going up like a ladder, more than ten or twenty feet long. I climbed up and took hold of the bristled top, clapping my hands, talking and laughing. Afterwards, I copied the methods of the old masters and gradually attained them myself" 余髫年便喜弄柔翰．先君子責以制舉之業，日無暇科，夜必篝燈著意摹寫．昆蟲草木翎毛花竹，無物不備，必至肖形而止．忽一夕，夢筆立如柱，直干雲漢，上有層級如梯，長可一二丈許．余登而據其毫端，鼓掌談笑．嗣後師法古人，往往自得. From *Free Immortal among Soughing Pines* (1629) in the collection of the Museum of Fine Arts, Boston. Translation by Thomas Lawton as modified by Eun-wha Park, "The World of Idealized Reclusion," 21.

37 For more on this famous scroll attributed to Lu Hong, see Zhuang Shen 莊申, "Tang Lu Hong Caotang shizhi tu juan kao" 唐盧鴻草堂十志圖卷考, *Lishi yuyan yanjiusuo jikan* 歷史語言研究所季刊 30 (1959): 615–79.

38 I refer to the blockbuster 1992 exhibition "The Century of Tung Ch'i-ch'ang," primarily organized by the late Wai-kam Ho. Chen Jiru was a frequent inscriber of Dong Qichang's painting and calligraphy and the author of many of the primary sources recording the facts of Dong's life.

39 For an excellent monograph documenting Chen's life, literary activities, and personae, see Jamie Greenbaum's *Chen Jiru (1558–1639): The Background to Development and Subsequent Uses of Literary Personae* (Leiden: Brill, 2007).

40 This is from the official document Chen presented to the local prefect in 1586, a year after failing the provincial exams for the second time. Cited from ibid., 18.

41 This was Huang Zongxi 黃宗羲 (1610–1695), describing an encounter that took place on West Lake at Hangzhou in 1628. Cited from ibid., xxxiv.

42 Ibid., xxxiv, 202–4.

43 Ibid., 27–28. The excursion was with the well-known literary figure Wang Shizhen 王世貞 (1526–1590), who recorded the occasion, and Xu Yisun 徐益孫 (act. c. 1580). Xu and Chen purchased the property together. In addition to building the shrine for the Lu brothers, they made deliberate allusion to another poet-recluse of the Wei-Jin period when they named the well on the property Jiaohua Jing (Well for Watering Flowers) after one owned by Pan Yue 潘岳 (247–300).

44 For an exception to this rule see Ren Daobin, "Ch'en Chi-ju as Critic and Connoisseur," in Wai-ching Ho, ed., *Proceedings of the Tung Ch'i-ch'ang International Symposium* (Kansas City: Nelson-Atkins Museum of Art, 1991), 9/1–9/25.

45 Dong Qichang describes his acquisition of the scroll in his first inscription. He mentions that prior to trading for it he had owned a copy, and on the basis of this had the image included in *Xihongtang tie*. See *Gugong shuhua lu* 故宮書畫錄 (Taipei: Guoli Gugong bowuyuan, 1965), 1:57.

46 Susan Bush, "Yet Again, 'Streams and Mountains without End'," *Artibus Asiae* 48, nos. 3/4 (1987): 197–223.

47 In an earlier catalogue entry for this painting, Wang Zhenghua draws attention to the similarities of this painting with Zhao Mengfu's *Water Village* (1302, collection of the Palace Museum, Beijing), a painting of some influence among people connected to Dong Qichang (who owned it), including Yang Wencong (cat. no. 19). Wang goes on to mention that Chen Jiru commented upon the similarity of the scenery depicted in *Water Village* to the outskirts of Songjiang. Richard M. Barnhart, et al., *The Jade Studio: Masterpieces of Ming and Qing Painting and Calligraphy from the Wong Nan-p'ing Collection* (New Haven, CT: Yale University Art Gallery, 1994), 104.

48 Ibid. Zhu Huiliang 朱惠良 first identified Chen's Hut of Vegetable Fragrance in her *Zhao Zuo yanjiu* 趙左研究 (Taipei: Guoli Gugong bowuyuan, 1979), 31n23.

49 Chen Jiru, *Taiping qinghua* 太平情話, *Baibu congshu jicheng* 百部叢書集成 ed. (Taipei: Yiwen yinshuguan, 1965–70), 2:12b.

50 This is described in Chen Jiru's chronological biography, in Greenbaum, *Chen Jiru*, 97.

51 From the fifth of six poems presented to Lu Ji by Pan Ni 潘尼. "Si Lu Ji chu wei Wu Wang langzhong ling" 賜陸機出為吳王郎中令, in *Wen xuan* 文選 (reprint, Taipei: Wenjin chubanshe, 1987), 24: 1156–58. In Pan's poem the object of envy are "the two palaces," a far cry from the "thatched hall" of the recluse that *wanluan* modifies as a title for Chen Jiru's site.

52 There are excellent discussions of this painting by Richard Vinograd in the catalogue entry for *The Wanluan Thatched Hall* in *The Century of Tung Ch'i-ch'ang* (vol. 1, 7–8) and in the very detailed study by Shou-ch'ien Shih, "Tung Ch'i-ch'ang's 'Wan-luan Thatched Hall' and the Innovation of his Painting Style," in *Proceedings of the Tung Ch'i-ch'ang International Symposium*, 13.1–13.28.

53 The term *shese* 設色, to add color, refers to a final stage for painting, in which tints might be added for visual appeal. The term has ancient origins, appearing in numerous classical sources and usually with implications of specialized, professional craft. Professionalism was antithetical to Dong Qichang's artistic position, and this makes the term's appearance here even more questionable.

54 Chen Jiru, alas, did not add any of his own thoughts to the painting. Other than Dong Qichang's title and three inscriptions, all of the remaining inscriptions were added by the Qing emperor Qianlong (Qing Gaozong 清高宗, r. 1735–1796).

55 The story regards the *qin* player Bo Ya and his friend, Zhong Ziqi, of the Spring and Autumn period. When Zhong died Bo broke his zither, swearing never again to play since the one who understood his sounds was gone. See Kenneth J. DeWoskin, *A Song for One or Two: Music and the Concept of Art in Early China* (Ann Arbor: University of Michigan Center for Chinese Studies, 1982).

56 See my *Mi Fu*, especially 194–211.

57 Dong singled out certain luminaries of the past as both models and challenges—Wen Zhengming 文徵明 (1470–1559) for painting, Zhao Mengfu for calligraphy, and Mi Fu for collecting. Evidence for the last of these is Dong's pride at having seen four "genuine" Li Cheng landscape paintings whereas Mi Fu had seen only two. See Celia Carrington Riely, "Tung Ch'i-ch'ang's Life (1555–1636)," in *The Century of Tung Ch'i-ch'ang*, vol. 2, 406–7.

58 The term *huayin* was used by Huang Tingjian 黄庭堅 (1045–1105) to describe Li Gonglin 李公麟 (c. 1041–1106), who "got lost in his painting among the many officials, from the start not expecting others to understand or not" 李侯畫隱百僚底，初不自期人誤知. Huang, "Yong Li Boshi mo Han Gan Sanma ci Su Ziyou yun jian Boshi jian ji Li Desu" 詠李伯時摹韓幹三馬次蘇子由韻簡伯時兼寄李德素, *Shangu ji* 山谷集 (*Siku quanshu* ed.), 2:8b. Cited from Eunwha Park, "The World of Idealized Reclusion," 95–96.

59 See note 25 above.

60 Nelson Wu, "Tung Ch'i-ch'ang: Apathy in Government and Fervor in Art," in *Confucian Personalities*, ed. Arthur F. Wright and Denis Twitchett (Stanford, CA: Stanford University Press, 1962), 260–93. Riely, "Tung Ch'i-ch'ang's Life," 387–457.

61 Dong Qichang's *Invitation to Reclusion at Jingxi* is in the Metropolitan Museum, New York. See *The Century of Tung Ch'i-ch'ang*, vol. 1, pl. 18. The friendship between Dong and Wu Zhengzhi, as well as the circumstances regarding this painting, are well described by Riely in "Tung Ch'i-ch'ang's Life," 411–15.

62 The work is now in the Morisada Hosokawa collection. Published in Suzuki Kei, ed., *Chūgoku kaiga sōgō zuroku*, vol. 4 (Tokyo: Tōkyō Daigaku Tōyō Bunka Kenkyūjo, 1983), 422–23.

63 The latter three artists were among the so-called Nine Friends of Painting, a coterie centered on Dong Qichang that also included Cheng Jiasui 程嘉燧 (1565–1644), Li Liufang 李流芳 (1575–1629), Bian Wenyu 卞文瑜 (c. 1576–1655), Wang Shimin, and Wang Jian 王鑑 (1598–1677), as made famous in a poem by Wu Weiye 吳偉業 (1609–1672).

64 See catalogue number 15 for identification of the poems. Only one remains unidentified.

65 Bai Jian 白堅, *Yang Wencong zhuan lun* 楊文驄傳論 (Shanghai: Shanghai renmin meishu chubanshe, 1990), especially 91–99.

66 *Water Village* is well reproduced in *Zhongguo lidai huihua* 中國歷代繪畫, vol. 4 (Beijing: Renmin meishu chubanshe, 1983), 22–27. Huang Gongwang's *Sand Marsh* is only known from reproductions in old Japanese publications and later copies, including an album leaf by Yun Shouping 惲壽平 (1633–1690) in the National Palace Museum, Taipei. This short composition by Huang has elicited no attention in modern scholarship, but it was well recognized and recorded in the seventeenth century. Dong Qichang mentions it in one of his inscriptions on Huang's *Dwelling in the Fuchun Mountains*.

67 Yang Wencong was the brother-in-law of Ma Shiying 馬士英 (c. 1591–1646), a person of profound influence at the loyalist Southern Ming court but also a problematic figure. The primary supporter of Zhu Yousong 朱由崧 (1607–1646), the newly enthroned emperor, Ma was also perceived as a supporter of the eunuchs and an opportunist whose tactics in court politics ultimately resulted in the disastrous defeat of the Ming forces at Nanjing. Ma's reputation had a profound effect on later perceptions of Yang, which were decidedly mixed. For Yang's rise through the Ministry of War, see Bai Jian, *Yang Wencong*, 164–65.

68 This happened in the eighth lunar month of 1646 at Pucheng (Fujian Province). Ibid., 168.

69 Frederick Wakeman, *The Great Enterprise: The Manchu Reconstruction of Imperial Order in Seventeenth-Century China* (Berkeley: University of California, 1985), 319–413. Lynn A. Struve, *The Southern Ming, 1644–1662* (New Haven, CT: Yale University Press, 1984), especially 15–45.

70 Presumably, Xiang Shengmo has in mind the early recluse Lu Tong, or Jieyu, the Wild Man of Chu, described in both the *Analects* and *Zhuangzi*.

71 Suicide's curious relationship with the concept of reclusion in early China is addressed by both Aat Vervoorn, *Men of the Cliffs and Caves* (page 47), and Alan Berkowitz, *Patterns of Disengagement* (pages 86 and 159).

72 Struve, *The Southern Ming*. See also Struve's *Voices from the Ming-Qing Cataclysm* for varied individual reflections on the dynastic transition.

73 For an excellent discussion of the complexities that attended the Ming-Qing transition in the context of painting, see Jonathan Hay, "The Suspension of Dynastic Time," in Hay, ed., *Boundaries in China* (London: Reaktion, 1994), 171–97.

74 See my *Mi Fu*, 196–98. It bears reminding that the writings, stories, and anecdotes of the Northern Song literati were particularly well studied in the late Ming. Su Shi and his inkstones were a frequent subject of the Yangzhou eccentric painter Huang Shen 黄慎 (1687–1768).

75 For informative discussions of Zhang's art, see Ho, *The Century of Tung Ch'i-ch'ang*, vol. 2, 118, and *The Jade Studio*, 143–45.

76 Stories regarding the woodcutter who happens upon a game of *weiqi* deep in the mountains commonly describe the unwitting passage of time. When he finally chooses to leave he discovers that the handle of his ax has rotted and centuries have passed. Ren Fang 任昉, *Shuyi ji* 述異記 (*Siku quanshu* ed.), *shang*:16a–b.

77 Chen Zuyan 陳祖言, "'Qiuping xiaoji, keyi yu da'—Qian Qianyi weiqi shi zhong fan Qing fu Ming de weici yinyu" 楸枰小技可以喻大——錢謙益圍棋詩中反清復明的微辭隱語, *Wenyi yanjiu* 文藝研究 5 (2009): 74–81.

78 Zheng Chenggong finally moved into the Yangzi River area about a year after Zhang Feng painted *Immortals' Secrets in a Stone Cave*, but his intentions for attacking Nanjing were well known in the summer of 1658. See Struve, *The Southern Ming*, 182–89. Qian Qianyi continued to use *weiqi* as a metaphor for contemporary affairs, and specifically for Zheng's military moves on the water around 1658–59. See Lawrence C. H. Yim, *The Poet-Historian Qian Qianyi* (London: Routledge, 2009), 130–31.

79 From Cheng Zhengkui's "Shixi xiaozhuan" 石溪小傳, cited from Xue Feng 薛鋒 and Xue Xiang 薛翔, *Kuncan* 髡殘 (Jilin: Jilin meishu chubanshe, 1993), 7.

80 James Cahill, "K'un-ts'an and his Inscriptions," in Alfreda Murck and Wen C. Fong, eds., *Words and Images: Chinese Poetry, Calligraphy, and Painting* (New York: Metropolitan Museum of Art; and Princeton: Princeton University Press, 1991), 514–16.

81 Cahill illustrates a number of these in "K'un-ts'an and his Inscriptions," figures 242–45. There is a large hanging scroll, depicting in close-up detail a monk or arhat seated on a mat in a cave, titled *Yanxue qi zhen* 巖穴棲真 (Realized one of cliffs and caves) in the National Palace Museum, Taipei. The painting is signed by Kuncan, with a short poetic inscription, but its authenticity remains to be determined.

82 Maggie Bickford, *Ink Plum: The Making of a Chinese Scholar-Painting Genre* (Cambridge: Cambridge University Press, 1996).

83 Jonathan Chaves has suggested through personal communication that Fang Yizhi may have intended an additional layer of meaning to "two or three," borrowing from the ancient text *Shang shu*: "If your Virtue is unified, then of your actions, none will fail to be auspicious. But if your Virtue is two- or three-faced, then of your actions, none will fail to be noxious" 德惟一，動罔不吉，德二三，動罔不凶. Lin Zhiqi 林之奇, *Shangshu quanjie* 尚書全解 (*Siku quanshu* ed.), 17:9a. If Fang is alluding to this passage then there is an embedded criticism of those in the *yimin* community who were wavering in their loyalty.

84 Yu Yingshi 余英時, *Fang Yizhi wanjie kao* 方以智晚節考 (Hong Kong: Xinya yanjiusuo, 1972).

85 For a brief though serious discussion of Fang Yizhi's painting, see Cahill, *The Distant Mountains*, 158–60. See also Rao Zongyi 饒宗頤, "Fang Yizhi zhi hualun" 方以智之畫論, *Xianggang Zhongwen daxue Zhongguo wenhua yanjiusuo xuebao* 香港中文大學中國文化研究所學報 7, no. 1 (1974).

86 The best guess for Bada's birth name is Zhu Tonglin (朱統鏊; alternate reading: Zhu Tongquan), which was determined by Li Dan and Wang Shiqing using various data and referencing elaborate principles utilized in the Ming dynasty for assigning names genealogically. Another name commonly assigned is Zhu Da 朱耷, but it is extremely unlikely that was his given name. See Wang Fangyu, "The Life and Art of Bada Shanren," in Wang, Richard M. Barnhart, and Judith G. Smith, eds., *Master of the Lotus Garden: The Life and Art of Bada Shanren (1626–1705)* (New Haven, CT: Yale University Art Gallery, 1990), 27–30. My narration relies heavily on Professor Wang's dedicated research, which summarizes the work of many scholars to provide the most comprehensive study of Bada's life and art.

87 Huang Anping's *Portrait of Geshan* (Bada Shanren) is in the collection of the Bada Shanren Memorial Museum, Nanchang. It was discovered around 1954 in the Fengxin Temple (Fengxin, Jiangxi Province). Reproduced in Wang and Barnhart, *Master of the Lotus Garden*, figure 12. See also the discussion by Wang, "The Life and Art of Bada Shanren," 37 and following.

88 From the biography written by Bada's contemporary, Shao Changheng. Cited in Wang, ibid., 41.

89 Ibid., 35.

90 For a more in-depth analysis of this aspect of Bada's paintings, see James Cahill, "The 'Madness' in Bada Shanren's Paintings," *Ajia bunka kenkyu*, no. 17 (March 1989): 119–43.

91 Wang, "The Life and Art of Bada Shanren," 41.

92 *Lunyu zhushu* 論語注疏 (*Siku quanshu* ed.), 18:4b. *Zhuangzi jinzhu jinshi*, 154; Watson, *The Complete Works of Chuang-tzu*, 66–67. Cited from Berkowitz, *Patterns of Disengagement*, 43. As Berkowitz points out, there is a suggestion of feigning stupidity, if not madness, in the *Shi jing*: "The stupidity of the common fellow is owed to natural debility; The stupidity of the wise man is owed to deliberate transgression." Ibid., 43.

93 Yao Silian's text on "Chushi" 處士 is included in *Liang shu* 梁書 (*Siku quanshu* ed.), 51:1b. Cited from Berkowitz, *Patterns of Disengagement*, 189–90, with an alternate translation of the phrase *daya zhi dao* 大雅之道, "the way of proper virtue."

94 From the biography by Shao Changheng; cited in Wang, "The Life and Art of Bada Shanren," 24.

95 The most significant threat to the Qing was the Revolt of the Three Feudatories led by Wu Sangui, which began in 1673 and ended eight years later. Wu was a primary supporter of the Manchus up until the Revolt. The final challenge to the Manchus was posed by the followers of Zheng Chenggong, who occupied Formosa (Taiwan) until Qing forces took the island in 1683.

96 See Richard Barnhart's introduction to Wang and Barnhart, *Master of the Lotus Garden*, especially pages 14–15.

97 *Zhuangzi jinzhu jinshi*, 487. Watson, *The Complete Works of Chuang-tzu*, 188–89.

98 Hui-Shu Lee, "The Fish Leaves of the Anwan Album: Bada Shanren's Journeys to a Landscape of the Past," *Ars Orientalis* 20 (1990): 69–85.

99 Hui-shu Lee, "Bada Shanren's Bird-and-Fish Painting and the Art of Transformation," *Archives of Asian Art* 44 (1991): 6–26.

100 Wang and Barnhart, *Master of the Lotus Garden*, 18.

101 The paintings are *Distant View from Shengjin Pagoda* (sometimes simply titled *Landscape*, 1681, collection unknown), and *Fishing by a Wintry Grove* (Palace Museum, Beijing), datable to circa 1681–83 on the basis of signature and seals. The former is illustrated in Wang and Barnhart, ibid., fig. 38. See also Zhang Xinzhi 張馨之, *Bada Shanren shanshui yanjiu* 八大山人山水研究 (Beijing: Wenhua yishu chubanshe, 2009), fig. 3. Wang Fangyu points out the existence of a landscape album leaf datable to circa 1689–90 that suggests continuity with Bada's mature landscape style of a few years later and probably reflects the very beginning of this development. Wang and Barnhart, *Masters of the Lotus Garden*, 70 and fig. 36.

102 According to Wang Fangyu, Bada Shanren relied upon the sale of his art for his livelihood, but his income must have been quite limited. His circle of acquaintances and friends included a wide range of individuals, including prominent Qing officials. See Wang, "The Life and Art of Bada Shanren," 57–64, and Wang Shiqing 汪世清, "Bada Shanren de jiaoyou" 八大山人的交友, in *Bada Shanren quanji* 八大山人全集, vol. 5 (Nanchang: Jiangxi meishu chubanshe, 2000), 1097–119.

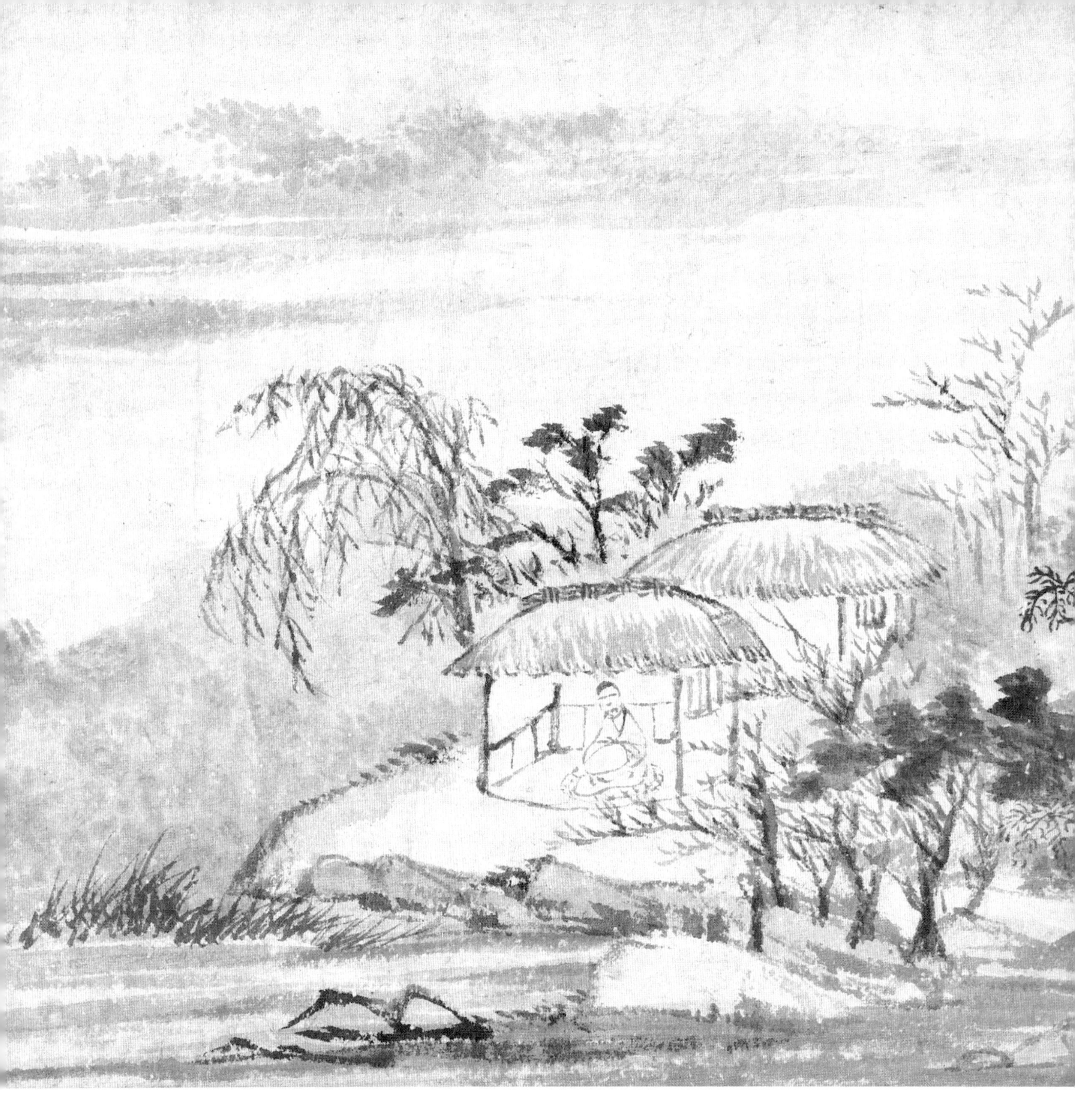

FIG. 18 Zhao Zuo, *Streams and Mountains without End* (detail), 1616 (cat. no. 13)

The Artful Life of the Late-Ming Recluse: Li Rihua and his Generation

Timothy Brook

On March 3, 1614, Chen Yong 陳墉 stepped out into the sleet to call on the eminent calligrapher and art collector Li Rihua 李日華 (1565–1635) at his home. Chen presented Li with a gift and begged for the favor of becoming his painting student. Li's first response was to refuse, but he let himself be persuaded after the young man's persistence. When Chen returned on March 19, Li gave him his first lesson. Before starting, he asked Chen to wait while he finished the painting he had just been working on, featuring a single boat in a snowscape. He then pulled twenty-odd paintings out of his own collection to explain the mistakes that a painter can make, taking Chen through the elements of landscape painting. The lesson ended up focusing on trees, which Li regarded as the hardest natural objects to paint. The teacher-student relationship must have moved onto solid ground quickly, for two months later Chen accompanied Li on a month-long journey to Mount Qiyun, the prominent Daoist retreat in Xiuning County to the west.[1]

We know about the otherwise unknown Chen Yong because Li recorded his pupil's visits in his diary. The only other time he appears between that first painting lesson and the trip to Qiyun is when he delivered a letter on April 22. The letter was from Huiyue 慧悦, a Buddhist monk who had gone into seclusion. This not uncommon form of religious exercise enabled a monk to remove himself from worldly distractions and deepen his understanding of the dharma. A monk in seclusion was not supposed to speak, but in this case seclusion did not rule out writing letters. Huiyue's letter was at least the second he wrote to Li during his seclusion. Li had opened their correspondence with a letter in which he contrasts the pilgrim who "wears out a thousand pairs of straw sandals trudging the roads" and the recluse who "shuts himself within the space of one woven rush mat," wondering whether it made any difference which the monk did. He suggests the pilgrim is like an itinerant trader and the recluse like a shopkeeper. Traveling salesman and shopkeeper avail themselves of different methods but share the same goal, which is to accumulate every penny they can lay their hands on to then go out and spend that treasure on wine, women, and song. It didn't matter the mode of commerce undertaken: the outcome is the same. The tone of Li's letter is playful, though the trope of wine, women, and song lends not a little pressure on Huiyue's decision to seclude himself, implying that he need not have gone to such an extreme. One may have expected a devout Buddhist like Li to admire the decision to withdraw from the world; yet Li was also a man whose pleasures ran to the things of this world—wine, women, and song noticeably among them—and he was not above poking fun at those who took themselves too seriously.

Huiyue replied to Li's letter in a similarly playful tone, reminding Li that his vow of poverty left him with nothing to waste on wine, women, and song. Li agreed, yet also wondered whether it might not be better that Huiyue show his upright conduct to the world rather than hide away. Huiyue's response was the letter Chen Yong delivered. Returning to Li's original trope of making money through commerce, Huiyue teases Li by asking why someone who has nothing to desire or depend on would want money. He turns to Li's second metaphor about hiding himself away by declaring that he is so thoroughly out of the marketplace of moral advocacy that nothing he could show would fetch a price. Then he reverts to the image of the pilgrim who wears out a thousand pairs of sandals with a verse that refuses Li's distinction between pilgrimage and seclusion:

> The rope on my straw sandals broken, I return to my hermitage;
> Hungry, I eat something; weary, I sleep.
> One affection arises, but where can it lodge?
> One nostril is open, but who does it tunnel into?
>
> 草鞋繩斷卻歸庵，飢即餐兮倦即眠.
> 一種胸懷何處善，半邊鼻孔向誰穿.

Some twenty days later, Li and Chen set off for the Daoist refuge on Mount Qiyun, more popularly known as Baiyue, the White Marchmount. They reached the prefectural capital of Huizhou on May 23. There the teacher called on an old classmate, now serving as the prefect, whom he would see several times over the course of the coming week. The following day, he and Chen were carried by chair-bearers thirty kilometers through the pouring rain, arriving in Xiuning County soaked to the skin. After a meal they continued another ten kilometers up to the base of the mountain, where they spent the night after drinking with another old friend. The next day they climbed to the main temple, performed a propitiatory rite, then retired to the temple residence where they admired a painting of a dead willow tree and water buffalo by Zhu Bang 朱邦 (act. c. 1500), a renowned drunkard who specialized in depicting water buffaloes. During the visit, Li was besieged by the Daoist priests to inscribe fans with his calligraphy. He dashed off over thirty, and even permitted Chen to do a few mountain sketches to satisfy them. The Daoists at the next monastery, overhearing that Li was visiting, sent over an acolyte barely sixteen years old to beg him for a painting. Captivated by the boy's beauty and elegance, Li dashed off a sketch of the mountain with a verse ending in this couplet:

> Trees enchain the mountain's waist, clouds enchain the trees;
> How could one know there are fairy spirits here like these?
>
> 樹鎖山腰雲鎖樹，那知個裡有神仙.

After visiting more sights and people the next day, Li and Chen went back down to Xiuning to indulge in a whirl of social calls that stretched over four or five days before finally heading back home to Jiaxing.

From this brief sketch of a season in the busy life of Li Rihua, one would not guess that this member of the late-Ming gentry thought of himself as a recluse, as someone who had withdrawn from the hectic world that defined the lives of his peers in official service. During the middle and later years of the Wanli era (1572–1620), when the court seemed rudderless, many sought to withdraw from public life, but many also sought to use the mechanisms of state administration to reform the realm according to a proactive vision of service known as *jingshi* 經世. The term is conventionally translated using the slightly archaic "statecraft," though a more literal translation of the embedded textile metaphor, "the warp of the age," gets closer to what those who subscribed to this ideal thought was their proper task as servants of the emperor: to consider every policy and practice of the state so as to improve the lives and morale of the people. In this vision of total involvement, there was no place for the recluse; and yet not a few officials found exits that they could take, if only temporarily, to survive the political maelstroms that regularly struck the court and neutralized their efforts to transform the world.

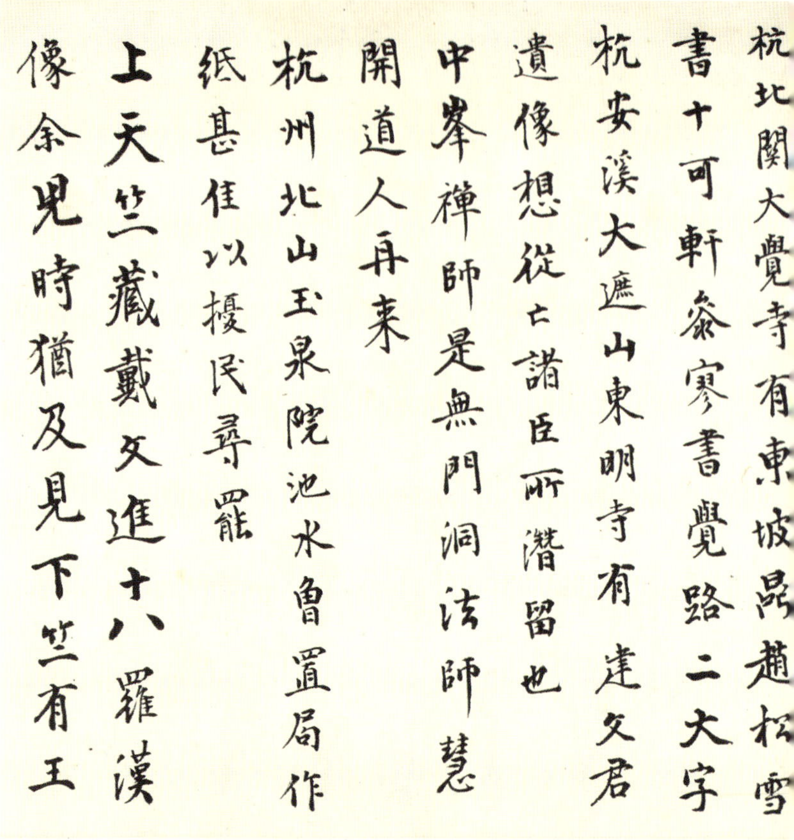

In the more difficult years of the Tianqi (1620–1627) and Chongzhen (1627–1644) eras still to come, the term for escaping from office was "choosing the Buddha."[2] For some it meant actually withdrawing into a Buddhist monastery, the one legitimate sanctuary from political life; for others, it simply meant leaving office. Some statecraft activists, such as the noted Hanlin academician Xu Guangqi 徐光啟 (1562–1633), disdained Buddhism as an unacceptable choice for the serious Confucian (he thought Christianity a better one), though even he sometimes chose reclusion, pleading ill health and removing himself to an experimental farm he ran in Tianjin whenever court politics became too difficult.

Li Rihua was born in 1565 and came of age during the opening decades of the Wanli reign.[3] He is less well known than many of the greatest artists of his age—among whom we may include Dong Qichang 董其昌 (1555–1636), Chen Jiru 陳繼儒 (1558–1639), and Chen Guan 陳裸 (1563–c. 1639), who are all represented in the current exhibition—but he stood at the center of the social and cultural world they defined. I focus on him in this essay because of the sources that survive to reveal his life to us. He did well to pass his provincial *juren* examination in 1591 and his national *jinshi* in 1592, which promptly launched him on a promising career. Rather than being relegated to the magistracy in some out-of-the-way county, as many a new graduate was, he was appointed to the post of prefectural judge of Jiujiang, the nexus of communication between the large and productive province of Jiangxi and the Yangzi River corridor linking the hinterland to the economic core on the Yangzi Delta. After six years of distinguished service, Li fell afoul of a superior. One of the charges, which cut rather a large schism through the mid-Wanli generation, was that he was devoted to Buddhism, an avocation that one faction of that generation regarded with suspicion. Though cleared of most charges, Li was demoted to lesser posts in the field. There he again acquitted himself well, notably in organizing flood-control work along the Yellow River, a classical statecraft concern. Fourteen years into his career, everything stopped when his mother died and he was obliged to return home to the Yangzi Delta to observe mourning for twenty-seven months.

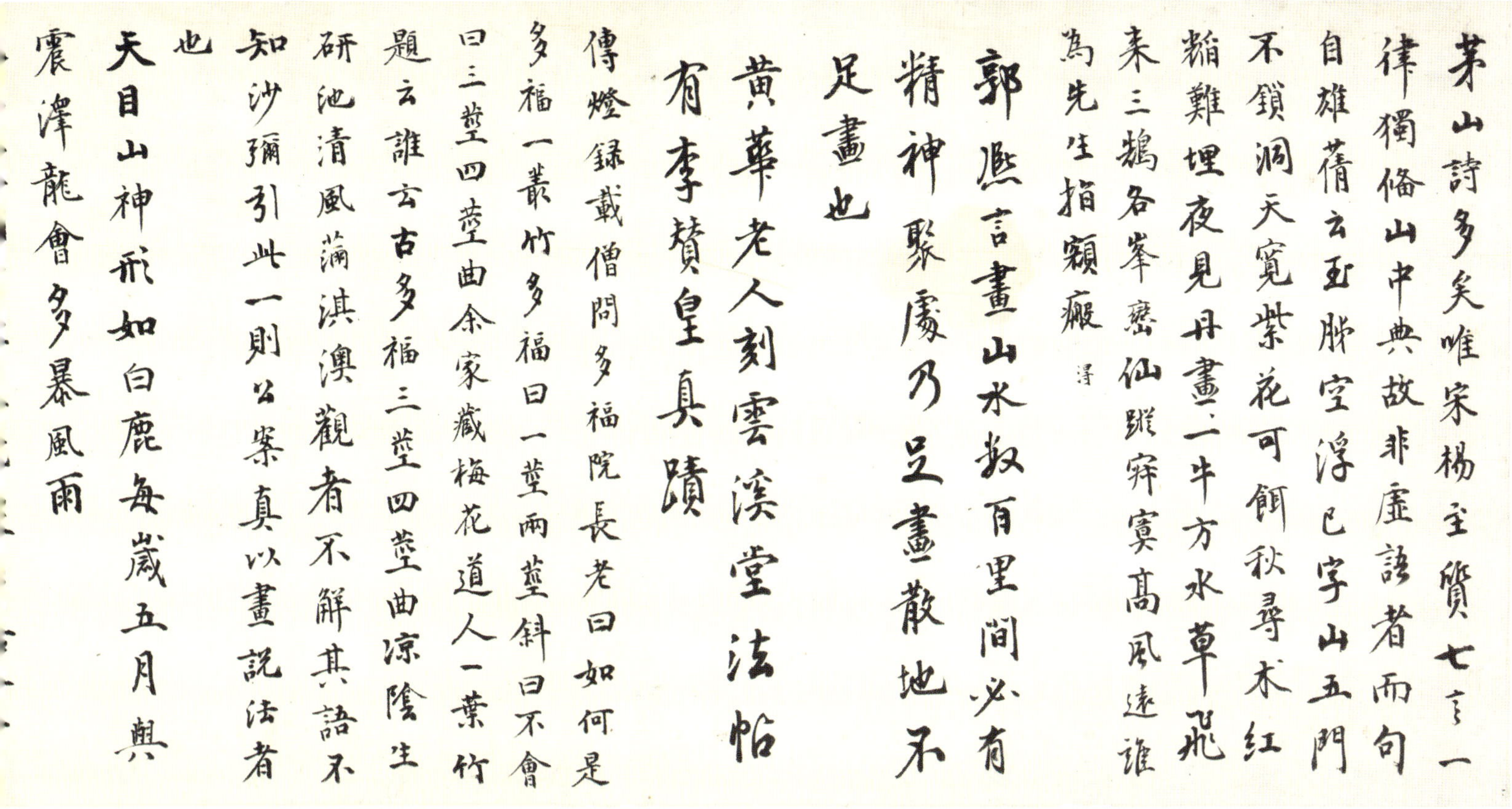

When the period of mourning for his mother expired toward the end of 1604, Li applied to the Ministry of Personnel for an extension to care for his aged father. As his father lived for another eleven years, there is some question as to whether the old man's health was sufficiently precarious to warrant Li's reclusion from public service. Filial piety may have been his motivation, but it also presented him with an acceptable ideological excuse not to re-enter the political turmoil of the time, which is precisely what Li wanted. The extension was renewed in 1611 and again in 1616. His father's death the following year furnished him with another twenty-seven months' absence from court. He used his own ill health to squeeze several more years' retirement beyond this. Even when he was ordered back into service in 1624 at the age of fifty-nine, he was able to finagle several local appointments that kept him out of Beijing during the reign of the eunuch establishment through the Tianqi era. After the Chongzhen emperor 崇禎 (r. 1627–1644) ascended the throne, Li submitted a memorial of proposals in the statecraft tradition that might have gained him an extraordinary appointment had he not fallen ill again. Except for one brief assignment, he continued his life of reclusion at home in Jiaxing until his death at the age of seventy.

FIG. 19 Li Rihua, *Notes from the Studio of Six Inkstones* (detail), 1626; Handscroll: ink on paper; 23.5 × 550 cm; Private collection

Thus it was that a man groomed for office in the Wanli era spent the first half of his career in the bureaucracy suffering the slings and arrows that fortune directed against righteous officials in those years, and the second half out of it, by circumstance to a large extent but also by choice as well. He mourned his mother and cared for his father, but he also enjoyed a life of leisure that enabled him to engage in the cultural and social pastimes of his generation free of the burden of public office: writing, painting, penning, versifying, gathering with like-minded friends, engaging in the local politics, traveling, visiting religious sites, and, most important of all for our purposes, keeping a diary. The eight years of diary entries that survive (from roughly 1609 to 1616) were published in the Republican period under the title *Weishui xuan riji* 味水軒日記 (Diary from the Pavilion for Tasting Water, 1929). The Pavilion for Tasting Water was a small structure on the family property where Li stored his art collection, painted, kept his diary, and received friends. The diary that carries its name reveals more about the fabric of daily life among the upper gentry of the late Ming era than any other surviving document from that period. In its pages, the statecraft official is limited to a few recollections of colleagues while in service; it is the recluse who takes center stage (fig. 19).

As the entries from the early spring of 1614 show, Li's withdrawal from government service, if it was reclusion, was of a highly social sort. It was not a physical withdrawal from the world. It included visits to Daoist mountains and Buddhist monasteries, to which some did indeed withdraw from worldly affairs, though these were not places to which Li was prepared to consign himself. As we have seen from his correspondence with the monk Huiyue, he was not even tempted by the notion. His reclusion in this regard was vicarious. He had an elderly father to care for and the affairs of a large family to manage; but even if he hadn't, one does not sense from his diary that he longed to escape his responsibilities.

The pose of recluse nonetheless suited Li, and he adopted it to the degree that suited his needs. Indeed, so long as he was outside the strict bounds of mourning, he needed the pose to demonstrate a purpose to his long vacation from office. According to his diary, he is challenged just once over this decision. The Vice-Minister of Personnel, whom Li identifies as his teacher, was expected to pass through Jiaxing in the summer of 1612 on his way home to visit his parents in southwest Zhejiang, and Li spent several days anxiously awaiting him, not knowing when he would arrive. His visit meant that Li had to put off a trip that he longed to take to a favorite haunt in the region, Stone Buddha Monastery. Finally on July 31, Vice-Minister Xiao 蕭侍郎 arrived; his first words to Li were: "You haven't come forward for an appointment for a decade. What is your intention?" Li replied, "What I have already written about this in my minor memorial is a sincere expression of my commitment."[4] After recording this exchange in his diary, Li noted that the Vice-Minister pondered his reply for some time without speaking. Li reveals nothing further. It is not difficult to suppose that his teacher was unhappy with the reply, yet he was unwilling to challenge Li any further. Li may have chosen this cryptic response as a way to avoid having to make a defense for his reclusion, which could have led him onto difficult ideological terrain. The problem was embedded in the Confucian model of public service, which counseled Confucian scholars to make themselves available for service to the state but allowed them to withdraw when the times were evil and the ruler had lost the Mandate of Heaven. Perhaps this is why the Vice-Minister did not press his protégé: he did not wish to hear an explicit argument against serving the Wanli emperor that might amount to treason. Tacitly at least they both let the matter rest, for Vice-Minister Xiao returned the courtesy of Li's greeting the following day by calling on him at his home, and the next night Li and three other local degree-holders hosted a banquet for him. The visit passed without further difficulty.

The "minor memorial" to which Li referred was his formal request to remain at home to care for his father, who had turned eighty. The court had forwarded this memorial to the Ministry of Personnel for deliberation on September 2 the previous year. On December 5 Li learned from the *Beijing Gazette* that the ministry's response had been approved by the emperor and issued three weeks earlier, though without knowing what that response was. The document reached him via the Jiaxing prefect's office on January 23. It was entirely positive, construing Li's filial devotion to his father as a commendable transformation of his loyalty to the emperor. The service waiver was good until his father died and the period of mourning completed. Li was mildly dismayed when he found a notice in the *Beijing Gazette* three years later that the Ministry of Personnel had put his name forward to serve as a bureau secretary for the Ministry of Rites in Nanjing, but no formal appointment was forthcoming.[5] He still had another four years of reclusion ahead of him (plus another four of illness beyond that) to keep him out of circulation.

Li was not alone in succeeding at avoiding government service. Occasionally when he heard of someone else who had done the same, he made a note of the man in his diary. For instance, on December 13, 1616, he commemorated the death of someone who worked with him in Henan the year before he himself left office. The man distinguished himself in flood-control work and was thus very much in the statecraft tradition. For his efforts he was rewarded with a promotion to Shaanxi Province not long after Li's departure from service, but he "loftily retired and did not take up the post."[6] Li's admiration is evident. Twenty days later, he used the same expression in describing a classmate to whom he had just written a letter. The man distinguished himself as a benevolent and effective magistrate, Li noted, but then "quit his post and went home to live as a recluse in the willow woods of his county, respected by all for having loftily retired."[7]

Political reclusion for Li Rihua, as for others of his inclination and status, was not a quiet life. The constant writing of letters and diary entries suggests as much. On some days he jotted down nothing more than the weather in his diary, leaving no clue as to how he passed the day. But more often he recorded a busy round of activities and outings and gatherings. Socializing was important to him, but that aside, more than any other type of activity, it was the production and consumption of art that occupied the center of his existence as a recluse from public service. No three days passed without Li either setting brush to paper or silk, gathering with like-minded friends to peruse his or their collections, or receiving an art dealer who wanted to show him his wares. All these encounters ended up in *Weishui xuan riji*, which is why we know more about the art market during these eight years, to say nothing of Li's collecting practices in particular, than at any other time in China before the twentieth century. Art was important to Li. It was the embodiment of high culture; it was his link to history; it was the expression of the values he held dear. As for reclusion, it was the medium in which the ideal found its purest expression. He could have imagined the monk Huiyue embodying that ideal when he went into religious seclusion, but instead Li teased him for making an extreme choice. Perhaps from the lofty position he occupied in the privileged society of the gentry, there was no realm other than art in which the recluse ideal could find its purest form.

Reclusion was a favorite theme in the paintings that Li and his friends produced and consumed, though that production and consumption was anything but reclusive. These men—and here I will speak particularly of Chen Jiru and Dong Qichang and secondarily of Chen Guan—formed a tight social network that positioned them as cultural and social leaders on the Yangzi Delta. Chen Guan lived in Suzhou, eighty-five kilometers to the north of Jiaxing, and was slightly outside the social unity of the other three. Chen Jiru and Dong Qichang lived in Huating, the seat of Songjiang Prefecture sixty-five kilometers northeast of Li's home. Though living only marginally closer to Jiaxing, Chen and Dong were close to Li.[8] Indeed, the bond among them became legendary. Xiang Shengmo 項聖謨 (1597–1658), grandson of Li's patron Xiang Yuanbian 項元汴 (1525–1590) and a friend to all three, retrospectively gathered them into a painting he produced with another artist in 1652. Now in the Shanghai Museum, *Venerable Friends* depicts a group of six elderly gentlemen in a garden replete with signs of reclusion (fig. 20).[9] The painting is supposed to depict a gathering in 1635, the year of Li's death. The work furnishes a glimpse of the leisured existence of the late-Ming elite world that artists of the early Qing felt they had lost. In admiration for this lost world, Xiang painted himself into the group.[10]

Through the diarized years, Chen Jiru visited Li in Jiaxing at least three times: once in 1611, once in 1612 to examine Li's painting collection, and once in 1616 to show him a book he had just published. Chen Guan did not come to visit, though on several occasions he sent paintings that he wanted Li to see.[11] Nor did Dong Qichang, even though he was nearby in Huating during these years.[12] Nonetheless, a token of their long relationship showed up on February 9, 1612, when a friend brought a fan that Li had painted years earlier, on which Dong later wrote an inscription extolling Li as the finest landscape painter in Jiaxing. Li returned the favor in a sense the following September when dealer Wang Danlin 王丹林 brought him a calligraphic album by Dong. Wang hoped Li would write an inscription, and Li obliged by writing a short piece crediting Dong's immense artistry to his Daoist sensibility, which enables him to withdraw from worldly cares and attain a resonance with nature itself.

This nesting of one's work within the work of the others was a common device, a gesture of mutual endorsement and affection. When a friend from Huating visited Li on November 24, 1610, bearing a painting of plum blossoms, Li discovered colophons by Dong Qichang and Chen Jiru and so happily acceded to the friend's request that he add his own.[13] The painting, which could have been in the style of Gao Jian's 高簡 (1634–after 1708) *Flowering Plum* (1708; cat. no. 57), no longer survives, but inscriptions by Li, Dong, and Chen do. The colophons authorized this scroll as a fine work of art, allowing it to enter the high cultural realm of which the three were guardians, to say nothing of raising its commercial value. The inscriptions by all three as well as the artist, dated between 1626 and 1628, are attached to a handscroll in the Los Angeles County Museum of Art,[14] the painter of which is none other Xiang Shengmo, friend to all three and the posthumous portraitist of two of them. What more appropriate painting for these men to praise than one titled *Invitation to Reclusion* (1625–26; cat. no. 1)? Their genre had triumphed. As if to underscore the point that important distinctions still had to be drawn—that aping the image of reclusion was not necessarily attaining the ideal of reclusion—Li reminds his reader that the common run of Yuan-landscape imitators merely pretend to "preserve the spirit of the untrammeled" without actually grasping what is at stake.

The theme of reclusion is strong for all four artists of the 1555–65 generation, perhaps in part because they had personal experience of alienation from the system of state power for which they trained. Of the three Jiaxing-Huating friends, Dong struggled with the exams the longest. The man who would eventually be regarded by many as the greatest calligrapher of the Ming era apparently started out with poor handwriting, the sine qua non of passing the exams, though eventually he reached the pinnacle of *jinshi* status in 1589. Li followed him in the next metropolitan examination in 1592. Chen dealt with the adversity of examination failure distinctively: he decided to give up the game in 1586, marking his decision with the dramatic and irreversible gesture of destroying his scholar's robes, possibly by burning them.[15] He would never go on to a career as an official, unlike Dong and Li, neither of whom ended up following a conventional course in their own careers. Dong was impeached in 1597 and returned home to Huating in 1599 to wait out his enforced retirement until 1621. As we have seen, Li would be sidelined by mourning five years later, but then take advantage of his circumstances to stay out of office for longer than Dong.

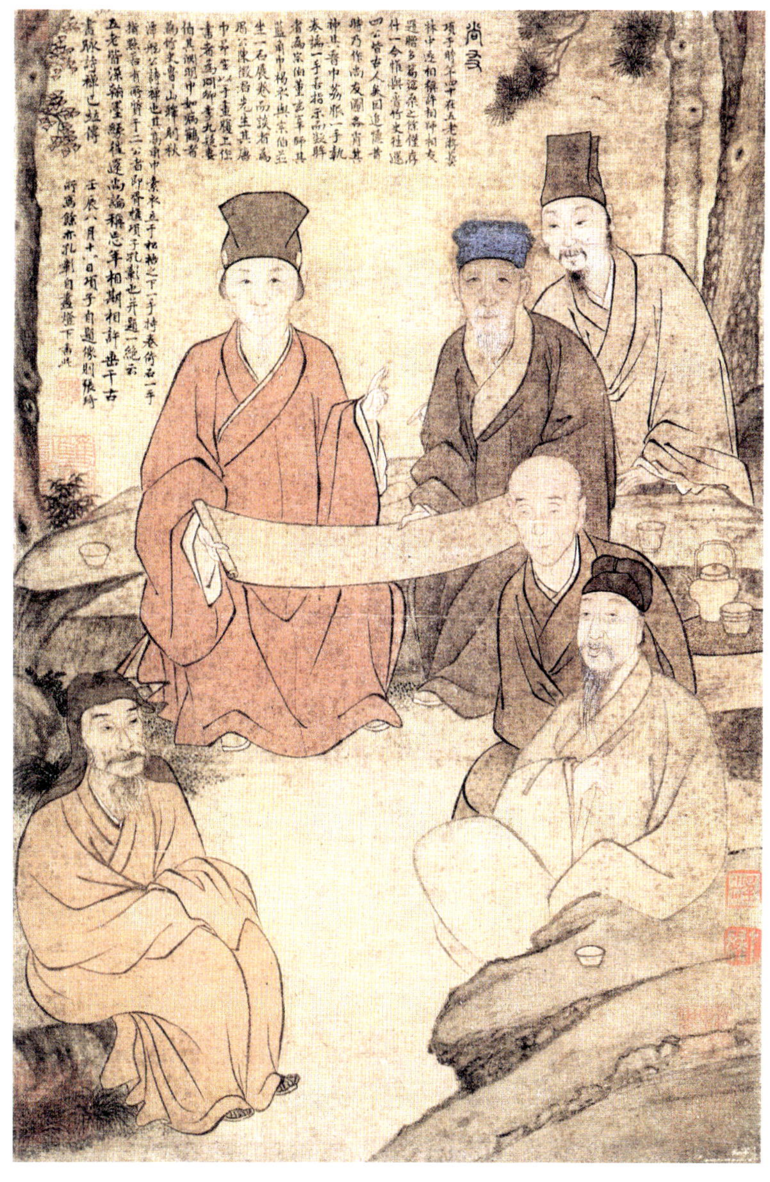

FIG. 20 Xiang Shengmo and Zhang Qi, *Venerable Friends*, 1652; Hanging scroll: ink and color on silk; 38.1 × 25.5 cm; Shanghai Museum. The sitters are (clockwise from upper left) Dong Qichang, Chen Jiru, Xiang Shengmo, Monk Qiutan, Li Rihua, and Lu Dezhi.

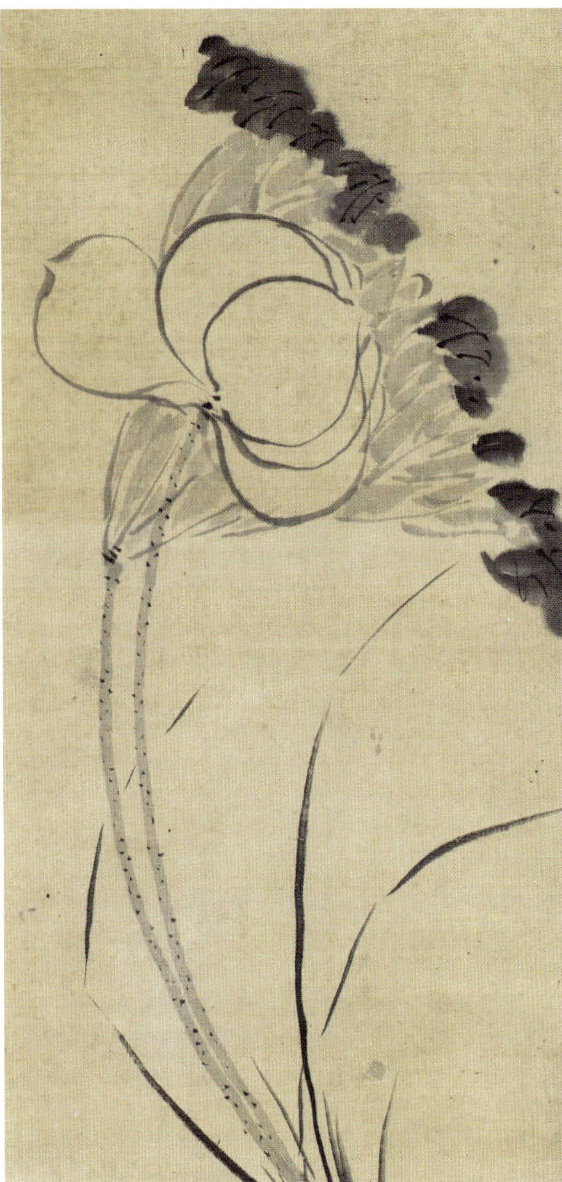

Not surprisingly then, they refer to and paint reclusion almost obsessively. The painting *Boat on a Snowy Landscape* that Li wanted to finish when student Chen Yong showed up fits the bill. So too does his solitary *Lotus* (cat. no. 10, fig. 21), in which the subject rises up from the mud without, following its classic Buddhist interpretation, being tainted by filth. Li also deployed his calligraphy—contrary to Dong's praise, Li is regarded today as a better calligrapher than painter—in this vein, for earlier on the same day that Dealer Wang asked him to inscribe an album of Dong's calligraphy, Li wrote a poem on a fan for someone he identified somewhat mysteriously as "a recluse who came down from the mountain." He matches the reclusive identity of his guest not so much with his style as with his images, which picture the main character of the poem sitting drunk among white stones in a forest and then, after eating, ascending a green mountain that faces a lake.[16]

The landscapes of Dong and the two Chens included in the exhibition share the theme of reclusion, not through metaphor in the mode of Li's lotus painting but through the representation of the landscape into which the recluse withdraws. The kind of place favored was mountainous upland, which lay somewhere below Heaven but above the workaday world of agriculture and commerce where most people spent their lives, trammeled by the cares of mundane existence. Chen Jiru's *Thatched Hut by Tall Pines* (cat. no. 11) depicts such a landscape, which provides a space for a sociable conversation between two self-designated recluses. Chen Guan in *Walking with a Staff over a Stream Bridge* (cat. no. 5) stages much the same setting.

These men did not invent the trope of landscape as the space of reclusion, which is a motif with a long history. They might look back as far as the Tang (618–907) for their progenitors, but they regarded the greatest landscape painters of reclusion to be the masters of the Yuan dynasty (1279–1368), notably Wang Meng 王蒙 (c. 1308–1385; famed as an eremite himself) and Huang Gongwang 黄公望 (1269–1354). Chen Guan revered both and was so keen to share their work with Li that he sent mountain paintings by both artists to him in 1609 so that he could see their work in the original.[17] Li was particularly taken with Wang's *Living in the Mountains* (1361), transcribing the text on the painting into his diary. Living in the mountains was a subject Wang painted over and over again during his career, which is why his oeuvre is regarded as the precursor of eremitic painting in the late Ming.[18] Li also admired Huang, whose influence he acknowledged in his own painting, also transcribing the texts on the painting that Chen Guan sent to him.[19] The aesthetic appreciation that Li and his cohort had for Huang and Wang is evident.[20] Their work was not just appreciated but much sought after—and therefore much faked. A Suzhou dealer who showed up on September 14, 1614, with paintings by Huang and Wang in his portfolio fared less well than he must have hoped. Li noted the two by Huang without further comment, but *Lofty Reclusion in the Pine Valley*, which the dealer attributed to Wang, elicits a blast of scorn. The theme was right, but the object itself was not: "the paper was thin and the ink excessive; nothing but a fake. It bore a colophon by Chen Lin: not worth talking about."[21]

The affinity that Li's group felt for the Yuan heightened their own sense of living in difficult times. And yet, from the distance that we stand from their time, the notion that they shared a common bond with these artists feels forced. As subjects of the Yuan dynasty, Wang and Huang lived under foreign occupation by the Mongols. This surely endowed their reclusion with a real-world significance that the late Ming, however politically troubled, could not command. The pressures for reclusion in this later time were not foreign occupation but factionalism, eunuch power, and an unbridled explosion of private wealth that was shattering the moral certainties on which earlier generations had been able to rely: serious matters, but of a lesser pitch.

Of the Wanli painters who absorbed and went beyond the Yuan masters, Dong Qichang is the master. In *The Wanluan Thatched Hall* (1597; fig. 8), which he dedicated to Chen Jiru, Dong situates the eponymous pavilion in a landscape that recalls Wang Meng but also leaves him behind. The pavilion sits empty in the middle distance, partially obscured among the folded rock formations that simultaneously loom over the site and protect it, tempting the potential recluse with a charmed space into which he might enter, just as the man in Li's poem did when in the final line he ascends the blue-green mountain. Though Dong praised Li on his fan as "taking refuge in and celebrating the pure and the distant, climbing to lofty places that he transforms into poetry, and never with recourse to the shortcuts of the mere artisan," none of Li's surviving landscapes comes near Dong's in conception or execution.[22] Within their circle perhaps, this didn't matter. The language of refuge, purity, distance, and loftiness they shared declared that they stood within the hermeneutic circle on which reclusion relied for its conceptual coherence; just to speak this language was to belong within its circle. Chen burned his gown after failing the exams, Dong was forced into retirement by envious colleagues, and Li prolonged his mourning to stay out of politics. Their experiences were disappointing to them, but their reclusion did not go much beyond a genteel

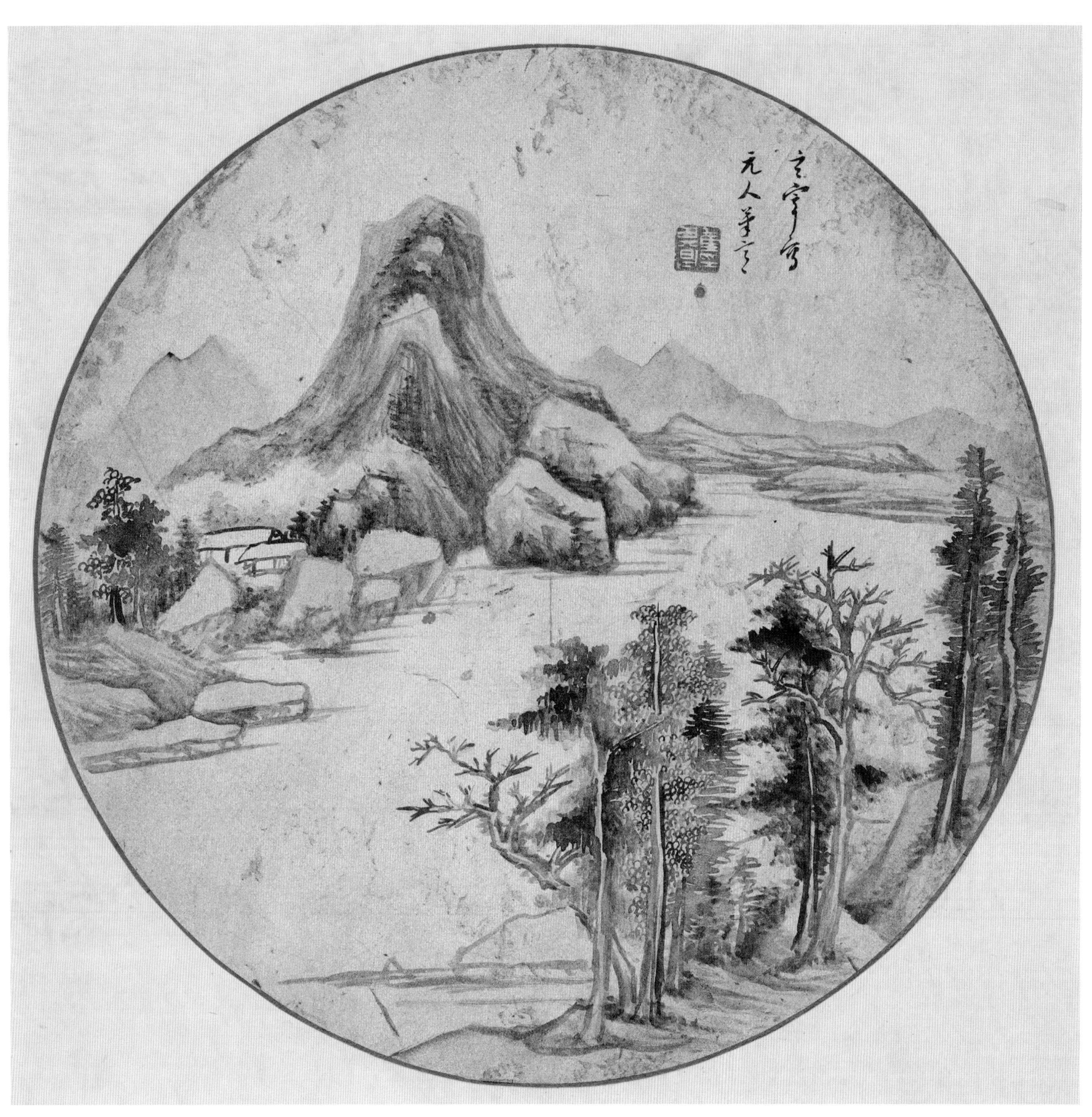

OPPOSITE: FIG. 21 Li Rihua, *Lotus* (detail; cat. no. 10)
ABOVE: FIG. 22 Dong Qichang, leaf from *Contemplating the Dao with Emotions Cleansed*, c. 1610 (cat. no. 8)

resentment of the way the world went. No cold wind of Mongol rule was blowing on their necks, only their anxiety to mark the status boundary they believed must separate them—as men of principle, as men of taste, as members of the greater gentry of Jiangnan—from the vulgar who grasped at power and wealth without a thought to righteousness. Their withdrawal from the world was more speech act than internal exile, more text than context.

The text of reclusion was for these artists both painterly and poetic, as on a painting by Dong a student brought to Li on June 8, 1613. Dated 1603, four years after Dong went home to Huating in disgrace, the painting was called *Autumn Mountains*—the quintessential reclusion subject. If it is anything like the painting we know by that name in the Cleveland Museum of Art, it depicts the approach to a hilly upland zone separate from the world of human affairs; indeed, it is so separate that it is entirely devoid of recluses or travelers. The narrow footbridge in the low foreground indicates that this is the way toward reclusion; but unlike *Wanluan Thatched Hall*, *Autumn Mountains* does not offer the prospective recluse any structure where he might imagine himself ensconced in this upland solitude. On the painting Dong transcribed a poem by the eminent Tang writer Bo Juyi 白居易 (772–846). The second half of the poem reads:

Who knows how brief a life can be here
Where we find ourselves between Heaven and earth?
Our hearts suffer the sorrows of a thousand years,
Our bodies are without a day of rest.
When will I be let loose from this sharp net
So long as this earth has shut me in?[23]

人生無幾何，如寄天地間.
心有千載憂，身無一日閒.
何時解塵網，此地來掩關.

The poem's final phrase, "shut in" (*yanguan* 掩關), is precisely the language of Buddhist seclusion that Li used in his first letter to Huiyue, in which he pictured the monk "shut within the space of one woven rush mat." The phrase covers both the reclusive ideal that Dong imagined and the real discipline of self-imposed seclusion that Li wondered was absolutely necessary for the cultivation of the self (fig. 23). I contrast the two usages here to bring out the contradiction I regard as intrinsic to the Wanli-era ideal of reclusion among an elite who in their daily practice were very much absorbed in weaving the warp of the age. To put it bluntly, absolute separation from the real world may have been what the literati of the Wanli era imagined they yearned for as they struggled to come to terms with the political turmoil and social transformation that was sweeping late-Ming society. But perfect seclusion was not really what they desired to put into practice nor even could have, had they tried. The upland was lovely to visit in real life, as Li and his student did when they had sedan chair-bearers carry them up the White Marchmount, but it was not a zone they chose to inhabit. Still, that did not discourage them from imagining it in their art. In fact, it may have pushed them to imagine it all the more intensely.

The occupation of the Yangzi Delta by the armies of the Manchu in 1645 changed all this. The idea of reclusion from the cares of this world came to have a much stronger valence for the elite; it also became a reality that some of them put into practice. Li Rihua's generation was safely dead a decade before the fall of the Ming dynasty. Li died in 1635, Dong the year after, Chen Guan sometime after 1638, and Chen Jiru in 1639. But their descendants lived through this traumatic time. Li's son, Li Zhaoheng 李肇亨, who is a constant presence in *Weishui xuan riji* as his father anxiously watches him make his way through the lower levels of the examination system, fled when the soldiers serving the new Qing dynasty (1644–1911) arrived in Jiaxing. He knew which direction to take: he fled to the hills. For Li Zhaoheng, the upland was not simply a place of mind. It was place into which he could seclude himself to avoid a far more dangerous world than his father ever had to confront. The family residence in Jiaxing managed to survive the takeover, but most of the family's wealth was lost. The cultural enterprise that the Pavilion for Tasting Water represented in any case became impracticable during the long shadow of loyalist resistance that the fall of the dynasty cast. Is it an irony that Li Zhaoheng ended up living what for his father had been only an imagined ideal by becoming a Buddhist monk, taking the dharma name of Changying 常瑩 and withdrawing to a monastery across the border in Songjiang? The son's skills as a painter were praised by Li's colleagues, or so the elder tells us in his diary, but few paintings survive.[24] The paintings in the exhibition by Ming-loyalist monks Bada Shanren 八大山人 (1626–1705) and Kuncan 髡殘 (b. 1612) hint at the changed social and cultural world in which Li the son painted a different engagement with the reclusionist ideal than Li the father ever experienced.

The contradiction inherent in Wanli-era reclusion, as an ideal put not into practice but only into art, in no way diminishes the power of the ideal and its importance to political recluses such as Li Rihua. This was an ideal that mattered to them. They circulated the ideal constantly within their cultural realm by writing about it and painting it and visiting it from time to time. It both expressed and influenced their orientation to the world and their sense of their own moral worth. We can hardly blame them for not disappearing into the zone of reclusion when the world around them was not designed for this to happen, or downgrade their posture as mere ideology even though the next generation would be forced to act it out.

A second break or contradiction between the ideal of reclusion that Li and others embraced and its practice is embedded in the fact that the ideal was not available to most people. The world from which Li withdrew was a very specific one: the world of service in the ranked bureaucracy. Entry into this world was carefully restricted, as it had to be when the principle of selection for service was not happily confined within an aristocracy but had to include anyone who could demonstrate merit. Those who had the talent and opportunity to demonstrate merit and become magistrates and ministers in the end were few. Those who chose to forego the power and privileges to which state service otherwise entitled them constituted an even tinier group. It set them off as men who chose moral autonomy over moral compromise; if only they could be recluses, there would not be many who would merit the distinction.

It was accordingly difficult for someone to earn the praise of his peers for withdrawing from the moral compromise of public service when one had neither degrees nor prospects, putting such service well beyond one's reach. But not impossible: this was in the end a cultural and not an administrative question. The day before Chen Yong showed up for his first lesson in landscape painting, Li had invited a friend to come over to his house and spend the evening together. The talk turned to a recluse, someone known only as Old Man Wang, who had been a neighbor in Li's friend's home village until his

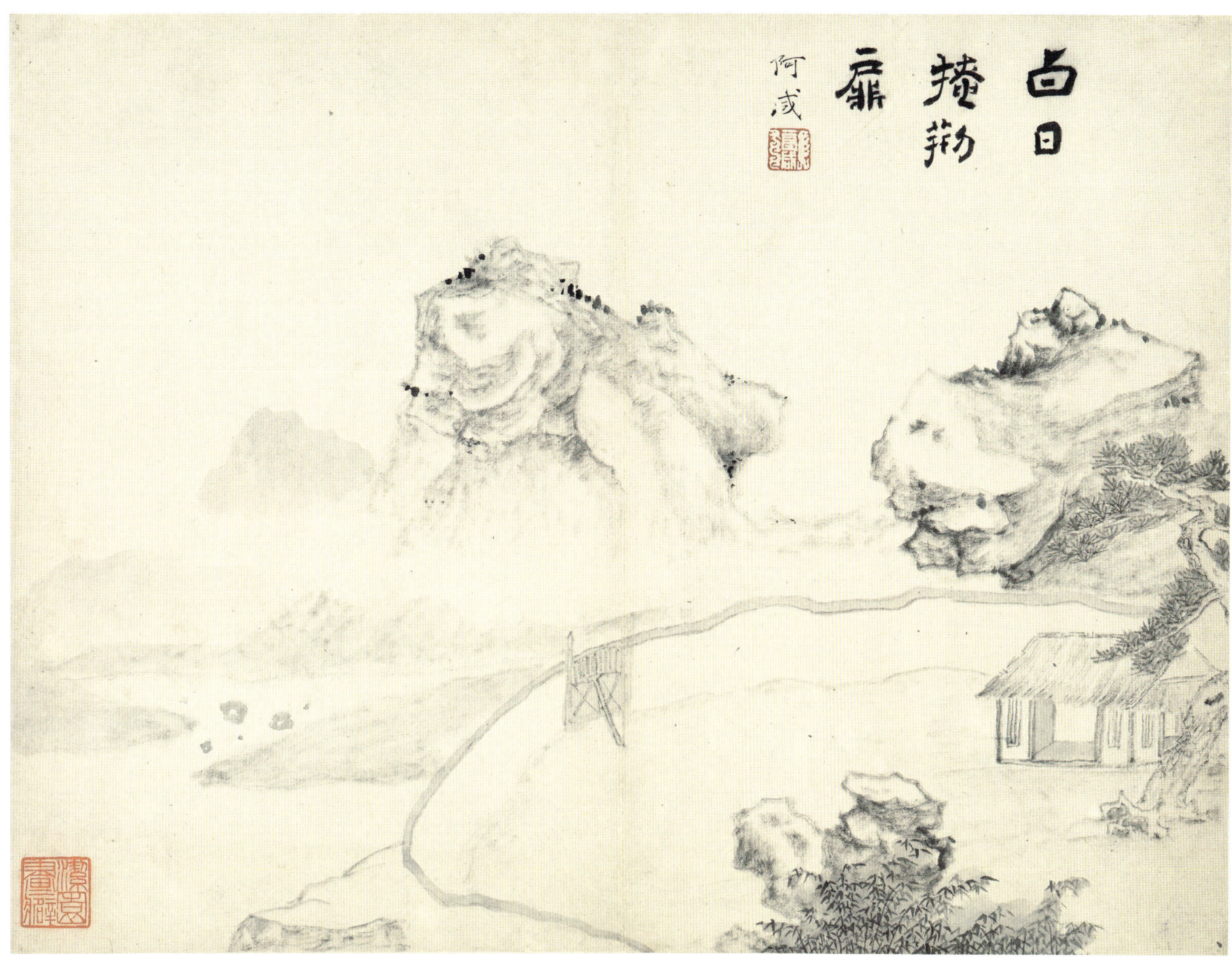

recent death past the age of eighty. As a boy, Wang had set out on the path toward government service and shown great promise, or so the retrospective story had it. But he abruptly quit school and "adopted the posture of the recluse," as Li phrases it. At the age of fifteen Wang had planted a plum tree in his courtyard. This tree he tended daily, trimming and pruning it to encourage its growth. By the time he was an old man, this tree had grown to a vast size, putting out tens of thousands of blossoms every spring that filled his residence with scent. "When the tree came into bloom," Li's friend recalled, "he opened his gate and let anyone come in and enjoy himself. If the visitor was a gentleman of elegance, then the old man prepared fine tea and liquor and treated his guest with boundless courtesy."

Li is thus presented, and in turn presents the reader of his diary, with the perfect recluse: the man who escaped from the examination system before ever becoming entangled in it, who preserved his own autonomy, and who toward the end of his life was free to immerse himself unselfconsciously in the serene aesthetic existence that reclusion promised. Li then writes that the man was known as the Plum Flower Station Master—at which point, at least for me, the illusion cracks. Old Man Wang had not devoted his life to reclusion after all, but had used the literacy of his early education to get a post as a courier station master. Station masters were government employees who occupied a narrow social stratum just below the titled gentry but above ordinary folk. So in fact Wang, in giving up one path to service, had turned to another; his reclusion was essentially no different from Li's. He expressed his reclusion through arborism rather than painting (that noted, Li was a keen flower gardener). Even then he was not so reclusive as keep his gate shut when the plum tree was in full bloom.

Li completes the diary entry about Old Man Wang by quoting an exchange for which he was remembered by those who knew him. He was once asked, "Why, sir, don't you ask your visitors for a poem on the plum blossoms, or have guests paint them on a scroll? Aren't you wasting a golden opportunity?" Wang knitted his brow, then replied enigmatically, "But if I did that, I would just be turning the plum blossoms into tumors." Li concludes: "Hearing this, people elevated him even higher."[25]

FIG. 23 Fang Hengxian, leaf from *Painting and Calligraphy*, after 1659 (cat. no. 39)

Li went along with the judgment. Thinking back to the plum painting that a Songjiang friend asked Li to inscribe in 1610, we might be tempted to say that Old Man Wang trumped the recluse professionals. Li, Dong, and Chen all willingly inscribed a painting that Wang in his loftiness might well have dismissed as nothing but a grossly failed transcription of a beauty that only the tree itself could embody. Indeed, if we adopt Wang's perspective, it is not hard to see the tight little blossoms in Gao Jian's *Flowering Plum* as looking more like tumors than flowers (see cat. no. 57). But this is the game in which the claim of reclusion always fails. For someone who is judged to be lofty and pure and refuses to sink to mere craftsmanship—Dong's evaluation of Li, which was so critical to literati identity—can always be outdone by someone else who is better positioned to perform literati ideals or better skilled to embody them in his calligraphy or painting.

The watchword, which Li uses in his account of Old Man Wang, is "elegance." If someone showed up during blossom time who was "a gentleman of elegance," then the qualifications were in place for the kind of social encounter that confirmed where the boundary between the truly elite and the merely ordinary was drawn. The elegant were served tea and wine, while the vulgar got nothing. Old Man Wang may not have consciously been playing this game of status, but his visitors undoubtedly were. Having spent a lifetime tending a plum tree that was like no other in his part of the county, Wang had proven himself to be the real thing: the real recluse, the real gentleman of elegance. In the tough competitive social atmosphere that prevailed in the late Ming, the greater gentry families felt themselves constantly under siege from lesser gentry and even merchant families. Elegance was the ineffable criterion that the elite used to safeguard entry into their ranks. It was a tough criterion to meet, especially when it defied clear definition.[26] But Li knew it when he saw it in the paintings he loved. And when he saw it, he also projected it onto the artist who created the work. He speaks of the painter Ni Zan 倪瓚 (1301–1374), for instance, as "the most elegant gentleman of the Yuan," an attribution meant for the person as well as the work.[27] One did not have to be a painter to be elegant, but one could not be a good painter unless one was; nor did reclusion ensure elegance, though it helped.

We should not be too hard on the circular reasoning through which Li Rihua and his peers relied to set themselves apart from the common run of humanity, or from the common run of degree-holding bureaucrats for that matter. We all elevate ideals that we leave under-scrutinized and rarely achieve. They provide the ideological ground that we can share with some and that we use to exclude others. These ideals may not actually be what we want to see brought into practice entirely, but they do serve to lend us an identity in the ongoing disagreement with the world that all of us, no matter who we are and what ideals we might wish to uphold, pursue. In the case of Li Rihua and his cohorts, reclusion was one of those ideals: rarely put into actual practice; difficult to carry out in the context of the everyday demands of life, work, and family; but powerful enough to motivate a system of discourse and image that endowed their lives with meaning. None of that generation could escape the ideal of reclusion. And they worked so assiduously at reproducing it that few artists of the next several generations could avoid imagining the world in any other way.

Li's reclusion was requited when a new emperor came to the throne after the fiascos of the late Wanli and Tianqi reigns. It came however at the moment that illness struck him in 1628, leaving him partly paralyzed and unable to resume the duties he had so successfully shirked through those difficult years. The irony of this situation was not diminished by the honor that Emperor Chongzhen bestowed on him. The emperor did not permit Li to retire, though he did grant him leave to recover, but he went further and honored Li for his long reclusion during the Wanli era by commending him for "preferring retirement out of filial consideration." The implied protest of Li's reclusion was thereby dissolved as a gesture of even greater loyalty to the dynasty. Li felt so vindicated by this commendation that he adopted the emperor's phrase, "preferring retirement" (*tianzhi* 恬致), as his sobriquet in his last years. It was a fitting description for a man who for two decades had mastered the art of secluding himself without actually giving up the privileges and the future that came with his status as a *jinshi* and his commitment to the duties of statecraft. Li was thus the perfect recluse, even in the eyes of the emperor for whom he should have been working. The only tragic flaw in this perfect narrative of service-cum-reclusion was time, which even autonomy could not stave off forever.

NOTES

1 The interactions between Li Rihua and Chen Yong are recorded in Li, *Weishui xuan riji* 味水軒日記 (Shanghai: Yuandong chubanshe, 1996), 367, 369–70, 377, 383–85. Li famously criticized Dong Qichang for being unable to paint trees; Kohara Hironobu, "Tung Ch'i-ch'ang's Connoisseurship in T'ang and Sung Painting," in *The Century of Tung Ch'i-ch'ang, 1555–1636*, ed. Wai-kam Ho, vol. 1 (Kansas City: Nelson-Atkins Museum of Art, 1992), 103n64.

2 Timothy Brook, *Praying for Power: Buddhism and the Formation of Gentry Society in Late-Ming China* (Cambridge, MA: Council on East Asian Studies, Harvard University Press, 1993), 122, 320.

3 Chaoying Fang's biography of Li Rihua appears in *The Dictionary of Ming Biography, 1368–1644*, ed. L. Carrington Goodrich and Chaoying Fang, vol. 1 (New York: Columbia University Press, 1976), 826–30. Li's social context is explored in Chu-tsing Li, "Li Rihua and his Literati Circle in the Late Ming Dynasty," *Orientations* 18, no. 8 (August 1987): 28–47. Two examples of his painting and one piece of calligraphy are reproduced in Chu-tsing Li and James C. Y. Watt, eds., *The Chinese Scholar's Studio: Artistic Life in the Late Ming Period* (New York: Thames and Hudson and the Asia Society, 1987), plates 3, 4c, and 5. The example of Li's calligraphy illustrated in fig. 19, a scroll containing excerpts of Li's *Liuyanzhai biji* 六研齋筆記 (Notes from the Studio of Six Inkstones), is fully illustrated and discussed by Bai Qianshen in Richard Barnhart et al., *The Jade Studio: Masterpieces of Ming and Qing Painting and Calligraphy from the Wong Nan-p'ing Collection* (New Haven, CT: Yale University Art Gallery, 1994), 115–18.

4 Li Rihua, *Weishui xuan riji*, 243.

5 Ibid., 188, 198, 204, 504–5.

6 Ibid., 554.

7 Ibid., 556.

8 The distances are taken from Huang Bian's 黄汴 (dates unknown) route book of 1570, *Yitong lucheng tuji* 一統路程圖記, reprinted in Yang Zhengtai 楊正泰, *Mingdai yizhan kao* 明代驛站考 (Shanghai: Shanghai guji chubanshe, 2006), 207, 278.

9 The painting is also reproduced in Li and Watt, eds., *The Chinese Scholar's Studio*, 144; see as well the discussion of the painting in Jamie Greenbaum, *Chen Jiru (1558–1639): The Background to Development and Subsequent Uses of Literary Personae* (Leiden: Brill, 2007), 183.

10 Dong Qichang and Chen Jiru are also featured in a similar group portrait from about this time, though without Li, by Huang Cunwu 黄存吾 (act. late seventeenth century), *Noble Gathering at Green Wood*, reproduced in Ho, *The Century of Tung Ch'i-ch'ang*, vol. 1, 4. A detail showing Li and Chen appears on page 2.

11 Chen Guan was in regular correspondence with Li, as he must have been with Chen Jiru. The three-way connection is apparent in a diary entry of 1611, when Li received from Chen Guan an essay by Chen Jiru commemorating a new shrine to Fang Xiaoru 方孝儒 (1357–1402), a high official executed by the Yongle emperor for remaining loyal to the nephew he overthrew. Fang was only rehabilitated in the Wanli era; the shrine was erected in part through the efforts of the Catholic convert Yang Tingyun. Li Rihua, *Weishui xuan riji*, 186–87.

12 This period is closely observed in Celia Carrington Riely, "Tung Ch'i-ch'ang's Life," in *The Century of Tung Ch'i-ch'ang*, vol. 2, 409–19. Li Rihua remains curiously silent about the much-publicized controversy surrounding Dong's son's kidnapping of Dong's maidservant/lover Lüying in April–May 1616. The silence may be because Li's recurring eye illness flared up on May 11 and he suspended writing in his diary until June 1; *Weishui xuan riji*, 526. The last reference of Dong in the diary appears to be April 7, though I have not yet confirmed this.

13 Li Rihua, *Weishui xuan riji*, 145, 198, 209, 227, 262, 549. For a later example from 1629, all three provide colophons for a painting by Du Qiong 杜瓊 (1396–1474) now in the Shanghai Museum; see Ho, *The Century of Tung Ch'i-ch'ang*, vol. 2, 564. For a calligraphic work by Zhao Mengfu 趙孟頫 (1254–1322) in the Shanghai Museum with colophons by Dong and Li though not Chen, see page 570.

14 All three colophons are transcribed and translated in Ho, *The Century of Tung Ch'i-ch'ang*, vol. 2, 110–12, and reproduced on pages 256–57; Li's phrase "preserve the spirit of the untrammeled" appears on page 112. The handscroll is reproduced in vol. 1, 310–11. Li's colophon can also be found in his collected writings, *Tianzhi tang ji* 恬致堂集 (reprint, *Siku jinhuishu congkan*; Beijing: Beijing chubanshe, 2000), 36.28.

15 Greenbaum, *Chen Jiru*, 18–19, 260–61. Chapter 2 of Greenbaum's book provides the best account thus far of what reclusion consisted of and signified in the late Ming era.

16 Li Rihua, *Weishui xuan riji*, 262.

17 Ibid., 51.

18 For comparable examples, see his *Reclusion in the Summer Mountains* of 1355; *Reading in the Spring Mountains*, and *Living in Reclusion in the Qingbian Mountains* of 1366. On the last of these paintings, see Richard Vinograd, "Family Properties: Personal Context and Cultural Pattern in Wang Meng's Pien Mountains of A.D. 1366," *Ars Orientalis* 13 (1982): 1–29.

19 The influence is attested in his *Landscape in the Manner of Huang Gongwang*, reproduced in James Cahill, *The Painter's Practice: How Artists Lived and Worked in Traditional China* (New York: Columbia University Press, 1994), 91. Cahill reproduces another Li Rihua landscape on page 106.

20 Zhao Mengfu was also appreciated for his landscapes, though Dong Qichang's evaluation of Zhao as a less inspired painter than the other Four Masters of the Yuan affected the views of his friends. Li was nonetheless keen to collect Zhao's work. He made a particular point of noting a poem of Zhao's in an album of Yuan calligraphy that one of his regular dealers brought to him on November 3, 1609, in which Zhao relates how he climbed a mountain to search out a recluse and, not finding him, wrote the poem instead; Li Rihua, *Weishui xuan riji*, 47.

21 Ibid., 258.

22 Ibid., 209.

23 Ibid., 313.

24 One painting by Li Zhaoheng is reproduced in Ho, *The Century of Tung Ch'i-ch'ang*, vol. 1, 302.

25 Li Rihua, *Weishui xuan riji*, 369.

26 The pressure to acquire ineffable markers of status distinction is part of the argument presented in my "Family Continuity and Cultural Hegemony: The Gentry of Ningbo, 1368–1911," in *Chinese Local Elites and Patterns of Dominance*, ed. Joseph Esherick and Mary Rankin (Berkeley: University of California Press, 1990), 38–41.

27 Li Rihua, *Weishui xuan riji*, 48.

約菴張學曾

"Traces buried among the market towns": Literary Expressions of Reclusion

Jonathan Chaves

1 The dichotomy between "going forth" to serve in the civil service bureaucracy and "withdrawing" to some degree of reclusive retirement is so essential in Chinese thought that it may be considered a timeless component of Chinese civilization. Nor is it a merely Daoist as opposed to Confucian concept; Confucius 孔子 (traditional dates 551–479 BC) himself famously declares in his *Lunyu* 論語 (Analects 7:11): "When they make use of you, then act; when they reject you, then hide away" 用之則行, 舍之則藏. He is speaking to Yan Hui 顏回 (sixth century BC), his favorite disciple. To "hide away" (*cang* 藏) implies withdrawal and reclusion of some kind, but with a readiness to re-emerge and serve when times improve. The dynamic of choice between these two courses of action will run throughout Chinese history and constitute a perennial theme in poetry and painting, as well as in other forms of expression.

In the era represented by the works in this exhibition, the later Ming and Qing dynasties, new importance would be given to this theme, partially under the pressure of the traumatic invasion of China in 1644 by the Manchus and their establishment of the Qing dynasty. Qian Chengzhi 錢澄之 (1612–1693)—a thinker and poet who was a friend or associate of several painters in this exhibition—provides an essential grounding for renewed interest in reclusion, one derived from the classic *Yi jing* 易經 (Book of changes) and thus, as shall be seen, rooted in the cosmological thinking fundamental to the Chinese worldview. But, in keeping with a familiar pattern in Chinese intellectual history, he is not asserting something new but rather rediscovering something ancient and giving it new meaning for the contemporary world.

Thus two generations before Qian, when Dong Qichang 董其昌 (1555–1636) added a second inscription to his *Landscape Evoking a Poem by Wang Wei* (1626; cat. no. 9), providing a poem of his own, he wrote:

Green forests burgeon with flourishing verdure,
Tall pines thrust above the forest crest:
That is why the Paths of Scholar Jiang
Are lovely, even without bamboo!

青林鬱蒙茸, 長松度林表.
所以蔣生逕, 無竹亦自好.

FIG. 24 Zhang Xuezeng, *Fisherman Recluse* (detail; cat. no. 25)

Every reader would immediately have recognized Scholar Jiang as Jiang Xu 蔣詡 (69 BC–17 AD), a Han-dynasty figure who, disgusted at the usurpation of power by the power-hungry Wang Mang 王莽 (45 BC–23 AD), withdrew to a humble residence in his hometown, cutting three paths through the brambles so as to allow visits by upright colleagues. So established does this literary allusion become that even the term "three paths" alone suffices to conjure up righteous reclusion.

Elsewhere Dong makes use of another classic allusion, this time to a prose work by the great Tang-dynasty thinker Han Yu 韓愈 (768–824), a man revered for his attempt to revive Confucian thought at a time of Buddhist and religious Daoist dominance at court. The key "Neo-Confucian" revivalists of the Northern Song dynasty (960–1127) and after would see him as the forerunner of their epochal movement, which in turn would spread beyond China's borders to Korea and Japan. In the year 801, Han composed the "preface" (*xu* 序) "Seeing Off Li Yuan on His Retirement to Pangu (Twisting Valley)" 送李愿歸盤谷序, which is followed by a poem in archaic meter praising Li's decision. Here Han describes the valley where Li was going as a virtual paradise on earth, where "the streams are sweet, and the soil rich, the plants and trees bursting with life, and the citizens few in number" 泉甘而土肥，草木藂茂，居民鮮少. Dong depicted the scene as an idyllic landscape and inscribed the complete text of the Han Yu work in a colophon, formatting the whole as a handscroll.[1]

In so doing, as with the Jiang Xu allusion, Dong was participating in an age-long tradition of employing precisely these allusions to conjure the atmosphere of reclusion. In his own colophon after the text, he notes that Han's composition was itself rooted in the tradition of the *Li sao* 離騷 (Encountering sorrow, fourth century BC) and other poems attributed to China's earliest recorded poet, the great Qu Yuan 屈原 (c. 340–278 BC), who is said to have written as a result of his own exile into reclusion in the far south of Hunan. There, despite the advice of a fisherman to "go with the flow" by remaining in pure withdrawal until he might once again go forth to serve in the admittedly "muddy" world, the stern Qu decided instead to commit suicide by jumping into a river.

As early as the Northern Song dynasty the Han Yu preface and poem were inspiring painters. Wen Tong 文同 (1019–1079), best known for his brilliant bamboo paintings but also for his landscapes, is known to have done a "Painting of Pangu Valley"[2] (now lost). By the Yuan dynasty (1279–1368), when China was commanded by a Mongol regime, Han's literary masterpiece took on even greater poignancy as now there was another, and deeper, reason to "withdraw." The important Southern Song poet and literary theorist Lü Benzhong 呂本中 (1084–1145) wrote a poem that was inscribed on a now-lost "Painting of Pangu Valley" by a certain Zhao Zuwen 趙祖文 (early twelfth century),[3] and his interpretation, centuries earlier than the late Ming–early Qing period, prepared the ground for what would become an important dimension in the reclusion theme:

> Young Chao sets his brush to silk to paint the "Twisting Valley":
> Ah, indeed, this was a time of perfect peace on earth!
> Today, up in those Taihang Mountains, how could it be so?
> The woodcutters who gather there are all barbarians now!
>
> 〈題趙祖文盤谷圖〉，趙郎落筆寫盤谷.
> 正是太平無事時，今日太行那有此.
> 滿山樵採盡胡[癡]兒.

Pangu Valley is in a part of northern China that, in 1126–27, fell into the hands of the Jurchen Tungus Jin dynasty (1115–1234); in Lü's day, the whole of northern China was thus under foreign occupation, a far cry from the Pangu thus characterized by Han in his poem:

> Tigers and leopards keep their distance:
> Here the dragon may hide away.
> Gods and spirits will protect you, Ah!
> Frightening away all inauspicious things.
>
> 虎豹遠跡兮蛟龍遁藏，鬼神守護兮呵禁不祥.

But now the "woodcutters," usually themselves emblems of peace and harmony, are "illegal aliens," Jurchen invaders!

Soon, of course, an even greater catastrophe would occur, the complete subjugation of China by a different alien regime, the Mongols. Pangu Valley would be elevated by one of the most important literary scholars and critics of the age, Fang Hui 方回 (1227–1307), to the position of the virtual embodiment of reclusion in literature. Presenting poems in categories determined by subject matter, Fang's important and enormously influential anthology of "regulated verse" (poems in eight lines that follow strict rules, such as syntactical and imagistic parallelism in the inner couplets)—*Yingkui lüsui* 瀛奎律髓 (The essence of regulated verse from the literary realm of paradise)—was influential in Japan as well as at home. His introduction to the section on *xianshi* 閒適, "Poems of Leisure,"[4] opens by quoting a section of Han's preface:

> You will live in a remote spot, at leisure, climb to high places for the view; sit all day among flourishing trees, wash in crystal streams to purify yourself; gather in the mountains wonderful things to eat, angle in the waters for fresh fish to dine on.
>
> 窮居而野處，升高而望遠．坐茂樹以終日，濯清泉以自潔．採於山，美可茹；釣於水，鮮可食.

Fang then comments,

> This describes to the full the flavor of "leisure," something poets must have, and cannot do without. And so the inspirations of mountain roaming, country rambling, residence in the plains or in the wilds, and the hidden, serene mysteries of reclusion and freedom are fully expressed in the poems herein selected.
>
> 此能極言閒適之味矣，詩家之所必有而不容無者也，凡山遊郊行，原居野處，幽寂隱逸之趣，於此所選詩備見之.

The very first poem Fang selected is in fact by Wang Wei 王維 (701–761), one of whose couplets inspired Dong Qichang's hanging scroll in this exhibition (cat. no. 9). For our late Ming–early Qing scholars, this long series of unfolding historical events would only add greater gravitas to the Han Yu text. No wonder Dong would found upon it one of his important works. The "Three Paths" and "Pangu Valley," of course, do not exhaust the iconic allusions emblematic of righteous reclusion. But they serve to demonstrate how poetry and painting shared a common heritage of these and would both deploy them to bring the important theme to the fore.

2 That the attractions of reclusion took on even greater appeal because of the fall of China into foreign hands is fully explicit in the writings of the Ming loyalists of the early Qing, whose numbers included several painters of the day. One of the most important and compelling of them was writer and painter Gui Zhuang 歸莊 (1613–1673), the great-grandson of Gui Youguang 歸有光 (1506–1571), one of the finest masters of prose style in the Ming dynasty. Gui Zhuang was stunned by the discovery of the previously lost *Xin shi* 心史 (History of the heart) by Song-dynasty loyalist (and orchid painter extraordinaire) Zheng Sixiao 鄭思肖 (Suonan 所南, 1241–1318). This book, found concealed in a dried-up well, fully and passionately expressed the feelings of despair and anger experienced by the literati when China was conquered by the Mongols in 1279. Reading the book, Gui of course immediately saw the application to his contemporary situation, and he wrote a long "ancient-style" verse as well as a set of no less than ten "regulated verse" poems all employing the same rhyme-words. In the seventh of these,[5] he explodes in indignation in some of the most powerful poetry written in his day:

> Those who drink koumiss and tear at raw lamb are simply not our kind!
> Ah, it is painful to gaze with grieving eyes upon these barbarians!
> But the soul of the hero who tried to assassinate Qin is still powerful today!
> And the bones of that lone official who returned to Chu have not yet dried away!
> Could we not start with partial security, recapturing the southeast?
> Then gradually pursue them back beyond the far northeast?
> Ah, Heaven's heart! If you are plotting for our victory,
> Let the spirit of fire rage and burn, never to be put out!

> 食酪披羶非我徒，難將愁眼向群胡.
> 椎秦壯士魂猶毅，復楚孤臣骨未枯.
> 焉得偏安收粵駱，漸看逐北涉狐奴.
> 天心倘為人謀勝，火德炎炎烈未渝.

Now this, far from being a call to reclusion, is a call to arms. But it serves, of course, to express with eloquence the feelings of the loyalists and others. Gui himself would in fact, like many others, don the black robes of a Buddhist monk, apparently without actual ordination, and thus withdraw from the world while hoping beyond hope that ancient heroes such as the pair alluded to in the second couplet of this poem might still appear on the scene, and expressing his true feelings as well in paintings of bamboo and other subjects.

While being what today might be called a "hawk," Gui was also a great advocate of reclusion as a way to express nobility of sentiment: indeed, we would be wrong to draw the line here at all. For a man thinking like Gui, boldness in battle and boldness in reclusion are *related*; both are expressions of a staunch and upright spirit (see cat. no. 25, fig. 24). The distinction is one of expediency. It would be foolish to attempt an uprising doomed to failure, as the ongoing tragedy of the "Southern Ming" resistance movement was demonstrating. So the wise loyalist increasingly would be expected to support the reclusion option. Gui expresses this matter with characteristic clarity in his 1672 colophon to *Wujun mingxian xiaoji* 吳郡名賢小紀 (Brief annals of the famous worthies of the Wu Region) by late-Ming scholar and calligrapher Wen Zhenmeng 文震孟 (1574–1636),[6] a text probably intended to accompany a similarly named collection of portraits of famous men of the Wu region, for which Gui also wrote a preface.[7] Gui was given a second chance in his life to examine this work, and found himself deeply moved by it:

> Reading his excellency's writing, we understand what he admired. In the case of scholars of noble achievement living in hidden reclusion, he inevitably featured them with glory; but in the case of those with public accomplishments achieved in the full light of day, such as Tutor Yao [Yao Guangxiao 姚廣孝 (1335–1418)] or Xu Wugong [Xu Youzhen 徐有貞 (1407–1472); both men powerful officials, the latter with military accomplishments], he actually expunged them, not including them at all! In judging the lines to be drawn in human relations, or the distinctions between what is correct and what is deviant, is this not to be very strict indeed!

> 讀公之序，知其所尚矣. 於潛隱之士有高行者必表章之，而顯赫如姚少師，徐武功，則黜而不載. 於人倫之際，邪正之辨，不亦嚴乎.

But it becomes clear that Gui *admires* this strictness:

> I once found a letter from this gentleman to my late father in an old basket; although it consisted of only a few columns of text, I have greatly treasured it, because a man like this gentleman is himself truly an outstanding example of a "famous worthy."

> 嘗於故簏中得公答先君書，雖數行猶寶藏之，蓋如公者，尤名賢之卓卓者云.

Thus for Gui, and others of his generation who thought as he did, in the absence of any realistic hope of a military uprising against the Manchus, reclusion was seen as the noblest of endeavors, implying, as it does, silent protest.

Understanding of the complexity of the concept of reclusion for Gui Zhuang's generation has recently been enhanced by the first modern publication of the collected works of scholar, thinker, poet, and man of letters Qian Chengzhi.[8] Proscribed during the "literary inquisition" of the mid-eighteenth century instituted by the Qianlong emperor 乾隆 (r. 1735–1796) because it was deemed excessively "anti-Manchu," Qian's prose writings, poems, and scholarly investigations of the classic *Yi jing* established him as a key theoretician of reclusion for his times. Characteristically for a Chinese thinker, he does not present his ideas in individual monographs but rather in nuggets of ideas placed in his various writings. By drawing upon Qian's newly available works, we come to understand that rather than a simple dichotomy between "service" and "reclusion," the men of the day were grappling with a *spectrum* of what might be called degrees of reclusion and trying to determine just how *much* and what *kind of* reclusion suited the current situation.

Qian's importance for the circles of interest to us in connection with the current exhibition is indicated by two facts alone. First, Qian Qianyi 錢謙益 (1582–1664), whose calligraphic handscroll in the exhibition (cat. no. 29) is a particularly important example of his work, was one of the leading cultural arbiters of the day; when he compiled an anthology of poetry by his disciples and close associates, *Wu zhi ji* 吾炙集 (An anthology of works by those close to me), he included more poems by Qian Chengzhi than by any other writer (it remains unclear whether the two men, both of the Qian clan, were in fact closely related). Secondly, Zhuo Erkan 卓爾堪 (1653–1712), one of the colophon writers on the Gong Xian 龔賢 (1619–1689) hanging scroll *Boating in the Breeze* (cat. no. 35), was also the compiler of the single most important anthology of poetry by Ming loyalists, *[Ming] Yimin shi* 明遺民詩 (Poems by [Ming] loyalists)—also, of course, proscribed under Qianlong—which included one hundred or more poems by only *three* poets, Qian Chengzhi among them.

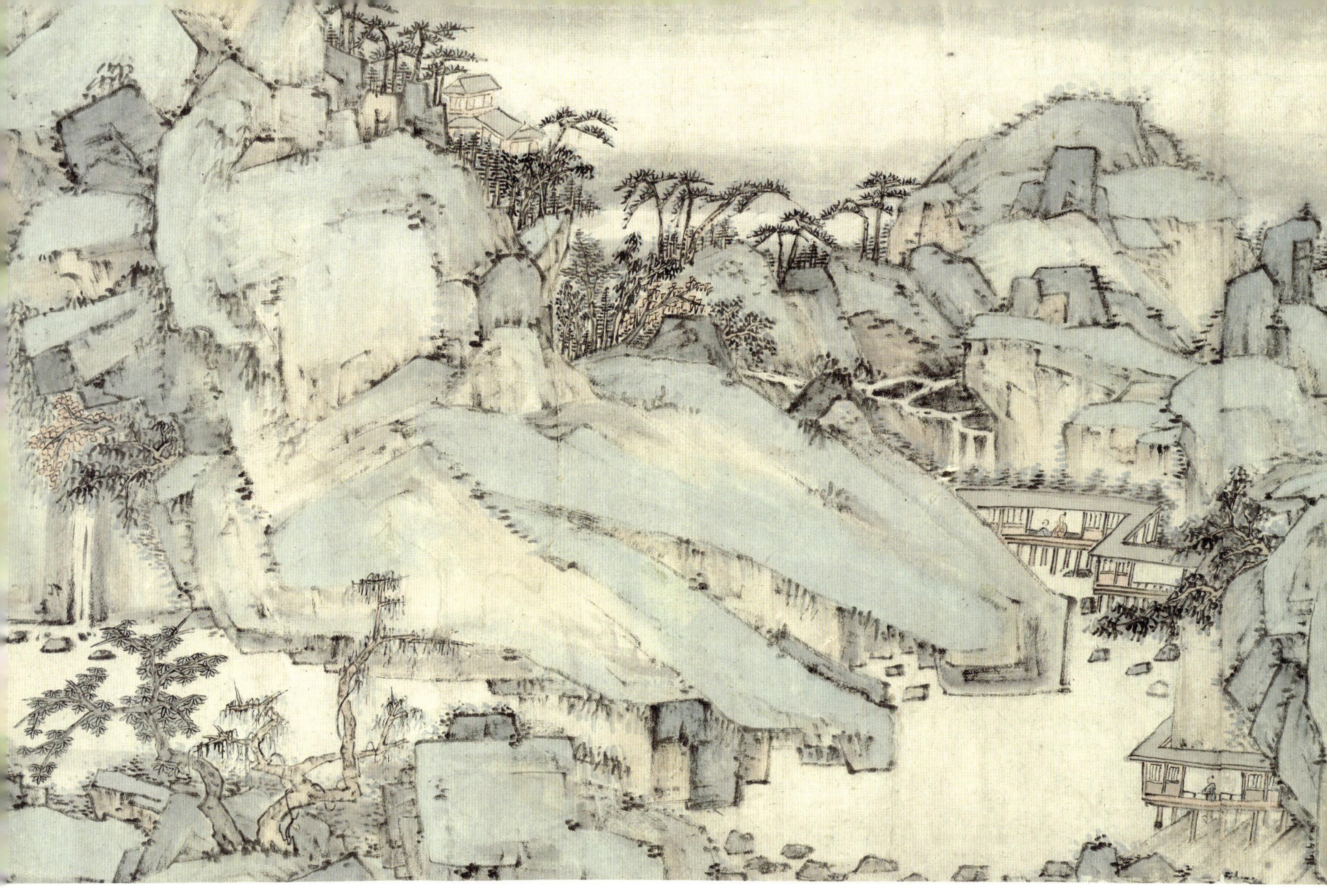

Even a cursory glance at Qian's collected writings will reveal his friendship with a number of the leading painters of the day, including several figures represented in this exhibition. Take for example his poem "Sent to Xiao Chimu Requesting a Painting" (1659)[9]—Xiao Chimu 蕭尺木 being the master painter Xiao Yuncong 蕭雲從 (1596–1673; cat. no. 24, fig. 25), a contributor to this exhibition and the founding father of the so-called Anhui School of painting that played a key role in the literati art world of the day, and of which Zha Shibiao 查士標 (1615–1698; cat. no. 49) was a major exponent. Qian characteristically and tellingly refers to Xiao as *chushi* 處士, "retired scholar" or "recluse" (or, in a specifically Buddhist context, "layman"). What is more, he openly refers to Xiao's apparent controverting of the literati amateur ideal by *selling* paintings! This is in fact an important theme: the idea that by candidly engaging in mercantile activity, one can register a protest. These are times when one should *hide away*; but ironically, by participating in the world of business (ordinarily held in contempt by the literati), one can express one's view that the times are wrong for "service."

"Sent to Xiao Chimu Requesting a Painting"

I am so fond of Recluse Xiao,
With his white hair, growing old beneath the Yangzi sky!
He has buried his traces among the market towns,
Shut his gate beside wind-driven waves.
He offers the monks just a bowl of rice,
Sells his paintings for a little spare change.
He promised to paint and send me some green mountains,
And he's owed them to me for ten years now!

〈寄蕭尺木索畫〉

吾憐蕭處士，白髮老江天.
埋跡市廛裡，閉門風浪邊.
供僧惟一飯，賣畫有閒錢.
許寫青山寄，欠來已十年.

Qian sees Xiao—the master painter frankly selling his work to make a living—as a type of recluse like himself, avoiding in his special way the "wind-driven waves," an ancient image for difficult times. Although he is living in "public," he might as well have "shut his gate," as he has *withdrawn* from the field of public service expected of a Confucian literatus. And although not a monk himself, he feels a bond with Buddhist monks whose reclusion is, of course,

FIG. 25 Xiao Yuncong, *Landscape* (detail), 1657 (cat. no. 24)

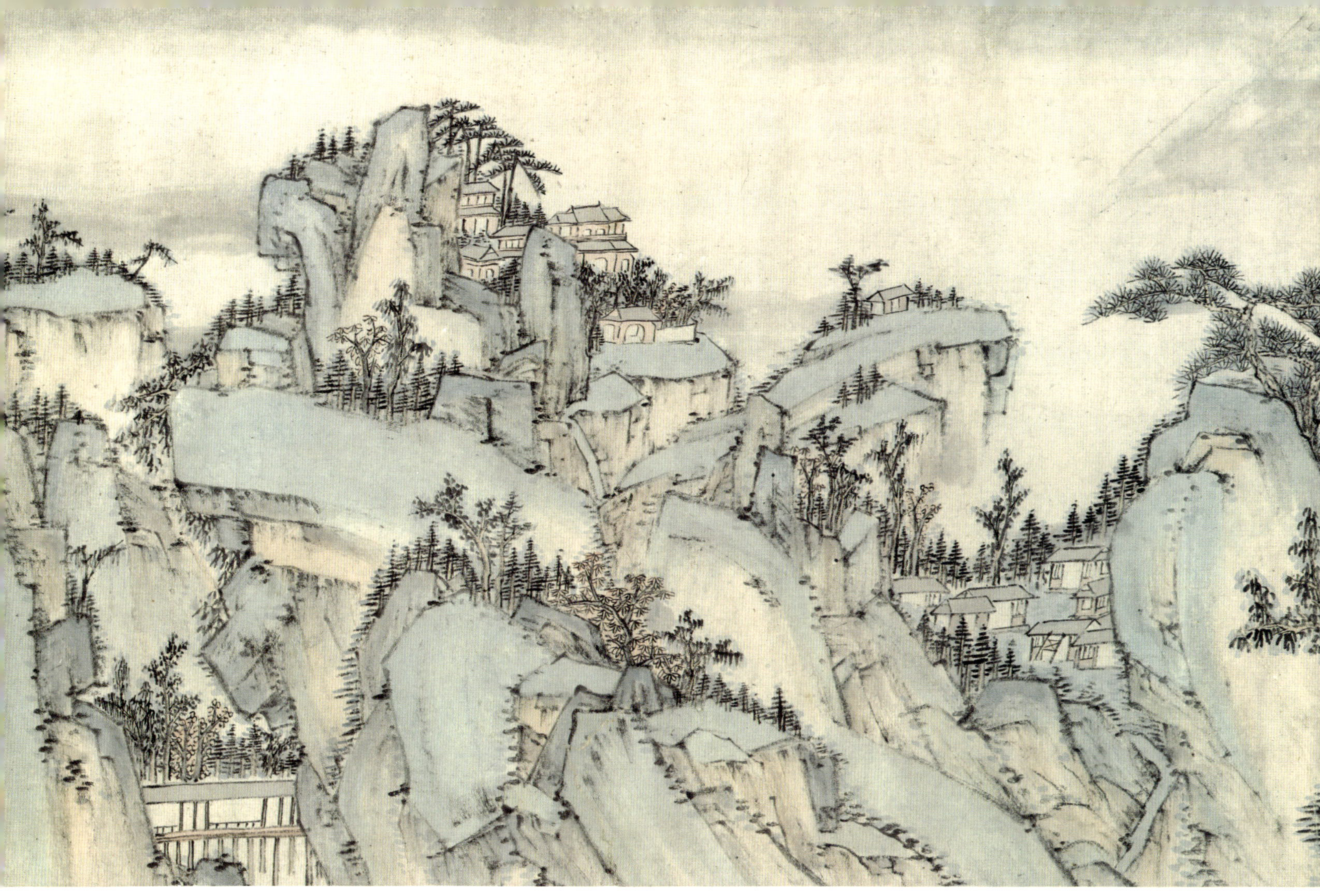

of a much more thorough variety. In a prose colophon attached to a handscroll at the Los Angeles County Museum of Art dated 1669 (just four years prior to his death), Xiao himself states, "For several years, when I've found myself at liberty, I have devoted my feelings entirely to mountains and gullies!" 數歲自放，唯縱情丘壑. Thus Xiao sees himself as a participant in the literati-cum-Buddhist world of withdrawal into nature, as if he were one of the tiny figures inhabiting the partially obscured pavilions depicted with such serenity in the painting itself.

That such men as Xiao and Qian should have associated intimately with noted Ming loyalists, or have been such "loyalists" themselves, is not surprising. Qian, in a poem penned one year after "Sent to Xiao Chimu Requesting a Painting," describes a gathering at the Nanjing home of perhaps the single finest of loyalist poets, Gu Yuzhi 顧與治 (or Mengyou 夢游, 1599–1660), whose portrait (now in the Nanjing Museum) by the great portrait painter Zeng Jing 曾鯨 (1564–1647; cat. no. 2)—with landscape elements added by Zhang Feng 張風 (d. 1662; cat. no. 30)—is one of the great masterpieces of Chinese portraiture (fig. 26).[10] Also present were no less than six other leading lights of the loyalist camp:

"On the third day of the first month of the year *gengzi* [1660], attending a gathering at the home of Gu Yuzhi, together with Shen Zhonglian, Yang Shangxian, Zeng Qingli, Fang Erzhi, Mei Shaosi, and Chen Boji"

Rain obscures the springtime city, although the way's not far:
On travelers' journeys, we gather here, to "praise the
pepper blossoms."
Deep in our cups, intoxicated, full of wanderers' feelings;
In this old house, dark and chill, a retired Recluse's home.
The new season—already we mourn the three days passed away;
Our temple hairs—altogether, turned gray for ten years.
Tomorrow morning must embark my boat, back to the mountains:
Sadness will kill me—the lonely cabin, moon-shadows slanting across.

〈庚子正三日沈仲連，楊商賢，曾青藜，方爾止，梅杓司，陳伯璣，同集顧與治宅〉

雨隔春城路未賒，客途相聚頌椒花.
深杯潦倒羈人興，老屋陰寒處士家.
時事又憐三日過，鬢毛總向十年華.
明朝便發還山櫂，愁煞孤篷月影斜.

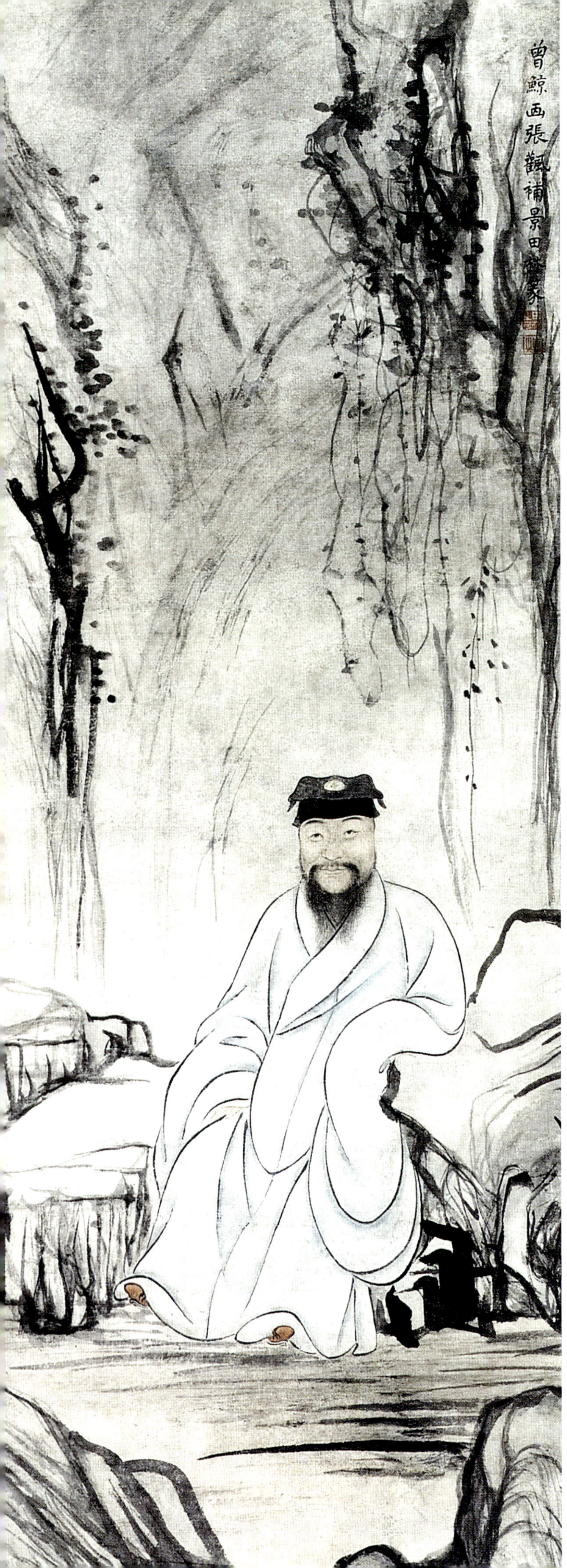

Gathered to "praise the pepper blossoms"—that is, the New Year, once famously celebrated by the wife (née Chen 劉臻妻陳氏, d. 156) of the feudatory Prince Liu Zhen in a eulogy in praise of pepper blossoms—these men are at the city home of Gu Mengyou, who, like Xiao Yuncong in the previous poem, is described as a *chushi*, even though he resides in the city of Nanjing. The poet, indeed, must leave tomorrow for "the mountains." Reclusion, again, comes in many forms.

Direct contact between Qian Chengzhi and contributors to this exhibition are easily established. Zhang Feng, who added the landscape details to Zeng Jing's portrait of Gu Mengyou, is one of the twenty-nine friends to whom Qian addressed a series of regulated-verse (eight-line) poems praising Zhang's artistry as a painter with a degree of directness unexpected in literati writing.[11] Ordinarily, painting tends to be presented as a "secondary" activity, the study of the classics and the writing of traditional poetry being presented by convention as primary:

> Men whose ink-work is as wonderful as yours are rare in this
> world of ours!
> Gazing at your "playful wanderings" makes me forget plotting
> and planning!
> Your purse may not be totally empty because of losing cash,
> But scrolls piled high produce enough for you to splurge on wine!
> Now, a guest from far, I must return, after staying over:
> Many times we've planned to travel—the time comes, we miss
> the date!
> At Pine Wind Pavilion, there is the stone known as Fields of Blue:
> You promised me to carve a seal from it, but so far it's never come!

> 墨妙如君世亦希, 看君游戲破忘機.
> 囊非正乏輸錢卻, 卷自成堆得酒揮.
> 遠客乍還經宿去, 貴遊屢約及期違.
> 松風閣上青天石, 許為鐫還竟不歸.

Although the precise allusion in the final couplet is unclear, Zhang certainly was a renowned seal carver, and Fields of Blue (or Qingtian soapstone, usually from Zhejiang) was particularly prized for the carving of seals.[12] Apparently Qian Chengzhi was waiting for a seal promised to him, as he was promised a painting from Xiao Yuncong! For our present purpose though, the most significant point is that painting *itself* is linked with reclusion here, in the sense that looking at a fine painting can inspire one temporarily to leave behind the "plotting and planning" of the ordinary world.

Of the major painters of the day, the one to whom Qian Chengzhi was closest was the monk Kuncan 髡殘 (b. 1612; cat. no. 37, fig. 27). Not only did Qian compose several poems to or about Kuncan, but he wrote a brief biographical account of him as well.[13] In this, he relates details of his own relationship with Kuncan:

> Whenever the two of us get together, we would happily chat. He would bring out tea and fruit, and keep me with him all day long. This became a regular habit of ours. The Master was born in the same year as I [1612], very tall and dazzling, his head as white as snow—and yet completely bald winter or summer. His body and limbs were barely able to tolerate cold or humidity, and he was often in pain,

FIG. 26 Zeng Jing and Zhang Feng, *Portrait of Gu Mengyou*; Hanging scroll: ink and color on paper; 105.4 × 45 cm; Nanjing Museum

suffering to a great degree. And for these reasons, he called himself "Kuncan" [Bald Remnant]. He was a man of noble and wonderful demeanor, and heavenly appearance. His understanding was simply transcendent. At a time when "clubbing and shouting" [modes of Chan/Zen instruction] were popular in the world, upon encountering such techniques, he would cover his ears and quickly run away. He would at times write poems which never followed the rules, and yet certain lines or phrases of his would often startle one out of one's ordinary way of thinking. And interspersed with these, he would paint landscapes and human figures of his own devising, completely transcending ordinary pathways.

I once said, "Shixi [Kuncan] has formed his own type of poetry, formed his own type of painting, and has even formed his own type of Chan [Zen]!"

He was very testy by nature, and intolerant, but he got along very well with me. Whenever I saw him, we would converse freely, and he would make the most remarkable jokes, holding nothing back! He once said to me, "When Mr. So-and-so writes, he tries to make sure that each and every line is incomprehensible to others. When you write, you try to make sure that each and every line is *comprehensible* to others, and this pleases me!"...

One day, he, Mr. Huoxi [unidentified], and myself together were en route to attend a vegetarian meal south of the city; I myself was wearing monk's garb. As we passed a small alleyway, we saw a lusty woman standing there, arms crossed, heavily and sloppily made up, eying the men going by. Once we had passed, the Master, as if protective of me, said, "How is it comprehensible that there are those in this world who are actually attracted to such a filthy thing as that?" I teased him, saying, "As I went by I did not see any *thing*! Why did you alone notice it?" The Master pointed at me and cursed, "You're too nasty!" With this, the three of us cracked up and burst out laughing! Alas, the friendly experiences of those times are still alive right before my eyes!

每予兩人至，則相與劇談，出茗果，留坐竟日，以為常. 師與予同年生，頎而皙，頭白如雪，冬夏一禿頂. 身臂少受寒濕，時作痛，甚厭苦之，因自號髡殘. 天姿高妙，見解超然. 當海內棒喝交馳之時，所過掩耳疾走. 時有吟誦, 都不入格，一言半句往往出人意表. 間以己意作山水人物，脫盡常蹊.
吾嘗謂石谿自成其詩，自成其畫，亦自成其禪也.
性卞急，不能容物，顧喜予率易. 予每見，輒縱談，諧謔雜出，無所隱諱. 嘗語予曰：某公為文，句句要人不解. 子為文，句句要人解...
一日，同藿溪及予同赴城南齋，予亦僧服，過小巷，有壯婦塗粉狼籍，叉手當門目之. 既過，師字予曰，世間有如此穢物，人偏好之，何可解也. 予嬈之曰：我過未見有物，汝何自獨見之. 師指罵曰：忒欺心. 三人相與絕倒大笑. 嗚呼！其一時情事聲容猶宛然在也.

The combination of Buddhist and literati interests characteristic of Kuncan as depicted here is perfectly conveyed by his masterpiece in this exhibition, *Temple on a Mountain Ledge* (1661; cat. no. 37, fig. 27). Here a Buddhist temple is not so much surrounded as embraced by mountains on all sides, but the front, in accordance with geomantic *fengshui* 風水 principles, is open to the panoramic view. The sacred man-made temple and the auspicious structures formed by nature's creative power exist in a perfect synergy.

Aside from the delightful portrait Qian Chengzhi provides of a friendship between two talented men of the period, he reveals that he too would actually wear Buddhist robes at times; indeed, Qian for a period of time was actually a monk himself. And yet, as shall be seen, his attitude towards Buddhism was conflicted in an interesting way.

3 When a Chinese scholar of any historical period raises ultimate questions about ontology and cosmology, he looks to the *Yi jing* for answers.[14] In keeping with the essentially cosmological nature of classical Chinese thought, it was understood that human affairs and the workings of the cosmos were in relation to each other, and were thus underpinned by the same primordial elements. These are represented by sixty-four "hexagrams" (groupings of six lines), themselves constituted of two of the eight "trigrams." The lines in question are of two types: solid (associated with the *yang* or male force) and broken (once, in the center, associated with the *yin* or female force). The workings of the entire cosmos were understood to consist of interactions between these, and the trigrams and hexagrams are emblematic of the various elemental forces and phenomena generated by this interaction of key polar powers.

At times of great tension, there would naturally occur revivals of interest in the *Yi jing*, and Qian Chengzhi—with his important work *Tianjian Yi xue* 田間易學 (Studies of the *Book of Changes* from amongst the fields)—established himself as one of its key scholars during the early Qing. In a poem praising a friend and fellow student of the classic called Mr. Zeng, whom he claims is a descendent of Confucius's disciple Zeng Xi 曾皙 (or Master Zeng, sixth century BC), Qian writes, "I too am one who studies the *Changes*, / Dedicated to the task with grim stubbornness!" 我亦學易者，執志苦拘牽.[15]

This important poem opens by reciting the origin of the Eight Trigrams, which were formed by the culture hero Fuxi: "Fuxi formed the Eight Trigrams; / Heaven and Earth have passed along their secrets" 宓羲作八卦，天地祕以宣. Thus the trigrams, and the hexagrams they in turn generate, go back to the very beginning of history and, indeed, of meaningful existence. They are the foundation stones of Being. "In their essence, they never move; / In their application, they are like a ring" 其體本不動，其用乃如環. Here Qian employs an important dichotomy in Chinese thought: between a thing's essence (*ti* 體, or basic structure) and its application or actual functioning in the world (*yong* 用, the same term used by Confucius to mean [when the powers that be] *make use of* you [you should serve]). (The distinction is reminiscent of the modern one between pure and applied science.) Thus the polarity of "service" and "withdrawal" actually parallels an alternation of working in the world (society) with renewed attention to the cultivation of one's essential self. Qian Chengzhi further asks that we "[p]lease observe the *Changes* from the Zhou [dynasty]: / Of the hexagrams, none is more honored than *Qian*" 請觀周世易，卦莫尊於乾. *Qian* is the name of the very first trigram and first hexagram, consisting of all-solid (and therefore all-*yang*) lines, whether three or six. These are interpreted one by one, starting from the bottom-most line and working up to the top-most in the *Yi jing* itself. And, as Qian next points out, "All six lines are denominated 'dragons': / And the very first is said to be in 'hiding'" 六爻以龍稱，其初即為潛. That is to say the dragon, taken to represent the scholar himself (or the subject, whoever he might be, of the divination undertaken), begins in hiding or hibernation. However, "The divine dragon does not show his head; / But how can he remain forever in the abyss?" 神龍不見首，豈必長在淵. Or eventually, as the times are propitious, he will emerge from hiding.

Qian Chengzhi's use of a *poem* to articulate philosophical concepts of such importance is entirely in keeping with one aspect of the Chinese poetic tradition, developed to its fullest point by the poets of the Song dynasty (960–1279) who were associated with the great Confucian revival of that period. The school of Song Confucianism known as Lixue 理學 (School of Principle)—associated especially with the brothers Cheng Hao 程顥 (1032–1085) and Cheng Yi 程頤 (1033–1107) and the preeminent leader of the school, Zhu Xi 朱熹 (1130–1200)—itself underwent an important revival in the early Qing, in large measure a response to the crisis of the day. The renewed interest in the *Yi jing* was itself a part of this development.

Tianjian Yi xue began as an act of filial piety, as Qian's father, Qian Zhili 錢志立 (act. late sixteenth–early seventeenth century), had begun the work. Qian Chengzhi recorded his father's ongoing research in a manuscript that was lost but later recovered, supplementing his father's uncompleted study with his own much more extensive composition.

Reclusion surfaces in particular in comments on hexagram number 33, *dun* or "withdrawal." (The character is written 遯, with which 遁, also read *dun*, may be considered interchangeable.) Closely related to this hexagram is number 12, *pi* (or *fou* 否) or "negativity." The hexagrams have this appearance:

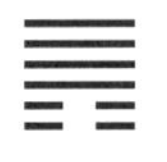

number 33

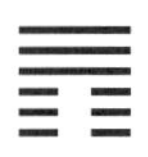

number 12

Reading the lines, as always from bottom up, it can be seen that the broken *yin* lines, here betokening weakening, are gradually encroaching; the situation, in other words, is deteriorating. Qian Chengzhi, who drew upon earlier scholars extensively throughout the book, in his comment on the first line of *dun* cites the Song thinker Cheng Yi to this effect:

> If one were to proceed, as there would be danger, it would be better *not* to proceed, but on the contrary to *hide away* in obscurity, thus avoiding the calamity. That is because in such a circumstance, it is better to take the rear position. Those among the ancients who occupied obscure and humble positions, seeking reclusion *within* the chaotic world and not actually leaving it behind, were many.[16]
>
> 往既有危，不若不往而晦藏，可免於災．處後故也．古人處微下，隱亂世而不去者多矣．

Here is a point of crucial importance for Qian and his entire generation: at a time of crisis, it is essential to find a *balance*—that is, a mode of reclusion that nevertheless puts one in the position of the dragon, which, while hiding now, may eventually rear his head again. This is precisely the point made by Xiang Shengmo 項聖謨 (1597–1658) in the opening couplet of his important poem-sequence on reclusion, inscribed as a colophon to the handscroll in this exhibition (cat. no. 1): "My entering the mountains is *not* to escape the world, / But simply to put ephemeral fame at a distance" 入山非辟世，端為遠浮名. And Xiang explicitly refers to hexagram number 33, citing the *Yi jing*, in the prose colophon to the third of what are in fact his three scrolls inspired by the theme "Summons to the Recluse" (see cat. no. 1)[17]: "The *Changes* states, 'heaven' with 'mountain' below yields *dun* (withdrawal)" 易曰：天下有山，遯.[18] This passage simply describes the structure of the hexagram, with the trigram for heaven (three solid lines) above the trigram for mountain (one solid above two broken lines) below. Wryly commenting on this, Xiang continues, "I indeed possess '[a desire for] withdrawal,' but lack any 'mountain' to which I might retire!" 謨固有遯而無山之可隱. Yet a third major painter, the great calligrapher and poet of the period Fu Shan 傅山 (1607–1684/85), opens the poem inscribed upon one of his landscapes with this remarkable line[19]:

> Beneath Heaven, there are mountains—the quintessence
> of *Reclusion* [*dun*].
>
> 天下有山遯之精.

Fu renders explicit here the implication that if "reclusion" is a hexagram, the principle of withdrawal is *innate* in the structure of the cosmos—in nature itself—and it is preeminently embodied in mountains.

The next stage of deterioration, represented by hexagram number 12, is itself poised against hexagram number 11, "positivity" or *tai* 泰, which precedes it in the overall sequence. Qian Chengzhi gives us a key insight in his comment under number 11, *negativity*: "The *negativity* or *positivity* of worldly evolutions is entirely connected to the sovereign's mind/heart: nothing else obtrudes" 世運之否泰全繫於君心，他無與也.[20] This is classic Confucian doctrine: the "Heavenly Mandate" (*tian ming* 天命) to rule depends on the moral caliber of the ruling house, as embodied in the emperor on the throne. He is the fulcrum between Heaven and Earth. Should his mind/heart not be morally sincere (*cheng* 誠), there will be a charismatic effect infecting the entire society that leads to Heaven's passing of the Mandate to a new dynasty. Conversely, if the emperor reflects true moral cultivation (*xiu* 修) in his person, he will facilitate harmonious relations between Heaven and man.

Thus grounding his philosophy of reclusion in the very hexagrams of the *Yi jing*, Qian was in a position to deploy these ideas in his poetic expressions of the theme, as we have already seen. One particularly fine example is the fifth poem from a group of five from 1659, "presented to" the noted Ming loyalist "Retired Scholar" or "Recluse Hu Xingqing" 胡星卿 (1597–1683).[21] After relinquishing a plan to commit suicide like many of his compatriots in the loyalist movement, Hu withdrew into a life of study and associated largely with Buddhist monks, according to his biographical "tomb inscription," which was written by Qian as well.[22] Hu's actions in fact demonstrated dramatically that for this generation, withdrawal into reclusion was in a sense an alternative choice for those who could not bring themselves to engage in the ultimate act of loyalist suicide.

FIG. 27 Kuncan, *Temple on a Mountain Ledge* (detail), 1661 (cat. no. 37)

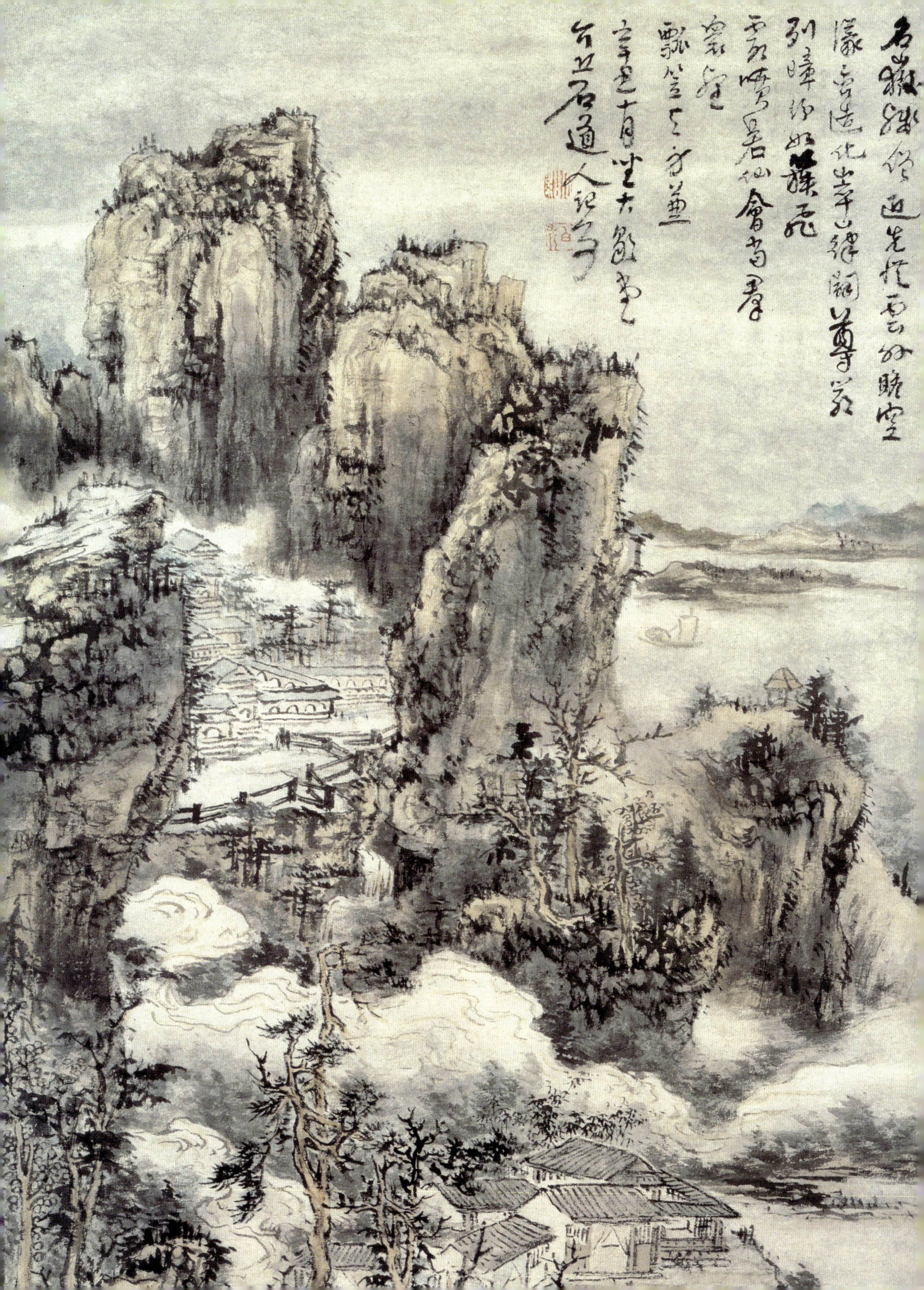

The sagely Way deteriorates day by day;
This man alone remains undimmed.
The Master perceives the great origin of things,
And his mind and actions never do betray it.
He has very little fear of standing alone,
Nor feels he any shame at *withdrawing* [*dun*] from the world.
He holds to virtue with the patience of Kṣānti;
In his studies, emulates the withdrawal of Laozi.
The humane one surely will be a man of courage:
How could the dust ever defile him?
And should he encounter a man of evil doctrine,
How passionately he will rebut him!
And who would guess that beneath his mild manners
The dragon nature persists eternally?

〈贈胡處士星卿〉

聖道日荒蕪，斯人固無昧.
夫子窺太初，心行果不背.
既鮮獨立懼，亦辭遯世悔.
德秉羼提忍，學遵老子退.
仁者必有勇，汶汶豈一概.
忽遇邪說人，辨論何慷慨.
豈知馴擾中，龍性固常在.

Here is high praise indeed, elevating Hu to the rank of perfect exemplars of true reclusion. It should be noted as well that in addition to the terminology drawn from the *Yi jing*, the Daoist master Laozi 老子 (traditional dates sixth century) and the Buddhist *bodhisattva* Kṣānti are used as parallels: all Three Teachings are at one in calling for reclusion.

But here we come to a challenging problem for Qian Chengzhi and his contemporaries. Given that proper reclusion is *balanced*—that if, in the words of Cheng Yi cited by Qian, one is "not actually to leave the world behind" entirely—where then is the line to be drawn? And we see Qian grappling somewhat uncomfortably with this difficult and ultimately unresolved question. We have noted that Qian actually joined the ranks of Buddhist monks for a period of time and, after reemerging into the lay world, would on occasion don a monk's robe (something, by the way, quite common among men of these circles). He clearly maintained close friendships with a number of monks, including the painter Kuncan, and seems always to have held a positive view of the religion. And yet when one particular Chan Master, the monk Langting 俍亭禪師 (1599–1665), asked him to write a preface to a work by him on the great Daoist thinker Zhuangzi 莊子 (fourth century BC), claiming Zhuangzi to have been a forerunner of Buddhism in China, Qian actually refused. In a letter to Langting he explains himself[23] in one of the most cogent statements on what might be called the "problem" of reclusion in the literature of the period. To summarize the rather complex argument, Qian insists that while "What you Buddhists speak of consists entirely of methods for leaving the world behind" 釋家所言皆出世法也, he claims that Zhuangzi never completely dismisses the ordinary world even as he transcends it. Because of this posture, Zhuangzi is better understood as representing a wing of the school of Confucius rather than as a forerunner of Buddhism. There may even be a hint of Han Yu's famous argument that the Chinese should actually reject Buddhism because of its foreign origins.

If the letter to Langting is taken to represent Qian's formal position on the proper balance to be maintained among the Three Teachings of Chinese thought—as well as between reclusion and service in general—virtually his entire body of poetry, perhaps unsurprisingly, presents a more informal, and sometimes even humorous, view of Buddhism and Daoism. An excellent example, and one of Qian's most delightful poems, is "Narrating My Drunkenness—Shown to All Chan Followers,"[24] which perfectly captures the paradoxical Chan Zen attitude towards attempts to discover truth, which are all based on the failure to recognize that one *already* possesses the Buddha nature. Qian indeed echoes the wording of the great Tang dynasty Chan poet Hanshan 寒山 (Cold Mountain; early ninth century?), using a phrase coined by his near contemporary, the Chan monk Mazu 馬祖 (709–788):

I send word to all pursuers of "humaneness":
Why so fond of this "humaneness"?
Return to the source! Know your own nature!
Your own nature itself is Buddha.

寄語諸仁者，仁以何為懷.
歸源知自性，自性即如來.

The "pursuers of 'humaneness'" would be the Confucians, and the Chan response to them was put aside your external searching for truth, you already have truth within. In his poem, Qian Chengzhi is in a sense putting on his "Buddhist" cap, even though in his letter to the monk Langting he had *castigated* Buddhism for being *too* otherworldly! It is apparent that Qian, representative again of his generation, is trying to find a balance between the Confucianism he reveres and the Buddhism he also appreciates. At the same time, he treats us to an amusing parody of the age-old Chinese tradition of associating wine with uplift and inspiration:

Last night, I came home drunk, alone, the last one back;
Out in the street, the moonlight shone, as bright as full daylight.
I told my friends, "No need at all to prop me up like this!
"I may be drunk, but in my heart I can't mistake the way!"
I clearly recall that I returned by way of the northern gate:
The gateman, Tso, held the door wide open, never had been closed.
The boy servant, asleep beneath the steps—I called him,
he didn't wake;
In front of the steps, flower-shadows danced all over my robe.
Loving these shadows, I sat right down and faced the
flowers themselves . . .
Until the young boy helped me up, to lie down in the
bamboo chamber. . .
But then, in the wee hours, I woke, sure I was lying on the stairs,
In the deserted courtyard, filled with wind and dew, feeling miserable.
I vaguely recalled the doorway lay somewhere along the wall:
Groping the wall, seeking the door—"Where is it, after all?"
How could I know that my body was already *inside* the door?
How could I somehow find the door to make my way within?
In a flash, I realized—and felt ashamed, yet glad:
To use the mind to find the mind must be the same as this!
I send word to my fellow-followers of the school of Chan:
"The householder, I've always been at home, inside my house!"

〈述醉示諸禪人〉

昨夜醉歸歸獨後，街頭月色清如晝.
同行不用更扶持，我醉心知路不謬.
分明記向北門歸，左氏門開未掩扉.
階下童子喚不醒，階前花影滿人衣.
愛此花影對花坐，小童扶入竹房臥.
半夜忽疑臥在階，空庭風露還愁大.
猶憶門櫳倚壁開，捫壁求門安在哉.
那知身在門以內，何處求門更入來.
翻然驚覺愧且喜，將心覓心一如此.
寄語同社參禪徒，主人原在儂屋裡.

Qian Chengzhi, like Xiang Shengmo, uses the very phrase "summons to/from reclusion" in the title to another poem, "A Poem Summoning Dicen *from* Reclusion—Drinking Heavily at the Home of Chen Mogong Together with Zuo Zizhi and Zuo Zihou" 滌岑招隱詩同左子直子厚飲陳默公樓上.[25] Chen Mogong, also known as Dicen, was yet another noted Ming loyalist, Chen Zhuo 陳焯 (act. seventeenth century). This poem presents the paradox of a recluse *within* a city. Of Chen we are told,

This country man abruptly came to town;
And where did he park his walking staff?
Neighboring on the homes of two or three old friends,
Cut off in a remote northwestern corner.

野人乍入市，振策何所投.
老友三兩家，僻在西北陬.

But Chen is able to feel like a recluse because:

At sunset, in the shadows of this corner of the city,
He goes on walks, and here he finds his freedom.
In the distance, he loves the view of forest copses, hidden,
Amongst their bends concealing a little hill.
My friend's an expert at lying in convalescence:
For a year thus he has lived in this little house.

日暮城隅隱，散步得自由.
遙愛林麓邃，曲折藏一丘.
我友善臥痾，經年居小樓.

And Chen has made the place even more "reclusive":

He's transplanted bamboo from his old mountain,
The fresh sprouts thriving as they grow.

移植故山竹，新梢頗修修.

Meanwhile, Qian reminisces:

How many friends survive now in these days?
Emerged, retired—not one really planned!
Those retired find sweet the solitude;
Those emerged go through vicissitudes.

存者今幾人，出處各不謀.
處者甘寂寞，出者亦沈浮.

Qian brings the poem to an unexpected close:

My hair—can it become black again?
Your illness—when will it ever heal?
Take elixir, and become an immortal?
—Could such a thing be really true at all?
Best thing is, to drink a lot of wine,
To whistle loud up on the western ridge!

我髮不可黑，子疾何時瘳.
服藥成神仙，此事真有否.
不如多飲酒，長嘯西山頭.

Here it would appear that Qian—playfully? seriously?—suggests that Chen leave his reclusive life, not to serve in government nor to trade it for the greater rigors of Buddhist monasticism, but for a *carpe diem* approach, to drink and enjoy his remaining days! And Qian elsewhere goes even further, intimating that he thinks it might be a good idea for Buddhists to allow themselve to drink wine! In the second poem from his series of twelve imitating the great Tao Qian's 陶潛 (365?–427) famed "Drinking Wine" poems,[26] Qian writes:

Why is it that the followers of Buddha
Do not allow a winecup in the hand?
Perhaps they'll say, "Once break this single vow,
And all the others?—Harder to maintain!"
Well, *my* mind leans towards going with what's natural:
There've never been any vows I could accept!
In fact, when I am all intoxicated,
Even the void entirely disappears!
Let me ask you students of the human heart:
Could *anyone* really live his life like this?

〈倣淵明飲酒二十首〉其二

如何學佛人，不許杯入手.
還言破此戒，諸戒亦難守.
我心任自然，本無戒可受.
方其酣醉時，虛空一何有.
試問學人心，有能如此否.

In fact, Qian's religiosity is broad enough to encompass not only the Three Teachings but veneration for folk religious gods as well. When his boat is unable to proceed because of excessively shallow waters, he joins his boatmen in offering prayers of remorse to the river god.[27] He prays as well at the shrine of one of the Eight Immortals, the immensely popular Lü Dongbin 呂洞賓 (eighth–ninth century).[28] And on one occasion, he hears the sounds of the ghosts of fighting soldiers emerging from a desert shrine to Guan Yu 關羽 (d. 219), the god of war.[29] At the same time, it should be noted that what might be dubbed "secular" modes of reclusion are also recognized by Qian, as in his poem to Xiao Yuncong previously discussed, implying that the practice of painting itself as a profession could be so interpreted, as well as numerous poems to "herbal doctors." One of these is like Qian, himself an ex-monk (who had been a member of the storied monastery at Gold Mountain Island in the Yangzi River) who now finds that "This remained the only course quite suitable to the times" 惟餘此道合時宜[30]—that course being to become a physician who sells herbal medicines, a very humble calling in traditional China.

Thus Qian, in his more formal mode, draws clear lines of distinction, while informally he seems to run the range from *carpe diem* through virtually every mode of religious or philosophical discourse available in his society. Yet we may find that the one theme running through them all is withdrawal—let us avoid the term "escape," because Qian's own examination of certain hexagrams in the *Yi jing* provides the sanction for the idea that this withdrawal, this "reclusion," is the *yin* to the *yang* of service, when the latter becomes suitable.

4 In 1646 the English Metaphysical poet Henry Vaughan (1621–1695), of course utterly oblivious to the fall of the Ming two years earlier, published one of the great monuments of English seventeenth-century literature, *Silex Scintillans* (The scintillating flintstone). In his preface, Vaughan calls upon poets to leave their preoccupation with shallow secular themes and to follow the example of the great George Herbert (1593–1633) in rededicating poetry to religion (that is, to Christianity).

One of the themes Vaughan celebrates is retirement, with two poems of that name.[31] In the first of these, he characterizes himself as a man called back from straying by God's "mild dove," who "Did show me home, and put me in the way." But he cautions those who would follow him:

> If then thou would'st unto my seat,
> 'Tis not the applause, and feat
> Of dust, and clay
> Leads to that way,
> But from these follies a resolved retreat.

The "seat" (home) of which he speaks may be metaphorical, rather than literally indicating a country retreat to which he has withdrawn, and in that regard something like one level of meaning of "Cold Mountain" in the Chan Buddhist poems of Hanshan—the phrase functioning there simultaneously as the poet's name, the name of his place of retreat, and a metaphor for a spiritual state. But Vaughan is clearly working with a dichotomy of being "in" or "withdrawn from" the world, with all its "follies." The "applause" of the latter may be tempting, but is ultimately empty.

In his second poem on the theme of retirement, added years later, Vaughan draws a line between the city (corrupt) and the countryside (the ideal place for reclusion):

> All various lusts in *cities* still
> Are found; they are the *thrones* of ill.
> The dismal *sinks* where blood is spilled,
> *Cages* with much uncleanness filled.
> But *rural shades* are the sweet fence
> Of piety and innocence.
> They are the *meek's* calm region, where
> Angels descend, and rule the sphere:
> Where heaven lies *leiger*, and the *Dove*
> Duly as *dew*, comes from above.
> If *Eden* be one earth at all,
> 'Tis that, which we the *country* call.

Chen Mogong, the Ming loyalist addressed by Qian Chengzhi in the poem "A Poem Summoning Dicen *from* Reclusion," "transplanted bamboo from his old mountain," undoubtedly to remind himself of the country even though he was living in a purposefully remote portion of the city as a "recluse." He would have agreed with Vaughan, as Qian would have done, about the greater closeness to paradise of the country, where one is more likely to encounter *leigers*—that is, ambassadors—from Heavenly realms, or the realms of the Immortals.

And so, at the same time, on two sides of the earth, two poets representative of their times and civilizations dreamed in common of *reclusion*, of distancing oneself from "inauspicious things," from the "follies" of this world.

NOTES

The use of BC/AD over BCE/CE in referencing chronological divisions reflects the personal preference of the author.

1 See the catalogue *Osaka Exchange Exhibition: Paintings from the Abe Collection and Other Masterpieces of Chinese Art* (Osaka: Osaka Municipal Museum of Fine Arts; and San Francisco: San Francisco Center of Asian Art and Culture, 1970), 64–65. For further discussion of the work, and a fine complete translation of the Han Yu text by Diana Chen, see Wai-kam Ho, ed., *The Century of Tung Ch'i-ch'ang* (Kansas City: Nelson-Atkins Museum of Art; and Seattle: University of Washington Press, 1992), vol. 1, plate 9, 152–53; and vol. 2, 15–16.

2 See the painting catalogue by Wu Sheng 吳升, *Da guan lu* 大觀錄 (1712), 13/6a–7b.

3 Lü Benzhong, *Donglai shiji* 東萊詩集, *Siku quanshu* 四庫全書 ed., 16/4a–b. For the reading "barbarians" (*hu'er*) in place of "wild men" (*chi'er*) in *Donglai shiji*, see the text of this poem as given in *Yuding lidai tihuashi lei* 御定歷代題畫詩類, *Siku quanshu* ed., 32/9a–b.

4 Fang Hui, *Yingkui lüsui* 瀛奎律髓, *Siku quanshu* ed., 23/1a–b.

5 Gui Zhuang, *Gui Zhuang ji* 歸莊集, vol. 1 (Shanghai: Guji chubanshe, 1984), 2–3, 12–13; for the poem translated here, see page 13.

6 Ibid., 275.

7 Ibid., 171–72. For more on Gui Zhuang as a poet and painter, see Jonathan Chaves, *Singing of the Source: Nature and God in the Poetry of the Chinese Painter Wu Li* (Honolulu: University of Hawaii Press, 1993), 16, 28–29, 188nn46–47, 189nn71–72 and 74; and Chaves, *The Chinese Painter as Poet* (New York: China Institute in America, 2000), 71–72.

8 The works of Qian Chengzhi were issued by Huangshan shushe, Hefei, in 1998 in seven primary volumes with some additional matter under the general title *Qian Chengzhi quan ji* 錢澄之全集. Consulted for the present study were vol. 1: *Tianjian Yi xue* 田間易學 (hereafter *TJYX*); vol. 5: *Tianjian shiji* 田間詩集 (hereafter *TJSJ*); and vol. 6: *Tianjian wenji* 田間文集 (hereafter *TJWJ*). Also consulted were vol. 3: *Zhuang Qu hegu* 莊屈合詁 (Zhuangzi and Qu Yuan jointly commented upon); and vol. 4: *Cangshange ji* 藏山閣集.

9 *TJSJ*, 108. See also page 19 for another poem to Xiao.

10 Ibid., 114. For the portrait, and for more on Gu Yuzhi or Mengyou, see Chaves, *The Chinese Painter as Poet*, 72–76.

11 *TJSJ*, 141–42.

12 For two examples, see Chu-tsing Li and James C. Y. Watt, eds., *The Chinese Scholar's Studio: Artistic Life in the Late Ming Period* (New York: Thames and Hudson and the Asia Society, 1987), fig. 70, E and F, and page 182.

13 For poems, see ibid., 72, 220, 264, etc. For the biographical sketch, see *TJWJ*, 422–24. For more on Kuncan, especially in terms of his writings, see James Cahill, "K'un-ts'an and His Inscriptions," in Alfreda Murck and Wen C. Fong, eds., *Words and Images: Chinese Poetry, Calligraphy, and Painting* (New York: Metropolitan Museum of Art; and Princeton: Princeton University Press, 1991), 513–34. See also Richard Pegg, "Kuncan: Man, Monk and Painter," *Oriental Art* 40, no. 4 (Winter 1994/95): 2–12.

14 For an excellent English translation of this classic, see Richard John Lynn, *The Classic of Changes—A New Translation of the* I Ching (New York: Columbia University Press, 1994). I have consulted Lynn for translations of the names of hexagrams and other matters.

15 *TJSJ*, 78.

16 *TJYX*, 399.

17 The complete colophon is recorded in Lu Xinyuan 陸心源, *Rangliguan guoyan lu* 穰梨館過眼錄 (1892), 31/5b, and translated by Eun-wha Park in her dissertation "The World of Idealized Reclusion: Landscape Painting of Hsiang Sheng-mo (1597–1658)" (University of Michigan, 1992), 96–98. I am indebted to Peter Sturman for this reference. (Note: there is some difference of interpretation between Park's version of the passage in question and my own.)

18 For the *Yi jing* passage with commentary, see Lynn, *The Classic of Changes*, 341 and 344n2.

19 Wu Yansheng 吳言生, ed., *Fu Shan ji* 傅山集, in the series *Zhongguo jiating jiben cangshu* 中國家庭基本藏書 (Taiyuan, Shanxi: Sanjin chubanshe, 2008), 15–16.

20 *TJYX*, 274.

21 *TJSJ*, 102–3.

22 *TJWJ*, 459–62.

23 *TJWJ*, 71–73.

24 *TJSJ*, 127.

25 Ibid., 30.

26 Ibid., 50.

27 Ibid., 483.

28 Ibid., 340.

29 Ibid., 304, second of the "Bamboo Branch" 竹枝詞 folk-style poems.

30 Ibid., 9; see also poems on pages 41–42, 259, 466, etc.

31 Alan Rudrum, ed., *Henry Vaughan: The Complete Poems* (paperback reprint, 1981; New Haven: Yale University Press, 1976), 222–23, 369. Italics in poems are Vaughan's own.

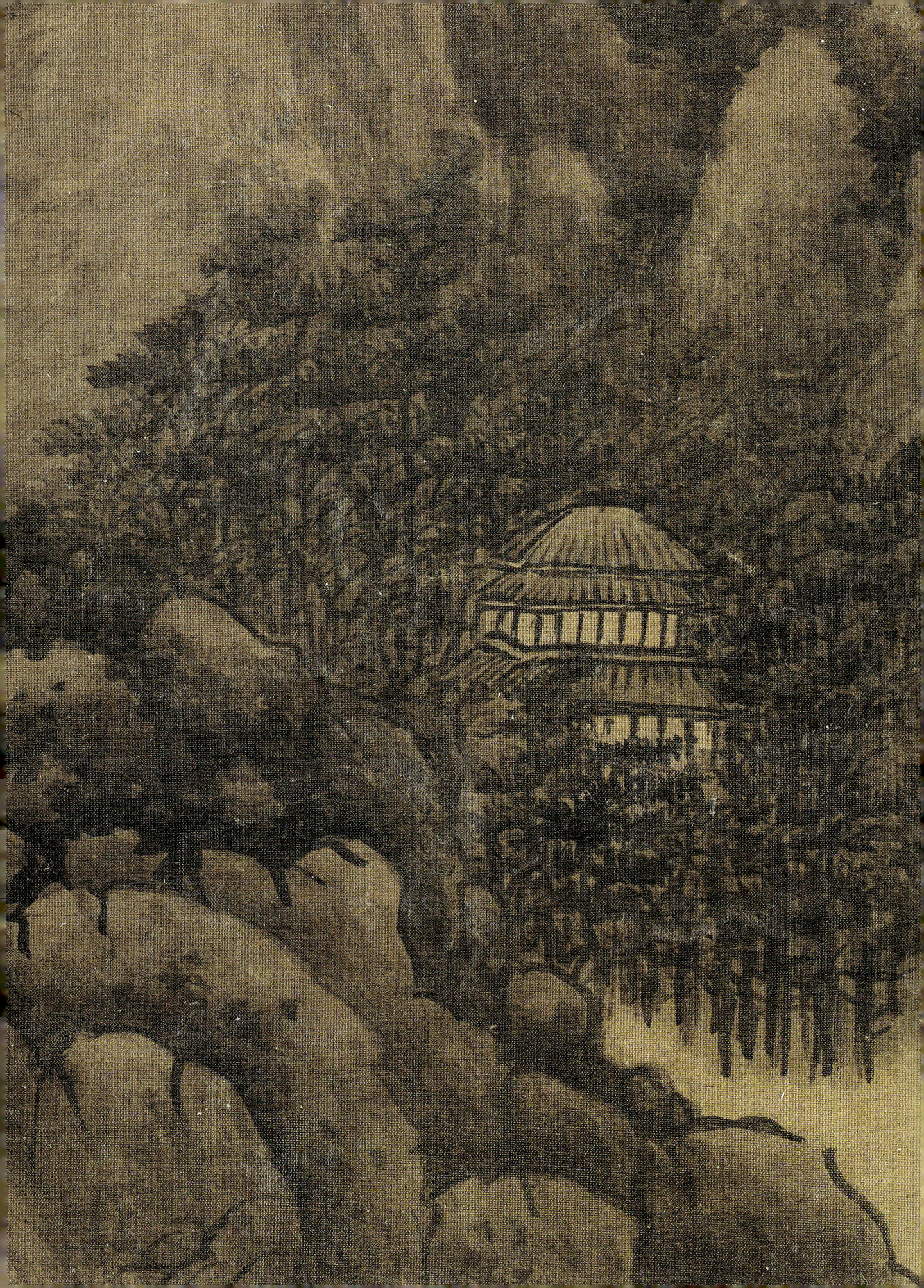

Posttraumatic Art: Painting by Remnant Subjects of the Ming

Jonathan Hay

The fall of the Ming dynasty (1368–1644) was experienced by most educated Chinese as a collective and personal trauma. Confucian education inculcated from childhood the idea that each individual had a family relation to the nation. The 1644 suicide by hanging of the last Ming emperor, Chongzhen 崇禎 (r. 1627–1644)—in response to the fall of the Ming dynasty to Chinese rebels—was therefore equivalent to the death of a father. The rebels themselves, however, would immediately fall in turn to the Manchus, who ruled China after 1644 as the Qing dynasty (1644–1911). The fall of the Ming dynasty thus also meant the loss of the nation. The trauma was double.

The Manchus did not invade the south of China until 1645. At that point, with resistance movements active in many parts there, no one knew whether the Qing dynasty would survive for ten years, let alone two hundred and fifty, but it was already clear that nothing could ever be the same again. In that year, Xiao Yuncong 蕭雲從 (1596–1673), an artist better known for his landscape paintings (cat. no. 24), created an image of a hanged man (fig. 29). It was part of a large series of designs for *Li sao tu* 離騷圖 (Illustrations to "Encountering Sorrow," 1645), a book of illustrations to a poem dating from the early third century BCE when China was not yet unified and states were continuously warring with each other. The original poem evokes a world of chaos and violence in one of those states, and Xiao's illustrations are clearly meant as indirect evocations of the horrors of war in his own time, and of the uncertainty of the future. Although Xiao's image of a hanged man does not directly represent the emperor's death and brings other possible real-life scenarios to mind as well, no educated man in 1645 could have viewed the image without being reminded of Chongzhen's fate.

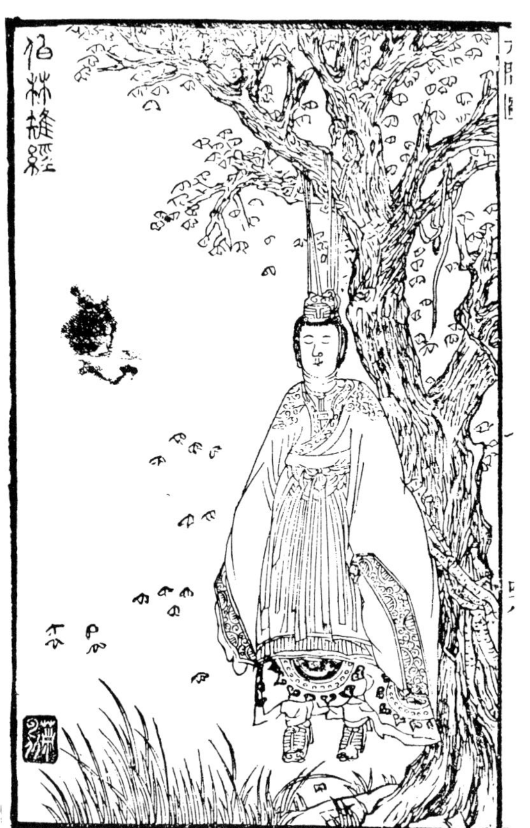

OPPOSITE: FIG. 28 Gong Xian, *Landscape* (detail), 1689 (cat. no. 36)
RIGHT: FIG. 29 Xiao Yuncong, "Suicide by Hanging," from *Li sao tu*; Woodblock prints. From Xiao Yuncong, *Li sao tu* (reprint, Taipei: Guoli Gugong bowuyuan, 1988), 48b.

For Chinese living after 1644, the fall of the Ming dynasty and their country's conquest by the Manchu Qing dynasty were the defining historical events of their lifetimes. Not only did the processes initiated in 1644 disastrously affect individual lives, but they also transformed the terms of political subjecthood for all those who lived through dynastic change. Subjecthood (an individual person's relation to the dynastic state) is at the heart of the present essay. Here I discuss the many different ways in which literati artists' convictions and sentiments about dynastic subjecthood affected their creative practice, conditioning their attempts to come to terms with what had happened and was happening around them. The trauma of what later came to be known as "the transformation" (*bian* 變) or "the chaos" (*luan* 亂) took infinite forms, at all levels of society. The artists generally sought to give voice to a wider suffering than their own, but in ways that were always mediated—and often muffled—by an obsession with answering the question: Of which dynasty am I the subject?

In dynastic subjecthood, two separate Chinese terms are in play. The first is *min* (民), often translated as "the people." Perhaps the most fundamental of this word's various meanings is the mass of the population subject to the emperor and for which he had responsibility. The *min* were divided into four categories that made up a socio-moral hierarchy: from top to bottom were scholars (the basis of the government), farmers, artisans, and finally merchants. However, political discourse also employed a second term, *chen* (臣), literally "servant" or "servitor." *Chen* was much narrower than *min* because it implied at least the possibility if not the reality of government service, and this made it particularly relevant to the educated elite. Referring to oneself in a signature or seal as a *chen* was one of the ways in which artists who remained loyal to the Ming advertised their fidelity, just as court painters working for the Qing emperors were obliged to preface their signatures with a *chen* character, there meaning "your loyal servant." Thus Xiang Shengmo 項聖謨 (1597–1658) signed his 1644 self-portrait, painted in the month following the Chongzhen emperor's suicide, "Xiang Shengmo from south of the Yangzi, a servitor in the wilderness" (cat. no. 20). And Gong Xian 龔賢 (1619–1689), a decade later, impressed a Ming loyalist seal reading "servitor Xian" on *Lofty Peak and Dense Woods* (cat. no. 34).

Broadly speaking, two normative conceptions of dynastic subjecthood had currency in the mid-seventeenth century. The first held that one's status, and thus also one's responsibilities, as political subject were determined by the dynasty under which one had been born. The opposing conception held that the Mandate of Heaven through which a ruling dynasty exercised power played the determining role. As long as the ruling dynasty's possession of the mandate was not seriously challenged, the two conceptions were not in contradiction and indeed were often not distinguished. However, when a dynasty fell, an entirely different kind of situation ensued because the dynasty under which one had been born no longer possessed the mandate. Of course, we have to bear in mind that not everyone at the time accepted that the Ming had lost the mandate in 1644; in fact, an armed Ming loyalist resistance continued as late as 1668. The "fact" that the Ming fell in 1644 was necessarily produced retrospectively.[1] Through the 1650s and even into the 1660s, an undeterminable number of the artists in this exhibition were no doubt still hoping for the restoration of the Ming empire.

During the first twenty-five years after 1644, when the Qing conquest still faced serious armed resistance, the two conceptions of subjecthood described above split apart. A fissure appeared between the sense of responsibility to the Qing dynasty's claim to the Mandate of Heaven, and responsibility to the Ming dynasty under which one was born. If the emperor's relation to his subjects was analogous to a father's relation to his family, how—in a culture that extolled filial piety—could one simply forsake one father for another? Yet, the counter-principle was equally strong. For the mandate was the guarantee of the flow of continuity (*tong* 通) traversing the change (*bian* again) of dynasties. In practical terms, it was the guarantee of the stability that made normal lives possible.

For the educated elite, these considerations were anything but theoretical since the mandate had its practical political realization in the state political apparatus. Government, after all, was the preferred career for those with a Confucian education. For those who privileged a mandate-defined definition of subjecthood, it was possible to conceive of entering Qing government, if not immediately (though a number did) then after a decent period of withdrawal. Others, however, defined their subjecthood in terms of the dynasty of their birth; for these men—at least for as long as they held true to their Ming roots—personal participation in Qing government was unthinkable. Both paths were entirely legitimate by their own lights, though obviously not by each other's, even if some individuals sought ways of reconciling the two and men on the two sides often respected each other's choices. Both paths also had long histories, with exemplars to follow as far back as the Three Dynasties of antiquity. In this essay, however, I shall be concerned only with the latter camp, that of the men who thought that to claim the name of a "left-over" or "remnant" subject of the Ming (*yimin*) entailed a corresponding disengagement from the Qing.

Xiang Shengmo's inscription to the aforementioned *Self-Portrait in Red Landscape*, dated to the fourth lunar month of 1644, dramatizes one man's immediate reaction to the fall of the Ming. "Sorrow and anger resulted in illness. Once I recovered, I sketched my likeness in ink and added the red painting" 悲憤成疾，既甦乃寫墨容，補以硃畫. Xiang felt the need to express viscerally his loyalty to the fallen dynasty, using red to allude to the name of the Ming dynastic family (fig. 30). He would not go on to commit suicide, or join the resistance, or become a monk; his lament was a private one, carefully concealed from the view of non-family members and according to family tradition subsequently kept for generations in the family temple. His two inscribed poems express his shame—at the insufficiency of the image he has painted and the words he has inscribed, and at the very sight of his own face. But the second poem ends on a note of resignation rather than defiance: "Though tear traces have been wiped away, grief remains; Daily hoping for the ascent of peace, my thoughts become foolishly obsessed" 啼痕雖拭憂如在，日望昇平想欲癡. It was precisely this desire for peace among the silent majority of the elite of southeast China that made it possible for the Manchu Qing to turn an occupation into accepted dynastic rule.

With its black-ink self-portrait standing out against the red landscape, Xiang's painting is visually disjunctive—a rare phenomenon in the history of Chinese painting, where unity was a preeminent aesthetic ideal. The opening lines of the inscription explain: "Remnant waters, leftover mountains—color still cinnabar red; / Murky heavens, darkened earth—shadow of a trifling body" 剩水殘山色尚朱，天昏地黑影微軀. Xiang's black-ink depiction, therefore, shows the mere shadow of an insignificant body that has taken into itself the murky heavens and darkened earth of a disjunctive moment of rebellion, war, and dynastic change. It is not irrelevant that the contrast of black and red was integral to literati culture. Black-printed books and ink-transcribed manuscripts were punctuated using red ink, with double inkstones existing for the purpose. And most monochromatic ink paintings bore seals of the artist impressed in red. In this more subtle sense, the painting affirms a specifically scholarly sense of unhappy destiny.

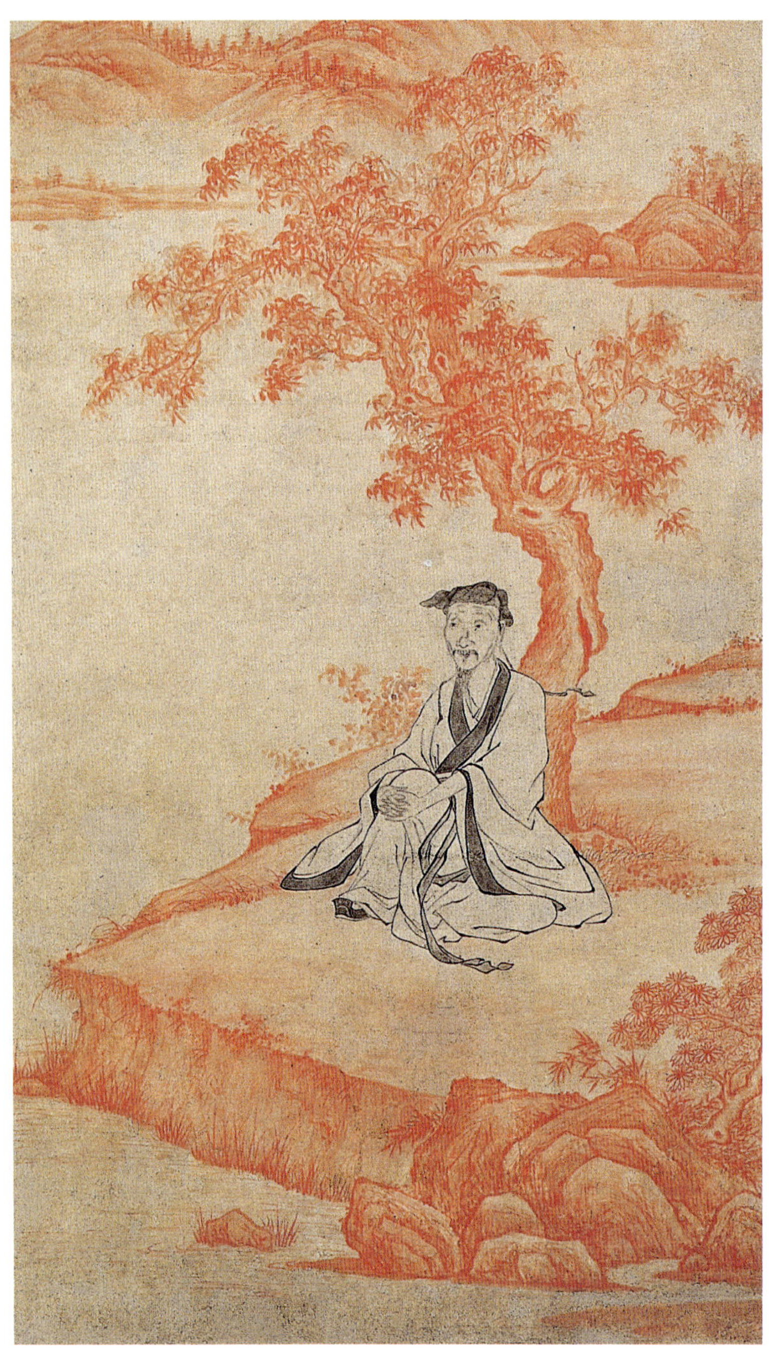

FIG. 30 Xiang Shengmo, *Self-Portrait in Red Landscape* (detail), 1644 (cat. no. 20)

THE SCREEN OF METAPHOR China's educated artists made sense of their post-1644 experience by filtering the raw facts of personal circumstances through a screen of metaphor. Temporally speaking, *yimin* (遺民), for which I shall use the translation "remnant subject," was the all-important term. A more tendentious interpretation as "loyalist" is common but has the disadvantage of narrowing the meaning down to a politically engaged, activist interpretation embraced by only a minority, even of those who considered being an *yimin* meant rejecting Qing service. Here I shall reserve the term "loyalist" for politically engaged *yimin*. For the majority of remnant subjects, the appellation *yimin* 遺民 was instead a way of giving contemporary relevance to the more common homophonous term 逸民, meaning "a subject who has fled" or more simply "a recluse." The two terms were inherently complicit, as one can see from an early seventeenth-century definition of the *yimin* (逸民) recluse: "Recluses are like the roots that survive after wilderness grass has been burned to ashes" 逸民如野燒草灰而根存.[2] Thus, although some remnant subjects were activist loyalists such as Fang Yizhi 方以智 (1611–1671; cat. no. 40), post-1644 any Ming-born self-proclaimed recluse could make the claim to be a remnant subject. This was the case in the 1660s for Fang's cousin Fang Hengxian 方亨咸 (act. c. 1647–1678; cat. no. 39), who had previously served as a Qing official between 1647 and 1657. Only in context, therefore, could one know what kind of remnant subject one was dealing with, and as the decades passed the context was easily lost. In a letter to Zhuo Erkan 卓爾堪 (1653–1712), commenting on the latter's now-famous 1690s compilation of poetry by remnant subjects, the Yangzhou-area loyalist Li Lin 李驎 (1634–1710) pointed out that not all of the remnant subjects selected by Zhuo were engaged Ming loyalists but were in some cases merely recluses—and even recluses by necessity rather than conviction.[3] The *yimin* world was a world of greys.

Corresponding to the temporal state of remnant subjecthood was the metaphoric space of internal exile known as the wilderness (*ye* 野)—thus Xiang Shengmo's self-description as a "servitor in the wilderness." As an ancient metaphor that took its meaning from opposition to the space of central power, *chao* (朝, literally "the court"), the wilderness was inherently political. While the exile in question could be non-metaphorically physical and geographic, as in the cases of banishment or flight, it more fundamentally referred to a self-displacement of consciousness—a disengagement from the sphere of political authority. In pictorial representation, many visual equivalents for this self-imposed social and mental exile in the wilderness were deployed. The most common included empty or isolated landscapes with wild prunus and ancient trees of all kinds, as well as depictions of specific places historically associated with exile.

The wilderness theme has a long and distinguished history in painting, one that may be as long as that of the pictorial representation and enactment of subjectivity. This history bequeathed to post-1644 remnant artists a broad range of wilderness subjects and styles. Some of these were associated with the loyalist end of the remnant-subject spectrum, because the fall of the Tang, the Northern Song, and the Southern Song had all led to intense loyalist contributions to painting under the immediately succeeding dynasties. Other themes and styles were associated with imposed or self-imposed exile. The latter can often be traced back to the late eleventh century and the literati artists who experienced geographic exile in the form of banishment. Complicating this latter part of the remnant subject's wilderness inheritance, however, was a development of the final century of the Ming dynasty, when political disintegration and the rapid development of urban commerce proceeded side by side.[4] During that extraordinary period of cultural experimentation, the wilderness had taken on a more complex social character, continuing to signify a space of exile from the orbit of imperial power but at the same time connoting a different kind of space—one of urban entrepreneurial opportunity and tastes. After 1644, however, literati reacted by purging the wilderness of the consumerist accretions that had adulterated its originally political meaning, allowing it to regain its character as a political space. Moreover, the exile connotations returned with intensified force, as we saw in the case of Xiang's 1644 self-portrait. This was to prove a temporary development, though, which would not survive the deaths of the final generation of Ming remnant subjects in the years on either side of 1710.

The transformation of 1644 being at once conquest by a foreign power and dynastic fall, remnant subjects focused now on one, now on the other, finding both equally painful. The Qing's conquest was the Ming's and their own defeat, leading to the loss of the nation. The fall of the Ming dynasty itself, meanwhile, was described in terms very different from the toppling action of our English metaphor. The dynasty was understood to have perished (*wang* 亡); indeed the Chinese nation itself as a sovereign entity had perished (*guowang* 國亡). This experience of dynastic death left remnant subjects with many questions that turned on the one hand around the possibility or impossibility of resistance, and on the other around the obligations of mourning.

Yang Wencong 楊文驄 (1597–1646) painted the handscroll *Water Village* (cat. no. 19, fig. 11) in the eleventh month of 1644. It is one of a number of surviving paintings produced in and around Nanjing during the brief period between the fall of Beijing in the third month of 1644 and the fall of Nanjing in the fifth month of 1645 that are pervaded by an eerie calm.[5] With Beijing in the hands of the Manchus, Nanjing became the capital of the Ming Hongguang 弘光 (1644–1645) regime, whose government Yang, formerly a Chongzhen-period official, joined, serving in the Ministry of War. Yang painted the scroll for a Hongguang Grand Secretary, Gao Hongtu 高弘圖 (1583–1645). From the artist's inscribed poems we learn that the view is of a peaceful watery landscape along the Xiang River in Hunan, invoking the ancient exile theme of the Xiao and Xiang Rivers. On one level, the painting is a dreamlike vision of retirement from court to the wilderness, of a longed-for self-imposed exile that had finally been attained after repeated petitions to retire. Yang advertises Gao's transitional situation through the combination of two Yuan-dynasty models, one by Zhao Mengfu 趙孟頫 (1254–1322), who had left the wilderness to serve the Mongols, the other by Huang Gongwang 黄公望 (1269–1354), who had kept his distance from the Mongol regime. The first of the artist's two poems comments admiringly on Gao's successive choices in the wake of Chongzhen's death to serve and then to withdraw:

> Sage sovereign, dragon-like, soared to reside at Fenghao [capital of the Zhou dynasty, here an indirect reference to Nanjing];
> With single-minded virtue, ruler and officials focused on the throne.
> The prime minister from Shandong [Gao Hongtu] personally seasoned the soup [i.e., formed the Hongguang government];
> Doubly bright [*alternatively*, Under the renewed Ming dynasty], sun [日] and moon [月, the two characters together make up the word ming (明)] illuminated the blue sky.
> [But] senior officials sat and argued behind yellow-painted doors,
> As the signal fires to the south went out, [the prime minister] shook his sleeves and left.
> With utmost respect and tender affection, I cherish Grand Secretary Gao;
> By imperial grace, like the Marquis of Ye to Mount Heng, he can retire to hermit life.[6]

> 聖主龍飛宅豐鎬，一德君臣凝大寶.
> 山東宰相手調羹，重明日月青天杲.
> 老臣坐論在黃扇，江表烽銷遑拂衣.
> 至尊繾綣惜高尚，鄴侯詔許衡山歸.

Yang affirms that Gao had fulfilled his loyalist obligation, and that it was the situation that failed him rather than the reverse. In such circumstances, as Tim Brook explains elsewhere in this volume, reclusion was an admirable moral choice. However, the painting and poem are not just a vision of reclusion but also a patriotic statement. This scroll is one of many paintings of the period that aligned the Chinese nation with the south of the country, echoing the geography of the Ming resistance.

DEFIANCE Educated to belong, at least potentially, to a national leadership class, China's literati could not but take the Ming defeat personally. Moreover, the Manchus quickly decreed that Chinese men wear their hair in the Manchu fashion as a way of forcing them to bear physically, as if branded, the sign of their humiliating new dynastic subjecthood. In response, many literati joined the Ming loyalist resistance and/or took the tonsure as Buddhist monks. Yang Wencong, for example, after helping to organize fortifications at Zhenjiang in late 1644, fought the Manchus at Quzhou in Zhejiang and later in Pucheng in Fujian, where he was captured and executed in 1645. Fang Yizhi is another artist who fought in the Southern Ming resistance, but he survived for a considerable time by becoming a monk. Fang was eventually arrested in 1671, suspected of rebellion, and died in custody by his own hand (see cat. no. 40). Gong Xian (cat. nos. 34–36) was active in the resistance during the 1640s. Although few details are known, Kuncan 髡殘 (b. 1612; cat. no. 37) is also thought to have participated in the Southern Ming resistance during the 1640s. Both the participants at the time and later the survivors once the resistance was defeated gave nationalist defiance symbolic form in writings and images. Here we have to remind ourselves that the art form we call literati painting (*wenrenhua* 文人畫) was not medium specific but rather was a culturally open practice, such that a single artwork could incorporate poetry, calligraphy, and painting proper, all of which mediated each other. For the educated man with some painterly skills, therefore, it was just as natural to express his defiance in this art form as it was for other literati to do so in poems or prose writings, or in the calligraphic transcription of appropriate texts.

Defiance was, however, dangerous. We have already seen that Xiang Shengmo's self-portrait was too explicit to be allowed to circulate outside the family. Artists dealt with this problem in a number of ways. Many stayed silent, especially prior to the 1680s, when one serious military threat to Manchu rule followed another. Even the die-hard loyalist Bada Shanren 八大山人 (1626–1705), according to Wang Fangyu, "seems to have refrained from expressing loyalist sentiments in his writings and art until the year 1682."[7] When he did start to express such sentiments, it was in densely allusive language that defied easy deciphering and in images of seemingly angry birds and fish whose meaning was brought by the viewer through context. Other artists preceded Bada in expressing their defiance obliquely by making their paintings either ambiguous or obscure, or both. This was easier to do when a painting was left uninscribed or when the inscription left the image unexplained.[8]

It would be a mistake to interpret this type of painting simply in autobiographical terms. The poetics of defiance also contributed to the larger strategic goal of exposing the gap between Qing authority and legitimacy. The Qing state could make its claim on the entirety of Chinese territory, but Hongren 弘仁 (1610–1664) shows us places where people live, unseen and elusive, beyond the authority of the state.[9] The art of the Ming court no longer existed, but an artist like Bada kept its themes alive.[10] The former Nanjing had been renamed Jinling, but for loyalists it remained the southern capital, its many Ming sites still available even as they took on newly imposed Qing names.[11]

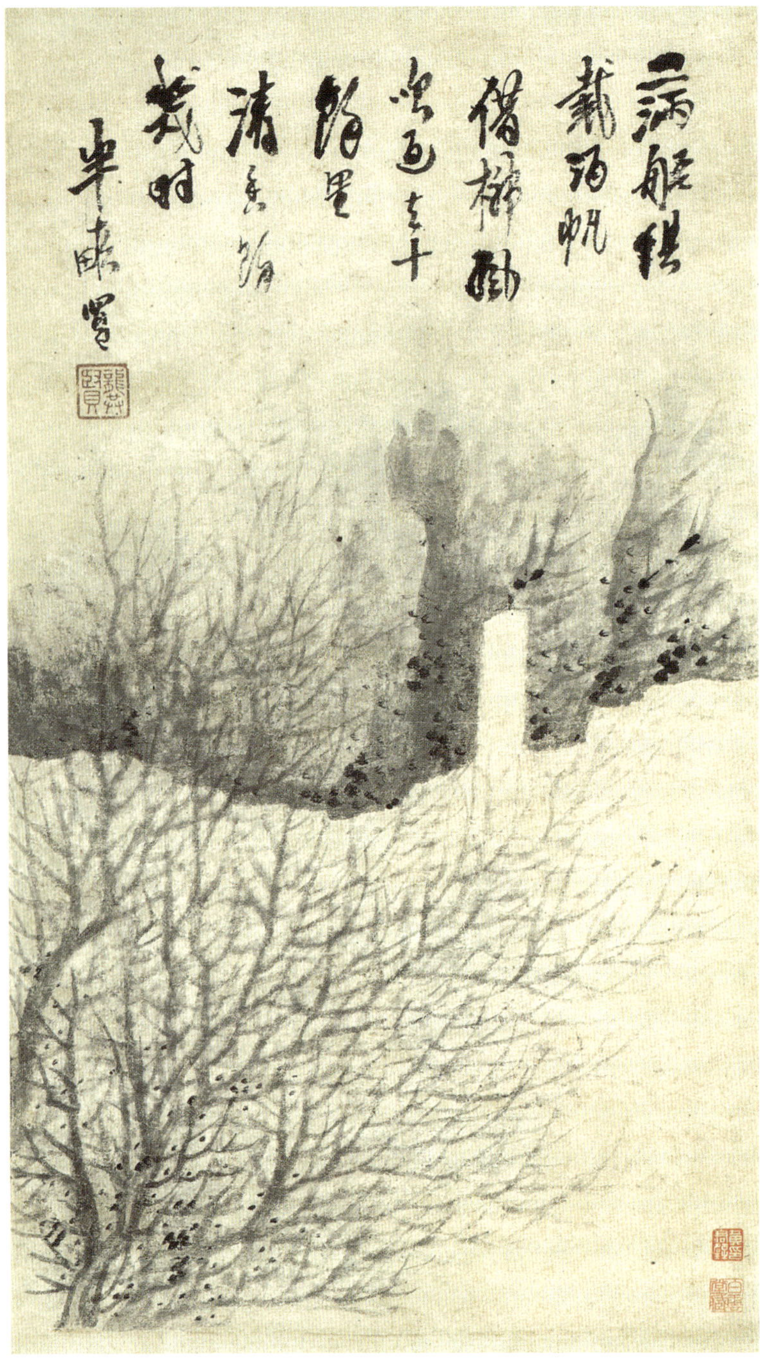

FIG. 31 Gong Xian, *Boating in the Breeze* (cat. no. 35)

Three works in the exhibition by Gong Xian—*Lofty Peak and Dense Woods*, *Boating in the Breeze*, and *Landscape*—show one artist's evolving stance on defiance over a period of almost forty years. In *Lofty Peak and Dense Woods* (cat. no. 34), a work of the 1650s, the tall foreground trees interfere with our view of a residence nestled within more trees in the foothills of an imposing mountain. As is the case for many of Gong's early hanging scrolls, human presence seems absorbed into the landscape itself, which confronts the viewer as a claustrophobic icon of reclusion. As one spends more time with the image, however, one discovers that its frontality is balanced by implications of narrative that run laterally across the picture surface. Near the bottom of the painting, an area of ground left as bare silk narrows as it threads its way between the trees. A little further up, cut off by the right-hand edge of the painting, is a gallery leading to and from the main part of the residence. Thus the buildings are, after all, accessible—though not to us, who are cast in the role of witness. Still further up, a twisting band of mist leads to the topmost peak, implying movement, if only spiritual or imaginary, between the residence and the mountaintop. The top half of the painting is modeled on the art of the monk-painter Juran 巨然 (act. c. 960–980), who was active during the troubled tenth century, initially under one of the Tang dynasty's successor states, the Southern Tang dynasty. The suggestion of a historical parallel with the Southern Ming is likely deliberate.

By the time Gong painted the much more intimate *Boating in the Breeze* (cat. no. 35, fig. 31) in the 1680s, he had long since returned to Nanjing and established himself as a leading professional artist. In the more relaxed political atmosphere following the Qing suppression of the Rebellion of the Three Feudatories, his art had become progressively more expansive and self-assured, as he settled into the public role of a principled but no longer active loyalist. His inscription is light-hearted, evoking a pleasure outing by boat; indeed, the painting may be an occasional work, executed during just such an outing. "The entire boat is laden with wine / Its billowing sail borrowing the breeze that passes through the willows. / After it has sailed another ten miles or more, / How long will [the wine's] pure fragrance have lasted?" 滿船俱載酒，帆借柳風吹，過去十餘里，清香餘幾時. The arresting visual image, though, freights these sentiments with melancholy. The willow has bare branches; the cliff is sheer rock; the shape of the sail, left as bare paper and silhouetted against the cliff, is reminiscent of a commemorative stone stele.

The latest of the three paintings, *Landscape* (cat. no. 36), dates from the year of Gong's death, 1689, which was also the year of the Kangxi emperor's 康熙 (r. 1661–1722) second visit to south China. In a conciliatory gesture, on this visit Kangxi poured libations at the mausoleum of the Ming founder, the Hongwu emperor 洪武 (r. 1368–1398), located at Mount Zhong just southeast of the city. For Gong, as for many Ming loyalists, this was an event that inspired mixed feelings. He responded by adding to the large number of landscape paintings by Nanjing artists that depict, without noting it in their inscriptions, Hongwu's mausoleum.[12] The many complexities of the painting are anchored by its character as a loyalist icon. The two-story structure of the mausoleum's stele hall, haloed by pines, nestles within a towering mountainscape transmuted from the low hills of Mount Zhong (fig. 28). Closer to us, empty residential buildings are framed by leafless, wintry trees. From all this our entry is barred by the expanse of water at the bottom of painting. Swaths of mist enter the landscape from both sides, intensifying the visual effect of a dystopian quasi-religious vision. And by summoning up memories of the monumental landscapes of the Five Dynasties, Song, and Yuan—an aspect of the painting that the artist underscores in his long inscription—Gong's masterwork identifies the lost Ming with the lost nation.

MOURNING THE MING LORD The majority of literati did not join the armed loyalist resistance. In the early years they were instead racked by paralyzing guilt and remorse, leading them often to withdraw from the world or, more rarely, to commit suicide. The context for suicide lay in the obligations attendant on a servitor (*chen* 臣) mourning for a lord (*zhu* 主). Evelyn Rawski has shown that although the official death ritual following the deaths of Ming and Qing emperors largely followed the pattern of family mourning (see below), this did not exclude a certain role for the practice of accompanying-in-death (*suizang* 隨葬).[13] Astonishing as it may seem, this archaic and barbaric practice, applied to palace concubines, remained active at the imperial level under the Ming until the second half of the fifteenth century, and its formal abolition in 1464 did not prevent it from continuing at the level of Ming princely burials.[14] In the mid-seventeenth century, various forms of accompanying-in-death were used in Manchu aristocratic burials, including that of the Qing emperor Shunzhi 順治 (r. 1644–1661) in 1660. The practice was finally abolished in 1673.[15] The suicide of the Chongzhen emperor in 1644 was not generally interpreted as an attempt to avoid a more unpleasant fate, but as a recognition of guilt or the loss of the mandate (interpretations varied). The emperor's suicide inspired a rash of suicides that were explicitly intended as accompaniment in death.[16] According to Frederick Wakeman, in Beijing "at least forty officials, many of them ranking ministers like Fan Jingwen 范景文 [1587–1644], committed suicide in the first few days following Chongzhen's death."[17] In the provinces, their example was followed by many others as the news spread. This martyrdom was in a sense the benchmark by which surviving loyalists measured their own demonstrations of loyalty. Zhang Dai's 張岱 (1597–c. 1684) commentary to the life of the Chongzhen emperor suggests something of the symbolic power of the idea of accompanying-in-death in loyalist consciousness: "When we scholar subjects [*shimin* 士民] turn our thoughts to the events of the third month of *jiashen* [1644], there is not one of us who is not so heartbroken that he could spit blood, and who does not think to himself that it would have been better to kill himself the same day as our late Emperor" 凡我士民，思及甲申三月之事，未有不痛心嘔血，思與我先帝同日死之之为愈也.[18]

It is from this point of view that some paintings by self-proclaimed loyalists can be understood as metaphoric representations of the Ming dynastic afterlife. Especially in the many loyalist representations of fantastic landscapes, the reference seems to be the wandering, unhappy *hun* (魂) soul roaming the dangerous cosmos in search of paradise. Many loyalist artists did wander the world during the first decades following 1644, fleeing from danger and scratching out a livelihood. As one of Gong Xian's poems has it: "Ten years in exile, my soul [*hun*] terrorized" 作客十年魂膽落.[19] In other cases, most obviously in depictions of the landscape around the former southern capital of Nanjing, the afterlife of the *po* (魄) soul that in contrast to the *hun* remained in the tomb residence seems the obvious point of reference. Just as a tomb contained depictions of a residence in order to provide the basis for the enactment of a continued comfortable existence in the afterlife, so too in painting we see the continuation of the Ming as a dematerialized, idealized, peaceable environment for men who considered themselves to be ghosts. It is striking, for example, how many loyalist painters—Hongren and Gong Xian being the most famous—omitted human figures from their landscapes. Houses, boats, and other signs of human presence such as fishing nets and well-tended fields make it clear that their landscapes are inhabited, but not by anyone that the ordinary viewer can see.

Other, more emblematic and self-referential loyalist images, notably depictions of the prunus, often catalyzed related poetic reflections. *Plum Blossoms and Pine* (after 1650; cat. no. 40, fig. 32) was painted by Fang Yizhi, a remnant subject who had donned monk's robes. Each painting in this set of four hanging scrolls bears an eight-line poem. The poem inscribed on an image of a prunus wreathed in white mist places us in Suzhou's Lingyan Monastery 靈巖寺:

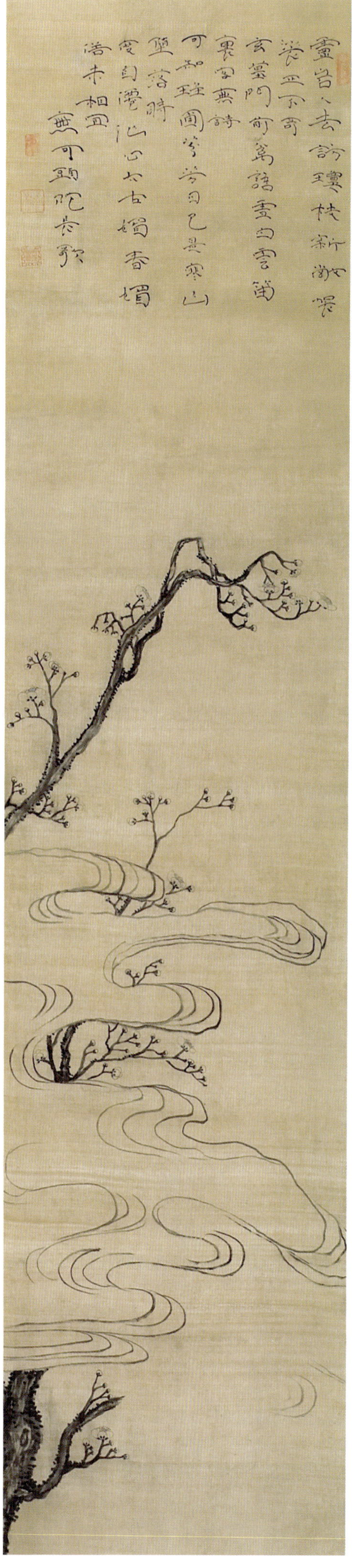

FIG. 32 Fang Yizhi, *Plum Blossoms and Pine* (detail), after 1650 (cat. no. 40)

At Lingyan Monastery after people have left, I seek out
jeweled branches;
Newly displayed monk's robes are not to be wondered at.
In front of the cemetery gates, birds chatter in the snow;
Amid the sounds of flutes that arrive through white mist,
this visitor has no poem to write.
I can see [now] that in the days when flowers bloomed
so fragrantly in paradise,
Blossoms were already falling in wintry mountains.
Taking stock, my heart belongs too much to the past
for me to become a transcendent;
Yet the enticements of spring and the vulgar world have
no purchase on me either.

靈岩人去訪瓊枝，新敞袈裟正不奇.
玄墓門前禽語雪，白雲笛裏客無詩.
可知瑆圃芬芳日，已是寒山墮落時.
度自僊仙心太古，媚春媚俗未相宜.

The artist here eloquently describes the limbolike existence of the loyalist subject compelled to live outside dynastic time, all too aware of the dead. The case of the loyalist Gui Zhuang 歸莊 (1613–1673), whose defiant poetry is discussed in Jonathan Chaves's essay, elucidates the kind of thinking underpinning landscape images, such as Gong Xian's *Landscape*, that evoke the same limbo. After participating in the loyalist resistance, Gui returned to his hometown of Kunshan, where he built a home for himself beside his father's grave. He inscribed his studio with words that included the comment: "on all four sides [this house] touches the earth of the lower world: how rare the living, how numerous the ghosts!" 四鄰接幽冥之宅，人何寥落鬼何多.[20]

While he did not usually literally accompany the emperor in death, the loyalist who renounced the world to become a monk, or who more simply refused to take the official examinations, symbolically fulfilled his ritual as well as his political responsibility to the lost dynasty through his lifetime commitment. If the self-penned epitaph of Zhang Dai stands as the preeminent literary expression of remorse, no visual artist gave more vivid voice to *yimin* feelings of guilt than Chen Hongshou 陳洪綬 (1599–1652; cat. nos. 21–23). Prior to the fall of the Ming, Chen had been a literati professional heavily engaged in the market who employed several assistants. He was famous for creating surprising and transgressive images that subverted the conventions of genres and styles. Post-1644, however, his work darkened. One interpretation of the later work would highlight its ironic and theatrical distancing of self. This device had previously functioned as a defensive mechanism against the moral compromise involved in the commercialization of literati self-expression. Now, though, it became the means by which the artist distanced himself from an earlier, pre-1644 self, exposed in the later paintings as morally deficient.

Album for Monk Yu (cat. no. 23) is one of a number of superb post-1644 albums (this one painted around 1650) in which Chen created melancholy interpretations of a range of diverse themes. Largely devoid of inscriptional commentary by the artist, the images are left to tell their own story. A single narcissus alludes to a subject closely associated with Zhao Mengjian 趙孟堅 (1199–c. 1264), a thirteenth-century artist whom seventeenth-century literati mistakenly believed to have created images of narcissi during the initial years of the Mongol conquest (cat. no. 23:5). A butterfly hovers over a spray of chrysanthemum that is paired with a stalk of bamboo; the fact that butterflies do not pollinate chrysanthemums makes this an image of futility (cat. no. 23:3). At the end of winter, an old prunus puts forth fresh blossoms, one of the most common self-images of the remnant subject (cat. no. 23:7). Three mynah birds, taking a rest from the squabbling that made them a Ming metaphor for court factionalism, sit on a tree branch (cat. no. 23:6); they have entered a painting that any educated viewer would have recognized as a reinterpretation of Su Shi's 蘇軾 (1037–1101) favorite theme of old trees, bamboo, and rocks: Su's visual metaphor for moral principles maintained in the face of adversity. One landscape explicitly evokes the restless style of Wang Meng 王蒙 (c. 1308–1385), who lived through the troubled transition between the Yuan and Ming dynasties (cat. no. 23:2); it takes a moment to notice a man in a skiff making his way out of the creek into open water as if emerging from hiding. A second landscape leaf painted, according to the inscription, in the recipient's library, "Reading History Pavilion" depicts a recluse picking his way through a lake landscape (cat. no. 23:4); the name of the library encourages us to see in this image a metaphor for the experience of reading history for its lessons. Finally, an aging recluse, archaically dressed, contemplates the falling leaves of autumn, as if seeing his remaining years slip away (cat. no. 23:1, fig. 33). Is this the artist? The recipient? It may be both, since Chen applies the word "old" (*lao* 老) repeatedly to both the recipient and himself. Among Chen's post-1644 style names was one, Belated Remorse, that corresponds well to the tone of this and similar albums.

MOURNING THE MING PARENT Gong Xian's *Landscape* is also a pictorial memorial to the death of the Ming dynasty, in which the tomb of the Ming founder comes to commemorate the dynasty's end. From this point of view, it is an image of mourning. Literati mourning of the death of the Ming was highly ritualized. While grieving for a lord provided one important model, familial mourning for parents was no less important. Gong's pictorial memorial did not just visualize the ghostly dynastic afterlife inhabited by Ming loyalists who had symbolically accompanied the emperor in death, it also enacted a particular moment in a process of mourning for the Ming dynastic parent. It was basic that mourning for parents should not go beyond a certain term. Although the term varied (for government officials it was twenty-seven months), the principle that it had to be brought to an end, declaring a symbolic return to normality, was inflexible. Thus the classical text, the *Liji* 禮記 (Book of rites), stipulates: "Three years are considered as the extreme limit of mourning; but though [his parents] are out of sight, a son does not forget them."[21] As we shall see, Gong's painting acknowledges in its own way that mourning the Ming dynastic parent had a limit, too—marked by the passing of Gong's generation.

Seen in terms of domestic, familial mourning, the dynastic transition emerges as a play of competing temporalities. The collaborating Chinese official in Qing government, through a restriction of the mourning period to the minimum length, was engaged in an operation of continuity that can be seen as maintaining the flow of dynastic time. It was possible, within the paradigm of familial mourning, for him to believe that by entering government under the Qing after a certain period, he was not simply being opportunistic but was fulfilling his ritual responsibility to the lost dynasty as well as his political responsibility to the new holder of the mandate.[22] The natural time lapse between the Ming military defeat and the Qing restoration of a functioning government took care of the mourning period. This course was not an easy one to choose, however. The collaborator was aware that he might be sacrificing his historical reputation—no small matter in a culture where the fortunes of the living were intertwined with those of the ancestors.

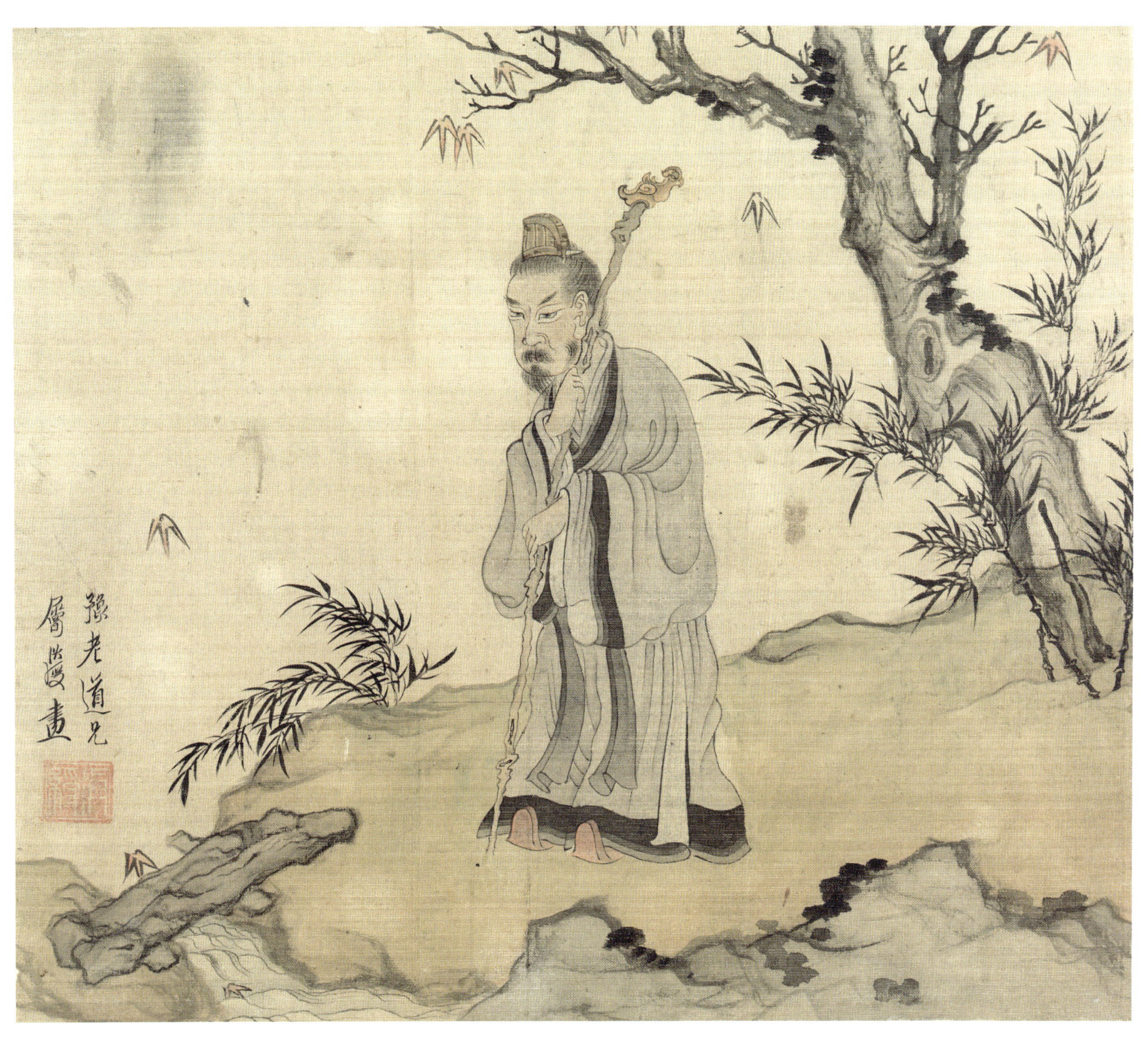

FIG. 33 Chen Hongshou, leaf from *Album for Monk Yu*, c. 1650 (cat. no. 23)

Among the painters represented in the exhibition, only Fang Hengxian (cat. no. 39) chose the path of collaboration, entering the Qing government in 1647, three years after the Ming fall. After 1660, however, following a period of banishment, Fang withdrew from public service. Like Cheng Zhengkui 程正揆 (1604–1676)—another artist who had served the Qing during the Shunzhi period—he subsequently supported himself as a professional artist in Nanjing, where the prefect, Zhou Lianggong 周亮工 (1612–1672), was a protector of remnant subject artists of all kinds. Five of the nine double leaves of Fang's album are a manifesto of the reclusive life: a man meditates in a cave; another wanders alone in a chilly wilderness environment; a house with no visible inhabitant stands within a compound whose outside gate is barred from within (fig. 23); a pile of vegetables extols the pleasures of a vegetarian diet; and a single lotus blossom blooms in its muddy pond, in an allusion to Zhou Dunyi's 周敦頤 (1017–1073) use of the lotus as an emblem of virtue. The opening double leaf, however, goes in a different direction, depicting an inscribed rock that had been an unwitting witness to dynastic change—a theme that Fang takes up again in the essay on an ancient coin that occupies the last three double leaves of the album. Both objects belonged to the wilderness. The rock stood "amidst wild grass growing in a deserted field" 於荒田蔓草間. The corroded coin, which he saw during the period of his banishment, had been found in the ground, amid the ruins of an old city wall.

In contrast to the collaborating official, the die-hard Ming loyalist extended the symbolic three years of mourning of the eldest son to cover his entire lifetime. If mourning always represents a calculated rupture with the normal socialized time of community or public life, the loyalist located himself within the disruption. He thus operated in a suspension of dynastic time, inhabiting and incarnating a limbo that one might call interdynastic in the sense that it stood outside Ming and Qing dynastic time.[23] As the drama progressed through the 1650s, 60s, and 70s, the hard line of even the most famous loyalists significantly softened. The decorum of mourning required that it not be taken to unreasonable lengths. The *Liji* stipulates: "The rites of mourning are the extreme expression of grief and sorrow. The graduated reduction of that expression in accordance with the natural changes (of time and feeling) was made by the superior men, mindful of those to whom we owe our being."[24] What is more, the Qing government took extremely seriously its ideological offensive aimed at loyalists and was able to further marginalize those who were most intransigent. The drama of the extraordinary *boxue hongci* 博學鴻詞 examination of 1679 entailed tempting loyalists with the possibility of exchanging their paradigms of ritual reference thirty-five years after the fall of the Ming, when passions had cooled. Some accepted, but others like Cheng Sui 程邃 (1607–1692; cat. no. 32) and Fei Erqi 費而奇 (act. 1678 or earlier–1701 or later) did not. Correspondingly, in the foreground of Fei's charming and expertly composed image of a rustic retreat in the mountains (cat. no. 33:1) is a stream flowing from a cave, a direct allusion to the story of the Peach Blossom Spring and its hidden self-sufficient community existing outside dynastic time (fig. 34). Five years after the *boxue hongci* examination, one of Kangxi's key actions was to pay his respects to the tomb of the Ming founder in Nanjing, as he did again in 1689—the act to which Gong Xian responds in *Landscape*.

Through the play of temporalities associated with different ritual options of mourning, the dynastic transition took on something of the character of a ritual narrative. In this narrative, instances of sordid opportunism aside, both loyalists and collaborators were necessary, and its emplotment had a certain inevitability corresponding to a consensus view of national destiny. As such it functioned as a ritual mechanism that, through the symbiotic engagements of loyalists and collaborators, ensured the stability of the society in the face of disaster. While the role of the collaborating official in such a process is clear enough, the loyalist's role is more obscure. In one direction, by personally assuming the burden of collective grief and shame, the community of remnant subjects freed the rest of literati society to return to normality. But equally important is the fact that the collaborator alone did not have the moral authority to create the symbolic *tabula rasa* without which the new dynasty could not pass from imposed authority to legitimacy.

This is where the loyalist—once he had abandoned military resistance—came in. Although the loyalist's refusal to recognize the Qing appears on its face to have prevented the new dynasty from acquiring legitimacy, the fact that this refusal (once the Southern Ming resistance had failed) took place within a context of mourning functioned as an implicit acknowledgment of the fact that dynastic death had occurred. Despite its negative character, this acknowledgment was crucial because its moral authority could not be challenged. A practical example of *yimin* use of their moral authority to acknowledge the Qing is the blessing that Huang Zongxi 黃宗羲 (1610–1695) gave the Qing-sponsored *Ming shi* 明史 (Ming history, completed 1739) by contributing materials and sending his son to participate in its compilation.[25] As soon as he gave up armed resistance, therefore, the loyalist was paradoxically condemned to collaborate, if only symbolically, with the collaborator in the normalization of Qing power. It is worth noting, in this light, that the political tensions between the two groups were not nearly as great in the late seventeenth century as is sometimes supposed. In the early Qing art world, it is the instances of intransigence that are unusual and notable.[26] Moreover, even the most committed loyalists took stock of the changing political situation. Part of what makes Gong Xian's *Landscape* such an important painting is the implicit acknowledgment it incorporates through its classicizing stability: that under Kangxi China had found peace again.

Mourning on the familial model found its pictorial expression within wilderness painting in a poetics of loss to which many styles made separate contributions. One common form was a desolate or melancholy mood already current in painting prior to 1644 but which was now recontextualized and inflected by the fall of the Ming. The Huizhou 徽州 wilderness vision as defined by Hongren, for example, took an archaizing mode of literati painting invented in the late Ming (see Song Jue's 宋珏 [1576–1632] album leaf, cat. no. 33:5) and applied it to the landscape of Huizhou and Mount Huang. By keeping the style free of color and stripping the trees of their leaves and the landscape of its people, Hongren, the loyalist monk, touched every scene with a wintry cool. Entirely different was the colorful but elegiac art of the great late-seventeenth-century painter of flowers and plants, Yun Shouping 惲壽平 (1633–1690). In Yun's hands, the late-Ming sensualist immersion in presentness was reframed by accompanying poems that introduce the distorting lens of memory, often by evoking images of palace life.

FIG. 34 Fei Erqi, "Recluse on a Pine Path," leaf from *Album of Landscapes by Famous Masters of the Late Ming–Early Qing* (cat. no. 33)

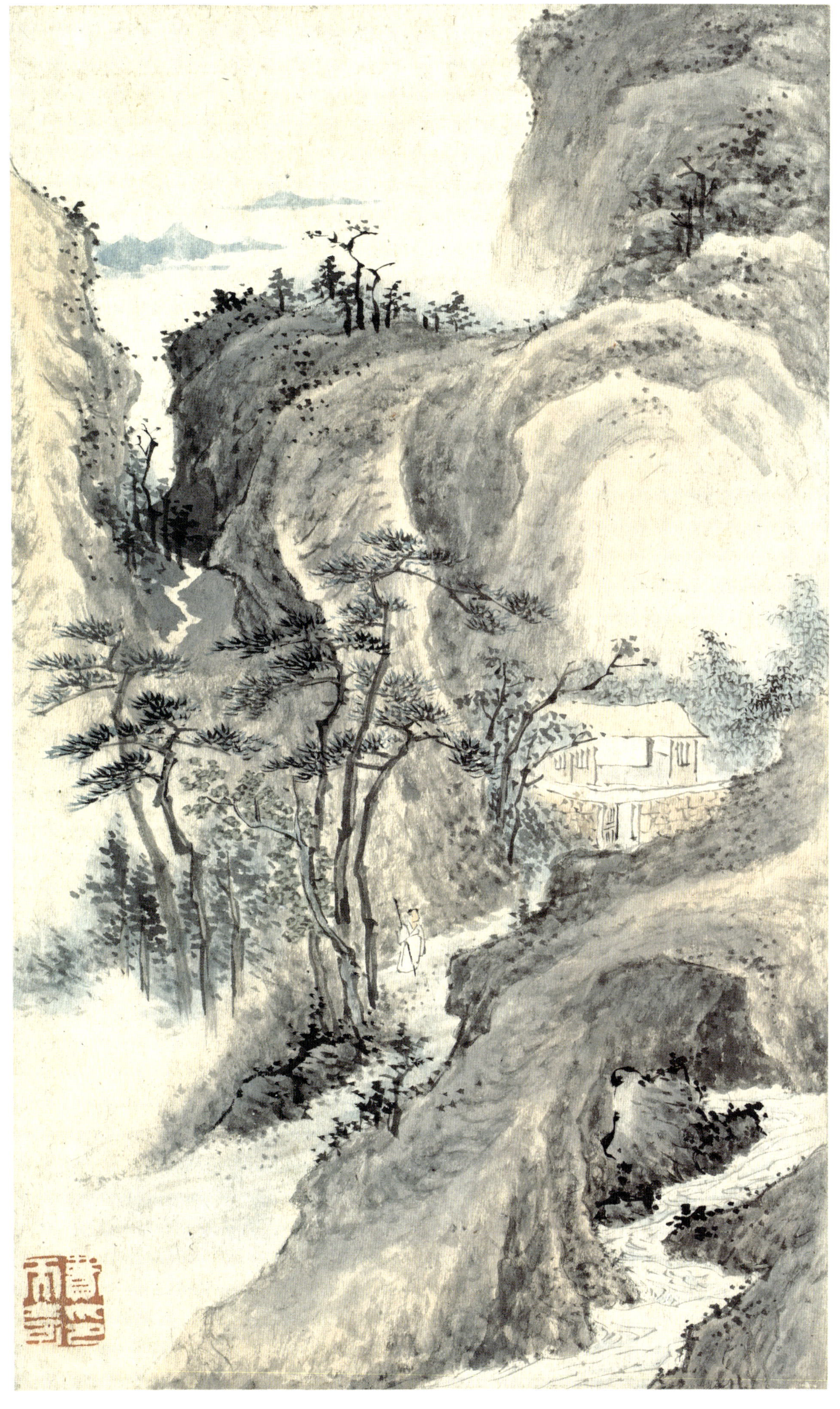

Yet another current of late-Ming painting had been the marriage of concrete particulars of place to poetic mood. This interest in a lyrical form of topographic depiction—originally associated with painters from Suzhou and Songjiang such as Shen Shichong 沈士充 (act. c. 1607–after 1640; cat. no. 17)—remained important in the late seventeenth century, when artists like the Nanjing-based Hu Yukun 胡玉昆 (act. c. 1640–1672) inflected the mood toward a poetics of loss and chose places for depiction accordingly. Four leaves by Hu are preserved in an album collection of works by otherwise unrelated artists (cat. no. 33). The places represented include ones of the deepest meaning to remnant subjects. The cemetery of Confucius and his descendants at Qufu in Shandong Province evoked the continuity of Han Chinese civilization (33:7). The area around Mount Tai, the sacred mountain of the east, also in Shandong, evoked both ancient battles and dynastic legitimacy (33:8). For the artist, the Temple of the Eastern Grove at Mount Lu in Jiangxi Province "calls to mind the worthies of old—summoning them [to government service] was hard!" 為想前賢難見招 (33:10, fig. 35). Eschewing the stylistic severity of his contemporary, Gong Xian, Hu used light color and delicate descriptive brushwork to exploit effects of light in the service of dreamlike, contemplative moods. His economical inscriptions provide just enough information to encourage melancholy reflection on recent events.[27]

For the few artists who were descendants of Ming princely households, familial mourning cut closer to the bone. One was Bada Shanren; another the monk Guofeng 過峰, who visited him in Nanchang in 1695. To commemorate the occasion and express his appreciation of the visit by this distant relative from faraway Yunnan Province, Bada painted for his visitor a folding fan (cat. no. 43, fig. 42). Through the golden space of the fan's surface, twenty-one tiny fish swim in a meandering line, forming a long chain of one-to-one connections much like the meeting that brought artist and recipient together. Although Bada reused a favorite, densely allusive poem from the previous year, it was one that took on new relevance on this occasion due to its Yunnan theme. It reads, in one possible translation:

> You come here to take pity on one who is haggard,
> Lingering—why, I wonder?—under the flowers for twenty
> or thirty days.
> To make Kunming Lake peaceful depends on the release of the fish.
> When the tree peony blooms, it is spring at Jinma.[28]
>
> 到此偏憐憔悴人，緣何花下兩三旬？
> 定昆明在魚兒放，木芍藥開金馬春.

As Richard Barnhart has noted, it was near Kunming Lake and Jinma Mountain that the last princely claimant to the Ming throne had died in 1662.[29] Inscribed on a fan for a fellow princely descendant, the poem could not but be taken as a commentary on the fates of this scattered group of men. The release of the fish is most obviously a reference to the annual Buddhist practice of buying fish in order to release them and thereby accumulate karma. Bada may have originally been alluding to the need for the Qing government not to pursue Ming loyalists, but here it is hard not to bring to mind Kangxi's 1668 order allowing "descendants of the Ming imperial family [to] return to their homes and restore their family name without recrimination."[30] Since Yongli 永曆 (r. 1646–1662) died in the spring, the final line speaks of a painful memory that for men like Bada and Guofeng was bound to recur every year on the anniversary of Yongli's death.[31]

LATECOMERS As the decades passed and the generations of older remnant subjects gradually disappeared, those who remained by 1700 were men who had been only children in 1644. By the 1690s, China was definitively a Qing nation led by a Manchu emperor who had earned widespread respect through his restoration of peace, stability, and prosperity. The dwindling loyalist community did not remain untouched by this evolution of the political situation. Even Bada underwent a change in attitude in his late years, seemingly letting go of his anger after 1694.[32] The very youngest remnant subjects were in a unique situation, since to all intents and purposes they had only known life under the Qing. In the world of artists, the most famous member of that final remnant-subject generation was Shitao 石濤 (1642–1707), who like Bada was born into a Ming princely household.

Yimin identity inspired conflicted feelings in Shitao during most of his life. He spent more than half a century as a Buddhist monk, initially to ensure his safety, then as a convinced religious professional pursuing a career, and finally during the first half of the 1690s in disillusionment at the failure of his ambitions as a Chan master. From the 1660s onwards, if not before, the monk's imperial identity was an open secret, making him like Bada a remnant subject of a very particular, charismatic kind. Shitao accepted the attention of his contemporaries yet pursued a contradictory path. His teacher Lü'an Benyue 旅庵本月 (d. 1676), and his teacher's teacher Muchen Daomin 木陳道忞 (1596–1674), were nationally prominent monks who had aligned themselves with the Qing court. Despite his Ming princely origins, or perhaps because of them, Shitao followed in their footsteps, engaging in a campaign to obtain the patronage of the Kangxi emperor. The campaign culminated in a sojourn between 1689 and 1692 in Beijing, where he was fêted by the high and mighty without in the end achieving his final goal of ensuring a sustained closeness to the throne. Rejected, entering his fifties, and disappointed in his longstanding ambition, he returned to the south in growing crisis, questioning his commitment to the life of the *sangha*.[33]

Having worked semi-professionally as an artist all his life, Shitao's obvious way out was to become a full-time professional artist as Bada had done in the 1680s. He eventually followed Bada's example, in the winter of 1696–97, but without fully returning to secular life. Instead, he proclaimed a Daoist identity even as he moved into his own house within the city of Yangzhou. During the final decade of his life, established as a professional artist in Yangzhou, Shitao embraced the role of a remnant subject and, more cautiously, of a Ming descendant. In 1697 he began to use regularly a seal whose meaning would have been cryptic for anyone not in the know, for it simply declared him to be the tenth-generation descendant of Zan, in reference to the founder of the Jingjiang princely lineage of the Ming, Zhu Zanyi 朱贊儀 (late fourteenth century). Not until 1701, at the age of sixty *sui*, did he feel able to sign a painting with his secular given name, Ruoji 若極. And only in 1702 did he begin to use a seal, declaring openly his Ming princely affiliation, that read "Jingjiang descendant" 靖江後人. By 1705 several other seals with related legends followed, but on present evidence he never once used his complete princely name of Zhu Ruoji 朱若極, probably out of a lingering fear that he might be considered a possible claimant to the Ming throne. For Shitao, the reengagement with his Ming family heritage at this point had little in common with the Ming loyalism of artists in earlier decades. For his contemporaries and men of a younger generation, however, he became a living monument of the Ming—a role that he increasingly embraced until his death in 1707.[34]

FIG. 35 Hu Yukun, "Tiger Stream Bridge at Mount Lu," leaf from *Album of Landscapes by Famous Masters of the Late Ming–Early Qing* (cat. no. 33)

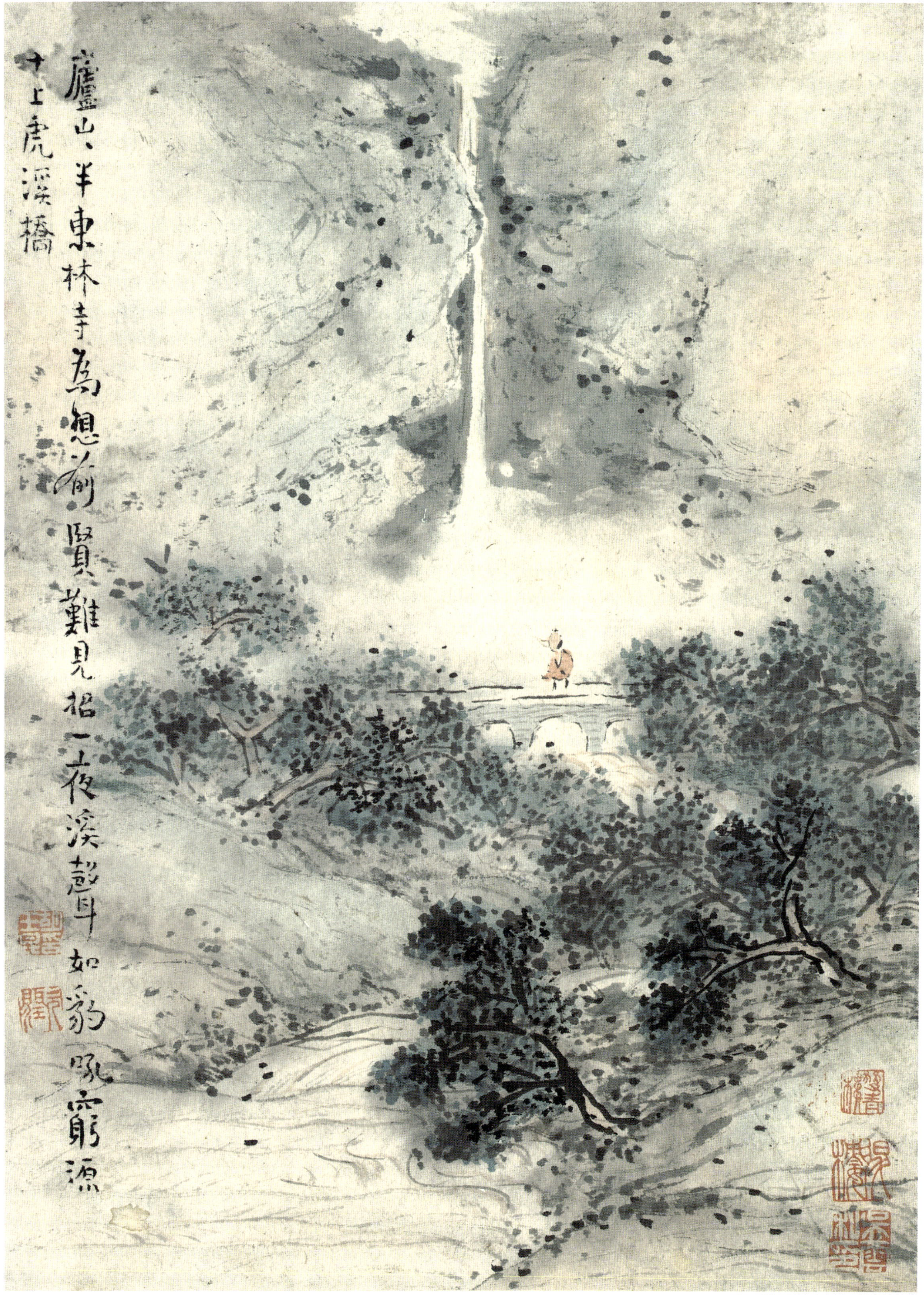
廬山山半東林寺為想前賢難見招一夜溪聲如豹吼窮源
十上虎溪橋

As late as the winter of 1693–94, Shitao was still insistent on maintaining a dual status as monk and artist. In the dedication to the twelve-scroll *Plants of Virtue and Rocks by Water (Sketching Bamboo)* (cat. no. 50, fig. 37), painted in Yangzhou during the early winter of 1693, he writes:

> I am by nature recalcitrantly myself and rarely get on with worldly society. It is only through brush and ink [that I do], expressing relaxed feelings and ancient ideas of virtue. When the monks of old said, "why not entrust one's true character to brush and ink?" this is what they meant.
>
> 予性懶真，少與世合．惟筆與墨，以寄閒情．古德云，何妨筆墨資真性，此之謂也．

Shitao knew that his art was desirable in part because of the moral capital of his social position as a monk. Indeed, he notes in the dedication that the patron had requested that he articulate a Buddhist vision for the image. Like many scholar-officials of the time, he squared this request with the requirements of a decorative commission by exploring the iconography of virtue in a work of ink alone on paper, with inscriptions to draw out his identification with his subjects. From right to left, bamboo and chrysanthemums give way to bamboo and hibiscus, then plantains and orchids, followed by pines and orchids, before concluding with bamboos alone. Rocks, grasses, and water tie together the overall composition into a coherent autumnal garden scene, appropriate to the wealthy residence in which the painting would have been displayed either as a set of scrolls on the wall or on a folding screen. Six inscriptions of varying lengths, tones, and calligraphic styles punctuate the composition, allowing the painting to be read as much as beheld. Drawing attention to the garden rock anchoring the first thematic section, Shitao presents himself first as an obsessive lover of rocks in the line of Mi Fu 米芾 (1052–1107/08), whose running script calligraphic style he also evokes. He then frames the second section with two short clerical-script inscriptions in scrolls four and six, one devoted to bamboo and the other pairing bamboo with hibiscus. He reverts to standard script for a poem on orchids and plantain in the cold wind of late autumn that announces the arrival of snow. Switching back to running script, he uses a couplet to turn the vignette of slightly more distant pines into a microcosmic mountainscape, complete with cliff and waterfall. Finally, by pairing the above-cited dedication on scroll eleven with the foreground bamboo, he manages to imply the virtue of the patron, whom he praises as possessing "a lofty simplicity." In this impressive work we see Shitao adapting to a southern clientele a mode of painting that he had previously perfected for the scholar-officials of the capital.

Shitao's doubts about his vocation as a monk, suppressed in *Plants of Virtue and Rocks by Water*, surfaced during the same period in the more intimate album format in works whose recipients were close friends. By late 1694, when he painted the *Landscapes for Huang Lü* (cat. no. 51), his self-questioning was at its height. Lacking his former sense of monastic purpose, he seems to have come to experience his itinerant circumstances as well-nigh intolerable, even as in characteristic fashion he confronted his situation head on in album after album. *Landscapes for Huang Lü* offers us leaves of itinerancy (the artist displacing himself to West Lake), of solidarity with a community of fellow artists, of a borrowed temple home, and of a sojourn as the guest of a private individual. The glory of the album, though, is the astonishing series of four leaves (cat. nos. 51:1, 3, 6, and 7; fig. 36) in which he visualizes destiny in terms of paths—paths that may or may not be mutually incompatible, that lead in different directions but may leave one back where one started, sometimes mutating along the way from the mundane to the transcendent. Rivers, streams, bridges, roadways, tracks between fields, cliffside paths, mountain ridges, and even clouds become the vehicles of the eye's restless narrative urge. The agents of destiny in these restless images are solitary figures—standing alone, floating in skiffs with the current, encountering strangers coming in the opposite direction—each one a surrogate for the artist who at this point was beginning to embrace belatedly a new identity as an *yimin* artist, an identity that within another two years would give him the courage to leave the security of monastic life and establish himself as a full-time professional artist in the city of Yangzhou.

The viability of a primary social identity as an artist is, in fact, the other great theme of this album, which would be followed by others, equally extraordinary, over the next two years. Here, as he engaged directly for the first time with the alternative social identity it offered, Shitao framed artistic identity in clearly political terms. The final, dedicatory leaf bears a long inscription in which Shitao identifies the practice of painting—"this Way"—with nine celebrated artists, living and deceased, to whom he pays homage and with whom he asserts his solidarity. All were remnant subjects like himself, here emblematically visualized as three leafless, wintry trees that frame the inscription. In this text, Shitao willingly assumes the role that others had long attributed to him but which he had resisted, of survivor and moral witness to history. As painting became his primary vocation, displacing Buddhism, it was fellow artists to whom Shitao looked as models. Of these nine men, five—Kuncan (cat. no. 37), Chen Shu 陳舒 (c. 1617–c. 1687), Hongren, Cheng Sui (cat. no. 32), and Bada Shanren (cat. nos. 41–48)—were well-known Ming loyalists. But the other four were not. Cheng Zhengkui served the Qing court from 1645 to 1657. Mei Qing 梅清 (1623–1697) sought repeatedly to pass the examinations under the Qing, and Mei Geng 梅庚 (1640–c. 1722; cat. no. 33:3) served briefly as a magistrate on the basis of a 1681 provincial-level *juren* degree. As for Zha Shibiao 查士標 (1615–1698; cat. no. 49), he had neither presented himself as a loyalist nor sought to enter Qing government. The heterogeneous political affiliations of these artists should not be taken as indicating an indifference to politics on Shitao's part; rather, they point to a distinctive political vision. Fifty years after 1644, with the legitimacy of Qing rule universally accepted, it was beginning to be possible to place openly the very different *yimin* responses to the fall of the Ming on the same footing. The litmus test of loyalism was finally starting to lose its relevance.

FIG. 36 Shitao, leaf from *Landscapes for Huang Lü*, 1694 (cat. no. 51)

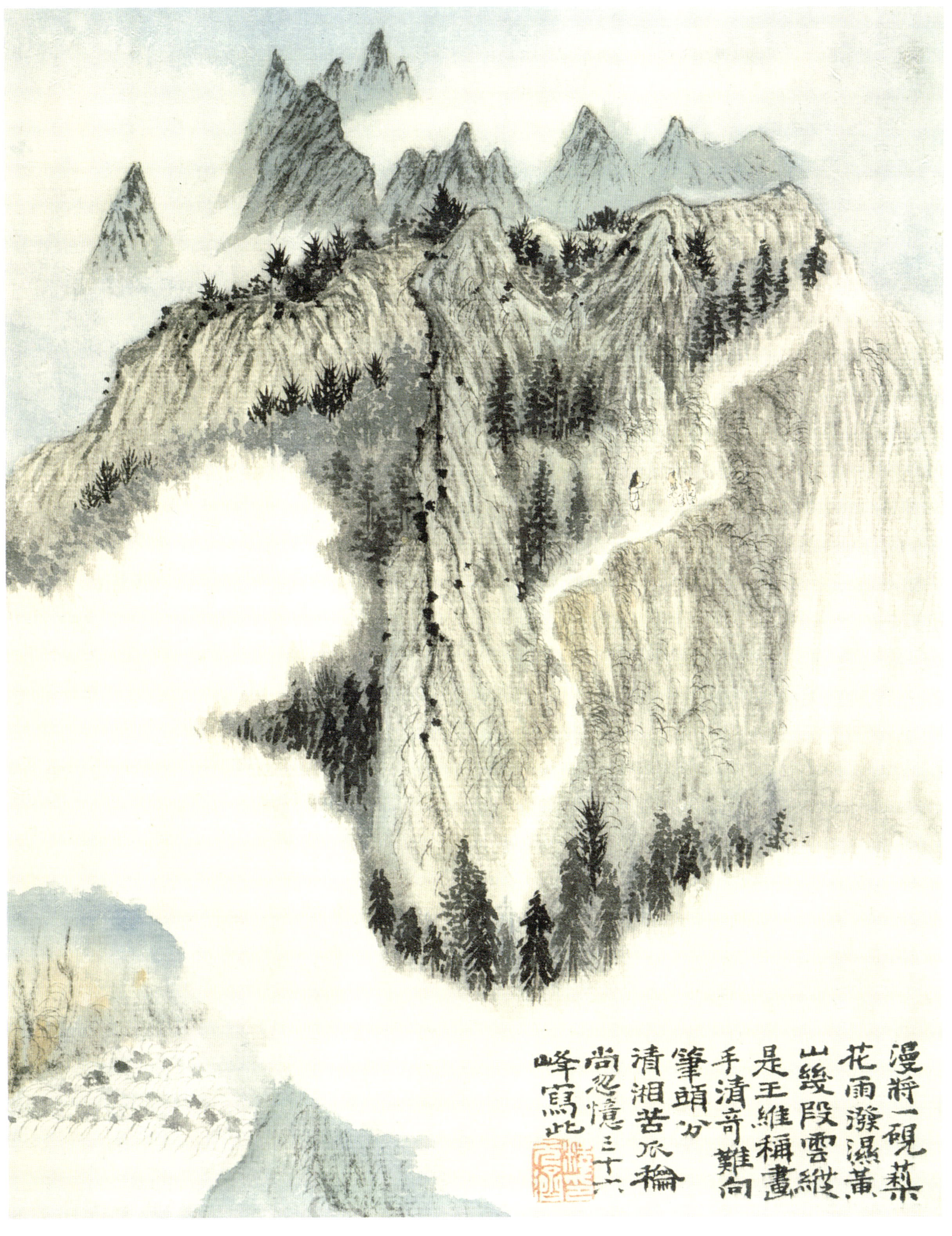
漫將一硯棃
花雨潑濕黃
山幾段雲縱
是王維稱畫
手清奇難向
筆頭分
清湘苦瓜龢
尚忽憶三十六
峰寫此

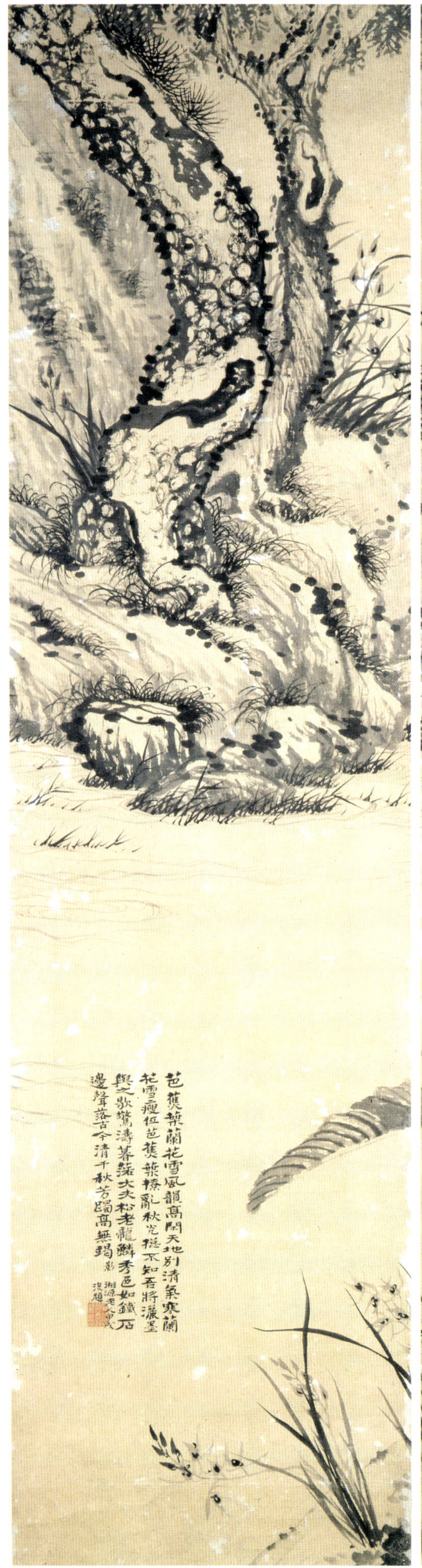
芭蕉葉蘭花雪風韻高閑天地別清氣寒蘭
花雪瘦伍芭蕉葉擦亂秋光搖不知吾將潑墨
與之歌驚濤暮蘇大夫松老龍鱗秀色如鐵石
邊聲落古今清千秋芳躅高無竭

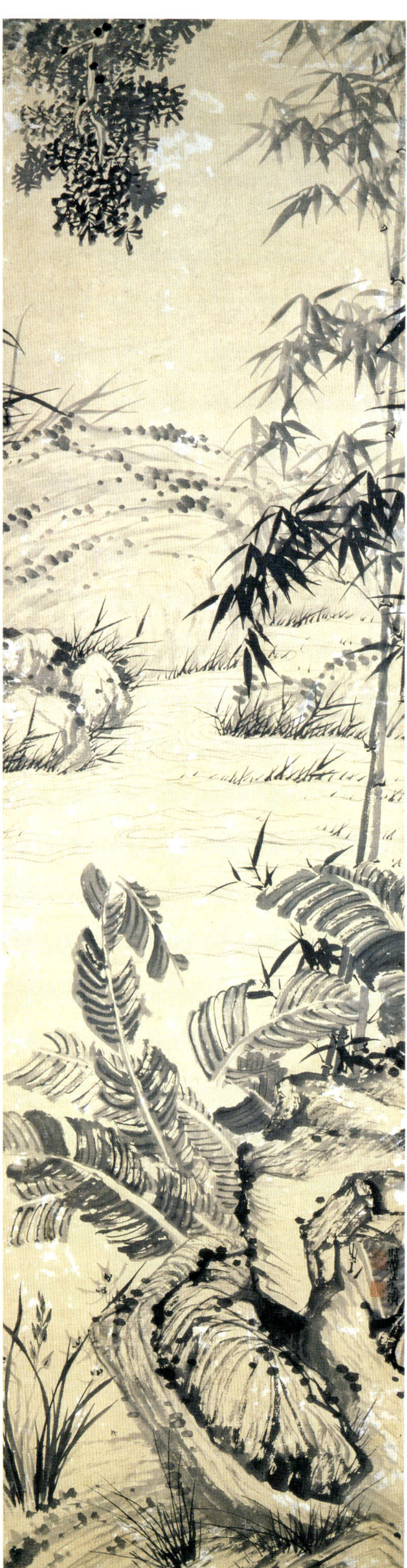

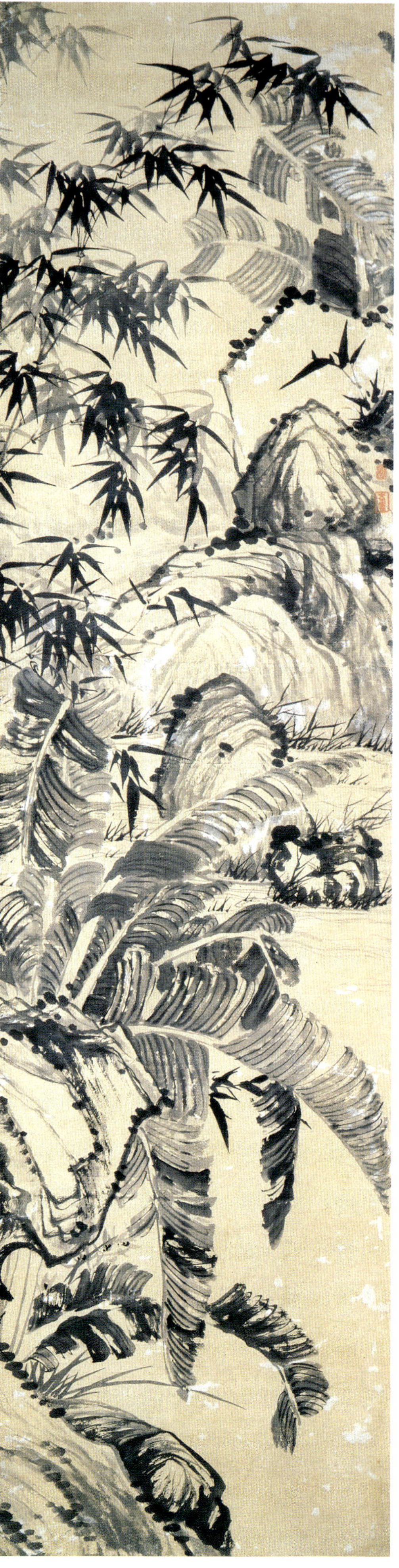

1 See Jonathan Hay, "The Suspension of Dynastic Time," in *Boundaries in China*, ed. Hay (London: Reaktion, 1994), 171–97.

2 Or "like the characters that continue to exist after the candle by which one was writing finally goes out" 亦復如夜書，燭滅而字在. These definitions, cited from Chen Jiru's 陳繼儒 (1558–1639) *Yimin shi* 逸民史, appear in Liang Weishu's 梁維樞 (1587–1662) 1655 *Yujian zunwen* 玉劍尊聞, 8/1a.

3 For a discussion, see Hay, *Shitao: Painting and Modernity in Early Qing China* (New York: Cambridge University Press, 2001), 100–1. The ambiguity could also be turned to rhetorical advantage. In the biography of the noted Ming loyalist Wang Fuzhi 王夫之 (1619–1692), written in 1705 by his follower Pan Zongluo 潘宗洛 (1657–1716, by then a Hanlin academician), Wang is described as "a remnant subject [here Pan uses an alternative and even stronger term, *yichen*] of the former Ming, and a recluse of our present dynasty" 故明之遺臣，我朝之逸民也. Jian Bozan 翦伯贊 and Zheng Tianting 鄭天挺, eds., *Zhongguo tongshi cankao ziliao, gudaibufen* 中國通史參考資料，古代部分 8 (Beijing: Zhonghua shuju, 1966): 248.

4 On the late Ming "opening"—what he terms the breakup of the epistemological field—see the important article by John Hay, "Subject, Nature, and Representation in Early Seventeenth-Century China," in Wai-ching Ho, ed., *Proceedings of the Tung Ch'i-ch'ang International Symposium*, 4.1–4.22.

5 Others include an album of landscapes by Zhang Feng 張風 (d. 1662), now in the Metropolitan Museum, discussed in Hay's "The Suspension of Dynastic Time," and an album of landscapes by Xiao Yuncong in the Zhilelou Collection.

6 The reference is to the Tang imperial advisor Li Mi (722–789), who was reluctantly permitted by Emperor Suzong to retire to Mount Heng as a hermit.

7 Wang Fangyu, "The Life and Art of Bada Shanren," in Wang, Richard Barnhart, and Judith G. Smith, eds., *Master of the Lotus Garden: The Life and Art of Bada Shanren (1626–1705)* (New Haven: Yale University Art Gallery, 1990), 54.

8 For discussions of such images by Zhang Feng and Gong Xian, see Hay, "The Suspension of Dynastic Time."

9 Although Hongren's paintings are not represented in this exhibition, one of his poems was transcribed by another artist, Zhang Xuezeng 張學曾 (act. c. 1633–1657), onto a landscape hanging scroll (cat. no. 25).

10 On Bada's treatments of Ming court themes, see Wang, Barnhart, and Smith, *Master of the Lotus Garden*, 198–201.

11 See Hay, "Ming Palace and Tomb in Early Qing Jiangning: Dynastic Memory and the Openness of History," *Late Imperial China* 20, no. 1 (June 1999): 1–48.

12 Hay, "The Suspension of Dynastic Time," 189–97; and "Ming Palace and Tomb."

13 Evelyn Rawski, "The Imperial Way of Death: Ming and Ch'ing Emperors and Death Ritual," in James L. Watson and Rawski, *Death Ritual in Late Imperial and Modern China* (Berkeley: University of California Press, 1988), 228–53.

14 See Huang Zhanyue 黄展岳, "Ming Qing huangshi de gongfei xunzang zhi" 明清皇室的宫妃殉葬制, *Gugong bowuyuan yuankan* 故宮博物院院刊, no. 1 (1988): 29–34. Huang seems to suggest that the practice extended in some cases to wives and concubines of the gentry.

15 Ibid.; and Rawski, "The Imperial Way of Death," 250.

16 In addition to the many suicides of eunuchs and other palace personnel (see Huang, "Ming Qing huangshi de gongfei xunzang zhi," 29), one can also note that of the hereditary noble Li Guozhen 李國楨 (d. 1644). According to Zhang Dai (other sources differ), having obtained assurances from Li Zicheng 李自成 (1606–1645) that the imperial tombs would not be destroyed and permission was granted to bury the emperor with the proper rites, Li Guozhen buried Chongzhen and then immediately killed himself. See Zhang, "Lie huangdi benji" 烈皇帝本記, in *Shikui shu houji* 石匱書後集.

17 Frederick Wakeman, *The Great Enterprise: The Manchu Reconstruction of Imperial Order in Seventeenth-Century China* (Berkeley: University of California Press, 1985), 269.

18 Zhang Dai, "Lie huangdi benji."

19 Cited in Liu Haisu 劉海粟, *Gong Xian yanjiu ji* 龔賢研究集, I (1989): 90.

20 Cited in a biography by Niu Xiu 鈕琇 (d. 1704). See *Gui Zhuang ji* 歸莊集, vol. 2 (Shanghai: 1983), 577.

21 *The Sacred Books of China: The Texts of Confucianism, Part III, The Li Ki, I–X*, trans. James Legge (reprint, 1968; Oxford: 1885), 124.

22 I exclude here those Ming officials who immediately took office under the Qing, since these were men for whom ideological legitimacy was not the primary concern.

23 For a more detailed argument, see Hay, "The Suspension of Dynastic Time."

24 *The Sacred Books of China*, 167.

25 See Wang Sizhi 王思治 and Liu Fengyun 劉風雲, "On the Evolution of Anti-Qing Attitudes among *Yimin* in the Early Qing Period" 論清初遺民反清態度的轉變, *Ming Qing shi* 明清史, 5 (1989): 33–42. The *Ming shi* could be described as the Ming dynasty's official epitaph.

26 One example is Bada's relationship with Song Luo 宋犖 (1634–1713) during the latter's tenure as governor of Jiangxi (see Wang, Barnhart, and Smith, *Master of the Lotus Garden*, 58–59, 120–23).

27 Quite different yet again was the conspicuous abandonment of restraint characterizing the paintings of certain wilderness artists, often proudly presented as madness (*chi* 癡), craziness (*kuang* 狂), or strangeness (*qi* 奇). Here there was a more radical displacement of experience. If *yimin* painting of this kind was heir to the transgressive tradition of late-Ming individualism, it also shared in wilderness painting's general commitment to the expression of "feelings for the former nation" (*guguo zhi qing* 故國之情). I wonder, though, whether in such lack of restraint there is not some echo of the alternative, Daoist ideological response to death as disorder (*luan* 亂). Whereas normative Confucian ritual aims at the restoration of order after the disorder that death represents, Daoist ritual restores order by embracing disorder.

28 Translation modified from that by Richard Barnhart in Wang, Barnhart, and Smith, *Master of the Lotus Garden*, 148, partly in the light of Hui-shu Lee's alternative translation in "The Fish Leaves of the Anwan Album: Bada Shanren's Journeys to a Landscape of the Past," *Ars Orientalis* 20 (1990): 69–85.

29 Wang, Barnhart, and Smith, *Master of the Lotus Garden*, 148.

30 Ibid., 54.

31 For a more detailed reading of this fan, to which my own is heavily indebted, see ibid., 160.

32 Ibid., 125.

33 For a detailed discussion of Shitao's life down to 1692, see Hay, "Zhu Ruoji's Destinies," in *Shitao*, 83–111.

34 For a more detailed discussion of this process, see Hay, "The Acknowledgment of Origins," in *Shitao*, 112–43.

FIG. 37 Shitao, three scrolls from *Plants of Virtue and Rocks by Water (Sketching Bamboo)*, 1693–94 (cat. no. 50)

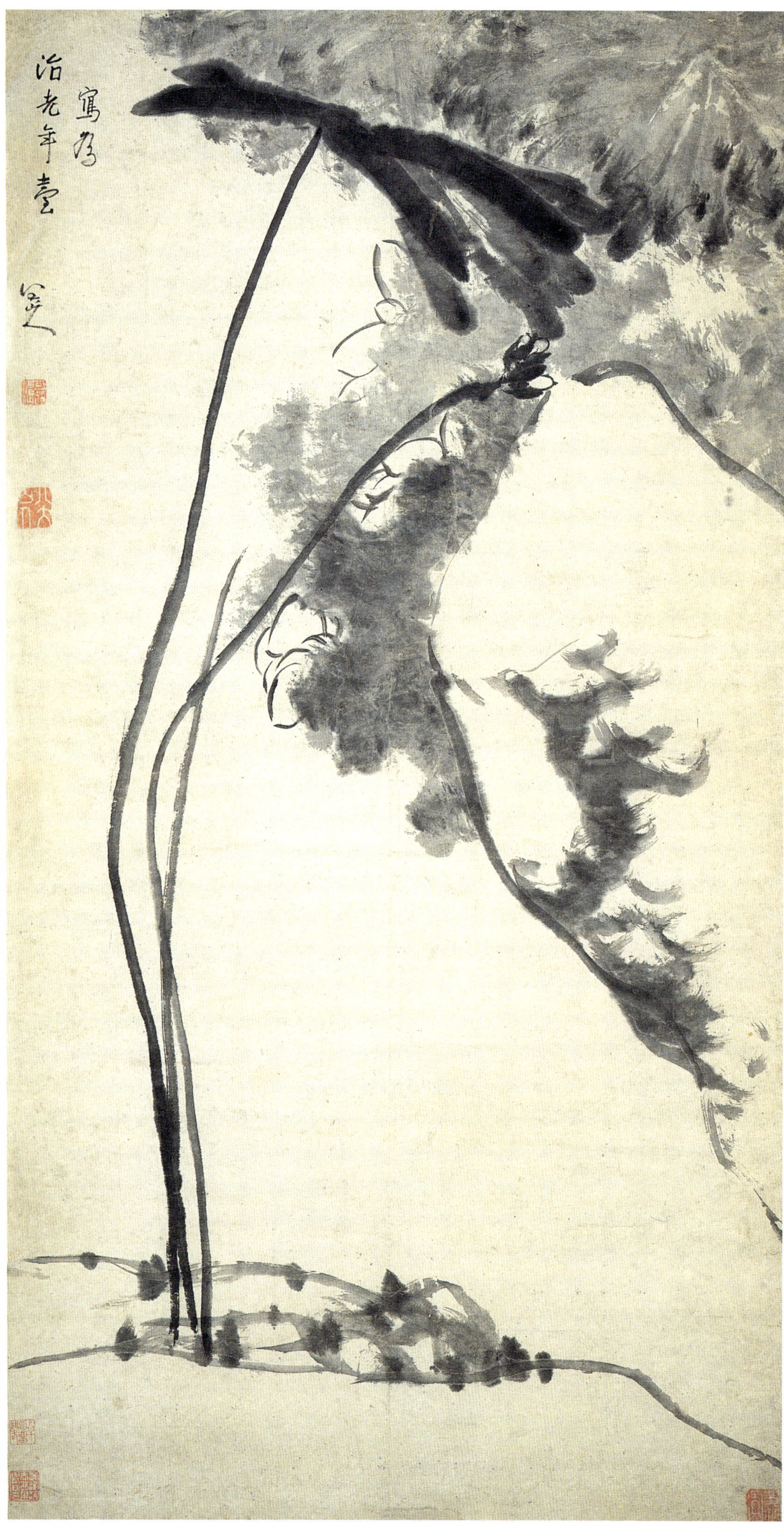

In the Lotus: Bada Shanren and the Heart of the *Yimin*

Hui-shu Lee

There probably has never been an artist so inviting and yet so distant as Bada Shanren 八大山人 (1626–1705). His images are alluring in their apparent simplicity, with equal doses of visual humor, wit, and a peerless mastery of brush and ink. However, behind the plants, flowers, and creatures with anthropomorphic expressions that served as his subject matter is a personal history defined by sorrow and alienation and a profoundly erudite mind capable of plumbing the remote and distant corners of China's deep literary and historical record. Bada often paired his paintings with texts that defy conventional reading and strike even the most educated of viewers as disjointed, puzzling, and frankly incomprehensible. A member of the Ming royal family, Bada Shanren (a sobriquet; his real name remains a matter of speculation) was a young adult when his dynasty was overthrown in 1644. He survived the transition by entering into the Buddhist community; for decades he suffered the psychological weight of having outlived his dynastic identity. Painting was his expressive outlet. While the images beckon, his texts repel. Or perhaps it is fairer to say that his texts simply seem impenetrable. Entry to this most hidden of seventeenth-century artists is not a simple matter.

Probably more than any other artist of the seventeenth century, even perhaps in the history of China, Bada Shanren embodied in his creative expression the idea of reclusion. As evident by the work of all of the painters in this exhibition, reclusion was a common subject for the seventeenth-century artist. For most, however, the intention was to communicate clearly a facet or image of the reclusive ideal. For Bada, however, the reality of reclusion was so much a part of his experience and inner mind that he took it a large step further. His art communicates—of this there is no doubt—but the viewer must follow a difficult path into a world where access is truly limited.

Twenty years ago professors Wang Fangyu and Richard Barnhart spearheaded a major project devoted to Bada Shanren.[1] That dedicated collective effort, which incorporated as well the earlier gains of other talented scholars, resulted in the prying open of many of the doors Bada had firmly shut. Nonetheless, a number of his subjects remained elusive; many of his cryptic poems were yet to be thoroughly researched and explained. The present exhibition offers an opportunity to continue the work on Bada Shanren, who is surely one of China's most extraordinary artists.

FIG. 38 Bada Shanren, *Lotus and Rock*, c. 1697 (cat. no. 44)

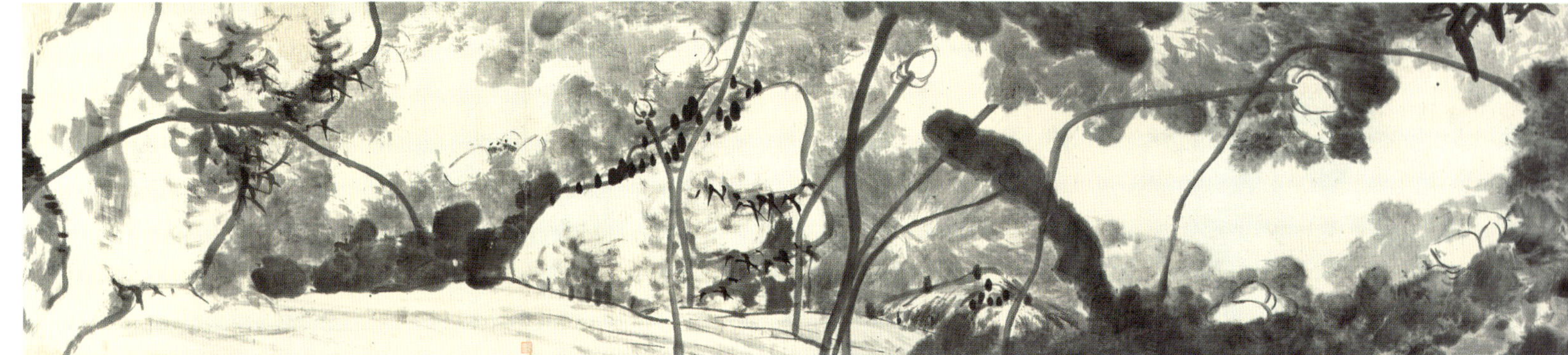

Specifically, my essay addresses Bada's paintings of lotus, represented by two important works in the exhibition: a leaf from the album *Golden Fish, Lotus Pods, Globefish, and Bamboo*, dated 1689, and the hanging scroll *Lotus and Rock* of some years later (cat. nos. 42 and 44). Among the many subjects that came alive under his vibrant brush, lotus was not only the most enduring, it was also the dearest. The subject emerged at the very beginning of his artistic career, and it was one of the very last subjects he painted before he died.[2] In addition, lotus appeared prominently in his seals and personal ciphers.[3] While his ingeniously crafted birds, fish, insects, animals, flowers, and plants can be considered personal reflections, metamorphoses, transformations, and personifications, it is only the lotus—"hold[ing] within itself virtue, redemption, and rebirth in another realm"[4]—that fully embodies the extraordinary life experience, memory, thought, and hope of Bada Shanren, Master of the Lotus Garden. Ultimately, lotus is the emblem for his life and art.

Among the many superb examples of Bada's lotus painting, one in particular stands out: *Flowers on the River* (1697, collection of the Tianjin Art Museum, figs. 39A–D), a striking, symphonic handscroll composition with lengthy song ballad that measures a staggering forty feet in length.[5] This painting is not included in the exhibition, but in many respects it is well represented by the aforementioned *Lotus and Rock*. Bada often repeated poems, compositions, and motifs in different paintings so that his individual works function holistically as integral pieces of a greater whole. Stylistically and iconographically, *Lotus and Rock* is so close to *Flowers on the River* that one must assume Bada intended the former to echo the complicated narrative inherent of the longer scroll. My goal is to present that narrative by first providing a close reading of the very challenging ballad that accompanies *Flowers on the River*. Gradually we will see how lotus forms but one part of a more complex iconography related to the all-important themes of loyalty and martyrdom. Painted at the age of seventy, *Flowers on the River* appeared when Bada was entering into a focused exploration of landscape as subject matter for his paintings. His turn to landscape in the 1690s has been interpreted as reflective of an attempt by the artist to find solace after reconciling with the reality of his existence as a loyalist survivor. In my view, *Flowers on the River*, combining lotus with landscape in a manner unusual if not unique in the artist's oeuvre, makes an important autobiographical statement that at once concludes his past while looking beyond.

FIG. 39A Bada Shanren, section 1 (from the right) of *Flowers on the River*, 1697; Handscroll: ink on paper; 46.6 × 1282 cm; Tianjin Art Museum

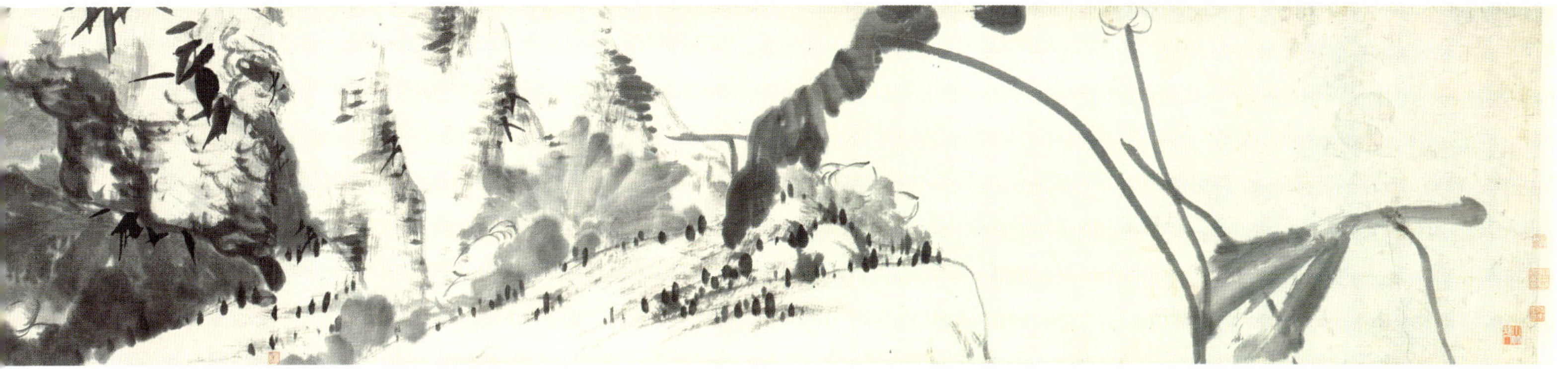

FLOWERS ON THE RIVER

> Mr. Huiyan asked me to paint this scroll. From the fifth month to the sixth, seventh till the eighth of the *dingchou* year [1697], lotus leaves and lotus flowers gradually emerged. Playfully I composed this song, *Flowers on the River*, altogether more than two hundred characters for his correction. [Signed] Bada Shanren.
>
> 蕙喦先生囑畫此卷，自丁丑五月，以至六，七，八月，荷葉，荷花落成，戲作河上花歌，僅二百餘字呈正．八大山人．

The brevity of Bada Shanren's matter-of-fact inscription at the end of *Flowers on the River* and the description of his lengthy song as "playfully composed" suggest a casual approach that the painting, at first glance, seems to support. Such is the mastery of the artist's handling of brush and ink that his forms possess an apparent impromptu power and bravado. However, Bada records that he worked on this scroll for some four months, a remarkably long period considering his style of painting—the relatively freestyle mode known as *xieyi* 寫意 ("writing or sketching of ideas")—and the artist's advanced age. Moreover, the painting includes much more than a few lotus leaves and flowers. His lotuses are integrated into a low-lying landscape that slowly reveals itself. This is a unique composition combining two subjects, lotus and landscape, that are never seen so elaborately intertwined in his other paintings. Clearly this is a serious, meticulously planned work.

Long Kebao 龍科寶 (1637–1723), a sympathetic townsman of Bada Shanren's native Nanchang in present-day Poyang County (Jiangxi Province), particularly praised Bada's painting of lotus, captivated by the manner in which he manipulated his brush seemingly by instinct to create multiple views of the leaves—tilted, swaying, twisted, half-frontal, from the underside. "[Their marvelous aspect] lies in his brushwork as no matter deep or shallow, it is always lively wielded and clearly distinguished" 在其用筆深淺皆活處辨之.[6] Bada's ability to make his lotus leaves demarcate space and direction is apparent right at the start of *Flowers on the River*. The scroll opens from the right with a prelude of swinging lotus stems, leaves, and a half-hidden bud against an empty background. The second lotus leaf, spread like a tilted canopy, brings the viewer into a densely packed rocky landscape filled with lotuses that rise and sway in a small lush valley. A large rock emerges in their midst, and then a second, even larger one breaks through the painting's upper border, tilted back to the right and hunkered over a last dipping lotus, its leaf formed with blobs of dark ink bowing down to the ground. This marks the conclusion of the painting's first section—a concerto of lotus leaves, stems, brushstrokes, and ink textures.

The lotuses momentarily retreat from view in the second section, which commences with a starkly painted willow trunk. The willow's arcing branches dramatically frame the waters of a serene pond against the backdrop of a vertical cliff. This closed, intimate space gives way to a series of large boulders interspersed with dark, abstract patches of plants. Slowly these come into focus as clusters of lotus leaves and stems. The pond is strategically placed at the center of the composition. From here the vista of lotus gradually evolves into a landscape dotted with other plants symbolic of reclusion and integrity—the fragrant orchid along the lower bank and the virtuous bamboo hanging from the rocky cliff. The last portion of the composition is filled with a dramatic cascade of water rushing from a deep valley into the foreground, scouring the boulders and providing an emphatic statement of closure.

Bada's words follow like musical notes sung in a long poetic ballad. His song has the aural qualities of a popular song, yet its allusions are so complex and his thoughts so apparently disjointed that little is understandable without extensive commentary and interpretation.

> Flowers on the river,
> One thousand leaves,
> Six Lad purchased drink, drunk without end,
> Ten thousand turns, one thousand spins, Six Lady Ding,
> Till the Herd Boy Star gazing north of the Milky Way.[7]
>
> Rain approaches Mount Wu, emerald canopy atilt,
> Pieces of clouds roil, Lake Kunming blackens.
> Presenting her with a bright pearl—it cannot be grasped,
> Painted all over my heart: a splotch of ink.
>
> Mr. Huiyan pitied me—old, with no chance for accomplishment.
> [Yet] once at Youquan, I played "fists" with Taibai [Li Bo].[8]
>
> Taibai said to me:
> > Lord Bowang,
> > Heavenly grand was he,
> > [In his] leaf-like skiff,
> > Beyond the edge of Heaven.[9]
> > Six Lady brandishing her sword dance ever forward,[10]
> > Reunited were they, in the eighth month, like Wu and Kuai.
> > The River Immortal was in the midst of painting a picture,
> > Belly propped, he sustained it over sixty feet,[11]
> > Hot or cold, done to the utmost, wearing the tall cap.

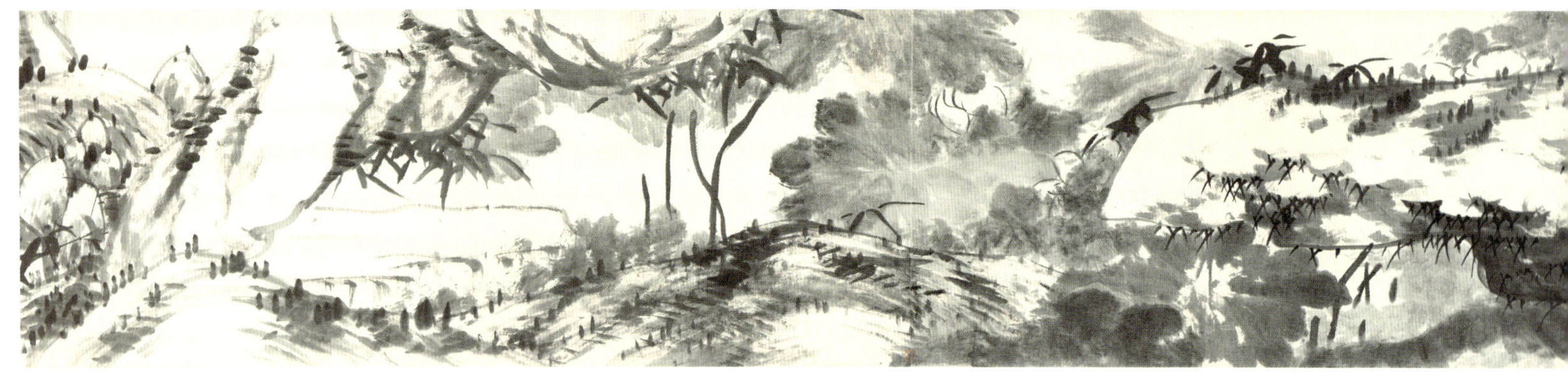

I said:

Mount Kuanglu deep, woods dense,
Since the Eastern Jin, yellow-capped Daoists have
 been equally many (as Buddhists).[12]
One hundred eight tallied thoughts go through my mind.[13]
Big diamond,
Petite jade,
Aren't they all just like those in the painting?
Being and non-being: a single lotus seed.
Alas! The whole world is within a lotus.
Why refine the cinnabar of immortality?[14]

Joyfully, I compose this ballad:

Flying cascades, passage upon passage, the flowers
 bloom in proper accord,
East, west, south, and north, are not all things the same?
The day of reunion, like twin buds, is hard to narrate,[15]
Till this day, I think of the man of Zhi Mountain.[16]

河上花，一千葉，
六郎買醉無休歇，
萬轉千迴丁六娘，
直到牽牛望河北.

欲雨巫山翠蓋斜，片雲捲去昆明黑.
餽爾明珠擎不得，塗上心頭共團墨.

蕙嵒先生憐余老大無一遇，
萬一由拳拳太白.

太白對予言:
博望侯，天般大，
葉如梭，在天外.
六娘劍術行方邁，
團圞八月吳兼會.
河上仙人正圖畫，
撐腸拄腹六十尺，
炎涼儘作高冠戴.

余曰:
匡盧山密林邇，
東晋黃冠亦朋比，
算来一百八顆念頭穿.
大金剛，小瓊玖，爭似圖畫中.
實相無相一顆蓮花子，
吁嗟世界蓮花裹.
還丹未.

樂歌行:
泉飛疊疊花循循，東西南北怪底同.
朝還並蒂難重陳，至今想見芝山人.

Bada Shanren's poem is in the literary genre of *gexing ti* 歌行體 (free-verse poetic ballad), derived from the ancient *yuefu* 樂府 (Songs of the music bureau), first compiled in the Han dynasty (206 BCE–220 CE). The genre reached its zenith in the Tang dynasty (618–907), when it was embraced by the great poets Li Bo 李白 (701–762) and Bo Juyi 白居易 (772–846), who immortalized it with a number of celebrated ballads. Significantly, the ballad form experienced a renaissance in the seventeenth century, due in large part to the eminent poet Wu Weiye 吳偉業 (also known as Wu Meicun, 1609–1672) and his allegorical "Yuanyuan qu" 圓圓曲 (Song of Yuanyuan) on the *femme fatale* Chen Yuanyuan 陳圓圓 (1624–1681) and the downfall of the Ming.[17] Due to its relatively free form in unregulated usage of three-, five-, and seven-character verse; variable rhymes; as well as emotional, narrative, and musical qualities, the *gexing* is celebrated as a free and vividly expressive form of poetic writing. As we know from other evidence, Bada especially admired the poet-immortal Li Bo, one of the early champions of the *gexing* genre. Hence, it is not surprising to find Bada utilizing it here, with Li playing the role of imaginary interlocutor. The fact that one of Li's sobriquets was Qinglian 青蓮 (Blue Lotus) makes his presence here all the more appropriate.

Bada's poem "Flowers on the River" is comprised of three parts: an elliptical description of lotus and lotus pond thickly woven with allusions, a fabled dialogue with Li, and a seven-character quatrain that returns attention to the painting while making obscure reference to something deep in the artist's mind. Following the poetic license of the ballad form, tenses in "Flowers on the River" shift from his present to the past and then to the present once more.[18] It opens with a high-spirited celebration of the lotus scene by alluding to exotic historical figures. Six Lad (Liulang, otherwise known as Zhang Changzong 張昌宗, d. 705) was the handsome male consort to the formidable Wu Zetian 武則天 (624–705), the one and only female emperor in the history of China. Liulang's beauty was likened to that of the lotus.[19] Six Lady Ding (Ding Liuniang 丁六娘, late sixth–early seventh century) was an alluring courtesan of the earlier Sui dynasty (581–618), renowned for her talent at composing *yuefu* ballads.[20] Bada implies that the lotus scene and poem born from his brush are as dazzling as the inebriated Liulang and as enchanting as the dancing, singing Liuniang. He also introduces through their anachronistic pairing and juxtaposition with the celestial Herd Boy, who forever yearns for the Weaving Maiden over the Milky Way, the theme of enduring, unrequited love.

TOP: FIG. 39B Bada Shanren, section 2 (from the right) of *Flowers on the River*, 1697

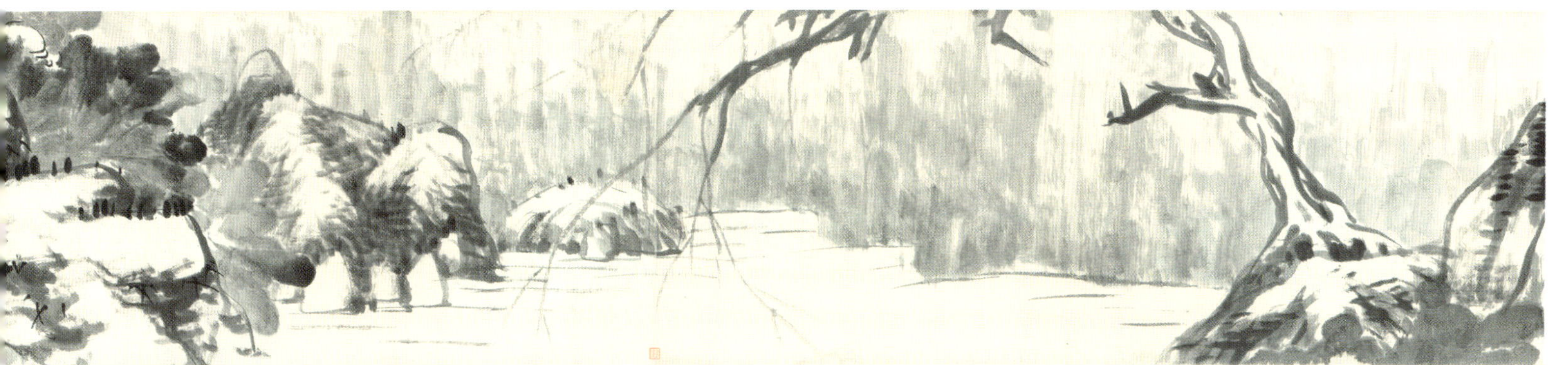

In the second stanza, Bada's song suddenly turns ominous. Rain approaches Mount Wu, one of the famous peaks in the Three Gorges region (Sichuan Province) along the upper reaches of the Yangzi River. Lake Kunming was a celebrated site for lotus located on the imperial grounds during the Han and Tang dynasties.[21] The "emerald canopy" describes a lotus leaf, the "bright pearl" a bead of water on its surface. But this is more than poetic description. Bada's carefully chosen images imply unfulfilled love, imperial collapse, and shattered promises. In legend, Mount Wu was associated with a female deity, and through a common trope the approaching rain consequently suggests an impending sexual encounter. However, the tilting of the emerald canopy, which by allusion refers to an imperial canopy, implies a breakdown of order.[22] The metaphorical reading of this line suggests a twist on an old theme from early China: failure of the loyal official to receive due recognition, not from the slander of jealous rivals but, in this case, because of dynastic collapse.[23] That idea is reinforced two lines down with a thinly disguised homophonic pun. "Bright pearl" (*mingzhu* 明珠) could symbolize an imperial token through a famous Tang-dynasty poem.[24] That concept is sharply highlighted by the suggested reference to the fallen Ming dynasty (明) ruled by the imperial Zhu (朱) clan, to which Bada belonged. In the preceding line is another contemporary reference. In addition to being a famous imperial lake in early times, Kunming referred to the city in Yunnan Province where Zhu Youlang 朱由榔 (r. 1646–1662), Prince of Gui and one of the last hopes for the restoration of the Ming, presided before being chased into Burma and ultimately killed.[25] The last line of the stanza brings the densely packed imagery and weighty allusions back to the painting and the innermost feelings of Bada Shanren.

The second part of Bada's ballad utilizes the narrative device of the interlocutor, with the eighth-century poet Li Bo playing the role of his partner in dialogue. Bada fancifully imagines a friendly meeting at Youquan, with the two engaged in hand (or fist) drinking games (Li was a known tippler).[26] The place is significant. Youquan is the ancient name of a county just south of Jiaxing (Zhejiang Province). The name was changed from Changshui (Long Water) by Qin Shihuangdi 秦始皇帝 (First Emperor of China, r. 246–210 BCE), after sending an army of workers to despoil the royal appearance of the area's beautiful lake; the emperor had been warned that a challenge to his throne would come from the area's geomantically favorable landscape.[27] A similar legend regarding Qin Shihuangdi's mutilation of a dragon-shaped lake figures prominently in another Bada poem that the artist added to his painting of a Mandarin fish on a leaf of the famous *Anwan Album* of 1694 (fig. 40):

Left and right, what is this water?
"It is named Qu'e" [the Grand Crooked].
I go on seeking the place where the source enters,
Perhaps there will be many beautiful clouds at sunset.[28]

左右此何水，名之曰曲阿.
更求淵注處，料得晚霞多.

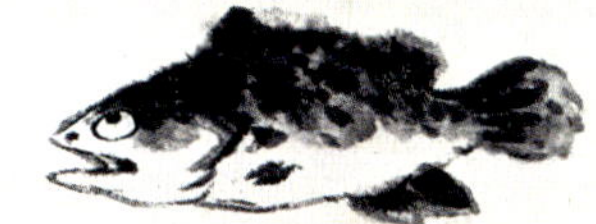

FIG. 40 Bada Shanren, "Mandarin Fish," leaf from *Anwan Album*, 1694; Album of twenty leaves: ink on paper; 31.7 × 27.5 cm each; Sen-oku Hakko Kan (Sumitomo Collection), Kyoto. From *Hachidai Sanjin, Bunjinga suihen* series, *Chūgoku hen* 6 (Tokyo: Chūō koronsha, 1986), pl. 28.

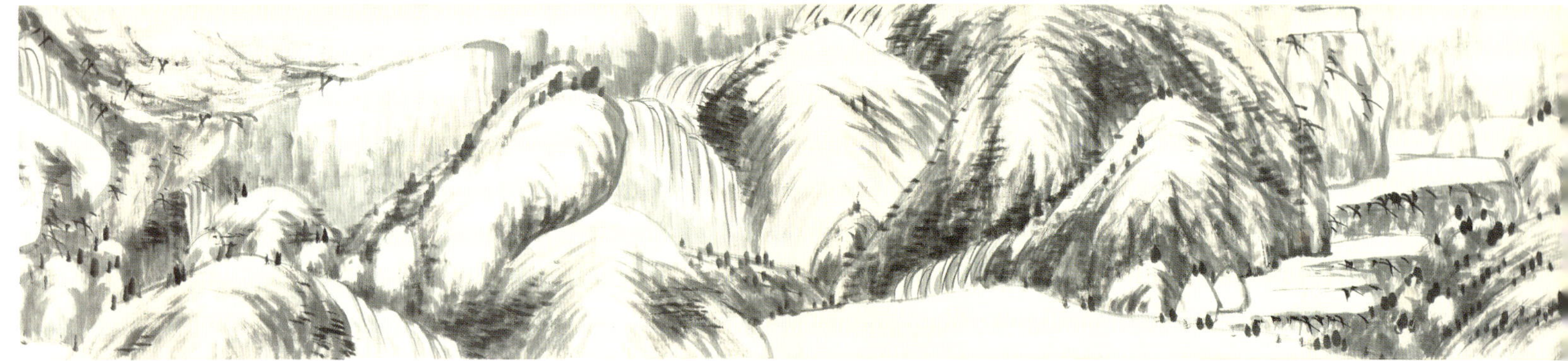

According to legend Lake Qu'e, located near Nanjing, was originally called Yunyang or Daze, both of which mean "great water." So named because of its long, beautiful shape that resembled a dragon, Qin Shihuangdi sent an army to divide the Great Water in two, "cutting the dragon at its waist" and turning its smooth, beautiful bank crooked after hearing that a "dragon" rival would emerge from the area and challenge his rule.[29] The disfigured lake, renamed Qu'e (The Grand Crooked), is the water in which Bada's fish swims, consigned ever to be "seeking its source." Both Youquan and Qu'e represent the scarring of a beautiful land by a tyrannical power to preempt the rise of a rightful king. This theme of violence and transformation follows throughout the rest of Bada's ballad, though always hidden below the surface of his playful language.

The "fist games" begin with Li Bo going first. Ever the unbridled immortal, Li expands the poem in space and time. He creates a fictional union between the great Han-dynasty explorer Zhang Qian 張騫 (Lord Bowang, 195–114 BCE)—whose journeys, according to legend, carried him across the Milky Way—and Six Lady. Given this woman's sword-dancing skills, it appears that Bada intended a reference not to the aforementioned Six Lady Ding but rather to Grand Lady Gongsun (Gongsun Daniang 公孫大娘), whose martial dancing was celebrated in poetry by both Li and Du Fu 杜甫 (712–770).[30] In Li's voice, Bada weds the two in the eighth month and juxtaposes them against another union. Wu and Kuai are not people but geographical sites, specifically the ancient kingdom of Wu (centered in Suzhou, Jiangsu Province) and Kuaiji, or modern-day Shaoxing (Zhejiang Province). The two were joined administratively by Qin Shihuangdi in the third century BCE, but Bada alludes to something far darker than an administrative partitioning of territory. Underlying his terse line is a reference to a particularly dramatic and grisly history of the region that took place during the fifth century BCE.[31] At the time Kuaiji was a part of Wu, but Wu was annexed by the rival state of Yue to the south in a war that had been forewarned by Wu Yuan 伍員 (better known as Wu Zixu 伍子胥, d. 484 BCE), a loyal minister and advisor to the King of Wu. Not only was Wu Zixu's counsel ignored but he was forced to commit suicide, his headless body tossed into the waters. Later generations associated the famed tidal bore, which comes rushing up the Qiantang River near Kuaiji, with the angry spirit of Wu Zixu,[32] and Bada's reference to the eighth month, when the tidal bore appears, points directly to Wu. As we shall see shortly, the early loyalist's presence is felt in other facets of Bada's poem as well.

Li Bo ends his cryptic comments by bringing attention to the painting. We presume that his River Immortal refers back to Bada putting his all into the long scroll. "Propping of the belly," necessary because of all that Bada had ingested, was a popular phrase used by Su Shi 蘇軾 (1037–1101) to describe mastery of thousands of volumes of writing—an apparent self-reflexive note on the artist's propensity for using obscure allusions.[33] Oblivious to heat and cold, the River Immortal is impervious to the up-and-down affairs of the world as he focuses on his painting. His response to Li seems to confirm the artist's attainment of a state of equanimity, unbothered by external matters. Situating himself in the religious landscape of Mount Lu (Kuanglu) in his native Jiangxi Province, Bada takes a stance of spiritual detachment that segues to the lotus's important role as a Buddhist symbol of purity, rising above the muck of the world. Apparent differences—Buddhist/Daoist, diamond/jade, being/non-being—lose significance, merging as one in the embrace of the lotus.

Finally, Bada ends his ballad with a seven-character quatrain. The ending verse mirrors the end of his painting, with rushing torrents of water flowing over the landscape. The flowers—the lotus—are set in orderly fashion in accordance with their place in nature. Bada juxtaposes this image with a statement of spiritual transcendence, in which all differences fade into the non-duality of Buddhist enlightenment. The last two lines, however, end his ballad with questions that seem to conflict the assertion of transcendence: "The day of reunion, like twin buds, is hard to narrate, / Till this day, I think of the man of Zhi Mountain." What reunion? Who is the man of Zhi Mountain that consumes Bada's thoughts?

My research into this ballad by Bada Shanren suggests that there are even more obscure allusions and layers of complexity. In fact, it is likely that we will never be certain where they end. One thing I think is fairly clear: the four months he spent working on this scroll must have mostly been focused not on the painting but rather on this ballad. This is literally a puzzle that was created as a kind of game for the recipient, Mr. Huiyan—hence Bada's reference to using "playful" and "joyful" language. Playful language aside, however, there is serious intent. In the summary that follows I attempt to focus on the basic themes that underlie his purpose for composing this painting and song.

There are a number of legendary and historical figures who show up in Bada's ballad, but it is apparent that the two most important are not mentioned directly by name. The first is the aforementioned Wu Zixu, ancient loyalist and tragic figure whose angry spirit metamorphosed into the Qiantang River tidal bore. Wu's spirit, in fact, hovers over Bada's entire ballad, beginning with its title. With good reason, a number of scholars have speculated that "Heshang hua" (Flowers on the river) alludes to an ancient Daoist recluse known as Heshang Gong 河上公, or Lord of the River.[34] We can add to this another layer of meaning that is more personal and playful: *heshang* 河上 (on the river) is a homophone for *heshang* 和尚 (Buddhist monk). In this case, the lotus literally (and appropriately) becomes "the monk's flower," and through this pun, ownership of painting and poem are claimed by Bada, who spent years in the Chan Buddhist community. There is yet another layer of meaning that is important. "Heshang" was originally an ancient song. Its title

FIG. 39C Bada Shanren, section 3 (from the right) of *Flowers on the River*, 1697

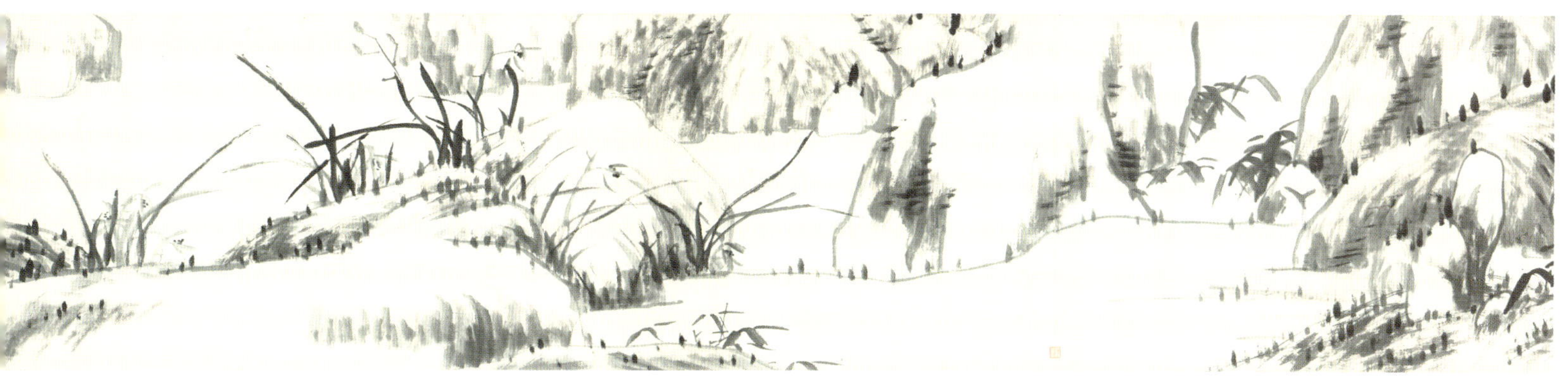

and a few lines were preserved in the Han-dynasty text *Wu Yue chunqiu* 吳越春秋, a compilation of early stories regarding the rise and fall of the Wu and Yue kingdoms. The specific passage involves a conversation in which Wu Zixu is asked why he places so much trust in a courtier named Bai Xi:

> Zixu responded, "My enmity is the same as Xi's. Have you not heard [these lines] from the song 'On the River'? 'Those who share an illness feel mutual compassion. Those who share an affliction help one another. Startled birds take wing, follow one another and gather. The water of swift rapids combines in flow. The steppe horse gazes into the northern wind, erect. The southern swallow faces the sun, bright. Who does not cherish those with whom we are close? Think sadly about those whom we miss?'"[35]
>
> 子胥曰：吾之怨與喜同．子不聞河上歌乎．「同病相憐，同憂相救．驚翔之鳥．相隨而集．瀨下之水，因復俱流．胡馬望北風而立，越燕向日而熙．誰不愛其所近，悲其所思者乎．」

The first two lines that Wu Zixu cites from "On the River" later became the catchphrase by which the song was known, following a longstanding tradition in which these *yuefu* were associated with specific themes. The song itself did not survive, and its very existence would have been forgotten if not for this record in *Wu Yue chunqiu*. In the seventeenth century it came to the attention of Ming *yimin* poets, who recognized in the underlying theme relevance to a fundamental issue of their own time—join forces with those of similar enmity and oppose the new Qing dynasty or forget one's origins and let loyalties fade.[36] There can be little question that Bada intended his ballad for *Flowers on the River* to be linked to the tragic figure of Wu Zixu. The ancient loyalist's comment on the expectation of unity among those who shared afflictions must have resonated deeply with Bada, who so persistently maintained his loyalty to the Ming and, so long after most had loosened their resolve, still sought fellow sufferers of like mind.

The second historical figure that haunts Bada Shanren's *Flowers on the River* scroll is the man of Zhi Mountain 芝山人, who brings the ballad to its close. Zhi Mountain is a common name that can refer to a number of places in China.[37] However, there is one site that must have been especially meaningful to Bada, one just east of his native Nanchang. Named after the discovery of *zhi* 芝 (fungus), which has immortal associations, the site is known for its beautiful scenery and a rare view of the famous Mount Lu, mentioned by Bada in his ballad, to the north across Lake Poyang.[38] The site was also associated with Jiang Wanli 江萬里 (1198–1275), Confucian statesman and mentor of Wen Tianxiang 文天祥 (1236–1283), the famous heroic loyalist who died at the hands of the Mongol conquerors of the Song dynasty.[39] A native of Jiangxi, Jiang served in high office under Emperors Lizong 理宗 (r. 1224–1264) and Duzong 度宗 (r. 1265–1274) before retiring at the advanced age of seventy-five in 1273. He retreated to Zhi Mountain in Raozhou and—in the following year, after Song armies lost critical battles at Xiangyang and Fancheng (Hubei Province)—had a pond dug in his rear garden that he named Zhishui 止水 (Still Water).[40] People did not know his intention until he announced to his disciples, "Gone is the momentum [of the great Song]! Though I no longer hold office, I shall be with my country in both life and death" 大勢不可支，余雖不在位，當與國爲存亡. When the Mongols took Raozhou, Jiang drowned himself in the pond. He was followed by his only son, kinsmen, and associates; the corpses piled up, one after the other.[41] As we learn from a poem Jiang wrote in anticipation of the end, the pond was filled with lotus:

> Constructed pavilion by the water—like being in a boat,
> Night rain storming, chaotically it beats the awnings.
> Lotus leaves observed at dawn appear as if never soaked,
> And make me suspect I was mistaken about those fifth-watch winds.[42]
>
> 結亭臨水似舟中，夜雨瀟瀟亂打篷.
> 荷葉曉看元不溼，卻疑誤聽五更風.

The impermeability of the lotus leaves, which show no sign of the night's stormy rain, implies strength and resolve. These qualities are added to the flower's purity and make the lotus a particularly appropriate symbol of personal integrity and loyalty. Rising from the mud to form perfect leaves and flowers, the lotus embodied the concept of being reborn in the Pure Land of the Buddha but was equally celebrated in Confucian teaching, especially after the Neo-Confucian scholar Zhou Dunyi 周敦頤 (1017–1073) wrote his famous "Ailian shuo" 愛蓮說 (My love of the lotus).[43] Jiang Wanli must have planned from the beginning for his Still Water to be a lotus pond, knowing well the potency of its symbolism when he made it his place of martyrdom. The taking of his life made Jiang a revered man among the loyalists of his time. It is noteworthy that among the thousands of Ming loyalists who took their lives in the early years of the Qing, many followed his example and drowned themselves. Perhaps Bada Shanren too contemplated suicide. As he admits in the final lines of his ballad, when he painted *Flowers on the River* at the age of seventy, the man of Zhi Mountain remained a constant presence in his mind.

With the identification of Jiang Wanli as the man of Zhi Mountain, we are now in a position to understand better Bada's *Flowers on the River* and, as a corollary, much of the hidden iconography he entrusted to his paintings of lotus. Returning to the long scroll, we follow the pendulum-like swings of his long-stemmed lotuses through the first section leading to the wintry willow that arches over the placid waters of what we now recognize to be Jiang Wanli's Zhishui, Still Water Pond—a moment of visual silence. The transition to the pond is a critical juncture in the scroll, arriving just before

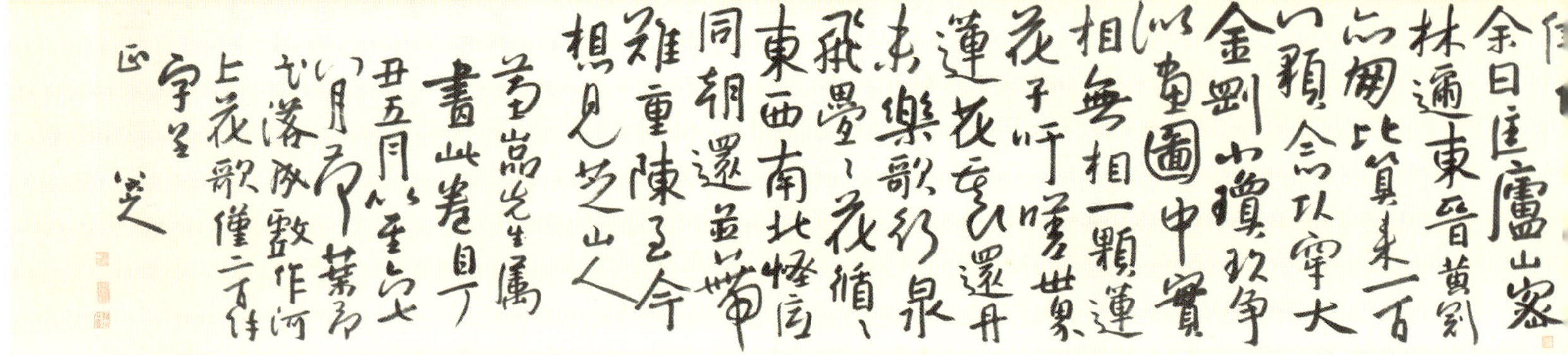

the center of the painting's composition. It is a classic convention in the handscroll format to place particular emphasis on this spatial and temporal moment, and Bada's painting delivers with the starkly painted willow backed by a wall-like cliff. Immediately preceding the willow is a large rock tilting to the right. Two lotuses arc across it—one with a long stem dipping back to the right, the other emerging from behind the rock, its stem mimicking (or perhaps doubling as) the rock's contour. Both are portrayed as fallen plants, with their leaves blending into the ground. Their movements echo the dipping branches of the willow, and once we recognize the identity of the pond it is hard not to associate their downward movements with the fate of Jiang and the other drowned loyalists.

Past the pond, lotuses reappear in the landscape, joined now by other plants of virtue. Bamboo appears first, peeking over and from under rocks. Eventually a few clumps of wild orchids rise by the meandering bank. Both are fraught with symbolic value, but given the context of this painting, one would associate the orchids in particular with Qu Yuan 屈原 (c. 340–278 BCE), the ancient paragon of loyalty who, spurned by his ruler, King Huai of Chu 楚懷王 (r. 328–288 BCE), drowned himself in the Miluo River after hearing of the capture of his capital by the rival state of Qin. In other poems, Bada expressed empathy with the Southern Song loyalist painter Zheng Sixiao 鄭思肖 (1241–1318), who specialized in orchids, and the Yuan-dynasty painter Wu Zhen 吳鎮 (1280–1354), a master of bamboo painting.[44] Did he have either or both in mind here? With Bada it is impossible to know the degree to which specific potential allusions may have been intended. He pokes fun at himself in his ballad, referring to a bellyful of knowledge, and, as he often repeated his poems and images from painting to painting, it is best to think of that store of knowledge as *always* relevant.

In this regard, the strange tilted rock that immediately precedes the willow in *Flowers on the River* may also have hidden iconographic meanings embedded in its twisted form. In his ballad, Bada brings up Youquan—the place where he met Li Bo and engaged in "fists." In a poem Bada composed for another painting, he associates Youquan with rock. It begins, "A piece of rock, this, Youquan" 塊石此由拳. As it is with so many of his poetic lines, there is no certain syntax, and one can read this in different ways, especially as he no doubt intended a play on the name Youquan. Thus, one reading would be "This rock is [literally] Youquan"; another could be "A piece of rock, this comes from [*you* 由] the fist [*quan* 拳]." I think Bada intended both—Youquan, the site of the Long Water destroyed by the tyrant Qin Shihuangdi, and the fist from which the guesses, wordplays, and other esoterica of Bada's drinking games are released. It is likely that one who was especially close to Bada would have been aware of his visual association of rock with Youquan and would have been reminded of this after encountering Youquan in the ballad. The song's context as a game to accompany drinking and its use of language, by Bada's own assertion, is playful, but such surface levity only deepens the anguish hidden within. This rock in *Flowers on the River*, looking very much like a clenched fist, has the potential of embodying an ancient tale of disfigured lands and lost hopes.

There is no question this scroll that took so much of Bada's time and effort was made for someone especially close to the artist. But who was the recipient, this Mr. Huiyan whom he addresses directly in the ballad as "one who pities me" (a pun on lotus, *lian* 蓮, and pity, *lian* 憐)? There are a number of references to Huiyan in his inscriptions of the mid- to late 1690s, but unfortunately his identity has not been established. What can be surmised is he was likely from Yangzhou, had ties to the Buddhist establishment, and was clearly connected to the *yimin* community, including Bada's distant cousin Shitao 石濤 (1642–1707; cat. nos. 50–51).[45] Moreover, Shitao suggests in one of his poems that Huiyan studied painting under Bada.[46] New evidence confirms this. In recent months a small fan landscape signed and sealed by Huiyan surfaced at auction (fig. 41).[47] Dated 1698, and thus painted only a year after *Flowers on the River*, Huiyan's sparse landscape distinctly reflects the influence of his teacher's style. We may not yet have a formal name to attach to Mr. Huiyan, but everything that we do know suggests an intimate kinship with Bada and reinforces the importance of Bada's scroll for him. *Flowers on the River*, in sum, is one of those rare works of art in which all evidence—visual, textual, and documentary—points to its exceptional place in a major master's oeuvre.

TRANSFORMATION AND TRANSCENDENCE In a study of Bada Shanren's painting of birds and fish that I authored many years ago, I drew attention to an unprepossessing handscroll by Bada dated 1693 in the Shanghai Museum that intersperses three texts with three rather modest images, two of fish and one of a pair of birds on a rock.[48] Probably because the texts outweigh the painted portions in more ways than one (they are dense with allusions), the scroll had attracted little attention. Careful analysis, however, revealed that the Shanghai *Birds and Fish*, like *Flowers on the River*, stands out as one of the key documents that help unlock the secrets of Bada's art. The scroll's overarching theme is transformation, expounding on concepts largely drawn from the early Daoist text *Zhuangzi*. A principal component of this is the ability of objects to speak metaphorically for human affairs: *ren shi wu shi* 人是物是 (as it is for humans, so it is for things). Bada uses this phrase at the end of his second inscription on the Shanghai *Birds and Fish* to summarize what essentially lies at the foundation of his art. He recalls the Southern Dynasties poet Shen Yue 沈約 (441–513), nicknamed Hidden Pocket (*yinnang* 隱囊) because of his extraordinary grasp of literary and historical knowledge. And he alludes to the indirect expression of hidden meanings and feelings through the use of metaphors and symbols such knowledge makes privy. Bada, in other words, talks about himself.

TOP: FIG. 39D Bada Shanren, section 4 (from the right) of *Flowers on the River*, 1697

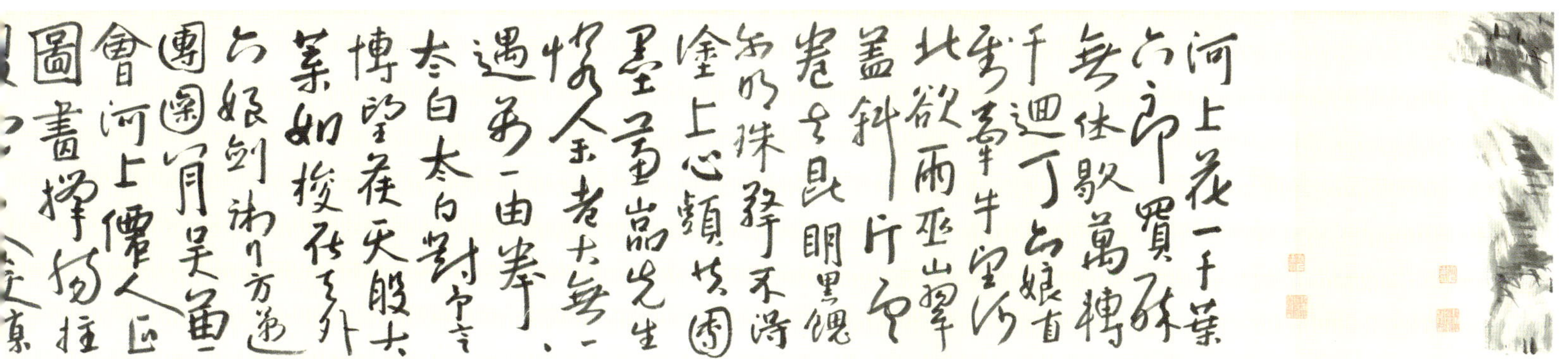

For Bada, transformation and transcendence are intricately related concepts. The former, especially through *Zhuangzi*, implies freedom and an opportunity to act. The most notable example, and one that Bada cited often, is the giant Kun fish that transforms into an even larger Peng bird to fly south and "realize great ambitions." As I wrote in my study of the Shanghai *Birds and Fish*, this iconography figures deeply in his painting of this subject from around 1689–92. However, just as the Peng depends on a giant wind to help it lift off, Bada was dependent on the right conditions for the transformation to lead to the realization of his goals—the restoration of the Ming. These conditions never came, and consequently his art of transformation largely remained a project of hopes unmet. We are reminded of his Mandarin fish (fig. 40)—an imperial fish apparently doomed to be forever swimming in the broken Lake Qu'e (Grand Crooked), seeking a source, an outlet, an end—some kind of resolution.[49]

If *Birds and Fish* is Bada's statement on transformation, with its focus on the interplay of humans and things, I would suggest that his *Flowers on the River* is an important statement on transcendence. Death, of course, represents the ultimate transcendence. The combined presence of Jiang Wanli's martyrdom and the lotus's symbolism establishes the theme. But short of death, it is apparent that Bada sought some measure of transcendence in the promise of landscape. As noted by Richard Barnhart, "Not until 1693 did he paint landscape consistently. The significance I would see in this development is that of the gradual creation of a new world to replace that which had been shattered in 1644. It took Bada fifty years to recover, fifty years to approach slowly the idea of acceptance, resignation."[50] Elsewhere, this is what I termed Bada's "serene lamentation" for his country and his lost world, a recurring overtone seen in many of his late works.[51] *Flowers on the River*, with its extended description of rocks, water, and plants, reflects his growing interest in landscape as a subject in the mid- to late 1690s. The cleansing of the landscape by the cascades at the end of the scroll implies landscape's promise of transcendence. Bada's turn to landscape late in life may not signify transcendence, but it certainly states his desire to achieve it.

The sampling of paintings by Bada Shanren in the exhibition includes superb examples of both his "things" and his landscapes. Of the former, fish occupy a particularly important position. They happily lent themselves to his penchant for humanizing creatures with wonderfully sentient expressions, as well as to his brush and ink skills. With just a few subtle brushstrokes and touches

FIG. 41 Huiyan, *Landscape*, 1698; Fan: ink on paper; 16.8 × 52.1 cm. From *Visual Feast: Classical Chinese Painting and Calligraphy* (China Guardian 2011 Autumn Auctions, November 12, 2011), cat. no. 823-3.

of variegated inkwash, Bada fully brought these creatures to life. Fish also paired well with his wordplay. As has been often noted, the sound for fish, *yu* 魚, is precisely the same as *yu* 餘 (leftover) that can be associated with the leftover or remnant status of the *yimin*. At a more basic level, fish is also the same sound and tone as the character for "I" or "me," *yu* 余. When Bada writes in his ballad on *Flowers on the River*, "Mr. Huiyan pities me," phonetically it is the same as "Mr. Huiyan pities fish." That is not the intended meaning in the ballad, but the confluence of pitiable people and fish appears frequently in his poems and paintings. One Bada poem of which he was especially fond, composed in 1694 and transcribed on a number of his compositions, is seen delicately written along the upper border of a fan painting created a year later titled *Small Fish* (cat. no. 43). Twenty-four minnow-like creatures, barely visible, swim in the shimmering, mica-surfaced paper below (fig. 42). The poem, in my translation, reads:

> Here comes the one who once was favored, now turned haggard;
> Why does he linger these many days under the flowers?
> Had Kunming remained the fish could be released;
> When the tree peony blossomed it was spring at Jinma.
>
> 到此偏憐憔悴人，緣何花下兩三旬.
> 定昆明在魚兒放，木芍藥開金馬春.

Here the character for pity (*lian* 憐) is used in a two-character compound to denote love and favor. Whether pity or favor, *lian* refers to a bestowal of emotion or sentiment born from empathy. The notion was especially applicable to fish, which were used as a sacrificial food in China. Through their symbolic release, fish were also the subject of the Buddhist good deed of saving a life. The helplessness of fish makes them pitiable; the joy associated with their carefree swimming enhances the tragedy of their capture and slaughter. Hence, the third line of Bada's poem on *Small Fish* specifically refers to "releasing the fish," coupling the image with places of significance to the Ming resistance in Yunnan—it was here that the last Ming prince, Zhu Youlang, was killed in 1662 after being captured by Wu Sangui 吳三桂 (1612–1678). Even by Bada's standards, the syntax and specific meaning of this short poem are challenging and defy certain reading. Nonetheless, the gist is clear—if the Ming had survived, the fish could be released. The identification of the fish with Bada and the *yimin* community is further supported by the fact that the dedicated recipient of this fan painting was a Yunnan monk who, like Bada, was surnamed Zhu and belonged to the Ming imperial family.[52] The painting of these twenty-four little fish is a lament for the destruction of the Ming loyalists' hopes in Yunnan.

Fish appear again in two of the four leaves that comprise an album dated 1689 (cat. no. 42, fig. 15): a magnificent puffer (or globe) fish who seems to be grinning as he looks upward, and four fish of less certain species earnestly swimming in formation from right to left. The other two leaves in the album depict lotus and red and black bamboo. Bada added poems to each of the leaves. Interestingly, the verse accompanying his four fish again brings up the image of something pitiable, but this time it is not the fish, which are too engaged with important matters to earn sympathy:

> The golden fish that used to carry wine,
> Have divided into equal camps, each in its corner.
> I paint a few sheets of pitiable water,
> At Xunyang twisting past two layers of mountains.
>
> 從來擔酒金魚子，戶牖平分是一端.
> 畫水可憐三五片，潯陽軋遍兩重山.

As gold and yellow are colors of nobility in China, golden-fish wine servers of a former time must refer to those of or close to the Ming court. These golden fish, however, are now divided into two camps. The key to this line is found in an anonymous, satirical poem presented to Bada's contemporary Wu Weiye on the occasion of Wu's departure for the north and a position in the government of the new dynasty:

> A thousand people seated on Thousand People Stone,
> Half for the Qing dynasty, half for the Ming.
> I send this to Scholar Wu of Loudong,
> The official of one dynasty who served the emperors of two.[53]
>
> 千人石上坐千人，一半清朝一半明.
> 寄與婁東吳學士，兩朝天子一朝臣.

This poem directly confronts the most sensitive problem of the Ming *yimin*—whether to remain a loyalist or reconcile with the new rulers. Bada entrusts the same idea to his golden fish, split into two camps, which are further represented by two layers of mountains. From his origins, his hometown of Xunyang, Bada and his golden fish follow the winding waters, always conscious of the opposing mountains on either side and the choices

ABOVE: FIG. 42 Bada Shanren, *Small Fish* (detail), 1695 (cat. no. 43)
OPPOSITE: FIG. 43 Bada Shanren, "Lotus Pods," leaf from *Golden Fish, Lotus Pods, Globefish, and Bamboo*, 1689 (cat. no. 42)

confronting them. I suspect that the frequent juxtaposition of binary subjects in Bada's poems—including a number in *Flowers on the River* (Wu/Kuai, Buddhist/Daoist, big diamond/petite jade, being/non-being)—ultimately relates to this all-important issue among the Ming *yimin* living in the second half of the seventeenth century.

"As it is for humans, so it is for things." The 1689 album shows Bada at the height of his text-image skills, each object paired with a densely meaningful poem that turns his "things" into reflections of himself and the *yimin* community. Of the four leaves, visually the least approachable is his lotus, but once deciphered, the accompanying verse adds another important piece to his personal development during the last decade of the 1690s (fig. 43). The image is not his customary lotus blossoms and leaves but rather the flower's late-season turn to seed-filled pods at the end of tough toppled stems.

> Upon seeing the heart of the lotus seed
> [I know] the lotus flower has roots.
> At Ruoye the lotus pod was clove open;
> In the painting: a dear young lord.[54]
>
> 一見蓮子心，蓮花有根柢.
> 若耶擘蓮蓬，畫裏郎君子.

It is striking that Bada repeats the character for lotus (*lian* 蓮) three times in this poem, and we are reminded of the artist's fondness for the homophonic *lian* that means "pity." That double entendre no doubt was intended in the first line, which could then be read "Upon seeing the lad's pitiable heart," suggesting Bada's origins through the "pitiable" flower's roots. Like fish, the lotus not only lent itself well to Bada's word games, it was also a subject with a rich store of historical allusions to mine. An important one appears in the third line. Ruoye refers to the area around modern-day Shaoxing (Zhejiang Province) and points to precisely the same area of Kuaiji that figures so prominently in the *Flowers on the River* ballad.[55] In fact, not only is it the same place but it also involves the same time and historical characters. It is said that Xi Shi 西施 (sixth–fifth century BCE), one of the great beauties of early Chinese history, plucked lotus on Ruoye Stream. Xi Shi had been sent from Wu to spy on Kuai's King Fuchai 夫差 (r. 495–473 BCE) by Kuai's rival and ultimate destroyer, Goujian 勾踐 (r. 496–465 BCE). It was partly because of Xi Shi's exhortations that Wu Zixu was put to death. Like a number of Bada's allusions, there may well be another layer to Ruoye. Early in the Ming dynasty there was a loyalist known as Ruoyexi Qiao 若耶溪樵 (the Woodcutter Recluse of Ruoye Stream), who retreated to Kuaiji after the young Emperor Hui 明惠帝 (r. 1398–1402) was murdered by his uncle; that uncle then became Emperor Chengzu 明成祖 (r. 1402–1424). There is a striking similarity between the Woodcutter Recluse of Ruoye Stream and Bada Shanren. He is said to have written things in the sand, which he immediately erased before others could see. Curious onlookers managed to catch a glimpse of their content and learned they were all words of loyalist sentiment.[56]

Although lotus pods were an unusual subject for painting, there is evidence that they possessed a metaphorical significance in the seventeenth-century *yimin* community that would explain Bada's interest. The problematic Wu Weiye, whose loyalties were questioned in the anonymous poem cited above, wrote a series of ten poems on objects that were clearly allegorical. The last

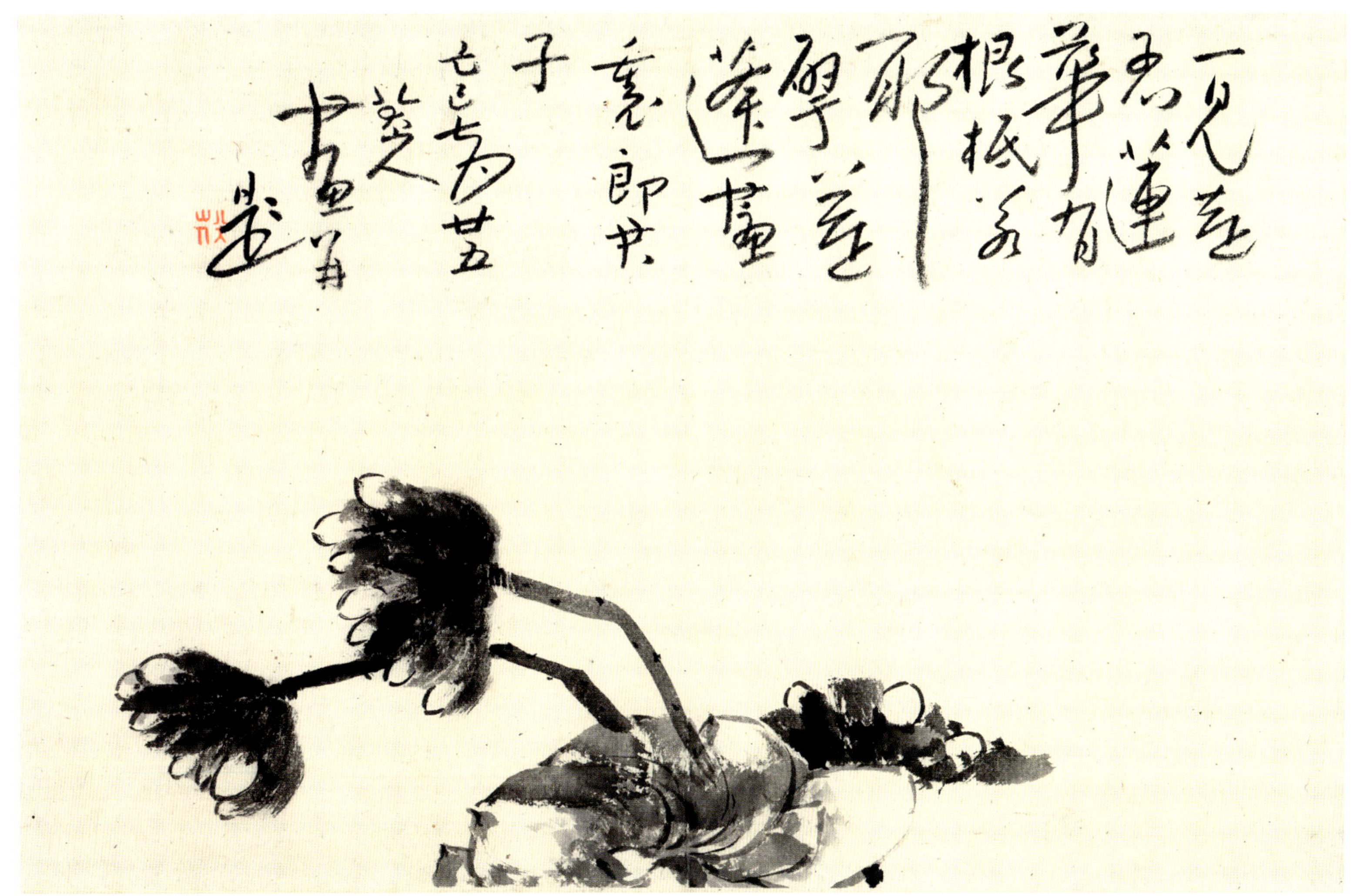

is titled "Lianpeng ren" 蓮蓬人 (Lotus pod man). Wu speaks of the lasting nature of the withering lotus and pod, bent over yet extraordinarily tough. In one line he contrasts the lasting durability of the old lotus with gentlemen who once, with bitter hearts, formed vows but today are scattered. He ends with praise for the lotus, always rising from the muck yet never stained.[57] Could there possibly be a better self-image for Bada Shanren, who remained deeply committed to his dynasty long after others had lost their resolve?

The last line of Bada's poem sounds self-referential: "In the painting: a dear young lord." *Langjun* 郎君 (young lord) is often used to address a promising young lad of high birth, so it would suit Bada, but only if he were writing retrospectively. This is possible, of course, but I suspect that there is another intended identification for *langjun*. Zhu Yihai 朱以海 (1618–1662), the Prince of Lu, established a rival regency in Shaoxing with the hope of sparking a restoration of the Ming from the eastern coast. From 1645 to 1659, loyalist supporters of Prince Lu launched many heroic sea battles against Qing troops along the Zhejiang coast, Zhoushan Island, and Taiwan, and even after the Prince of Lu's death in 1662 the Ming restoration movement was carried on by Zheng Chenggong 鄭成功 (1624–1662) and his son. It was not until 1683 that resistance was fully extinguished, along with any hope of a restoration of the Ming.[58] This smaller but persistent force of resistance led by Prince Lu that began in the ancient region of Kuaiji provides a compelling explanation for Bada's frequent citation of the area and allusion to the loyalism of Wu Zixu. The violence applied to Bada's lotus pod, cleaved or ripped open (*bo* 擘), matches the tragic end of both the Prince of Lu, who died on the island of Quemoy off the Fujian coast, and his loyal followers. It also echoes the angry martyrdom of Wu Zixu thousands of years earlier.

The harsh realities of geopolitical struggles in Wu Zixu's time, which highlighted individual acts of loyalty and betrayal, must have resonated with the Ming loyalists of the seventeenth century. Wu, for example, died not at the hands of enemies but was betrayed by a man he had once recommended and his own king.[59] Fuchai, the King of Wu, lost his kingdom because of his own failings, swayed by treacherous voices and unable to recognize sage counsel. Historians agree that in the end, the real tragedy of the Ming restoration movement was that its failure did not lie in a shortage of dedicated, talented loyalists willing to sacrifice themselves for the cause but in the rifts and clashes among members of the Ming royal house and loyalists alike, which resulted in fragmented, weakened efforts unable to withstand the unified forces of the Manchu.[60] Under the surface humor of Bada's fish and lotus pods, under the word games and puzzles, seethe an anger and sadness that become apparent once the accompanying poems to his "things" are decoded. This is precisely what his contemporary admirer and chronicler Shao Changheng 邵長蘅 (1637–1704) noted:

> Many people know of Mountain Man [Shanren], but actually no one really knows him. In his innermost being he is at once ebullient and melancholy, and because he is unable to release these tensions, he is like a bubbling spring blocked by a large rock, or a fire smothered by a wet blanket. If Mountain Man could meet with such men as Fang Feng [1240–1321], Xie Ao [1249–1295], and Wu Siqi [1238–1301; all loyalists after the fall of the Song to the Mongols], they would throw their arms around him and weep together in anguish until their voices were gone. I am ashamed that I am not such a man.[61]
>
> 世人多知山人，然竟無知山人者．山人胸次汩渤鬱結，別有不能自解之故，如巨石窒泉，如濕絮之遏火，無可如何…假令山人遇方鳳，謝翱，吳思齊輩，又當相扶攜慟哭至失聲．愧予非其人也．

In the 1690s Bada Shanren appears to have attempted his own transformation, from tortured loyalist to transcendent—one who would seek acceptance of the world as it had evolved since 1644. If *Flowers on the River* is indicative, that shift in mentality may have involved a subtle change of emphasis in his lotus iconography—away from the Zhejiang coast and the angry tidal bore of Wu Zixu to his home in Jiangxi and the Still Water of the Southern Song loyalist Jiang Wanli. A pond where a mass ritual suicide took place hardly seems indicative of a turn to a more serene state of mind, but perhaps Bada was attracted to Jiang's unwavering resolve and action. In any case, is it our place to question his self-description of "joyfully" composing the ballad on *Flowers on the River*? Do we question the evident relief that fills the first line of his quatrain, "Flying cascades, passage upon passage, the flowers bloom in proper accord"? There are no lotus pods being clove here, only a marvelous field of graceful stems, flowers, and leaves: each, as Bada describes, a place for the world to take refuge.

Lotus and Rock (cat. no. 44, fig. 38), painted for an unidentified Master Zhilao, appears to be a smaller version of the grander image presented in *Flowers on the River*. A date of two to three years earlier (c. 1694–95) has been suggested by scholars, though there really is nothing to preclude a date closer to 1697. The visual link to *Flowers on the River* is strong, and consequently this tall handsome scroll of lotus forming a sheltering cloud over a tilted rock is best understood as a statement offering shared serenity and the hope for transcendence.

One last poem Bada wrote on a number of occasions will conclude this discussion of his lotus by pointing to the landscapes that dominated his late practice of painting (fig. 44).

> Rain gathering—the boat has no place to anchor;
> Clouds moving—I reside my studio in the lotus.
> At this moment, I exhaust my gaze toward the south;
> It has already turned into a landscape of Wan Mountain.[62]
>
> 雨蓄舟無處，雲行閣在芙．
> 此時南盡望，已是皖山圖．

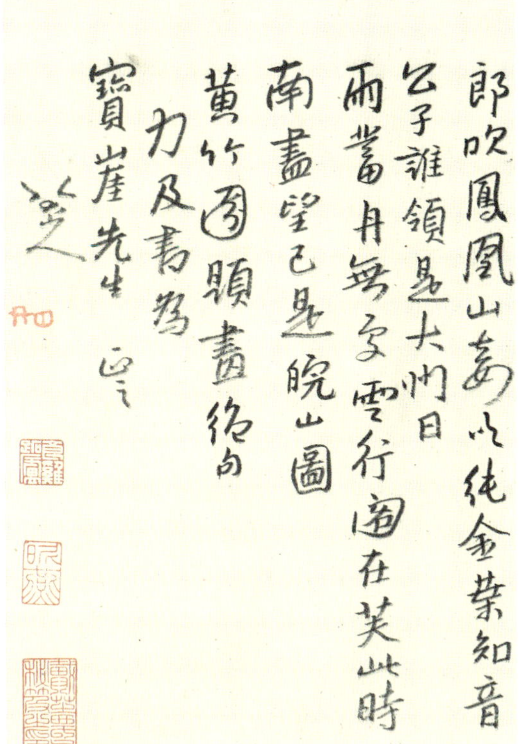

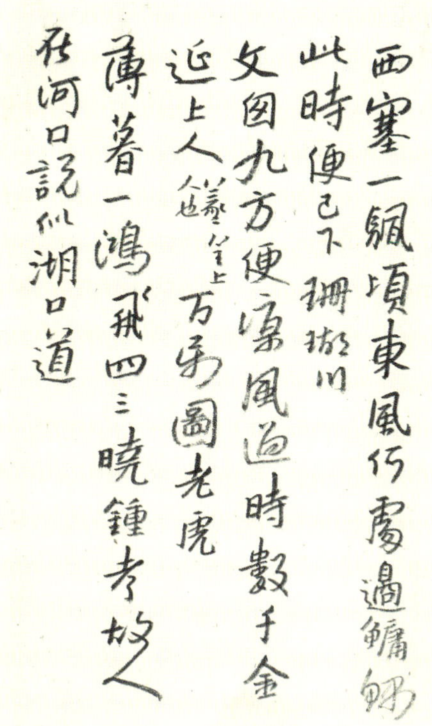

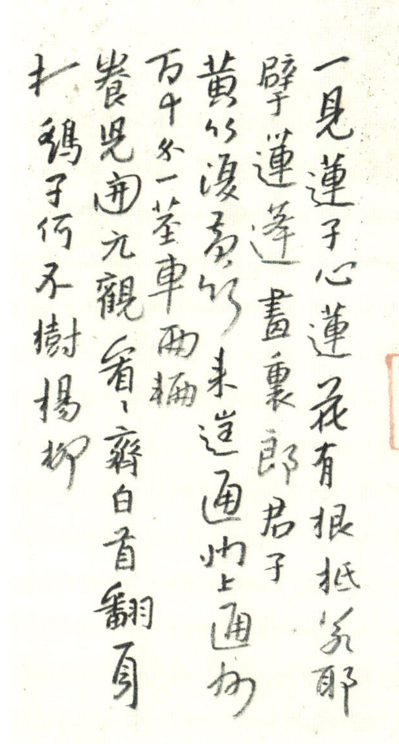

Bada uses the image of the floating boat assailed by rain as a self-image, perhaps describing his past: the storm of dynastic transition and the decades-long period in which he, like a vagrant cloud, resided in the Buddhist community, symbolized by the lotus. However, this image of residing in the lotus was clearly not limited to his earlier life as a monk. That phase of his life ended in 1680. Over a decade later, in the early to mid-1690s, he used two seals that echo the second line in the poem: *zaifu* (在芙, "in the lotus") and *zaifu shanfang* (在芙山房, "mountain studio in the lotus"). It is apparent that Bada intended the idea of residing in the lotus to suggest something more in line with what we find in his *Flowers on the River* and *Lotus and Rock*: lotus as refuge, a place to find serenity. The last two lines transition to landscape. His "gaze toward the south," an allusion to *Zhuangzi*'s story of the giant Peng and its grand ambition of flying to the extreme south, has come to an end, replaced by a *wanshan tu* (皖山圖, "picture of Wan Mountain"). Wan Mountain refers to a celebrated mountain located in Anhui Province that in early times was singled out as the southern *yue* 岳, or sacred peak. Significantly, one of the most famous poets to praise the mountain in verse was Bada's imaginary drinking partner, Li Bo.[63] However, I suspect that Bada is also using the mountain's name for a pun. Wan 皖, which literally means "fair" or "bright," is a homophone for *wan* 晚 (late). Read this way, his poem suggests the distant view of a late-afternoon mountain filled with diminishing twilight and fleeting beauty. Sentimental and serene, the late mountain echoes the title *Anwan*, "to comfort the late years," that graces one of his most famous albums of 1694. It also resonates with the ending line of the poem on his Mandarin fish, which is one of the paintings in the *Anwan Album* (fig. 40): "Perhaps there will be many beautiful clouds at sunset." Ultimately, however, we must turn to Li's poem on Wan Mountain, "On the River, Gazing at Wangong Mountain" 江上望皖公山, as the link between Bada and the great Tang poet was too strong for this not to have played a role in Bada's verse. Li's poem is a simple statement of unadulterated love for the mountain, but he fears that they exist in different spheres of spirituality. Hence, in the closing stanza, a pledge is made between mountain and man:

> Silently, I pledge from a distance;
> My heart longs to go there but I am yet unable.
> Wait until I cultivate the cinnabar;
> Then my footsteps will return me to this place.[64]
>
> 默然遙相許，欲往心莫遂.
> 待吾還丹成，投跡歸此地.

Li's plan for transcendence involved the Daoist art of refining cinnabar to achieve immortality. We are reminded of the end of Bada's response to Li in his *Flowers on the River* ballad: "Alas! The whole world is within a lotus. / Why refine the cinnabar of immortality?" Transcendence, Bada Shanren's ultimate goal, was indelibly linked to lotus. He resides within and gazes out toward those late landscapes—images of paradise that have supplanted the old ambitions of this most stalwart of loyalists.

FIG. 44 Bada Shanren, Couplets for Paintings, three leaves from *Combined Album of Painting and Calligraphy: Grieving for a Fallen Nation*, c. 1693–96; Album of four leaves of painting and eleven leaves of calligraphy: ink on paper; 24.5 × 16.2 cm each with slight variations; Freer Gallery of Art, Smithsonian Institution, Washington, DC: Bequest from the collection of Wang Fangyu and Sum Wai, donated in their memory by Mr. Shao F. Wang, F1998.54.8,.9,.10

1 The project resulted in an exhibition devoted to Bada Shanren organized by the Yale University Art Gallery (January–March 1991); it opened earlier at the Asian Art Museum, San Francisco (August–October 1990). The accompanying catalogue, frequently cited below, is Wang Fangyu, Richard Barnhart, and Judith G. Smith, eds., *Master of the Lotus Garden: The Life and Art of Bada Shanren (1626–1705)*. Some of the work that I did for the project was published separately in two articles: "The Fish Leaves of the Anwan Album: Bada Shanren's Journeys to a Landscape of the Past," *Ars Orientalis* 20 (1990): 69–85; and "Bada Shanren's Bird-and-Fish Painting and the Art of Transformation," *Archives of Asian Art* 44 (1991): 6–26.

2 An album of lotus dated 1665, formerly in the Wang Fangyu and Sum Wai collection, is now in the Freer Gallery of Art. Lotus is the subject of a hanging scroll, dated autumn 1705, in the collection of the Palmer Museum of Art, Pennsylvania State University. See *Master of the Lotus Garden*, 83–85 (cat. no. 1, fig. 45) and 214–16 (cat. no. 72, fig. 130). See as well Joseph Chang et al., *In Pursuit of Heavenly Harmony: Paintings and Calligraphy by Bada Shanren from the Estate of Wang Fangyu and Sum Wai* (Washington, DC: Freer Gallery of Art, 2003), 30–37 (cat. no. 1).

3 These include *zaifu* 在芙 (in the lotus), *zaifu shanfang* 在芙山房 (mountain studio in the lotus), and *Heyuan* 何園 (lotus garden). The chronology of Bada's extant lotus paintings is well established and individual paintings discussed in *Master of the Lotus Garden*, especially 32, 74–75, 83–84, 88, 115–18, 120, 123, 137, 146, 148, 156–57, 214–15.

4 Barnhart, introduction to *Master of the Lotus Garden*, 17.

5 The exact dimensions of the scroll are 47 centimeters by 12.92 meters. See *Yiyuan duoying* 藝苑掇英, no. 19 (1983): 20–29, for a full illustration.

6 Long Kebao, "Bada Shanren huaji" 八大山人畫記, in Wang Fangyu 王方宇, comp., *Bada Shanren lunji* 八大山人論集 (Taipei: Guoli Bianyiguan Zhonghua congshu bian shen wei yuan hui, 1984–85), 529. Long singles out lotus together with pine and rock as Bada's "three excellences."

7 Lad Six refers to Zhang Changzong, Six Lady Ding a courtesan of the Sui dynasty. See discussion below and notes 19, 20.

8 Bada Shanren is creating a fanciful fiction—imagining himself in dialogue with the Tang poet Li Bo. He plays with the language in this line, repeating the second character of Youquan (just south of modern-day Jiaxing, Zhejiang Province), which means "fist." The term is often used for hand-or-fist guessing games that accompany drinking. Bada is said to have been fond of such games, though he was not a strong drinker. His contemporary biographer, Shao Changheng, describes: "[Bada] was also fond of the [drinking] game of 'hiding in the fist.' When he won he would laugh 'ya-ya,' and when he lost a few times he would use his fist to pound the winner and laugh even more. When drunk he would often burst into tears" 又喜藏鉤拇陣之戲. 賭酒勝，則笑啞啞：數負，則拳勝者背，笑愈啞啞不可止. 醉則往往欷歔泣下. Shao Changheng, "Bada shanren zhuan" 八大山人傳, in Wang Fangyu, *Bada shanren lunji*, 527. The significance of Youquan is explained in my discussion of the poem.

9 Lord Bowang refers to Zhang Qian, famed explorer of the Han dynasty. According to legend he followed the Yellow River to its source and reached the celestial Milky Way, where he met the astral Herd Boy and Weaving Maiden.

10 Here Ding Liuniang, or Six Lady, has adopted the sword dancing skills of Gongsun Daninang, or Lady Gongsun 公孫大娘 (eighth century), immortalized in verse by Li Bo and Du Fu. See discussion below.

11 The phrase *chengchang zhufu* (撐腸拄腹, literally "propping the gut and supporting the stomach") refers to having a great capacity, with the implication that Bada will utilize his great store of knowledge and ability in making the painting. The phrase is borrowed from a poem by Su Shi. Su Shi, "Shi yuan jiancha" 試院煎茶, in *Dongpo shiji zhu* 東坡詩集註 (*Siku quanshu* ed.), 7:9a–b.

12 Mount Kuanglu refers to Mount Lu, the most celebrated scenic mountain in Bada's home province of Jiangxi. Mount Lu has a long history of association with both Buddhists and Daoists since the time of Huiyuan 慧遠 (341–416).

13 One hundred eight refers to both Buddhist and Daoist prayer beads (rosaries) and simply means numerous.

14 Being and non-being refers to the fundamental view of the illusion of duality in Buddhism. *Huandan* (還丹, literally "returning cinnabar"), in the practice of Daoist alchemy, refers to the pursuit of immortality.

15 Twin buds describes the auspicious phenomenon of two flowers growing from a single stem. In usage it can refer to a harmonious couple.

16 A reference to Jiang Wanli, as discussed below.

17 With regard to the development of the *gexing* as a literary genre, see Wang Li 王莉, "Lun gexing ti de yuanqi ji qi zai xian Tang de liubian—cong Han yuefu xing ti geshi dao gexing ti" 論歌行體的緣起及其在先唐的流變——從漢樂府"行"題歌詩到"歌行體", in *Shanxi Shida xuebao* 山西師大學報 34, no. 2 (March 2007): 101–4; and Xue Tianwei 薛天緯, *Tangdai gexing lun* 唐代歌行論 (Beijing: Renmin wenxue chubanshe, 2006). For studies of Wu Weiye's poetry and songs, see Kang-i Sun Chang, "The Idea of the Mask in Wu Wei-yeh (1609–1671)," *Harvard Journal of Asiatic Studies* 48, no. 2 (December 1988): 289–320; and Wai-yee Li, "History and Memory in Wu Weiye's Poetry," in Wilt Idema, Wai-yee Li, and Ellen Widmer, eds., *Trauma and Transcendence in Early Qing Literature* (Cambridge, MA: Harvard University Asia Center, 2006), 99–148.

18 Regarding this convention in the Chinese ballad, see Hans Frankel, "The Chinese Ballad 'Southeast Fly the Peacocks'," *Harvard Journal of Asiatic Studies* 34 (1974): 262.

19 Liu Xu 劉昫, *Jiu Tang shu* 舊唐書 (*Siku quanshu* ed.), 90:13b.

20 For the four surviving ballads of Lady Ding's original ten, see Guo Maoqian 郭茂倩, *Yuefu shiji* 樂府詩集 (*Siku quanshu* ed.), 79:8b–9b.

21 On the surface, Kunming alludes to the famous royal Kunming Pond of the Han and Tang dynasties, a famous site for lotus and celebrated in well-known poems by Du Fu and Han Yu 韓愈 (768–824) in particular. Bada probably had the seventh of Du's famous "Autumn Sentiments" in mind when he composed his ballad. Du Fu, "Qiu xing" 秋興, in *Ji qianjia zhu Du Gongbu shiji* 集千家註杜工部詩集 (*Siku quanshu* ed.), 15:28b–29a. Equally important is Han's "Qujiang hehua xing" 曲江荷花行 (Song on the lotus of Qujiang), in Han Yu, *Wubaijia zhu Changli wenji* 五百家注昌黎文集 (*Siku quanshu* ed.), 7:8a–9a.

22 The allusion is from the first poem of Du Fu's "Yong huai" (詠懷, Singing of my emotions): "Once again the Western Capital collapsed, / The emerald canopy was lost amidst the flying dust" 西京復陷沒，翠蓋蒙塵飛. Du Fu, *Ji qianjia zhu Du Gongbu shiji*, 19:24b–25a.

23 The model for the unrecognized loyal official was Qu Yuan, author of the *Li sao* 離騷, (Encountering sorrow). See David Hawkes, *The Songs of the South* (Hammondsworth: Penguin, 1985), 67–95.

24 This is Han Yu's poem, cited in note 21.

25 Xie Guozhen 謝國楨, *Nan Ming shilue* 南明史略 (Shanghai: Shanghai renmin chubanshe, 1957), 185–90. Later in this essay I present another poem by Bada Shanren that refers to Kunming.

26 See note 8.

27 *Shuijing zhu* 水經注 (*Siku quanshu* ed.), 29:10a. Yue Shi 樂史, *Taiping huanyu ji* 太平寰宇記 (reprint, Beijing: Zhonghua shuju, 2007), 1914–15.

28 I discuss this painting and poem in detail in my "The Fish Leaves of the Anwan Album."

29 Yue Shi, *Taiping huanyu ji*, 1763.

30 Bada's fascination with the legend of Zhang Qian riding his skiff over the Milky Way in the eighth month is evidenced in a poem on grapes. See Wang Zidou 汪子豆, *Bada Shanren shichao* 八大山人詩鈔 (Nanchang: Jiangxi renming chubanshe, 1986), 69a. It appears that Bada specifically had Li Bo's ballad on the cursive writing of the monk-calligrapher Huaisu 懷素 (737–799) in mind when he brought up Grand Lady Gongsun, as he transcribed it a number of times on other paintings. Li Bo, "Caoshu gexing" 草書歌行, in *Li Taibai wenji* 李太白文集 (*Siku quanshu* ed.), 6:15a–b.

31 Yue Shi, *Taiping huanyu ji*, 1819, 1921–927.

32 The folktale and legend of Wu Zixu as Lord of the Tidal Bore, with a shrine erected to commemorate his loyalty by the Qiantang River, were well established by the Song dynasty as recorded in Li Fang 李昉, *Taiping Guangji* 太平廣記 (*Siku quanshu* ed.), 291:6a–b. As for the original record regarding Wu Zixu's death, see Zhao Ye 趙曄, *Wu Yue chunqiu* 吳越春秋 (reprint, Nanjing: Jiangsu guji chubanshe, 1986), 52–66.

33 See note 11.

34 See for example, Zhu Liangzhi 朱良志, *Bada Shanren yanjiu* 八大山人研究 (Hefei: Anhui jiaoyu chubanshe, 2010), 285. Heshang Gong, also known as Heshang Zhangren 河上丈人 (Elder on the river), was an ancient Daoist recluse credited with transmitting the Daoist text *Laozi*. Ge Hong 葛洪, *Shenxian zhuan* 神仙傳 (*Siku quanshu* ed.), 8:9a–10a. Notably, Heshang Zhangren is associated with the lotus and the pursuit of immortality in a quatrain by the Tang poet Wang Changling 王昌齡 (698–c. 756): "The Elder on the River rides on his ancient wooden skiff; / He attains the cinnabar (of immortality) with only the blue lotus flower"

河上老人坐古槎，合丹只用青蓮花. *Yuding Quan Tang shi* 御定全唐詩 (*Siku quanshu* ed.), 143:15a. Wang's poem is often called *Heshang ge* 河上歌 (Song on the river). Given the confluence of images and language, including Li Bo's sobriquet as Blue Lotus, it is certain that Bada was aware of Wang's poem and intended Daoist connotations.

35 Zhao Ye, *Wu Yue chunqiu*, 28–29.

36 Qian Qianyi 錢謙益 (1582–1664) brings this up in his preface to a series of poems he wrote after reading four verses by Wu Weiye, "Du Meicun gongzhan yanshi yougan shu hou" 讀梅村宮詹豔詩有感書後: "With regard to the song 'On the River,' listeners either respond as those who share an illness feel mutual compassion, or simply think of it as sharing the same bed but having different dreams and have a good laugh" 河上之歌，聽者將同病相憐，抑或以為同牀各夢，而輾爾一笑也. Qian Qianyi, *Muzhai youxue ji* 牧齋有學集 (Shanghai: Shanghai guji chubanshe, 1996), 116.

37 *Zhi* (芝, magic fungus) is associated with the Daoist pursuit of immortality and thus is a relatively common name for mountains in China. Scholars in the past have come up with different identifications. Wan Zhaofeng, for example, brings attention to a Zhi Mountain in Shandong Province, and Zhu Liangzhi attaches it to a place in Nanjing. See Wan Zhaofeng 萬兆鳳, "Shi Bada Shanren tihuashi 'heshang hua ge'" 釋八大山人題畫詩河上花歌, in *Bada Shanren quanji* 八大山人全集, vol. 5 (Nanchang: Jiangxi meishu chubanshe, 2000), 1282; and Zhu Liangzhi, *Bada Shanren yanjiu*, 292 and note 3. Both of these scholars downplay the significance of "man of Zhi Mountain," considering it a self-reference by Bada.

38 Xie Min 謝旻, *Jiangxi tongzhi* 江西通志 (*Siku quanshu* ed.), 11:33b.

39 Wen Tianxiang met Jiang and received his blessing in 1273. See Wen's biography in Tuotuo 脫脫, *Song shi* 宋史 (reprint, Beijing: Zhonghua shuju, 1985), 418:12534; and Richard Davis, *Wind against the Mountain: The Crisis of Politics and Culture in Thirteenth-Century China* (Cambridge, MA: Harvard University Press, 1996), 58–59.

40 Jiang's naming of his suicide pond Zhishui was a conscious allusion to a passage from the chapter "De chong fu" 德充符 (The sign of virtue complete) in *Zhuangzi*, which reads, "Men do not mirror themselves in running water—they mirror themselves in still water. Only what is still can still the stillness of other things" 人莫鑑於流水而鑑於止水，唯止能止眾止. *Zhuangzi jinzhu jinyi* 莊子今註今譯 (reprint, Taipei: Taiwan shangwu yinshuguan, 1984), 160. Translation by Burton Watson, *The Complete Works of Chuang Tzu* (New York: Columbia University Press, 1968), 69.

41 For Jiang Wanli's biography and martyrdom, see Tuotuo, *Song shi*, 416:12523–25; *Jiangxi tongzhi*, 4:18b, 19a; and Davis, *Wind against the Mountain*, 78–79.

42 Recorded in Li E 厲鶚, *Songshi jishi* 宋詩記事 (*Siku quanshu* ed.), 68:21b–22a. The poem was titled "Shuiting" (水亭, Water pavilion), but is also known by the title "Lotus."

43 Zhou Dunyi 周敦頤, *Zhou Yuangong ji* 周元公集 (*Siku quanshu* ed.), 2:1b–2a. Bada transcribed this essay in a calligraphy hanging scroll dated around 1698. See *Fine Chinese Paintings* (New York: Sotheby's, December 6, 1989), 82. He also frequently copied the Tang calligrapher Chu Suiliang's 褚遂良 (596–658) *Shengjiao xu* 聖教序 (Preface to the sacred teachings), a text that eulogizes lotus.

44 Bada reminisced on Zheng Sixiao in an inscription to his striking image of *Old Plum* (1682): "When I painted these plum blossoms I thought about Zheng Sixiao; / How can a monk be like those who gathered ferns?" [referring to the ancient sages Boyi and Shuqi, who refused the food of the new dynasty] 梅花畫裏思思肖，和尚如何如采薇. In a painting of orchids, Bada recalled Wu Zhen: "Sketching bamboo, sketching orchids, Wu Zhonggui [Wu Zhen]" 寫竹寫蘭吳仲圭. *Master of the Lotus Garden*, fig. 26 and p. 54; cat. no. 3, fig. 47c, and p. 87.

45 Including *Flowers on the River*, Huiyan appears at least four times in Bada's writings. According to Wang Shiqing, these are dated 1694–96, 1697, 1699, and 1701. Wang Shiqing 汪世清, "Bada Shanren de jiaoyou" 八大山人的交友, in *Bada Shanren quanji* 八大山人全集, vol. 5, 1113, 1119nn103, 105, 106. The earliest record of Huiyan appears in Bada's inscription to his landscape in the Huang Gongwang–style datable to 1694–96. In this informative inscription, Bada describes Huiyan as being of Guangling, another way of describing Yangzhou, and refers to Huiyan's commission of a large blue-and-green landscape by Shitao through their intermediary, Cheng Jing'e 程京萼 (1645–1715), who was a patron and occasional intermediary for both Bada and Shitao. Ibid., 1113. The painting is now in the collection of the Shanghai Museum and is published in *Zhiren wufa: Gugong, Shangbo zhencang Bada Shitao shuhua jingpin* 至人無法：故宮、上博珍藏八大石濤書畫精品 (Macao: Aomen yishu bowuguan, 2004), pl. 29. In a letter of 1699 that Bada wrote to a Yangzhou Buddhist priest, he praises highly a Shitao painting commissioned by Huiyan. See Wang Shiqing, "Bada Shanren de jiaoyou," 1113, 1119n103. This letter is now in the collection of the He Chuangshi shufa yishu jijinghui (Taipei).

46 This is in a poem that Shitao inscribed onto his own landscape (formerly in the collection of Wu Hufan). Wang Shiqing, "Bada Shanren de jiaoyou," 1119n106.

47 China Guardian 2011 Autumn Auctions, November 12, 2011; the fan was published in the accompanying catalogue *Visual Feast: Classical Chinese Painting and Calligraphy*, cat. no. 823–3.

48 See Lee, "Bada Shanren's Bird-and-Fish Painting and the Art of Transformation," especially 9–14.

49 The last line in the poem accompanying the Mandarin fish tempers that gloomy prospect with a note of resignation that is almost serene: "Perhaps there will be many beautiful clouds at sunset."

50 Barnhart, *Master of the Lotus Garden*, 18.

51 Lee, "The Fish Leaves of the *Anwan* Album," 69–85.

52 I discuss this poem at some length in ibid., especially pages 72–74.

53 Recorded in Liu Xianting 劉獻廷, *Guangyang zaji* 廣陽雜記, in *Congshu jicheng jianbian* 叢書集成簡編, vol. 737 (Taipei: Shangwu yinshuguan, 1966), 1:9. Loudong refers to Taicang (Jiangsu Province).

54 This is a revised translation from what I previously had written for *Master of the Lotus Garden*, 115. The poem appears in at least two other places: on the 1690 handscroll *Lotus and Birds* (Cincinnati Museum of Art) and as one of eight poems transcribed in the *Combined Album of Painting and Calligraphy: "Grieving for a Fallen Nation"* (c. 1693–96) in the Freer Gallery of Art. For the former, see *Master of the Lotus Garden*, fig. 59; for the latter, see Joseph Chang, et al., *In Pursuit of Heavenly Harmony: Paintings and Calligraphy by Bada Shanren from the Estate of Wang Fangyu and Sum Wai* (Washington, DC: Freer Gallery of Art, 2003), cat. no. 8, leaf 8, poem 1.

55 Ruoye belongs to Kuaiji County of Shaoxing District. See *Taiping huanyu ji*, 1927, 1930.

56 Ruoyexi Qiao was paired with Monk Yunmen 雲門 as the two recluses of Kuaiji. Ruoyexi Qiao often wrote in the sand with reeds, immediately erasing the words, and Monk Yunmen burnt his poems to conceal his feelings. Zhang Tingyu 張廷玉, et al., *Ming shi* 明史 (*Siku quanshu* ed.), 143:19b. Their secrecy in writings and behavior were similar to Bada in many ways.

57 Wu Weiye, "Lianpeng ren" 蓮蓬人, in *Meicun jiacang gao* 梅村家藏稿 (*Sibu congkan* ed.), 16:8a–b.

58 Xie Guozhen, *Nan Ming shilue*, 107–22, 197–212.

59 Wu Zixu was betrayed by the same Bai Xi whom Wu claimed he trusted because of their shared experiences. See above, notes 32 and 35.

60 For good general discussions about the problems of the Ming *yimin*, see Lynn A. Struve, *The Southern Ming, 1644–1662* (New Haven, CT: Yale University Press, 1984); He Guanbiao 何冠彪, "Lun Ming yimin zhi chuchu" 論明遺民之出處, in He, ed., *Ming mo Qing chu xueshu sixiang yanjiu* 明末清初學術思想研究 (Taipei: Xuesheng shuju, 1991), 53–124; and He, *Sheng yu si: Ming ji shidaifu de jueze* 生與死：明季士大夫的抉擇 (Taipei: Lianjing chubanshe, 1997), especially 15–23. See also Wai-yee Lee's introduction to *Trauma and Transcendence in Early Qing Literature*, 1–70.

61 *Master of the Lotus Garden*, 19, translation by Matthew Kercher with modification by the author. On the influence of the Song loyalists on the seventeenth century, see Jennifer W. Jay, *A Change in Dynasties: Loyalism in Thirteenth-Century China* (Bellingham, WA: Western Washington University, 1991), 261. For discussion of the individual Song loyalists Xie Ao, Fang Feng, and Wu Siji, see Zhou Quan 周全, *Song yimin zhijie yu wenxue* 宋遺民志節與文學 (Taipei: Dongwu daxue, 1991), 56–71; appendix, 7, 20.

62 For an alternative translation, see *Master of the Lotus Garden*, 140. Here I took a very different reading in some of the key words, especially with regard to *wanshan tu*. Instead of reading it as "picture of Bright Mountain," I think the adjective *wan* is a crucial linguistic pun for "being late"; thus "landscape of late mountains" would be a self-reflective metaphor for this late stage of Bada's life and a sense of resignation. This is from the last poem in a series of eight on three album leaves which form part of the *Combined Album of Painting and Calligraphy*, dated c. 1693–96. See *Heavenly Harmony*, 60–63 (cat. no. 8, leaf 10, poem 8), and *Master of the Lotus Garden*, 103 (cat. no. 7, fig. 51, leaf b), 115–18 (cat. no. 15, fig. 59), and 139–40 (cat. no. 30, fig. 75). The poem is also inscribed on a calligraphy hanging scroll in semi-cursive style; see Wang Zhaowen, ed., *Bada Shanren quanji*, 3:628 (cat. no. 196).

63 Yue Shi, *Taiping huanyu ji*, 2474.

64 Li Bo, *Li Taibai wenji* 李太白文集 (*Siku quanshu* ed.), 18:7a–8b. 皖公山 (Wangong shan) is the same as Wang Mountain.

Catalogue of the Exhibition

NOTE TO THE READER

Literati painting is almost by definition inflected by language and writing, which appears in the form of accompanying poems and inscriptions written by the artist and/or admiring friends and later viewers. This documentation is an essential part of the objects in the exhibition. Excerpts that appear in the catalogue section provide a taste of these literary accompaniments. Fuller transcriptions and translations, limited to those of the artist and his or her near contemporaries, follow on pages 276 to 307. Unless otherwise noted, translations are by the individual catalogue entry contributors. Characters for all Chinese names that appear in the entries can be found in the Names and Dates of Historical Figures on pages 310 to 312.

CONTRIBUTORS

Birgitta Augustin **BA**
Seokwon Choi **SWC**
Julia H. Cross **JHC**
Jonathan Hay **JH**
Ka-yi Ho **KYH**
Meichih T. Ho **MH**
Philip K. Hu **PKH**
Nathaniel Kingdon **NK**
Theeng T. Kok **TTK**
Hui-shu Lee **HSL**
Oh Mee Lee **OML**
Lihong Liu **LL**
Kathy Yim-king Mak **KYM**
Ying-chen Peng **YCP**
Feng Qin **FQ**
Yoonjung Seo **YJS**
Peter C. Sturman **PCS**
Hye-shim Yi **HSY**
Jiayin Zhang **JYZ**
Meimei Zhang **MMZ**
Yunshuang Zhang **YSZ**

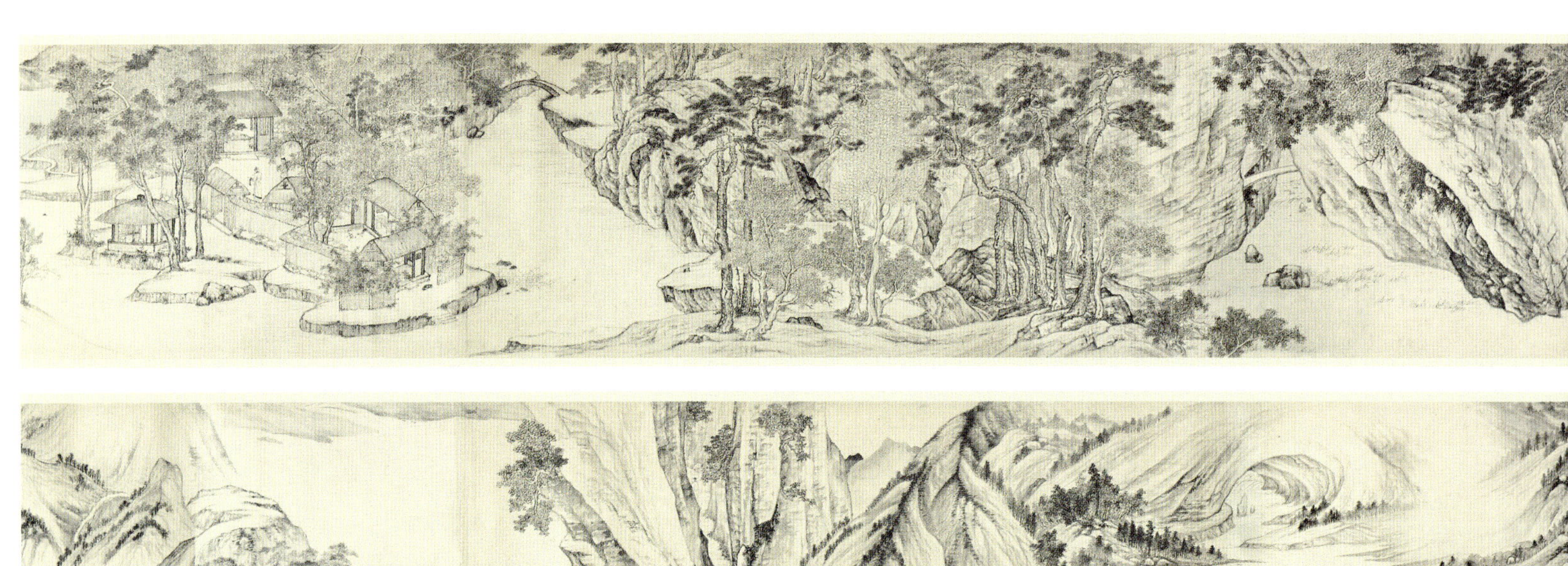

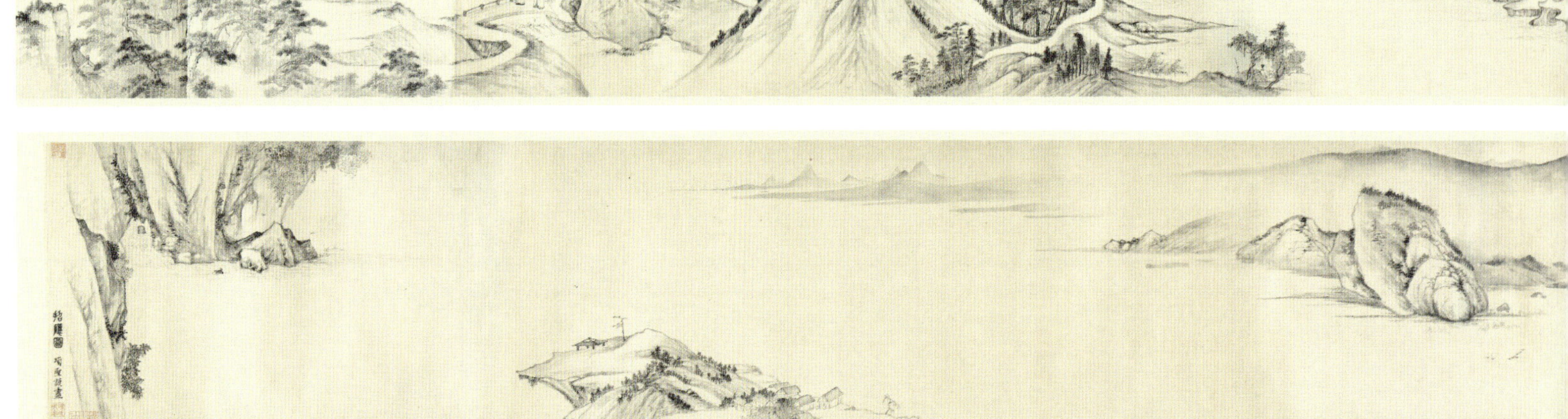

1 **Xiang Shengmo** 項聖謨
1597–1658

Invitation to Reclusion **招隱圖卷**
1625–26
Los Angeles County Museum of Art
Los Angeles County Fund

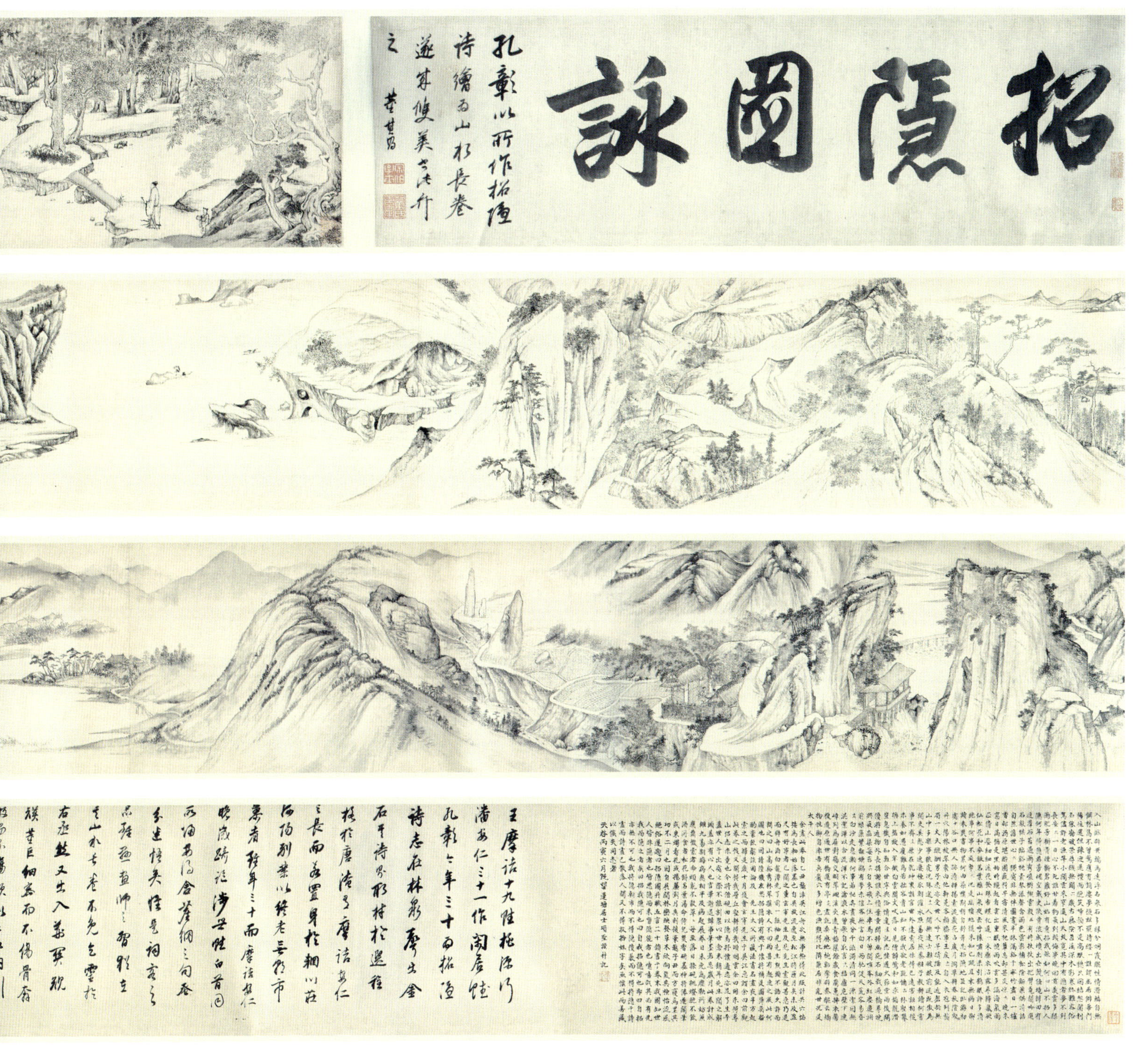

Entering the mountain is not avoiding the world,
But a deep desire to be far from floating fame.
Streams and stones so blue-green,
Mists and evening clouds unleash my emotions.
The submerged fish knows not to take the bait;
Forest birds have never been startled.
Surely I will dream of dissolving all dust . . .

Xiang Shengmo's deep engagement with the theme of reclusion arose from his family background, social network, personal inclination, and timing. A native and lifelong resident of Jiaxing (Zhejiang Province), Xiang was born to one of the wealthiest clans in this prosperous area just southwest of Songjiang in the heart of the Yangzi River Delta. A distant ancestor of the beginning of the Yuan dynasty named Xiang Hongdu lived as a recluse on a nearby hill called Mount Xu.[1] Xiang's grandfather was Xiang Yuanbian, who possessed an unparalleled collection of painting and calligraphy. That collection was especially rich in Yuan-dynasty painting, providing a pictorial survey of images idealizing reclusion; it also brought Xiang into close contact with Dong Qichang, who had been a frequent visitor to Xiang Yuanbian's household, and his close friend Chen Jiru. Chen in particular helped popularize the image of the recluse in the late Ming. A disaffected intellectual frustrated by the examination system and the constraints of official service during the Wanli reign (1572–1620), Chen adopted the posture of the recluse and then capitalized on the image's attraction through his professional literary activities (see cat. nos. 11–12).

Xiang's own attempts at an official career appear to have been halfhearted at best. By the late 1620s he had largely devoted himself to painting, thereby choosing a professional route that somewhat paralleled Chen's as a lettered talent who espoused the values of reclusive living.[2] When Xiang initiated this extraordinarily ambitious scroll in 1625 at the age of only twenty-eight, the subject of reclusion was more popular than ever, as it coincided with the unchecked power at the court by the eunuch Wei Zhongxian and the persecution of high scholar-officials.

Immediately following his long landscape, Xiang Shengmo added twenty self-composed poems and then a lengthy inscription explaining the painting's circumstances. His sources of inspiration were the "Zhaoyin" (Beckoning the recluse) poems composed by the Wei-Jin period (220–420) writers Zuo Si and Lu Ji. Zuo's and Lu's verses celebrate the pleasures of rustic living, using the conceit of the poet/protagonist seeking a recluse, or man of the hills, who can lead him into the landscape. Xiang's composition shows the progress of a white-robed, staff-bearing gentleman who wanders into a densely compacted scene of unclear passage. As the landscape opens to the left, constricting cliffs give way to waterways, attractive villas, and expansive scenes. Past the midway point we encounter the gentleman on a bridge holding hands with a dark-shirted fellow. This is the "beckoned" recluse. His extended arm points the way ever deeper into the landscape. In a sense, both the recluse and the white-robed gentleman are the artist's avatars, acting as the guide and the guided. The landscape, in turn, evokes a paradise that is both known and awaiting discovery. Xiang's twenty poems and the ending comments to his inscription mirror the dual nature of his reclusion—expressing emotions that range from the euphoric to the wistful. To describe his landscape, Xiang used a painstakingly meticulous mode of depiction evocative of the realism of Song-dynasty professional painters. As one colophon writer noted, however, his primary model was likely to have been *Views from a Thatched Hut*, attributed to Lu Hong of the eighth century (see fig. 5). One of the great treasures of Xiang Yuanbian's collection, Lu's scroll was a direct, as well as extraordinarily early, pictorial commentary on reclusion.

Xiang Shengmo's *Invitation to Reclusion* was clearly a work of singular importance to the youthful artist. As he describes in his long inscription, Dong Qichang monitored its progress from an early stage, adding unusual pressure that must have ensured redoubled efforts on the part of the painter. Later, Dong added a handsome title frontispiece as well as an inscription. Chen Jiru and Li Rihua added colophons as well, thus creating a weighty body of commentary from three of the seventeenth century's most significant arbiters of taste. Later Xiang would revisit the beckoning-the-recluse theme with two more long scrolls of the same title, the second circa 1640 and the third completed in the first (lunar) month of 1644, two months before the fall of the capital to rebel forces.[3] In the chaos of the following years Xiang lost and then later regained

For inscriptions and other documentation, see pages 277–79 in this catalogue.

1 One of Xiang Shengmo's sobriquets was the Woodcutter of Mount Xu 胥山樵, which indicates an awareness of the family legacy. Biographical information on Xiang is largely drawn from Eun-wha Park, "The World of Idealized Reclusion," 7–42. I am also indebted to Park's detailed discussion of the various scrolls by Xiang related to the reclusion theme. Other useful sources are Li Chu-tsing, "Xiang Shengmo zhi zhaoyin shihua," 531–59; Li, "The Literati Life," in Li and James C. Y. Watt, eds., *The Chinese Scholar's Studio*, especially 45–51; and Wai-kam Ho, ed., *The Century of Tung Ch'i-ch'ang*, vol. 2, 110–12.

2 This is from Xiang's inscription to his *Untrammeled Immortal among Soughing Pines* of 1629 (Museum of Fine Arts, Boston). Park, "The World of Idealized Reclusion," 21; and Wai-kam Ho, ed., *The Century of Tung Ch'i-ch'ang*, vol. 2, 113.

3 The second *Invitation to Reclusion* scroll is in the collection of the National Palace Museum, Taipei. Painted with ink and color on silk, it is missing any poems that might have originally accompanied it. See *Gugong shuhua tulu* (2001), vol. 20, 3–8. The third *Invitation to Reclusion* scroll, no longer extant, is recorded in Lu Xinyuan 陸心源, *Rangliguan guoyan lu* 穰梨館過眼錄, in *Zhonguo lidai shuhua yishu lunzhu congbian* 中國歷代書畫藝術論著叢編 (reprint, Beijing: Zhongguo da baike quanshu chubanshe, 1997), 31: 4a–12a.

4 Lu, *Rangliguan guoyan lu*, 31: 4a–b.

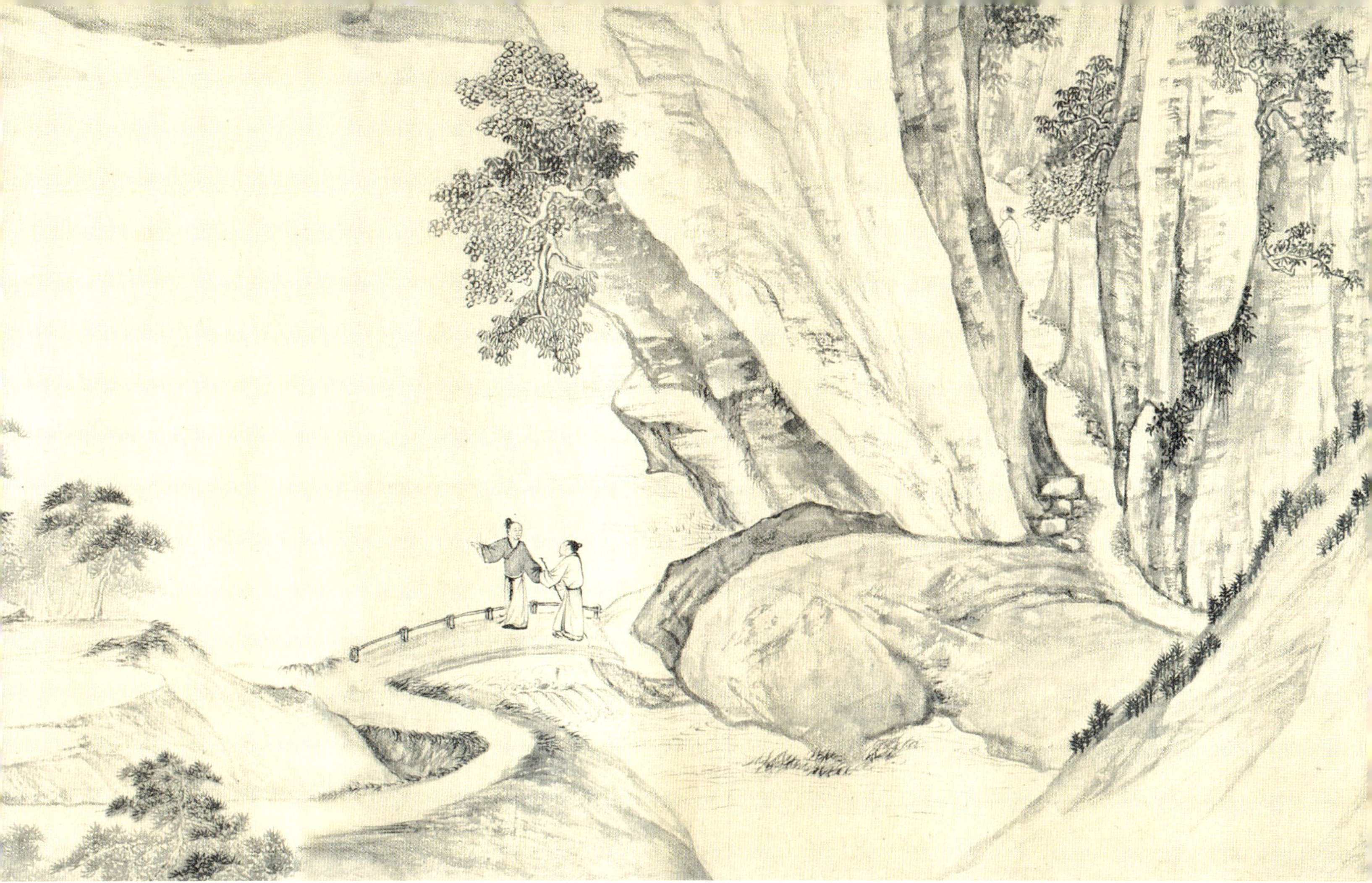

his third *Invitation to Reclusion* scroll. He added an inscription late in 1647 that describes the loss of his city, home, and possessions to the pillaging of Manchu troops two years earlier:

> In the following year [1645], to the south of the Yangzi River, both soldiers and people were swept around in great disorder, and infantry and cavalry crisscrossed the country. On the twenty-sixth day of the leap sixth month, the city of He [Jiaxing] fell, pillaging fires burning up the sky. By myself, I could only carry my mother and flee with my wife and children to somewhere far from the city. Thus my home fell apart. All the famous calligraphic works and paintings that my brothers and I had inherited from my grandfather and some of those dispersed in other hands were lost, half being trampled over and half being turned into ashes.[4]
>
> 明年夏，自江以南，兵民潰散，戎馬交馳，於閏六月廿有六日，禾城既陷，劫火熏天．余僅孑身負母並妻子遠竄．而家破矣．凡余兄弟所藏祖君之遺法書名畫，與散落人間者，半為踐踏，半為灰燼．

Knowledge of Xiang Shengmo's real-life travails adds poignancy to this earlier vision of escape, painted when reclusion was an ideal to be described for the appreciation of respected elders and like-minded colleagues. **PCS**

In this rare painting by the noted portraitist Zeng Jing, the Suzhou scholar and poet Pan Qintai is depicted standing, wearing a white cotton robe and grasping a bamboo staff: the precise image of a non-degree holder and recluse as imagined and lived in late-Ming China. Zeng applied only minimal color to his subject's face and hand, thus highlighting his subject's lofty status as one removed from worldly affairs. The black of his informal headgear and shoes accents his form and provides a triangular stability that enhances Pan's iconic image, isolated against empty space. Surrounding the figure are the inscriptions of seven renowned scholar-artists from the Jiangnan region (Yangzi River Delta), including Chen Jiru (cat. nos. 11–12), Li Liufang, and Chen Guan (cat. no. 5). These inscriptions largely employ the *zan* 贊 (encomium) literary form to extol Pan's elegant taste, artistic achievement, and rustic life. With these inscribed encomia by living contemporaries, the portrait becomes a pictorial and literary homage to the subject.

Pan Qintai's upright posture, informal attire, and staff are reminiscent of earlier portrait paintings that celebrate famous scholars out of office, such as the famous poet-recluse Tao Yuanming, who famously retired from office to become a gentleman farmer, and Su Shi, whose first period of political exile was perceived as a triumph of personal integrity over circumstance. As illustrated by the 1363 *Portrait of Yang Zhuxi in a Landscape*, a collaborative work by Wang Yi and Ni Zan, the figure with staff had been established for centuries as one of the iconographic representations of reclusion in portrait painting.[1] In his inscription to *Portrait of Pan Qintai*, Lin Yunfeng honors Pan by comparing his virtues to Tao's noble mind. Zeng Jing accomplishes the same in his portrait of Pan by including visual motifs like the white cotton robe, black informal headgear, and sandals. With such literary and art historical references, this portrait effectively embodies the reclusive life of the late Ming scholar.

The meticulous detail in the treatment of the facial features is the defining feature of Zeng Jing's style of portraiture. Zeng's extant portraits show discernible differences in posture, accompanying objects, and background setting, but they share a unique coloring in the depiction of faces. This novel technique received critical acclaim from Ming and Qing critics. Jiang Shaoshu, for example, in his history of painting *Wusheng shishi* described Zeng's portrait images as possessing several layers of tones.[2] Pan's upper eyelids are painted darker than the other parts of the face to emphasize his deep-set eyes, and the volume of his nose is indicated by a smooth gradation of flesh tones. Together with this rich coloring, Zeng utilized ink lines to define Pan's facial features and beard, while the robe is sparingly delineated with a minimal number of calligraphic lines. The critic Zhang Geng underlined the linear aspect of Zeng's style in *Guochao huazheng lu*: "[Zeng] first finished the ink lines, then added color washes in order to suit the age of the subject, yet the spirit is already transmitted through the ink framework" 墨骨既成，然後傅彩，以取氣色之老少，其精神早傳於墨骨中矣.[3] Reconciling color washes with ink lines, Zeng's technique became a popular stylistic idiom for portrait painting throughout the late Ming and Qing periods.

Zeng Jing is a seminal figure in the history of Chinese portraiture for his association with the flourishing of informal portraits of contemporary figures, which broke away from the long-standing tradition of ancestral portraits. Considering that ancestral portraits were produced mainly as iconic reminders of forebears for use in ancestral rites, Zeng's portraits suggest an important shift in the function of the portrait from a ritual object to one for aesthetic appreciation. Bearing laudatory inscriptions by contemporary scholar-artists, his portraits were commissioned and appreciated by leading cultural figures of the day, such as Dong Qichang, Chen Jiru, Ge Yilong, and Wang Shimin. Like Pan, Zeng's sitters were mostly depicted as non-degree holders and were praised in inscriptions for their reclusion. Circulated among the Jiangnan elite, of which Dong and Chen were pivotal figures, Zeng's portraits spoke to the increasing self-awareness and shared sense of identity of the politically marginalized literati in the turbulent era of the late Ming. The fame of a prolific portraitist like Zeng Jing indicated the Jiangnan literati's concern with visual self-fashioning during a time of political decline and social uncertainty. Though little additional documentation on Pan Qintai survives, by virtue of Zeng's portrait and his contemporaries' inscriptions viewers are still able to remember Pan's reclusive life.[4]
SWC

For inscriptions and other documentation, see page 280 in this catalogue.

1 For *Portrait of Yang Zhuxi in a Landscape* in the collection of the Palace Museum, Beijing, see Richard Vinograd, *Boundaries of the Self*, fig. 14.

2 Jiang Shaoshu 姜紹書, *Wusheng shishi* 無聲詩史, in *Zhongguo shuhua quanshu* 中國書畫全書 (Shanghai: Shanghai shuhua chubanshe, 2000), vol. 4, 857. See also James Cahill, *The Distant Mountains*, 213–14.

3 Zhang Geng 張庚, *Guochao huazheng lu* 國朝畫徵錄, in *Zhongguo shuhua quanshu*, vol. 10, 437.

4 A later copy of this 1621 portrait is housed in the Shanghai Museum. See Marshall Pei-sheng Wu, *The Orchid Pavilion Gathering*, vol. 1, 122–23.

2 Zeng Jing 曾鯨
1564–1647

Portrait of Pan Qintai **潘琴台像**
1621
University of Michigan Museum of Art
Museum purchase made possible by the Margaret Watson Parker Art Collection Fund

Mr. Pan is fond of hidden solitude. Never seeking wealth, he is always content. His heart is like still water, his form like arid wood. He wears white cotton robes and dwells in a yellow thatched hut. His body is in peaceful repose; his dreams are pure and sound. He is a man of a thousand books and a song of the qin zither. . .

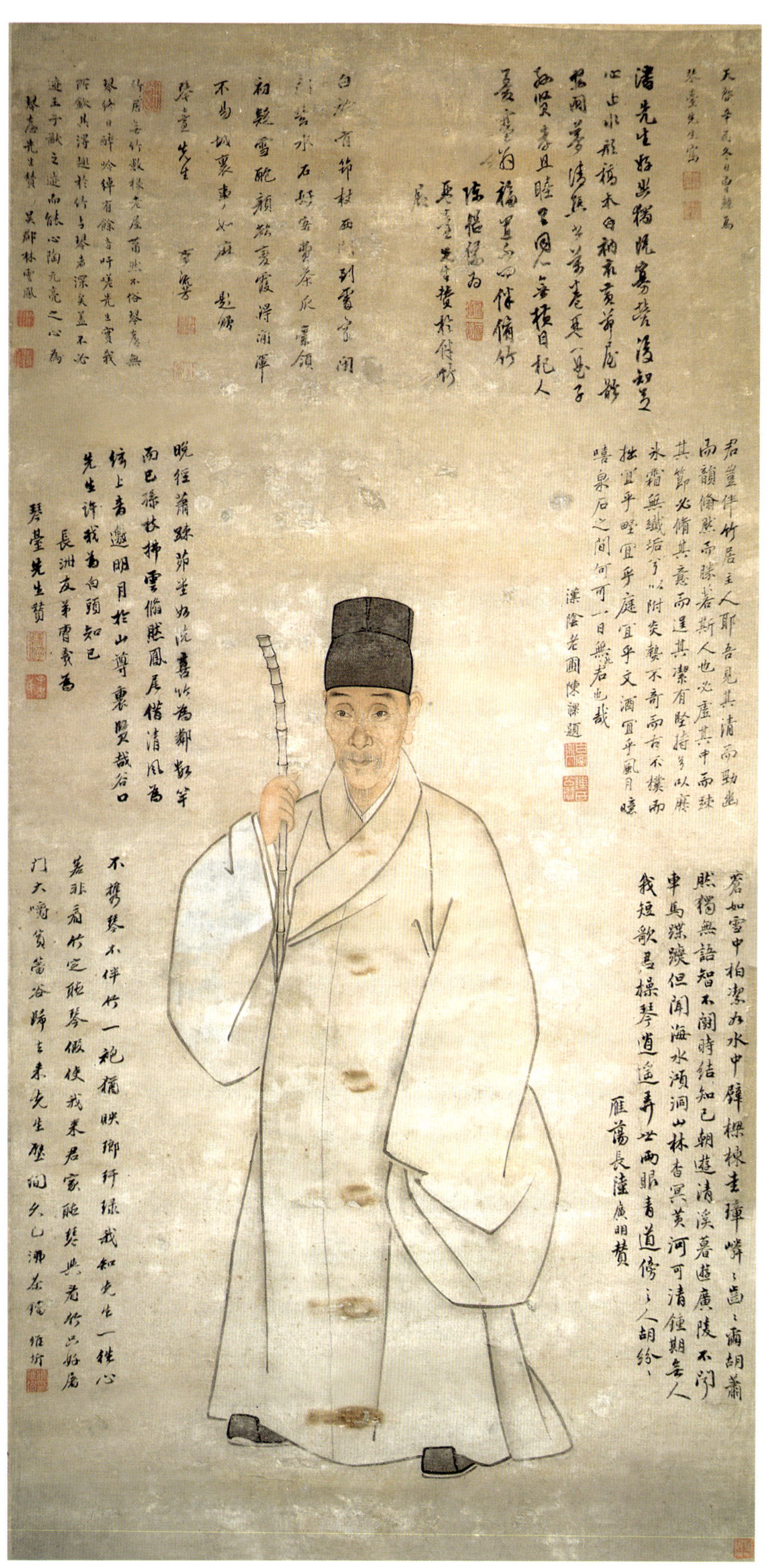

This previously unrecorded work, which recently resurfaced from a Japanese collection, sheds light on the early-seventeenth-century landscape-painting style of an important artist from northern China whose works are rarely seen. A native of Beijing, Mi Wanzhong was better known as a calligrapher in his lifetime and during the earlier part of the Qing dynasty, celebrated as one of the Four Great Calligraphers of the Late Ming.[1] After obtaining his *jinshi* (presented scholar) degree in 1595, he served as county magistrate in Yongning (Henan Province) and Tongliang (Sichuan Province) before being appointed to the more desirable magistracy of Liuhe County (Jiangsu Province), on the north bank of the Yangzi River in relative vicinity to Nanjing.[2] While stationed in this heartland of Chinese calligraphy and painting, Mi must have had numerous opportunities to view famous collections around the city of Nanjing.

The painting's narrative begins at lower right, where a pathway leads past bamboo groves to a fence and open gate. Tall leafy trees anchor the lower part of the composition, and their slight tilt to the right leads the viewer's eye to the main subject—a thatch-roofed pavilion on stilts overlooking a stream. Here a lone scholar sits with an open book on a low table, but his attention is focused on a precipitous waterfall that is mirrored by a large, billowing rock formation topped by a grove of trees. A pathway continues upward via a series of steps to a flat area with two small thatched structures. Further up at upper right, a temple clings precariously to the mountainside, echoing the human presence below. The diagonal thrust of the promontories and the billowing rock formation serve as the visual focus of topographical interest. This painterly strategy serves the theme of reclusion well, relegating the human elements in a subordinate position to the grandeur of the natural world. The top of the scroll is graced by Mi Wanzhong's inscription, dedicating the painting to the unidentified Xuanmiao (Mystical and Vast)[3]—a sobriquet with Daoist connotations that suits the painting's theme.

In formal terms, the billowing structural elements of this landscape recall those by the Northern Song master Yan Wengui. However, the vertical composition and calligraphic brushwork appear to be indebted to later Yuan and Ming interpretations of the Yan style, as exemplified by the well-known painting *Spring Dawn over the Elixir Terrace* by Suzhou artist Lu Guang.[4] The painting's strongly vertical proportion is fairly common among the works of mid- and late-Ming artists. Given that the width is close to the height of sheets of paper used for standard-sized handscrolls, this kind of format may be likened to a horizontal handscroll rotated ninety degrees. Their modest size and similarity to handscrolls when rolled up meant that such paintings could be taken out to be viewed occasionally in intimate surroundings of the scholar's studio. They may be contrasted against very tall and wide hanging scrolls, also popular during this time, which were displayed for extended periods of time in the main halls of Chinese mansions.

Sometime during the early nineteenth century, the painting came into the possession of the collector Qian Tianshu in Pinghu, Zhejiang Province, perhaps also passing into the collection of the connoisseur Zhang Shouxian from Gui'an in the same province.[5] In the early twentieth century, Mi Wanzhong's painting came to the attention of the eminent Japanese painter, calligrapher, seal-carver, and collector Nagao Ko, who was also responsible for the title slip on the scroll and for the inscription on the wooden box in which the scroll is stored. Nagao, along with his fellow countryman Kawai Senro, had joined the Xiling Seal Society (Xiling yinshe 西泠印社) upon its founding in 1904 at West Lake, Hangzhou; it is thus likely that he acquired this painting in Zhejiang sometime during the final years of the Qing dynasty.[6] **PKH**

For inscriptions and other documentation, see page 281 in this catalogue.

1 The other three were Dong Qichang, Xing Tong, and Zhang Ruitu.

2 According to the *Liuhe xian zhi* 六合縣志 (Gazetteer of Liuhe County), Mi Wanzhong was well liked and came to be known by locals as "benevolent and enlightened, compassionate and kind, as well as clever and like a doting mother" 仁明慈惠，兼水鏡慈母之心. See *Jiangnan tongzhi* 江南通志, compiled by Zhao Hong'en 趙弘恩, et al., in *Yingyin Wenyuange Siku quanshu* 景印文淵閣四庫全書 (Taipei: Taiwan Shangwu yinshuguan, 1983–86), 113:22a.

3 The second character of the recipient's sobriquet (*hao*) is given as *miao* 渺, but this character is interchangeable with the more commonly used character *miao* 妙, meaning marvelous.

4 The undated (c. 1369) work is in the collection of the Metropolitan Museum of Art, New York, and is illustrated in Wen C. Fong, *Beyond Representation*, pl. 114.

5 In Zhang Shouxian's inscription along the lower left edge in two columns of very small regular script, he writes that "Zhang Han 張瀚 [1510–1593] and Lu Shidao 陸師道 [1517–1574] both had the sobriquet Xuanmiao 玄渺 and both were from the same period as Youshi 友石 [Mi Wanzhong], but which of them [the sobriquet refers to] is not known." Since the painting was done in 1609, the recipient could neither have been Zhang Han nor Lu Shidao, as both were already dead for some time by then.

6 Coincidentally, Nagao adopted for himself the sobriquet Shiyin 石隱 ("Stone Recluse" or "Rock Recluse"), which had also been used by Mi Wanzhong in his signatures and seals. This choice may well have been inspired by Nagao's knowledge and understanding of the late-Ming artist through this fine painting in his collection.

3 **Mi Wanzhong** 米萬鍾
1570–1628

Reading in a Pavilion by a Stream
溪亭讀書圖
1609
Private collection

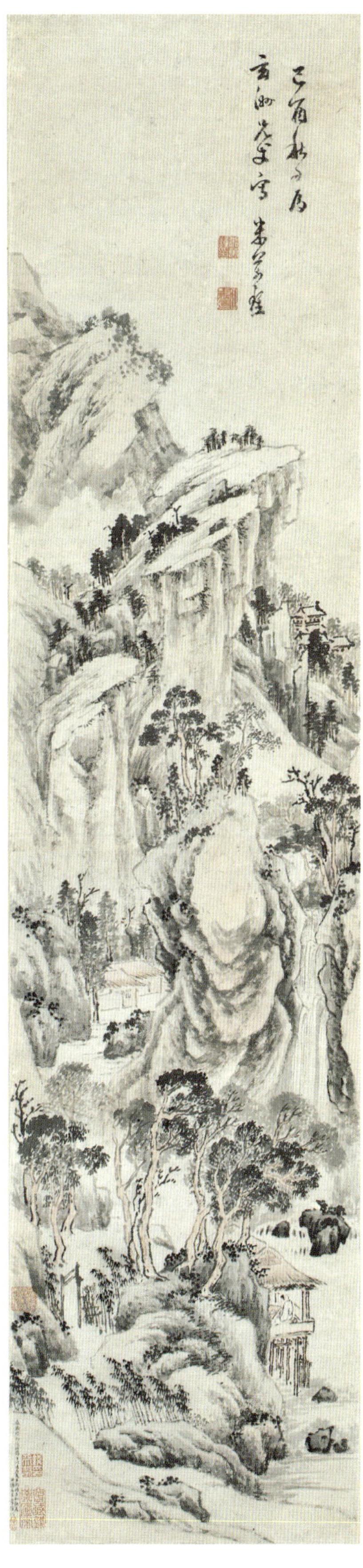

This monumental landscape is the most important surviving painting by Mi Wanzhong. In the lower section, an impressive group of tall pine trees front a flat-topped terrace on a rocky promontory. The middle ground, with cascading landforms topped with trees depicted at a reduced scale to indicate recession in space, features a solitary figure holding a staff crossing a bridge and approaching a hermitage tucked away at the left. There are numerous stylistic references in the painting to various masters of the Five Dynasties period and Yuan dynasty, as well as the more recent Wu School masters Shen Zhou and Wen Zhengming.[1] However, while Mi made liberal use of historical models, he did not over-intellectualize the painting. As James Cahill has pointed out, this "handsome, essentially eclectic picture does not, in fact, assert its style at all but simply presents its subject for the viewer's enjoyment and imaginary participation."[2] Mi Wanzhong's work appeared at a time when Chinese painting was dominated by his older contemporary Dong Qichang (cat. nos. 8–9) and the Songjiang School. Mi and Dong may well have crossed paths in the early 1600s in Nanjing during the course of their official careers, but artistically they were apart. Dong presented a radical transformation of his Song and Yuan models and a willful denial of unity and clarity in compositional structure. In contrast, Mi preferred a more conservative approach that highlighted naturalistic modes of representation, with carefully applied layered ink tones and pale washes.[3]

Although the first two characters of Mi Wanzhong's poem are lost due to damage to the scroll, the gist of his verse, with its celebration of reclusive living, is clear. The lower of the two seals following his signature reads *Hutian shiyue you* 壺天十岳友 (Friend of the ten peaks in a miniature heaven).[4] The "miniature heaven" has clear Daoist associations, with the "ten peaks" referring to those found on the ten mythical Daoist isles. This allusion takes on greater meaning given that the painting was made during the brief Tianqi period (1620–1627), during which Wei Zhongxian, a powerful and corrupt palace eunuch, instigated much factional strife in and out of court. Wei coveted Mi Wanzhong's collection of art and antiquities and periodically asked him to part with his treasured items. The eunuch also sent his representatives to negotiate the purchase of Mi's suburban estate, the Shao Garden in Haidian. Mi always politely rebuffed these efforts, but the enmity that resulted led to trumped-up charges and a narrow escape from a death sentence.[5] Mi sympathized with the political principles espoused by the Donglin party that was firmly aligned against Wei. Like many other literati of his time, Mi abhorred the "living shrines" (*shengci* 生祠) dedicated to Wei, scores of which were being erected in Hangzhou, Nanjing, Suzhou, and Beijing in 1626 and 1627.[6] Mi would not visit any of the shrines and declined all requests for his calligraphy to adorn them.[7] He was subsequently impeached by one of Wei's henchmen and removed from the civil service (*xiaoji* 消籍, literally "struck off the register").

Landscape was made in the summer of 1625, roughly half a year before the onset of Mi Wanzhong's troubles. By then, many high officials had been purged, and Mi may well have sensed his own impending fate as a victim of factional politics.[8] After Wei Zhongxian's suicide at the end of 1627, Mi was politically rehabilitated, but he succumbed to illness and died soon after in 1628. It was against this historical backdrop that great effort was put into producing a *magnum opus*. This painting thus serves as a key example of the transmission of Wu School style in the late Ming, even as Songjiang-based styles and artistic discourse became predominant. Mi, a northerner from Beijing, was able to continue the great Suzhou-based tradition by infusing it with new life and vitality. His elegant pictorial synthesis may be seen as a successful attempt in counterbalancing the theory-driven, but often aesthetically wanting, artistic visions of Dong Qichang during the early seventeenth century. **PKH**

For inscriptions and other documentation, see page 281 in this catalogue.

1 The "alum-headed" rocks on the towering peak resemble those found in several famous works, including *Layered Peaks and Dense Forests* attributed to Juran, *Autumn Mountains* by Wu Zhen, and *Hermit Fisherman of Huaxi* by Wang Meng (all in the collection of the National Palace Museum, Taipei). A similar lone figure in a landscape is seen in the National Palace Museum's *Walking with a Staff* by Shen Zhou. The tall trees in the foreground with the distinctive textural treatment of the trunks are stylistically related to those rendered by Wen Zhengming in paintings such as *Pine Forest and Waterfall* of 1527–31 in the National Palace Museum.

2 James Cahill, *The Distant Mountains*, 168.

3 Mi Wanzhong occasionally ventured into more "eccentric" types of painting under the influence of his friend and teacher Wu Bin, a professional painter active in Nanjing and Beijing. This painting, however, has more in common with the Suzhou master Zhang Hong than Wu Bin. For more on Zhang's naturalistic approach to representing landscape, see James Cahill, *The Compelling Image*, 1–35.

4 This seal is reproduced in Victoria Contag and Wang Chi-ch'ien, *Seals of Chinese Painters and Collectors of the Ming and Ch'ing Periods, Reproduced in Facsimile Size and Deciphered*, rev. ed. (Hong Kong: Hong Kong University Press, 1966), 649, no. 83a, seal impression no. 14. However, the accompanying transcription of the seal's legend contains an error: the last character of the phrase (at the lower left corner) should be *you* 友 (friend) and not the homophonous 有 (to have) as printed.

5 See fascicle 19 of Xue Gang 薛岡, comp., *Tianjue tang wenji* 天爵堂文集 (1632), reprinted in *Siku weishou shu ji kan* 四庫未收書輯刊, ser. 6, no. 25 (Beijing: Beijing chuban she, 1997), 445–688; and Han Dacheng 韓大成 and Yang Xin 楊欣, *Wei Zhongxian zhuan* 魏忠賢傳 (Beijing: Renmin chuban she, 1997), 269.

6 For the widespread construction of these shrines and their locations, see Miao Di 苗棣, *Wei Zhongxian zhuanquan yanjiu* 魏忠賢專權研究 (Beijing: Zhongguo shehui kexue chuban she, 1994), 163–68; and Han and Yang, *Wei Zhongxian zhuan*, 273–80, and app. 1, 322–25.

7 Among the prominent officials who did agree to offer their calligraphic skills for the establishment of such shrines dedicated to Wei Zhongxian were the grand secretaries Shi Fenglai and Zhang Ruitu. Shi and Zhang respectively wrote the stele inscription and the principal name plaque for the so-called Pude Shrine between the shrines to Guan Yu and Yue Fei on the banks of West Lake in Hangzhou. Despite his infelicitous actions, Zhang Ruitu is remembered as one of the Four Great Calligraphers of the Late Ming, along with Dong Qichang, Xing Tong, and Mi Wanzhong.

8 For instance, one of the so-called Six Martyrs, Yang Lian, a senior vice censor-in-chief, had impeached Wei Zhongxian in a memorial, but was subsequently arrested and died in imprisonment on the twenty-fourth day of the seventh lunar month of 1625, after many continuous days of flogging. For a detailed study of disastrous factional politics during the Tianqi period, see John W. Dardess, *Blood and History in China*.

4 Mi Wanzhong 米萬鍾
1570–1628

Landscape 山水軸
1625

Iris & B. Gerald Cantor Center for Visual Arts
at Stanford University
Committee for Art Acquisitions Fund

. . . In a thatched cottage beyond the bridge,
who is it secluded in the bamboo,
Never tiring of the short vines that split open
the deepening mists?

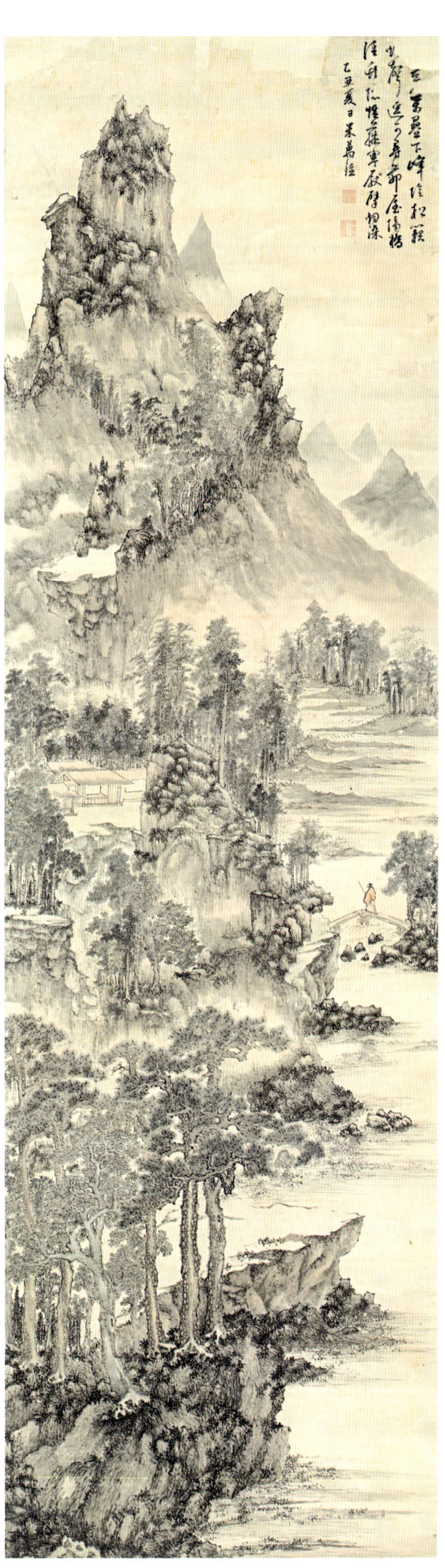

A native of Suzhou, Chen Guan demonstrates in this painting his affiliation with his city's artistic heritage (commonly referred to as the Wu School), specifically with its patriarch, the reclusive painter Shen Zhou of earlier in the dynasty.[1] Chen's blunt wet texturing and manner of painting heavily shaded boulders and foliage clearly echo Shen's signature style. The scroll's composition adds another stylistic connection to earlier Wu School painting: the sense of verticality created by the tall trees that extend their branches into the middle level of the painting. At the center stand two gentlemen scholars on a bridge crossing a stream. The image of the wandering scholar bearing a staff on a bridge, probably first inspired by fan and album-leaf painting of the Southern Song (1127–1279), is a motif commonly seen in Shen's paintings as well as the work of his Wu School followers. However, whereas Shen typically painted the figure trudging alone through the landscape, Chen portrays his socially engaged with a companion. Many of Chen's hanging-scroll compositions present tall, intricately structured landscapes that overshadow the figures within.[2] In contrast, the gentlemen on the bridge in this painting are the center of attention, amplified in scale and rendered with considerable detail in the clothing and the facial features of the staff-bearer. This central figure facing forward is recognizable as a recluse, as he shares the dress typically adopted by hermits or sages.[3] Turning to face his companion with a gentle expression, he acts as a guide, leading the way to the casual pleasures of landscape beyond the bridge.

Chen Guan was actively engaged in literati circles and commercial art activities in the city of Suzhou from about 1610 to 1640.[4] His father maintained a considerable social network with many of the prominent Wu School painters, providing Chen with substantial training in literature and art.[5] Chen's paintings generally reveal strong stylistic connections with Wen Zhengming, Shen's pupil and the single most influential figure in Wu School painting during the sixteenth century. Historical accounts of Chen's painting confirm the affiliation, listing Wen along with Zhao Boju of the Southern Song and Zhao Mengfu of the Yuan as stylistic precedents.[6]

While Chen Guan's artistic development was deeply rooted in the literati traditions of the Wu School, this painting's focus on narrative elements, with relatively large and carefully drawn figures, ties it to the work of sixteenth-century painters who were openly professional, such as Zhou Chen, Tang Yin, Qiu Ying, and Chen's contemporary Li Shida. Chen Zhenhui, who was one of Chen Guan's patrons, recounts that his art was popular among eminent men, who "sought him as a guest and to acquire his paintings."[7] With its theme of the lofty recluse and companion, and its style emulating the revered Shen Zhou, *Walking with a Staff over a Stream Bridge* matches well Chen Zhenhui's suggestion that Chen Guan's primary audience was the educated elite of Suzhou. The ideal that Chen Guan presents in this painting was one that he also pursued in his life: his later years were spent in seclusion at Tiger Hill, located outside of the city walls of Suzhou, where he "passed his time composing and chanting poems."[8] **KYM**

For inscriptions and other documentation, see page 281 in this catalogue.

1 Historical documents record Chen Guan's original given name as Zan 瓚 and his style name (*zi*) as Shuguan 叔祼; later his given name and *zi* were changed to Guan 祼 and Chengjiang 誠將, respectively. See Xu Qin 徐沁, *Ming hua lu* 明畫錄, in *Huashi congshu* 畫史叢書 (Taipei: Wenshizhe chubanshe, 1974), vol. 2, 1166; and Jiang Shaoshu 姜紹書, *Wusheng shi shi* 無聲詩史 (*Huashi congshu* ed.), vol. 2, 1027.

2 For example Chen Guan's *Gazing at a Waterfall* (1630), discussed by James Cahill in *The Distant Mountains*, 32. See also Marsha Smith's discussion of the painter's *Landscape with Cranes* (1638) in "The Wu School in Late Ming, I: Conservative Masters," in James Cahill, *The Restless Landscape*, 45.

3 For related imagery see the articles by Susan E. Nelson, "On Through to the Beyond," 23; and "Intimations of Immortality in Chinese Landscape Painting of the Fourteenth Century," 275.

4 Smith, "The Wu School in Late Ming, I," 45; and Cahill, *The Distant Mountains*, 32. According to a recorded inscription of unverifiable authenticity, the painter was born in 1563. See Ellen Johnston Laing, "Biographical Notes on Three Seventeenth-Century Chinese Painters," 109. See also Liu Qiaomei 劉巧楣, "Wan Ming Suzhou huihua," 27–31.

5 For a detailed analysis of Chen Guan's family background and life, see Liu, "Wan Ming Suzhou huihua," 27–31, and Laing, "Biographical Notes," 107–9. According to Xu Qin's *Ming hua lu*, Chen enjoyed reading such classic literature as the *Li sao* and *Wen xuan*.

6 Jiang, *Wusheng shi shi*. Regarding stylistic connections between Chen Guan, Wen Zhengming, and Song and Yuan masters, see Marshall Pei-sheng Wu, *The Orchid Pavilion Gathering*, vol. 1, 94.

7 Chen Zhenhui 陳貞慧, *Shanyang lu* 山陽錄, reprinted in Zhang Chao 張潮, ed., *Zhaodai congshu* 昭代叢書 (n.p.: Shikaitang kan ben, 1876), vol. 45, *wu ji*, 13b–14a. Cited in Laing, "Biographical Notes," 108.

8 Chen, *Shanyang lu*, 13b–14a (Laing, ibid., 108–9).

5 Chen Guan 陳祼
1563–c. 1639

Walking with a Staff over a Stream Bridge
溪橋策杖圖
Santa Barbara Museum of Art
Gift of N. P. Wong Family

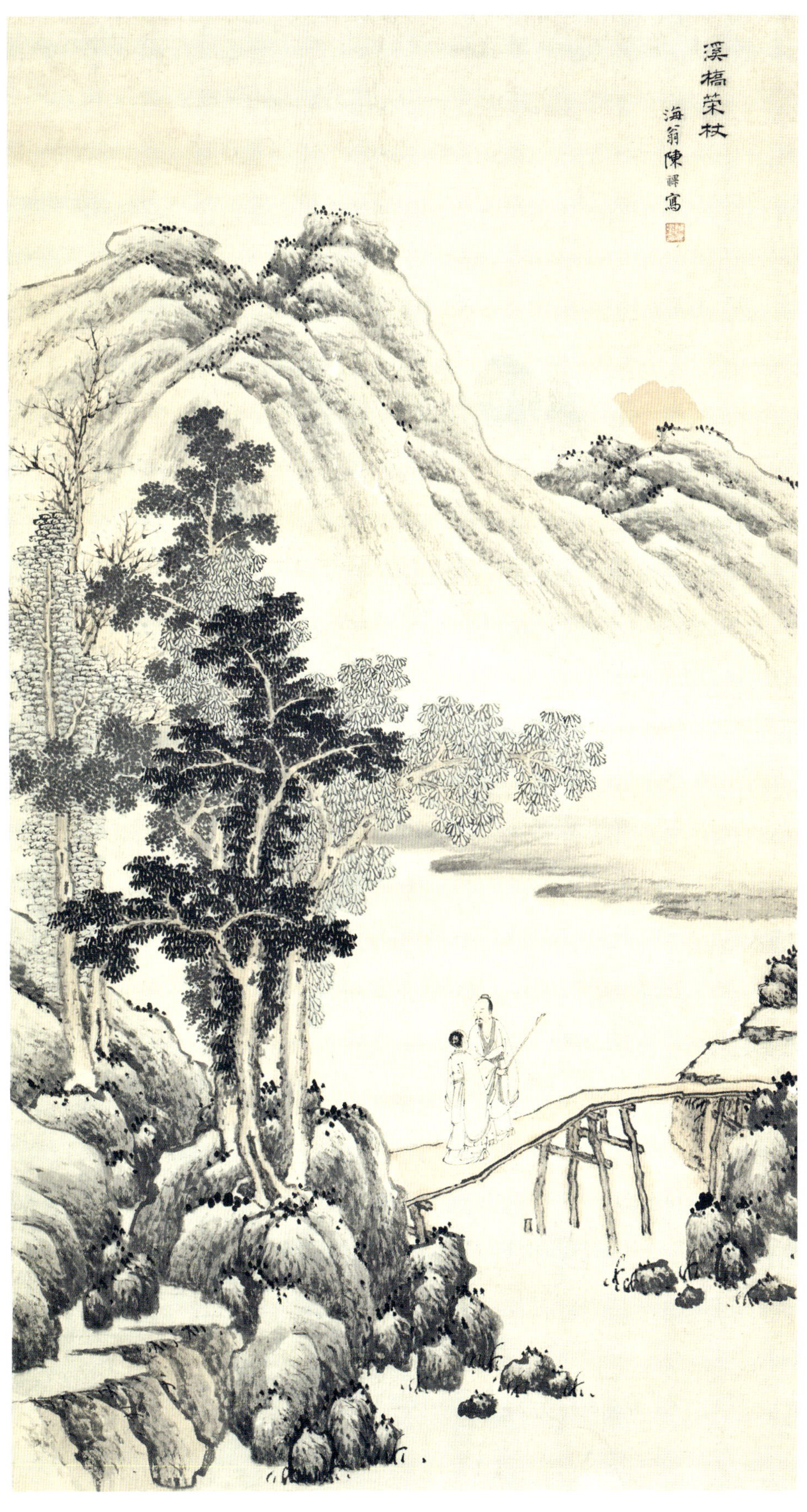

Little is known about the late-Ming Suzhou painter Sun Zhi. Dated works and historical records suggest that he was active in the late Jiajing (1521–1567) and Wanli (1572–1620) periods, and that his landscape painting shows the influence of Wen Zhengming.[1] Others state that he pursued the more unbridled style of Tang Yin but could not surpass him.[2] Interestingly, the influences of both Wen and Tang are evident in this small landscape fan. Sun was actively engaged in the cultural circles of Suzhou and nearby areas. He was one of three painters who created a series in 1601 for the late-Ming collector Wang Aijing,[3] and his extant album *Illustration of Renowned Spots of West Lake* 西湖紀勝圖, depicting twelve different scenes at Hangzhou, is provided with twin frontispieces by two of the more celebrated literati of the day, Mo Shilong and Zhou Tianqiu.[4]

The landscape depicted in this fan presents a quiet bay free of human intrusion except for a single, small boat. The boat appears to be headed for the empty pavilion nestled amongst trees in the foreground at the left. The pavilion, reminiscent of those painted by the famous Yuan-dynasty literati artist Ni Zan, is walled off from other human structures by a towering cliff and thus suggests remoteness and solitude. A gushing waterfall further emphasizes the pavilion's isolation, which appears to be accessible only to the approaching ferry. The quiet of the distant mountain shaped solely by ink wash gradually transitions into forceful movements through the use of long and gestural texture strokes in the middle of the fan. Dark outlines added to the cliff top provide visual highlights, while the ink dots scattering around the cliff serve as musical notes that resonate with the foliage in the foreground. As a result, the painting exhibits a rhythmic reverberation and sense of spontaneity that contrasts with the delicacy and exactitude seen in a number of Sun Zhi's other works.[5]

The eremitic landscape was a popular theme among Suzhou painters of the mid-Ming period, especially those alluding to Tao Yuanming's two famous writings on the ideals of reclusion, "Home Again" and "The Peach Blossom Spring."[6] All of the major Wu School painters—including Shen Zhou, Wen Zhengming, Qiu Ying, and Lu Zhi—painted landscapes that explore and celebrate the ideals of reclusion. Some of them developed new modes, including the use of shorthand motifs, to suggest the deep literary traditions that were so familiar. Peach trees and an empty boat by a cave, for example, would immediately call to mind Tao's "The Peach Blossom Spring" without the need to elaborate the story's narrative.[7]

Sun Zhi also created a range of landscape paintings that explore the theme of escapist landscape. His fan leaf *Fisherman Recluse amid Stream and Mountain* of 1589 in the Suzhou Museum follows the Yuan-dynasty model of depicting hermitic life by portraying a fisherman-recluse under a tree.[8] The undated *Jade Cave and Peach Blossoms* (National Palace Museum, Taipei) utilizes symbolic images to create an otherworldly landscape.[9] In contrast, his *Stream and Mountain in the Mood of Autumn* of 1579 (Shanghai Museum) and this fan painting create what might be called a more secular version of the reclusive landscape through the use of relatively ordinary symbols and the narrative implied by the composition.[10]
KYM

For inscriptions and other documentation, see page 281 in this catalogue.

1 Early records of Sun Zhi are found in Jiang Shaoshu 姜紹書, *Wusheng shi shi* 無聲詩史, in *Huashi congshu* 畫史叢書 (Taipei: Wenshizhe chubanshe, 1974), vol. 2, 1003; and Xu Qin 徐沁, *Ming hua lu* 明畫錄, in *Huashi congshu*, vol. 2, 1184. One of his earliest extant paintings is *Plum Blossoms and Narcissus* of 1559 (National Palace Museum, Taipei), reproduced in *Gugong shuhua tulu* (1989), vol. 8, 129.

2 Yu Jianhua 俞劍華, ed., *Zhongguo meishujia reming cidian* 中國美術家人名辭典 (Shanghai: Shanghai renmin meishu chubanshe, 1981), 683.

3 The other two painters were his contemporaries, Zhou Zhimian and Zhang Longzhang. Sun Zhi's painting was later inscribed by the poet and calligrapher Wang Zhideng and Lu Shiren. This painting series was recorded by Wang Aijing's son, Wang Keyu 汪砢玉, in *Shanhu wang* 珊瑚網 (Shanghai: Shanghai Guji chubanshe, 1991), 792–93.

4 This album is in the Tianyige Museum, Ningbo. For a color reproduction, see *Zhongguo huihua quan ji* (1997), vol. 15, pl. 139–50. For the two frontispieces of the album written by Mo Shilong and Zhou Tianqiu, see *Zhongguo gudai shuhua tumu* (2001), vol. 11, 287. Mo came from a noted literati family in Huating and was close to Dong Qichang. See L. Carrington Goodrich and Chaoying Fang, eds., *The Dictionary of Ming Biography*, vol. 2, 1073. Zhou, a close disciple of Wen Zhenming, was particularly known for his calligraphy and was a close friend of Wang Zhideng. Goodrich and Fang, 1363.

5 Sun Zhi's meticulous style, generally associated with the style of Wen Zhengming, is seen in his *Plum Blossom and Narcissus* of 1559 (see note 1) and *A Snowy Journey to a Friend's Home* of 1595 (Suzhou Museum). The latter is reproduced in *Suzhou bowuguan cang Ming Qing shuhua*, 81.

6 Susan E. Nelson, "On Through to the Beyond," 23.

7 Ibid., 35–41.

8 Reproduced in *Zhongguo gudai shuhua tumu*, vol. 6, 43.

9 Reproduced in *Gugong shuhua tulu*, vol. 8, 131.

10 *Stream and Mountain in the Mood of Autumn* is reproduced in *Mingdai huihua* 明代繪畫, *Zhongguo meishu quanji* 中國美術全集 (Shanghai: Shanghai renmin meishu chubanshe, 1988), vol. 7, 195.

6 **Sun Zhi** 孫枝
Act. late sixteenth–early seventeenth century

Landscape 山水扇面
Santa Barbara Museum of Art
Anonymous Gift

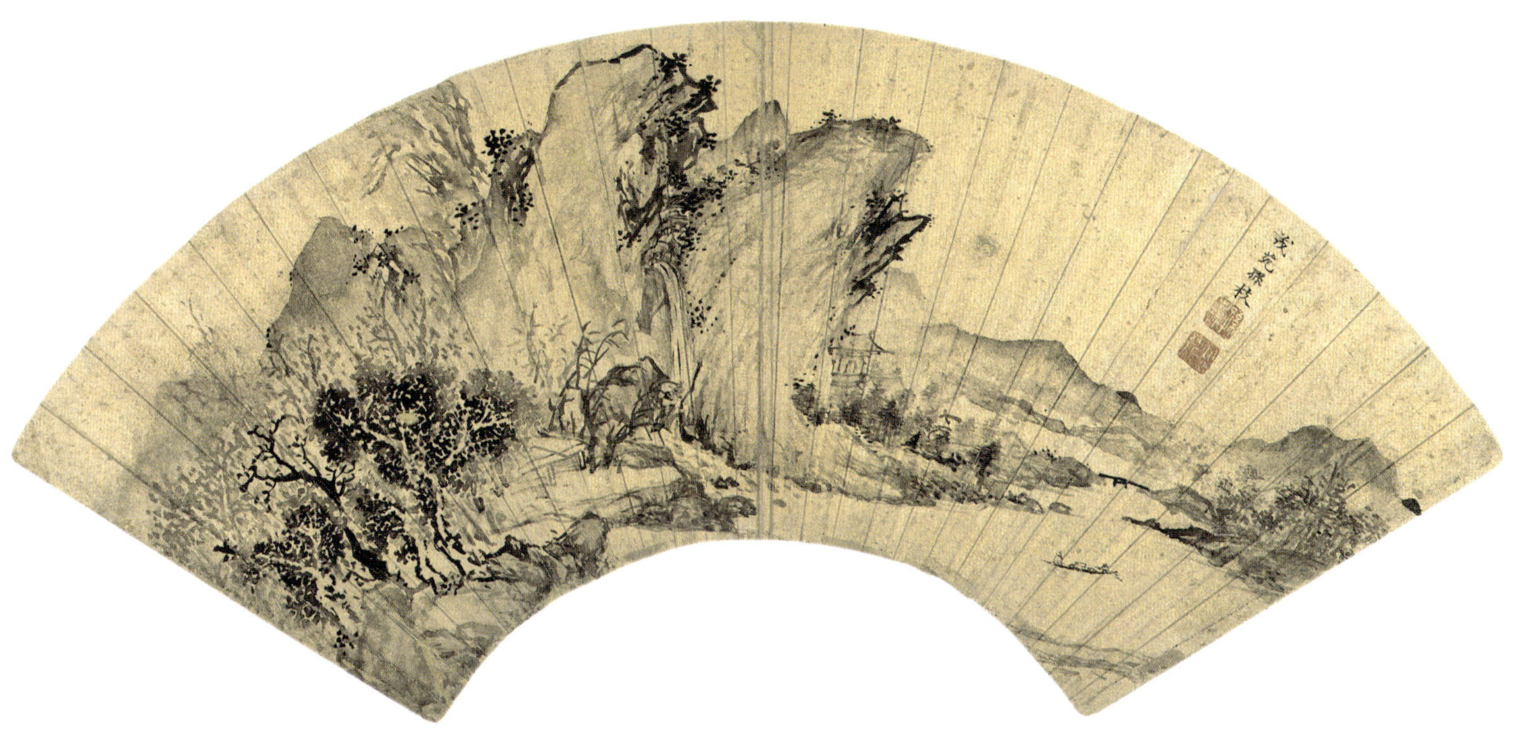

Yuan Shangtong's couplet, with its description of a house located past stone cliffs deep in autumn woods, helps the viewer read a narrative into the painting it accompanies. The traveler with walking staff at the far right approaches a stream and bridge amongst a copse of trees. His destination is the dwelling, with a single waiting figure, under pines perched on a rocky outcrop above a stream-crossing causeway at the left. The couplet's description of the stream as "ancient" creates a sense of remoteness to the landscape, which the artist skillfully conveys by suggesting an indeterminate distance between the foreground trees and the scene that appears to the left behind the large rock. The seated hermit awaiting the traveler's arrival presumably is Longji, Yuan's "elder in poetry," to whom the fan is dedicated. A popular style name in the late Ming period, this specific Longji remains unidentified. If this painting is any guide, however, he fully embraced the ideal of reclusion that was popular at this time.[1]

In an article published in 1991, art historian Yang Xin questioned the validity of the single painting that others had used to establish Yuan Shangtong's date of birth to 1570 and pointed instead to another composition, *Withered Tree, Cold Crows* (Shanghai Museum), as a more trustworthy source. Yuan dated the Shanghai scroll to 1661 and referred to himself as "seventy-two [*sui*]," which would mean he was born in 1590.[2] His last dated painting, *Peach Garden Utopia* (Palace Museum, Beijing), confirms that he was still active in 1666.[3] Surviving works by Yuan Shangtong suggest a painter capable of remarkably diverse subject matter, including landscapes, birds and flowers, and genre scenes, all of which he painted in a style that showcases rough, energetic brushwork. A native of Suzhou (Jiangsu Province), Yuan's early work, including this lovely fan painting and a landscape in the hanging-scroll format also dated 1638,[4] shows the distinct influence of the late-Ming Suzhou painter Zhang Hong, who employed a staccato, almost pointillistic brush technique that suggests atmosphere and emphasizes textural effect more than calligraphic brushwork.[5] That style is particularly useful in a painting like this, pairing with the suggestive couplet to describe a scene that is deep in poetic feeling.

JHC

For inscriptions and other documentation, see page 281 in this catalogue.

1 An album of paintings by various artists dedicated to a Longji (also unidentified) and focused on the theme of chess-playing came up for auction at China Guardian (Jiade), Beijing, in November 2009. The paintings and texts from that album date from 1665 to 1672.

2 Yang Xin 楊新, "Yuan Shangtong shengnian bianxi," 71.

3 Wu Yangmu 吳養木, *Zhongguo gudai huajia cidian* 中國古代畫家辭典 (Hangzhou: Zhejiang renmin chubanshe, 1999), 348–49. See also Yu Jianhua 俞劍華, *Zhongguo meishujia renming cidian* 中國美術家人名辭典 (Shanghai: Shanghai renmin meishu chubanshe, 1981), 757.

4 Titled simply *Landscape*, the hanging scroll is in the collection of the Beijing Cultural Relics Store. Similar to the Santa Barbara Museum of Art fan, this painting by Yuan Shangtong also bears a poetic couplet.

5 Zhang Hong's paintings and their distinctive approach to representing the world are discussed by James Cahill, *The Compelling Image*, 1–35.

7 Yuan Shangtong 袁尚統
1590–1666 or later

Landscape 石壁秋林圖
1638
Santa Barbara Museum of Art
Anonymous Gift

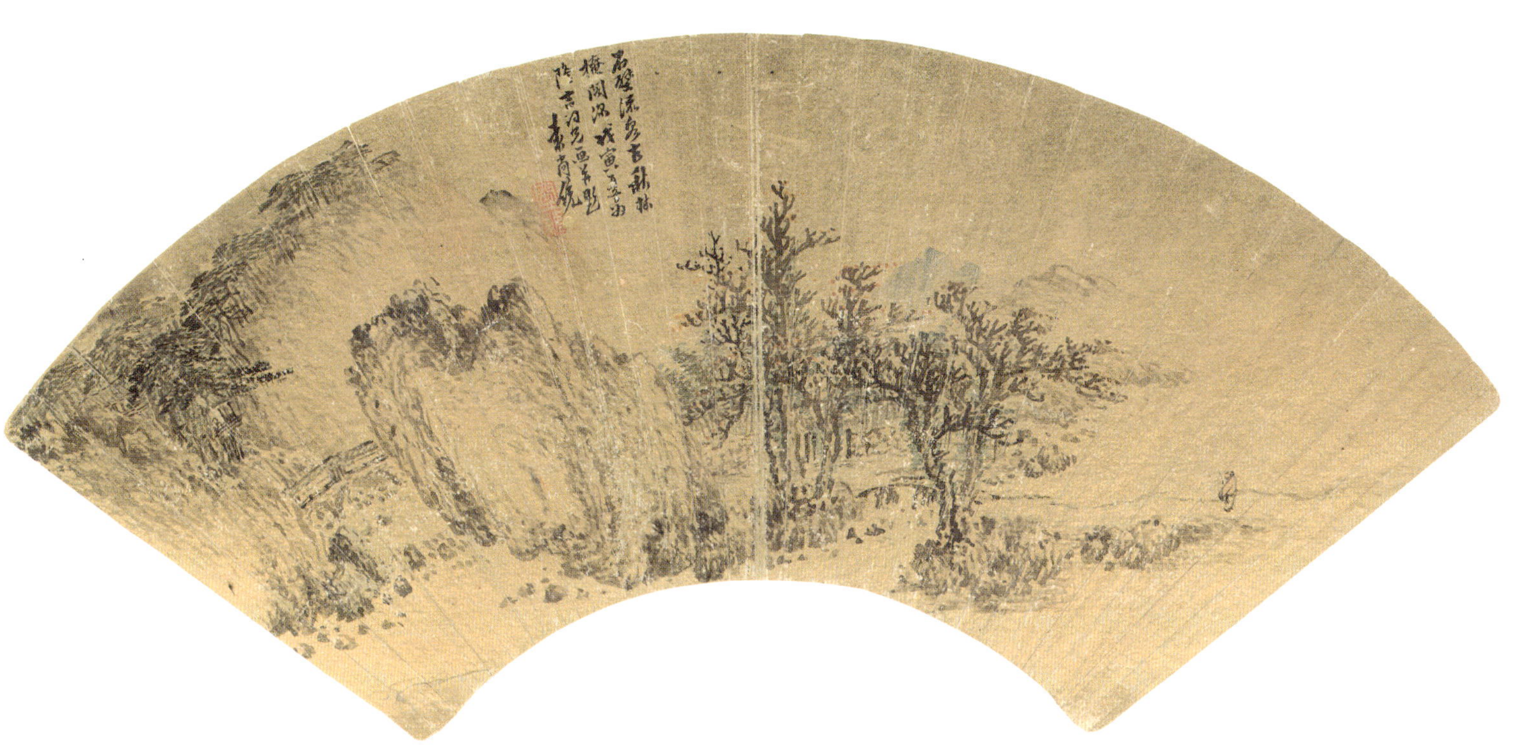

Stone cliff—flowing stream is ancient;
Autumn grove—shuttered house is deep.

In 1610, Dong Qichang returned to his adopted hometown of Huating after a term of only forty-five days as Surveillance Vice Commissioner of Fujian.[1] Out of favor at court and disenchanted with provincial politics, he would not accept another official assignment until he was recalled to court by Emperor Guangzong ten years later. During the first year of his retirement from politics, he produced an album of paintings and calligraphy on rounded fans, now in the Hsü-pai Chai (Low Chuck Tiew) collection.[2] Similarly rounded fans on gold leaf, an unusual format favored by Dong, as well as corresponding seals and thematic and textual agreements suggest that the album *Contemplating the Dao with Emotions Cleansed* was also created around 1610.[3] These works mark a productive three-year period in which Dong, financially secure and much sought after as a connoisseur of painting, committed his attention to painting and consolidating his style.[4] This album represents an incisive study of the ideas of reclusion and antiquarianism that he explored during this period.

Many of the albums Dong Qichang produced in his retirement can be understood as sets of exercises after earlier painters. In 1611, he produced an album of seven landscape paintings in the manner of old masters, each leaf focusing on a particular historical painter.[5] The fourth leaf in the *Contemplating the Dao* album, "Brush Ideas of Yuan," combines the Yuan master Huang Gongwang's method of modeling mountains through layered strokes with a sparse composition in the style of his contemporary Ni Zan. In the accompanying leaf of calligraphy Dong augments the Yuan theme by transcribing a poem Ni's contemporary Bian Tong had originally inscribed on Ni's *Autumn Mountains* of 1363, a painting that Dong owned.[6] In the third leaf, Dong expounds on the different manner of painting trees by two tenth-century masters: Li Cheng's twisted trees versus Dong Yuan's pioneering "luxurious twigs and upright trunks." Elsewhere, Dong Qichang recommends the methods of Dong Yuan and Zhao Mengfu for painting trees. However, he also notes that "for dead branches, one follows Li Cheng."[7] Significantly, Dong Qichang uses the same description for Dong Yuan's tree schema in leaf eight from the Low Chuck Tiew album.[8] Although the inscriptions on the facing leaves of the *Contemplating the Dao* album are intended as related but separate texts rather than as captions describing the accompanying images, we can understand the relatively bare, crooked trees in the foreground as close to Li Cheng, whereas the trees with luxuriant foliage and straight trunks appear closer to the Dong Yuan style. These albums are not purely studies of the ancient masters, but the intimate size and format lends itself to a close examination of specific compositional and stylistic formulae that Dong associated with things he had seen and masters he admired.

Dong Qichang's turn away from public affairs in favor of a reclusive, scholarly lifestyle is evident in other works from this period. For example, he painted *Invitation to Reclusion at Jingxi* in 1611 for his close friend Wu Zhengzhi, a highly educated scholar who was similarly resigned to a period of semi-retirement outside of the court.[9] We can imagine that the retreat from the profane world that Dong imagines for his friend reflects his own introspective mood at this time. He stretches the four characters of his title, *Contemplating the Dao with Emotions Cleansed*, across two double leaves of the album. This bold introduction to the paintings reminds us just how passionately he reveled in his reclusion. The second painted leaf in the album, "Solitary Temple among Misty Peaks," again picks up on the eremetic theme. A partially hidden set of temple buildings, touched by a strand of fog, represent the ideal setting in which to contempla te the Dao. As in the other leaves in the album, Dong employs a simple composition, with the temple buildings and coastline following parallel diagonal lines and a distinct absence of superfluous elements such as bridges or pavilions. Only two leaves in the album contain buildings. It is this simplicity of form and sense of peace in nature that permeates the album and distinguishes it from others of the period.

Dong Qichang further explains his motivation for creating the album in the ending inscription he wrote in his outstanding calligraphy (see fig. 9). He cites the famous Song-dynasty scholar Ouyang Xiu, who wrote in his "Calligraphy Exercises": "To have a clean desk beside a bright window, and to have a brush, inkstone, paper, and ink, all of high quality, is one of life's greatest pleasures" 明牕净儿，筆硯紙墨皆極精良，亦自是人生一樂事.[10] Dong's citation of Ouyang not only emphasizes his enduring love of painting and calligraphy, it also explicitly associates his artistic outlook with that of one of the most admired scholars of the past. Like Dong, Ouyang valued internal meaning in painting and rejected technical achievements as characteristic of mere artisan painters.[11] In Ouyang, Dong found an ideal figure to speak to both his artistic practice and theoretical outlook during a truly unfettered period of his career. **NK**

For inscriptions and other documentation, see pages 281–82 in this catalogue.

1 Celia Carrington Riely, "Tung Ch'i-ch'ang's Life," in Wai-kam Ho, ed., *The Century of Tung Ch'i-ch'ang*, vol. 2, 411.
2 Reproduced in *The Century of Tung Ch'i-ch'ang*, vol. 1, pl. 13.
3 Accompanying Dong's inscription are three seals: *Taishi shi*, *Dong Qichang yin*, and *Xuanshang zhai*. The first two are seen on his *Water Village and Mountain Colors* (see *The Century of Tung Ch'i-ch'ang*, vol. 2, 291–90), possibly the work of a ghost-painter. The third seal is used in the Low Chuck Tiew album.
4 James Cahill, "Tung Ch'i-ch'ang's Painting Style: Its Sources and Transformations," in *The Century of Tung Ch'i-ch'ang*, vol. 1, 63. Dong would lose his estate and much of his collection to an angry mob in 1616, and there are few extant paintings from 1613 leading up to the event. Riely, "Tung Ch'i-ch'ang's Life," 418.
5 Cahill, "Tung Ch'i-ch'ang's Painting Style," 63.
6 Zhao Qimei 趙琦美, *Zhaoshi Tiewang shanhu* 趙氏鐵網珊瑚 (*Siku quanshu* ed.), 14:30a. Dong often cited this poem and used it on his own paintings, though here he changed (perhaps inadvertently) the very first character from *yun* (clouds) to *lin* (trees or forest).
7 This is from Dong Qichang's *Hua zhi* 畫旨, translated in Mae Anna Quan Pang, "Wang Yüan-Ch'i (1642–1715) and Formal Construction in Chinese Landscape Painting," 56, 102.
8 "Landscape painters' use of luxuriant twigs on upright trees originated with Dong Beiyuan (Dong Yuan)." *The Century of Tung Ch'i-ch'ang*, vol. 2, 23.
9 Riely, "Tung Ch'i-ch'ang's Life," 413.
10 Ouyang Xiu 歐陽修, "Xue shu wei le" 學書為樂, *Wenzhong ji* 文忠集 (*Siku quanshu* ed.), 130: 3a. Translation by Ronald Egan, *The Literary Works of Ou-yang Hsiu (1007–72)*, 198.
11 Ibid.

8 **Dong Qichang** 董其昌
1555–1636

Contemplating the Dao with Emotions Cleansed 澄懷觀道圖
C. 1610
Private collection

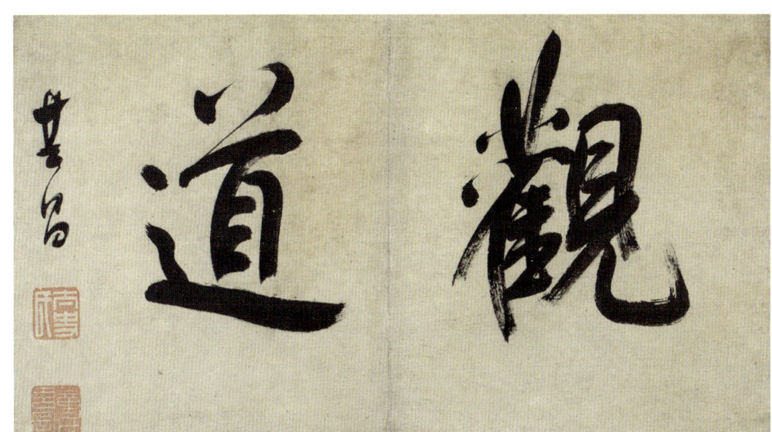

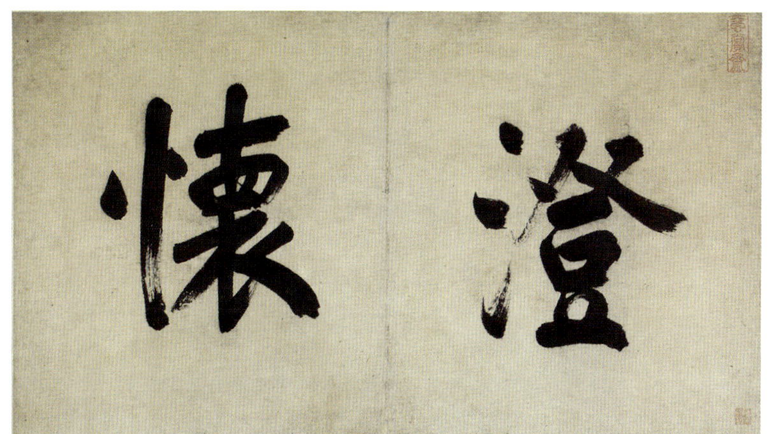

FRONTISPIECE

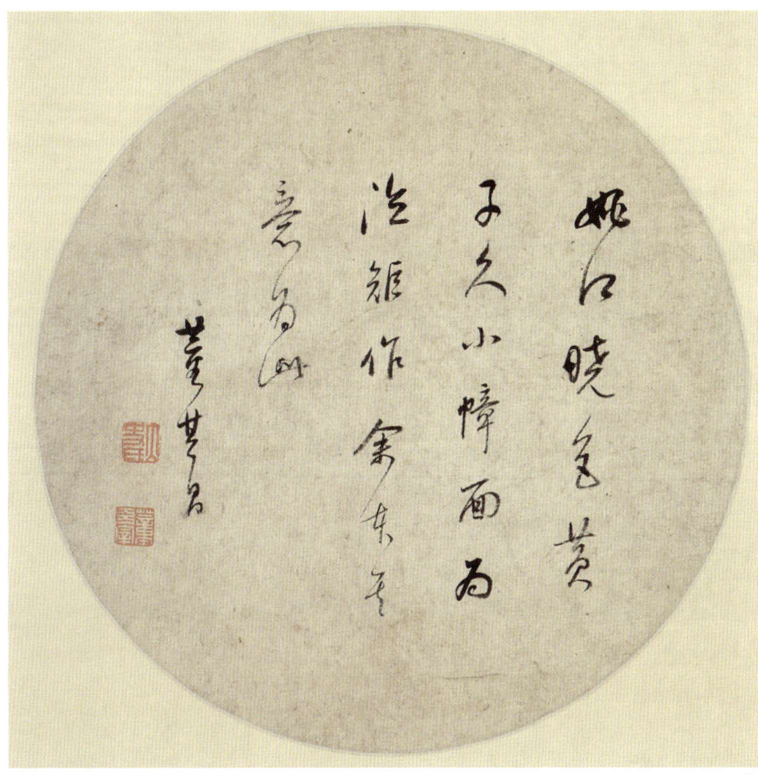

2a

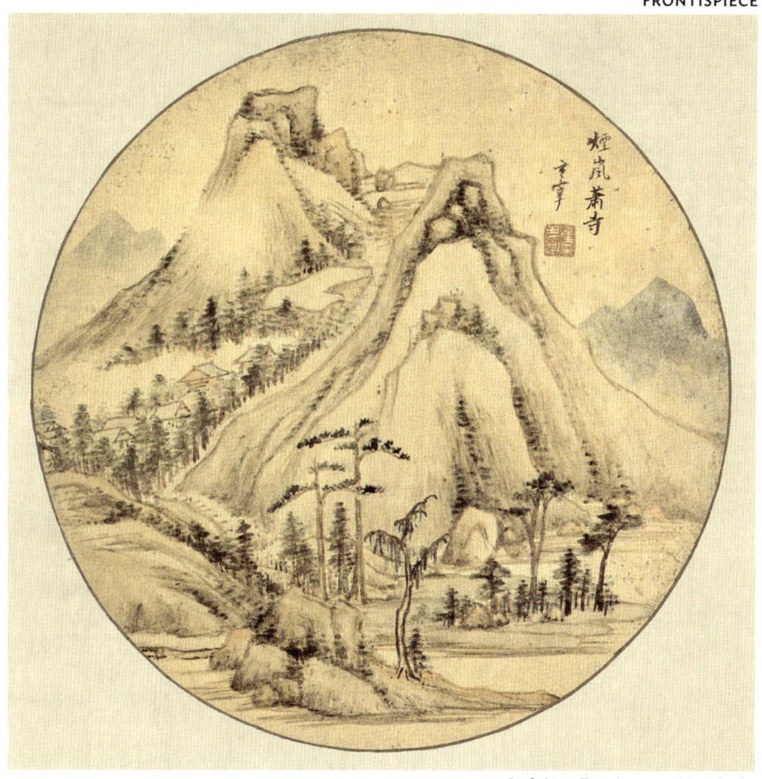

2 Solitary Temple among Misty Peaks

Morning View of Yao River, *a small composition Huang Zijiu [Huang Gongwang] painted for Deju. I painted this after Huang's idea.*

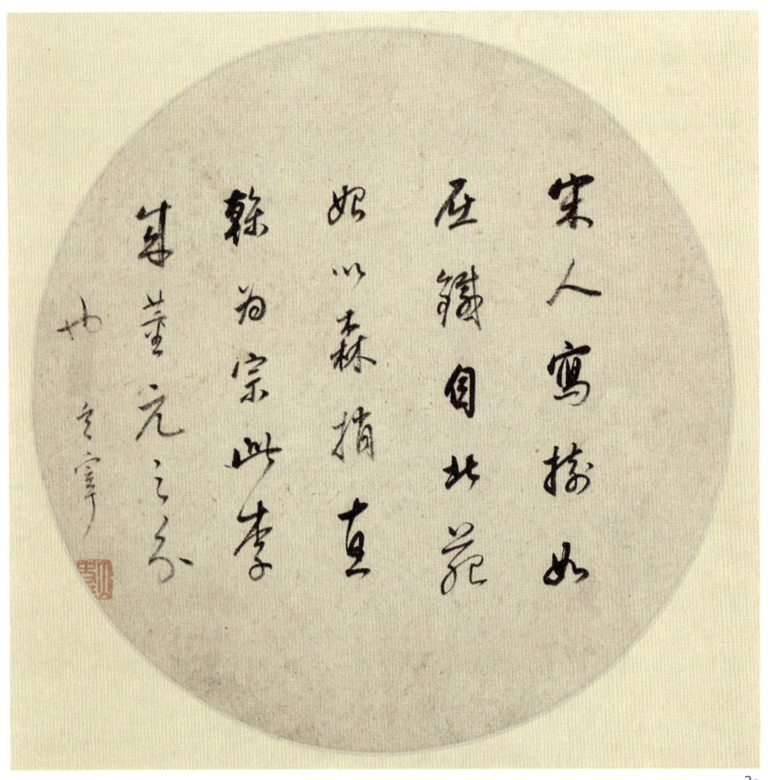

3a

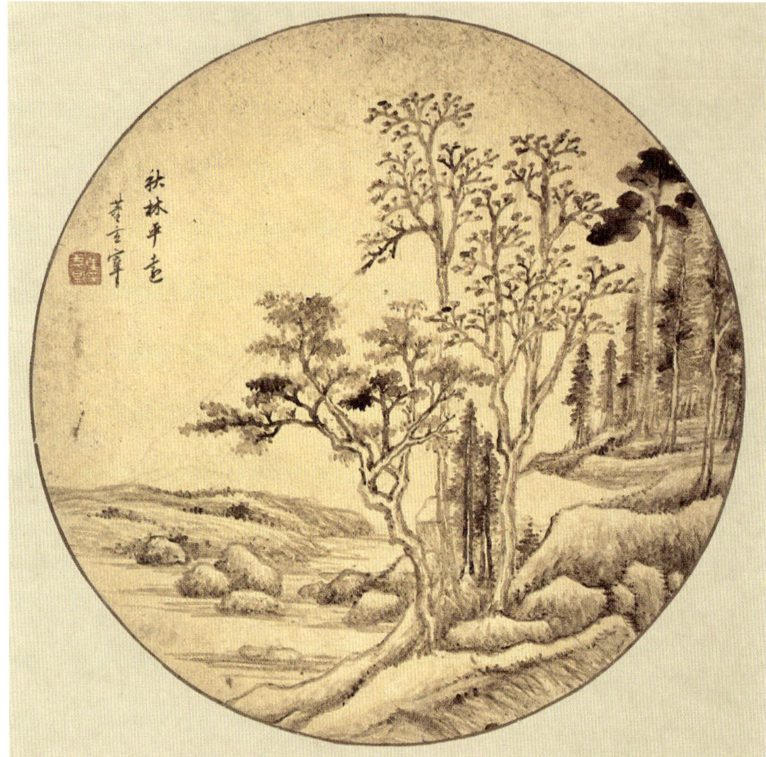

3 Autumn Grove, Level Distance

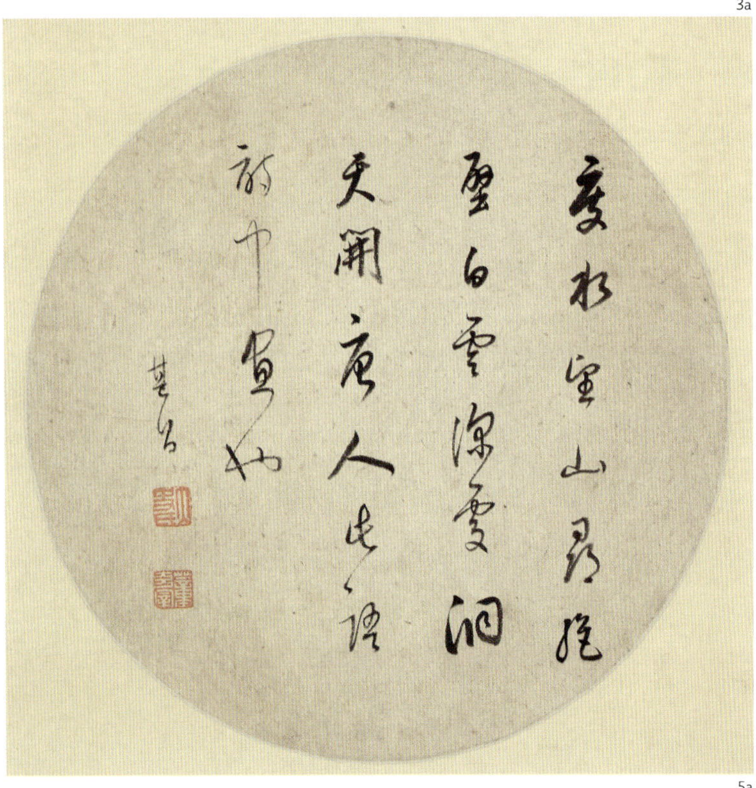

5a

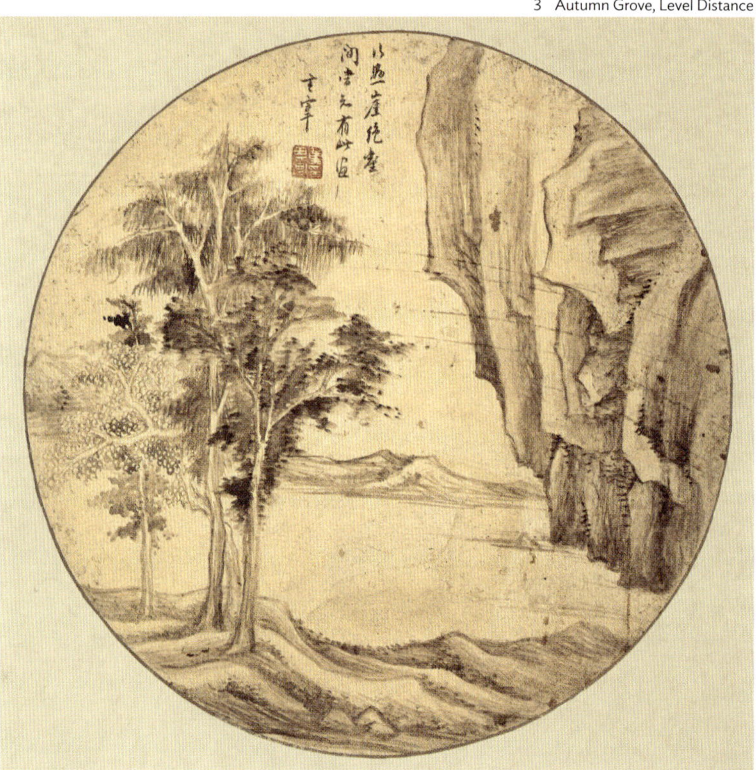

5 When you walk among the cliffs, then you will understand this painting.

Dong Qichang's concluding inscription for this album is reproduced in fig. 9, page 31.

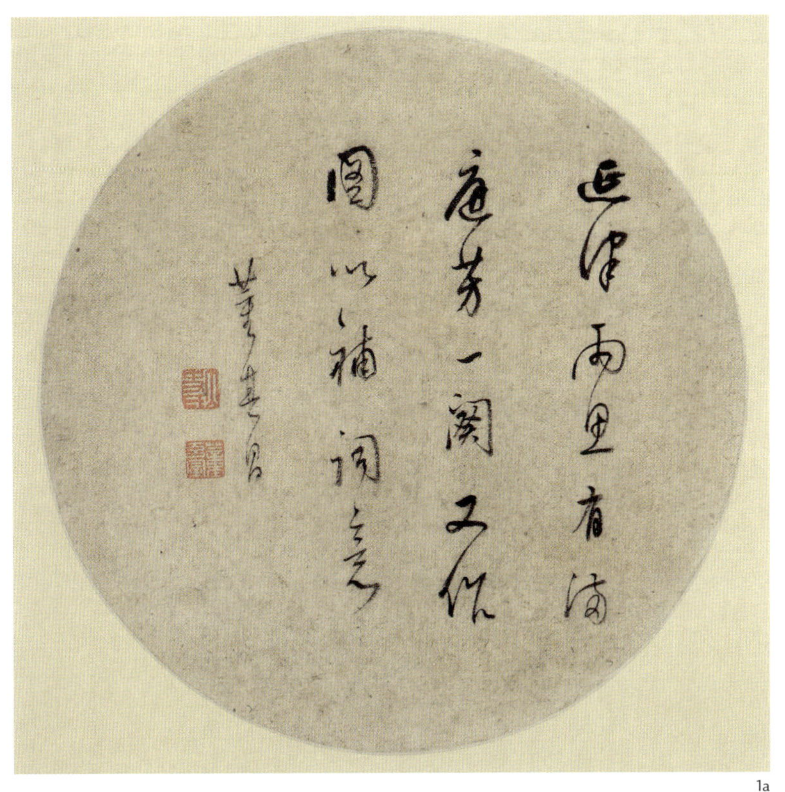

1a

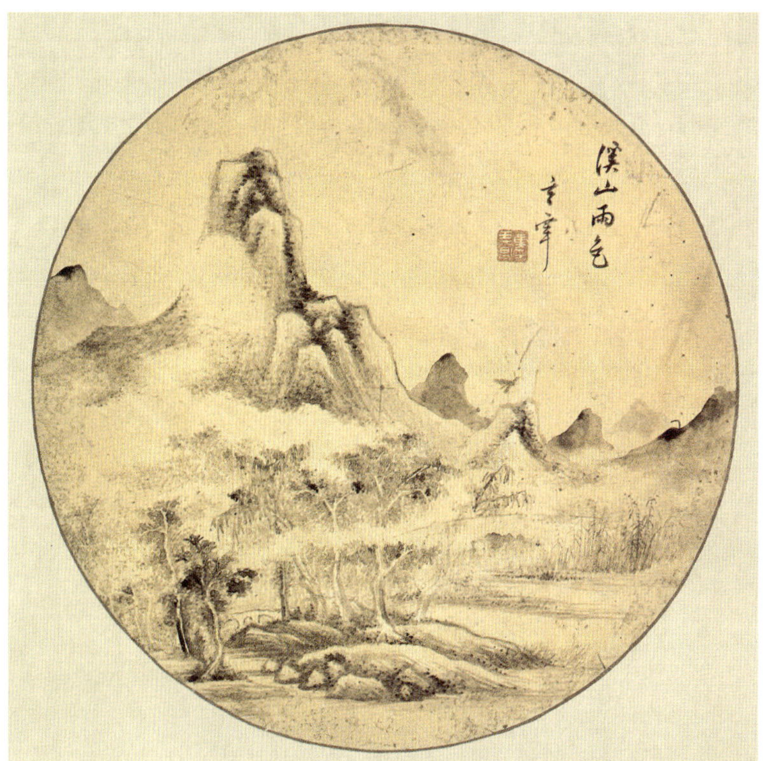

1 Streams and Mountains in Rain

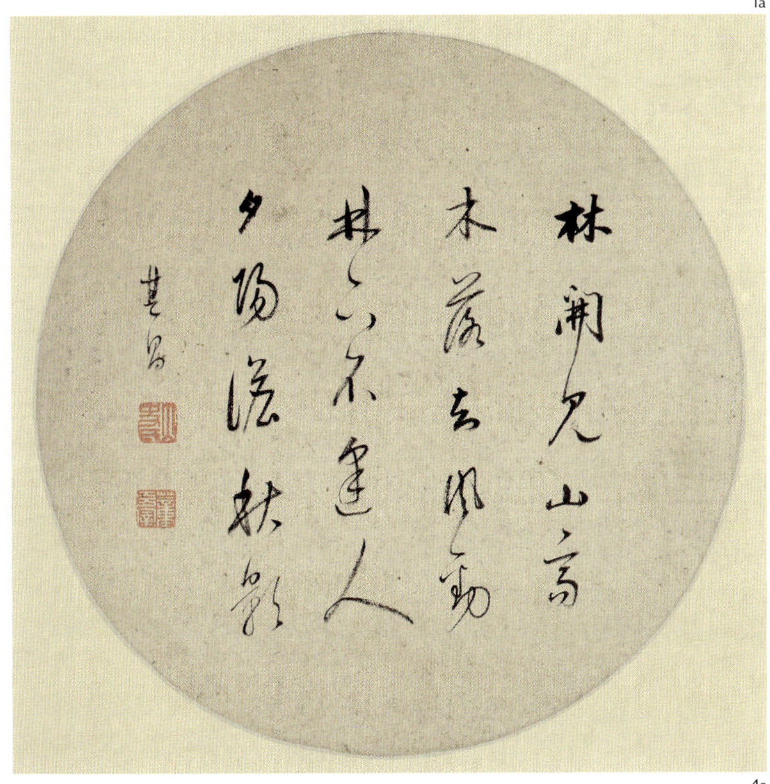

4a

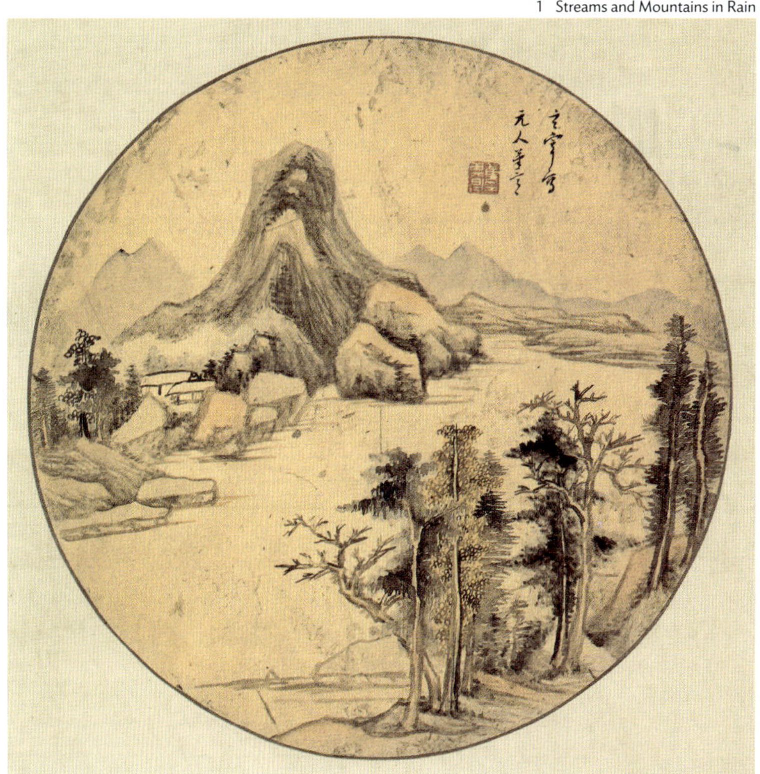

4 Xuanzi sketches the brush ideas of Yuan.

The factional struggles that plagued late-Ming politics affected Dong Qichang's career choices as well as his preference of painting themes. He resigned from office several times in order to avoid political persecution. In 1626 Dong retired for the third time; this would last until he was summoned to the court again in 1631.[1] Shortly after the 1626 retirement, Dong painted two compositions after Wang Wei's poems on the theme of reclusion. One is *A Painting after the Wangchuan Quatrains*, based on Wang's well-known poems expressing the pleasure of living a reclusive life in his Wangchuan Villa.[2] The other is the present painting, which evokes the last two lines of Wang's seven-character regulated verse, "On a Spring Day, Passing Xinchang Village and Seeking but not Finding Recluse Lü with Pei Di." The couplet had become a popular theme of reclusion in painting no later than the Yuan period, when Wang Meng illustrated the same couplet in a painting now in the Cleveland Museum of Art.[3] Dong was aware of Wang Meng's use of the Wang Wei couplet, but his own rendition is quite different.[4] Whereas Wang Meng depicted a recluse seated in contemplation in a cottage under pine trees, Dong visualized the spirit of the couplet in his 1626 scroll by simply rooting an old pine tree with dragon-scale–like bark in the very center of his foreground.

The layering of visual and textual images in Dong Qichang's painting fills it with various meanings. In his second inscription, he states that the painting's scenery matches the depiction of a different poem he had added to earlier paintings.[5] One such example is extant—a hanging scroll titled *Landscape in the Manner of Dong Yuan* (1625) in the Rietberg Museum.[6] Noting how the scenery of *Landscape Evoking a Poem by Wang Wei*, with its tall pine tree protruding beyond the foreground, was suggestive of this other poem he had illustrated in the past, Dong decided to add it again. There were also visual resonances that may have encouraged him to add the second poem: Dong probably remembered the cone-shaped mountain, the houses at the foot of the mountains, the pine tree in the foreground, and the mountain ranges rendered in Huang Gongwang's style that he used in *Landscape in the Manner of Dong Yuan* a year earlier.

Dong Qichang's *Hua zhi* (The purport of painting) records one of his theories of the development of literati painting:

> In Chan Buddhism there is a Southern and a Northern school, which first separated in the Tang period [618–907]; in painting, a similar division into a Southern and a Northern school also appeared in the Tang period. . . The Southern School began with Wang Mojie [Wang Wei], who first used a light ink-wash technique, transforming the outline method; it was transmitted by Zhang Zao, Jing [Jing Hao], Guan [Guan Tong], Dong [Dong Yuan], Ju [Juran], Guo Zhongshu, the two Mis, father and son [Mi Fu and Mi Youren], down to the Four Great Masters of the Yuan.[7]

Under the belief that the Southern School's styles were those that literati painters should follow, Dong pursued his art based on these selected models. Since Wang Wei played an important role in initiating the use of ink strokes, which was characteristic of literati painting, it was natural for Dong to utilize Wang's style while visualizing his couplet. In *Landscape Evoking a Poem by Wang Wei*, the sharp, twisted cliffs and rocks in the middle ground, and the striking contrast between textured and blank areas along the conjunctions of mountain ranges, suggest the naïve, antique style that Dong believed to belong to Wang Wei.[8]

Identifying Wang's brushwork was an important step in Dong Qichang's development of his painting style. In the ninth month of 1597, after years of searching, Dong finally confirmed his understanding of Wang's style through *Wangchuan Villa after Wang Wei*, a painting attributed to Guo Zhongshu in Gao Shenfu's collection. Right after this visit, Dong painted *The Wanluan Thatched Hall* (fig. 8) for his close friend Chen Jiru using meticulously repeated short, round strokes, which he considered to be the true method of Wang Wei.[9] Years later, after decades of experimentation, Dong confidently embodied the spirit of Wang in a more theoretically comprehensive way, utilizing the motifs and brush modes of later Southern School followers, such as Huang Gongwang, to emphasize the connections within the lineage. Combining multiple masters' representative techniques into one piece, such as we see in *Landscape Evoking a Poem by Wang Wei*, marked the maturity of Dong's art. **KYH**

For inscriptions and other documentation, see page 282 in this catalogue.

1 Ren Daobin 任道斌, *Dong Qichang xinian*, 230–31; Zhang Tingyu 張廷玉, et al., *Ming shi* 明史, in *Jingyin Wenyuange Siku quanshu* 景印文淵閣四庫全書 (Taipei: Taiwan Shangwu yinshuguan, 1983), vol. 301, 866. For Dong's activities in 1631, see Ren, *Dong Qichang xinian*, 267–72.

2 Ren, *Dong Qichang xinian*, 234. The location of *A Painting after the Wangchuan Quatrains* is unknown.

3 For Wang Meng's painting, see Wai-kam Ho, et al., *Eight Dynasties of Chinese Painting*, 136.

4 Dong left a colophon on the album (now dispersed) that originally included Wang Meng's painting after the same couplet. Ibid. For a record of that album see Wang Keyu 汪砢玉, *Shanhu wang* 珊瑚網, in *Jingyin Wenyuange Siku quanshu* (Taipei: Taiwan Shangwu yinshuguan, 1983), vol. 818, 835.

5 The five-character quatrain was compiled in Dong Qichang, *Rongtai ji shiji* 容台集 詩集, in *Siku quanshu cunmu congshu jibu* 四庫全書存目叢書集部 (Jinan: Qilu shushe, 1997), vol. 171, 599.

6 Reproduced in Wai-kam Ho, ed., *The Century of Tung Ch'i-ch'ang*, vol. 1, pl. 52.

7 Dong Qichang, *Rongtai ji bieji*, 723. Translation after Wen Fong, *The Century of Tung Ch'i-ch'ang*, vol. 1, 47–48.

8 The blank strips applied along the mountain ranges echo a famous painting attributed to Wang Wei that Dong Qichang regarded as genuine. See Shih Shou-chien, "Tung Ch'i-ch'ang's 'Wan-luan Thatched Hall' and the Innovation of His Painting Style," 13.1–13.28.

9 Ibid. For a Chinese version of this article see Shi Shouqian, "Dong Qichang Wanluan caotang tu ji qi gexin huafeng" 董其昌〈婉孌草堂圖〉及其革新畫風, *Zhongyang yanjiuyuan lishi yuyan yanjiusuo jikan* 中央研究院歷史語言研究所集刊 65, no. 2 (1994): 307–32.

9 Dong Qichang 董其昌
1555–1636

***Landscape Evoking a Poem by Wang Wei* 右丞詩意圖**
1626
Private collection

Evoking Youcheng's poetic idea:
Behind the closed door [I] have written books for months and years;
Pines planted long ago have all grown old with dragon scales.

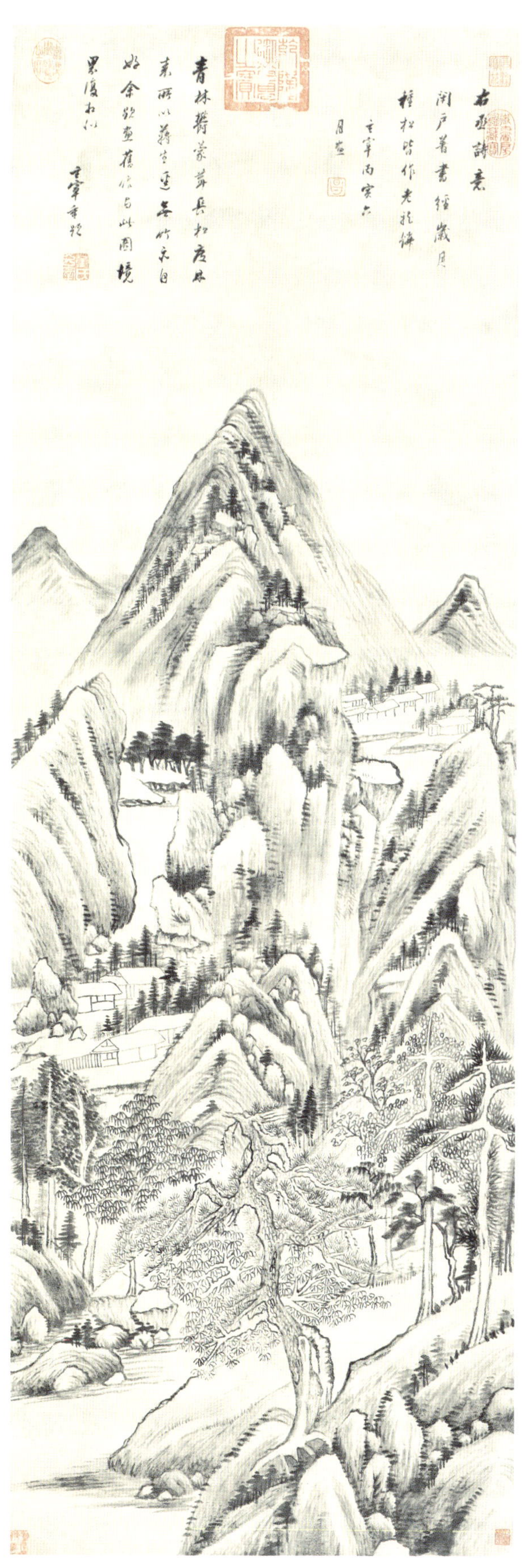

Among his many roles—including able official, filial son, erudite scholar, avid collector, and humble artist—Li Rihua is perhaps best considered as art theorist and connoisseur. He is one of a select few whose writings compete in depth with those of Dong Qichang, who happened to be a close acquaintance. However, because of the scarcity of his work and a lack of recognition of many of his writings, Li's accomplishments of the seventeenth-century art scene have seldom been mentioned. It is only recently that scholars have begun to reexamine his comments on art, which have long been overshadowed by his forceful and prolific friend.[1]

Born to a gentry family of Jiaxing (Jiangsu Province), Li Rihua developed a strong early interest in antiquity and began to collect art while preparing for the imperial examinations.[2] Though he met his father's expectations of passing the exams and serving as an honest official, he aspired to a simple, scholarly life. A well-known group portrait of 1652 jointly painted by Xiang Shengmo and Zhang Qi titled *Venerable Friends* documents the influential literati circle to which Li belonged (fig. 20).[3] Li's writings on art, including *Liuyanzhai biji* (Notes from the Studio of Six Inkstones; see fig. 19) and *Weishui xuan riji* (Diary from the Pavilion for Tasting Water), provide rich material for the reconstruction of artistic activities in seventeenth-century literati circles.[4] More importantly, they were the forum for his astute and often highly opinionated criticisms. For example, while Li agreed with Dong Qichang that the Wu School of Suzhou had declined into a state of commercial mediocrity, he also criticized the Songjiang School led by Dong, contending that the Songjiang painters were so obsessed with the arrangement of calligraphic traces that their landscape paintings failed to present the realistic forms of trees and rocks.[5]

In this painting of lotus, Li Rihua depicts a wind-blown blossom backed by a large leaf painted in dual tones to differentiate its two sides. The interplay between Li's couplet and image is clever. His inscription transforms the lotus into a beautiful woman, whose appearance is reflected on the water and whose fragrance reaches people from afar. The key to this sensual experience is the breeze that blows the lotus and carries its fragrance everywhere; as if to emphasize this, Li left the character for "fragrance," *xiang* 香, at the bottom of the first line in closest proximity to his image. This is a casual work by the artist, but it still displays his four desiderata for painting: form (*xing* 形), movement (*shi* 勢), resonance (*yun* 韻), and character or nature (*xing* 性). According to Li's ideal, capturing the object's form is the basis for a painting, to which should be added an element of liveliness by depicting movement. An exceptional artist, however, will go beyond this and find a way to capture the more abstract qualities that define the essence of his subject.[6] To help put his words into practice Li planted on his property such favored plants as pine trees, bamboo, and plums for observation.[7] While there are some realistic touches to Li Rihua's *Lotus*, its abbreviated depiction suggests that the painter here was more interested in the poetic and essential qualities of his subject. **YCP**

For inscriptions and other documentation, see page 282 in this catalogue.

1 Lin Yixin 林逸欣, "Li Rihua huihua jiancang pinwei zhi yanjiu."
2 Tan Zhenmo 譚貞默, "Ming Zhongyi daifu Taipusi shaoqing Li Jiuyi xiansheng xingzhuang" 明中議大夫太僕寺少卿李九疑先生行狀, in Tan Xinjia 譚新嘉, ed., *Biyi sanji* 碧漪三集, collected in *Congshu jicheng san bian* 叢書集成三編 (Taipei: Xinwenfeng chubanshe, 1997), vol. 60, 529a.
3 The group portrait includes Dong Qichang, Li Rihua, Chen Jiru, Lu Dezhi, Xiang Shengmo, and the monk Qiutan and is in the collection of the Shanghai Museum. See Chu-tsing Li, "The Literati Life," in Li and James C. Y. Watt, eds., *The Chinese Scholar's Studio*, 37–38, pl. 1.
4 Li Rihua 李日華, *Liuyanzhai biji* 六研齋筆記, in *Biji xiaoshuo daguan* 筆記小說大觀 (Taipei: Xinxing shuju, 1985), vol. 38; *Weishui xuan riji* 味水軒日記 (Shanghai: Yuandong chubanshe, 1996). The former records Li Rihua's comments on art he collected or saw; the latter is a diary of Li's activities in local literati circles when he resided in Jiaxing from 1609 to 1616. These works were extensively utilized by Craig Clunas to observe the changing view toward the sixteenth-century Wu school master Wen Zhengming in the seventeenth-century art market. Clunas, *Elegant Debts*.
5 Li Rihua, *Liuyanzhai biji*, 6:370. Lin Yixin, "Li Rihua huihua jiancang pinwei zhi yanjiu," 40–41.
6 Li Rihua, *Liuyanzhai sanbi* 六研齋三筆, in *Biji xiaoshuo daguan san jiu bian* 筆記小說大觀 三九編 (Taipei: Xinxing, 1985), no. 2, 2:512.
7 Li Rihua, *Zitaoxuan zazhui* 紫桃軒雜綴, in *Siku quanshu cunmu congshu* 四庫全書存目叢書 (Tainan: Zhuangyan wenhua, 1995), no. 108, 1:12. Lin Yixin, "Li Rihua huihua jiancang pinwei zhi yanjiu," 36.

10 Li Rihua 李日華
1565–1635

Lotus 荷花圖軸
Private collection

The beautiful lady's appearance reflects
on the water clearly;
Her fragrance scents people from afar.

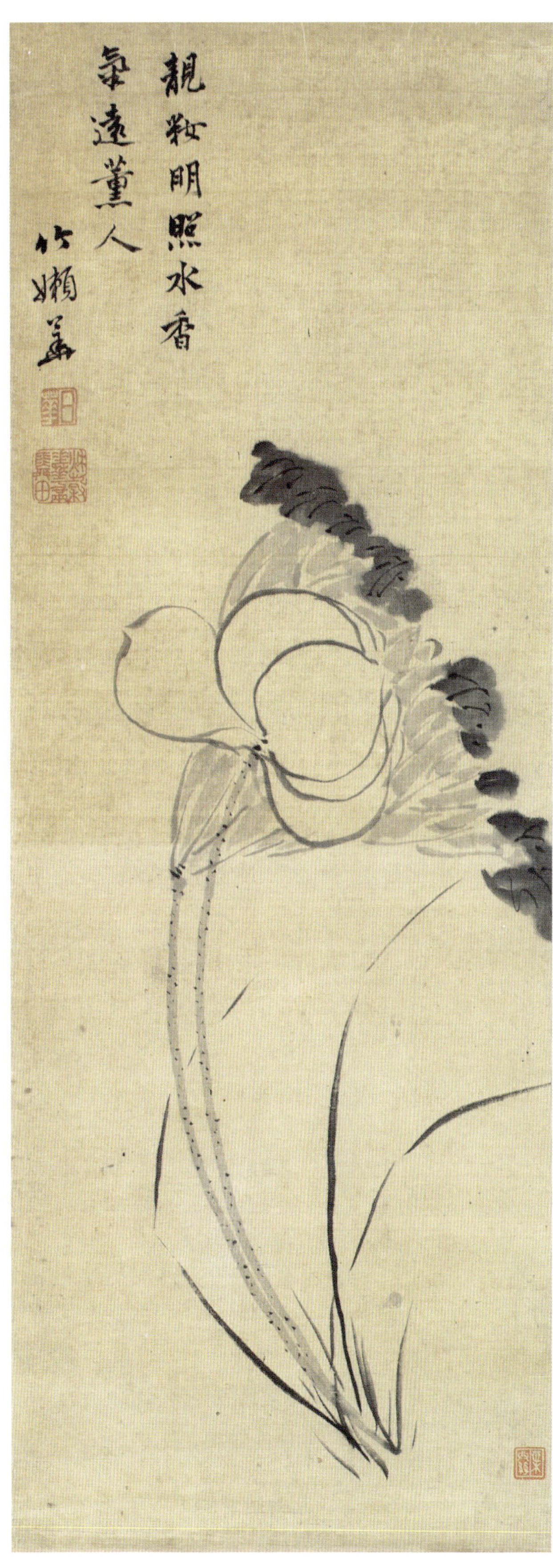

Although Chen Jiru's use of the term *xie*, "to write" or "sketch," in his signature for *Thatched Hut by Tall Pines* is common among late Ming-dynasty literati painters and usually carries little meaning, it is appropriate for this casually painted scene of a rustic hut in a garden setting. Since the establishment of a literati theory for painting in the eleventh century, much had been made of the potential relationship between calligraphy and painting. As reflected by Su Shi's famous statement that the scholar-artist need not learn how to paint, as he already knows how to handle the brush through writing, there was an early perception that quality in painting, as it was in calligraphy, was inextricably linked to the quality of its maker. Personal expressive qualities associated with the calligrapher's handling of the responsive brush were gradually transferred to painting, with a consequent valuation of brushwork over descriptive appearance. *Thatched Hut by Tall Pines* exemplifies the true scholar-amateur tradition: a simple composition created by one who had little training as a painter, a painting that opens itself up to a process of reading by a viewer whose primary interest would be in the person of Chen Jiru.

Chen Jiru was one of the most prominent men of his generation. A native of Songjiang (Jiangsu Province)—the same area whence hailed his lifelong friend, the artist and high official Dong Qichang—Chen passed the *xiucai* 秀才 (licentiate) examination but never proceeded with an official career. In a celebrated act, he burned his scholar's robes at the age of twenty-seven or twenty-eight and adopted the leisurely life of a lofty hermit. A recent study has shown that the burning of one's robes was a common social gesture among first-degree holders to symbolize one's refusal to hold office.[1] Chen Jiru was the most celebrated example of the time. Shortly thereafter, he wrote a petition to the Prefect of Songjiang that revealed his motivation:

> To participate in worldly affairs produces clamor; to dissociate from worldly affairs results in peace. To support one's parents through office holding or by personal attendance amounts to the same thing... Spending one's life in calculation is as unreal as the image of a flower in the mirror. I intend to take the rest of my life into my own hands and spend it happily, communing with nature.[2]

Far from a true recluse, Chen earned a livelihood by teaching privately, composing books on cultural matters, and writing epitaphs and birthday congratulations.[3] He earned the high praise and lifelong friendship of Dong Qichang, who built a studio for Chen titled the Laizhong Tower (literally "Come Zhong Tower," Zhong being the first character of Chen's style name, Zhongchun 仲醇). The writer Wang Shizhen, another paramount cultural figure of the late Ming, also highly valued Chen's literary and intellectual talents (Chen was given the honor of composing Wang's tomb epitaph). Often invited to serve in office, Chen habitually declined for reasons of ill health.[4] Most of his time was spent in an idyllic residence he built in the eastern She Hills of his native district, where he planted pines and firs. On the land adjoining his home he transplanted some one hundred old plum trees, from which, no doubt, he gained inspiration for his many paintings of blossoming prunus.[5] Late in his life his popularity was such that "the hermit's abode became a market," as a constant stream of visitors, it is said, emerged from a mile-long line of moored boats in front of his welcoming hall.

For inscriptions and other documentation, see page 283 in this catalogue.

1 Ch'en Kuo-tung, "Temple Lamentation and Robe-burning—Gestures of Social Protest in Seventeenth-Century China," 33–52. The original article was first published in *Xin shixue* 新史學 3, no. 1 (March 1992): 69–94. A more recent monograph on Chen Jiru by Greenbaum provides an excellent overall study of Chen's life, his publishing activities, and his image. Jamie Greenbaum, *Chen Jiru (1558–1639)*.

2 Cited from Ch'en, "Temple Lamentation and Robe-burning," 37. Translation by Greenbaum with minor revisions. See also Greenbaum, *Chen Jiru*, 18.

3 In addition to Greenbaum's monograph, see the entry on Chen Jiru (Ch'en Chi-ju) by Fang Chao-ying in Arthur Hummel, ed., *Eminent Chinese of the Ch'ing Period*, vol. 1, 83–84. The fact that publishers often borrowed Chen's name for marketing books of questionable worth is a clear indication of his fame.

4 *Ming shi* 明史 (Beijing: Zhonghua shuju ed., 1974), 298: 7631–632.

5 Jiang Shaoshu 姜紹書, *Wusheng shishi* 無聲詩史, in *Zhongguo shuhua quanshu* 中國書畫全書 (Shanghai: Shanghai shuhua chubanshe, 2000), 4: 853–54.

11 Chen Jiru 陳繼儒
1558–1639

Thatched Hut by Tall Pines 長松草堂圖
Santa Barbara Museum of Art
Gift of N. P. Wong Family

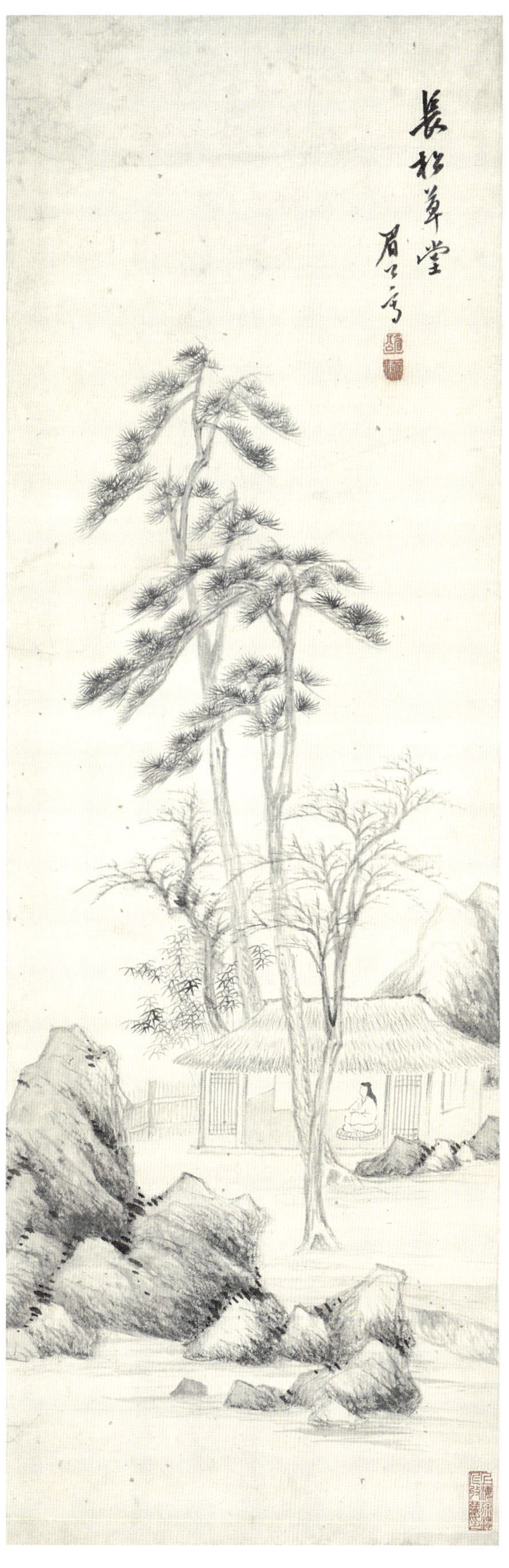

Chen Jiru was a noted connoisseur of art and owned a considerable collection of calligraphy, paintings, ancient bronzes, and jades.[6] Like Dong Qichang, with whom he shared many an occasion devoted to the close examination of prized objects, Chen's approach to art practice was entirely predicated on the privilege of being able to learn directly from earlier masterpieces. In this regard, his repute as a high-minded man of letters was essential, earning him easy access to the major art collections in the Jiangnan region. Not surprisingly, he echoed Dong's theory of the Northern and Southern Schools (professional versus literati painting) and shared his aesthetic criteria, much of which was borrowed from calligraphy. Painting, like calligraphy, should be "even and light" (*pingdan* 平淡) and aspire to naturalness. An artist's work should transcend the mundane and be without any trace of worldliness. One's intrinsic character will be presented through the painting; hence there is a strong emphasis on casualness, which allows the genuine self to appear, and brushwork, that trusted medium for personal display. Harmony, sparseness, evenness: these are the qualities that Chen sought to exhibit in his paintings, qualities that, in turn, would reflect the state of peaceful equilibrium he had attained in his transcendent lifestyle.

In all likelihood, Chen Jiru's training as a painter was fairly limited, as his paintings lack the maturity and polish that is readily apparent in his calligraphy, which was his true forte (see cat. no. 12). As a youth, he learned to paint together with Dong, very possibly learning from fellow townsmen Gu Zhengyi and Mo Shilong.[7] Another possible influence was the painter Zhao Zuo, who was also of Songjiang and is known to have been close to Chen (see cat. no. 13). *Thatched Hut by Tall Pines* lacks the variety of brushwork seen in the work of the more professional Zhao and pales in sheer visual interest, but its composition and motifs reflect a common Songjiang School style, if not influence. The painting, in any case, perfectly represents Chen Jiru, literally describing a lofty hermit seated in meditation with quiet, unassertive brushwork learned from the study of such Southern School luminaries as the Yuan-dynasty painters Wu Zhen and Ni Zan.

A last note of interest to this painting is the collector's seal of Xu Weiren. Xu was a prominent collector of nineteenth-century Shanghai—a comrade of such other noted aficionados of art and antiquity as Liang Tongshu, Wang Xuehao, Chen Hongshou (1768–1822), and Zhang Tingqi—and an amateur artist in his own right. Like Chen Jiru, Xu was a calligrapher first, mastering the various scripts before beginning to learn how to paint orchids, bamboo, and landscapes at the age of thirty-eight. No doubt Chen Jiru served as an inspiration from the past, the kind of paragon of literati ideals that helped sustain the tradition of amateur painting in late imperial China to which Xu Weiren and countless others subscribed. **PCS**

6 For a good overview of Chen Jiru's activities as a collector and critic, see Ren Daobin, "Ch'en Chi-ju as Critic and Connoisseur," 9.1–9.25.

7 In an inscription to his own painting, recorded in his collected writings, Chen mentions that he painted with Dong Qichang in his youth. Ren Daobin, ibid., 9–16, note 2. For the suggestion that Chen studied with Gu Zhengyi and Mo Shilong, see Chu-tsing Li and James C. Y. Watt, eds., *The Chinese Scholar's Studio*, 151.

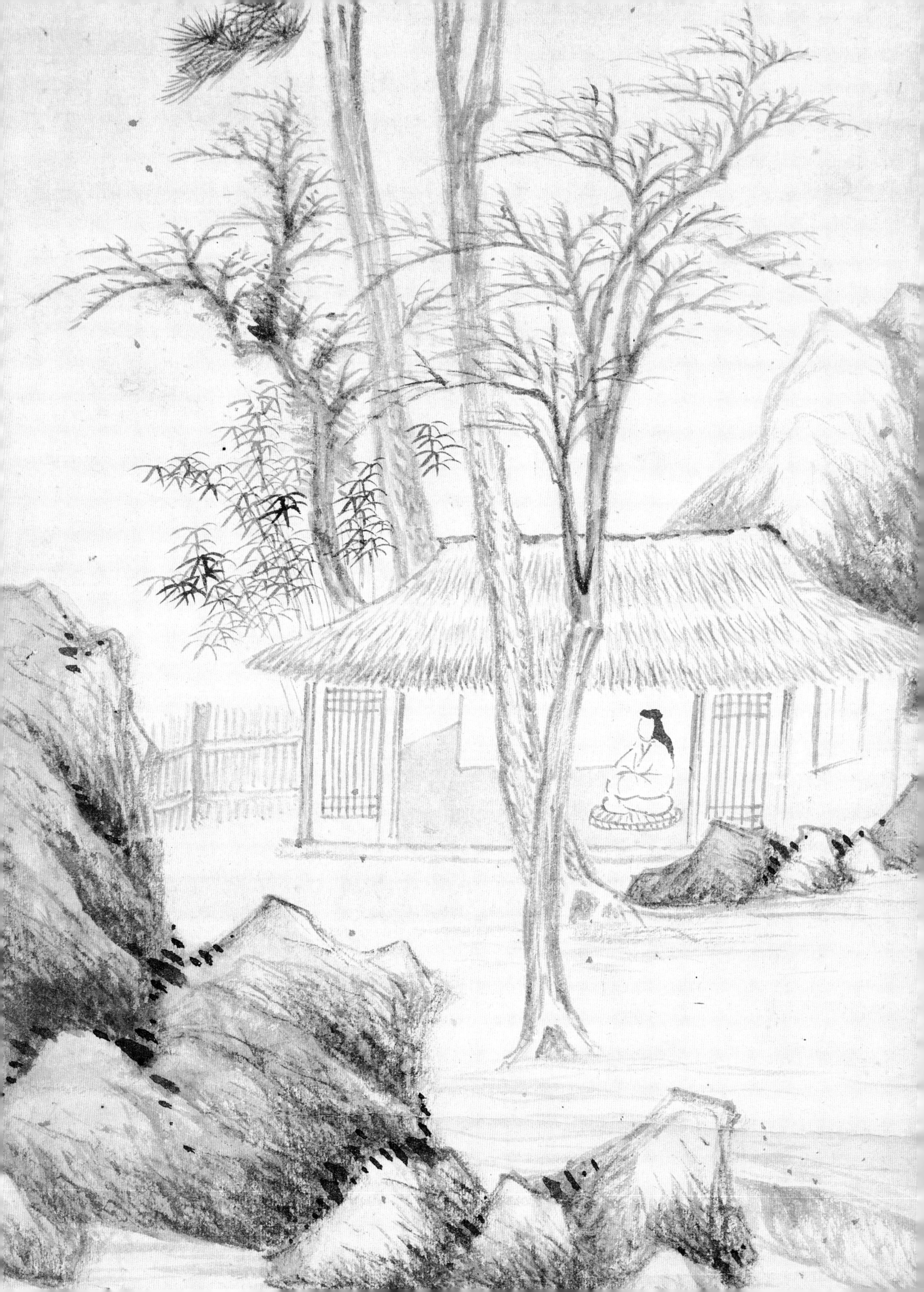

4

3

8

7

12 Chen Jiru 陳繼儒 1558–1639

Zhang Heng's "Returning to the Field"
張衡《歸田賦》
Calligraphy in semi-cursive script
Private collection

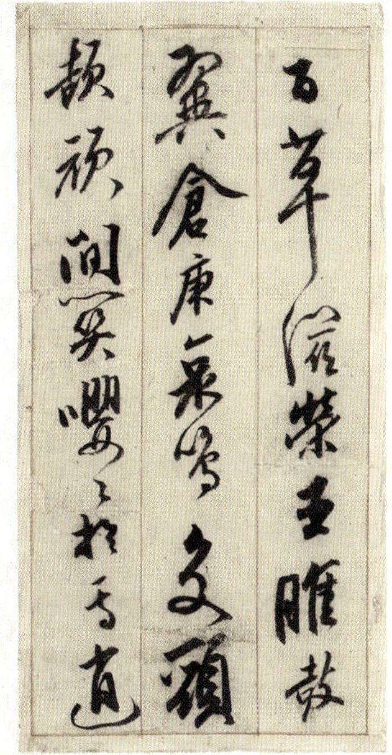

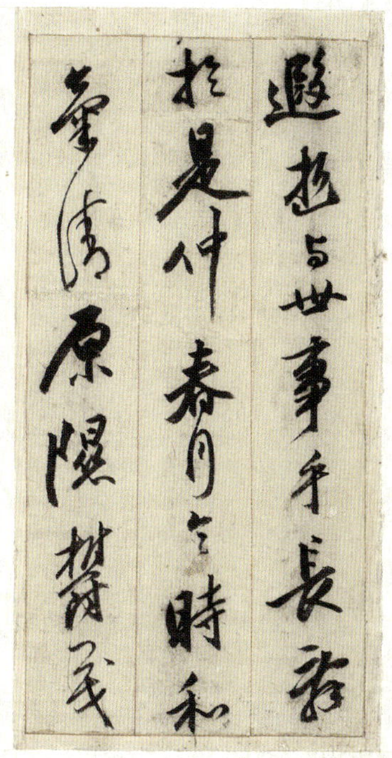

2

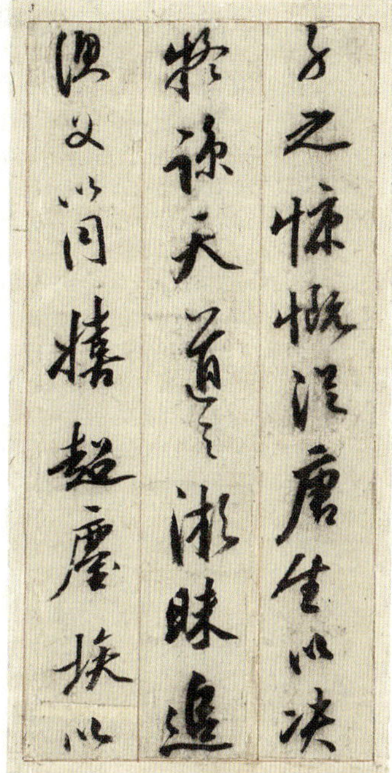

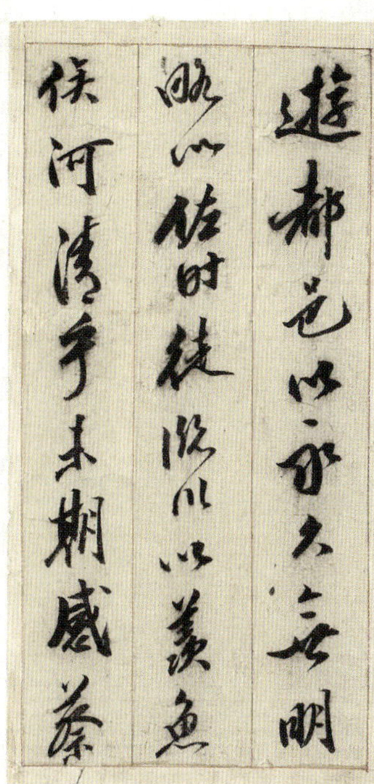

1

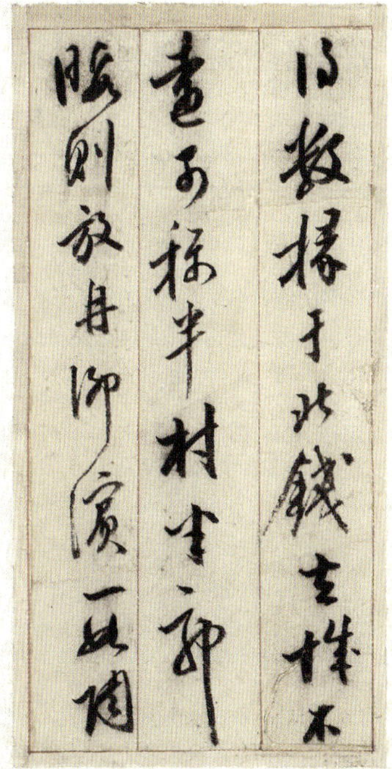

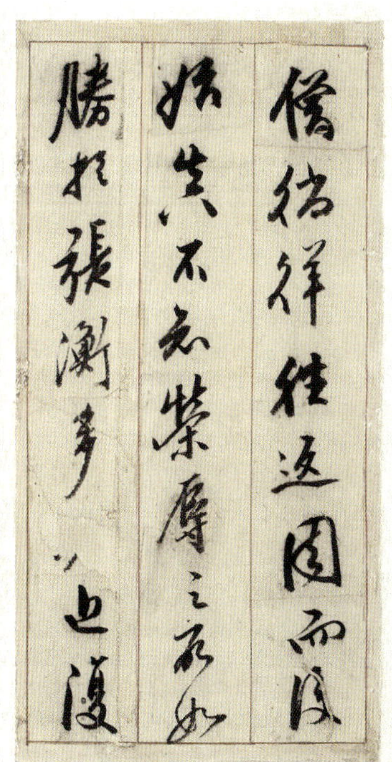

6

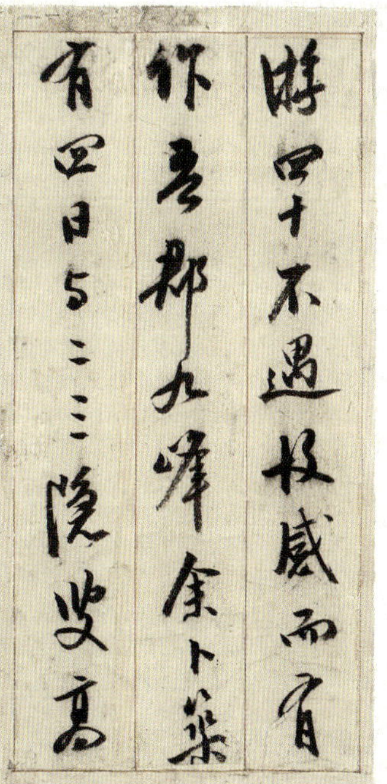

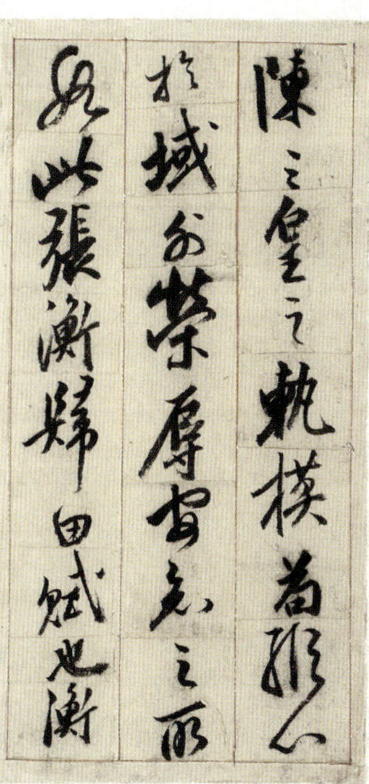

5

This is Zhang Heng's "Returning to the Field." Having served at official posts for forty years without being honored, Zhang Heng was moved to compose this piece. My hometown is in the Nine Peaks region, where I have had four structures built. Day after day, I entertain myself together with two or three intimate recluses or monks, whiling away the entire day then starting all over again. Under these circumstances, I truly know nothing about honor or disgrace, and in this regard I am far better than Zhang Heng . . .

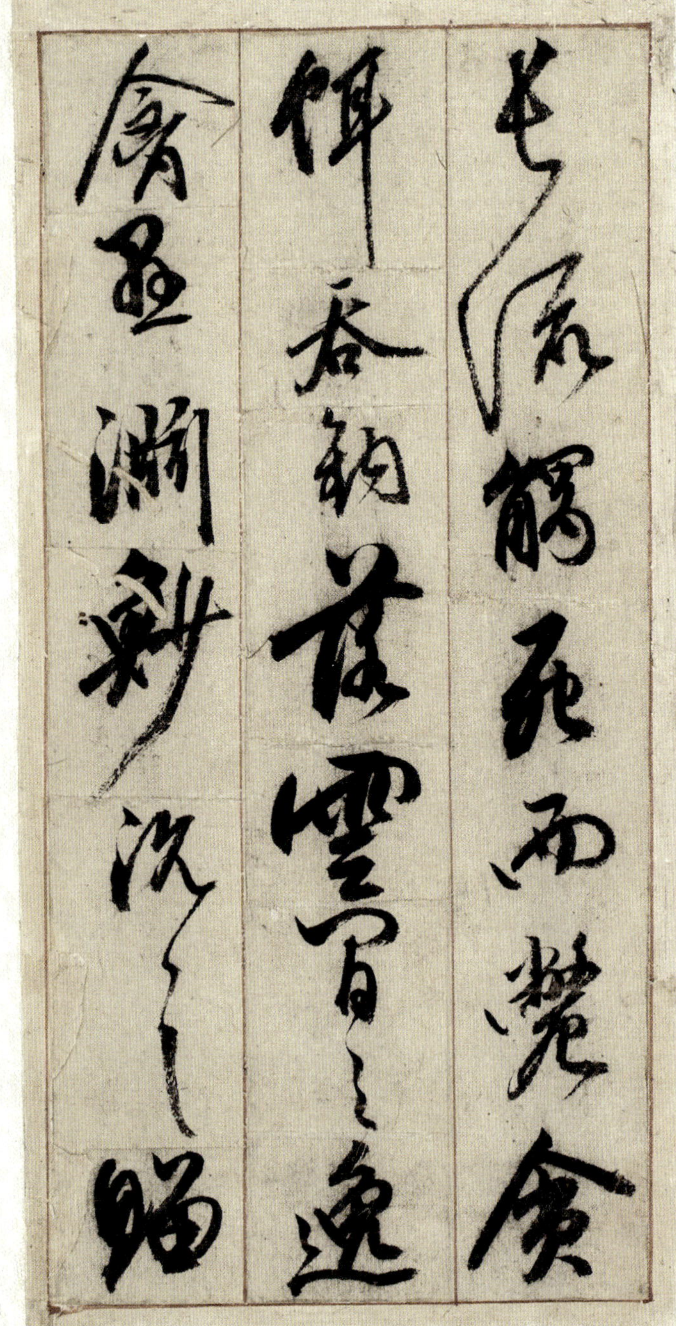

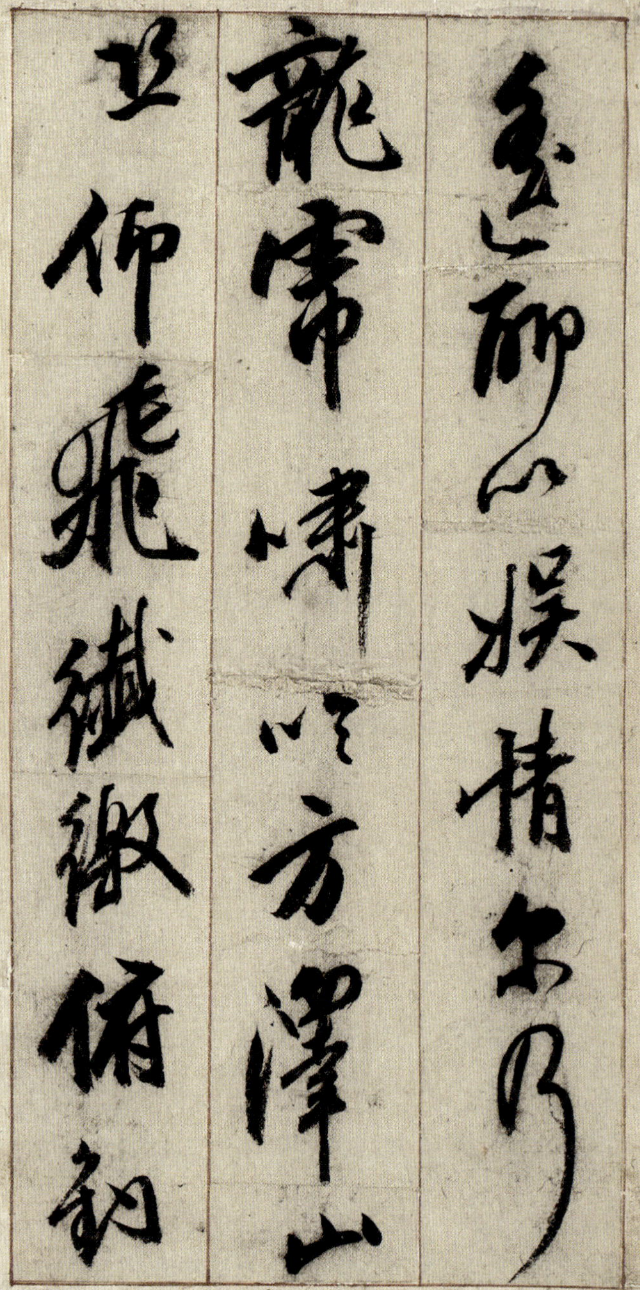

Together, the content and calligraphy of this album come together to create a work that perfectly commemorates Chen Jiru's life as a celebrated scholar and recluse of his time. The text is a transcription of Zhang Heng's famous rhapsody (*fu* 賦) *Returning to the Field*, one of the earliest known poetic writings in Chinese literature to extol the virtues of retirement and reclusion.[1] Unlike Zhang, who requested to retire only after serving at the court and facing the enmity of political rivals, Chen rejected the path to an official career despite the reputation of his literary talents and frequent requests to assume such duties. In the lengthy inscription that he added to his transcription (see page 283), Chen claims a status above that of Zhang, who for decades had concerned himself with obtaining official recognition. Nonetheless, while Zhang's *Returning to the Field* eulogizes the scenery of the natural world and extols the pursuits of a retirement far from worldly affairs, Chen's reclusion, as he describes in his inscription, flourishes with social outings, acquaintances, and the accumulation of personal properties dotting the landscape.

Based on Chen Jiru's mention of his four structures in the Nine Peaks region, this album can be dated between 1610, when he moved from his retreats in the Mount Kun area to Mount She in the Nine Peaks region, and 1621, when at least eight of his personal properties were located there.[2] His record of four structures, as well as his mentioning of a recent purchase of additional studios in Beiqian—"half urban, half rural"—highlight not only his wealth and interest in landholdings but also his ease with a form of reclusion not particularly distant from the manners of urban life. At the same time, his association with place and the famous recluses before him is important. Tao Zongyi and Cao Zhibo of the Yuan dynasty, both of whom are singled out as models in Chen's description, had settled in the same region and had close affinities with Chen's ideal of reclusion. Tao repeatedly refused official appointments and instead chose a life of letters and tutoring. Cao, like Chen, not only refused to serve at court but also possessed significant landholdings. He was also an important painter and friend of the greatly admired Huang Gongwang—a fact that must have been known to Chen, who was a keen student of the Yuan artistic and literary scene.[3]

Performed in an informal setting among friends and acquaintances as a gift in return for a painting of his studio, Chen Jiru's calligraphy is at once bold and elegant. The album format is suggestive of the model calligraphy compendia (*fatie* 法帖), which Chen espoused for practicing brush control and character composition and would have been a major source for his own study of calligraphy, especially that of the Song-dynasty masters Su Shi and Mi Fu. As with the Song masters, whom he so admired and whose theories and styles he embraced, Chen believed in copying and borrowing from ancient predecessors as a step to developing and displaying his own style of writing. His concern, however, was less about the development of a personal style than of showing his capacity for synthesizing preferable traits as a style, and the means and display of his self-cultivation. In comparison to another superb example of his calligraphy represented in this exhibition, his inscription to Xiang Shengmo's *Invitation to Reclusion* written a few years later (see cat. no. 1), Chen's calligraphy in this album reveals more of an effort to impart variations of brushwork, texture, and character composition, all in keeping with the album's function as a showcase for his ability as a creative calligrapher. His brush, elegant and blunt, pulls and turns the ink into a style beautifully perfected and descriptive of Chen Jiru, the learned and sophisticated recluse. **OML**

For inscriptions and other documentation, see page 283 in this catalogue.

1 James R. Hightower, "The *Fu* of T'ao Ch'ien," 90.

2 *Nianpu* 年譜, in *Chen Meigong xiansheng quanji* 陳眉公先生全集 (Huating: Chen shi, 1628), fu, 21b–22a.

3 Tao Zongyi was a literary scholar of the late Yuan-dynasty from Huangyan (Zhejiang). After failing the imperial examination in 1348, purportedly because of his unfavorable political commentary, he turned to studying the classics and calligraphy with scholars of renown. By the end of the Yuan he was living in Huating, where Chen Jiru also settled, and accepted students with whom he could share his broad learning while also tending to the fields. In 1396, he refused an official appointment. The author of such well-known texts as *Zhuogeng lu* 輟耕錄 (Notes taken after setting aside the plow) and *Shushi huiyao* 書史會要 (Essentials of the history of calligraphy), Tao's literary activities and successes, as well as his association with Huating, provided an important precedent for Chen. William Nienhauser Jr., ed., *The Indiana Companion to Traditional Chinese Literature*, vol. 1, 769–70. The earlier Cao Zhibo was also from Huating. A well-known painter, Cao is said to have amassed great wealth through his agricultural activities. Early in his career, he refused positions in the capital, preferring to live on his extensive landholdings in Songjiang. See Richard M. Barnhart, et al., *Three Thousand Years of Chinese Painting*, 166.

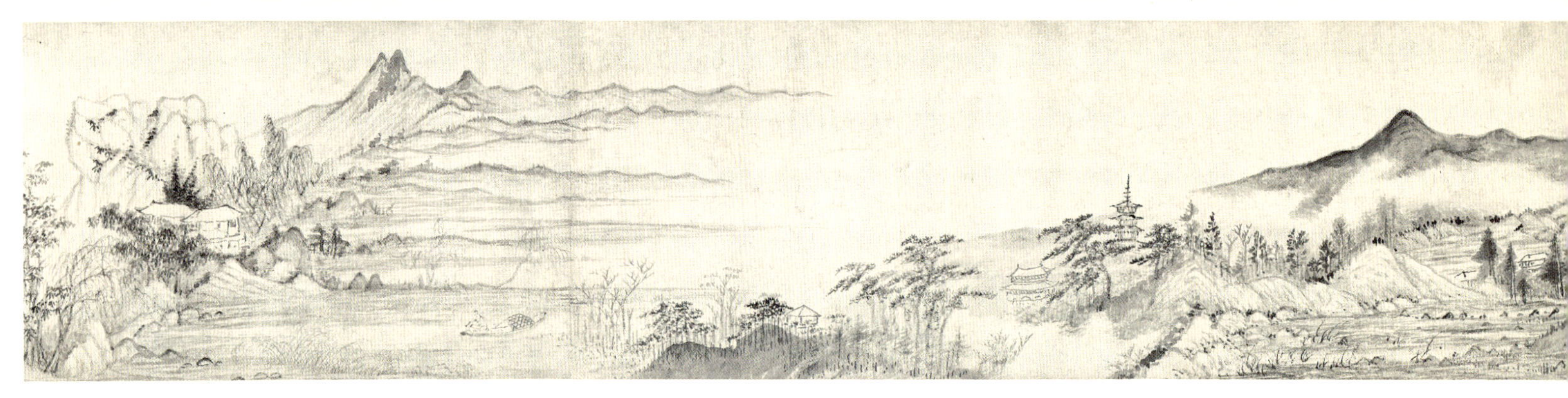

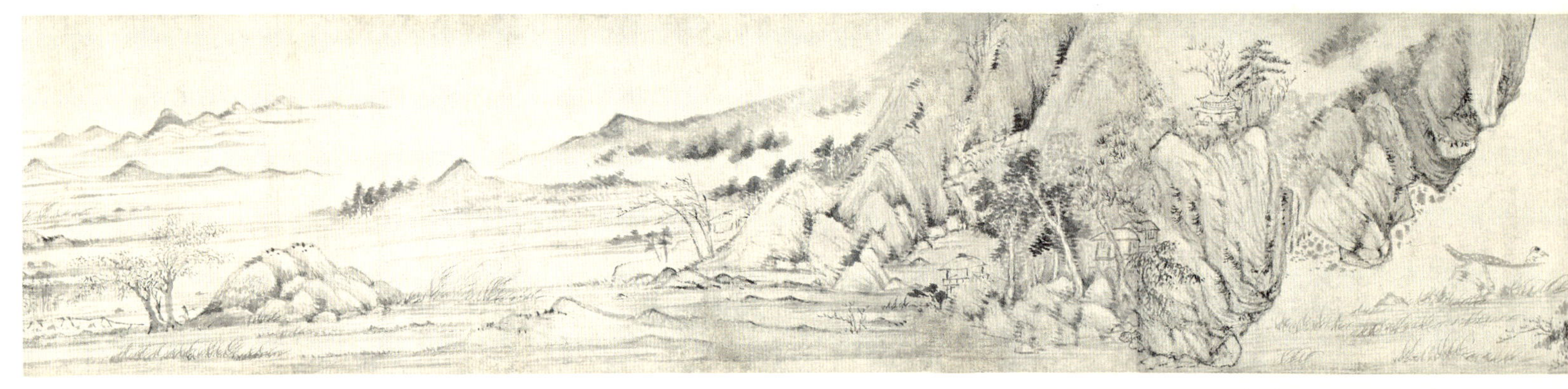

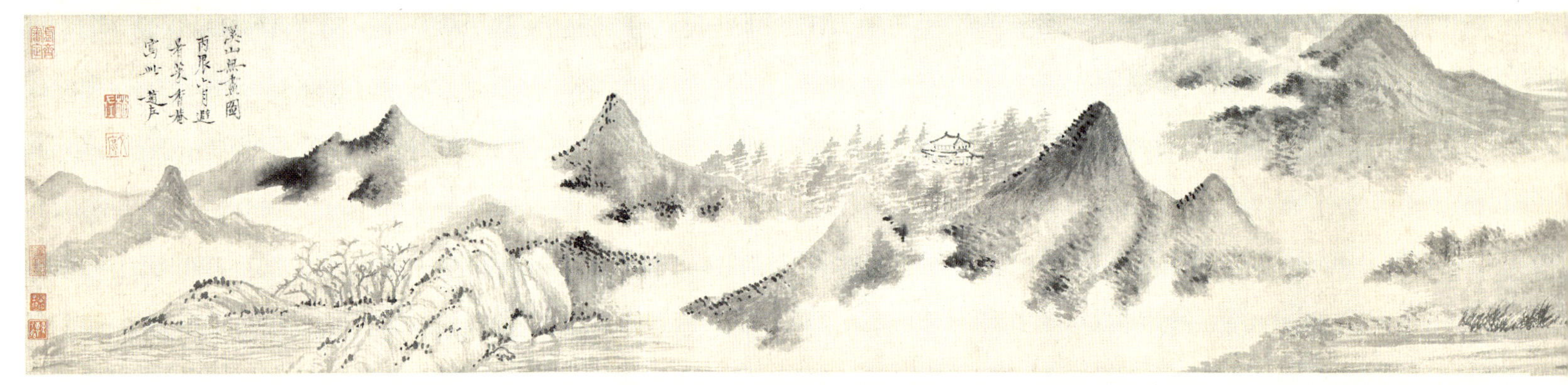

13 Zhao Zuo 趙左
C. 1570s–1633 or later

Streams and Mountains without End 溪山無盡圖卷
1616
Private collection

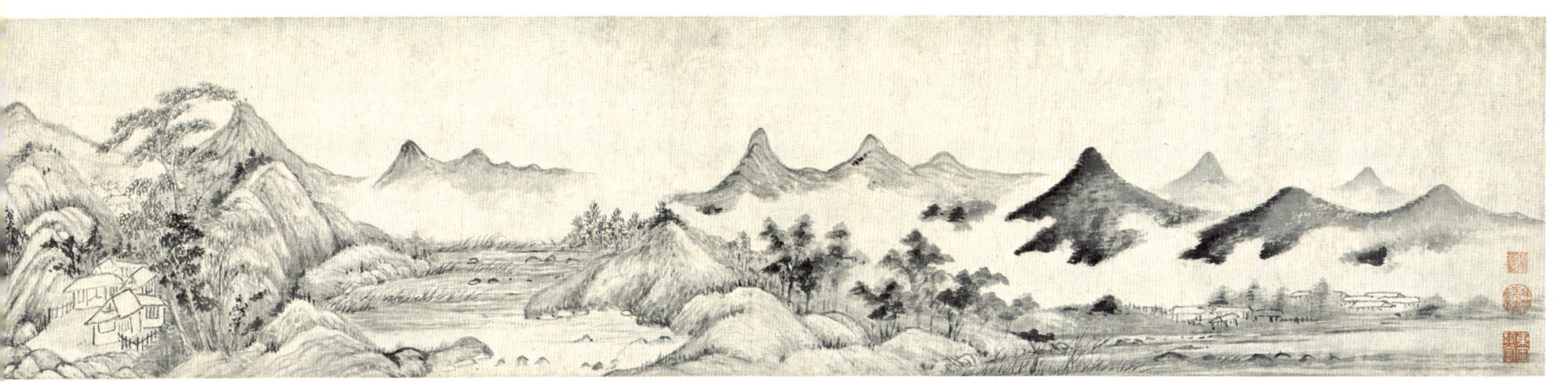

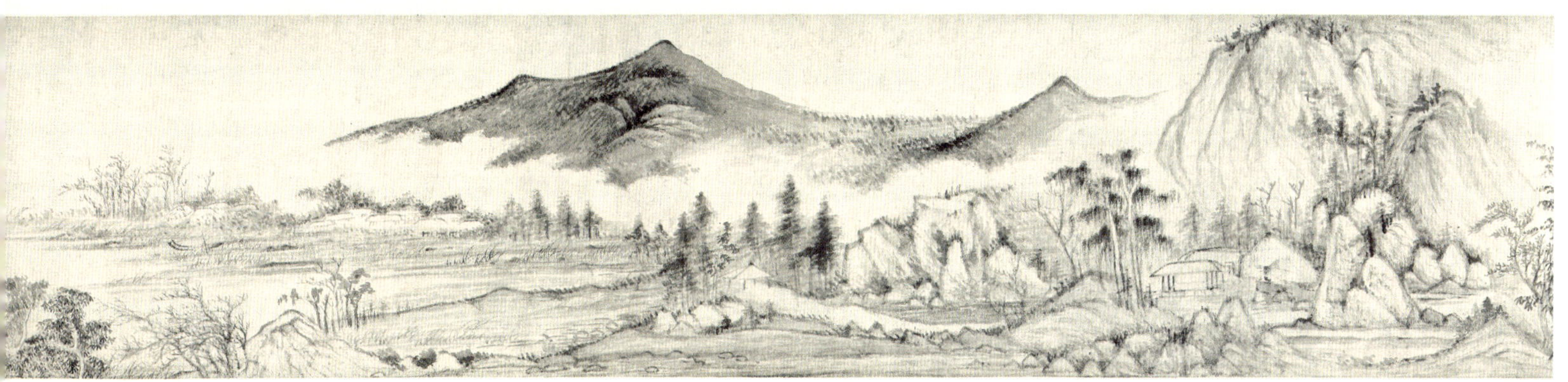

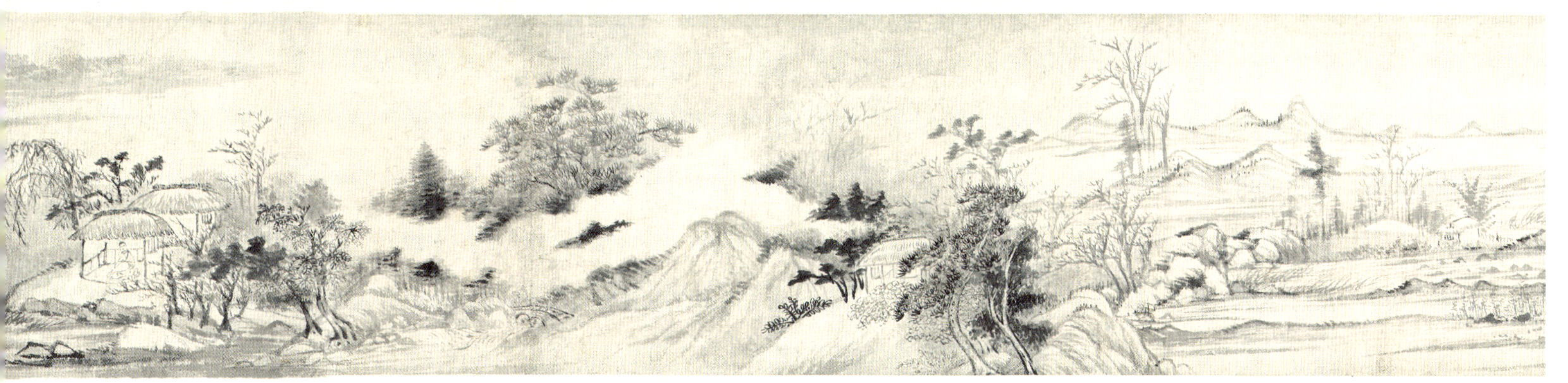

Zhao Zuo pursued the path of a career official through preparation for the civil service examinations, and as a young man his skill in the literary arts was already noted. However, like many educated men of the Wanli era (1572–1620), he was discouraged from following this ambition and by about 1610 turned to his skill as a painter to make a living.[1] Zhao's ties to his native Huating (Songjiang, present-day Shanghai area) were intrinsic to his identity as a painter. He was acquainted with Gu Zhengyi, a key figure in the development of a local style of landscape painting, studied under Song Xu, and also befriended Dong Qichang (cat. nos. 8–9), the famed literary recluse Chen Jiru (cat. nos. 11–12), and Song Maojin, all of whom influenced his personal life and artistic career. Collectively these artists became known as the Huating or Songjiang School. Their identity was to a large degree established through a regional rivalry with the painters of Suzhou, only fifty miles away. Emphasizing brushwork (*bi* 筆), with its strong associations of careful study of past masters, the Huating artists and their critical supporters saw themselves as rejuvenating the art of painting with a sense of purpose and direction.[2]

In many respects, *Streams and Mountains without End* epitomizes the Huating School's emphasis on brushwork. According to its short inscription, Zhao Zuo painted the lengthy handscroll while staying as a summer guest in the Hut of Vegetable Fragrance, which has been identified as a property owned by Chen Jiru.[3] Supporting the inscription's suggestion of locality is a resemblance between the low-lying hills wrapped in mists and the scenery of the Songjiang area. Zhao carefully composed the landscape, utilizing open spaces to form transitional segments and modulating shades of ink to create depth and pictorial accents. The painting begins with a balanced view of near, middle, and distant scenes before rhythmically opening and contracting to take the viewer deeply into the distance and then forward. The overall sparseness of the landscape allows the viewer to appreciate these movements and focus on Zhao's treatment of individual passages and motifs. Ultimately, the diversity and expert handling of his brushwork become readily apparent. Approaching the end of the scroll, as the landscape again moves in to highlight the foreground area, the viewer encounters a prominently displayed set of two simple thatched huts with a bearded figure seated within (see fig. 18). This is likely to be the master of the Hut of Vegetable Fragrance, Chen Jiru, the artist's friend and patron.

Art historian Zhu Huiliang divides Zhao Zuo's extant paintings into three periods: an early phase (before 1615) in which most works tend to be imitational after the great masters; a middle stage (1615–20), when the influence of Dong Qichang was especially strong; and a late phase (after 1620) of synthesis and maturity.[4] *Streams and Mountains without End* belongs to the very productive middle period. In the same year this painting was produced, Zhao finished several others in a variety of formats and styles.[5] Of particular note with this scroll is his heavy reliance on the Mi family style of cloudy mountains derived from the Song-dynasty literati painters Mi Fu and Mi Youren. A moist brush is extensively employed, so that the trees, sandbars, and even the contour of the mountains blur. The Mi dots have replaced the hemp-fiber texturing method of Huang Gongwang, which is more foregrounded in Zhao's earlier work, as the predominant means to express layers and shades in the mountains. In line with Mi Fu's own description, Zhao's painting pursues an impressionistic likeness that was considered appropriate for the landscape of the Jiangnan region.[6] Chen Jiru is known to have been a great admirer of Mi Fu, both for his calligraphy and painting. By painting the landscape of Chen's Hut of Vegetable Fragrance in a style that deliberately evokes Mi Fu, Zhao Zuo appears to be honoring the aesthetic preferences of his host. **JYZ**

For inscriptions and other documentation, see page 284 in this catalogue.

1 What little is known of Zhao Zuo's biography is largely drawn from local gazetteers and Mao Xianshou's 毛先壽 preface to a collection of Zhao's writings, "Zhao Wendu Dayu an ji xu" 趙文度大愚庵集序. See Zhu Huiliang 朱惠良, *Zhao Zuo yanjiu*, 23–24, 40. See also the entry on this painting by Wang Cheng-hua in Richard M. Barnhart, et al., *The Jade Studio*, 103.

2 On the Suzhou-Songjiang rivaly, see James Cahill, *The Distant Mountains*, 27–30.

3 Zhu, *Zhao Zuo yanjiu*, 31n23.

4 Ibid., 55–56.

5 For the paintings that Zhao Zuo finished between 1615 and 1617, see Zhu, *Zhao Zuo yanjiu*, 81.

6 Mi Fu wrote, "I do not attend to fine detail; rather I just capture the general likeness" 不取細意，似便已. Cited in Peter C. Sturman, "Mi Youren and the Inherited Literati Tradition," 189.

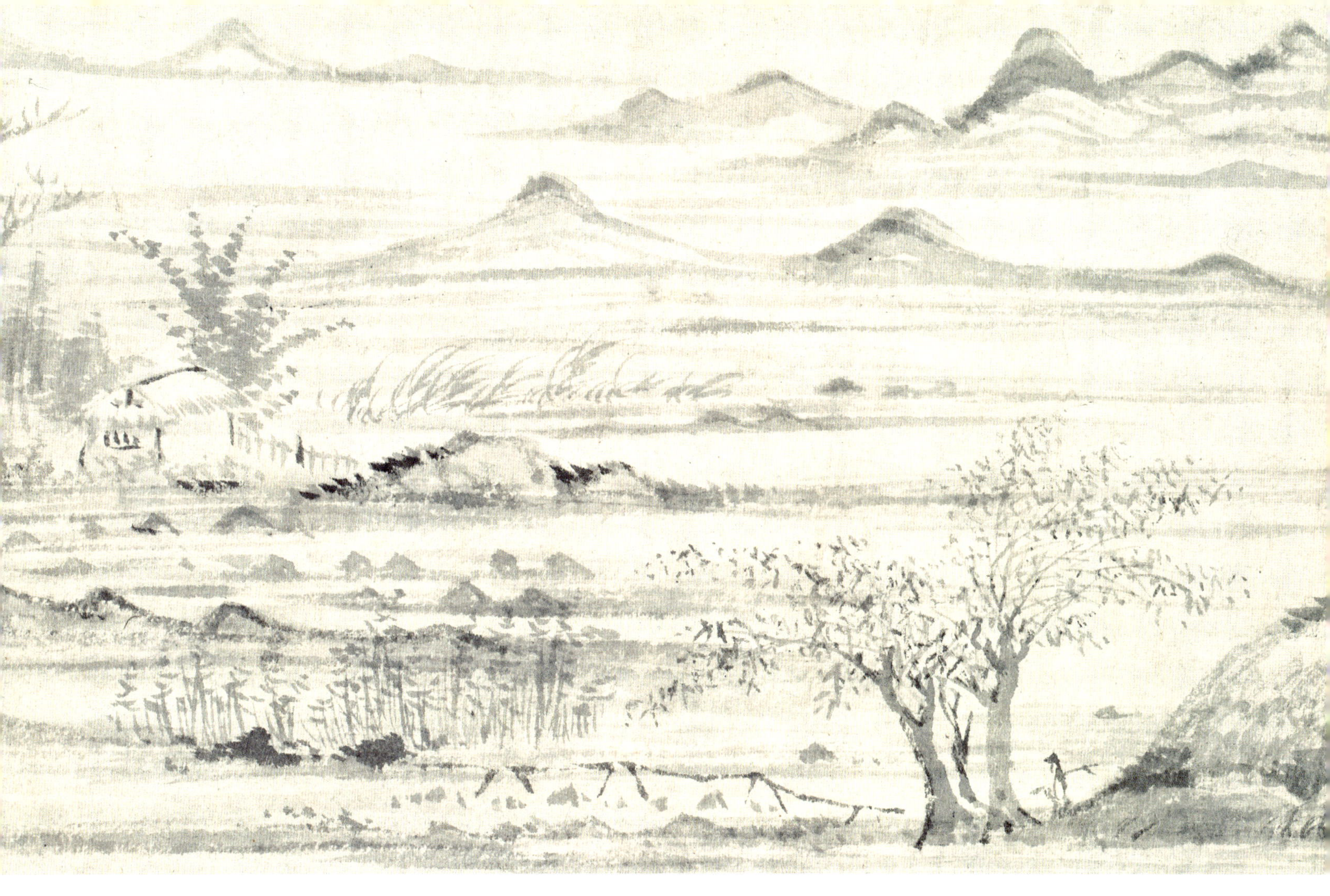

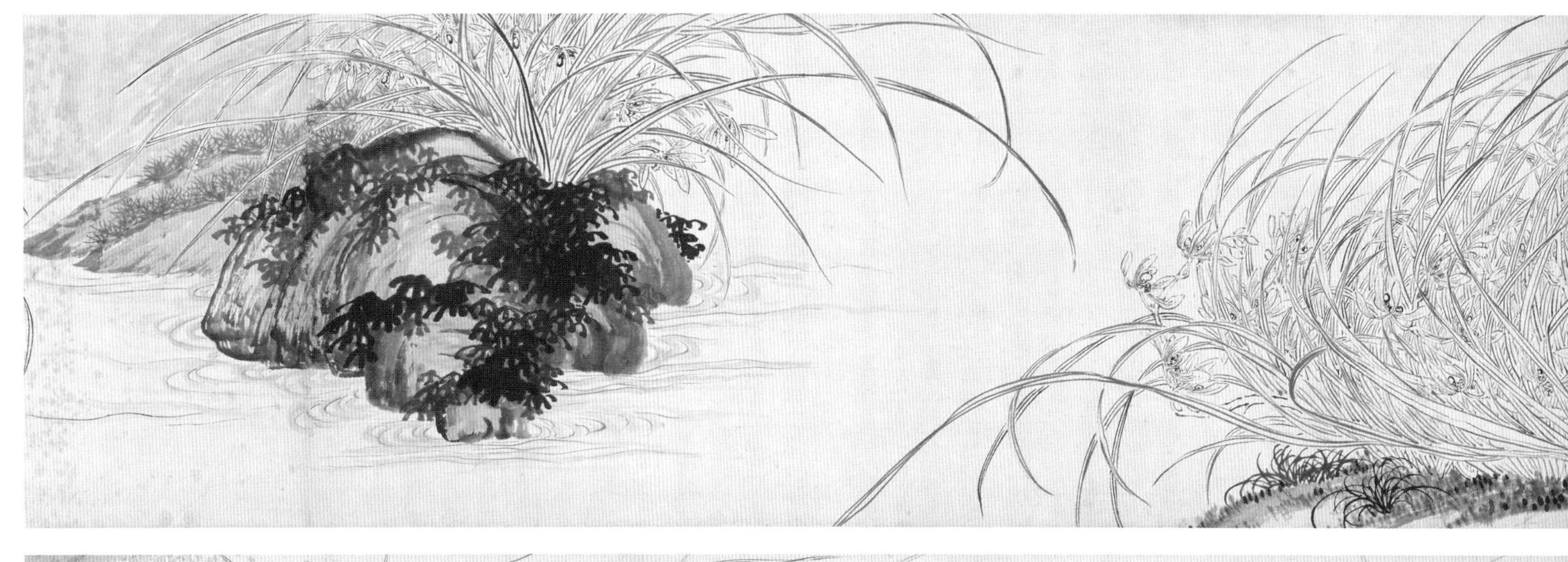

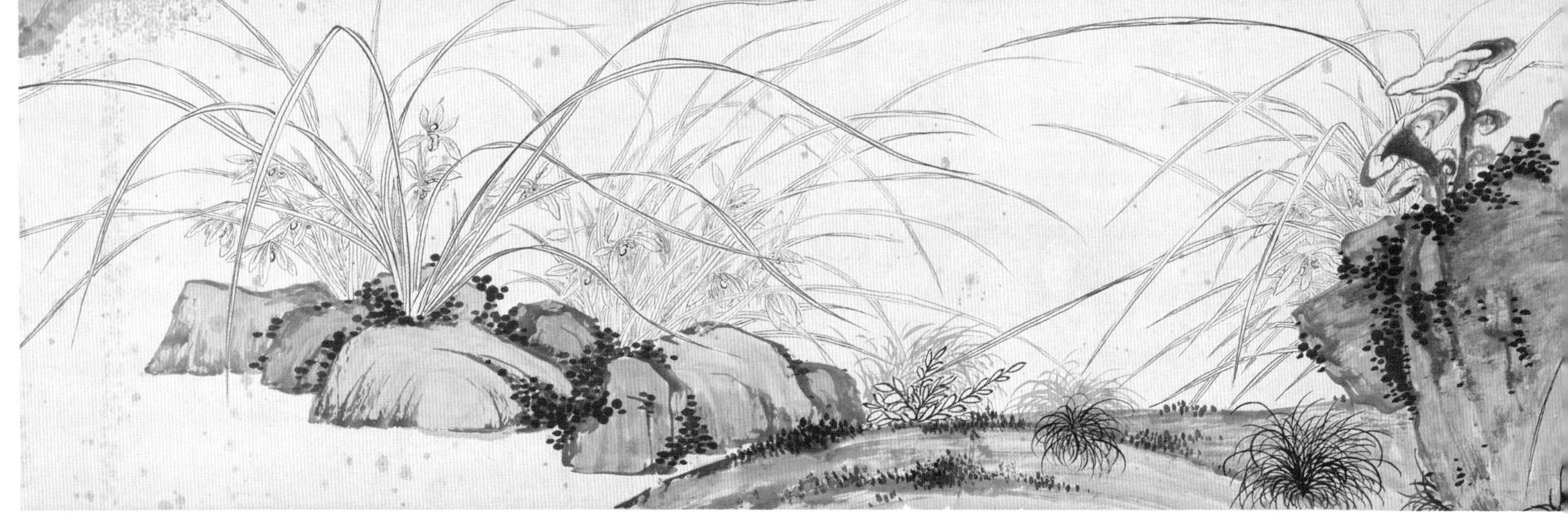

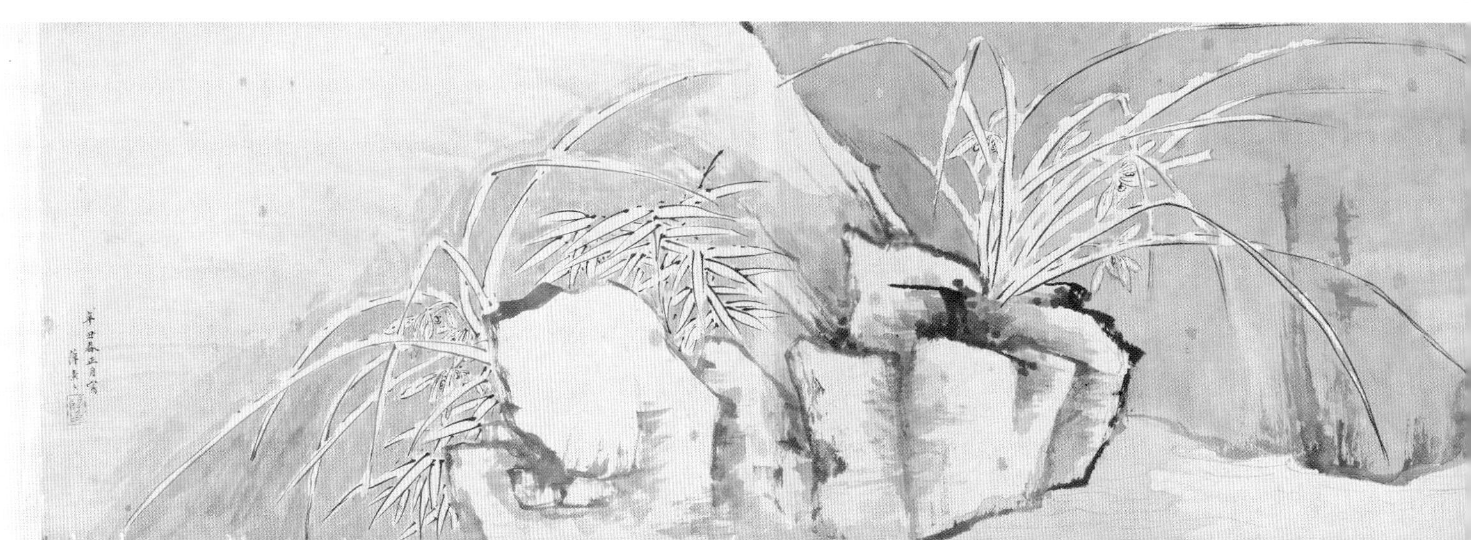

14 **Xue Wu** 薛五
C. 1564–c. 1637

Wild Orchids 蘭石圖卷
1601
Honolulu Museum of Art
Purchase

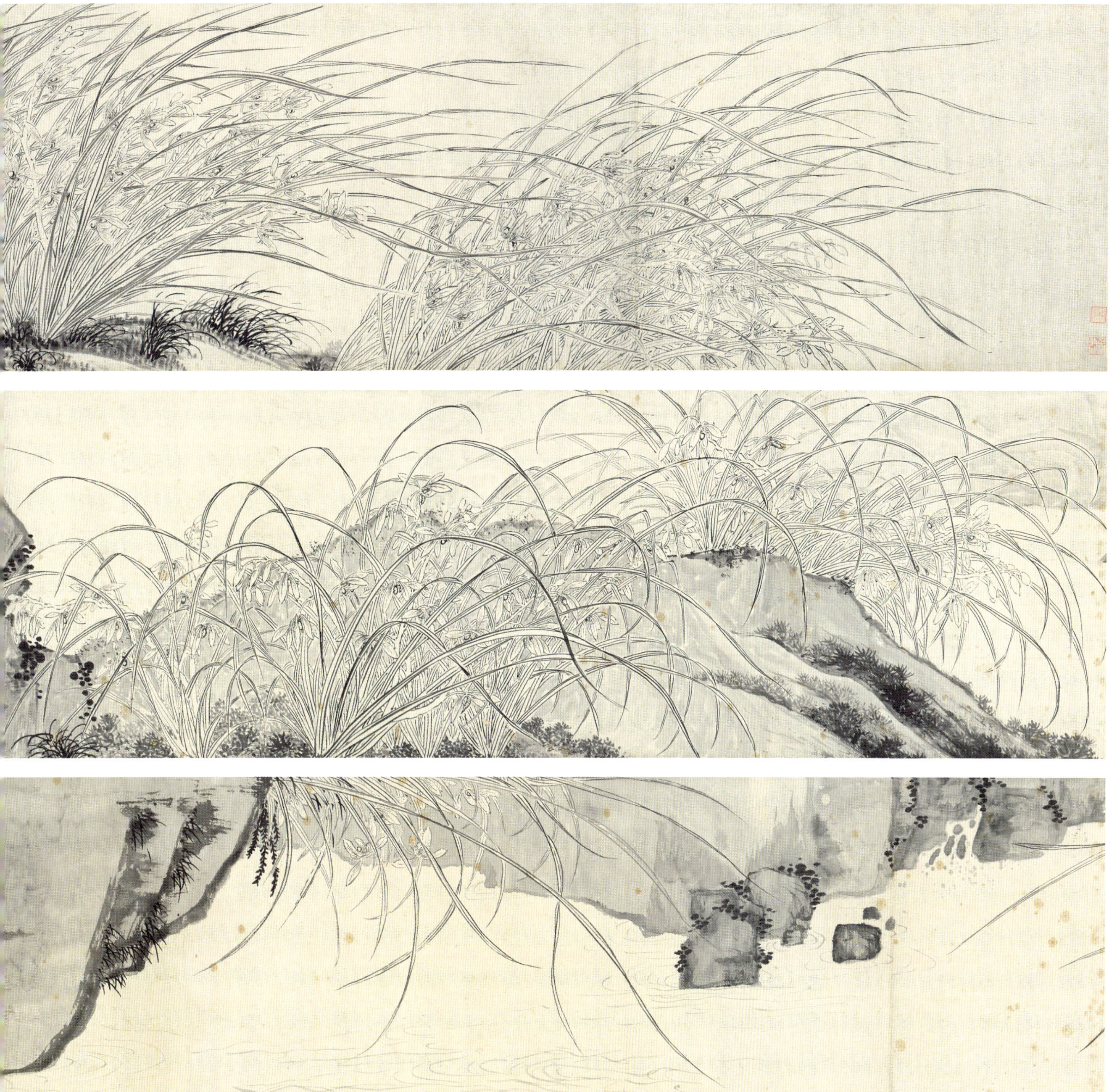

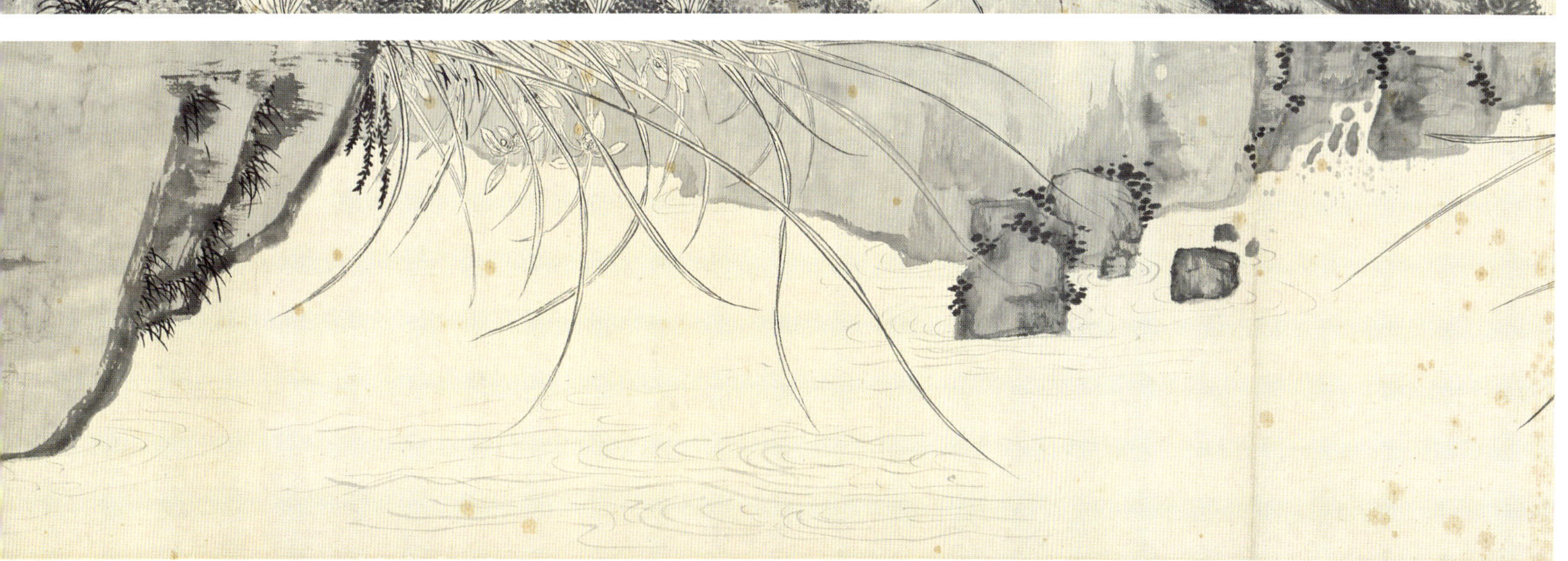

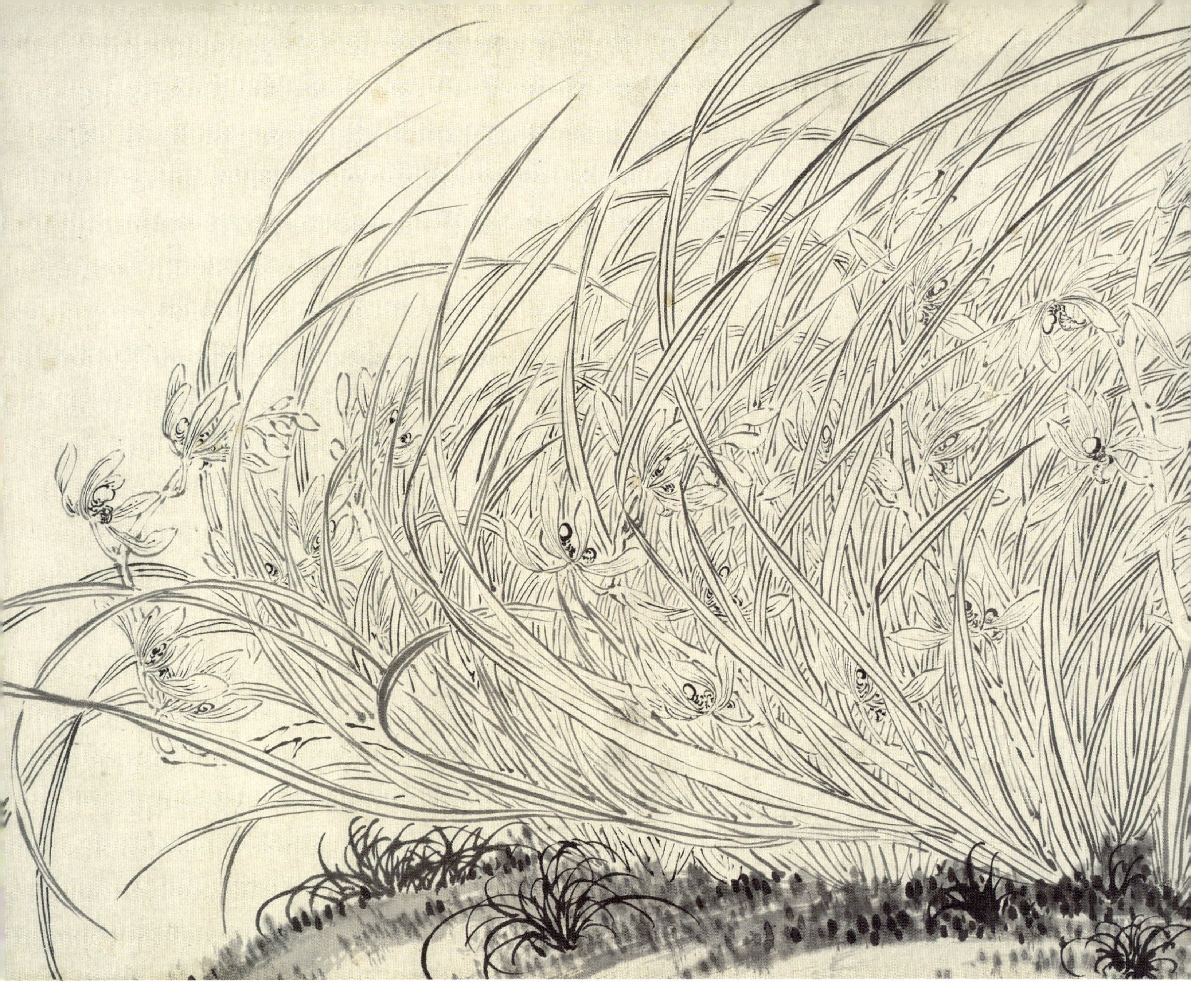

Xue Wu was the rare female artist of dynastic China who specialized in a broad spectrum of the arts. A talented young woman of Wu (Suzhou, Jiangsu Province), she was trained as a courtesan and became famous in literati circles by the name Xue Susu during the Wanli reign (1572–1620). Late-Ming courtesans were known for using their artistic and literary training to entertain their literati clientele and sometimes even participated in their circles. Xue's adopted name, Susu 素素 (plain and pure), may well reflect this cultural phenomenon, as it suggests the aesthetic realm of high literary culture. Nonetheless, her remarkably well-rounded achievements in poetry, painting, calligraphy, small ball games (*danshu* 彈術), and equestrian arts make her an exceptional figure.[1] Xue's mastery of small standard-script calligraphy and bird-and-flower subjects in painting was typical of most of the talented courtesans who gained the attention of connoisseurs. Atypically, however, she was also capable of painting landscapes and figures. Her natural skill with the brush was lauded. It is said that whether painting landscape, orchid, or bamboo, her brush would descend with fast, sweeping movements, none of which failed to enter the divine 山水，蘭竹下筆迅掃，無不意態入神.[2] Despite such formidable talent, Xue Susu's life did not end happily. Her transient relationships with men led to several short marriages, including one with Shen Defu, a famous scholar, collector, and author. After becoming one of Shen's concubines, she painted a famous self-portrait titled *Lady Playing the Flute*. The relationship concluded for reasons unknown today, and the talented courtesan artist ended up as an elder concubine to a rich Suzhou merchant, painting images of the Buddhist deity bodhisattva as a devotional object for couples who wished to pray for offspring.[3]

In order to bring variety and rhythm to this long handscroll, Xue Susu painted a meandering brook and rocks with numerous orchids growing along the banks. Through the extended, curving lines of the orchid leaves, she portrayed a breeze blowing from the left of the scroll. The fine and stable lines demonstrate the artist's achievement in the small standard script, as both require good control of the brush's tip. Such dense lines remind one of the Yuan literati artist Zhao Mengjian's narcissus paintings. Overall, *Wild Orchids* is a well-organized handscroll. The artist played between contrasting visual effects to complicate the simple subjects of orchid and rock. For instance, she painted the orchids with neat outline drawing, or *baimiao* 白描, and inkwash to depict the texture of the rocks. She also used different degrees of ink tones to suggest space. Consequently, there are two pairs of contrast in the handscroll: dense-spacious and dark-light.

The handscroll provides a rare glimpse of the Ming courtesan's art. To paint such long, extending lines, the artist had to wave her arm widely instead of restricting the movement to her wrist. One can imagine the visual pleasure the performative nature of this painting would have provided the audience, captivated by the sight of a beautiful courtesan displaying her skill. The subject is of interest, too. Orchid is arguably the most common subject among works by courtesan painters because this symbol of the gentleman can represent high self-regard, a characteristic that the cultured courtesan often addressed. Orchids do not require a long time to paint and thus are well suited for entertaining literati clientele.[4] Moreover, the handscroll was a popular format for courtesan painters, as the artist and guests could always add more paper and continue the performance by adding inscriptions for the occasion.[5] For these reasons, this work by Xue Susu demonstrates the particular performativity and materiality of this unique genre. **YCP**

For inscriptions and other documentation, see page 284 in this catalogue.

1 Jiang Shaoshu 姜紹書, *Wusheng shi shi* 無聲詩史, in *Lidai yishu shiliao congkan shuhua bian* 歷代藝術史料叢刊 書畫編 (Shanghai: Huadong shufan daxue chubanshe, 2009), 6:5b. Xue Susu's poems are now lost. For the reconstruction of some of her writings, see Daria Berg, "Cultural Discourse on Xue Susu," 171–200.

2 Hu Yinglin 胡應林, *Jiayi shengyan* 甲乙剩言, in *Ming Qing biji shiliao congkan* 明清筆記史料叢刊 (Beijing: Zhongguo shudian, 2000), no. 32, 138.

3 Qian Qianyi 錢謙益, *Liechao shiji xiaozhuan* 列朝詩集小傳 (Shanghai: Gudian wenxue chubanshe, 1957), 775; and Bian Yongyu 卞永譽, ed., *Shigutang shuhua huikao* 式古堂書畫匯考 (Taipei: Zhongzhong shuju, 1958), vol. 4, 542.

4 Tao Yongbai 陶詠白 and Li Shi 李湜, *Shiluo de lishi*, 50.

5 Ibid., 63.

These eight small landscape paintings by the poet, calligrapher, and painter Shao Mi recall earlier masters.[1] Their names, written into the pictorial space, are part of image and narrative. The accompanying poems by Yuan poets inscribed by Shao in his distinct, crisply written cursive script complement the scenes. Distinctly varying in mood, the paintings range from sparse, almost abandoned settings in dry brushwork to leisurely, rich, even-colored atmospheres. For the most part they depict men in solitary contemplation, conversation, or enjoyment of nature; where no figures are present, there are at least signs of human life, such as an empty pavilion or dwellings under a steep cliff. Throughout Shao explores the classical idiom of the recluse.

A native of Changzhou, near Suzhou, Shao Mi was praised for the "delicate and emaciated" style reflecting his personality. Burdened with feeble health since childhood and unable to take the civil service examination, he was "a pure spirit and a very thin but warped man who did not like to meet vulgar people" and was allegedly obsessed with cleanliness and order. In this he resembled his idols, the Song calligrapher Mi Fu and the Yuan painter Ni Zan.[2] As a poet he is said to have followed the recluse poet Tao Yuanming, as a calligrapher Mi Fu's cursive and Yu Shinan's standard scripts. His painting studies are said to have begun with Jing Hao and Guan Tong, before he moved on to the styles of the acclaimed masters Tang Yin and Wen Zhengming of his native Suzhou area. Tang's and Wen's refined styles of elegantly colored and densely layered compositions were soon eclipsed by the newly developing Songjiang School around the paragon connoisseur and artist Dong Qichang, who is said to have paid Shao the ultimate compliment by comparing him with the Four Masters of the Yuan, who were idolized by the Songjiang painters. Shao was grouped together with Dong (cat. nos. 8–9) as one of the Nine Friends of Painting.[3] The present album is very much in line with Dong's theories. It is painted mostly in monochromatic ink on paper with abbreviated calligraphic brushwork and flat compositions and pays homage to the old masters.

The leaves are dedicated to painters of times of upheaval or significant changes. Artists of the Song and Ming dynasties are not invoked. Shao Mi's earliest references are to the beginning of landscape painting and its establishment as a subject of its own, with the names of two masters of the late Tang and early Five Dynasties: Jing Hao from the north (two compositions) and Sun Wei from the south. Four leaves invoke the Four Masters of the late Yuan dynasty: Ni Zan, Wu Zhen, Huang Gongwang, and Wang Meng. A fifth refers to another late Yuan painter, Ma Wan. Jing Hao's large vertical paintings of rock formations with tiny dwellings nestled in steep valleys may have inspired Shao (leaf 1). Jing was a theorist and "patriarch of the northern landscape tradition." In his treatise on landscape painting, *Bifa ji* (A note on the art of the brush), Jing describes a mysterious meeting deep in the landscape with a sage who reveals the secrets of painting.[4] In leaf 7, Shao's two figures conversing while crossing a bridge seemingly enter a mystical world of hanging rocks and clouds. Sun Wei was a mural painter, celebrated for instance for his "dragons in water." Leaf 2's strong blue, red, and green hues might refer to those typical colors of Tang landscape scroll and wall painting. Today Sun is known for part of what is believed to be a depiction of the Seven Worthies of the Bamboo Grove, a group of scholars who retreated during the turmoil at the fall of the Wei (220–265) and the beginning of the Western Jin (265–316) dynasty and were prototypes for recluses thereafter.[5]

The four leaves dedicated to the Yuan-dynasty masters are characterized by elements associated with their personal styles. Many artists retreated to the countryside of Jiangnan in southeast China during the rule of the Mongols, cultivating a life of intellectual seclusion, expressed in style or idiom. The empty pavilion in leaf 3 is found in some of Ni Zan's landscapes, as are the almost leafless trees and the bamboo behind the hut. The two figures sitting in the partly hidden boat in leaf 4 may recall Wu Zhen's many paintings of fishermen. In leaf 5, a solitary figure, perhaps a Daoist (as we may guess from his hair knot), sits on a small hillock. The landscape morphology is typical for Huang Gongwang, and the characters on the painting, *Yi feng dao ren* (Daoist of the Single Peak), stand for his

For inscriptions and other documentation, see pages 284–85 in this catalogue.

1 For an entry on this album without translations of the poems, see Richard Barnhart, et al., *The Jade Studio*, 133–37. Shao Mi's signatures resemble those on a landscape album dated 1642. See *Zhongguo shuhuajia yinjian kuanshi* 中國書畫家印鑒款識 (Shanghai: Wenwu chubanshe, 1987), vol. 1, 633–34.

2 Information on Shao Mi drawn from Zhang Geng 張庚, *Qingchao hua zheng lu* 清朝畫徵錄, in *Meishu congshu* 美術叢書 (Taipei, 1956–65), vol. 2, 560; Ellen Johnston Laing's biography of Shao in L. Carrington Goodrich and Chaoying Fang, eds., *The Dictionary of Ming Biography*, 1166; Osvald Siren, *Chinese Painting, Leading Masters and Principles*, vol. 4, 32; James Cahill, *The Distant Mountains*, 59–60; and Ellen Johnston Laing, "'Riverside' by Liu Yüan-ch'i and 'The Waterfall on Mt. K'uang-Lu' by Shao Mi," 1–16. A recent analysis of Shao Mi's biography offers a birth date of 1598. See Lu Lin 陸林, "Wan Ming shuhuajia Shao Mi shengnian xinshuo," 67–71.

3 On Shao's calligraphy studies, see *Liu yi zhi yilu* 六藝之一錄 (*Siku quanshu* ed.), 373:13b–14a; on his painting studies, see Zhang, *Qingchao hua zheng lu*, 560. Dong Qichang's comment is cited by Cahill, *The Distant Mountains*, 60n25.

4 Kiyohiko Munakata, *Ching Hao's Pi-Fa-Chi*. No extant originals by Jing Hao are known. For a discussion of a painting attributed to Jing, see Jonathan Hay, "'Travelers in Snow-Covered Mountains,'" 85–91.

5 On Sun Wei, see Li Jian 李廌, "Deyutang hua pin" 德隅堂畫品, in *Zhongguo shuhua quan shu* 中國書畫全書 (Shanghai: Shanghai shuhua chubanshe, 1993), vol. 1, 990–94. The painting of the Seven Worthies of the Bamboo Grove belongs to the Shanghai Museum.

15 Shao Mi 邵彌
C. 1595–1642

Paintings in the Styles of Earlier Masters with Accompanying Poems of the Yuan Dynasty 倣宋元八家山水詩冊
Private collection

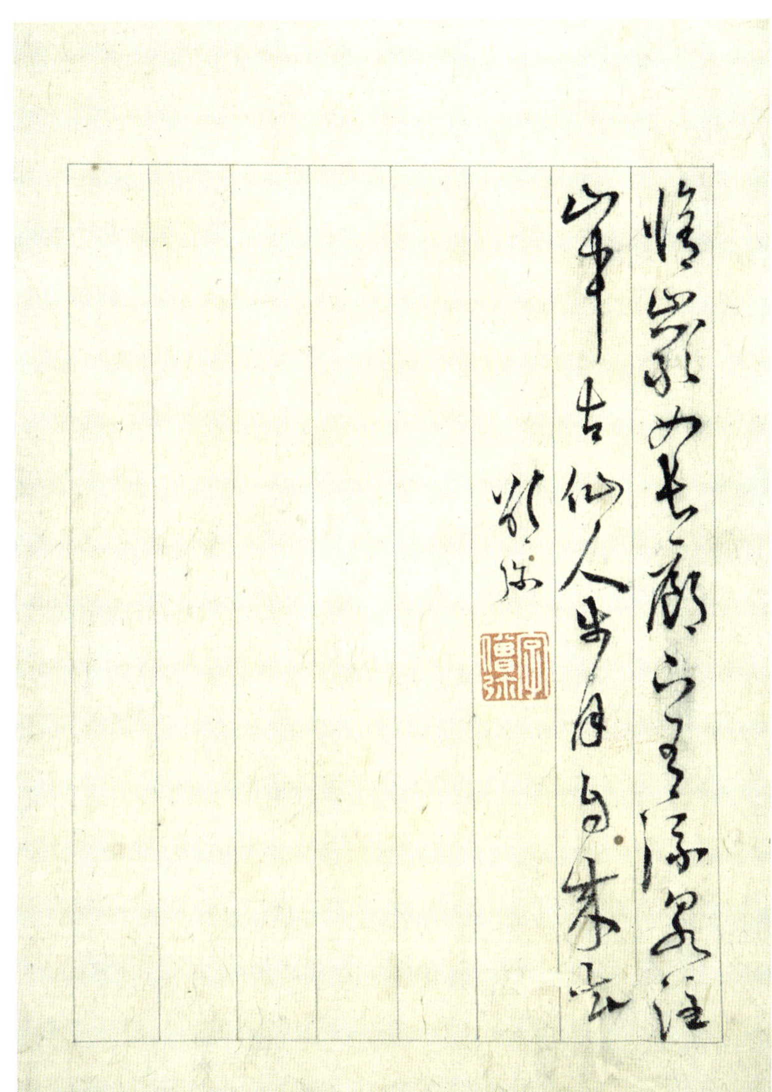
7a

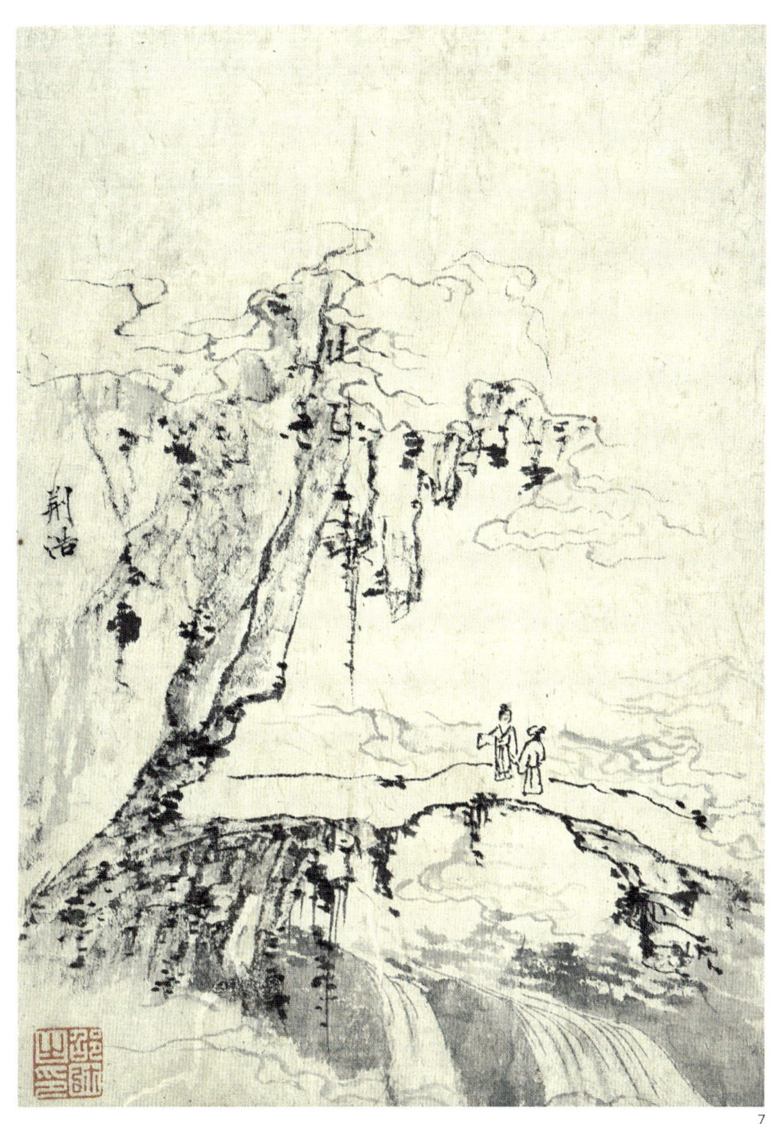
7

A long cliff like a covered corridor,
Below a flowing spring pouring down.
Amidst the mountains ancient immortals,
Who pace the moon and wander to and fro.

Daoist name. In leaf 8, the large trees on a rising slope in front of two thatched huts and the wavering texture strokes may remind us of Wang Meng's densely foliated and wooded scenes. The four characters on the upper right read *Huangheshan qiao* (Woodcutter of the Yellow Crane Mountain). Shao seems to follow Wang's habit of inscribing his paintings with their titles and his sobriquet in seal script. Finally, leaf 6 is dedicated to Ma Wan. The latest of all represented painters and a close follower of Huang Gongwang, Ma might be seen here as bridging the Yuan masters and the Songjiang painters.

Although stylistic inspirations for Shao Mi's paintings reach back as far as the Tang and Song dynasties, the verses that complement his landscapes all appear to be drawn from the writings of famous poets of the Yuan-dynasty period, including Zhao Mengfu, Chen Lü, He Zhong, and Li Xiaoguang (the verse accompanying leaf 4 remains unidentified). Shao gives no explanation for his choices. They might have been casually drawn from a favorite volume of collected Yuan poetry. Or perhaps the decision to illustrate Yuan writers was more deliberate—an effort to harmonize the eremitic sentiments of the fourteenth century with a broader sweep of art historical models. In any case, written in ruled columns, which add a formal note to the album, Shao Mi's energetic cursive calligraphy resonates with the vital lines of his paintings. The paintings, in turn, share the poems' aura of transcendence. **BA**

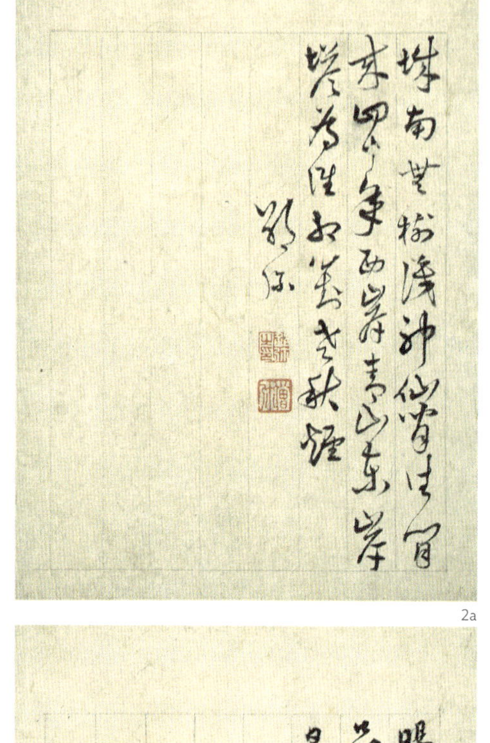

2a

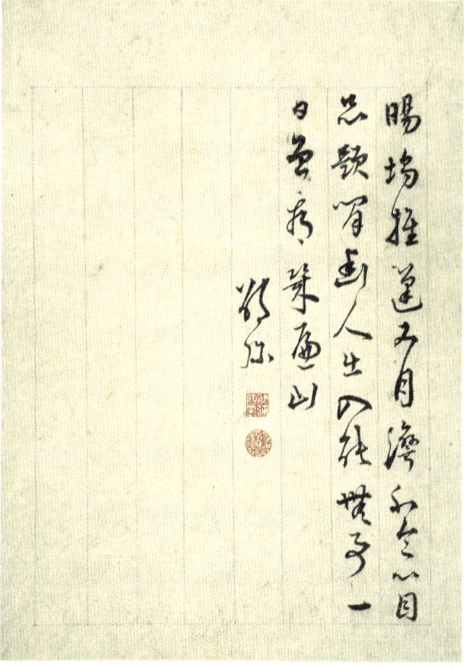

4a

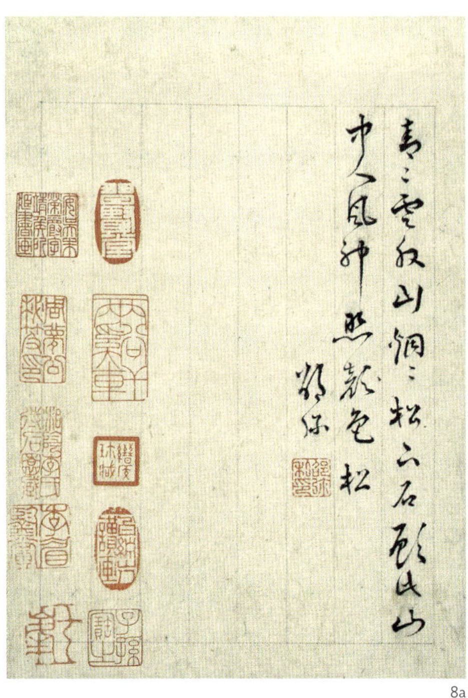

8a

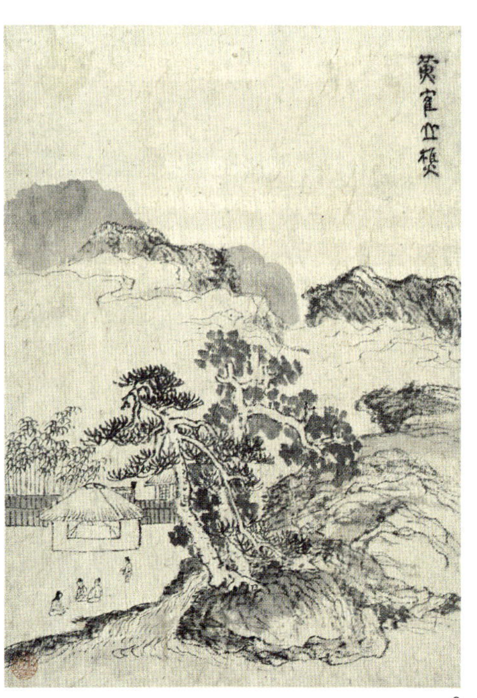

8

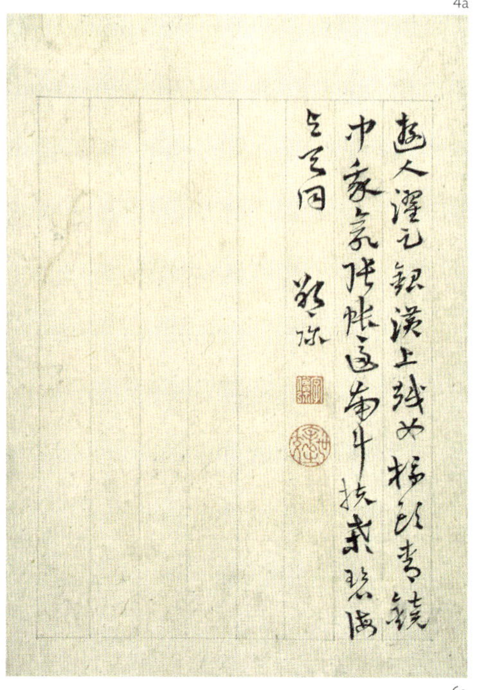

6a

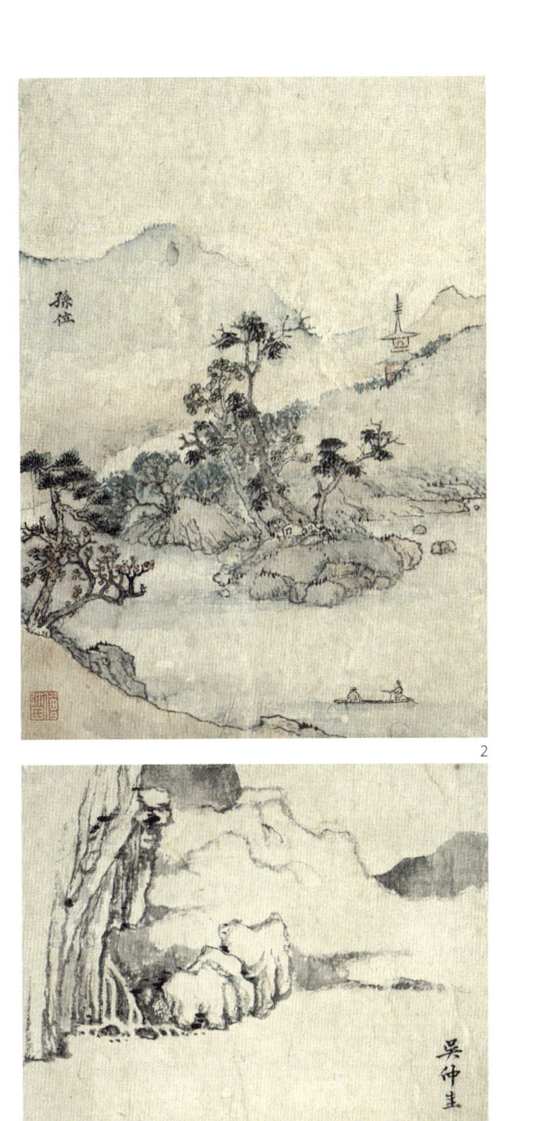

2

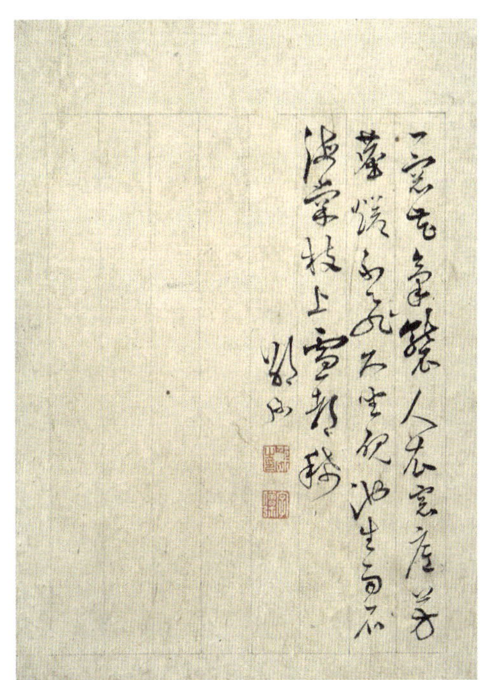

1a

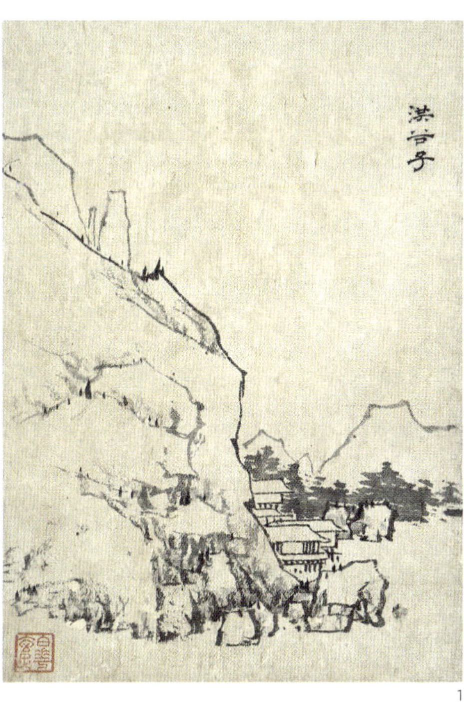

1

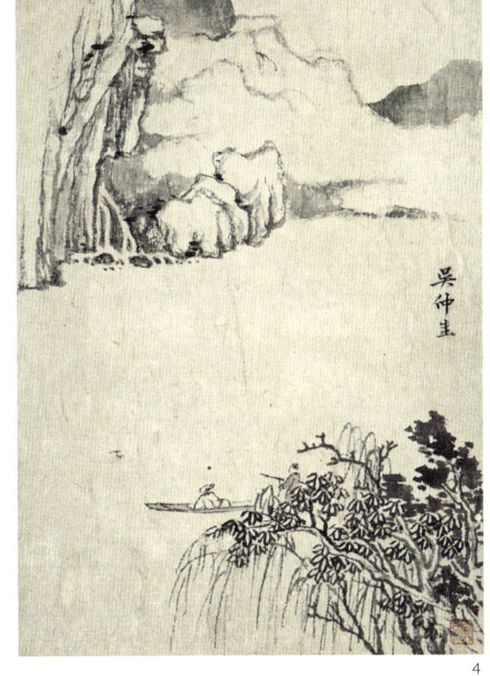

4

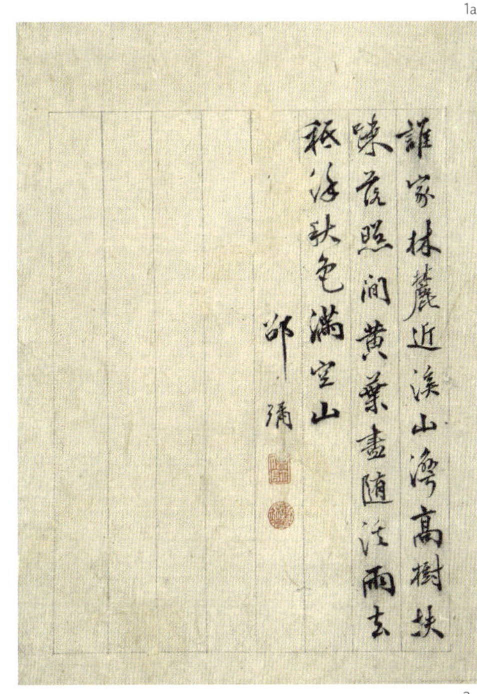

3a

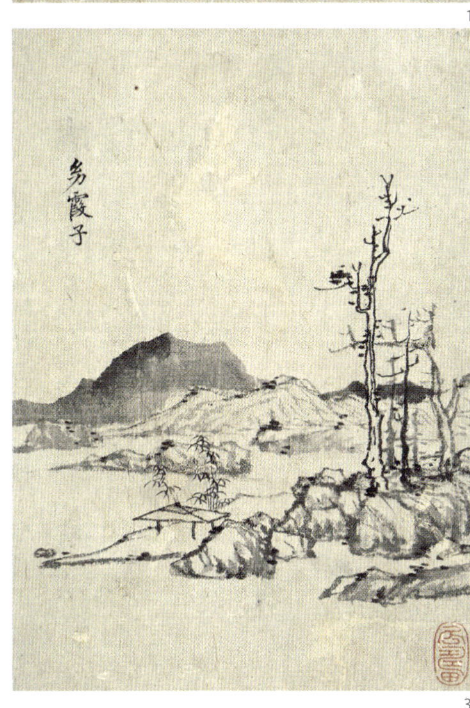

3

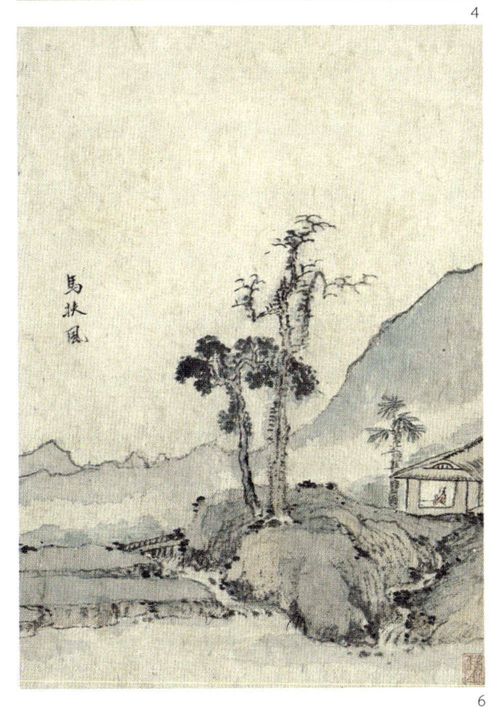

6

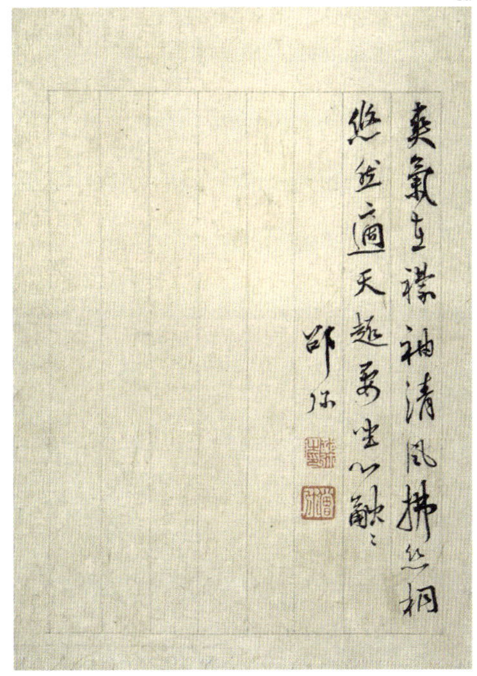

5a

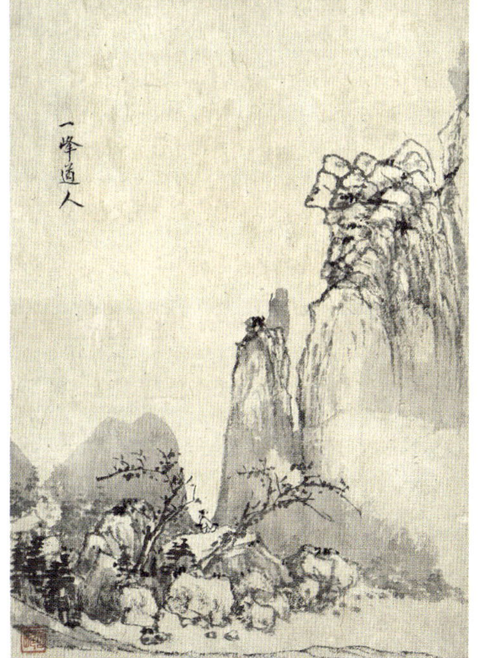

5

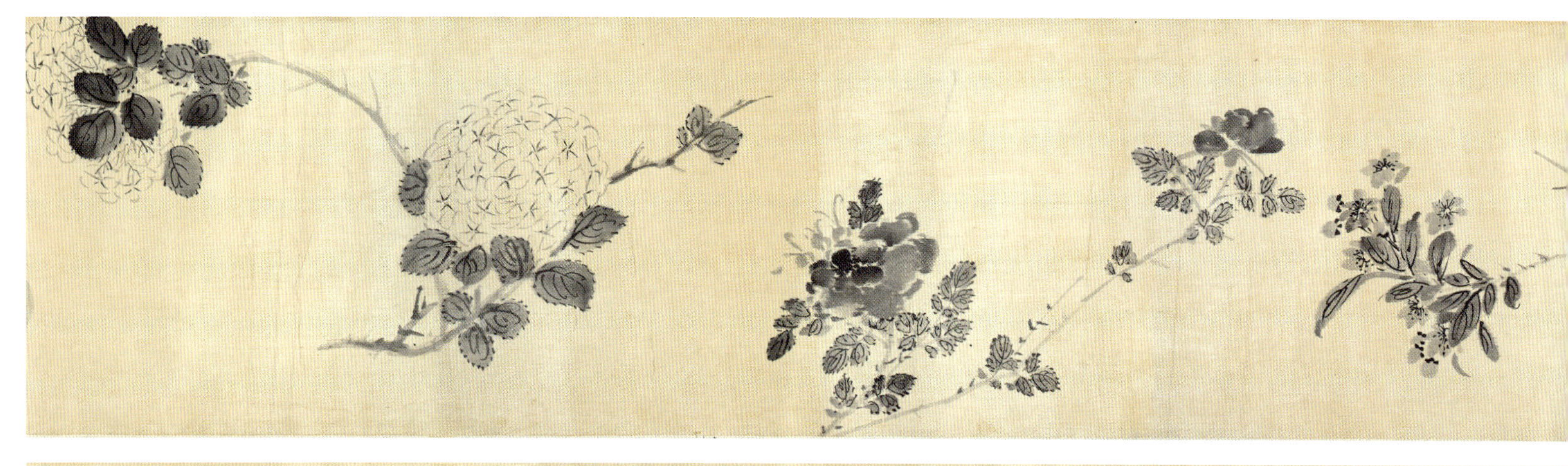

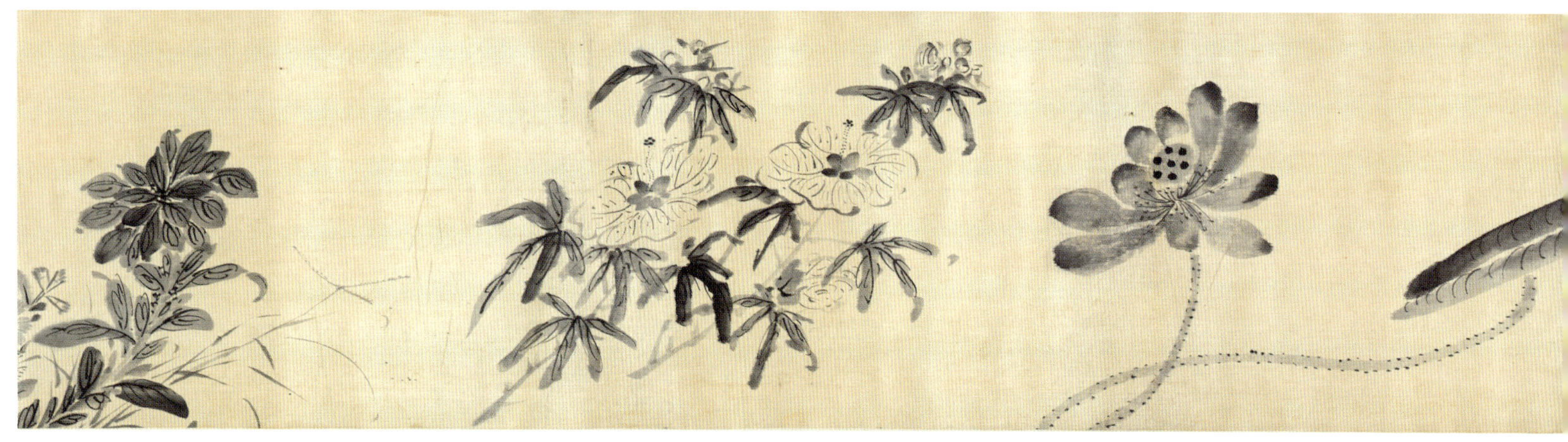

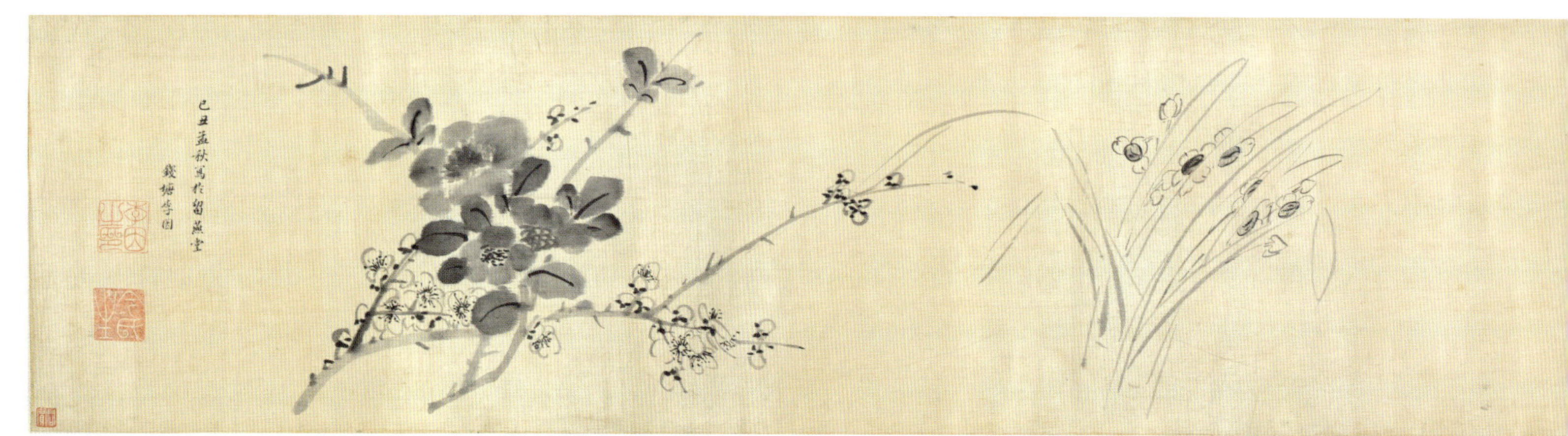
己丑孟秋寫於留燕堂
錢塘李因

16 **Li Yin** 李因
C. 1611–1685

Flowers of the Four Seasons 四季花卉圖卷
1649
Honolulu Museum of Art
Partial Gift of Mr. and Mrs. Mitchell Hutchinson

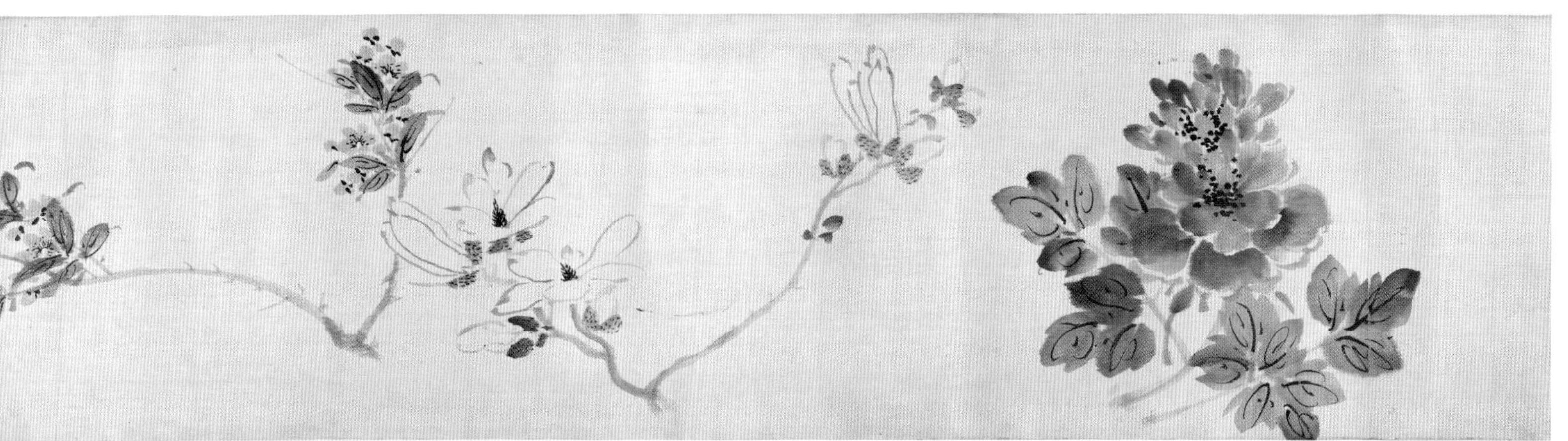

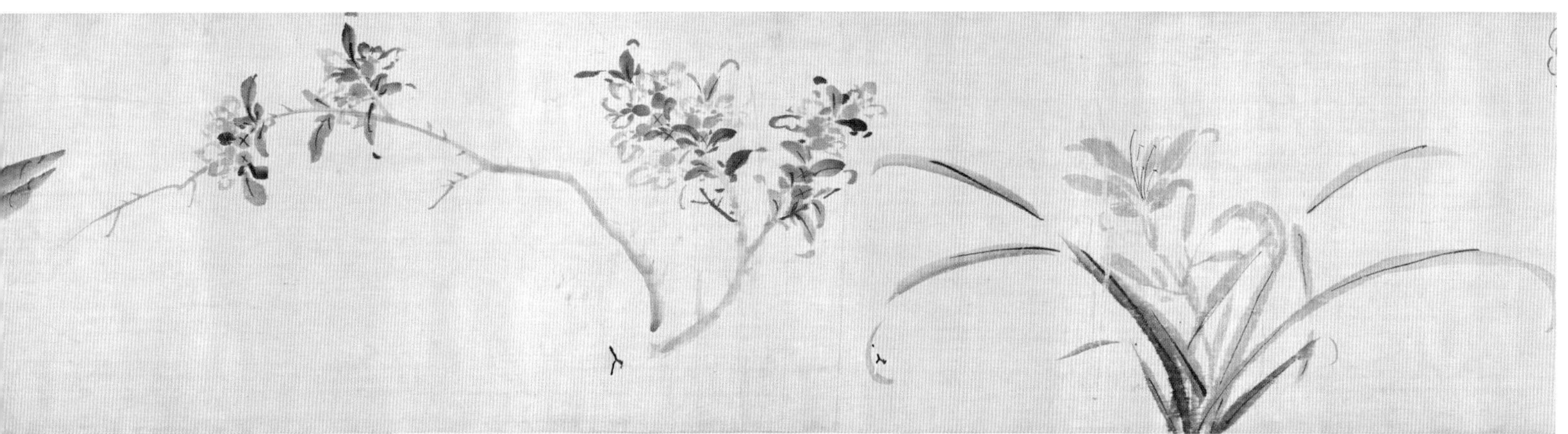

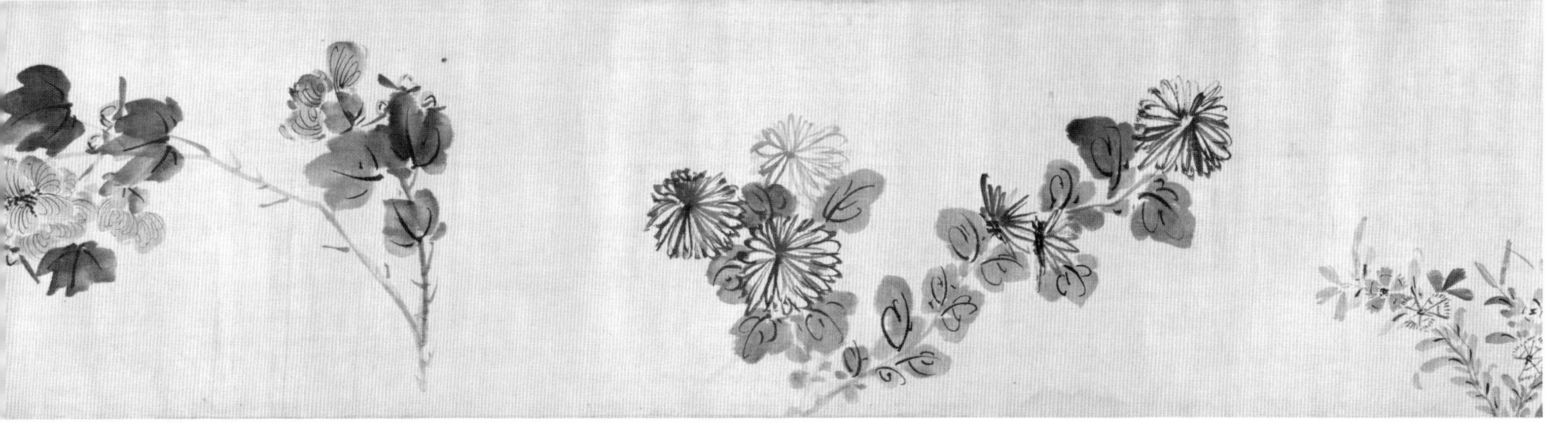

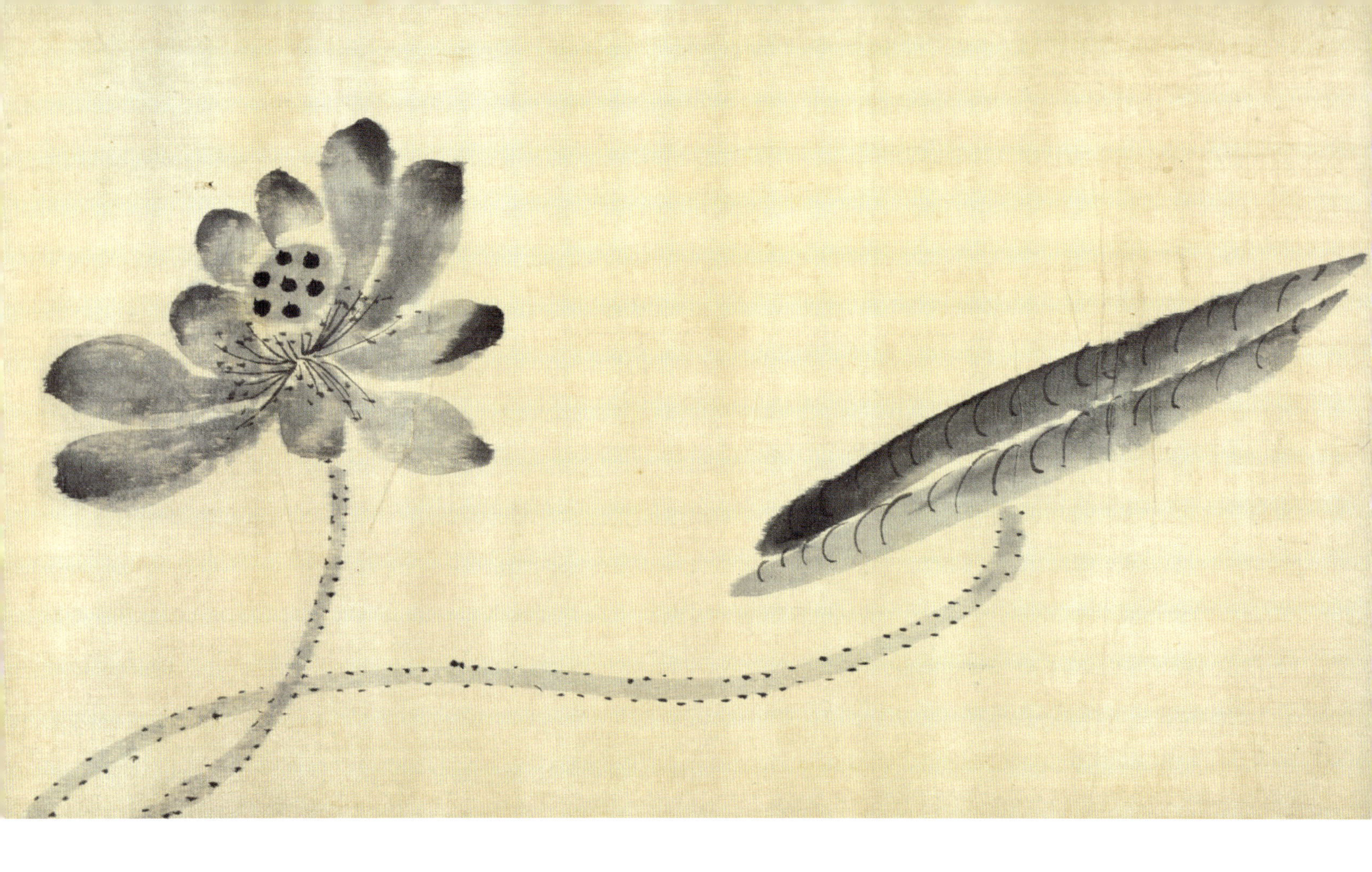

Li Yin is one of a handful of woman painters who earned the praise of male connoisseurs in Chinese art history. According to her biography, written by the famous seventeenth-century scholar and philosopher Huang Zongxi, she was born into a poor family of Hangzhou (Zhejiang Province), a situation that did not prevent her from learning poetry and painting. A single line of poetry that she composed in her youth—"One branch, I wish, could delay its opening till late in spring" 一支留待晚春開—garnered the admiration of the scholar-painter Ge Zhengqi, who brought her in as his concubine. When Ge passed the metropolitan examination in 1628 and began to serve as a high official, she was introduced to his literati circle. After her husband's untimely death, Li lived in Haichang (Zhejiang Province) and painted to earn a living. Her works were so popular that some forty painters of her time were said to forge her work.[1]

Like other gentry-women painters, Li Yin followed the tastes of the Ming literati. Naturally, Ge Zhengqi was encouraging. He provided the following record of her choice of models in a preface he wrote for a book of her collected verse, *Zhuxiao xuan shichao* 竹笑軒詩鈔 (Poetry of the Studio of Laughing Bamboo):

> Shi'an [Li Yin] only copied the work of the Two Mis, and she captured their style with great subtlety. This is what is called being nurtured by mists and clouds... However, to go no further than painting bamboo groves in the wind and bamboo shoots in the rain is the same as tasting only meat from the ding vessel. Why not learn the legacy of Master Baiyang? She thereupon carved his image with aloe wood to honor him and excelled at his style.[2]
>
> 是庵獨摹大小米，具體而微，所謂以煙雲供養也...
> 然止風篁雨籜，嘗鼎一臠耳，盍為白陽先生遺跡乎.
> 遂刻沈香而事之，悉臻堂奧.

Ge Zhengqi specifies the Song-dynasty father-and-son literati painters Mi Fu and Mi Youren as Li Yin's initial models, but the two Mis were only known for cloudy mountain landscapes. Ge implies that Li was encouraged to expand her repertoire by looking at the work of Chen Chun (sobriquet Baiyang), who not only painted landscapes in the Mi style but also specialized in flowers. Both the Mi-style landscape and Chen's flower paintings, often done with expressive ink wash, were highly appreciated in the Jiangnan region as exemplars of the literati painting tradition.[3] Ge was so proud of his concubine's flower paintings that he gave an example of her work to Li Rihua (cat. no. 10), one of the most important connoisseurs of the time. Li Rihua responded with the compliment that the artist "throws away the embroidery pattern book, as she comprehends the spirit of flowers" 拋將綉譜領花神.[4]

Flowers of the Four Seasons, painted a few years after Ge Zhengqi's death in 1645, well displays Li Yin's mastery of Chen Chun's style of monochrome ink flowers. The long handscroll of fifteen flowers begins with peony and proceeds with magnolia, peach blossom, China rose, hydrangea, daylily, cape jasmine, lotus, abelmosk, dianthus *chinensis*, chrysanthemum, hibiscus, narcissus, and a bouquet of plum and camellia, roughly following their sequence of seasonal bloom. There is no sign of hesitancy in her brushwork, the branches and leaves forming a visual rhythm of expert strokes and varied ink tones that do full justice to Chen's legacy of capturing the spirit of his floral subjects. It was this quality in Li's flower paintings that earned her the praise "mysterious and light to a marvelous degree" 幽淡欲絕.[5] Her scroll—so closely allied with the literati tradition of ink flower painting and so capable in its demonstration of the artist's control of brush and ink—represents the art of the gentry woman at its highest level in seventeenth-century China. **YCP**

For inscriptions and other documentation, see page 285 in this catalogue.

1 Huang Zongxi 黄宗羲, "Li Yin zhuan" 李因傳, in *Nanlei wending qian ji* 南雷文定前集 (Hefei: Huangshan shushe, 2008), *juan* 10, 9–10. Translation of Li Yin's poetic line by Marsha Weidner, et al., *Views from Jade Terrace*, 102.

2 Cited from He Junhong 赫俊紅, *Danqing qipa*, 78.

3 Chen Chun's flower paintings were sometimes praised as surpassing the work of his mentor, Wen Zhengming. Wang Zhideng 王穉登, *Wujun danqing zhi* 吳郡丹青志, in *Congshu jicheng chubian* 叢書集成初編 (Shanghai: Shangwu yinshuguan, 1935), vol. 1655, 4–5. See also Chen Baozhen 陳葆真, *Chen Chun yanjiu* 陳淳研究 (Taipei: Guoli Gugong bowuyuan, 1978), 84–86.

4 Li Rihua 李日華, *Liuyanzhai sanbi* 六研齋三筆 (Hefei: Huangshan shushe, 2008), 2:15.

5 Chen Weisong 陳維崧, *Furen ji* 婦人集 (Shanghai: Shangwu yinshuguan, 1936), 36:24.

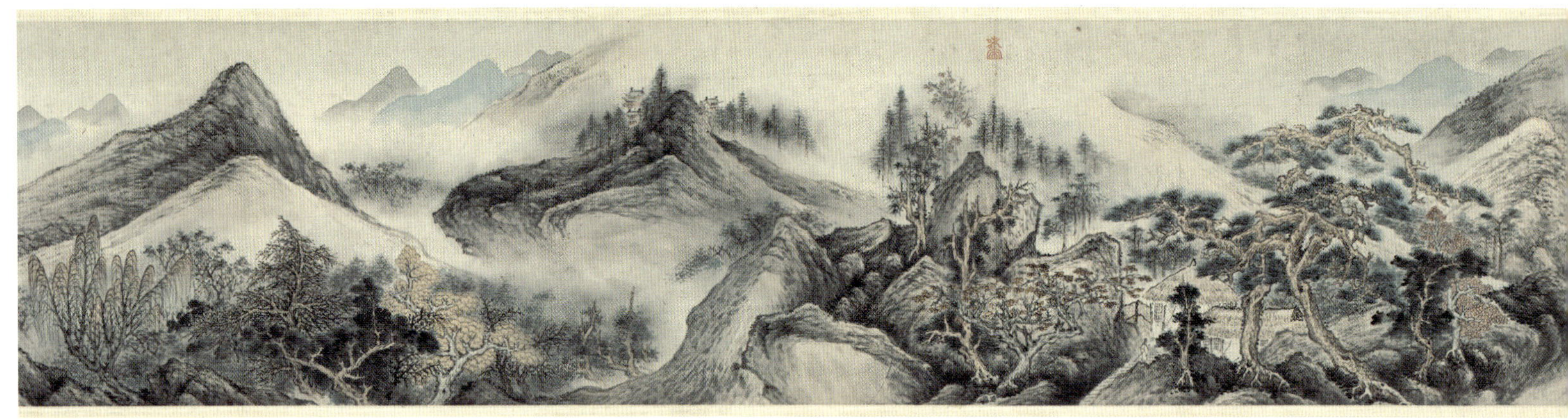

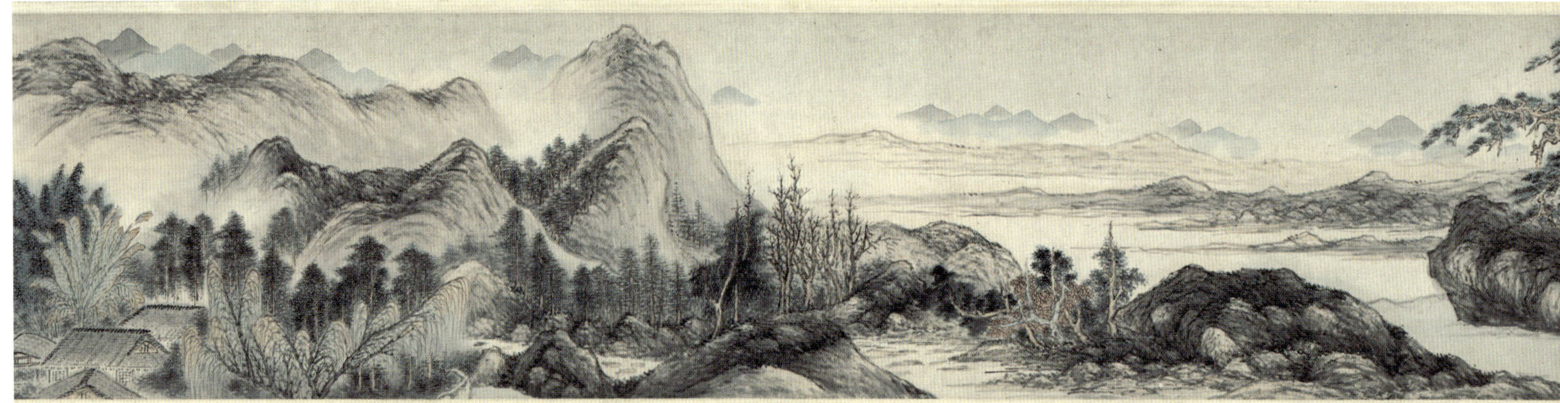

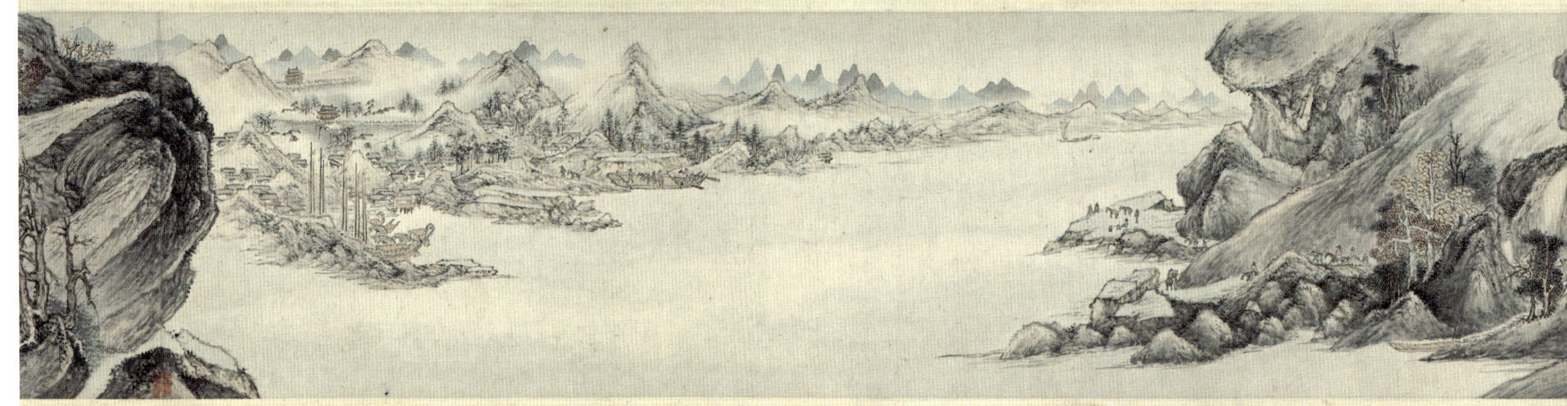

宋元人長卷以山水為第一然畫山
水非身歷道路胸有書卷者未能結
構今攷趙大年尚有上陵田々消々宋元
佳蹟寥々無幾即明之王孟端沈石田文
徵仲唐六如長卷亦不易得沈子居擅名
於明末雖無出人之處而筆墨海潤饒有
秀致此溪山小卷丘壑連綿山橋野店有
數百里境界閒窗觀之可以永日因加裝
潢出入自隨庶髴于居昔日經營苦心
也康熙壬午正月六日風日晴朗古梅盛
開立春在初八日然去冬久晴全無寒冽數
十年所少與大兒輿展閱書後別有一卷與
大兒藏之侍萊衣人高士奇

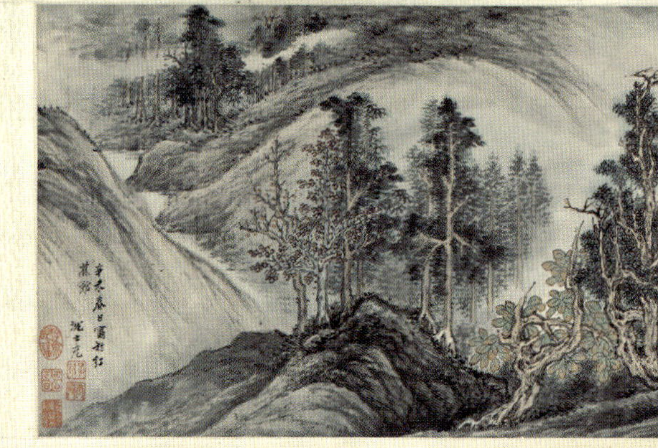

17 **Shen Shichong** 沈士充
Act. c. 1607–after 1640

Landscape **山水長卷**
1631
Private collection

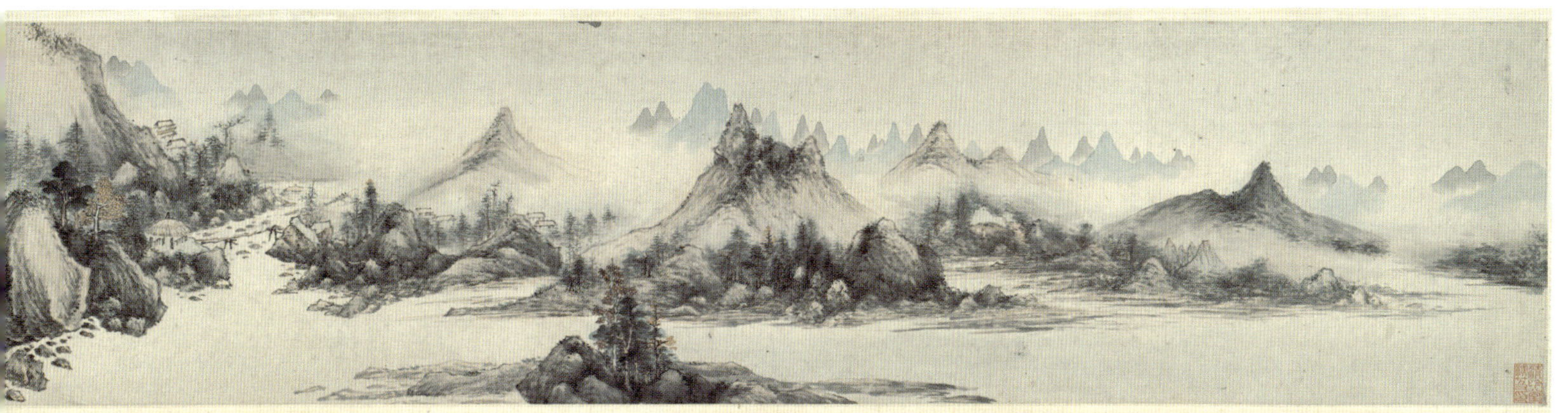

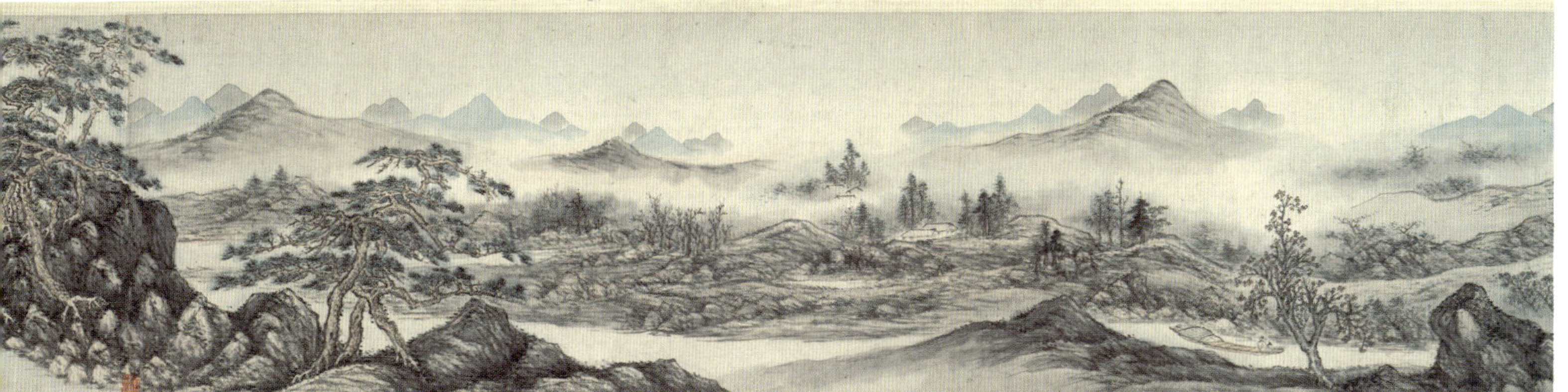

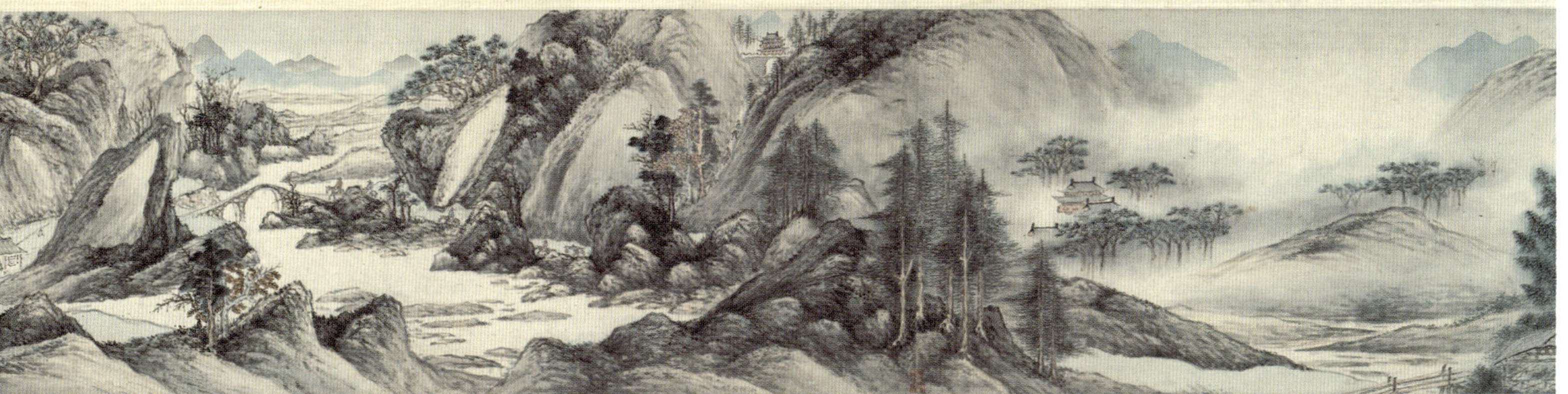

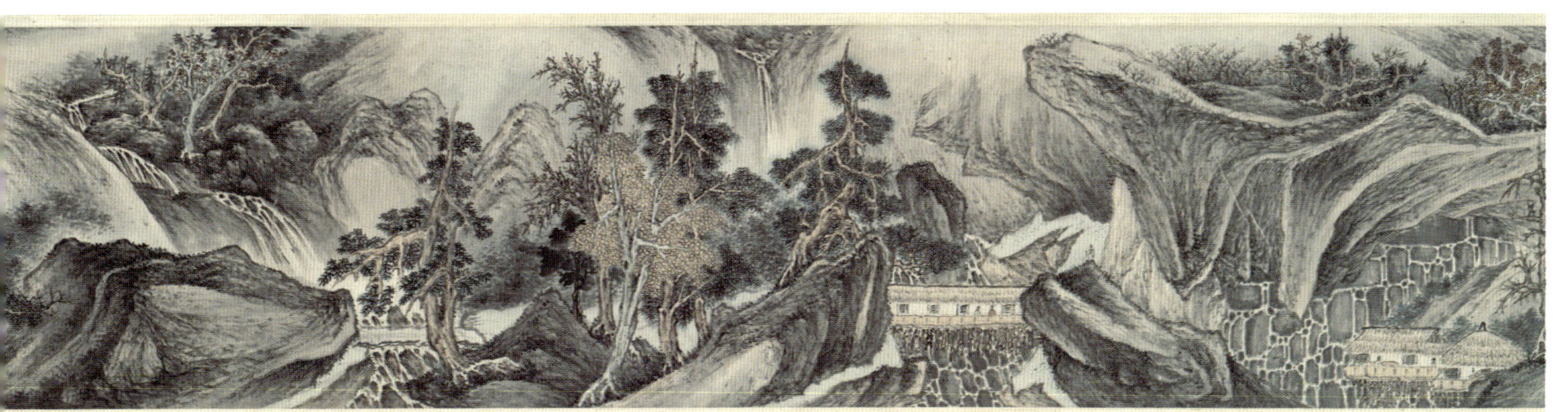

Shen Shichong was active in the Songjiang district (present-day Shanghai municipality) during the first half of the seventeenth century. His earliest known dated painting, *Dwelling in the Mountains* (1605), presents an incisive, linear manner of depicting mountains with great clarity.[1] In contrast, the present long handscroll is a superb example of Shen's mature style, in which misty scenes contrast with empty space, and softly modulated ink and blunt, dry, short brushstrokes are often used to structure the forms. Compared to his early work, Shen's later paintings show greater sophistication of compositional structure along with a more spontaneous use of brush and ink, as well as subtler color schemes.[2] In his colophon following the painting, the late-seventeenth-century collector and connoisseur Gao Shiqi ungenerously describes Shen's art as lacking any "truly original features," and yet he rightly points out the great difficulty of composing an extremely long handscroll of landscape. Gao stressed that a convincing compositional structure was not easy to achieve unless the painter had personally traveled and read widely. In this painting, Shen's extraordinary command of spatial organization and morphology seems to be his most salient accomplishment.

Shen Shichong appears to have structured the landscape in three segments: hermitage in a rustic village; journey to a city in conjunction with an urban view; and sightseeing in the suburbs. Although viewed section by section, the landscape is unified by consistently proceeding viewpoints. The pictorial space is gradually pulled from a distant scene of waters and serried mountains at the beginning of the scroll into an intermediary space accommodating the narrative of the journey to the city before ending in a close-up view of dramatic scenery. Interestingly, at the points marking the transitions between the three segments, Gao Shiqi placed one of his seals, *Jiangcun sanshi nian jingli suo ju* (Gathered as part of Jiangcun's efforts over thirty years), as if to draw attention to the compositional shifts.[3]

Shen Shichong is considered a first-generation member of the so-called Yunjian School, referring to painters active in the Songjiang region. He studied painting with Song Maojin and Zhao Zuo (cat. no. 13); Song's paintings are rare, and what exists suggests that his style is restrained and limited in scope. Shen's independence is suggested by an inscription Song added to a scroll of 1610 by Shen: "Although Ziju [Shen] learned painting under my guidance, he is capable of directly learning from masters of the past on his own" 子居雖出余門，而自能直造古人.[4] That scroll comprises fourteen vignettes of landscape combined with inscriptions written by contemporaries. In each painting Shen claims to interpret one master of the Song or Yuan dynasties. Another long handscroll, also of 1610 titled *Peach Blossom Spring*, features a blue-green landscape. According to Dong Qichang's colophon, Shen there emulated a painting of the same subject by Zhao Boju that was circulating in southern Jiangsu at the time.[5] Bringing canonical values from the past into newly adopted styles as part of a larger claim to artistic authenticity was characteristic of seventeenth-century Songjiang painters and critics. In this regard, Shen, like his older townsman Zhao Zuo, was very much in line with the theories of Dong, for whom both Shen and Zhao occasionally acted as ghost painters.[6]

In an inscription to a painting by Shen Shichong dated 1628, Fan Yunlin criticized the painters of his native Suzhou, who viewed the Songjiang painters as their rivals, by pointing out that the Songjiang painters tended to learn from masters of the past, unlike recent Suzhou painters who only knew how to learn from a single master, Wen Zhengming.[7] It is evident from the present scroll, however, that by 1631 Shen was not averse to utilizing Suzhou styles. His manner of painting trees in the third section resembles that of the same Wen Zhengming, who cast such a great shadow over later Suzhou painters. Moreover, in this painting Shen took over one of the standard sixteenth-century themes of Suzhou artists: the long handscroll depicting an experience of the environs of a city. In other words, however strong the polemics of Dong Qichang's approach to painting may have been in Songjiang circles, clearly Shen was a masterful painter in his own right and on his own terms. *Landscape* demonstrates his powerful representational skills and an open approach that privileges sight, sound, and mood over theory. **LL**

For inscriptions and other documentation, see page 285 in this catalogue.

1 Wang Shiqing, "Dong Qichang de jiaoyou" 董其昌的交友, in Wai-kam Ho, ed., *The Century of Tung Ch'i-ch'ang 1555–1636*, vol. 2, 465. The painting, in the collection of the Shanghai Museum, is reproduced in *Zhongguo gudai shuhua tumu* (1990), vol. 3, 329.

2 The painting is stylistically close to another handscroll, *Thatched Hall in a Pine Grove* (Shanghai Museum), dated 1626. Reproduced in Ho, *The Century of Tung Ch'i-ch'ang*, vol. 1, pl. 86.

3 Although the seal in both cases marks the joins between two of the pieces of paper used for the painting, Gao did not mark all of the joins in the handscroll.

4 In the collection of the Palace Museum, Beijing. Reproduced in *Zhongguo gudai shuhua tumu* (1986), vol. 1, 13–15.

5 In the collection of the Palace Museum, Beijing. Reproduced in Ho, *The Century of Tung Ch'i-ch'ang*, vol. 1, pl. 85. See also Xu Lisha 徐麗莎, "Wan Ming zhiye huajia Shen Shichong de yishu licheng," 37–70; and Wang Cheng-hua's catalogue entry on this painting in Richard M. Barnhart, et al., *The Jade Studio*, 125.

6 See Wang, "Dong Qichang de jiaoyou."

7 Lu Shihua 陸時化, *Wu Yue suo jian shuhua lu* 吳越所見書畫錄 (Shunde: Deng shi, 1910), 5:62. For a translation of this passage, see Susan Bush, *The Chinese Literati on Painting*, 174–75.

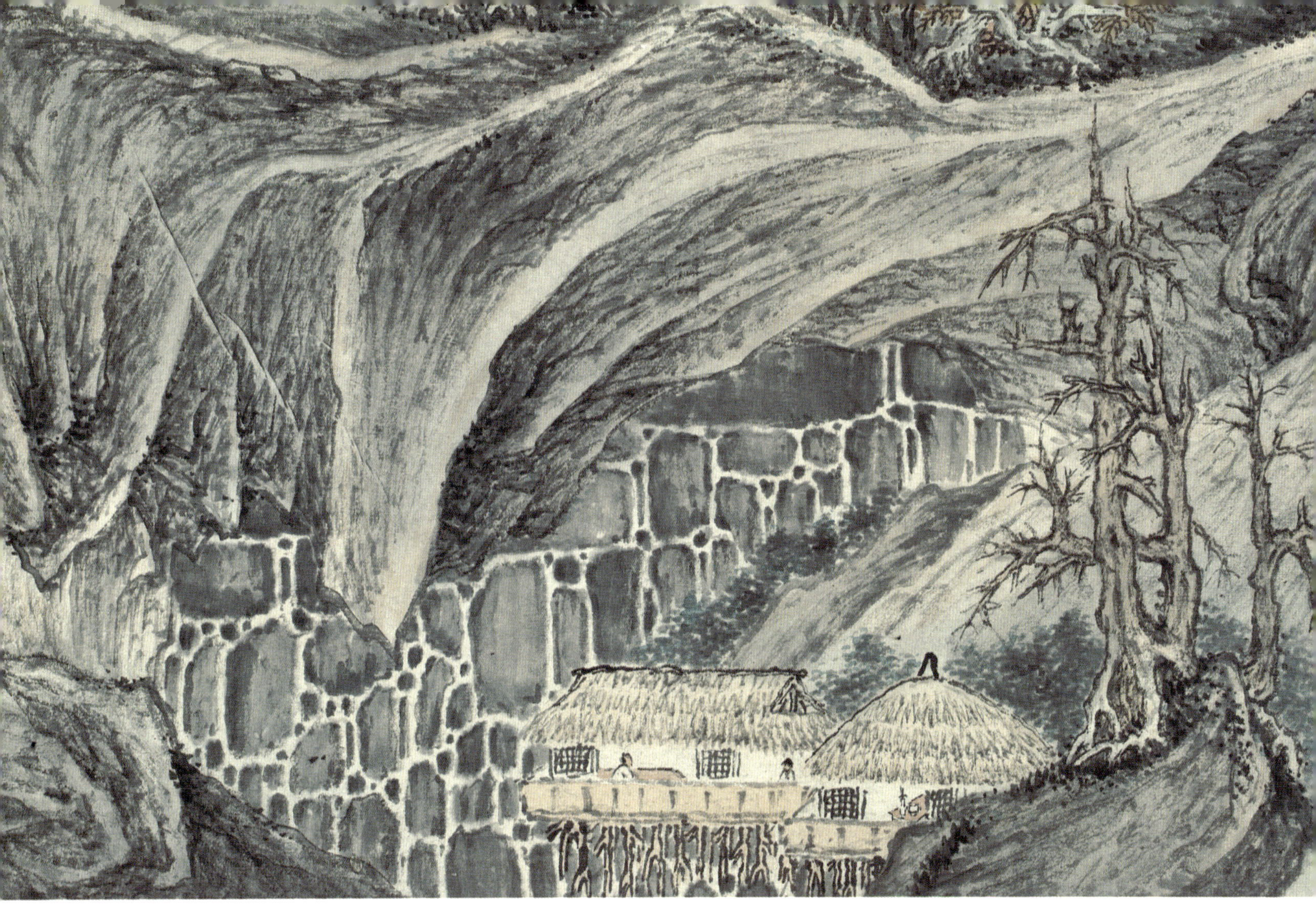

Yang Wencong's colorful handscroll of mist-covered rolling hills by a waterway begins with two figures on a small path. Entering the landscape from the right along a foothill in the foreground, their path will take them past a fisherman in a boat and across a small arched bridge to houses nestled against a large hill surrounded by several trees. Past the hill the landscape is devoid of any human presence. Immediately following the painting is an inscription by Chen Yuanlong, who speaks knowingly of the recipient of Yang's painting—someone with the sobriquet Yunqing, which literally means Lord Cloud. The identity of Yunqing is not known, though it is evident that Yang created this image of landscape specifically for him.[1] Not only does the landscape's cloudy atmosphere suit Yunqing's name but, according to Chen's inscription, the specific style of the painting—*mogu* 沒骨, or "boneless"—was something that Yunqing himself practiced in landscape painting. The boneless style was a very particular mode that privileged color and washes over calligraphic line and was associated with an especially early period of Chinese painting history. As the twentieth-century connoisseur Wu Hufan added in his later inscription to the scroll, Yang's paintings in the boneless style were virtually unknown. The meaningful confluence of content and style for the recipient points to the extraordinary care Yang took in painting *Cloudy Valley*.

Yang Wencong was a prominent official, poet, and painter of the late Ming period. He was a native of Guiyang (Guizhou Province), but spent most of his life in Nanjing. After obtaining his *juren* (provincial graduate) degree in 1618, he was appointed director of studies in Songjiang. While holding this post, he began to study painting with Dong Qichang (cat. nos. 8-9). His association with Dong later led to his being counted as one of the Nine Friends of Painting by the poet Wu Weiye.[2] Though recognized as a follower of Dong, Yang was praised as exceeding his teacher by the influential Nanjing collector and connoisseur Zhou Lianggong in his famous treatise on painting, *Du hua lu*.[3] Yang was actively involved in politics during the final decades of the Ming dynasty. In 1644, he became magistrate of Nanjing on the recommendation of his brother-in-law, Ma Shiying. The following year, he obtained the position of secretary of the Board of War and subsequently was promoted to the position of assistant military intendant in Jiangsu Province. After Manchu armies captured Nanjing, he fled to Fujian. He was captured there and executed for refusing to transfer his loyalty to the Qing.[4]

In an inscription to one of Yang Wencong's paintings, Dong Qichang wrote that Yang attained the vigorous brushstrokes of the Song masters and the elegance of the Yuan. Dong also commended Yang for reaching the artistic realms of the Song-dynasty painters Juran and Huichong.[5] Other biographies state that Yang developed his painting from Juran and Huichong and attained the achievements of Huang Gongwang and Ni Zan.[6] Most of Yang's extant paintings attest to his persistent interest in the styles of the Yuan masters, especially Ni Zan, Zhao Mengfu, and Huang Gongwang.

Cloudy Valley differs markedly in its application of color, painterly rendering of forms, and small touches of the anecdotal, adopting the archaistic conventions of the boneless style. That style was first associated with Zhang Sengyao of the Liang dynasty (502–557) and then developed by Yang Sheng of the Tang (618–907). As Chen Yuanlong explains in his inscription, the *mogu* style was associated with the Tang masters, but the real source of inspiration for Yang Wencong was Dong Qichang, whose exploration of early landscape styles reached back to this most archaistic of models. There are at least two extant paintings by Dong in the *mogu* style: *Boneless Landscape after Yang Sheng* (1615) and *White Clouds and Red Trees after Zhang Sengyao* (1628).[7] Dong's pronounced reference to such early painters as Yang Sheng and Zhang Sengyao announces that his mastery and knowledge of the tradition was not limited to the better-known masters of the Southern School lineage that he commonly touted. In the same vein, Yang Wencong's motivation for using this style is related to his pursuit of antiquity and an endeavor to expand art-historical knowledge. However, compared to the bold colors and decorative nature of Dong's *mogu* landscapes, Yang's *Cloudy Valley* emphasizes poetic atmosphere through a softer touch of the brush and a subtle gradation of colored wash. Mountains tinted in muted hues of blue and greenish ocher are accentuated by red and blue dots representing foliage. Misty clouds surrounding the mountains enhance the poetic qualities. Yang's two small figures at the start of the scroll enliven the scene and convey the delightfulness of a life in reclusion. In these elements, his landscape differs from Dong's textually based *mogu*-style landscape painting. Here, one can find both Yang's indebtedness to Dong and his creativity as a literati painter of the seventeenth century. **YJS**

For inscriptions and other documentation, see page 286 in this catalogue.

1 Two figures of artistic talent known to have the sobriquet Yunqing are Mo Shilong and Han Yunjun. Mo's association with Dong Qichang makes him particularly suitable, but neither Mo's nor Han's dates work with Yang Wencong's period of activity.

2 In his "Ode to the Nine Friends of Painting," Wu Weiye ranked Yang Wencong with Dong Qichang and Wang Shimin. The other "friends" are Cheng Jiasui, Zhang Xuezeng, Bian Wenyu, Shao Mi, Li Liufang, and Wang Jian.

3 Zhou Lianggong 周亮工, *Du hua lu* 讀畫錄, in *Huashi congshu* 畫史叢書 (Shanghai: Shanghai renmin meishu chubanshe, 1982), 3:37.

4 Arthur W. Hummel, et al., *Eminent Chinese of the Ch'ing Period*, 895–96. Yang Wencong's activities at the Southern Ming court and his former alliance with the Fushe circle appear in the play *Tao hua shan* (The Peach blossom fan), written by Kong Shangren in 1699.

5 Wai-kam Ho, ed., *The Century of Tung Ch'i-ch'ang*, vol. 2, 480; and Bai Jian 白堅, *Yang Wencong zhuan lun*, 103.

6 Xu Qin 徐沁, *Ming hua lu* 明畫錄 (Taipei: Yiwen chubanshe, 1968), 5:1; and Jiang Shaoshu 姜紹書, *Wusheng shi shi* 無聲詩史, *Huashi congshu* ed., 7:130.

7 *Boneless Landscape after Yang Sheng* (Nelson-Atkins Museum of Art) is illustrated in *The Century of Tung Ch'i-ch'ang*, vol. 1, pl. 25. *White Clouds and Red Trees after Zhang Sengyao* is in the National Palace Museum, Taipei. For Dong Qichang's two inscriptions on these paintings, see *The Century of Tung Ch'i-ch'ang*, vol. 2, 36.

18 Yang Wencong 楊文驄
1597–1646

Cloudy Valley 雲壑圖
Private collection

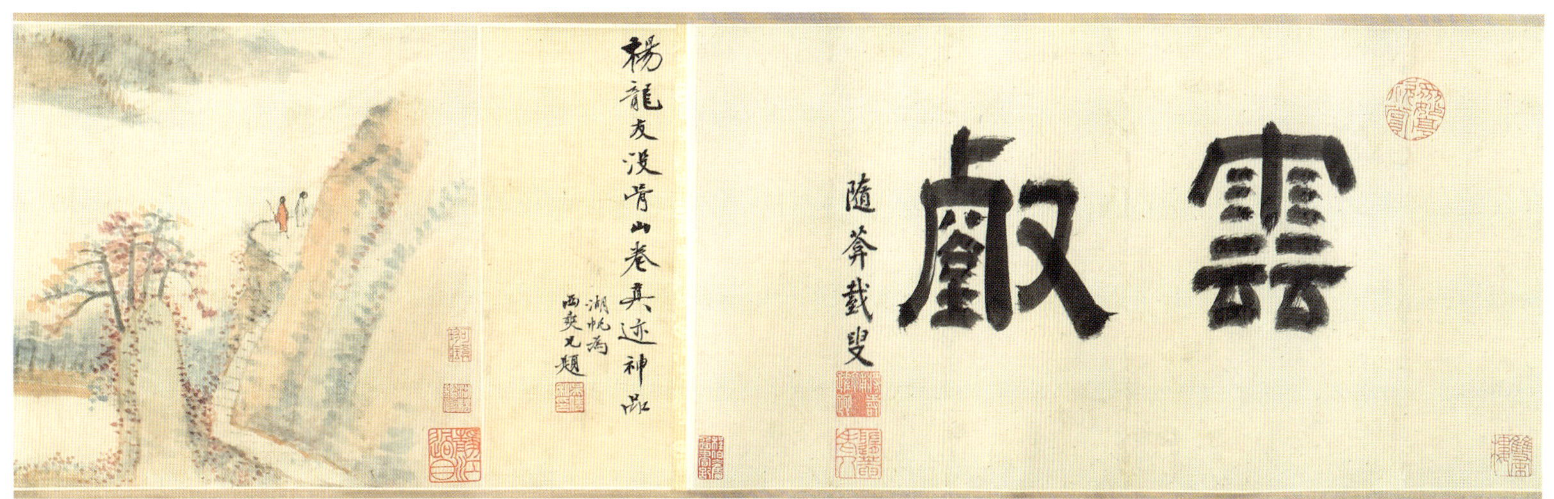

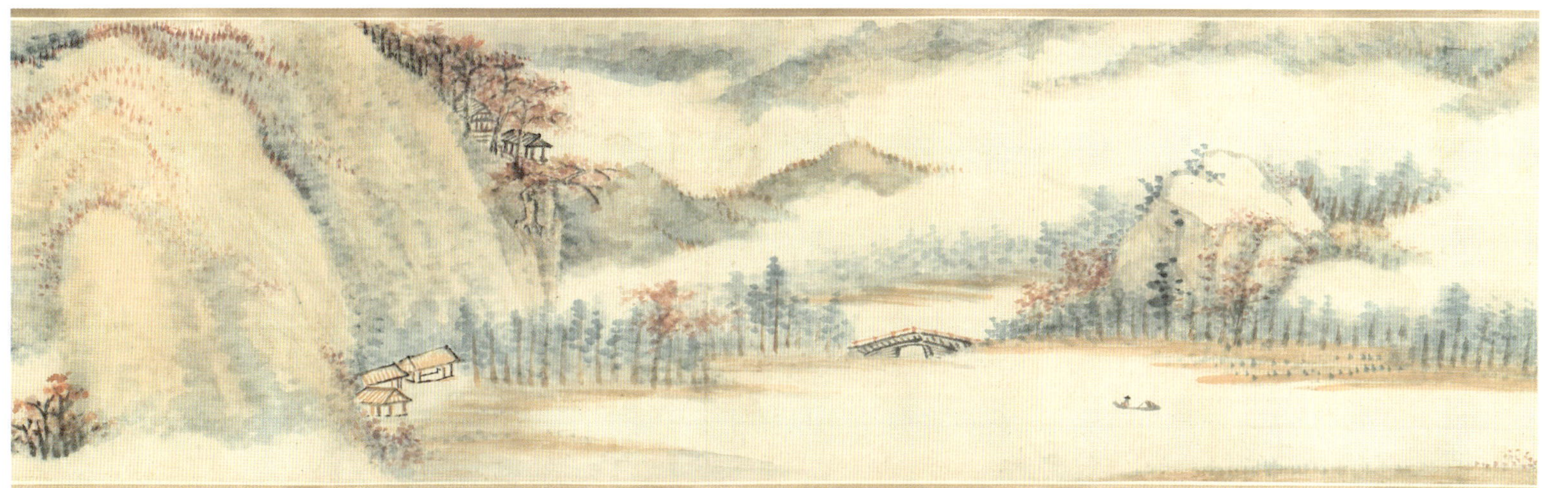

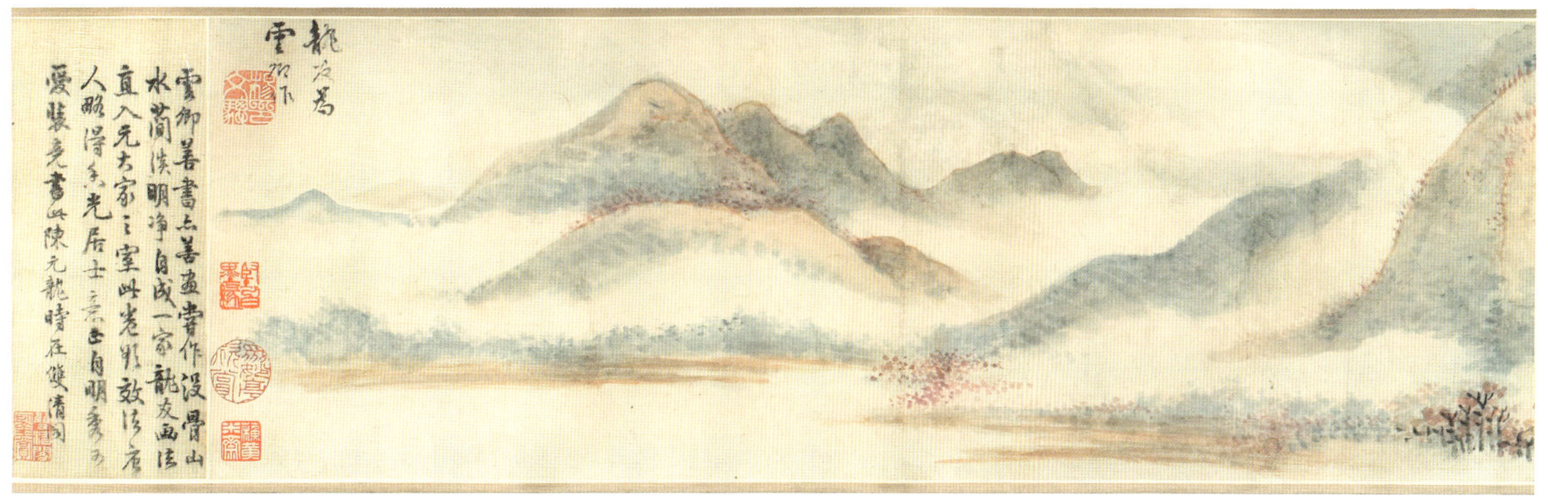

When Yang Wencong painted this delicate handscroll, his country was in disarray. Beijing had been sacked by a rebel force, and the Chongzhen emperor was dead by his own hand. A portion of the Ming court had reassembled in Nanjing (Jiangsu Province), but Manchu armies, now occupying the north, posed a serious threat to the newly enthroned Emperor Hongguang, and the fate of the dynasty was in doubt. Under these tumultuous circumstances, Yang, serving as a high official for the Southern Ming court, painted this scroll for Gao Hongtu, one of the Grand Secretaries and a moderating force among an increasingly divided group of senior officials. Although greatly respected, even preferred, by Hongguang, Gao repeatedly requested to retire in late 1644 due to his unhappiness with factional fighting at the court. His request was finally granted in the tenth lunar month, one month before Yang Wencong painted *Water Village* and added his poem. Nanjing fell to Manchu troops a few months later and Hongguang was captured. After learning of this stunning defeat, Gao committed suicide in a remote temple in Kuaiji (Shaoxing, Zhejiang Province) by refusing to eat.[1] A year later, Yang would share a similar fate. Stationed in Quzhou (Zhejiang Province), he fought against the Manchus until forced to retreat to Pucheng (Fujian Province), where he was defeated. Because he refused to surrender, Yang was executed along with thirty-six members of his family.[2]

Despite Yang Wencong's patriotic end, his life was viewed with great ambiguity. The son of a prominent official, he enjoyed the privileges of a classical education and cultivated a circle of affluent friends including artists, poets, and officials. He was deeply associated with members of the Restoration Society—a group of scholar-officials committed to strengthening the dynasty.[3] However, at odds with the Restoration Society were his family ties, most notably those with his brother-in-law, Ma Shiying, who was associated with a clique at the court led earlier by the notorious eunuch Wei Zhongxian. Under the leadership of Ma and Ruan Dacheng, the Eunuch Party played a dubious role in weakening the already decaying Ming court. Yang maintained a delicate balance by befriending Restoration Society members while at the same time accepting promotions from Ma. Consequently, there is much disagreement on the subject of Yang's legacy. Some later representations portray him as a despicable traitor; others view his sacrificial death as a redeeming sign of his patriotism.[4] Interestingly, Gao Hongtu, the recipient of *Water Village*, was deeply opposed to Ma and insisted on retiring precisely because of his rising influence. The painting is thus a tangible memento reflecting Yang's difficult position between the two political camps.

Yang Wencong's *Water Village* well reflects the guidance he received in matters of painting from Dong Qichang. According to Yang's inscription, the landscape combines the influence of two highly celebrated fourteenth-century paintings, Zhao Mengfu's *Water Village* of 1302 and Huang Gongwang's undated *Sand Marsh*. The former is one of Zhao's best-known landscapes, currently housed in Beijing's Palace Museum. Dong owned this scroll, which certainly makes it possible, if not likely, that Yang personally viewed and studied it. In any case, Zhao's composition was one favored by Yang, who painted a free-form rendition of it a few years earlier in 1638.[5] In contrast to Zhao's *Water Village*, Huang's *Sand Marsh* (*Shaqi tu* 沙磧圖) is a largely forgotten painting, known only by photos in old publications (see fig. 12). In the seventeenth century, however, Huang's short landscape was often mentioned and occasionally copied.[6] The general topographical resemblance of Zhao's and Huang's two paintings, both descriptive of the marshy water country of the Jiangnan region south of the Yangzi River, made it natural for Yang to combine them for his own painting. Nonetheless, while he adopted qualities from the two fourteenth-century masters, Zhao's and Huang's influence was more intuitive than literal. Capturing his impressions of the earlier paintings, Yang configured them into a personal vision of an idyllic landscape for his retiring friend Gao Hongtu.

Yang Wencong's *Water Village* was deeply admired by later viewers, who added laudatory inscriptions praising the artist's courage in the trying times that immediately followed his making of the painting in late 1644. Also of interest are the seals of Song Luo, a prominent scholar, official, and connoisseur who was known to have sought the company of old Ming loyalists in the generation that followed Yang.[7] **FQ**

For inscriptions and other documentation, see pages 286–87 in this catalogue.

1 For Gao Hongtu's biography, see *Ming shi* 明史, in *Qingdai zhuanji congkan* 清代傳記叢刊 (Taipei: Mingwen shuju, 1985–86), vol. 67, 136. See also Lynn A. Struve, *The Southern Ming*, 20, 33; and Frederick Wakeman, *The Great Enterprise*, 364–65.

2 Bai Jian 白堅, *Yang Wencong zhuan lun* 楊文驄傳論 (Shanghai: Shanghai renmin meishu chubanshe, 1990), 168.

3 Liu Yazhang 劉亞璋, "Wan Ming wenren huajia Yang Wencong kaolue," 31.

4 Bai, *Yang Wencong zhuan lun*, 1. The well-known dramatic work *Peach Blossom Fan* by Kong Shanren offers a dramatized version of the struggles between the Restoration Society and the Eunuch Party. Yang Wencong appears in the play as a weak official who wavers between the two sides. When the heroine of the play refuses a forced marriage by committing suicide, specks of her blood splatter a fan; Yang uses his brush to add ink, turning the specks into peach blossoms. For an English translation, see Chen Shih-hsiang and Harold Acton, tr., *The Peach Blossom Fan*. See also Richard E. Strassberg, *The World of K'ung Shang-jen*, especially 246–51, 269–70.

5 Zhao Mengfu's *Water Village* is reproduced in *Zhongguo lidai huihua: Gugong bowuyuan canghua ji* 中國歷代繪畫：故宮博物院藏畫集, vol. 4 (Beijing: Renmin meishu chubanshe, 1983), 22–27. For thoughts on the influence of this scroll in the seventeenth century, see Wang Cheng-hua's entry on Zhao Zuo's *Streams and Mountains without End* in Richard M. Barnhart, et al., *The Jade Studio*, 104. Yang Wencong's 1638 rendition is the first part of a handscroll titled *Collective Landscapes by Four Sages* for Yang Bu. See cat. no. 25 for Zhang Xuezeng's *Fisherman Recluse*, note 4. Yang's painting is separately reproduced in Xu Bangda 徐邦達, comp., *Zhongguo huihua shi tulu* 中國繪畫史圖錄 (Shanghai: Shanghai renmin meishu chubanshe, 1981), vol. 2, 662.

6 In December 2010, a scroll of poems and inscriptions by Qing-dynasty writers titled *Qing mingxian shihan juan* 清名賢詩翰卷 was auctioned by the Poly International Auction Company in Beijing; it appears to have originally been a part of Huang Gongwang's *Sand Marsh*.

7 Song Luo was governor of both Jiangxi (1688–1692) and Jiangsu (1692–1705). He sought the company of Bada Shanren, who spurned him. See Wang Fangyu, Barnhart, and Judith G. Smith, eds., *Master of the Lotus Garden*, 58–59 (where he is called Song Lao).

19 Yang Wencong 楊文驄 1597–1646

Water Village 水村圖 1644

Private collection

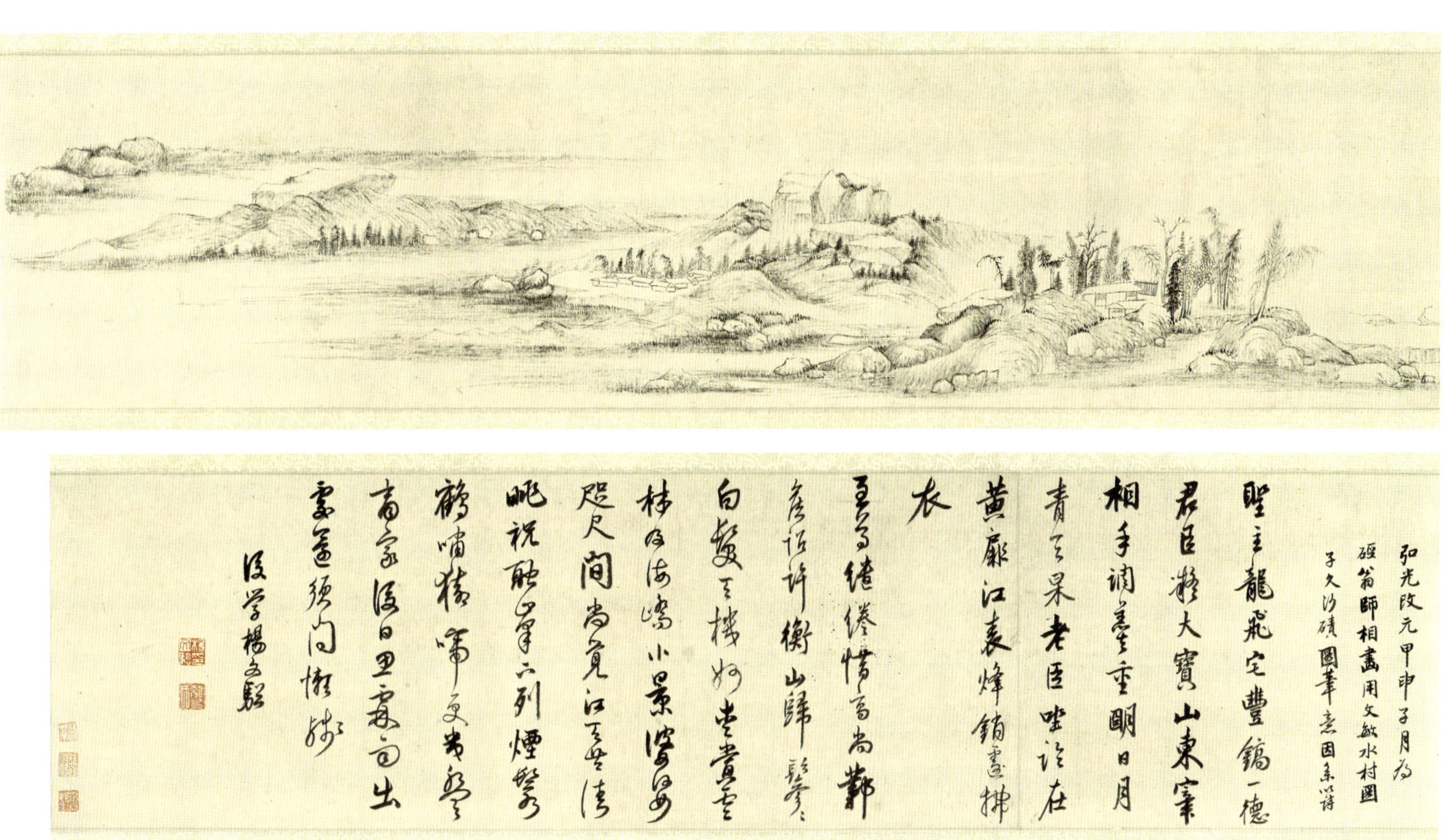

. . .This small scene delicately unfurls within the space of a foot;
So that together we can purely gaze at rivers and sky.
Under Zhurong Peak arrayed mists coil;
Crane calls, monkey howls—how many vales and mountains? . . .

Hearing that rebel forces had captured the Ming capital at Beijing and the Chongzhen emperor had committed suicide, Xiang Shengmo chose this moment of national trauma to compose a self-portrait. In a manner that appears to be unprecedented, he painted himself in black ink seated in a crimson landscape. He sits under a tree, gently resting clasped hands on an upraised knee as if enjoying nature. The red landscape, however, creates a distinctly dissonant note. The key to the color's symbolism is made clear at the very beginning of Xiang's first poem. In it he looks back in time to a famous precedent—the Tang-dynasty poet Du Fu, who similarly experienced the threat of dynastic collapse—and echoes one of Du's most famous lines: "The country is broken, mountains and rivers remain" 國破山河在.[1] However, Xiang cleverly turns the meaning around: the landscape is in pieces but it remains cinnabar red, *zhu* 朱. This same character *zhu* was the surname of the Ming imperial family, and his line could thus read, "Remnant waters, leftover mountains, but its color is still Ming." Defiantly, Xiang thus affirms loyalty to his dynasty and insists on its continued existence. According to Jiang Gusun, who owned *Self-Portrait in Red Landscape* earlier in the twentieth century and commissioned the many inscriptions on its outer mounting, the survival of this remarkable scroll was due to the fact that it was a hidden image for most of its history, kept in the Xiang family temple in Jiaxing (Zhejiang Province) until nine years after the fall of the Qing dynasty in 1911.[2]

As Xiang's first dated self-portrait, this image of 1644 heralds a visual and thematic strategy in which red pigment and the imagery of reclusion are used to express loyalist sentiment and the eremitic ideal.[3] In his *Tall Tree in the Wind* (Palace Museum, Beijing) of circa 1649, Xiang portrayed himself in a red robe under a withered tree, referencing the same symbolic meaning of red. In his *Free Immortal of Soughing Pines* (Jilin Provincial Museum) of 1652, the artist depicts himself as a Daoist hermit walking beneath the pines.[4] In *Self-Portrait in Red Landscape* the concept of reclusion is almost overshadowed by the unnatural red landscape with its overt statement of loyalty to the dynasty, but there are important visual clues. He alludes to that most famous of all recluse-poets, Tao Yuanming, by depicting himself wearing the translucent gauze headgear that was associated with Tao and other free spirits of the Six Dynasties period. He also includes what appears to be a shrub of chrysanthemums, Tao's hallmark, in the lower right corner.[5] Xiang abandoned the pursuit of government service and aspired to the ideal life of a recluse from an early age. The theme of eremitism was his abiding interest, exemplified by the subject of "summoning the recluse," which he painted a number of times (see cat. no. 1). The third of Xiang's *Summoning the Recluse* scrolls was painted just a few months before this painting, in the first lunar month of 1644.[6] Intriguingly, he refers to this series at the end of his first poem on this scroll. Now denying the need of "summoning the recluse" to show Xiang Shengmo the way into reclusion, he affirms that he has already achieved his goal.

The late Ming period witnessed a considerable increase in portrait production among the Jiangnan literati, though these were almost always commissioned to professional portraitists. With regard to Xiang's self-portraits, it is important to note his close association with the famed portraitist Zeng Jing and his disciples. For example, Xiang added the landscape to Zeng's portrait of Dong Qichang (Shanghai Museum). In 1652 with Zhang Qi, one of Zeng's followers, Xiang collaborated in a group portrait of eminent Jiangnan intellectuals titled *Venerable Friends* (Shanghai Museum, fig. 20).[7] In the same year, he collaborated with Zeng's disciple Xie Bin on *A Carefree Immortal among Waves of Pines* (Palace Museum, Beijing).[8] Another portrait of Xiang painted in 1646 (Wango Weng collection) possesses a very similar facial depiction to that seen in *Self-Portrait in Red Landscape*, though it is unclear if this was painted by Xiang or a professional portraitist.[9] Considering these collaborations and their stylistic affinities, it is possible that Zeng or his followers contributed to the depiction of Xiang's visage in this painting. In any case, there is no doubt that Xiang Shengmo designed the pictorial scheme to construct his visual persona and that his extraordinary enthusiasm for self-fashioning resulted in one of the most striking self-images in the history of Chinese portraiture. **SWC**

For inscriptions and other documentation, see page 287 in this catalogue.

1 Du Fu 杜甫, "Chun wang" 春望, in *Du shi xiangzhu* 杜詩詳注 (*Siku quanshu* ed.), 50:4b. Du wrote this in response to the An Lushan Rebellion of 756. The terms "remnant waters" and "leftover mountains" in Xiang's first line were probably derived from another poem by Du: "Pei Zheng Guangwen you He Jiangjun shanlin shishou" 陪鄭廣文遊何將軍山林十首, in ibid., 2:56b.

2 Li Chu-tsing (Li Zhujin 李鑄晉), "Xiang Shengmo zhi zhaoyin shihua," 547.

3 Kela Shang, "Visualizing Social Spaces," 211–16. For an overview of Xiang's self-images, see Richard Vinograd, *Boundaries of the Self*, 36–40.

4 *Free Immortal of Soughing Pines* recalls an earlier scroll of 1629 of the same title (Museum of Fine Arts, Boston) in which Xiang Shengmo portrayed his old estate. Here the natural setting not only conveys the reclusive ideal; it also represents a nostalgic longing for the past.

5 Illustrations to Tao Yuanming's *Returning Home*, modeled after Li Gonglin, were once in Xiang Yuanbian's collection. See Eun-wha Park, "The World of Idealized Reclusion," 187.

6 Ibid., 38–39.

7 *Venerable Friends* includes, among others, Dong Qichang, Chen Jiru, Li Rihua, and Xiang himself. See Chu-tsing Li and James C. Y. Watt, eds., *The Chinese Scholar's Studio*, 144.

8 James Cahill, *The Distant Mountains*, 214–15.

9 Ibid.

20 Xiang Shengmo 項聖謨 1597–1658

Self-Portrait in Red Landscape

朱色自畫像圖軸

1644

Collection of Shitou Shuwu

Remnant waters, leftover mountains—
color still cinnabar red;
Murky heavens, darkened earth—
shadow of a trifling body.
A flame ignites in my crimson heart,
and I daub the ocher red;
But from this dry brush only careless words—
I am ashamed to paint pictures.
Men of mark are few and desolate;
who is there to depict?
Valley clouds obscured in shadow—
as if an ignorant fool.
In a change of heart, I laugh at my three
"summons to the recluse";
Who would have believed that I was already
one with the wild man?...

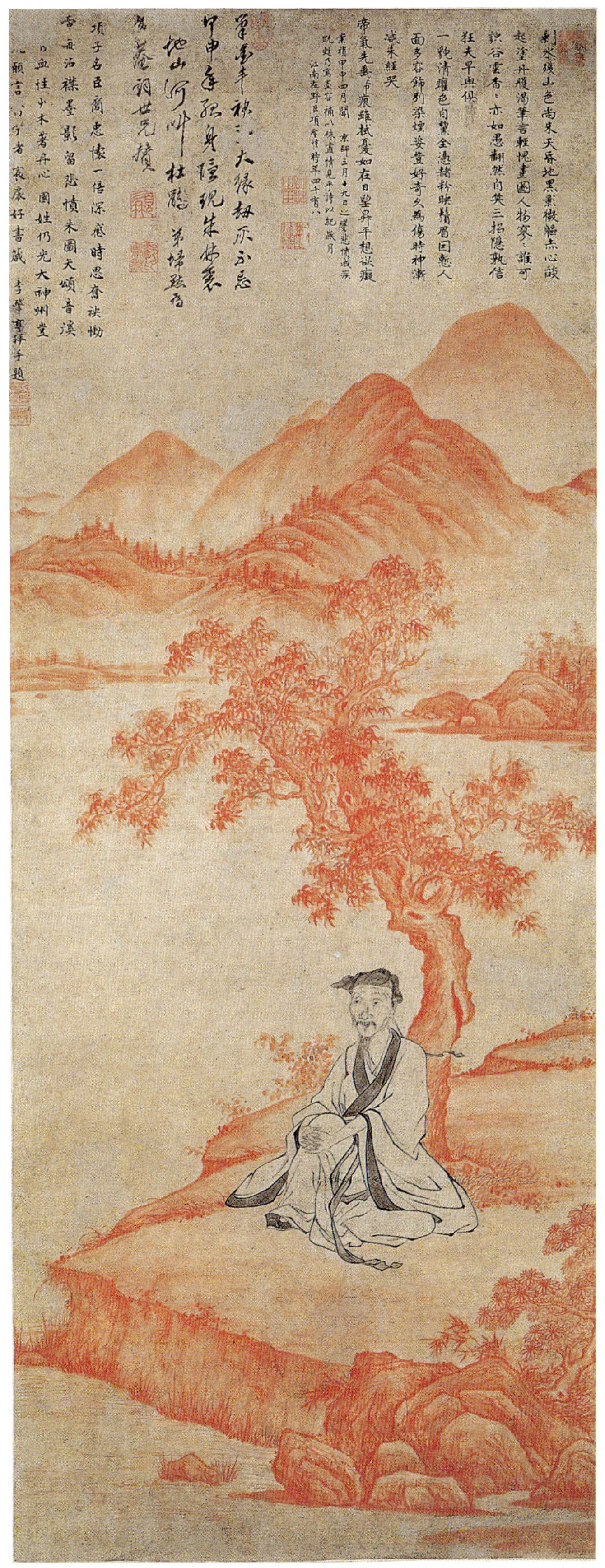

Chen Hongshou's inscription specifies that he painted this tall colorful scroll at a repository for Daoist scriptures. A number of Chen's works are similarly signed as painted at Daoist institutions and possess Daoist overtones (see also cat. no. 23). The mystical scene is a ritual site located deep in the mountains, as signified by the background peaks striped by bands of white mist. Strangely patterned pines and a bizarre Taihu rock together with other plants frame a foreground setting in which a central figure in a red robe stares intently at a minute female figure emerging from a gourd on the ground to offer a cup that presumably is filled with the elixir of immortality. Surrounding attendants with strange features and garb stand respectfully behind and to the side, one holding a vase of chrysanthemums and day lilies, another holding what appears to be a *qin* (zither) wrapped in brocade. On the long table behind the seated figure are set a crackled-glaze ceramic wine bowl with stacked cups, what appear to be carved images of a pig and elephant, a bronze vessel, and a shallow white jade dish holding peaches and lotus root. The various fruits and flora are associated with longevity and health in popular Daoism.

A similar version of this painting in Zurich's Rietberg Museum was interpreted by Chu-tsing Li as an illustration of the Daoist master and alchemist Tao Hongjing and his patron, Emperor Wu of the Liang dynasty (502–557).[1] Tao was a key practitioner and theoretician of the Shangqing 上清 (Highest Purity) sect of Daoism who devoted himself to alchemical experiments and to the compilation of Daoist scriptures. Under Emperor Wu's patronage, he established Maoshan (Mount Mao, Jiangsu Province) as the center of Shangqing Daoism, building hundreds of temples and altars. According to Li's reading of the Rietberg painting, the seated figure—essentially identical to the figure in this painting—is Emperor Wu, who has come to Tao's retreat on Maoshan to obtain an elixir of immortality. Li identifies a single figure standing behind, occupying the position of the two figures here, as Tao. On the basis of this study, the iconography of this painting too has been associated with Tao Hongjing and Emperor Wu.[2] However, if any figure is to be identified with Tao in this painting it should be the central seated gentleman, whose white and red robe with dark trim matches a standard portrayal of the Prime Minister of the Mountains, as Tao was famously called.[3]

Chen Hongshou's antique style heightens the painting's mystic ambience and harmonizes with its ancient Daoist theme. In constructing the natural setting, he used washes of deep colors, adopting the archaic "blue-and-green" style of landscape painting developed during the Tang dynasty. This archaistic manner of decorative coloration, a style that the amateur literati painters practiced only rarely, is typical of Chen's works in the 1630s.[4] The heavily colored landscapes of this period attest to Chen's artistic training under Lan Ying (cat. nos. 26–27), a professional painter active in Hangzhou, and to his turn to professionalism by this time.[5] Along with bright colors, the paintings of this archaic style feature repetitive, formulaic, and ordered brushwork in the depiction of landscape. In contrast, Chen employed fine and detailed brushwork for the figures. The curvilinear delineation of facial features heralds the mature style of his later works, while the angular contours of the garments characterize the earlier style exhibited in his woodblock illustrations.[6]

It is natural that Tao Hongjing—a Daoist master, recluse, and artist—made an attractive subject for Chen Hongshou, who had a great interest in both Daoism and reclusion.[7] Chen, who descended from a scholar-official family in Zhejiang Province, made several attempts during the late Ming to obtain a high government post but failed at the civil service examinations.[8] Moreover, he lost his family property during the Manchu invasion. These personal misfortunes forced him to make a living by selling paintings while wandering around the Hangzhou area. Tao's close relationship with the court—his worldly success while maintaining a reputation of being a man of the hills—was an attractive model to many. The recipient of this painting remains unknown, but Chen's paintings of similar subjects were often produced on the occasion of a birthday.[9] Indeed, Chen made many paintings involving themes of longevity and Daoism, which points to the commemorative function and marketable value of his *Immortal Conveying Longevity* and other works in a similar vein. **SWC**

For inscriptions and other documentation, see page 288 in this catalogue.

1 Chu-tsing Li, *A Thousand Peaks and Myriad Ravines*, vol. 1, 26–29, and vol. 2, fig. 4.

2 The identification was repeated for the Christie's sale of this painting, lot 202 (Sale 7908), June 1994.

3 See the anonymous fourteenth-century portrait of Tao Hongjing in the National Palace Museum, Taipei, reproduced in Stephen Little, *Taoism and the Arts of China*, cat. no. 38. For a late-Ming image of Tao in a woodblock-printed book, see Hong Zicheng 洪自誠, ed., *Huixiang lie xian zhuan* 繪像列仙傳 (reprint, Shanghai: Saoye shanfang, 1887), 4/4–7.

4 For example, see Chen's *Landscape in the Blue-and-Green Manner* of 1633 (Metropolitan Museum of Art) and *Lady Xuanwen Jun Giving Instructions on the Classics* of 1638 (Cleveland Museum of Art). These two paintings are reproduced in Wan-go Weng 翁萬戈, *Chen Hongshou: His Life & Art*, vol. 2, 76–78, 97–99. Another excellent example is *A Tall Pine and a Daoist Immortal* of 1635 (National Palace Museum, Taipei), reproduced in James Cahill, *The Distant Mountains*, color plate 18.

5 See Cahill, *The Distant Mountains*, 203–6.

6 Tamara Heimarck Bentley, "Authenticity in a New Key," 21–25.

7 For Tao Hongjing's life as a recluse, see Alan J. Berkowitz, *Patterns of Disengagement*, 209–15.

8 For Chen Hongshou's biography, see Shi-yee Liu, "An Actor in Real Life," 6–44.

9 On Chen's painting for birthday celebrations, see Anne Burkus-Chasson, "Elegant or Common?," 279–300.

21 **Chen Hongshou** 陳洪綬
1599–1652

Immortal Conveying Longevity 壽者仙人圖
1638
Private collection

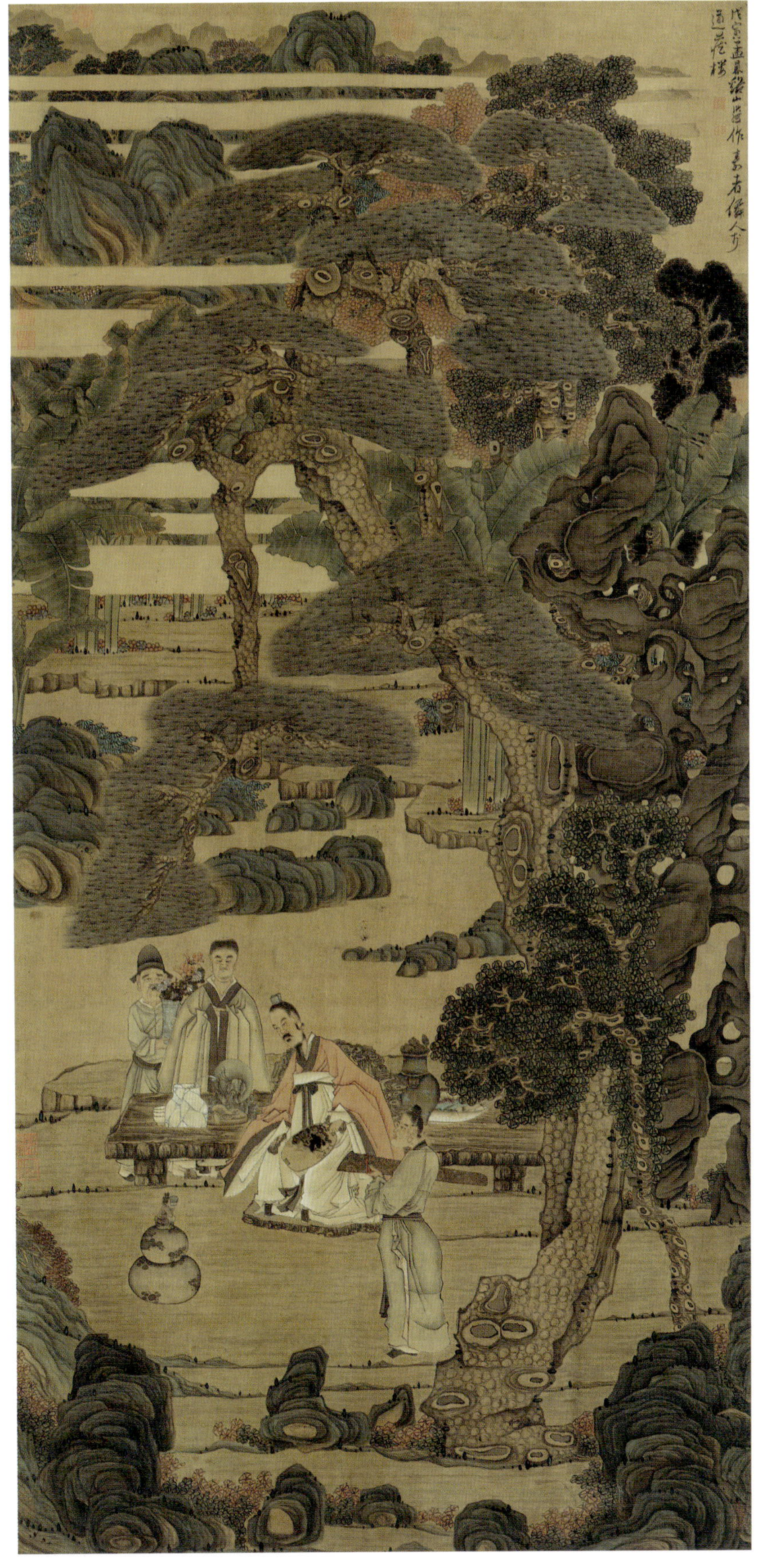

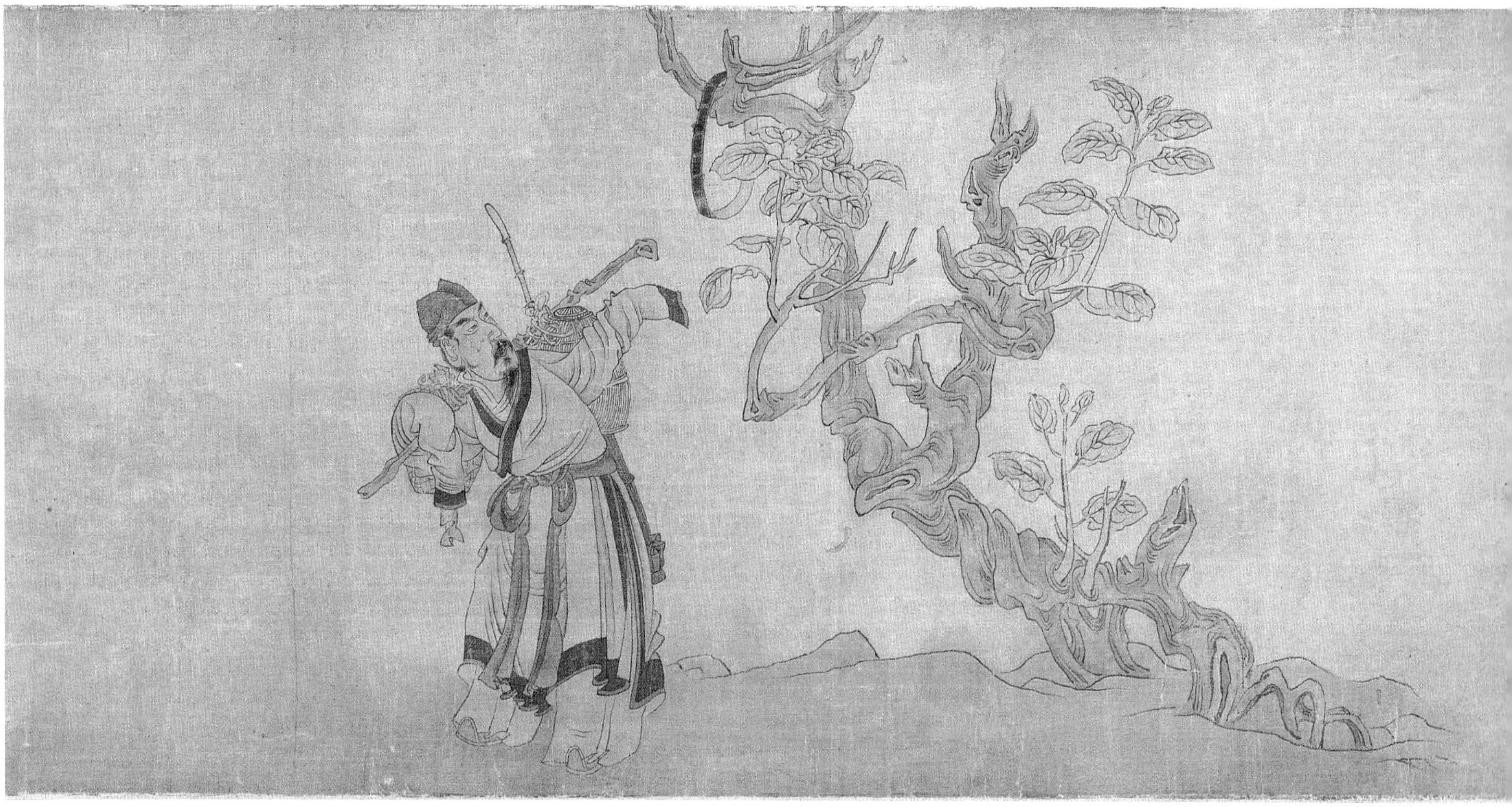

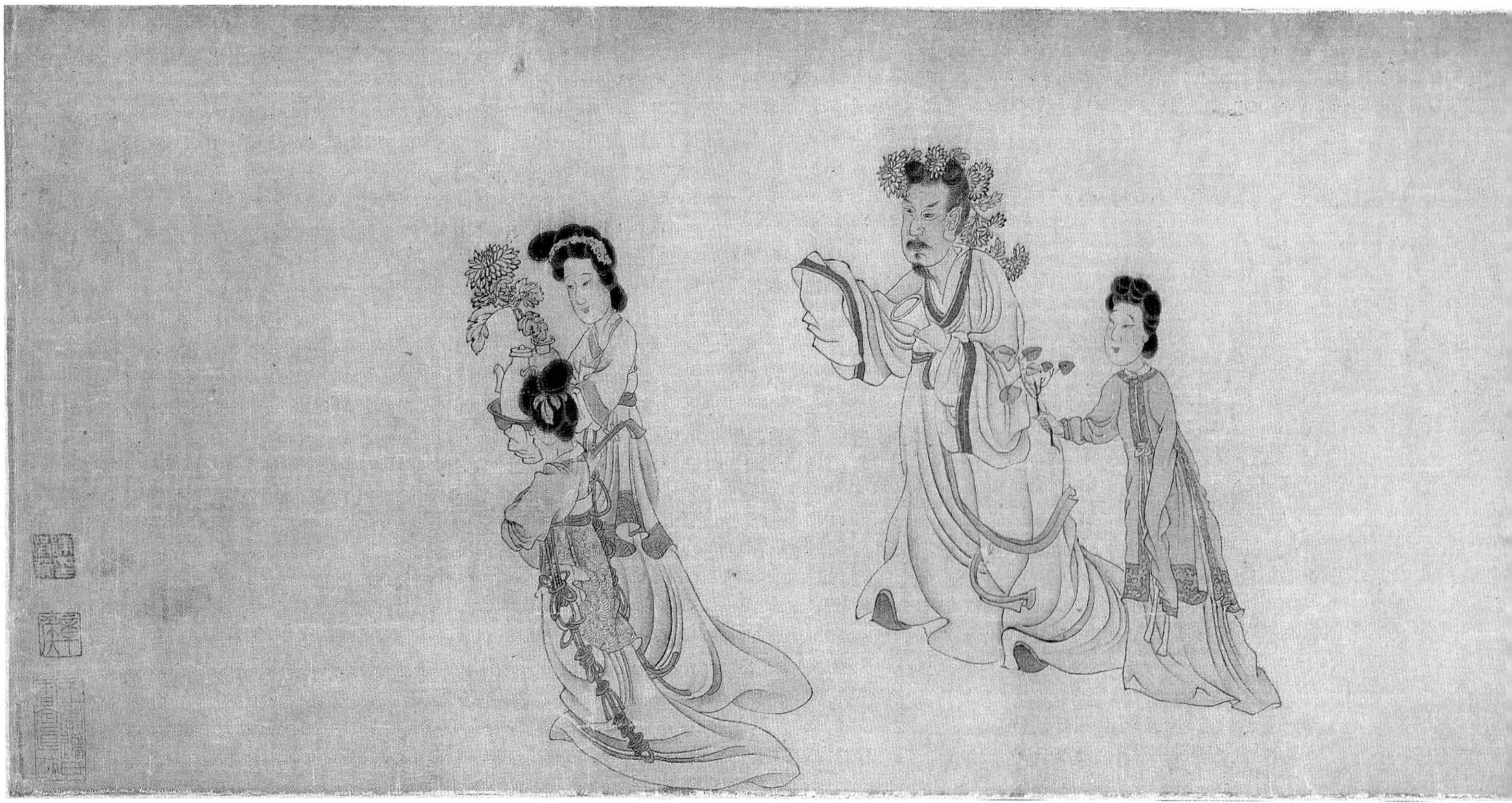

22 Chen Hongshou 陳洪綬 1599–1652

Historical Figures 史實人物圖卷

Collection of Shitou Shuwu

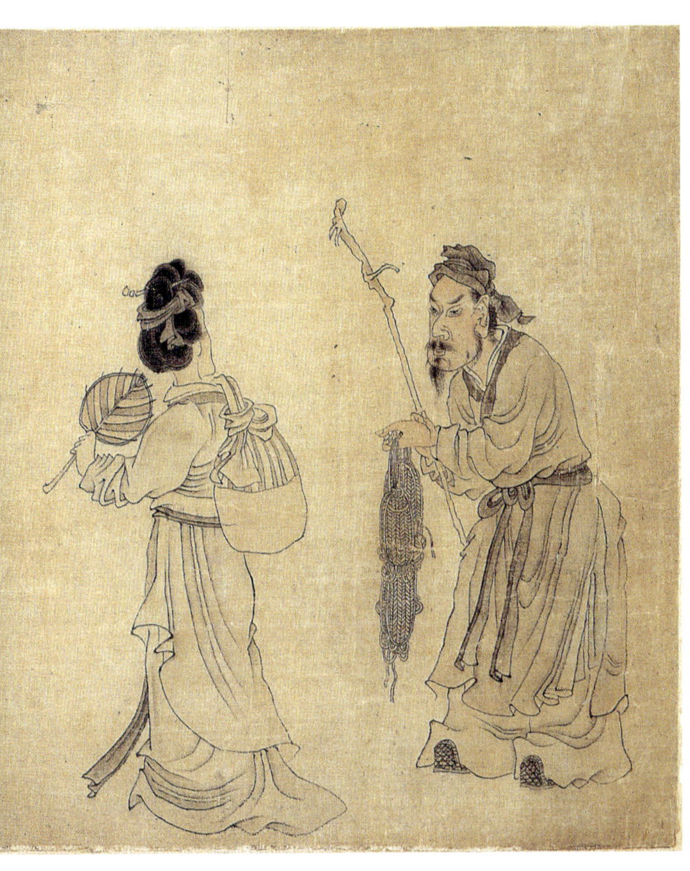

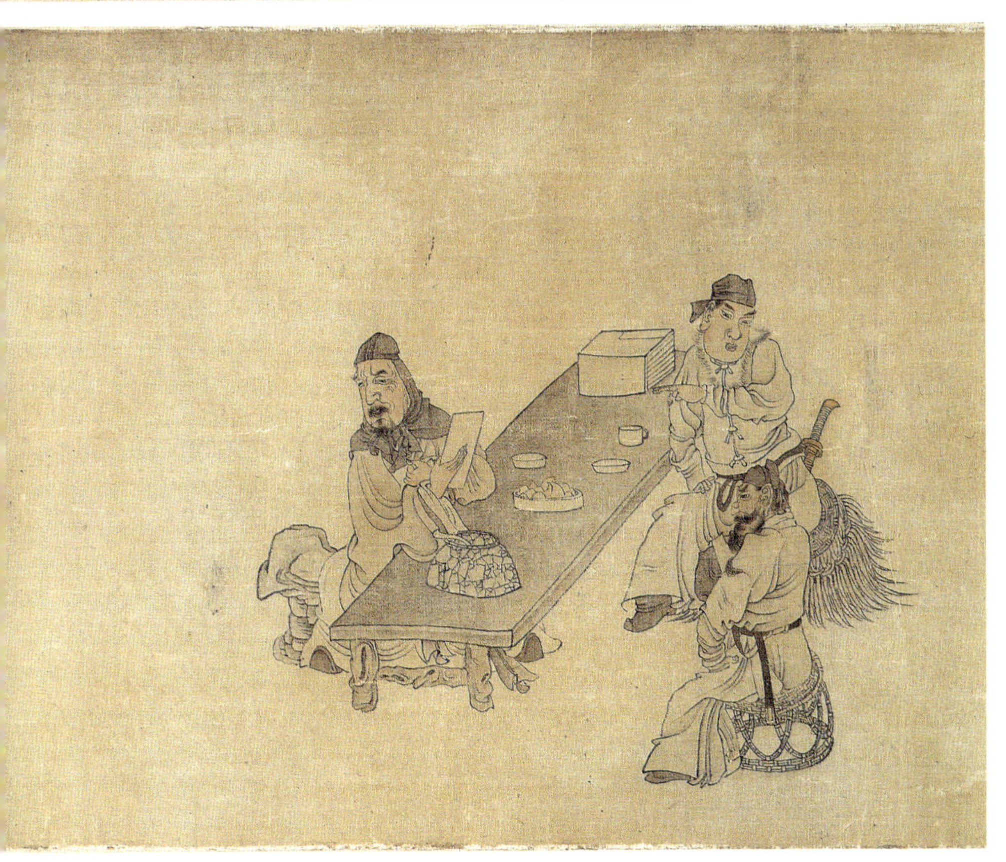

Chen Hongshou's figure paintings encompass a range of subjects, including both historical and fictional characters, contemporary scholars, and self-portraits. This handscroll appears to depict scenes of a reclusive life, one of the artist's major themes. Utilizing an archaic composition for narrative illustration characteristic of the pre-Tang period, Chen depicts four different vignettes in one continuous tableau. The style of painting is equally archaic, evoking the early master Gu Kaizhi with fine-line drawing and muted colors. Rendered against a blank background, the illustration emphasizes costume, gesture, and the interactions between the figures. The heightened theatricality of the four scenes recalls Chen's other forte: illustrations for printed novels and plays.

Because the painting lacks explanatory inscriptions and appears somewhat truncated, it is possible that *Historical Figures* is not complete.[1] Compounding the difficulty of identifying the content, the iconography of the depicted scenes does not conclusively correspond with known precedents. Absent specific documentary or visual information, there is a natural tendency to associate the imagery with the renowned poet Tao Yuanming (also known as Tao Qian), the most celebrated recluse of the Six Dynasties period in the minds of later literati, specifically for his famous poem "Home Again!" (Indeed, this is how a later collector labeled the painting.) More discriminating analysis has isolated the second and fourth scenes as illustrations of Tao's life.[2] The second scene, featuring a belt casually tossed over a tree branch, suggests a passage from Tao's biography—"He untied his official belt and gave up the post"—that alludes to the recluse's renouncement of his role in public affairs.[3] The fourth scene depicts a figure wearing a chrysanthemum wreath. Tao was associated with chrysanthemums and was portrayed elsewhere with this kind of garland by Chen.[4] However, despite these correspondences, the identification of Tao with these two scenes is not certain. Reference to removing or hanging up an "official belt" is found frequently in early literature, used as a trope for freedom or reclusion. Moreover, there are other elements in this scene, such as the wicker basket slung over the gentleman's pole, that are not standard motifs in Tao's iconography. Similarly, in the long pictorial tradition of representing Tao Yuanming, he almost never appears with the kind of alluring female attendants that appear in the fourth scene.[5] In extant illustrations of his "Returning Home," he is typically depicted as a lofty recluse and wearing a unique head scarf, which is not seen in this scroll.[6]

It is possible that the scroll describes another, or multiple, early recluses or simply alludes to the life of Chen Hongshou himself and his contemporaries. While the hedonistic lifestyle exhibited in the fourth scene conflicts with Tao's image as a paragon of unworldly reclusion, it corresponds well with literary descriptions of the artist as a libertine who could neither drink nor sleep without women.[7] The scene may depict Chen in the guise of Tao, possibly on the occasion of the Double Ninth Festival, enjoying wine and chrysanthemums as Tao did.[8] Contrasting with this image of festiveness, the other three scenes present a more austere picture. There are few clues to identify the figures, but the scenes seem to encapsulate different phases of the reclusive life. The second scene illustrates the key moment of the recluse's withdrawal from public life, as he tosses his official belt into a tree. The contrast between reclusion and officialdom is also drawn in the third scene, where the recluse receives a visit from an armed military officer and a government official, both of whom wear the characteristic belt. In the first scene the recluse may be trying to trade sandals for provisions in the woman's bundle. Poverty was an abiding emblem of the recluse.[9]

For inscriptions and other documentation, see page 288 in this catalogue.

1 See Huang Yifen's 黃逸芬 catalogue entry for the painting in *Yuemu*, vol. 2, 48. Chen Hongshou's two seals appear at the end of the scroll.
2 Ibid., 48.
3 A. R. Davis, *T'ao Yüan-ming (AD 365–427)*, vol. 2, 171.
4 For the representation of chrysanthemum flowers associated with Tao, see Susan E. Nelson, "Revisiting the Eastern Fence," 437–60.
5 I am grateful for the input of Professor Jonathan Chaves about the symbolism of the official belt, and to Professor Susan Nelson, who considers it unlikely that the figure in the fourth scene is Tao due to the presence of accompanying women.
6 In one canonical illustration of Tao's "Returning Home" by Li Gonglin, Tao is shown wearing his "wine-straining" headscarf even in the scene where he is farming.
7 This is a noted element in the biographies of Chen Hongshou by Mao Qiling and Zhu Yizun. For annotated translations of these two biographies, see Anne Gail Burkus, "The Artefacts of Biography in Ch'en Hung-Shou's 'Pao-Lun-T'ang Chi'," vol. 2, 422–43.
8 Tao Yuanming's preface to his poem "Living in Retirement on the Ninth Day" records that the wine-loving poet ate chrysanthemums since no wine was left. Davis, *T'ao Yüan-ming*, vol. 1, 43–45.
9 According to Yan Yanzhi's description, Tao Yuanming also chose a life of poverty and wove shoe strings. For the translation of Yan's funeral elegy for Tao, see Davis, *T'ao Yüan-ming*, vol. 1, 243–49.
10 Hongnam Kim, *The Life of a Patron*, 75–86.
11 See Kohara Hironobu, "An Introductory Study of Chen Hongshou, Part II," 67–83.
12 Chu-tsing Li, *A Thousand Peaks and Myriad Ravines*, vol. 1, 29–40.
13 This point is emphasized by James Cahill and Richard Vinograd in their writings on Chen's figure painting. Cahill, *The Distant Mountains*, 248–62; and Vinograd, *Boundaries of the Self*, 30–36.

Many of Chen Hongshou's pictures of historical recluses postdate the fall of the Ming, and most of them reflect his own or his peers' strong interest in reclusion. He painted *Scenes from the Life of Tao Qian* (1650, Honolulu Museum of Art) as an attempt to awaken the moral values of reclusion in his friend Zhou Lianggong, who chose to serve the new Qing regime.[10] Chen's commentaries on these illustrations of Tao's life were largely drawn from his own experiences. His album *Sixteen Views of Seclusion* (1651, National Palace Museum, Taipei), which depicts a variety of recluse-poets and historical figures including Tao, Du Fu, and Su Shi, is also regarded as a commentary on Chen's personal experience of reclusion in 1646 (see fig. 13).[11] In the scroll *The Four Pleasures of Nan Shenglu* (1649, Rietberg Museum, Zurich), Chen depicted his friend Nan wearing chrysanthemum sprigs, suggesting that he was like Tao Yuanming.[12] In the same way, Chen could feature the chrysanthemum here in the fourth scene to suggest Tao-like nobility. The interweaving of past and present in the other works mentioned suggests that the elusive *Historical Figures* may be best understood as a melding of themes from Chen's own life and classical narratives of reclusion.[13] **SWC**

Upon receiving a request from the Daoist monk Tang Yu, Chen painted this exquisite album of assorted subjects at a Daoist temple on Mount Wu, a hill by West Lake at Hangzhou. The first leaf portrays an old hermit with staff strolling amidst falling foliage. The remaining paintings of landscapes, flora, and fauna together form a personal world for Tang to explore. A fisherman, a wandering recluse, and a waterfowl in the three landscape scenes add a sense of remoteness, satisfying the Daoist's identification with the natural world. The other leaves depict a butterfly hovering above branches of chrysanthemum and bamboo, narcissus by a rock, a trio of perching birds in a wintry scene, and a plum tree with flowering branches. Among Chen's post-1644 works are a few comparable albums similarly composed of figure, landscape, and bird-and-flower subjects.[1] For Chen Hongshou, the album of miscellaneous subjects appears to have been the perfect format for presenting his versatility, skill, and sophistication, as well as his familiarity with earlier painting traditions.

Indeed, *Album for Monk Yu* showcases Chen's attraction to archaic styles and subjects. The hermit of the first leaf is portrayed in exaggerated form, with elongated face, slanted eyes and eyebrows, and flowing robe that reflect the artist's extensive study of ancient figure-painting masters from Gu Kaizhi of the Jin to Li Gonglin of the Song. Many of Chen's figure paintings depict celebrated hermits of antiquity, a favorite being the Eastern Jin recluse-poet Tao Yuanming (see cat. no. 22). The hermit in *Album for Monk Yu* resembles Chen's typical manner of portraying Tao, and the subject's inclusion at the beginning makes a powerful statement about the archaistic and eremitic values present throughout the album and presumably shared by Tang Yu.

The bird-and-flower leaves in the album evoke the styles of Song-dynasty masters, in particular Southern Song court painters of the twelfth and thirteenth centuries.[2] The artistic legacy of Northern Song scholar-artist Su Shi is evoked in the sixth leaf depicting trees, bamboo, and rocks. The chrysanthemum and bamboo of the third leaf represent the "broken branch" type of composition popularized during the Southern Song (1127–1279). Also thematically connected to the past, the selected flowers—chrysanthemum, plum, and narcissus—allude to the classical scholar-hermits Tao Yuanming, Lin Bu, and Zhao Mengjian, respectively.[3] Chen's image of a butterfly would have been recognized as a symbol of the ancient Daoist philosopher Zhuangzi, who dreamed of transforming into a butterfly.

In the album's three landscape paintings, Chen depicted autumnal lake scenery with a low horizon, which Southern Song painters especially favored.[4] Having studied with the famed landscape painter Lan Ying (cat. nos. 26–27), Chen was well aware of the landscape styles of the local Zhejiang tradition. His late-life residency by Hangzhou's West Lake, where the Southern Song court painters flourished, no doubt accentuated his appreciation for the fan and album-leaf landscapes by the Southern Song professional masters. Chen painted a number of lake-scenery landscapes in antique styles that resemble the three leaves in *Album for Monk Yu*. Some were presented to his friend Tang Jiujing, whom Wan-go Weng has speculated was the same person as the recipient of this album, the monk Tang Yu.[5]

Zhou Lianggong, who was one of Chen Hongshou's major patrons, once wrote: People "do not know that Chen's every brushstroke is based on precedent" 不知其筆筆有來歷.[6] Shortly before his death, Chen himself wrote a statement which encapsulates his distinctive archaism: "I, Old Lotus, therefore exhort the 'illustrious gentlemen' to study old masters and to examine Song painting exhaustively so as to arrive in the end at Yuan. I exhort the professional artists to model themselves on the Song masters but entreat them also to include Tang styles [in their studies]. If you truly immerse your mind in the Way, you will attain to the True Lineage [of painting]" 老蓮願名流學古人，博覽宋畫僅至於元．願作家法宋人乞帶唐人．果深心此道，得其正脉.[7] Chen clearly favored Song and pre-Song styles, and he openly denigrated the theories of Dong Qichang, the foremost artist and theorist of the late Ming who championed Yuan literati painting over that of the Song professionals. *Album for Monk Yu*, with its clear ties to the Southern Song court painters of an earlier Hangzhou, epitomizes Chen's unique interpretation of antique styles and his penchant for antiquity, asserting an alternative archaism to rival the dogmatic classicism of Dong.[8] **SWC**

For inscriptions and other documentation, see page 288 in this catalogue.

1 One that is particularly close, titled *Paintings after Ancient Masters* (Cleveland Museum of Art), was also created for a Daoist monk, thus supporting the hypothesis that the subjects of *Album for Monk Yu* were specifically chosen with the recipient in mind. The Cleveland album and a related album in the Nanjing Museum are reproduced in Wan-go Weng, *Chen Hongshou*, vol. 2, 276–307.

2 Anne Gail Burkus discusses the influence of Song painting on Chen's bird-and-flower painting in "The Artefacts of Biography," vol. 1, 314–23. For depicting birds, Chen singled out in particular Emperor Huizong of the Northern Song as a model. This appears in one of the leaves of the aforementioned Cleveland album.

3 In 1651 Chen painted these three flowers with the title *Three Hermits* and included an inscription that refers to Tao, Lin, and Zhao. Weng, *Chen Hongshou*, vol. 2, 262–63.

4 Chen states that he followed the landscape styles of Li Tang, Zhao Boju, and Zhao Lingrang in an album in the Palace Museum, Beijing. See Weng, *Chen Hongshou*, vol. 2, 158–65.

5 See Weng, *Chen Hongshou*, vol. 1, 88–89; vol. 2, 241; and vol. 3, 185.

6 Cited in Hongnam Kim, "Chou Liang-kung and his 'Tu-hua-lu' (Lives of Painters)," vol. 2, 42.

7 Chen Hongshou, *Baolun tang ji* 寶綸堂集, in *Qingdai shiwen ji huibian* 清代詩文集彙編 (Shanghai: Shanghai guji chubanshe, 2009), vol. 11, 694. Translation from Cahill, *The Distant Mountains*, 265.

8 Wen Fong sees Chen's art as primitive archaism, compared to Dong Qichang's classicism. See Wen C. Fong, "Archaism as a 'Primitive' Style," 89–109.

23 Chen Hongshou 陳洪綬
1599–1652

Album for Monk Yu 唐豫老雜畫冊
C. 1650
Honolulu Museum of Art
Purchase

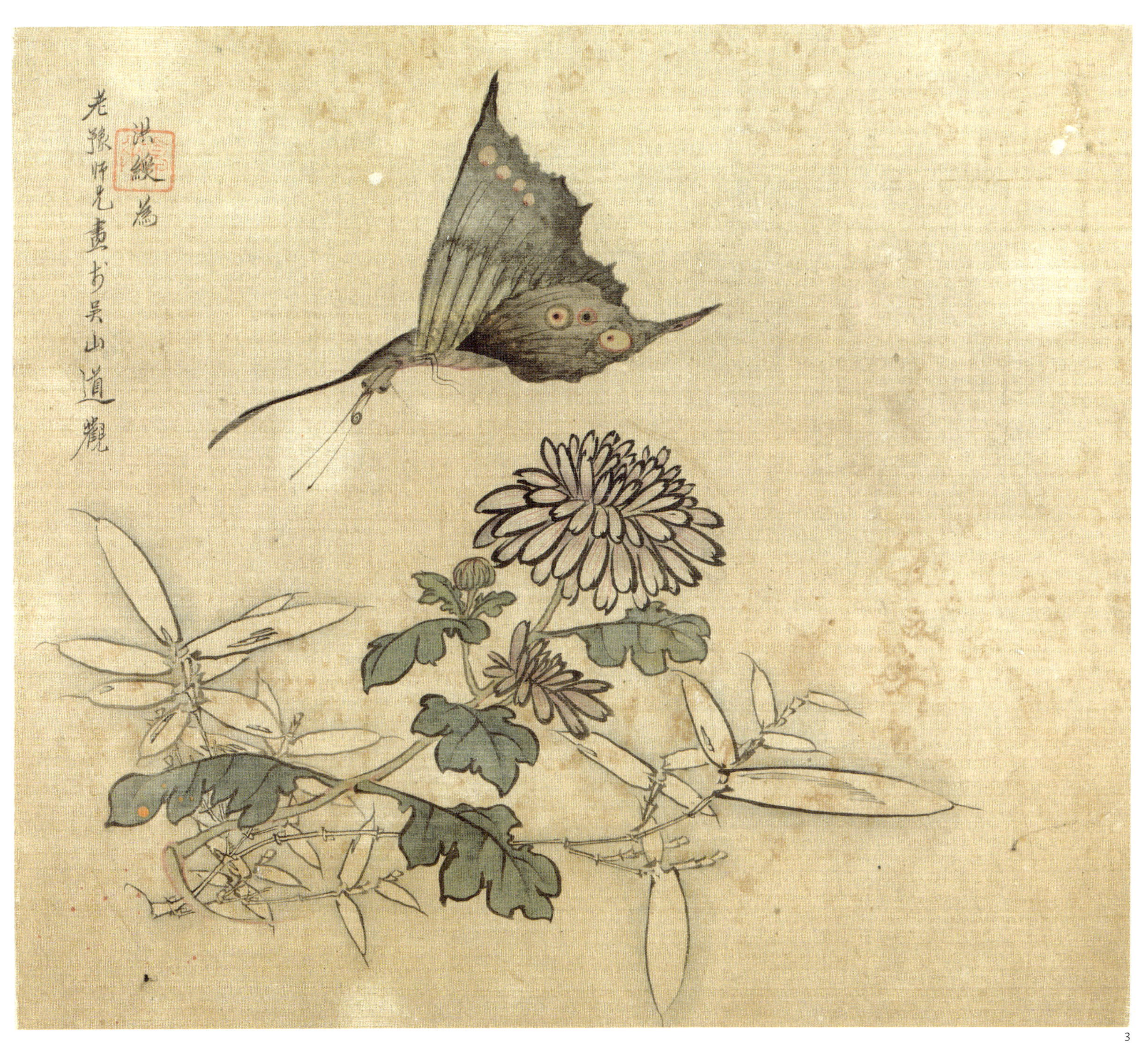

3

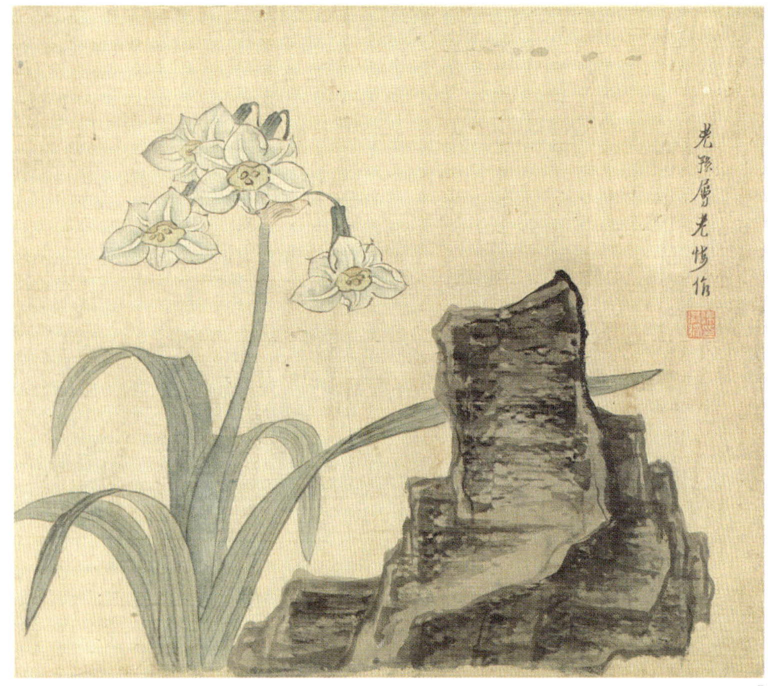

5

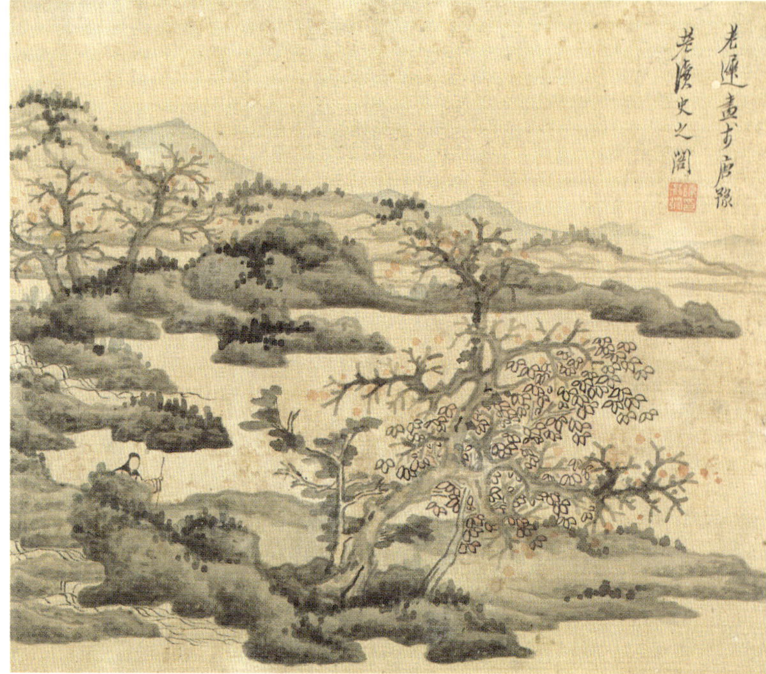

4

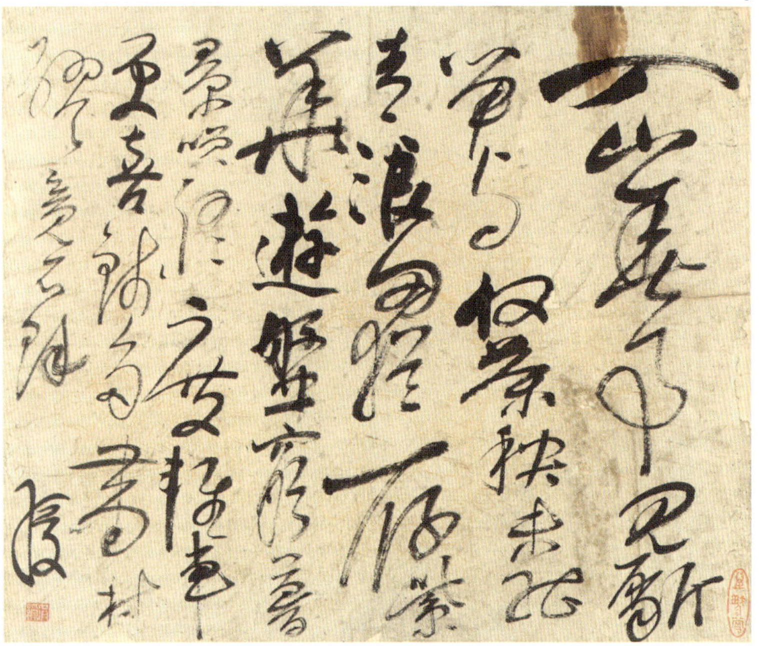

9

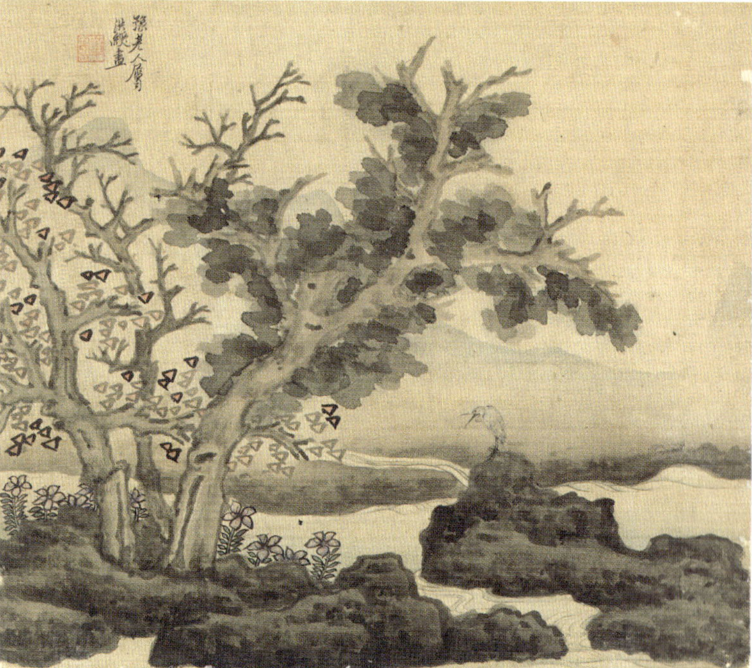

8

Entering the mountains, spring matters are presented:
Cut bamboo shoots and harvest tea.
Rice seedlings not yet ready to form green waves,
Fields still possess purple florescence.
Carousing throughout the evening scene,
With laughing chatter our light carriage passes.
Even happier with lots of cash to carry,
Village wine in the end all consumed!

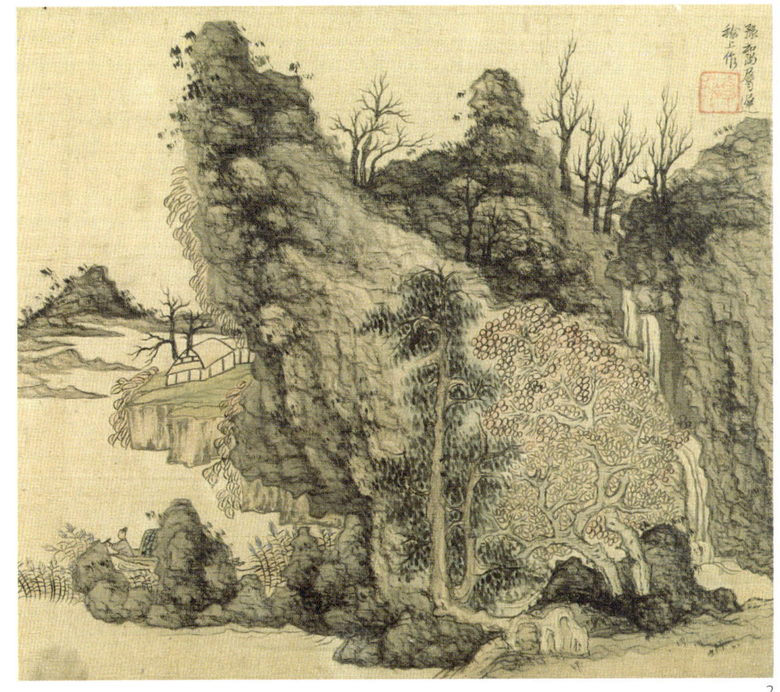

2

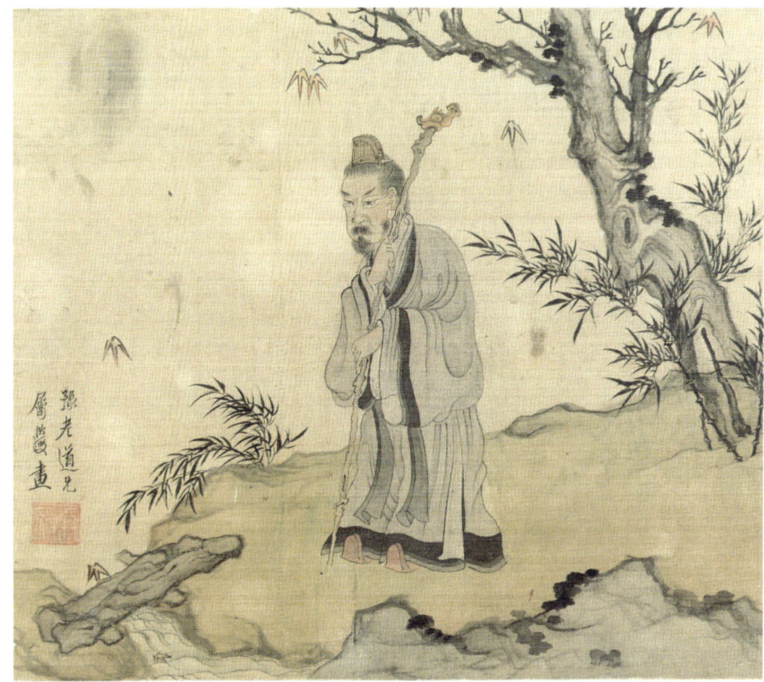

1

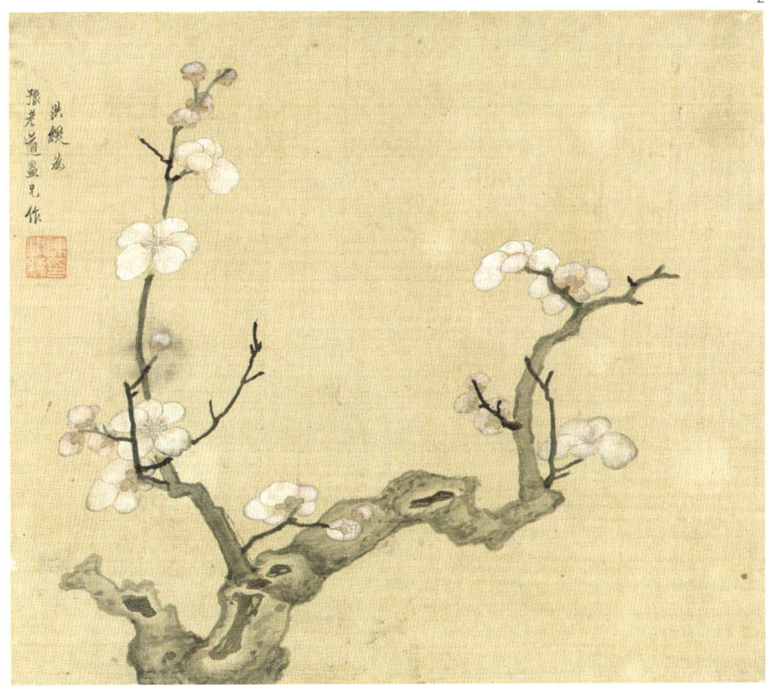

7

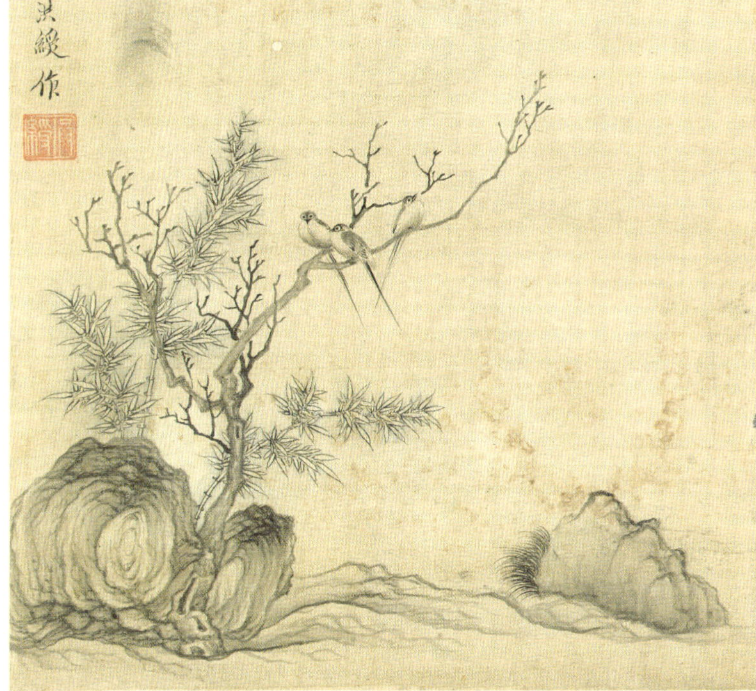

6

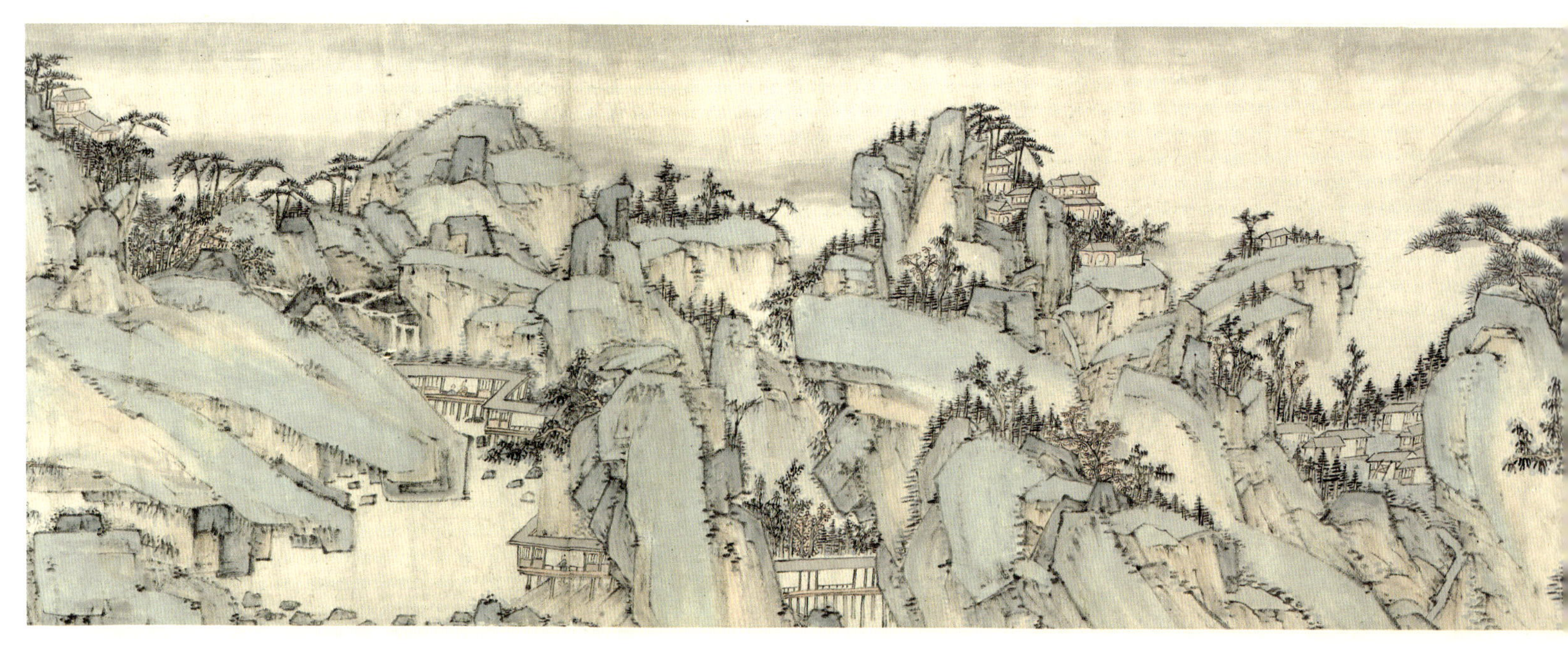

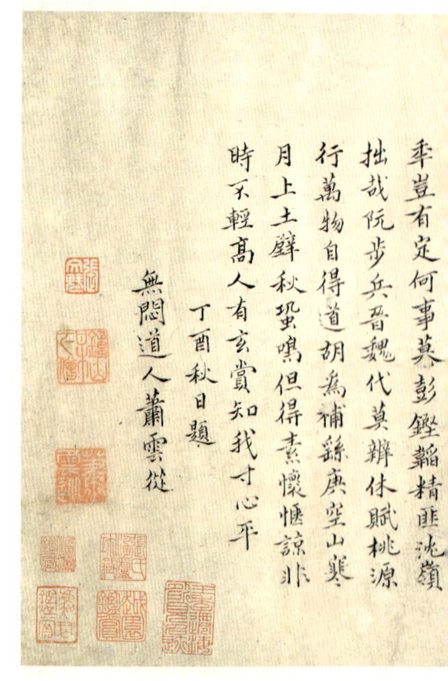
秊豈有定何事羨彭鏗錙精匪沈嶺
拙哉阮步兵晉魏代莫辨休賦桃源
行萬物自得道胡為補綠庾空山寒
月上土壁秋蛩鳴但得素懷愜諒非
時不輕高人有玄賞知我寸心平
丁酉秋日題
無悶道人蕭雲從

24 Xiao Yuncong 蕭雲從
1596–1673

Landscape 設色山水圖卷
1657
Private collection

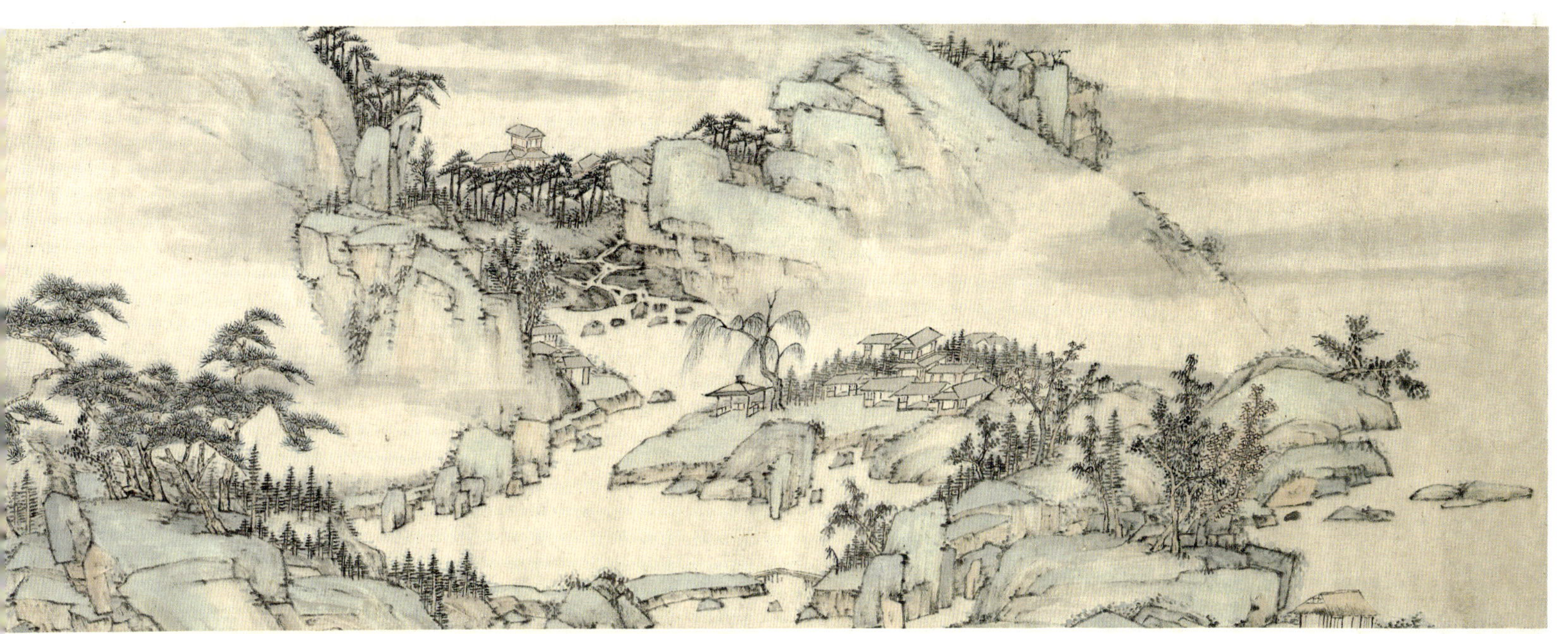

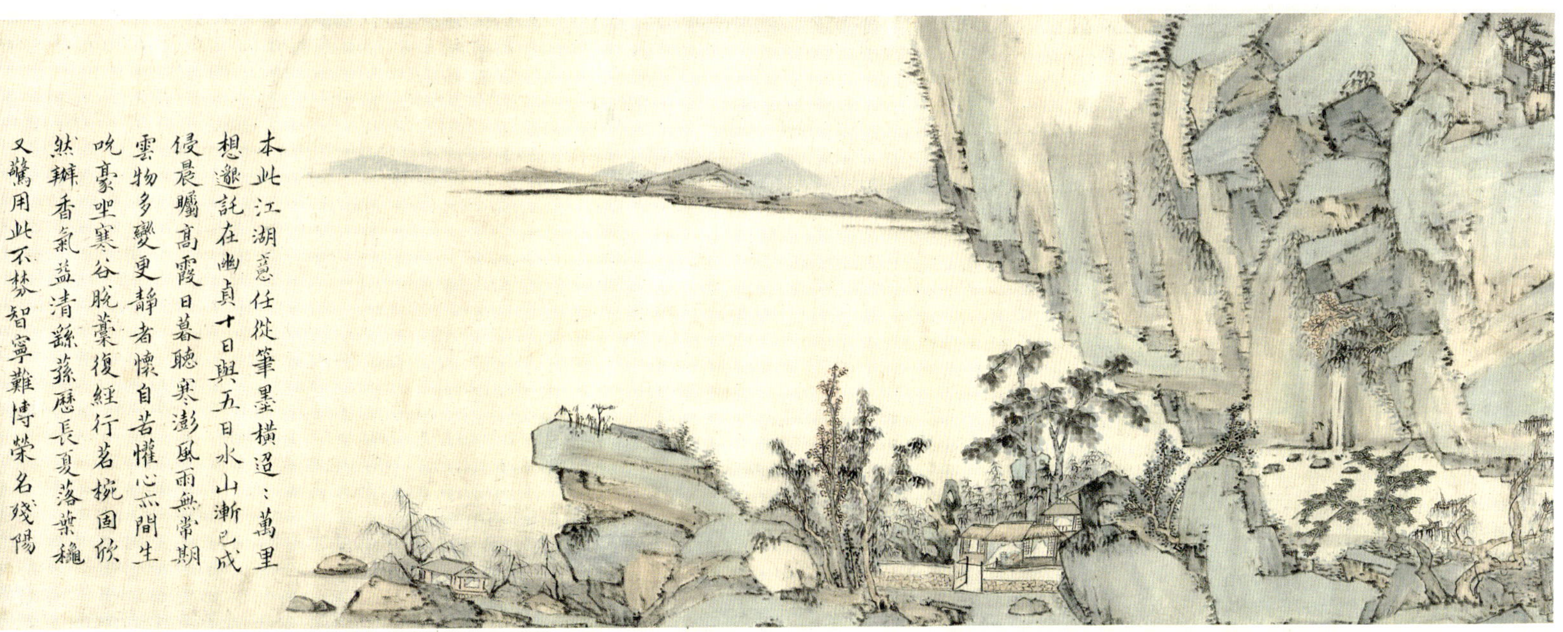

Rooted in my feelings for river and lake,
I release my brush and ink to freely flow!
Far, far, thoughts of ten thousand miles:
Distantly entrusted to a realm of chaste reclusion
"Ten days" then "five days":
Rivers and mountains gradually taking form.
At crack of dawn I gaze at towering mists;
At sunset listen to the cold gurgling of streams.

Wind and rain have no fixed seasons;
Cloud-forms have many permutations.
In quietude, yet I harbor suffering;
Even happy, I question this life of ours.
Sucking my brush, I sit in the chilly valley;
Draft completed, go out for a stroll again...

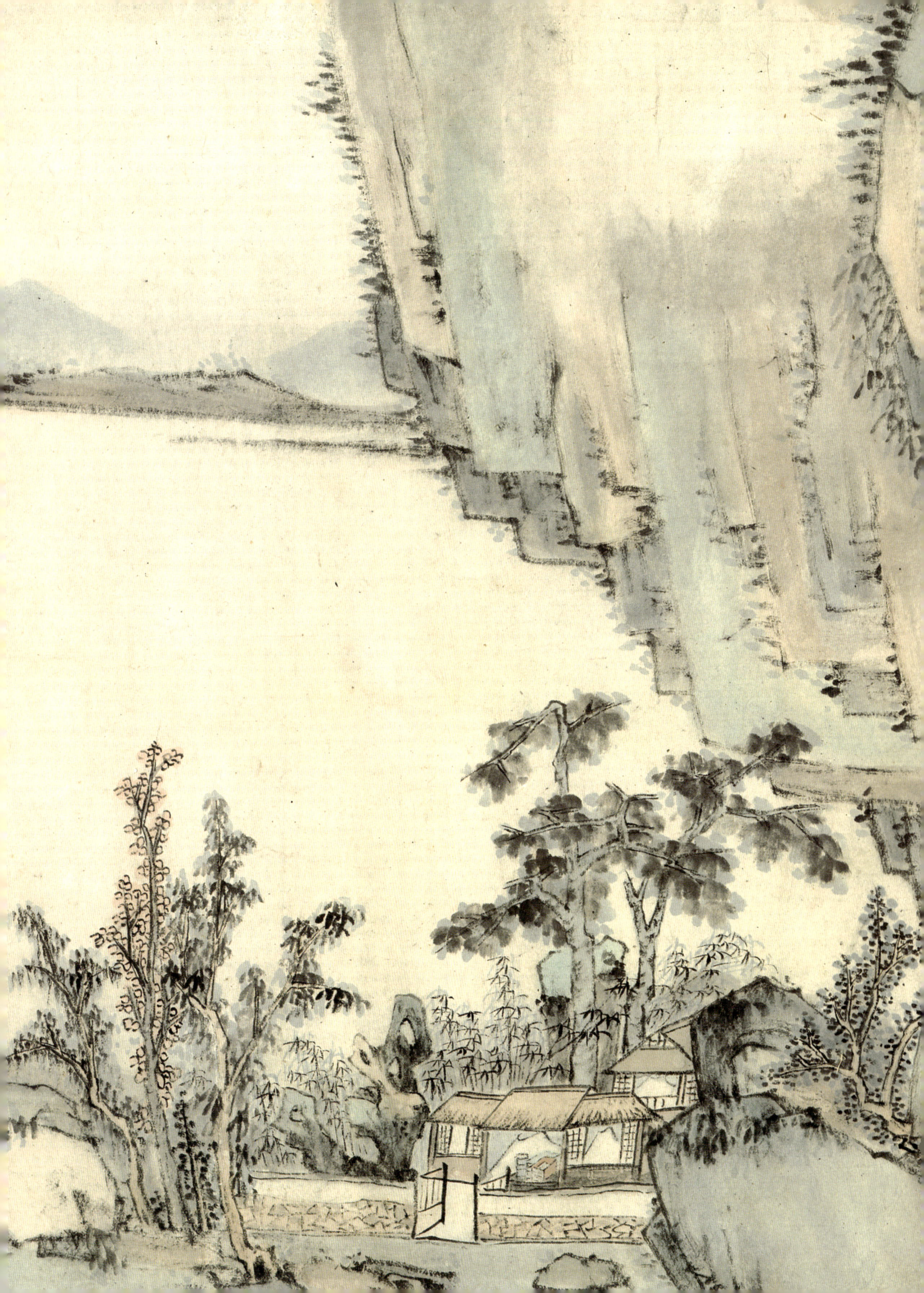

Xiao Yuncong's ambitions to initiate a career as an official were first thwarted by his failure to pass the first-level examinations in the late years of the Ming dynasty and then destroyed by the cataclysmic events of 1644. Fleeing from Manchu troops a year later, Xiao abandoned his home at Wuhu (Anhui Province) and relied upon his artistic skills to survive.[1] He illustrated a number of printed books, including *Illustrations to "Encountering Sorrow"* (*Li sao tu* 離騷圖, fig. 29) of 1645 and *Illustrations of Taiping Prefecture* (*Taiping shanshui tu* 太平山水圖) of 1648.[2] While his woodblock illustrations were influential, most of his fame was gained from landscape paintings created during the 1650 and 60s. Possessing strong loyalist sentiment, Xiao developed a particular skill in depicting panoramic views of mountains and rivers that carried the viewer into an ideal world removed from the difficult reality of the early years of the Qing. As his poem on this delicate landscape of 1657 reveals, painting offered an opportunity to escape, a chance to create a place of chaste reclusion and distant thoughts.

On an album of paintings depicting the scenery of Yellow Mountain (Huangshan, Anhui), Xiao Yuncong wrote, "Traveling to mountains and rivers seems to be my destiny" 山水之遊，似有前緣.[3] The natural scenery near the Yangzi River of Anhui where he was born provided him with much of the artistic inspiration for his landscape paintings. In the late Ming, traveling to scenic places became a trend, and subsequently the production of topographical landscapes and travel accounts grew in popularity among scholar-artists. This was particularly true in southern Anhui, where a group of artists collectively known as the Xin'an School drew from the local scenery for inspiration and subject matter, especially Yellow Mountain.[4] This included Xiao Yuncong, whose keen interest in depicting his hometown's natural environs is evidenced in *Illustrations of Taiping Prefecture*, for which he made forty-three designs of regional landscapes.

In this handscroll composition mountain peaks rise and fall, intermingled with rushing streams and cascading waterfalls before giving way to a river vista at the end. A variety of trees, mostly pines, are scattered throughout the landscape. Houses, pavilions, and a temple complex nestle comfortably in the hills and valleys. Where the mountain ends at the riverbank, Xiao displays a scholar's abode surrounded by bamboo, *wutong* (firmiana) trees, and a few oddly shaped Lake Tai garden rocks. The open gate leads us further to the left, where a final riverside pavilion sits by willow trees next to Xiao Yuncong's long poem. In contrast to the unpopulated landscapes of other Anhui painters, such as Hongren and Zha Shibiao (cat. no. 49), Xiao often introduces human presence into his scenes. This landscape possesses an elegant, comfortable tone colored by a distinctively cool palette of blue, green, and ocher washes. The brushwork is dry and light, emulating in mood the distinctive style of the Yuan-dynasty master Ni Zan (see fig. 4), who was revered by the Anhui painters. Xiao's use of the blue-green mode, together with his stylized approach to rendering landscape forms, adds an archaistic touch that helps transform the Anhui scenery into an idealized portrayal of nature.[5]

The serenity of the landscape transitions into a solemn, poignant poem, written in Xiao's refined, small standard-script calligraphy based on a classical style associated with the fourth-century master Wang Xizhi.[6] The poem conveys nostalgic sentiments, utilizing the autumnal season as a reminder of the inevitable passage of time. Although Xiao is unspecific, we can be certain that what grieves him, his "inner suffering," must be the fate of the Ming dynasty. Mention of the renowned recluse Ruan Ji of the historic Wei-Jin dynastic transition reflects on Xiao's own experience as a "leftover subject" (*yimin*) of the Ming dynasty.[7] Most telling is Xiao's allusion to Tao Yuanming's famous story of the Peach Blossom Spring. This is a recurring theme in Xiao's approach to landscape—the suggestion of an idyllic, timeless place removed from the ills of the present. Xiao Yuncong's determined creation of a landscape that offers solace and escape in a vernacular that also recalls the familiar landscape of the Yangzi River area must have provided a source of comfort to his *yimin* compatriots while also eliciting a sense of nostalgia and longing for their lost world. **SWC**

For inscriptions and other documentation, see page 289 in this catalogue.

1 Xiao Yuncong's home Plum Blossom Studio (Meizhu) was destroyed by the Qing army, and his anguish over this tragic event is well expressed in his poem "Moving My Residence" ("Yiju shi" 移居詩) in Huang Yue 黃鉞, comp., *Xiao Tang erlao yishi hebian* 蕭湯二老遺詩合編, in *Yi zhai ji* 壹齋集 (Wuhu: Xu shi, 1859–63), 5a.

2 For a detailed study of the Taiping illustrations, see Seojeong Shin, "Illustrations of Taiping Prefecture (1648)." For *Illustrations of "Encountering Sorrow"*, see Xiao Yuncong, *Li sao tu*, in *Mingdai banhua congkan* 明代版畫叢刊 5 (Taipei: Guoli Gugong bowuyuan, 1988).

3 Cited in Shin, "Illustrations of Taiping Prefecture," 47.

4 James Cahill, "Huang Shan Paintings as Pilgrimage Pictures," 246–92. The Anhui School was the primary subject of a 1981 exhibition and catalogue, *Shadows of Mt. Huang*, edited by Cahill. For Xiao Yuncong's 1656 depiction of a place he had visited, see Chu-tsing Li, *A Thousand Peaks and Myriad Ravines*, vol. 1, 172–79.

5 On Xiao's study of the ancient paintings, see Huang Yue 黃鉞, *Huayou lu* 畫友錄, in Yu Anlan 于安瀾, ed., *Huashi congshu* 畫史叢書 (Taipei: Wenshizhe chubanshe, 1974), 1–17.

6 Xiao was also a prolific poet, and most of his paintings bear his own poems. Some of them were collected in *Xiao Tang erlao yishi hebian*.

7 By using the seal of his sobriquet *Zhongshan meixia seng* (A monk under the plum tree in Mount Zhong), Xiao implies his identity as a loyalist. Mount Zhong, where the Ming founder's mausoleum is located, was a symbolic place for the Ming loyalists.

The solitary fisherman plying his line in a secluded waterway removed from the dust of worldly affairs is one of the oldest and most familiar of all images of reclusion in China, but rarely is it so effectively presented as in this hanging scroll by Zhang Xuezeng. Hidden under a hat, his back to the viewer, and facing the open expanse of a lake, the angler focuses solely on his fishing rod and the simple task of catching dinner. Or not: one of the common conceits associated with the sage-fisherman of Daoist lore is that his detachment is so profound that there is no concern about the fruits of his labor. Much of the effectiveness of Zhang's presentation resides in the poetic inscription he added at the upper left. The cited "new lines" by a Master Jian succinctly capture the allure of the fisherman-recluse as well as the reverence with which he was held. Poem and painting assign an ideal existence to the fisherman's simple boat. Living the life of emotional detachment, fortune and misfortune are meaningless, the passage of time as well. To whom can the fisherman-recluse be compared? The strength of his moral superiority exceeds the power of a great warrior.

Master Jian in all likelihood refers to Jianjiang, better known by his Buddhist name Hongren.[1] One of the most important painters of the Ming-Qing transition, and the leading figure among artists collectively known as the Xin'an School associated with southern Anhui Province, Hongren is believed to have been a staunch loyalist of the fallen Ming dynasty. He was also a noted poet. Although the two lines cited by Zhang are not recorded in what remains of Hongren's literary works, their description of a fisherman whose moral strength surpasses that of a mighty general accords with the sentiments of a Ming loyalist living in the traumatic years of the early Qing.[2]

Relatively few details are known regarding Zhang Xuezeng's life, and, as earlier connoisseurs often remarked, his paintings are rarely encountered. Compounding the paucity of material and textual remains is the fact that Zhang deeply subscribed to the orthodox theories of Dong Qichang (cat. nos. 8–9), resulting in paintings that to modern viewers often appear too constrained by adherence to past models to merit attention. However, there is no question that Zhang was one of the more significant painters of his time. He was famously grouped with Dong and a number of his followers as one of the Nine Friends of Painting by the noted poet Wu Weiye.[3] Wu's label implies a social orientation to this set of late-Ming painters. The recent emergence of a handscroll titled *Collective Landscapes by Four Sages* 四賢山水合卷 corroborates this perspective. The scroll comprises four small landscapes by late-Ming painters, including three of the Nine Friends—Wang Shimin, Yang Wencong, and Zhang Xuezeng (the fourth is by Yun Xiang).[4] The four individual scenes were all painted in 1638 for Yang Bu. Zhang Xuezeng's inscription describes a serendipitous encounter of old friends Yang Bu and Yang Wencong at the home of Yun Xiang while traveling between Beijing and the Yangzi River area (Wang Shimin, another comrade, added his scene two months later). Zhang appears as a socially connected scholar-official busily engaged with his official career in the very late years of the Ming. What makes this collective work particularly interesting is a second inscription added by Zhang seventeen years later in 1655. The world had been turned upside down; Yang Wencong and Yun Xiang were already dead, and Zhang had accepted the position of prefect of Suzhou in 1654, serving the new Qing dynasty. He wanted to meet with Yang Bu, who was living in reclusion in the environs of Suzhou, but Yang, resolute in his loyalty to the Ming, refused to enter the city. It was only after Zhang relinquished his post the following year that the two old friends were able to meet and Zhang could revisit this memento of friendship and artistic ideals from before the fall of the dynasty and add his second inscription. *Collective Landscapes by Four Sages* and its inscriptions provide a valuable perspective on Zhang Xuezeng. At first willing to work with the Manchu court, he felt conflicted and after only a year resigned from his position. In all likelihood, *Fisherman Recluse* was painted around this time, circa 1655.[5] As such, Zhang's "inspiration" was not simply a matter of appreciating Hongren's poetic talents. The fisherman's solitude and moral strength must have been genuine ideals.

Fisherman Recluse is a paean to the masters of Yuan-dynasty painting, none revered more than Wu Zhen, who often utilized the image of the fisherman to express the ideal of existing among rivers and lakes in a "leaf-like" skiff untarnished by the affairs of the world. Like the other "Friends of Painting," Zhang Xuezeng was especially familiar with Yuan-dynasty styles and felt comfortable exploring their nuances. The overall density of Wu's wet mode of brushwork is balanced by both the range of textures and an effective use of the paper's open expanse. Simple on the surface, the painting's familiar theme belies Zhang's deep engagement with his subject. It is a noteworthy reflection of the painting's quality that in the eighteenth century it was owned by Miao Yuezao, one of the most discerning of collectors active in the mid-Qing dynasty. **MH/PCS**

For inscriptions and other documentation, see page 289 in this catalogue.

1 Hongren is often referred to as Master Jian by later figures, such as Huang Binhong, who was repeating earlier precedents. The earliest biographical records of Hongren, written by contemporaries, typically refer to him as Great Master, Lord Jian 大師漸公, or Master Jianjiang 漸江師. See Wang Shiqing 汪世清, *Jianjiang ziliao ji*, 3–16.

2 For a collection of Hongren's extant poetry see Wang, ibid., 29–57. Hongren left his native Shexian (Anhui) after the fall of the city to the Manchus in 1645. His close association with Wang Muri, who was a noted loyalist, and their journey that year to Fujian, where one of the Ming princes had established an independent regime, strongly imply Hongren's loyalty to the Ming. See Jason C. Kuo, *The Austere Landscape*, 3–4.

3 In addition to Dong, the others are Cheng Jiasui, Li Liufang, Bian Wenyu, Yang Wencong, Wang Shimin, Wang Jian, and Shao Mi.

4 See the catalogue for the Xiling yinshe 西泠印社 spring auction of 2007, titled *Zhongguo shuhua gudai zuopin zhuanchang* 中國書畫古代作品專場 (Hangzhou, 2007), no. 138.

5 Zhang Xuezeng's calligraphy, which is primarily based on the style of Su Shi, presents a rougher, less delicate appearance in the inscription of 1655 compared to that of 1638 on the scroll for Yang Bu. Supporting a date of circa 1655 for *Fisherman Recluse* are Zhang's *Landscape After Dong Yuan* of 1654, reproduced in Richard M. Barnhart, et al., *The Jade Studio*, cat. no. 35; and *Landscape in the Manner of Wu Zhen* (Palace Museum, Beijing), also of 1654, reproduced in Wai-kam Ho, ed., *The Century of Tung Ch'i-ch'ang*, vol. 1, pl. 106.

25 Zhang Xuezeng 張學曾
Act. c. 1633–1657

Fisherman Recluse **山水軸**
Private collection

Reincarnated, mystifying return: a single
fisherman's skiff;
Don't speak of fortune or misfortune; don't record
the years.
The general at the head of his troops wears
a thousand layers of armor,
But these cannot match in strength the half collar
of the [fisherman's] green coir jacket.

Reciting these pure new lines of Master Jian,
I cannot help but be inspired. Thus I have sketched
this in order to find outlet for my stimulation.

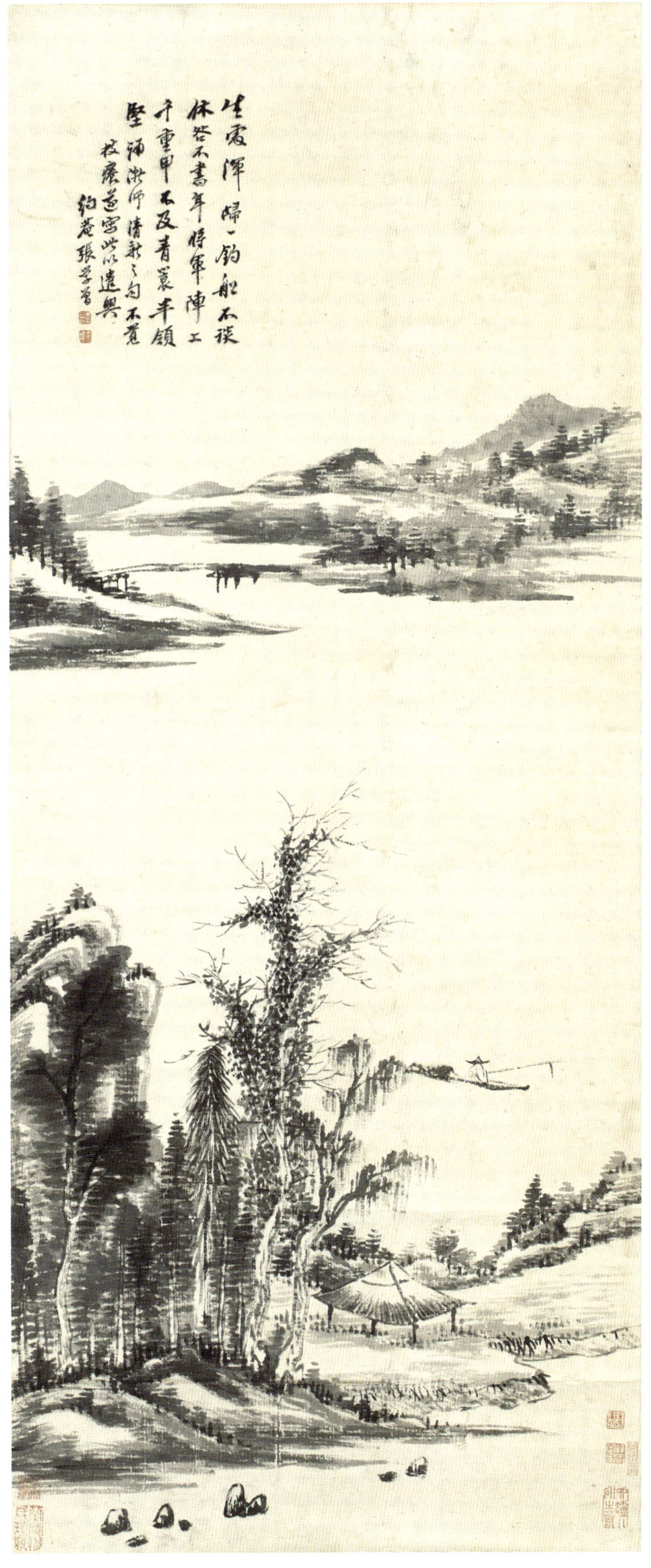

Lan Ying's awkward historical position as a painter bridging the professional and amateur worlds in China is well exemplified by this late and impressive landscape in the style of Huang Gongwang (sobriquet Dachi [Great Fool]). An inventive and highly prolific painter, Lan produced hundreds of skilled, polished paintings in a variety of genres. In content and style, however, many of his paintings, including this landscape, reveal an approach that aspired to the literati tradition as it had come to be defined during the artist's lifetime.

Born and raised in Hangzhou, a city that had been associated with the practice of painting at its highest level of professionalism since the twelfth century when it was home to the Southern Song imperial court, Lan began by learning from local professionals the Song academic painting style as it had developed over the centuries. He proceeded to travel widely, broadening his knowledge of various artistic styles and ultimately becoming acquainted with the prominent literati artists of Suzhou and Songjiang, most notably Dong Qichang (cat. nos. 8–9) and Chen Jiru (cat. nos. 11–12).[1] The latter two impressed upon Lan the importance of the Yuan-dynasty masters, as well as an approach to the practice of painting that entailed assiduously studying and copying genuine works by the old masters and applying the lessons learned to one's own efforts. His association with this circle, and his growing reputation as a master painter, must have provided access to important private collections in the Jiangnan region, including Suzhou, Songjiang, and Hangzhou. By the 1620s and 30s, his own mature style of painting was fully recognized and admired, and he was especially productive during the last decade of the Ming dynasty. There is evidence that suggests Lan became a Daoist recluse in the early years of the Qing dynasty, but whatever reclusion he practiced ultimately did not affect his overall production.[2] By the end of his lifetime he had established a highly successful atelier, which included his son, Lan Meng, and two grandsons, Lan Shen and Lan Tao, as well as numerous students.[3]

While Lan Ying expressed a healthy latitude in his practice of imitating the ancients (*fanggu* 仿古), extant works reveal that the Huang Gongwang style was one that he practiced regularly (and occasionally with spectacular success) throughout his career.[4] Lan Ying was familiar with Huang's masterpiece *Dwelling in the Fuchun Mountains* (National Palace Museum, Taipei), which had been owned by Dong Qichang, but Lan's later work, including this painting in the vertical format, may well have been more influenced by another well-known Huang composition. In the facing inscription to a leaf in Huang's style for an album of 1655 titled *Contemplating the Dao with Emotions Cleansed*, Lan writes that he studied Huang's *Stone Cliff at Heavenly Pond*, a composition known today from later copies.[5] Discussing the art of composing a landscape, Lan begins the inscription with the following observation: "When painters of the Song and Yuan composed landscapes, they focused on having the hills and valleys tightly dense and the mountains and peaks precipitous. Mists and clouds were not simply to suggest empty spaces, but rather the emphasis was on their enwrapping of trees and foliage" 宋元諸畫家作山水章法，意在丘壑遵密，峰巒峻峭，寫煙雲不輕為空隙，強以繞掩林莽.

This passage well encapsulates Huang Gongwang's reputation as a painter who could grasp the full sweeping grandeur of landscape and re-create its spatial dimensions on silk or paper. Something of that ability is demonstrated in *Stone Cliff at Heavenly Pond*, which brings the viewer's eye down into a wooded mountain valley before climbing a magnificent, snaking set of serried hills. Lan Ying's *Autumn Landscape in the Style of Huang Gongwang* preserves the general idea of Huang's composition, though in an abbreviated form. The broad, shifting movements of Huang's mountain forms are duplicated, as well as such notable motifs as the stilt-raised dwellings, textured slopes of hemp-fiber strokes, and clumping boulders. Most of the landscape elements are pushed to the right side of the scroll, which opens up the left side's distant view necessary for highlighting the two seated figures in the foreground. These figures, which add a thoughtful intimacy to the painting, are one of Lan's primary additions to the interpretation.[6] This narrative element is a standard feature in Lan's landscape paintings and no doubt suited the tastes of his many patrons, who had come to expect such self-identifying figures through the work of the Suzhou literati masters Shen Zhou and Wen Zhengming, as well as their many followers. Lan Ying's other addition is the casualness of his brush mode, approaching what is often characterized as *xieyi* 寫意, "the sketching of ideas." Relaxed and unpretentious in appearance yet executed with remarkable proficiency, Lan's brushwork melds the ostensibly antithetical worlds of the amateur scholar and the skillful professional. **YJS / PCS**

For inscriptions and other documentation, see page 289 in this catalogue.

1 Lan Ying traveled to Guangdong, Fujian, and a number of northern provinces before returning to the Jiangnan region, where he gained the esteem of Dong Qichang, Chen Jiru, and Sun Kehong, among others. His paintings from the 1630s bear colophons by Dong, Chen, Yang Wencong, and other late-Ming cognoscenti of the Songjiang reigon. Yan, *Lan Ying yu fanggu huihua*, 6–13; L. Carrington Goodrich and Chaoying Fang, eds., *Dictionary of Ming Biography, 1368–1644*, vol. 1, 786; and *Kaikodo Journal* 19 (Spring 2001): 270.

2 Lan Ying figures prominently in the well-known play *Peach Blossom Fan*, written by Kong Shangren in 1699. In it, he departs in 1645 to study the Dao in Clouds' Roost Hills, east of Hangzhou. Howard Rogers points out that after 1645, Lan signed a number of paintings "Lan the Daoist." *Masterworks of Ming and Qing Painting*, 148.

3 Forty years after Lan Ying's death, Gao Qipei, the renowned finger-painting specialist, commented on the successive generations of master painters that flourished in the region, including the earlier Zhe School painters Dai Jin and Lü Ji, leading up to Lan and his various followers. Ibid.

4 Lan Ying's biographers comment on the importance of the Huang Gongwang style in his art. See, for example, Xu Qin 徐沁, *Ming hua lu* 明畫錄 (Taipei: Yiwen yinshuguan, 1968), 5:5; and *Tuhui baojian xuzuan* 圖繪寶鑑續纂 (*Huashi congshu* ed.), 2:14. Lan writes of having studied Huang's style for almost thirty years in inscriptions he added to handscroll paintings modeled after Huang of 1638 and 1639. Yan, *Lan Ying yu fanggu huihua*, 6. See also James Cahill, *The Distant Mountains*, 181.

5 *Zhongguo gudai shuhua tumu* (1986), vol. 1, 17. The painting is in the Palace Museum, Beijing.

6 Another rendition of this theme painted in the same year, 1656, came up in a recent auction (China Guardian, Beijing, Autumn 2009, no. 1546). For this painting, titled *Pure Conversation in Pine Valley*, Lan Ying used the style of Li Cheng rather than Huang Gongwang.

26 Lan Ying 藍瑛
1585–1664 or later

Autumn Landscape in the Style of Huang Gongwang 法大癡老人山水
1656

Santa Barbara Museum of Art
Gift of Peggy Maximus

Modeled after the painting of Dachi [Huang Gongwang] on an autumn day of the bingshen *year [1656] at the Chengqu Thatched Hall.*

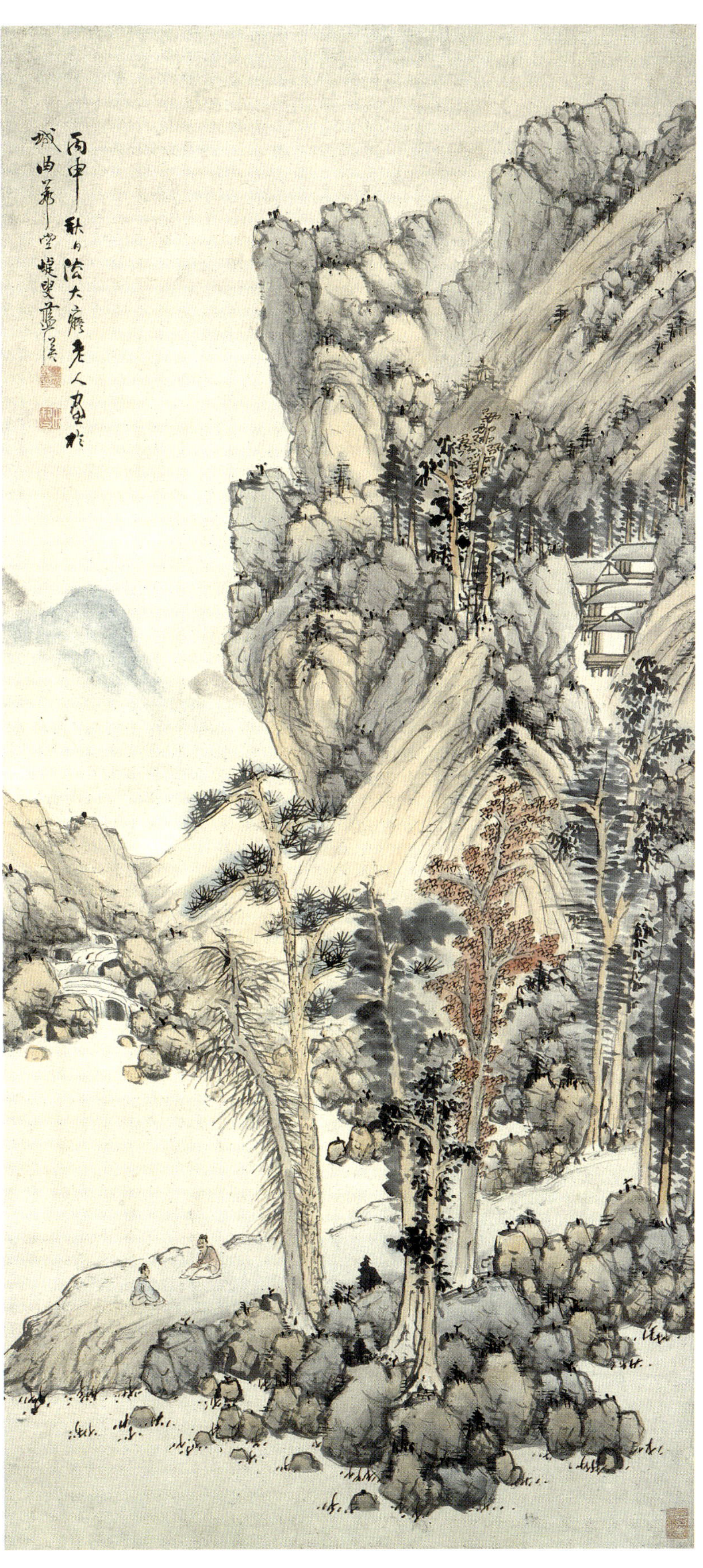

In this painting Lan Ying presents an image of an isolated ornamental rock, colorfully tinted with green and ochre pigments that accompany the modulated textures of the artist's brilliant brush and ink. The left side of the rock possesses an interesting tension between the colors, which provide a sense of spatial recession, and the strong ink contours, which pull the image forward from the two-dimensional surface of the paper. The variety of the painting's brushwork—its speed, textures, and dynamics—lies at the core of Lan's presentation: a small but compact display of literati aesthetics.

According to Lan Ying's inscription at the upper left, the rock depicted was originally owned by the great literati artist and connoisseur Mi Fu of the Song dynasty. Mi's Bao-Jin Studio (Studio for Treasuring the Jin) was named after the prized Jin-dynasty (265–420) painting and calligraphy that he assiduously collected over many decades.[1] Traces of Mi's residences, located in Zhenjiang (Jiangsu Province), still existed in the seventeenth century. More significantly, the rich lore of Mi's experiences with art lived on in the many anecdotes recorded in popular miscellany.[2] A number of these recounted his passion for unusual rocks, including a particularly popular one in which he, when serving in office in Wuwei (Anhui Province), encountered a specimen so wonderful that he kowtowed to it and said, "I have been longing to meet Elder Brother Rock for twenty years" 吾欲見石兄二十年矣.[3] It is unlikely that Lan Ying was depicting a genuine rock that had once been owned by Mi, but whether actual or imaginary, the subject of his painting possessed historical layers that provided meaning for a scholarly audience.

Lan Ying was one of a number of painters who depicted garden and ornamental rocks in the seventeenth century, reflecting a general interest in rocks as objects of appreciation and collecting in late-Ming China. Rocks were almost always included as high-status objects in popular contemporary writings that ranked collectible things.[4] For example, in Li Rihua's *Weishui xuan riji* 味水軒日記 (Diary from the Pavilion for Tasting Water), "strange rocks of a rugged and picturesque type" were numbered sixteenth in his ranking of antique objects, and Wen Zhenheng allotted one chapter to explain "water and rocks" in his *Zhang wu zhi* 長物志 (Treatise on superfluous things).[5]

Rocks were important objects that could represent, like painting and calligraphy, an owner's taste. The primary aesthetic criteria to appreciate rocks are neatly demonstrated in Lan's rock painting: leanness (*shou* 瘦), surface texture (*zhou* 皺), and foraminate structure (*lou/tou* 漏/透).[6] The rock in this painting reveals a narrow-waisted, contorted configuration; wrinkles (depicted with dry brush textures); and five differently sized cavities. Eroded and sculpted by nature's forces, rocks were thought to possess condensed natural energy within,[7] and the three aesthetic criteria were thought of as qualities of this inner force. Leanness describes the state in which the interior power retains visible control over the exterior configuration, so that the form of the rock exhibits energy's pattern. Similarly, the wrinkle patterns on the surface of the rock provide visual form to erupting energy from the rock's interior. The foraminate structure draws the viewer into that interior. By presenting through brushwork that bespeaks scholar-painting intentions a rock that clearly embodies these aesthetic criteria and possesses historical reference to Mi Fu, Lan Ying demonstrated the particular taste that was so highly valued in the antiquarian culture of the period. **HSY**

For inscriptions and other documentation, see page 290 in this catalogue.

1 Xiang Shang 向尙, "Wuwei Baojinzhai beitie moji kaolu" 無爲寶晉齋碑帖墨蹟考錄, *Journal of Chaohu College* 巢湖學院學報, vol. 92 (2008): 69–73.

2 A number of these are discussed and translated in Peter C. Sturman, *Mi Fu*, 212–24.

3 Fei Gun 費袞, *Liangxi manzhi* 梁溪漫志, in *Wenyuange Siku quanshu* 文淵閣四庫全書 (Taipei: Taiwan Shangwu yinshuguan, 1983–86), vol. 116, 735. See Sturman, *Mi Fu*, 224, for a translation of another version of this anecdote. According to Edward Schafer, Emperor Huizong inherited a number of Mi Fu's rocks and installed them in his Genyue Park. Edward H. Schafer, "Cosmos in Miniature," 24–26.

4 Craig Clunas, *Superfluous Things*, 8–39.

5 Ibid., 41 and 105.

6 John Hay, "Structure and Aesthetic Criteria in Chinese Rocks and Art," 5–22.

7 Lothar Ledderose, "The Earthly Paradise," 165–83.

27 Lan Ying 藍瑛
1585–1664 or later

***Rock* 寶晉齋石**
Private collection

One of the rocks from the collection of the Bao-Jin Studio.

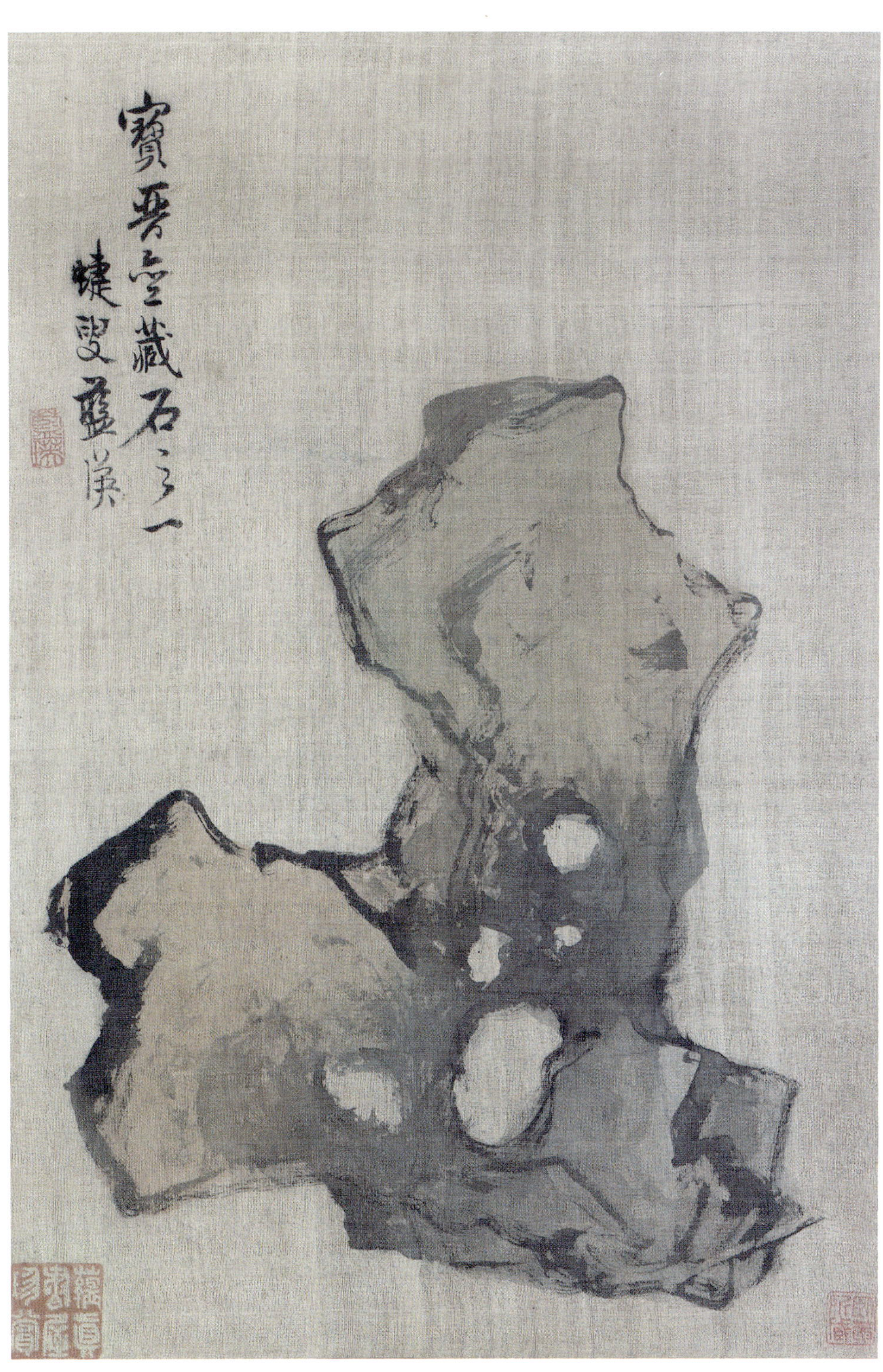

To date, no other painting by the seventeenth-century artist Zhang Zhengyue has surfaced, making this handsome blue-green–style landscape an extremely rare object. He is a largely unknown figure, and vexing problems remain in establishing his exact identification. For example, while there is no recorded entry on Zhang Zhengyue in standard biographical resources for the Qing dynasty, there are for Zhang Zhenyue 張振岳; Zhenyue appears in one of the artist's seals on this painting, where it may indicate a style name (*zi* 字) or sobriquet (*hao* 號).[1] Either the artist changed his name, substituting Zheng 正 for Zhen 振, or the few texts that comment on Zhang Zhengyue record his sobriquet as given name (Songgao, which appears in another seal on the painting, is recorded as the artist's style name). Another question concerns the place of origin that Zhang records with his signature on this painting. Xiangxi presumably refers to the Xiang River, which would make Zhang Zhengyue a native of the lush southern landscape of Hunan or Jiangxi Province. Yet the texts record Zhang Zhenyue as a native of Xiaoshan, the prefecture northwest of Shaoxing in Zhejiang Province.[2]

Such discrepancies are not unusual for a relatively unknown painter, especially one whose primary status may have been as a professional. Biographical information is rarely recorded in detail for those who were not officials or notable men of letters, and what is recorded is often mistaken—such as the character of a name or a place of origin. We can hypothesize that while Zhang's ancestral roots were further south, his family hailed in more recent generations from Xiaoshan, just across the river from the city of Hangzhou. Proximity to Hangzhou would have allowed for him to be introduced to the luminous heritage of professional painting that had flourished in the city since the twelfth century. The short accounts of Zhang all record that he was a contemporary of Lan Ying, the most prominent of the seventeenth-century Hangzhou professionals (cat. nos. 26–27). Lan admired Zhang and described his paintings thus: "Clear peaks and abrupt cascades, stream ravines and precipitous cliffs, reed villages and [hideaway] peach blossom caves, willow banks and streamside fishermen" 晴嵐絕澗，深谷危巖，葦村桃洞，柳岸漁溪. Tao Yuanzao, author of *Yuehua jianwen* (Paintings of Yue seen and heard) in which Lan's statement is recorded, added: "These are all scenes not easily captured by the poet. His breath-resonance is marvelous; had he not studied the ancients, he would not be able to reach such a level" 皆詞人難狀之景，氣韻絕佳，非學古何能至此.[3] In writing poetry, Zhang is said to have studied the great Tang-dynasty writers Li Bo and Du Fu. Modeled after Wang Xizhi, Zhang's calligraphy especially excelled at the small-sized standard script. He was also an excellent player of the *qin* zither, and was said to have been a person of unbending integrity.

This brief but tantalizing résumé meshes nicely with his landscape. A number of the foreground details, including the brightly colored trees and rocky cascade, are stylistically related to Lan Ying's attractive and highly influential manner of painting. The exaggerated rock and mountain forms, as well as the grand expanse of the scene, owe much to Wu Bin, who is credited with reviving the monumental landscape form in Nanjing a generation earlier. Clearly Zhang Zhengyue was a practiced master of the genre, with results that sweep the viewer up in the majesty and mystery of an imagined landscape. The blue-green color scheme, a well-established indicator of archaistic value through its association with landscape paintings of a thousand years earlier, heightens the paradisiacal quality of the mountainscape. A scholar with a staff approaching a small temple complex at the lower center of the composition provides the central focus. One pathway over a small bridge implies passage along the left side of the painting, eventually leading to the miniscule pavilion precariously set on a distant precipice. Along the right side of the painting is a small mountain village, where travelers and pack animals pass. The journey here wends its way past a towering waterfall to another temple nestled amongst trees in the cloudlike peaks.

Although practically nothing is known of Zhang Zhengyue and his patrons, a few observations can be offered concerning the artist and this painting in the context of its time. First, as Zhang was known to be a contemporary of Lan Ying, and as the painting was made in his seventy-fifth year, we can assign it a tentative date in the period between 1650 and 1670. This would place it somewhere in the first decades following the fall of the Ming dynasty in 1644 and directly in the transition period prior to the firm establishment of the new Qing dynasty by the Manchus. These were troubled times, when loyalties were tested and those who revealed active ties to the fallen Ming did so at considerable risk. Given this context, the comment that Zhang was a man of unbending integrity may well refer to unspoken loyalist sentiment. The painting's description of a journey to temple complexes in the mountainous backwoods resonates with the fact that in the decades immediately following the fall of the Ming such Buddhist establishments provided safe haven for those who sought either spiritual solace or anonymity in the face of mortal danger. The painting's subject of escape from the problems of this world would no doubt have assuaged the pain and frustration of clients who witnessed a world turned upside down. The painting's blue-green veneer accentuates the theme of removal by suggesting temporal displacement, and yet the unreality often associated with the blue-green landscape style is countered here by compelling qualities of movement and vision. It is easy to be drawn into this hideaway world and believe in its purity and charm. **PCS**

For inscriptions and other documentation, see page 290 in this catalogue.

1 Feng Jinbo 馮金伯, *Guochao huashi* 國朝畫識 (Shanghai: Zhonghua shuju, 1933), *juan* 5:8a; *Guochao qixian leizheng chubian* 國朝耆獻類徵初編 (Taipei: Mingwen shuju, 1985), 426:49a–b; and Tao Yuanzao 陶元藻, *Yuehua jianwen* 越畫見聞, *Huashi congshu* ed. (reprint, Shanghai, 1982), 26.

2 Compounding the problem of identification is the record of another Zhang Zhenyue, who was known as a talented writer. *Guochao qixian leizheng chubian*, 429:21a–b. This Zhang Zhenyue is recorded with yet another character for Zhen but possessing the same style name, Songgao. He was a student of Xiong Bolong and is described as remarkably talented but lax in behavior and addicted to alcohol. Given some of the recorded information on the painter, these appear to be different individuals.

3 Tao, *Yuehua jianwen*, 26.

28 Zhang Zhengyue 張正嶽
B. c. 1590

Mountain Landscape 青綠山水
Santa Barbara Museum of Art
Gift of Mr. and Mrs. George Griffiths

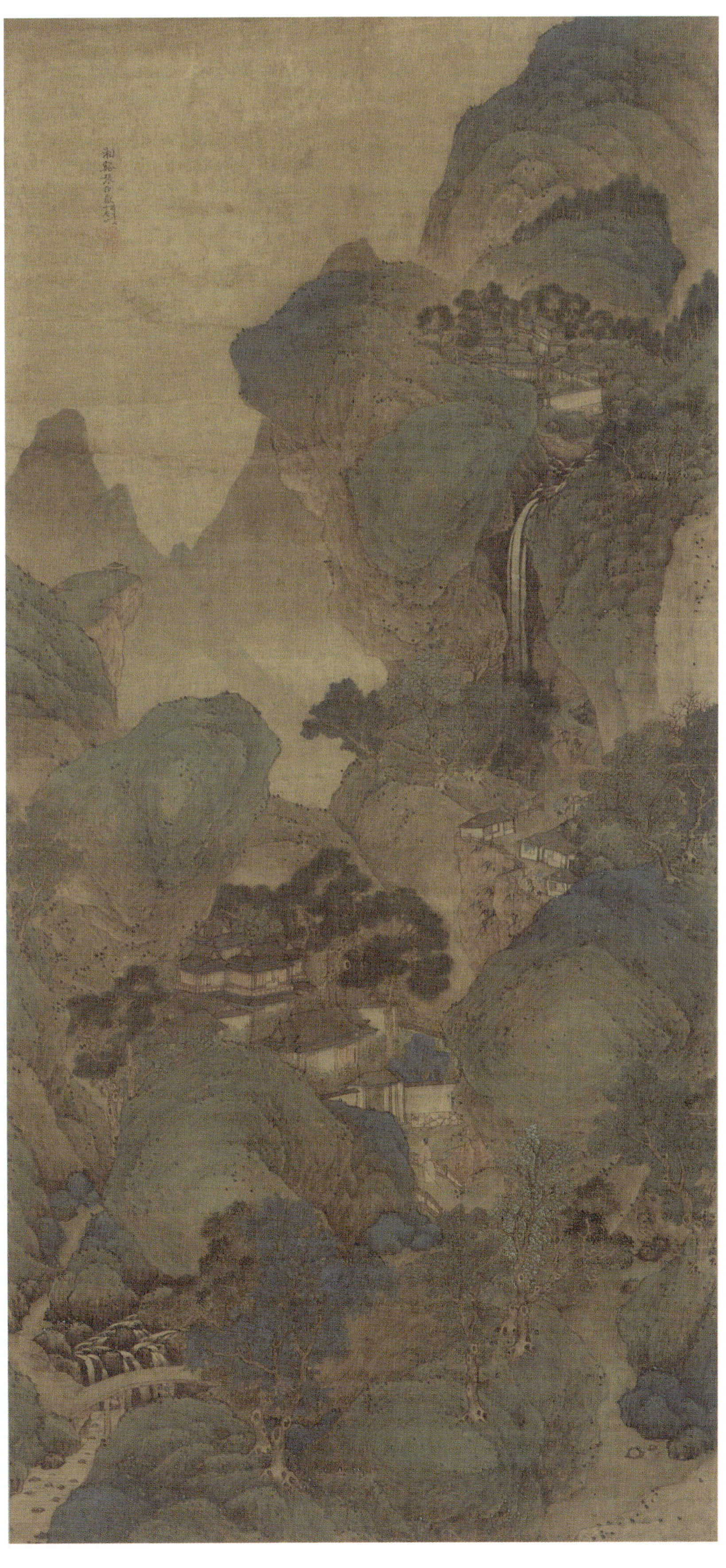

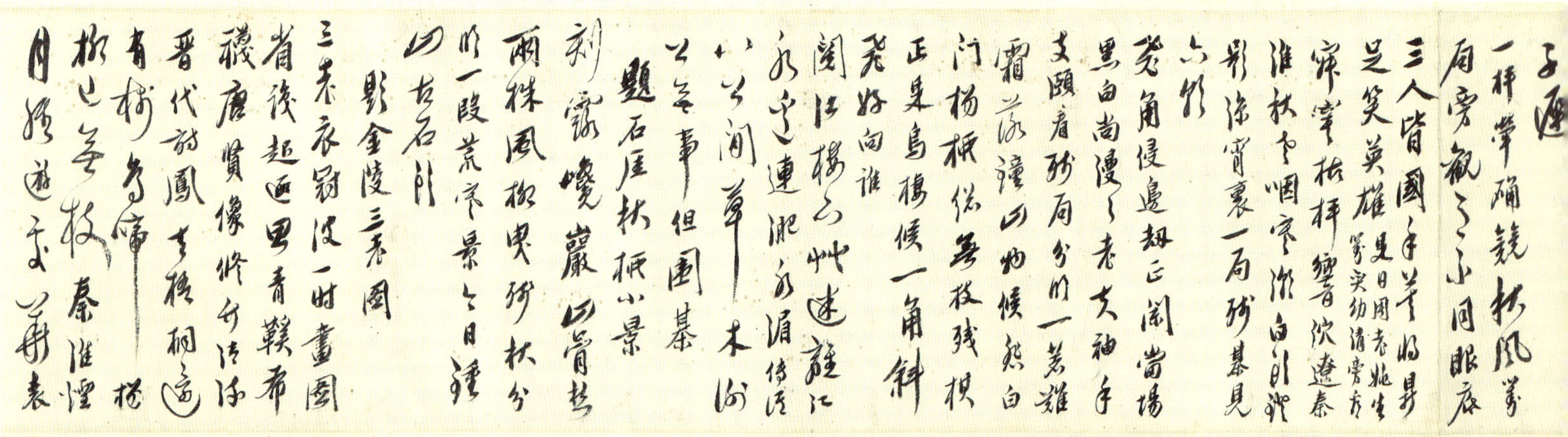

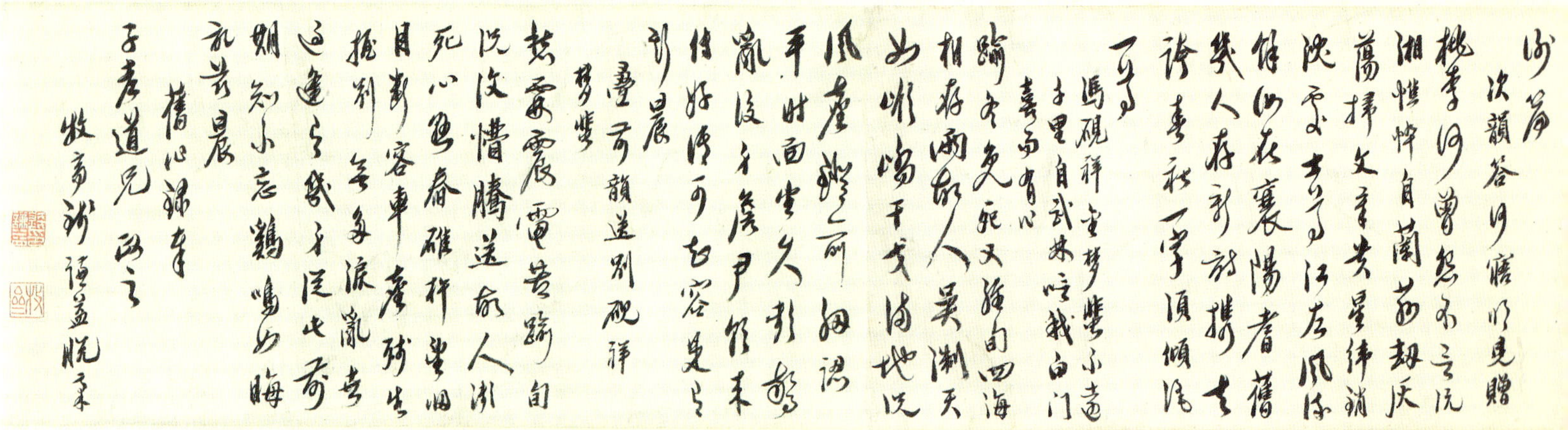

29 Qian Qianyi 錢謙益
1582–1664

Poems 行書詩卷
Calligraphy in semi-cursive script
Private collection

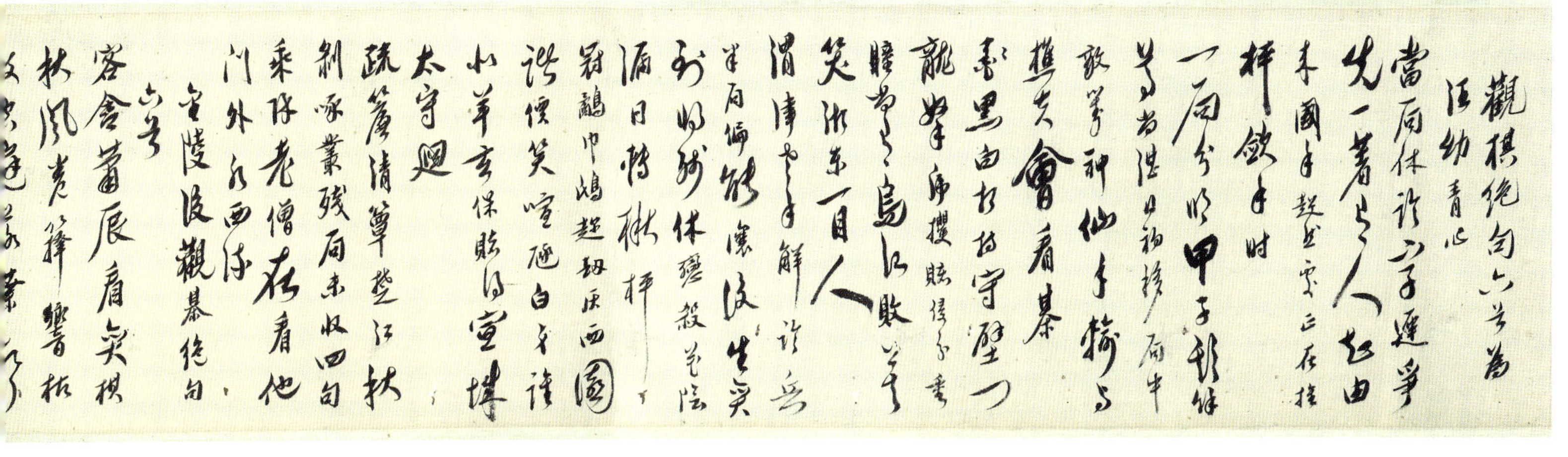

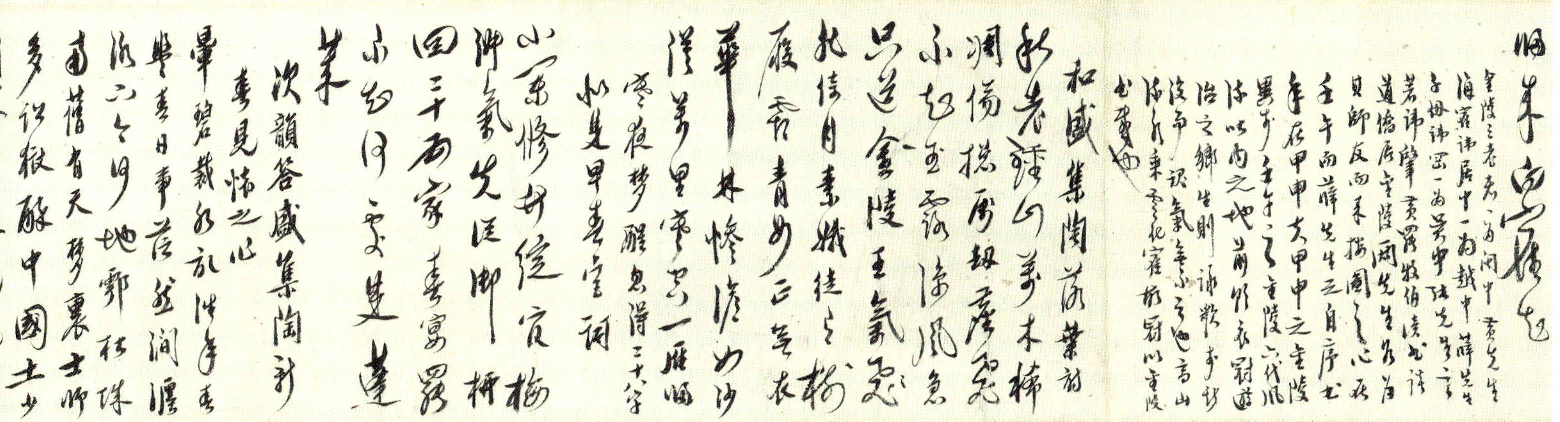

***Six Quatrains on Watching a Game of* Weiqi,**
for the correction of Wang Youqing

...The chess board clearly lays out events that last sixty years:
Wine still bubbling in lingering vessels, the sun just starts to set.
Those immortals hands which are playing a game of chess
All lose the game to those gatherers of bundles of firewood.

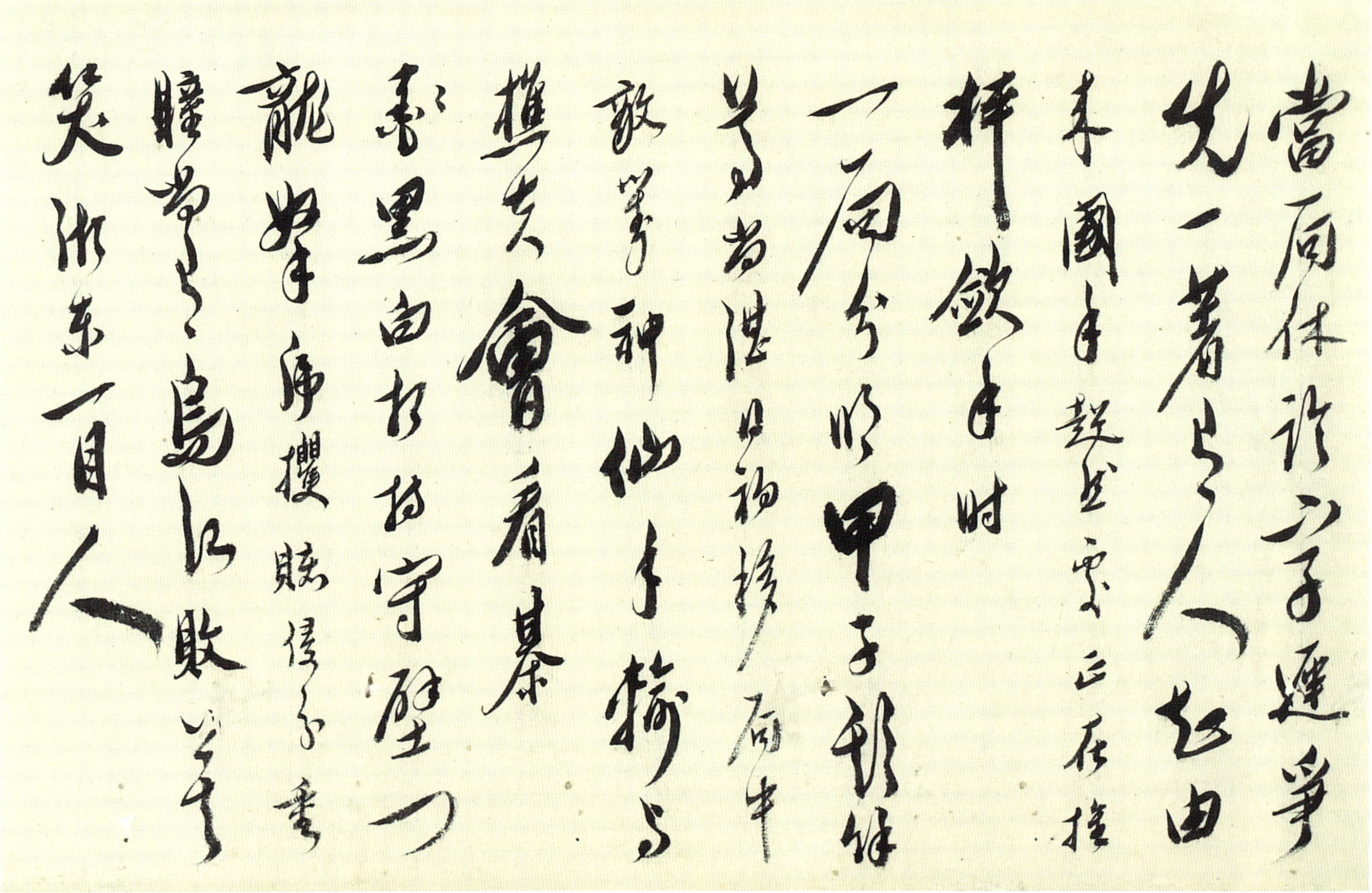

An important scholar, poet, and high official during the Ming-Qing transition, Qian Qianyi was also a controversial figure because of his choice of action during the critical moment of the Manchu conquest. In addition to being a leading literary figure, he enjoyed high repute as one of the leaders of the Donglin Party opposed to the entrenched powers of the eunuchs at the late Ming court. However, 1645 brought a turning point in Qian's life; when the Ming collapsed he was among the first to surrender to the Manchus. As his writings show, the decision to capitulate rather than commit suicide was one that he bitterly regretted for the rest of his life. Although he worked hard to compensate for his actions, aiding the Ming restoration movement by helping with the resources and communication of different local powers and sent to prison for his relation with Huang Yuqi, a leader in the movement, he never lost the reputation of being "an official of two dynasties." Later scholars continued to criticize Qian's character even while they admired his scholarship and literary work, which was banned and largely destroyed during Qianlong's reign (1735–1796). Another well-known, even celebrated, aspect of his life was his relationship with Liu Rushi, a famous courtesan of Nanjing.[1]

As this scroll of Qian Qianyi's poems well demonstrates, the multi-faceted scholar and literary figure also excelled at calligraphy. The ten compositions were all originally included in the second collection of his work, *Youxue ji* 有學集, which was printed in 1664 and featured his literary work from after 1645. More precisely, the poems on this scroll are from the first section of verses (titled *Qiuhuai shiji* 秋槐詩集) from 1645 to 1648. They are varied in subject matter and at first seem to make a random group. A closer look, however, shows that they are all deeply reflective on the sad history Qian experienced firsthand. For example, a number of the poems focus on the desolation of Jinling (Nanjing), site of the Southern Ming government before the Manchus took the city in 1645 and highly symbolic as the seat of earlier dynastic courts. The two sets of six quatrains on *weiqi* (chess) that open the scroll seem unrelated. Yet, as Chen Zuyan and others have noted, *weiqi* was used to comment metaphorically on military strategy during the early critical years of Ming resistance. Qian composed the poems in the fall of 1648, when the fighting was fierce and hope remained high, and his choice of images and allusions are highly meaningful.[2] The Jinling poems comment not only on the tragedy of his dynasty but also his personal life and inner world. They should date from 1648, the year Qian was held in custody in Jinling and lived on the bank of the Qinhuai River after being implicated with Huang Yuqi. Living here, in a city so deeply layered in history, must have inspired the poet to express his profound melancholy. The scroll's poems thus prove to be all of one critical moment in Qian's life, when hope and despair coexisted: a chess match whose outcome remained undetermined.

Qian Qianyi's semi-cursive calligraphy is elegant and alluring, fully embodying the classical tradition as inherited from Song- and Yuan-dynasty models. Like his older contemporaries, Dong Qichang (cat. nos. 8–9) and Chen Jiru (cat. nos. 11–12), he was able to gain access to valuable genuine works, which supplemented study of the earlier great masters of the tradition through compendia of rubbings (*fatie* 法帖). At the core of the classical tradition was the writing of Jin-dynasty calligraphers such as Wang Xizhi, but Ming writers often combined this with the study of Song-dynasty masters. Qian was no exception—his calligraphy reveals the study of both Mi Fu and Su Shi. With its balanced, beautiful compositions and easy, graceful brushwork, Qian's writing has a slightly feminine tone that is not out of keeping with the image of a romantic scholar. It also bears a curious resemblance to the calligraphy of the Yuan-dynasty master Zhao Mengfu (who was similarly criticized for collaborating with a conquering force), though there is no evidence of direct study. However one is inclined to judge Qian Qianyi, this scroll demonstrates that in addition to his literary skills he was an extremely accomplished calligrapher. Its fluidity, applied to its scholarly structure, results in calligraphy that feels at once natural and learned. This, in turn, brings these highly emotional poems to vivid life. **MMZ**

For inscriptions and other documentation, see pages 290–92 in this catalogue.

1 For Qian Qianyi's biography, see in particular Ge Wanli 葛萬里, *Muzhai xiansheng nianpu* 牧齋先生年譜, (reprint, Beijing: Beijing tushuguan chubanshe, 1999); Pei Shijun 裴世俊, *Sihai zongmeng wushi nian*; and Lawrence C. H. Yim's *The Poet-Historian Qian Qianyi.*

2 Chen Zuyan, "The Art of Black and White," 643–54. See also Chen Zuyan 陳祖言, "'Qiuping xiaoji, keyi yu da,'" 74–81; and Yim, *The Poet-Historian Qian Qianyi*, 130–31.

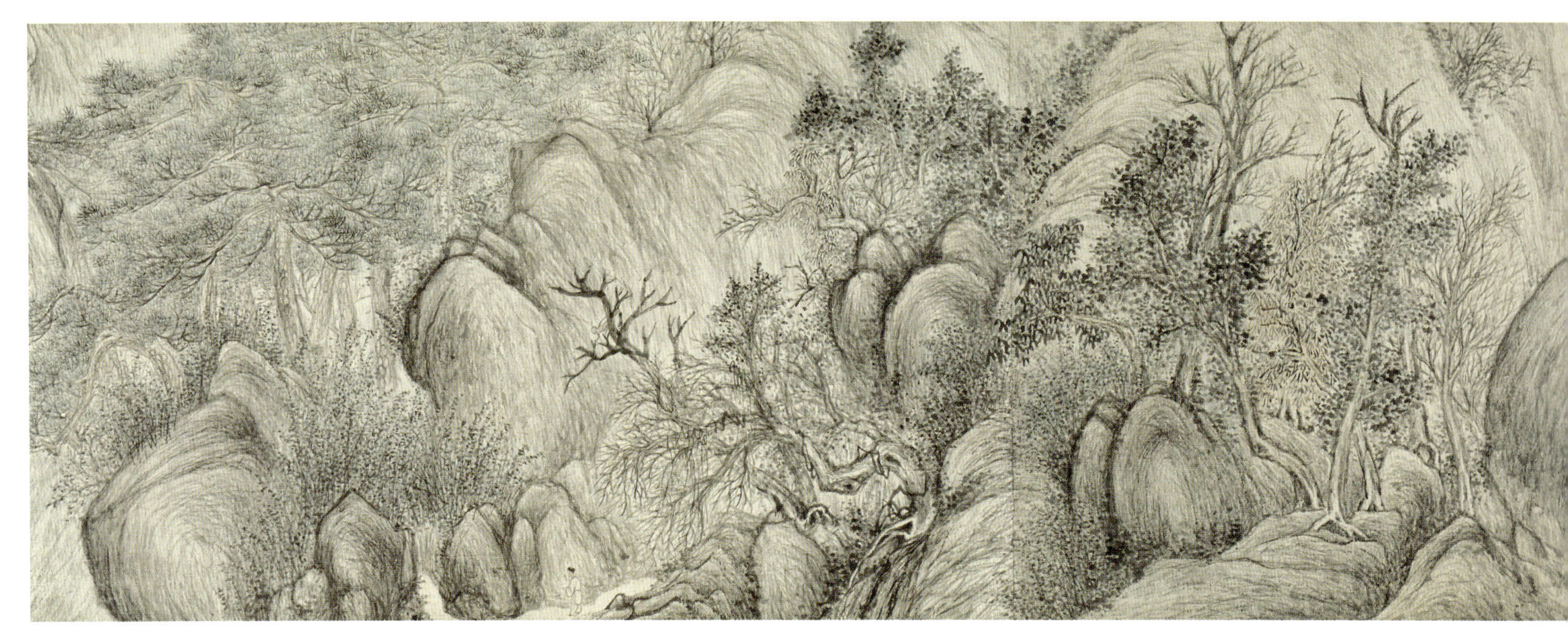

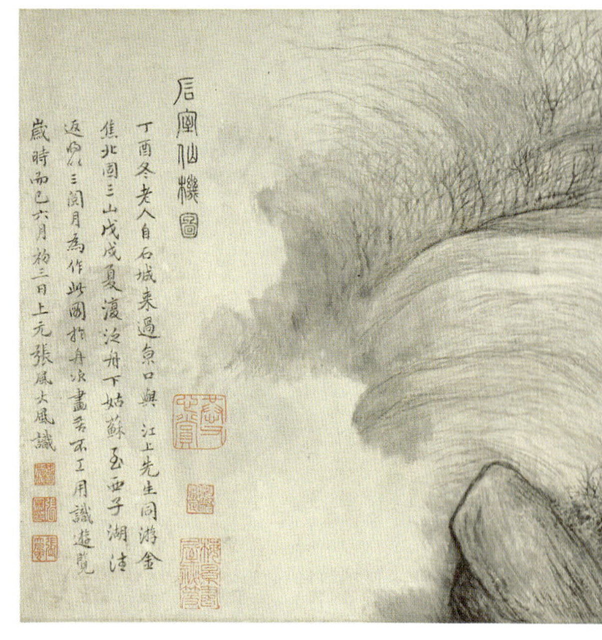

石室仙機圖
丁酉冬老人自石城來過京口與 江上先生同游金
焦北固三山戊戌夏復泛舟下姑蘇至西子湖津
返吳以三閱月為作此圖於舟次畫殊不工用識遊覽
歲時而已六月初三日上元張風大風識

30 Zhang Feng 張風
D. 1662

Immortals' Secrets in a Stone Cave
石室仙機圖卷
1658
Private collection

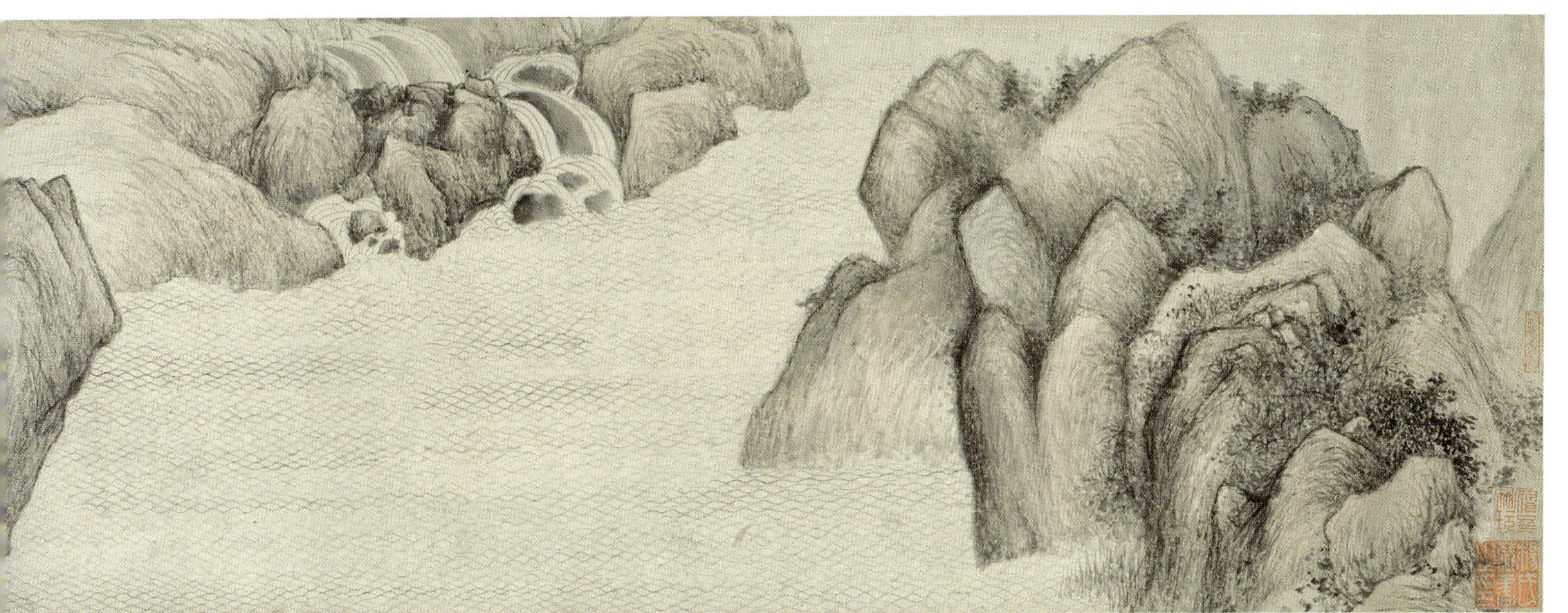

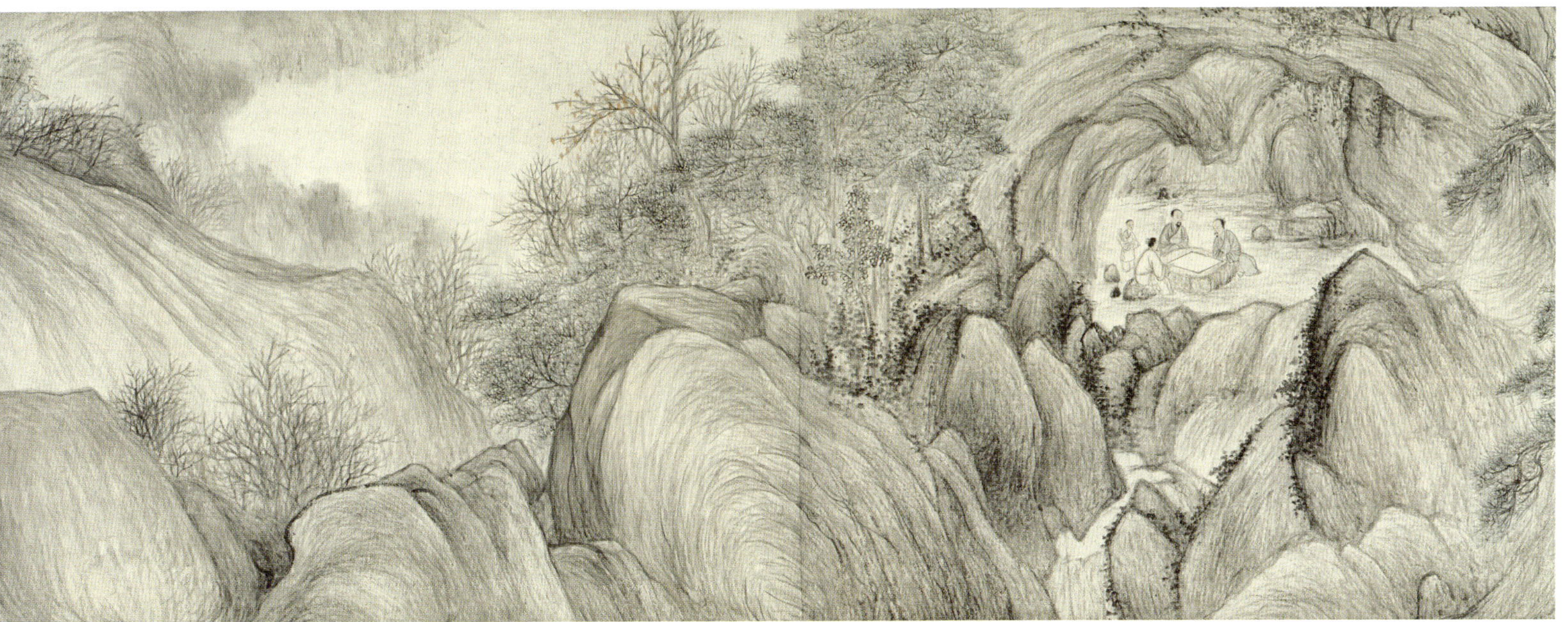

Immortals' Secrets in a Stone Cave. In the winter of the dingyou *year [1657], this old man traveled from Shicheng [Nanjing] to Jingkou [Zhenjiang]. There, in the company of Master Jiangshang [Da Chongguang], we sojourned to the three hills, Jin, Jiao, and Beigu. In the summer of the* wuxu *year [1658], again we traveled by boat down to Gusu [Suzhou] and eventually to West Lake [at Hangzhou]. Traveling back and forth, it has been almost three months. As this painting was made during the boat trip, it was difficult to accomplish and not very skillful—something only useful as a record of our sightseeing during this time.*

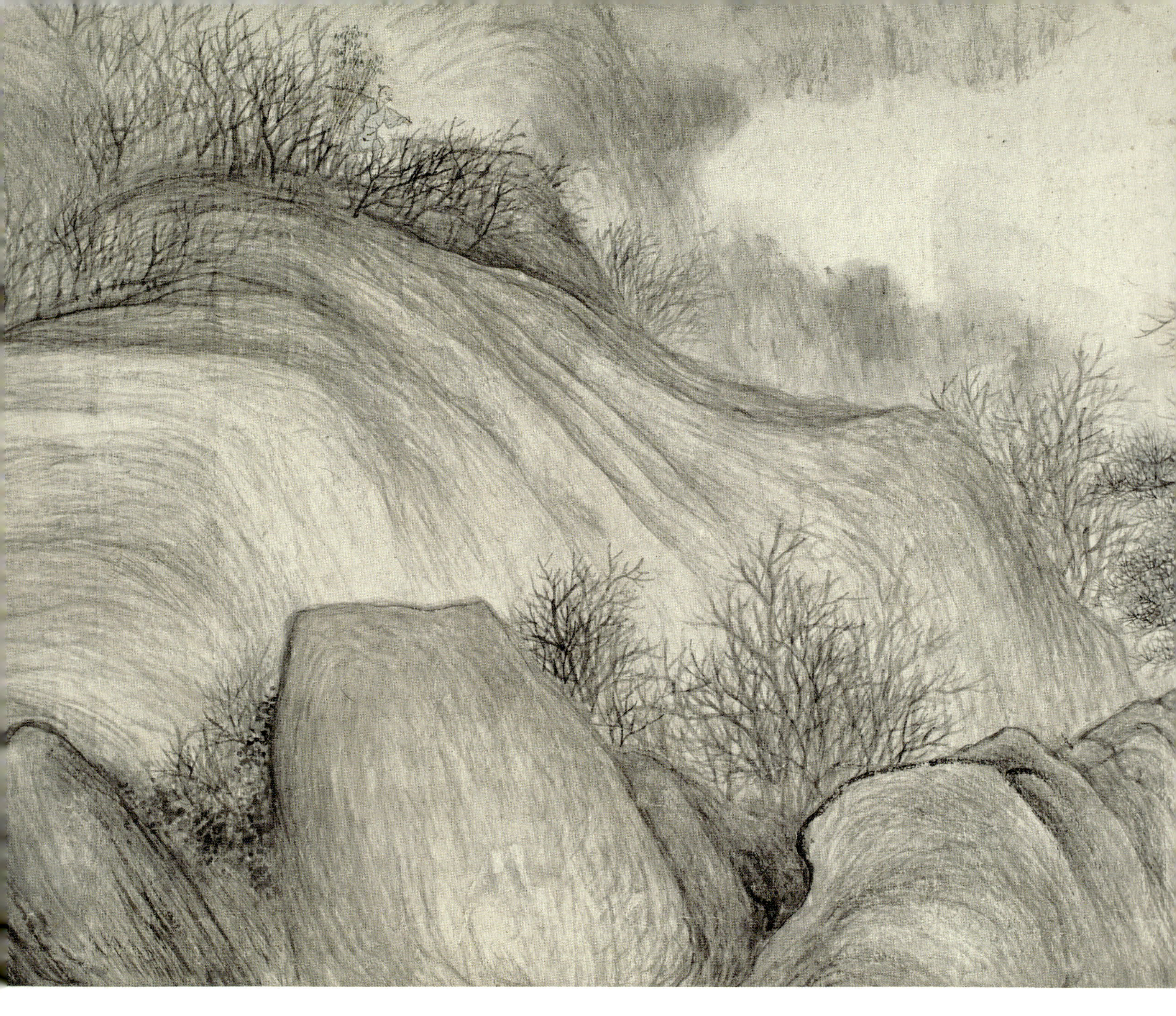

On the surface, Zhang Feng's *Immortals' Secrets in a Stone Cave* presents itself as a fanciful record of a sightseeing trip. As his inscription describes, Zhang traveled from Nanjing down the Yangzi River to the nearby city of Jingkou (Zhenjiang, Jiangsu Province), where he met up with his friend Da Chongguang (cat. no. 31), a native of the area. The two then visited the three famous "mountains" of Jingkou—Jinshan, Jiaoshan, and Beigushan (Jinshan and Jiaoshan were hilly islands in the Yangzi just off the city's shore; Beigushan is a promontory facing the Yangzi with historic sites). Zhang's travels continued some months later, eventually bringing him and Da through Suzhou to Hangzhou.[1]

The painting records their outing, but of what exactly? On the one hand, the three hills of Jingkou were famous for a plentitude of Daoist temples and grottoes as well as a deep cultural history, but there is nothing in Zhang's inscription to identify the scene that he paints with any specific site in the Yangzi landscape between Nanjing and Hangzhou. Rather, as his title pronounces, he creates a landscape of otherworldly activities. In a stone cave deep in the heart of the landscape, two figures and an observer are engaged in *weiqi* 圍棋, a game of wits and strategy akin to chess (fig. 14). Access is difficult. Entrance into another world through a restricted or difficult entryway has a long history in China, with the cavern customarily providing transcendental passage.[2] Moreover, the game of *weiqi* is deeply associated with the timelessness of this otherworld. In the renowned supernatural tale "Lanke shan" 爛柯山 (Mountain of the rotting ax handle), a woodcutter who encounters two immortals playing *weiqi* deep in the mountains is so transfixed that unbeknownst to him decades pass and his ax handle disintegrates with age.[3] Zhang alludes to the immortal nature of his *weiqi* players by including an acolyte holding a feather fan. A woodcutter enters the scene from the left, well hidden among the wilderness brambles.

The apparent whimsy of Zhang Feng's landscape masks the difficult realities of the time. His paintings, commonly featuring historical or reclusive figures wandering or meditating alone in a remote landscape, suggest a sense of personal trauma. Zhang's father served the Ming court as a senior military officer and committed suicide after losing a battle in 1611. His elder brother continued the family's military career, serving as a battalion commander during the Chongzhen reign (1627–1644). During this period Zhang passed the entry-level government student examination but was unable to pursue an official career because of the fall of the dynasty. Demonstrating loyalty to the Ming, he burned his exam books and followed the example of his elder brother to become a Daoist, leading a reclusive life and painting remote, often barren, landscapes.[4] Zhang's escape into Daoism, however, did not preclude clandestine engagement with other loyalists. That is especially evident from *Immortals' Secrets in a Stone Cave*, a painting whose escapist subject subversively comments on contemporary affairs. The game of *weiqi* has a long history of association with political and military figures because of its conceptual affiliations with warfare through the deployment of sequential strategies based on retreat and attack. For this reason, Zhang Feng's contemporary, the noted scholar and poet Qian Qianyi, wrote verses on *weiqi* to allude to military resistance of the Manchu forces in the chaotic early years of the Qing dynasty (see cat. no. 29).[5] Clearly Zhang has similar intentions here: the date of his painting coincided with the rise of loyalist expectations for Zheng Chenggong to stage a naval counterattack in the lower reaches of the Yangzi.[6]

Immortals' Secrets in a Stone Cave presents an image of another world, but one that mirrors through allusion and style the chaotic landscape of the early Qing. Zhang Feng structures a landscape of dry and foreboding forms and few clues of access to its inner depths, where immortals plot their strategies. Pine trees grow here—emblems of longevity and strength and suitable markers of the cave's entrance to a paradisiacal realm. In Zhang's hands, however, the grotto seems to suggest less a passage into an idealized world than a respite from the brutalities of the wilderness, where secret thoughts and goals can still be embraced. **KYM**

For inscriptions and other documentation, see page 292 in this catalogue.

1 Zhang Feng mentions his summer trip to Suzhou with Da Chongguang in an inscription to calligraphy by Zhu Yunming dated the fifth lunar month of 1658. See Rao Zongyi 饒宗頤, "Zhang Dafeng ji qi jiashi," 65. For a description and map of the three hills recorded in the seventeenth century, see Yang Erzeng 楊爾曾, *Hainei qiguan* 海內奇觀, 8:15–18; reprinted in *Zhongguo gudai banhua congkan er bian* 中國古代版畫叢刊二編 (Shanghai: Shanghai guji chubanshe, 1994), vol. 8, 193–99. Today Jinshan is connected to land and is no longer an island.

2 Franciscus Verellen, "The Beyond Within," 271. See also Rolf A. Stein, *The World in Miniature.*

3 Recorded in *Shuyi ji* 述異記, commonly ascribed to Ren Fang. Cited from Liu Shancheng 劉善承, ed., *Zhongguo weiqi*, 276.

4 Zhang Geng 張庚, *Guochao huazheng lu* 國朝畫徵錄, 1:18, in *Huashi congshu* 畫史叢書 (Taipei: Wenshizhe chubanshe, 1974), vol. 3, 1266. The most thorough examination of Zhang's life is Rao's "Zhang Dafeng ji qi jiashi." See also He Yaoguang 何耀光, *Zhilelou shuhua lu*, 54; Wai-kam Ho, ed., *The Century of Tung Ch'i-ch'ang*, vol. 2, 118; Liu Heping's entry on this painting in Richard M. Barnhart, et al., *The Jade Studio*, 145; and Jonathan Hay, "The Suspension of Dynastic Time," 171–82.

5 For an analysis of Qian Qianyi's *weiqi* poems, see Chen Zuyan 陳祖言, "'Qiuping xiaoji, keyi yu da,'" 74–81. For military associations with *weiqi*, see He Yunbo 何雲波, *Weiqi yu Zhongguo wenhua*, 290–94.

6 See Peter Sturman's essay elsewhere in this catalogue.

The negative space of this relatively broad hanging scroll helps to illuminate Da Chongguang's calligraphy. The characters, like the floating immortal islands that Da describes in his poem, seem to be in a state of flux, marking yet not confined to the paper they occupy. Achieving clarity of form and empty space was a goal that Da sought in the painting of landscape. As he explains in his treatise on painting, *Hua quan*: "Emptiness is difficult to paint, but when the substantial scenery is clear then the scenery of the void becomes manifest. . . If the composition is muddled then where there is painting can be like so many extra warts, but when substance and emptiness mutually reinforce then even where there is no painting all is marvelous scenery" 空本難圖，實景清而空景現... 位置相戾，有畫處多屬贅疣；虛實相生，無畫處皆成妙境.[1] The careful balance of positive form and negative space applies equally well to Da's calligraphy.

Da Chongguang is considered one of the four great calligraphers of the early Qing dynasty, along with Jiang Chenying, Wang Shihong, and He Zhuo. He developed his style of writing by first copying the works of Dong Qichang. Later he turned to earlier calligraphers for study, such as the Song-dynasty masters Mi Fu and Su Shi, whose work embodied the literati ideal of expressing individuality while still being founded in tradition.[2] Like Dong Qichang, Chen Jiru, and the Song calligraphers, Da displays a mastery of his models and a confidence in unleashing their inspiration through a bold semi-cursive script. Mi Fu, in particular, is an important model for this calligraphy. Upon Mi's style Da adeptly created a nearly three-dimensional ebb and flow of characters with a fluid, versatile brush, leaving rounded marks that seem to at once float on the paper and expand into the space of the scroll.

Both the calligraphy and the poem of this scroll portray Da Chongguang's state of retirement in the foothills of Maoshan, located to the southeast of Zhenjiang in Jiangsu Province. Turning to Daoism after speaking out against the greed and lawlessness of officialdom, Da settled where centuries before him Mi Fu had also enjoyed much of his retired life and was later enshrined. Just north of the city proper is the island called Jiaoshan, surrounded by the waters of the Yangzi River. Named after Jiao Guang, a recluse of the late Eastern Han (25–220) who sought refuge on the island's secluded peak as he repeatedly declined invitations to serve the court, Jiaoshan also became known as Floating Jade Mountain because of its greenery, which seems to float on the waters.[3]

The beauty of the landscape, the rich history of the area, and Mi Fu in particular all provide meaning to Da Chongguang's poem and calligraphy. Foremost, however, is the presence of the calligrapher himself. In a text on calligraphy Da used somatic metaphors to convey the transference of life and energy from calligrapher to his writing:

> The handling of the brush resides in the horizontal stroke; the character's stance relies upon the vertical stroke. The unfurling of the energy is seen in the diagonal *pie* [left] and *na* [right] strokes. The connectivity of the tendons resides in the brush's twists and turns. The continuity of the arteries lies in the subtle ligatures. The stability of bone structure and flesh resides in the fullness [of heavy ink]. The disclosure of unique flavor lies in the hooks and dots.[4]
>
> 筆之執使在橫畫. 字之立體在豎畫. 氣之舒展在撇捺. 筋之融結在紐轉. 脈絡之不斷在絲牽. 骨肉之調停在飽滿. 趣之呈露在勾點.

The poem ends with a robust writing of the character *wu* 無, which ironically means "emptiness" (second to last character, third column from the right). This assertively written character in particular seems to embody the presence of the calligrapher—engaged by the scene and its history, but also ready to drift away or dissolve in the passing of time personified by the mighty Yangzi River. **OML**

For inscriptions and other documentation, see page 293 in this catalogue.

1 Da Chongguang, *Hua quan* 畫筌 (reprint, Taipei: Yiwen yinshuguan, 1966), 12–13.
2 Wang Youfen, et al., *Chinese Calligraphy*, 340–41.
3 Jiaoshan has many cliff inscriptions of considerable age carved in its rock faces. One of the most famous of these, much admired since the Song dynasty, is the *Yihe ming* 瘞鶴銘, or "Eulogy on Burying the Crane," which at one time was thought to have been written by Wang Xizhi.
4 Da Chongguang, *Shu fa* 書法, in Huang Binhong 黃賓虹 and Deng Shi 鄧實, eds. *Zhonghua meishu congshu* 中華美術叢書 (reprint, Nanjing: Jiangsu guji chubanshe, 1986), vol. 1, 4a.

31 Da Chongguang 笪重光
1623–1692

Floating Jade Mountain **行書詩軸**
Calligraphy in semi-cursive script
Santa Barbara Museum of Art
Gift of N. P. Wong Family

Floating Jade Mountain surges upward,
water floats on every side!
Jiao Cliff's pine trees tower high,
just like the Isles of Paradise!
This panorama of the Yangzi River,
continuous, past and present:
With such wild waves, could anyone pole
a boat out there right now?

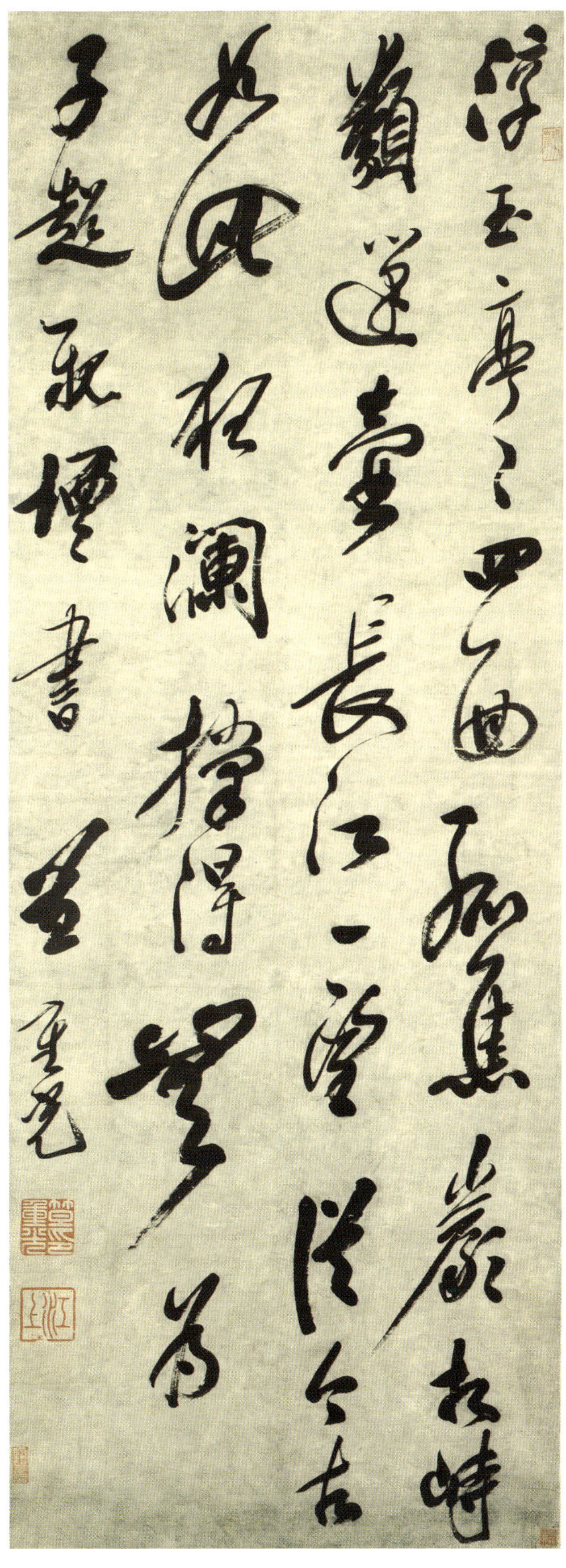

A versatile intellectual whose life bridged the Ming-Qing transition, Cheng Sui had a high reputation in classics, literature, epigraphy, painting, and calligraphy during his lifetime.[1] In his preface to Cheng's anthology, *Xiaoran yin*, Zhang Xun compared Cheng to the two ancient recluses Xiang Chang and Pang De, who refused the call to serve at the Eastern Han court, and explained that Cheng's decision to live a reclusive life was not a narcissistic withdrawal from political turmoil but the result of his indifference to fame.[2] Cheng's self-effacing personality is also reflected in his analysis of his own painting, in which he admits to being prone to excessive embarrassment (*kuipi* 愧癖) and keen on hiding his clumsiness from the view of others.[3] Judging from his extant work, his self-consciousness may have been a factor in the development of such a light and meticulous manner of brushwork.[4]

In *Tall View of Streams and Mountains*, one of his few extant monumental paintings, Cheng Sui created a tranquil, secluded refuge away from worldly turbulence in a grand setting. Starting at the lower left corner, a path along the riverbank beckons the viewer, zigzagging to a compound of three cottages on the other side of the stream. Although no figures are shown, this is an ideal environment for reclusive living, abutting a clear mountain stream and surrounded by flourishing trees and bamboo. Upright mountains and a recessive valley create an impressive backdrop, with the complexity of Cheng's rock formations enhancing the liveliness of the central portion of the painting. Arrayed trees lining the mountain gently introduce the horizontal spread of distant mountains at the top. A mountain village emerges here among the trees at the upper right, its small size accentuating the massive cliffs behind. A cottony mist rests lightly on this upper portion, providing a gentle, heavenly cap to the high vista.

Cheng Sui demonstrates not only a utopian vision in *Tall View of Streams and Mountains* but also his understanding of an orthodox way of painting. We know from his collected works that Zhang Xun, the recipient of the painting, was a close friend who like him secluded himself after the fall of the Ming dynasty.[5] According to Zhou Lianggong, Zhang's own early paintings were indistinguishable from those of Cheng.[6] Though Zhang's extant paintings are few, one work, *Tranquil Serenity of Streams and Mountains* (Sen-oku Hakko Kan, Kyoto), shows characteristics of the "high distance" composition that constitutes the theme of *Tall View of Streams and Mountains* and is the focal point of Cheng's inscription.[7] Cheng makes a point of distinguishing his and Zhang's use of this compositional type from the Jiangdong (Suzhou) painters, who painted in a "sweet and vulgar" manner, echoing a criticism voiced by many who were influenced by Dong Qichang.[8] In his youth, Cheng resided in Huating (Songjiang, Jiangsu Province) and studied under Dong's lifelong friend Chen Jiru.[9] The influence of Dong through Chen Jiru and other Dong followers is apparent in certain characteristics shared between Cheng Sui's landscapes and the Huating School, such as the use of multiple units of rocks to create the movement of mountains.

Also notable in Cheng's landscapes are signs of the influence of Dong's theory of the Southern School, the lineage of earlier literati painters that Dong promoted above all others. Qian Qianyi once praised Cheng as the reincarnation of Wang Meng, one of the key figures in that lineage.[10] Although Cheng's brushwork in *Tall View of Streams and Mountains* is much sparer than that of Wang, the repeatedly applied short lines along the mountain tops create an effect similar to Wang's busily textured rock surfaces. Cheng also managed to create lushness with a dry brush, which is an innovative transformation of Wang's dense style. Most important, Cheng's depiction of the life of seclusion, composed as a winding journey deep into the mountains, recalls a number of Wang's renditions of the theme in the high distance format.[11] Although undated, there is evidence to suggest that *Tall View of Streams and Mountains* belongs to the early years of the Qing dynasty, circa 1650, when both the influence of the Huating School and the impetus to create a compelling image of reclusion were strong.[12] **KYH**

For inscriptions and other documentation, see page 293 in this catalogue.

1 For Cheng Sui's biography, see Chen Ding 陳鼎, *Liuxi wai zhuan* 留溪外傳, in *Siku quanshu cunmu congshu shibu* 四庫全書存目叢書史部 (Jinan: Qilu shushe, 1997), vol. 122, 512. See also Li Zhigang 李志綱, "Cheng Sui yanjiu," 39–84; and Chen Sandi 陳三弟, "Cheng Sui zhi jiaoyou kaoyi," 85–100.

2 For Zhang Xun's preface, see Cheng Sui, *Xiaoran yin* 蕭然吟, in *Siku jinhui shu congkan jibu* 四庫禁燬書叢刊集部 (Beijing: Beijing chubanshe, 2000), vol. 116, 475–76.

3 Zhou Lianggong, *Duhua lu* 讀畫錄, in Yu Anlan 于安瀾, *Huashi congshu* 畫史叢書 (Shanghai: Shanghai shuhua, 1962), 36.

4 Chen Sandi, "Cheng Sui zhi jiaoyou kaoyi," 49.

5 Zhang Xun was a native of Jingyang (Shaanxi Province) and passed the metropolitan examination in 1643. See Zhao Hongen 趙洪恩, et al., *Jiangnan tongzhi* 江南通志, in *Jingyin Wenyuange Siku quanshu* 景印文淵閣四庫全書 (Taipei: Taiwan shangwu yinshu guan, 1983), vol. 511, 904. Cheng Sui, *Xiaoran ji* 蕭然集, in *Qing dai shiwenji huibian* 清代詩文集彙編 (Shanghai: Shanghai guji chubanshe, 2009), vol. 21, 475.

6 Zhou, *Duhua lu*, 37. Zhou cites Cheng Sui praising Zhang Xun and Cheng Zhengkui as the best painters of his time.

7 Reproduced in Suzuki Kei 鈴木敬, ed., *Chūgoku kaiga sōgō zuroku*, vol. 3, no. JM 13–30.

8 Dong Qichang, *Rongtai ji bieji* 容台集別集, in *Siku quanshu cunmu congshu jibu* 四庫全書存目叢書集部 (Jinan: Qilu shushe, 1997), vol. 171, 742.

9 Cheng Sui wrote a poem on trying to locate Chen Jiru's tomb. Cheng, *Xiaoran ji*, 638. His maternal uncle, Cheng Yuanxun 程元勳, was an important collector and a friend of Dong Qichang. See Huang Binhong 黄賓虹, "Gou daoren yishi fu gou daoren yizhu," vol. 2, 327. Li, "Cheng Sui yanjiu," 83n96.

10 Cheng Sui, *Xiaoran ji*, 600. The tenth-century painter Juran, another important figure in the Southern School lineage, is also mentioned as a source of study for Cheng Sui. Zhang Geng 張庚, *Guochao huazheng lu* 國朝畫徵錄, in *Xuxiu Siku quanshu* 續修四庫全書 (Shanghai: Shanghai guji chubanshe, 2002), vol. 1067, 110.

11 Notably Wang Meng's *Dwelling in the Qingbian Mountains* of 1366 (Shanghai Museum).

12 See Huang Yifen's catalogue entry for *Tall View of Streams and Mountains* in *Yuemu*, vol. 2, 88–89.

32 Cheng Sui 程邃
1607–1692

Tall View of Streams and Mountains
溪山高遠圖軸
Collection of Shitou Shuwu

Painters of the Jiangdong region revere "level distance" [compositions of landscape], but this path has increasingly hastened towards the light and shallow. Only my friend, Mr. Zhigong, is able to utilize the strength of "high distance" to revitalize the declined learning. I, too, have been engaged in such matters, which the two of us discuss from time to time. By chance I imitate [Zhigong's] manner but dare not compete.

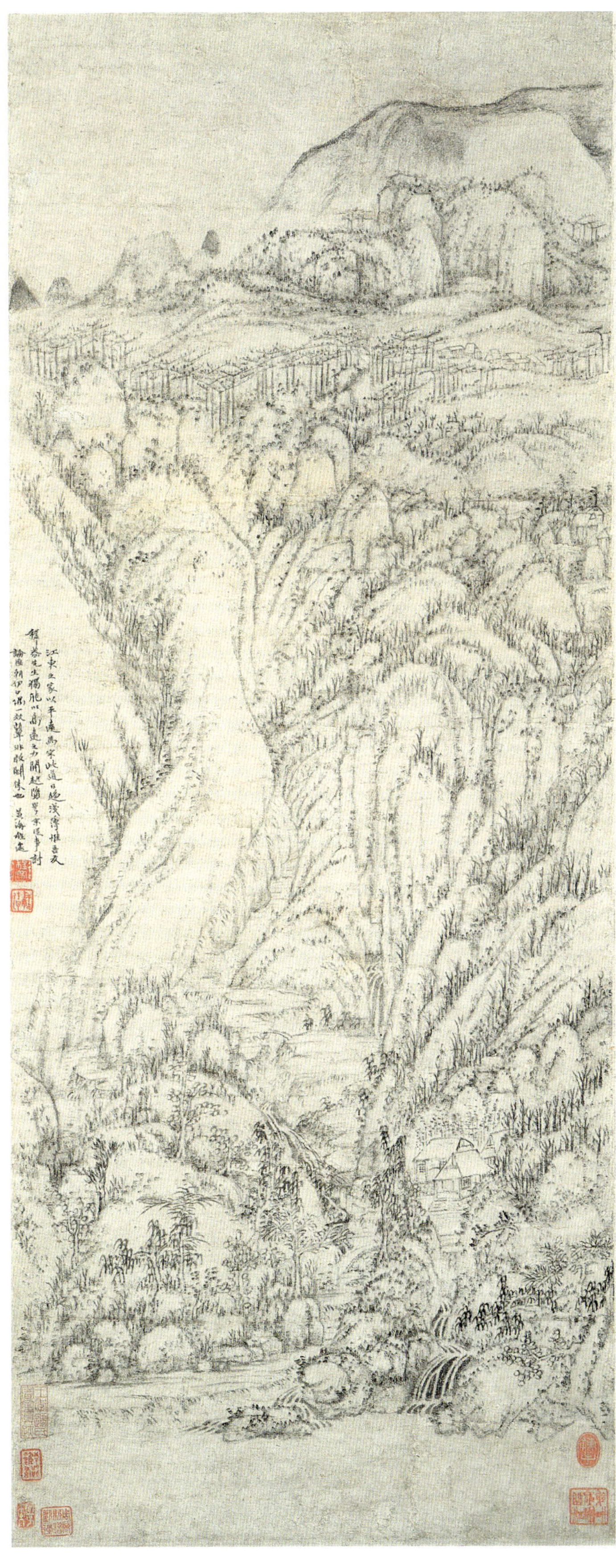

This album consists of ten landscape leaves painted by five artists from different places and backgrounds in south China who were active from the last quarter of the sixteenth century to the first two decades of the eighteenth century. Hu Yukun is the major contributor with four leaves, followed by Fei Erqi and Song Jue with two each; Mei Geng and Gu Ningyuan each painted one. Though the sizes of the leaves belonging to the last two artists are the same, the rest vary, indicating different provenances. Moreover, only Hu Yukun's leaves bear the seals of prominent nineteenth-century collector Wu Yun. The album was evidently assembled in its present form by a later collector sometime before 1961, when Pang Guojun, a reputed calligrapher and connoisseur from the circle of Wu Hufan, added texts on the facing leaves. Pang thoughtfully adjusted the sizes of his calligraphic leaves in order to match the corresponding paintings. Each features a five- or seven-character line poem written in large characters, followed by a note that provides commentary ranging from biographical and art-historical information on the artist to historical notes related to the painted scene.

Two of the artists, Song Jue and Gu Ningyuan, were active during the late-Ming period. Song, originally from Putian in Fujian Province, sojourned in Nanjing and traveled around the lower Yangzi region for most of his career until his death. A leading carver of both seals and bamboo, he was also famous for his clerical-script calligraphy, which is seen in his title to leaf 6 of the album. His simple but powerful landscape compositions demonstrate his skill at creating spatial arrangements that are economical and precise, drawing on the seal-carver's familiarity working with the limited surfaces of seals; they map motifs onto well-designed surfaces, creating tranquil, still, impressionistic images that incorporate identifiers of place. Gu Ningyuan was from an old Suzhou family of officials but never pursued government office. He was a writer, antique collector, and painting theorist. His conspicuously classicizing paintings are modeled on previous masters with great analytical care. Leaf 4 bears an inscription in seal script, stating that his model was Cao Zhibo, a prominent Yuan-dynasty painter from Songjiang (Jiangsu Province). The landscape, devoid of human presence, seems like an imaginary place. Stylistically, it is notable for the consistent use of lateral dots to define vegetation and bamboo groves. In this painting Gu seems to address a local Songjiang tradition that was taken up by Dong Qichang and perhaps can be attributed to Dong's predecessor, Cao Zhibo.

Of the three early-Qing painters represented, Fei Erqi is the least known today as an artist. A prominent poet and scholar in the Ming loyalist community, he was summoned to sit for the court-sponsored *boxue* (extensive learning) examination in 1678. As a painter, he specialized in flower paintings and landscape. The two rare examples of his work in this album (leaves 1 and 2) share the theme of the rustic retreat. In the first, the artist renders the wilderness thoughtfully by choosing a seemingly random view and pulling the monumental ridges off to the margins, thereby creating a convincingly real place of reclusion. In leaf 2 trees dominate the picture, their dots and lines orchestrated with graphic rhythm. A gentleman in a boat, oblivious to the viewer's gaze, is shown somewhat distantly from the rear. He seems to be returning to the thatched huts on the far shore, a realm that is elusive, austere, yet peaceful.

Mei Geng was a native of Xuancheng in Anhui Province. A relative of the more famous Mei Qing, he was an accomplished painter in his own right, known also as a poet and calligrapher.[1] While influenced by his relative's dynamic compositions, Mei Geng's paintings also show an awareness of the washes and inky gradations of the leading Nanjing painter, Gong Xian (cat. nos. 34–36). Mei's painting in this album (leaf 3) is notable for a pictorial conceit in which the crown of a pine is bifurcated, with one part stretching toward the sky while the other droops down to the ground. The former resonates with the precipitous cliffs, from which a waterfall springs, while the latter echoes the mountain stream rushing down to the river. Mei's style name was Tingshan Weng (The Old Man Listening to Mountains), which prompted Pang Guojun, in his accompanying inscription, to suggest that the seated figure is a self-portrait.

The remaining four leaves (7 through 10) were painted by Hu Yukun, a Nanjing painter closely associated with the influential collector Zhou Lianggong.[2] The leaves, bearing his own inscriptions, depict particular places he had visited: the Confucian Grove (7), Muling Road in Shandong Province (8), Chestnut Village (9), and Mount Lu in Jiangxi Province (10). Because leaf 9 resembles one from another album dated 1652, it has been suggested that Hu's leaf, and by extension the three other paintings included in this album, may have been executed around the same time.[3] The paintings and inscriptions go beyond mere topographic reference to incorporate variously a sense of his life's journey, or of historical realities that resonate with post-conquest political circumstances. Muling Pass (Muling Guan 穆陵關), for example, had repeatedly been a military battlefield over thousands of years; the battle between the Qi and Lu states during the Warring States period was particularly famous. This rich context lends emotional depth in each case to the rather somber pictorial atmosphere, which is fairly consistent over the four leaves. **LL**

For inscriptions and other documentation, see pages 293–4 in this catalogue.

1 The kinship of the two Meis is a matter of debate. Howard Rogers identifies Mei Geng as a cousin of Mei Qing. See *Kaikodo Journal* 17, no. 11, 80.

2 Hongnam Kim, *The Life of a Patron*, 50–53.

3 Paul Moss, ed., *This Single Feather of Auspicious Light*, 504. The 1652 album appeared at auction at Sotheby's, New York, November 1993.

33 Song Jue 宋珏
1576–1632

Gu Ningyuan 顧凝遠
1595 or earlier–1654

Hu Yukun 胡玉昆
Act. c. 1640–1672

Fei Erqi 費而奇
Act. 1678
or earlier–1701 or later

Mei Geng 梅庚
1640–c. 1722

Album of Landscapes by Famous Masters of the Late Ming–Early Qing
明清名家山水冊
Private collection

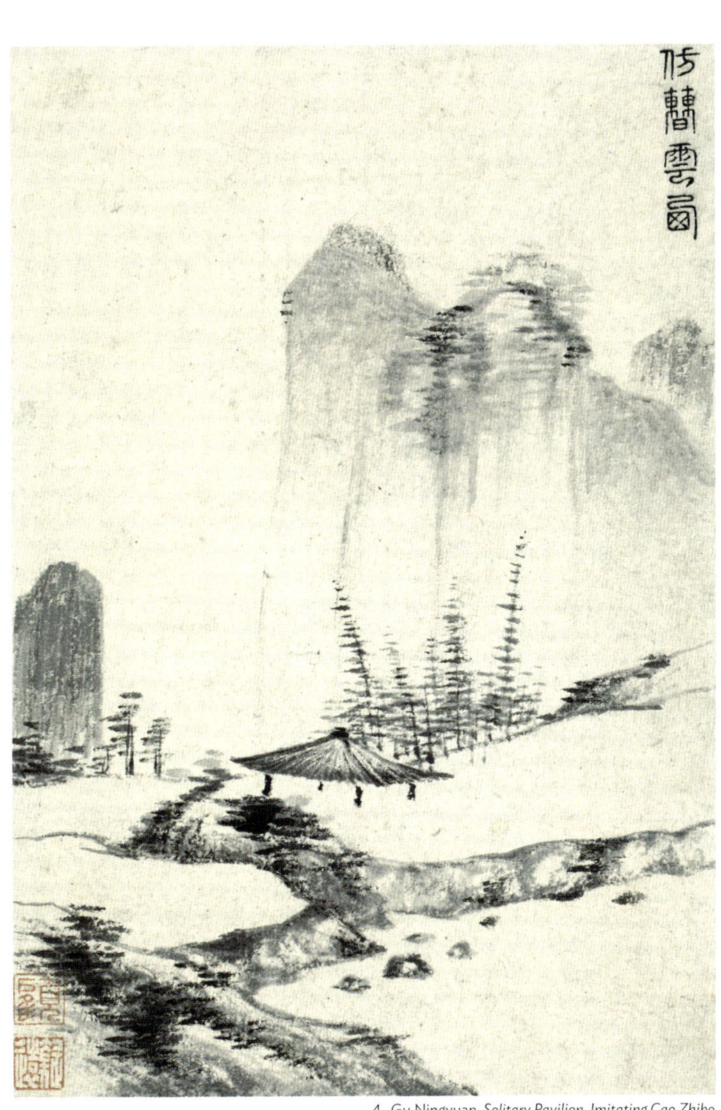

4 Gu Ningyuan, *Solitary Pavilion, Imitating Cao Zhibo*

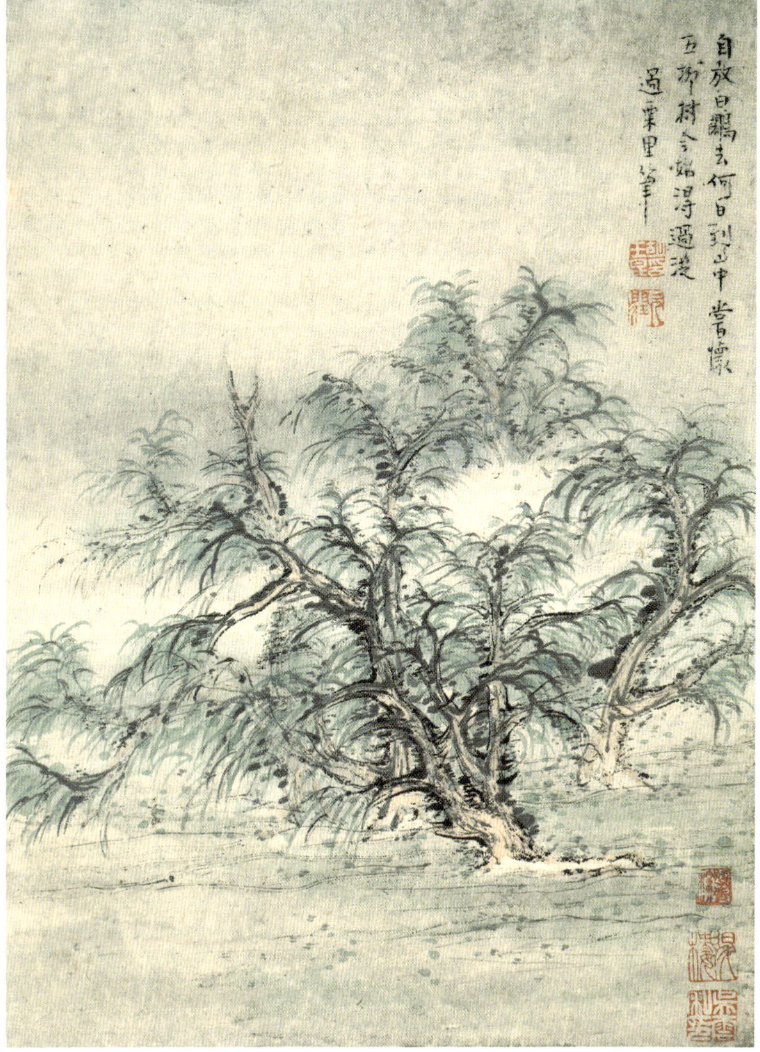

9 Hu Yukun, *The Five Willows at Chestnut Village*

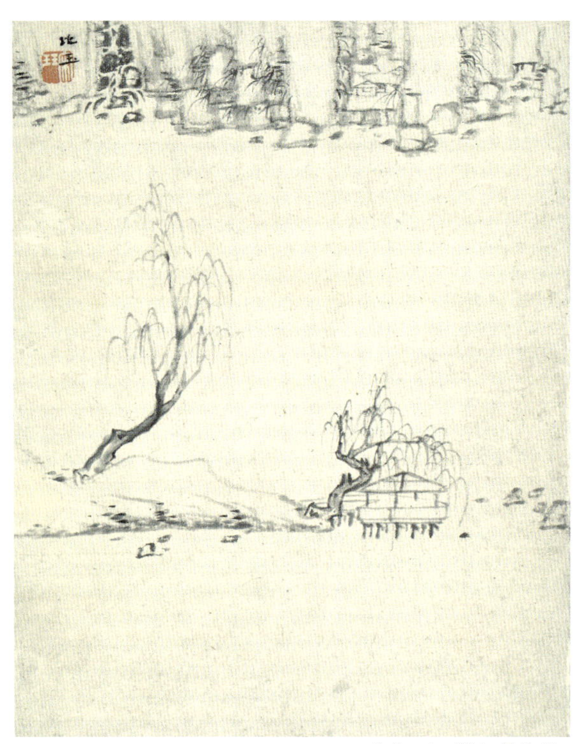

5 Song Jue, *Waterside Pavilion*

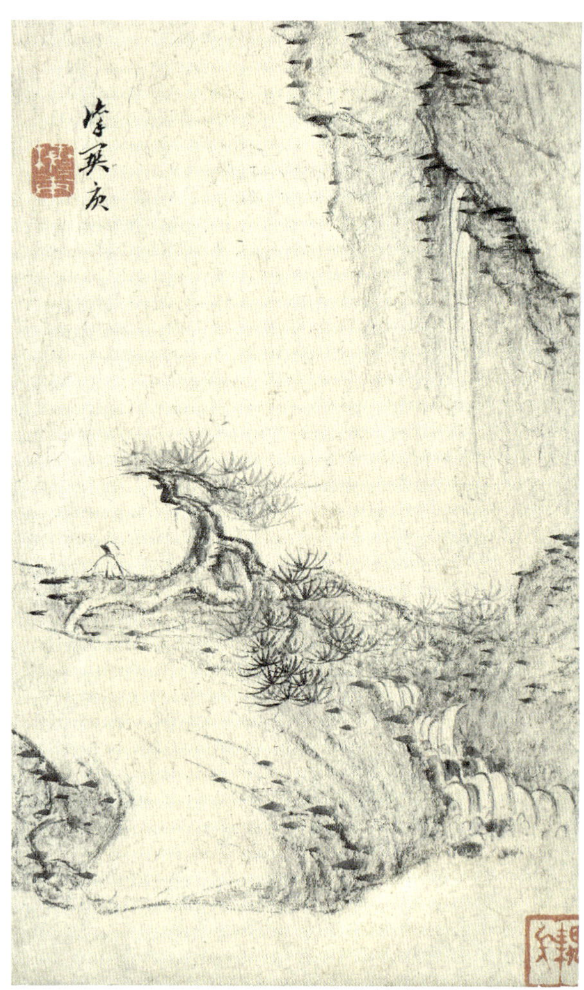

3 Mei Geng, *Gazing at a Waterfall*

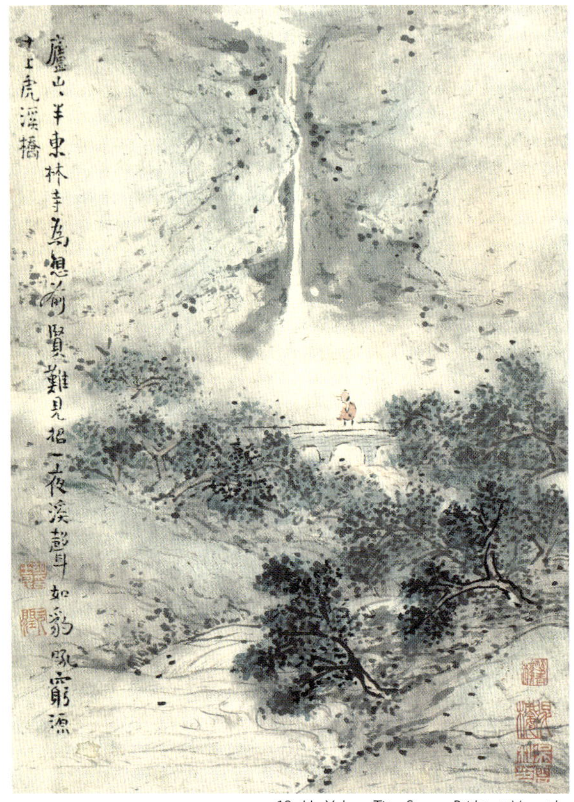

10 Hu Yukun, *Tiger Stream Bridge at Mount Lu*

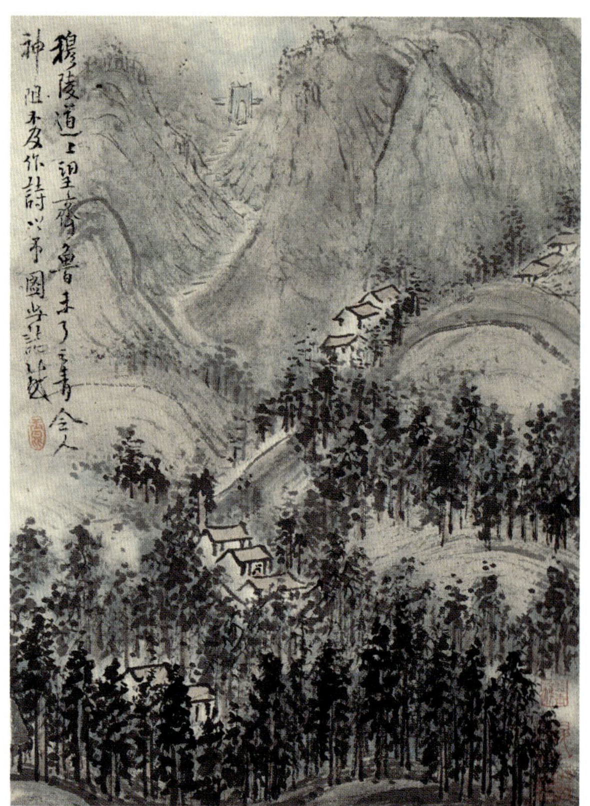

8 Hu Yukun, *On Muling Road*

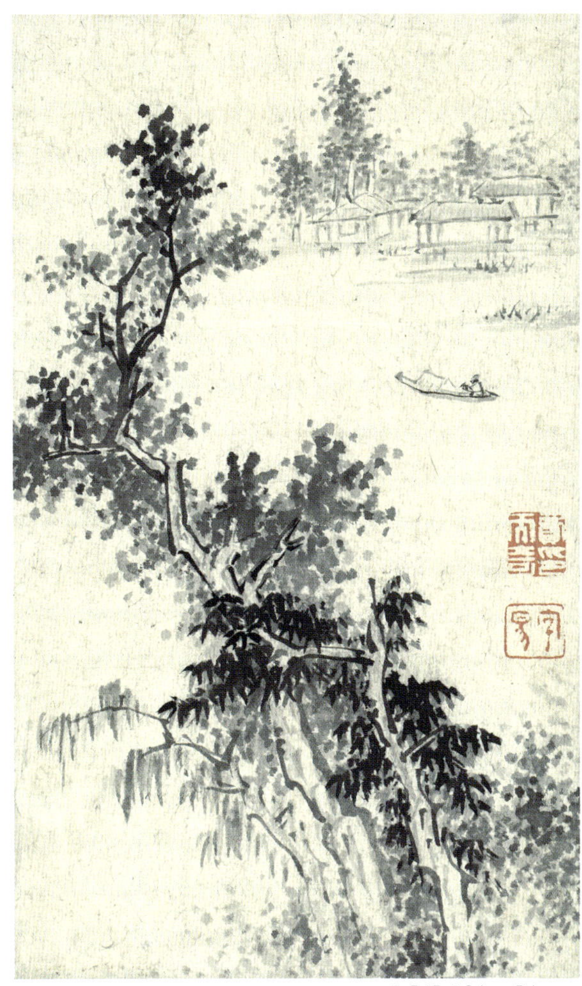

2 Fei Erqi, *Solitary Fisherman*

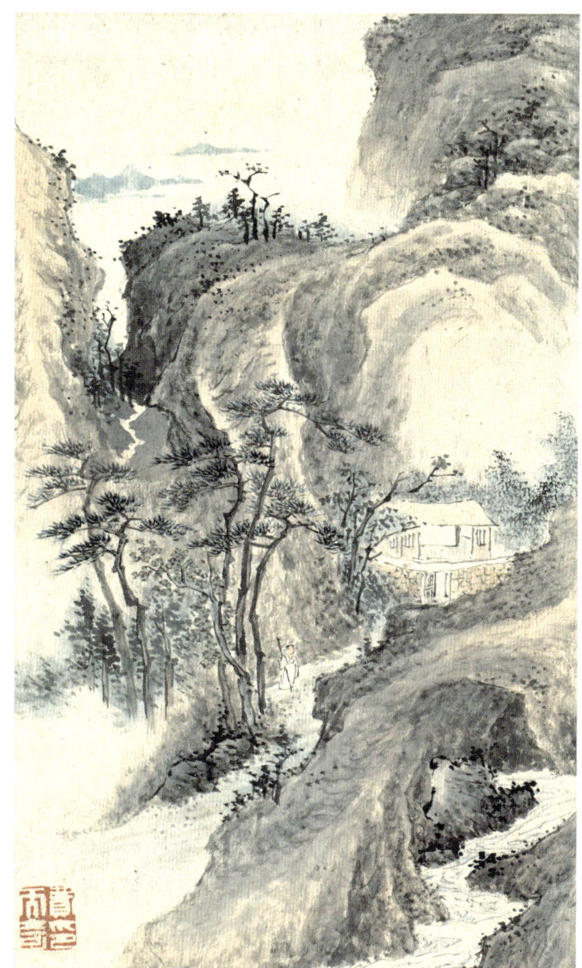

1 Fei Erqi, *Recluse on a Pine Path*

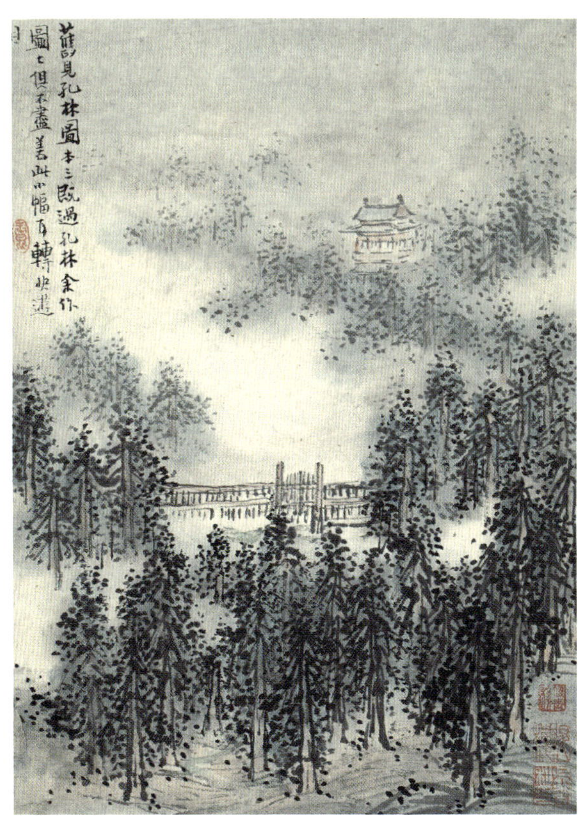

7 Hu Yukun, *The Confucian Grove*

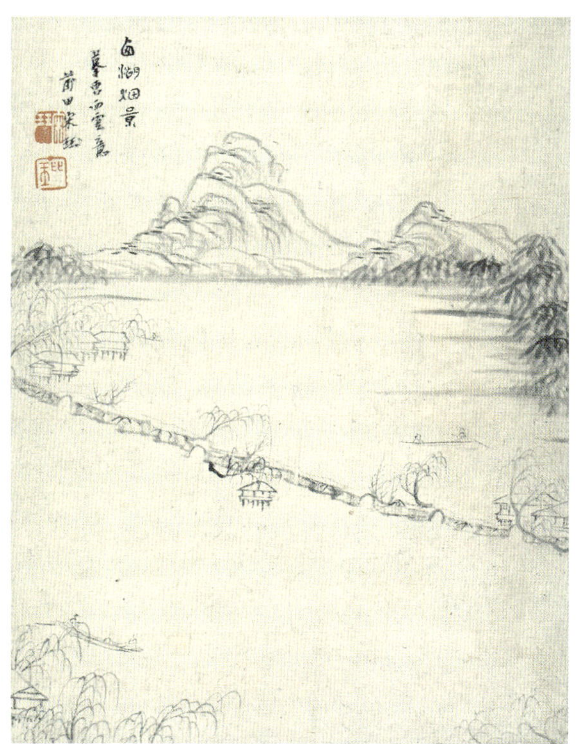

6 Song Jue, *Misty Scene at West Lake*

Gong Xian, one of the major individualist painters of the seventeenth century, was a prolific artist whose dramatic and haunting landscapes are among the most readily recognizable among all Chinese painters. Gong was born to a prominent clan in Kunshan (Jiangsu Province) but moved to Nanjing at an early age and identified strongly with this major urban center. Little is directly stated about his early life and background, though it has been surmised that he was raised as a young scholar under privileged circumstances in Nanjing; there is reference to him learning directly from Dong Qichang (cat. nos. 8–9), which appears to have occurred through the mentorship of Yang Wencong (cat. nos. 18–19) when Gong was thirteen years of age.[1] Such associations bespeak precocious talent and help to explain a number of shared points between Gong's later work and Dong's well-established views on orthodoxy and painting.[2]

In Nanjing during the 1630s Gong Xian was involved with poetry and painting clubs and was a member of the Fushe Restoration Society that sought government reform. The Manchu conquest affected him deeply. In addition to being the seat of the Southern Ming provisional court, Nanjing was close to Yangzhou, the site of an infamous razing by Manchu troops just before they took Nanjing in the fifth month of 1645. Judging from exchanged poems from both before and after 1645, most of Gong's acquaintances were devoted anti-Manchu activists. Gong may have avoided this characterization, but his movements during the early years of the Qing dynasty strongly imply sympathy, if not a direct tie, to underground resistance. Around 1666 he returned to the Nanjing area after having lived in Yangzhou for over a decade, establishing residence in a place on Qingliang Mountain he named the Half-Acre Garden. He resided there in reclusion, much as he had from the fall of the Ming, supporting himself by teaching painting, selling his poems and paintings, editing poetic anthologies, and enjoying culture and leisure with his circle of fellow Ming loyalists until his death in 1689.[3]

The monumentality of *Lofty Peak and Dense Woods*, together with its seals and signature, suggests a date in the 1650s, when Gong Xian moved away from his earlier abbreviated style to an intense and melancholic but dynamic image in an extraordinarily tall format of landscape. Two of his works from the period, *Mountain Landscape* (Shitou Shuwu collection, Taipei; dated 1655) and *Landscape in the Style of Dong Yuan and Juran* (Cleveland Museum of Art, c. 1650), provide context.[4] This is a scale of painting that presented distinct challenges, but for the ambitious painter the large vertical format also allowed experimentation with compositional arrangement and the rendering of depth, recession, and tone through layers of brushstrokes. All three paintings display a three-part composition, with a screen of trees in the foreground, hills in the middle ground, and towering mountains in the background, but the density of the forest in particular distinguishes *Lofty Peak and Dense Woods*. Encircling a mysterious dwelling with an air of energy and tension, the trees seem at once foreboding and protective. The mountain forms in this painting reference the style of Juran and relate closely to what is seen in *Landscape in the Style of Dong Yuan and Juran*.

Gong Xian's paintings often reveal the artist as preoccupied by the fate of Ming loyalists, and these earlier landscapes in the monumental format should be considered with that in mind. The 1650s were a period of great uncertainty, when hopes for the revival of the Ming dynasty were embraced by the *yimin*. One of the seals on *Lofty Peak and Dense Woods*—*chen Xian*, or "subject [Gong] Xian"—indicates Gong's continued alliance with the Ming court. Most of the artist's paintings depict mountain landscapes, but monumental landscapes of this stature are rare and seem to refer back to the imperial monumental landscapes of the Song, another dynasty that fell to foreign forces. On *Mountain Landscape* of 1655 he inscribed the following poem:

> Layered ridges, gathered peaks like thousands
> of statesmen's tablets;
> Darkly, throughout the day they fill the
> upper scene.
> I am suddenly startled by arriving rain under-
> neath the waterfall;
> Carrying wine, I intend to view them from
> the traveler's path.[5]
>
> 烈巘攢峰千萬笏，蒼然盡日在眉端.
> 忽驚雨至飛泉下，攜酒還從閣道看.

The likening of lofty peaks with the statesmen's tablets, indicative of imperial authority, suggest a metaphorical use of the natural landscape to proclaim lasting values that transcend the turmoil of the time. The majestic background of *Lofty Peak and Dense Woods* conveys a similar image of everlasting grandeur. Gong Xian embeds it in a realm of strangeness and novelty (*qi* 奇) that was both the hallmark of Nanjing taste and the artist's personal vision. **TTK**

For inscriptions and other documentation, see page 294 in this catalogue.

1 For a thorough examination of Gong Xian's biography, see Chung-lan Wang, "Gong Xian (1619–1689)."

2 See, for example James Cahill, "Hung-jen and Kung Hsien: Nature Transfigured," in *The Compelling Image*, 168–83. Wang discusses the relationship between Gong Xian and Yang Wencong in "Gong Xian (1619–1689)," 26 and following.

3 Gong Xian was first and foremost a poet, admired by his contemporaries for verses modeled after Tang-dynasty styles. Ibid., 116 and following. His poetry was published in at least four separate collections arranged by period.

4 *Mountain Landscape* is reproduced in *Yuemu*, pl. 31. For *Landscape in the Style of Dong Yuan and Juran* see Wai-kam Ho, et al., *Eight Dynasties of Chinese Painting*, cat. no. 213.

5 Translation based on that of Jerome Silbergeld, "Political Symbolism in the Landscape Painting and Poetry of Kung Hsien (c. 1620–1689)," 205.

34 Gong Xian 龔賢
1619–1689

Lofty Peak and Dense Woods **崇巖密林**
Los Angeles County Museum of Art
Mr. and Mrs. Allan C. Balch Fund

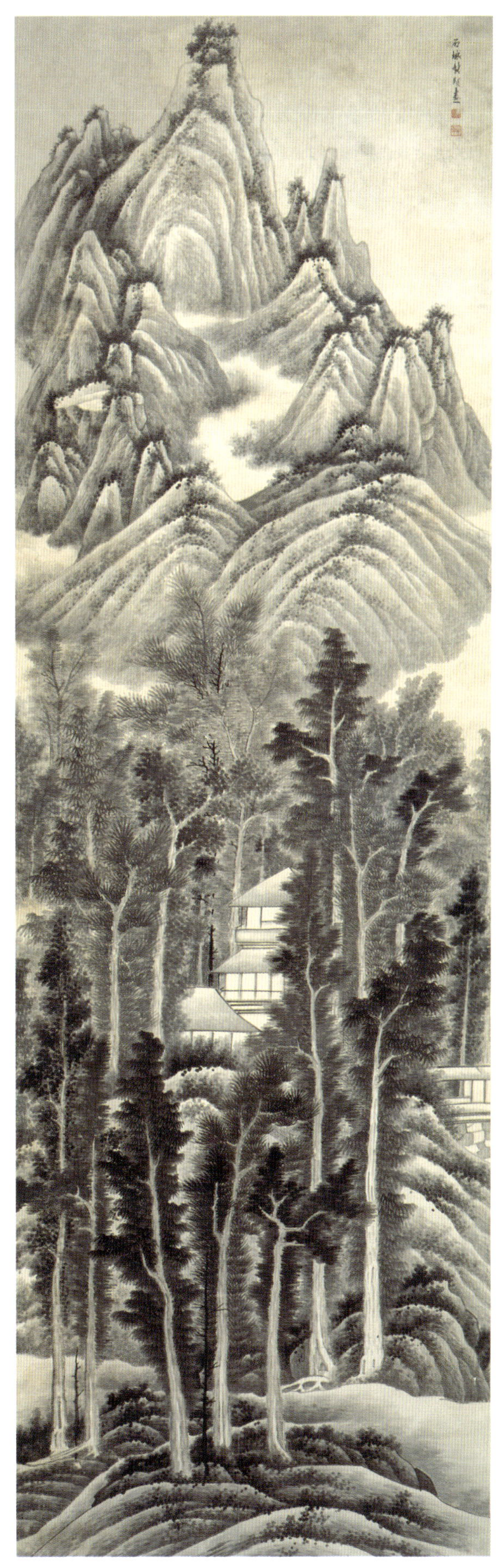

As it is for many of Gong Xian's paintings, an informed reading of *Boating in the Breeze* reveals personal meanings that add much to what at first appears a simple landscape scene. The sail is hardly recognizable, nor are the trees immediately identifiable as willows. Contrasting sharply with the typically feminine portrayals of graceful, windblown trees seen in paintings throughout a long pictorial tradition, the willows here extend their branches upward with short, thin tendrils extending one from the other to create a subtle weblike pattern. Common associations for the graceful willow include feminine beauty, romance, friendship at parting, and, somewhat negatively, short-lived or shallow success. For Gong Xian, the willow represented something more complex. Describing and depicting it frequently in writings and instructional manuals and on paintings, he used it as a kind of personal motif to encompass self-doubt, suffering, pride, and virtue. He expounded on his interpretation of the motif in one painting of the late 1650s in particular, *Uncultivated Willows in Early Winter*.[1] As Jerome Silbergeld explains in his essay about Gong's fascination with the willow, it was a metaphor for upholding morality even in difficult, chaotic conditions. Although of weak wood above ground and plain in appearance, the willow tree sinks strong roots in watery environments where other trees, such as the pine and cypress—more common metaphors for morality—would rot. The symbolism was especially meaningful to the Ming *yimin*, who remained loyal and virtuous to the fallen dynasty and now lived in reclusion under foreign rule.[2]

The willow in this painting comes from Gong Xian's mature period. Earlier in his career, as evident in the aforementioned *Uncultivated Willows in Early Winter*, he painted the trees with a rough, harsh appearance; trunks and branches jut forth like sharp spines, and the brushwork is similarly dark and stiff. The effect is prickly, perhaps not unlike his attitude towards the Qing government as he and the *yimin* adjusted to the harsh winter of foreign rule. By the 1670s, Gong's situation had stabilized following his return to Nanjing. His return to the city suggests a resignation after so many years of absence hoping for the return of the Ming. In comparison, the abundant growth of the willows in *Boating in the Breeze* perhaps can be interpreted as indicating survival through several winters and the artist's self-assurance of his status. A sense of regained pride and confidence, embodied by the flourishing of the trees' branches, is echoed in his poetic inscription. The boat carrying wine is a metaphor for a drunken Gong Xian, who has managed to survive by borrowing the strength of the uncultivated willows. However, there is also a suggestion of dissatisfaction. The character translated here as "clear" in the final line is *qing* 清, the same used for the Manchu dynasty.[3] Gong, the Ming loyalist, is rhetorically asking how long Qing rule will last. The painting does not seem to provide much of an answer. Like Gong's ghostly sail, we are confined to a narrow strip of middle-ground water by the cliff on the opposite bank. Gong Xian seems to lament that the situation is limited and constrained.

Especially noteworthy are the inscriptions above and below the painting, written in 1697 and 1698 by well-known *yimin* residing in Yangzhou. This was less than a decade after Gong had died, and it is likely that all of the inscribers had known the artist. Zha Shibiao (cat. no. 49), who resided in Yangzhou from the 1670s, in particular was a close friend of Gong Xian's as was Shitao (cat. nos. 50–51), whom he frequently entreated to visit his Half-Acre Garden. By the time the inscriptions were added there was no hope for a restoration of the former dynasty. The writers, rather, looked at *Boating in the Breeze* as a personal image of their former comrade. **TTK**

For inscriptions and other documentation, see pages 294–95 in this catalogue.

1 Collection unknown. See Jerome Silbergeld, "Kung Hsien's Self-Portrait in Willows," fig. 10.
2 Ibid., 27–31.
3 Jerome Silbergeld, "Political Symbolism in the Landscape Painting and Poetry of Kung Hsien (c. 1620–1689)," 127–28.

35 Gong Xian 龔賢
1619–1689

Boating in the Breeze 柳風片帆圖
Private collection

A full boat, completely laden with wine;
The sail borrows the willow's breeze and billows.
Sailing mile upon mile,
How long will the clear fragrance last?

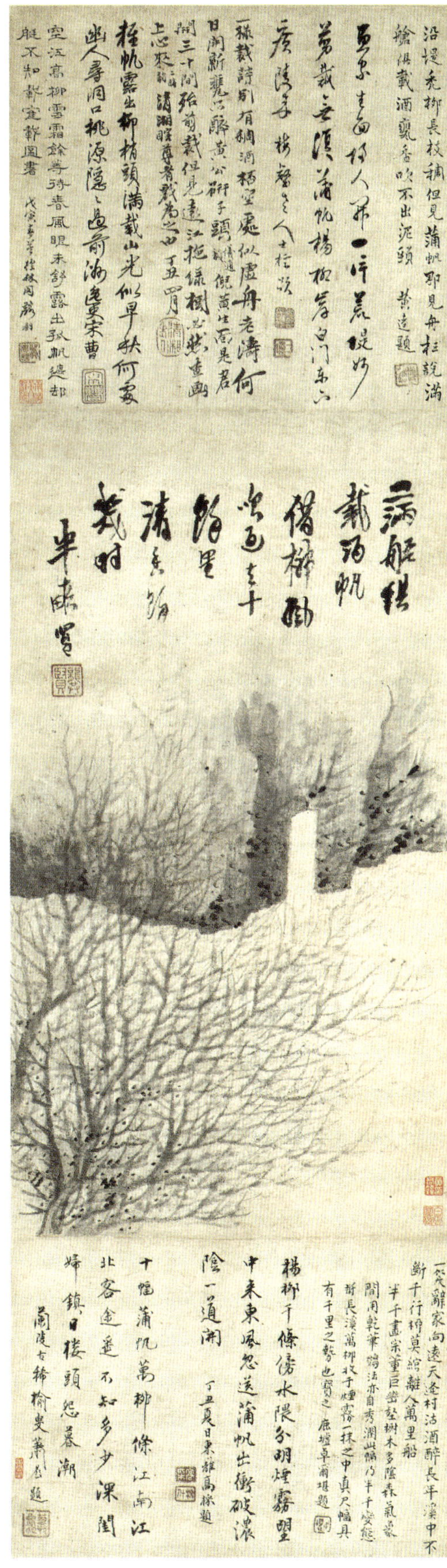

Painted four months before his death, *Landscape* is Gong Xian's last known dated painting. The inscription is appropriately retrospective, reflecting on his lifelong intellectual approach to painting. As he notes in the inscription, he hoped to reach the "untrammeled" class—a category of painting traditionally recognized as being both distinct and superior to the common ranks. Paintings of the Song and Yuan dynasties represented the classical tradition to Gong; they were the foundation upon which any painter who adhered to the principles laid down earlier in the seventeenth century by Dong Qichang would build one's art. Gong suggests that by moving beyond their rules one might achieve a level of accomplishment that is essential and personal. At the core of his inscription is an affirmation of literati painting. He references literature and calligraphy—the primary arts of the scholar—and, with his allusion to Su Shi's description of Wen Tong's painting as a "leftover skill," points directly to the association of one's art with the virtue of the artist. Gong ends with a description of Wang Fu and Shen Zhou—two Ming-dynasty painters whose approach to painting fits his development as well. Shen was an especially important predecessor, singled out by Gong elsewhere as the embodiment of Dong Qichang's "great synthesis."[1]

In his paintings of the 1680s, Gong Xian returned to the abbreviated style of his earliest paintings of the 1650s, and this would help lead to a new synthesis of his own.[2] He emphasized Shen Zhou's interpretations of Dong Yuan and Juran, two painters he referenced throughout his life.[3] In contrast to his earlier works of the 1660s and 70s, Gong used lighter brushstrokes in *Landscape*, although they are no less dense. The individual brushstrokes seem to meld into one another in moist layers that are associable with the style of Dong Yuan. Rather than emphasize texture and surface pattern, he focused on modeling three-dimensional forms using carefully calculated and applied calligraphic strokes in the descriptive form of Shen Zhou. The awkwardness found in his earlier *Lofty Peak and Dense Woods* (cat. no. 34) has been replaced by a surer handling of composition, depiction of depth and recession, and modeling. The outcroppings of rock on the mountains demonstrate Gong's interpretation of the alum-rock accumulations of Juran.

Landscape is far more welcoming than Gong's early paintings in the monumental mode, where chaotic compositions often obstructed orderly exploration. Here the viewer enters the landscape by crossing placid waters to access the shore at the lower left, then heads toward a cluster of three humble, thatched-roofed buildings flanked by a copse of bare-branched trees. A more formal two-story timber structure nestles half-hidden in the trees above the hills and mist in the middle ground. The mountains behind seemingly enwrap it in security. *Landscape* lacks the intensity and drama of the earlier monumental landscapes. The rocks no longer warp and thrust violently and sharply in all directions but have been softened and weathered—perhaps Gong's personal commentary on his age and change in political stance over time.[4] Nonetheless, even if this painting suggests some kind of reconciliation with his fate, there should be no questioning the power of Gong's fundamental convictions: with quiet modesty the painting asserts a continued trust in the permanence and monumentality of a landscape rooted in tradition. Whereas the structure of his landscapes in prior decades created plausible fantasy, the scene here seeks a subtle balance more firmly planted in reality. **TTK**

For inscriptions and other documentation, see page 295 in this catalogue.

1 A lengthy inscription on Shen Zhou's significance is found on a leaf in an album of 1683 in the Osaka Municipal Museum of Art. Gong Xian ends it with the ultimate compliment, likening Shen to Confucius. See Chung-lan Wang, "Gong Xian (1619–1689)," 311–12.

2 Ibid., 313; and William Ding Yee Wu, "Kung Hsien," 182–83.

3 Wu, "Kung Hsien," 182–83.

4 Jerome Silbergeld, "Political Symbolism in the Landscape Painting and Poetry of Kung Hsien (c. 1620–1689)," 116.

36 Gong Xian 龔賢
1619–1689

Landscape 山水軸
1689

Honolulu Museum of Art
Purchase

In painting, one must first make an orderly arrangement of the principles of the Song and the Yuan. Afterwards, by relaxing [the principles' binds] one's work will be of the untrammeled class. Although a painting may be composed of just a few scattered strokes, if the Six Laws are complete within, and if the spirit of literature and the standards of calligraphy are both present, then one knows that this painting is the "leftover" skill of a talented person and not some laughable effortby a specialist hoping to stand out from the chaotic masses. Mengduan [Wang Fu] and Qinan [Shen Zhou] in later years amused themselves with the styles of Ni [Ni Zan] and Huang [Huang Gongwang] while remaining grounded in the fundamentals of Dong [Dong Yuan] and Ju [Juran]. My teachers! My teachers! I have made this silk [painting and inscription] in order to set forth the intentions of my brush.

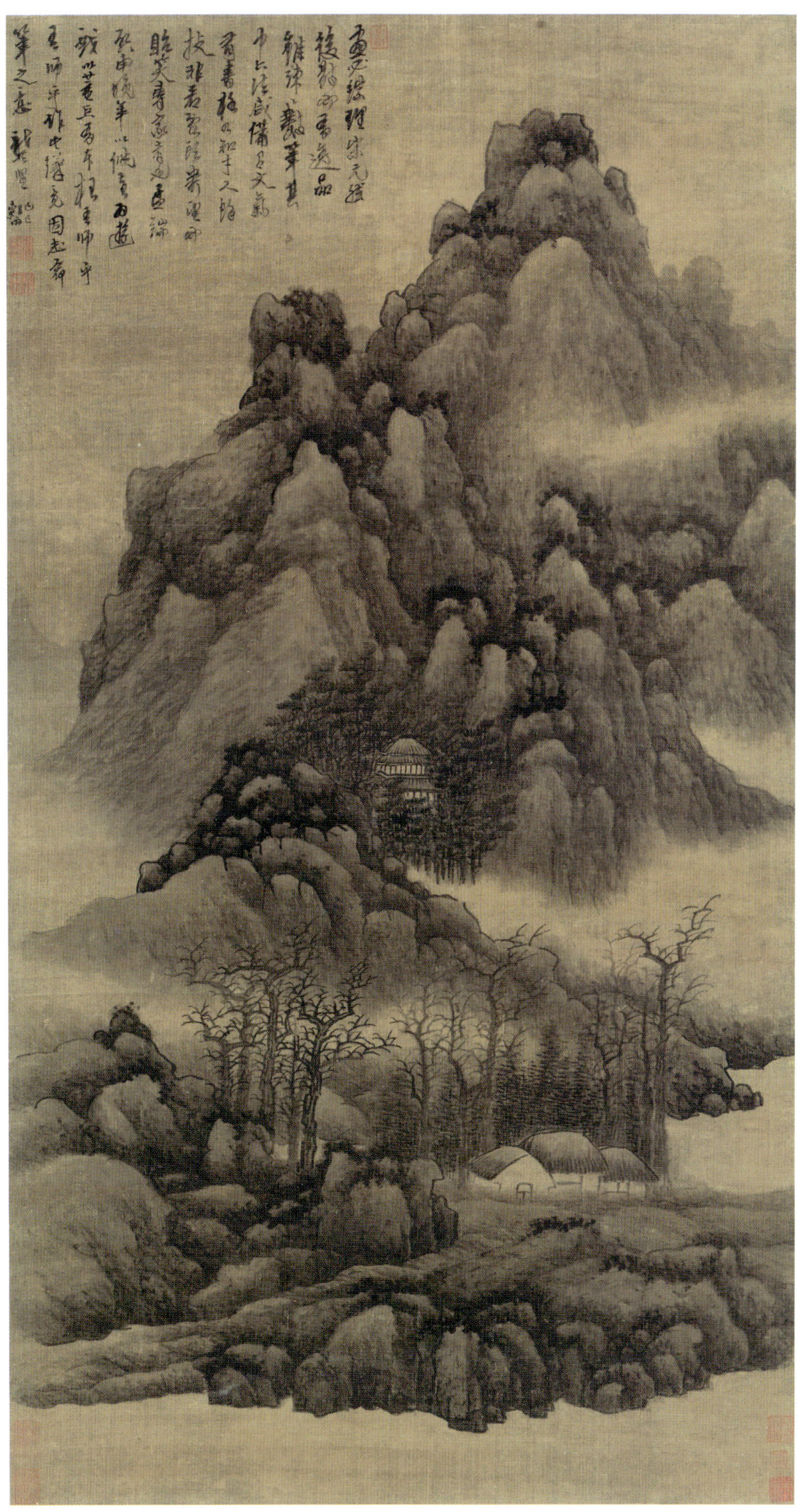

Painted in Kuncan's quarters at Youqi Temple near Nanjing, this painting of 1661 depicts the surroundings of a mountain temple, which was the Buddhist monk-painter's favorite subject. His poem at the upper right, written in a rough and casual hand, describes his journey into the mountainous landscape of the painting. Juxtaposing the lofty and misty mountain with the reclusive monk, Kuncan expresses his quest for enlightenment through communion with nature. Matching the poetic praise of nature's grand scene, he paints a landscape in which towering mountains are exalted. Nestled within, the temple complex is depicted as a Buddhist retreat, its seclusion emphasized by a wooden fence, waterfall, and mist. A rustic dwelling is depicted below, a single fisherman in his boat by the bank—Kuncan, perhaps? On a promontory upstream overlooking the river the artist added an isolated pavilion that faces a lone sailboat and distant shores. Like the "flying mists" of the poem, a swirling mist rises from the river and encircles the scene, emanating the mystique of nature.

Kuncan painted landscapes almost exclusively, most of them depicting scenes similar to *Temple on a Mountain Ledge*.[1] This was the world Kuncan knew. Committed to Buddhism prior to the fall of the Ming dynasty in 1644, the monk spent years wandering among mountain temples, which served as places of refuge for Chan Buddhist monks and Ming loyalists alike. Kuncan was both. He settled in Nanjing in 1654 and studied under the Chan master Juelang Daosheng. A few years later he became the abbot of the Youqi Temple, a sub-temple of the Baoen Monastery, where he spent the rest of his life.[2] The temple environments around Nanjing inspired him to paint and meditate on landscapes. After his journey to Huangshan (Yellow Mountain, Anhui Province) in 1659, he seems to have become increasingly fascinated by the majestic scenery of mountains.[3] During the 1660s, his most productive period, he often painted views of Baoen Monastery as well as other temples around Nanjing.

Settling in Nanjing was significant to Kuncan's development as an artist, as here he became closely associated with the painters Cheng Zhengkui and Gong Xian (cat. nos. 34–36) as well as the prominent patron Zhou Lianggong.[4] Cheng and Zhou, both of whom wrote biographies of Kuncan, had celebrated painting collections that provided material for Kuncan's study.[5] Moreover, Cheng and Gong had both studied under the leading theorist and painter Dong Qichang (cat. nos. 8–9) and provided Kuncan with a vital connection to the literati painting tradition as interpreted through Dong's ideas. In particular, Kuncan practiced the painting styles of Mi Fu, Huang Gongwang, and Wang Meng, all key figures in Dong's lineage of preferred masters he labeled the Southern School. Among these influences, the Yuan painter Wang Meng is the most salient to Kuncan's *Temple on a Mountain Ledge*.[6] The compositional density and tactile richness of the painting, common also to Kuncan's other hanging scrolls, are drawn from Wang's style, though Kuncan has thoroughly transformed the Yuan master's mode into his own visual language that highlights an exquisite interplay of brushstrokes and coloring.

A fine example of Kuncan's artistic maturity in the 1660s, *Temple on a Mountain Ledge* typifies the signature style he developed through his extensive study of the old masters. Owing to this stylistic indebtedness, he is often considered less individualistic than some other contemporary monk-painters, notably Hongren, Bada Shanren (cat. nos. 41–48), and Shitao (cat. nos. 50–51). However, by synthesizing the work of preceding masters and integrating it with a deeply personal, spiritual experience of landscape, Kuncan developed a style distinct from his contemporaries. His *Temple on a Mountain Ledge* embodies his meditative and artistic practices, as well as the religious and cultural richness of Nanjing in the aftermath of the dynastic transition. **SWC**

For inscriptions and other documentation, see page 295 in this catalogue.

1 Richard Pegg, "Kuncan: Man, Monk and Painter," 6–8.
2 Ibid., 2–5.
3 An important marker for this development is Kuncan's *Journey to Mount Huang* of 1660 in the Shanghai Museum. See Wai-kam Ho, ed., *The Century of Tung Ch'i-ch'ang*, vol. 1, pl. 118.
4 Pegg, "Kuncan," 8–11; and Zhu Wanzhang 朱萬章, *Shixi*, 27–37.
5 Cheng Zhengkui 程正揆, "Shixi xiaozhuan" 石谿小傳, *Qingxi yigao* 青溪遺稿, in *Qingdai shiwen ji hui bian* 清代詩文集彙編 (Shanghai: Shanghai guji chubanshe, 2009), vol. 20, 268–69. Zhou Lianggong 周亮工, "Shiqi heshang" 石谿和尚, *Duhua lu* 讀畫錄, in *Baibu congshu jicheng* 百部叢書集成 39, no. 8 (Taipei: Yiwen yinshuguan, 1965–70), 2:8b–9b. Kuncan often painted for Zhou Lianggong. See Hongnam Kim, *The Life of a Patron*, 115–16.
6 Cheng Zhengkui and other seventeenth-century critics noted Kuncan's stylistic indebtedness to the Yuan masters. See Zhang Geng 張庚, *Guochao huazheng lu* 國朝畫徵錄, in *Zhongguo shuhua quanshu* 中國書畫全書 (Shanghai: Shanghai shuhua chubanshe, 2000), vol. 10, 445–46.

37 **Kuncan** 髡殘
B. 1612

Temple on a Mountain Ledge 群峰古寺
1661
Asia Society, New York
Mr. and Mrs. John D. Rockefeller 3rd Collection

Famous mountains! I, Monk Can, approach,
First viewing them from beyond the clouds.
That vast expanse encompasses Creation,
That lofty majesty displays great dignity!
Rows of peaks, like clustered bamboo,
Flying mists, as if spit out by Immortals!
Soon I will be amongst those myriad ravines,
Gourd and bamboo hat as my companions.

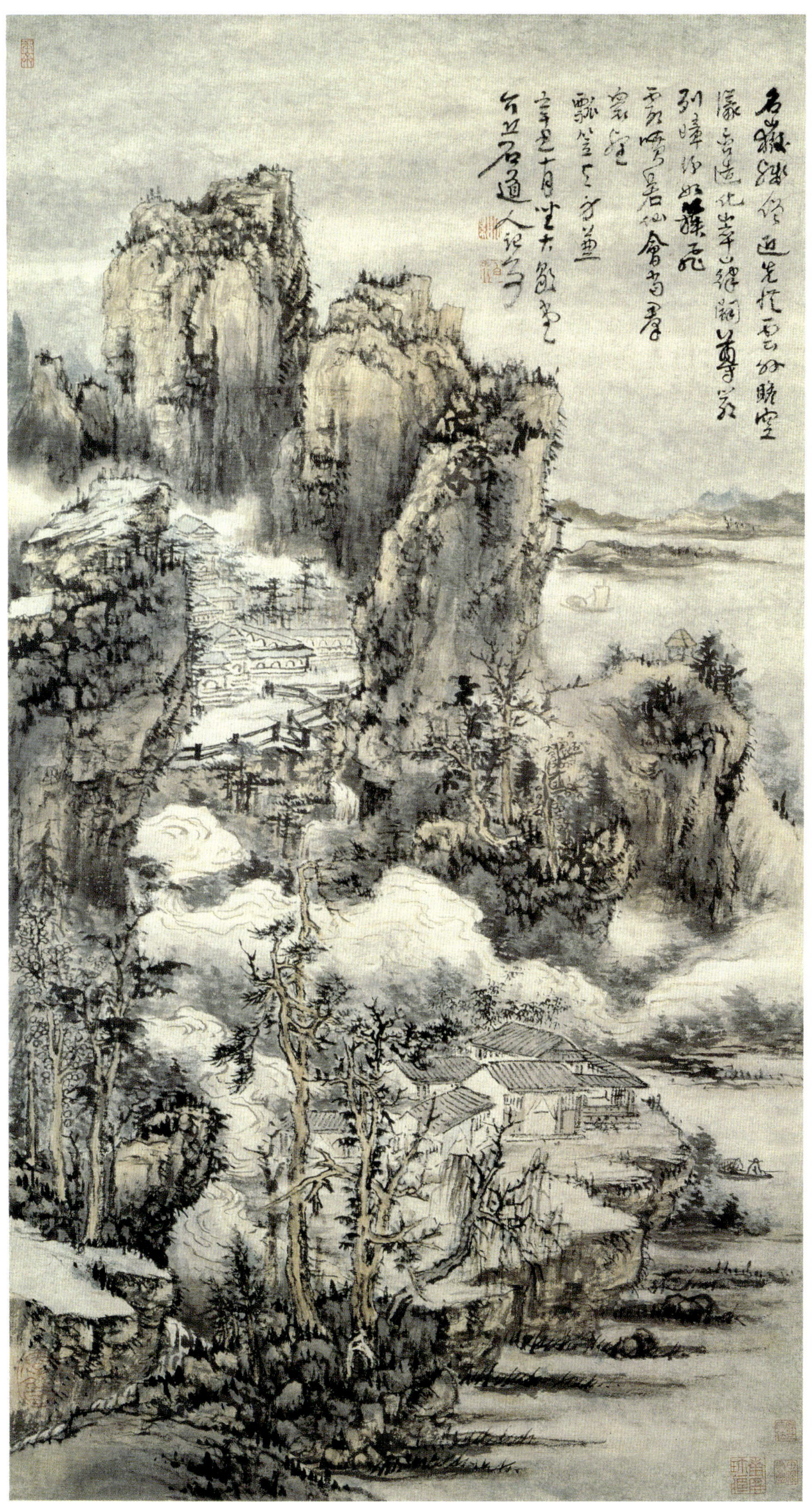

This painting of Mount Qinyuhang by the noted Ming loyalist Xu Fang depicts a scenic place in the western suburbs of Suzhou (Jiangsu Province). The scroll is one of an original set of twelve collectively titled *The Twelve Surpassing Scenes of the Mountains of Wu* (*Wu shan zui-sheng shier tu* 吳山最勝十二圖) depicting Mount Lingyan 靈岩山, Lianhua Grotto 蓮花洞, Shangsha Village 上沙, Mount Hua 華山, Heavenly Pond 天池, Mount Qinyuhang 秦餘杭山 (also called Yang Mountain 陽山), Arrow Peak 箭闕, Zhu Embankment 竺塢, Hu Mountain Bridge 虎山橋, Tong Ravine 銅坑, Mount Dengwei 鄧尉山, and Qishier Peak Pavilion 七十二峰閣. According to his inscription on the landscape of Mount Dengwei, Xu Fang painted this series in the third lunar month of 1672. The conditions of the individual scrolls, now scattered among various collections, show great variance, suggesting that either the set was split up some time ago or the extant scrolls represent more than one set. The latter is a distinct possibility, since it is evident that Xu painted this set more than once; another version of the Mount Qinyuhang composition is in the collection of the Anhui Provincial Museum.[1] Moreover, in precisely the same year (1672), Xu Fang painted an album titled *Twelve Surpassing Scenes of the Mountains of Wu* (*Wu shan mingsheng shier tu* 吳山名勝十二圖), utilizing compositions that are closely related to the hanging scroll set(s), despite the very different size and format.[2] It is clear that this particular subject, comprising individual scenes of the local landscape around Suzhou (Wu) with strong topographical references, was Xu's signature work. The particular scene represented in this scroll must have been especially meaningful to him: he went by the sobriquet Recluse of Mount Qinyuhang (Qinyu shanren 秦餘山人).

A native of Suzhou, Xu Fang passed the highest level of examination and earned the *jinshi* (presented scholar) degree in 1642.[3] Three years later, however, the Ming succumbed to Manchu forces and Xu's father—Xu Qian, an officer of the Ming court—took his own life to die a martyr. Xu Fang wished to follow, but Xu Qian prevented him by saying, "I have no choice but to die, but it would be acceptable for you to live as a farmer, buried away from the world" 吾固不可以不死，若長為農夫以沒世可也.[4] Xu Fang closely followed his father's words and lived the remainder of his life as a recluse. As he wrote in the preface of his collected works, *Juyitang ji* 居易堂集, for twenty years after the fall of the Ming he would not step into the city, and for twenty more years he would not even leave his house. He was thus labeled one of the "three (great) loyalists" 海內三遺民, together with Chao Mingsheng of Jiaxing and Shen Shoumin of Xuancheng.[5] In reclusion, Xu and his family suffered from poverty and illness. In succession his two sons and daughter died of hunger and cold, and Xu himself almost died of illness in 1658. Nonetheless, he steadfastly refused to keep company with the Qing officials who reached out to him. After recovering, he was framed for tax evasion, which drove him to live as a fugitive without a definite residence for five years. Mount Qinyuhang, the subject of this painting, served as one of his temporary dwellings in the Suzhou area, where he lodged at the home of his relative Zhang Dezhong in 1663. In the same year, Xu's close friend and teacher, the monk Hongchu, built a rustic residence for him in Shangsha Village, between Mount Tianping and Mount Lingyan.[6] Xu lived there in seclusion for the remainder of his life.

Although he only lived for a year on Mount Qinyuhang, Xu Fang identified with the site, and his sobriquet as its mountain man or recluse is significant. Mount Qinyuhang was well known as the first site of reclusion for Zhidun, a famous monk of the Eastern Jin (317–420).[7] It was also the last place of refuge for Fuchai, the King of Wu who was defeated by the state of Yue, lost his state and life, and was buried on the mountain.[8] Thus, Mount Qinyuhang represented both the pleasure of being a recluse and the sorrow of losing one's country. Moreover, the mountain's name alludes to the escape from a tyrannical state. As told in the famous "Peach Blossom Spring" of Tao Yuanming, refugees fled the disturbances of the Qin dynasty (221–207 BCE) by retreating to a hidden valley. Qinyuhang literally means "crossing over of the remnants of Qin."[9] The mountain, named after the Peach Blossom Spring utopia, was Xu's personal emblem of reclusion.

The inscriptions that Xu Fang added to his *Twelve Surpassing Scenes* are unusually matter-of-fact—more of the nature of gazetteer descriptions than the belles-lettres writing associated with the literati. The descriptive narrative style suits the ostensibly topographical function of the paintings, yet the landscapes themselves are rendered in a decidedly personal manner. Xu's painting style is sometimes traced back to the tenth-century Juran, but the primary precedent is clearly Shen Zhou, who not only painted in a similarly blocky style but also was associated with works of Suzhou's topography.[10] Through a stylistic as well as thematic association with Shen Zhou, the paragon of Ming Suzhou culture, Xu subtly states his allegiance to the local landscape unrelated to the reality of post-Qing conquest. More importantly, by painting scenes that were tied to his personal experiences during the many decades that he lived in the environs of Suzhou, Xu Fang was able to reframe the mountains of Wu as his own living space and a representation of his existence as a loyalist and recluse. In this respect, the topographical narratives help assert his identity as inextricable from the timeless fact of Suzhou's real landscape. **YSZ**

For inscriptions and other documentation, see pages 295–96 in this catalogue.

1 Reproduced in *Zhongguo gudai shuhua tumu* (1993), vol. 12, 235. The Anhui Provincial Museum scroll possesses the same inscription in what appears to be an identical style, but the two paintings vary in composition. Both paintings appear to be genuine works, which would then suggest the existence of different sets.

2 Reproduced in *Xu Sizhai Wu shan mingsheng shier tu* 徐俟齋吳山名勝十二圖 (Shanghai: Youzheng shuju, 1919).

3 For Xu Fang's biography, see Li Yuandu 李元度, *Guochao xianzheng shilue* 國朝先正事略 (Changsha: Yuelu shushe, 1991), 45:1164–65; *Qing shi gao* 清史稿 (Beijing: Zhonghua shuju, 1977), 50:13846–48; and Luo Zhenyu 羅振玉, "Xu Sizhai xiansheng nianpu" 徐俟齋先生年譜, in *Qingchu mingru nianpu* 清初名儒年譜 (Beijing: Beijing tushuguan chubanshe, 2006), vol. 9, 83–212. See also Chen Sandi 陳三弟, "Xu Fang yanjiu," 76–86; and Wen Shiliang 溫世亮, "Ming yimin Xu Fang yanjiu."

38 Xu Fang 徐枋 1622–1694

Mount Qinyuhang 秦餘杭山圖 Datable to 1672

Private collection

Mount Yang is the chief mountain in the commandery. Another name for it is Mount Qinyuhang. It is also called Mount Sifei [Four-Flying], since the mountain range is endless and the four sides all look like they are in flight. Thus, one can imagine how grand and steep it is. Many of the mountains of Wu are outstanding in appearance, but none has ever compared to Mount Qinyu. The dangerously narrow hill paths wind into the void with countless turns. Halfway up the side of the mountain, there is a temple. Several bends further up, there is the site of Master Zhi's religious practices, which is the old Manjusri Temple. In the past, this temple together with the temples on Mount Zhixing and Mount Hua were called the three legs of the tripod [being the most important]. In front of the temple, there is a terrace. Handsomely erect, facing the clouds, and of immeasurable height, it is called the Cliff of Self-Sacrifice. Turning left from the cliff and passing the Buddhist temple, there is the Terrace of Heavenly Wind. The two terraces face one another. They are also cliffs. Nowadays it is called Osmanthus Terrace. Within, the terrace is level and expansive. Above it rises the Peak of Incessant Clouds. Under the peak, there is a pond and a spring. The peak rises several meters above the ground and is a couple hundred feet in width. Grand and majestic, it is just like a screen. The loftiness and steepness, as well as the unevenness, up and down, all defy description. Various sorts of trees prosper in the stone cracks. Red, yellow, purple and emerald [their leaves and blossoms] do not wither in any season. They flicker brightly, scattered among the green cliffs and peaks. How marvelous it is!

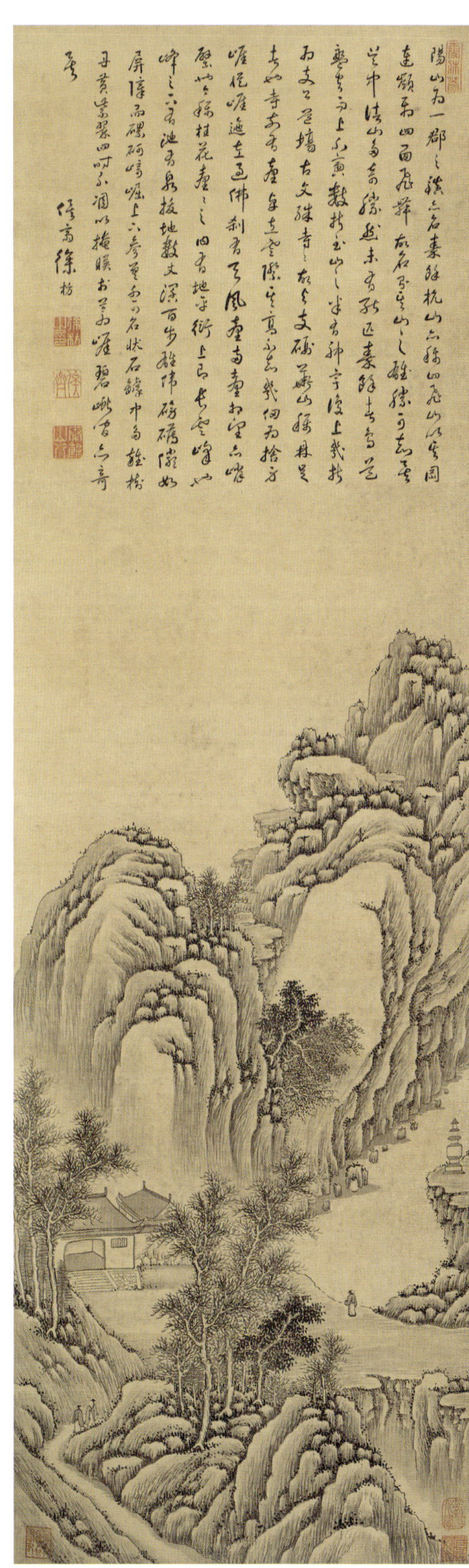

4 *Qing shi gao*, 501:13847.

5 For the biographies of Chao Mingsheng and Shen Shoumin, see Li, *Guochao xianzheng shilue*, 45:1165–67.

6 Ibid.

7 Huijiao 慧皎, *Gaoseng zhuan* 高僧傳 (Beijing: Zhonghua shuju, 1992), 159.

8 Zhao Ye 趙曄, *Wuyue chunqiu* 吳越春秋, in *Wuyue chunqiu quanyi* 吳越春秋全譯, ed. Zhang Jue 張覺 (Guiyang: Guizhou renmin chubanshe, 1993), 5:228, 229n2, 232.

9 Bada Shanren and other Ming loyalists employed the historical lessons of both the Wu-Yue conflict of the Spring and Autumn period and the Qin conquest to comment on contemporary affairs. See Hui-shu Lee's essay in this catalogue.

10 For one example of this kind of topographical image associated with Shen Zhou, see his *Famous Sights of Wu*, reproduced in Wai-kam Ho, et al., *Eight Dynasties of Chinese Painting*, cat. no. 152. Zhang Geng describes Xu's style as "arranging landscape in a steady and well-balanced way, rather than focusing on strange and marvelous expression." Zhang Geng 張庚, *Guochao hua zheng lu* 國朝畫徵錄 (facsimile reprint of 1739 ed.), 1:9a. See also Sun Fuxuan 孫福軒, "Xu Fang huaxue sixiang lun," 67–74.

Fang Hengxian was born of a renowned clan in Tongcheng, Anhui Province. He settled in Nanjing during the late years of the Ming dynasty and established a reputation as a painter, collector, and art critic.[1] Unlike his cousin Fang Yizhi (cat. no. 40), who remained staunchly loyal to the Ming, Fang Hengxiang served the Qing court from 1647 to 1657, though this ended with a period of banishment to Shenyang (Liaoning Province) in the far northeast.[2] By the time he returned from his travails in 1660, he had lost all interest in an official career and dedicated the remainder of his life to artistic pursuits.[3]

These nine leaves of painting and calligraphy have been passed down as a group since 1915, when the collector Chen Kuilin documented them in his catalogue *Baoyuge shuhua lu* 寶迂閣書畫錄 (the current sequence follows that in Chen's catalogue).[4] It is apparent, however, that even then the album was incomplete. A hanging scroll by the artist in the Palace Museum (Beijing) titled *Strange Rocks of the Palace City in Bianliang* (right) is composed of two leaves of precisely the same measurements as the leaves in this album.[5] The bottom leaf of that scroll features two ornamental rocks said to have been remnants from Emperor Huizong's famed Genyue Park, each chiseled with a name said to have been composed by Huizong's own hand. The upper leaf is a calligraphic transcription by Liu Gao of an oft-copied text composed by the Southern Song official and literary figure Luo Dajing.[6] Luo's text, sometimes titled "Dwelling in the Mountains," praises a life of reclusion. Narrating his daily life, Luo describes first the silence of living in such seclusion that no one knocks at his door, continues with a leisurely stroll along a mountain path to a stream, and then returns home to enjoy a meal made with root vegetables. He ends by quoting Su Shi on sitting quietly in meditation.

This literary account of a reclusive existence precisely matches what is depicted in four leaves of *Painting and Calligraphy*, making it all but certain that Liu Gao's transcription originally belonged. Since the remaining leaves of this album—one depicting a lotus, three featuring a text on "An Old Coin," and one portraying in text and image a rock purported to have belonged to Shen Yue—as well as the Beijing leaf (depicting the two strange rocks of Bianliang underneath Liu Gao's transcription) are all of uniform size, it is logical to assume that they all were originally of one album.[7]

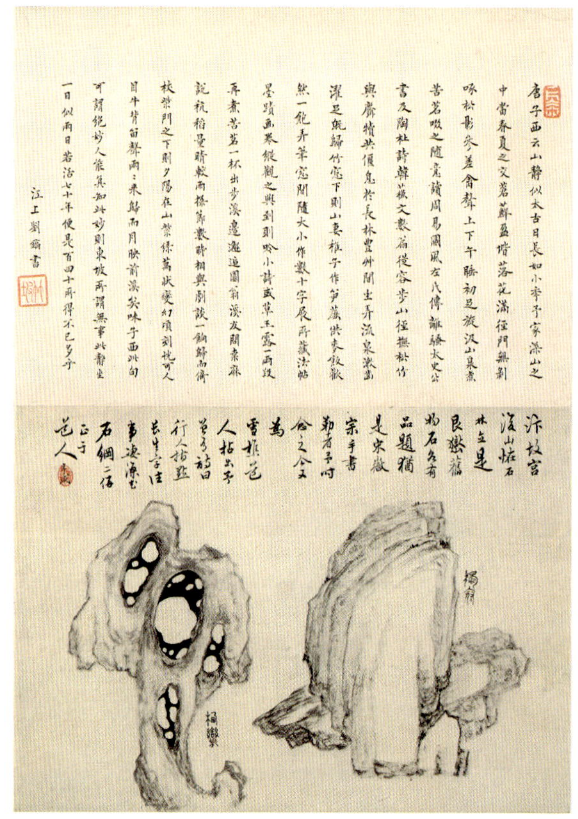

Fang Hengxian, *Strange Rocks of the Palace City in Bianliang*; Hanging scroll: ink on paper; 58.4 × 39.1 cm; Palace Museum, Beijing

There are a number of unanswered questions regarding this album as well as the small hanging scroll in the Palace Museum. Who, for example, was Liu Gao? Was his transcription of the Luo Dajing text specifically written for Fang Hengxian?[8] On his painting of the strange rocks of Bianliang, Fang added a short inscription suggesting that the painting was for someone whose sobriquet was Xueqiao daoren 雪樵道人 (Woodcutter-of-the-Snow Daoist), yet this name does not appear in any of the inscriptions on the leaves of the album; only an uncle is mentioned, found in Fang's inscription on the leaf depicting root vegetables. Who was this snowy woodcutter? Xueqiao daoren has not been identified, but another painting by Fang that recently appeared at auction suggests a potential explanation for some of the issues surrounding the album. That hanging scroll depicts a single strange rock that is precisely the same in appearance as one of the rocks in *Strange Rocks of the Palace City in Bianliang*. Not only is the rock the same, right down to its seal-script label (Qiluan 棲鸞, Roosting Phoenix), the painting also includes exactly the same inscription with reference to Xueqiao daoren.[9] It appears that this was a favored subject of Fang, one that he recycled

For inscriptions and other documentation, see page 296 in this catalogue.

1 See the informative entry for Fang Hengxian's *Landscape of Mount Yuelu* in *Kaikodo Journal* (Autumn 1996), cat. no. 17.

2 Hongnam Kim, "Chou Liang-kung and his 'Tu-hua-lu' (Lives of Painters)," 167.

3 Zhou Lianggong 周亮工, *Du hua lu* 讀畫錄, in *Qingdai zhuanji congkan* 清代傳記叢刊 (Taipei: Mingwen shuju, 1985–86), vol. 71, 36–37. Fang is said to have emulated Huang Gongwang's style in his landscape paintings. See Yu Jianhua 俞劍華, ed., *Zhongguo meishujia renming cidian* 中國美術家人名辭典 (Shanghai: Shanghai renmin meishu chubanshe, 1981), 43.

4 Chen Kuilin 陳夔麟, *Baoyuge shuhua lu* 寶迂閣書畫錄, in *Lidai shuhua lu jikan* 歷代書畫錄輯刊 (Beijing: Beijing tushuguan chubanshe, 2007), vol. 13, 525–28.

5 Shan Guoqiang 單國強, ed., *Jinling zhujia huihua* 金陵諸家繪畫, in *Gugong bowuyuan cang wenwu zhenpin quanji* 故宮博物院藏文物珍品全集 (Hong Kong: Shangwu yinshuguan, 1997), vol. 10, 75.

6 Luo Dajing 羅大經, *Helin yulu* 鶴林玉露 (Beijing: Zhonghua shuju, 1983), 304. Luo's text was often transcribed by later compilers and artists. Liu Gao's identity remains uncertain, though there was an official of this name active in the late Ming.

7 The possibility of the album once having more leaves, now missing, should also be considered.

8 From its publication in *Jinling zhujia huihua* it appears that Liu's transcription is written on a different kind of paper from Fang Hengxian's painting below.

39 **Fang Hengxian** 方亨咸
Act. c. 1647–1678

Painting and Calligraphy **書畫冊**
After 1659
Private collection

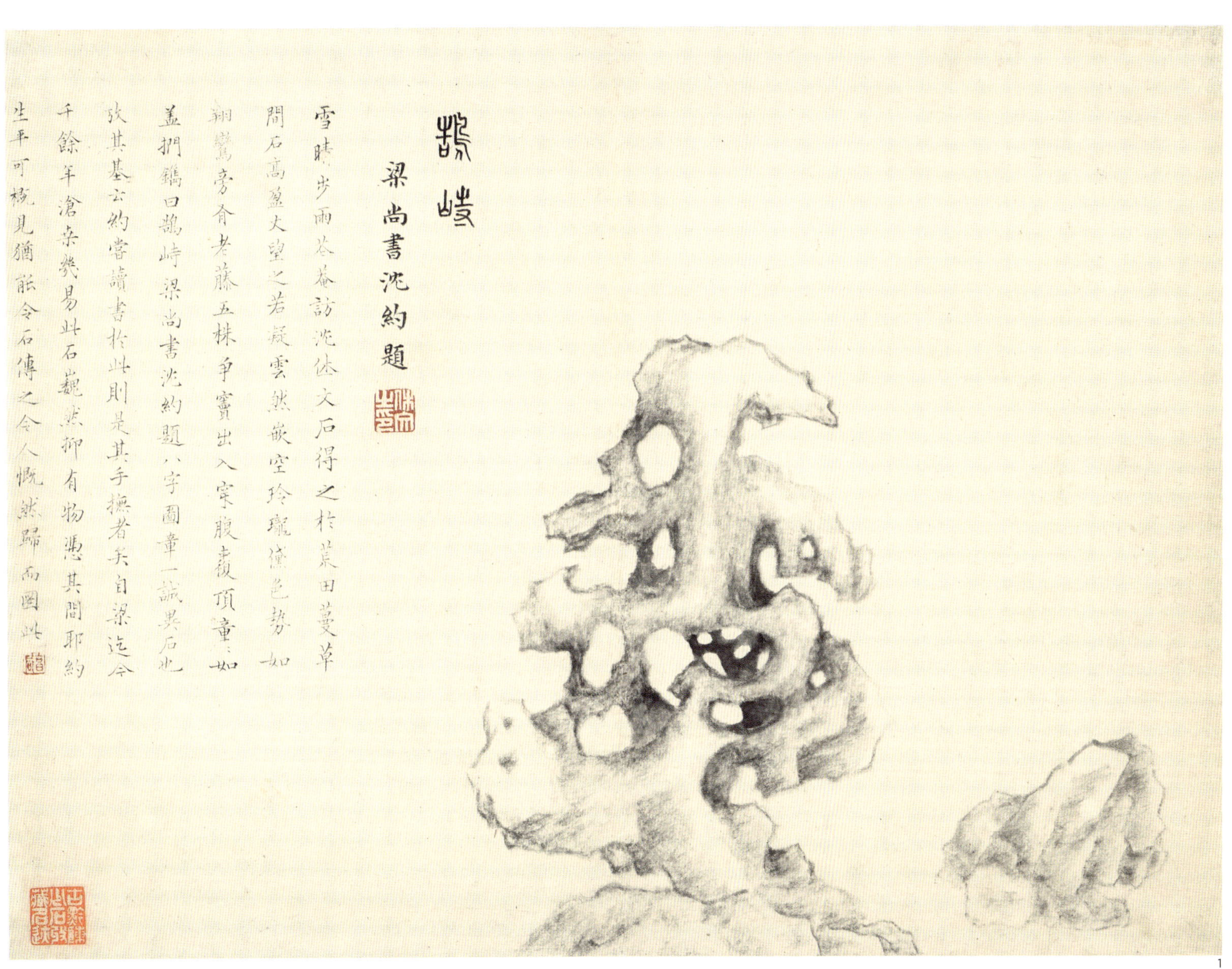

1

Straight and Erect. Inscribed by the Imperial Secretary, Shen Yue, of the Liang Dynasty.

The sky cleared after snow, and I strolled to Yuhua'an [Studio of Rain and Flowers] to seek Shen Xiuwen's [Shen Yue's] rock. I found it amidst wild grass growing everywhere in a deserted field. . .

a number of times in different formats, including its original inscription. Such flexibility helps explain the eclectic nature of this album. At a glance their subjects seem rather disparate, but when considered as an ensemble it is apparent that there is deep, personal meaning.

After the leaves related to Luo Dajing's text on reclusion, which form a discrete unit within the album, those featuring the two strange rocks from Huizong's Genyue, Shen Yue's rock, and the old coin from Huizong's reign (described in poem and preface) are all related as presenting ancient objects that Fang Hengxian encountered. Furthermore, they express the common theme of surviving dynastic change. The objects from the Huizong period reminded Fang of the sorrowful fall of the Northern Song. However, he appreciates their longevity, their ability to survive the vicissitudes of history. Shen Yue's rock survived even longer, but the focus here, perhaps, was more on the person than the object. Shen himself symbolized survival through dynastic change since he was the unusual politician who served three successive dynasties: the Song (420–479), Qi (479–502), and Liang (502–557). These rock paintings and preface with poem can be regarded as a series of works to express the same idea.

The overall theme of *Painting and Calligraphy* seems to reflect the painter's internal conflict as a leftover subject of the Ming dynasty. After the Qing dynasty was established, Fang Hengxian chose to survive by serving in the government rather than to resist. However, it could not have been a decision without regret, especially for someone like Fang, whose family produced a number of Ming loyalists.[10] Sorrowful, he expressed his regret indirectly by lamenting the fall of the Northern Song. After his exile to the northern borderlands, he seems to have reconsidered the wisdom of surviving through collaboration. In his poem on the coin, which he first composed at this time, he remarks that if the coin had been in the right place to be used, it would not have existed until this day; thus, there should be no grief in being lost and isolated. As the discarded coin keeps its shape intact, Fang might have hoped to survive by withdrawing from political affairs. With these autobiographical references, it is clear that Fang Hengxian's album is an extraordinarily personal comment on reclusion in the early years of the Qing. His use of the intimate form of his given name, A'xian 阿咸, as a signature on two of the leaves suggests that the album was intended as personal correspondence. **HSY**

9 The hanging scroll appeared in the fall 2010 auction held by Jiade (Guardian Auction House), Beijing.

10 In addition to Fang Yizhi, Fang Hengxian's uncle Fang Wen was also a member of the Fushe Restoration Society. Kim, "Chou Liang-kung and his 'Tu-hua-lu' (Lives of Painters)," 167.

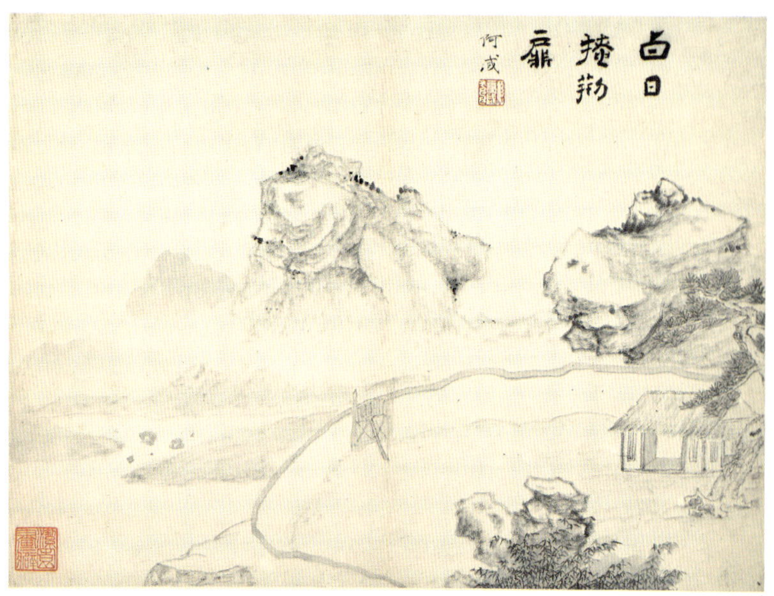

4

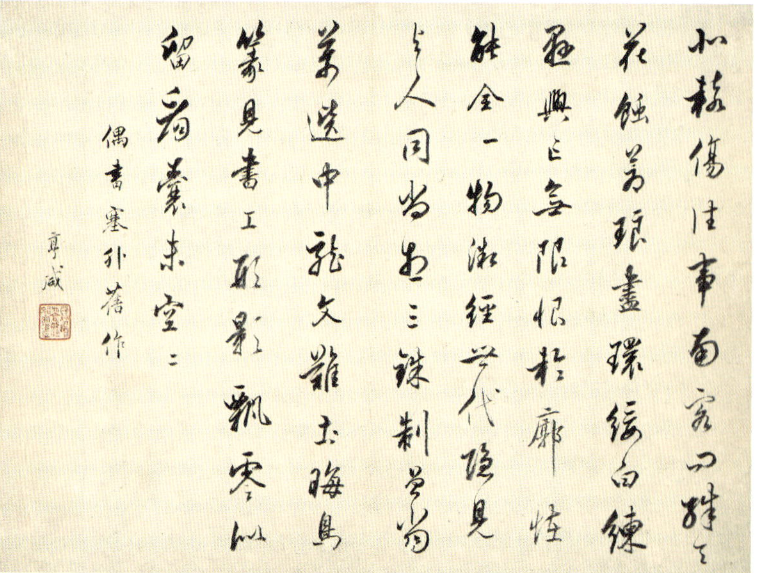

9

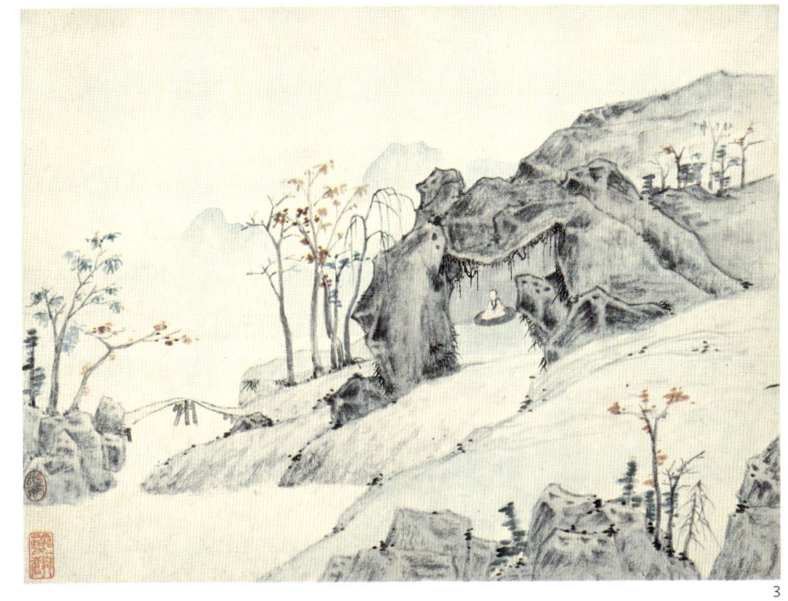

3

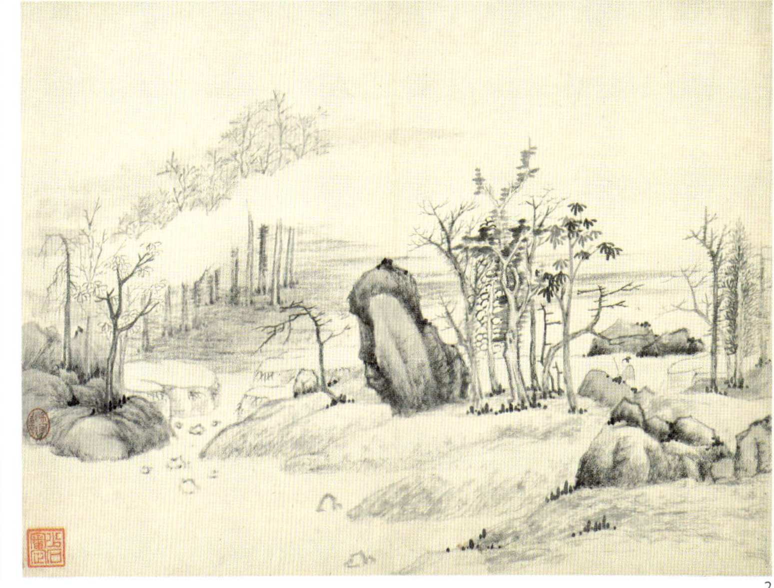

2

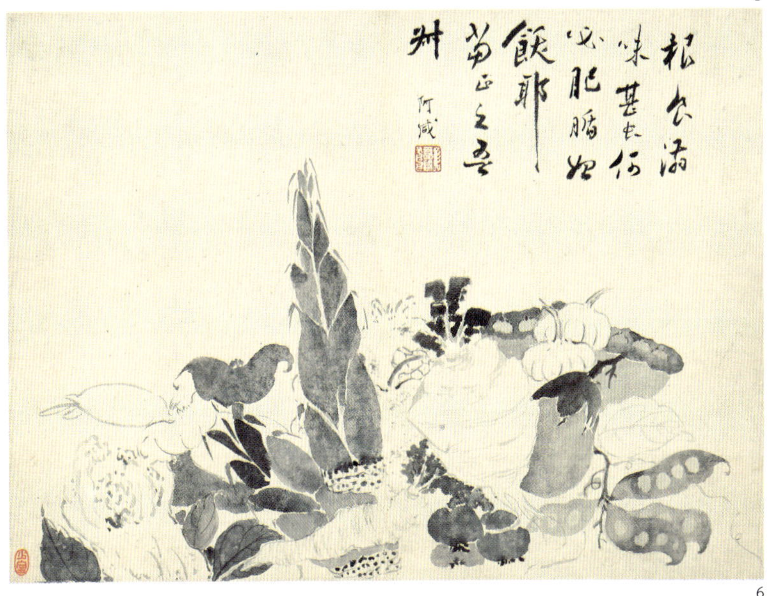

6

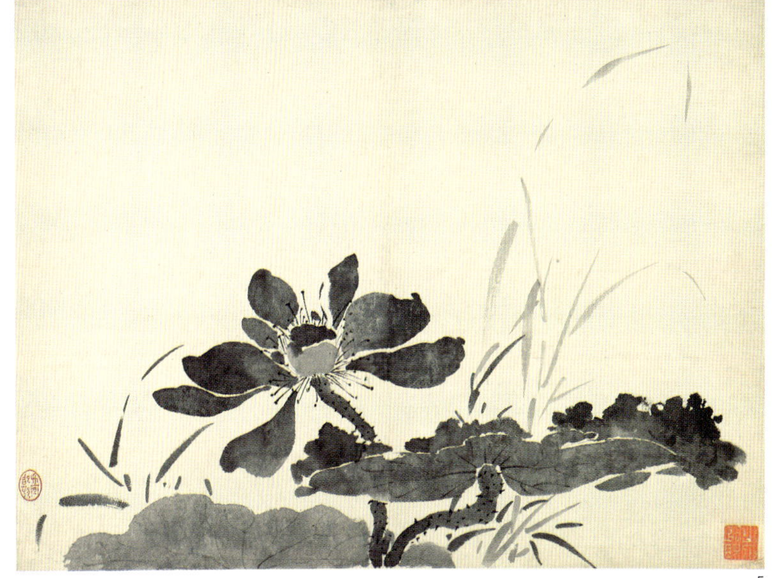

5

8

7

Fang Yizhi is one of the most intriguing, as well as mysterious, figures among the Ming loyalists. Better known for his wide-ranging scholarship than for artistic achievement, he is considered one of the most important thinkers of the seventeenth century.[1] Born into a well-known scholarly family in Tongcheng (Anhui Province), Fang received a broad education in literature, art, philosophy, and even Western science, frequently traveling with his father, Fang Kongzhao, who served as Grand Coordinator of the Huguang Circuit.[2] Fang Kongzhao was impeached and imprisoned in Beijing on false charges in 1639. Fang Yizhi managed to save his father and won first rank in the imperial examination in 1640, but his promising political career was cut short by the fall of the capital to Li Zicheng in 1644 and the subsequent Manchu conquest. He briefly joined the Southern Ming regime in Nanjing and then independently led resistance against the Manchus. After the last force of the Ming regime was destroyed, he was captured and forced to collaborate or become a monk. He chose the latter out of loyalty to the fallen dynasty, but his commitment to the Buddhist *sangha* was limited, as he continued writing and associating with literati in the south. In 1671 Fang was arrested and accused of being involved in the mysterious "Yue'an" 粵案 (Yue case), possibly a plot to overthrow the Qing dynasty. On the way to Beijing for interrogation, he died under mysterious circumstances. It is now assumed that he committed suicide at Huangkongtan (Jiangxi Province), the site where the Southern Song loyalist Wen Tianxiang took his own life battling the Mongols four centuries earlier.[3]

Multitalented, Fang Yizhi excelled at poetry, music, painting, calligraphy, and even the writing of popular stories.[4] Records show that he was a productive artist but, because of his loyalist activities, efforts were made during the Qing to destroy his writings and other traces. *Plum Blossoms and Pine*, an undated set of four hanging scrolls, is thus an exceedingly rare example of Fang's work. His signatures, using names adopted after joining the Buddhist community, indicate that the set was completed after 1650, as does the paintings' strongly expressive style, which shares much with certain strains of Ming loyalist art. Each scroll presents branches of plum blossoms together with a poem. The long, narrow painting surface of the scrolls posed a particular compositional challenge, which Fang met by accentuating the angular nature of the plum branches. The boldness of his compositions is matched by the highly idiosyncratic style of "gold wire" clerical script calligraphy he employed for the writing of his poems.[5] The effect is both archaic and strange. In an album depicting nine different rocks that the artist painted in 1670, he experimented with nine kinds of textures, and in this set too it is apparent that he paid attention to the reductive textures of his objects. Fang once praised the Yuan painter Huang Gongwang's devotion to the observation of nature. It seems, however, that after taking the tonsure Fang turned toward a more abstract form of representation, painting with dry dark ink to aim more for expressiveness than likeness.[6]

Plum blossoms, *meihua*, are a subject deeply packed with metaphoric meaning in both the literary and painting traditions. Associated with purity and integrity because of their chaste and early seasonal appearance, plum blossoms were used to describe both women of ethereal beauty and scholars of upright character. Since the Northern Song period (960–1127), the plum became a favored subject for literati painting because of its strong symbolic qualities.[7] Fang Yizhi utilized these fully, finding in the plum genre an ideal medium with which to express his loyalist sentiments in a manner that is extraordinarily novel.

There is no obvious visual order to the four scrolls, which customarily are viewed (or read) from right to left. Similarly, there is no clear-cut sequence to the poems.[8] No doubt, the disjointed quality of both image and text was intended, as it leads the viewer into the discomfortable world that Fang inhabited. The poems tap into the rich lore of *meihua* and use allusions that well demonstrate Fang's broad knowledge. At the same time there are suggestive references to the Ming loyalist's condition that provide both a poignancy and edge. The pairing of Lin Bu and Zhao Yi in one poem, for example, poses the quintessential hermit—the plum-loving Lin—against the lesser-known Zhao, who served three separate regimes, thereby highlighting the choice of reclusion or collaboration with the Manchus that every remnant subject of the Ming faced.[9] The plum blossoms are sometimes female embodiments of desire, such as the loyal wives of the legendary Shun, who underlie the reference to Lord Mountain. Other times they are clearly meant to symbolize the community of *yimin* monks and scholars to which Fang belonged. Throughout the poems, the theme of loyalty pervades, as well as thoughts of transcendence. The scroll of plum and pine makes a fitting last statement. The "bright moon" that planted the plum is a clear reference to the fallen dynasty (Ming 明 means bright). The chaste and ephemeral flowers, seeking friendship in the enduring pine, are the artist-poet himself. **YCP / PCS**

For inscriptions and other documentation, see page 297 in this catalogue.

1 Williard Peterson, *Bitter Gourd*, 12–13. Fang Yizhi's *Tongya*, a comprehensive collection of glosses, is particularly important for its demonstration of the author's encyclopedic knowledge. Fang Yizhi 方以智, *Tongya* 通雅, in *Siku quanshu zhenben sanji* 四庫全書珍本三集 (Taipei: Shangwu yinshu guan, 1972), vol. 201–210.

2 Ren Daobin 任道斌, *Fang Yizhi nianpu*, 8.

3 Yu Yingshi 余英時, *Fang Yizhi wanjie kao*.

4 Zhou Lianggong 周亮工, *Duhua lu* 讀畫錄, in *Congshu jicheng chubian* 叢書集成初編 (Shanghai: Shanghai guji chubanshe, 1936), vol. 1657, 17–18.

5 *Plum Blossoms and Pine* are reproduced and discussed in Paul Moss, ed., *This Single Feather of Auspicious Light*, 442–457. Moss reproduces as well one of Fang Yizhi's landscape paintings with a similar example of this style of calligraphy. Ibid, 448.

6 Rao Zongyi 饒宗頤, "Fang Yizhi zhi hualun," 124.

7 Maggie Bickford, *Ink Plum*.

8 An alternate sequence switches scrolls 1 and 2. The logic behind this order is the rooting of the plum's trunk at the lower right corner of scroll 2 together with Fang Yizhi's placement of his seals along the lower right border, both of which suggest to some that this scroll was intended to be at the far right.

9 Zhao Yi was an official of the Later Qin (384–417) before being captured first by the Xia (407–431), then by the Northern Wei (386–534). Instead of dying out of loyalty to the Later Qin, Zhao dutifully served the Xia and the Northern Wei, eventually winning the respect of the Northern Wei emperor Taiwu. Wei Shou 魏收, *Weishu* 魏書, in *Jingyin Siku quanshu* 景印四庫全書 (Taipei: Shangwu yinshuguan, 1983), vol. 262, 51:1–2a.

40 Fang Yizhi 方以智
1611–1671

Plum Blossoms and Pine 梅華松圖軸
After 1650

Private collection

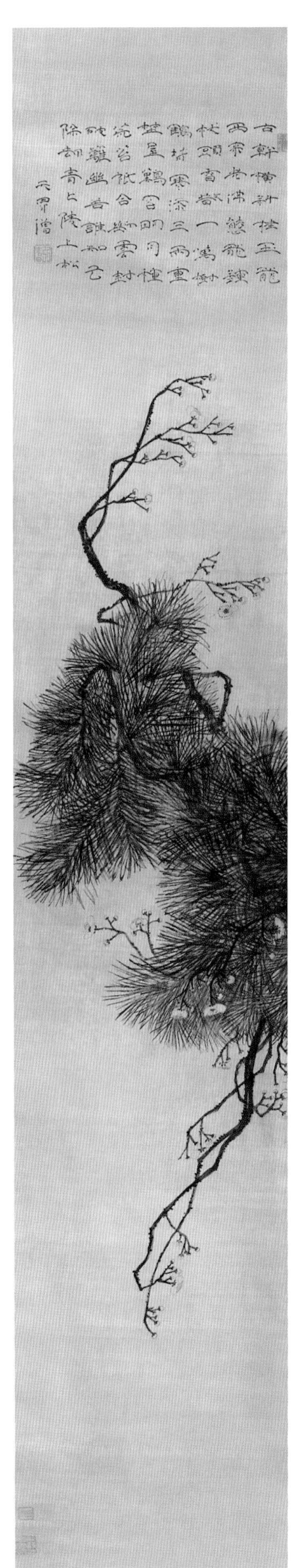

4

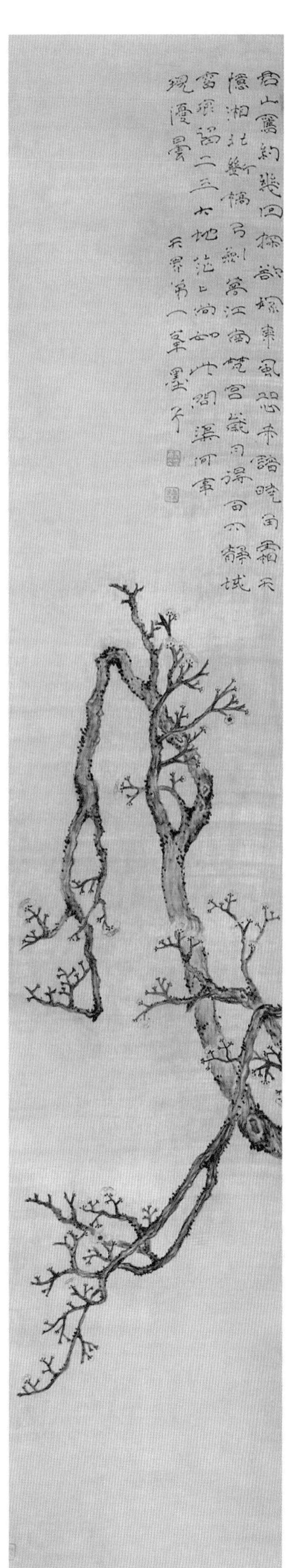

3

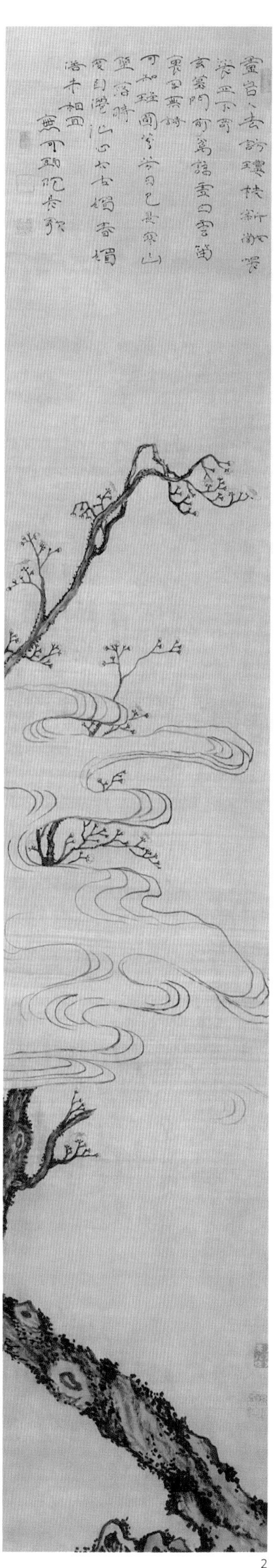

2

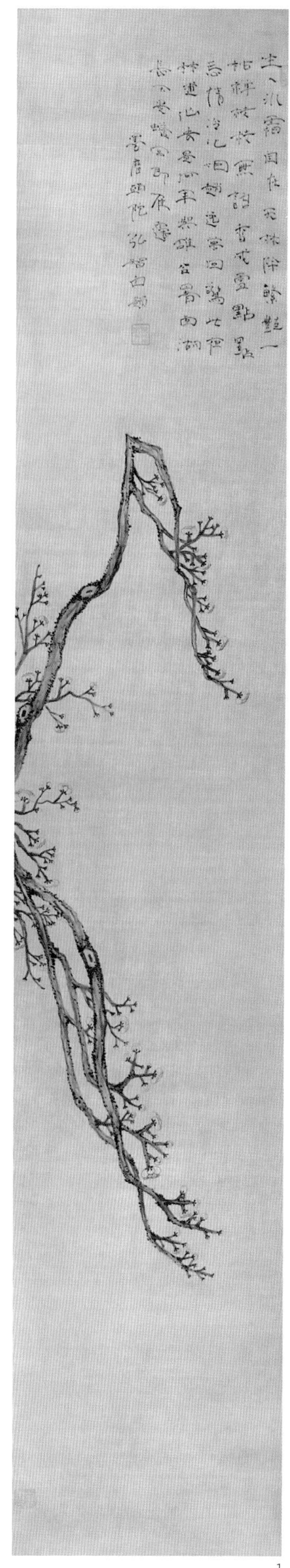

1

Three different kinds of flowers protrude from the edges of a dramatically split-open cliff in Bada Shanren's scroll, filling the void between jutting rock faces. Although quite different in appearance from one another, the flowers are all called *haitang*, commonly translated as "crabapple." Two peek out from the back of the upper cliff and dangle down. The third, painted with darker ink, grows out from the lower cliff and cuts across the foreground space. The composition is striking, almost claustrophobic, drawing the viewer into a world of jagged forms with a gravitational pull softened only by the delicacy and texture of the flowers' petals and leaves. The artist's poetic inscription at the upper left further constricts the painting's space. Filled with abrupt, unexplained images, the poem adds to the painting's feeling of compression.

Crabapple Blossoms provides a particularly visceral introduction to Bada Shanren, an artist of extraordinary talent but also unusual complexity and mystery. A member of a branch of the Ming imperial family that resided in Nanchang (Jiangxi Province), Bada, as he was later known, was eighteen when his dynasty fell. The young man, whose true name remains a matter of conjecture, disappeared into the Buddhist community near Nanchang in order to survive and eventually was recognized as a brilliant priest. He remained with the Buddhist church for more than three decades until around 1680, when he took the very difficult step of transitioning into secular life. In anticipation of this move, the Ming scion, who remained fiercely loyal to the lost dynasty, exhibited bizarre behavior with the intention of appearing mad. The years leading to 1684, when the artist adopted the name Bada Shanren (Eight Great Mountain Man) by which he would be known the rest of his life, was a period of instability and deep emotion. This is precisely when *Crabapple Blossoms* was painted. He signed it Geshan, "this sole mountain," a name with Buddhist connotations. The seal underneath, *he fu* 何負, is known to appear only on this single painting. Its meaning, "To what degree have I disappointed?," alludes to the anguish he felt as he attempted to find a place in Qing civil society.[1]

As it is with all of Bada Shanren's paintings, the path to understanding the artist's thoughts and intentions leads through the difficult texts that accompany his images. In this short poem, he mentions four different kinds of flowers: the *xifu* (Sichuan) and *chuisi* (hanging silk) crabapples; *ditang* (*Kerria rosaceae*, also known as *Pleniflora*), which he calls here *tangdi*[2]; and lotus. The last appears by allusion: Ruoye (Kuaiji, Zhejiang Province) was renowned for its lotus and famously celebrated in the Tang dynasty (618–907) by poet Li Bo, whom Bada especially admired.[3] The first line of Bada's poem equates the Sichuan crabapple, considered the most beautiful of all of the *haitang*, with the *ditang* flower. In part he did this because of his love of playing with language—Jiangxi people called the Sichuan crabapple *tangdi*—but there is also a hidden layer of meaning that refers to his royal identity. The Sichuan crabapple had been associated with royal beauty since the time of the Tang dynasty; the *ditang* flower is a deep yellow, *huang* 黃, a color that Bada frequently used to allude to his imperial background because of the homophonic *huang* 皇 (imperial).

The flower in the foreground of Bada's painting appears to be the Sichuan crabapple. Just above and behind is the *chuisi* crabapple. This flower's bloom is described in traditional texts as being like a petite lotus because of its delicate long stem and dense body of petals.[4] This helps to explain the second line of Bada's poem, in which the *chuisi* crabapple is equated with lotus. The critical line, however, is the third: "Ruoye, within the four seas, all are brothers." Ruoye presumably refers back to lotus, but Bada adds another layer of meaning. The great beauty of antiquity, Xi Shi (Shi of the West), hailed from Ruoye. Xi Shi points us toward the last line of the poem to her antithesis, the ugly Dong Shi (Shi of the East), who imitated to ill effect one of Xi Shi's particular mannerisms.[5] Bada's third line also points back to the previous line. One of the chapters in the classic *Shi jing* (Book of odes) is titled "Changdi" after the *ditang* flower. The underlying theme of this set of *Shi jing* poems is the unity of brotherhood.[6] Bada appears to be suggesting that lotus and *haitang* are the same, and if they can unite then there will be harmony among all of the floral beauties.

There have been some noted interpretations of the poem in *Crabapple Blossoms*, including one that reads it in the context of Bada Shanren's personal family life.[7] The reading proposed here is strictly political. Two events that shook Bada's world close to the time he left the Buddhist community for secular life were the special examination, *boxue hongci* 博學鴻詞, sponsored by the Manchu court in 1679 to lure old loyalists out and invite their participation in the new dynasty, and Emperor Kangxi's triumphant tour of the south in 1684, which was intended to make a statement of Qing unification. Old loyalties to the Ming were fading, driving a wedge in the *yimin* (remnant people) community. The theme of divided loyalties appears frequently in Bada's poems and paintings, and *Crabapple Blossoms* gives every appearance of being a particularly sharp rendition. The division of flowers, all *haitang* of a sort, points to the internal rifts within the brotherhood of Ming loyalists. In typical fashion, Bada used his extraordinary command of the classical literary tradition to find and expand upon a subject that was not only applicable to his condition but also possessed the possibility of multiple layers of meaning. The last of these pertains to the third set of flowers hovering at the top of his composition to the immediate right of his poem. These flowers are identifiable from their appearance in a leaf of an album by Bada dated 1684 as yet another type of *haitang* flower—the autumn crabapple (*qiu haitang* 秋海棠), which in fact is no crabapple at all but rather a begonia (*Begonia evansiana*).[8] In the poem that Bada added to accompany that album leaf it is clear that he intended the flower as a self-image. It fits perfectly here too: the crabapple that blooms out of season—or, in other words, "does not accord with the times"—is the displaced Dong Shi, who longs for harmony among her more attractive brethren, divided by a fracture in the landscape. **HSL**

For inscriptions and other documentation, see page 297 in this catalogue.

1 For a thorough introduction to Bada Shanren, see Fangyu Wang, Richard M. Barnhart, and Judith G. Smith, eds., *Master of the Lotus Garden*.

2 The *ditang* flower was originally called *changdi* 常棣 in its early appearance in the *Shi jing* 詩經 (Book of odes). *Tangdi* 棠棣 is another variation. See Ouyang Xiu 歐陽修, *Shi benyi* 詩本義 (*Siku quanshu* ed.), 6:5b–6a.

3 Bada uses the character *hu* 滸 instead of *fu* 府 for the *xifu* crab apple. He often used alternative characters to create an added layer of ambiguity. *Tangdi* was commonly called *ditang*. For Ruoye, Li Bo, and lotus, see my essay elsewhere in this catalogue. The *ye* in Ruoye is again an alternative character; it is commonly written as 耶.

4 Wang Xiangjin 王象晉, *Guang qunfang pu* 廣群芳譜 (*Siku quanshu* ed.), 35:1b.

5 During the Spring and Autumn period the two Shi families lived on either side of the stream that passed through Ruoye. The Shi clan of the west produced one of China's legendary beauties; bothered by discomfort in her chest she often held her hand there and knit her brows. This was imitated by a less attractive maiden from the Shi clan of the east, with a result that was both affected and comical. Peng Dayi 彭大翼, *Shantang sikao* 山堂肆考 (*Siku quanshu* ed.), 113:12a–b.

6 Ouyang Xiu, *Shi benyi*, 6:5b–6a.

7 Wang Fangyu published a number of articles in which he argues for the reading of painting and poem as a comment on Bada's unhappy marital status. See Wang Fangyu 王方宇, "Guanyu Bada Shanren hunyin de wenti" 關於八大山人婚姻的問題, *Gugong xueshu jikan* 故宮學術季刊 5, no. 1 (Autumn 1987): 77–85; and Wang Fangyu, "Geshan kuan Bada Shanren Haitang tuzhou tishi he Bada Shanren de hunyin wenti" 個山款八大山人海棠圖軸

41 Bada Shanren 八大山人 1626–1705

Crabapple Blossoms 海棠春秋圖 C. 1684

Private collection

Xifu crabapples—*tangdi* blossoms;
Chuisi crabapples—*Tang Ruoye* [lotus].
Ruoye, within the four seas, all are brothers;
Longing for harmony, this ugly Dong Shi
    is still without abode.

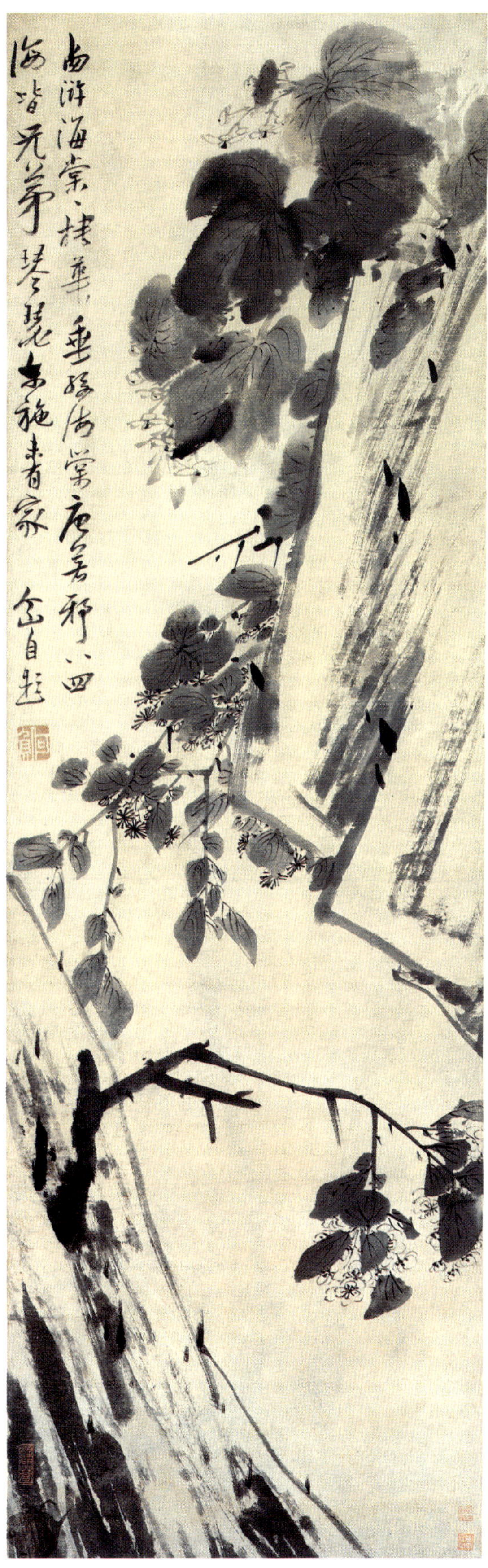

題詩和八大山人的婚姻問題, *Gugong wenwu yuekan* 故宮文物月刊 8, no. 6 (September 1990): 86–91. For a recent rebuttal, see Zhu Liangzhi 朱良志, *Bada Shanren yanjiu*, 157–59, 392–408.

8 This is leaf e from the former Chen Wen Hsi (Chen Wenxi) *Album of Flowers, Rabbit, and Other Subjects*. See *Master of the Lotus Garden*, 98, cat. no. 5e.

The unusual configuration of this album by Bada Shanren, comprising four leaves of two different sizes, raises questions regarding how these paintings with poetic inscriptions were originally intended to be viewed. Were the similarly sized pairs—*Globefish* and *Bamboo*, and *Lotus Pods* and *Golden Fish*—of two different albums? Were there other leaves, now lost? Do these four compositions together form a single consistent theme? Three of the four leaves can be precisely dated to 1689: *Globefish* in the sixth lunar month, *Lotus Pods* the following month, and *Golden Fish* in the tenth.[1] Coordinating the dates with the measurements of the individual leaves answers few questions, as the two that are closest in date are of different sizes. There may well have been some sequential order that would explain how these four diverse images were meant to be read. On the other hand, knowing what we do about the artist's approach to both painting and poetic composition encourages a more holistic perspective. Bada painted a wide variety of subjects throughout his life, and he combined them in ways that are often puzzling. Even if originally of different albums, these four leaves of disparate subjects speak cohesively about his personal concerns, and they present a rich display of his conceptual and artistic abilities during an important phase of his life.

The overarching principle, as Bada himself explained in an inscription on another painting of a few years later, is what he called *renshi wushi* 人是物是: "as it is for humans, so it is for things."[2] The basis of this idea goes to the very roots of the Chinese literary tradition, in which objects of the natural world—"things"—are used to express human traits and values through metaphor and allusion. However, while the use of objects to speak for human affairs in poetry was entirely commonplace, Bada took the practice to places where few, if any, had ever tread before. His borrowings and allusions are often recondite, drawn from different corners of the vast literary tradition. Moreover, he deployed them with a terse poetic style in which the syntax is sometimes left deliberately ambiguous. He also frequently created puns, taking advantage of Chinese's openness to homophonic play. The results are texts that puzzle and provoke. His "things" may speak of human affairs, but they do so in a language that is entirely of his fashioning.

Of these four leaves, the poem on *Golden Fish* is perhaps the least opaque. Fish were one of Bada Shanren's favorite subjects because their perceived vulnerability created an easy association with the plight of the Ming-dynasty loyalists. That association is strongly implied in this verse by their golden (royal or noble) hue and the suggestion of lost status. Echoing the theme of division that Bada explores in *Crabapple Blossoms* (c. 1684, cat. no. 41), the poem describes the rift between those leftover Ming subjects who maintained their loyalty and those who were willing to accept the Qing dynasty. Bada's poem accompanying his amusing *Globefish* is less easy to grasp because of his use of characters that can be substituted with homophones (*huang* 黄 "yellow" for *huang* 皇 "imperial," and *ya* 牙 "teeth" for *ya* 芽 "sprouts"). Is it a dish for "yellow teeth" (Bada poking fun at himself), a dish for "imperial teeth" (another self-reference), or a dish of "yellow sprouts" (immortal fare)? He may well have intended all of these readings. Though terse, his poems often possess multiple layers of meaning through the use of homophones and allusions. The one thing of which we can be certain is behind that toothy grin is a complex set of ideas and associations that somehow tie his imperial background and status as a loyalist with the deliciousness (as well as danger) of the globefish.[3]

The other two leaves of this album, *Bamboo* and *Lotus Pods*, similarly allude to Bada Shanren's imperial background and loyalist sentiments. *Bamboo*—two delicate sprigs, one painted in black, the other red—shows Bada once again presenting a dichotomous image. Here, however, the duality may be to evoke a historical allusion. The Xiang River (Hunan Province) was the site of one of the earliest displays of imperial loyalty: this was where Ehuang and Nüying, the wives of the sage-ruler Shun, committed suicide out of despair for their lost husband. Their tears are said to have caused the spots on the famous bamboo of the region. Bamboo, *zhu* 竹, has the same sound as the surname of the Ming imperial family, Zhu 朱. The red pigment Bada used for the short right branch deepens the association with the fallen dynasty, as the character for the surname Zhu literally means "red" or "crimson" (see also cat. no. 20). As for the dragonflies in the last line of Bada's poem, one would assume that the image was

For inscriptions and other documentation, see page 298 in this catalogue.

1 The *Bamboo* leaf is undated, though its signature is consistent with a 1689 date. Until recently, these four album leaves were mounted together in handscroll format.

2 I refer to the second of three inscriptions on Bada Shanren's *Birds and Fish* of 1693 in the Shanghai Museum. The painting is illustrated and discussed in my "Bada Shanren's Bird-and-Fish Painting and the Art of Transformation," 6–26.

3 Ibid., 14–16. See also Fangyu Wang, Richard M. Barnhart, and Judith G. Smith, eds., *Master of the Lotus Garden*, 102–4.

42 Bada Shanren 八大山人
1626–1705

Golden Fish, Lotus Pods, Globefish, and Bamboo **竹, 蓮蓬, 河豚, 金魚子合冊**
1689
Private collection

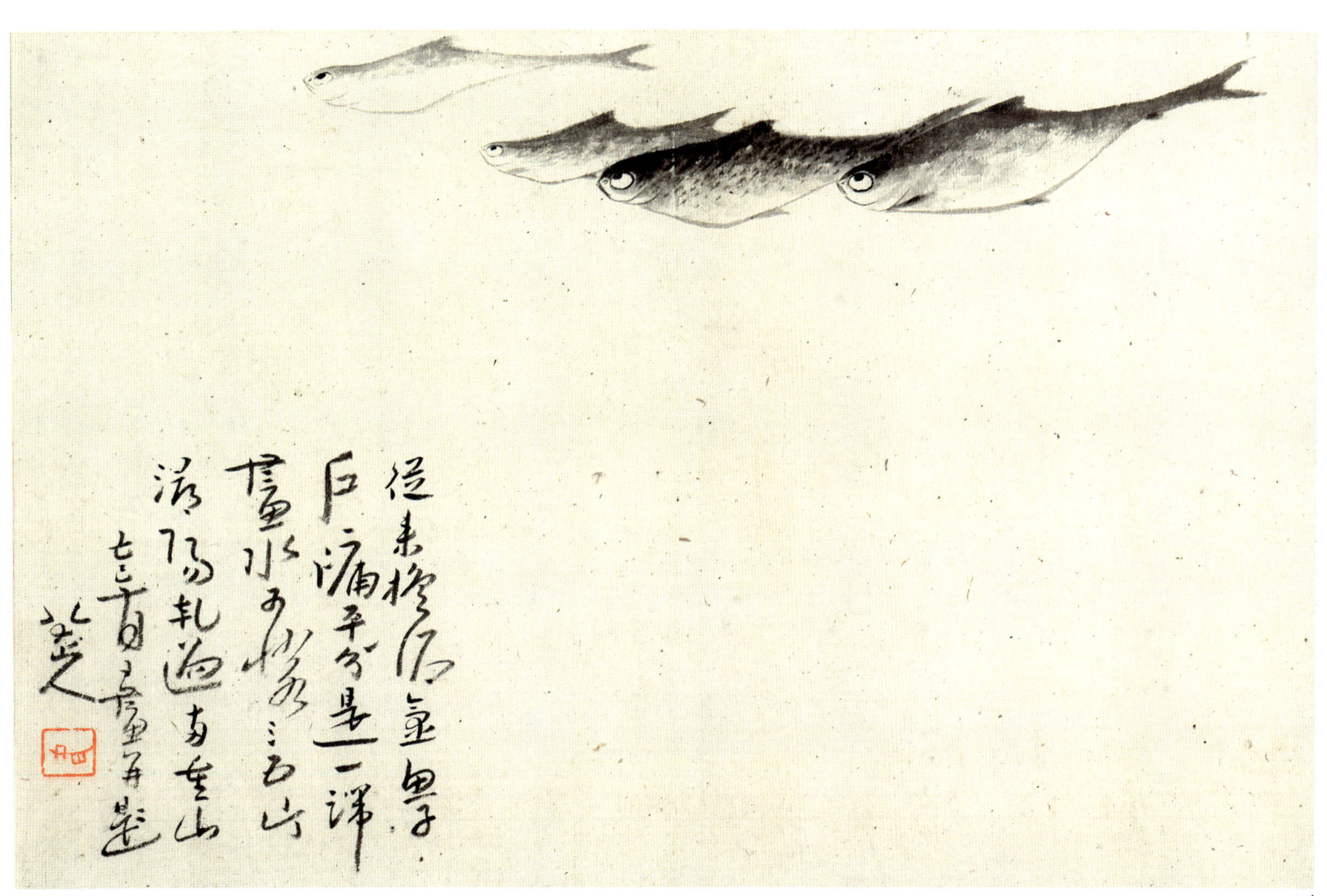

4

4. GOLDEN FISH
The golden fish that used to carry wine,
Have divided into equal camps, each in its corner.
I paint a few sheets of pitiable water,
At Xunyang twisting past two layers of mountains.

inspired by the formal qualities of the bamboo, whose leaves resemble the insect's wings. However, there is an important allusion buried within. A late Ming text of miscellaneous records includes the following passage:

> There are giant dragons that molt on the banks of Lake Tai. From the scales emerge insects that instantaneously transform into red dragonflies. People who capture them become severely ill. People today see the red dragonflies and call them "scales of the dragon." They also call them "descendants of the dragon." For this reason they dare not harm them.[4]
>
> 有大龍蛻於太湖之湄，其鱗甲中出蟲，頃刻化為蜻蜓朱色．人取之者病瘧．今人見蜻蜓朱色者，謂之龍甲，又謂之龍孫，不敢傷之．

Surely, Bada had this curious folktale in mind when he painted *Bamboo*. The placement of his inscription on this leaf is noteworthy. His poem seemingly hovers like a third sprig (or dragonfly) balanced between the black and red bamboo; his red seal overlaying the black ink of his signature creates another echo with the painted forms. Bada literally inscribes himself as a "descendant of the dragon" (emperor), cultivating the Daoist's cinnabar of immortality but, like a dragonfly in mid-air, not yet home.

As I discuss *Lotus Pods* in some detail in my essay on Bada Shanren's lotus painting elsewhere in this catalogue I will avoid repeating my explanation of the wordplay and allusions that underlie this unusual image. Suffice it to say the image and poem were important to Bada: extant works demonstrate that he repeated them numerous times.

Between the time Bada Shanren painted *Golden Fish* and *Lotus Pods*, during the ninth lunar month of 1689, he had completed a long ambitious scroll titled *Fish and Ducks* (Shanghai Museum) that includes among its denizens very similar renditions of this album's globefish and school of golden fish. Considered together, album and scroll provide a vivid glimpse into Bada's artistic concerns toward the very end of the 1680s. His presentation of "things" reaches an extraordinary level of both complexity and virtuosity. At the same time, he integrates them in the exploration of the broader conceptual themes of transformation, transcendence, and immortality. In many respects, the four leaves collected in this album provide a critical entryway into the last stage of his remarkable life and art. **HSL**

4 The text, *Wuchen zachao* 戊辰雜鈔 by Xu Bangzuo 徐邦佐, was compiled during the Chongzhen reign (1627–1644) and exists only in partial form. See *Yuding Yuanjian leihan* 御定淵鑑類函 (*Siku quanshu* ed.), 437: 7a.

1. GLOBEFISH

Fine rain drizzling in Yellow Bamboo Village,
A light boat bobbing in mounds of water
and clouds.
How can one get [satisfied with] a meal for the
Yellow Teeth [the immortal's yellow sprouts]?

2. BAMBOO

Painting bamboo [in ink] and cinnabar,
Cultivating the cinnabar, not yet home.
For now, above the Xiang River,
Dragonflies have not yet radiated the rosy clouds.

3. LOTUS PODS

Upon seeing the heart of the lotus seed
[I know] the lotus flower has roots.
At Ruoye the lotus pod was clove open;
In the painting: a dear young lord.

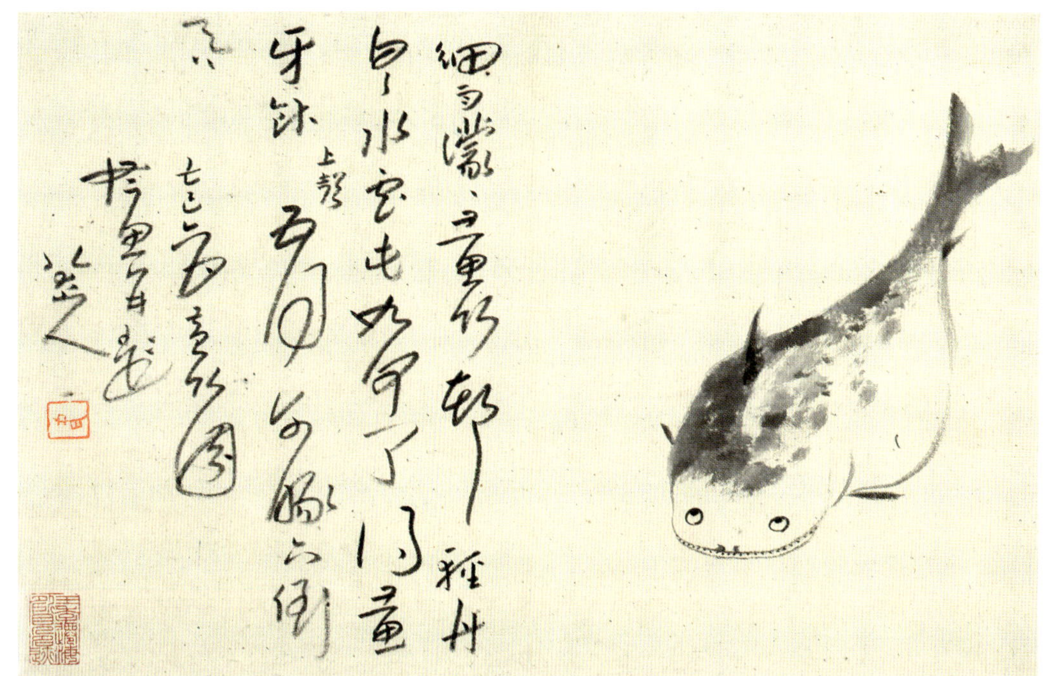

1

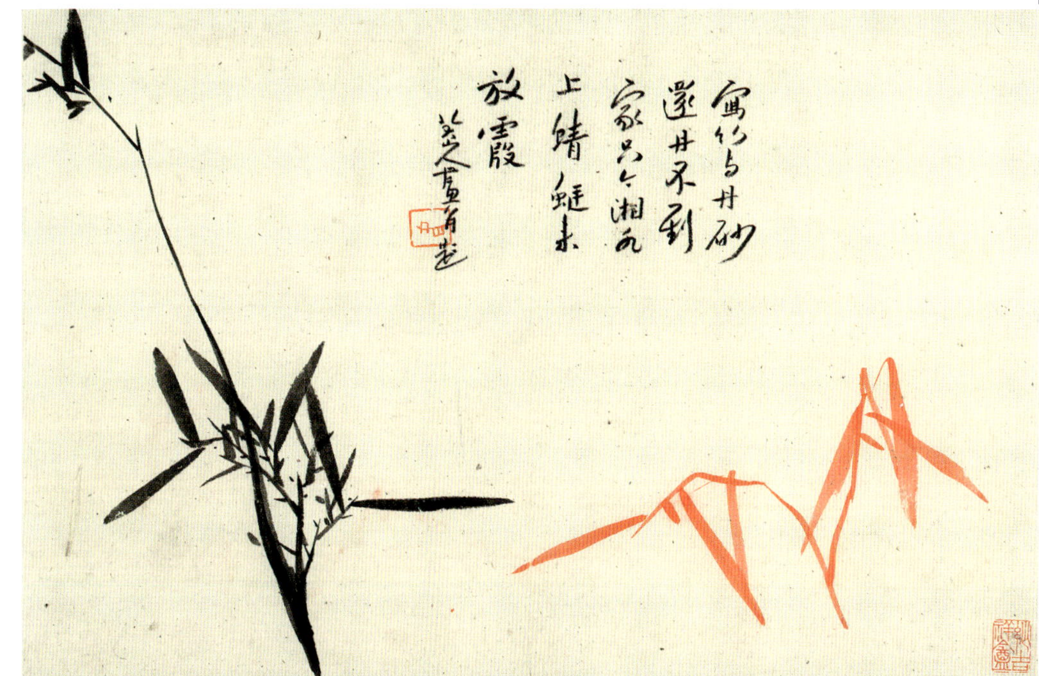

2

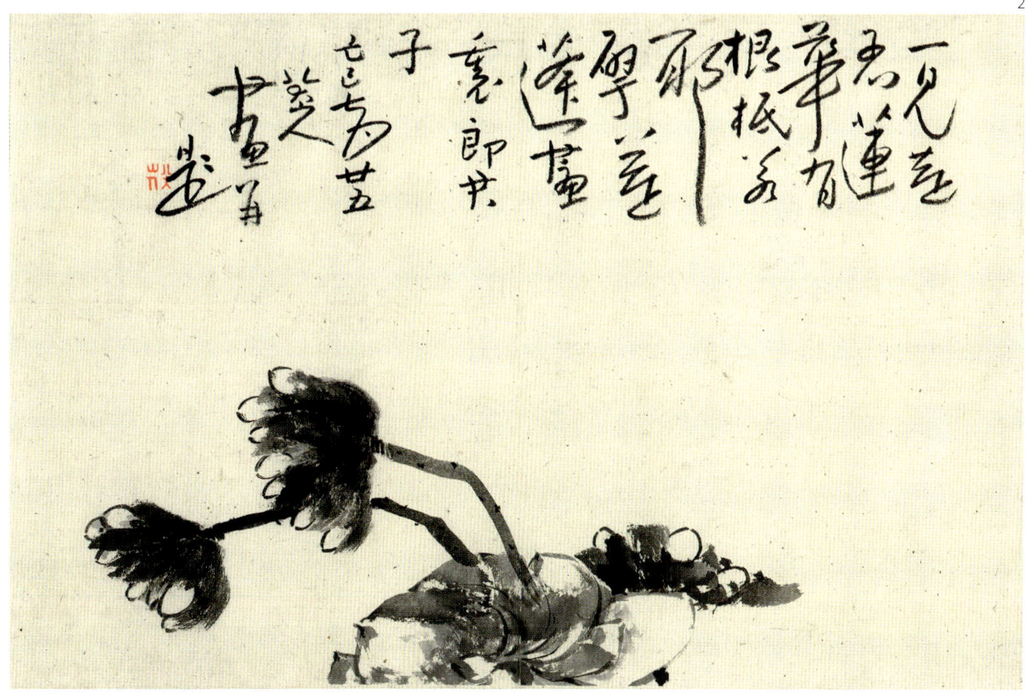

3

The poem that Bada Shanren added to this charming, shimmering fan of twenty-four tiny fish has the distinction of being both one of his most important as well as one of his most challenging. We know it was important because he used it repeatedly in the mid-1690s: among his extant paintings there are at least four others, all from 1694–95, with what might be called the Haggard Fish verse. One of these is a leaf in the famous *Anwan Album*—the image of a single small fish adrift in the middle of the composition accompanied only by Bada's poem and signature at the upper right. Another album leaf dated summer 1695 presents seven small fish very much like the twenty-four in this fan. The other two are hanging scrolls, one of a single fish swimming alone with the poem, the other a more complicated composition of two fish underneath a large floating rock upon which perch three birds.[1] In the two hanging scrolls the fish are painted on a larger scale, though typologically all of these fish appear to be the same—what I have identified elsewhere as the Yellow Fish, or Yellow-Cheek Fish.[2] The word for yellow was one of Bada's favorite for puns, as it is a precise homophone with the character meaning "imperial" (see cat. nos. 41–42). Whether one or many, it is clear that his "haggard fish" were intended as a self-image tied to his imperial origins and his identity as a member of the scattered remnants of Ming loyalists still swimming in the waters of the early Qing.

Both the syntax and meaning of Bada's poem are typically elusive. The haggard one once favored must refer to the plight of the *yimin* loyalists, who linger somewhat indolently under flowers. The second half of Bada's poem is far less direct, juxtaposing Kunming (various possible identifications), the releasing of fish, tree peony, Jinma (gold horse), and spring in a confusing manner. There have been various attempts to explain the puzzle. My own interpretation has Bada's focus on the geography of Yunnan Province and the fate of the last ruler of the Southern Ming, Zhu Youlang (Prince of Gui), who fled to the far southwest where he was eventually captured and executed in 1662. Kunming was the site of his execution; it is also the name of a lake near a mountain called Jinma that had distinct Buddhist associations. Bada appears to overlay the releasing of fish—a Buddhist ritual of compassion—with the fate of Zhu Youlang, who of course was not released. The first character of the third line, *ding* 定 ("certainly" or "to set"), is particularly strange in what appears to be garbled syntax. I suspect that Bada intended a particularly obscure definition here in which *ding* refers to the name of a star. In its original context, the Ding star, when occupying its proper position in the sky, signals the optimum conditions for the building of an imperial palace. This interpretation does not improve the poem's syntax, but it adds another layer of meaning, which may explain why Bada used it to begin the pivotal third line. The original allusion, drawn from the *Shi jing* (Book of odes), refers to the relocation of an imperial capital after the state of Wei was invaded by the barbarian Di tribes from the north in the seventh century BCE.[3] This was a lesson from the ancient past that certainly would have resonated with the circumstances and hopes of the Ming loyalists so many centuries later. The tree peony is also known as the "parting flower," presented to friends when separating. It blooms in the fourth month, which happens to be precisely the time of year when Zhu Youlang was executed in Kunming, putting an end to the hopes of a restoration of the Southern Ming.

Bada Shanren provided no lexicon for the reading of his poems, leaving many lines, phrases, even individual characters open to conjecture. Interpretations are virtually endless given the complexity and depth of the Chinese literary tradition, and this greatly complicates the problem of reading his art. However, there is no question that Bada had the ability and inclination to devise densely packed word puzzles. In this regard, the short comment he added following his poem on *Small Fish* is telling. We know from elsewhere that the monk Guofeng, the presumed recipient of this fan, like Bada was surnamed Zhu and originally of the Ming imperial family.[4] By specifying that he composed the poem a year earlier and that he went over it again with someone who shared the same history and concerns, Bada reveals how central these difficult texts are to his art. In the case of *Small Fish*, his poem gently dances across the upper border of the fan, echoing the delicate images of the pitiable fish that wander across the silvery mica-coated surface of the paper. The lightness of this exquisite object, clearly a special gift for someone dear to Bada, belies the gravity of its embedded message. **HSL**

For inscriptions and other documentation, see page 298 in this catalogue.

1 The *Anwan Album*, dated summer 1694, is in the Sumitomo Collection, Sen-oku Hakko Kan (Kyoto, Japan). The 1695 album leaf is in the collection of the Mushakoji Saneatsu Memorial Hall (Tokyo, Japan). The single-fish hanging scroll (eighth lunar month, 1694) is in the Wang family collection; the whereabouts of *Birds, Fish and Rock* (fifth lunar month, 1694) is unknown. All of these paintings are reproduced and discussed in my "The Fish Leaves of the Anwan Album," 69–85. The discussion here is drawn from my more detailed research presented in this article. *Small Fish* is also included and discussed in Fangyu Wang, Richard M. Barnhart, and Judith G. Smith, eds., *Master of the Lotus Garden*, 160–61.

2 Lee, "The Fish Leaves of the Anwan Album," 71.

3 "Ding zhi fanzhong" 定之方中, in *Maoshi zhushu* 毛詩注疏 (*Siku quanshu* ed.) 4:28b–30b.

4 Li Yeshuang 李葉霜, "Bada Shanren yu Yunnan Guofeng," 205–10.

43 Bada Shanren 八大山人
1626–1705

Small Fish 小魚群扇面
1695
Private collection

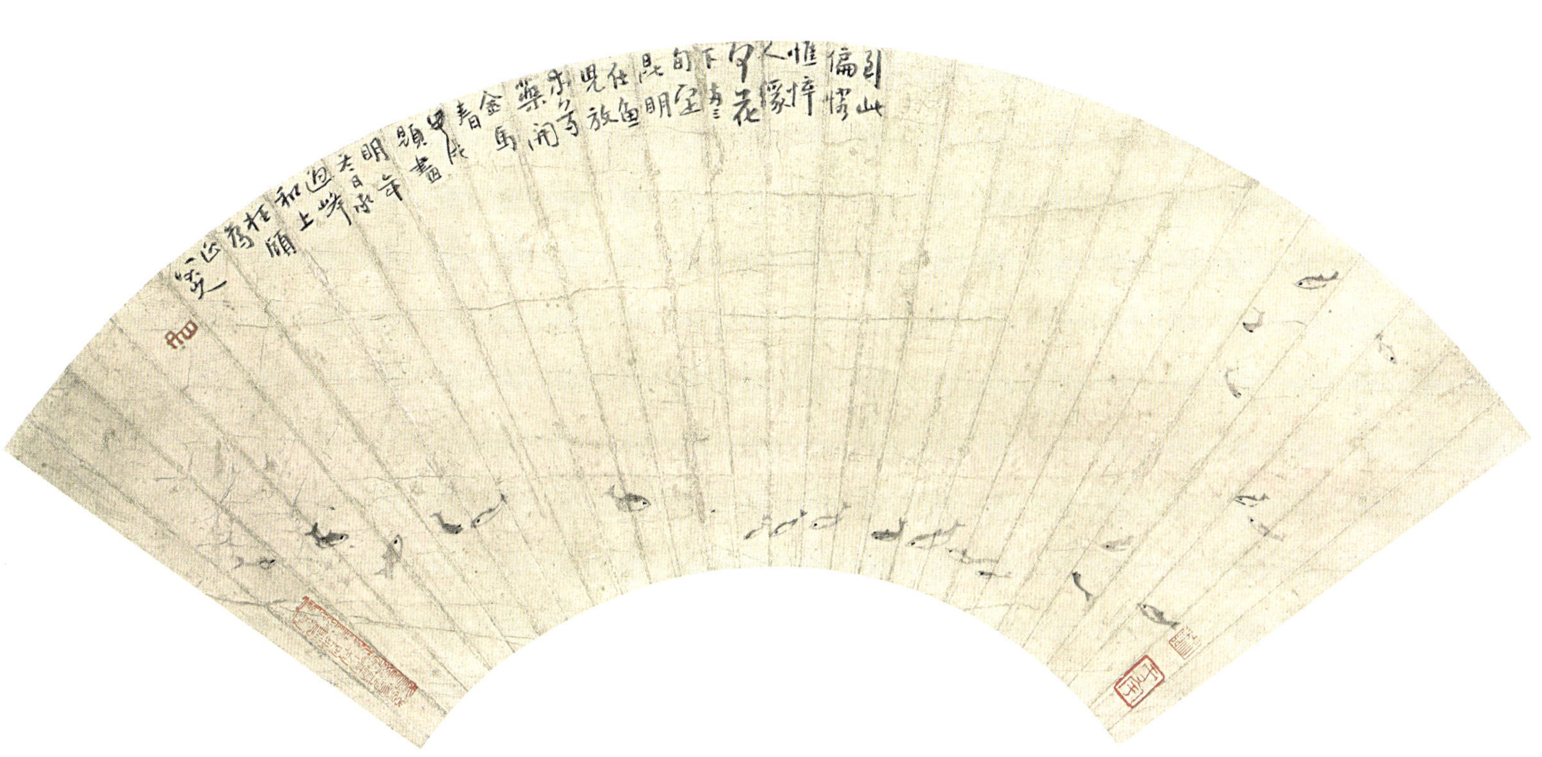

Here comes the one who once was favored, now turned haggard;
Why does he linger these many days under the flowers?
Had Kunming remained the fish could be released;
When the tree peony blossomed it was spring at Jinma.

This poem was composed in the jiashu *year [1694]. In the winter of the next year the monk Guofeng looked it over for me.*

Among Bada Shanren's many subjects, lotus stands out as both the most enduring and dearest. Paintings of lotus emerged at the very beginning of his artistic career, as evidenced by an album of lotus datable to circa 1665, and they were among the last works he painted, as we know from a large hanging scroll dated autumn 1705. In addition, lotus appears prominently in his seals and personal ciphers: *zaifu* 在芙, "in the lotus"; *zaifu shanfang* 在芙山房, "Mountain Studio in the Lotus"; and *Heyuan* 何園, "Lotus Garden."[1] Bada's interest in lotus is attributable to a number of factors. Foremost is the plant's symbolic role in Buddhism: rising from the muck, the lotus unfurls large beautiful leaves and exquisite flowers over a pond's surface, thereby suggesting transcendence of the world of illusion and rebirth into a purer realm where enlightenment can be attained. The promised purity of the lotus was equally applicable in the Confucian sphere, in which moral officials distanced themselves from the grit of politics. Bada's "in the lotus" signals a particularly hermitic embrace of the flower. Borrowing from notions of escape into another world, typified by the phrase *huzhong tian* 壺中天 (paradise in a pot),[2] he enwraps himself in the lotus's moral and spiritual shield to maintain his purity in a world transformed by the loss of his dynasty.

In his own time, Bada Shanren's lotus paintings were singled out by fellow townsman Long Kebao as one of his "three excellences" (the other two were pine and rock) for their sheer bravado of brushwork and form. After seeing a mural of Bada's lotus at the Beilan Monastery and witnessing a live painting performance in a private gathering, Long praised Bada's lotus with the following comment:

> [Bada's] lotus painting is especially fantastic. Its excellence lies not in the flowers but the leaves. Each is lively and vibrant. There are some that distinctively rise from the side like uplifted canopies, and some that sway and twist like banana leaves. One leaf is blown by the wind and reveals a half-frontal, half-side view. There are those that display the back in reverse and the frontal sides entirely. It lies in his brushwork, as no matter deep or shallow all are lively wielded and clearly distinguished. . .[3]
>
> 蓮尤勝，勝不在花，在葉．葉葉生動，有特出側見如擎蓋者，有委折如焦者，有含風一葉而正見側出各半者，有反正各全露者，在其用筆深淺皆活處辨之．

Long Kebao was indeed discerning in pointing out the pictorial uniqueness of Bada Shanren's lotus painting, as one quickly notes that it focuses almost exclusively on the display, movement, and variation of the leaves but not on the lotus flowers, which are always shielded and guarded, as if in hiding. Long's description suggests a three-dimensional quality to Bada's lotus leaves that is less readily apparent. Rather, paintings such as *Lotus and Rock* demonstrate that Bada relished the opportunity afforded by the lotus's striking form to create a rich array of ink textures and calligraphic strokes that accentuate the picture plane. It is only with a more focused viewing that spatial relationships begin to appear. Subtle but effective, these are worked out in a shallow stage. In the center of *Lotus and Rock* are three stalks of lotus, one topped by dark wet leaves, one by a lotus pod (see cat. no. 42), and one by nothing at all. Particularly skillful are the dark forms of his canopylike lotus leaves connecting the short dedicatory inscription at the upper left to the rock that looms upward from the right. Radically foreshortened, these leaves typify the pictorial challenge Bada faced balancing the formal abstractions of brush and ink with the creation of a lotus-world that lures in the viewer.

A date of 1694–95 was previously suggested for *Lotus and Rock* on the basis of Bada's signature and seals.[4] However, neither precludes a slightly later date of circa 1697, which I suggest here because of the clear stylistic relationship between this painting and Bada's long 1697 handscroll *Flowers on the River* (Tianjin Art Museum, fig. 39). *Lotus and Rock* was probably intended to function as an abbreviated version of *Flowers on the River*. The latter possesses an extraordinarily complex ballad that brings the reader through a series of word games and allusions to tales of ancient treachery, loyalty, martyrdom, and transcendence.[5] *Lotus and Rock* is left unburdened by such heavy matters. On the other hand, it is fair to assume that the painting's recipient, the unidentified Master Zhilao, was privy to the complexities of Bada's lotus iconography. **HSL**

For inscriptions and other documentation, see page 298 in this catalogue.

1 The 1665 album, formerly in the Wang Fangyu and Sum Wai collection, is now in the Freer Gallery of Art. The 1705 hanging scroll is in the collection of the Palmer Museum of Art, Pennsylvania State University. See Wang, Richard M. Barnhart, and Judith G. Smith, eds., *Master of the Lotus Garden*, figs. 45, 130. |For the seals see page 249.

2 The phrase, still in use today, is derived from the Han-dynasty story of an immortal's sojourns to a world that magically exists in a container.

3 Long Kebao 龍科寶, "Bada Shanren huaji" 八大山人畫記, compiled in Wang Fangyu 王方宇, *Bada Shanren lunji*, 529. For a slightly different translation, see Wang, Barnhart, and Smith, *Master of the Lotus Garden*, 137. For more on Long, see Zhu Liangzhi 朱良志, *Bada Shanren yanjiu*, 611–12.

4 Wang, Barnhart, and Smith, *Master of the Lotus Garden*, 156–57.

5 See my essay "In the Lotus: Bada Shanren and the Heart of the *Yimin*" elsewhere in this catalogue.

44 **Bada Shanren** 八大山人
1626–1705

Lotus and Rock 墨荷圖軸
C. 1697
Collection of Shitou Shuwu

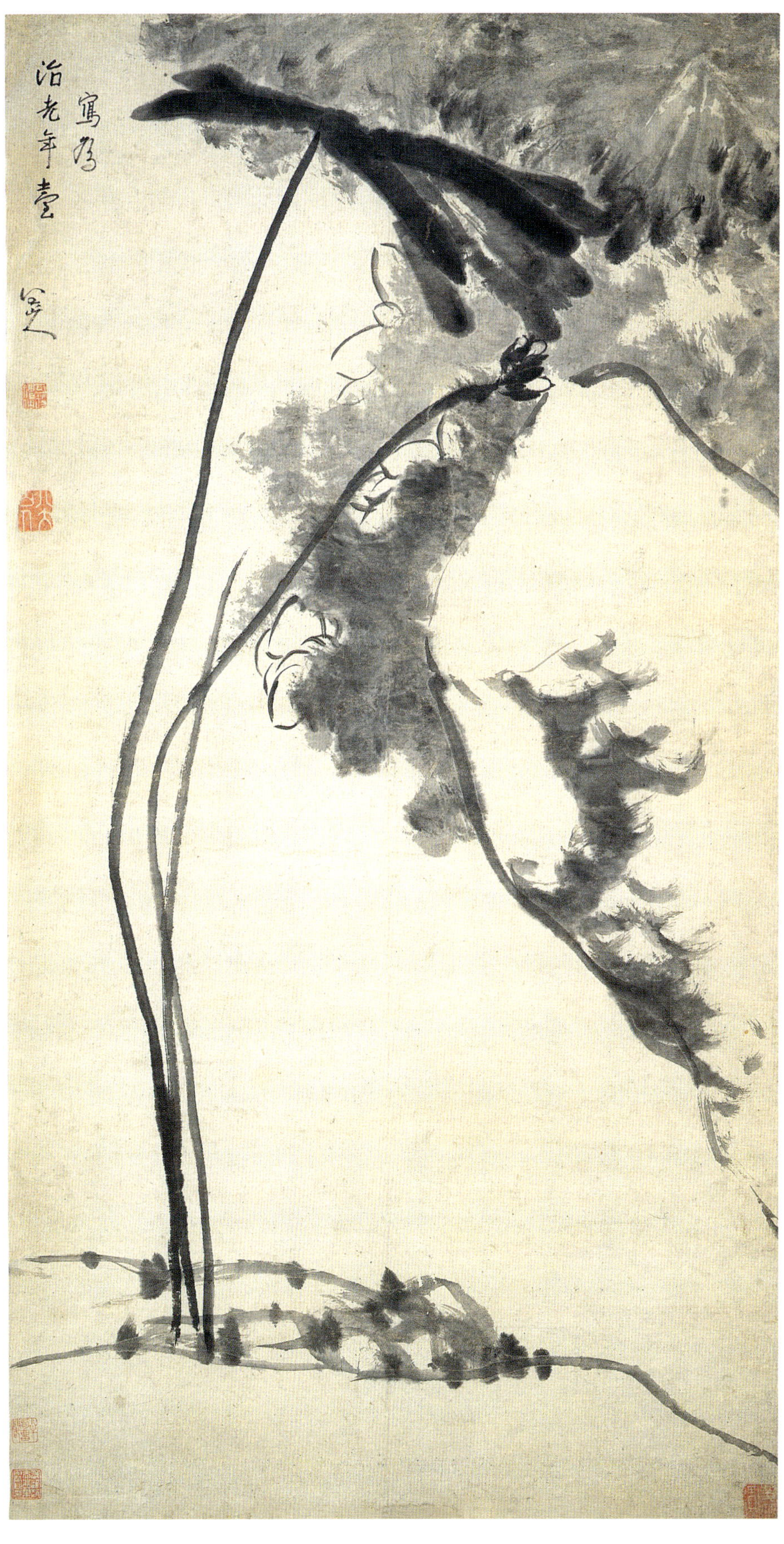

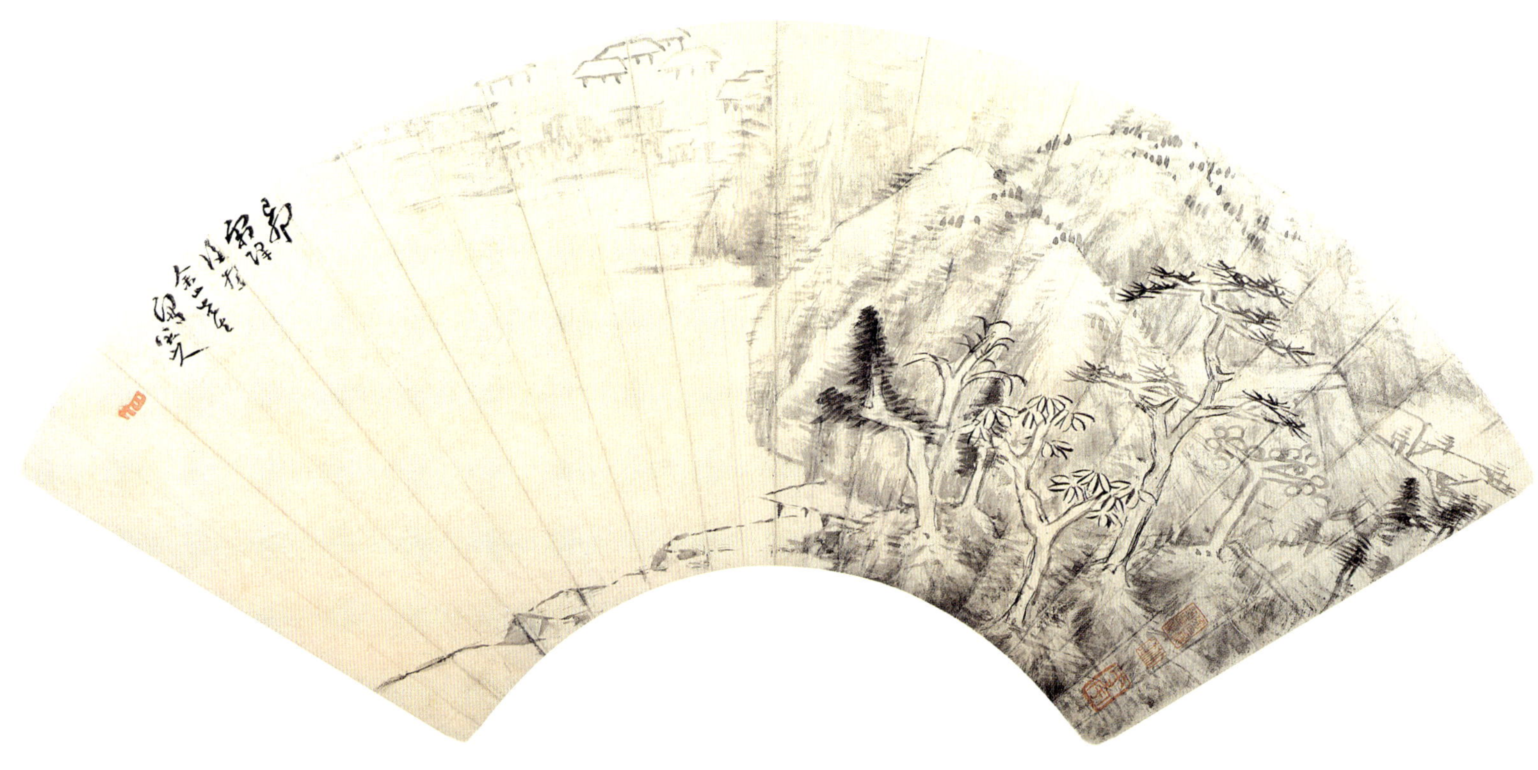

Landscape for Yushan 贈余山山水
Sketched for Mr. Yushan after frost in the jimao *year [1699].*

Bada Shanren 八大山人
1626–1705

45 ***Landscape for Yushan***
贈余山山水扇面
1699
Private collection

46 ***Landscape*** 山水扇面
C. 1705
Private collection

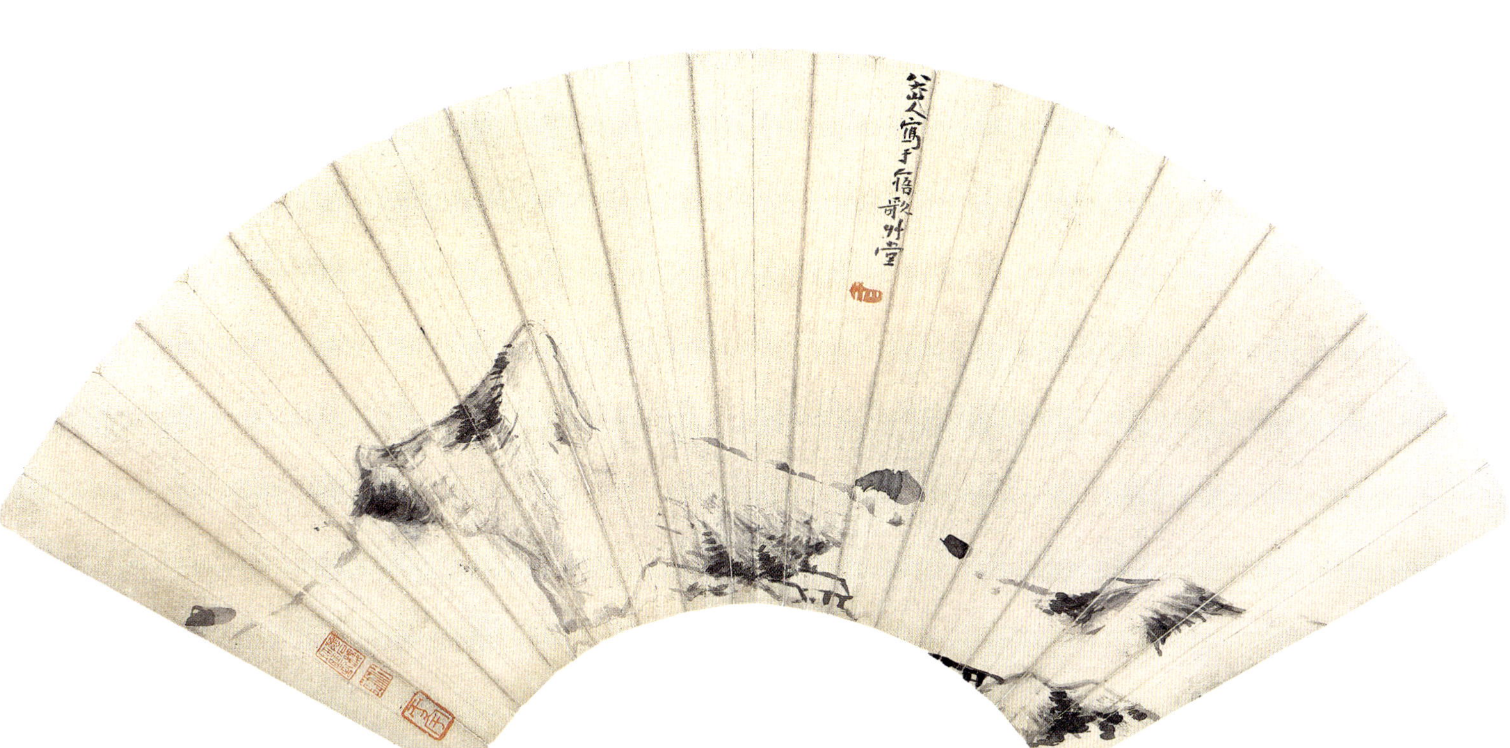

Landscape 山水扇面
Sketched by Bada Shanren at the Wuge Thatched Hall.

With subtle charm, these two fan paintings capture the depth of sentiment Bada Shanren directed toward landscape late in his life. Landscapes are almost entirely absent from his oeuvre until the early 1690s, a fact that is both notable and strange. Landscape was the one subject definitively associated with the concepts of escape, hiding, purity, and moral integrity that together encapsulate reclusion, and after the Manchu conquest its pertinence to the expression of Ming *yimin* sentiment was unquestioned. As had occurred many times in the past, the loss of a center with which a loyal subject could identify was a powerful incentive to fashion and explore a surrogate, idealized world for imagined dwelling. Conversely, through mood or metaphor a painter might create a scene reflective of the darkened reality in which he and his community lived. Bada's apparent decision to avoid painting landscape for so many decades thus stands out, as does his decision to immerse himself in its description for the last twelve years of his life. Richard Barnhart has suggested that the turn to landscape in the 1690s reflects a degree of acceptance of the fact that his old world would not be restored. A measure of peace seems to have accompanied Bada's resignation, and this, in turn, may have allowed him to begin the construction of his own personal world of rivers and mountains.[1]

That world, viewed through the dozens of individual scrolls, album leaves, and fans extant today, reveals a realm distinct in character yet profoundly multi-faceted and thoughtful. Bada Shanren's landscape fan of 1699 presented to Yushan is an excellent example.[2] The scene is light and airy, with landscape elements woven in fine textures on the right and an open expanse of water on the left. The viewer is drawn to Bada's foreground trees, deliberately reductive in form to frank, childlike images that denote innocence and purity. A more careful look reveals subtle elements: a pavilion for viewing on the shore facing Bada's inscription at the upper left, the barest suggestion of roofs at the upper right leading to another body of water, and a small village of simple, geometric structures, pale and alluring at the top of the fan. Bada composed his landscape as a counter-clockwise journey to follow the contours of the fan, from plateaued shore to pavilion, past the trees, and then deeper still to far-off vales that ultimately lead to a remote village that floats like a distant, unattainable dream. Bada probably intended his landscape to evoke the Yuan-dynasty master Ni Zan (fig. 4), both through the lightness of his brushwork and the motif of the foreground pavilion. The allusion adds another layer of meaning, but it is so skillfully subsumed into the fabric of the landscape that one barely notices.

Landscapes are meant to be journeys. They provide visual pathways in suggested space, and the eye's movement alone provides a kind of psychological release. There is evidence that nearly two decades earlier, circa 1681–83, Bada began to experiment with the subject of landscape, but from what we can see of those efforts, the effect is different (see fig. 16).[3] The elements of these earlier paintings are juxtaposed rather than integrated. This may reflect Bada's long-practiced skill at presenting individualized subjects that always seem to say more with less, often accompanied by densely allusive poems. The late landscapes are less commonly paired with texts, but when they are the texts are often transcriptions of earlier writings that seem intended to provide more of a tonal complement than an iconographic puzzle.[4] More concerned with journey and mood, these landscapes nonetheless still demonstrate Bada's recognition of the power of reductive form. Man-made structures in particular—pavilions and dwellings—are simplified and often given pronounced, iconic presence, as if to express his desire to accentuate human existence in a realm of greater meaning.

It is hard to imagine a painting that demonstrates this with more poignancy than the second fan, simply titled *Landscape*. Signature and seal suggest a date as late as 1705, the last year of Bada's life. Descending along the line of one of the fan's original staves is Bada's artfully placed inscription explaining that the landscape was sketched at the Wuge Thatched Hall. This is the name of Bada's own studio in his late years. There can be little doubt that the building depicted directly beneath is one and the same, though the rendition is of an idealized space more descriptive of Bada's state of mind than the actual studio.[5]

For inscriptions and other documentation, see page 298 in this catalogue.

1 See Richard Barnhart's introduction to Fangyu Wang, Barnhart, and Judith G. Smith, eds., *Master of the Lotus Garden*, 18. Barnhart and Wang both note that the emergence of Bada Shanren's mature landscapes circa 1693–94 was likely to have been part of a gradual process, pointing in particular to an album of landscapes in a private collection datable to circa 1689–90. Ibid., 70, fig. 36. Hui-shu Lee touches upon this change in Bada's attitude in her "The Fish Leaves of the Anwan Album" and in her essay elsewhere in this catalogue.

2 The commentary accompanying this fan's publication in *Diyan caotang zhencang huaji*, 60–61, identifies Yushan's surname as Zheng 鄭.

3 See note 101 of my essay elsewhere in this catalogue.

4 A good example is an album in the Asian Art Museum, San Francisco, in which individual landscape leaves are paired with Bada's transcriptions of verses by a number of Tang poets. See Wang, Barnhart, and Smith, *Master of the Lotus Garden*, 181–83. Bada's poem on his 1681 *Landscape* (see previous note) is more in keeping with the kinds of textual puzzles we are accustomed to seeing on his paintings of other subjects.

5 Wang Fangyu describes the Wuge Thatched Hall as a "small room that Bada occupied in Nanchang in the last years of his life." Ibid., 32. See also Joseph Chang, et al., *In Pursuit of Heavenly Harmony*, 9.

6 "Kao pan" 考槃. Translation by James Legge (with punctuation slightly modified), *The Chinese Classics* (reprint of Hong Kong University of Press reissue, Taipei: Southern Materials Center, 1983), vol. 4, 93–94.

In this final stage of Bada's life and art it took but a few strokes from his brush to describe a scene at once economical and complete. Dark strokes describe a rustic bridge leading to a dwelling sited in perfect geomantic harmony. Borrowing from the natural lines of the fan's folds, it seemingly radiates a mysterious light. Bada adopted the name of his studio, which can be translated as "Singing upon Awakening," from a poem in the *Shi jing* (Book of odes), China's most ancient collection of verse. The original poem, written in archaic, simple phrases, captures the essence of reclusion and is worth citing in full to pair with Bada's landscape. Together they suggest that in the recesses of his mind, the artist finally found some measure of long-deserved equilibrium.

He has reared his hut by the stream in the valley,
—That large man, so much at his ease.
Alone he sleeps and wakes and talks.
He swears he will never forget [his true joy].

He has reared his hut in the bend of the mound,
—That large man, with such an air of indifference.
Alone he sleeps and wakes and sings.
He swears he will never pass from this spot.

He has reared his hut on the level height,
—That large man, so self-collected.
Alone he sleeps and wakes and sleeps again.
He swears he will never tell [of his delight].[6]

考槃在澗，碩人之寬.
獨寐寤言，永矢弗諼.
考槃在阿，碩人之薖.
獨寐寤歌，永矢弗過.
考槃在陸，碩人之軸.
獨寐寤宿，永矢弗告.

PCS

The complexity of Bada Shanren's texts combined with his strikingly reductive approach to representation may leave the viewer with an impression that his art is primarily conceptual. In fact, few painters could match Bada's technical skills. The "strength of his brush" (*bili* 筆力), a vital aesthetic shared between calligraphy and painting primarily referring to the integrity of one's brush-strokes, is peerless, and his ability to use those strokes to describe objects so convincingly is equally impressive. Less obvious, perhaps, is a sensuality that he was capable of imparting to his paintings. This is never more apparent than with his paintings on satin, a luxurious though difficult material that he seems to have particularly relished. These eight album leaves presenting different images of landscape are a wonderful example of the visceral touch that seemed to flow naturally and unconsciously from the artist's feelings to a manifestation in images of depth and beauty. As others have noted, the eight landscapes also suggest style-consciousness, deliberately evoking the manners of earlier masters. Sensuality and style-consciousness are not mutually exclusive. However, it is the rare artist who succeeds in somehow combining that sense of personal feeling with the formal challenges posed by the dictums of Dong Qichang's orthodoxy.

When Bada finally turned to the subject of landscape in the early 1690s, it is evident that Dong Qichang's theory of the Southern School was of significant influence and that Dong himself was an important filter. One noted album of six leaves by Bada presents him faithfully copying a series of landscapes by Dong, right down to his original inscriptions and signatures. These inscriptions, in turn, point to Dong's sources in the great luminaries of his Southern School: Dong Yuan, Huang Gongwang, and Ni Zan, among others.[1] Landscapes by Bada frequently invoke these same names—brief statements of allegiance to an earlier master's "brush-mode" in a textual format largely standardized by the orthodox followers of Dong Qichang. There is, however, nothing particularly standard in Bada's interactions with antiquity. Typically, he incorporates a common motif or loose rendition of a composition or modeling stroke that is traceable to an artist like Huang Gongwang or Ni Zan, but in such a manner that his own subjectivity dominates. His self-assurance is surely due to the fact that he was already so accomplished as a painter, and certain of who he was as a person, by the time he turned his brush to depicting landscape. In many respects Bada resembles another acclaimed "individualist," Gong Xian, who also was keen to attach himself to the pantheon of established literati artists gathered under the label of Southern School (see cat. no. 36). Both Bada and Gong recognized in Dong's lineage a pillar of constancy that was embedded deeply in the cultural bedrock and partially offset the loss of their dynasty. Where Bada differed from Gong was his enviable freedom when engaging the ancient styles. Gong's heaviness contrasts markedly with Bada's obvious delight.

In an earlier study Chou Ju-hsi drew specific attention to this album's relationship with Southern School styles, noting in particular how the original sequence of the leaves, as recorded in a nineteenth-century record, alternated paintings suggestive of the Mi style (Mi Fu and Mi Youren) with others.[2] Besides Mi father and son, certainly the artist whose seventeenth-century interpretation is most notably present is Huang Gongwang (see leaves B, F, G). Yet, without accompanying explanatory texts, how do we gauge the significance of these stylistic markers? Were they truly intended, or simply the result of momentary whims? This question can be answered in part by a landscape leaf from another album (whereabouts currently unknown) whose composition is strongly related to leaf A of the Honolulu album.[3] These two leaves clearly allude to the wet, misty landscape style associated with the Song-dynasty painters Mi Fu and Mi Youren. On the other leaf, however, is a short inscription: "Regarding the style of the Mi family, this mode is number one" 米家畫法，此品為第一. Bada's comment should be equally applicable to leaf A of this album, and consequently we are justified in presuming that his use of earlier styles here was intended to make a statement of sorts. How precisely one interprets that statement is less clear. Perhaps the last leaf (H) holds a clue. The large, ghostlike building nestled at the base of a majestic peak and fronted by foreground pines resembles structures identified by Jonathan Hay in paintings by other *yimin* artists as symbolizing the imperial tomb for the first Ming emperor at Mount Zhong outside of Nanjing.[4] The suggested linkage of Bada's familial and dynastic roots with the permanence he associated with the Southern School painters would help to explain the depth of sentiment presented by each of these exquisite landscapes.

PCS

For inscriptions and other documentation, see page 299 in this catalogue.

1 The album, which may not be complete, was formerly in the collection of Wang Fangyu and Sum Wai. It is discussed and partially illustrated in Wang, Richard M. Barnhart, and Judith G. Smith, eds., *Master of the Lotus Garden*, 178–81. See also Joseph Chang, et al., *In Pursuit of Heavenly Harmony*, cat. no. 12 and pages 150–51. Dong Qichang's original album does not appear to be extant.

2 Ju-hsi Chou, "A Landscape Painting Album by Chu Ta," 36–47.

3 Leaf 3 from the undated album pairing calligraphy and painting, *Shuhua hebei ce* 書畫合璧冊, is reproduced in Zhang Xinzhi 張馨之, *Bada Shanren shanshui yanjiu*, 245.

4 Hay, "The Suspension of Dynastic Time," especially 194–95. See also Hay's essay elsewhere in this catalogue.

47 **Bada Shanren** 八大山人
1626–1705

Landscapes 山水冊
C. 1702–03
Honolulu Museum of Art
Gift of Robert Allerton

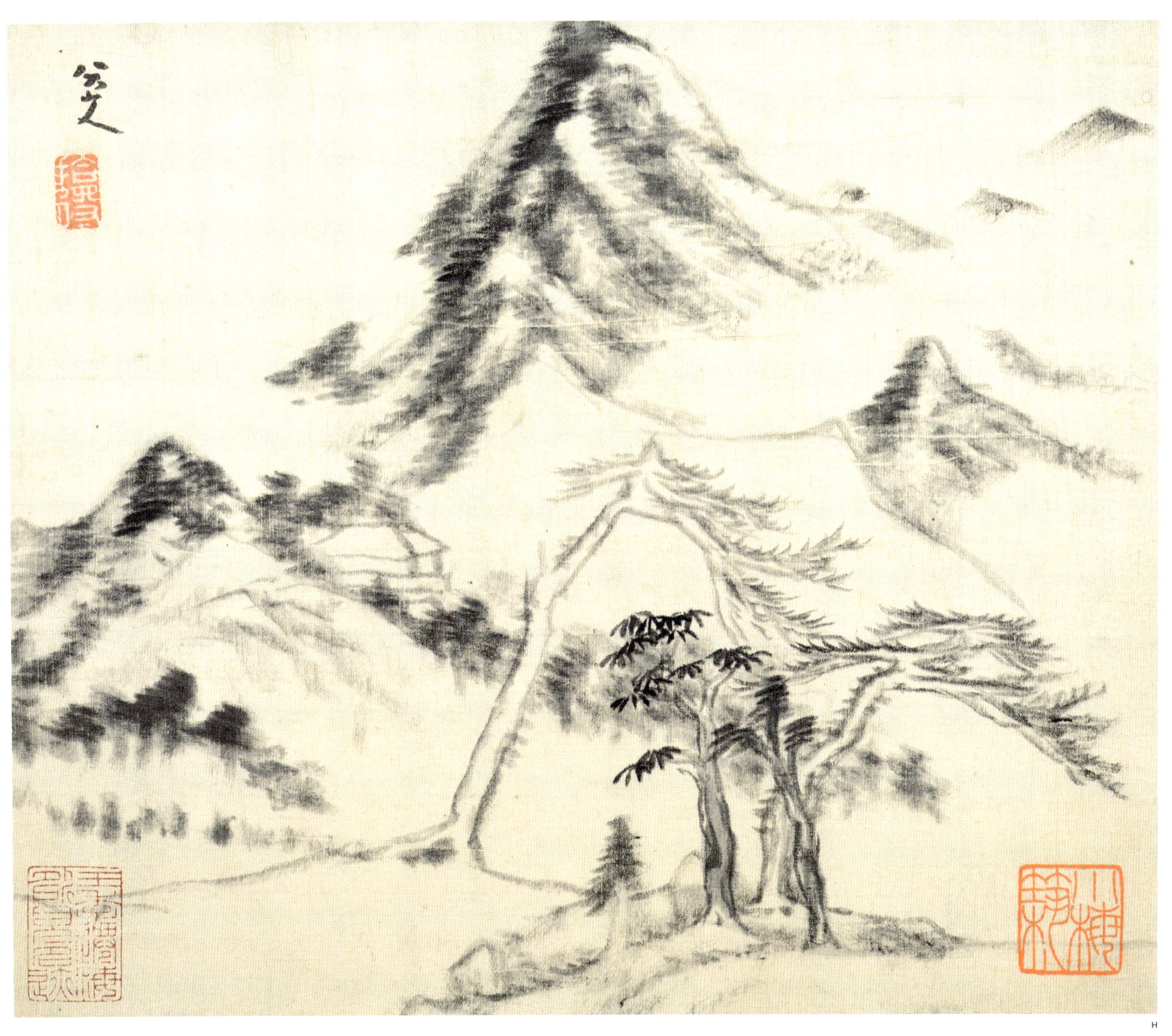

H

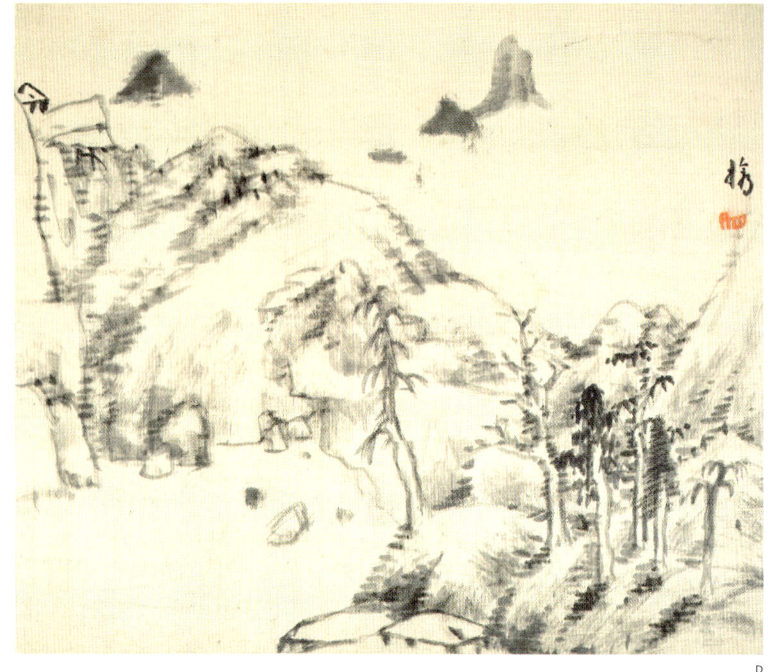

D

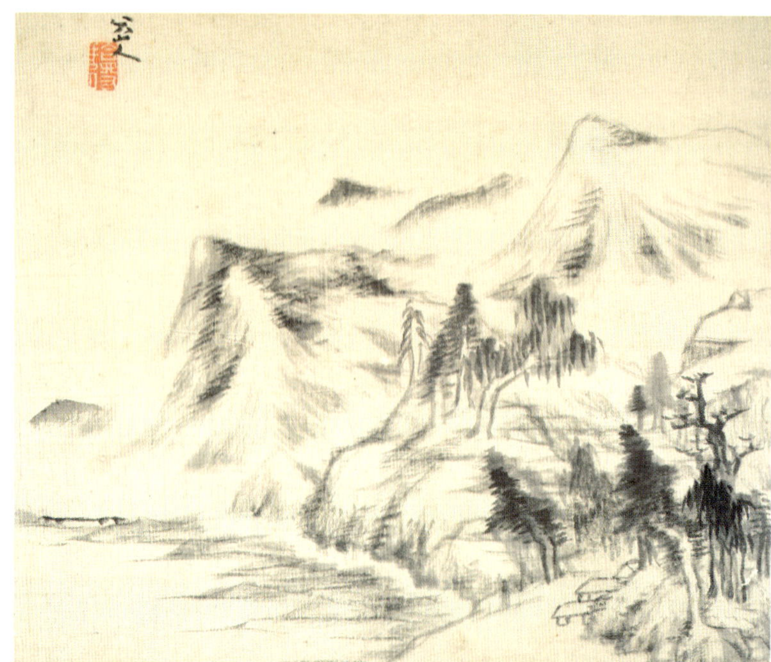

C

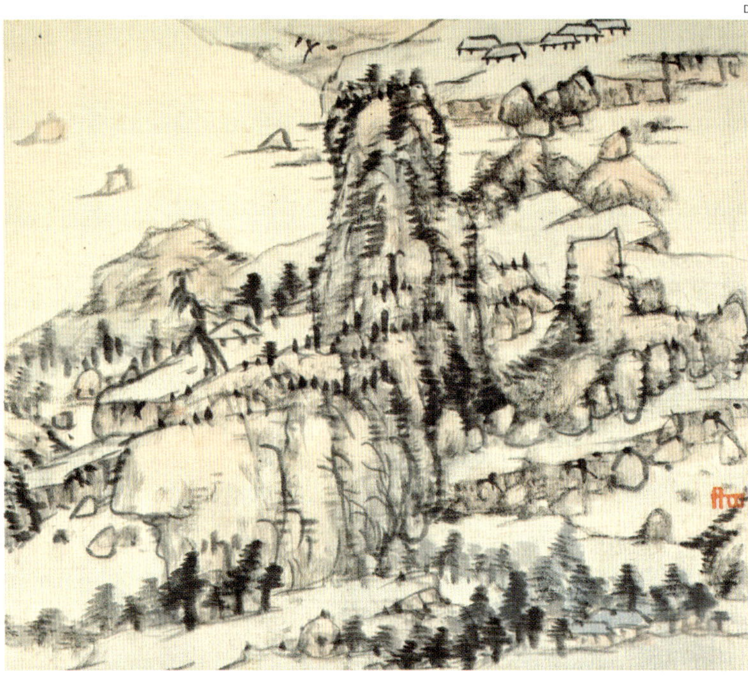

G

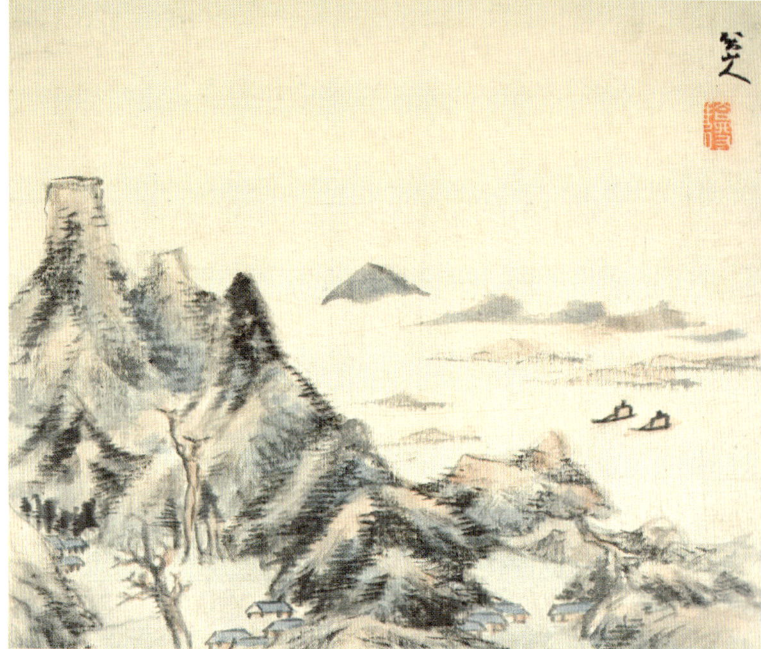

E

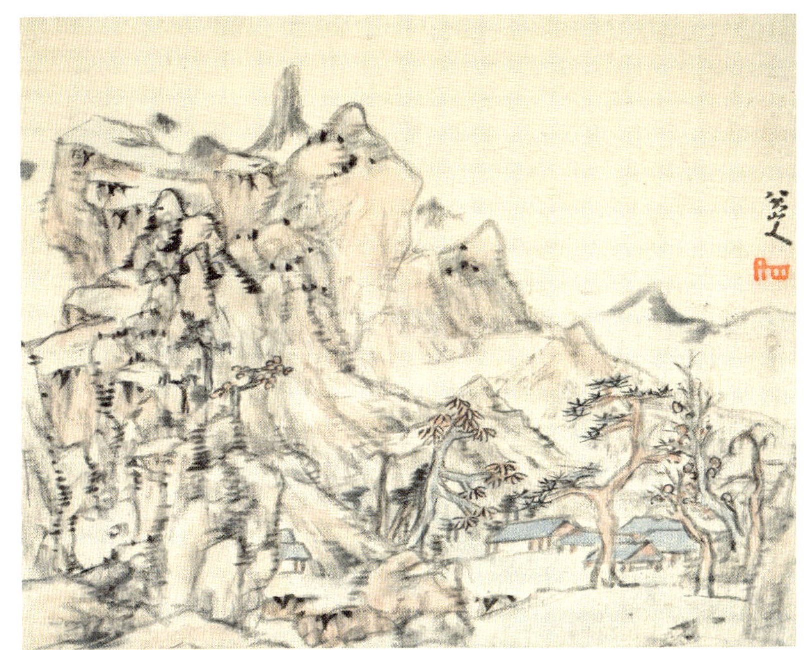

B

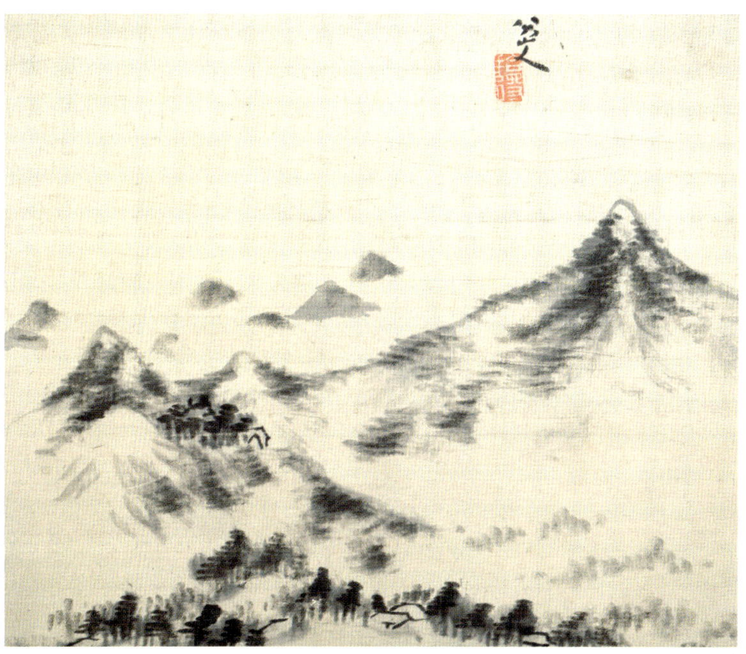

A

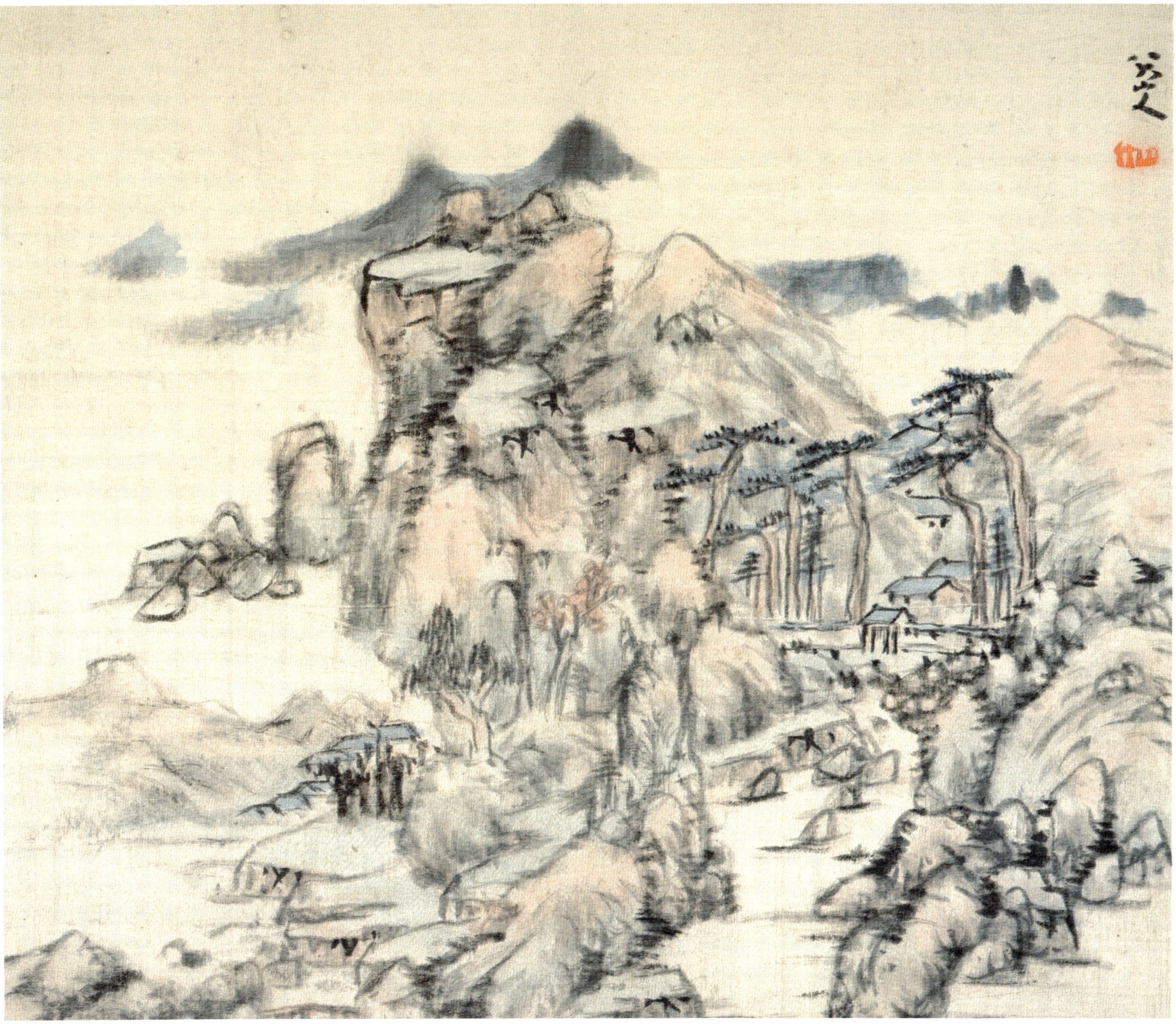

F

The title slip for this tall landscape by Bada Shanren, written by the prominent twentieth-century calligrapher Zhang Longyan, reads: "Landscape following the ancients" 循古山水. Zhang's inscription on the painting's silk mounting explains further, noting the deep devotion with which Bada followed Dong Qichang in landscape painting, often singling out such masters of the Southern School lineage as the tenth-century Dong Yuan; the eleventh-century eccentric Mi Fu, who was associated with misty mountains; and Great Fool (Dachi 大癡) Huang Gongwang of the Yuan. None of these earlier painters is specified on the scroll; Bada signed only his name and the character *xie* 寫, "to write or sketch." Still, Zhang's comments are perceptive. Dong Yuan, Mi Fu, and Huang Gongwang are all evoked in this sweeping vista of a rising mountain, and in the seamless blending of their influences we are shown how well Bada mastered Dong Qichang's ideal of creating a "great synthesis" (*dacheng* 大成) after imbibing deeply from the lessons of earlier painters.

Had Bada added an earlier model's name as a source of inspiration for this landscape it almost certainly would have been Dong Yuan's. Dong was one of the least known of the early landscape masters, but he was a key lynchpin in Dong Qichang's Southern School because of Mi Fu's powerful advocacy of his style of painting in the eleventh century and Dong Yuan's perceived influence on such Yuan-dynasty masters as Zhao Mengfu, Huang Gongwang, and Wu Zhen, all of the Jiangnan region (Yangzi River Delta, which Dong Yuan was noted for painting). Dong Qichang felt a particular affinity because of their shared surnames. Seventeenth-century painters like Bada Shanren understood Dong Yuan primarily through Dong Qichang. Dong Qichang's perspective, however, was skewed by the somewhat random nature of his encounters with Dong Yuan attributions. One of these, largely ignored today, appears to have been especially important: a tall hanging scroll titled *Traveling among Streams and Mountains* 溪山行旅.[1] Many of Dong Qichang's renditions of the earlier Dong's style invoke the large, darkly foliaged foreground trees of this particular attribution, and that appears to be what ultimately lies behind this tall landscape on satin by Bada. Bada's landscape paintings that specifically designate Dong Yuan as a model typically foreground similar trees and set them into a landscape of softly mounded hillocks and plentiful mists. The closest example is an undated scroll titled *After Beiyuan's (Dong Yuan) Landscape* in the collection of the Museum of Far Eastern Antiquities (Stockholm).[2] Both hanging scrolls separate the foreground knoll from a rising sweep of serpentine mountain forms that build in height and distance. The present *Landscape* differs slightly by creating more separation from foreground to background. This, together with a more systematic build-up of textured slopes and boulders, provides the background mountains with a greater sense of monumentality. The assemblage of forms, motifs, and textures are predominantly Yuan, Huang Gongwang specifically; the majestic vision, however, is pure Song.

As Bada began to explore the subject of landscape in the 1690s he was drawn to some of its most ancient and fundamental associations, including the longing, promise, and nonattainability of immortality. He referenced the immortal island of Penglai, seen from a distance yet unreachable. He described the utopian paradise of the Peach Blossom Spring, gained by the wayward fisherman but ultimately lost.[3] Monumental landscapes of the tenth and eleventh centuries in particular—with their convincing, sublime renderings of far-off mountains—come closest to capturing the essence of what landscape represented. Whether or not Bada had the opportunity to see such paintings, he appears to be re-creating that experience with this painting. In this regard, his choice of seals to accompany his signature is most apt: *Kede shenxian* 可得神仙, or "immortality is attainable." **PCS**

For inscriptions and other documentation, see page 299 in this catalogue.

1 Dong Yuan's *Traveling among Streams and Mountains* is reproduced in Xu Bangda 徐邦達, *Zhongguo huihua shi tulu* 中國繪畫史圖錄 (Shanghai: Renmin meishu chubanshe, 1981), vol. 1, 77. The painting is said to be in the Ogawa collection, Kyoto, Japan. Despite the fact that it was considered to be only half a painting, this Dong Yuan attribution was much celebrated in the seventeenth century, earning the moniker "Half a piece of Jiangnan." See Yin Ji'nan 尹吉男, "'Dong Yuan' gainian de lishi shengcheng," 92–101.

2 Reproduced and discussed in Fangyu Wang, Richard M. Barnhart, and Judith G. Smith, eds., *Master of the Lotus Garden*, 164–66. A related example is in the Beijing Palace Museum, reproduced in *Zhiren wufa*, vol. 1, cat. no. 22.

3 The Penglai reference is seen on one of the two landscape leaves in the *Anwan Album* (Sen-oku Hakko Kan, Kyoto, Japan). Bada painted the Peach Blossom Spring and transcribed Tao Yuanming's story in a scroll dated 1696 (Beijing Palace Museum). See *Zhiren wufa*, vol. 1, cat. no. 25.

48 **Bada Shanren** 八大山人
1626–1705

Landscape 山水軸
C. 1697–1700
Private collection

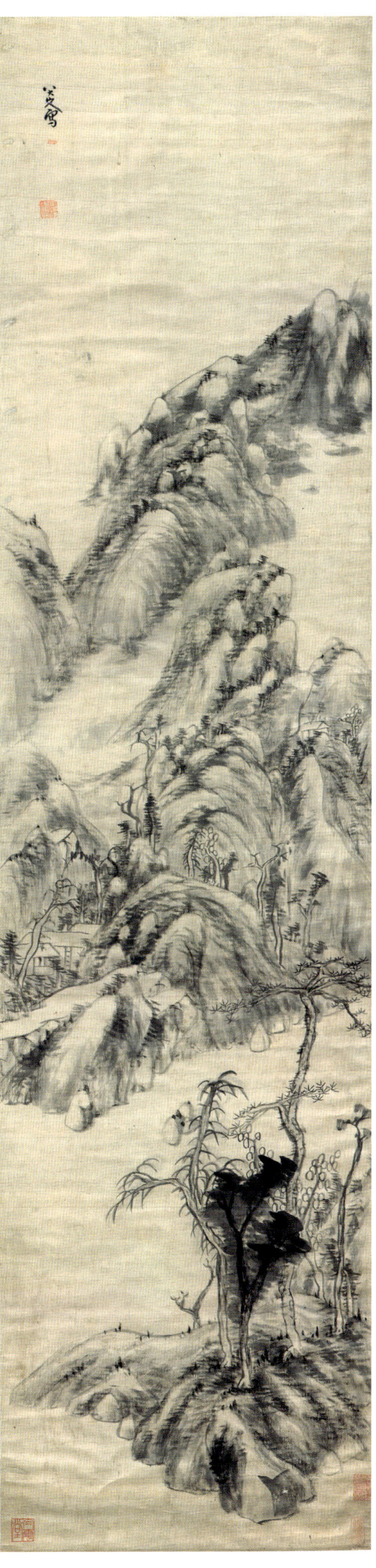

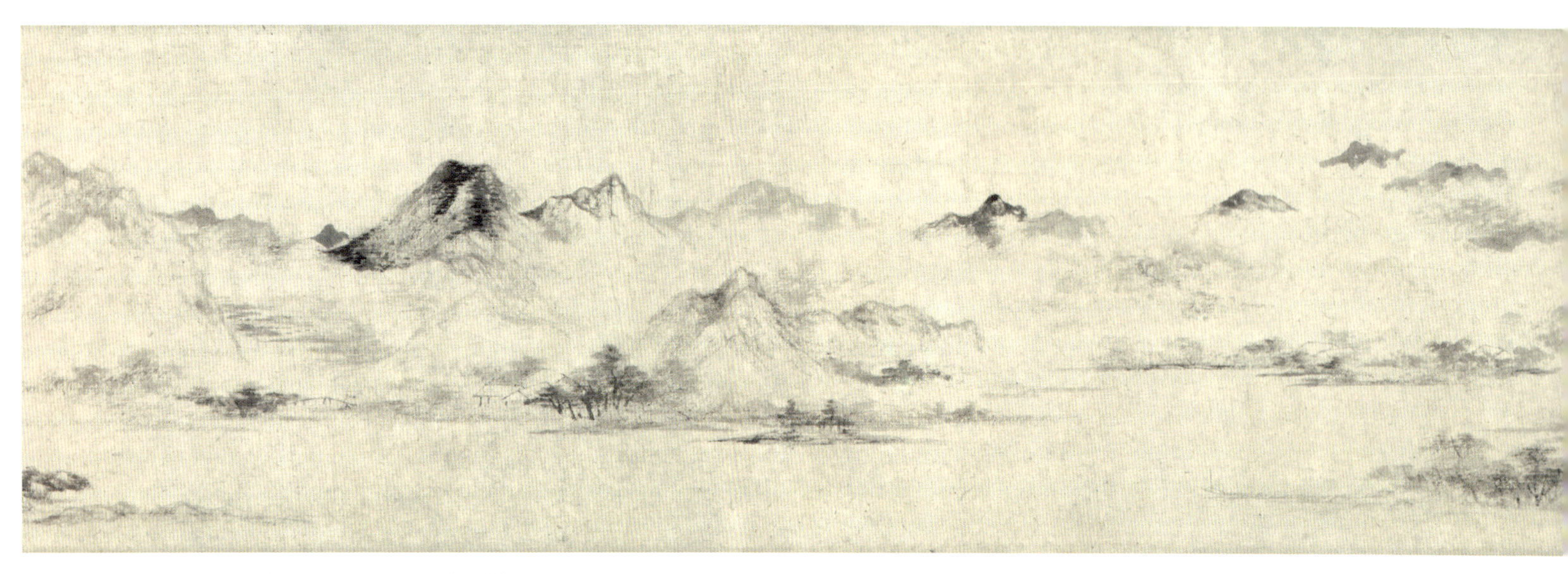

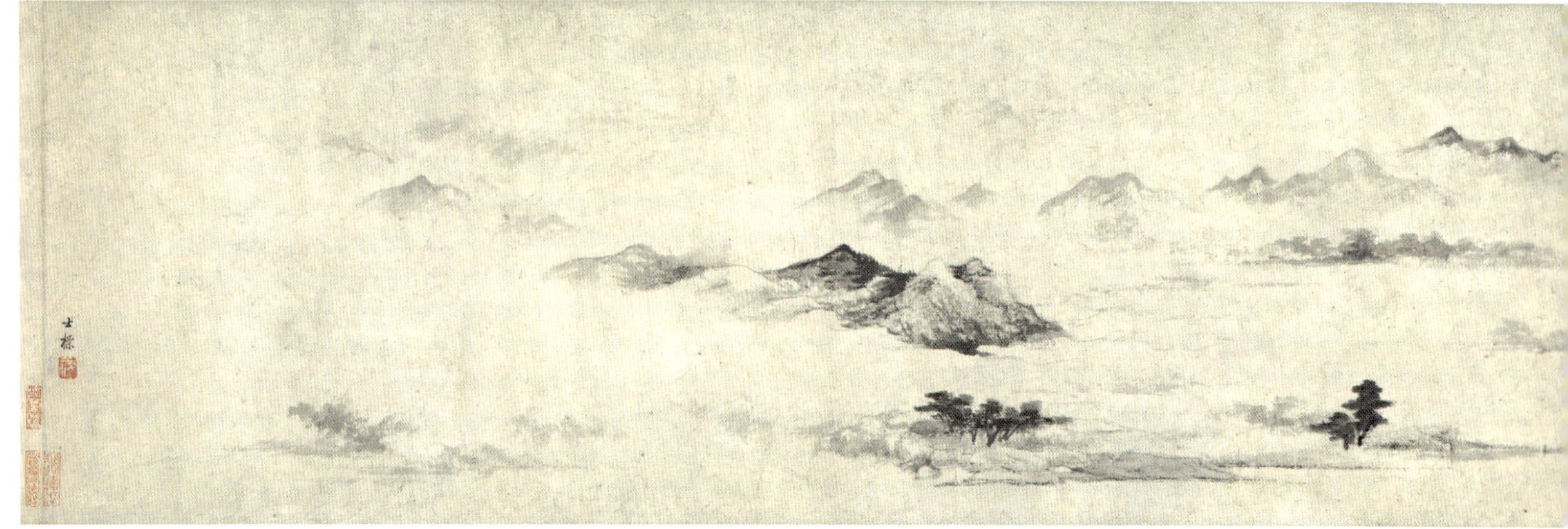
士標

49 Zha Shibiao 查士標
1615–1698

Scenery of the Xiao and Xiang after Mi Youren 瀟湘圖卷
Private collection

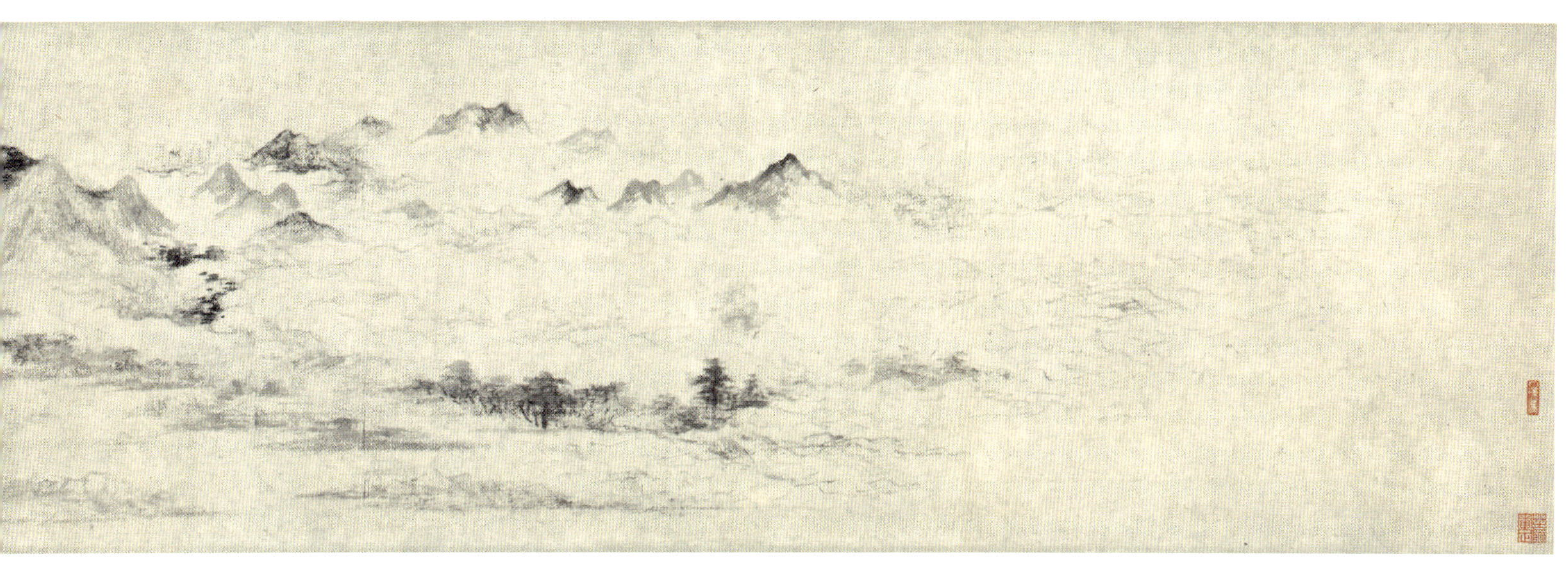

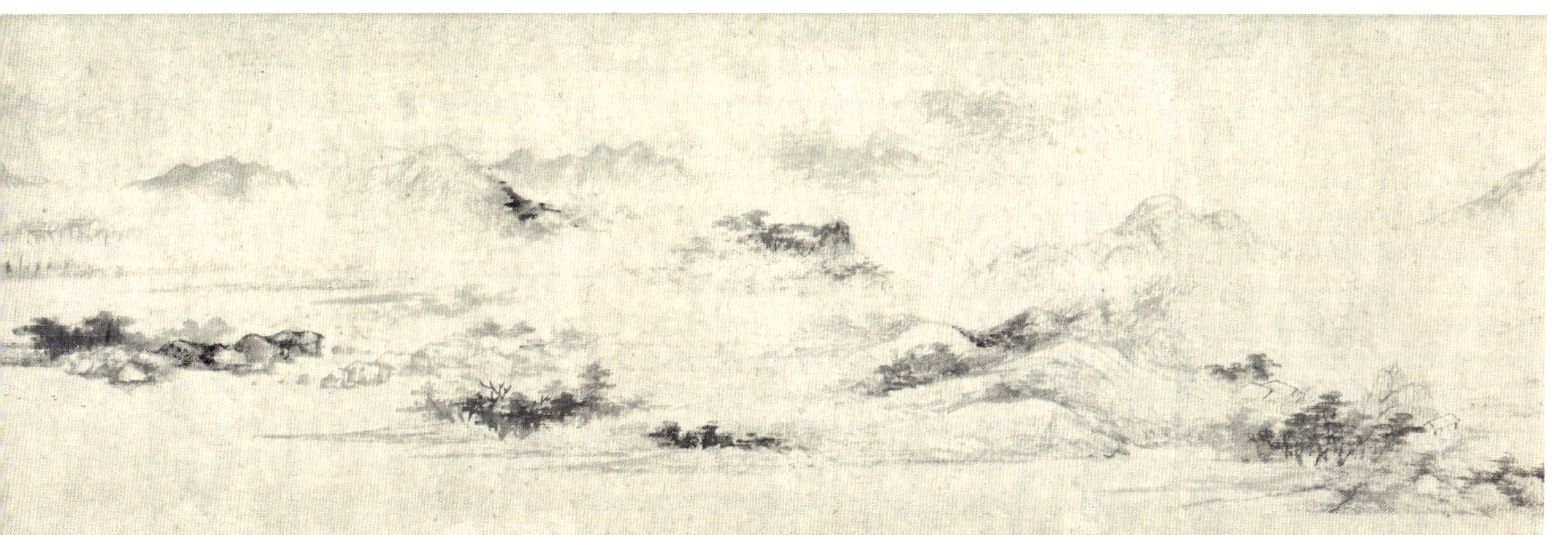

Born into a wealthy family of Xiuning (Anhui Province), Zha Shibiao studied for the civil service exam under the Ming but abandoned any office-holding ambitions after the establishment of the Manchu regime. Although he did not fight against the Manchu army, he pledged allegiance to the Ming and refused to serve the Qing court, instead devoting his energies to literary and artistic pursuits. Zha was later grouped with his contemporaries Hongren, Sun Yi, and Wang Zhirui as the Four Masters of Xin'an, named after the old geographical designation of the area in southern Anhui Province that includes Xiuning and Shexian.[1] In addition to being influenced by the local scenery of Huangshan (Yellow Mountain), the Xin'an painters were noted for their emulation of the sparse, clean style associated with the Yuan-dynasty master Ni Zan (fig. 4).

Approximately twenty-five years after the collapse of the Ming, Zha Shibiao moved to Yangzhou (Jiangsu Province), where he spent most of the remainder of his life. His painting style subsequently changed, evolving away from an almost exclusive adherence to Ni Zan to a more comprehensive approach. The two Mis—Mi Fu and his son, Mi Youren—especially the distinctive mode of painting cloudy mountains that the younger Mi in particular developed, became an important source for Zha from around 1670 until the end of his life. The city of Zhenjiang (Jiangsu Province), a short trip across the Yangzi River from Yangzhou, was where Mi Fu established the family residence in the late eleventh century, and six hundred years later there were still material remains that kept this important cultural figure's legacy very much alive.[2] This may well have been a factor in Zha's interest in the Mi style after establishing residency in Yangzhou. He traveled frequently between Yangzhou, Nanjing, and Zhenjiang, and his circle of friends included Da Chongguang (cat. no. 31), who was closely associated with the Zhenjiang area.

While the undated *Scenery of the Xiao and Xiang after Mi Youren* is consistent with Zha Shibiao's other works in the Mi family style of his Yangzhou period, it stands out as a particularly beautiful and naturalistic rendition.[3] Zha's accompanying letter to the recipient, Yiweng, which is mounted to the scroll following the misty landscape, provides some interesting information that helps explain the quality of the painting. Zha uses exceedingly polite, formal language, written with the same kind of care that his delicate scenery reveals. Though Yiweng has not been identified, he clearly was important to Zha. Moreover, he seems to have been very specific regarding this commission. Cognizant of a famous scroll by Mi Youren that was known at the time as *Xiao Xiang* (Shanghai Museum), Yiweng apparently requested that Zha re-create the scroll by painting an extended landscape and adding the numerous inscriptions by Mi and other early writers that follow Mi's painting.[4] It is unlikely that Zha had access to Mi's painting, but the inscriptions were well known.[5] In his transcriptions, Zha employs a uniform style of calligraphy that recalls the Mi family style but is quite different from the various hands that contributed to Mi Youren's *Xiao Xiang*. Zha emphasizes Yiweng's knowledge and skill as a connoisseur of old paintings—a clear signal that Mi Youren's painting had meaning to Yiweng.

Scenery of the Xiao and Xiang after Mi Youren was executed on a fibrous and absorbent paper, proper for the misty and watery Mi style. The scene opens with dense clouds and waters, gradually extending to barely discernible mountains in the middle- and background, along with blurred riverbanks and trees in the foreground. Space plays a significant role in this painting, as it suggests the massive nature of the clouds and vastness of the water and serves to create a misty aura. Balance is another concern. The painter left a large amount of space in the opening and closing sections and arranged most of the motifs in the middle part of the scroll. Zha Shibiao's painting clearly evokes Mi Youren's style, but whereas most Ming and Qing landscapes in that style exaggerate its conventions, in accord with the general perception that Song painting was realistic, Zha seems determined to hide the standard motifs and brush modes in a setting that approximates the way things appear and feel.

It is difficult to know what Mi Youren's painting may have meant to Yiweng. Perhaps it was, as Zha Shibiao's inscription suggests, simply a reflection of the connoisseur's interest. Or perhaps Yiweng shared Zha's loyalist sentiments and saw in Mi's painting, with its various inscriptions of the early Southern Song period, an earlier paragon of cultural survival during a similar period of difficult dynastic transition. If this were the case, Zha's *Scenery of the Xiao and Xiang after Mi Youren* is best understood as a melding of the real with the ideal, past and the present, firmly set upon a foundation of the Mi family cultural legacy.
JYZ / PCS

For inscriptions and other documentation, see page 299 in this catalogue.

1 James Cahill, ed., *Shadows of Mt. Huang*.

2 Mi Fu's famous studio, Haiyue An (Studio of Oceans and Mountains), was rebuilt during the Wanli reign (1572–1620). Mi's tomb, along with many eulogistic descriptions, existed by the Helin Temple just south of the city. See Peter C. Sturman, *Mi Fu*, 1–4.

3 Reproduced and documented in Paul Moss, ed., *Scrolling Images*. My translation of the documentation accompanying this scroll is based on this publication.

4 The painting is known today as *White Clouds along the Xiao and Xiang* 瀟湘白雲圖. See Peter C. Sturman, "Mi Youren and the Inherited Literati Tradition," 395–442, 485–94. The inscriptions that Zha Shibiao transcribes are listed and summarized on pages 486–90.

5 Mi Youren's painting was probably in the collection of Wang Yongning when Zha Shibiao painted this scroll. The inscriptions are recorded in a number of seventeenth-century catalogues, such as Bian Yongyu's 卞永譽 *Shigutang shuhua huikao* 式古堂書畫彙考 of 1682.

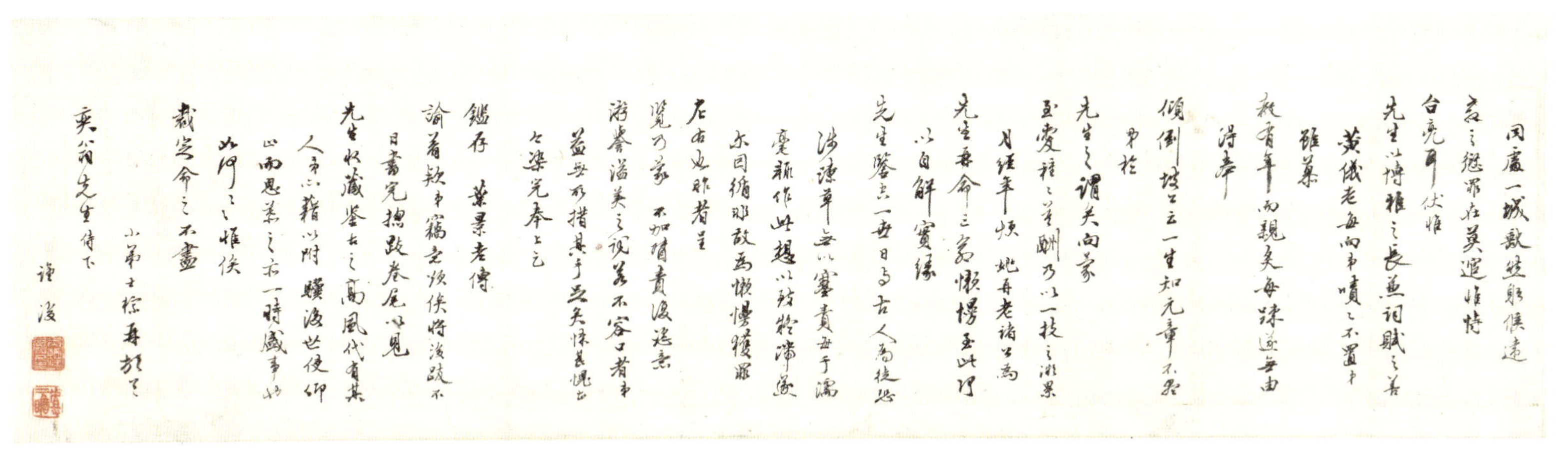

LETTER BY THE ARTIST TO THE RECIPIENT, YIWENG

Although we live in the same town, I have not yet paid you a visit because of my indolence. My fault of missing your teaching cannot be evaded. Hopefully I can gain your forgiveness for my negligence. Mr. Huang Yi has often spoken to me of your erudition and literary talent. Although I have admired you for years, I have failed to pay you a visit in person and thus we have not met. Lord Slope [Su Shi] once said that for his entire life he had not known Yuanzhang [Mi Fu] thoroughly. This can also be applied to me with regard to you. I have always received your favor yet have not reciprocated. Now, this one insignificant skill of mine—for several months, almost a year already—numerous friends have reminded me of your order. So indolent! How can I excuse myself? It is because you are such a fine connoisseur, daily in step with the masters of old. I fear that my work will appear slovenly, that I will have nothing with which to fulfill my responsibility. Each time I am ready to apply ink and brush I begin to think like this. I do not intend to slack off, procrastinate, and furthermore offend you. The other day when I showed you this painting, unfinished, not only did you not criticize it, but you praised it with such excessive compliments. I feel even more surprised and flattered. With much reverence and humility, I completed the painting and venture to present it to you for your criticism and collection. Mr. Ye Jing has given me your instructions for the inscriptions. I hope to finish writing them in the next few days. With the inscriptions added to the end, these will demonstrate that your connoisseurship and knowledge of the past is indeed lofty and far-reaching. I too will benefit from the galloping of your reputation to later generations. This makes one look forward with anticipation—a splendid event of our times. How does that sound? Let's wait for the judgment of generations yet to come.

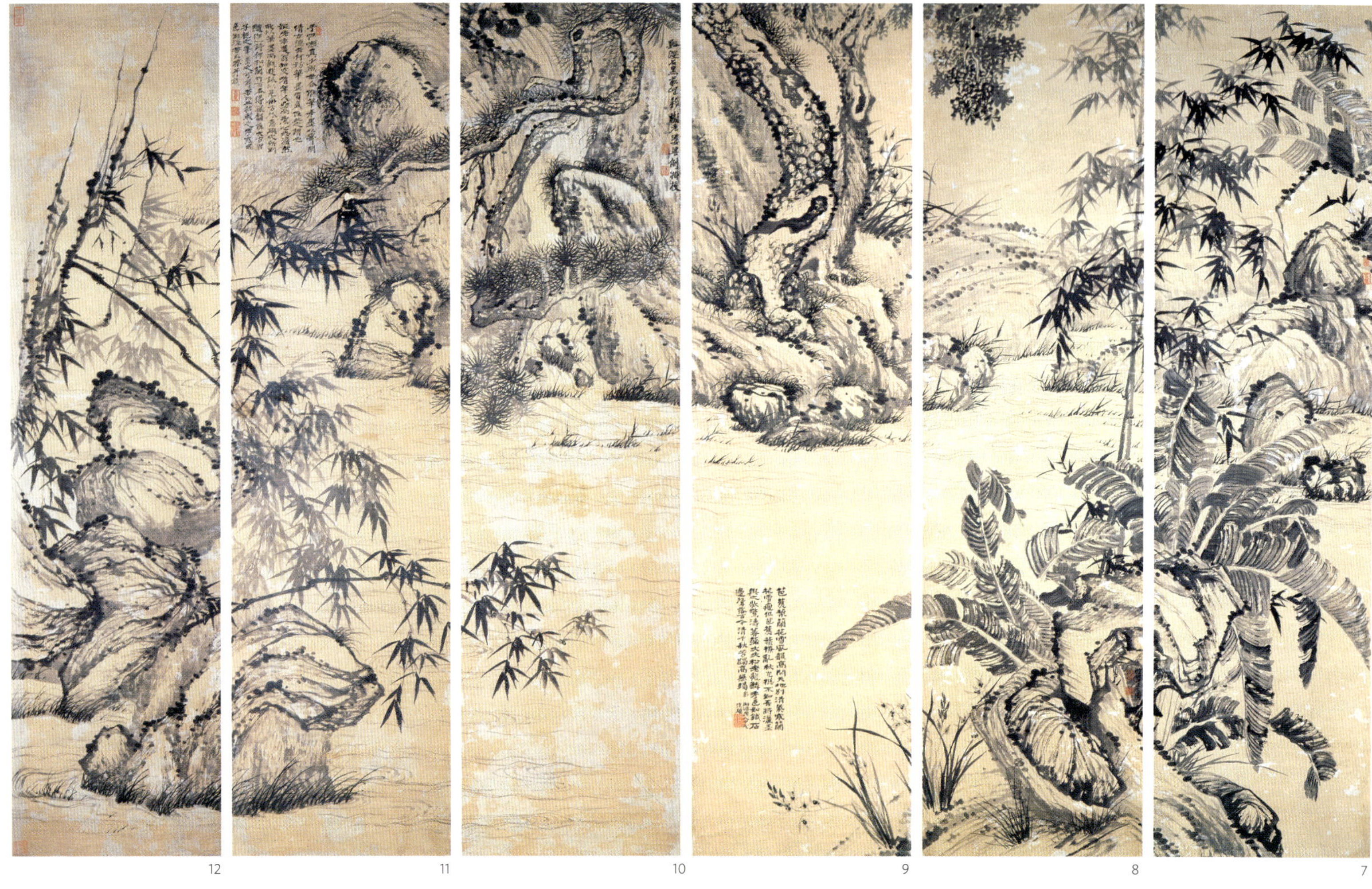

50 Shitao 石濤
1642–1707

Plants of Virtue and Rocks by Water (Sketching Bamboo) **寫竹通景十二屏**
1693–94
National Palace Museum, Republic of China (Taiwan)

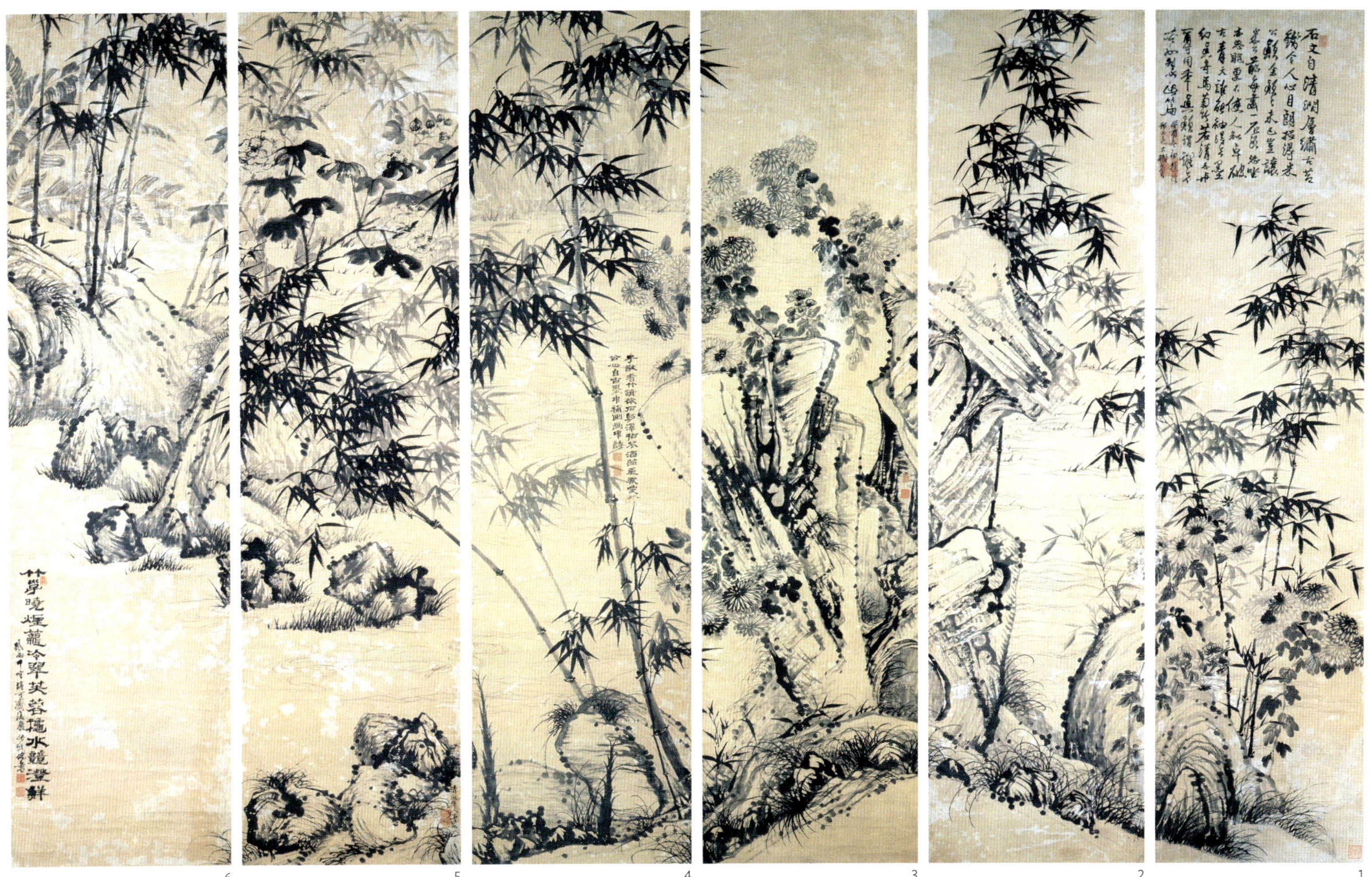

The patterning of the rocks is naturally clear and smooth,
The old moss is layered like silk brocade.
The sight makes a person's heart and eyes bright,
And summons up the craziness of Master Mi [Mi Fu].
My own craziness is endless,
So how can I defer to Master Mi?
Each time you painted a rock
You forgot to sit down, forgot to sleep.
You did not even remember to let people know
That your brilliance stood out against the blue sky of ancient times.
Who now is able to wave his sleeves
And conjure truly extraordinary visions from ink?
These chrysanthemums and bamboo will stand for my pure ambitions:
Consider me of the same stripe as you.
Who is the truly crazy one, would you say,
After the effort I have put into creating this vision?

Shitao orchestrated this vast composition from five representational units, each of which depicts a garden element on the banks of a central pond. The combination of the cropping of the garden elements by the painting's edges and the openings left between elements at either end of the scene lets us understand that both pond and garden extend far beyond the boundaries of the painting, and that we are seeing the garden from deep within. From right to left, we pass from angular to twisting rhythms; from chrysanthemums to hibiscus to orchids; from bamboo to plantains to pines and back to bamboo; and from grass script to clerical to standard to running script, finally returning to standard script. An ensemble of rocks dominates the right half of the composition, while a miniature landscape of pines and waterfall occupies the left half.

Although Shitao's name has often been associated with small-scale formats, from a very early point in his career he painted large sets of paintings that were intended to be mounted together on folding screens or hung side by side on the wall to make up a single mural-sized composition.[1] In this respect, he was not unusual among the artists of his milieu. Gong Xian in Nanjing, Bada Shanren in Nanchang, and Zha Shibiao in Yangzhou all created large-scale works of this kind, usually in ink alone. The continuous multi-scroll composition evolved during the tenth century from the earlier multi-panel screen. From the tenth century onwards, the two formats coexisted, with highpoints of popularity first under the Northern Song dynasty (960–1127), and later during the late Ming–early Qing period. Continuous composition multi-panel screens and multi-scroll sets were much produced during Shitao's lifetime in Yangzhou, where they became a specialty of the Yuan family workshop of decorative painters on silk. It was in counterpoint to (and in competition with) their brightly colored works that Shitao, like Zha Shibiao, painted similarly large monochrome compositions, which he preferred to execute on paper.[2]

Plants of Virtue and Rocks by Water is one of several works that Shitao painted in the same studio, the Hall of the Great Tree (Dashu Tang), probably located within Yangzhou's Jinghui Monastery.[3] He completed the painting itself in the early winter of 1693, as attested by the poem dated to that moment on scroll 1, at the far right of the composition. A matching dedication at the far left, on scroll 11, mentions that after completing the painting the artist added a poem, referring to the inscription on the first scroll. It is likely, therefore, that the work was originally presented to the recipient with just these two inscriptions; the remaining inscriptions would have been added later. Two are explicitly identified as later inscriptions: scroll 9's text bears a date of 1694, and scroll 6's states that the artist was then staying in the Danke Studio. The most plausible scenario is that the artist added all the later inscriptions during a visit to the recipient's residence during 1694. Shitao chose different script types, styles, and scales for his various calligraphic interventions. In this way he turned what was no doubt a request difficult to decline into an opportunity to showcase another aspect of his artistic talent. At a time when he was inching toward full-time professionalism, such self-advertisement had its uses.[4]

Shitao describes the as-yet-unidentified recipient, Jilao, in literati terms as a man of lofty simplicity and placid temperament. This does not mean, though, that the man's primary social identity was necessarily a literati one. The dedication does not include the honorific acknowledgment due to a present or former government official, and the man may not have been a member of the local gentry either, given that so few of Shitao's known commissions can be linked to that group of Yangzhou-area society. The artist's major market was among Yangzhou's "Confucian merchants" (*rushang* 儒商), businessmen of considerable education and cultural sophistication hailing in the main from Huizhou in Anhui Province. Decorum usually dictated that a dedication to a merchant patron pass over the recipient's commercial activities in order to highlight a parallel literati cultural identity that was often well deserved. Certainly, a painting of this scale can only have been intended for an imposing residence, where it would have served to extend the atmosphere and cultural

For inscriptions and other documentation, see page 300 in this catalogue.

1 One such set of paintings dating from 1671 is composed of separate landscape compositions on silk. The set was executed for presentation as a birthday gift to the then-prefect of Huizhou, Cao Dingwang, and today is in the Jicui Yuan Museum, Fujian. See *Shitao shuhua quanji*, vol. 2, pl. 415.

2 Shitao's preference for paper over silk is clearly stated in a letter from 1702 or later. See Jonathan Hay, *Shitao*, 334, appendix two, letter no. 15.

3 Shitao also used this studio name during an earlier Yangzhou stay, in the late 1680s. It should be noted, however, that to the best of my knowledge the two names (Jinghui Monastery and Hall of the Great Tree) do not appear together on any single work.

4 For more on this subject, see my essay elsewhere in this catalogue.

5 Hay, *Shitao*, 334.

connotations of the residence's garden elements into a reception hall. Such halls were highly formal, dominated by the symmetry not only of the architectural envelope but also of the placement of furniture and display objects. The artist would have had this eventual physical setting in mind when he boldly invoked in his inscriptions and in his pictorial execution a contrasting craziness (*dian* 顛) classically associated with the Song literati calligrapher, connoisseur, and painter Mi Fu.

The modern art historian is tempted to interpret the work principally in relation to Shitao's self-fashioning. But there can be no doubt that the artist intended this garden scene to be understood as a metaphor for the human qualities and cultural sophistication of the recipient. Equally, the owner who placed this massive painting in his reception hall would have expected the painting to be taken as evidence of his own open-minded taste, and of the breadth of his social connections. An additional dimension of meaning derives from the artist's celebrity. In 1693, Shitao was nationally famous as an artist of extraordinary talent and achievement, as a descendant of the Ming imperial family, and also as a Chan master who did part of his teaching through painting. A painting on this scale from one of the most famous artists of the day was something of a trophy. The artist, well aware that the value of the commission to the patron far exceeded the decorative function of the painting, would undoubtedly have insisted on appropriate remuneration. In a letter written circa 1702 or later, he wrote: "If someone wants a continuous scene, it means standing on a scaffold or a bench, stretching my arm and craning my neck to reach the painting, up and down, always moving about or standing. For painting in these conditions I charge fifty taels per screen."[5] Although in 1693 he may not yet have been able to charge such a high price, it was important commissions such as *Plants of Virtue and Rocks by Water* that allowed Shitao to accumulate the capital necessary to acquire his own residence in Yangzhou just a few years later. **JH**

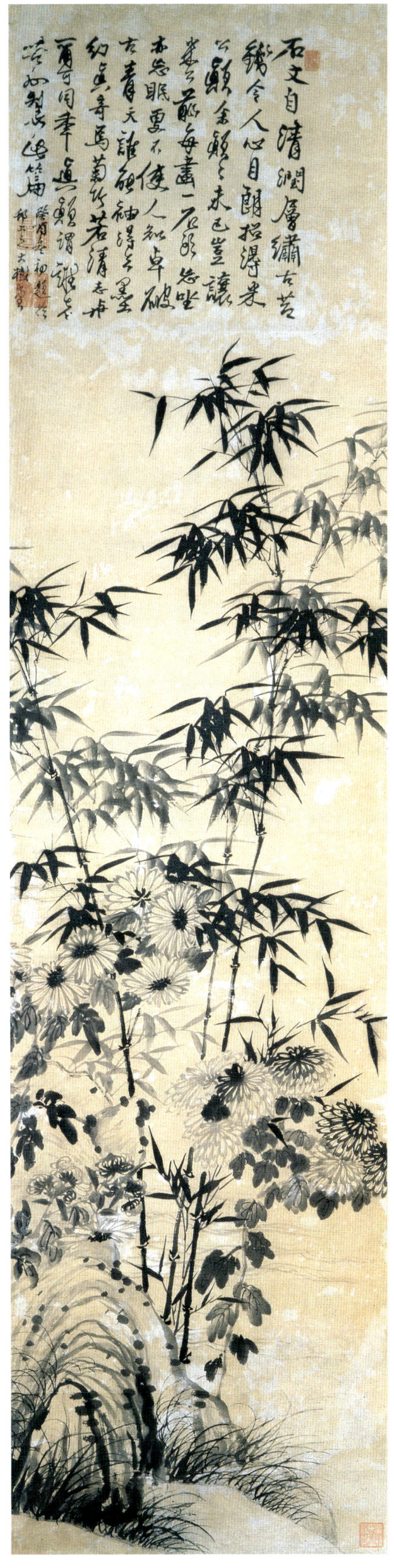

Zhu Ruoji, better known by his Buddhist names Shitao and Yuanji, was born to a distant branch of the Ming imperial family. Orphaned in 1645, he was rescued from death by a loyal retainer and found refuge in the Buddhist community, which provided intellectual, artistic, and spiritual nurturing for many decades. After an extensive period in Xuancheng (Anhui Province), where he lived in proximity to the inspiring landscape of Mount Huang and became an acknowledged Chan Buddhist master, Shitao moved to Nanjing in 1680 and expanded his social circle to include Qing officials as well as Ming loyalists. He moved to the commercial city of Yangzhou in 1687 and was encouraged to journey to the capital at Beijing and seek patronage after meeting with Kangxi during the Qing emperor's second inspection tour of 1690.

This album was painted in the autumn of 1694, commissioned in Yangzhou by Huang Lü, who originally hailed from Shexian (Anhui Province) and lived in Nanchang (Jiangxi Province). The years 1693 and 1694 were a period of great ambivalence for Shitao. His stay in Beijing at the beginning of the 1690s had not been successful, and he had returned to the south in 1692, eventually moving to the Yangzhou area in the spring of 1693. While living at the Jinghui Monastery in Yangzhou, he contemplated leaving behind his lifelong status as a Buddhist monk; indeed, within a few years (early 1697 at the latest) he would acquire his own house in the city.

The eight paintings in this album are formally audacious and highly original. The inscriptions convey a self-conscious emphasis on being present in the here and now, as well as a refusal to follow existing stylistic paths. Shitao's long inscription to the final leaf cites nine painter-contemporaries who, according to him, understood painting in his era. In the first sentence—"Those who enter the Dao of painting through the common gateway are hardly worth treasuring"—he quotes a well-known Chan saying used by a master to criticize a pupil who does not seek enlightenment through his inner ability but relies on outside forces. Shitao then employs several critical categories to define the appreciable qualities of artists who, to the contrary, follow their own paths, including lofty antiquity (*gaogu* 高古), untrammeled purity (*qingyi* 清逸), dry sparseness (*ganshou* 乾瘦), dripping moistness and exceptional sense of antiquity (*linli qigu* 淋漓奇古), and heroic expansiveness (*haofang* 豪放). His assessment aligns him with a section of the contemporary art world, but then he separates himself with the statement, "Only I cannot grasp these ideas and so my painting is vacant and hollow (*kongkong dongdong*), dumb and mute (*mumu momo*) like this."[1] We can associate the meanings of the two onomatopoetic phrases with Shitao's experience of being a Chan monk, and can perhaps understand them as an analogy to the inward meditative practice of Chan. By using Chan principles to explain the practice of painting, Shitao seems to say that a painter should be aware of his own ideas and manifest them in paintings, so that he can make a unique reputation in his own era. That the self is present in the here and now is palpably a Chan idea, and Shitao wittily deploys it to support his mapping of a modern art world surrounding him. The accompanying image visualizes his philosophical thinking. Three bare trees grow in the middle of nowhere, each with its own character. A few grasses around their trunks impart a sense of a particular place. The trees seem to represent both the material and the immaterial, being at once metaphysically meaningful and formally functional.[2]

The landscapes of the other leaves present Shitao's personal vision but also specific memories. Most obvious is leaf 1, in which he painted his memories of Mount Huang from the 1660s and 70s. A meandering path coils around the waist of the mountain ridges, suggesting a journey in space, in the imagination, and in memory. Another inviting path is depicted in leaf 7. Beyond a line of reeds, a man walks along a path that is flanked by water. The path is almost like a bridge linking him to an islet, where rocky mounds and trees are depicted; it also echoes the bridge on the other side. Here, Shitao's persistence and self-denial are metaphorically visualized in strikingly poetic form. In the inscription, he asks: "Who is there who would share with me the ups and downs of this vast world?" He continues by saying that he is who he is, faults and all, and then tells us that his inkstone had long been in disuse, so that his just-written and out-of-practice poems had to be torn apart in front of a visitor. The painting stages his self-declared self-absorption in an image of poetic solitude.

For inscriptions and other documentation, see pages 300–01 in this catalogue.

1 Jonathan Hay, *Shitao*, 256. Hay's translation.

2 The transference from method to no-method is also revealed in Shitao's inscription on leaf 3, in which he associates the methods of painting with those of calligraphy. When the painter understands these methods he or she will no longer focus on the association. He explains by using a parallel association between calligraphy and martial arts. When the Tang calligrapher Zhang Xu comprehended that the practice of calligraphy could be inspired from sword dancing, he did not actually see a sword dancer. Shitao places obvious emphasis on the painter's individual agency in creating paintings. Both his comprehension of principles and personal experiences played roles in his exceptional creativity.

51 Shitao 石濤 1642–1707

Landscapes for Huang Lü 贈黃律山水冊 1694

Los Angeles County Museum of Art
Los Angeles County Fund

LEAF 7

Who is there who would share with
me the ups and downs of this vast world?
Old and without a thing, I've become
stubborn and crotchety.
I didn't realize my inkstone had become
so overgrown with weeds.
In front of guests I tear up my poems
written while drunk.

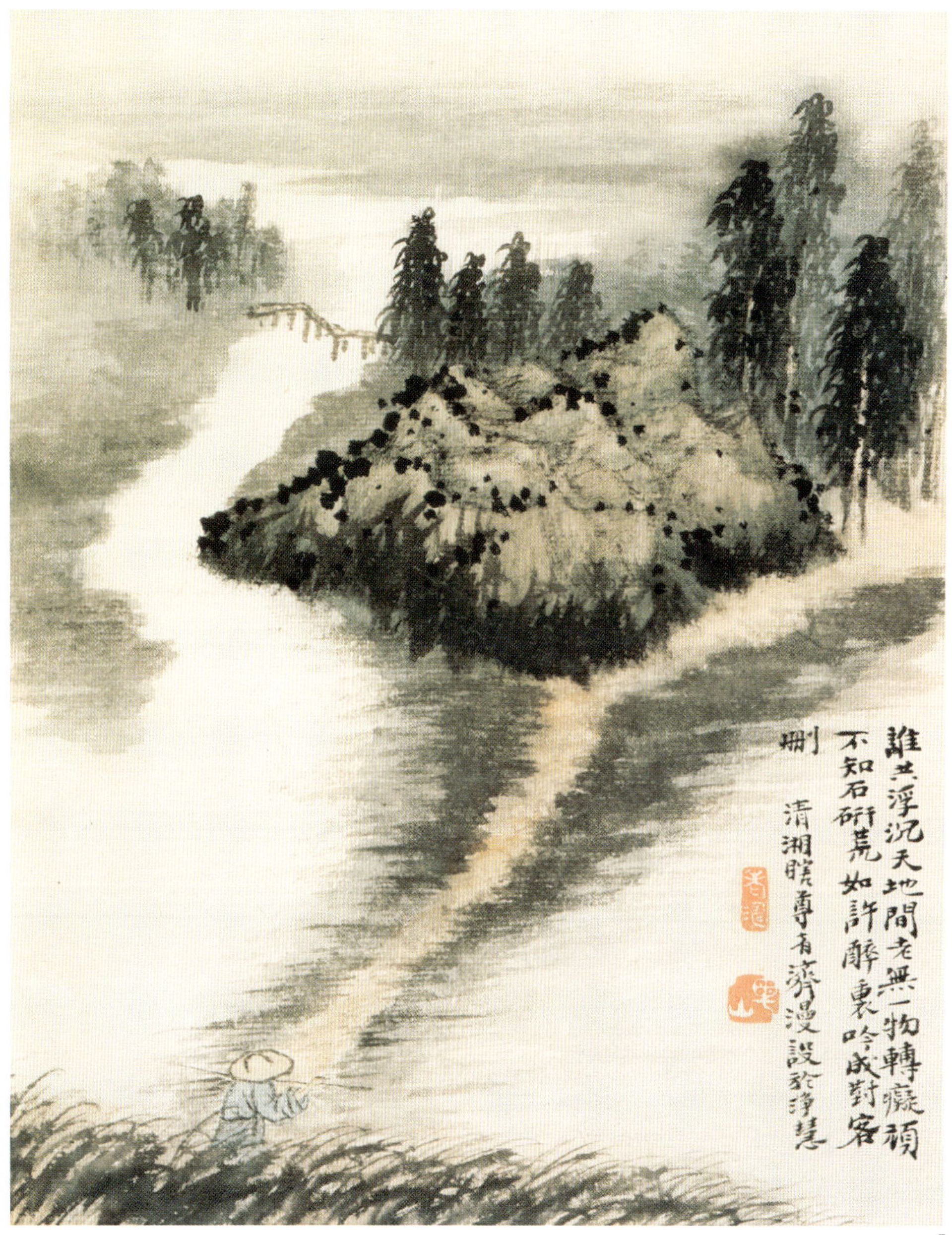

7

The "ups and downs of this vast world" is a reference to destiny, which is also evoked by the strong sense of journeying in leaves 4 and 6. In both we see a man traveling on a boat on a river among mountains, with residences located along the way. In leaf 4, a larger figure stands contrastingly in front of a thatched hut, which is nestled in the crook of an encompassing boulder. The boat seems to be carried along by the downward-flowing water, creating a strong tension with the stability of the reclusive residence. A close-up view of travel is depicted in leaf 2. A gentleman rows a skiff on a slightly rippling lake; a tree on the shore is blown in the other direction. The wind stirs the scene, adding a sense of the passage of time, of aging, of coming and going. What is to be valued in the endless movement of life is true ease, like the rhythmic movement of the oar.

Although white-haired, as Shitao writes in his inscription, a peaceful place like the one depicted in leaf 5 makes him carefree. In this painting, a two-courtyard complex of two-story houses is nestled in a pine forest. A gentleman looks out through a window in the rear building. Ribbonlike clouds hover over the forest and cultivated fields, contributing to the comforting effect. Shitao writes: "Every year when spring arrives, I'll gaze out from the window, alone." This peaceful and pleasant place is visually substantiated by tightly layered depictions of the pines, the grounds, and detailed houses. Yet the clouds left in reserve contrast strikingly with the scene, triggering a contradiction in the viewer's imagination. This meticulously realized place is like a dream, deceptively fictional. **LL**

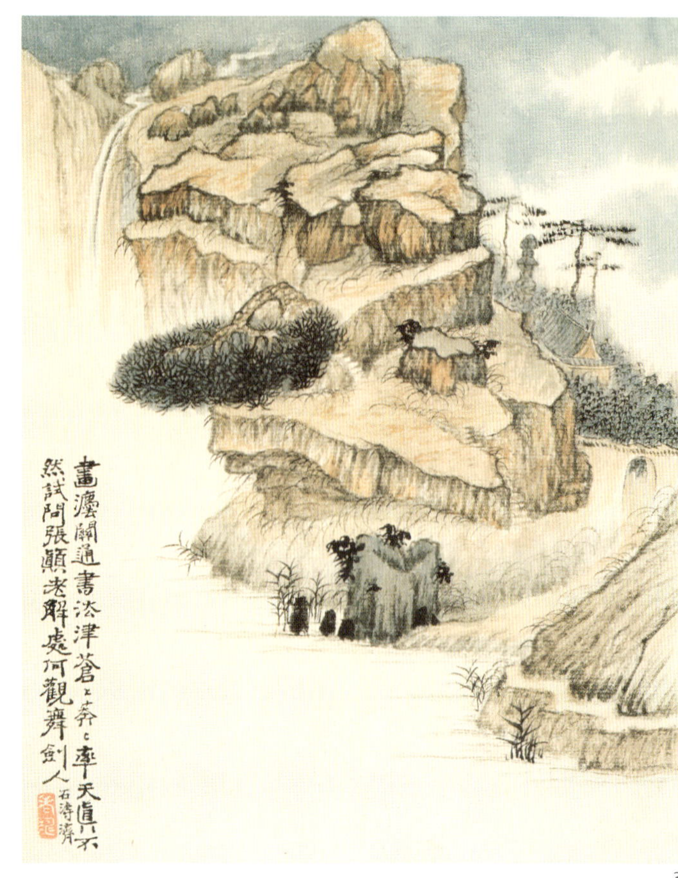

3

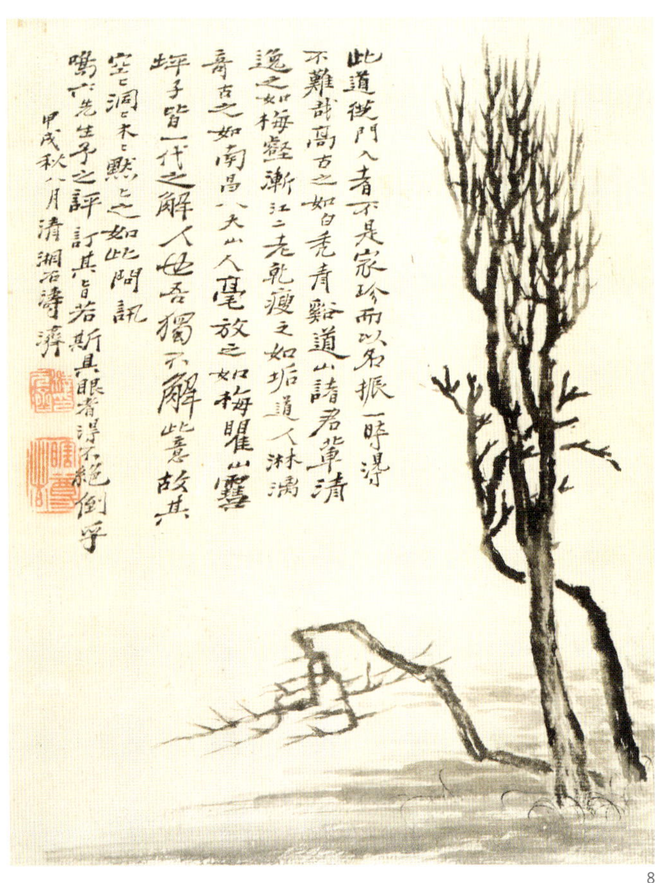

8

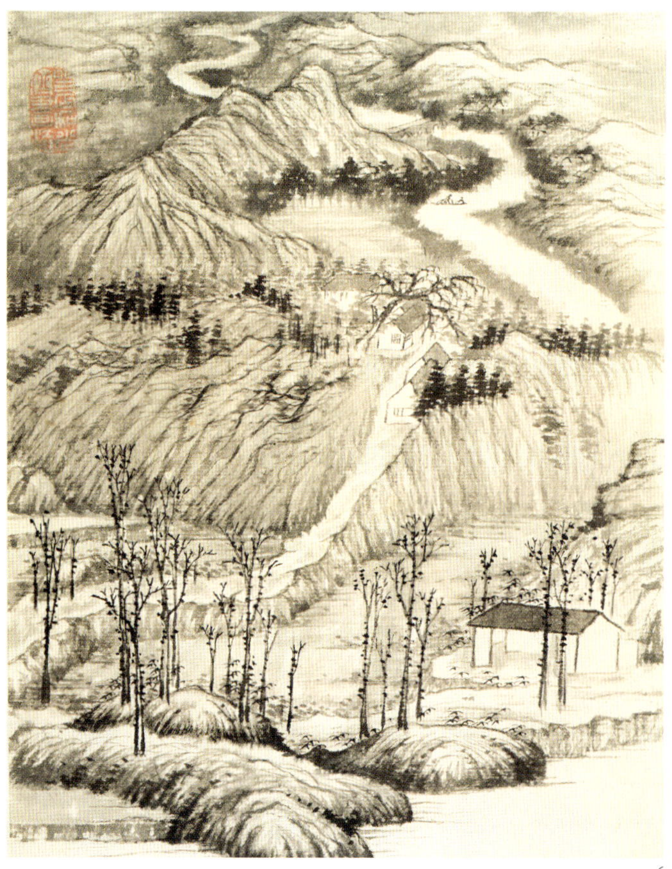

6

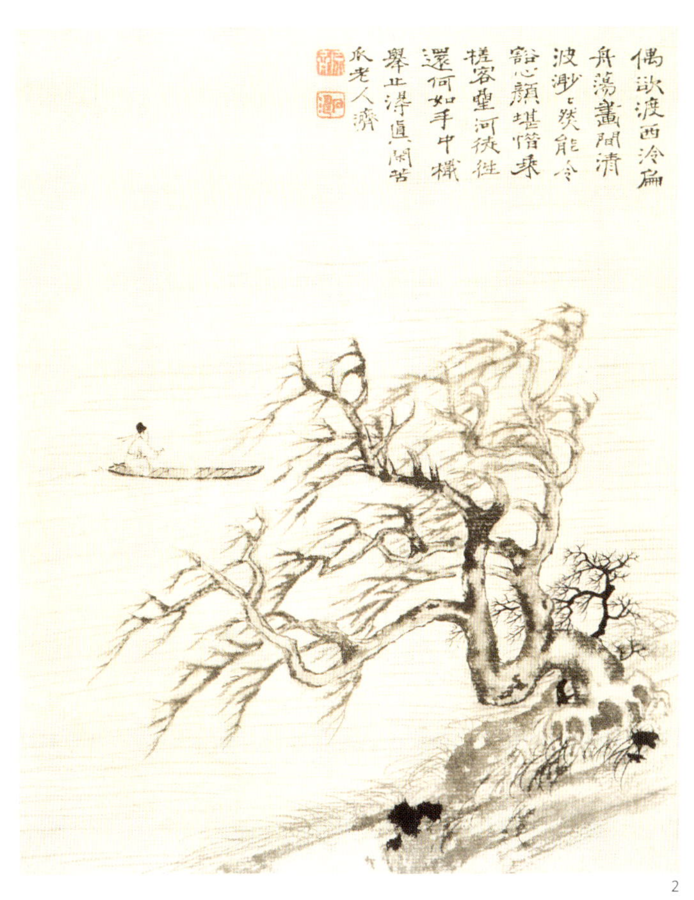

2

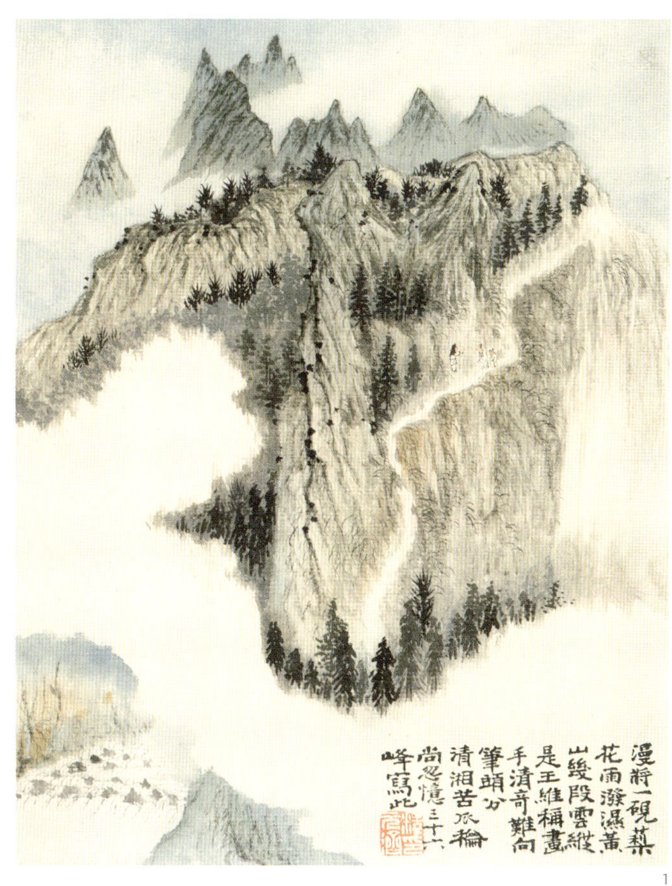

1

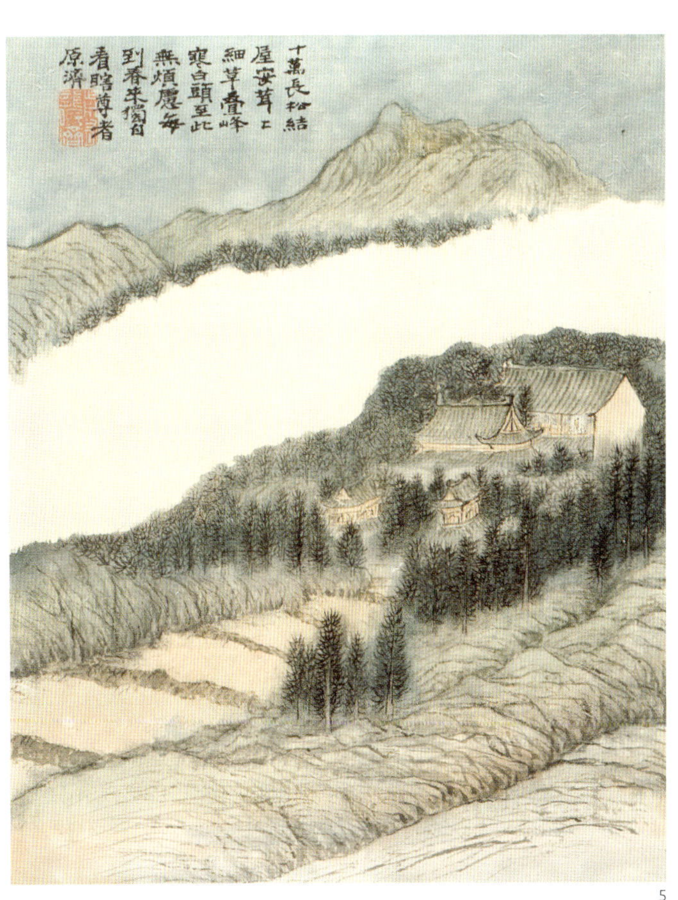

5

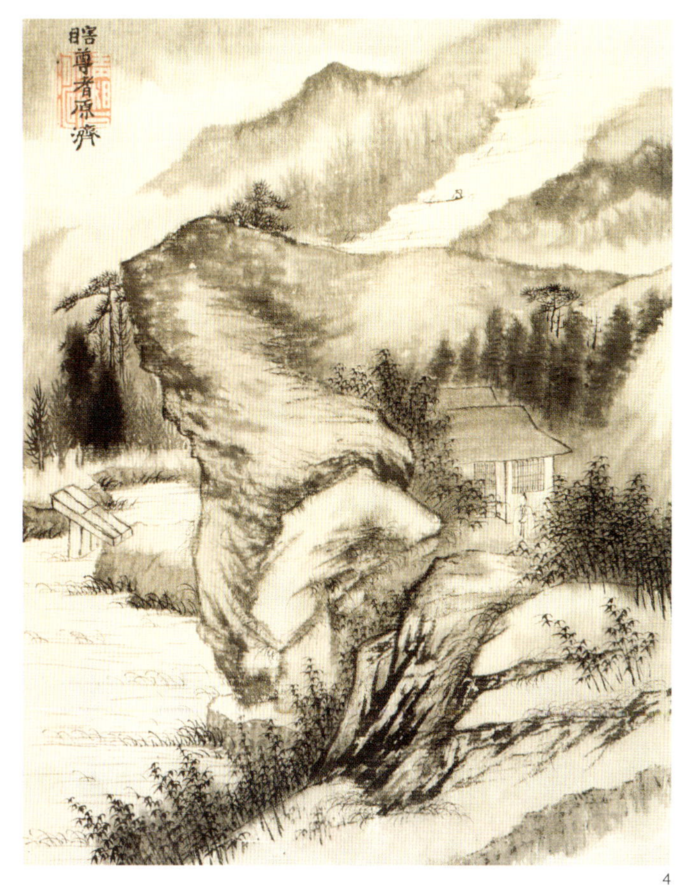

4

This album by Lu Wei possesses an inscription of 1701 by Wang Danlin explaining the interesting and somewhat spontaneous process by which the album evolved into its present state. Traveling south on a boat twelve years earlier in the company of his friend Yingru (Tao Ersui), Wang took out the album for the two to critique and enjoy. When they reached Guabu (near Nanjing, Jiangsu Province), Wang asked Tao, who was an accomplished poet, to compose verses for each of Lu's paintings.[1] Tao wrote his poems, dated 1689, on a separate leaf for the album. In 1701 Wang presented the album to a third friend, Ren Tangong, upon Ren's parting from the capital. The two friends looked over the album, just as Tao and Wang had a number of years earlier. As Wang explains in his inscription, he, Tao, and Ren were all friends who had passed the exams together in 1691, and, in that moment, he felt as if all three were enjoying the album together. At that time, Wang embellished the album by adding to each of Lu's paintings poems of his own, all of which echo the original poems written by Tao twelve years earlier. The two-character titles written in clerical script on each album leaf set the poetic themes. Presumably, these were written by Lu when he composed the paintings, though it is also possible they were added later by Wang, responding to the subject matter of the images.

Whether or not Lu Wei designated the poetic titles, the images are full of "poetry ideas" (*shiyi* 詩意), as evidenced by Tao Ersui's and Wang Danglin's verses. The last leaf, presenting the archetypal image of the humble scholar-official riding off on a donkey in search of poetic lines, encapsulates the album's theme. The poems, like the album leaves, express ideas conducive to thoughts of leisure, away from the busy life of the court official.[2] One example, the reclusive fisherman, was especially popular and appears frequently in Lu's work. In the leaf *Returning Fishermen*, two anglers boat across a river in a wooden skiff, the figure with the single oar seemingly smiling while his companion folds the nets.[3] The day's work done, they return to their village of thatch-roofed houses, snuggled among hills and bamboo in the waning light of gathering dusk. This captivating image reflects the ideals of the fisherman-recluse at peace on the tranquil water. Equally charming is *Transporting a Rock*, showing three men vigorously punting a lean boat that transports an irregular rock destined for a scholar's garden. Wang's poem reads in part, "Mysterious inspiration to be sent to a garden / It is here that Duke Wei sobers up from wine." This refers to the Tang-dynasty scholar Li Deyu, who is said to have had a stone in his garden that he embraced when drunk in order to steady himself.

Landscapes of Poetic Ideas presents Lu Wei working in a delicate manner, with a soft, misty treatment of forms, flowing spaces, gentle scenery, and occasional hints of naturalism—all in line with the poetic theme. His style suggests influence from Zhao Zuo (cat. no. 13), an earlier native of Songjiang, whence Lu hailed.[4] Inspiration likely also came from Southern Song fan and album-leaf painting, which were often paired with poetic texts and titles. In some of Lu's painting the soft suffused atmosphere so prevalent in this album is combined with bold, darkly delineated trees for a striking effect. The novelty of his paintings matched a reputation for being highly unconventional. He only sold his paintings when out of cash and rice, which prospective buyers would know by climbing a temple tower near his home to see if any smoke arose from his hearth by noon. He thus earned the nickname Crazy Lu (Lu Chi 陸癡).[5] **JHC**

For inscriptions and other documentation, see pages 301–03 in this catalogue.

1 Tao is the author of two collections of poetry that have survived to the present time: *Xilu shi* 息廬詩 and *Zunzhu ji* 遵渚集. For more on Tao see Tan Jiading 譚嘉定, ed., *Zhongguo wenxuejia da zidan* 中國文學家大字典 (Taipei: Shijie shuju, 1985), 1435.

2 These sorts of recluse scenes often portray the prototype retiree and poet Tao Yuanming. See James Cahill, *The Painter's Practice*, 18, 20.

3 The aloof fisherman and left-behind fishing nets are common identifiers of a recluse. However, in literati painting it can be difficult to distinguish whether the fisherman is a "scholar-turned-recluse" or in fact a professional fisherman. See Jonathan Chaves, *The Chinese Painter as Poet*, 49.

4 James Cahill, *The Distant Mountains*, 82.

5 Yu Jianhua 俞劍華, *Zhongguo meishujia renming cidian* 中國美術家人名辭典 (Shanghai: Shanghai renmin meishu chubanshe, 1981), 983. Weng Fanggang 翁方綱, *Fuchuzhai shiwen ji* 復初齋詩文集 (Beijing: Wenwu chubanshe, 1982), 16:11b–12b. See also Cahill, *The Painter's Practice*, 53–54, where he notes that although Lu's compositions were likely strange in his time and place, to "foreign eyes their (probably Western-inspired) illusionism makes them curiously un-exotic."

52 Lu Wei 陸暐
Act. late seventeenth century

Landscapes of Poetic Ideas 山水詩意冊
Before 1689
Private collection

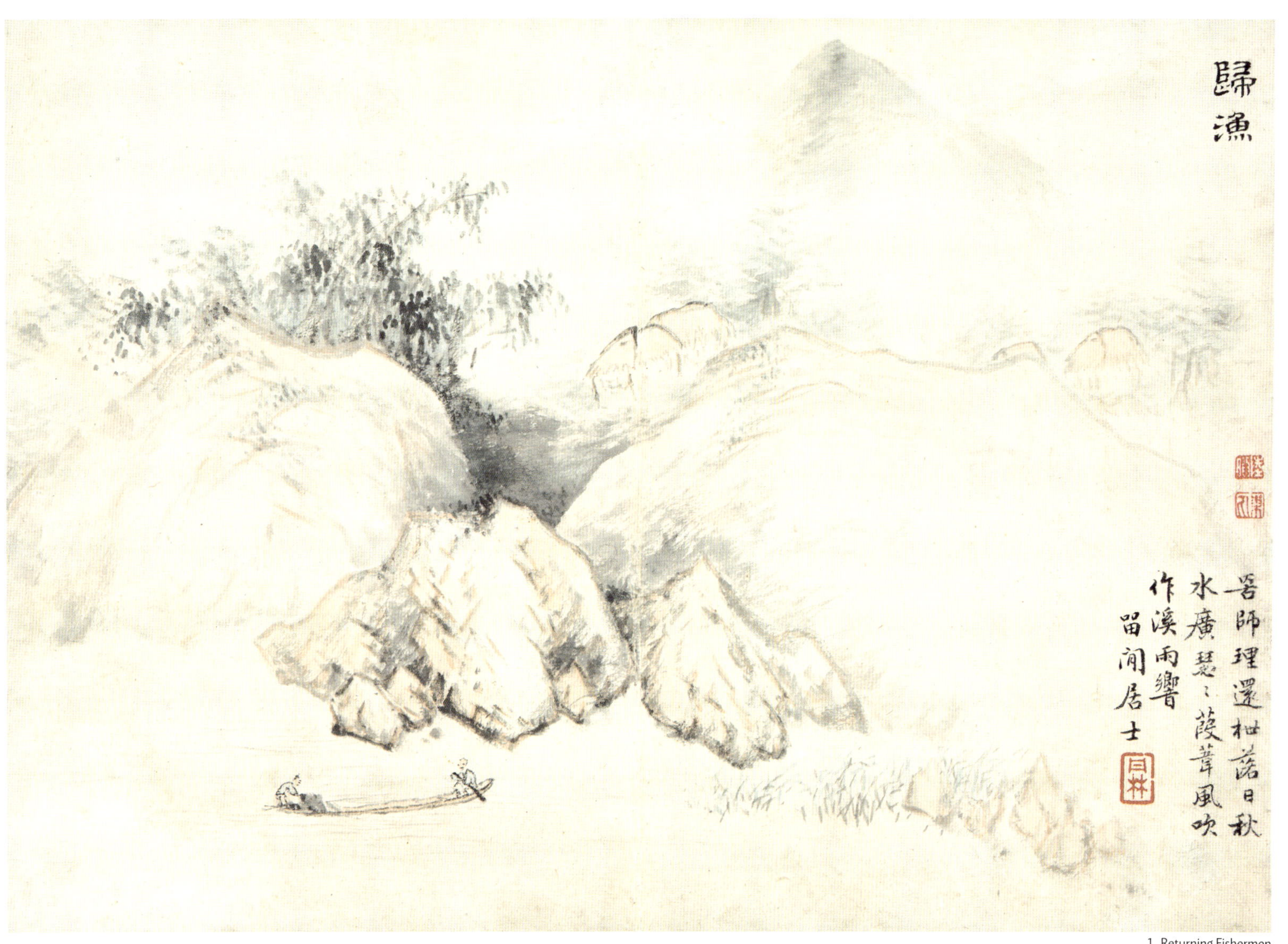

1 Returning Fishermen

Master of the nets folds them away, long oar returning,
As the sun sets on the broad autumn waters.
The wind rustles the reeds;
Blowing on the stream, it makes the sound of rain.

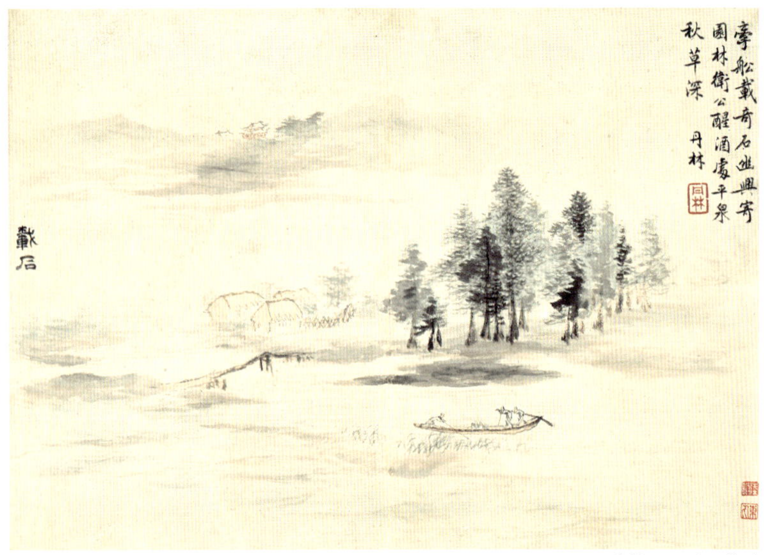

6 Transporting a Rock

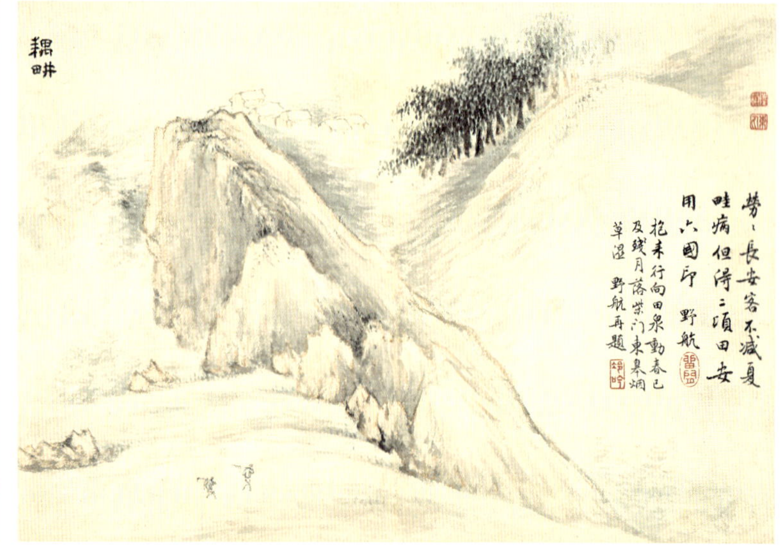

4 Plowing Side by Side

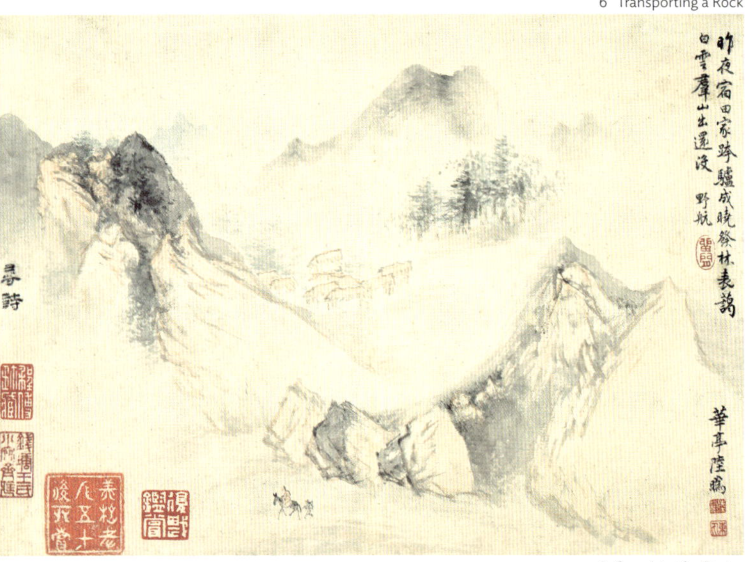

8 Searching for Poetry

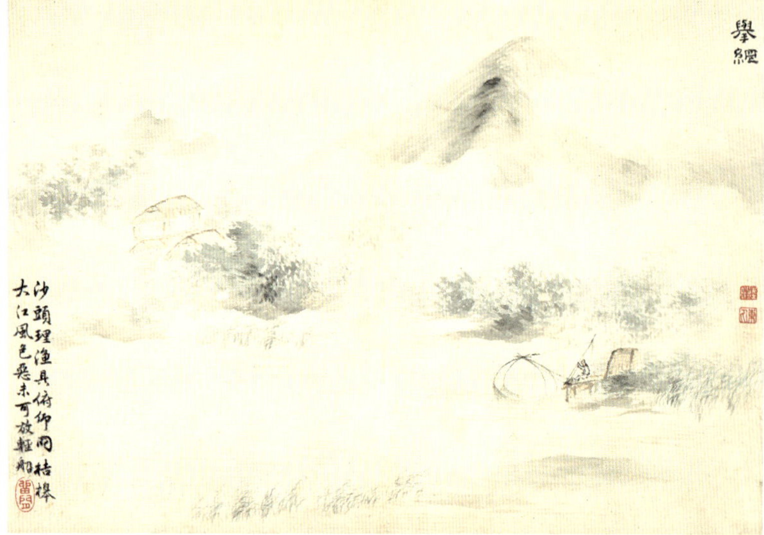

7 Casting the Nets

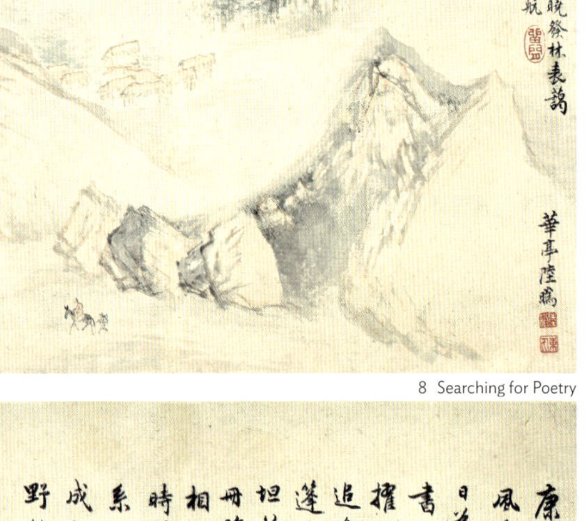

10 Inscription by Wang Danglin, 1701

9 Poems by Tao Ersui, 1689

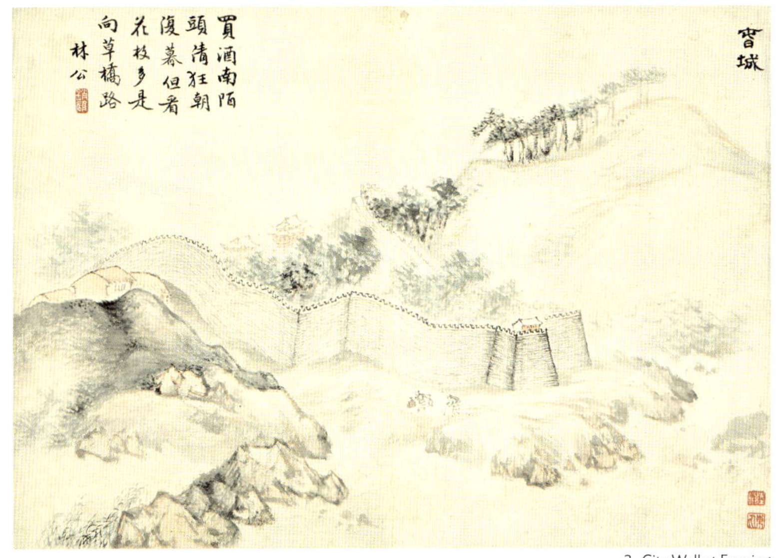

3 City Wall at Evening

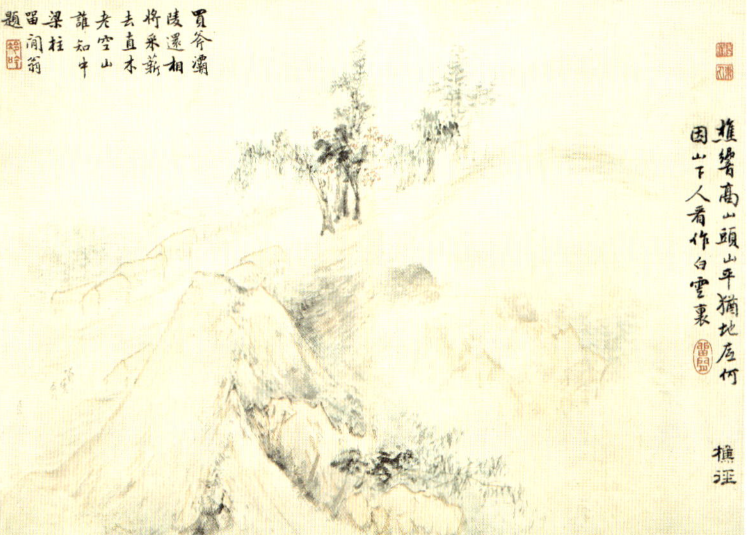

2 The Woodcutters' Path

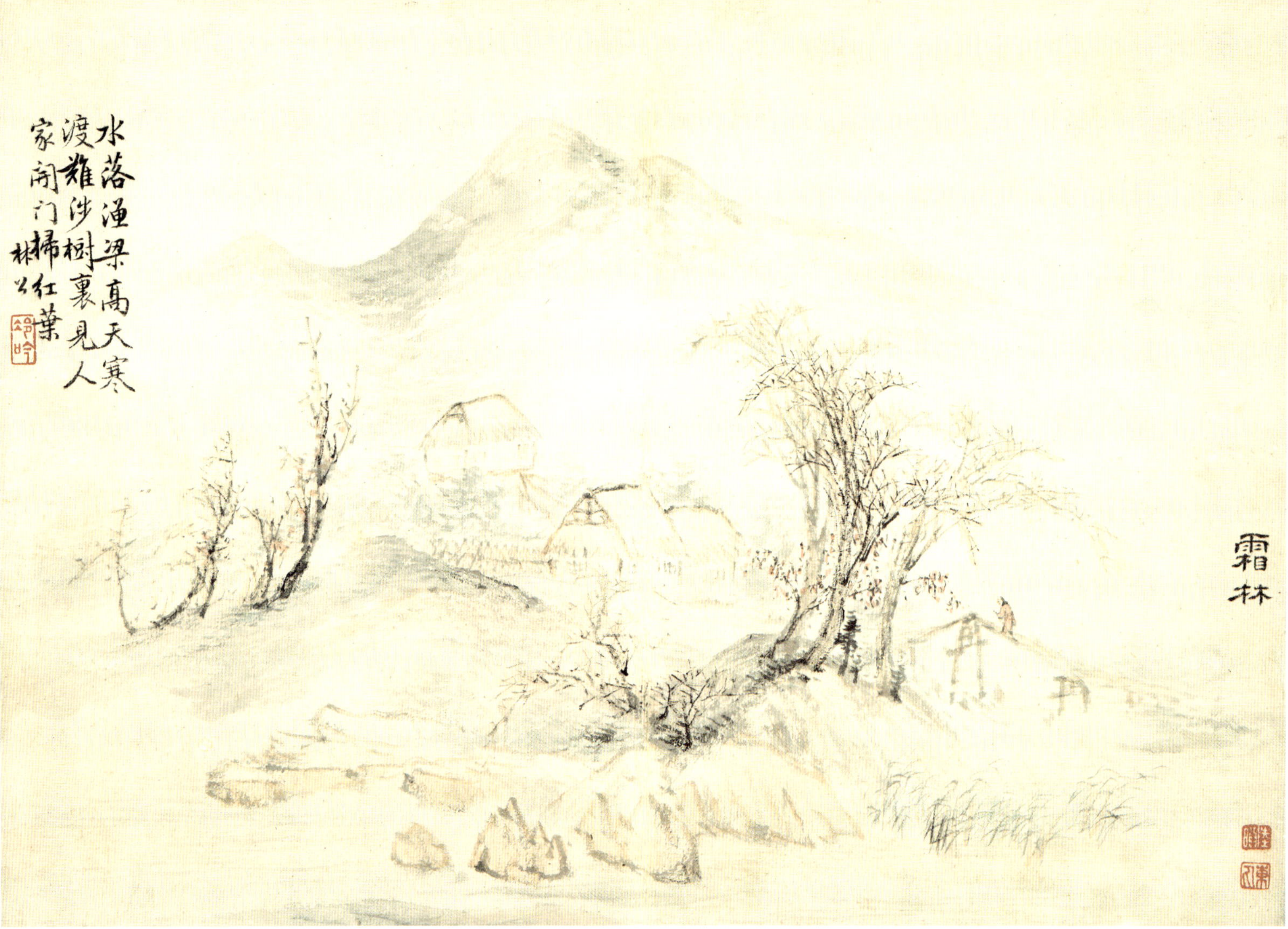

5 Frosty Woods

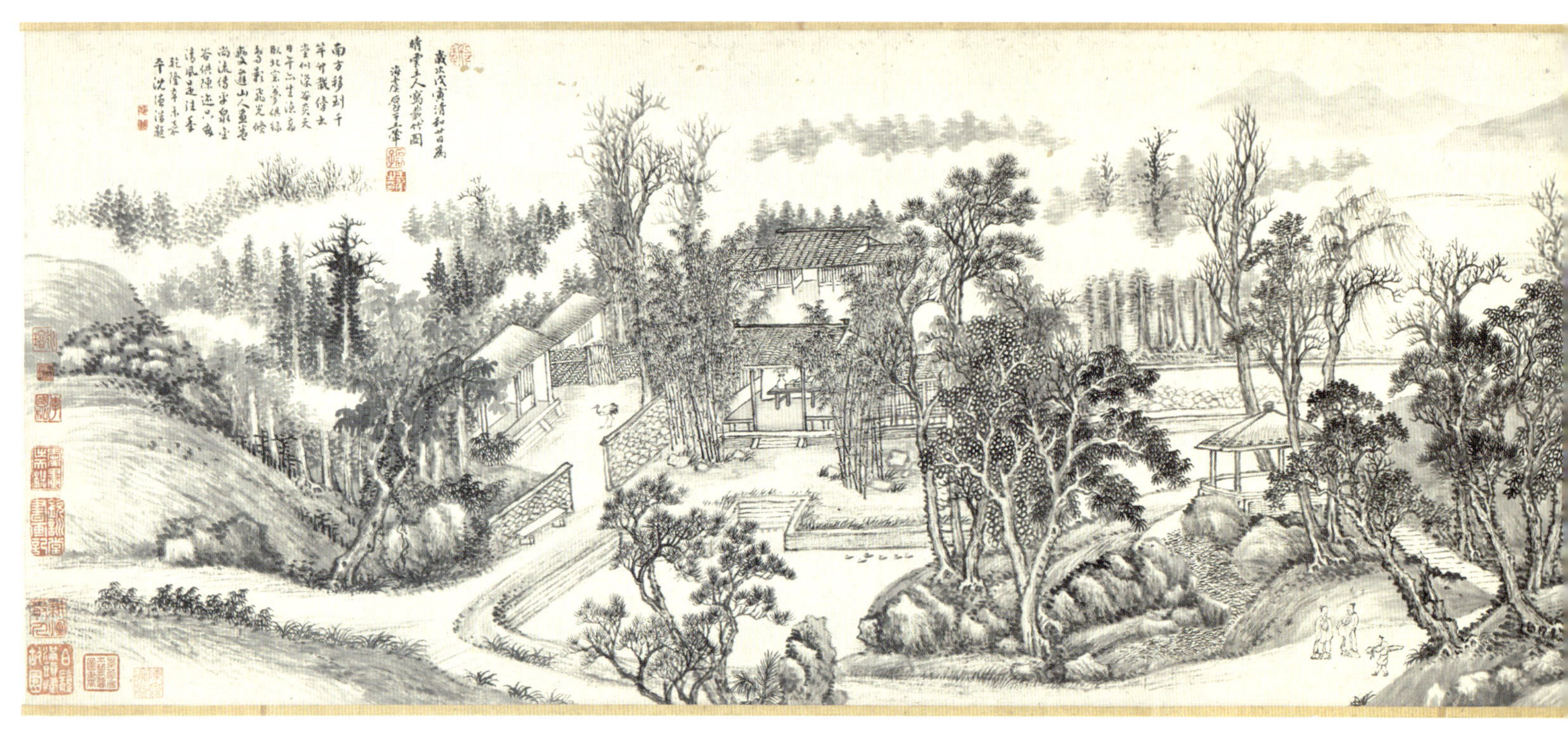

53 Wang Hui 王翬
1632–1717

***Transporting Bamboo* 載竹圖卷**
1698
Private collection

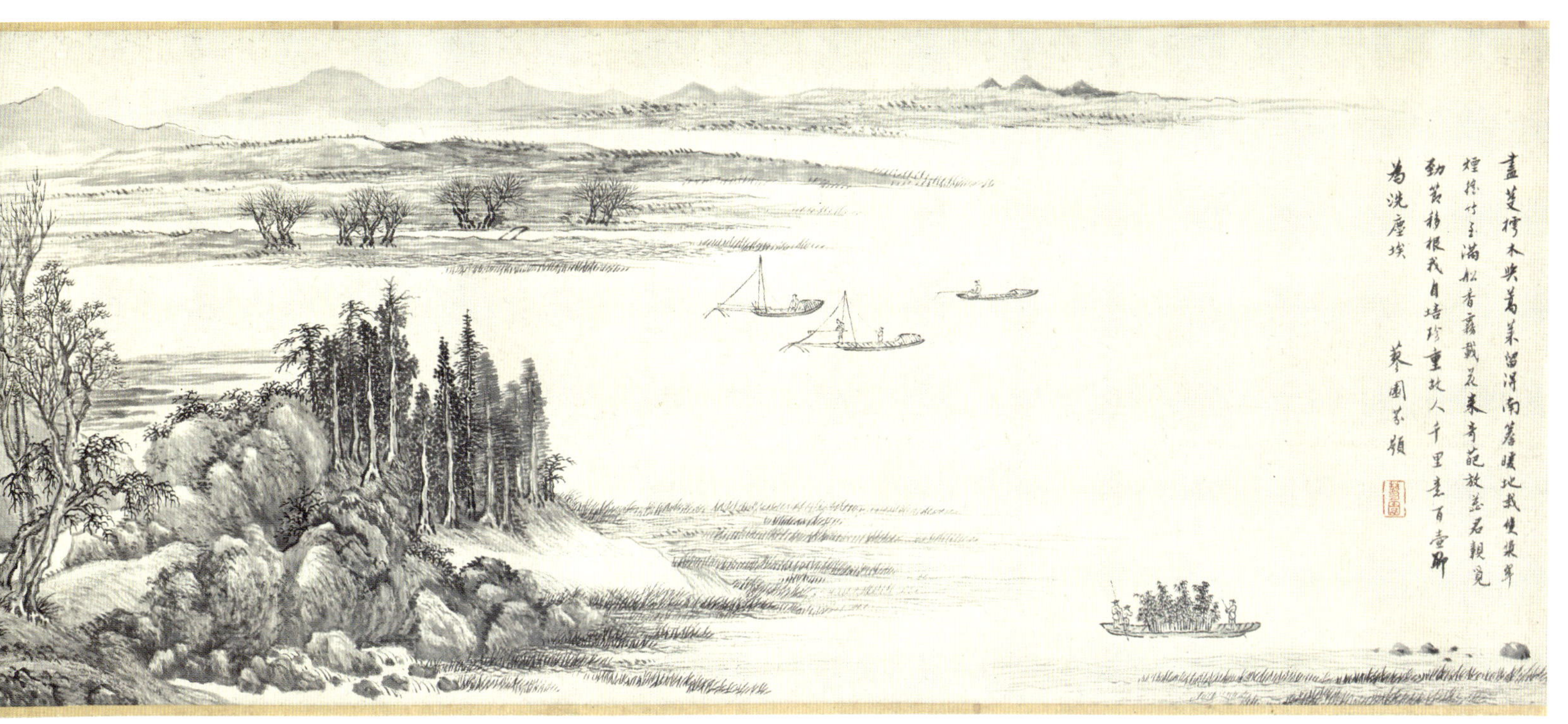

I weeded out the useless trees and wild grass,
Left the warm ground under the southern eaves to be planted.
A pair of oars with emerald green mists sculled bamboo back,
The whole boat with fragrance carried flowers here.
Special flowers in bloom were found by you in person;
Firm bamboo joints being transplanted were nurtured by myself.
I treasure this long distance goodwill from my old friend;
With hundreds of wine pots, just to wash away the dust.

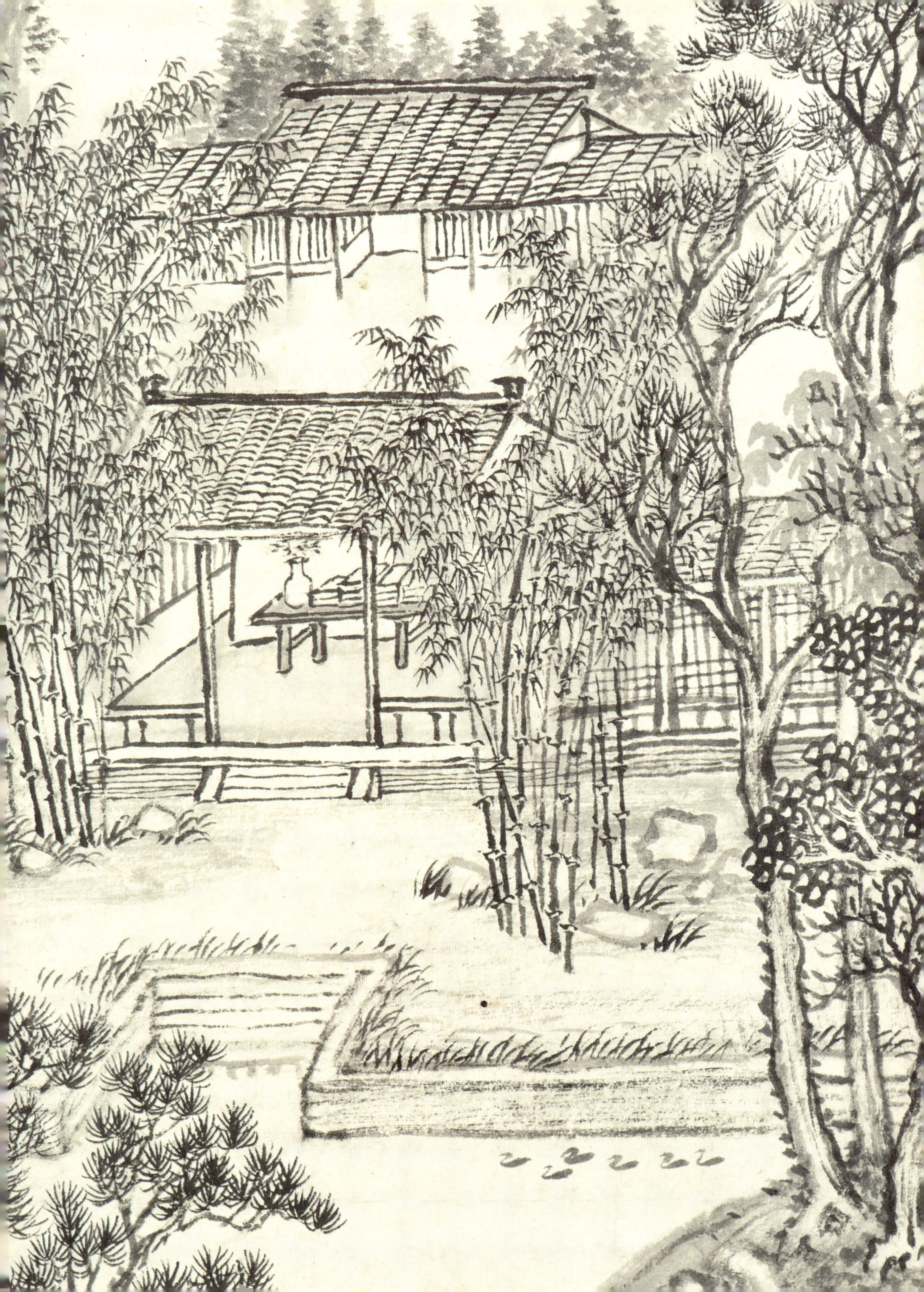

Wang Hui was an important representative of the orthodoxy that developed from the theories of Dong Qichang (cat. nos. 8–9) and came to dominate much of the later history of Chinese painting. A major factor in the rise of the orthodox approach was the Qing court's patronage of Wang to oversee the production of paintings depicting Emperor Kangxi's southern inspection tour in 1691. Wang's involvement with the court led to his association with many powerful Manchu officials who became his patrons.[1] *Transporting Bamboo* is a prime example of such patronage, one of a number of paintings that he produced for the high-ranking Suo Fen. The scroll commemorates the construction of Suo's studio and the great pains he undertook to embellish it with the refined value attached to the literati appreciation of bamboo. Suo was a devoted lover of the plant; although he had planted countless bamboo, he was disappointed because of the absence of excellent species in the northern clime of the capital. Huang Ding, a prominent painter who worked with Suo, went south in search of specimens and eventually brought back by boat such prized examples as Square, Purple, and Xiang Consorts bamboos. According to one of Suo's inscriptions, the moment he planted the new bamboo there was a timely rain that helped it flourish. Wang Hui, who was his guest at the time, depicted the story in this painting.

The story artfully utilizes the handscroll format, unrolling from right to left. At the beginning, a small boat fully loaded with young bamboo draws the viewer's attention and points toward the shore, which gradually reveals an elegant villa surrounded by trees, hills, and clouds. A studio sits in the center flanked by lush bamboo, which, diachronically, would appear to represent the successful efforts of the planting of the young transplants. The whole painting, from right to left, describes a dynamic process of transporting bamboo and bringing it to a flourishing state. The painting is a wonderful expression of reclusive literati taste, to which Wang Hui was very much attuned. With such well-calculated details as a vase with bamboo and stacks of books in the studio as well as a crane just outside, the artist created a residence of pure ideals, removed from the concerns of worldly affairs.

When Wang painted *Transporting Bamboo*, however, Suo Fen's life was hardly so placid. Suo was the son of Suoetu, one of the highest officials of the late seventeenth century. Suoetu was the uncle of Empress Xiaocheng and assisted the young Emperor Kangxi gain his imperial position by killing the imperious official Oboi. He became more and more powerful and built an extremely close relationship with the heir apparent, Empress Xiaocheng's son Yinreng. Suo Fen benefited from his father's rise with a successful early career,[2] but Suoetu did not remain in favor. In 1708, five years after Suoetu's execution, Suo was sentenced to death when Yinreng's title of heir apparent was rescinded. Kangxi believed that Suo had conspired with Yinreng to take revenge for Suoetu. In brief, Suo's whole life was strongly connected with various political struggles.[3]

Suo Fen's writings were banned by Kangxi, and there are few extant materials related to him today.[4] Nonetheless, there are still some clues that allow us to reconstruct the lifestyle in his Studio of Clear Clouds, which is so idyllically portrayed in Wang Hui's painting. In the writings of Boerdu and Yueduan, both of whom were royal princes and inscribers on *Transporting Bamboo*, there are several poems that mention the Studio of Clear Clouds.[5] These poems show that many high officials and royal princes were deeply immersed in purely literary activities, such as composing poems and appreciating paintings in the studio. These facts echo the reclusive and literati tastes reflected in both the painting and the lengthy set of inscriptions that follow. From 1698, when the picture was painted, to 1828, seventeen people added inscriptions. Most of the inscribers were high officials and/or royal princes. By the inscriptions, Suo Fen's intimate friends—including Boerdu, Heyi, Yueduan, Suoerbi, and Tuo Xian—all represented him as a cultivated recluse with an obsession for bamboo. Moreover, some of them implied that they also owned such places of escape and leisure, although not as elegant as Studio of Clear Clouds. In this way, although very much a part of court life, they eagerly and successfully built distinct spaces to identify themselves as literati and to display their ideals of reclusion. Wang Hui often used his talents to provide paintings of these rustic idylls. Two that are particularly close in style to *Transporting Bamboo* are *West Studio* (1697) and *Hall of Lofty Pines* (1703), painted for the scholar-officials Wu Jing and Li Du'ne, respectively.[6] These paintings were essential mediums that allowed such officials to act the role of recluses at the court. **YSZ**

For inscriptions and other documentation, see pages 303–04 in this catalogue.

1 For an introduction to Wang Hui's art, see Wen C. Fong, Chin-Sung Chang, and Maxwell K. Hearn, *Landscapes Clear and Radiant*, which includes Hearn's essay "Art Creates History: Wang Hui and *The Kangxi Emperor's Southern Inspection Tour*," 129–85. For Wang's association with Manchu officials, see Marshall Wu (Wu Peisheng 武佩聖), "Wang Hui ke jingshi qijian zhi jiaowang yu huihua huodong," 607–27.

2 Boerdu, Suo Fen's good friend and relative by marriage, mentions in a poem that Suo received his important official position when he was only about twenty years old. Boerdu 博爾都, "He Su'an taipu," 賀素菴太僕, *Wenting shiji* 問亭詩集 (Beijing: Beijing chubanshe, 1997), vol. 8, 6:9a.

3 The story of the Suo family and this painting by Wang Hui is recounted by Marshall Wu, "History Hidden in a Chinese Scroll," in Richard M. Barnhart, et al., *The Jade Studio*, 43–50. See also Marshall Wu, "A-er-hsi-p'u and His Painting Collections," 61–74.

4 Suo Fen's collected writings, *Qingyun shuwu gao* 晴雲書屋稿, were named after his studio. Deng Zhicheng 鄧之誠, comp., *Qingshi jishi chubian* 清詩紀事初編 (Taipei: Mingwen shuju, 1985), 636.

5 Boerdu, "Su'an Qingyun shuwu cheng tong Wu Tianzhang Chen Shuyi Shen Kezi yanji fen yun" 素菴晴雲書屋成同吳天章陳叔毅沈客子宴集分韻, *Wenting shiji*, vol. 8, 6:7a. Yueduan 岳端, "Guo Qingyun shuwu guan Mi Nangong Xiaoxiang yeyu tu mancheng changge sanshou cheng Su'an biaodi Fen" 過晴雲書屋觀米南宮蕭湘夜雨圖漫成長歌三首呈素菴表弟芬, *Yuchisheng gao* 玉池生稿, in *Qingdai shiwenji huibian* 清代詩文集彙編 (Shanghai: Shanghai guji chubanshe, 2009), vol. 225, 97–98.

6 *West Studio* (collection of the Shanghai Museum) is reproduced in *Si Wang huaji* 四王畫集 (Shanghai: Shanghai shuhua chubanshe, 1992), pl. 64. *Hall of Lofty Pines* (Cleveland Museum of Art) is reproduced in Wai-kam Ho, et al., *Eight Dynasties of Chinese Painting*, 323–33.

Jiang Shijie's sparsely painted scene is a typical rendition of a Ni Zan landscape: a foreground knoll hosts a group of trees and an empty pavilion on a riverside bank, with low hills in the background. Jiang's emulation of Ni's style (fig. 4) extended to his calligraphy, written along the fan's upper edge with the precise, elegant, "bent-ribbon" strokes of the fourteenth-century master. The only point of departure from Ni's signature style is Jiang's brushwork, which lacks Ni's flinty dryness and reveals an affinity with the other highly regarded Yuan master, Huang Gongwang. Jiang Shijie's oeuvre clearly shows that Ni Zan was his principal model for painting; almost all of the former's extant works follow the latter's easily recognizable compositions and calligraphic style.[1] Jiang seems to have viewed several of Ni's paintings in person and possibly owned one or more.[2] It is not an exaggeration to state that Jiang's absorption in the master's style was a lifelong artistic pursuit.

Jiang Shijie was born into a renowned Ming loyalist family from Laiyang (Shandong Province).[3] His father, Jiang Cai, served the Ming court and was exiled to Xuanzhou (Anhui Province) after the Manchu conquest in 1644 because of a forthright statement of loyalty to the deceased Emperor Chongzhen.[4] After the Ming collapsed, Jiang Cai settled in Suzhou, where he remained loyal to the fallen dynasty until his death. He wore his exile proudly, calling himself the Old Soldier of Xuanzhou (*Xuanzhou laobing* 宣州老兵), and is said to have purchased the old residence of Wen Zhenmeng, one of the most upright of late Ming officials, as a statement of personal alliance and integrity.[5] Jiang Shijie inherited the house and the *yimin* identity from his father. According to biographical records, he lived as a recluse and spent his life keeping the ancestral hall of his father and uncle, Shrine of the Two Jiangs (Er Jiang Ci 二姜祠), at a place called Herun (at Huqiu, or Tiger Hill, Suzhou).[6] However, his *yimin* identity seems to have been determined more by filial piety than political creed. He associated closely with people serving the Qing court, such as Wang Wan and Wu Qi. Moreover, although described as a "recluse," he neither seriously withdrew from the human world nor lived a simple and frugal life, as evidenced by the scale of the house, Yipu 藝圃, that he inherited from his father.[7]

Jiang Shijie's reclusion may have been more a state of mind than fact. Nonetheless, this was the core of his understanding of himself. His sobriquet was Herun 鶴澗, and one of his most frequently used seals is *Huqiu Herun* 虎丘鶴澗, a clear reference to his father. In his inscription to a painting of 1705 he wrote, "Getting old in this cold season, I have withdrawn to Huqiu, where I have maintained the ancestral hall for more than twenty years" 老矣歲寒時，余避蹟虎丘，灑掃先祠二十餘年.[8] By the end of the seventeenth century, the symbolic use of Ni Zan's style as an expression of literati eremitism was well established.[9] In Jiang Shijie's case, there was a personal dimension to the style, in which reclusion was also a statement of family heritage. **HSY**

For inscriptions and other documentation, see page 304 in this catalogue.

1 Perhaps the finest example of Jiang Shijie's Ni Zan style is *Sound of the Stream in a Single Valley*, a large hanging scroll dated 1707 in the Shanghai Museum. See *Zhongguo gudai shuhua tumu* (1990), vol. 5, 115.

2 According to Jiang Shijie's inscription on *High Mountains and Flowing Streams* of 1705, the artist spent time viewing Ni Zan's *Landscape of Mt. Yayi*, hung on the wall of his Jiancao Studio. See Gu Wenbin 顧文彬 and Gu Linshi 顧麟士, *Guoyun lou shuhua ji, xu ji* 過雲樓書畫記、續記 (Nanjing: Jiangsu guji chubanshe, 1999), 145–46.

3 *Zhongguo meishujia renming cidian* 中國美術家人名辭典 (Shanghai: Shanghai renmin meishu chubanshe, 1981), 582.

4 Yamamoto Teijiro 山本悌二郎, *Ming mo minzu yiren zhuan* 明末民族藝人傳, in *Qingdai zhuanji congkan* 清代傳記叢刊 (Taipei: Mingwen shuju, 1985–86), vol. 68, 932–36.

5 Li Huiyi 李惠儀, "Shibian yu wanwu," 40–41. Wen Zhenmeng was particularly known for a scathing memorial he wrote in 1622 criticizing corruption and ineptitude at the court of Emperor Xizong. At the time, Wen had just achieved number-one ranking in the palace examinations and was serving as senior compiler in the Hanlin Academy. See John W. Dardess, *Blood and History in China*, 39–40.

6 Feng Jinbo 馮金伯, *Guochao huashi* 國朝畫識, in *Qingdai zhuanji congkan* (1985), vol. 71, 485–86.

7 Li, "Shibian yu wanwu," 41–42.

8 Gu and Gu, *Guoyun lou shuhua ji*, 145–46.

9 James Cahill, *Shadows of Mt. Huang*, 7–15.

54 Jiang Shijie 姜實節
1647–1709

Landscape **山水扇面**
1701
Santa Barbara Museum of Art
Anonymous Gift

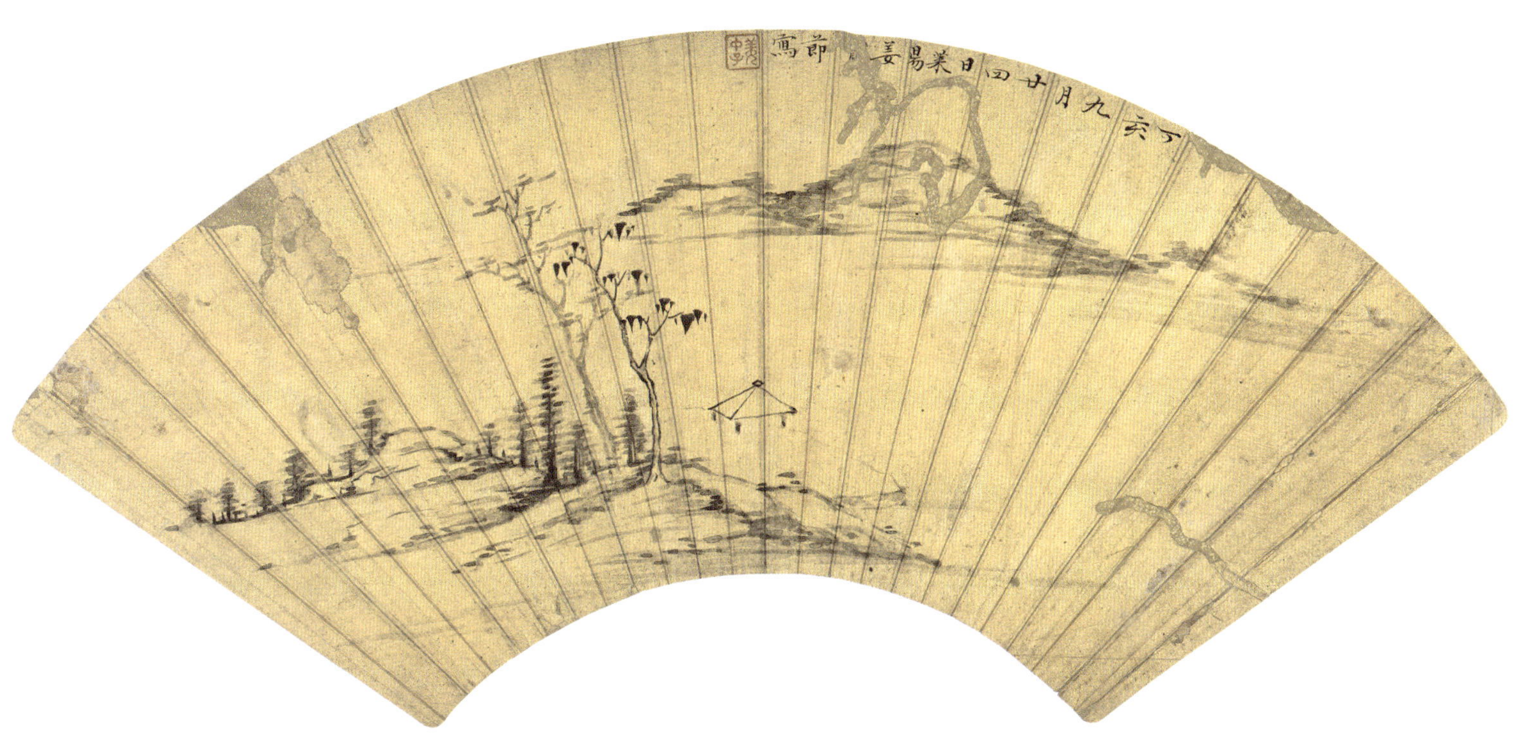

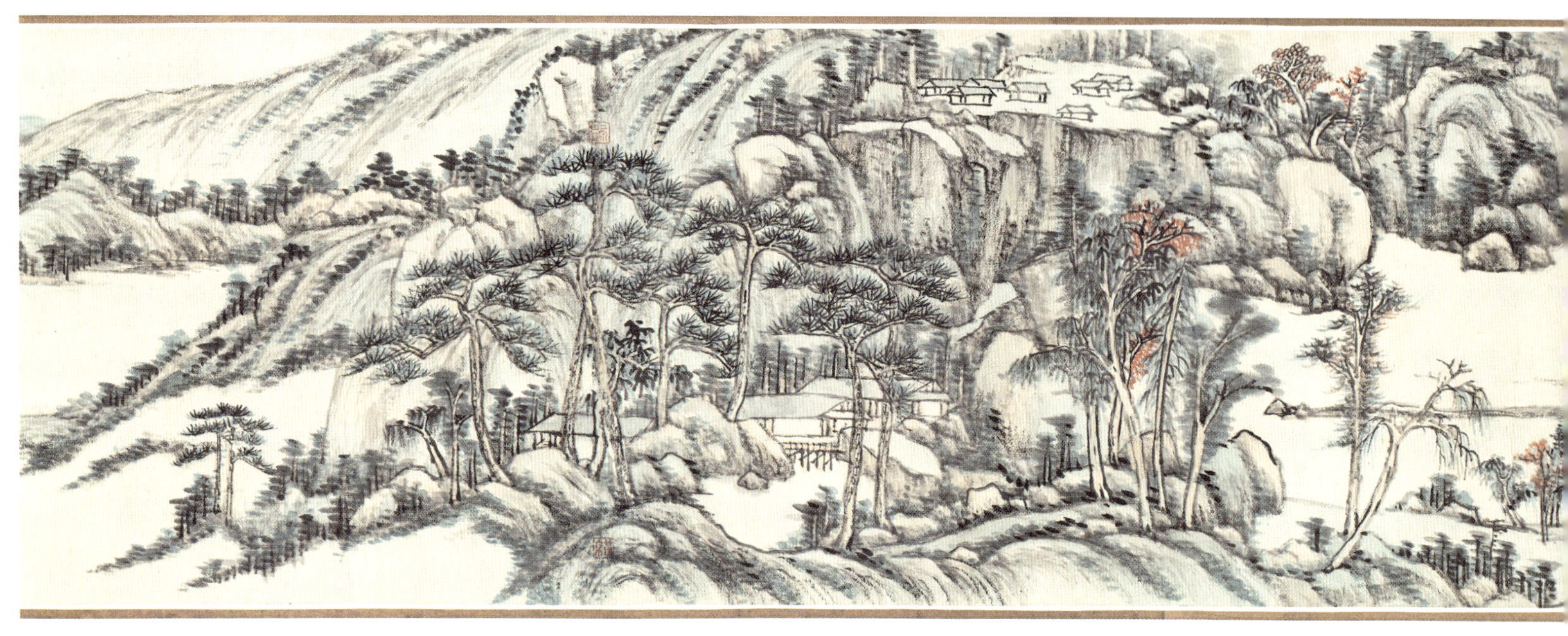

古人畫長卷命意精深立格高遠五日一山十日
一水遲之歷年而後成故能脫盡凡近毫筆不
匠心而出如子久富春山卷是也余慕
子恩婁先生之爽 先生亦酷嗜余畫中秋後攜過
寓論奧析理洞微余於此道夢夢不間有會心處
即信筆揮灑遂成此卷歷月而成未能極深研
幾豈能入古人之室聊以見命云爾
康熙甲申小春三日題於穀詒堂
婁東王原祁

55 Wang Yuanqi 王原祁
1642–1715

Autumn Mountains after Huang Gongwang 仿大癡秋山圖卷
1704

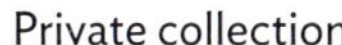
Private collection

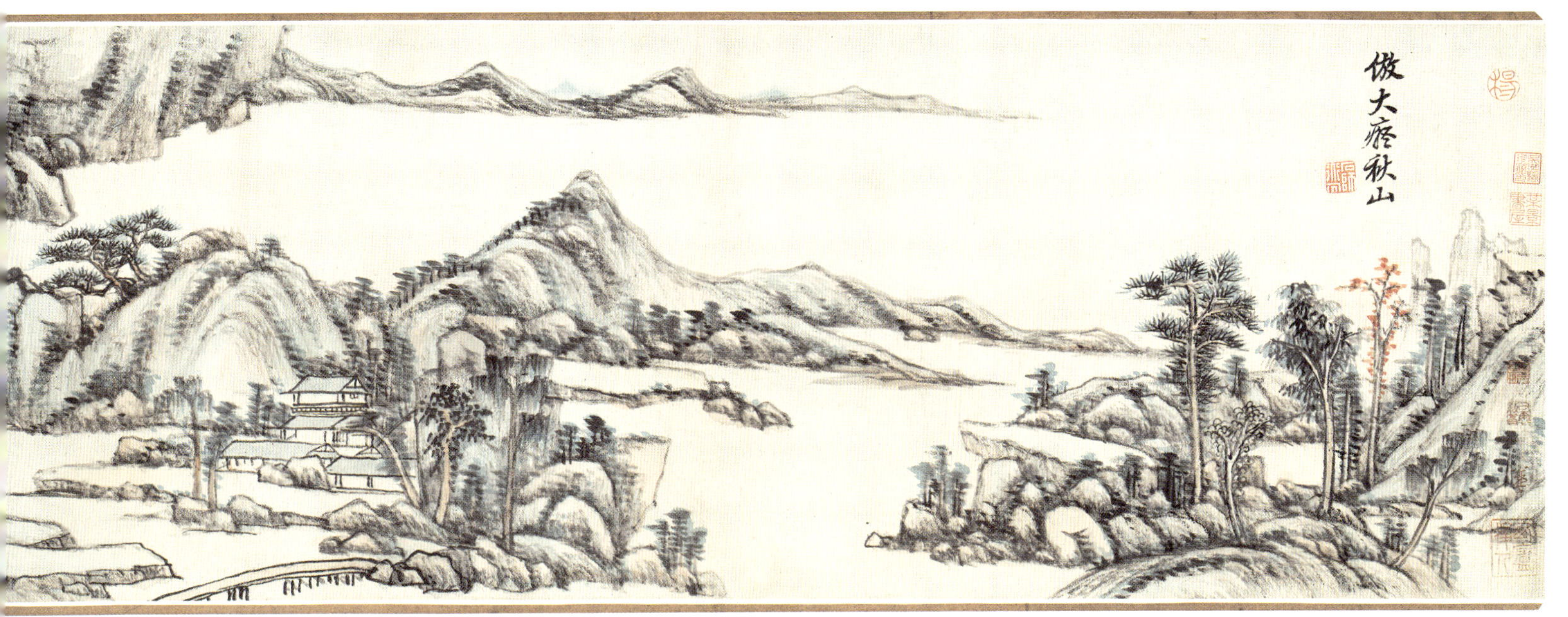

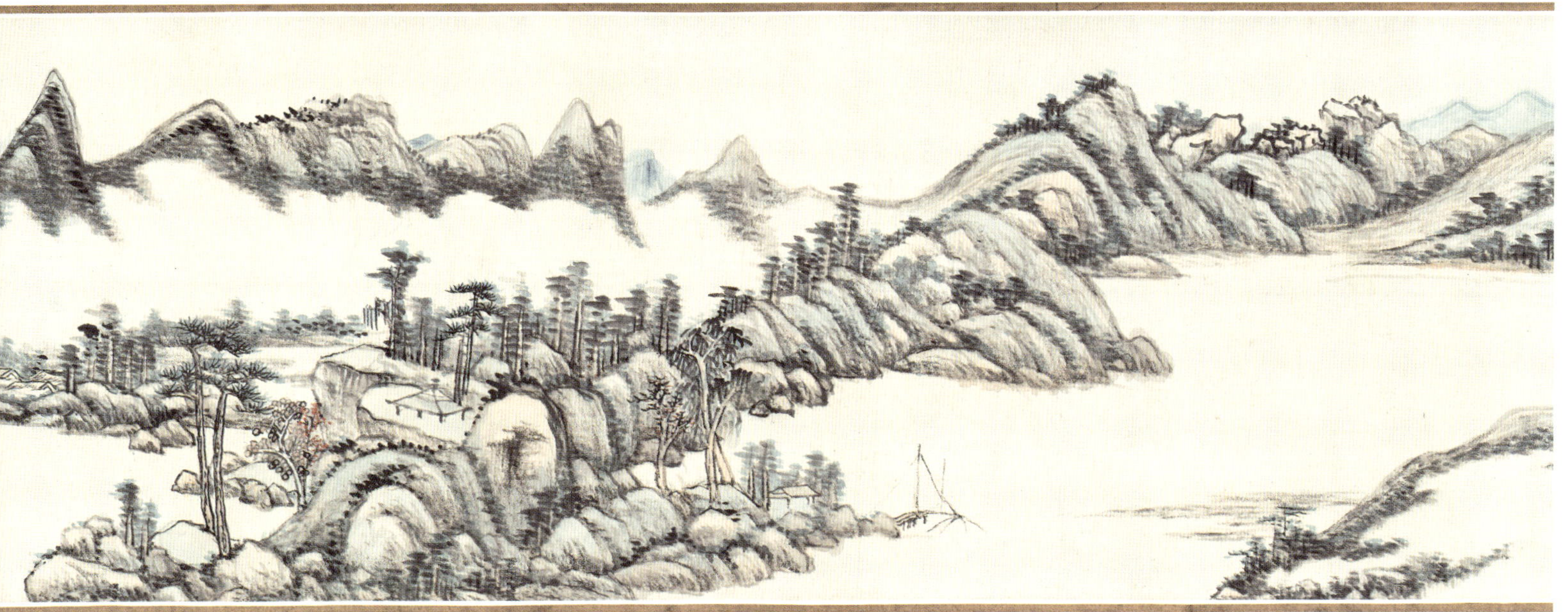

When the ancients painted long handscrolls they marshaled their conceptions with depth and refinement and established styles that were lofty and distant. Five days to paint a mountain, ten days to paint a river, slowly, gradually, it took years before the painting would be completed. It is for this reason that they were able to shed completely the superficial habits of their contemporaries—not a single brushstroke would be lacking the utmost skill…

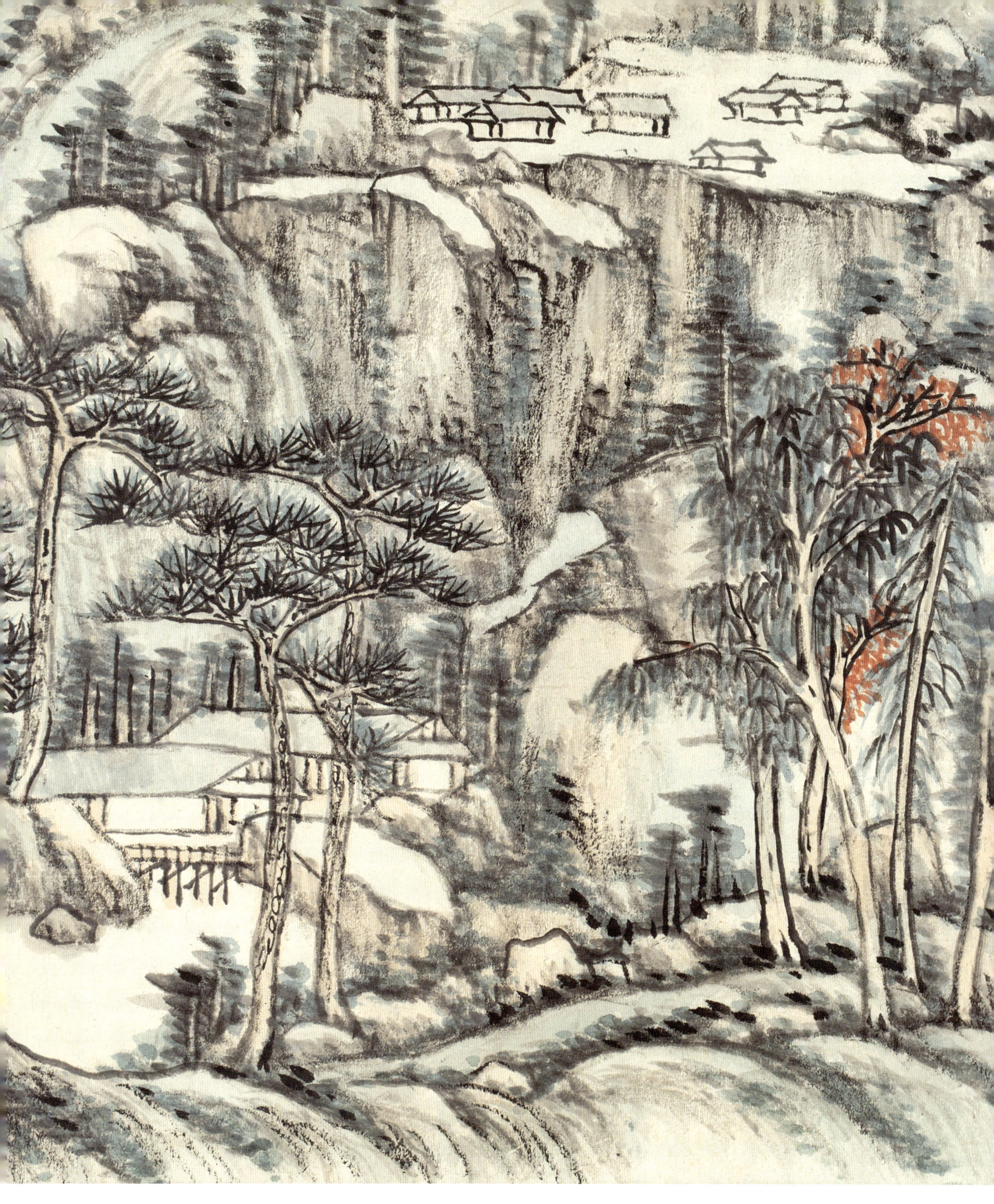

Wang Yuanqi's family enjoyed high prestige in both politics and painting since the time of his great-great-grandfather, Wang Xijue, who served the Ming court as a Senior Grand Secretary. Wang Yuanqi's grandfather was Wang Shimin, who rose to prominent official positions late in the Ming and was a noted painter and calligrapher closely associated with Dong Qichang. Wang Yuanqi continued the family legacy with an impressive official career that led him to the capital at Beijing, where he served as an important cultural leader both in and out of the court.[1] Benefiting from Wang Shimin's personal instruction, as well as the family's rich collection of art, Wang Yuanqi received solid training in painting by studying masters of the past, especially those who represented the proper lineage according to Dong Qichang's theories.

Of the various painters Wang Yuanqi emulated, none was as important as Huang Gongwang. As Wang once stated in a summary of his painting career, "What I learn is Dachi [Huang Gongwang], and what I transmit is Dachi" 所學者大癡也，所傳者大癡也.[2] Wang frequently made specific reference to Huang's well-known masterpiece *Dwelling in the Fuchun Mountains* (1347–50).[3] In the inscription on *Autumn Mountains after Huang Gongwang*, Wang describes how Huang constructed his painting at a leisurely pace, "spending five days to paint a mountain, ten days to paint a river." Wang completed this painting in a month—far quicker than the three years Huang took to complete *Dwelling in the Fuchun Mountains*—but the implication of his inscription is that each stroke, each passage, must be done with care and thought.

The composition of *Autumn Mountains* loosely follows *Dwelling in the Fuchun Mountains*. The landscape proceeds as a journey through ideal Jiangnan scenery, meandering along a river by a series of upright cliffs, past rustic hermitages, and ultimately ending with cloudy mountains painted in the style of Mi Fu. This is an example of Wang Yuanqi's light-colored landscape style, also inspired by Huang Gongwang, in which washes of ocher brown and light green are intricately blended with "hemp-fiber" ink strokes and dots to make densely textured forms.[4] Wang used dry ink strokes, subtly rubbed onto the surface of the mountains, to provide a final touch of solidity and help accentuate the rhythms of the ink. Red-leaved trees stand out in the green-and-brown toned landscape, signifying the fall season. According to his inscription, Wang painted this for his chess friend Lou Zien in the tenth month. Wang implies that the painting's autumn scenery was inspired by Lou's chess skills, which is an elegant way of stating the closeness of their friendship.

In the twentieth century, *Autumn Mountains after Huang Gongwang* was owned by the eminent collector and connoisseur Wu Hufan, who added a number of inscriptions to the scroll. In one, Wu references an *Autumn Mountains* by Huang Gongwang that, because of lavish praise from Dong Qichang, was avidly sought by Wang Shimin and Wang Hui (cat. no. 53).[5] Wu consequently believed that Wang Yuanqi must have studied Huang's *Autumn Mountains* and captured its "shape and spirit" (*xingshen* 形神). However, on another painting also titled *Autumn Mountains after Huang Gongwang* painted by Wang three years later (1707), the artist wrote that he had not had a chance to see Huang's *Autumn Mountains*, and only speculated about its appearance through his understanding of Huang's style.[6] That understanding would have been informed by Huang's text "Secrets of Landscape Painting" ("Xie shanshui jue" 寫山水訣), which describes placing buildings on the slopes of mountains to impart life, using trees with red leaves to manifest an autumnal theme, and arranging mountain ridges into twisting, interchanging forms that carry momentum.[7] The last example was further developed into Wang Yuanqi's "dragon vein" (*longmai* 龍脈) theory, one of the critical principles in his own "Ten Articles on Painting" ("Lun hua shize" 論畫十則).[8] **KYH**

For inscriptions and other documentation, see pages 304-05 in this catalogue.

1 Wang Yuanqi was summoned to serve the Kangxi emperor in 1700. Wang Yuanqi 王原祁, *Wang Sinnong tihua lu* 王司農題畫錄, in Zhao Yichen 趙詒琛, ed., *Jiaxu congbian* 甲戌叢編 (Taipei: Yiwen yinshuguan, 1972), vol. 1, 4. As the emperor's artistic advisor, Wang was directly involved in the compilation of the *Peiwenzhai shuhua pu* 佩文齋書畫譜 (The encyclopedia of calligraphy and painting of Peiwenzhai).

2 Wang Yuanqi, *Lutai tihau gao* 麓臺題畫稿, in Huang Binhong 黃賓虹 and Deng Shi 鄧實, eds., *Meishu congshu* 美術叢書 (Taipei: Yiwen yinshuguan, 1975), 569.

3 In the collection of the National Palace Museum, Taipei. See *Shanshui hebi.*

4 For Wang Yuanqi's innovation in light-colored landscapes, see Shen Wang, "Wang Yuangqi and the Orthodoxy of Self-Reflection in Early Qing Landscape Painting," 171–85.

5 Yun Ge 惲格, *Ouxiang guan ji* 甌香館集, in Wang Yunwu 王雲五, et al., *Congshu jicheng chubian* 叢書集成初編 (Taipei: Shangwu yinshu, 1935), 260–62.

6 This painting is a hanging scroll in the National Palace Museum, Taipei. Reproduced in *Shanshui hebi*, pl. 5–36; the inscription is transcribed on page 352.

7 James Cahill, *Hills Beyond a River*, 86–88.

8 For a translation of Wang's description of the dragon vein in landscape painting, see Roderick Whitfield, ed., *In Pursuit of Antiquity*, 185–86. See also Susan Bush, "Lung-mo, K'ai-ho, and Ch'i-fu."

Following the lead of his grandfather, Wang Shimin, Wang Yuanqi was deeply immersed in the tradition of the Yuan-dynasty masters; among these he favored Huang Gongwang and Ni Zan above all others.[1] The elder Wang had been a student of Dong Qichang (cat. nos. 8–9), and Wang Yuanqi attempted to share in that association with the great master by also referring to Dong as teacher.[2] Dong's influence is apparent here: more than simply an imitation of Huang and Ni, this painting reflects the specific method of appropriating and manipulating techniques espoused by Dong and his lineage.

In his inscription, Wang Yuanqi explains that inspiration came from a leisurely conversation with a friend and nephew regarding a collaborative effort by Huang Gongwang and Ni Zan. Huang and Ni are known to have attended the same literary gatherings at the home of Cao Zhibo, and they exchanged compliments on colophons to their paintings, but the specific painting to which Wang refers is unknown.[3] However, Wang emphasizes that his painting is not a copy of an existing painting but an attempt to capture the spirit of the Yuan masters. His method of appropriating the manner of Ni and Huang follows directly from Dong Qichang's theory of imitation. Dong established his method on the brushstrokes and forms of a specific lineage of ancient masters, but he criticized painters who blindly copied without innovation. He summed up the idea of *fang* 仿 (imitation) as "following a method but doing away with its shortcomings."[4] Wang Yuanqi echoes this sentiment in his inscription, differentiating his approach from those of "facile habits," which must refer to painters who superficially imitate a manner without adequate understanding or substance. In this respect, Wang asserts his commitment to the true teachings of Dong—basing his style on the Yuan masters but also seeking to create something individual and innovative.

Wang Yuanqi's paintings in the style of Ni Zan all contain the wide expanse of water, skeletal trees, and dialogue between foreground and distant landmasses characteristic of Ni's signature landscape compositions (see fig. 4). Wang identifies "rhythmic regulations" in the spacing of forms, and it is appropriate to understand Ni's two landmasses as beats separated by a rest. In *Landscape in the Manner of Huang Gongwang and Ni Zan*, a third beat, the landmass that enters from the right in the middle ground, adds density with a persistent building of rocky forms that continues both forward and backward. This is associated with Huang Gongwang's style. Underlying this preoccupation with formal development was Wang's desire to infuse his landscapes with "life-breath" (*qishi* 氣勢), which he saw as the vital counterpart to a landscape's composition. Central to Wang's idea of life-breath is the "dragon vein" (*longmai* 龍脈), a conduit by which energy can circulate throughout the landscape: "[The dragon vein] may be slanted or straight, whole or fragmented, broken or continuous, hidden or manifested."[5] In Wang's paintings, in particular those based on Huang's example, this geomantic concept is often manifest as continuous mountain ranges that curve from the top of the composition to the bottom like great vertebrae. In *Landscape in the Manner of Huang Gongwang and Ni Zan*, the sloping mountain in the background, as well as the visual continuity between fore-, middle, and background by way of rocks that appear to bridge the river, may relate to the dragon vein. Wang also emphasizes a sense of "opening and closing" and "rising and falling" to facilitate life-breath. He writes, "Rising and falling moves from near to far... calling and responding by leaning and tilting."[6] The mountain in the background slopes to the left while the large rock on the foreground landmass tilts to the right. This sense of "rising and falling" is further enhanced by the way in which the buildings on the right appear to tilt upward in relation to the distant shore, which is perfectly horizontal to the picture frame.

Perhaps Wang Yuanqi's greatest innovation within the orthodoxy that followed from Dong Qichang is his use of color. In his writings he criticized his contemporaries, whose colors float over their landscape forms without serving any structural function.[7] In contrast, Wang applies color in conjunction with layered hemp-fiber brushstrokes to infuse his rocky forms with a convincing three-dimensionality. Although he acknowledges the Yuan masters in his title, Wang constructs this painting to express his own artistic theories and a more immediate lineage in Wang Shimin and Dong Qichang. **NK**

For inscriptions and other documentation, see page 305 in this catalogue.

1 Wang Yuanqi was especially tutored in the style of Huang Gongwang: "In my youth, I heard the teachings of my late grandfather... What I studied was the style of Huang Gongwang." Cited in Mae Anna Quan Pang, "Wang Yüan-Ch'i (1642–1715) and Formal Construction in Chinese Landscape Painting," 3. Wang Shimin was especially proud of his grandson's grasp of Huang's style. See Max Loehr, *The Great Painters of China* (New York: Harper and Row, 1980), 319.

2 "I was at the same time privately admiring the old gentleman Dong [Qichang] and taking him as my teacher." Cited in Pang, "Wang Yüan-Ch'i," 4.

3 Ibid., 157.

4 Cited in ibid., 99.

5 Ibid., 17.

6 Wang Yuanqi, *Yuchuang manbi* 雨窗漫筆, cited in ibid., 18.

7 "Colors will then be brought to life by 'chi'; they will neither float on the surface nor be congested." Wang, *Yuchuang manbi*, cited in ibid., 23.

56 Wang Yuanqi 王原祁
1642–1715

Landscape in the Manner of Huang Gongwang and Ni Zan
仿黃公望倪瓚山水圖

1709

Private collection

From the time I was a young man to the approach of old age I have studied Zijiu [Huang Gongwang] and Yunlin [Ni Zan], taking as my guiding principle the elimination of the air of facile habits. I have studied these two for a long time, yet while I understand [this principle] I have not been able to put it into practice. These two masters once painted a collaborative work, but after all these years I have yet to achieve a copy of its general idea. In the tenth month of the jichou year [1709], my nephew Qiwang [Wang Zhan] came from Luhe, and after finishing with his business at the court delayed his return. While drinking with old Mr. Tanren in his residence, by chance our conversation turned to the Six Laws and they inquired about the small-scale work by Ni and Huang. With the sudden arrival of inspiration I did this painting. I do not seek a formal resemblance, not to mention the complexity or simplicity [of its composition]. Rather, I seek the points of correspondence between its breath-resonance and my heart and in this way almost get close. Do the lofty and clear-minded consider it thus or not?

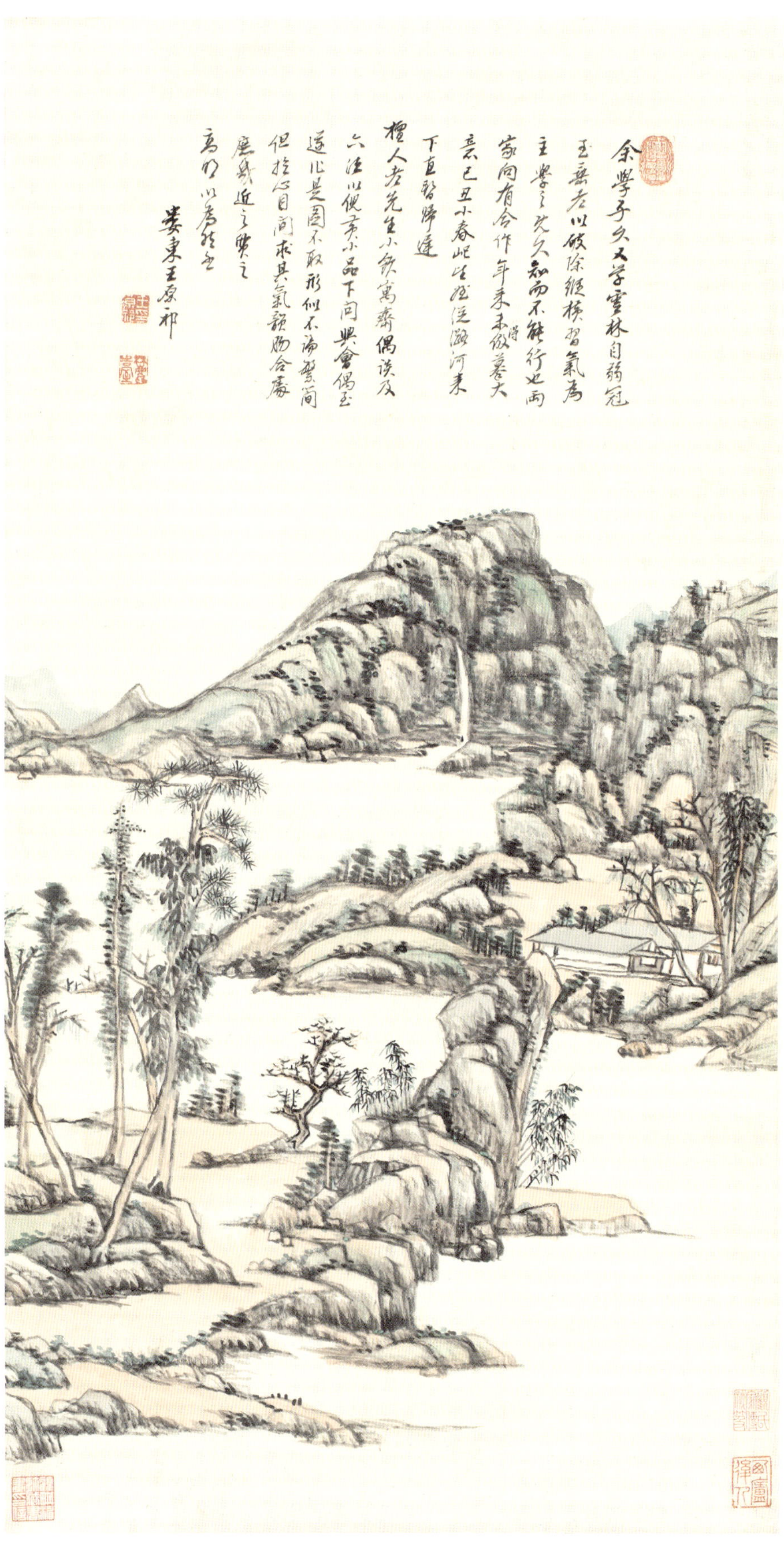

Precious plum blossoms just awakened or still enclosed in round, hardly visible buds shyly decorate and elegantly contrast with prominently gnarled, twisted branches in Gao Jian's album of twelve leaves.[1] First to bloom while the weather is still cold, the plum is regarded as a sign of purity and renewal, loneliness and eremitism. In this album, partial views in monochrome ink or light color are accompanied by poetic inscriptions and accentuated with red seals. Appealing in their casualness and variety of length, the texts effectively counterbalance the images and anchor the dynamic, shifting movements of the angular plum branches. Written in a careful, delicate rendition of the formal standard (*kai*) script by an unidentified calligrapher, the texts add a vital literary component with a decidedly feminine touch.[2] Gao Jian, a native of Suzhou (Jiangsu Province), was already seventy-four years of age when he painted this album. A poet and painter admired for possessing "books in his breast," he incorporated his scholarship in his paintings, which focused both on landscapes in the manner of the Yuan masters and plum blossoms, which he occasionally painted in collaboration with other artists.[3]

Poems focused solely on plum blossoms were composed during the Six Dynasties period, and Tang-dynasty eremitic poetry on this theme often "strikes a note of neglect and isolation." Both Tao Yuanming and Wang Wei connected plum blossoms to the hermit's retreat in their poetic writings, and the Northern Song poet-recluse Lin Bu, who retired to grow plum trees at West Lake near Hangzhou, turned the plum and the hermit into a composite poetic image.[4] This image was then visualized by court painters of the Southern Song in small-scale fans and album leaves with a lyrical, atmospheric mood, of which Ma Yuan's *Moments of the Flowering Plum* is the oldest extant example.[5] After the fall of the Song dynasty in 1279, the plum became an emblem for the dislocated scholar or loyalist. Whether from the Southern Song to Yuan, or from the Ming to the Qing, plum blossoms possessed particular significance for those who experienced dynastic transition.

In the Qing dynasty, the *Mustard Seed Garden Manual of Painting* (1701) compendium included a plum-painting manual, versions of which had already been published in the Song and Yuan dynasties. While the Song and Yuan manuals used a literary approach and, as Maggie Bickford notes, "took the life cycle of the plum as their program, presenting archetypical configurations of flowering plums surmounted by poetic rubrics and followed by quatrains,"[6] the Qing dynasty manual treats the plum genre in a more analytical, encyclopedic way. Painting albums of plum blossoms, sometimes as collaborative works, became popular again around the time Gao Jian produced this album. Rather than treat the plum as an object of analysis, Gao attempted to revive the genre's poetic aspect. The combination of still-closed and already-opened blossoms appears to emphasize change and transformation. Contrasting rough bark with delicate petals, he promotes the purity and elegance of the blossoms. In leaf 3 he presents the plum together with bamboo, another symbol for the scholar-recluse because of its pliancy and ability to endure the cold of winter. Prompted by the poem, we view the dark, shadowy branch of a plum painted in wet ink and bluish bamboo leaves by its side as bathed in moonlight.

Although some of the poems have been identified as verses by earlier writers, others may have been composed by Gao or the collaborating transcriber (note the first poem's beginning: "From of old, I've had a 'plum blossom craze': As soon as it's spring, I start writing poems."). A number of famous plum-blossom authors are represented, including Lin Bu, Su Shi, and the song-lyric writer Jiang Kui, all of whom were associated with West Lake, as well as the Yuan poet Guo Yuheng, author of an anthology consisting entirely of poems on the plum. The poems emphasize the "supreme moment" just before it blooms, introduce subtle fragrance into the picture (1), equate man with the plum blossom (3), and repeat the poetic image of the hermit (7): "From ancient times, love of plum blossoms has been suited to us hermits." **BA**

For inscriptions and other documentation, see pages 305–07 in this catalogue.

1 Gao Jian's *Flowering Plum* was originally in the Cathay Art Museum collection and is reproduced in Suzuki Kei, *Chūgoku kaiga sōgō zuroku*, vol. 2, 36–37.

2 Gao Jian's signature on the last leaf shows clearly that the calligraphy of the texts was added by someone else, whose sobriquet appears to have been Ganzhu (Deep Purple Pearl) and, judging from another seal (*Wumen*), hailed from Suzhou. This may have been a female writer, or a male calligrapher who adopted a somewhat feminine style of writing to suit the subject matter.

3 Feng Jinbo 馮金伯, *Guochao hua shi, Moxiang ju hua shi* 國朝畫識, 墨香居畫識 (Moxiangju: 1794), 4:25. Gao Jian's horizontal landscape *Discourse on Poetry* (Metropolitan Museum of Art), dated 1698 and mounted together with an essay, and an album titled *Landscapes* in the Chih Lo Lou collection (Hong Kong) depicting the poems of Tao Yuanming testify to his involvement in poetry and his passion for visualizing it. For the latter, see *Nobility and Virtue*, pl. 73. Also in the Chih Lo Lou collection is the long horizontal landscape painting *Rivers and Mountains without End* of 1678 (*Nobility and Virtue*, pl. 72). Another example of his plum blossom painting, dated 1699 and said to be in the manner of Tang Yin, is recorded in *Midian zhulin Shiqu baoji* (Taipei: Guoli Gugong bowuyuan, 1971), 629. Gao Jian painted the leaf *Blossoming Plum* for a collaborative album dated 1663–64. Published in Suzuki Kei, *Chūgoku kaiga sōgō zuroku, Zokuhen* 中國繪畫總合圖錄，續編 (Tokyo: Tōkyō Daigaku Tōyō Bunka Kenkyūjo, 1998–99), vol. 1, 90. For a vertical painting of plum by Gao, see Suzuki Kei, *Chūgoku kaiga sōgō zuroku*, vol. 4, 286.

4 Maggie Bickford, ed., *Bones of Jade, Soul of Ice*, 22–23.

5 Ibid., fig. 5a–f.

6 Ibid., 125.

57 Gao Jian 高簡
1634–after 1708

***Flowering Plum* 梅華詩畫冊**
1708
Santa Barbara Museum of Art
Museum purchase with funds provided by the Wallis Foundation

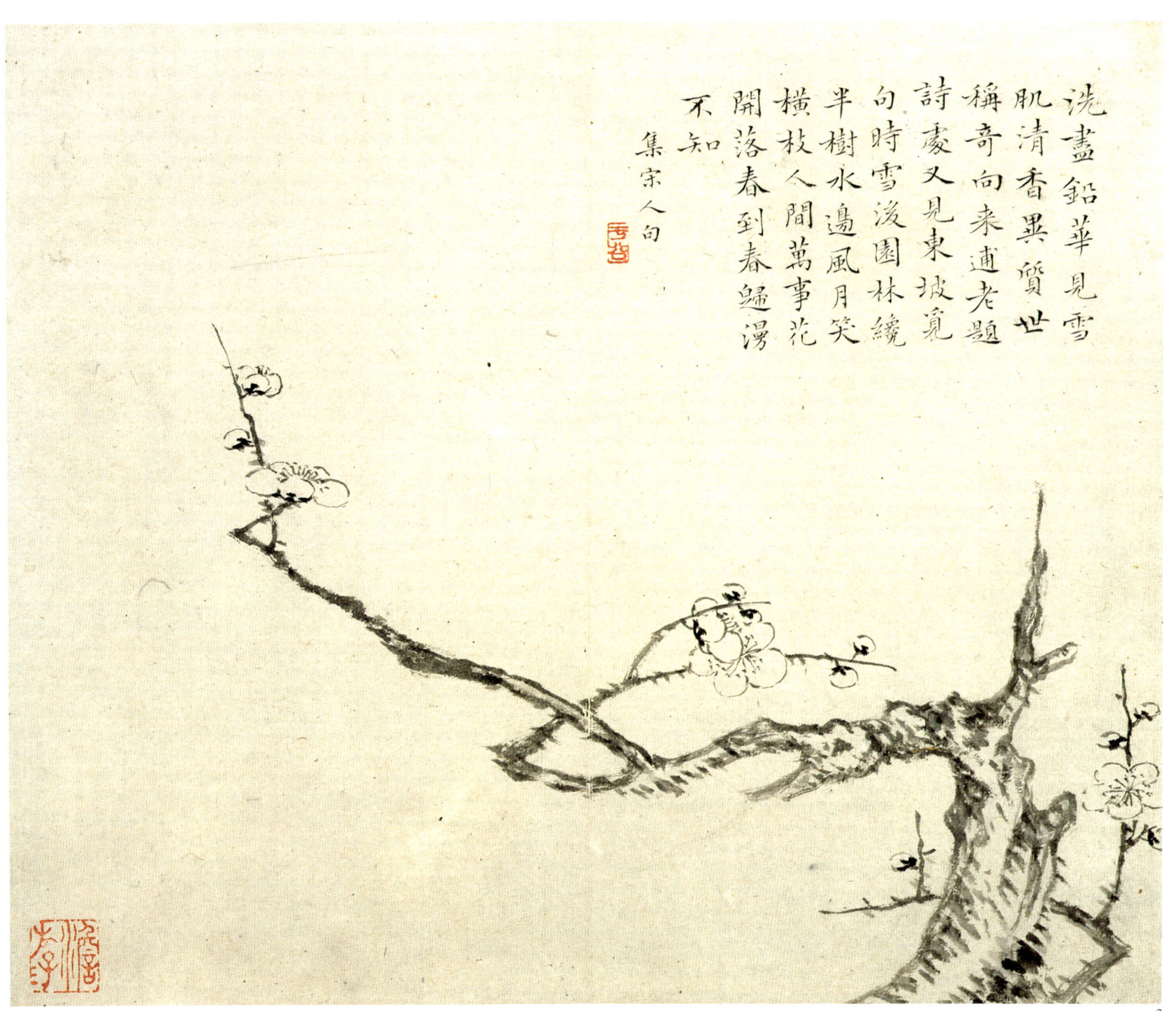

2

Wash off the white makeup, reveal the snowy flesh!
Pure perfume, wondrous substance—called marvelous by the world.
The place where old [Lin] Bu used to inscribe his verses,
Also saw Dongpo [Su Shi] seeking lines.
After snow, out in the garden, they cover just half a tree;
Beside the stream, in wind-swept moonlight, smiling from slanting branches.
In the human world, everything resembles flowers: blooming, fading.
Spring arrives, spring returns; we hardly ever notice.

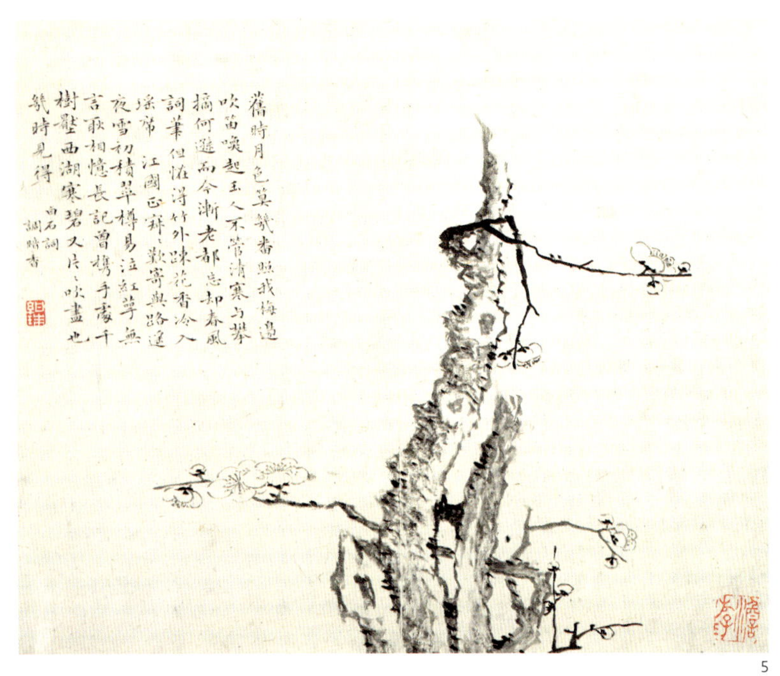

5

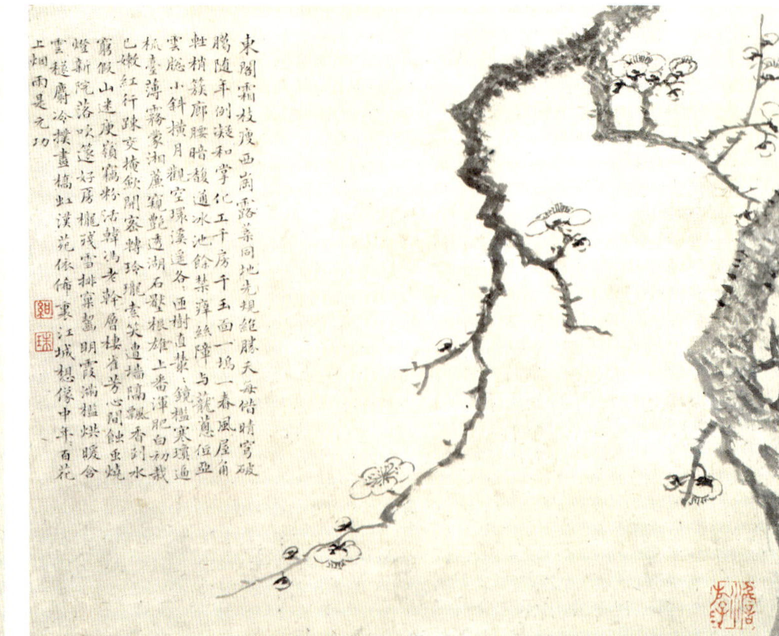

4

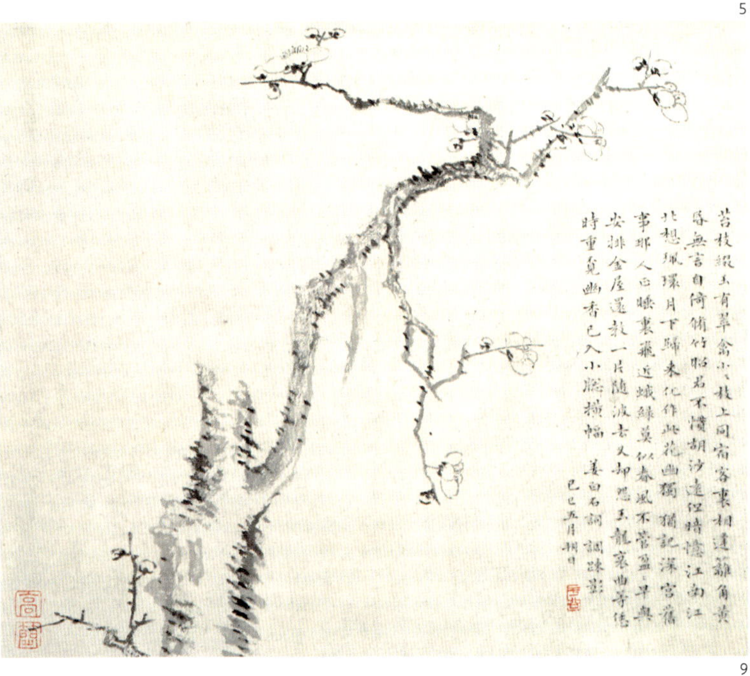

9

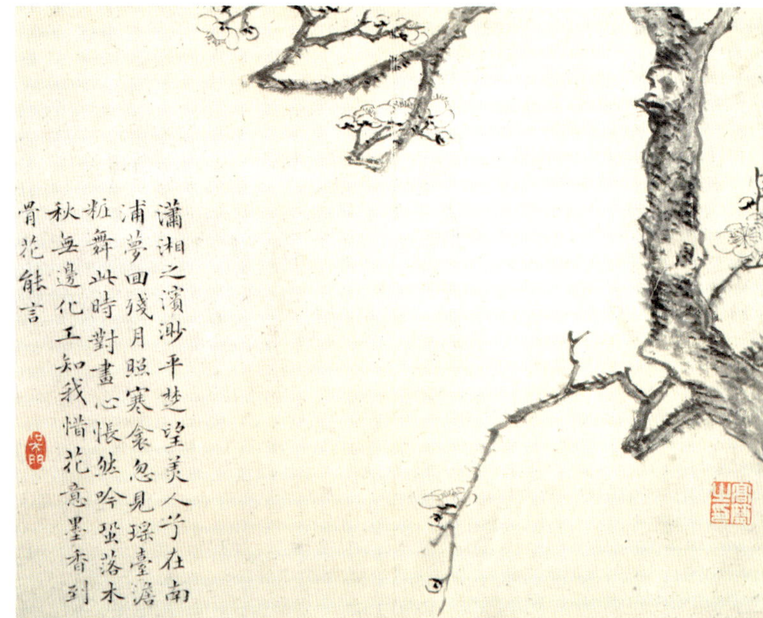
瀟湘之濱渺平楚望美人兮在南
浦夢回殘月照寒衾忽見瑤臺瀉
粧舞此時對畫心悵然吟蛩落木
秋無邊化工知我惜花意墨香到
骨花能言

8

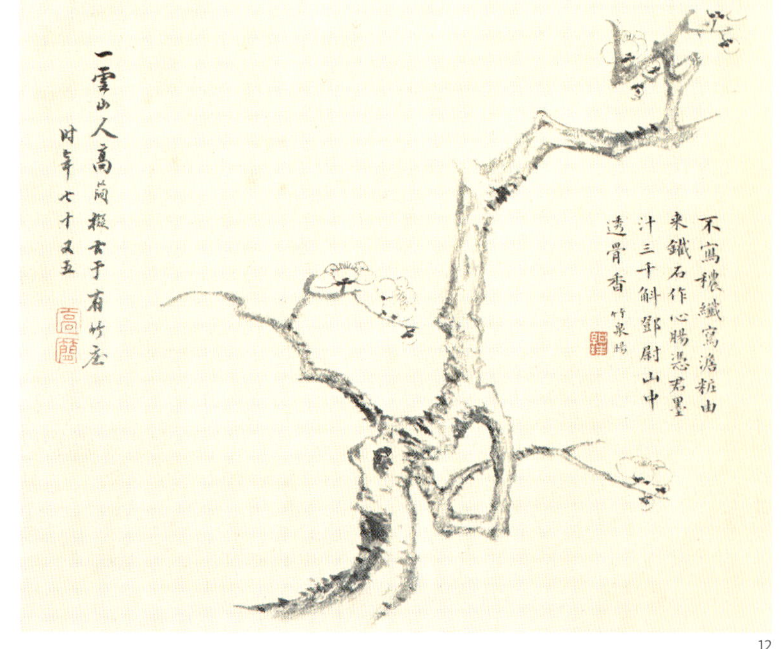
不寫穠纖寫澹粧由
來鐵石作心腸憑君墨
汁三千斛鄧尉山中
透骨香
一雲山人高簡擬古于有竹居
時年七十又五

12

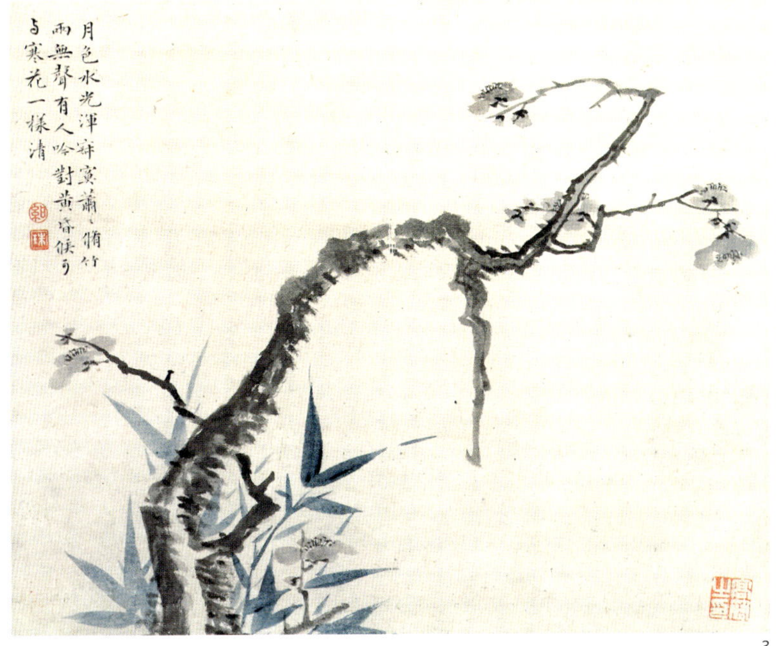

3

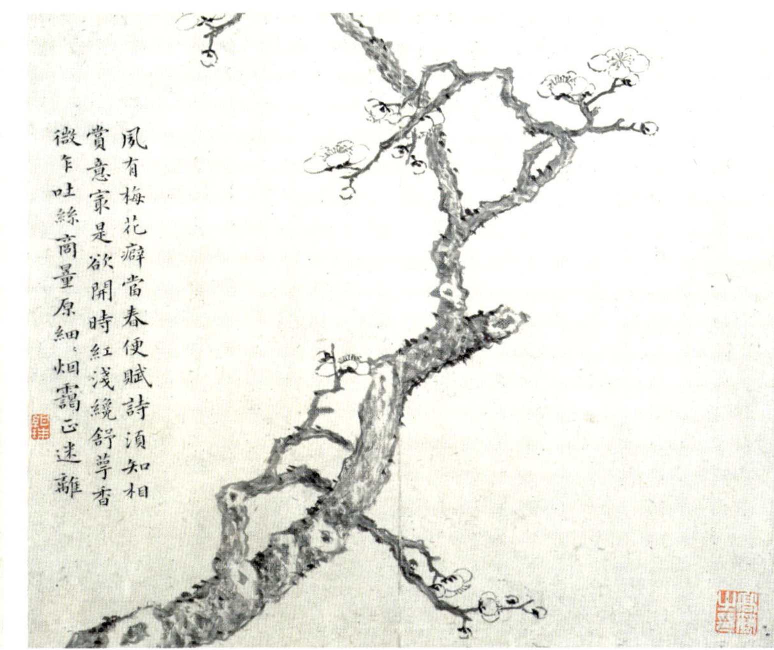

1

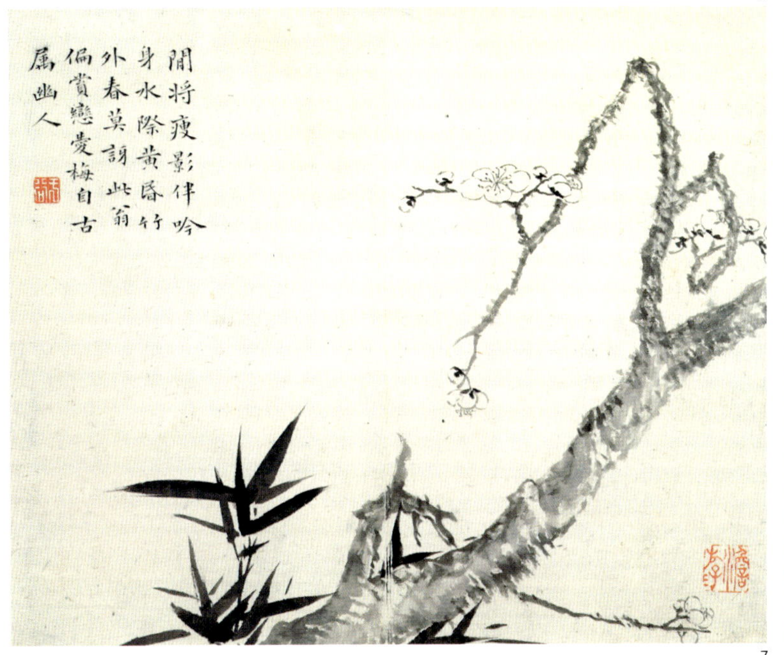

7

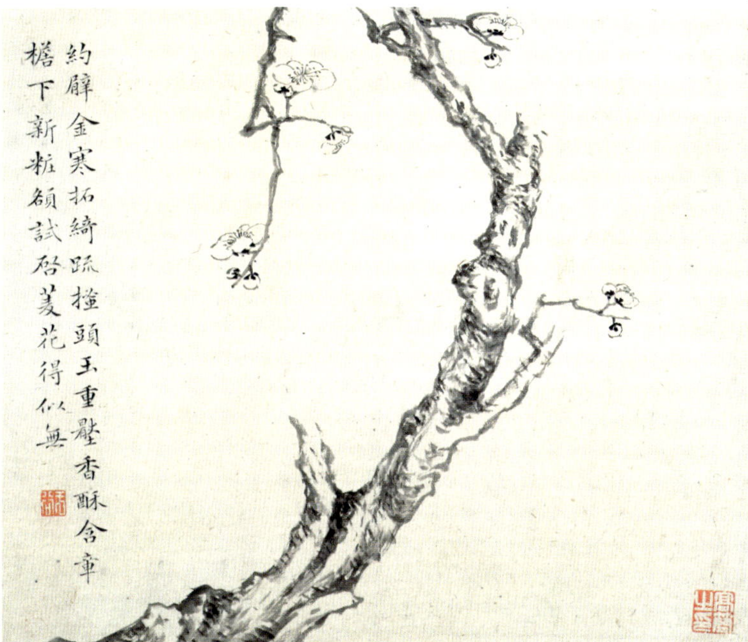

6

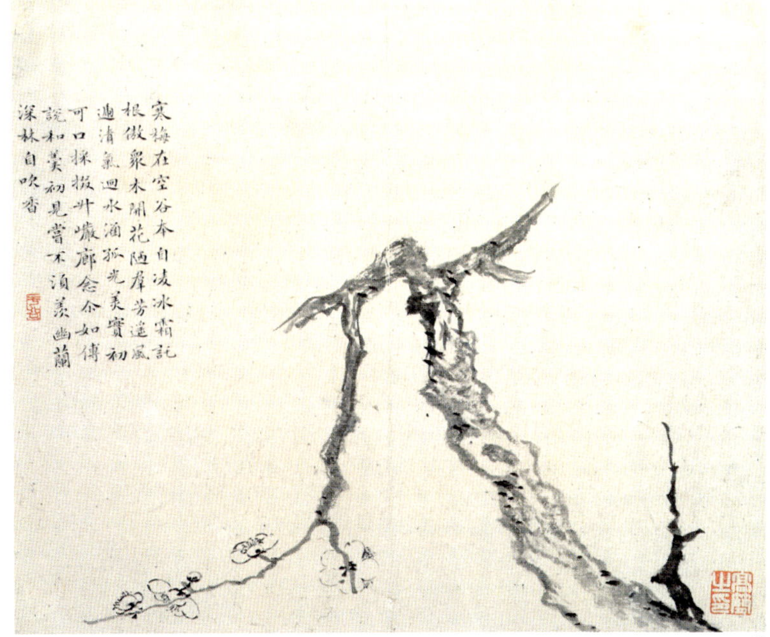

11

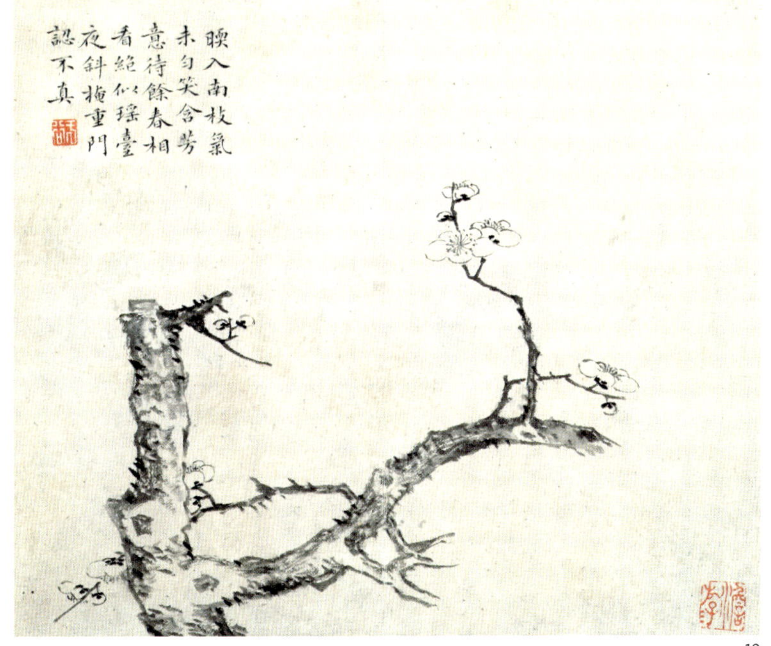

10

Inscriptions and Documentation

CAT. NO. 1

XIANG SHENGMO 項聖謨 1597–1658

Invitation to Reclusion 招隱圖卷, 1625–26

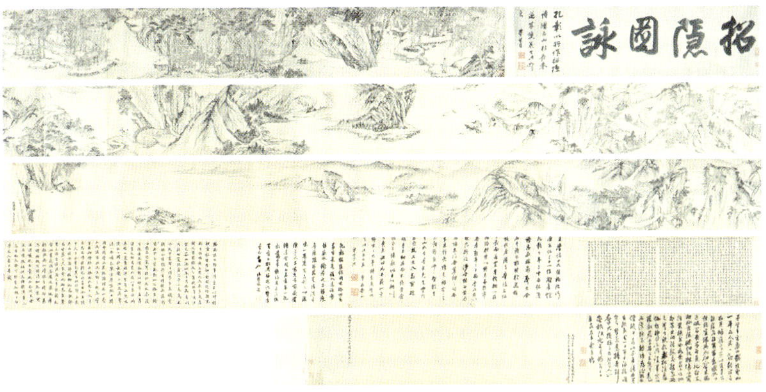

Handscroll: ink on paper; 26.7 × 1320.8 cm (10 ½ × 520 inches); Los Angeles County Museum of Art, Los Angeles County fund (60.29.2)

FRONTISPIECE BY DONG QICHANG

Painting and Chanting an Invitation to Reclusion. Kongzhang has painted a long landscape to accompany his poems on the theme of inviting the recluse and thus made a double beauty. Written as a foreword, [Signed] Dong Qichang.

《招隱圖詠》. 孔彰以所作招隱詩, 繪為山水長卷, 遂成雙美. 書此弁之. 董其昌.

SEALS: *Zongbo xueshi* 宗伯學士, *Dong shi Xuanzai* 董氏玄宰.

SIGNATURE OF THE ARTIST

Invitation to Reclusion, painted by Xiang Shengmo. 招隱圖, 項聖謨畫.

SEAL: *Xiang shi Kongzhang* 項氏孔彰.

INSCRIPTIONS BY THE ARTIST

Entering the mountain is not avoiding the world,
But a deep desire to be far from floating fame.
Streams and stones so blue-green,
Mists and evening clouds unleash my emotions.
The submerged fish knows not to take the bait;
Forest birds have never been startled.
Surely I will dream of dissolving all dust;
Henceforward no thoughts of an official career.[1] (1)

入山非辟世, 端為遠浮名.
泉石多綠兮, 烟霞縱性情.
潛鱗自無餌, 林鳥不曾驚.
應有銷塵夢, 從此罷請纓. (一)

Who says reclusive living need be remote?
At the rush gate there is little traffic.
Not only are the civilities for greeting and parting few,
Gone as well are laughing and crying faces.
It is not for the steadiness of lofty sleep,
Rather, thoughts of engagement are idle.
Profit and fame can be seen for what they are,
Neither glory nor dishonor ever my concern. (2)

誰謂幽居僻, 蓽門稀往還.
但疏迎送禮, 而絕笑啼顏.
不是高眠穩, 只因結想閒.
利名能勘破, 榮辱總無關. (二)

Old vines provide straight shade;
The stream is deep, tree shade is cool.
In the end no allowance for vulgar carriage;
At most permit the fisherman's rod.
The small pavilion is made narrow by arriving clouds;
Distant mountains are released broadly by the sky.
In this setting there is a recluse,
Whose dreams do not reach to the capital. (3)

歲古藤陰直, 溪深木影寒.
終難容俗駕, 儘許老漁竿.
小閣雲來窄, 遙山天放寬.
其中有隱者, 夢不到長安. (三)

If for a day the heart is not stilled,
Who will gladly don the fisherman's gear?
To the end, matters of regret are late;
Glancing back, clouds to envy are many.
Green rain nourishes fragrant trees;
Azure mists break emerald vines.
Fine mountains begin to have a notion,
And summon me... How about it?! (4)

一日心不死, 誰甘著釣蓑.
到頭悔事晚, 回首羡雲多.
綠雨肥芳樹, 青烟斷碧蘿.
好山始有意, 招我欲如何. (四)

If the mountains do not summon me to reclusion,
Then when would I become a Lord Recluse?
Fragrant souls emptily fill the histories,
The bones of knights-errant form graves in waves.
Leave the world for a bounty of surpassing scenes;
Return to the fields and escape the crowd.
Stone moss is elegant after rain;
Cliff trees shimmer lined by clouds. (5)

山不招人隱, 何年得隱君.
芳魂空載史, 俠骨浪成墳.
出世饒佳境, 歸田有逸群.
石苔過雨秀, 巖樹襯雲紋. (五)

At times grasping staffs we go out,
Arms about shoulders, idly seeking poems.
Or choose stones to slap down for chess,
Approach streams where we set down our plain zithers.
Waterfall sounds hold the mood of rain;
Cloud shadows add to the pine's shade.
Fresh fruit feeds our pure talk;
Naturalness quiets the worldly heart. (6)

有時扶扙[杖]出, 把臂覓閒吟.
選石敲棋子, 臨溪枕素琴.
瀑聲含雨色, 雲影補松陰.
新菓供清話, 自然澹世心. (六)

Being alone is not being without companion:
Books and scrolls, by chance, take half the bed.
Across the stream: a thousand acres of bamboo;
Throughout the day: a brazier of incense.
Village wine, it turns out, works well for getting drunk;
Garden vegetables provide an early taste.
A pure wind arrives, and, pillowed on a bamboo basket,
I've completely forgotten extremes of heat and cold. (7)

獨處非無伴, 圖書恰半牀.
隔溪千畝竹, 盡日一爐香.
村酒原堪醉, 園蔬得早嘗.
清風來枕簞, 忘却甚炎涼. (七)

Dawn comes and fills the window,
Though it's still the time of sweet dark slumber.
I arise in time to see clouds emerge;
Return to sleep with memories of blowing rain.
Clouds largely hold the ocean mist;
Rain perfectly adorns the mountains' appearance.
Ever so lightly, flowers open by the stream;
Amid the wonderful fragrance, the butterfly's dream is late.[2] (8)

曉來窗日滿, 猶是黑甜時.
纔起看雲出, 重眠憶雨吹.
雲多涵海氣, 雨正倩山姿.
細細溪花發, 殊香蝶化遲. (八)

Picking herbs, my robes dampen with dew;
Seeking the road home, I have the urge to become an immortal.
Pine flowers harmonize the grain rice,
Tea leaves brew in mountain stream water.
Night goes, beckoning the cries of the gibbon;
Morning comes, inviting the crane's slumber.
So many pure outstanding matters;
Which of these would not extend one's years?! (9)

采藥衣沾露, 尋歸氣欲仙.
松花和麥飯, 茗葉釀山泉.
夜去呼猿嘯, 朝來引鶴眠.
許多清絕事, 何事不延年. (九)

How special, this place for hidden roosting!
Since old, few have known of it.
I take advantage of these illness-free days,
And casually read books from before the great burning.
Encumbered by objects—what are the roots of this stain?
Great aspirations slowly unfurl from the self.
Forgotten already: the place from which I was summoned to reclusion;
Directly remembered: the start of the reclining journey.[3] (10)

況是幽棲地, 從來知已疏.
且乘無病日, 聊讀未焚書.
物累何由染, 襟期稍自舒.
並忘招隱地, 直記臥游初. 處 (十)

In the mouth of the valley no sign of people;
A pure shimmering highlights an unsullied stream.
Cliffside flowers divine years and months;
Cave grasses distinguish spring from autumn.
Shaded gully abuts the cinnabar cave;
Bright forests are covered in a coat of green.
Who cares about high officials in carriages?
Their faces and postures set to serve nobles.[4] (11)

谷口無人跡, 清輝揚素流.
巖花占歲月, 洞草辨春秋.
陰壑臨丹穴, 陽林被翠裘.
由他軒冕客, 顏膝事王矦. (十一)

From the time one enters the ranks of the robe and cap,
Whiskers and eyebrows, a grown gentleman.
To indulge in rewards—that's a young man's goal,
Not to mention receiving worldly acclaim.
But later the wondering begins:
Can one ever escape bending at the waist?
In the mountains there are many things that gladden the heart,
More so when wolves and tigers follow different paths. (12)

自入衣冠列, 鬚眉一丈夫.
縱酬男子志, 亦受世人呼.
不早躊躇及, 能逃磬折無.
山中多樂事, 狼虎況殊途. (十二)

In this world there are no men of accomplishment;
Oh, so hard to break the delusions before our eyes!
Already proud to be an idle clerk,
Who would be distressed to lack an untrammeled wife?
Cultivating melons, in the morning I water;
Notating the *Book of Changes*, at night I burn the vine staff.
My sons are taught both tilling and reading;
When were these two matters not of equal worth?[5] (13)

人間無達士, 難破眼前迷.
既傲為閒吏, 奚愁少逸妻.
種瓜朝灌水, 點易夜然藜.
稚子教耕讀, 何嘗事不齊. (十三)

Originally of Heaven and Earth,
So who would guess an encounter beyond this world?
Living alone was not my intention;
Keeping harm at a distance, it just naturally followed.
I was not raised to pass my days as a fool;
And it is hard to adopt the manner of being clumsy.
Green mountains, understanding, do not reject;
I want to grow old in utter indolence. (14)

原在乾坤裡，誰言世外逢.
索居非得已，遠害詎相從.
未養如愚度，難為若拙容.
青山知不拒，我欲老疏慵.（十四）

Clambering up forested cliffs,
Leisurely I enter shady green glens.
Amid white clouds I hear dogs barking;
As the sun sets I spot a returning monk.
Orioles harmonize, as if seeking to rhyme;
The dragon submerges—plans put in wait?
I know myself the difficulty of fitting into this world;
Can it be due to an aversion to common emotions? (15)

林壑攀躋上，盤旋入翠微.
白雲聞犬吠，落日見僧歸.
鶯和如求韻，龍潛豈息機.
自知難合世，寧與俗情違.（十五）

Long I set my will to live remotely;
Thatched hut opens after rain.
In my carefree sojourns I dodge material concerns;
Formal bows no longer a concern for who arrives.
The servant boy casually sweeps piles of leaves,
And deftly plants secluded flowers among rocks.
Crossing the bridge in search of a late-day mood,
My sandal-teeth are stained green by the moss. (16)

託志棲遲久，茆堂雨後開.
優游逃物外，長揖謝誰來.
積葉童閒掃，幽葩石細栽.
過橋尋晚興，屐齒染莓苔.（十六）

Since coming to live on this riverside rock,
I no longer hear the clamor of horse and cart.
Beyond the peaks, red dust is distant;
In front of the isles, green water plants flourish.
Strangely, I dislike seagull dreams,
And have never trusted in the "silent guest."
The sun presses on its westward journey;
The mien of barren wilds changes to sunset.[6] (17)

自來矶上住，車馬不聞喧.
峰外紅塵遠，洲前綠藻繁.
翻嫌鷗有夢，未信客無言.
白日西馳促，天荒容易昏.（十七）

Hurriedly, rapids flow over white sand;
What's the reason for this busy rush?
Day and night split the forward current;
Murky and clear stem from a single source.
Unsoiled because there's no mixing in the unsoiled;
Turbid as it joins the turbid flow.
Do you not remember the Canglang waters?
And a song whose words it inspired?[7] (18)

白沙走急瀨，何事若忙奔.
晝夜分前派，濁清同一源.
潔因無混潔，渾以合流渾.
不記滄浪水，曾歌自取言.（十八）

I built my hut under a precipitous cliff,
Where connected peaks form a screen.
Facing ridges crisscross, brightly verdant;
Meandering streams narrow, distantly blue.
Rice and grain aplenty to eat year after year;
Orchids finger my robes with their fragrance.
A web of roads reaches into the world;
But here there is bridge and pavilion. (19)

結廬危壁下，連嶂列為屏.
對嶺交明翠，迴溪夾遠青.
稻粱餘歲食，蘭蕙拂衣馨.
複道原通世，有橋還有亭.（十九）

Having exhaustively discussed grounds for mulberry and hemp,
With the Peach Blossom Spring we study the escape from Qin.
Freely speaking, we clarify the nature of things,
And marshal ourselves to personal genuineness.
Cliffs and caves greatly add complexion,
Fishermen and woodcutters are neighbors.
Nesting in reclusion—it is not for outside chaos;
How much more so a man of Great Peace. (20)

盡說桑麻地，桃溪學辟秦.
縱云矯物性，聊自率吾真.
巖穴多增色，漁樵得比鄰.
巢居非亂世，況是太平人.（二十）

I painted this scroll because in the autumn of the *yichou* year [1625], as my boat was arriving at Wujiang [Jiangsu Province], there were a few matters that needed my attention. I found this sheaf of paper in a total of six lengths, made it into a long handscroll, and began to apply brush and ink. From Wu [Suzhou] I set sail and slowly wound my way to Songjiang. In a month's time I [still] had completed less than a foot of the painting. An idler had already reported [about the painting] to Mr. Dong Xuanzai [Dong Qichang], and thus when I went to visit, Mr. Dong urgently pressed me to show him. I returned to the boat, moored at White Dragon Lake, and completed the first length of the scroll. Putting it in my sleeve, I went to see Mr. Dong again. He regarded it, nodded his head without saying a word, and then after a while finally remarked: "The mountains are high, the valleys are beautiful. The forests are green and breezes caress the robes. The man does not look back and very much has an air of transcendence. What exactly is this painting?" I replied, "Because I read the poems on the invitation to reclusion by Lu Ji and Zuo Si I was very much inspired and painted this piece as an accompaniment." It was already evening and he invited me for dinner. In the midst of unbridled drinking our conversation became animated, and the discussion turned to the many famous works of calligraphy and painting in my grandfather's collection. It was midnight before I arose and bade farewell, bringing the scroll back with me.

In the tenth month of that year I once again met Mr. Xuanzai at Wujiang. Impatiently, he asked, "Since the last time I saw your scroll, how many layers of mountains and valleys have you opened, and how many fields of mists and clouds have you tilled?" I replied, "As I have not found a mountain-seeking companion, it is yet unfinished. Now I am only interested in farming my inkstone as a recluse. Expressing what is in my breast to attain my ideals—that would be enough for this life. Many people reach the point of making a decision to leave the world behind only to find they are unable to cut off their ties because they cannot leave worldly things behind."[8] When the gentleman heard this he smiled, understanding and sharing my sentiments. Our talk finished, we said goodbye. I returned home and attended to the matters of brush and ink, so concentrated in my work that I lost track of the passage of time. When the end was finally in sight, nine months had already passed, during half of which I was either sick or depressed. Moreover, when I was able to get up from my bed and stretch out the painting, I was often prevented from working on it by worldly matters, in addition to having to answer requests [for paintings] from various people. Troubled by all of these worrisome matters, I dared not [paint] for fear of being loose and careless. Only after the sun was down would I clean the inkstone and adjust the lamp. I abstained completely from alcohol and ate only pine-flower cakes and tea-leaf soup. Then I ordered the servant to burn incense and grind the ink. When exhaustion neared I would put down the brush. Sometimes I would then [go out strolling] with a candle in hand to look at flowers or roll up the curtain to face the moon. If refreshed, I would pick up the brush once more. I usually worked until midnight before going to bed. If the time were added up, it amounted to a period close to two months.

Now when I look at it, I can see that the forests and hills are bright and smiling, grasses and trees are happy and growing, the air is lively and the spirit is pleasant, all being far from vulgarity. I then gave it the title *Invitation to Reclusion*, and composed twenty poems of five-character lines with the same rhymes and wrote them down at the end of the scroll. I well realize that many people in the world are not recluses, and that they want to be recluses but are unable. Alas! There must have been others who became recluses before me. I say, "Please summon me for reclusion." I say: "I shall summon myself to reclusion." I can just say: "It is alright for me to summon myself for reclusion." I want to be a recluse of the city but cannot. I want to retreat into mountains and rivers but cannot. I want to retreat into poems and paintings, but they have been scattered around in the world, making it impossible for me to collect the names of those who own them. Thus, I must keep this in my arms and store it well in order to wait for one who shares my ideal. On the sixteenth day of the sixth month of the *bingyan* year of the Tianqi reign [1626], the Hermit of the Lotus Pond, Xiang Shengmo, wrote this.

余畫此卷，因乙丑秋涉吳江，舟次無事，檢得此紙，計共六幅，接為長軸，始落筆也.自吳放流，遶至松江，將匝月矣，未及盈尺.有好事者已聞之董玄宰先生.及見先生，索觀甚急，乃退而辟舟，泊白龍潭，先了前一紙袖見.先生點頭不語，久許而問之曰："山高溪秀，林翠撲衣，人不回顧，甚有超逸之風.此何圖也？"曰："因讀陸機，左思招隱詩，有興于懷，將補是圖."薄暮留酌，豪飲劇談.因論及先王大父所藏法書名畫，夜半方起，索之而歸.是歲十月，復會玄宰先生於吳江.急謂余曰："前觀此卷之後，又開得幾層丘壑，耕得幾項煙云？"余曰："因未得尋山侶，志未竟也.今將借硯田以隱焉.抒懷適志，亦足了生平.蓋世人於出處之際，不能割裂，以世念未銷耳."先生聞之解頤，蓋亦有心人也.言畢，謝退.歸事筆墨，若忘歲月.此卷計成，雖九易朔晦，病愁相半.及病起展卷，日未免為塵鞅所妨，兼應酬徵索者命，煩亂不敢草草.每至落日，滌硯挑燈，絕不飲酒，所食者松花餅茗葉湯.命侍兒焚香研墨，神將倦，隨擱筆；或秉燭看花，或捲簾對月，爽則援毫，越子丑而方寢焉.累其功不二月也.因自展閱，林巒映發，草木欣向，氣爽神怡，流風絕俗.遂題曰《招隱圖》，并賦五言二十韻，書於卷末.我固知世人皆非隱者也，皆思隱而未肯者也.噫嘻哉！其必有先我而隱之者矣.曰招我隱可也；曰自我招隱可也；即曰自招亦無不可也.我將隱朝市，而不得；隱陵藪，而不得；將隱於詩畫，而詩畫已散落人間，又不得收拾姓字矣.亟懷此而善藏，以俟夫同志者.天啟丙寅六月既望，蓮塘居士項聖謨并記.

ADDITIONAL INSCRIPTIONS[9]

DONG QICHANG (1555–1636)

Wang Mojie [Wang Wei] wrote his "Peach Blossom Poems" at the age of nineteen, and Pan Anren [Pan Yue] composed his "Poems on Leisure" when he was thirty-one. Now Kongzhang writes his "Invitation to Reclusion Poems" at the age of thirty. With his will set among forests and springs, his sounds emerge strong and firm. The material for his poems comes from the *Wenxuan*, and the metrical form from Tang verses. Thus, his poems combine the best features of both Mojie and Anren and create the feeling of living in [Wang Wei's] Wangchuan Villa and [Pan Yue's] Heyang Retreat for the rest of his life, without the distraction of the cities. Even though he is at the age of thirty, his lines, "Hoary head is what everybody will eventually become; there is no completely secure earthly net," show that he is already well aware of the rugged perils one might have to face late in life, such as those that befell Mojie and Anren. However, although the characters of the poets are different, the practices of the painters are the same. Xiang's long landscape handscroll, while having some ideas from Youcheng [Wang Wei], also derives from Jing [Jing Hao] and Guan [Guan Tong] and is modeled after Dong [Dong Yuan] and Ju [Juran]. It is meticulous but does not hurt its bone structure; it is free but does not harm its spirit resonance. Thus, it does not seem to take the Wangchuan as its ultimate goal, but goes far beyond. In the future, when he reaches full maturity like Wei Suzhou [Wei Yingwu] and Li Xigu [Li Tang], how will his poetry and painting be? On the basis of this youthful work we can look forward with great expectations. Inscribed by Dong Qichang.

王摩詰十九賦《桃源行》，潘安仁三十一作《閒居賦》．孔彰今年三十為《招隱詩》，志在林泉，聲出金石．其詩則取材於《選》，程格於唐．淹有摩詰，安仁之長，而若置身於輞川莊，河陽別業以終老，無朝市慕者．雖年三十，而摩詰，安仁晚歲踦距涉世，賦「白首同所歸，安得舍塵網」之句，蚤分迷悟矣．惟是詞客之品雖懸，畫師之習猶在．其山水長卷，不免乞靈於右承，然又出入荊，關，規模董，巨．細密而不傷骨，奔放而不傷韻．似未以輞川為竟者．他時如韋蘇州，李晞古之大年，詩畫更當何若？以此為少年之筆，為券可也．董其昌題．

SEALS: *Zongbo xueshi* 宗伯學士, *Dongshi Xuanzai* 董氏玄宰.

CHEN JIRU (1558–1639)

Kongzhang's *Invitation to Reclusion* in both poetry and painting combines four lengths of Song paper to form a long handscroll. The road leads into winding paths, sharp turns, high peaks, thatched huts, and deep caves, all so clean that no dust can be found. Also there are vegetables and mushrooms in the valley that taste pure and desirable. When the scroll is unrolled, all desire for fame and profit drains away. Among the famous paintings in the collection of Mr. Zijing [Xiang Yuanbian], Lu Hong's *Thatched Hut* ranked the very first. Kongzhang's handling of the brush has captured the strange and precarious compositions of this Tang painter. There is no need for him to match horns with the masters of the last dynasty. Inscribed by Chen Jiru.

孔彰《招隱》詩圖，宋紙四番，遂成長卷．路入迂詰，勢轉嶺欹．綿茆穴土，鮮潔無塵，餐谷茹芝，清淡有味．一展卷間，名利之心，汲除盡矣．子京先生家藏盧鴻《草堂圖》，為名畫第一．孔彰落筆，極得其奇險位置處，不願與勝國諸賢摩壘相角也．陳繼儒題．

SEAL: *Meigong* 眉公.

LI RIHUA (1565–1635)

In matters of painting, masters of the last dynasty attained the "heart-prints" of Dong and Ju [Dong Yuan and Juran]. Loosely applying and smearing the ink, they all achieved a resonance of spirit. Only in composition were they more cautious about originating [novel concepts]. Huang [Huang Gongwang] and Wang [Wang Meng] were more innovative in this respect; their works of this kind, however, are still quite rare. [This is because] composition for painting is analogous to elaborate description for prose. If one's breast is not steeped in broad experience, able to ingest mountains and seas and thus spit out sun and moon, then even if produced by a master of beautiful fabrics like the Weaving Maid, it still would not be a simple matter. Nowadays, painting habits are getting worse. They have descended into barren emptiness, lost in the fog of the strange and fantastical. It has become so bad that trees are painted without order and depth and rocks are sketched with neither front nor back. Pushed, such painters hide behind the Yuan style, claiming to reside in "the untrammeled." This kind of habit passes on from teacher to pupil and is impossible to rein in.

My friend Xiang Kongzhang [Xiang Shengmo], a youthful scion of a famous family, has devoted himself to this art in his spare time from his studies. One day he showed me this scroll. It is beautifully and skillfully done, powerful and primordial like a lofty peak. The forms of the mountains and aspects of the waters constantly change from section to section, in a length of some thirty to forty feet. Its brushwork is modeled after Hongyi's [Lu Hong] *Thatched Hut*, Mojie's [Wang Wei] *Wangchuan*, Guan Tong's *Cliff Paths in Snow*, and Yingqiu's [Li Cheng] *Wintry Forests*. Not a single stroke follows the narrow path of the Southern Song painters, yet there is no lack of vividness or vitality. This is the mainstream of painting. Kongzhang's grandfather, Mr. Zijing [Xiang Yuanbian], was a great collector and discerning connoisseur. His collection of paintings both past and present was number one in the world. I once saw his own paintings *Guo Wu Practicing Alchemy on Mount Jiao* and *Wu Zuoqing Sailing in the Peach Blossom River*, both more than two feet long and each unusual. Now this scroll, so monumental and splendid, is about three times as long. Truly the Wuwa [Gansu Province] horses are justly famed for their dragon-seeds. During this decline of the art of painting, the ground has been defiled by the devil's saliva, which spreads out like a spider web, entrapping any painter who tries to escape. Kongzhang alone seems to have been able to overcome such pitfalls with his forceful ideas and intuitive understanding. Can we not recognize him as a rising hero? As we are natives of the same hometown and our families have known each other for generations, I feel that my praise and admiration for his work should count double that of Dong and Chen. [Signed] the first day of the last month of winter, *dingmao* year of the Tianqi reign [1628], Li Rihua, a friend from Baizhu.

勝國諸公繪事，得董巨心印，縱橫塗抹，皆有神韻．獨於作圖，不輕自任．唯黄，王有之，亦不多見．蓋繪之有圖，猶文之有賦，非胸次淹宏，苞茹山海，吐吞日月，而又出以天孫七襄組麗之手，未易為也．今天下畫習日繆，率多荒穢空疏，怪幻慌惚．乃至作樹無復行次，寫石不分背面．動以元格自掩，曰：「我存逸氣耳」．相師成風不復可挽．吾友項孔彰，以妙年名裔，讀書之餘，篤意此道．一日出示此卷，精工美麗，雄渾乍崿．山態水情，段段轉換．長幾三四丈．其筆法一本鴻乙《草堂》，摩結《輞口》，關同《雪棧》，營丘《寒林》諸蹟，無一毫入南渡蹊徑．而生動之趣，未嘗不在，此繪林正脈也．孔彰大父子京先生，博雅精鑒，所蓄古今名蹟甲天下．余嘗見先生所作《郭五遊焦山煉丹圖》，《鄔佐卿桃花放棹圖》，皆盈二尺有奇．而此卷巨麗，實三倍之，信渥涯之多龍種也．當此畫道凋落，魔涎灑地，布網粘綴，無一得脫之時，而英思神悟，超然獨得如孔彰，可不謂崛起之豪歟．余忝同里世交，其嘆服稱快，又陪於陳，董二先生也．天啟丁卯季冬朔日白苧友人李日華識．

SEALS: *Li Rihua yin* 李日華印, *Junshi* 君實.

ADDITIONAL INSCRIPTIONS by Yu Yan 俞彥 (seventeenth century), dated 1628; Fei Nianci 費念慈 (1855–1905), dated 1889.

NOTES

1 Literally, "end all requests for a military assignment," using a phrase that alludes to Zhong Jun of the Han dynasty, who eagerly sought a position of grave responsibility but died at the age of only twenty. See Tao Zongyi 陶宗儀, *Shuofu* 說郛 (*Siku quanshu* ed.), 14 *xia*: 13b–14a. Xiang Shengmo's allusion to Zhong is particularly apt considering his own youthful age when he painted this scroll.

2 Literally, "butterfly's transformation." This is an allusion to the well-known passage from the *Zhuangzi*, in which Zhuangzi dreams happily of being a butterfly, awakens but then wonders if he is Zhuangzi who has awakened or a butterfly now dreaming of being Zhuangzi. *Zhuangzi jinzhu jinshi* 莊子今註今譯, ed. Wang Yunwu 王雲五 (Taipei: Taiwan Shangwu yinshuguan, 1975), 101. Xiang Shengmo suggests not only the charm of the rain-filled scene but also its seemingly timeless quality.

3 The "great burning" refers to the efforts of the first emperor of the Qin dynasty (221–207 BCE), Qin Shihuangdi, who beginning in 213 BCE condemned to flame earlier writings of the Hundred Schools of Thought in an effort to control knowledge and ideas. "Reclining journey" is a common trope used to describe a painted representation of landscape.

4 The "unsullied stream" (*suliu* 素流) of the second line can refer to water as well as people, in the sense of followers of pure mind but poor circumstances.

5 The third and fourth lines allude to the first of Guo Pu's *Roaming Immortal* poems: "The Qiyuan had its haughty clerk, / Master Lai had his untrammeled wife" 漆園有傲吏，萊氏有逸妻. Guo Pu 郭璞, "Youxian shi qishou" 遊仙詩七首, in *Wenxuan* 文選 (Taipei: Wenjin chubanshe, 1987), 21:1019. The haughty clerk of the Qiyuan (Lacquer Garden) refers to Zhuangzi. Master Lai 老萊, also known as Lao Laizi 老萊子 and one of the Twenty-Four Paragons of Filial Piety, lived the life of a recluse-farmer at Mengshan when invited to court by the King of Chu. Though Laizi was inclined to accept the offer, his wife steadfastly insisted on pursuing the life of reclusion. "Cultivating melons" (line 5) should refer to Shao Ping, former high official of the Qin, who chose to live as a recluse and grow melons outside the eastern gate of the capital Chang'an early in the Western Han rather than serve the new dynasty. See Sima Qian 司馬遷, *Shiji* 史記 (*Siku quanshu* ed.), 53:5a. Burning the vine staff (line 6) is an allusion to the scholar Liu Xiang of the Eastern Han. Collating books all day long in the Tianlu Tower, he would not halt even after daylight passed. One night an old man dressed in yellow robes climbed the steps of the tower with a vine staff, the tip of which magically flamed when the old man blew upon it, thus providing the diligent scholar with light to continue his work. See Wang Jia 王嘉, *Shiyi ji* 拾遺記 (*Siku quanshu* ed.), 6:10b.

6 "Clamor of horse and cart" refers to a famous line from the fifth of Tao Yuanming's "Poems on Drinking." "Seagull dreams" point to aspirations of reclusion; disliking it is unexpected. The poet seems to suggest that he is past dreaming of reclusion since he is already living in it. As for a speechless or "silent guest," this commonly refers to one transfixed by the beauty of the landscape. In one poem included in a text recording traces of the Six Dynasties period, sober guests facing a beautiful scene are silent while drunken ones chat noisily. See "Shangxin ting" 賞心亭, in Zhang Dunyi 張敦頤, *Liuchao shiji bianlei* 六朝事跡編類 (*Siku quanshu* ed.), 1:52b. If Xiang had this text in mind his line would echo the poem's earlier reference to the wine-loving Tao and suggest that his reclusion is a non-sober affair. The "barren wilds," *tianhuang* 天荒, of the poem's last line could be a euphemism to describe unrealized human talent due to a lack of ability or opportunity to pass the examinations.

7 A reference to a lad described by Mengzi 孟子, who sang a song describing how he washed the tassels of his hat in the Canglang's waters when clean and his feet when the waters were muddy. *Mengzi zhushu* 孟子注疏 (*Siku quanshu* ed.), 7 *shang*: 18b.

8 To farm one's inkstone means to apply oneself devotedly as an artist or writer.

9 Translations modified from those of Chu-tsing Li and Wai-kam Ho in Ho, ed., *The Century of Tung Ch'i-Ch'ang*, vol. 2, 110–12.

CAT. NO. 2

ZENG JING 曾鯨 1564–1647

Portrait of Pan Qintai 潘琴台像, 1621

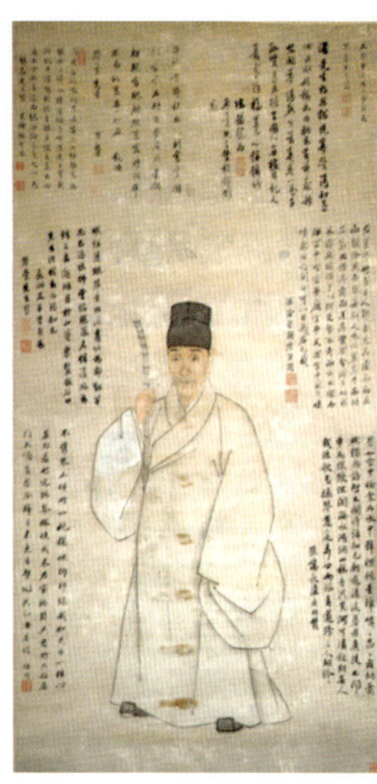

Hanging scroll: ink and color on paper; 116.6 × 58.5 cm (45 7/8 × 23 inches); University of Michigan Museum of Art, Museum purchase made possible by the Margaret Watson Parker Art Collection Fund, 1966/1.110

SIGNATURE OF THE ARTIST

On a winter day in the *xinyou* year of the Tianqi reign [1621], Zeng Jing sketched for Mr. Qintai.

天啟辛酉冬日，曾鯨爲琴台先生寫.

SEALS: *Zeng Jing zhi yin* 曾鯨之印, *Bochen* 波臣.

INSCRIPTIONS

CHEN JIRU (1558–1639)

Mr. Pan is fond of hidden solitude. Never seeking wealth, he is always content. His heart is like still water, his form like arid wood. He wears white cotton robes and dwells in a yellow thatched hut. His body is in peaceful repose; his dreams are pure and sound. He is a man of a thousand books and a song of the *qin* zither. His fine sons and grandsons are amiable and filial. Always agreeable, they never exchange angry looks. He needs neither those groundless worries of the man of Qi nor the unexpected luck of an old man on the frontier, because he has the companionship of the slender bamboo.[1] [Signed] Chen Jiru extols Mr. Qintai at the Accompanying Bamboo Hermitage.

潘先生，好幽獨．既寡營，復知足．
心止水，形槁木．白衲衣，黃茆屋．
體安閑，夢清熟．書萬卷，琴一曲．
子孫賢，孝且睦．有同心，無橫目．
杞人憂，塞翁福．置不勿，伴修竹．
陳繼儒爲琴臺先生，贊于伴竹居.

SEALS: *Meigong* 眉公, *Yi fu ru* 一腐儒.

LI LIUFANG (1575–1629)

Clothed in white cotton robe he holds
a bamboo staff,
Arriving at West Lake he makes a home.
Gate closed, he arranges rocks by his
garden ponds;
An attentive host, he serves plenty of tea
and melon.
While his white collar is clean as fresh snow,
His face, wine-flushed, is like changing
evening mists.
Attaining leisure is certainly not so easily
come by;
The affairs of the city are like [tangled] hemp.

Inscribed and presented to Mr. Qintai, [Signed] Li Liufang.

白衲有笻杖，西湖到處家.
閉門營水石，好客費瓜茶.
素領初疑雪，酡顏欲變霞.
得閑渾不易，城裡事如麻.
題贈琴臺先生，李流芳.

SEALS: *Li Liufang yin* 李流芳印, *Li Changheng* 李長蘅.

LIN YUNFENG (SIXTEENTH–SEVENTEENTH CENTURY)

His "Bamboo Retreat" has no bamboo, only a cluster of old huts; yet how tasteful they appear. His *qin* [zither] table is without a *qin*, all day long his drunken poetic chants, like music lingering in midair. Oh, how I admire this gentleman! How profoundly he has gained enjoyment from the bamboo and his *qin*! He does not need to model himself after the traces of Wang Ziyou [Wang Huizhi]—his heart is already similar to that of Tao Yuanliang [Tao Yuanming].[2] [Signed] Extolling Mr. Qintai, Lin Yunfeng of Wujun [Suzhou].

竹居無竹，數椽老屋，蕭然不俗．琴臺無琴，終日醉吟，綽有餘音．吁嗟先生，實我所欽．其得趣于竹與琴者，深矣．蓋不必跡王子猷之蹟，而能心陶元亮之心．為琴台先生贊，吳郡林雲鳳.

SEALS: *Lin Yunfeng yin* 林雲鳳印, *Ruofu shan* 若撫山.

CHEN GUAN (1563–C. 1639)

Are you not Master of Accompanying Bamboo Hermitage? I see that you are pure and resolute, elegant and refined, cultivated and outstanding. A person like you must be empty within and of lofty morals. You must cultivate your intentions to present such purity. Through tenacity, you survived the ice and frost [of misfortune]. You are free of the fine dust [of pollution] yet still remain near to the fiery reins of power. Not eccentric, yet ancient. Not simple, yet "clumsy." [Your nature] is suited to the field, suited to the court, suited to cultural pursuits and wine, suited to wind and moon. Ah! Among rocks and streams, how could a day be spent without this gentleman?[3] [Signed] Chen Guan, The Old Gardener of Hanyin.

君豈伴竹居主人耶．吾見其清而勁，幽而韻，修然而勝．若斯人也，必虛其中，而疏其節，必修其意，而呈其潔．有堅持兮，以歷冰霜．無纖垢兮，以附炎勢．不奇而古，不樸而拙．宜乎畦，宜乎庭．宜乎文酒，宜乎風月．噫嘻．泉石之間，何可一日無此君也哉．漢陰老圃，陳裸題.

SEALS: *Baishi Daoren* 白室道人, *Chen Gongzan shi* 陳公瓚氏.

CAO XI 曹羲 (SIXTEENTH–SEVENTEENTH CENTURY)

In the evening the path is deserted. The thatched hut appears as if recently cleansed. You enjoy living by bamboo; even a few stalks will do. Their young branches brush the clouds, refined like the tail of a phoenix. You borrow the pure [bamboo] breeze and turn it into the sounds of your zither. You invite the radiant moon to nestle within a rustic drinking cup. Virtuous are you, Mr. Gukou! Allow me to be your close friend until our heads turn white. [Signed] Extolling Mr. Qintai, younger brother Cao Xi of Changzhou.

晚徑蕭疏，茆堂如洗．喜竹爲鄰，數竿而已．孫枝拂雲，修然風尾．借清風爲弦上音，邀明月於山尊裡．賢哉谷口先生，許我爲白頭知已．長州友弟曹羲，爲琴台先生贊.

SEALS: *Luofu* 羅浮, *Zidai shi* 子岱氏.

LU GUANGMING 陸廣明 (SIXTEENTH–SEVENTEENTH CENTURY)

Majestic as a juniper in snow, unsullied like a [white] jade disc under water. [Like] a wooden beam or pillar, jade tally or scepter, precipitous and serried. Why do you stand alone in silence? [Because your] wisdom does not struggle against the times; you only forge intimate friendships. At dawn you amble by clear streams; in the evening saunter through Guangling [Yangzhou]. You hear not the comings and goings of horses and carriages, but rather hear the sound of the rolling sea. Mountains and forests are deep and mysterious, and the Yellow River may run clear, but there will never be another Zhong Qi [to comprehend your music].[4] Allow me to sing a short song while you strum the *qin*. Carefree sporting with the world, your two eyes clear, while passersby scurry about oblivious. [Signed] The Elder of Yandang, Lu Guangming extols.

蒼如雪中柏，潔如水中璧．梁棟圭璋，嶙嶙齒齒．爾胡蕭然獨無語．智不鬥時，結知已．朝遊清溪，暮遊廣陵．不聞車馬蹀躞，但聞海水澒洞，山林杳冥，黃河可清，鍾期無人．我短歌，君操琴．逍遙弄世兩眼青，道旁之人胡紛紛．雁蕩長陸廣明贊.

FENG WEIQI 馮維圻 (SIXTEENTH–SEVENTEENTH CENTURY)

Not carrying his *qin*, not accompanying bamboo, his robe still reflects the plant's jade green. I understand the longings of this gentleman's heart: if not the sight of bamboo, then it is the sounds of his *qin*. If I were to come to the gentleman's home and listen to the music from his *qin* and regard his bamboo, [being uncouth,] the elegant and rare bamboo from the Yandang Valley would be wasted on me, like a vagabond drooling over meat at a butcher's shop. Come, let us retire from public life. The teapot at your house has long been boiling. [Signed] Weiqi.[5]

不攜琴，不伴竹，一袍猶映琅玕綠．我知先生一往心，若非看竹定聽琴．假使我來君家聽琴與看竹，只好屠門大嚼篔簹谷．歸去來，先生壁間久已沸茶鐺．維圻.

SEALS: *Feng Weiqi yin* 馮維圻印.

Additional SEALS: *Tongyuan* 通園; *Huaigong jiancang* 淮恭鑒藏.

notes

1 "Form like arid wood" recalls the attributes of the superior man in the Daoist classic *Zhuangzi*, which exalts the detached, "out-of-body" manner of the sage whose spirit wanders through the universe. The "man from Qi" worried incessantly of the sky falling; the "old man of the frontier" had no concern for wealth or fame. These two allusions are from the early classic texts *Liezi* 列子 and *Huainanzi* 淮南子. See Liang Xiaopeng 梁小鵬, *Liezi* (Beijing: Zhonghua shuju, 2005), 16–19; and John S. Major, et al., *The Huainanzi: A Guide to the Theory and Practice of Government in Early Han China* (New York: Columbia University Press, 2010), 728–29.

2 Wang Huizhi was especially fond of bamboo. Tao Yuanming was the recluse-poet admired above all others by later literati. For Wang's love of bamboo, see Richard B. Mather, trans., *Shih-shuo Hsin-yü: A New Account of Tales of the World*, 2nd. ed. (Ann Arbor: Center for Chinese Studies, University of Michigan, 2002), 430.

3 The last line alludes to Wang Huizhi's famous quote regarding bamboo (see the previous note). Chen Guan is referring specifically to Pan Qintai, but with obvious identification with the other gentleman (bamboo) also intended.

4 Zhong Qi, otherwise known as Zhong Ziqi, was the one person who truly understood the zither playing of Yu Boya. When Zhong died, Boya broke his zither, vowing never to play again now that the one who "understood the sounds" was no longer. This anecdote was especially popular during the late Ming. See Feng Menglong, *Stories to Caution the World: A Ming Dynasty Collection*, vol. 2, translated by Yang Shuhui and Yang Yunqin (Seattle: University of Washington Press, 2005), 7–20.

5 Transcriptions and translations modified from Marshall Wu, *The Orchid Pavilion Gathering*, vol. 1, 115–17.

CAT. NO. 3

MI WANZHONG 米萬鍾 1570–1628
Reading in a Pavilion by a Stream
溪亭讀書圖, 1609

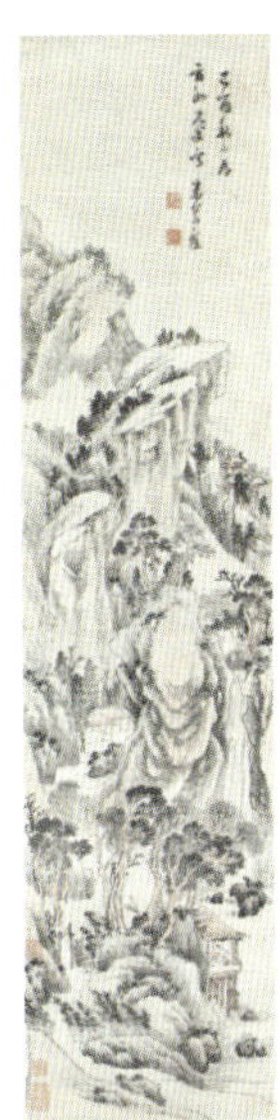

Hanging scroll: ink and light color on paper; 105.1 × 24.8 cm (41 ⅜ × 9 ¾ inches); Private collection

INSCRIPTION BY THE ARTIST
On an autumn day in the *jiyou* year [1609], sketched for elder brother Xuanmiao. [Signed] Mi Wanzhong.

己酉秋日，為玄渺兄丈寫．米萬鍾.

SEALS: *Mi Wanzhong yin* 米萬鍾印, *Zhongzhao shi* 仲詔氏.

ADDITIONAL INSCRIPTION by Zhang Shouxian 章綬銜 (1804–1875), in which Zhang speculates about the identity of the painting's recipient.

ADDITIONAL SEALS: *Qian Tianshu* 錢天樹, *Qian Tianshu yin* 錢天樹印, *Zeng cang Qian Menglu jia* 曾藏錢夢盧家 (Qian Tianshu 錢天樹, 1778–1841); *Zibo* 仔百, *Dixi Zhang Zibo zhanshang* 荻谿章紫伯珍賞 (Zhang Shouxian 章綬銜, 1804–1875).

Title slip and additional inscriptions on storage boxes by Nagao Ko 長尾甲 (1864–1942).

CAT. NO. 4

MI WANZHONG 米萬鍾 1570–1628
Landscape 山水軸, 1625

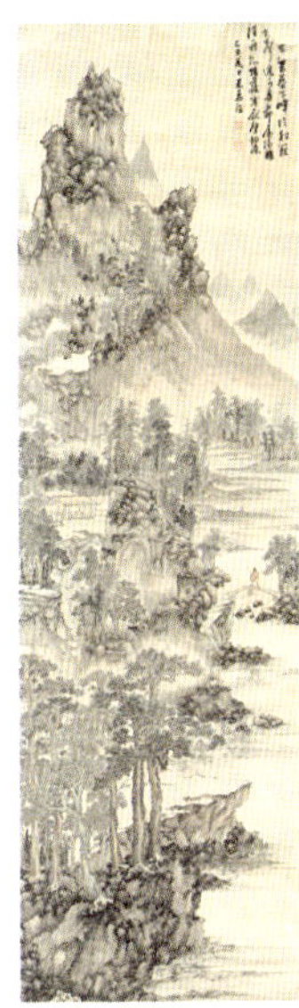

Hanging scroll: ink and light color on paper; 344.2 × 102.2 cm (135 ½ × 40 ¼ inches); Iris & B. Gerald Cantor Center for Visual Arts at Stanford University, Committee for Art Acquisitions Fund

INSCRIPTION BY THE ARTIST
[*illegible*] myriad layers, in the shade of the lower peaks,
Amidst the soughing of pines and sounds of streams, a path can be found.
In a thatched cottage beyond the bridge, who is it secluded in the bamboo,
Never tiring of the short vines that split open the deepening mists?
A summer day in the *yichou* year [1625], [Signed] Mi Wanzhong.

_ _萬疊下峰陰，松籟谿聲逕可尋.
茆屋隔橋誰竹隱，短藤寧厭擘煙深.
乙丑夏日米萬鍾.

SEALS: *Mi Wanzhong zi Zhongzhao* 米萬鍾字仲詔, *Hutian shiyue you* 壺天十岳友.

CAT. NO. 5

CHEN GUAN 陳裸 1563–c. 1639
Walking with a Staff over a Stream Bridge
溪橋策杖圖

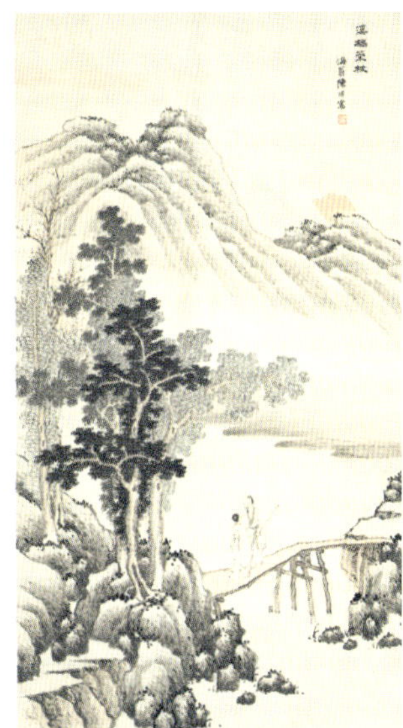

Hanging scroll: ink and color on paper; 91.4 × 51.1 cm (36 × 20 ⅛ inches); Santa Barbara Museum of Art, Gift of N. P. Wong Family, 1995.63.5

TITLE AND SIGNATURE
Walking with a Staff over a Stream Bridge, sketched by Haiweng, Chen Guan.

溪橋策杖，海翁陳裸寫.

SEAL: *Chen Guan zhi yin* 陳裸之印.

CAT. NO. 6

SUN ZHI 孫枝 act. late sixteenth–early seventeenth century
Landscape 山水扇面

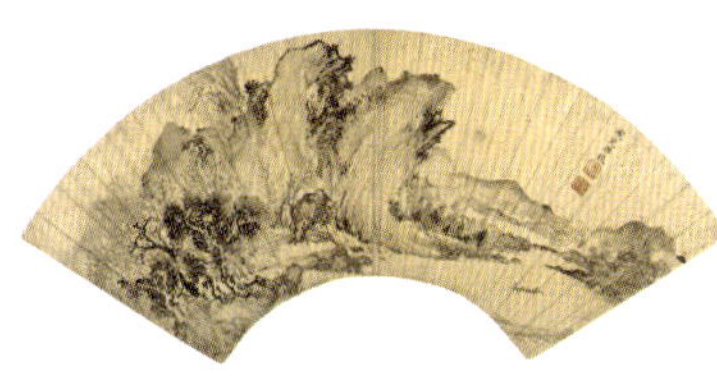

Fan remounted as an album leaf: ink on gold paper; 22.2 × 48.9 cm (8 ¾ × 19 ¼ inches); Santa Barbara Museum of Art, Anonymous gift, 1992.82.3

SIGNATURE OF THE ARTIST
Maoyuan Sun Zhi 茂苑孫枝.

SEALS: *Sun Hualin* 孫華林, *Zhao xing* 兆行.

CAT. NO. 7

YUAN SHANGTONG 袁尚統
1590–1666 or later
Landscape 石壁秋林圖, 1638

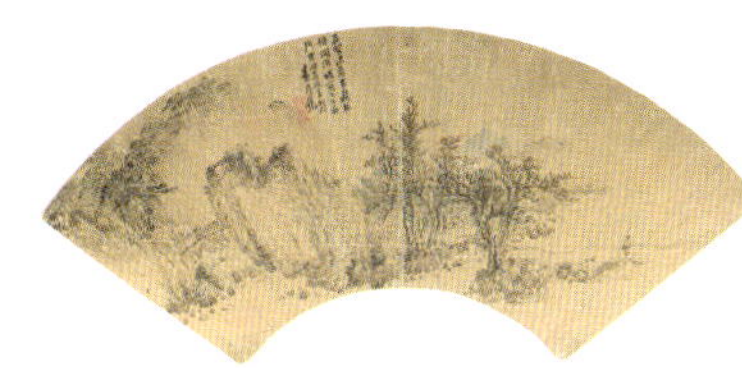

Fan remounted as an album leaf: ink and color on gold paper; 22.2 × 48.9 cm (8 ¾ × 19 ¼ inches); Santa Barbara Museum of Art, Anonymous gift, 1992.82.1

INSCRIPTION BY THE ARTIST
Stone cliff—flowing stream is ancient;
Autumn grove—shuttered house is deep.
On a summer day in the *wuyin* year [1638], painted and inscribed for my elder in poetry, Longji. [Signed] Yuan Shangtong.

石壁流泉古，秋林掩閣深．戊寅夏日為隆吉詞兄畫並題．袁尚統.

SEAL: *Shangtong* 尚統.

CAT. NO. 8

DONG QICHANG 董其昌 1555–1636
Contemplating the Dao with Emotions Cleansed 澄懷觀道圖, c. 1610

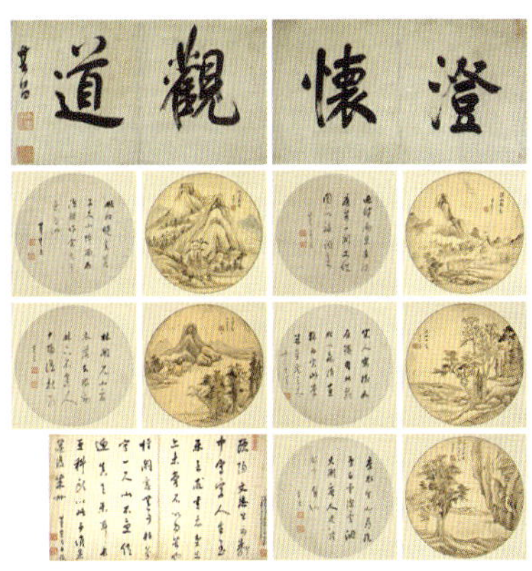

Album of sixteen leaves consisting of five circular paintings in ink and color on gold paper and five corresponding inscriptions on plain paper, frontispiece, and inscription by the artist; 40.1 × 38.1 cm (17 ¾ × 15 inches) each; Private collection

FRONTISPIECE BY THE ARTIST
Contemplating the Dao with Emotions Cleansed 《澄懷觀道》.

SEALS: *Xuanshang zhai* 玄賞齋, *Taishi shi* 太史氏, *Dong Xuanzai Shi* 董玄宰氏.

Leaf 1
Streams and Mountains in Rain. [Signed] Xuanzai [Dong Qichang].

溪山雨色. 玄宰.

SEAL: *Dong Qichang yin* 董其昌印.

Leaf 1a
At Yan Ford, according to thoughts in the rain, I composed a lyric to the tune of "Manting fang" [Fragrance filling the hall]. Furthermore, I painted this to supplement the meaning of the lyric. [Signed] Dong Qichang.

延津雨思, 有滿庭芳一闋. 又作圖以補詞意. 董其昌.

SEALS: *Taishi shi* 太史氏, *Dong Xuanzai* 董玄宰.

Leaf 2
Solitary Temple among Misty Peaks. [Signed] Xuanzai.

煙嵐蕭寺. 玄宰.

SEAL: *Dong Qichang yin* 董其昌印.

Leaf 2a
Morning View of Yao River, a small composition Huang Zijiu [Huang Gongwang] painted for Deju. I painted this after Huang's idea.[1] [Signed] Dong Qichang.

姚江曉色, 黃子久小幛面爲德矩作. 余本其意爲此. 董其昌.

SEALS: *Taishi shi* 太史氏, *Dong Xuanzai* 董玄宰.

Leaf 3
Autumn Grove, Level Distance. [Signed] Xuanzai.

秋林平遠. 玄宰.

SEAL: *Dong Qichang yin* 董其昌印.

Leaf 3a
Song painters painted trees as twisted iron. Starting from Beiyuan [Dong Yuan], lush tips and straight trunks became the mainstream. This is the difference between Li Cheng and Dong Yuan. [Signed] Xuanzai.

宋人寫樹如屈鐵, 自北苑始以森梢直榦爲宗, 此李成董元之分也. 玄宰.

SEAL: *Taishi shi* 太史氏.

Leaf 4
Xuanzai sketches the brush ideas of Yuan.

玄宰寫元人筆意.

SEAL: *Dong Qichang yin* 董其昌印.

Leaf 4a
Trees part, revealing the height
 of mountains;
Leaves fall and the strength of wind
 is noticed.
In the forest grove, no sign of people;
The setting sun lightly casts the
 autumn shadows.
[Signed] Qichang.

林開見山高, 木落知風勁. 林下不逢人, 夕陽澹秋影. 其昌.

SEALS: *Taishi shi* 太史氏, *Dong Xuanzai* 董玄宰.

Leaf 5
When you walk among the cliffs, then you will understand this painting. [Signed] Xuanzai.

行懸崖絕壑間, 當知有此畫. 玄宰.

SEAL: *Dong Qichang yin* 董其昌印.

Leaf 5a
Crossing the water, gazing at mountains,
 I search for steep cliffs;
Deep amid white clouds, an unearthly
 scene is revealed.
This Tang couplet is "painting in poetry."[2]
[Signed] Qichang.

度水望山尋絕壁, 白雲深處洞天開. 唐人此語詩中畫也. 其昌.

SEAL: *Taishi shi* 太史氏, *Dong Xuanzai* 董玄宰.

INSCRIPTION BY THE ARTIST
Ouyang Wenzhong [Ouyang Xiu] said, "To be in a state of calm and write calligraphy is the utmost pleasure of life." As for pursuing the goals of calligraphy from the dust [of the world], has this not always been a kind of suffering? Idle by a window and without matters of concern, grasping a brush to sketch a foot-long mountain, free from any kind of outside pressure—that is true pleasure! On a long summer day and hatless, I engage in these matters to dispel the heat and compose this album. Dong Qichang inscribes.

歐陽文忠公云, 靜中寫字, 人生至樂. 至求書志坌出, 亦未嘗不以爲苦也. 惟閑窓無事, 拈筆寫一尺山, 不受促迫, 眞是樂耳. 長夏科頭, 以此事消暑, 遂復成册. 董其昌自題.

SEAL: *Taishi shi* 太史氏; *Dong Qichang yin* 董其昌印; *Xuanshang zhai* 玄賞齋.

ADDITIONAL DOCUMENTATION: Inscription by Liang Zhangju 梁章鉅 (1775–1849), dated 1846, with seal: *Tui'an shending* 退庵審定.

ALBUM COVER
The album was part of Yan Shiqing's 顏世清 (1873–1929) Hanmu Tang 寒木堂 collection and was presented to a diplomat named Longfeng 龍峰 (unidentified) in 1923.

NOTES
1 Wang Hui painted a leaf after the same Huang Gongwang painting in his album *Tuhui ce* (National Palace Museum, Taipei), but there is little compositional resemblance with Dong's album leaf. See *Gugong shuhua tulu*, vol. 23, 368.

2 From the poem "Ti Hexi Qiandong" 題合溪乾洞 by Yu Hu 于鵠 (act. c. 780). *Wenyuan yinghua* 文苑英華 (*Siku quanshu* ed.), 161: 6a. Dong Qichang changes the third character *pang* 旁 (next to) to *wang* 望 (gazing).

CAT. NO. 9

DONG QICHANG 董其昌 1555–1636
Landscape Evoking a Poem by Wang Wei
右丞詩意圖, 1626

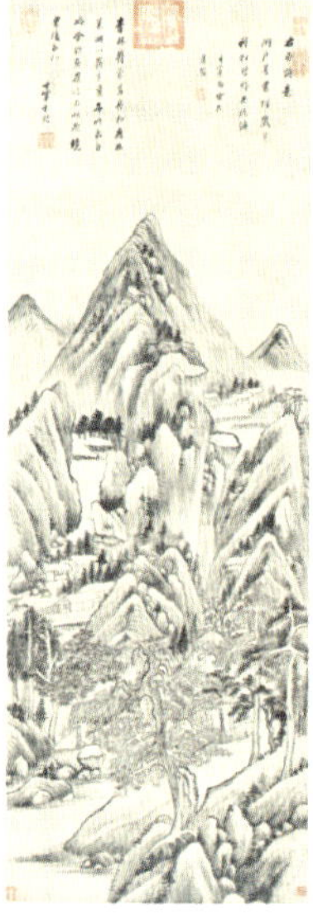

Hanging scroll: ink on paper;
141.6 × 47.9 cm (55 ¾ × 18 ⅞ inches);
Private collection

INSCRIPTIONS BY THE ARTIST
Evoking Youcheng's poetic idea:
Behind the closed door [I] have written
 books for months and years.
Pines planted long ago have all grown old
 with dragon scales.[1]
Xuanzai [Dong Qichang] painted in the sixth month of the *bingyin* year [1626].

《右丞詩意》. 閉戶著書經歲月, 種松皆作老龍鱗. 玄宰丙寅六月畫.

SEAL: *Chang* 昌.

Green trees grow in thick profusion;
Tall pines surge above the trees.
In a place like this, the paths of Mr. Jiang,
Are beautiful even without bamboo.
This is an inscription that I inscribed on a painting in the past. Its meaning is similar to this painting. Xuanzai inscribes again.[2]

青林鬱蒙茸, 長松度林表.
所以蔣生逕, 無竹亦自好.
余題畫舊作, 與此圖境界復相似.
玄宰重題.

SEAL: *Dong shi Xuanzai* 董氏玄宰.

ADDITIONAL SEALS: *Shiqu baoji* 石渠寶笈, *Yushufang jiancang bao* 御書房鑑藏寶, *Qianlong yulan zhi bao* 乾隆御覽之寶 (Emperor Qianlong, r. 1735–1796); *Jiaqing yulan zhi bao* 嘉慶御覽之寶 (Emperor Jiaqing, r. 1796–1820); *Xianxian Ji shi zhencang* 獻縣紀氏珍藏 (Ji Yun 紀昀, 1724–1805); *Zheng'an shending* 正闇審定 (Deng Bangshou 鄧邦述, 1868–1939).

NOTES
1 Wang Wei, "Chunri yu Pei Di guo Xinchang li fang Lü yiren buyu" 春日與裴廸過新昌里訪呂逸人不遇, *Wang Youcheng ji jianzhu* 王右丞集箋注 (*Siku quanshu* ed.), 10:22b–23a.
2 Translation after Liu Heping, in Richard Barnhart, et al., *The Jade Studio*, 114.

CAT. NO. 10

LI RIHUA 李日華 1565–1635
Lotus 荷花圖軸

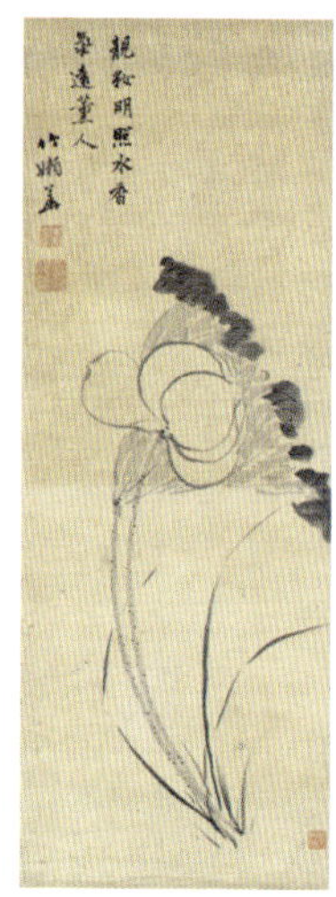

Hanging scroll: ink on satin;
70.5 × 26 cm (27 ¾ × 10 ¼ inches);
Private collection

INSCRIPTION BY THE ARTIST
The beautiful lady's appearance reflects on the water clearly; her fragrance scents people from afar. [Signed] Painted by Zhulai.

靚粧明照水, 香氣遠薰人. 竹嬾畫.

SEAL: *Rihua* 日華.

CAT. NO. 11

CHEN JIRU 陳繼儒 1558–1639

Thatched Hut by Tall Pines 長松草堂圖

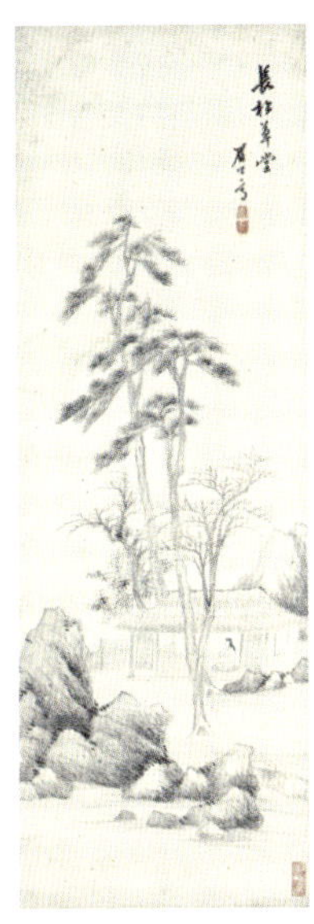

Hanging scroll: ink on paper;
91.4 × 30.8 cm (36 × 12 ⅛ inches);
Santa Barbara Museum of Art,
Gift of N. P. Wong family, 1995.63.4

TITLE AND SIGNATURE BY THE ARTIST

Thatched Hut by Tall Pines,
sketched by Meigong.

長松草堂，眉公寫.

SEALS: *Meigong* 眉公, *Yi furu* 一腐儒.

ADDITIONAL SEAL: *Shanghai Xu Weiren shoucang yin* 上海徐渭仁收藏印 (Xu Weiren 徐渭仁, d. 1853).

CAT. NO. 12

CHEN JIRU 陳繼儒 1558–1639

Zhang Heng's "Returning to the Field"
張衡《歸田賦》

Calligraphy in semi-cursive script

Album of sixteen leaves: ink on paper;
23.2 × 11.8 cm (9 ⅛ × 4 ⅝ inches) each;
Private collection

TRANSCRIPTION AND INSCRIPTION BY THE ARTIST

In the city I have lingered for a long while,
Without wise strategies to assist the times.
To no avail I look out over the stream and admire the fish,
Waiting in vain for the river to run clear.
I am moved by the fervor of Cai Ze,
Whose doubts Master Tang resolved.[1]
The profound ways of Heaven are unfathomable;
I shall emulate the fisherman by sharing his joys.
And surpass the dust of the world through distance and time,
I bid a final farewell to worldly affairs.

On a typical mid-spring day,
When the weather is fine and the air clear.
Highlands and lowlands are burgeoning,
All the plants luxuriant.
The king osprey drums its wings,
The oriole wails mournfully.
With necks entwined they fly up and down,
Guan, guan, ying ying [chirp-chirp, twitter-twitter].
Among such I roam,
For the pleasure it gives me.
Like a dragon chanting in the great marsh,
A tiger roaring in the mountain.
Gazing up, I release the thin silk bow thread,
Looking down, I fish in the ever-flowing stream.
Colliding with the arrow and killed,
Greedy for the bait and caught by the hook.
The loitering bird drops from the clouds;
The shark fish dangles then sinks in the depths.
Meanwhile, the bright sun inclines to the west,
Followed by the charioteer of the moon.
Entranced by the supreme pleasure of wandering,
Even though the sun is setting, I forget my weariness.
I take to heart the admonition handed down by Laozi,
And desire to quickly return to my thatched cottage.
I pluck the five-stringed zither with my deft fingers,
And recite the works of the Duke of Zhou and Confucius.
I brandish brush and ink to invoke elegance,
Expounding upon the models of the Three Emperors.
If I indulge my heart beyond this realm,
Where would I recognize the semblance of honor and disgrace?[2]

This is Zhang Heng's "Returning to the Field." Having served at official posts for forty years without being honored, Zhang Heng was moved to compose this piece. My hometown is in the Nine Peaks region, where I have had four structures built. Day after day, I entertain myself together with two or three intimate recluses or monks, whiling away the entire day then starting all over again. Under these circumstances, I truly know nothing about honor or disgrace, and in this regard I am far better than Zhang Heng.[3] Recently, I bought a few more houses in Beiqian. Not far from the city, one could say it is half urban, half rural. When I have free time I amuse myself by boating along the lake, just like the stories of Tao Nancun [Tao Zongyi] and Cao Yunqi [Cao Zhibo]. After returning home, I see a tall tree, clear stream, and flowers and bamboo enclosing my dwelling. On the earthen wall framing the door hangs a couplet: "The pool bending in half resembles the crescent moon; A pair of embracing trees form a gateway." This couplet is a true portrayal of the scene of my residence. On the twentieth day of the eighth month, Zhang Shiqing and I returned together from Zuili [Jiaxing, Zhejiang Province]. He has painted "Thatched Hut" for me. In return, I transcribe Zhang Heng's "Returning to the Field." As I write, Yu Bocheng from Zuili, Zhou Gongmei from Wujiang, the poet monks Qiutan and Lianru and others are present.[4] Mei Daoren [Chen Jiru] records.

遊都邑以永久，無明略以佐時.
徒臨川以羨魚，俟河清乎未期.
感蔡子之慷慨，從唐生以決疑.
諒天道之微昧，追漁父以同嬉.
超塵埃以遐逝，與世事乎長辭.

於是仲春月令，時和氣清，原隰鬱茂，
百草滋榮.
王雎鼓翼，鶬鶊哀鳴，交頸頡頏，關關嚶嚶.
於焉逍遙，聊以娛情.

尔乃龍虎嘯吟，方澤山丘.
仰飛纖繳，俯釣長流. 觸矢而斃，貪餌吞鉤.
落雲間之逸禽，懸淵鯊沉之鰡.
于時曜靈俄景，繼以望舒. 極盤遊之至樂，
雖日夕而忘劬.
感老氏之遺誡，將迴駕乎蓬廬. 彈五絃之妙指，詠周，孔之圖書. 揮墨以奮藻，陳三皇之軌模. 苟縱心於域外，榮辱安知之所如.

此張衡《歸田賦》也. 衡游四十不遇，故感而有作. 吾郡九峰，余卜築有四，日與二三隱叟高僧徜徉往返，周而復始，眞不知榮辱之所如，勝於張衡多也. 近復得數椽于北錢，去城不遠，可稱半村半郭，暇則放舟泖濵，一如陶南村曹雲栖故事. 歸則偉木淸流，花竹回匝. 衡門土壁，門榜一聯云："曲池剛半偏多月，老樹成雙便設門." 盖實境也，時仲秋二十日，同張世卿歸自醉李，爲余作《草堂圖》，余書《歸田賦》酬之. 在坐者醉李郁伯承，吳江周公美，詩衲秋潭，蓮儒二公也. 眉道人又記.

SEALS: *Meigong* 眉公, *Chen Jiru yin* 陳繼儒印.

NOTES

1 Cai Ze 蔡澤 of the Warring States period only began a successful official career after hearing from the physiognomist Tang Ju 唐舉 that he would live another forty-three years.

2 Translation after those of James Hightower and Liu Wu-chi. See Hightower, "The *Fu* of T'ao Ch'ien," 90–92; and Liu, *An Introduction to Chinese Literature*, 54.

3 Zhang Heng pursued an official post and returned to the fields after not obtaining one. In contrast, Chen Jiru was famous for making a public demonstration of burning his scholar's robes and not pursuing an official career.

4 Qiutan was a monk poet and important figure in the social group portrayed by Xiang Shengmo in his *Venerable Friends* (1652). Lianru's courtesy name was Baishishan nazi 白石山衲子. Zhang Shiqing, Yu Bocheng and Zhou Gongmei are unidentified.

CAT. NO. 13

ZHAO ZUO 趙左 c. 1570s–1633 or later
Streams and Mountains without End 溪山無盡圖卷, 1616

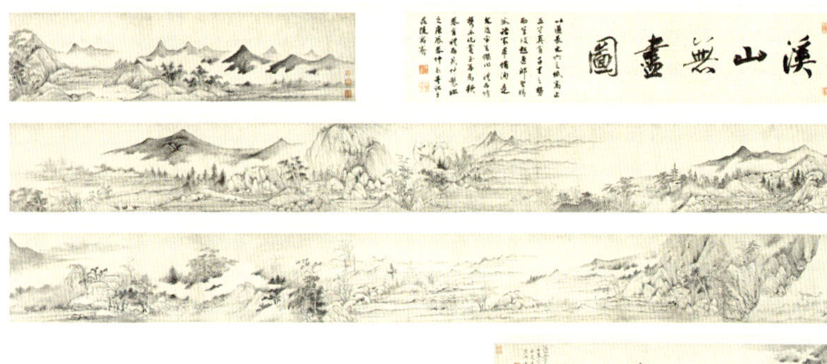

Handscroll: ink on paper; 19.1 × 515 cm (7 ½ × 202 ¾ inches); Private collection

FRONTISPIECE
By Wang Gong: *Streams and Mountains without End* 《溪山無盡圖》, with an inscription dated 1820.

SEALS: *Wang Gong zhiyin* 汪恭之印, *Zhuping jushi* 竹坪居士, *Kuangran tianzhen* 曠然天真.

INSCRIPTION BY THE ARTIST
Streams and Mountains without End. Painted in the sixth month of the *bingchen* year [1616], escaping summer heat at the Hut of Vegetable Fragrance. [Signed] Zhao Zuo.

《溪山無盡圖》. 丙辰六月避暑菜香庵寫此. 趙左.

SEALS: *Zhao Zuo* 趙左, *Wendu* 文度.

ADDITIONAL SEALS: *Lan po jing yan* 蘭坡經眼, *Jin Chuansheng* 金傳聲 (Jin Chuansheng, mid-nineteenth–early twentieth century); *Xuzhai jianzang* 虛齋鑑藏, *Laichen xinshang* 萊臣心賞, *Xuzhai shending* 虛齋審定, *Pang Laichen zhenshang yin* 龐萊臣珍賞印 (Pang Yuanqi 龐元濟, 1864–1949); *Dongpu zhenshang* 東圃珍賞, *Weixian zhuren shuhua zhang* 味閒主人書畫章.

CAT. NO. 14

XUE WU 薛五 c. 1564–c. 1637
Wild Orchids 蘭石圖卷, 1601

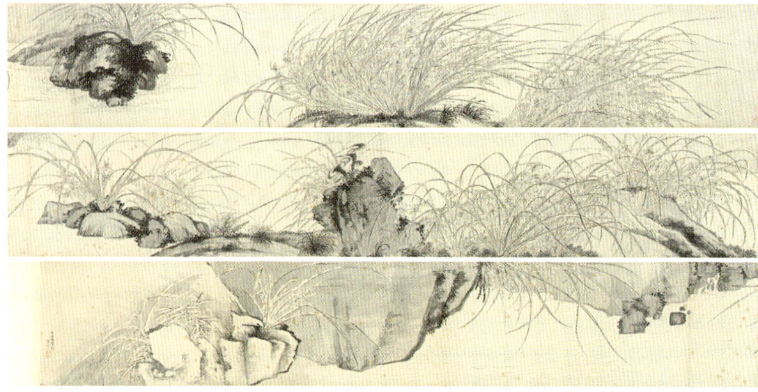

Handscroll: ink on paper; 32.1 × 594.4 cm (12 ⅝ × 234 inches); Honolulu Museum of Art, Purchase 1952 (1667.1)

SIGNATURE OF THE ARTIST
First [lunar] month of spring, *xinchou* year [1601], sketched by Xue Susu.

辛丑春正月寫 薛素素.

SEAL: *Xue yin* 薛印.

ADDITIONAL SEALS: *Zheng'an shending* 正闇審定, *Zheng'an shoucang* 正闇收藏 (Deng Bangshu 鄧邦述, 1868–1939).

CAT. NO. 15

SHAO MI 邵彌 c. 1595–1642
Paintings in the Styles of Earlier Masters with Accompanying Poems of the Yuan Dynasty
倣宋元八家山水詩冊

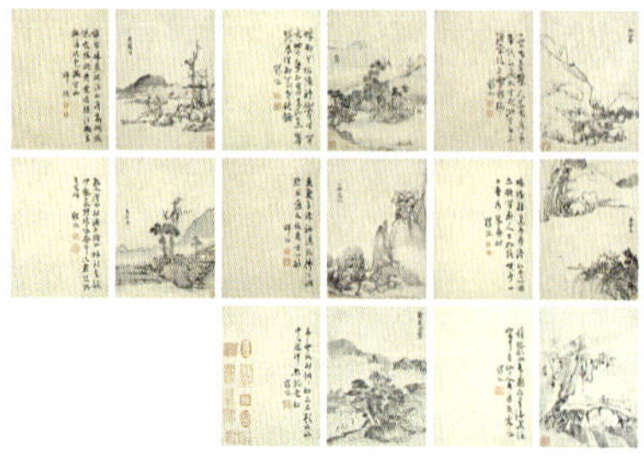

Album of eight leaves of painting and eight leaves of calligraphy: ink or ink and color on paper; 24.1 × 17.5 cm (9 ½ × 6 ⅞ inches) each; Private collection

INSCRIPTIONS BY THE ARTIST

Leaf 1
[Titled] Hongguzi 洪谷子 [Master of the Broad Valley, Jing Hao]

SEAL: *Baihua xuan zi* 白花玄子.

Leaf 1a
A window full of flower fragrance striking the clothes of men,
Inside the window, fragrant pollen has not flown away.
Long seated by the inkstone pool, where rain-flower stones appear,
The snow on crabapple branches is already sparse.[1]
[Signed] Shao Mi.

一窗花氣襲人衣, 窗底芳塵煖不飛.
久坐硯池生雨石, 海棠枝上雪都稀.
邵彌.

SEALS: *Shao Mi zhi yin* 邵彌之印, *zi Seng Mi* 字僧彌.

Leaf 2
[Titled] Sun Wei 孫位

SEAL: *Seng Mi shi* 僧彌氏.

Leaf 2a
South of the city none of the trees recognizes [me] the divine immortal,
Who leisurely has been coming and going for forty years.
On the west shore blue mountains, on the east shore a pagoda;
On whose behalf are they facing each other in the aged autumn mist?[2]
[Signed] Shao Mi.

城南無樹識神仙, 閒往閒來四十年.
西岸青山東岸塔, 為誰相對老秋烟.
邵彌.

SEALS: *Shao Mi zhi yin* 邵彌之印, *Seng Mi* 僧彌.

Leaf 3
[Titled] Huanxiazi 幻霞子 [Master of Illusory Mists, Ni Zan]

SEAL: *Gua shou* 瓜疇.

Leaf 3a
Whose home is in the woods near the bay of the stream,
Where tall trees mix full and sparse in the day's setting light?
[Now] their yellow leaves all gone with the rain and the stream,
Only the remaining autumn colors fill the remote mountains.[3]
[Signed] Shao Mi.

誰家林麓近溪灣, 高樹扶疏落照間.
黃葉盡隨溪雨去, 秖餘秋色滿空山.
邵彌.

SEALS: *Seng Mi* 僧彌, *Zhong se gua* 種色瓜.

Leaf 4
[Titled] Wu Zhonggui 吳仲圭 [Wu Zhen]

SEAL: *Seng Mi* 僧彌.

Leaf 4a
Rising sun over the cove, [the boatmen] pushes the boat toward Youyue Bay,
Do not casually make assessments on leisure,
The secluded man can be without worries,
On a single day, he has seen whole ranges of mountains.[4]
[Signed] Shao Mi.

暘塢推蓬又月灣, 不令心目品題閑.
幽人出入能無事, 一日曾看幾遍山.
邵彌.

SEALS: *Shao Mi zhi yin* 邵彌之印, *Zhong se gua* 種色瓜.

Leaf 5
[Titled] Yifeng daoren 一峰道人 [Daoist of the Single Peak, Huang Gongwang]

SEAL: *Seng Mi* 僧彌.

Leaf 5a
Refreshing air playing over garment and sleeves,
A clear breeze lightly touches the zither strings.
A carefree manner suits naturalness,
Casually seated, my heart is at ease.[5]
[Signed] Shao Mi.

爽氣在襟袖, 清風拂絲桐.
悠然適天趣, 晏坐心融融.
邵彌.

SEALS: *Shao Mi zhi yin* 邵彌之印, *Seng Mi* 僧彌.

Leaf 6
[Titled] Ma Fufeng 馬扶風 [Ma Wan]

SEAL: *Seng Mi* 僧彌.

Leaf 6a
The wanderer bathes his feet in the
Milky Way;
The Yue Maiden combs her hair in the
bronze mirror.
I wish to open the curtains and approach
the Southern Dipper,
So that [I can look toward] the mystic
islands in the green sea accompanying
the sky.[6]
[Signed] Shao Mi.

遊人濯足銀潢上，越女梳頭青鏡中.
我欲張帳逼南斗，扶桑碧海與天同.
邵彌.

SEALS: *Zi Seng Mi* 字僧彌, *Shibiao zhi jiao* 世表之交.

Leaf 7
[Titled] Jing Hao 荊浩

SEAL: *Shao Mi zhi yin* 邵彌之印.

Leaf 7a
A long cliff like a covered corridor,
Below a flowing spring pouring down.
Amidst the mountains ancient immortals,
Who pace the moon and wander
to and fro.[7]
[Signed] Shao Mi.

脩巖如長廊，下有流泉注.
山中古仙人，步月自來去.
邵彌.

SEAL: *Zi Seng Mi* 字僧彌.

Leaf 8
[Titled] Huangheshan qiao 黃鶴山樵
[Woodcutter of Yellow Crane Mountain,
Wang Meng]

SEAL: *Zhong se gua* 種色瓜.

Leaf 8a
Deep blue clouds beyond mountains,
Brightly glistening: stones below pines.
Look at these people living
in the mountains,
Whose elegant demeanor reflects the
pines' color.[8]
[Signed] Shao Mi.

青青雲外山，炯炯松下石.
顧此山中人，風神照色松.
邵彌.

SEAL: *Shao Mi si yin* 邵彌私印.

ADDITIONAL SEALS: *Jin hou xinshang* 緝侯心賞, *Jin hou zhencang* 緝侯珍藏, *Anwu Zhu Rongjue zi Jinghou suocang shuhua* 安吳朱榮爵字靖侯所藏書畫, *Liangxi xuan* 兩溪軒, *Xixian tang* 習賢堂 (Zhu Rongjue 朱榮爵, nineteenth century); *Baizhu shanren du hua* 白紵山人讀畫; *Zi zun bao zhi* 子孫寶之 (Shen Yuyuan 沈玉垣, Qing dynasty); *Zhou Menggong mi ji yin* 周夢公秘笈印 (Zhou Qingyun 周慶雲, 1864–1933); *Xiangyin Li shi Daishiyuan cang* 湘陰李氏待石園藏 (Li Heng 李桓, 1827–1891); *Ji mei jian shang* 季眉鑒賞 (Wang Chuantao 王傳燾, 1903–1978); *Yu'an xinshang* 禺盦心賞 (He Yu'an 何禺盦); *Qifeng* 七峯.

Album label by Yuan Kewen 袁克文 (1890–1931) dated 1915.

NOTES

1 Chen Lü 陳旅, "Fu ning chun xiao yin" 賦凝春小隱, *Anyatang ji* 安雅堂集 (*Siku quanshu* ed.), 1:10b. Shao Mi reversed the order of Chen's *shiyu* 石雨 to *yushi* 雨石, possibly working from a variant text. *Yushi* can refer to a type of stone with mottled pattern prized by collectors. All translations are by the author.

2 He Zhong 何中, "Yuzhang deng zhou zuo" 豫章登舟作, *Zhifeitang gao* 知非堂稿 (*Siku quanshu* ed.), 6:16a.

3 Chen Lü, "Ti Gao shi suo cang hua tu er shou" 題高氏所藏畫圖二首, *Anyatang ji*, 1:13b–14a. Shao Mi's transcription is a variant of Chen's poem as recorded in the *Siku quanshu*. Shao also added the character *shan* 山 by mistake in the first line. He signaled his mistake with a small dot to the right.

4 Author unknown.

5 Zhao Mengfu 趙孟頫, "Ti Zhou xiucai ci shan tang" 題周秀才此山堂, *Songxuezhai ji* 松雪齋集 (*Siku quanshu* ed.), 5:17a–b. This is the second half of Zhao Mengfu's poem.

6 Second half of the poem "Yue shang" 越上 by Li Xiaoguang, recorded in *Yuan yin* 元音 (*Siku quanshu* ed.), 9:24a. In the last two lines, some of Shao's characters differ from the *Siku* version, which reads, "I wish to set sail and ascend to the Southern Dipper, / So that [I could look toward] the mystic islands in the green sea and communicate with the sky."

7 Zhao Mengfu, "Changlang yan" 長廊岩, *Songxuezhai ji*, 5:12b.

8 This is the first half of Zhao Mengfu's poem "Ti Zhou xiucai ci shan tang." See note 5. Shao corrected one character in the last line of the poem by placing a dot next to it and reversed the last two characters of the *Siku* version of this poem.

CAT. NO. 16

LI YIN 李因 c. 1611–1685

Flowers of the Four Seasons 四季花卉圖卷, 1649

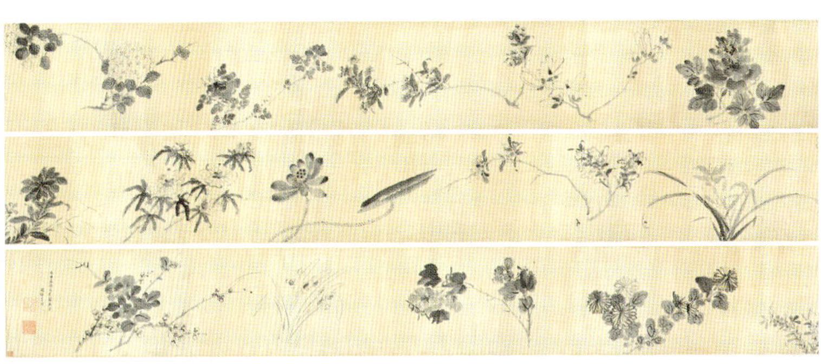

Handscroll: ink on satin; 25.4 × 581 cm (10 × 228 ¾ inches); Honolulu Museum of Art, Partial gift of Mr. and Mrs. Mitchell Hutchinson, 1994 (7855.1)

FRONTISPIECE
By Huang Junshi (b. 1934): Leftover Tones of Baiyang. [Signed] *Junshi*. 白陽遺韵. 君實.

SEAL: *Huang shi Junshi* 黃君實氏.

INSCRIPTION BY THE ARTIST
Sketched in the Hall of Remaining Swallows in the first month of autumn in the *xinchou* year [1649], Li Yin of Qiantang.

己丑孟秋寫於留燕堂，錢塘李因.

SEALS: *Li Yin zhi yin* 李因之印, *Jinsheng shi* 今生氏.

Additional undated inscription and seals by Huang Junshi.

CAT. NO. 17

SHEN SHICHONG 沈士充 act. c. 1607–after 1640

Landscape 山水長卷, 1631

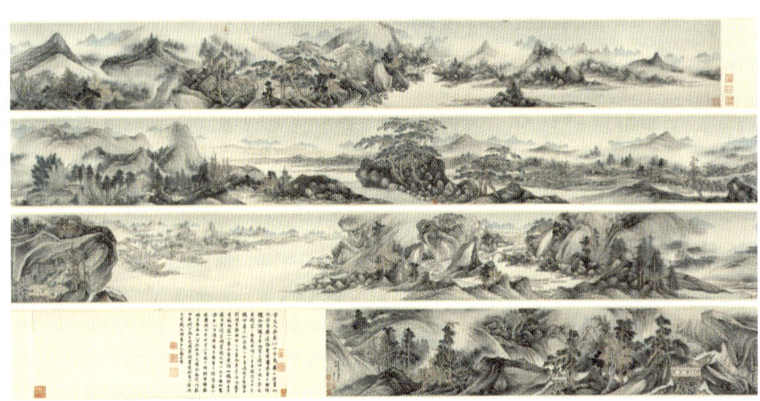

Handscroll: ink and color on paper; 21.9 × 692.2 cm (8 ⅝ × 272 ½ inches); Private collection

INSCRIPTION BY THE ARTIST
Spring of the *xinwei* year [1631], I painted this at Red Plantains Mansion. [Signed] Shen Shichong.

辛未春日寫于紅蕉館，沈士充.

SEALS: *Ziju* 子居, *Shichong* 士充.

ADDITIONAL SEALS: *Keyi yong ri* 可以永日, *Jiangcun sanshi nian jingli suo ju* 江邨三十年精力所聚, *Qingyintang miji yin* 清吟堂秘笈印, *Zhu chuang* 竹窗, *Mao song qingquan chen suo xu ye* 茂松清泉臣所須也, *Gao Zhanshi* 高詹事, *Jiangcun Shiqi zhi zhang* 江村士奇之章, *bu yi san gong yi ci ri* 不以三公易此日 (Gao Shiqi 高士奇, 1645–1704); *Cunzhai yanfu* 存齋眼福, *Lingnan dongdao binbei shizhe* 嶺南東道兵備使者, *Cunzhai you cheng Qianyuan* 存齋又稱潛園, *Qianyuan shuhua zhi yin* 潛園書畫之印 (Lu Xinyuan 陸心源, 1834–1894); *Shutong guoyan* 叔同過眼, *Gui'an Lu Shusheng kao cang jinshi shuhua yin* 歸安陸樹聲考藏金石書畫印 (Lu Shusheng 陸樹聲, act. late nineteenth century).

ADDITIONAL INSCRIPTION
By Gao Shiqi, dated 1702, in which he comments at length on the painting and mentions that he just had it remounted.

CAT. NO. 18

YANG WENCONG 楊文驄 1597–1646
Cloudy Valley 雲壑圖

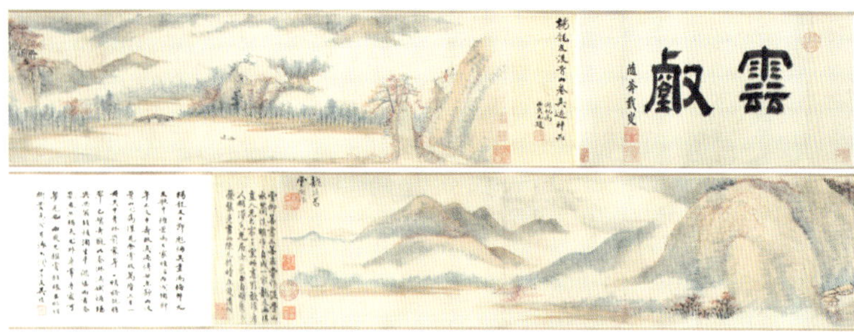

Handscroll: ink and color on paper; 23.5 × 195.3 cm (9 ¼ × 76 ⅞ inches); Private collection

FRONTISPIECE
By Wang Zhuan 王撰 (1623–1709): *Cloudy Valley*. [Signed] Suian diesou.

《雲壑》. 隨菴戴叟.

SEALS: *Jiangshou bu cuotuo* 將壽補蹉跎, *Suian laoren* 隨菴老人.

INSCRIPTION BY THE ARTIST
Made for Yunqing by Longyou [Yang Wencong].

龍友爲雲卿作.

SEAL: *Yang Wencong yin* 楊文驄印.

ADDITIONAL INSCRIPTION
Yunqing excelled not only in calligraphy but also painting. In the past he painted boneless-style landscapes. Simple, light, clear, and bright, he established his own style. Longyou's painting style directly entered the chamber of the Yuan masters, [though] in this painting he modeled himself after the style of the Tang painters and rather captured Dong Qichang's idea. It truly is outstandingly refined and adorable. Having finished mounting the painting I wrote this. [Signed] Chen Yuanlong at the Shuangqing Pavilion.

雲卿善書亦善畫, 嘗作沒骨山水, 簡淡明净, 自成一家. 龍友畫法直入元大家之室. 此卷欲效法唐人, 略得香光居士意, 正自明秀可愛, 裝竟書此. 陳元龍時在雙清閣.

SEAL: *Shuangqingge jianshang* 雙清閣鑒賞.

ADDITIONAL INSCRIPTIONS
By Wu Hufan 吳湖帆 (1894–1968), the second dated 1954. Wu identifies the owner of the painting as Xishuang 西爽 (Huang Xishuang 黃西爽, 1906–1967). In the second, longer inscription, Wu comments on the scarcity of Yang Wencong's paintings and remarks that this is the sole example he had seen of Yang's work in the boneless style.

ADDITIONAL SEALS: *Zhongmiaoting xinshang* 眾妙亭欣賞, *Su-Huang-Mi zhai* 蘇黃米齋 (Zhao Weiqing 趙渭卿, nineteenth–twentieth century); *Jianbai moyuan* 堅白墨緣 (Wu Changshuo 吳昌碩, 1844–1927); *Jingjiang guo mu* 靜江過目 (Zhang Renjie 張人傑, 1877–1950); *Hufan jianshang* 湖帆鑒賞, *Wu Qian siyin* 吳倩私印, *Wu Hufan yin* 吳湖颿印 (Wu Hufan); *Kean zhencang* 可菴珍藏, *Cheng Bofen tushu ji* 程伯奮圖書記, *Shuang-Song lou* 雙宋樓 (Cheng Qi 程琦, 1911–2002).

CAT. NO. 19

YANG WENCONG 楊文驄 1597–1646
Water Village 水村圖, 1644

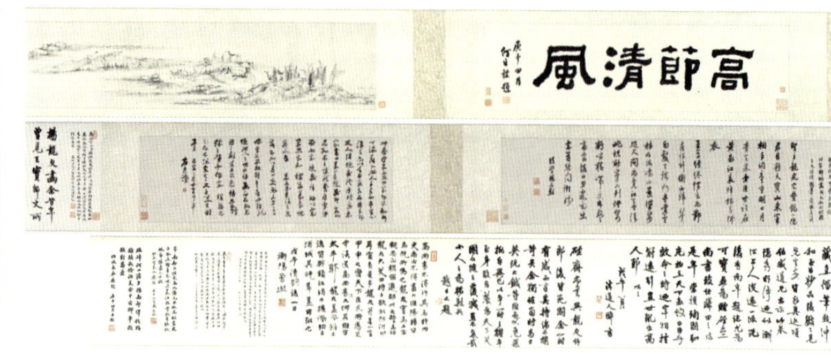

Handscroll: ink on paper; 24.8 × 199.4 cm (9 ¾ × 78 ½ inches); Private collection

FRONTISPIECE
By He Weipu 何維樸 (1844–1925): *Pure Winds of Lofty Character*. [Signed] In the fourth month of the *gengshen* year [1920], inscribed by He Weipu.

《高節清風》. 庚申四月何維樸題.

SEAL: *Weipu siyin* 維樸私印.

INSCRIPTION BY THE ARTIST
In the eleventh [lunar] month of the *jiashen* year [1644], beginning with the Hongguang reign, I painted this for the Grand Preceptor Master Keng utilizing the brush-ideas of Wenmin's *Water Village* and Zijiu's *Sand Marshes*.[1] For this reason I also present this poem:

Sage sovereign, dragon-like, soared to reside at Fenghao,
Of one heart and mind, lord and officials focused on the throne.
The prime minister from Shandong personally seasoned the soup;
Doubly bright, moon and sun illuminated the blue sky.
[But] senior officials sat and argued behind yellow-painted doors;
As the signal fires to the south went out, he shook his sleeves and left.[2]
With great respect and affection, I cherish Grand Secretary Gao;
By imperial grace, the Marquis of Ye can retire to Mount Heng.[3]
White hair unbound, attuned to Nature's mysteries:
He loves the cloudy forests and seaside mountain ranges.
This small scene delicately unfurls within the space of a foot;
So that together we can purely gaze at rivers and sky.
Under Zhurong Peak arrayed mists coil;
Crane calls, monkey howls—how many vales and mountains?
The house of Gao in later days will cherish its imperial bounties;
But to escape now in reclusion you must still ask the Lazy Scavenger.[4]
[Signed] Your follower in studies, Yang Wencong.

弘光改元, 甲申子月, 為硜翁師相畫, 用文敏水村圖, 子久沙磧圖筆意. 因系以詩.

聖主龍飛宅豐鎬, 一德君臣凝大寶.
山東宰相手調羹, 重明日月青天杲.
老臣坐論在黃扉, 江表烽銷遽拂衣.
至尊繾綣惜高尙, 鄴侯詔許衡山歸.
鬖鬖白髮天機妙, 愛賞雲林及海嶠.
小景婆娑咫尺間, 尙覺江天共清眺.
祝融峯下列煙鬟, 鶴嘯猿啼更幾盤.
高家後日思霖雨, 出處還須問懶殘.
後學楊文驄.

SEALS: *Yang Wencong* 楊文驄印, *Longyou shi* 龍友氏.

ADDITIONAL INSCRIPTIONS
By Gao Fenghan 高鳳翰 (1683–1749) dated 1746; Cheng Xuexun 程學恂 (1873–1951) dated 1918; Li Ruiqing 李瑞清 (1867–1920) dated 1918; Zeng Xi 曾熙 (1861–1930) dated 1918; Shijun 世駿 (unidentified, but a nephew of Cheng Xuexun) dated 1918; Zhu Yifan 朱益藩 (1861–1937) dated 1918; Wu Qingchi 吳慶坻 (1848–1924) dated 1920; Wu Shijian 吳士鑒 (1868–1934), dated 1920. At this time (1918–20), the painting was owned by Cheng Xuexun (referred in the various inscriptions by his sobriquet Bozang 伯臧).

ADDITIONAL SEALS (PARTIAL): *Song Luo* 宋犖, *Song Luo shending* 宋犖審定 (Song Luo, 1634–1713); *Gao Fenghan* 高鳳翰 (Gao Fenghan); *Yu'an moyuan* 甂闇墨緣, *Xinjian Cheng shi Beizhuang suocang shuhua jinshi zhi ji* 新建程氏北莊所藏書畫金石之記, *Yingshi lou* 影史樓 (Cheng Xuexun); *Meian zhuren* 梅盦主人, *Amei* 阿梅, *Qingdao ren* 清道人 (Li Ruiqing); *Laoran guan* 老髯觀 (Zeng Xi).

NOTES
1 The Hongguang reign was due to begin with the first month of the *yiyou* year (1645); Yang Wencong is anticipating the new beginning, announcing the new reign a couple of months early. Master Keng is Gao Hongtu,

the painting's recipient. Xiangshi 相師 (Grand Preceptor) was a term used in the Song dynasty and is here used to honor Gao's high court position. Wenmin is Zhao Mengfu. Zijiu is Huang Gongwang.

2 Fenghao was an early capital of the Zhou dynasty, southwest of present-day Xi'an (Shaanxi Province). Yang Wencong uses it here as an honorific way of describing the Southern Ming's new seat of power in Nanjing. The prime minister from Shandong refers to Gao Hongtu, who was a native of Jiaozhou (near Qingdao, Shandong Province). "Seasoning the soup" is a metaphor for good governance. "Doubly bright" (重明) puns the Ming dynasty. Yellow-painted doors refer to the halls of important court deliberations. To shake one's sleeves is a sign of frustration and action.

3 The Marquis of Ye refers to Li Mi, a notable scholar and official of the Tang dynasty who lived for twelve years as a recluse on Mount Heng in Hunan Province and was especially renowned for possessing an extensive personal library. It is unclear if Gao Hongtu had any specific plans to retire to the Mount Heng area. More likely, Yang Wencong was simply attracted to the model Li provided for Gao as a high-ranking official and learned scholar who retired (temporarily) for the hermit's life. The fact that Li returned to the court and attained his highest position late in his life makes the model especially apt, as it suggests that Gao's retirement, too, is temporary.

4 Zhurong is the tallest peak of Mount Heng. The Lazy Scavenger, Lancan, is a nickname given the Tang-dynasty monk Mingcan. Lancan, so named because he was lazy and content to eat whatever was left over, was a close friend of Li Mi.

CAT. NO. 20

XIANG SHENGMO 項聖謨 1597–1658

***Self-Portrait in Red Landscape* 朱色自畫像圖軸, 1644**

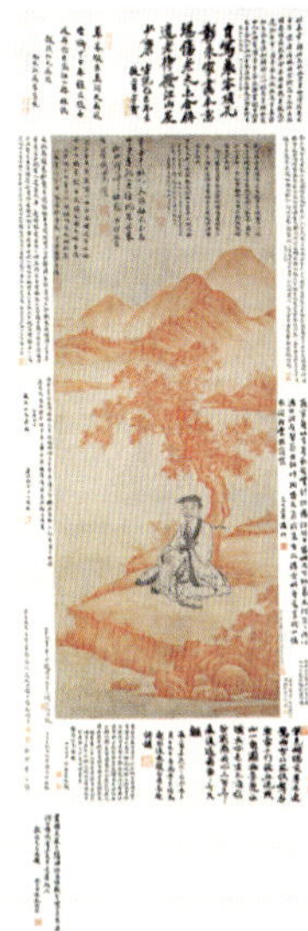

Hanging scroll: ink and color on paper; 151.4 × 56.7 cm (59 ⅝ × 22 ⅜ inches); Collection of Shitou Shuwu

INSCRIPTION BY THE ARTIST

Remnant waters, leftover mountains—color still cinnabar red;
Murky heavens, darkened earth—shadow of a trifling body.
A flame ignites in my crimson heart, and I daub the ocher red;
But from this dry brush only careless words—I am ashamed to paint pictures.
Men of mark are few and desolate; who is there to depict?
Valley clouds obscured in shadow—as if an ignorant fool.
In a change of heart, I laugh at my three "summons to the recluse";
Who would have believed that I was already one with the wild man?

Pure but gaunt visage, color dark and sallow,
Relies entirely on red pigment to make beard and eyebrows glow.
Because I am ashamed of my face, adornments are many;
Separately coloring my wispy figure, is that anything unusual?
Long lamenting the times, my spirit has diminished;
Before crying for the emperor, my energy had already lagged.
Though tear traces have been wiped away, grief remains;
Daily hoping for the ascent of peace, my thoughts become foolishly obsessed.

In the fourth month, *jiashen* year of the Chongzhen reign [1644], I learned of the catastrophe in the capital that took place on the nineteenth day of the third month. Sorrow and anger resulted in illness. Once recovered, I sketched my likeness in ink and then added the vermilion painting. My feelings are expressed in the poem to record the year and month. [Signed] The Official in the Wilds of Jiangnan, Xiang Shengmo, at the age of 48.

剩水殘山色尚朱，天昏地黑影微軀.
赤心餤起塗丹雘，渴筆言輕愧畫圖.
人物寥寥誰可貌，谷雲杳杳亦如愚.
翻然自笑三招隱，孰信狂夫早與俱.

一貌清臞色自黧，全憑赭粉映鬚眉.
因慚人面多容飾，別染煙姿豈好奇.
久為傷時神漸減，未經哭帝氣先垂.
啼痕雖拭憂如在，日望昇平想欲癡.

崇禎甲申四月聞京師三月十九日之變，悲憤成疾，既甦乃寫墨容，補以硃畫，情見乎詩以紀歲月. 江南在野臣項聖謨時年四十有八.

SEALS: *Yanyulou bian diao ao ke* 煙雨樓邊釣鰲客, *Cao zhuo zhi chen* 艸拙之臣, *Xiang Kongzhang shu shi hua* 項孔彰書詩畫.

ADDITIONAL INSCRIPTIONS

TAN ZHENMO 譚貞默 (1590–1665)

Spirit and manner of brush and ink [unite?] in great fate;
Amid the ashes of the plundering, he does not forget the *jiashen* year [1644].
A solitary figure appears from reclusion amidst the crimson forest;
Around the world, over mountains and rivers, cries the [mournful] cuckoo.
Younger brother Saomo eulogizes for elder brother in verse Yian [Xiang Shengmo].

筆墨丰神_大緣，刧灰不忘甲申年.
孤身隱現朱林裏,(天)地山河叫杜鵑.
弟埽默爲易菴 詞世兄贊.

SEALS: *Yao shan* 樂山, *Ran* 髯, *Tan Zhenmo yin* 鄭鼎默印.[1]

LI ZHAOHENG 李肇亨
(SEVENTEENTH CENTURY)

Master Xiang, progeny of illustrious officials,
His loyalty is thus doubly deep.
Moved by the times, his thoughts are of sleeve-shaking anger;
Mourning the emperor, daily he soaks his robes with tears.
Ink image records his grief and ire;
Red picture presents the sounds of his hymn.
Streams and mountains preserve his blood and character;
Grasses and trees mark his red heart.
The imperial surname still shines in glory,
So how can our divine land sink and perish?
Ardently he thinks of his royal presence;
In the imperial audience gladly writing admonitions.
Li Zhaoheng bows with clasped hands and inscribes.

項子名臣裔，忠懷一倍深.
感時思奮袂，慟帝每沾襟.
墨影留悲憤，朱圖矢頌音.
溪(山存)血性，草木著丹心.
國姓仍光大，神州豈(陸沉).
願言(當宁)者，宸扆好書箴.
李肇亨拜手題.

SEALS: *Li Zhaoheng yin* 李肇亨印, *Zuiou* 醉鷗.

ADDITIONAL INSCRIPTIONS ON THE MOUNTING

By Zheng Xiaoxu 鄭孝胥 (1860–1938), Jin Rongjing 金蓉鏡 (1855–1929), Feng Junmu 馮君木 (1873–1931), Wu Hufan 吳湖帆 (1894–1968), Guo Lanxing 郭蘭祥 (1885–1938), Guo Lanzhi 郭蘭枝 (1887–1935), Zhao Shigang 趙時棡 (1874–1945), and Chu Deyi 褚德彝 (1871–1942), all dated 1929; Wang Naizheng 王乃徵 (1861–1933) and Bai Jian 白堅 (b. 1883), dated 1933; Ye Gongzhuo 葉恭綽 (1881–1968), Xia Jingguan 夏敬觀 (1875–1953), Chen Shi 陳詩 (1864–1942), and Deng Bangshu 鄧邦述 (1868–1939), dated 1935; Kong Decheng 孔德成 (1920–2008) and Li Xuangong 李宣龔 (1876–1953), dated 1943; Chen Zengshou 陳曾壽 (1878–1949) and Qian Xiongxiang 錢熊祥 (1875–1966), dated 1948. There are also undated inscriptions by Fei Longding 費龍丁 (1880–1937), Feng Chaoran 馮超然 (1882–1954), and Li Pang 李滂 (act. early twentieth century).

ADDITIONAL SEALS ON THE MOUNTING: *Ye qi an sou* 夜起庵叟 (Zheng Xiaoxu); *Zi yan* 自嚴 (Jin Rongjing); *Feng Junmu* 馮君木 (Feng Junmu); *Hufan* 湖颿 (Wu Hufan); *Shang zhai* 尙齋 (Guo Lanxiang); *Qi ting* 起庭 (Guo Lanzhi); *Song chuang* 松窗 (Chu Deyi); *Zizai tang* 自在堂, *Yuhu* 玉虎 (Ye Gongzhuo); *Jingguan* 敬觀, *Xuean* 吷庵 (Xia Jingguan); *Hechai shanren* 鶴柴山人 (Chen Shi); *Zheng an* 正闇 (Deng Bangshu); *Kong Decheng* 孔德成 (Kong Decheng); *Fanshuang guan* 緐霜館, *Xuangong* 宣龔, *Ba ke* 拔可 (Li Xuangong); *Shou* 壽 (Chen Zhenshou); *Chaoran* 超然 (Feng Chaoran); *Jiang Zuyi* 蔣祖詒, *Gu sun jiancang* 穀孫鑑藏 (Jiang Zuyi 蔣祖詒, 1902–1973).

NOTE

1 For this inscription, I am indebted to Dr. Han-yun Chang and Dr. Hui-ju Chuang for identifying the inscriber and seals.

CAT. NO. 21

CHEN HONGSHOU 陳洪綬 1599–1652
Immortal Conveying Longevity 壽者仙人圖, 1638

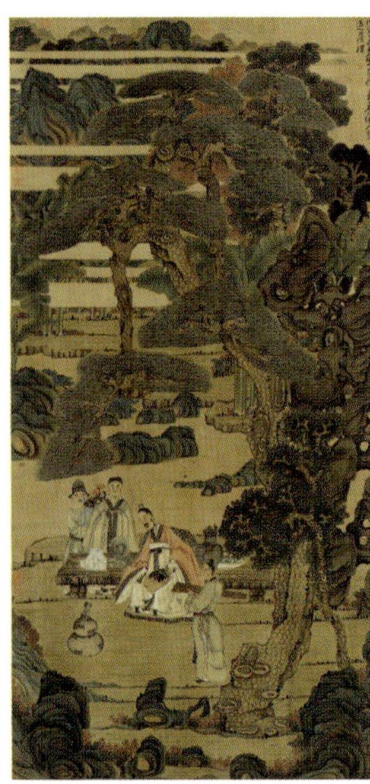

Hanging scroll: ink and color on silk; 200 × 98.5 cm (78 ¾ × 38 ¾ inches); Private collection

INSCRIPTION BY THE ARTIST
In mid-spring of the *wuyin* year [1638], *Immortal Conveying Longevity* painted by Hongshou of Xishan at the Daozang Lou [Tower for Daoist Scriptures].

戊寅孟春，溪山洪綬作壽者仙人於道藏樓.

SEALS: *Hongshou* 洪綬, *Zhanghou* 章侯.

ADDITIONAL SEALS: *Fanglin zhuren jianshang* 芳林主人珍藏, *Danruzhai shuhua yin* 淡如齋書畫印 (Yinli 胤禮, 1697–1738); *Qianlong yulan zhi bao* 乾隆御覽之寶, *Shiqu baoji* 石渠寶笈, *Qianlong jianshang* 乾隆鑒賞, *Sanxitang jingjian xi* 三希堂精鑒璽, *Yizisun* 宜子孫 (Emperor Qianlong, r. 1735–1796); *Wang Jiqian shi shending zhenji* 王季遷氏審定真跡, *Wang Jiqian haiwai suojian mingji* 王季遷海外所見名跡 (Wang Jiqian 王季遷, 1907–2003).

TITLE LABEL by Zhang Longyan 張隆延 (1909–2009).

CAT. NO. 22

CHEN HONGSHOU 陳洪綬 1599–1652
Historical Figures 史實人物圖卷

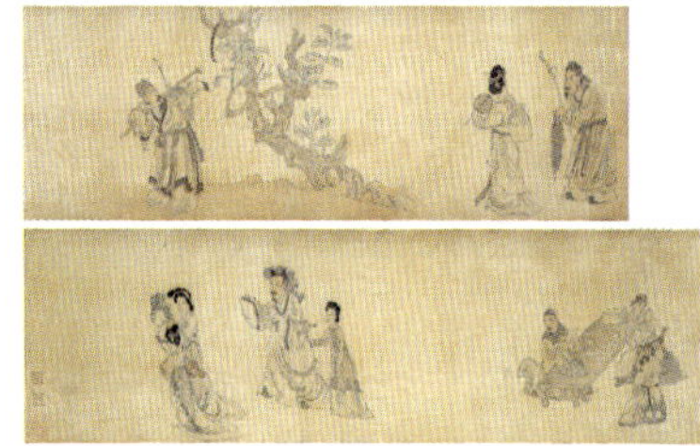

Handscroll: ink and color on silk; 27.5 × 171 cm (10 ⅞ × 67 ⅜ inches); Collection of Shitou Shuwu

SEALS OF THE ARTIST: *Chen Hongshou yin* 陳洪綬印, *Zhanghou* 章侯.

ADDITIONAL SEAL: *Wang Jiqian shi shending zhenji* 王季遷氏審定真跡 (Wang Jiqian 王季遷, 1907–2003).

OUTER SLIP: Chen Hongshou's "Home Again!", a divine work 陳洪綬歸去來圖神品.

CAT. NO. 23

CHEN HONGSHOU 陳洪綬 1599–1652
Album for Monk Yu 唐豫老雜畫冊, c. 1650

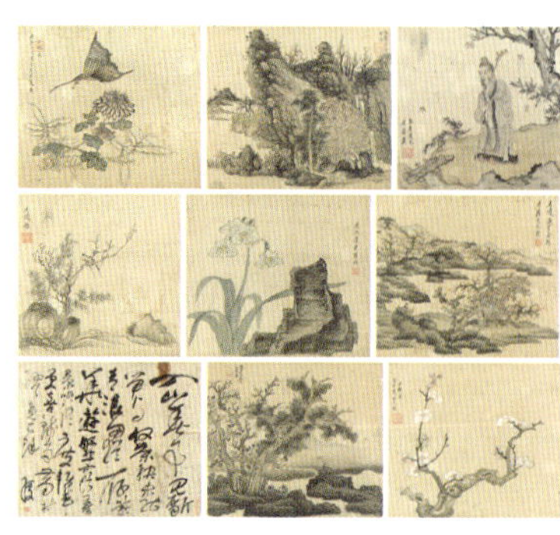

Album of eight leaves of paintings, one leaf of poetic inscription by the artist, and nine leaves of additional inscriptions: ink and color on silk; 25.7 × 29.7 cm (10 ⅛ × 11 ¾ inches) each, with slight variations; Honolulu Museum of Art, Purchase, 1966 (3420.1)

Leaf 1
INSCRIPTION BY THE ARTIST
Requested by Old Daoist monk Yu, painted by Hongshou.

豫老道兄屬，洪綬畫.

SEAL: *Hongshou* 洪綬.

Leaf 2
INSCRIPTION BY THE ARTIST
Requested by Monk Yu, painted on Chi [Late] Bridge.

豫和尚屬，遲橋上作.

SEAL: *Zhanghou* 章侯.

Leaf 3
INSCRIPTION BY THE ARTIST
Painted by Hongshou for Old Master Yu at the Daoist temple on Mount Wu.

洪綬爲老豫师兄畫於吳山道觀.

SEAL: *Zhanghou* 章侯.

Leaf 4
INSCRIPTION BY THE ARTIST
Painted by Old Late at Old Tang Yu's Reading History Pavilion.

老遲畫於唐豫老讀史之閣.

SEAL: *Chen Hongshou yin* 陳洪綬印.

Leaf 5
INSCRIPTION BY THE ARTIST
Requested by Old Yu, painted by Old Regret.

老豫屬，老悔作.

SEAL: *Chen Hongshou yin* 陳洪綬印.

Leaf 6
INSCRIPTION BY THE ARTIST
Painted by Hongshou. 洪綬作.

SEAL: *Hongshou* 洪綬.

Leaf 7
INSCRIPTION BY THE ARTIST
Hongshou painted for older brother Daoist Yu.

洪綬為豫老道盟兄作.

SEAL: *Chen Hongshou yin* 陳洪綬印.

Leaf 8
INSCRIPTION BY THE ARTIST
Requested by Old Yu, painted by Hongshou.

豫老人屬，洪綬畫.

SEAL: *Zhanghou* 章侯.

Leaf 9
INSCRIPTION BY THE ARTIST
Entering the mountains, spring matters
are presented:
Cut bamboo shoots and harvest tea.
Rice seedlings not yet ready to form
green waves,
Fields still possess purple florescence.
Carousing throughout the evening scene,
With laughing chatter our light
carriage passes.
Even happier with lots of cash to carry,
Village wine in the end all consumed!
[Signed] Shou.

入山春事見，斷筍與收茶.
秧未能青浪，田猶存紫華.
游盤窮暮景，笑語度輕車.
更喜錢多帶，村醪竟不餘．綬.

SEAL: *Hongshou* 洪綬.

ADDITIONAL SEAL: *Wan yi zhen shang* 萬鈦珍賞.

Seven leaves follow, each with poems by Ni Dai 倪岱 and Wang Tingji 王廷楫 (both act. eighteenth century). Following are two leaves with colophons by Wang Tingji dated 1757, Jiang Wangyou 將王猷 (act. eighteenth century), and Tian Shifa 田實發 (act. eighteenth century) dated 1730. It is apparent from the order of these inscriptions that Tian's leaf was shifted to the rear when Wang Tingji added his poems and inscription. Seals of each of these writers accompany their colophons.

ALBUM COVER
Chen Zhanghou's Marvelous Work. In the collection of Pingsheng.[1]
《陳章侯妙跡》，缾生藏.

NOTES
1 Pingsheng is a sobriquet of the Qing scholar Weng Tonghe.

CAT. NO. 24

XIAO YUNCONG 蕭雲從 1596–1673

Landscape 設色山水圖卷, 1657

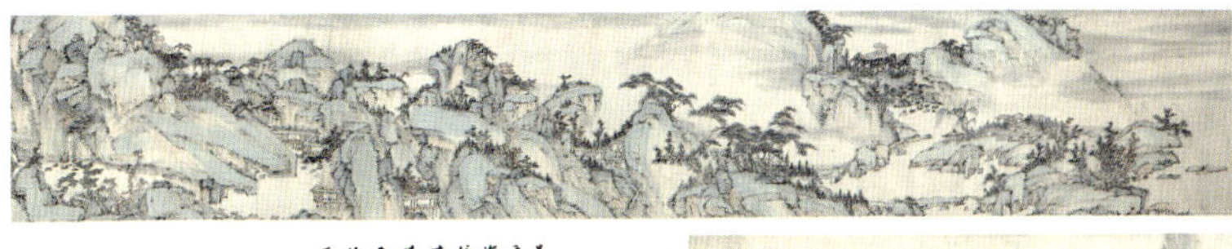

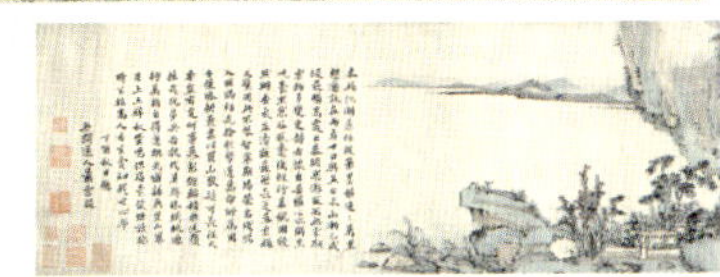

Handscroll: ink and color on paper;
28.5 × 254.5 cm (11 ¼ × 100 ⅛ inches);
Private collection

INSCRIPTION BY THE ARTIST

Rooted in my feelings for river and lake,
I release my brush and ink to freely flow!
Far, far, thoughts of ten thousand miles:
Distantly entrusted to a realm of
 chaste reclusion
"Ten days" then "five days"[1]:
Rivers and mountains gradually taking form.
At crack of dawn I gaze at towering mists;
At sunset listen to the cold gurgling
 of streams.
Wind and rain have no fixed seasons;
Cloud-forms have many permutations.
In quietude, yet I harbor suffering;
Even happy, I question this life of ours.
Sucking my brush, I sit in the chilly valley;
Draft completed, go out for a stroll again.
I am indeed pleased with my cups of tea;
The leaves' fragrance brings great purity.
Burgeoning flora lasts the long summer
Until once more, falling leaves startle
 us in autumn.
Following this, wisdom will not be thwarted:
What difficulty in earning a glorious name?
Late daylight enters the western quarter,
A lovely glow collects about my little lamp.
My fate has been consigned to the
 wild brambles,
Exerting strength just to plow and grow.
I sell my paintings so I can "buy a mountain":
Hair let down, then off on my long
 wanderings!
Is it not that one's allotted years are fixed?
Why ever should we envy Peng Keng's
 longevity?[2]
Hiding his light, disappearing deep
 in the mountains,
Clumsy indeed was Infantryman Ruan![3]
If the Jin and Wei cannot be distinguished
 from one another,
Don't bother writing a poem on Peach
 Blossom Spring![4]
Let the ten thousand creatures each find its
 right way:
Why bother trying to divine your lifespan?
From the deserted mountain the cold
 moon rises,
In the earthen walls the autumn crickets sing.
I only strive to have simple feelings:
It's not at all that the times are not easy.
Should a man of wisdom secretly appreciate
 my meaning,
There being one who really knows me; my
 heart will be at peace.
Inscribed on an autumn day of the *dingyou* year [1657]. [Signed] Wumen daoren Xiao Yuncong.[5]

本此江湖意, 任從筆墨橫.
迢迢萬里想, 邈託在幽貞.
十日與五日, 水山漸已成.
侵晨矚高霞, 日暮聽寒澎.
風雨無常期, 雲物多變更.
靜者懷自苦, 歡心亦問生.
吮豪坐寒谷, 脫槀復經行.
茗碗固欣然, 瓣香氣益清.
繇蓀歷長夏, 落葉穐又驚.
用此不棼智, 寧難博榮名.
殘陽入西隅, 紹光拾短檠.
蓬蒿命所属, 用力僅勝耕.
賣畫以買山, 散髮可長征.
天季豈有定, 何事慕彭鏗.
韜精匪沈嶺, 拙哉阮步兵.
晉魏代莫辨, 休賦桃源行.
萬物自得道, 胡為補繇庚.
空山寒月上, 土壁秋蛩鳴.
但得素懷愜, 諒非時不輕.
高人有玄賞, 知我寸心平.
丁酉秋日題. 無悶道人蕭雲從.

SEALS: *Zhongshan meixia seng* 鐘山梅下僧, *Xiao Yuncong* 蕭雲從.

ADDITIONAL SEALS: *Yuqin jianshang* 虞琴鑒賞 (Yao Jingying 姚景瀛, 1867–1961); *Yueyuan jianshang* 越園鑒賞, *Yu Shaosong* 余紹宋, *Yueyuan* 越園 (Yu Shaosong 余紹宋, 1883–1949); *Zhang Wenkui* 張文魁, *Zhang shi Hanlu zhencang* 張氏涵廬珍藏, *Hanlu jiancang* 涵廬鑒藏 (Zhang Wenkui 張文魁, 1905–1967); *Wang Jiqian haiwai suojian mingji* 王季遷海外所見名跡 (Wang Jiqian 王季遷, 1906–2002).

ADDITIONAL INSCRIPTION by Yu Shaosong dated 1947.

NOTES

1 This phrase alludes to Du Fu's "A Song Playfully Inscribed on Wang Zai's Landscape Painting." For a translation, see William Hung, *Tu Fu: China's Greatest Poet* (Cambridge, MA: Harvard University Press, 1952), vol. 1, 169–70.

2 Peng Keng (Peng Zu) was a legendary figure who was believed to have lived for over 800 years.

3 Ruan Ji was a Wei-dynasty poet and renowned for his reclusion as a member of the Seven Sages of the Bamboo Grove. In the poem Xiao addresses him as "Bubing" (infantryman), alluding to Ruan's brief military service. "Clumsy" here is probably intended as a positive attribute, following the Daoist philosophy of Laozi and Zhuangzi.

4 Jin and Wei refer to what is commonly called the Wei-Jin period of the third and fourth centuries. Xiao Yuncong is probably alluding to the dynastic transition of his own time, perhaps pointing to those who quickly changed loyalties and aligned with the Qing. For the collaborators there is no need for a Peach Blossom Spring—referring to Tao Yuanming's classic story of the Chinese utopia.

5 Translation by Jonathan Chaves, with minor revisions.

CAT. NO. 25

ZHANG XUEZENG 張學曾 act. c. 1633–1657

Fisherman Recluse 山水軸

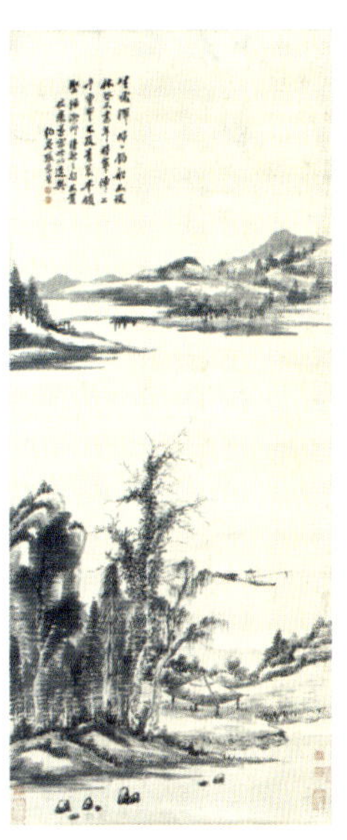

Hanging scroll: ink on paper;
118.1 × 50.2 cm (46 ½ × 19 ¾ inches);
Private collection

INSCRIPTION BY THE ARTIST

Reincarnated, mystifying return: a single
 fisherman's skiff;
Don't speak of fortune or misfortune; don't
 record the years.
The general at the head of his troops wears
 a thousand layers of armor,
But these cannot match in strength
 the half collar of the [fisherman's] green
 coir jacket.
Reciting these pure new lines of Master Jian, I cannot help but be inspired. Thus I have sketched this in order to find outlet for my stimulation. [Signed] Yuean, Zhang Xuezeng.

生處渾歸一釣船, 不談休咎不書年.
將軍陣上千重甲, 不及青蓑半領堅.
誦漸師清新之句, 不覺技癢. 遂寫此以遣興.
約奄張學曾.

SEALS: *Xuezeng* 學曾, *Erwei* 爾唯.

ADDITIONAL SEALS: *Lanling Miao shi zhencang* 蘭陵繆氏珍藏 (Miao Yuezao 繆曰藻, 1682–1761); *Yang feng qingmi* 陽風清秘, *Jin shou sheng zui jiu wu* 金壽生最舊物, *Xiang _ shending* 相_審定, *Xin lu bayan zhi zhai* 心鑪八研之齋, *Mu hui jing yan* 慕會經眼.

CAT. NO. 26

LAN YING 藍瑛 1585–1664 or later

Autumn Landscape in the Style of Huang Gongwang 法大癡老人山水, 1656

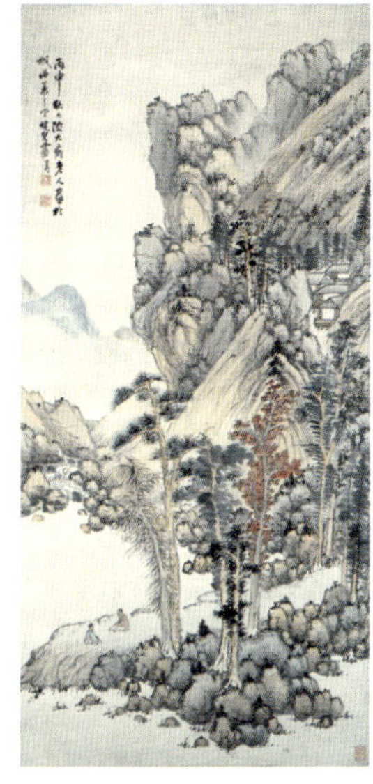

Hanging scroll: ink and color on paper;
128.9 × 61 cm (50 ¾ × 24 inches);
Santa Barbara Museum of Art,
Gift of Peggy Maximus, 1997.42

INSCRIPTION BY THE ARTIST

Modeled after the painting of Dachi [Huang Gongwang] on an autumn day of the *bingshen* year [1656] at the Chengqu Thatched Hall. [Signed] Diesou Lan Ying.

丙申秋日, 法大癡老人畫於城曲茆堂.
蜨叟藍瑛.

SEALS: *Lan Ying zhiyin* 藍瑛之印, *Tianshu fu* 田叔父.

ADDITIONAL SEAL: *Taixia Li shi Boquan zhencang zhi yin* 太下李氏博泉珍藏之印.

CAT. NO. 27

LAN YING 藍瑛 1585–1664 or later

Rock 寶晉齋石

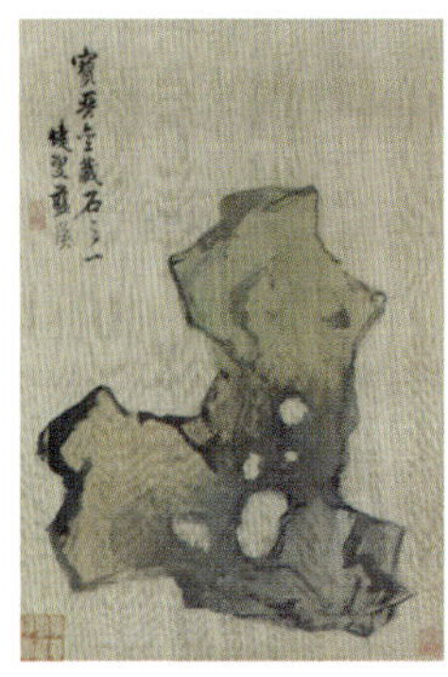

Hanging scroll: ink and color on silk; 34.3 × 23.5 cm (13 ½ × 9 ¼ inches); Private collection

INSCRIPTION BY THE ARTIST

One of the rocks from the collection of the Bao-Jin Studio. [Signed] Diesou, Lan Ying.

寶晉齋藏石之一，蜨叟藍瑛.

SEAL: *Lan Ying* 藍瑛.

ADDITIONAL SEALS: *Woan suocang* 臥菴所藏 (Zhu Zhichi 朱之赤, seventeenth century); *Yunzhen shuwu zhen shang* 蘊真書屋珍賞.

CAT. NO. 28

ZHANG ZHENGYUE 張正嶽

b. c. 1590

Mountain Landscape 青綠山水

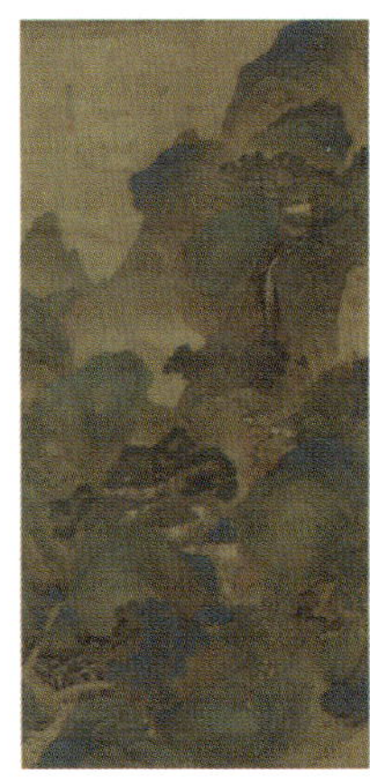

Hanging scroll: ink and color on silk; 95.9 × 47.6 cm (37 ¾ × 18 ¾ inches); Santa Barbara Museum of Art, Gift of Mr. and Mrs. George Griffiths, 1999.49

INSCRIPTION BY THE ARTIST

Zhang Zhengyue of Xiangxi, painted at the age of seventy-six [*sui*].

湘谿張正嶽，時年七十有六.

SEALS: *Zhenyue* 振岳, *Songgao* 崧高.

CAT. NO. 29

QIAN QIANYI 錢謙益 1582–1664

Poems 行書詩卷

Calligraphy in semi-cursive script

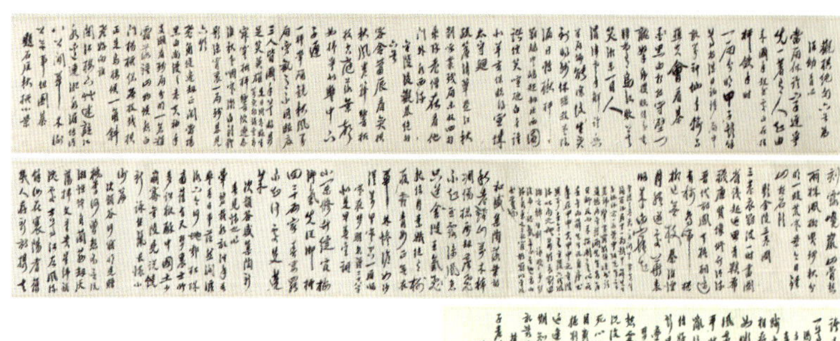

Handscroll: ink on paper; 30.5 × 478.2 cm (12 × 188 ¼ inches); Private collection

INSCRIPTION BY THE ARTIST

These old works were transcribed and presented to my friend Zilao for correction. Completed by Muzhai, Qian Qianyi.

舊作錄奉子老道兄正之. 牧齋謙益脫稿.

SEALS: *Qian Qianyi yin* 錢謙益印, *Muzhai* 牧齋.

POEMS[1]

1

"Six Quatrains on Watching a Game of *Weiqi*, for the correction of Wang Youqing"[2]

Facing the board, do not worry about being slow to move:
Striving to get ahead, one wrong move will be seen through by people!
From ancient times, the real superiority of national masters
Has shown at moments when they folded their hands and refused to touch the board.

觀棋絕句六首為汪幼青作

當局休論下子遲，爭先一著有人知.
由來國手超然處，正在推枰斂手時.

The chess board clearly lays out events that last sixty years:
Wine still bubbling in lingering vessels, the sun just starts to set.
Those immortal hands which are playing a game of chess
All lose the game to those gatherers of bundles of firewood.[3]

一局分明甲子期，餘尊尚湛日初移.
局中敵對神仙手，輸與樵夫會看棊.

The black and the white hold each other at bay, behind their defensive walls;
Dragons claw, tigers scratch, staking all on the next *qinfen* incursion.
Even the man of double-pupils suffered defeat at the River of Wu;
Don't laugh at the man with just one eye in the region East of River Xiang![4]

黑白相持守壁門，龍拏虎攫賭侵分.
重瞳尚有烏江敗，莫笑湘東一目人.

The old man at the Wei River ford is good at strategy[5]:
Halfway through the game, he's able to retreat, preparing for renewed life.
When the enemy seems about to scatter, don't become too fond of killing:
Setting sunlight, seeping through flowered shade, can reverse the entire board.

渭津老手解論兵，半局偏能讓後生.
弈到將殘休戀殺，花陰漏日轉楸枰.

Capped like snipe and turbaned like owls, rushing towards utter destruction!
In the Western Garden, wrangling over prices, laughing raucously!
In poverty, who compares today with Yang Xuanbao of old?
And yet we see he won the position of Xuancheng Magistrate by a game of chess![6]

冠鷸巾鴟趁劫灰，西園諸價笑喧豗.
白身誰似羊玄保，賭得宣城太守回.

Wide-spaced blinds, fresh, clean mats, autumn along the Yangzi in Chu;
"Click-clack," clustered, dispersed, the game has not yet ended.
The old monk is here, "with four verses of advancing and receding":
He just watches the river outside the gate as it flows to the west.[7]

疏簾清簟楚江秋，剝啄叢殘局未收.
四句乘除老僧在，看他門外水西流.

2

"Latter Six Quatrains on Watching a Game of *Weiqi* at Jinling (Nanjing)"

Guest quarters, a sad dawning, watching a game of chess:
Autumn wind bends the bamboo, making withered branches creak.
In the empty courtyard, falling leaves—making sounds like being swept,
Resemble those chess pieces slowly dropped onto the board.

後觀棊絕句六首

客舍蕭辰看奕棋，秋風卷籜響枯枝.
空庭落葉聲如掃，爭似盤中下子遲.

A chess board, with sounds of falling pieces of chess, rivaling the autumn wind,
Two players, one onlooker, all of different minds.
The three one sees, each one of them is a national master!
Do not mock these heroes for dividing the empire into three tripod legs![8]
[Poet's prose note:] On this day, Old Chou and Young Yao were playing *weiqi* while Youqing watched.

一枰犖确競秋風，對局旁觀意不同.
眼底三人皆國手，莫將鼎足笑英雄.
是日周老，姚生對弈，幼青旁看.

Sorrowful, lonely, the withered board sounds out in desolation;
Along [Nanjing's] Qinhuai River, autumn ages, cold tides gurgle below.
White-haired, shadows thrown by lamps, wrapped in this chilly night,
On this little board filled with scattered pieces I see the Six Dynasties.

寂莫枯枰響泬寥，秦淮秋老咽寒潮.
白頭鐙影涼宵裏，一局殘棊見六朝.

The enemy's *feijiao* have penetrated the frontier, *jie* draws to a close![9]
Upon the field, the whites and the blacks are still spread all around.
For me, an old man, hands in sleeves, propping chins, just looking...
Clearly, the endgame renders difficult even a single move.

飛角侵邊劫正闌，當場黑白尚漫漫.
老夫袖手支頤看，殘局分明一著難.

Frost has settled on Mount Zhong, the season filled with sadness;
At White Gate the willow trees are stripped bare of their branches.
The scattered endgame looks just like a flock of crows settled down to roost:
To which one corner would they fly on the slant?[10]

霜落鍾山物候悲，白門楊柳總無枝.
殘棊正是烏棲候，一角斜飛好向誰.

Beneath River-Viewing Tower, plants grow in confusion;
The Yangzi's waters flow and flow, joining the banks of River Fei.
They tell of the tranquil plants and trees out there, on Eight Duke Mountain:
Now, Master Xie has nothing to do but concentrate on *weiqi*.[11]

閱江樓下草迷離，江水遙連淝水湄.
傳語八公閒草木，謝公無事但圍棊.

3
"Inscribed on the Small-Scene Painting *Autumn Willows by a Rocky Cliff*"

You've carved out here a craggy cliff—
mountain-bone so sad!
And two wind-driven willow trees, trailing
in the lingering autumn.
Clearly, this little slice of desolate,
cold scenery
Shows the ancient rock formations
of Mount Zhong today!

題石厓秋柳小景

刻露巉巖山骨愁，兩株風柳曳殘秋.
分明一段荒寒景，今日鍾山古石頭.

4
"Inscribed on the Painting *Three Elders of Jinling*"

Three elders, dressed in robes and caps, and
from another era:
Examining this painting now gives rise to
distant thoughts.
Greenish sandals, cotton stockings: portraits
of Tang-dynasty worthies;
Tall bamboo, crystal stream—as in
Jin-dynasty poems!
The phoenix has departed, yet the *wutong*
tree remains;
Crows are cawing, willows with no branches.
The Qinhuai River, mist and moon, a place
I've been before;
Returning to the carved columns, white
cranes are aware.[12]

[Poet's prose note:] The Three Elders of Jinling are Master Huang Haihe from Min [Fujian Province], given name Juzhong [1562–1644], Master Xue Qianren from Yue [Zhejiang Province], given name Gang [b. 1561], and Master Zhang Xuanzhu of Wu, given name Zhaohuang. When they finished their government positions, they read books, discussed the Dao, setting up residence in Jinling. Two of the gentlemen came here for relatives and friends. This painting was done in the *renwu* year [1642], but Master Xue's self-written preface is dated the *jiashen* year [1644]. Jinling in *jiashen* was different from the Jinling of *renwu*. This is the place where the literary talents of the Six Dynasties flourished, where the grandees of previous reigns in their caps and gowns came to rule and reside. When alive they sang songs here, and when dead their spirits and breath still remained. A place of high mountains and flowing water, where they ride the clouds transformed into cranes—so [the painting was] crowned Jinling to express their feelings.

題金陵三老圖

三老衣冠彼一時，畫圖省識起遐思.
青鞵布襪唐賢像，修竹清流晉代詩.
鳳去梧桐還有樹，烏啼楊柳已無枝.
秦淮煙月經遊處，華表歸來白鶴知.

金陵三老者，一為閩中黃先生海鶴，諱居中. 一為越中薛先生千仞，諱岡. 一為吳中張先生玄著，諱肇黃. 罷牧伯，讀書談道，僑居金陵. 兩先生各為其師友而來. 按圖之作在壬午，而薛先生之自序，書年在甲申. 夫甲申之金陵，異於壬午之金陵. 六代風流吐內之地，前朝衣冠遊冶之鄉，生則詠歌於斯，沒而魂氣無不之也. 高山流水，乘雲化鶴，故冠以金陵，書感也.

5
"Echoing Sheng Jitao's Poem on Falling Leaves"

As autumn ages at Mount Zhong, ten
thousand trees grow sparse;
This withering and dying always recalls
the flying dust of war.
We do not heed the jade-like dew chilling in
brisk wind;
We only note that the kingly vapors of Jinling
are fading.
For leaning upon there on the moon, pure
Chang'e has only a tree;
Treading upon the frost, Blue Maiden has no
robes to wear.
A blooming grove, turned sad and sere, just
like a barren desert:
For ten thousand miles, cold void above,
a single goose returning.[13]

和盛集陶落葉詩

秋老鍾山萬木稀，凋傷總屬劫塵飛.
不知玉露涼風急，只道金陵王氣飛.
倚月素娥徒有樹，履霜青女正無衣.
華林慘澹如沙漠，萬里寒空一雁歸.

6
"On a Cold Night, Waking from a Dream, Suddenly Twenty-Eight Characters Came to Me, Resembling a Palace Poem on Early Spring"

By a small fence with tall bamboo, official
plums burst in bloom,
This pure aura first returned by way of
imperial willows.
Twenty-five households concluding
spring banquets;
I wonder which might be the magic
isle Penglai?

寒夜夢醒忽得二十八字似是早春宮詞

小闌修竹綻官梅，淑氣先從禦柳回.
二十五家春宴罷，不知何處是蓬萊.

7
"Replying to a Poem Sent to Me by Sheng Jitao on Thoughts of New Year, Following His Rhymes"

A blend of green stitched with red,
I remember years passed;
Spring platter on New Year's Day, feelings
at a loss.
What is the place under Jian, Fa, and Luo?
At Hudu, south of the walls, there was
heaven in the past.
The Magistrate in my dreams is always
judging disputes;
My country's land, when I am drunk, appears
less collapsed.
Conversing with you in Jinling, forgive this
new poem;
Sonorous and beautiful, long I cherish the
work of Little Xie.[14]

次韻答盛集陶新春見懷之作

暈碧裁紅記往年，春盤春日事茫然.
澗瀍雒下今何地，鄠杜城南舊有天.
夢裏士師多訟獄，醉中國土少崩騫.
金陵見說饒新詠，佳麗長懷小謝篇.

8
"Replying to a Poem Sent to Me by He Wuming, Following His Rhymes"

Peach and plum—when have they ever
resented their own silence?
Yuan and Xiang Rivers—desolate since the
master of orchid and iris.
The dust of era's end sweeps all before it,
literature remains worthy;
Stars and constellations may dissolve or sink,
but the retired scholar is still noble.
Of the poetic world of the Yangzi Delta, only
you and I are left;
Of our old friends from Xiangyang, how
many remain alive?
Take your new poems to the Spring Sacrifice,
there to boast of them:
For each character you will have to pour
another toast in wine.[15]

次韻答何寤明見贈

桃李何曾怨不言，沅湘憔悴自蘭蓀.
劫灰蕩掃文章貴，星緯消沈處士尊.
江左風流餘汝在，襄陽耆舊幾人存.
新詩攜去誇春社，一字須傾酒一樽.

9
"Feng Yanxiang and Jin Mengfei, Not Considering One Thousand *Li* Too Far, Have Come from Wulin to Express Condolences for Our White Gate (Nanjing). Overjoyed, I Have Composed This."

I got through winter avoiding death, and now
another ten days;
Within the four seas, surviving together,
two old friends.
Wu and Zhe are now as if separated by vast
mountain ranges;
Shields and spears fill the land, not to
mention wind-blown dust!
In lamplight peering closely I recognize these
faces of old;
Seated long, I am amazed by news of your
post-disaster lives.
Zhanyin was here at dawn, bringing
happy news:
Who would have known we could have a day
like this?![16]

馮研祥金夢蜚不遠千里，自武林唁我白門，喜而有作

逾冬免死又經旬，四海相存兩故人.
吳浙(各)天如嶺嶠，干戈滿地況風塵.
燈前細認平時面，坐久頻驚亂後身.
詹尹朝來傳好語，可知容是有斯晨.

10
"Repeating the Rhymes of the Former Poem, Seeing Off Yanxiang and Mengfei"

Miserable rain, earth-shaking lightning—
we've suffered more than ten days;
How much worse, confused by sorrow,
I must see off my old friends!
On the brink of death, my heart hangs like
a pestle above the mortar;
Gazing toward their return, my sight is cut off
by the dust behind their carriage.
In this lingering life, holding hands in parting,
few tears left to weep;
In this world of chaos, how many remain for
get-togethers now?
Though henceforth our earlier vows I know
we won't forget,
When the cock crows in the darkness, we will
remember this morning.

疊前韻送別研祥夢蜚

愁霖震電苦逾旬，況複懵騰送故人.
瀕死心懸舂碓杵，望歸目斷客車塵.
殘生握別無多淚，亂世遭逢有幾身.
從此前期知不忘，雞鳴如晦記茲晨.

ADDITIONAL INSCRIPTIONS by Zhao Huaiyu 趙懷玉 (1747–1823) dated 1784; Zhang Weiping 張維屏 (signed Hanqiao 酣樵, 1780–1859) dated 1840; Xu Tongbo 徐同柏 (1775–1854); and Li Zuoyu 李佐禹 dated 1871.

ADDITIONAL SEALS: *Weixin* 味辛 (Zhao Huaiyu); *Peidun* 培敦 (Zhang Weiping); *Xu Shouzang* 徐壽臧 (Xu Tongbo).

NOTES

1 The translations that follow are modified from those of Jonathan Chaves with the exception of poem 7, which had not been translated. There are some differences between the texts of this handwritten scroll and the same poems collected in Qian Qianyi's *Youxue ji* 有學集.

2 Wang Youqing 汪幼青 (Wang Yilian) was a master chess player as well as acquaintance of Qian Qianyi.

3 This refers to an ancient story recorded in *Shuyi ji*, in which a man named Wang Zhi 王質 went inside a mountain and watched two boys playing chess. By the time the game was over, Wang's axe handle had decayed and hundreds of years had passed. Ren Fang 任昉, *Shuyi ji* 述異記 (*Siku quanshu* ed.), *shang*, 16a–b.

4 *Qinfen* refers to a technique of *weiqi*, in which one puts a chess piece in the opponent's field to break and occupy it. The man of double-pupils refers to Xiang Yu, heroic general after the downfall of the Qin empire. He was defeated by Liu Bang and committed suicide on the banks of the Wu River. The man with one eye refers to Xiao Yi, emperor of Liang, who defeated the rebel army of Hou Jing.

5 The old man refers to Lü Shang, who helped King Wen of Zhou defeat the Shang and establish the Zhou Dynasty. King Wen discovered him fishing at the Wei River.

6 The West Garden refers to the dwelling place of Zhang Rang, powerful and corrupt eunuch at the court of Emperor Ling of Han, who sold official positions and wrangled over prices. Yang Xuanbao was awarded the position magistrate of Xuancheng by winning a chess game with an emperor.

7 The last two lines all refer to stories regarding the monk Yixing included in Duan Chengshi's 段成式 *Youyang zazu* 酉陽雜俎 of the Tang dynasty. He did not know how to play *weiqi* at first, but became expert after watching just one game played by a national master and claimed that he could teach others how to play with just four verses. Yixing could also predict the future. One day, he heard a monk's voice and correctly predicted that the monk would become his disciple and the river outside the gate would change direction to flow westward.

8 A reference to the Three Kingdoms period (220–265), when hegemony was contested by the powers of Wei, Shu, and Wu.

9 *Feijiao* and *jie* are technical terms of *weiqi* referring to specific moves and strategy.

10 Mount Zhong is a famous site in the city of Nanjing, the place where the first Ming emperor Zhu Yuanzhang was buried. White Gate refers to the Xuanyang Gate in Nanjing, oftentimes used as a synecdoche for the city. The last line also refers to the *feijiao* technique (see last poem), in which one moves diagonally across the board.

11 The River-Viewing Tower was built by decree of the first Ming emperor, Zhu Yuanzhang, who also wrote a record of it titled "Yuejiang lou ji" 閱江樓記. This poem alludes to a famous battle between the Eastern Jin and Former Qin that took place in 383 at the Fei River (Anhui Province). Despite numerical superiority, the Former Qin was decisively defeated. On a pivotal day of the battle, the leader of the Former Qin troops observed Jin's army during the night and suspected that there were troops in ambush under the plants and trees of Eight Duke Mountain. Master Xie refers to Xie An, who was prime minister of Jin at the time of the battle and led his state through a major crisis. Playing chess with guests when news of the victory arrived at his house, he did not display particular emotion.

12 The fourth line alludes to the famous gathering of literati in 353 at the Orchid Pavilion near Shaoxing (Zhejiang) during the Spring Purification Festival to compose poems and enjoy wine. Carved or ornamental columns were used to mark important sites, usually with imperial significance, such as tombs.

13 Sheng Sitang 盛斯唐 (style name Jitao) was a poet-friend of Qian Qianyi active in the early years of the Qing dynasty. Kingly vapors refer to the fact that Jinling (Nanjing) served as the capital for a number of earlier dynasties. Chang'e is the legendary goddess of the moon, where she resides accompanied only by a jade rabbit and cassia tree. The Blue Maiden is the goddess of frost and snow.

14 Spring platter refers to an offering dish with an artful display of delicacies composed for the first day of the New Year. It is apparent that Qian's poem (and probably Sheng Sitang's original verse) alludes to the opening lines of a poem by Yuan Haowen titled "Spring Day": "At the local shrine ingenuity of the spring platter competes / Cut red, blend of green aids the seasonal mood" 里社春盤巧欲爭，裁紅暈碧助春情. Yuan Haowen 元好問, "Chun ri" 春日, *Yishan ji* 遺山集 (*Siku quanshu* ed.), 8:2a. Jian, Chan, and Luo are all places that have been mentioned in the *Book of Documents*. Hudu was a lovely place near Chang'an (Xi'an), the site of Han Xuandi's (r. 74–49 BCE) tomb and, according to common sayings of the Tang dynasty, only one and a half feet from heaven. In the last line Qian Qianyi likens his friend Shen Sitang to Xie Huilian, a poet of the (Liu) Song dynasty.

15 The first line alludes to the saying "Peaches and plums do not have to talk, yet the world beats a path to them," which means that true gentlemen attract admiration naturally without self-praise. The master of orchid and iris refers to the famous poet and loyalist Qu Yuan, associated with poems of the *Chu ci* (Songs of the south), many of which include these and other fragrant plants in their narratives. "Friends from Xiangyang (Hubei Province)" is an allusion to a line in a poem by Du Fu: "In the past there was Master Pangde, / Who never entered prefectural service. / Of my old friends from Xiangyang, / Only the recluse cultivates his integrity severely" 昔者龐德公，未曾入州府．襄陽耆舊間，處士節獨苦. Du Fu 杜甫, "Qianxing wushou" 遣興五首, *Jiujia zhu Du shi* 九家集注杜詩 (*Siku quanshu* ed.), 5:16b.

16 Feng Yanxiang, native of Jiaxing (Zhejiang Province), shared with Qian Qianyi an interest in collecting calligraphy, rubbings, and antiquities. Wulin refers to Hangzhou (Zhejiang Province). Zhanyin was a diviner of the Warring States period.

CAT. NO. 30

ZHANG FENG 張風 d. 1662

Immortals' Secrets in a Stone Cave **石室仙機圖卷, 1658**

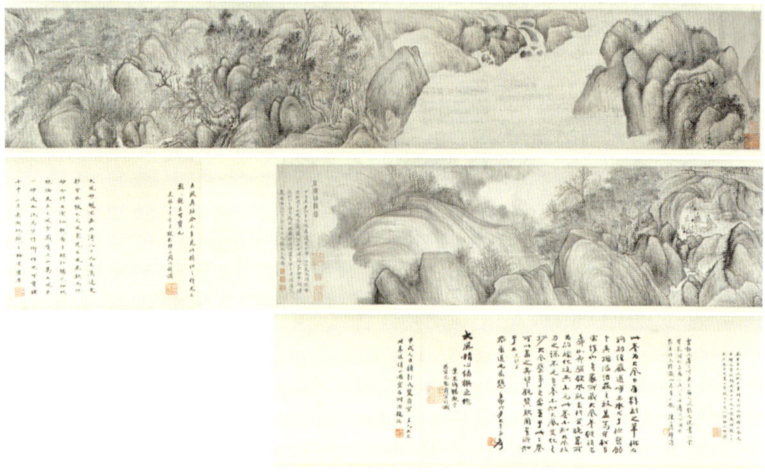

Handscroll: ink and color on paper; 24.1 × 221 cm (9 ½ × 87 inches); Private collection

TITLE AND INSCRIPTION BY THE ARTIST *Immortals' Secrets in a Stone Cave*. In the winter of the *dingyou* year [1657], this old man traveled from Shicheng [Nanjing] to Jingkou [Zhenjiang]. There, in the company of Master Jiangshang [Da Chongguang], we sojourned to the three hills, Jin, Jiao, and Beigu. In the summer of the *wuxu* year [1658], again we traveled by boat down to Gusu [Suzhou] and eventually to West Lake [at Hangzhou]. Traveling back and forth, it has been almost three months. As this painting was made during the boat trip, it was difficult to accomplish and not very skillful—something only useful as a record of our sightseeing during this time. [Signed] third day of the sixth [lunar] month, Zhang Dafeng of Shangyuan.

《石室仙機圖》. 丁酉冬，老人自石城來過京口，與江上先生同游金，焦，北固三山. 戊戌夏，復泛舟下姑蘇，至西子湖. 往返將以三閱月，為作此圖於舟次，畫苦不工，用識遊覽歲時而已. 六月初三日，上元張風大風識.

SEALS: *Zhichang jushi* 知嘗居士, *Zhang Feng yin* 張風印, *Zhang Dafeng* 張大風.

ADDITIONAL INSCRIPTIONS: Zhou Zuorong 周作鎔 (nineteenth century), dated 1882; Wu Hufan 吳湖帆 (1894–1968) twice, the first dated 1932; Chen Ziqing 陳子清 (d. 1946); Zhang Daqian 張大千 (1899–1983), dated 1932; Ye Gongchuo 葉恭綽 (1881–1968); He Cheng 何澄 (1880–1946), dated 1934.

ADDITIONAL SEALS: *Yangshi cangshu zhi yin* 楊氏藏書之印 (possibly Yang Yizeng 楊以增, 1787–1855); *Zhizhai miwan* 質齋秘玩 (possibly Xiao Peiyuan 蕭培元, 1816–1873); *Hufan jiancang* 湖颿鑑, *Hufan shending* 湖颿審定, *Meiying shuwu biji* 梅景書屋祕笈, *Wu Wan baocang* 吳萬寶藏, *Wu Hufan yin* 吳湖颿印 (Wu Hufan); *Gongfu xin shang* 恭父心賞 (Peng Gongfu 彭恭父, act. early twentieth century); *Zhou Zuorong yin* 周作鎔印 (Zhou Zuorong); *Chen Ziqing* 陳子清 (Chen Ziqing); *Ji ai zhi yin* 季爰之印 (Zhang Daqian); *Ye Gongchuo yin* 葉恭綽印 (Ye Gongchuo); *He Cheng zhi yin* 何澄之印 (He Cheng).

CAT. NO. 31

DA CHONGGUANG 笪重光 1623–1692

Floating Jade Mountain 行書詩軸

Calligraphy in semi-cursive script

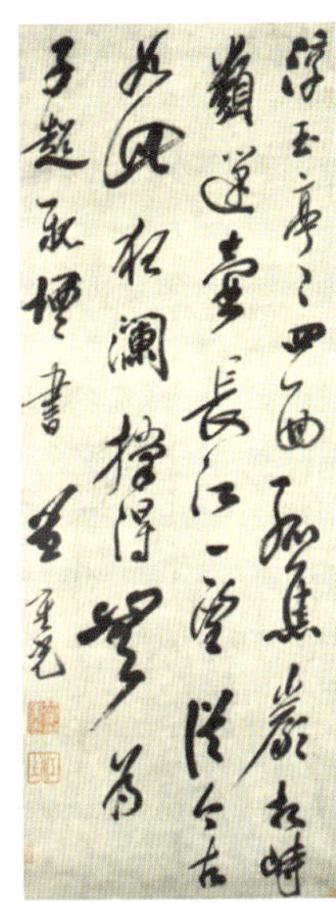

Hanging scroll: ink on paper;
142.2 × 52.7 cm (56 × 20 ¾ inches);
Santa Barbara Museum of Art,
Gift of N. P. Wong family, 1995.63.7

INSCRIPTION BY THE ARTIST

Floating Jade Mountain surges upward,
water floats on every side!
Jiao Cliff's pine trees tower high, just like the
Isles of Paradise!
This panorama of the Yangzi River,
continuous, past and present:
With such wild waves, could anyone pole
a boat out there right now?[1]
For Zichao, Qiuyan, [Signed] Da Chongguang.

浮玉亭亭四面孤,
焦巖松峙類蓬壺.
長江一望縱今古,
如此狂瀾撐得無.
為子超, 秋煙 書 笪重光.

SEALS: *Da Chongguang yin* 笪重光印, *Jiang shang* 江上.

ADDITIONAL SEALS: *Zhang Zezhi yin* 張澤之印 (Zhang Shanzi 張善孖, 1882–1940); *Dafengtang changwu* 大風堂長物, *Huanzhu shanfang* 環竹山房 (Zhang Daqian 張大千, 1899–1993).

NOTE

1 Translation by Jonathan Chaves.

CAT. NO. 32

CHENG SUI 程邃 1607–1692

Tall View of Streams and Mountains

溪山高遠圖軸

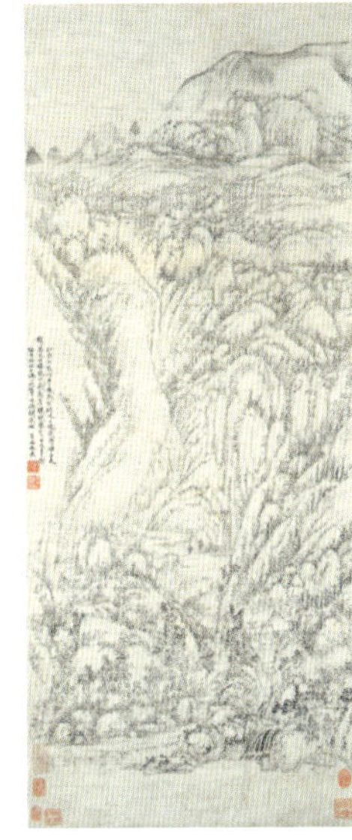

Hanging scroll: ink on paper;
102.8 × 41.9 cm (40 ½ × 16 ½ inches);
Collection of Shitou Shuwu

INSCRIPTION BY THE ARTIST

Painters of the Jiangdong region revere "level distance" [compositions of landscape], but this path has increasingly hastened towards the light and shallow. Only my friend, Mr. Zhigong, is able to utilize the strength of "high distance" to revitalize the declined learning. I, too, have been engaged in such matters, which the two of us discuss from time to time. By chance I imitate [Zhigong's] manner but dare not compete. [Signed] Huanghai Cheng Sui.

江東之家以平遠為宗, 此道日趨淡薄, 惟吾友稺恭先生, 獨能以高遠之力開起墮學. 余從事討論, 匪朝伊夕, 偶一效顰, 非敢鬬勝也. 黃海程邃.

SEALS: *Cheng Sui* 程邃, *Muqian* 穆倩.

ADDITIONAL SEALS: *Wang shi Jiqian shending zhenji* 王氏季遷審定真跡 (Wang Jiqian, 1907–2002); *Zuili* 檇李; *Gonggen ying_ qujiang* 躬耕應_曲江; *__ suiyou* __雖幼; *Yi zisun* 宜子孫; *Zhou __ jieguan guo* 周__借觀過.

CAT. NO. 33

SONG JUE 宋珏
1576–1632

GU NINGYUAN 顧凝遠
1595 or earlier–1654

HU YUKUN 胡玉昆
Act. c. 1640–1672

FEI ERQI 費而奇
Act. 1678 or earlier–1701 or later

MEI GENG 梅庚
1640–c. 1722

Album of Landscapes by Famous Masters of the Late Ming–Early Qing 明清名家山水冊

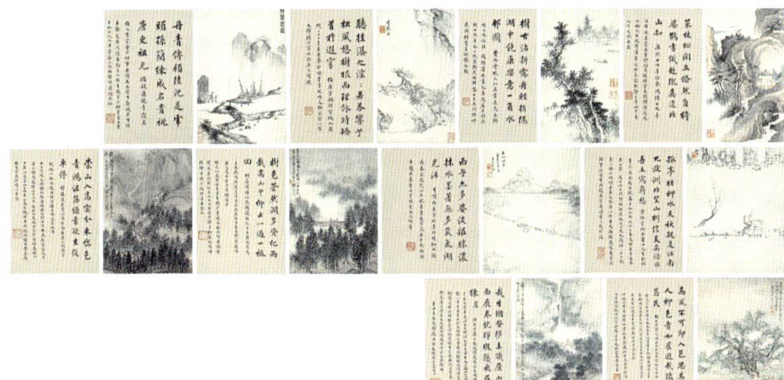

Album of ten leaves of painting, facing calligraphy by Pang Guojun (1885–1966); Private collection

Leaf 1
Fei Erqi, *Recluse on a Pine Path*
Ink and color on paper;
19.7 × 12.1 cm (7 ¾ × 4 ¾ inches)

SEAL OF THE ARTIST

Fei Erqi yin 費而奇印.

Leaf 2
Fei Erqi, *Solitary Fisherman*
Ink on paper; 19.7 × 12.1 cm
(7 ¾ × 4 ¾ inches)

SEALS OF THE ARTIST

Fei Erqi yin 費而奇印, *Ziyi* 字易.

Leaf 3
Mei Geng, *Gazing at a Waterfall*
Ink on paper; 19.5 × 11.7 cm
(7 ¾ × 4 ⅝ inches)

SIGNATURE OF THE ARTIST

Geng 庚.

SEALS: *Mei Geng* 梅庚, *Ouchang* 耦長.

Leaf 4
Gu Ningyuan, *Solitary Pavilion, Imitating Cao Zhibo*
Ink on paper; 17.2 × 11.9 cm
(6 ¾ × 4 ¾ inches)

TITLE

In Imitation of Cao Yunxi [Cao Zhibo]
仿曹雲西.

SEALS: *Gu* 顧, *Ningyuan* 凝遠.

Leaf 5
Song Jue, *Waterside Pavilion*
Ink on paper; 18.1 × 14.5 cm
(7 ⅛ × 5 ¾ inches)

SIGNATURE OF THE ARTIST

Biyu 比玉.

SEAL: *Song Jue* 宋珏.

Leaf 6
Song Jue, *Misty Scene at West Lake*
Ink on paper; 18.1 × 14.5 cm
(7 ⅛ × 5 ¾ inches)

TITLE AND SIGNATURE OF THE ARTIST

Misty Scene at West Lake, after Cao Xiyun [*sic*: Cao Zhibo]. [Signed] Song Jue of Putian.

西湖煙景, 摹曹西雲意. 莆田宋珏.

SEALS: *Song Jue* 宋珏, *Biyu* 比玉.

Leaf 7
Hu Yukun, *The Confucian Grove*
Ink and color on paper;
20.8 × 15.3 cm (8 ¼ × 6 inches)

INSCRIPTION OF THE ARTIST

In the past, I saw three paintings of the Confucian Grove. Now I have been to the Confucian Grove myself and thus made this painting. When the painting was finished it was not perfect, but since it is just a small leaf it serves to capture what was seen by my wanderer's eyes.

舊見孔林圖本三, 既過孔林, 余作圖. 圖俱, 不盡善. 此小幅耳, 轉映遊目.

SEAL: *Yukun* 玉昆.

Leaf 8
Hu Yukun, *On Muling Road*
Ink and color on paper;
20.8 × 15.3 cm (8 ¼ × 6 inches)

INSCRIPTION OF THE ARTIST
On Muling Road, I gaze toward Qi and Lu. The unending black [mourning] traces haunt my mind. I was unable to compose a poem of lamentation, so this painting will have to serve to commemorate this scene!

穆陵道上望齊魯，未了之青，令人神阻，未及作詩以弔，圖當志哉！

SEAL: *Yukun* 玉昆.

ADDITIONAL SEALS: *Tuilou* 退樓, *Wu Yun zhi yin* 吳雲之印 (Wu Yun, 1811–1883); *Fangqing lou* 芳青樓.

Leaf 9
Hu Yukun, *The Five Willows at Chestnut Village*
Ink and color on paper;
20.8 × 15.3 cm (8 ¼ × 6 inches)

INSCRIPTION OF THE ARTIST
Once the white crane is released,
On what day will he arrive in
the mountains?
So long I've yearned for the five
willow trees;
Today, for the first time, I get to pass them.
Brushed while visiting Chestnut Village.

自放白鶴去，何日到山中.
嘗懷五柳樹，今始得過從.
過栗裏筆.

SEALS: *Hu Yukun yin* 胡玉昆印, *Yuanrun* 元潤.

ADDITIONAL SEALS: *Tuilou* 退樓, *Wu Yun zhi yin* 吳雲之印 (Wu Yun); *Fangqing lou* 芳青樓.

Leaf 10
Hu Yukun, *Tiger Stream Bridge at Mount Lu*
Ink and color on paper;
20.8 × 15.3 cm (8 ¼ × 6 inches)

INSCRIPTION OF THE ARTIST
Halfway up Mount Lu is the Temple of the
Eastern Grove;
It calls to mind the worthies of old, but
summoning them is hard!
All night long the stream sounds with
a leopard's roar;
Only after reaching the source can one
surmount Tiger Stream Bridge.

廬山山半東林寺，為想前賢難見招.
一夜溪聲如豹吼，窮源才上虎溪橋.

SEALS: *Hu Yukun yin* 胡玉昆印, *Yuanrun* 元潤.

ADDITIONAL SEALS: *Tuilou* 退樓, *Wu Yun zhi yin* 吳雲之印 (Wu Yun); *Fangqing lou* 芳青樓.

ALBUM TITLE SLIP by Pang Guojun: *Album of Landscapes by Famous Masters of the Late Ming-Early Qing*. Treasure of the discerning Douwen. Autumn, *xinchou* year [1961], Pang Guojun inscribes the title slip.

《明季清初名家山水合冊》.
斗文鑒家秘笈之一. 辛丑秋龐國鈞題籤.

SEALS: *Pang Guojun yin* 龐國鈞印, *Hengshang* 蘅裳.

ADDITIONAL SEALS of Pang Guojun on facing leaves of calligraphy: He 鶴, E'an 莪闇, E'an qishi yihou suozuo 莪闇七十以後所作, Hengshang 蘅裳, Guojun da li 國鈞大利, Pang Guojun 龐國鈞.

CAT. NO. 34

GONG XIAN 龔賢 1619–1689
Lofty Peak and Dense Woods 崇巖密林

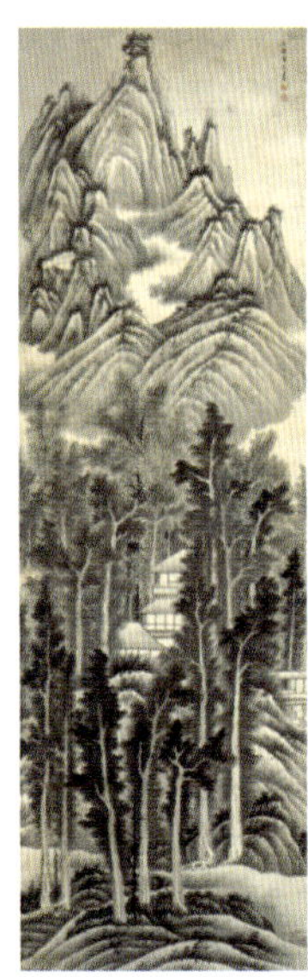

Hanging scroll: ink on paper;
264.2 × 85.1 cm (104 × 33 ½ inches);
Los Angeles County Museum of Art,
Mr. and Mrs. Allan C. Balch Fund (M.54.27)

SIGNATURE OF THE ARTIST
Painted by Gong Xian of Shicheng. 石城龔賢畫.

SEALS: *Chenxian* 臣賢, *Banqian* 半千.

CAT. NO. 35

GONG XIAN 龔賢 1619–1689
Boating in the Breeze 柳風片帆圖

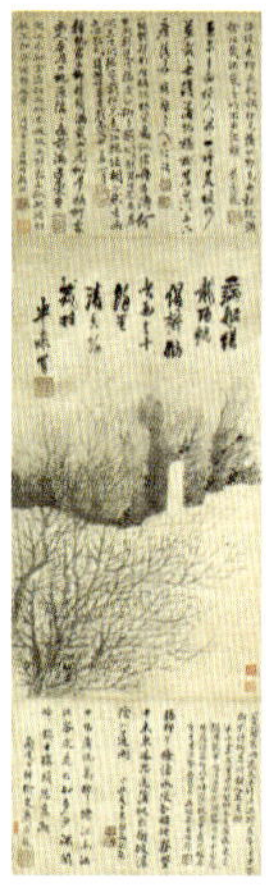

Hanging scroll: ink on paper;
104.5 × 30.5 cm (41 ⅛ × 12 inches);
Private collection

INSCRIPTION BY THE ARTIST
A full boat, completely laden with wine;
The sail borrows the willow's breeze
and billows.
Sailing mile upon mile,
How long will the clear fragrance last?
[Signed] Banmou Xian.

滿船俱載酒，帆借柳風吹.
過去十餘里，清香餘幾時.
半畝賢.

SEAL: *Gong Xian* 龔賢.

ADDITIONAL INSCRIPTIONS ON MOUNTING
HUANG KUI (SEVENTEENTH CENTURY)
Along the bank bare are willows, branches
long and dense;
Suddenly I spot a rush sail, but where might
be the boat?
Don't bother reporting the hold is laden
with wine;
The fragrance in the urn cannot get past the
mud seal.
Huang Kui inscribes.

沿堤禿柳長枝稠，但見蒲帆那見舟.
枉說滿艙俱載酒，甕香吹不出泥頭.
黃逵題.

SEAL: *Yibu* 儀逋.

ZHA SHIBIAO (1615–1698)
On the painting's raw surface the man of old
opened the scene:
A piece of desolate riverside marvelously cut
from the fabric.
Headless, a rush sail by willow bank;
East, under White Gate, Guangling arrives.[1]
Old Man Meihe, Shibiao, inscribes.

畫裡生面故人開，一片荒堤妙剪裁.
無頭蒲帆楊柳岸，白門東下廣陵來.
梅壑老人士標題.

SEALS: *Erzhan* 二瞻, *Zha Shibiao yin* 查士標印.

SHITAO (ZHU RUOJI, 1642–1707)
Similarly, I "cut" a poem, but with a different
density;
The emptiness of my wine cup resembles the
vacant boat.
When will [I] Old Tao, open a brand new vat?
I only get drunk on Sir Huang's inkstone top.
[Rhyming Yibu's verse]
New aspects of Ni and Huang are opened
by the gentleman,
Nigh on thirty years he practically cut
and tailored.
But in order to see the distant river with
green trees in tow,
It is necessary to examine the painting with
serious intent. [Rhyming Eryan's verse]
Playfully done by the Qingxiang Blind Arhat
in the fourth [lunar] month of the *dingchou*
year [1697].

一樣裁詩別有稠，酒梧空處似虛舟.
老濤何日開新甕，只醉黃公研子頭.
[儀逋韵]
倪黃生面是君開，三十年間殆剪裁.
但見遠江拖綠樹，必然查畫上心來.
[二瞻韵]
清湘瞎尊者戲為之也. 丁丑四月.

SEAL: *Qing xiang laoren* 清湘老人.

SONG CAO (1620–1701)
An airy sail shows itself by the willow tops;
Fully carrying the mountains' glow, it seems
like early autumn.
Where will the recluse seek the
cave's opening?
Peach Blossom Spring, deeply hidden, just
past the front isles.
[Signed] The Remnant Historian Song Cao.

輕帆露出柳梢頭，滿載山光似早秋.
何處幽人尋洞口，桃源隱隱過前洲.
逸史宋曹.

SEAL: *Song Cao* 宋曹.

ZHUO ERKAN (1653–1712)
With a laugh the poet faces toward
distant Heaven,
Encounters a village, buys wine, and is drunk
the year round.
Along the stream, unbroken, a thousand rows
of willows;
Don't hold back the traveler and his
thousand-mile boat.
Banqian's [Gong Xian] paintings are modeled after Dong [Yuan] and Ju[ran], and his hills, valleys, and woods largely partake of deep, shady atmosphere. Interspersed are places where he used a dry brush, [resulting in] texturing that is also elegant and rich. In this painting Banqian displays a different manner, with ten thousand willows gathered by a long stream in a patch of mist and fog. Truly, this small painting has the force of a thousand miles. Treasure it. Inscribed by Zhuo Erkan of Luxu.

一笑辭家向遠天，逢村沽酒醉長年.
溪中不斷千行柳，莫縮離人萬里船.
半千畫宗董巨，巒壑樹木，多陰森氣象.

間用乾筆，皴法亦自秀潤. 此幅乃半千變態，將長溪萬柳收于煙霧一抹之中. 真尺幅具有千里之勢也. 寶之. 鹿墟卓爾堪題.

SEAL: *Erkan* 爾堪.

GAO CAI (ACT. LATE SEVENTEENTH–EARLY EIGHTEENTH CENTURY)

A thousand willow branches set by the water's cove,
Clearly dividing the mist, they enter my gaze.
The eastern wind suddenly sends out a rush sail;
Bursting through the thick haze, it opens up a path.
On a summer day in the *dingchou* year [1697], inscribed by Dongli Gao Cai.

楊柳千條傍水隈，分明煙霧望中來. 東風忽送蒲帆出，衝破濃陰一道開. 丁丑夏日，東籬高採題.

SEALS: *Gao Cai* 高采, *Meisheng* 枚升.

XIAO CHEN (ACT. LATE SEVENTEENTH–EARLY EIGHTEENTH CENTURY)

Ten sheets of rush sail, ten thousand willows,
South-of-the-river, north-of-the-river, the traveler's route is remote.
Who knows how many wives from the deep chambers,
All day, atop their towers, resent the evening tides.
Inscribed by the seventy-year old Yusou, Xiao Chen of Lanling.

十幅蒲帆萬柳條，江南江北客途遙.
不知多少深閨婦，鎮日樓頭怨暮潮.
蘭陵古稀楡叟蕭晨題.

SEAL: *Xiao Chen yin* 蕭晨印.

MIN LINSI (1628–1704)

On tall willows by a deserted river, snow and frost in excess;
Awaiting the spring breeze, my eyes cannot gaze far.
Suddenly a lone sail is revealed, shielding a small boat;
Who knows if it carries a crane or carries paintings and calligraphy.
[Signed] Late spring, *shuyan* year [1698], Tanlin Min Linsi.[2]

空江高柳雪霜餘，等待春風眼未舒.
露出孤帆遮却艇，不知載隺載圖書.
戊寅春暮，檀林閔麟嗣.

SEAL: *Min Binlian shi* 閔賓連氏.

ADDITIONAL SEALS: *Nanhai Huang Junbi cang* 南海黃君璧藏, *Huang Junbi yin* 黃君璧印, *Baiyun tang cang* 白雲堂藏, *Baiyun tang* 白雲堂 (Huang Junbi, 1898–1991).

NOTES

1 White Gate refers to Nanjing. Guangling refers to the *Guangling san* 廣陵散, a celebrated *qin* (lute) musical piece notably performed by Xi Kang. According to tradition, Xi played the melody one last time before being executed for political reasons. The *Guangling san* became a trope for the idea of life and art prematurely ended, with distinct loyalist associations.

2 Min Linsi's inscription, though placed in the middle of the others, is dated last. It probably came after that of Xiao Chen, written where there was still some room among the other colophons.

CAT. NO. 36

GONG XIAN 龔賢 1619–1689

Landscape **山水軸, 1689**

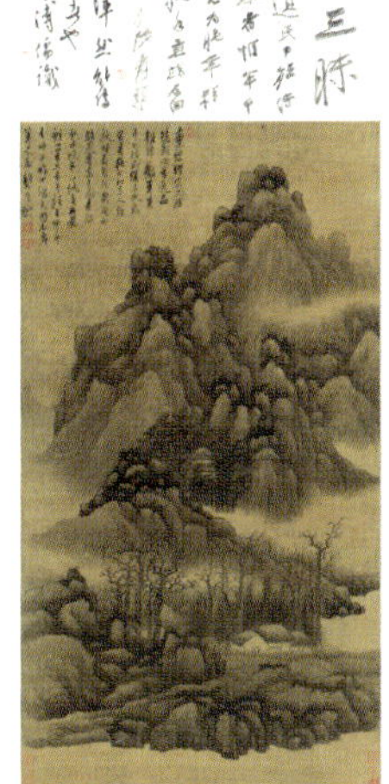

Hanging scroll: ink on silk;
137.8 × 54.8 cm (54 ¼ × 21 ⅝ inches);
Honolulu Museum of Art, Purchase, 1957 (2295.1)

INSCRIPTION BY THE ARTIST

In painting, one must first make an orderly arrangement of the principles of the Song and the Yuan. Afterwards, by relaxing [the principles' binds] one's work will be of the untrammeled class. Although a painting may be composed of just a few scattered strokes, if the Six Laws are complete within, and if the spirit of literature and the standards of calligraphy are both present, then one knows that this painting is the "leftover" skill of a talented person and not some laughable effort by a specialist hoping to stand out from the chaotic masses. Mengduan [Wang Fu] and Qinan [Shen Zhou] in later years amused themselves with the styles of Ni [Ni Zan] and Huang [Huang Gongwang] while remaining grounded in the fundamentals of Dong [Dong Yuan] and Ju [Juran]. My teachers! My teachers! I have made this silk [painting and inscription] in order to set forth the intentions of my brush. [Signed] Gong Xian, early spring, 1689.[1]

畫必綜理宋元，然後散而為逸品. 雖疏疏數筆，其中六法咸備，有文氣，有書格，乃知才人餘技非若亂頭叢，望而貽笑專家者也. 孟端，啓南晚年以倪黃為遊戲，以董巨為本根. 吾師乎，吾師乎. 作此縑竟，因志命筆之意. 龔賢. 己巳穀雨.

ADDITIONAL INSCRIPTIONS WITH SEALS ON MOUNTING by Zhang Daqian 張大千 (1899–1983) dated 1946 and Pu Ru 溥儒 (1896–1963).

NOTE

1 Translation after Chung-lan Wang, "Gong Xian (1619–1689)," 308–9, with amendments.

CAT. NO. 37

KUNCAN 髡殘 b. 1612

Temple on a Mountain Ledge **群峰古寺, 1661**

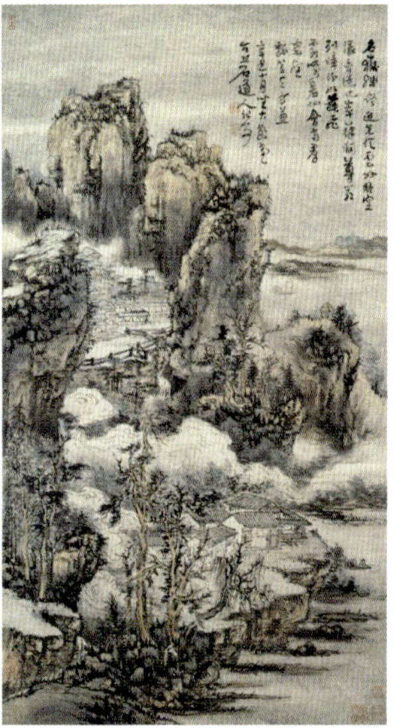

Hanging scroll: ink and color on paper;
85.9 × 48.3 cm (33 ¾ × 19 inches);
Asia Society, New York, Mr. and Mrs. John D. Rockefeller 3rd Collection 1979.124

INSCRIPTION BY THE ARTIST

Famous mountains! I, Monk Can, approach,
First viewing them from beyond the clouds.
That vast expanse encompasses Creation,
That lofty majesty displays great dignity!
Rows of peaks, like clustered bamboo,
Flying mists, as if spit out by Immortals!
Soon I will be amongst those myriad ravines,
Gourd and bamboo hat as my companions.
In the tenth month of the *xinchou* year [1661], sitting in the Daxie Hall,
Jieqiu, the Stone Monk records.

名嶽殘僧近，先從雲外瞻.
空濛含造化，崒嵂闢尊嚴.
列嶂紛如簇，飛霞噴若仙.
會當群眾壑，瓢笠與身兼.
辛丑十月坐大歇堂，介丘石道人記事.

SEALS: *Shixi* 石谿, *Baitu* 白禿.

ADDITIONAL SEALS: *Yuzhai* 玉齋, *Nanping zhencang* 南屏珍藏 (Wong Nan-p'ing 王南屏, 1924–1985); *Guanwu zhencang* 冠五珍藏, *Tianxi shuwu* 田溪書屋 (He Guanwu 何冠五, twentieth century); *Haomeng* 好夢 (Zhang Daqian 張大千, 1899–1983).

CAT. NO. 38

XU FANG 徐枋 1622–1694

Mount Qinyuhang **秦餘杭山圖, datable to 1672**

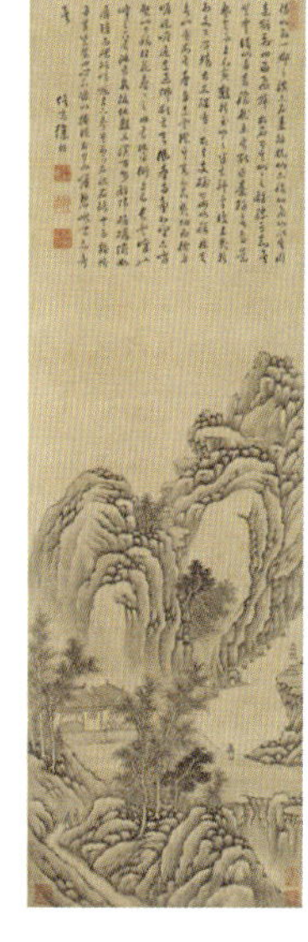

Hanging scroll: ink on silk;
156.2 × 48.9 cm (61 ½ × 19 ¼ inches);
Private collection

INSCRIPTION BY THE ARTIST

Mount Yang is the chief mountain in the commandery. Another name for it is Mount Qinyuhang. It is also called Mount Sifei [Four-Flying], since the mountain range is endless and the four sides all look like they are in flight. Thus, one can imagine how grand and steep it is. Many of the mountains of Wu are outstanding in appearance, but none has ever compared to Mount Qinyu. The dangerously narrow hill paths wind into the void with countless turns. Halfway up the side of the mountain, there is a temple. Several bends further up, there is the site of Master Zhi's religious practices, which is the old Manjusri Temple. In the past, this temple together with the temples on Mount Zhixing and Mount Hua were called the three legs of the tripod [being the most important]. In front of the temple, there is a terrace. Handsomely erect, facing the clouds, and of immeasurable height, it is called the Cliff of Self-Sacrifice. Turning left from the cliff and passing the Buddhist temple, there is the Terrace of Heavenly Wind. The two terraces face one another. They are also cliffs. Nowadays it is called Osmanthus Terrace. Within, the terrace is level and expansive. Above it rises the Peak of Incessant Clouds. Under the peak, there is a pond and a spring. The peak rises several meters above the ground and is a couple hundred feet in width. Grand and majestic, it is just like a screen. The loftiness and steepness, as well as the unevenness, up and down, all defy description. Various sorts of trees prosper in the stone cracks. Red, yellow, purple and emerald [their leaves and blossoms] do not wither in any season. They flicker brightly, scattered among the green cliffs and peaks. How marvelous it is! [Signed] Sizhai, Xu Fang.

陽山爲一郡之鎮，亦名秦餘杭山，亦稱四飛山，以其岡連嶺屬，四面飛舞故名，則其山之雄勝可知矣．吳中諸山多奇勝，然未有能匹秦餘者．鳥道盤空而上，不啻數折．至山之半有神宇，復上幾折，爲支公道場古文殊寺．寺故與支硎，華山稱鼎足者也．寺前有臺，卓立雲際，其高不知幾仞，爲捨身崖．從崖迤左，過佛剎，有天風臺，兩臺相望，亦峭壁也，今稱桂花臺．臺之內有地平衍．上即長雲峰也．峰之下有池有泉．拔地數丈，闊百步．雄偉磅礴，儼如屏障，而磥砢崎崛，上下參差，不可名狀．石罅中多雜樹，丹黃紫翠，四時不凋，以掩暎於蒼崖碧巘間，亦奇矣．
俟齋徐枋．

SEALS: *Xuechuang'an* 雪床庵, *Xu Fang zhi yin* 徐枋之印, *Sizhai* 俟齋, *Qinyu shanren* 秦餘山人, *Lishan lishui jian* 笠山笠水間, *Juyi tang yin* 居易堂印, *Xu Bozi Sizhai huaji* 徐伯子俟齋畫記.

CAT. NO. 39

FANG HENGXIAN 方亨咸 act. c. 1647–1678
Painting and Calligraphy 書畫冊, after 1659

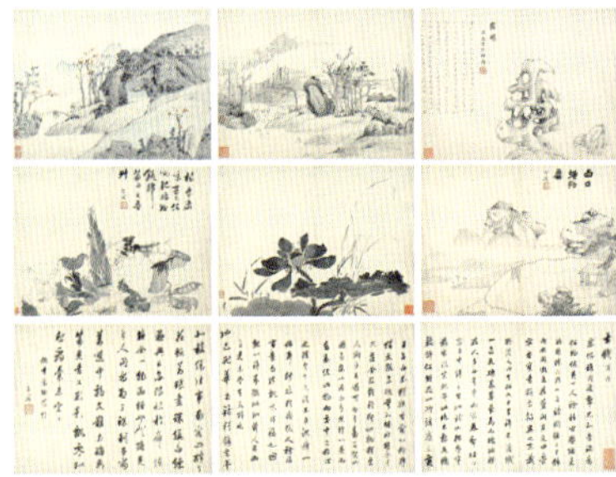

Album of nine leaves: ink and color on paper; 29.2 × 39.1 cm (11 ½ × 15 ⅜ inches); Private collection

INSCRIPTIONS OF THE ARTIST

Leaf 1
Straight and Erect. Inscribed by the Imperial Secretary, Shen Yue, of the Liang Dynasty. [One seal masquerading as that of Shen Yue] *Xiuwen zhi yin*.
The sky cleared after snow, and I strolled to Yuhua'an [Studio of Rain and Flowers] to seek Shen Xiuwen's [Shen Yue's] rock. I found it amidst wild grass growing everywhere in a deserted field. The height of the rock was roughly one *zhang* [about ten feet]. Gazing at it, it was like congealed clouds. The hollows were exquisite. The color was dark, and its manner was like a soaring phoenix. Beside the rock were five old vines, competing with one another in and out of the hollows, piercing through the abdomen and covering the top. Overgrown branches and leaves seemed to be wrapping and stroking it. The rock was engraved with eight characters, "Straight and Erect, inscribed by the Imperial Secretary, Shen Yue, of the Liang dynasty," followed by a seal. Indeed, it was a fantastic rock. I further investigated the base. It was inscribed, "[Shen] Yue once studied here." His hand must have stroked this rock! It has been more than a millennium since the Liang dynasty. The world has changed several times, and yet the rock still stands majestically. Is it because of a spirit within? The facts of [Shen] Yue's life are more or less known. Or this rock can also transmit it, and make people sigh in reflection.
I returned and painted this.

《鵠峙》梁尚書沈約題.「休文之印」.
雪晴步雨花菴訪沈休文石，得之於荒田蔓草間．石高盈丈．望之若凝雲，然嵌空玲瓏，黛色，勢如翔鸞，旁有老藤五株争竇出入，穿腹覆頂，童童如蓋捫．鎸曰：鵠峙，梁尚書沈約題，八字，圖章一．誠異石也．考其基云：約嘗讀書於此．則是其手撫者矣！自梁迄今千餘年，滄桑幾易，此石巍然，抑有物憑其間耶．約生平可概見，猶能令石傳之，令人慨然．歸而圖此．

SEAL: *Hengxian* 亨咸.

ADDITIONAL SEAL: *Guqian Chen Shaoshi shoucang mingji* 古黔陳少石收藏名跡.

Leaf 2
SEAL: *Fangshi shaocun* 方氏邵邨.

ADDITIONAL SEAL: *Shaoshi shending* 少石審定.

Leaf 3
SEAL: *Fangshi shaocun* 方氏邵邨.

ADDITIONAL SEAL: *Kuilin* 夔麟.

Leaf 4
The thatched door remains closed during the day. [Signed] *A'xian.*

白日掩荊扉．阿咸.

SEAL: *Hengxian* 亨咸.

ADDITIONAL SEAL: *Jieyuan huapi* 潔園畫癖.

Leaf 5
SEAL: *Fangshi shaocun* 方氏邵邨.

ADDITIONAL SEAL: *Shaoshi guoyan* 少石過眼.

Leaf 6
The taste of root vegetables is quite enduring. Why is it necessary to eat meat to get satiated? This is for my uncle's correction. [Signed] *A'xian.*

根食滋味甚長，何必肥腯始飫耶．當正之吾叔．阿咸.

SEAL: *Hengxian* 亨咸.

ADDITIONAL SEAL: *Shaoshi* 少室.

Leaves 7–9
An Old Coin, with Preface
In the border areas, it was the custom to use money made of leather, so they did not know what a green [bronze] coin was. By chance, I saw a person with this thing ostentatiously hanging from his belt. Examining it, I realized that it was an old coin. Its diameter was over two *cun* [inches]. Its edge and hole were exquisite, its patina encrusted deep green. The inscription read *Chongning chongbao*, "Treasure of the Chongning reign" [1102–1106], in writing similar to the ancient clerical script. I found it unusual and wondered whence it came. A person accompanying me said, "Over sixty *li* away there is an old city wall. Rubble and thick grass cover the district but the ruins of the wall still exist. Many people farm there. After the spring rains, they plow the field and often find something in the soil—all coins like this." *Chongning* was the name of one of Song Huizong's reigns, but this area did not belong to the Song territory where coin smelting took place, so how could it reach here? Perhaps during the Jingkang change [1126, when the Northern Song fell to the Jin], a plain-clothed member of the defeated royal family still carried the *chongbao* as a symbol of sovereignty? It is regrettable that texts provide no clues regarding the origin of this wall. The hardy spindle trees have long withered and golden bowls are difficult to trace. How is it that this object still appears in the human realm? Its travails are lamentable but its longevity deserves celebrating. Because of this I ruminate: because they are used, teeth waste away, yet the *chu* tree, because its timber is useless, enjoys a long life. If this object had been buried would tomb robbers have let it remain buried for long? Had it been smelted down in the blaze of a furnace, could it have become an adornment for this man's belt? Don't say that being discarded with no one to depend upon is not a blessing. Hence I write this poem to add to the fact that in the past there was someone who had wandered here, not beyond Heaven's pale.

This area no longer a part of the realm,
Yet the coin still bore a Song year.
Northern axles—heart-rending matters
of the past[1];
Southern travelers question the territory
beyond their reach.
Completely corroded to a deep jade green,
The circular coin suspended with a white
silk string.
The rise and fall [of a dynasty] is cause
for endless grief,
Yet, strangely, the shape of the coin
is preserved.
An object so small passed down generation
after generation;
Its emergence and hiding so much like
a person.
I still recall the making of the *sanzhu* coins,[2]
Which would be chosen from out of
ten thousand.
Thus, the soil would not easily obscure its
dragon design,
And its bird seal script would present the
calligrapher's skill.
The coin's form and shadow are as if lost
in time,
Yet it remains to fill a purse.
Casually I transcribe an old piece that I composed in the past while in the border regions. [Signed] Hengxian.

古錢，幷序.
塞俗雜用皮幣，不知青錢爲何物．偶見一人襘裆間壓綏者的然，探之乃一古錢，圜徑二寸餘，肉好周緻，土花蒼潤．其文曰：崇甯重寶．書類古隸，異之不識．所從人曰：去此六十里許有舊城一區，瓦礫蓁莽蒙焉，而壖垣猶在．人多田其中，雨過春犂，往往從土中得之，皆此錢也．按崇甯爲宋徽宗紀年，此地不隸瓦橋鼓鑄，何能及此？抑靖康之變王子白衣猶挾重寶以狩耶．惜文獻無徵莫知城始．然冬青久落，金盌難稽，何此物猶出人間乎？其遇可悲其壽可賀也．因念齒以用而自焚，樗以棄而多壽．使此物向處中土，椎埋之徒豈令久没？不過洪爐一焰耳，何能猶周旋人襘裆間哉？勿謂飄零非福也．因紀以詩益徵此地前人有遊之者，未嘗在天外也.
地已非華土，錢猶鑄宋年.
北轅傷往事，南客問殊天.
花蝕蒼琅盡，環綏白練懸.
興亡無限恨，輪廓怪能全.
一物微經世代，隱現與人同.
尙想三銖制，曾當萬選中.
龍文難土晦，鳥篆見書工.
形影飄零似，留看囊未空.
偶書塞外舊作．亨咸.

SEAL: *Longmian Fang Hengxian Shaocun tuhua yin* 龍眠方亨咸邵邨圖畫印.

ADDITIONAL SEAL ON LEAF 7: *Baoyu ge shuhua ji* 寶迂閣書畫記 (Chen Kuilin 陳夔麟, 1855–1928).

NOTES

1 Northern axles refer to carts being brought to the north. The phrase was used in reference to the capture of Song Huizong and his son, Song Qinzong, and their journey to Jin territory, where they ultimately perished.

2 The *sanzhu* coins were minted at the start of Emperor Han Wudi's reign (141–87 BCE).

CAT. NO. 40

FANG YIZHI 方以智 1611–1671

Plum Blossoms and Pine 梅華松圖軸, after 1650

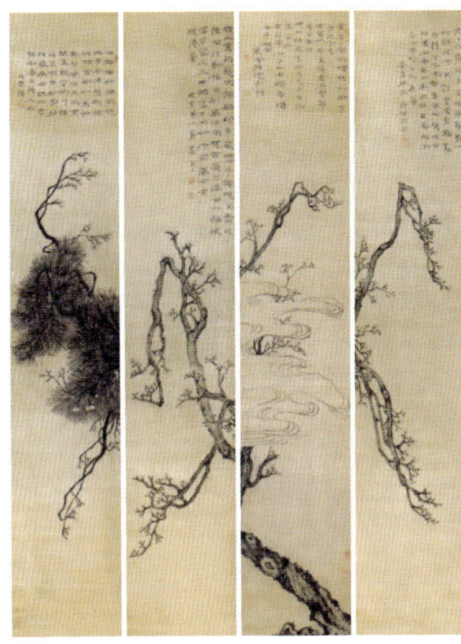

Four hanging scrolls: ink on satin;
210.5 × 38.1 cm (82 ⅞ × 15 inches) each;
Private collection

Scroll 1

Freshly, freshly, growing icy, frosty here in this natural realm,
Sweeping away the resplendent and sensual, a withered Chan monk.
Sturdy branches in utter silence, fragrance forming snow;
Petal on petal, dispassionate, coldness transformed to mist.
Zhao Yi's dream returns, startling this night;
Lin Bu, transformed and gone—what year would that have been?
With whom do the blossoms reside, here at West Lake, for many a long age?
If not in the toad's moon palace then to distant lands where wild geese migrate.[1]
[Signed] Inscribed by me, Monk Moli Hongzhi.

生生冰霜自在天，抹除繁艷一枯禪.
祛祛無語香成雪，點點忘情冷化烟.
趙逸夢回驚此夜，林逋仙去是何年.
與誰合署鹵湖長，不是蟾宮即雁邊.
墨歷頭陀弘智自題.

SEALS: *Qulu woyou* 曲廬臥遊, *Wu wo xiang* 無我相, *Yu jing ze ping yu xin* 欲靜則平於心.

Scroll 2

People gone from Spirit Cliff, I go to visit the jeweled branches;
Newly displaying their monks' robes—not to be wondered at.
Before the gates of the Dark Tomb, birds chatter in the snow;
Flute music in white clouds, the guest is without poem.
And so I realize the days of fragrant bloom out in the immortal's realm
Is a time when, on cold mountains, the blossoms have already fallen.
I think within, I'd like to become an Immortal, but my heart is too ancient,
Enticed by spring, enticed by the common world, just not suitable at all.[2]
[Signed] Monk Wuke's long poem.

靈岩人去訪瓊枝，新敞袈裟正不奇.
玄墓門前禽語雪，白雲笛裏客無詩.
可知瑝圃芬芳日，已是寒山堕落時.
度自僊仙心太古，媚春媚俗未相宜.
無可頭陀長歌.

SEALS: *Fushan yuzhe* 浮山愚者, *Wuxian qin* 無弦琴, *Ci zhi wei ziqian* 此之謂自謙, *Tianqiu dafu _zhang* 天求大夫 _章, *Yaodi toutuo* 藥地頭陀. One seal undeciphered.

Scroll 3

An old appointment at Lord Mountain; how many times have I gone searching?
She wishes to marry the eastern wind but I fear familiarity is lacking.
Dawn Horns in the Frosty Sky—I remember North-of-Xiang River;
Bow and sword at Broken Bridge—I dream of South-of-the-Yangzi.
In Buddhist temples down through the years I've drawn the "106";
In precincts of serenity, amid traces of snow, remain two or three.
The vast earth so full of confusion still like this;
I ask others: what will make the Udumbara flower appear?[3]
[Signed] Mozi, number one peak in the heavenly realm.

君山舊約幾回探，欲嫁東風恐未諳.
曉角霜天憶湘北，斷橋弓劍夢江南.
梵宮歲月得百六，靜域雪痕留二三.
大地茫茫尚如此，問渠何事現優曇.
天界第一峯墨子.

SEALS: *Zhi* 智, *Yu tian wei tu* 與天為徒. Two partial seals: *Fang* 方, *Wu you bei* 吾又悲.

Scroll 4

Its ancient trunk slants crosswise—a fragrant jade dragon;
Or an old Buddha arrived from the West, manner old and feeble.
From his staff head fragrance scatters, covering ten thousand trees;
Straddling a crane [so high], the cold is doubled, tripled!
By the rustic hut it is hard to describe, cultivated by the bright moon;
Only wild moss suits it, sealed tight by cut-off clouds.
By broken fence in a hidden valley, who acts as understanding friend?
Not counting this green, green pine tree atop a hill?
[Signed] Monk Tianjie.

古幹横斜桂玉龍，西來老佛態龍鍾.
杖頭香散一萬樹，鶴背寒添三兩重.
埜屋難容明月種，荒苔祇合斷雲封.
破籬幽谷誰知己，除却青青陵上松.
天界僧.

SEALS: *Hongzhi* 弘智, *Fushan yuzhe* 浮山愚者, *Xipao* 繫匏, *Yu jingzhe ping yu xin* 欲靜者平於心.

NOTES

1 Translations for the inscriptions on the four paintings are amended from those by Jonathan Chaves in Moss, *This Single Feather of Auspicious Light*, 450–56. Lin Bu was the eleventh-century hermit of West Lake who was known for his love of plum blossoms. Whereas Lin never served his own state, Zhao Yi, described as a bookish recluse, was captured and served under the enemy for the common people's sake (see also page 222, note 9). By pairing these two historical figures, Fang Yizhi perhaps expressed his wish of serving neither the remnant Ming resistance nor the conquering Qing regime.

2 Spirit Cliff and Dark Tomb (Mountain) both refer to scenic sites in the vicinity of Suzhou. Dark Tomb Mountain was especially known for its plum blossom trees. The mountain is named because of the tomb of a fourth-century official, Yu Taixuan (*xuan* 玄 translates as "dark" or "mysterious," which is adopted here because of the parallel with the "spirit" of Spirit Cliff). Yu is said to have been so kind as to have moved birds and animals—hence the chattering birds in this line. See *Taiping yulan* 太平御覽 (*Siku quanshu* ed.), 922:6b.

3 Fang Yizhi uses a wealth of allusions to compose a poem that is deeply suggestive of loyalist sentiment, beginning with one of legendary times. Lord Mountain, located within Lake Dongting in Hunan Province, is named after the "lords of the Xiang," King Shun's loyal wives Ehuang and Nüying, who sought his whereabouts and died in the region. "Dawn Horn in the Frosty Sky" is the title of a *ci* (song lyrics) tune. Fang is almost certainly alluding specifically to a song written to this tune by Fan Chengda on the subject of plum blossoms that praises their enduring character in a metaphoric manner. See *Quan fang bei zu ji* 全芳備祖集 (*Siku quanshu* ed.), 1:53a–b. Broken Bridge is a well-known feature on West Lake at Hangzhou where the plum-loving recluse Lin Bu resided. "Bow and sword" is an allusion to the mourning of one's lost lord. The fifth line of Fang's poem utilizes the symbolism of the *Yi jing* 易經 (Book of changes) to highlight the bad fortune (the number 106) of the Ming *yimin*, or remnant subjects. Fang may have intended an additional layer of meaning to "two or three" in line 4, borrowing from the ancient text *Shang shu*: "If your Virtue is unified, then of your actions, none will fail to be auspicious. But if your Virtue is two- or three-faced, then of your actions, none will fail to be noxious" 德惟一，動罔不吉，德二三，動罔不凶. Lin Zhiqi 林之奇, *Shangshu quanjie* 尚書全解 (*Siku quanshu* ed.), 17:9a. If Fang is alluding to this passage, then there is an embedded criticism of those in the *yimin* community who were wavering in their loyalty. The last line's Udumbara blossom (a flower embedded within its fruit and consequently unseen) was used in Buddhist discourse to suggest events of rare occurrence. Fang uses it to express his despair over the current situation, wondering when an auspicious age will return.

CAT. NO. 41

BADA SHANREN 八大山人 1626–1705

Crabapple Blossoms 海棠春秋圖, c. 1684

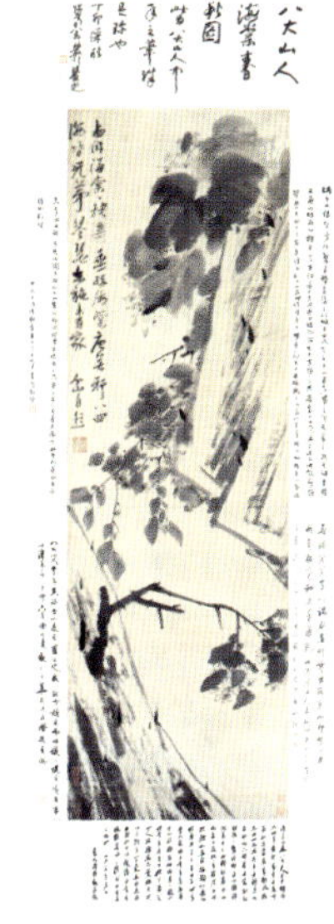

Hanging scroll: ink on paper;
119.5 × 38.5 cm (47 × 15 ¼ inches);
Private collection

INSCRIPTION BY THE ARTIST

Xifu crabapples—*tangdi* blossoms;
Chuisi crabapples—Tang Ruoye [lotus].
Ruoye, within the four seas, all are brothers;
Longing for harmony, this ugly Dong Shi is still without abode.
Inscribed by Geshan.

西湝海棠棠棣華，垂絲海棠唐若邪.
若邪四海皆兄弟，琴瑟東施未有家.
个山自題.

SEAL: *Hefu* 何負.

ADDITIONAL SEALS: *Qingxiang laoren* 清湘老人 (Shitao, 1642–1707); Tang Yun shending 唐雲審定 (Tang Yun, 1910–1993); *Diyan caotang* 滌硯草堂, *Deng Shixun cang* 鄧仕勳藏 (Deng Shixun, b. twentieth century).

TITLE AND ADDITIONAL INSCRIPTIONS WITH SEALS ON OUTER MOUNTING by Xie Zhiliu 謝稚柳 (1910–1997), Xu Bangda 徐邦達 (1911–2012), Qigong 啟功 (1912–2005), Liu Jiuan 劉九庵 (1915–1999), and Wang Fangyu 王方宇 (1913–1997).

SEALS: *Zhiliu* 稚柳, *Xie* 謝 (Xie Zhiliu); *Bangda shending* 邦達審定, *Xu Bangda yin* 徐邦達 (Xu Bangda); *Qigong* 啟功, *Yuanbai* 元白 (Qigong); *Liu* 劉, *Jiuan* 九庵 (Liu Jiuan); *Fangyu* 方宇 (Wang Fangyu).

OUTER LABEL WRITTEN by Xiao Ping 蕭平 (b. 1942).

CAT. NO. 42

BADA SHANREN 八大山人
1626–1705
Golden Fish, Lotus Pods, Globefish, and Bamboo 竹，蓮蓬，河豚，金魚子合冊, 1689

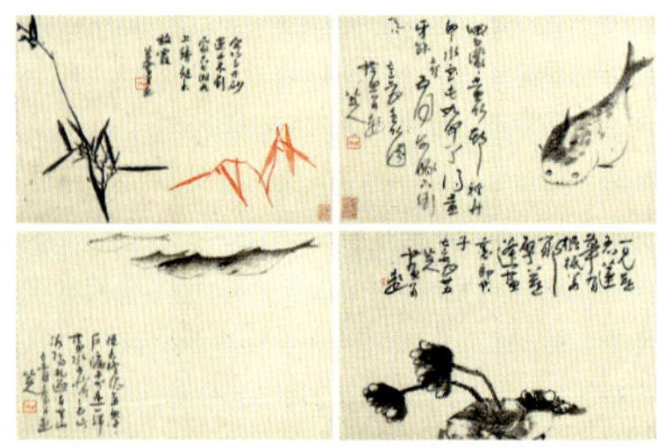

Album of four leaves: ink and color on paper; *Golden Fish* and *Lotus Pods*: 29.8 × 28.3 cm (11 ¾ × 11 ⅛ inches), *Globefish* and *Bamboo*: 29.8 × 46.6 cm (11 ¾ × 18 ⅜ inches); Private collection

INSCRIPTIONS BY THE ARTIST

1. Globefish
Fine rain drizzling in Yellow
Bamboo Village,
A light boat bobbing in mounds of water
and clouds.
How can one get [satisfied with] a meal
for the Yellow Teeth [the immortal's
yellow sprouts]?
In the fifth month the river pig is swallowed
upside down!
Painted and inscribed at the Yellow Bamboo Garden in the sixth month of the *jisi* year [1689], Bada Shanren.

細雨濛濛黄竹村，輕舟勺勺水雲屯.
如何了得黄牙飯，五月河豚下倒吞.
己巳六月黄竹園畫并題，八大山人.

SEAL: *Bada Shanren* 八大山人.

2. Bamboo
Painting bamboo [in ink] and cinnabar,
Cultivating the cinnabar, not yet home.
For now, above the Xiang River,
Dragonflies have not yet radiated the
rosy clouds.
Painted and inscribed by Bada Shanren.

寫竹與丹砂，還丹不到家.
只今湘水上，蜻蜓未放霞.
八大山人畫并題.

SEAL: *Bada Shanren* 八大山人.

3. Lotus Pods
Upon seeing the heart of the lotus seed
[I know] the lotus flower has roots.
At Ruoye the lotus pod was clove open;
In the painting: a dear young lord.[1]
Painted and inscribed by Bada Shanren, twenty-fifth day of the seventh month, *jisi* year [1689].

一見蓮子心，蓮花有根柢.
若耶擘蓮蓬，畫裏郎君子.
己巳七月二十五，八大山人畫并題.

SEAL: *Bada Shanren* 八大山人.

4. Golden Fish
The golden fish that used to carry wine,
Have divided into equal camps, each in its
corner.
I paint a few sheets of pitiable water,
At Xunyang twisting past two layers of
mountains.[2]
Painted and inscribed in the tenth month of the *jisi* year [1689], Bada Shanren.

從來擔酒金魚子，戶牖平分是一端.
畫水可憐三五片，潯陽軋過兩重山.
己巳十月畫并題，八大山人.

SEAL: *Bada Shanren* 八大山人.

ADDITIONAL SEAL: *Miao jixiang an* 妙吉祥庵 (Huang Shanshou 黄山壽, 1855–1919).

NOTES

1 This is a revised translation from what I previously had written for *Master of the Lotus Garden*, 115. The poem appears in at least two other places: on the 1690 handscroll *Lotus and Birds* (Cincinnati Museum of Art) and as one of eight poems transcribed in the *Combined Album of Painting and Calligraphy: "Grieving for a Fallen Nation"* (c. 1693–96) in the Freer Gallery of Art (fig. 43). For the former, see *Master of the Lotus Garden*, fig. 59; for the latter, see Joseph Chang, et al., *In Pursuit of Heavenly Harmony*, cat. no. 8, leaf 8, poem 1.

2 Xunyang refers to the region around the city of Jiujiang in Jiangxi Province where the Yangzi River passes.

CAT. NO. 43

BADA SHANREN 八大山人
1626–1705
Small Fish 小魚群扇面, 1695

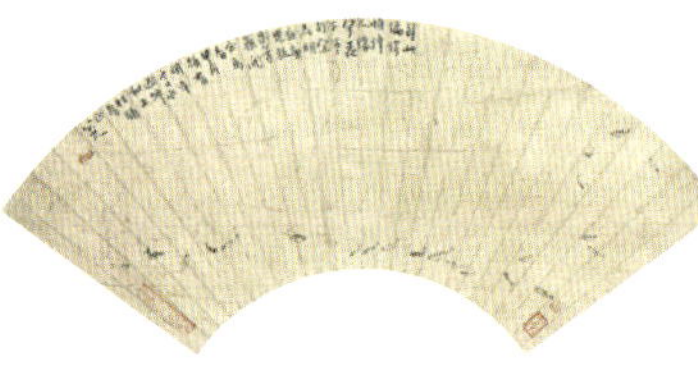

Folding fan mounted as an album leaf: ink on mica-surfaced (*yunmu*) paper; 16.7 × 49.5 cm (6 ⅝ × 19 ½ inches); Private collection

INSCRIPTION BY THE ARTIST

Here comes the one who once was favored,
now turned haggard;
Why does he linger these many days under
the flowers?
Had Kunming remained the fish could
be released;
When the tree peony blossomed it was
spring at Jinma.
This poem was composed in the *jiashu* year [1694]. In the winter of the next year the monk Guofeng looked it over for me.

到此偏憐憔悴人，緣何花下兩三旬.
定昆明在魚兒放，木芍藥開金馬春.
甲戌題畫，明年冬日承過峰和上枉顧為正.

SEAL: *Bada Shanren* 八大山人.

ADDITIONAL SEALS: *Dafengtang Jianjiang Kuncan Xuege Kugua moyuan* 大風堂漸江髡殘雪个苦瓜墨緣 (Zhang Daqian, 1899–1983); *Fangyu* 方宇 (Wang Fangyu 王方宇, 1913–1997); *Shixun* 仕勳 (Deng Shixun 鄧仕勳).

CAT. NO. 44

BADA SHANREN 八大山人
1626–1705
Lotus and Rock 墨荷圖軸, c. 1697

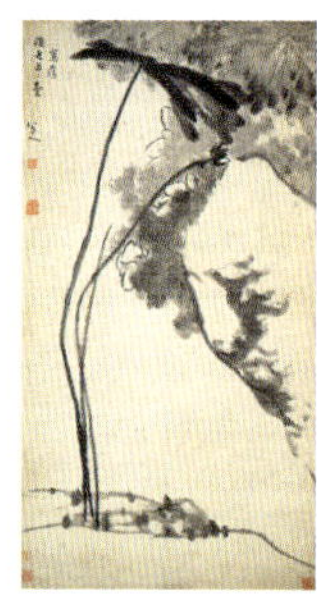

Hanging scroll: ink on paper; 127.5 × 67.6 cm (50 ¼ × 26 ⅝ inches); Collection of Shitou Shuwu

INSCRIPTION BY THE ARTIST

Sketched for Zhi, the Elder. [Signed] Bada Shanren.

寫為治老年臺. 八大山人.

SEALS: *Huangzhuyuan* 黄竹園, *Kede shenxian* 可得神仙, *Bada Shanren* 八大山人.

ADDITIONAL SEALS: *Banjuliuge* 半句留閣, *Wujin Zhao Qufei Yaonong cangyin* 武進趙去非藥農藏印 (Zhao Yuhuang 趙燏黄, 1883–1960).

CAT. NO. 45

BADA SHANREN 八大山人
1626–1705
Landscape for Yushan 贈余山山水扇面, 1699

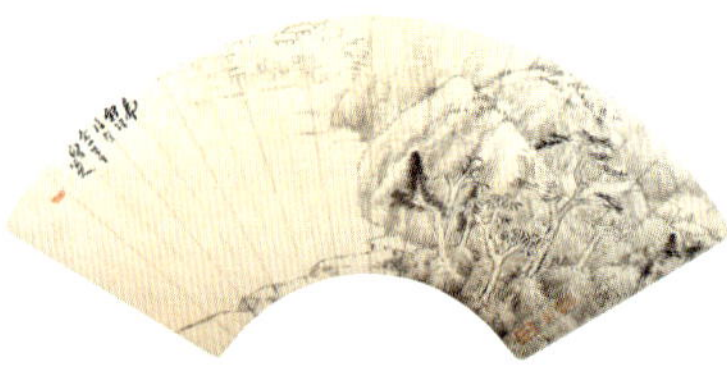

Folding fan mounted as an album leaf: ink on paper; 18 × 53 cm (7 ⅛ × 20 ⅞ inches); Private collection

INSCRIPTION BY THE ARTIST

Sketched for Mr. Yushan after frost in the *jimao* year [1699]. [Signed] Bada Shanren.

己卯霜降後為余山先生寫. 八大山人.

SEAL: *Bada Shanren* 八大山人.

ADDITIONAL SEALS: *Fangyu* 方宇 (Wang Fangyu 王方宇, 1913–1997); *Shixun* 仕勳, *Huaishilou zhencang ji* 懷石樓珍藏記 (Deng Shixun 鄧仕勳, b. twentieth century).

CAT. NO. 46

BADA SHANREN 八大山人
1626–1705
Landscape 山水扇面, c. 1705

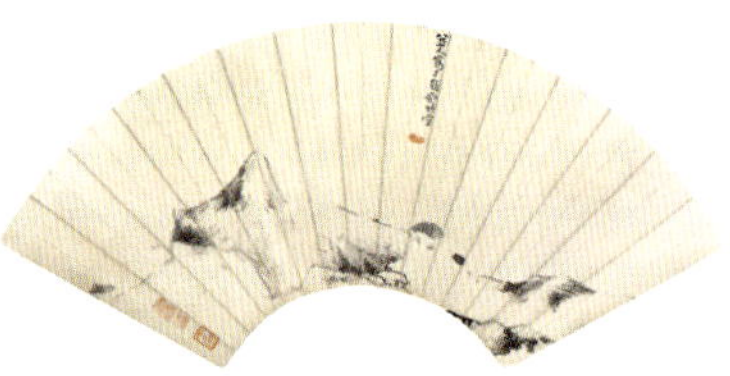

Folding fan mounted as an album leaf: ink on paper; 18 × 50 cm (7 ⅛ × 19 ¾ inches); Private collection

INSCRIPTION BY THE ARTIST

Sketched by Bada Shanren at the Wuge Thatched Hall.

八大山人于寤歌草堂.

SEAL: *Bada Shanren* 八大山人.

ADDITIONAL SEALS: *Fangyu* 方宇 (Wang Fangyu); *Shixun* 仕勳, *Huaishilou zhencang ji* 懷石樓珍藏記 (Deng Shixun).

CAT. NO. 47

BADA SHANREN 八大山人
1626–1705
Landscapes 山水冊, c. 1702–03

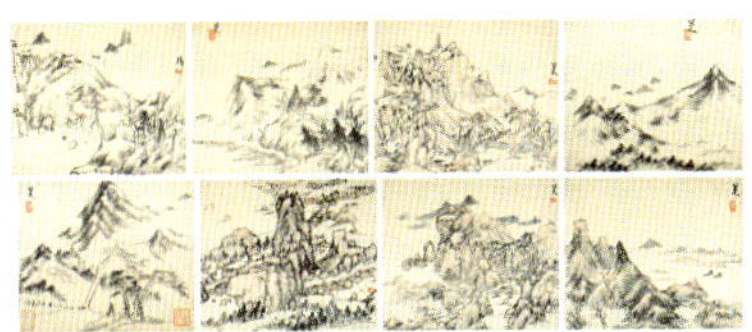

Album of eight leaves: ink and color on satin; 23.5 × 27.8 cm (9 ½ × 10 ⅞ inches) each, with slight variations; Honolulu Museum of Art, Gift of Robert Allerton, 1959 (2561.1)

SIGNATURES AND SEALS OF THE ARTIST

Leaf A
Bada Shanren 八大山人. *Shi de* 拾得.

Leaf B
Bada Shanren 八大山人. *Bada Shanren* 八大山人.

Leaf C
Bada Shanren 八大山人. *Shi de* 拾得.

Leaf D
Shi de 拾得. *Bada Shanren* 八大山人.

Leaf E
Bada Shanren 八大山人. *Shi de* 拾得.

Leaf F
Bada Shanren 八大山人. *Bada Shanren* 八大山人.

Leaf G
Bada Shanren 八大山人 (seal only).

Leaf H
Bada Shanren 八大山人. *Shi de* 拾得.

ADDITIONAL SEALS on leaf H: *Wang Jiqian haiwai suojian mingji* 王季遷海外所見名跡 (Wang Jiqian 王季遷, 1907–2003); *Xiao mei xin* 小梅薪.

CAT. NO. 48

BADA SHANREN 八大山人
1626–1705
Landscape 山水軸, c. 1697–1700

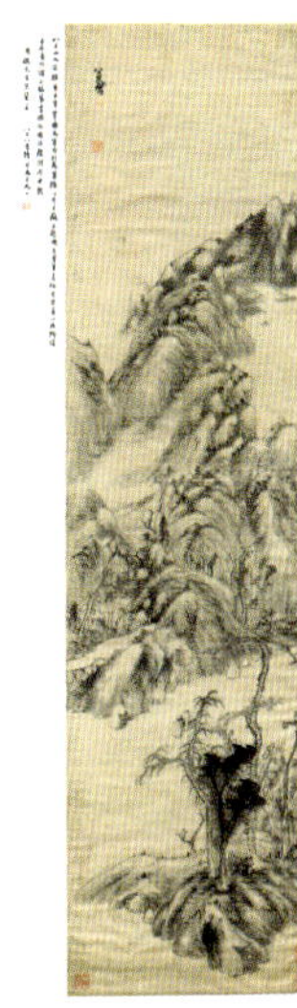

Hanging scroll: ink on satin; 186 × 47 cm (73 ¼ × 18 ½ inches); Private collection

INSCRIPTION BY THE ARTIST
Sketched by Bada Shanren.

八大山人寫.

SEALS: *Bada Shanren* 八大山人, *Kede shenxian* 可得神仙, *Yaozhu* 遙屬.

ADDITIONAL SEALS: *Baiyun tang* 白雲堂 (Huang Junbi 黃君璧, 1898–1991); *Wang Jiqian haiwai suojian mingji* 王季遷海外所見名跡 (Wang Jiqian 王季遷, 1907–2003).

ADDITIONAL INSCRIPTION dated 1999 on the outer mounting by Zhang Longyan 張隆延 (1909–2009).

SEAL: *Longyan* 隆延.

TITLE SLIP WRITTEN by Zhang Longyan.

CAT. NO. 49

ZHA SHIBIAO 查士標 1615–1698
Scenery of the Xiao and Xiang after Mi Youren 瀟湘圖卷

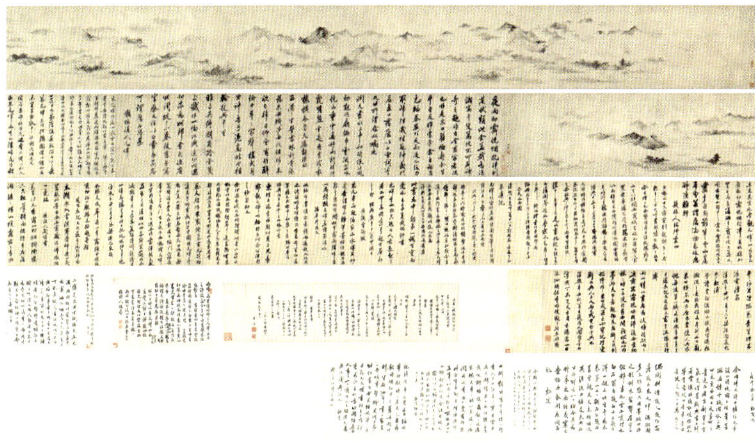

Handscroll: ink on paper; 25.4 × 315.6 cm (10 × 124 ¼ inches); Private collection

SIGNATURE OF THE ARTIST
Shibiao 士標.

SEAL: *Erzhan* 二瞻.

Following the painting are Zha Shibiao's transcriptions of many of the inscriptions mounted with Mi Youren's *White Clouds along the Xiao-Xiang*, a famous scroll now in the collection of the Shanghai Museum.

LETTER BY THE ARTIST TO THE RECIPIENT, YIWENG
Although we live in the same town, I have not yet paid you a visit because of my indolence. My fault of missing your teaching cannot be evaded. Hopefully I can gain your forgiveness for my negligence. Mr. Huang Yi has often spoken to me of your erudition and literary talent. Although I have admired you for years, I have failed to pay you a visit in person and thus we have not met. Lord Slope [Su Shi] once said that for his entire life he had not known Yuanzhang [Mi Fu] thoroughly.[1] This can also be applied to me with regard to you. I have always received your favor yet have not reciprocated. Now, this one insignificant skill of mine—for several months, almost a year already—numerous friends have reminded me of your order. So indolent! How can I excuse myself? It is because you are such a fine connoisseur, daily in step with the masters of old. I fear that my work will appear slovenly, that I will have nothing with which to fulfill my responsibility. Each time I am ready to apply ink and brush I begin to think like this. I do not intend to slack off, procrastinate, and furthermore offend you. The other day when I showed you this painting, unfinished, not only did you not criticize it, but you praised it with such excessive compliments. I feel even more surprised and flattered. With much reverence and humility, I completed the painting and venture to present it to you for your criticism and collection. Mr. Ye Jing has given me your instructions for the inscriptions. I hope to finish writing them in the next few days. With the inscriptions added to the end, these will demonstrate that your connoisseurship and knowledge of the past is indeed lofty and far-reaching. I too will benefit from the galloping of your reputation to later generations. This makes one look forward with anticipation—a splendid event of our times. How does that sound? Let's wait for the judgment of generations yet to come. Younger brother Shibiao bows his head again for Yiweng and respectfully inscribes.

同處一城，缺然躬候，違教之愆，罪在莫逭，惟恃台亮耳．伏惟先生以博雅之長，兼詞賦之善，黃儀老每向弟嘖嘖不置．弟雖慕教有年，而親炙每疎，遂無由得奉傾倒．坡公云，一生知元章不盡．余於先生之謂矣．向蒙至愛，種種莫酬．乃以一技之微，累月經年，煩姚再老諸公為先生再命三命，懶慢至此，何以自解．實緣先生鑒空一世，日與古人為徒，恐涉潦草，無以塞責，每於濡毫輒作此想．以致疑滯，遂爾因循，非故為懶慢，獲罪左右也．昨者呈覽乃蒙不加督責，復恣意游譽，溢美之詞若不容口者，余益無所措其手足矣．悚甚愧甚，今染完奉上，乞鑒存．葉景老傳諭著款，余竊意欲俟將後跋不日書完，總跋卷尾，以見先生收藏鑒古之高風，代有其人．弟亦藉以附驥後世．使仰止而思慕之，亦一時盛事也．如何如何．惟俟裁定命之．不盡．小弟士標再頓首奕翁先生侍下．謹後．

SEALS: *Shibiao siyin* 士標私印, *Zha Erzhan* 查二瞻.

ADDITIONAL INSCRIPTION by Li Hou 李侯 (Li Zaixian 李在銑, 1818–1902) dated 1886, and six inscriptions by Yan Shiqing 顏世清 (1873–1929).

ADDITIONAL SEALS: *Zhuolu Li shi zhencang* 涿鹿李氏珍藏, *Rujing lu* 入境廬, *Li Zaixian yin* 李在銑印, *Zhihe* 芝核 (Li Hou).

NOTE

1 Su Shi wrote this to Mi Fu in the last year of his life. See Sturman, *Mi Fu*, 177–78.

CAT. NO. 50

SHITAO 石濤 1642–1707

Plants of Virtue and Rocks by Water (Sketching Bamboo) 寫竹通景十二屏, **1693–94**

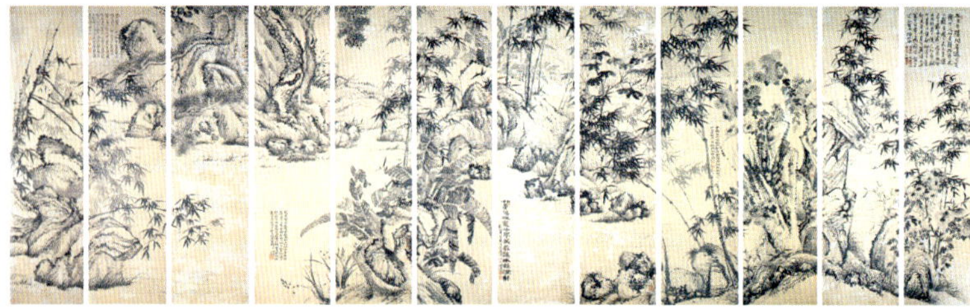

Set of twelve hanging scrolls: ink on paper; 195 × 49 cm (76 ¾ × 19 ¼ inches) each; National Palace Museum, Republic of China (Taiwan)

INSCRIPTIONS BY THE ARTIST

Scroll 1

The patterning of the rocks is naturally clear and smooth,
The old moss is layered like silk brocade.
The sight makes a person's heart and eyes bright,
And summons up the craziness of Master Mi [Mi Fu].
My own craziness is endless,
So how can I defer to Master Mi?
Each time you painted a rock
You forgot to sit down, forgot to sleep.
You did not even remember to let people know
That your brilliance stood out against the blue sky of ancient times.
Who now is able to wave his sleeves
And conjure truly extraordinary visions from ink?
These chrysanthemums and bamboo will stand for my pure ambitions:
Consider me of the same stripe as you.
Who is the truly crazy one, would you say,
After the effort I have put into creating this vision?
Inscribed in the Hall of the Great Tree in Hanshang [Yangzhou] at the beginning of winter in the *guiyou* year [1693].

石文自清潤，層繡古苔錢.
令人心目朗，招得米公顛.
余顛顛未已，豈讓米公前.
每畫一石頭，忘坐亦忘眠.
更不使人知，卓破古青天.
誰能袖得去，墨幻真奇焉.
菊竹若清志，與爾可同年.
真顛謂誰者，苦心製此篇.
癸酉冬初題於邗上之大樹堂.

SEALS: *Xia zunzhe* 瞎尊者, *Qingxiang Shi daoren* 清湘石道人, *Shanguoyue zhi zi Tiantongzhai zhi sun Yuanji zhi zhang* 善果月之子天童忞之孫原濟之章.

Scroll 4

When Ziyou [Wang Huizhi] saw bamboo, he was so moved he had to lean on a rock;
When Pengze [Tao Yuanming] picked flowers, he filled his cup with wine.
I love these two gentlemen for their naturally archaic character
And so, from ink, I extract a pictorial poem.

子猷看竹情依石，彭澤拈花酒滿卮.
我愛二公心自古，墨中補出畫中詩.

SEALS: *Gaohuangzi Ji* 膏肓子濟, *Qingxiang Shitao* 清湘石濤.

Scroll 5

[Signed] Qingxiang laoren Shitao 清湘老人石濤.

SEAL: *He ke yiri wu ci jun* 何可一日無此君.

Scroll 6

Bamboo shoots in morning mist, cold and lush in the basket;
Hibiscus by an autumn pond, vying in freshness with the clear still water.
Sitting in Danke Studio in windy and rainy weather, I unrolled this scroll again and wrote something on a whim.

竹子曉煙籠冷翠，芙蓉秋水競澄鮮.
風雨中坐澹可齋，復展此紙偶書.

SEALS: *Xiaosheng ke* 小乘客, *Kugua heshang* 苦瓜和尚, *Shitao* 石濤.

Scroll 9

A plantain extends its leaves
Over snow-like orchids;
A mood of lofty relaxation takes me out of this world.
The clear air is crisp.
The orchids are like snow:
Their attenuated silhouettes bow before the plantain leaves
Waving wildly about in the play of autumn light.
I match the scene with splashed ink until, my efforts exhausted,
I am astonished by a sight like "billowing waves at dusk."[1]
Below the great ancient pine
With its allure of dragons and kylins, the shadows are dark as old iron.
Beside the rocks, sounds of flowing water ring out with the same clear purity as in ancient times.
For a thousand autumns men of inexhaustible loftiness have left their traces.
In the *jiaxu* year [1694], Qingxiang laoren inscribed again.

芭蕉葉,
蘭花雪,
風韻高閑天地別.
清氣寒,
蘭花雪,
瘦低芭蕉葉,
撩亂秋光總不知.
吾將灑墨與之歇,
驚濤暮落.
大夫松老,
龍麟秀色影如鐵.
石邊聲落古今清.
千秋芳躅高無竭.
湘源老人甲戌復題.

SEAL: *Sibai feng zhong ruoli weng tushu* 四百峰中箬笠翁圖書.

Scroll 10

In the deep spring, rocks appear black in the shadows of the peak.
From the old tree a branch descends, as if dancing.

谿深石黑前峰影，樹老婆娑倒掛枝.

SEALS: *Xia zunzhe* 瞎尊者, *Shitao* 石濤.

Scroll 11

I am by nature recalcitrantly myself and rarely get on with worldly society. It is only through brush and ink [that I do], expressing relaxed feelings. When monks of old said: "Why not entrust one's true character to brush and ink?" this is what they meant. My elder in the Dao, Jilao, has been my close friend for years. He is a man of lofty unstained character and calm temperament. So I took up brush and ink and drew on my wanderings and poem-chanting to make visible where my unworldly excitement led me, subsequently composing a poem. Leaning pines, orchids, bamboo, and rocks: each has attained a rhythmic resonance. Only by viewing them with gentlemanly generosity will the handling of brush and ink seem satisfactory. Should one judge the result in terms of craftsmanlike skill, I will be embarrassed. [Signed] Bitter Gourd, Ji, from Xiangyuan, adds this inscription.

予性懶真，少與世合．惟筆與墨以寄閑情．古德云：何妨筆墨資真性？此之謂也．姬老年道翁知交有年，人品高潔，心志澹然．故以筆墨而假遊詠，以見余方外意興之所到，隨作一詩．俾松蘭竹石各得風韻，惟大方君子視之筆墨之可耳．若以工拙較之，寧無愧色．湘源苦瓜濟并識.

SEALS: *Qian you Longmian Ji* 前有龍眠濟, *Lao Tao* 老濤, *Kugua heshang* 苦瓜和尚, *He ke yiri wu ci jun* 何可一日無此君.

ADDITIONAL SEALS: *Zhongxinglu zhu shoucang jinshi shuhua zhi zhang* 中行廬主收藏金石書畫之章, *Zhongxinglu* 中行廬, *Yuejun jiancang shuhua* 岳軍鑒藏書畫 (Zhang Qun 張群, 1889–1990).

NOTE

1 The allusion is to Du Fu's poem "Dong shen" 冬深 (In deepest winter).

CAT. NO. 51

SHITAO 石濤 1642–1707

Landscapes for Huang Lü 贈黃律山水冊, **1694**

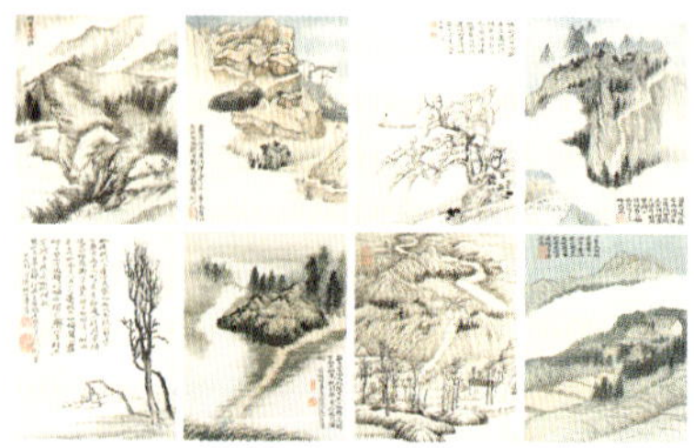

Album of eight leaves of painting: ink and color on paper; 27.9 × 22.2 cm (11 × 8 ¾ inches); Los Angeles County Museum of Art, Los Angeles County fund (60.29.1a–h)

INSCRIPTIONS BY THE ARTIST

Leaf 1

Casually, I took ink made with the tears of a beauty.
And splashed forth Mount Huang amid the clouds.
Even for Wang Wei, so praised as a painter,
The purity and uniqueness [of poetry] was hard to extend to the brush.
Written by Monk Bitter Gourd of Qingxiang upon a sudden recollection of the thirty-six peaks of Mount Huang.[1]

漫將一硯梨花雨，潑濕黃山幾段雲.
縱是王維稱畫手，清奇難向筆頭分.
清湘苦瓜和尚忽憶三十六峰寫此.

SEAL: *Shi Yuanji yin* 釋元濟印.

Leaf 2

I had a random wish to cross over to Xiling,[2]
And my boat floated into this painting.
Where clear ripples form an endless expanse,
Opening my mind and relaxing my face.
One should pity the traveler on a raft,
[Like Zhang Qian,] in vain moving back and forth along a river of stars.[3]
Why not be like the paddle in his hand.
And in the rhythmic motion find true ease?
Old Man Bitter Gourd, Ji.

偶欲渡西泠，扁舟蕩畫間.
清波渺渺然，能令豁心顏.
堪惜乘槎客，星河徒往還.
何如手中楫，舉止得真閑.
苦瓜老人濟.

SEALS: *Yuanji* 原濟, *Shitao* 石濤.

Leaf 3

At the ford where painting's methods join those of calligraphy,
The deep blue water surges naturally and spontaneously.
Otherwise, ask Crazy Old Zhang about this;
When you understand, you won't need to watch a dancer with a sword.[4]
Shitao Ji.

畫法關通書法津，蒼蒼莽莽率天真.
不然試問張顛老，解處何觀舞劍人.
石濤濟.

SEAL: *Lao Tao* 老濤.

Leaf 4
[Signed] The Blind Arhat, Yuanji 瞎尊者原濟.

SEAL: *Lao Tao* 老濤.

Leaf 5
Peaceful is the house that's built among
a hundred thousand tall pines,
Between lushly growing grass and layers
of cold peaks.
White-haired, I arrived here without the
slightest care;
Every year when spring arrives, I'll gaze
out from the window, alone.
The Blind Arhat, Yuanji.

十萬長松結屋安，茸茸細草疊峰寒.
白頭至此無煩慮，每到春來獨自看.
瞎尊者原濟.

SEAL: *Qian you Longmian Ji* 前有龍眠濟.

Leaf 6
SEAL: *Kugua heshang Ji huafa* 苦瓜和尚濟畫法.

Leaf 7
Who is there who would share with me
the ups and downs of this vast world?
Old and without a thing, I've become
stubborn and crotchety.
I didn't realize my inkstone had become
so overgrown with weeds.
In front of guests I tear up my poems
written while drunk.
The Blind Arhat from Qingxiang, Ji, while residing at the Monastery of Purity and Intelligence.

誰共浮沉天地間，老無一物轉癡頑.
不知石研荒如許，醉裏吟成對客刪.
清湘瞎尊者濟漫設於淨慧.

SEALS: *Lao Tao* 老濤, *Yueshan* 粵山.

Leaf 8
Those who enter the Dao of painting through the common gateway are hardly worth treasuring, yet they gain fame in their time without difficulty. [In contrast are those who display] a lofty antiquity like Baitu [Kuncan], Qingxi [Cheng Zhengkui], and Daoshan [Chen Shu], those with an untrammeled purity like the two venerables Meihuo [Zha Shibiao] and Jianjiang [Hongren], those with a dry sparseness like Goudaoren [Cheng Sui], those with a dripping moistness and exceptional sense of antiquity like Bada Shanren of Nanchang, or those with a heroic expansiveness like Mei Qushan [Mei Qing] and Xuepingzi [Mei Qing's brother Mei Geng]—these are the ones who understood painting for our era. I alone cannot grasp its meaning so my work is empty and vacuous, dumb and inexpressive just like this. I would like to ask Mr. Mingliu for criticism of these opinions. Will not discerning people fall over laughing at them? Written during autumn in the eighth [lunar] month of the *jiaxu* year [1694].

此道從門入者，不是家珍，而以名振一時，得不難哉. 高古之如白秃，青谿，道山諸君輩，清逸之如梅壑，漸江二老，乾瘦之如垢道人，淋漓奇古之如南昌八大山人，豪放之如梅瞿山，雪坪子，皆一代之解人也. 吾獨不解此意，故其空空洞洞，木木默默之如此. 問訊鳴六先生，予之評訂，其旨若斯，具眼者，得不絕倒乎. 甲戌秋八月清湘石濤濟.

SEALS: *Shi Yuanji yin* 釋元濟印, *Xia zunzhe* 瞎尊者.

NOTES

1 Translations by Richard E. Strassberg, with slight modifications.

2 Xiling refers to Xiling Bridge, connecting Gushan (Solitary Isle) at West Lake in Hangzhou.

3 Zhang Qian was the Han-dynasty explorer who reputedly followed the Yellow River upstream toward its source and eventually paddled into the Milky Way.

4 Crazy Zhang refers to Zhang Xu, renowned practitioner of wild cursive calligraphy. The sword dance of Lady Gong Sun was a celebrated source of inspiration for wild cursive scribblers.

CAT. NO. 52

LU WEI 陸暐 act. late seventeenth century

Landscapes of Poetic Ideas **山水詩意冊, before 1689**

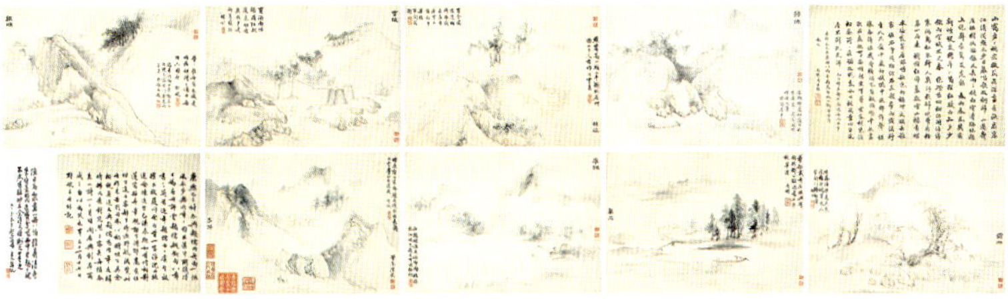

Album of eight leaves of painting and two leaves of calligraphy: ink and light color on paper; 23.2 × 33 cm (9 ⅛ × 13 inches) each; Private collection

Leaf 1
"Returning Fishermen" 歸漁

SEALS OF THE ARTIST
Lu Wei 陸暐, *Dongren* 東人.

INSCRIPTION BY WANG DANLIN (ACT. C. 1700)
Master of the nets folds them away,
long oar returning,
As the sun sets on the broad autumn
waters.
The wind rustles the reeds;
Blowing on the stream, it makes the sound
of rain.
[Signed] The Recluse of Liuxian (Wang Danlin).

罟師理還枻，落日秋水廣.
瑟瑟葭葦風，吹作溪雨響.
留閒居士.

SEAL: *Danlin* 丹林.

Leaf 2
"The Woodcutters' Path" 樵徑

SEALS OF THE ARTIST
Lu Wei 陸暐, *Dongren* 東人.

INSCRIPTIONS BY WANG DANLIN
The sounds of the woodcutter on the high
mountain peak
Echo where the mountain is as level
as the ground.
Why do the people at the foot
of the mountain
Believe that the sound is coming from
among the white clouds?

樵響高山頭，山平猶地底.
何因山下人，看作白雲裏.

They've bought new axes in Baling,
then returned[1];
Together they will go gather firewood.
As for the straight trees that grew old
in the desolate mountains,
Did they ever think they could become
pillars and beams?
[Signed] Inscribed by the old man Recluse Liuxian.

買斧灞陵還，相將采薪去.
直木老空山，誰知中梁柱.
居士留閒翁題.

SEALS: *Liuxian* 留閒, *Lengyin* 冷吟.

Leaf 3
"City Wall at Evening" 昏城

SEALS OF THE ARTIST
Lu Wei 陸暐, *Dongren* 東人.

INSCRIPTION BY WANG DANLIN
Having bought wine along the southern
path,
From dusk to dawn they were uninhibited.
But look at the abundant flower branches;
This is the way to the verdant bridge.
[Signed] Master Lin.

買酒南陌頭，清狂朝復暮.
但看花枝多，是向草橋路.
林公.

SEAL: *Xiaoxiong* 銷雄.

Leaf 4
"Plowing Side by Side" 耦畊

SEALS OF THE ARTIST
Lu Wei 陸暐, *Dongren* 東人.

INSCRIPTIONS BY WANG DANLIN
Hardworking are these men of Chang'an,
Their pains of working in the summer
fields do not diminish.
All one needs is two *qing* of land;
What use are the seals of the Six States?[2]
[Signed] Yehang.

勞勞長安客，不減夏畦病.
但得二頃田，安用六國印.
野航.

Shouldering their plows they head for
the fields,
The ice has melted and the streams flow—
spring has arrived!
A persistent waning moon sinks behind
the humble wooden gate,
The misty grass on the eastern bank
is moist.
[Signed] Yehang inscribes again.

抱耒行向田，泉動春已及.
殘月落柴門，東皋烟草濕.
野航再題.

SEALS: *Liuxian* 留閒, *Lengyin* 冷吟.

Leaf 5
"Frosty Woods" 霜林

SEALS OF THE ARTIST
Lu Wei 陸暐, *Dongren* 東人.

INSCRIPTION BY WANG DANLIN
The tide descends, the fishing weir stand high;
The sky is cold, the water must be hard to ford.
Homes are visible amidst the trees;
They open their doors to clear away the red leaves.
[Signed] Master Lin.

水落漁梁高，天寒渡難涉.
樹裏見人家，開門掃紅葉.
林公.

SEAL: *Lengyin* 冷吟.

Leaf 6
"Transporting a Rock" 載石

SEALS OF THE ARTIST
Lu Wei 陸暐, *Dongren* 東人.

INSCRIPTION BY WANG DANLIN
Pulling the boat along to transport a fantastic rock,
Mysterious inspiration to be sent to a garden.
It is here that Duke Wei sobers up from wine,
A steady stream, deep among autumn grasses.[3]
[Signed] Danlin.

牽舩載奇石，幽興寄園林.
衛公醒酒處，平泉秋草深.
丹林.

SEAL: *Danlin* 丹林.

Leaf 7
"Casting the Nets" 舉絡

SEALS OF THE ARTIST
Lu Wei 陸暐, *Dongren* 東人.

INSCRIPTION BY WANG DANLIN
On the sand-spit he prepares his fishing gear,
Moves up and down like the water-drawing pendulum.[4]
The weather looks bad on the Yangzi River,
Can't set out in a little fishing boat.

沙頭理漁具，俯仰同桔槔.
大江風色惡，未可放輕船.

SEAL: *Liuxian* 留閒 .

Leaf 8
"Searching for Poetry" 詩尋

SIGNATURE OF THE ARTIST
"Lu Wei of Huating" 華亭陸暐.

SEALS: *Lu Wei* 陸暐, *Dongren* 東人.

INSCRIPTION BY WANG DANLIN
Last night, I lodged at a farmer's house,
Setting out at daybreak straddling my donkey.
The tips of the woods are covered in white misty clouds;
Mountain ranges appear then disappear.[5]
[Signed] Yehang.

昨夜宿田家，跨驢成曉發.
林表藹白雲，羣山出還沒.
野航.

SEAL: *Liuxian* 留閒.

ADDITIONAL SEALS: *Fukan jianshang* 復戡鑑賞 (Zhu Yifang 朱義方 [Zhu Fukan 朱復戡], 1902–1989); *Meiduo laoren wushi hou suoshang* 美柮老人五十後所賞; *Cheng Fu zhencang* 程傅珍藏; *Qiantang Wang shi Xiaowan zhai cang* 錢塘王氏小宛齋藏.

Leaf 9
POEMS BY TAO ERSUI (ACT. C. 1692)
Mountain mists vast and gray, tree-shadows all faint;
Deep among the autumn reed blossoms is the gate of a fisherman's hut.
The cold river is clear, shallow, and few are the fish that come;
At sunset, singing, he gathers his nets and returns.

山靄蒼蒼樹影微，荻花深處有漁扉.
寒江清淺魚來少，日暮唱歌收網歸.

Pathway by a tangled bank where strange trees grapple;
Sickles at their waists, two or three men depart in a group.
Among the white clouds, there is a path: please, don't lightly climb it!
Up there, on steep, overgrown cliffs tigers and lynxes are plenty.

一道奔厓恠樹扶，腰鐮人去兩三俱.
白雲有路休輕上，絕壁蒙茸足虎貙.

Spring rain, spring wind, how many new gusts come?
By the misty embankment, the result: grass like a cushion!
Scarlet-red, creamy-white—can you imagine how much?
Folks locked up in the cities—*they* see nothing of spring.

春雨春風幾番新，煙堤贏得草如茵.
猩紅膩白知多少，鏁向空城不見春.

On a precipitous ledge, twisting, turning, a tiny path appears;
Like ocean waves coldly dripping, ten thousand pine trees mourn.
Traveler, don't be surprised if the woodcutters are late returning:
They've been watching a game of chess up there.

絕磴盤回細路開，海濤寒瀉萬松哀.
行人莫訝樵歸晚，曾看枯棊一局来.

The trees deploy a brocade of red, reed catkins float like snow;
The mountains cluster, verdant spirals, the river links with mist.
Thatched hut, eyes bright, autumn scene so fine;
So, leaning on his bamboo staff, whose house is he off to now?

樹鋪紅錦蘆飄雪，山擁青螺水接霞.
茅屋眼明秋色好，楖卬更欲去誰家.

Fantastic rocks compete for the name of "Sober-up Stone"!
This long skiff is dragging one along, down the shallow stream.
The owner simply loves that the stream flows calmly:
Just listen to the middle flow, the whispering, gurgling sound.

恠石爭憐醒酒名，長艘牽向淺溪行.
主人只愛平泉好，試聽中流邪許聲.

Green ripples, spring pond, how many layers of waves?
On the front of a raft, fishing baskets, on a little shelf, a lamp.
A thousand slivers of fish you've taken—Sir, you must be happy!
Will it be necessary, tomorrow morn, to lower the nets again?!

綠漲春潭浪幾層，槎頭笭箵椴頭燈.
千絲盡取君應快，可要明朝更下罾.

Forms of clouds, colors of trees, calmly overlapping;
Toiling, toiling, an exhausted donkey braves the dawn mist.
This day I open the painting and take a look once more;
Windswept dust will never sully this Pond for Washing Flowers![6]

雲容樹色澹相糸，得得疲驢犯曉嵐.
今日披圖重回首，風塵不到浣花潭.

In the second month of winter of the *jisi* year [1689], we were returning south from the capital by boat. When we reached Guabu, my elder Chishu [Wang Danlin] brought out an album of eight leaves and asked me to write poems for them. I have written a quatrain for each of them, and moreover request his corrections. [Signed] Tao Ersui of Nancun.

己巳仲冬，都下南還，舟次瓜步，赤抒長兄出畫册八幀索題，爲各賦一斷句，并請教定. 南邨陶爾穟.

SEALS: *Chen* 臣, *Sui* 穟.

Leaf 10
INSCRIPTION BY WANG DANLIN
In the second month of winter of the *jisi* year of the Kangxi reign [1689], Yingru and I headed south in the same boat. But we happened to be delayed by a windstorm at Guabu [Jiangsu Province]. As we had nothing to do, we took out an album from the luggage that Lu Riwei had painted for me, to critique and enjoy together.[7] Yingru composed eight quatrains, which he wrote out on a separate piece of paper. In recent years, Yingru was sent from Shangyu [Zhejiang Province] to govern over Jiazhou [Jiaxian, Shaanxi Province]. As for me, I have grown white-haired in my single official position, drifting about in the West Chamber [Central Drafting Office]. As I thought back to these old times, I suddenly found myself feeling happy, as if we were enjoying ourselves, face to face, with Yingru again beside the window of our cabin, brush and inkstone deployed for our pleasure: how could it not be so? The Presented Scholar Ren Tangong of Gaomi [Shandong Province] has been residing here in the capital. He happened to visit me at my Rustic Boating Studio, and looked over this album. Yesterday, he came again to say farewell, and so I have decided to present [the album] to him as a gift. Tangong and I see eye to eye, with no disagreements. Moreover, he, Yingru, and I are friends who passed the exams in the same year. As he was preparing to depart, I opened the album upon my desk, and it was as though we three friends were all together again! So, on each leaf I composed a poem or two, all casual expressions reflecting inspirations born of a life of leisure. I hope he will not laugh at me. [Dated] the seventeenth day of the eleventh month of the *xinsi* year [1701], recorded by Yehang, Wang Danlin.

康熙己巳仲冬，與潁儒同舟南，一阻風瓜步，無所事事，因出篋中所攜陸日爲畫册評賞. 潁儒題斷句八章，書之簡首. 邇年潁儒由上虞令，被擢出牧葭州. 余白首一官，浮沈西掖. 追念陳迹，忽已浹辰，欣如昔時，相對篷窓，拈弄筆硯，詎可得耶. 高密任坦公進士 客都下時，過野航流覽此册. 昨來告别，因舉以相贈. 坦公與余相視莫逆，又與潁儒爲同年友. 歸時拂几展對，宛然三客矣. 每幀各系小詩一二首，皆閒居興到率爾成之，勿以爲笑也. 辛巳十一月十七日，野航王丹林記.

SEALS: *Wang Danlin* 王丹林印, *Chishu* 赤抒, *Yehang* 野航 (Wang Danlin).

ADDITIONAL INSCRIPTION by Cheng Jiarui 程甲銳 (1918–2003) dated 1962.

NOTES

1 Baling refers to present-day Xi'an (Shaanxi Province).

2 The first line alludes to a passage in *Mengzi*. See *Mengzi zhushu* 孟子注疏 (*Siku quanshu* ed.), 6:2a. The last line refers to a comment made by Su Qin, a political strategist of the Warring States period: "If all I had were two *qing* [about 33 acres] of land by the walls of Luo, what use would I have for the seals of the Six States?" *Gujin shiwen leiju* 古今事文類聚 (*Siku quanshu* ed.), 36:4a. It is said that at the peak of Su's career he persuaded the leaders of the six kingdoms of Chu, Han, Zhao, Yan, Wei, and Qi to unite against the emperor of Qin. Thereupon, Su donned robes decorated with the crests of the six states.

3 This is an allusion to the Tang-dynasty scholar Li Deyu (the Duke of Wei), who had a "stone for sobering up from wine" in his garden that he would lean on when drunk to sturdy himself. Ouyang Xiu 歐陽修, *Xin Wudai shi* 新五代史 (*Siku quanshu* ed.), 45:3b–4a. See also James Cahill, *The Distant Mountains*, 261.

4 In *Zhuangzi* this is used as a metaphor for one's natural ability to adjust to the vicissitudes of life, moving up and down with the flow like a water-drawing pendulum. *Zhuangzi zhu* 莊子注 (*Siku quanshu* ed.), 5:30a.

5 For a study of the iconography of the donkey rider and his relationship to poetry, see Peter C. Sturman, "The Donkey Rider as Icon."

6 Pond for Washing Flowers is a variation of Flower-Washing Stream, which is where the Tang-dynasty poet Du Fu lived while in Chengdu (Sichuan Province). See ibid., 48.

7 Wang Danlin refers to Lu Wei 陸暐 as Lu Riwei 陸日為. The unusual character for his given name, *Wei*, has frequently resulted in the mistaken assumption that it is in fact two characters, *ri* 日 and *wei* 為. It has also been suggested that Riwei was the artist's sobriquet.

CAT. NO. 53

WANG HUI 王翬 1632–1717

Transporting Bamboo 載竹圖卷, 1698

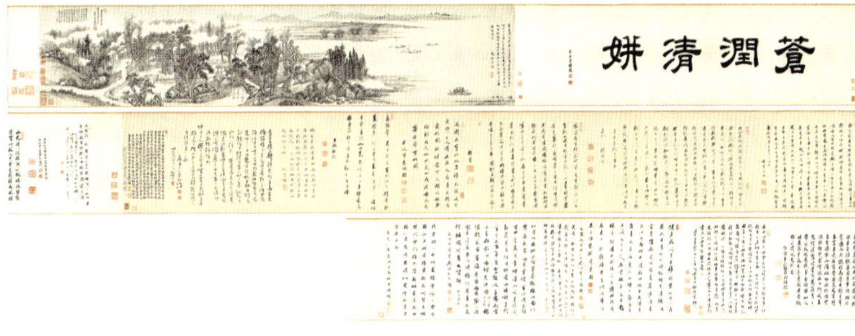

Handscroll: ink on paper;
34.9 × 170.2 cm (13 ¾ × 67 inches);
Private collection

FRONTISPIECE

By Zhang Ruoai 張若靄 (1713–1746): *Vigorous, Moist, Pure, and Beautiful*. Zhang Ruoai respectfully inscribes.
《蒼潤清妍》. 張若靄謹題.

SEALS: *Lianxue* 鍊雪, *Qinglan jushi* 晴嵐居士.

INSCRIPTION BY THE ARTIST

On the twentieth day of the fourth month of the *wuyin* year [1698], I painted *Transporting Bamboo* for Master Clear Clouds. [Signed] Master of the Stone Valley, Wang Hui, of Haiyu. 歲次戊寅清和廿日, 爲晴雲主人寫載竹圖. 海虞石谷子王翬.

SEALS: *Shangxia qiannian* 上下千年, *Shigu zi* 石谷子, *Wang Hui zhi yin* 王翬之印, *Baifa mantou gui guyuan* 白髮滿頭歸故園, *Gengyan sanren* 耕煙散人.

ADDITIONAL INSCRIPTIONS

SUO FEN (D. 1708)

I weeded out the useless trees and wild grass,
Left the warm ground under the southern eaves to be planted.
A pair of oars with emerald green mists sculled bamboo back,
The whole boat with fragrance carried flowers here.
Special flowers in bloom were found by you in person;
Firm bamboo joints being transplanted were nurtured by myself.
I treasure this long-distance goodwill from my old friend;
With hundreds of wine pots, just to wash away the dust.
[Signed] Fen of the Liao [Smartweed] Garden.

盡芟樗木與蒿萊, 留得南簷暖地栽.
雙槳翠煙搖竹至, 滿船香霧載花來.
奇葩放蕊君親覓, 勁節移根我自培.
珍重故人千里意, 百壺聊爲洗塵埃.
蓼園芬題.

SEAL: *Liaoyuan* 蓼園.

By nature I love bamboo most. Whenever I pass fallow gardens or deserted temples, if several bamboo are planted there, I spend the whole day facing them. It is pleasant for my heart and I forget to go back home. To the east of my residence I recently built a studio of three rooms. The vacant spaces to its south and north are very broad. I planted thousands of bamboo in person, but still am not tired. However, the northern area suffers from coldness and lacks other species. The only bamboo plentiful alternates green and yellow colors, and these are limited to one or two *zhang* in height. Only the Guanyin [Hedge] Bamboo from the Chonghua Temple is a superior type. I was able to buy some clumps in the past, but now it has become an imperial good and can no longer be obtained. My guest Huang Zungu and I have known each other for ten years, and he knows that I am obsessed with bamboo.[1] He travels hundreds of miles to buy and transport by boat Square Bamboo, Purple Bamboo, and Xiang Consorts Bamboo as presents for me. By good fortune, when I planted them I encountered a steady rain. Thus, the bamboo shoots grew immediately. They were tall and grew into groves. This indeed satisfied my long-cherished ambition. At that time Master Stone Valley was present, so he painted these scenes into a handscroll. I wrote a short record myself. On the thirteenth day of the fifth [lunar] month, *wuyin* year of the Kangxi reign [1698], [Signed] Master Clear Clouds.

余性最愛竹. 每過荒園廢寺, 凡栽數枝者, 必相對終日, 怡然神樂而忘歸. 宅東新築書屋三間, 南北隙地頗寬敞. 手種千餘竿, 殆不知倦. 然北地苦寒, 更無他種, 獨多青黃相間, 僅一, 二丈. 惟崇化寺觀音竹乃佳品, 昔年曾購得數叢, 今已爲官物, 不復可得. 客有黃君尊古, 與余交十年, 識余有此癖, 不遠數千里, 買舟載方竹, 紫竹, 湘妃斑竹以贈. 種時幸逢霖雨, 且即生笋, 修然成林, 良可謂愜吾之宿願矣. 適石谷在坐, 因寫爲卷. 余自作短記. 時在康熙戊寅五月十三日也. 晴雲主人.

SEALS: *Liaoyuan* 蓼園, *Chen Fen zhi yin* 臣芬之印, *Su'an* 素菴.

BOERDU (1649–1708)

One who is fond of mountains still fears the steepness of sheer cliffs;
One who is fond of water is afraid of swirling waves and turbulence.
These "fondnesses" are not as good as being fond of flower and bamboo,
Whose fragrance and verdant color can immediately gladden the heart.
The north has bamboo but no fine species;
Their forms like reed and wormwood, soft and downy.
A guest transports bamboo from south of the Yangzi;
Elegant, reaching for the sky, they grow with promise.
Their rustling sounds are indeed adorable,
Transplanted among flowers and within the stone railings.
Red jade reflecting the sun, they add beauty to the dawn's rosy haze;
Like green jasper embracing mist, they condense the evening vapors.
Who knows when they suffered from their lovesickness?
Till this day the tear stains remain.[2]
The owner sometimes sits among them,
His heart purged of all worries, playing his zither.
Their shadows cross the windows, swaying in the pure moonlight;
Sounds flying on the tips of trees invite the pure wind.
The old man Stone Valley is indeed heroic,
His brush seizes the power of Creation—not something made by man!
Their luxuriousness is no less than the groves of Weichuan[3];
Facing [the painting], it cleanses my heart and spirit.
I own lofty pines one hundred feet tall:
Canopies hanging lightly east of Hui Stream.
With bamboo staff in hand, I walk slowly seeking verses,
The appearance seems to be the same as that among the bamboo.
Inscribed for my old relative Su'an, seeking his instruction. [Signed] Boerdu.

好山者恐歷懸岩斷壁之巑岏, 好水者恐涉盤渦澒洞之波瀾.
不若好花與好竹, 芳香青翠令人一見愁心歡.
北地有竹無佳種, 形類葦艾何茸茸.
客自江南載得來, 秀色參天成把拱.
蕭蕭瑟瑟真堪愛, 移植花隙石欄內.
赤瓊映日麗朝霞, 綠玉含烟凝暮靄.
不知何代相思苦, 至今淚點依然在.
主人有時坐其中, 胸絶萬慮調絲桐.
影橫窗外搖素月, 聲飛樹杪來清風.
石谷老叟誠豪雄, 筆奪造化非人工.
莪莪豈減渭川上, 教余對之心神空.
我有百尺之喬松, 偃蓋冉冉惠溪東.
扶筇緩步尋詩句, 彷彿音容與此同.
題呈素菴老親台並求教政. 博爾都.

SEALS: *Songxia qingzhai* 松下清齋, *Xiusheng* 朽生, *Boerdu yin* 博爾都印, *Wenting* 問亭, *Donggao yufu* 東皋漁父, *Fuguo jiangjun* 輔國將軍.

HEYI (1643?–1720?)

At my residence I also have tens of bamboo, but their color is yellow and their stems soft—decidedly not worthy of appreciation. Bamboo in the north is almost all like this. One day I came to the Studio of Clear Clouds and saw emerald bamboo filling the steps.

Upon observation I found that they all were precious species that I had never seen before. Pure wind filled the woods; their green shade covered the mats. At that moment I began to understand the subtlety of bamboo. I asked him where it came from, and [Master Clear Clouds] answered that they were transported from south of the Yangzi River. I sighed and said, "You indeed are one worthy of the label 'bamboo-obsessed'!" I always appreciate that Su'an is relaxed, serene, and indifferent to fame. Fond of reading and good at composing poems, he is keen on elegant literary pursuits. Now he has had bamboo transported from hundreds of miles away and planted them around his studio. How refined! Moreover, he invited Master Wang Stone Valley to make a painting. Thus it is that elegant people do elegant things! [Signed] Heyi.

余家亦有竹數十竿，色黃幹茸，殊不足觀．北地大概皆此類耳．一日至晴雲書屋，見翠竹盈堦，察之皆名種，皆從所未見者．淸風滿林，綠陰盈簟，始知竹之妙也．問其何所得之，云自江南載至．余嘆曰：眞可謂有竹癖者也．余常愛素菴閑靜恬逸，喜讀書，工於詩，好爲韻事．今不遠數千里載竹植於齋中，韻矣．乃更囑王子石谷爲之圖，則又韻人而爲韻事也．赫奕．

SEALS: *Songyue yechuang xu* 松月夜窗虛, *Heyi zhi yin* 赫奕之印, *Danshi* 澹士.

YUEDUAN (1671–1704)

Reclusive bamboo of the south country is not found in the north;
Continuously, roots were moved to the capital.
The owner loves their [virtuous] nodes reaching to the sky,
Painting histories will pass this down as *Transporting Bamboo*.
This species should be called Royal Groom bamboo,
So that in the future it can match nicely with Grandee pine.[4]
I only worry that one day in the midst of a thunderstorm,
Ten thousand shoots, one thousand canes—all will transform into dragons.
Inscribed by Master of the Jade Pond, Yueduan.

南國幽篁北地無，移根迢遞至京都．
主人憐此參天節，畫史傳爲載竹圖．
此種當呼太僕竹，他年好對大夫松．
只愁一夜逢雷雨，萬籜千竿盡化龍．
玉池生岳端題．

SEALS: *Yuchi sheng* 玉池生, *Yueduan siyin* 岳端私印, *Zi yue Jianshan* 字曰兼山, *Songjian caotang* 松間草堂, *Yufeng* 御風.

SUOERBI (SEVENTEENTH–EIGHTEENTH CENTURY)

With lofty interest he's always admired Ziyou's sagacity,[5]
[So] he bought bamboo from the south of the Yangzi, spending his salary.
A pair of oars sculling emerald, moon of a thousand *li*;
Ten thousand canes carrying green, mists of a single stream.
Just planted by his studio—like being in the mountains;
Suddenly surprised that Xiao-Xiang was moved to in front of the door.[6]
I am so envious of my relative, this crazy Royal Groom,
Pure winds will be further transmitted by this painting.
Younger brother Bi respectfully inscribes.

高情常慕子猷賢，買竹江南破俸錢．
雙櫓翠搖千里月，萬竿青帶一溪烟．
乍栽書院如山裏，忽訝瀟湘在檻前．
羡殺吾家狂太僕，淸風猶有畫圖傳．
弟弼拜題．

SEALS: *Suoerbi yin* 索爾弼印, *Tongya* 桐崖, *Qingsong daoren* 青松道人.

TUO XIAN (SEVENTEENTH–EIGHTEENTH CENTURY)

Crane-white hair to his shoulders, the Old Painting Master,
Painted *Transporting Bamboo* seated in utter ease.
It was three thousand *li* between south of the Yangzi and north of Ji,[7]
In frigid rains and cold mists, some tens of branches.
Shadows scattered on the evening window and swayed in the pure moonlight;
Emerald-dense at the close of spring, dropping into the jade wine cup.
The owner has separated from the bustling world for a long time,
Facing this and casually chanting, he can thoroughly enjoy himself.
Tuo Xian inscribes.

鶴髮垂肩老畫師，圖成載竹坐淋漓．
江南薊北三千里，冷雨寒煙數十枝．
影散晚窗搖素月，翠濃春盡落瑤卮．
主人久已紛華絕，對此閑吟好自怡．
託賢題．

SEAL: *Tuo Xian zhi zhang* 託賢之章.

ADDITIONAL INSCRIPTIONS WITH SEALS by Li Kai 李鍇 (1686–1755) dated 1747, Yongjing 永瑆 (1712–1787) dated 1747, Shen Deqian 沈德潛 (1673–1769) dated 1751, Yinxi 胤禧 (1711–1758) dated 1752, Li Shizhuo 李世倬 (d. 1770), Hongzhan 弘瞻 (1733–1765), Wu Songliang 吳嵩梁 (1766–1834) dated 1825, Li Zonghan 李宗瀚 (1770–1832) dated 1825, Bao Guixing 鮑桂星 (1764–1826), Gu Chun 顧蒓 (1765–1832) dated 1825, and Zeng Yu 曾燠 (1760–1831) dated 1828.[8]

TITLE SLIP by Zhang Ruoai: "Wang Shigu's Transporting Bamboo." Collected by the Baozhen Studio. Inscribed by Zhang Ruoai. 王石谷載竹圖．葆眞書屋珍藏．張若靄題籤．

SEALS: *Ruo* 若, *Ai* 靄, *Baozhen shuwu* 葆眞書屋.

NOTES

1 Zungu was the courtesy name of Huang Ding. Huang was considered an excellent painter in the Kangxi period.

2 A reference to the Xiang Bamboo, whose mottled pattern is said to be caused by the tears of the maidens Ehuang and Nüying, who pined for their lost husband, the legendary ruler Shun.

3 Weichuan was the place famous for the prosperity of bamboo groves that covered one thousand *mu*.

4 *Taipu*, Royal Groom, is one of Suo Fen's official titles. *Dafu* pine refers to a tree on Mount Tai that was granted the official title *dafu* (Grandee of the ninth order) by Qin Shihuangdi.

5 Ziyou was the courtesy name of Wang Huizhi, who was famous for his deep love of bamboo.

6 Xiao-Xiang is the area of the Xiao and Xiang Rivers in Hunan Province, where the Xiang Bamboo in particular was from.

7 Ji should refer to Jiqiu, a site outside of Beijing.

8 For some of this documentation refer to Richard M. Barnhart, et al., *The Jade Studio*, 181–82.

CAT. NO. 54

JIANG SHIJIE 姜實節 1647–1709

Landscape **山水扇面, 1701**

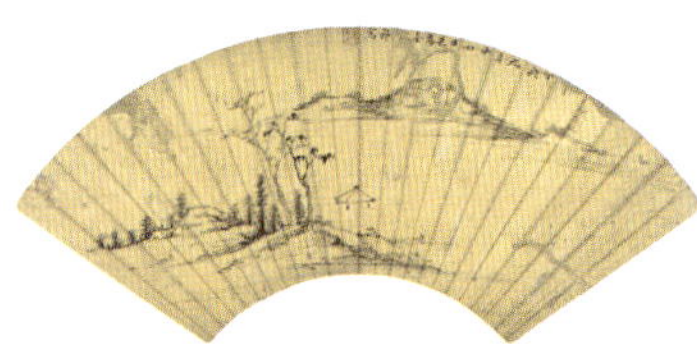

Fan mounted as an album leaf: ink on gold paper; 22.2 × 48.9 cm (8 ¾ × 19 ¼ inches); Santa Barbara Museum of Art, Anonymous gift, 1992.82.2

INSCRIPTION BY THE ARTIST

On the twenty-fourth day of the ninth [lunar] month, *dinghai* year [1701], sketched by Jiang Shijie of Laiyang.

丁亥九月廿四日．萊陽姜實節寫．

SEAL: *Jiang Zhongzi* 姜中子.

CAT. NO. 55

WANG YUANQI 王原祁 1642–1715

Autumn Mountains after Huang Gongwang **仿大癡秋山圖卷, 1704**

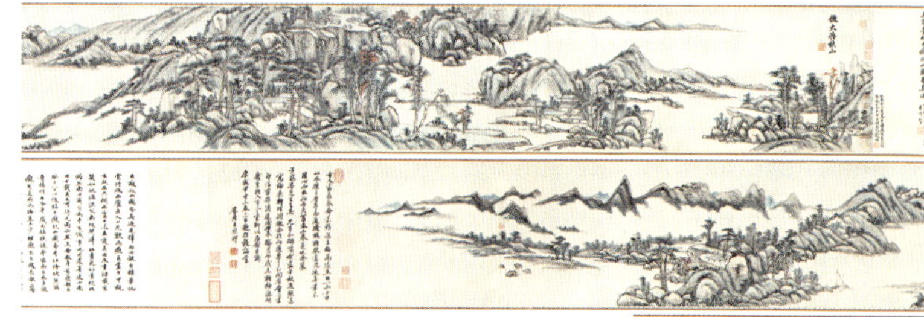

Handscroll: ink and color on paper; 31.1 × 334 cm (12 ¼ × 131 ½ inches); Private collection

TITLE BY THE ARTIST

Autumn Mountains after Dachi [Huang Gongwang] 仿大癡秋山.

SEAL: *Shishi daoren* 石師道人.

INSCRIPTION BY THE ARTIST

When the ancients painted long handscrolls they marshaled their conceptions with depth and refinement and established styles that were lofty and distant. Five days to paint a mountain, ten days to paint a river, slowly, gradually, it took years before the painting would be completed. It is for this reason that they were able to shed completely the superficial habits of their contemporaries—not a single brushstroke would be lacking the utmost skill. Zijiu's [Huang Gongwang] *Dwelling in the Fuchun Mountains* is like this.

I admire Mr. Lou Zien's talent in *yi* [chess], and Mr. Lou loves my paintings. After mid-autumn, I frequently went to his place. His analysis of *yi* is profound and precise. When it comes to the Dao of *yi* I am a bit dense, but occasionally there are things that I intuit. Consequently, trusting in this spirit, I painted this scroll, taking more than a month to complete it. I am not able to exhaust the deepest, most subtle principles, so how can I enter into the chamber of the ancients? Thus, I only name the work after [Huang's painting]. Tenth [lunar month] of the *jiashen* year of the Kangxi reign [1704], inscribed at Guyi Hall. [Signed] Wang Yuanqi of Loudong.

古人畫長卷，命意精深，立格高遠．五日一山，十日一水，遲遲歷年而後成，故能脫盡凡近，無筆不匠心而出，如子久富春山卷是也．余慕子恩婁先生之奕，先生亦酷嗜余畫．中秋後頻過寓，論奕析理洞微．余於此道夢夢，亦間有會心處．即信奉揮灑，遂成此卷，踰月而成．未能極深研幾，豈能入古人之室，聊以名命之爾．康熙甲申小春三日題於穀詒堂，婁東王原祁．

SEALS: *Wang Yuanqi yin* 王原祁印, *Lutai* 麓臺.

ADDITIONAL SEALS OF THE ARTIST: *Xilu houren* 西廬後人, *Maojing* 茂京, *Yu shuhuatu liuyu ren kan* 御書畫圖留與人看.

ADDITIONAL INSCRIPTIONS by Wu Hufan 吳湖帆 (1894–1968), two of which are dated 1951. Wu Hufan speaks of the rarity of excellent handscrolls by Wang Yuanqi, of which this counts as one that he particularly treasures. He also comments on references to Huang Gongwang's *Autumn Mountains*.

ADDITIONAL SEALS: *Hufan* 湖颿, *Qianan* 倩盦, *Wu Hufan zhencang yin* 吳湖颿珍藏印, *Meiying shuwu* 梅景書屋, *Hufan jianshang* 湖颿鑑賞, *Wu hufan* 吳湖颿印, *Dachi Fuchun shan tu yijiao renjia* 大癡富春山圖一角人家, *Hufan changshou* 湖颿長壽 (Wu Hufan); *Haichang Qian jngtang cang* 海昌錢鏡塘藏 (Qian Jingtang 錢鏡塘, 1908–1983); *Erquan shanren* 二泉山人; *Yinyun biji* 尹雲祕笈.

CAT. NO. 56

WANG YUANQI 王原祁 1642–1715

Landscape in the Manner of Huang Gongwang and Ni Zan 倣黃公望倪瓚山水圖, 1709

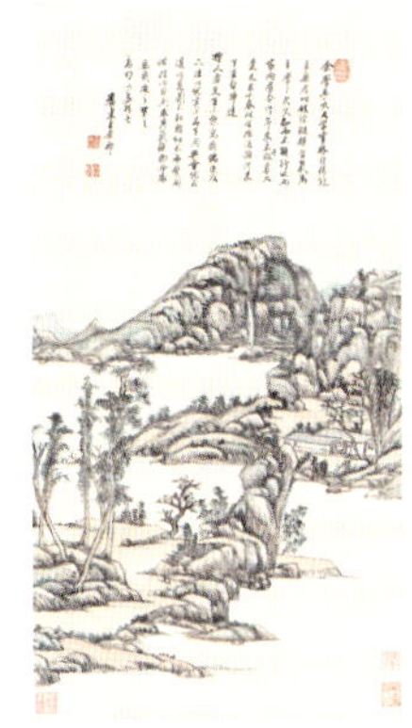

Hanging scroll: ink and color on paper; 89.2 × 47.6 cm (35 ⅛ × 18 ¾ inches); Private collection

INSCRIPTION BY THE ARTIST

From the time I was a young man to the approach of old age I have studied Zijiu [Huang Gongwang] and Yunlin [Ni Zan], taking as my guiding principle the elimination of the air of facile habits. I have studied these two for a long time, yet while I understand [this principle] I have not been able to put it into practice. These two masters once painted a collaborative work, but after all these years I have yet to achieve a copy of its general idea. In the tenth month of the *jichou* year [1709], my nephew Qiwang [Wang Zhan] came from Luhe, and after finishing with his business at the court delayed his return. While drinking with old Mr. Tanren in his residence, by chance our conversation turned to the Six Laws and they inquired about the small-scale work by Ni and Huang. With the sudden arrival of inspiration I did this painting. I do not seek a formal resemblance, not to mention the complexity or simplicity [of its composition]. Rather, I seek the points of correspondence between its breath-resonance and my heart and in this way almost get close. Do the lofty and clear-minded consider it thus or not? [Signed] Wang Yuangqi of Loudong.

余學子久又學雲林，自弱冠至垂老，以破除縱習氣為主．學之既久，知而不能行也．兩家向有合作，年來未得倣摹大意．己丑小春，屺望姪從潞河來，下直暫歸遲．檀人老先生小飲寓齋，偶談及六法以倪黃小品下問．興會偶至，遂作是圖，不取形似，不論繁簡，但於心目間求其氣韻脗合處庶幾近之．質之高明以為然否．婁東王原祁．

SEALS: *Wang Yuanqi* 王原祁, *Lutai* 麓臺, *Yu shuhua tu dan yu ren kan* 御書畫圖單與人看, *Xilu houren* 西廬後人.

ADDITIONAL SEALS: *Gu shi jia biji* 顧氏家祕笈, *Gu Gengmei zhencang shuhua yinxin* 顧耕湄珍藏書畫印信.

CAT. NO. 57

GAO JIAN 高簡 1634–after 1708

Flowering Plum 梅華詩畫冊, 1708

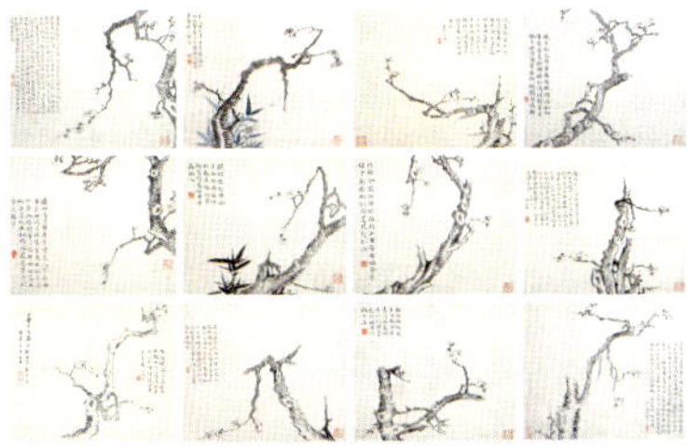

Album of twelve leaves: ink and color on paper, 21.6 × 26 cm (8 ½ × 10 ¼ inches); Santa Barbara Museum of Art, Museum purchase with funds provided by the Wallis Foundation, 2002.45.1–12

Leaf 1

From of old, I've had a "plum blossom craze";
As soon as it's spring, I start composing poems.
Please realize, for the supreme moment of highest appreciation,
Is when they are about to bloom.
Pale red, the calyx just unfolds,
Subtly fragrant, the fine threads [stamens] are sprouting.
Tender buds are naturally delicate,
Cloudy mist just so vague.[1]

夙有梅花癖，當春便賦詩．
須知相賞意，最是欲開時．
紅淺纔舒萼，香微乍吐絲．
商量原細細，烟靄正迷離．

SEAL OF THE CALLIGRAPHER
Gan Zhu 紺珠.

SEAL OF THE ARTIST
Gao Jian zhi yin 高簡之印.

Leaf 2

Wash off the white makeup, reveal the snowy flesh!
Pure perfume, wondrous substance—called marvelous by the world.
The place where old Bu used to inscribe his verses,
Also saw Dongpo seeking lines.
After snow, out in the garden, they cover just half a tree;
Beside the stream, in wind-swept moonlight, smiling from slanting branches.
In the human world, everything resembles flowers: blooming, fading.
Spring arrives, spring returns; we hardly ever notice.
Collecting the lines of Song poets.[2]

洗盡鉛華見雪肌，清香異質世稱奇．
向來逋老題詩處，又見東坡覓句時．
雪後園林纔半樹，水邊風月笑横枝．
人間萬事花開落，春到春歸漫不知．
集宋人句．

SEAL OF THE CALLIGRAPHER
Yu gu 于谷.

SEAL OF THE ARTIST
Danyou 澹游.

Leaf 3

Moonlight glitters on water—all is perfectly quiet,
Wind whispers through tall bamboo—rain falls without sound.
Someone chants poems after dusk,
This can be as pure as the chilly blossoms.

月色水光渾寂寞，蕭蕭脩竹兩無聲．
有人吟對黄昏候，可與寒花一樣清．

SEALS OF THE CALLIGRAPHER
Gan 紺, *Zhu* 珠.

SEAL OF THE ARTIST
Gao Jian zhi yin 高簡之印.

Leaf 4

At the Eastern Pavilion, frosted branches, sparse,
At the Western Ridge, dew-laden leaves, similar.
The earth, predetermines supremely distinct,
The sky, always lends its clarity of its vault.
Winter solstice, following yearly custom,
Congealed harmony controlling the work of transformation.
A thousand households—a thousand jade faces,
On a single embankment—a single breath of spring.
At the house's corner, young tips of flowers make a cluster,
In the corridor's center, concealed fragrance passes through.
At frozen pond—still warnings about catching cold!
Silk curtains join verdant grass.
[Behind] the hanging branches, the cloud window looks small,
[Below] the slanting branches, the moon pavilion appears empty.
Circling streams, spread in the distance,
Surrounding trees, clustered all in rows.
Cold jade drawing close to the mirror,
Thin mist blurring the toilette stand.
Through bamboo blinds from the Xiang River,[3] we peer at infiltrating beauty,
Rocks obtained from lakes pressing on their roots heroically.
Those first bloomed are white and fleshy,
Those recently planted, are already tender red.
Sparse in rows, yet intertwining, covering each other,
Blooming densely and then turning exquisite.
Seek their smiles? Blocked by walls,
Their floating fragrance, reach the end of the lake.
This rock garden, resembles the Ridge of Yu!
Their stolen white powder might bring Han Ping to life!

In the old tree, sparrows rest in tiers,
Its fragrant flower cores give lodge to
parasites.
Lighting the lanterns in the new courtyard,
Playing the flute in the lovely chambers.
Lingering snow gnarls on the rows of nests,
Evening glow fills the balustrade.
Warmth holds the musk-scent of cloud-
like grains;
Coldness buffets the rainbow over the
painted bridge.
As if they were appearing in the gardens
of the Han,
Or in imagination in Jiangcheng![4]
Year after year, best of the hundred flowers,
In mist and rain, the primordial act of
creation.

東閣霜枝瘦，西崗露葉同.
地先規絕勝，天每借晴穹.
破臘隨年例，凝和掌化工.
千房千玉面，一塢一春風.
屋角輕稍簇，廊腰暗馥通.
冰池餘禁瘞，絲障與籠蔥.
低亞雲窗小，斜橫月觀空.
環溪遙各各，匝樹直叢叢.
鏡檻寒瓊逼，梳臺薄霧蒙.
湘簾窺豔透，湖石壓根雄.
上番渾肥白，初栽已嫩紅.
行疎交掩斂，開密轉玲瓏.
索笑遭牆隔，飄香到水窮.
假山迷瘐嶺，竊粉活韓馮.
老幹層棲雀，芳心間蝕蟲.
燒燈新院落，吹篴好房櫳.
殘雪排窠鬣，明霞滿檻烘.
暖含雲楼麝，冷撲畫橋虹.
漢苑依稀裏，江城想像中.
年年百花上，煙雨是元功.

SEALS OF THE CALLIGRAPHER
Gan 紺, *Zhu* 珠.

SEAL OF THE ARTIST
Danyou 澹游.

Leaf 5
The moonlight of the old days,
How many times, has shown upon me
Playing the flute by the plum trees?
I called my jade lady to rise,
Ignoring the chill, to pick the blossoms
with me.
He Xun is now aging,
His pen, once spring wind, is wholly
forgotten.
He's only bemused by the few flowers
past the bamboos,
Whose cold fragrance enters the banquet
hall.

The River Country
Is just now lonely and still.
I sigh that the road is too long to send a
blossom,
And the evening snow begins to pile up.
Tears freely drop in front of the green
wine pot;
The red calyxes are speechless, disturbed
by mutual thoughts.
Long shall I remember the places where
we held hands:
A thousand trees press against the West
Lake's cold green.
Petal by petal, all blown away,
When shall I see them again?[5]

Ci lyric by Baishi [Jiang Kui], to the tune of "Anxiang" [Hidden fragrance].

舊時月色，算幾番照我，梅邊吹笛?
喚起玉人，不管清寒與攀摘.
何遜而今漸老，都忘卻，春風詞筆.
但怪得竹外疏花，香冷入瑤席.
江國，正寂寂.
嘆寄與路遙，夜雪初積.
翠尊易泣，紅萼無言耿相憶.
長記曾攜手處，千樹壓，西湖寒碧.
又片片，吹盡也，幾時見得?

白石詞，調暗香.

SEAL OF THE CALLIGRAPHER
Gan Zhu 紺珠.

SEAL OF THE ARTIST
Danyou 澹游.

Leaf 6
The golden armlet feels cold, when
pushing open the elaborately carved
windows,
Heavy emerald hairpins pressing down
fragrant lustrous hair.
The newly adorned forehead under the
eave of the Hanzhang Palace,[6]
Trying to open the waternut blossom-
shaped mirror but why (I see) nothing?[7]

約辟金寒拓綺疎，搔頭玉重壓香酥.
含章檐下新粧額，試啟菱花得似無.

SEAL OF THE CALLIGRAPHER
Yu gu 于谷.

SEAL OF THE ARTIST
Gao Jian zhi yin 高簡之印.

Leaf 7
Leisurely taking these sparse reflections
as companion to my chanting self,
Nightfall at the water edge, spring beyond
the bamboo grove.
Do not wonder that this old man is
inclined to feel attached to them,
From ancient times, the esteem
of plum blossoms has been suited
to us hermits.[8]

閒將瘦影伴吟身，水際黃昏竹外春.
莫訝此翁偏賞戀，愛梅自古屬幽人.

SEAL OF THE CALLIGRAPHER
Yu gu 于谷.

SEAL OF THE ARTIST
Danyou 澹游.

Leaf 8
Along the banks of Xiao and Xiang, vast
over the expanse of Chu,
I gaze upon these lovely ladies, Ah! there
on the southern bank.
In a dream I return to (night when)
crescent moon illuminates my cold
blanket,
Suddenly I see them on a jasper terrace,
dancing in pale makeup.
At this time, faced with this painting,
heart full of sad feelings,
Chanting crickets, falling leaves—autumn
without limit!
The Master of Transformation knows my
cherishing of these flowers:
Their ink fragrance reaches the bones, and
the flowers are able to speak![9]

瀟湘之濱渺平楚，望美人兮在南浦.
夢回殘月照寒衿，忽見瑤臺澹粧舞.
此時對畫心悵然，吟蛩落木秋無邊.
化工知我惜花意，墨香到骨花能言.

SEAL OF THE CALLIGRAPHER
Wumen 吳門.

SEAL OF THE ARTIST
Gao Jian zhi yin 高簡之印.

Leaf 9
Mossy branches decked with jade;
Tiny, tiny bluebirds
Roost on them together.
When wandering we meet—
By the corner of the fence in the dusk,
Without a word she leans on slender
bamboos.
Unaccustomed to the remote
barbarian sands,
Zhaojun secretly longed for the
Yangzi's climes.
Surely it is her jade waistband
That returns on moonlit nights,
Transformed into this blossom, so solitary.

The old palace tale still comes to mind:
When that beauty was asleep,
One blossom fluttered to her black moth
eyebrows.
Don't be like the spring wind,
Careless of beauty,
But early prepare a gold chamber for it.
If one lets all the petals drift with
the current,
He shall resent hearing the sad tune for
the Jade Dragon.
If one waits till then to find the subtle
fragrance,
It will have entered the horizontal scroll
over the small window.[10]

Ci lyric by Jiang Baishi [Jiang Kui], to the tune of "Shuying" [Sparse shadows]. First day of the fifth month, *jisi* year.

苔枝綴玉，有翠禽小小，枝上同宿.
客裏相逢，籬角黃昏，無言自倚脩竹.
昭君不慣胡沙遠，但暗憶江南江北.
想珮環月下歸來，化作此花幽獨.
猶記深宮舊事，那人正睡裏，飛近蛾綠.
莫似春風，不管盈盈，早與安排金屋.
還教一片隨波去，又卻怨，玉龍哀曲.
等恁時，重覓幽香，已入小窗橫幅.

姜白石詞．調疏影．己巳五月朔日.

SEAL OF THE CALLIGRAPHER
Yu gu 于谷.

SEALS OF THE ARTIST
Gao 高, *Jian* 簡.

Leaf 10
Warmth enters the southern branches,
weather not yet balanced:
Smiles holding a promise of fragrance,
awaiting the rest of spring.
Gazing at each other, this most resembles
the night at Jasper Terrace:
Slantwise covering the doubled gates, so
hard to recognize.[11]

暖入南枝氣未勻，笑含芳意待餘春.
相看絕似瑤臺夜，斜掩重門認不真.

SEAL OF THE CALLIGRAPHER
Yu gu 于谷.

SEAL OF THE ARTIST
Danyou 澹游.

Leaf 11
The cold plums in the secluded valley:
By nature, braving the ice and frost.
Clutching with their roots, prouder than
ordinary trees,
Blossoming with flowers putting others
to shame.
A distant wind brings pure freshness;
In twirling ripples surges the solitary moon.
Fine fruits just [turn ripe] and become
delicious,
To collect them we only have to climb the
cliff-top corridors.
I consider you are like Fu Yue:
Only when mixed in the broth is your
taste known!
No need to envy the solitary orchid,
Deep in the woods [the plum blossoms]
breathing out the fragrance alone.[12]

寒梅在空谷，本自淩冰霜.
託根傲眾木，開花陋羣芳.
遙風遞清氣，迴水涵孤光.
美實初可口，採掇升巖廊.
念爾如傅說，和羹初見嘗.
不需羨幽蘭，深林自吹香.

SEAL OF THE CALLIGRAPHER
Yu gu 于谷.

SEAL OF THE ARTIST
Gao Jian zhi yin 高簡之印.

Leaf 12
Not depicting heavy adornment,
depicting pale makeup,
From ancient times, iron and stone
constitute the heart of this tree!
We can depend on three thousand gallons
of your ink,

To produce bone-penetrating fragrance
from the Mountain of Dengwei![13]

On a fine day at the Bamboo Springs.

不寫穠纖寫澹粧，由來鐵石作心腸.
憑君墨汁三千斛，鄧尉山中透骨香.
竹泉暘.

SIGNATURE OF THE ARTIST
Yiyun shanren, Gao Jian, imitating the ancients at Bamboo Villa, at the age of seventy-five. 一雲山人高簡擬古于有竹庄. 時年七十又五.

SEALS OF THE ARTIST
Gao 高, *Jian* 簡.

NOTES

1 Translations revised from those of Jonathan Chaves unless otherwise noted. I would like to thank Mei Fado for proof-reading and commenting on my revisions. Any remaining errors are mine.

2 This poem, a collection of individual lines on plum blossoms by different authors, was originally pieced together by Guo Yuheng in the Yuan dynasty. Guo Yuheng 郭豫亨, *Meihua zizi xiang qianji* 梅花字字香前集 (*Siku quanshu* ed.), 12a–b. Old Bu refers to the poet-recluse Lin Bu. Dongpo is Su Shi. Lines from poems by both of these writers are included in this mélange.

3 In modern Hunan Province.

4 The modern city of Wuhan.

5 *Ci* lyric to the tune of "Anxiang" (Hidden fragrance) by Jiang Kui. Translation by Lin Shuen-fu, *The Transformation of the Chinese Lyrical Tradition*, 137–38. He Xun was a sixth-century poet known for his love of plum blossoms.

6 This is an allusion to the plum blossom petal falling on the forehead of Princess Shouyang, the daughter of Emperor Wudi of the Liu-Song, and becoming a "plum blossom ornament." Shuen-Fu Lin, in Cai Zong-qi ed., *How to Read Chinese Poetry: A Guided Anthology* (New York: Columbia University Press, 2004), 295.

7 Chen Qi 陳起, "Meihua" 梅花, *Jianghu xiaoji* 江湖小集 (*Siku quanshu* ed.), 69:8b.

8 Gao Qi 高啟, "He Lou xiucai kan mei" 和婁秀才看梅, *Da quan ji* 大全集 (*Siku quanshu* ed.), 18:12a–b.

9 Chen Tai 陳泰, "Meihua wuyou tu" 梅花五友圖 (partial), *Suoan yiji* 所安遺集 (*Siku quanshu* ed.), 9b–10a.

10 *Ci* lyric to the tune of "Shuying" (Sparse shadows) by Jiang Kui. Translation by Lin, *The Transformation of the Chinese Lyrical Tradition*, 172. Zhaojun is Wang Zhaojun, the Han-dynasty beauty who was sent to the northern frontiers to marry a Xiongnu chieftain.

11 Feng Zizhen 馮子振, "Ban kai mei" 半開梅, *Meihua baiyong* 梅花百詠 (*Siku quanshu* ed.), 9a–b. This is one of a hundred verses on plum blossoms by Feng. The title of this verse is "Half-opened Plum Blossoms." Jasper Terrace is a possible reference to the Daoist deity Queen Mother of the West (Xiwangmu 西王母), who held annual banquets for the Immortals at the Terrace residence inaccessible to ordinary mortals.

12 Han Ju 韓駒, "Ti Meilan tu ershou" 題梅蘭圖二首, *Lingyang ji* 陵陽集 (*Siku quanshu* ed.), 2:1a. Fu Yue was a semi-legendary minister under Emperor Wu Ding of the Shang dynasty. This emperor is said to have remarked that Fu was as important to his regime as "salt and plum" were as seasonings to the sacrificial broth.

13 Dengwei Mountain southwest of Suzhou was famous for the beauty of its plum blossoms.

List of Artists

BADA SHANREN 八大山人
1626–1705
Cat. nos. 41–48

CHEN GUAN 陳祼
1563–c. 1639
Cat. no. 5

CHEN HONGSHOU 陳洪綬
1599–1652
Cat. nos. 21–23

CHEN JIRU 陳繼儒
1558–1639
Cat. nos. 11 and 12

CHENG SUI 程邃
1607–1692
Cat. no. 32

DA CHONGGUANG 笪重光
1623–1692
Cat. no. 31

DONG QICHANG 董其昌
1555–1636
Cat. nos. 8 and 9

FANG HENGXIAN 方亨咸
Act. c. 1647–1678
Cat. no. 39

FANG YIZHI 方以智
1611–1671
Cat. no. 40

FEI ERQI 費而奇
Act. 1678 or earlier–1701 or later
Cat. no. 33

GAO JIAN 高簡
1634–after 1708
Cat. no. 57

GONG XIAN 龔賢
1619–1689
Cat. nos. 34–36

GU NINGYUAN 顧凝遠
1595 or earlier–1654
Cat. no. 33

HU YUKUN 胡玉昆
Act. c. 1640–1672
Cat. no. 33

JIANG SHIJIE 姜實節
1647–1709
Cat. no. 54

KUNCAN 髡殘
B. 1612
Cat. no. 37

LAN YING 藍瑛
1585–1664 or later
Cat. nos. 26 and 27

LI RIHUA 李日華
1565–1635
Cat. no. 10

LI YIN 李因
C. 1611–1685
Cat. no. 16

LU WEI 陸暐
Act. late 17th century
Cat. no. 52

MEI GENG 梅庚
1640–c. 1722
Cat. no. 33

MI WANZHONG 米萬鍾
1570–1628
Cat. nos. 3 and 4

QIAN QIANYI 錢謙益
1582–1664
Cat. no. 29

SHAO MI 邵彌
C. 1595–1642
Cat. no. 15

SHEN SHICHONG 沈士充
Act. c. 1607–after 1640
Cat. no. 17

SHITAO 石濤
1642–1707
Cat. nos. 50 and 51

SONG JUE 宋珏
1576–1632
Cat. no. 33

SUN ZHI 孫枝
Act. late 16th–early 17th century
Cat. no. 6

WANG HUI 王翬
1632–1717
Cat. no. 53

WANG YUANQI 王原祁
1642–1715
Cat. nos. 55 and 56

XIANG SHENGMO 項聖謨
1597–1658
Cat. nos. 1 and 20

XIAO YUNCONG 蕭雲從
1596–1673
Cat. no. 24

XU FANG 徐枋
1622–1694
Cat. no. 38

XUE WU 薛五
C. 1564–c. 1637
Cat. no. 14

YANG WENCONG 楊文驄
1597–1646
Cat. no. 18 and 19

YUAN SHANGTONG 袁尚統
1590–1666 or later
Cat. no. 7

ZENG JING 曾鯨
1564–1647
Cat. no. 2

ZHA SHIBIAO 查士標
1615–1698
Cat. no. 49

ZHANG FENG 張風
D. 1662
Cat. no. 30

ZHANG XUEZENG 張學曾
Act. c. 1633–1657
Cat. no. 25

ZHANG ZHENGYUE 張正嶽
B. c. 1590
Cat. no. 28

ZHAO ZUO 趙左
C. 1570s–1633 or later
Cat. no. 13

Names and Dates of Historical Figures

B

Bada Shanren 八大山人 (1626–1705)
Bai Xi 白喜 (6th–5th century BCE)
Bian Tong 卞同 (act. 14th century)
Bian Wenyu 卞文瑜 (c. 1576–1655)
Bo Juyi 白居易 (772–846)
Boerdu 博爾都 (1649–1708)
Boyi 伯夷 (11th century BCE)

C

Cao Dingwang 曹鼎望 (1618–1693)
Cao Zhibo 曹知白 (1272–1355)
Chao Mingsheng 巢鳴盛 (1611–1680)
Chaofu 巢父 (legendary)
Chen Chun 陳淳 (1483–1544)
Chen Duxiu 陳獨秀 (1879–1942)
Chen Guan 陳裸 (1563–c. 1639)
Chen Hongshou 陳洪綬 (1598–1652)
Chen Hongshou 陳鴻壽 (1768–1822)
Chen Jiru 陳繼儒 (1558–1639)
Chen Lü 陳旅 (1287–1342)
Chen Qi 陳起 (act. 13th century)
Chen Shu 陳舒 (c. 1617–c. 1687)
Chen Tai 陳泰 (act. 1279–1320)
Chen Yong 陳墉 (act. 17th century)
Chen Yuanlong 陳元龍 (1652–1736)
Chen Yuanyuan 陳圓圓 (1624–1681)
Chen Zhenhui 陳貞慧 (1604–1656)
Chen Zhuo 陳焯 (act. 17th century)
Cheng Hao 程顥 (1032–1085)
Cheng Jiasui 程嘉燧 (1565–1644)
Cheng Jing'e 程京萼 (1645–1715)
Cheng Sui 程邃 (1607–1692)
Cheng Yi 程頤 (1033–1107)
Cheng Zhengkui 程正揆 (1604–1676)
(Emperor) Chengzu of Ming 明成祖 (r. 1402–1424)
(Emperor) Chongzhen of Ming 明崇禎 (r. 1627–1644)
Chu Suiliang 褚遂良 (596–658)
Confucius 孔子 (traditional dates 551–479 BCE)

D

Da Chongguang 笪重光 (1623–1692)
Dai Jin 戴進 (1388–1462)
Ding Liuniang 丁六娘 (late 6th–early 7th century)
Dong Qichang 董其昌 (1555–1636)
Dong Yuan 董源 (10th century)
Du Fu 杜甫 (712–770)
Du Qiong 杜瓊 (1396–1474)
(Emperor) Duzong of Song 宋度宗 (r. 1265–1274)

F

Fan Chengda 范成大 (1126–1193)
Fan Jingwen 范景文 (1587–1644)
Fan Yunlin 范允臨 (1558–1641)
Fang Feng 方鳳 (1240–1321)
Fang Hengxian 方亨咸 (act. c. 1647–1678)
Fang Hui 方回 (1227–1307)
Fang Kongzhao 方孔炤 (1590–1655)
Fang Wen 方文 (1612–1669)
Fang Xiaoru 方孝儒 (1357–1402)
Fang Yizhi 方以智 (1611–1671)
Fei Erqi 費而奇 (act. 1678 or earlier–1701 or later)
Feng Yanxiang 馮研祥 (17th century)
Feng Zizhen 馮子振 (1257–1348)
Fu Shan 傅山 (1607–1684/85)
(King) Fuchai 夫差 (r. 495–473 BCE)

G

Gao Hongtu 高弘圖 (1583–1645)
Gao Jian 高簡 (1634–after 1708)
Gao Qi 高啟 (1336–1374)
Gao Qipei 高其佩 (1660–1734)
Gao Shenfu 高深甫 (1573–1620)
Gao Shiqi 高士奇 (1645–1704)
(Emperor) Gaozong of Song 宋高宗 (r. 1127–1162)
Ge Yilong 葛一龍 (1567–1640)
Ge Zhengqi 葛徵奇 (d. 1645)
Gong Xian 龔賢 (1619–1689)
Gongsun Daniang 公孫大娘 (8th century)
(King) Goujian 勾踐 (r. 496–465 BCE)
Gu Kaizhi 顧愷之 (c. 344–406)
Gu Ningyuan 顧凝遠 (1595 or earlier–1654)
Gu Yuzhi 顧與治 (1599–1660)
Gu Zhengyi 顧正誼 (act. c. 1575–1597)
Guan Tong 關仝 (10th century)
Guan Yu 關羽 (d. 219)
(Emperor) Guangzong of Ming 明光宗 (r. 1620)
Gui Youguang 歸有光 (1506–1571)
Gui Zhuang 歸莊 (1613–1673)
Guo Pu 郭璞 (276–324)
Guo Xi 郭熙 (c. 1000–c. 1090)
Guo Yuheng 郭豫亨 (act. early 14th century)
Guo Zhongshu 郭忠恕 (d. 977)
Guofeng 過峰 (act. c. 1695)

H

Han Ju 韓駒 (d. 1135)
Han Yu 韓愈 (768–824)
Han Yunjun 韓雲俊 (1750–1777)
Hanshan 寒山 (early 9th century?)
He Xun 何遜 (d. c. 534)
He Zhong 何中 (1265–1322)
He Zhuo 何焯 (1661–1722)
Heyi 赫奕 (1643?–1720?)
Hongchu 弘儲 (1605–1672)
(Emperor) Hongguang of the Southern Ming 南明弘光帝 (r. 1644–1645)
Hongren 弘仁 (Jianjiang 漸江, Jiang Tao 江韜, 1610–1664)
Hongwu 洪武 (Emperor Ming Taizu 明太祖, r. 1368–1398)
Hou Jing 侯景 (d. 552)
Hu Shi 胡適 (1891–1962)
Hu Xingqing 胡星卿 (1597–1683)
Hu Yukun 胡玉昆 (act. c. 1640–1672)
(King) Huai of Chu 楚懷王 (r. 328–288 BCE)
Huaisu 懷素 (737–799)
Huang Bian 黃汴 (act. 16th century)
Huang Binhong 黃賓虹 (1865–1955)
Huang Cunwu 黃存吾 (act. early 17th century)
Huang Ding 黃鼎 (1660–1730)
Huang Gongwang 黃公望 (1269–1354)
Huang Lü 黃律 (act. late 17th century)
Huang Shen 黃慎 (1687–1768)
Huang Tingjian 黃庭堅 (1045–1105)
Huang Yuqi 黃毓棋 (1579?–1648)
Huang Zongxi 黃宗羲 (1610–1695)
Huichong 惠崇 (c. 965–1017)
(Emperor) Huidi of Ming 明惠帝 (r. 1398–1402)
Huiyuan 慧遠 (341–416)
Huiyue 慧悅 (act. early 17th century)
(Emperor) Huizong of Song 宋徽宗 (r. 1100–1125)

J

Jiang Cai 姜埰 (1607–1673)
Jiang Chenying 姜宸英 (1628–1699)
Jiang Kui 姜夔 (c. 1155–1221)
Jiang Shaoshu 姜紹書 (1573–1638)
Jiang Shijie 姜實節 (1647–1709)
Jiang Wangyou 蔣王猷 (act. 18th century)
Jiang Wanli 江萬里 (1198–1275)
Jiang Xu 蔣詡 (69 BCE–17 CE)
Jiao Guang 焦光 (1st century)
Jing Hao 荊浩 (c. 880–c. 940)
Juelang Daosheng 覺浪道盛 (1592–1659)
Juran 巨然 (act. c. 960–980)

K

Kangxi 康熙 (Emperor Shengzu of Qing 清聖祖, r. 1661–1722)
Kawai Senro 河井仙郎 (1871–1945)
Kong Shangren 孔尚任 (1648–1718)
Kuncan 髡殘 (b. 1612)

L

Lan Meng 藍孟 (1644–1722)
Lan Shen 藍深 (late 17th–18th century)
Lan Tao 藍濤 (late 17th–18th century)
Lan Ying 藍瑛 (1585–1664 or later)
Langting 俍亭禪師 (1599–1665)
Laozi 老子 (traditional dates 6th century)
Li Bo 李白 (701–762)
Li Cheng 李成 (919–967)
Li Deyu 李德裕 (787–849?)
Li Du'ne 勵杜訥 (1628–1703)

Li Gonglin 李公麟 (c. 1041–1106)
Li Guozhen 李國楨 (d. 1644)
Li Lin 李驎 (1634–1710)
Li Liufang 李流芳 (1575–1629)
Li Mi 李泌 (722–789)
Li Rihua 李日華 (1565–1635)
Li Shida 李士達 (act. c. 1589–1620)
Li Tang 李唐 (act. c. 1100–1150)
Li Xiaoguang 李孝光 (1280–1350)
Li Yin 李因 (c. 1611–1685)
Li Zhaoheng 李肇亨 (17th century)
Li Zicheng 李自成 (Li Hongji 李鴻基, 1606–1645)
Liang Tongshu 梁同書 (1723–1815)
Liang Weishu 梁維樞 (1587–1662)
(Emperor) Liang Wudi 梁武帝 (r. 502–549)
Liangting 佷亭 (1599–1665)
Lin Bu 林逋 (967–1028)
Lin Yunfeng 林雲鳳 (16th–17th century)
(Emperor) Lingdi of Han 漢靈帝 (r. 168–189)
Liu An 劉安 (c. 179–122 BCE)
Liu Gao 劉鎬 (unknown)
Liu Xiang 劉向 (c. 77–6 BCE)
Liu Zhen 劉臻 (d. 156)
(Emperor) Lizong of Song 宋理宗 (r. 1224–1264)
Long Kebao 龍科寶 (1637–1723)
Lou Zien 婁子恩 (act. late 17th–18th century)
Lü Benzhong 呂本中 (1084–1145)
Lu Dezhi 魯得之 (1585–after 1660)
Lü Dongbin 呂洞賓 (8th–9th century)
Lu Guang 陸廣 (c. 1300–after 1371)
Lu Hong 盧鴻 (act. first half 8th century)
Lu Ji 陸機 (261–303)
Lü Ji 呂紀 (act. late 15th– early 16th century)
Lu Tong 陸通 (Jieyu 接輿, 6th–5th century BCE)
Lu Wei 陸暐 (act. late 17th century)
Lu Zhi 陸治 (1496–1576)
Lü'an Benyue 旅庵本月 (d. 1676)
Luo Dajing 羅大經 (1196–1242)

M

Ma Shiying 馬士英 (c. 1591–1646)
Ma Wan 馬琬 (c. 1310–1378)
Ma Yuan 馬遠 (act. c. 1190–after 1225)
Mao Qiling 毛奇齡 (1623–1716)
Mazu 馬祖 (709–788)
Mei Geng 梅庚 (1640–c. 1722)
Mei Qing 梅清 (1623–1697)
Mi Fu 米芾 (1052–1107/08)
Mi Wanzhong 米萬鍾 (1570–1628)
Mi Youren 米友仁 (1074–1151)
Mingzan 明瓚 (8th century)
Mo Shilong 莫是龍 (1537–1587)
Muchen Daomin 木陳道忞 (1596–1674)

N

Nagao Ko 長尾甲 (1864–1942)
Ni Dai 倪岱 (act. 18th century)
Ni Zan 倪瓚 (1301–1374)
Niu Xiu 鈕琇 (d. 1704)

O

Oboi 鼇拜 (d. 1669)
Ouyang Xiu 歐陽修 (1007–1072)

P

Pan Ni 潘尼 (3rd century)
Pan Qintai 潘琴台 (act. late 16th–early 17th century)
Pan Yue 潘岳 (247–300)
Pan Zongluo 潘宗洛 (1657–1716)
Pang De 龐德 (d. 219)

Q

Qian Chengzhi 錢澄之 (1612–1693)
Qian Qianyi 錢謙益 (1582–1664)
Qian Tianshu 錢天樹 (1778–1841)
Qian Zhili 錢志立 (act. late 16th–early 17th century)
Qianlong 乾隆 (Emperor Gaozong of Qing 清高宗, r. 1735–1796)
(Emperor) Qinzong of Song 宋欽宗 (r. 1125–1126)
Qiu Ying 仇英 (c. 1494–c. 1552)
Qiutan 秋潭 (1558–1630)
Qu Yuan 屈原 (c. 340–278 BCE)

R

Ren Fang 任昉 (460–508)
Ren Tangong 任坦公 (act. late 17th–early 18th century)
Ruan Dacheng 阮大鋮 (1587–1646)
Ruan Ji 阮籍 (210–263)
Ruoyexi qiao 若耶溪樵 (act. late 14th–early 15th century)

S

Shao Changheng 邵長蘅 (1637–1704)
Shao Mi 邵彌 (c. 1595–1642)
Shao Ping 召平 (act. late 3rd–early 2nd century BCE)
Shen Defu 沈德符 (1578–1642)
Shen Shichong 沈士充 (act. c. 1607–after 1640)
Shen Shoumin 沈壽民 (1607–1675)
Shen Yue 沈約 (441–513)
Shen Zhou 沈周 (1427–1509)
Sheng Sitang 盛斯唐 (act. 17th century)
(Emperor) Shenzong of Ming明神宗 (r. 1572–1620)
Shi Fenglai 施鳳來 (1563–1642)
(Emperor) Shihuangdi of Qin 秦始皇帝 (r. 246–210 BCE)
Shitao 石濤 (Zhu Ruoji 朱若極, 1642–1707)
(Princess) Shouyang 壽陽公主 (383–444)
Shun 舜 (traditional dates 23rd–22nd centuries BCE)
(Emperor) Shunzhi of Ming 明順治 (r. 1644–1661)
Shuqi 叔齊 (11th century BCE)
Sima Qian 司馬遷 (c. 145–86 BCE)
Song Jue 宋珏 (1576–1632)
Song Luo 宋犖 (1634–1713)
Song Maojin 宋懋晉 (c. 1559–after 1622)
Song Xu 宋旭 (1525–after 1605)
Su Qin 蘇秦 (380–284 BCE)
Su Shi 蘇軾 (1037–1101)
Sun Kehong 孫克弘 (1533–1611)
Sun Wei 孫位 (act. late 9th century)
Sun Yi 孫逸 (d. c. 1658)
Sun Zhi 孫枝 (act. late 16th–early 17th century)
Suo Fen 索芬 (d. 1708)
Suoerbi 索爾弼 (17th–18th century)
Suoetu 索額圖 (d. 1703)

T

Taigong Wang 太公望 (Lü Shang 呂尚, 11th century BCE)
(Emperor) Taiwu of the Northern Wei 北魏太武帝 (r. 423–452)
(Emperor) Taizong of the Tang 唐太宗 (r. 627–649)
(Emperor) Taizu of the Ming 明太祖 (r. 1368–1398)
Tan Zhenmo 譚貞默 (1590–1665)
Tang Jiujing 唐九經 (act. 17th century)
Tang Yin 唐寅 (1470–1523)
Tao Ersui 陶爾穟 (act. c. 1692)
Tao Hongjing 陶弘景 (456–536)
Tao Yuanming 陶淵明 (Tao Qian 陶潛, 365?–427)
Tao Yuanzao 陶元藻 (1716–1801)
Tao Zongyi 陶宗儀 (1329–c. 1412)
Tian Shifa 田實發 (act. 18th century)
Tuo Xian 託賢 (17th–18th century)

W

Wang Aijing 汪愛荊 (act. late 16th–early 17th century)
Wang Changling 王昌齡 (698–c. 756)
Wang Danlin 王丹林 (act. c. 1612)
Wang Danlin 王丹林 (act. c. 1700)
Wang Fu 王紱 (1362–1416)
Wang Fuzhi 王夫之 (1619–1692)
Wang Gong 汪恭 (late 18th–early 19th century)
Wang Hui 王翬 (1632–1717)
Wang Huizhi 王徽之 (act. 338–386)
Wang Jian 王鑑 (1598–1677)
Wang Mang 王莽 (45 BCE–23 CE)
Wang Meng 王蒙 (c. 1308–1385)
Wang Muri 汪沐日 (1605–1679)
Wang Shihong 汪士鋐 (1658–1723)
Wang Shimin 王時敏 (1592–1680)
Wang Shizhen 王世貞 (1526–1590)
Wang Tingji 王廷楫 (act. 18th century)
Wang Wan 汪琬 (1624–1691)
Wang Wei 王維 (701–761)

Wang Xianzhi 王獻之 (344–388)
Wang Xijue 王錫爵 (1534–1614)
Wang Xizhi 王羲之 (303–361)
Wang Xuehao 王學浩 (1754–1831)
Wang Yi 王繹 (1333–after 1362)
Wang Yilian 汪一廉 (d. 1662)
Wang Yongning 王永寧 (17th century)
Wang Yuanqi 王原祁 (1642–1715)
Wang Zhideng 王穉登 (1535–1612)
Wang Zhirui 汪之瑞 (d. c. 1660)
Wei Yingwu 韋應物 (737–c. 792)
Wei Zhongxian 魏忠賢 (1568–1627)
Wen Tianxiang 文天祥 (1236–1283)
Wen Tong 文同 (1019–1079)
Wen Zhengming 文徵明 (1470–1559)
Wen Zhenheng 文震亨 (1585–1654)
Wen Zhenmeng 文震孟 (1574–1636)
Weng Tonghe 翁同龢 (1830–1904)
(King) Wu of Zhou (Zhou Wuwang 周武王, d. 1043 BCE)
Wu Bin 吳彬 (act. c. 1591–1626)
Wu Hufan 吳湖帆 (1894–1968)
Wu Jing 吳暻 (b. 1662)
Wu Qi 吳綺 (1619–1694)
Wu Sangui 吳三桂 (1612–1678)
Wu Siqi 吳思齊 (1238–1301)
Wu Weiye 吳偉業 (Wu Meicun, 1609–1672)
Wu Yuan 伍員 (Wu Zixu 伍子胥, d. 484 BCE)
Wu Zetian 武則天 (624–705)
Wu Zhen 吳鎮 (1280–1354)
Wu Zhengzhi 吳正志 (d. c. 1619)
(Emperor) Wudi of Han 漢武帝 (r. 141–87 BCE)
(Emperor) Wudi of Liu-Song 劉宋武帝 (r. 420–423)

X

Xi Kang 嵇康 (223–262)
Xi Shi 西施 (6th–5th century BCE)
Xiang Chang 向長 (act. c. 9–25)
Xiang Hongdu 項宏度 (d. c. 1295)
Xiang Shengmo 項聖謨 (1597–1658)
Xiang Yu 項羽 (232–202 BCE)
Xiang Yuanbian 項元汴 (1525–1590)
Xiao Yi 蕭繹 (Emperor Liang Yuandi 梁元帝, 508–554)
Xiao Yuncong 蕭雲從 (1596–1673)
(Empress) Xiaochengren 孝誠仁皇后 (1654–1674)
Xibo Chang 西伯昌 (King Wen of Zhou 周文王, 1099–1050 BCE)
Xie An 謝安 (320–385)
Xie Ao 謝翱 (1249–1295)
Xie Bin 謝彬 (b. 1602)
Xie Huilian 謝惠連 (397–433)
Xing Tong 邢侗 (1551–1612)
Xiong Bolong 熊伯龍 (1617–1669)
(Emperor) Xizong of Ming 明熹宗 (r. 1620–1627)
Xu Fang 徐枋 (1622–1694)
Xu Guangqi 徐光啟 (1562–1633)
Xu Qian 徐汧 (1597–1645)
Xu Weiren 徐渭仁 (d. 1853)
Xu Yisun 徐益孫 (act. c. 1580)
Xu You 許由 (legendary)
Xu Youzhen 徐有貞 (1407–1472)
(Emperor) Xuandi of Han 漢宣帝 (r. 74–49 BCE)
Xue Wu 薛五 (Xue Susu 薛素素, c. 1564–c. 1637)

Y

Yan Hui 顏回 (6th century BCE)
Yan Wengui 燕文貴 (act. late 10th century)
Yan Yanzhi 顏延之 (384–456)
Yang Bu 楊補 (1598–1657)
Yang Lian 楊漣 (1571–1625)
Yang Sheng 楊昇 (8th century)
Yang Wencong 楊文驄 (1597–1646)
Yang Xuanbao 羊玄保 (371–464)
Yao 堯 (traditional dates 23rd–22nd centuries BCE)
Yao Guangxiao 姚廣孝 (1335–1418)
Yao Silian 姚思廉 (557–637)
Yinreng 胤礽 (1675–1767)
Yixing 一行 (683–727)
(Emperor) Yongli of the Southern Ming 南明永曆帝 (r. 1646–1662)
Yu Shinan 虞世南 (558–638)
Yu Taixuan 郁泰玄 (4th century)
Yuan Haowen 元好問 (1190–1257)
Yuan Shangtong 袁尚統 (1590–1666 or later)
Yueduan 岳端 (1671–1704)
Yun Shouping 惲壽平 (1633–1690)
Yun Xiang 惲向 (1568–1655)
Yunmen 雲門 (act. late 14th–early 15th century)

Z

Zeng Jing 曾鯨 (1564–1647)
Zeng Xi 曾晳 (6th century BCE)
Zha Shibiao 查士標 (1615–1698)
Zhang Changzong 張昌宗 (d. 705)
Zhang Dai 張岱 (1597–c. 1684)
Zhang Dezhong 張德仲 (b. 1594)
Zhang Feng 張風 (d. 1662)
Zhang Geng 張庚 (1685–1760)
Zhang Heng 張衡 (78–139)
Zhang Hong 張宏 (1577–c. 1652)
Zhang Longzhang 張龍章 (act. c. 1560–1600)
Zhang Qi 張琦 (act. mid-17th century)
Zhang Qian 張騫 (195–114 BCE)
Zhang Rang 張讓 (d. 189)
Zhang Ruitu 張瑞圖 (1570–1641)
Zhang Sengyao 張僧繇 (act. c. 500–550)
Zhang Shouxian 章綬銜 (1804–1875)
Zhang Tingqi 張廷濟 (1768–1848)
Zhang Xu 張旭 (act. 713–740)
Zhang Xuezeng 張學曾 (act. c. 1633–1657)
Zhang Xun 張恂 (c. 1643–1682)
Zhang Zao 張璪 (late 8th–early 9th century)
Zhang Zhengyue 張正嶽 (b. c. 1590)
Zhao Boju 趙伯駒 (d. c. 1162)
Zhao Lingrang 趙令穰 (act. c. 1070–1100)
Zhao Mengfu 趙孟頫 (1254–1322)
Zhao Mengjian 趙孟堅 (1199–c. 1264)
Zhao Yi 趙逸 (late 4th–early 5th century)
Zhao Zuo 趙左 (c. 1570s–1633 or later)
Zhao Zuwen 趙祖文 (early 12th century)
Zheng Chenggong 鄭成功 (Koxinga, 1624–1662)
Zheng Sixiao 鄭思肖 (Suonan 所南, 1241–1318)
Zheng Yuanxun 鄭元勳 (1598–1645)
Zhidun 支遁 (314–366)
Zhong Jun 終軍 (c. 133–before 112 BCE)
Zhou Chen 周臣 (act. c. 1500–1535)
Zhou Dunyi 周敦頤 (1017–1073)
Zhou Lianggong 周亮工 (1612–1672)
Zhou Tianqiu 周天球 (1514–1595)
Zhou Zhimian 周之冕 (1521?–after 1606)
Zhu Bang 朱邦 (act. c. 1500)
Zhu Tonglin 朱統鏊 (alternate reading: Zhu Tongquan; cf. Bada Shanren)
Zhu Xi 朱熹 (1130–1200)
Zhu Yihai 朱以海 (1618–1662)
Zhu Yizun 朱彝尊 (1629–1709)
Zhu Youlang 朱由榔 (Prince of Gui 桂王; see Yongli)
Zhu Yousong 朱由崧 (see Hongguang)
Zhu Yuanzhang 朱元璋 (see Taizu of the Ming)
Zhu Yunming 祝允明 (1460–1526)
Zhu Zanyi 朱贊儀 (late 14th century)
Zhuo Erkan 卓爾堪 (1653–1712)
Zhuangzi 莊子 (4th century BCE)
Zuo Si 左思 (c. 253–c. 307)

Photography Credits

Credits for thumbnail images on pages 277–307 are identical to those for the larger images that appear in the Catalogue of the Exhibition (pages 112–275).

Brian Forrest: Jacket, 12, 27, 31, 32–34, 38–39, 50, 52–53, 56, 57, 59, 83, 87, 89, 119, 123, 127, 129–31, 133, 135, 137, 139, 140–42, 144–45, 147, 153–55, 160–61, 163, 165, 167, 185, 196–98, 201, 205–7, 217, 219–21, 245–47, 257–62, 265, 267–70, 273–75, 320; Photography by Bryan Toro: 2, 62; Photo © 2012 Museum Associates/LACMA: 16–17, 91, 112–13, 115, 209, 253–55; Palace Museum, Beijing: 20, 44, 218; Photo Courtesy of the National Palace Museum, Republic of China (Taiwan): 23, 25, 26, 37, 92, 249, 251; Photography by Chiu Lem: 42, 66–67, 105, 171, 180–82, 227, 229, 243; Shanghai Museum: 55; Nanjing Museum: 68; Susumu Wakisaka, Idemitsu Museum of Arts, Tokyo: 71, 215; Courtesy of the Honolulu Museum of Art: 76, 85, 148–50, 156–58, 177–79, 213, 239–41; Courtesy of Shitou Shuwu: 80, 94, 169, 172–73, 203, 233; Tianjin Art Museum: 96–103 (top); Freer Gallery of Art, Smithsonian Institution: 107; Courtesy of the University of Michigan Museum of Art: 117; Iris & B. Gerald Cantor Center for Visual Arts at Stanford University: 121; Photography by Scott McClaine: 187; Courtesy of Sydney L. Moss Ltd., London, Photographer Ken Adlard, UK: 189, 192–94; Photo Courtesy of MegaVision: 191, 318; and James Chen Studio: 223.

Selected Bibliography

Allan, Sarah. "The Identities of Taigong Wang in Zhou and Han Literature." *Monumenta Serica* 30 (1972–73): 57–99.

Bada Shanren quanji 八大山人全集. Edited by Wang Chaowen 王朝聞. 5 vols. Nanchang: Jiangxi meishu chubanshe, 2000.

Bai Jian 白堅. *Yang Wencong zhuan lun* 楊文驄傳論. Shanghai: Shanghai renmin meishu chubanshe, 1990.

Barnhart, Richard M. *Painters of the Great Ming: The Imperial Court and the Zhe School*. Dallas: Dallas Museum of Art, 1993.

———, et al. *The Jade Studio: Masterpieces of Ming and Qing Painting and Calligraphy from the Wong Nan-p'ing Collection*. New Haven: Yale University Art Gallery, 1994.

———, Yang Xin, et al. *Three Thousand Years of Chinese Painting*. New Haven: Yale University Press, 1997.

Bauer, Wolfgang. *China and the Pursuit of Happiness: Recurring Themes in Four Thousand Years of Chinese Cultural History*, trans. Michael Shaw. New York: Seabury Press, 1976.

Bentley, Tamara Heimarck. "Authenticity in a New Key: Chen Hongshou's Figurative Oeuvre, 'Authentic Emotion,' and the Late Ming Market." Ph.D. diss., University of Michigan, 2000.

Berg, Daria. "Cultural Discourse on Xue Susu, A Courtesan in Late Ming China." *International Journal of Asian Studies* 6, no. 2 (2009): 171–200.

Berkowitz, Alan. "Courting Disengagement: 'Beckoning the Recluse' Poems of the Western Jin." In Paul W. Kroll and David R. Knechtges, eds., *Studies in Early Medieval Chinese Literature and Cultural History, in Honor of Richard B. Mather and Donald Holzman*, 81–116. Provo, UT: T'ang Studies Society, 2003.

———. *Patterns of Disengagement: The Practice and Portrayal of Reclusion in Early Medieval China*. Stanford, CA: Stanford University Press, 2000.

———. "Topos and Entelechy in the Ethos of Reclusion in China." *Journal of the American Oriental Society* 114, no. 4 (October–December 1994): 632–38.

Bickford, Maggie. *Ink Plum: The Making of a Chinese Scholar-Painting Genre*. Cambridge: Cambridge University Press, 1996.

———, et al. *Bones of Jade, Soul of Ice: The Flowering Plum in Chinese Art*. New Haven: Yale University Art Gallery, 1985.

Bokenkamp, Stephen R. "The Peach Flower Font and the Grotto Passage." *Journal of the American Oriental Society* 106, no. 1 (January–March 1986): 65–77.

Brook, Timothy. "Family Continuity and Cultural Hegemony: The Gentry of Ningbo, 1368–1911." In Joseph Esherick and Mary Rankin, eds., *Chinese Local Elites and Patterns of Dominance*, 27–50. Berkeley: University of California Press, 1990.

———. *Praying for Power: Buddhism and the Formation of Gentry Society in Late-Ming China*. Cambridge, MA: Council on East Asian Studies, Harvard University Press, 1993.

———. "Xu Guangqi in his Context: The World of the Shanghai Gentry." In Catherine Jami, Pieter Engelfriet, and Gregory Blue, eds., *Statecraft and Intellectual Renewal in Late Ming China: The Cross-Cultural Synthesis of Xu Guangqi*, 72–98. Leiden: Brill, 2001.

Brotherton, Elizabeth. "Li Kung-lin and Long Handscroll Illustrations of T'ao Ch'ien's 'Returning Home'." Ph.D. diss., Princeton University, 1992.

Burkus, Anne Gail. "The Artefacts of Biography in Ch'en Hung-shou's 'Pao-lun-t'ang chi'." 2 vols. Ph.D. diss., University of California, Berkeley, 1987.

Burkus-Chasson, Anne. "Elegant or Common? Chen Hongshou's Birthday Presentation Pictures and His Professional Status." *Art Bulletin* 76, no. 2 (1994): 279–300.

Bush, Susan. *The Chinese Literati on Painting: Su Shih (1037–101) to Tung Ch'i-Ch'ang (1555–1636)*. Cambridge, MA: Harvard University Press, 1971.

———. "Lung-mo, K'ai-ho, and Ch'i-fu: Some Implications of Wang Yuan-ch'i's Three Compositional Terms." *Oriental Art* 8, no. 3 (Autumn 1962): 120–27.

———. "Yet Again, 'Streams and Mountains without End'." *Artibus Asiae* 48, no. 3/4 (1987): 197–223.

Cahill, James. *The Compelling Image: Nature and Style in Seventeenth-Century Chinese Painting*. Cambridge, MA: Harvard University Press, 1982.

———. *The Distant Mountains: Chinese Painting of the Late Ming Dynasty, 1570–1644*. New York: Weatherhill, 1982.

———. "The Early Styles of Kung Hsien." *Oriental Art* 16, no. 1 (Spring 1970): 51–71.

———. *Hills Beyond a River: Chinese Painting of the Yüan Dynasty, 1279–1368*. New York: Weatherhill, 1976.

———. "Huang Shan Paintings as Pilgrimage Pictures." In Susan Naquin and Chün-fang Yü, eds., *Pilgrims and Sacred Sites in China*, 246–92. Berkeley: University of California Press, 1992.

———. "K'un-ts'an and his Inscriptions." In Alfreda Murck and Wen C. Fong, eds., *Words and Images: Chinese Poetry, Calligraphy, and Painting*, 513–34. New York: Metropolitan Museum of Art; and Princeton: Princeton University Press, 1991.

———. "The 'Madness' in Bada Shanren's Paintings." *Ajia bunka kenkyu*, no. 17 (March 1989): 119–43.

———. *The Painter's Practice: How Artists Lived and Worked in Traditional China*. New York: Columbia University Press, 1994.

———. *Parting at the Shore: Chinese Painting of the Early and Middle Ming Dynasty, 1368–1580*. New York: Weatherhill, 1978.

———. *The Restless Landscape: Chinese Painting of the Late Ming Period*. Berkeley: University Art Museum, 1971.

———, ed. *Shadows of Mt. Huang: Chinese Painting and Printing of the Anhui School*. Berkeley: University Art Museum, 1981.

Chang, Joseph, Qianshen Bai, and Stephen Allee. *In Pursuit of Heavenly Harmony: Paintings and Calligraphy by Bada Shanren from the Estate of Wang Fangyu and Sum Wai*. Washington, D.C.: Freer Gallery of Art, 2003.

Chang, Kang-i Sun. "The Idea of the Mask in Wu Wei-yeh (1609–1671)." *Harvard Journal of Asiatic Studies* 48, no. 2 (December 1988): 289–320.

Chaves, Jonathan. *The Chinese Painter as Poet*. New York: China Institute in America, 2000.

———. *Singing of the Source: Nature and God in the Poetry of the Chinese Painter Wu Li*. Honolulu: University of Hawaii Press, 1993.

Chen Duxiu 陳獨秀. "Wenxue geming lun" 文學革命論 (Discourse on a revolution in literature). In *Chen Duxiu zhuzuo xuan* 陳獨秀著作選 (Selected writings of Chen Duxiu), 260–61. Shanghai: Shanghai renmin chubanshe, 1993.

Ch'en, Kuo-tung. "Temple Lamentation and Robe-Burning—Gestures of Social Protest in Seventeenth-Century China." Translated by James Greenbaum. *East Asian History*, nos. 15/16 (June–December 1998): 33–52.

Chen Sandi 陳三弟. "Cheng Sui zhi jiaoyou kaoyi" 程邃之交游考譯 (Study of Cheng Sui's acquaintances). *Duoyun* 朵雲 46 (June 1997): 85–100.

———. "Xu Fang yanjiu" 徐枋研究 (Research on Xu Fang). *Qingshi yanjiu* 清史研究, no. 1 (1997): 76–86.

Chen, Shih-hsiang, and Harold Acton, trans. *The Peach Blossom Fan: T'ao-hua-shan*. Berkeley: University of California Press, 1976.

Chen Zuyan 陳祖言. "The Art of Black and White: Wei-ch'i in Chinese Poetry." *Journal of the American Oriental Society* 117, no. 4 (1997): 643–54.

———. "'Qiuping xiaoji, keyi yu da'—Qian Qianyi weiqi shi zhong fan Qing fu Ming de weici yinyu" 楸枰小技、可以喻大——錢謙益圍棋詩中反清復明的微辭隱語 (Hidden meanings related to the Ming restoration in the poetry on *weiqi* by Qian Qianyi). *Wenyi yanjiu* 文藝研究, vol. 5 (2009): 74–81.

Cheng, François. *Shitao (1642–1707): La saveur du monde*. Paris: Éditions Phébus, 1998.

Chou, Ju-hsi. "A Landscape Painting Album by Chu Ta." *Journal of the Honolulu Academy of Arts* 2 (1977): 36–47.

The Classic of Changes—A New Translation of the I Ching as Interpreted by Wang Bi. Translated by Richard John Lynn. New York: Columbia University Press, 1994.

Clunas, Craig. *Elegant Debts: The Social Art of Wen Zhengming, 1470–1559*. Honolulu: University of Hawaii Press, 2003.

———. *Superfluous Things: Material Culture and Social Status in Early Ming China*. Urbana and Chicago: University of Illinois Press, 1991.

Dardess, John W. *Blood and History in China: The Donglin Faction and its Repression, 1620–1627*. Honolulu: University of Hawaii Press, 2002.

Davis, A. R. *T'ao Yüan-ming (AD 365–427): His Works and Their Meaning*. 2 vols. Cambridge: Cambridge University Press, 1983.

Davis, Richard. *Wind against the Mountain: The Crisis of Politics and Culture in Thirteenth-Century China*. Cambridge, MA: Harvard University Press, 1996.

DeWoskin, Kenneth J. *A Song for One or Two: Music and the Concept of Art in Early China*. Ann Arbor: University of Michigan Center for Chinese Studies, 1982.

Diyan caotang zhencang huaji 滌研草堂珍藏畫集 (Masterpieces from the Diyan Caotang collection). Hong Kong: Ailianju yishu chubanshe, 2008.

Edwards, Richard. "The Painting of Tao-chi: Postscript for an Exhibition." *Oriental Art*, new series, 14, no. 4 (Winter 1968): 261–70.

———. *The Painting of Tao-chi, 1641–circa 1720*. Ann Arbor: University of Michigan Museum of Art, 1967.

Egan, Ronald. *The Literary Works of Ou-yang Hsiu (1007–72)*. Cambridge: Cambridge University Press, 1984.

Fong, Wen C. "Archaism as a 'Primitive' Style." In Christian F. Murck, ed., *Artists and Traditions: Uses of the Past in Chinese Culture*, 89–109. Princeton, NJ: Princeton University Press, 1976.

———. *Beyond Representation: Chinese Painting and Calligraphy 8th–14th Century*. New York: Metropolitan Museum of Art, 1992.

———, et al. *Images of the Mind: Selections from the Edward K. Elliot Family and John B. Elliot Collections of Chinese Calligraphy and Painting at the Art Museum, Princeton University*. Princeton: Art Museum, Princeton University, in association with Princeton University Press, 1984.

———, Chin-Sung Chang, and Maxwell K. Hearn. *Landscapes Clear and Radiant: The Art of Wang Hui (1632–1717)*. New York: Metropolitan Museum of Art, 2008.

———, James C. Y. Watt, et al. *Possessing the Past: Treasures from the National Palace Museum, Taipei*. New York: Metropolitan Museum of Art, 1996.

Frankel, Hans. "The Chinese Ballad 'Southeast Fly the Peacocks.'" *Harvard Journal of Asiatic Studies* 34 (1974): 248–71.

Fu Shen 傅申. "Ming Qing zhi ji de xiebi goule fengshang yu Shitao de zaoqi zuopin" 明清之際的渴筆勾勒風尚與石濤的早期作品 (An aspect of mid-seventeenth century Chinese painting: The "dry linear" style and the early work of Shitao). *Journal of the Institute of Chinese Studies of the Chinese University of Hong Kong* 8, no. 2 (1975): 579–616.

Ganza, Kenneth Stanley. "The Artist as Traveler: The Origin and Development of Travel as a Theme in Chinese Landscape Painting of the Fourteenth to Seventeenth Centuries." Ph.D. diss., Indiana University, 1990.

Goodrich, L. Carrington, and Chaoying Fang, eds. *The Dictionary of Ming Biography, 1368–1644*. 2 vols. New York: Columbia University Press, 1976.

Greenbaum, Jamie. *Chen Jiru (1558–1639): The Background to Development and Subsequent Uses of Literary Personae*. Leiden: Brill, 2007.

Gugong shuhua lu 故宮書畫錄 (Records of painting and calligraphy in the National Palace Museum). Taipei: Guoli Gugong bowuyuan, 1965.

Gugong shuhua tulu 故宮書畫圖錄 (Pictorial records of painting and calligraphy in the National Palace Museum). 25 vols. Taipei: Guoli Gugong bowuyuan, 1989–2006.

Hawkes, David. *The Songs of the South: An Anthology of Ancient Chinese Poems by Qu Yuan and Other Poets*. Harmondsworth: Penguin, 1985.

Hay, Alan John. "Huang Kung-wang's 'Dwelling in the Fu-ch'un Mountains': The Dimensions of a Landscape." Ph.D. diss., Princeton University, 1978.

———. *Kernels of Energy, Bones of Earth: The Rock in Chinese Art*. New York: China Institute, 1985.

———. "Structure and Aesthetic Criteria in Chinese Rocks and Art." *RES: Anthropology and Aesthetics* 13 (Spring 1987): 5–22.

———. "Subject, Nature, and Representation in Early Seventeenth-Century China." In Wai-ching Ho, ed., *Proceedings of the Tung Ch'i-ch'ang International Symposium*, 4.1–4.22. Kansas City: Nelson-Atkins Museum of Art, 1992.

Hay, Jonathan. "Ming Palace and Tomb in Early Qing Jiangning: Dynastic Memory and the Openness of History." *Late Imperial China* 20, no. 1 (June 1999): 1–48.

———. *Shitao: Painting and Modernity in Early Qing China*. New York: Cambridge University Press, 2001.

———. "The Suspension of Dynastic Time." In John Hay, ed., *Boundaries in China*, 171–97. London: Reaktion, 1994.

———. "'Travelers in Snow-Covered Mountains': A Reassessment." *Orientations* 39, no. 8 (November–December 2008): 85–91.

He Guanbiao 何冠彪. "Lun Ming yimin zhi chuchu" 論明遺民之出處 (Discussion of political positioning among the Ming *yimin*). In He, ed., *Ming mo Qing chu xueshu sixiang yanjiu* 明末清初學術思想研究 (Research on scholastic thought during the late Ming and early Qing), 53–124. Taipei: Xuesheng shuju, 1991.

———. *Sheng yu si: Ming ji shidaifu de jueze* 生與死：明季士大夫的抉擇 (Life and death: The literati and their choices at the end of the Ming). Taipei: Lianjing chubanshe, 1997.

He Junhong 赫俊紅. *Danqing qipa: Wanming Qingchu de nüxing huihua* 丹青奇葩：晚明清初的女性繪畫 (Women's painting of the late Ming–early Qing). Beijing: Wenwu chubanshe, 2008.

He Yaoguang 何耀光. *Zhilelou shuhua lu: Ming yimin zhi bu* 至樂樓書畫錄：明遺民之部 (Painting and calligraphy by Ming *yimin* of the Zhilelou collection). Hong Kong: Heshi Zhilelou, 1973.

He Yunbo 何雲波. *Weiqi yu Zhongguo wenhua* 圍棋與中國文化 (*Weiqi* and Chinese culture). Beijing: Renmin chubanshe, 2001.

Hightower, James R. "The *Fu* of T'ao Ch'ien." In John L. Bishop, ed., *Studies in Chinese Literature*, 45–72. Cambridge, MA: Harvard University Press, 1965.

Ho, Wai-kam, ed. *The Century of Tung Ch'i-ch'ang, 1555–1636*. 2 vols. Kansas City: Nelson-Atkins Museum of Art, in association with the University of Washington Press, 1992.

———, et al. *Eight Dynasties of Chinese Painting: The Collections of the Nelson Gallery-Atkins Museum, Kansas City, and the Cleveland Museum of Art*. Cleveland: Cleveland Museum of Art, 1980.

Hu, Philip K. "The Paradise Landscape of Yangshuo: A Monumental Painting by Mi Wanzhong." *Cantor Arts Center Journal* 2 (2000–01): 6–21.

Hu, Shih. *The Chinese Renaissance: The Haskell Lectures, 1933*. New York: Paragon, 1963.

Huang Binhong 黃賓虹. "Gou daoren yishi fu gou daoren yizhu" 垢道人軼事附垢道人遺著 (Activities and writings of Cheng Sui). In *Huang Binhong wenji shuhua bian* 黃賓虹文集書畫編 (Shanghai: Shanghai shuhua chubanshe, 1999), vol. 2, 327.

Hummel, Arthur, ed. *Eminent Chinese of the Ch'ing Period*. 2 vols. Washington, D.C.: U.S. Govt. Printing Office, 1943–44.

Jang, Scarlett Ju-yu. "Issues of Public Service in the Themes of Chinese Court Painting." Ph.D. diss., University of California, Berkeley, 1989.

Jay, Jennifer W. *A Change in Dynasties: Loyalism in Thirteenth-Century China*. Bellingham: Western Washington University, 1991.

Kim, Hongnam. "Chou Liang-kung and his 'Tu-hua-lu' (Lives of Painters): Patron-Critic and Painters in Seventeenth-Century China." 2 vols. Ph.D. diss., Yale University, 1985.

———. *The Life of a Patron: Zhou Lianggong (1612–1672) and the Painters of Seventeenth-Century China*. New York: China Institute in America, 1996.

Kohara, Hironobu. "An Introductory Study of Chen Hongshou, Part I." Trans. Anne Burkus. *Oriental Art* 32, no. 4 (1986–87): 398–410; "Part II," *Oriental Art* 33, no. 1 (1987): 67–83.

Kuo, Jason C. *The Austere Landscape: The Paintings of Hung-jen*. Taipei and New York: SMC Publishing, 1991.

Laing, Ellen Johnston. "Biographical Notes on Three Seventeenth-Century Chinese Painters." *Renditions*, no. 6 (Spring 1976): 107–10.

———. "'Riverside' by Liu Yüan-ch'i and 'The Waterfall on Mt. K'uang-lu' by Shao Mi." *University of Michigan Museum of Art Bulletin*, new series, vol. 5 (1970–71): 1–16.

Ledderose, Lothar. "The Earthly Paradise: Religious Elements in Chinese Landscape Art." In Christian Murck and Susan Bush, eds., *Theories of the Arts in China*, 165–83. Princeton, NJ: Princeton University Press, 1983.

Lee, Hui-shu. "Bada Shanren's Bird-and-Fish Painting and the Art of Transformation." *Archives of Asian Art* 44 (1991): 6–26.

———. "The Fish Leaves of the Anwan Album: Bada Shanren's Journeys to a Landscape of the Past." *Ars Orientalis* 20 (1990): 69–85.

Legge, James, trans. *The Sacred Books of China: The Texts of Confucianism, Part III, The Li Ki, I–X*. Delhi: Motilal Banarsidass, 1968.

Li, Chu-tsing (Li Zhujin 李鑄晉). "Li Rihua and his Literati Circle in the Late Ming Dynasty." *Orientations* 18, no. 8 (August 1987): 28–47.

———. *A Thousand Peaks and Myriad Ravines: Chinese Paintings in the Charles A. Drenowatz Collection*. 2 vols. Ascona: Artibus Asiae, 1974.

———. "Xiang Shengmo zhi zhaoyin shihua" 項聖謨之招隱詩畫 (Xiang Shengmo's poetry and painting on the theme of "summoning the recluse"). In *Zhongwen daxue Zhongguo wenhua yanjiusuo xuebao* 中文大學文化研究所學報 8, no. 2 (1976): 531–59.

———, and James C. Y. Watt, eds. *The Chinese Scholar's Studio: Artistic Life in the Late Ming Period*. New York: Thames and Hudson and the Asia Society, 1987.

Li Huiyi 李惠儀. "Shibian yu wanwu—luelun Qing chu wenren de shenmei fengshang" 世變與玩物——略論清初文人的審美風尚 (Amusements after dynastic change: Brief discussion of aesthetic tastes of the literati in the early Qing). *Zhongguo wenzhe yanjiu jikan* 中國文哲研究集刊, vol. 33 (2008): 40–41.

Li, Wai-yee. "History and Memory in Wu Weiye's Poetry." In Wilt Idema, Wai-yee Li, and Ellen Widmer, eds., *Trauma and Transcendence in Early Qing Literature*, 99–148. Cambridge, MA: Harvard University Asia Center, 2006.

Li Yeshuang 李葉霜. "Bada Shanren yu Yunnan Guofeng" 八大山人與雲南過峰 (Bada Shanren and Guofeng of Yunnan). In Wang Fangyu 王方宇, ed., *Bada Shanren lunji* 八大山人論集, 205–10. Taipei: Guoli Bianyiguan Zhonghua congshu bian shen wei yuan hui, 1984–85.

Li Zhigang 李志綱 (Lee Chi Kwong). "Cheng Sui yanjiu" 程邃研究 (Research on Cheng Sui). *Duoyun*, vol. 46 (June 1997): 39–84.

Lin, Shuen-fu. *The Transformation of the Chinese Lyrical Tradition: Chiang K'uei and Southern Sung Tz'u Poetry*. Princeton, NJ: Princeton University Press, 1978.

Lin Yixin 林逸欣. "Li Rihua huihua jiancang pinwei zhi yanjiu" 李日華繪畫鑑藏品味之研究 (Research on Li Rihua's collecting and taste in paintings). Master's thesis, Graduate Institute of Art Studies, National Zhongyang University, Taiwan, 2003.

Little, Stephen, and Shawn Eichman. *Taoism and the Arts of China*. Chicago: Art Institute of Chicago, 2000.

Liu Qiaomei 劉巧楣. "Wan Ming Suzhou huihua" 晚明蘇州繪畫 (Painting in Suzhou in the late Ming). Master's thesis, Department of History, National Taiwan University, 1989.

Liu Shancheng 劉善承, ed. *Zhongguo weiqi* 中國圍棋 (Chinese *weiqi*). Chengdu: Sichuan kexue jishu chubanshe, 1985.

Liu, Shi-yee. "An Actor in Real Life: Chen Hongshou's *Scenes from the Life of Tao Yuanming*." Ph.D. diss., Yale University, 2003.

Liu, Wu-chi. *An Introduction to Chinese Literature*. Bloomington: Indiana University Press, 1966.

Liu Yazhang 劉亞璋. "Wan Ming wenren huajia Yang Wencong kaolue" 晚明文人畫家楊文驄考略 (Research on the late-Ming literati painter Yang Wencong). *Yishu tansuo* 藝術探索 19, no. 1 (February 2005): 31–34.

Lu Lin 陸林. "Wan Ming shuhuajia Shao Mi shengnian xinshuo" 晚明書畫家邵彌生年新說. Zhongguo dianji yu wenhua 中國典籍與文化 4 (2003): 67–71.

Lu, Suh-fen. "A Study on Tseng Ching's Portraits." Master's thesis, University of Michigan, 1986.

Lü Xiao 呂曉. *Kuncan huihua yanjiu* 髡殘繪畫研究 (Research on the paintings of Kuncan). Nanchang: Jiangxi meishu chubanshe, 2010.

Ma Jige 馬季戈. *Zeng Jing yu Bochen pai* 曾鯨與波臣派 (Zeng Jing and the Bochen School). Jinan: Shandong meishu chubanshe, 2004.

Mather, Richard. "The Controversy over Conformity and Naturalness during the Six Dynasties." *History of Religions* 9, nos. 2/3 (November 1969–February 1970): 160–80.

Miller, Harry. *State versus Gentry in Late Ming Dynasty China, 1572–1644*. New York: Palgrave Macmillan, 2009.

Moss, Paul. *This Single Feather of Auspicious Light: Old Chinese Painting and Calligraphy*. London: Sydney L. Moss, 2010.

———, ed. *Scrolling Images: Chinese Painting and Calligraphy in Handscroll Format*. London: Sydney L. Moss, 1991.

Mote, Frederick. "Confucian Eremitism in the Yüan Period." In Arthur F. Wright, ed., *The Confucian Persuasion*, 202–40. Stanford, CA: Stanford University Press, 1960.

Munakata, Kiyohiko. *Ching Hao's Pi-Fa-Chi: A Note on the Art of Brush*. Ascona: Artibus Asiae Publishers, 1974.

Murck, Alfreda. *Poetry and Painting in Song China: The Subtle Art of Dissent*. Cambridge, MA: Harvard University Press, 2000.

Murray, Julia. *Mirror of Morality: Chinese Narrative Illustration and Confucian Ideology*. Honolulu: University of Hawaii Press, 2007.

Nelson, Susan E. "Intimations of Immortality in Chinese Landscape Painting of the Fourteenth Century." *Oriental Art* 33, no. 3 (1987): 275–92.

———. "On Through to the Beyond: The Peach Blossom Spring as Paradise." *Archives of Asian Art*, vol. 39 (1986): 23–47.

———. "Revisiting the Eastern Fence: Tao Qian's Chrysanthemums." *Art Bulletin* 83, no. 3 (2001): 437–60.

Nie Chongzheng 聶崇正. *Zeng Jing* 曾鯨. Taipei: Jinxiu chuban shiye gufen youxian gongsi, 1996.

Nienhauser, William H., Jr., ed. *The Indiana Companion to Traditional Chinese Literature*. 2 vols. Bloomington: Indiana University Press, 1986.

Nobility and Virtue: A Selection of Late Ming and Early Qing Paintings and Calligraphies from the Chih Lo Lou Collection. Hong Kong: Kangleji wenhua shiwushu, 2010.

Osaka Exchange Exhibition: Paintings from the Abe Collection and Other Masterpieces of Chinese Art. Osaka: Osaka Municipal Museum of Fine Arts; and San Francisco: San Francisco Center of Asian Art and Culture, 1970.

Ouyang, Zhongshi, Wen C. Fong, et al. *Chinese Calligraphy*. New Haven: Yale University Press, 2008.

Pang, Mae Anna Quan. "Wang Yüan-ch'i (1642–1715) and Formal Construction in Chinese Landscape Painting." Ph.D. diss., University of California, Berkeley, 1976.

Park, Eun-wha. "The World of Idealized Reclusion: Landscape Painting of Hsiang Sheng-mo (1597–1658)." Ph.D. diss., University of Michigan, 1992.

Pegg, Richard. "Kuncan: Man, Monk and Painter." *Oriental Art* 40, no. 4 (Winter 1994–95): 2–12.

Pei Shijun 裴世俊. *Sihai zongmeng wushi nian: Qian Qianyi zhuan* 四海宗盟五十年：錢謙益傳 (Biography of Qian Qianyi). Beijing: Dongfang chubanshe, 2001.

Peterson, Willard J. *Bitter Gourd: Fang I-Chih and the Impetus for Intellectual Change*. New Haven: Yale University Press, 1979.

Porter, Bill. *Road to Heaven: Encounters with Chinese Hermits*. San Francisco: Mercury House, 1993.

Rao Zongyi 饒宗頤. "Fang Yizhi zhi hualun" 方以智之畫論 (Fang Yizhi's discussions on painting). *Xianggang Zhongwen daxue Zhongguo wenhua yanjiusuo xuebao* 香港中文大學中國文化研究所學報 7, no. 1 (1974): 113–31.

———. "Zhang Dafeng ji qi jiashi" 張大風及其家世 (Zhang Feng and his family background). *Xianggang Zhongwen daxue Zhongguo wenhua yanjiu xuebao* 香港中文大學中國文化研究所學報 8, no. 1 (1976): 51–70.

Rawski, Evelyn. "The Imperial Way of Death: Ming and Ch'ing Emperors and Death Ritual." In James L. Watson and Evelyn S. Rawski, eds., *Death Ritual in Late Imperial and Modern China*. Berkeley: University of California Press, 1988.

Ren Daobin 任道斌. "Ch'en Chi-ju as Critic and Connoisseur." In Wai-ching Ho, ed., *Proceedings of the Tung Ch'i-ch'ang International Symposium*, 9.1–9.25. Kansas City: Nelson-Atkins Museum of Art, 1991.

———. *Dong Qichang xinian* 董其昌系年. Beijing: Wenwu chubanshe, 1988.

———. *Fang Yizhi nianpu* 方以智年譜 (Fang Yizhi chronology). Hefei shi: Anhui jiayu chubanshe, 1983.

Riely, Celia Carrington. "Tung Ch'i-ch'ang's Ownership of Huang Kung-wang's 'Dwelling in the Fu-ch'un Mountains': With a Revised Dating for Chang Ch'ou's *Ch'ing-ho shu-hua fang*." *Archives of Asian Art*, vol. 28 (1974–75): 57–76.

Rogers, Howard, and Sherman E. Lee. *Masterworks of Ming and Qing Painting from the Forbidden City*. Honolulu: Honolulu Academy of Arts, 1989.

Schafer, Edward H. "Cosmos in Miniature: The Tradition of the Chinese Garden." *Landscape* 12, no. 3 (1963): 24–26.

Shang, Kela. "Visualizing Social Spaces: Site and Situation in Xiang Shengmo's (1597–1658) Art." Ph.D. diss., Stanford University, 2007.

Shanshui hebi: Huang Gongwang yu Fuchun shanju tu tezhan 山水合璧：黃公望與富春山居圖特展 (Landscapes reunited: Special exhibition of Huang Gongwang's *Dwelling in the Fuchun Mountains*). Taipei: Guoli Gugong bowuyuan, 2011.

Shih, Shou-chien. "Tung Ch'i-ch'ang's 'Wan-luan Thatched Hall' and the Innovation of his Painting Style." In Wai-ching Ho, ed., *Proceedings of the Tung Ch'i-ch'ang International Symposium*, 13.1–13.28. Kansas City: Nelson-Atkins Museum of Art, 1992. Chinese version: 石守謙.〈董其昌婉孌草堂圖及其革新畫風〉.《歷史語言研究所集刊》65, no. 2 (1994): 307–32.

Shin, Seojeong. "Illustrations of Taiping Prefecture (1648): A Printed Album of Landscapes by the Seventeenth-Century Literati Artist, Xiao Yuncong (1596–1673)." Ph.D. diss., University of Maryland, College Park, 2006.

Shitao shuhua quanji 石濤書畫全集 (Painting and calligraphy of Shitao). Tianjin: Tianjin renmin meishu chubanshe, 1995.

Silbergeld, Jerome. "Kung Hsien: A Professional Chinese Artist and His Patronage." *Burlington Magazine* 123, no. 940 (July 1, 1981): 400–10.

———. "Kung Hsien's Self-Portrait in Willows, with Notes on the Willow in Chinese Painting and Literature." *Artibus Asiae* 42, no. 1 (1980): 5–36.

———. "The Political Landscapes of Kung Hsien, in Painting and Poetry." *Journal of the Institute of Chinese Studies of the Chinese University of Hong Kong* 8, no. 2 (December 1976): 50–73.

———. "Political Symbolism in the Landscape Painting and Poetry of Kung Hsien (c. 1620–1689)." Ph.D. diss., Stanford University, 1974.

Siren, Osvald. *Chinese Painting, Leading Masters and Principles*. 7 vols. New York and London: Ronald Press, 1956–58.

Stein, Rolf A. *The World in Miniature: Container Gardens and Dwellings in Far Eastern Religious Thought*. Stanford, CA: Stanford University Press, 1990.

Strassberg, Richard E. *The World of K'ung Shang-jen: A Man of Letters in Early Ch'ing China*. New York: Columbia University Press, 1983.

Struve, Lynn A. *The Southern Ming, 1644–1662*. New Haven: Yale University Press, 1984.

———. *Voices from the Ming-Qing Cataclysm: China in Tigers' Jaws*. New Haven: Yale University Press, 1993.

Sturman, Peter C. "The Donkey Rider as Icon: Li Cheng and Early Chinese Landscape Painting." *Artibus Asiae* 55, nos. 1/2 (1995): 43–97.

———. *Mi Fu: Style and the Art of Calligraphy in Northern Song China*. New Haven: Yale University Press, 1997.

———. "Mi Youren and the Inherited Literati Tradition: Dimensions of Ink-Play." Ph.D. diss., Yale University, 1989.

Sun Fuxuan 孫福軒. "Xu Fang huaxue sixiang lun" 徐枋畫學思想論 (Discourse on Xu Fang's painting and thought). *Xin meishu* 新美術, no. 5 (2007): 67–74.

Suzhou bowuguan cang Ming Qing shuhua 蘇州博物館藏明清書畫 (Ming-Qing paintings and calligraphies in the collection of the Suzhou Museum). Beijing: Wenwu chubanshe, 2006.

Suzuki Kei 鈴木敬, ed. *Chūgoku kaiga sōgō zuroku* 中国絵画総合図録 (Comprehensive illustrated catalogue of Chinese paintings). 4 vols. Tokyo: Tōkyō Daigaku Tōyō Bunka Kenkyūjo, 1983.

Swartz, Wendy. *Reading Tao Yuanming: Shifting Paradigms of Historical Reception (427–1900)*. Cambridge, MA: Harvard University Asia Center, 2008.

Tang Yin, Wang Yangming, Mo Shilong, Xing Tong, Chen Jiru 唐寅，王陽明，莫是龍，邢侗，陳繼儒. Edited by Liu Zhengcheng 劉正成. *Zhongguo shu fa quanji* 中國書法全集 series, vol. 52. Beijing: Rongbaozhai chubanshe, 2005.

Tao Yongbai 陶詠白 and Li Shi 李湜. *Shiluo de lishi: Zhongguo nüxing huihua shi* 失落的歷史：中國女性繪畫史 (History forgotten: Women painters of China). Changsha: Hunan meishu chubanshe, 2000.

Tenckhoff, Diana. "Cha Shih-piao (1615–1698): The Yangchou Traveler." Ph.D. diss., University of Kansas, 2002.

Tseng, Yu-ho. "A Report on Ch'en Hung-shou." *Archives of the Chinese Art Society of America* 13 (1959): 75–88.

Verellen, Franciscus. "The Beyond Within: Grotto-Heavens (*Dongtian*) in Taoist Ritual and Cosmology." *Cahiers d'Extreme-Asie* 8 (1995): 265–90.

Vervoorn, Aat. "Boyi and Shuqi: Worthy Men of Old?" *Papers on Far Eastern History* 28 (September 1983): 1–22.

———. *Men of the Cliffs and Caves: The Development of the Chinese Eremitic Tradition to the End of the Han Dynasty*. Hong Kong: Chinese University Press, 1990.

Vinograd, Richard. *Boundaries of the Self: Chinese Portraits 1600–1900*. Cambridge: Cambridge University Press, 1992.

Wakeman, Frederick. *The Great Enterprise: The Manchu Reconstruction of Imperial Order in Seventeenth-Century China*. 2 vols. Berkeley: University of California, 1985.

Wan Zhaofeng 萬兆鳳. "Shi Bada Shanren tihuashi 'heshang hua ge'" 釋八大山人題畫詩河上花歌 (Interpreting Bada Shanren's ballad for "Flowers on the River"). In *Bada Shanren quanji* 八大山人全集 5: 1282.

Wang, Chung-lan. "Gong Xian (1619–1689): A Seventeenth-Century Nanjing Intellectual and His Aesthetic World." Ph.D. diss., Yale University, 2005.

Wang Fangyu 王方宇. *Bada Shanren lunji* 八大山人論集 (Collected essays on Bada Shanren). Taipei: Guoli Bianyiguan Zhonghua congshu bian shen wei yuan hui, 1984–85.

———, Richard M. Barnhart, and Judith G. Smith, eds. *Master of the Lotus Garden: The Life and Art of Bada Shanren (1626–1705)*. New Haven: Yale University Art Gallery, 1990.

Wang, Shen. "Wang Yuangqi and the Orthodoxy of Self-Reflection in Early Qing Landscape Painting." Ph.D. diss., University of Pennsylvania, 2010.

Wang Shiqing 汪世清. "Bada Shanren de jiaoyou" 八大山人的交友 (Acquaintances of Bada Shanren). In *Bada Shanren quanji* 八大山人全集 5: 1097–119.

———. *Jianjiang ziliao ji* 漸江資料集 (Hongren materials). Hefei: Anhui renmin chubanshe, 1984.

———. *Juan huai tiandi zi you zhen: Wang Shiqing yiyuan chayi buzheng sankao* 卷懷天地自有真：汪世清藝苑查疑補證散考 (Essays by Wang Shiqing). 2 vols. Taipei: Shitou chuban, 2006.

Wang Youfen, et al. *Chinese Calligraphy*. New Haven: Yale University Press, 2008.

Watson, Burton, trans. *The Complete Works of Chuang Tzu*. New York: Columbia University Press, 1968.

———. *Records of the Historian: Chapters from the Shih Chi of Ssu-ma Ch'ien*. Reprint, New York: Columbia University Press, 1969.

Weidner, Marsha, et al. *Views from Jade Terrace: Chinese Woman Artists 1300–1912*. New York: Rizzoli, 1988.

Wen Shiliang 溫世亮. "Ming yimin Xu Fang yanjiu" 明遺民徐枋研究 (Research on the Ming loyalist Xu Fang). Master's thesis, Suzhou University, Suzhou, 2010.

Weng, Wan-go (Weng Wan'ge 翁萬戈). *Chen Hongshou: His Life and Art*. 3 vols. Shanghai: Shanghai renmin meishu chubanshe, 1997.

———. "*A Tall Pine and Daoist Immortal:* An Examination of a Painting Attributed to Chen Hongshou." In Judith G. Smith and Wen C. Fong, eds., *Issues of Authenticity in Chinese Painting*, 170–86. New York: Metropolitan Museum of Art, 1999.

Whitfield, Roderick, and Wen C. Fong. *In Pursuit of Antiquity: Chinese Paintings of the Ming and Ch'ing Dynasties from the Collection of Mr. and Mrs. Earl Morse*. Princeton: Art Museum, Princeton University, 1969.

Wilson, Marc F. "Kung Hsien: Theorist and Technician in Painting." *Nelson Gallery and Atkins Museum Bulletin* 4, no. 9 (1969).

Wu, Marshall (Wu Peisheng 武佩聖). "A-er-hsi-p'u and His Painting Collections." In Chu-tsing Li, James Cahill, and Wai-kam Ho, eds., *Artists and Patrons: Some Social and Economic Aspects of Chinese Painting*. Lawrence, KS: Kress Foundation Department of Art History, University of Kansas; Kansas City: Nelson-Atkins Museum of Art, in association with University of Washington Press, 1989.

———. *The Orchid Pavilion Gathering: Chinese Painting from the University of Michigan Museum of Art*. 2 vols. Ann Arbor: University of Michigan, 2000.

———. "Wang Hui ke jingshi qijian zhi jiaowang yu huihua huodong" 王翬客京師期間之交往與繪畫活動 (Wang Hui's associations and painting activities during his period in the capital). In *Qingchu si Wang huapai yanjiu lunwen ji* 清初四王畫派研究論文集 (Collection of research essays on the Four Wangs of the early Qing), 607–27. Shanghai: Shanghai shuhua chubanshe, 1993.

Wu, Nelson. "Tung Ch'i-ch'ang: Apathy in Government and Fervor in Art." In Arthur F. Wright and Denis Twitchett, eds., *Confucian Personalities*, 260–93. Stanford, CA: Stanford University Press, 1962.

Wu, William Ding Yee. "Kung Hsien." Ph.D. diss., Princeton University, 1979.

———. "Kung Hsien's Style and His Sketchbooks." *Oriental Art* 16, no. 1 (Spring 1970): 72–80.

Xie Guozhen 謝國楨. *Nan Ming shilue* 南明史略 (Short history of the Southern Ming). Shanghai: Shanghai renmin chubanshe, 1957.

Xu Lisha 徐麗莎. "Wan Ming zhiye huajia Shen Shichong de yishu licheng" 晚明職業畫家沈士充的藝術歷程 (Artistic career of the late Ming professional painter Shen Shichong). *Jiuzhou xuelin* 九州學林 5, no. 4 (Winter 2007): 31–70.

Yan Juanying 顏娟瑛. *Lan Ying yu fanggu huihua* 藍瑛與仿古繪畫 (Lan Ying and the imitation of ancient paintings). Taipei: Guoli Gugong bowuyuan, 1980.

Yang Xin 楊新. *Si seng huihua* 四僧繪畫. Hong Kong: Shangwu yinshuguan, 1999.

———. *Xiang Shengmo* 項聖謨. Shanghai renmin meishu chubanshe, 1982.

———. "Yuan Shangtong shengnian bianxi" 袁尚統生年辨析 (Analysis of the birth date of Yuan Shangtong). *Wen wu* 文物, no. 7 (1991): 68–71.

Yim, Lawrence C. H. *The Poet-Historian Qian Qianyi*. London and New York: Routledge, 2009.

Yin Ji'nan 尹吉男. "'Dong Yuan' gainian de lishi shengcheng" '董源'概念的歷史生成 (The formation of the historical conception of Dong Yuan). *Wenyi yanjiu* 文藝研究, no. 2 (2005): 92–101.

Yu Yingshi 余英時. *Fang Yizhi wanjie kao* 方以智晚節考 (Study of Fang Yizhi's late years). Hong Kong: Xinya, 1972.

Yuemu: Zhongguo wanqi shuhua 悅目：中國晚期書畫 (Enchanting images: Paintings and calligraphies from late imperial China). 2 vols. Taipei: Shitou chuban youxian gongsi, 2001.

Zhang Xinzhi 張馨之. *Bada Shanren shanshui yanjiu* 八大山人山水研究 (Research on the landscape painting of Bada Shanren). Beijing: Wenhua yishu chubanshe, 2009.

Zhiren wufa: Gugong, Shangbo zhencang Bada Shitao shuhua jingpin 至人無法：故宮、上博珍藏八大石濤書畫精品 (Masters without rules: Paintings and calligraphies of Bada Shanren and Shitao from the collections of the Palace Museum and Shanghai Museum). 2 vols. Macao: Aomen yishu bowuguan, 2004.

Zhongguo gudai shuhua tumu 中國古代書畫圖目 (Pictorial index of classical Chinese paintings and calligraphies). 24 vols. Beijing: Wenwu chubanshe, 1986–2001.

Zhongguo huihua quan ji 中國繪畫全集 (Comprehensive collection of Chinese paintings). 30 vols. Beijing: Wenwu chubanshe, 1997–2001.

Zhou Jiyin 周積寅. *Zeng Jing de xiaoxiang hua* 曾鯨的肖像畫 (Zeng Jing's portrait painting). Beijing: Renmin meishu chubanshe, 1981.

Zhou Quan 周全. *Song yimin zhijie yu wenxue* 宋遺民志節與文學 (Loyalty and literature of the Song *yimin*). Taipei: Dongwu daxue, 1991.

Zhu Huiliang 朱惠良. *Zhao Zuo yanjiu* 趙左研究 (Research on Zhao Zuo). Taipei: Guoli Gugong bowuyuan, 1979.

Zhu Liangzhi 朱良志. *Bada Shanren yanjiu* 八大山人研究 (Research on Bada Shanren). Hefei: Anhui jiaoyu chubanshe, 2010.

Zhu Wanzhang 朱萬章. *Shixi* 石谿 (Kuncan). Shijiazhuang: Hebei jiaoyu chubanshe, 2006.

Zhuang Shen 莊申. "Tang Lu Hong Caotang shizhi tu juan kao" 唐盧鴻草堂十志圖卷考 (Study of Lu Hong's *Ten Views of a Thatched Hall*). *Lishi yuyan yanjiusuo jikan* 歷史語言研究所季刊 30 (1959): 615–79.

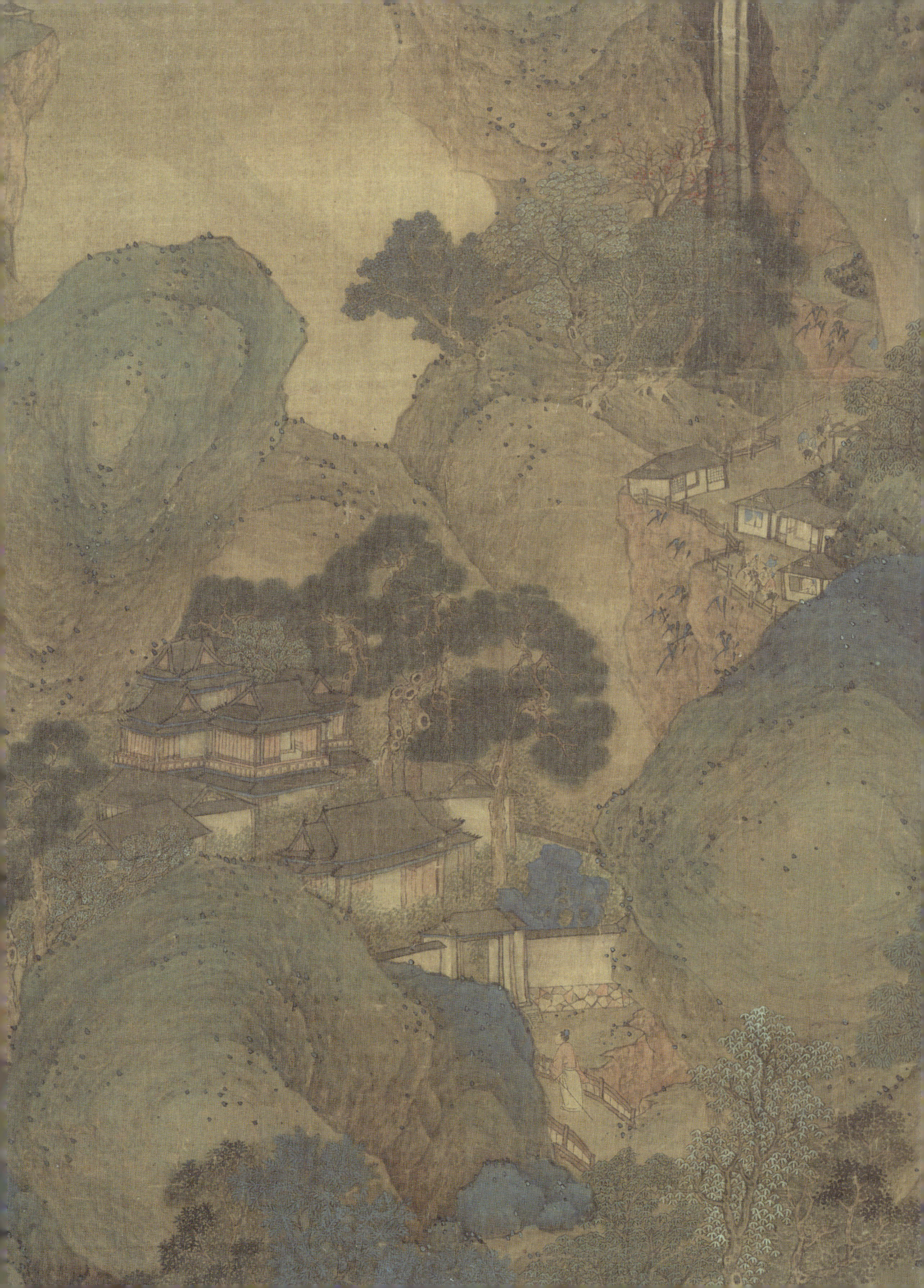

2012–13 Board of Trustees
Santa Barbara Museum of Art

Zhang Zhengyue, *Mountain Landscape*
(detail; cat. no. 28)

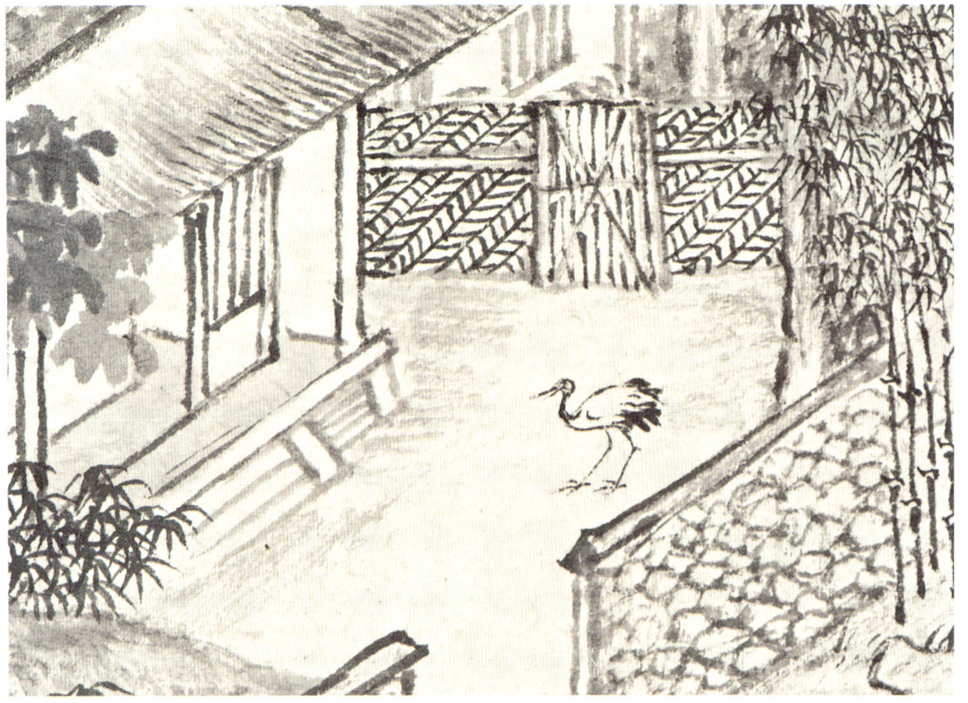

This catalogue accompanies the exhibition *The Artful Recluse: Painting, Poetry, and Politics in Seventeenth-Century China*, organized by Susan S. Tai in collaboration with Peter C. Sturman and presented at the Santa Barbara Museum of Art, Santa Barbara, California, October 20, 2012–January 20, 2013, and the Asia Society, New York, March 5–June 2, 2013.

This exhibition and catalogue are made possible by the China Guardian Auctions Co., Ltd.; SBMA Women's Board; Robert and Mercedes Eichholz Foundation; Dr. Albert E. and Antoinette Gump Amorteguy Asian Publications Endowment; Cecille and Michael Pulitzer Foundation; Victor K. Atkins Jr.; Natalia and Michael Howe; Siri and Bob Marshall; The Charles Bloom Foundation; The Rong-Wu Foundation; Capital Group, Inc., Asian Lecture Endowment; Robert and Christine Emmons; Bruce G. Wilcox; Chen Chite; Amy Chu-hua O'Dowd; Pamela Melone; The Metropolitan Center for Far Eastern Art Studies, Kyoto; E. Rhodes and Leona B. Carpenter Foundation; and the Santa Barbara Museum of Art's Friends of Asian Art.

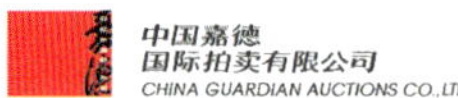

Critical support for the Asia Society Museum presentation of *The Artful Recluse* comes from The Partridge Foundation, a John and Polly Guth Charitable Fund.

Published in 2012 by the Santa Barbara Museum of Art and DelMonico Books, an imprint of Prestel, a member of Verlagsgruppe Random House GmbH

Santa Barbara Museum of Art
1130 State Street
Santa Barbara, CA 93101
www.sbma.net

Prestel Verlag
Neumarkter Strasse 28
81673 Munich
Germany
TEL +49 89 4136 0
FAX +49 89 4136 2335

Prestel Publishing Ltd.
4 Bloomsbury Place
London WC1A 2QA
United Kingdom
TEL +44 20 7323 5004
FAX +44 20 7636 8004

Prestel Publishing
900 Broadway, Suite 603
New York, NY 10003
TEL 212 995 2720
FAX 212 995 2733
E-MAIL sales@prestel-usa.com
www.prestel.com

ISBN 978-3-7913-5272-5

Library of Congress Cataloging-in-Publication Data

The artful recluse : painting, poetry, and politics in seventeenth-century China / edited by Peter C. Sturman, Susan S. Tai ; essays by Peter C. Sturman, Timothy Brook, Jonathan Chaves, Jonathan Hay, Hui-shu Lee.
pages cm
This catalogue accompanies the exhibition The Artful Recluse: Painting, Poetry, and Politics in Seventeenth-Century China, organized by Susan S. Tai in collaboration with Peter C. Sturman and presented at the Santa Barbara Museum of Art, Santa Barbara, California, October 20, 2012–January 20, 2013, and the Asia Society, New York, March 5–June 2, 2013.
Includes bibliographical references and index.
ISBN: 978-3-7913-5272-5 (hardcover)
1. Arts and society—China—History—17th century—Exhibitions. 2. Recluses—China—Exhibitions. 3. China—Intellectual life—Exhibitions. I. Sturman, Peter Charles. II. Tai, Susan. III. Santa Barbara Museum of Art. IV. Asia Society.
NX180.S6A7516 2012
700.951'09032—dc23

2012030768

COPY EDITOR Jane Hyun
CHINESE LANGUAGE COPY EDITORS Han-yun Chang and Seokwon Choi
DESIGNERS Lorraine Wild, Xiaoqing Wang, and Amy Fortunato, Green Dragon Office, Los Angeles
PROJECT MANAGERS Michelle R. Sullivan and Sydney L. Hengst
PRODUCTION SUPERVISION The Actualizers, New York
EXHIBITION DESIGNER Joseph Cochand, Joseph Cochand Design
COLOR SEPARATIONS AND PRINTING SYL Creaciones Gráficas, Barcelona, Spain

COVER
Zhang Feng, *Immortals' Secrets in a Stone Cave* (detail), 1658 (cat. no. 30)

COVER INSIDE FLAP, CASE FRONT, AND PAGE 1
Frontispiece by Dong Qichang (detail) from Xiang Shengmo, *Invitation to Reclusion*, 1625–26 (cat. no. 1). Orientation of original text has been changed.

FRONTISPIECE
Yang Wencong, *Cloudy Valley* (detail; cat. no. 18)

ABOVE
Wang Hui, *Transporting Bamboo* (detail), 1698 (cat. no. 53)

Typeset in Ideal Sans and SimSun

Printed and bound in Spain